DECISION
Graduate
School
GUIDES

GRADUATE PROGRAMS IN

# Psychology
## 2004

THOMSON

PETERSON'S

Australia • Canada • Mexico • Singapore • Spain • United Kingdom • United States

**About The Thomson Corporation and Peterson's**

With revenues of US$7.8 billion, The Thomson Corporation (www.thomson.com) is a leading global provider of integrated information solutions for business, education, and professional customers. Its Learning businesses and brands (www.thomsonlearning.com) serve the needs of individuals, learning institutions, and corporations with products and services for both traditional and distributed learning.

Peterson's, part of The Thomson Corporation, is one of the nation's most respected providers of lifelong learning online resources, software, reference guides, and books. The Education Supersite[SM] at www.petersons.com—the Internet's most heavily traveled education resource—has searchable databases and interactive tools for contacting U.S.-accredited institutions and programs. In addition, Peterson's serves more than 105 million education consumers annually.

For more information, contact Peterson's, 2000 Lenox Drive, Lawrenceville, NJ 08648; 800-338-3282; or find us on the World Wide Web at www.petersons.com/about.

ISSN 1528-5979
ISBN 0-7689-1194-X

Printed in Canada

10  9  8  7  6  5  4  3  2  1     05  04  03

# Table of Contents

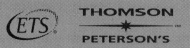
The *Decision Guides* are a collaborative effort between Peterson's and Educational Testing Service (ETS) and the Graduate Record Examinations (GRE) Board. This collaboration builds upon Peterson's survey research and publication capabilities and the GRE Program's long-term relationship with the graduate education community, including administration of the Graduate Record Examinations. This collaboration enables a greater range of potential graduate students to access comprehensive information as they make decisions about pursuing graduate education. At the same time, it enables institutions to achieve greater promotion and awareness of their graduate offerings.

The graduate and professional programs in this *Decision Guide* are offered by colleges, universities, and professional schools and specialized institutions in the United States and U.S. territories. They are accredited by U.S. accrediting bodies recognized by the Department of Education or the Council on Higher Education Accreditation. Most are regionally accredited.

This volume is divided into nineteen sections that represent the subject fields in which graduate degrees in psychology are offered: Psychology-General; Addictions/Substance Abuse Counseling; Clinical Psychology; Cognitive Sciences; Counseling Psychology; Developmental Psychology; Experimental Psychology; Forensic Psychology; Genetic Counseling; Health Psychology; Human Development; Industrial and Organizational Psychology; Marriage and Family Therapy; Rehabilitation Counseling; School Psychology; Social Psychology; Sport Psychology; Thanatology; and Transpersonal and Humanistic Psychology.

## How Information Is Organized

Graduate program information in this *Decision Guide* is presented in profile form. The format of the profiles is consistent throughout the book, making it easy to compare one institution with another and one program with another. Any item that does not apply to or was not provided by a graduate unit is omitted from its listing. The following outline describes the profile information.

**Identifying Information.** In the conventional university-college-department organizational structure, the parent institution's name is followed by the name of the administrative unit or units under which the degree program is offered and then the specific unit that offers the degree program. (For example, University of Notre Dame, College of Arts and Letters, Division of Humanities, Department of Art, Art History, and Design, Concentration in Design.) The last unit listed is the one to which all information in the profile pertains. The institution's city, state, and postal code follow.

**Awards.** Each postbaccalaureate degree awarded is listed; fields of study offered by the unit may also be listed. Frequently, fields of study are divided into subspecializations, and those appear following the degrees awarded. Students enrolled in the graduate program would be able to specialize in any of the fields mentioned.

**Part-Time and Evening/Weekend Programs.** When information regarding the availability of part-time or evening/weekend study appears in the profile, it means that students are able to earn a degree exclusively through such study.

**Postbaccalaureate Distance Learning Degrees.** A postbaccalaureate distance learning degree program signifies that course requirements can be fulfilled with minimal or no on-campus study.

**Faculty.** Figures on the number of faculty members actively involved with graduate students through teaching or research are separated into full- and part-time as well as men and women whenever the information has been supplied.

**Students.** Figures for the number of students enrolled in graduate and professional programs pertain to the semester of highest enrollment from the 2001–02 academic year. These figures are divided into full- and part-time and men and women whenever the data have been supplied. Information on the number of students who are members of a minority group or are international students appears here. The average age of the students is followed by the number of applicants, the percentage accepted, and the number enrolled for fall 2001. This section also includes the number of degrees awarded in calendar year 2001. Many doctoral programs offer a terminal master's degree if students leave the program after completing only part of the requirements for a doctoral degree; that is indicated here. All degrees are classified into one of four types: master's, doctoral, first-professional, and other advanced degrees. A unit may award one or several degrees at a given level; however, the data are only collected by type and may therefore represent several different degree programs.

**Degree Requirements.** The information in this section is also broken down by type of degree, and all information for a degree level pertains to all degrees of that type unless otherwise specified. Degree requirements are collected in a simplified form to provide some very basic information on the nature of the program and on foreign language, thesis or dissertation, comprehensive exam, and registration requirements. Some units may also provide a short list of additional requirements, such as fieldwork or internships. Information on the median amount of time required to earn the degree for full-time and part-time students is presented here. For complete information on graduation requirements, contact the graduate school or program directly.

**Entrance Requirements.** Entrance requirements are divided into the levels of master's, doctoral, first-professional, and other advanced degrees. Within each level, information may be provided in two basic categories, entrance exams and other requirements. The entrance exams use the standard acronyms used by the testing agencies, unless they are not well known. Other entrance requirements are quite varied, but they often contain an undergraduate or graduate grade point average (GPA). Unless otherwise stated, the GPA is calculated on a 4.0 scale and is listed as a minimum required for admission.

**Application.** The standard application **deadline,** any nonrefundable application **fee,** and whether electronic applications are accepted may be listed here. Note that the deadline should be used for reference only; these dates are subject to change, and students interested in applying should contact the graduate unit directly about application procedures and deadlines.

**Expenses.** Cost of study may be quite complex at a graduate institution. There are often sliding scales for part-time study, a different cost for first-year students, and other variables that make it impossible to completely cover the cost of study for each graduate program. To provide the most usable information, figures are given for full-time study for a full year where available and for part-time study in terms of a per-unit rate (per credit, per semester hour, etc.) **if** these costs are reported to be the **same** as the parent institution. If specific program costs have been reported as different from the parent institution, the reader is advised to contact the institution for expense information. Because expenses are always subject to change, this is good advice at any time.

**Financial Support.** This section contains data on the number of awards administered by the institution and given to graduate students during the 2001–02 academic year. The first figure given represents the total number of students enrolled in that unit who received financial aid. If the unit has provided information on graduate appointments, these are broken down into three major categories: *fellowships* give money to graduate students to cover the cost of study and living expenses and are not based on a work obligation or research commitment, *research assistantships* provide stipends to graduate students for assistance in a formal research project with a faculty member, and *teaching assistantships* provide stipends to graduate students for teaching or for assisting faculty members in teaching undergraduate classes.

In addition to graduate appointments, the availability of several other financial aid sources is covered in this section. *Career-related internships* or *fieldwork* offer money to students who are participating in a formal off-campus research project or practicum. *Federal Work-Study* is made available to students who demonstrate need and meet the federal guidelines; this form of aid normally includes 10 or more hours of work per week in an office of the institution or off campus in a nonprofit agency. *Tuition waivers* are routinely part of a graduate appointment, but units sometimes waive part or all of a student's tuition even if a graduate appointment is not available. *Institutionally sponsored loans* are low-interest loans available to graduate students to cover both educational and living expenses. The availability of grants, scholarships, traineeships, unspecified assistantships, and financial aid to part-time students is also indicated here.

Some programs list the financial aid application deadline and the forms that need to be completed for students to be eligible for financial aid. There are two forms: FAFSA, the Free Application for Federal Student Aid, which is required for federal aid; and the CSS Financial Aid PROFILE.

**Faculty Research.** Each unit has the opportunity to list several keyword phrases describing the current research involving faculty members and graduate students. Space limitations prevent the unit from listing complete information on all research programs. The total expenditure for funded research from the previous academic year may also be included.

**Unit Head and Application Contact.** The head of the graduate program for each unit is listed with the academic title and telephone and fax numbers and e-mail addresses, if available. In addition to the unit head, many graduate programs list separate contacts for application and admission information. Unit Web sites are provided, if available. If no unit head or application contact is given, you should contact the overall institution for information.

## For Further Information

Many programs offer more in-depth, narrative style information that can be located at www.petersons.com/gradchannel. There is a notation to this effect at the end of those program profiles.

# How This Information Was Gathered

The information published in this book was collected through *Peterson's Annual Survey of Graduate and Professional Institutions*. Each spring and summer, this survey is sent to more than 1,800 institutions offering postbaccalaureate degree programs, including accredited institutions in the United States and U.S. territories. (See article entitled "Accreditation and Accrediting Agencies.") Deans and other administrators provide information on specific programs as well as overall institutional information. Peterson's editorial staff then goes over each returned survey carefully and verifies or revises responses after further research and discussion with administrators at the institutions.

While every effort is made to ensure the accuracy and completeness of the data, information is sometimes unavailable or changes occur after publication deadlines. The omission of any particular item from a directory or profile signifies either that the item is not applicable to the institution or program or that information was not available.

# The Admissions Process

Generalizations about graduate admissions practices are not always helpful because each institution has its own set of guidelines and procedures. Nevertheless, some broad statements can be made about the admissions process that may help you plan your strategy.

## General Requirements

Graduate schools and departments have requirements that applicants for admission must meet. Typically, these requirements include undergraduate transcripts (which provide information about undergraduate grade point average and course work applied toward a major), admission test scores, and letters of recommendation. Most graduate programs also ask for an essay or personal statement that describes your personal reasons for seeking graduate study. In some fields, such as art and music, portfolios or auditions may be required in addition to other evidence of talent. Some institutions require that the applicant have an undergraduate degree in the same subject as the intended graduate major.

Most institutions evaluate each applicant on the basis of the applicant's total record, and the weight accorded any given factor varies widely from institution to institution and from program to program.

## Admission Tests

The major testing program used in graduate admissions is the Graduate Record Examinations (GRE) testing program, sponsored by the GRE Board and administered by Educational Testing Service, Princeton, New Jersey.

The Graduate Record Examinations testing program consists of a General Test and eight Subject Tests. The General Test measures verbal reasoning, quantitative reasoning, and analytical writing skills. It is offered as a computer-adaptive test (CAT) in the United States, Canada, and many other countries. In the CAT, the computer determines which question to present next by adjusting to your previous responses. Paper-based General Test administrations are offered in some parts of the world.

The computer-adaptive General Test consists of a 30-minute verbal section, a 45-minute quantitative section, and a 75-minute analytical writing section. In addition, an unidentified verbal or quantitative section that doesn't count toward a score may be included and an identified research section that is not scored may also be included.

The paper-based General Test consists of two 30-minute verbal sections, two 30-minute quantitative sections, and a 75-minute analytical writing section. In addition, an unidentified verbal or quantitative section that doesn't count toward a score may be included.

The Subject Tests measure achievement and assume undergraduate majors or extensive background in the following eight disciplines:

- Biochemistry, Cell and Molecular Biology
- Biology
- Chemistry
- Computer Science
- Literature in English
- Mathematics
- Physics
- Psychology

The Subject Tests are available at regularly scheduled paper-based administrations at test centers around the world. Testing time is approximately 2 hours and 50 minutes. You can obtain more information about the GRE tests by visiting the GRE Web site at www.gre.org or consulting the *GRE Information and Registration Bulletin*. The *Bulletin* can be obtained at many undergraduate colleges. You can also download it from the GRE Web site or obtain it by contacting Graduate Record Examinations, Educational Testing Service, Princeton, NJ 08541-6000, telephone 1-609-771-7670.

If you expect to apply for admission to a program that requires any of the GRE tests, you should select a test date well in advance of the application deadline. Scores on the computer-adaptive General Test are reported within ten to fifteen days; however, if you choose to handwrite your essay responses on the analytical writing section, score reporting will take approximately six weeks. Scores on the paper-based General Test and the Subject Tests are reported within six weeks.

Another testing program, the Miller Analogies Test (MAT), is administered at more than 600 licensed testing centers in the United States, Canada, and other countries. Testing time is 50 minutes. The test consists entirely of analogies. You can obtain the *Candidate Information Booklet*, which contains a list of test centers and instructions for taking the test, by calling The Psychological Corporation, Controlled Test Center, at 1-800-622-3231.

Check the specific requirements of the programs to which you are applying.

# Factors Involved in Selecting a Graduate School or Program

Selecting a graduate school and a specific program of study is a complex matter. Quality of the faculty; program and course offerings; the nature, size, and location of the institution; admission requirements; cost; and the availability of financial assistance are among the many factors that affect one's choice of institution. Other considerations are job placement and achievements of the program's graduates and the institution's resources, such as libraries, laboratories, and computer facilities. If you are to make the best possible choice, you need to learn as much as you can about the schools and programs you are considering before you apply.

The following steps may help you narrow your choices.

- Talk to alumni of the programs or institutions you are considering to get their impressions of how well they were prepared for work in their fields of study.
- Remember that graduate school requirements change, so be sure to get the most up-to-date information possible.
- Talk to department faculty and the graduate adviser at your undergraduate institution. They often have information about programs of study at other institutions.
- Visit the Web sites of the graduate schools in which you are interested to request a graduate catalog. Contact the department chair in your chosen field of study for additional information about the department and the field.
- Visit as many campuses as possible. Call ahead for an appointment with the graduate adviser in your field of interest and be sure to check out the facilities and talk to students.

**Tips for Minority Students:** Indicators of a university's values in terms of diversity are found both in its recruitment programs and its resources directed to student success. Important questions: Does the institution vigorously recruit minorities for its graduate programs? Is there funding available to help with the costs associated with visiting the school? Are minorities represented in the institution's brochures or Web site or on their faculty rolls? What campus-based resources or services (including assistance in locating housing or career counseling and placement) are available? Is funding available to members of underrepresented groups?

At the program level, it is particularly important for minority students to investigate the "climate" of a program under consideration. How many minority students are enrolled and how many have graduated? What opportunities are there to work with diverse faculty and mentors whose research interests match yours? How are conflicts resolved or concerns addressed? How interested are faculty in building strong and supportive relations with students? "Climate" concerns should be addressed by posing questions to various individuals, including faculty members, current students, and alumni.

Information is also available through various organizations, such as the Hispanic Association of Colleges and Universities (HACU), and publications, such as *Black Issues in Higher Education* and *Hispanic Outlook* magazine. There are also books devoted to this topic, such as *The Multicultural Student's Guide to Colleges* by Robert Mitchell.

# When and How to Apply

You should begin the application process at least one year before you expect to begin your graduate study. Find out the application deadline for each institution (many are provided in the profile section of this volume). Go to the institution Web site and find out if you can apply online. If not, request a paper application form. Fill out this form thoroughly and neatly. Assume that the school needs all the information it is requesting and that the admissions officer will be sensitive to the neatness and overall quality of what you submit. Do not supply more information than the school requires.

The institution may ask at least one question that will require a three- or four-paragraph answer. Compose your response on the assumption that the admissions officer is interested in both what you think and how you express yourself. Keep your statement brief and to the point, but, at the same time, include all pertinent information about your past experiences and your educational goals. Individual statements vary greatly in style and content, which helps admissions officers to differentiate among applicants. Many graduate departments give considerable weight to the statement in making their admissions decisions, so be sure to take the time to prepare a thoughtful and concise statement.

If recommendations are a part of the admissions requirements, choose carefully the individuals you ask to write them. It is generally best to ask current or former professors to write the recommendations, provided they are able to attest to your intellectual ability and motivation for doing the work required of a graduate student. It is advisable to provide stamped, preaddressed envelopes to people being asked to submit recommendations on your behalf.

Completed applications, including references and transcripts and admission test scores, should be received at the institution by the specified date.

Be advised that institutions do not usually make admissions decisions until all materials have been received. Enclose a self-addressed postcard with your application, requesting confirmation of receipt. Allow at least 10 days for the return of the postcard before making further inquiries.

If you plan to apply for financial support, it is imperative that you file your application early.

# How Admission Decisions Are Made

The program you apply to is directly involved in the admissions process. Although the final decision is usually made by the graduate dean (or an associate) or by the faculty admissions committee, recommendations from faculty members in your intended field are important. At some institutions, an interview is incorporated into the decision process.

# A Special Note for International Students

In addition to the steps already described, there are some special considerations for international students who intend to apply for graduate study in the United States. All graduate schools require an indication of competence in English. The purpose of the Test of English as a Foreign Language (TOEFL) is to evaluate the English proficiency of people who are nonnative speakers of English and want to study at colleges and universities where English is the language of instruction. The TOEFL is administered by Educational Testing

Service (ETS) under the general direction of a policy board established by the College Board and the Graduate Record Examinations Board.

The TOEFL is administered as a computer-based test throughout most of the world and is available year-round by appointment only. It is not necessary to have previous computer experience to take the test. The test consists of four sections—listening, reading, structure, and writing. Total testing time is approximately 4 hours.

The TOEFL is offered in the paper-based format in areas of the world where computer-based testing is not available. The paper-based TOEFL consists of three sections—listening comprehension, structure and written expression, and reading comprehension. Testing time is approximately 3 hours. The Test of Written English (TWE) is also given. TWE is a 30-minute essay that measures the examinee's ability to compose in English. Examinees receive a TWE score separate from their TOEFL score. The

*Information Bulletin* contains information on local fees and registration procedures.

Additional information and registration materials are available from TOEFL Services, Educational Testing Service, P.O. Box 6151, Princeton, New Jersey 08541-6151. Telephone: 1-609-771-7100. E-mail: toefl@ets.org. World Wide Web: http://www.toefl.org.

International students should apply especially early because of the number of steps required to complete the admissions process. Furthermore, many United States graduate schools have a limited number of spaces for international students, and many more students apply than the schools can accommodate.

International students may find financial assistance from institutions very limited. The U.S. government requires international applicants to submit a certification of support, which is a state-ment attesting to the applicant's financial resources. In addition, international students *must* have health insurance coverage.

# Financial Support

The range of financial support at the graduate level is very broad. The following descriptions will give you a general idea of what you might expect and what will be expected of you as a financial support recipient.

## Fellowships, Scholarships, and Grants

These are usually outright awards of a few hundred to many thousands of dollars with no service to the institution required in return. Fellowships and scholarships are usually awarded on the basis of merit and are highly competitive. Grants are made on the basis of financial need or special talent in a field of study. Many grants not only cover tuition, fees, and supplies but also include stipends for living expenses with allowances for dependents. However, the terms of each grant should be examined because some do not permit recipients to supplement their income with outside work. Fellowships, scholarships, and grants may vary in the number of years for which they are awarded.

In addition to the availability of these funds at the university or program level, many excellent fellowship programs are available at the national level and may be applied for before and during enrollment in a graduate program. A listing of many of these programs can be found at the Council of Graduate Schools' Web site: http://www.cgsnet.org/ResourcesForStudents/fellowships.htm.

## Assistantships and Internships

As described here, many graduate students receive financial support through assistantships, particularly involving teaching or research duties. It is important to recognize that such appointments should not be simply employment relationships but rather should constitute an integral and important part of a student's graduate education. As such, the appointments should be accompanied by strong faculty mentoring and increasingly responsible apprenticeship experiences (these are often lacking for teaching assistantships). The specific nature of these appointments in a given program should be factor considered in selecting that graduate program.

## Teaching Assistantships

These usually provide a salary and full or partial tuition remission, and they may also provide health benefits. Unlike fellowships, scholarships, and grants, which require no service to the institution, teaching assistantships require recipients to provide the institution with a specific amount of undergraduate teaching, ideally related to the student's field of study. Some teaching assistants are limited to grading papers, compiling bibliographies, or monitoring laboratories. At some graduate schools, teaching assistants must carry lighter course loads than regular full-time students.

## Research Assistantships

These are very similar to teaching assistantships in the manner in which financial assistance is provided. The difference is that recipients are given basic research assignments in their disciplines rather than teaching responsibilities. The work required is normally related to the student's field of study; in most instances, the assistantship supports the student's thesis or dissertation research.

## Administrative Internships

These are similar to assistantships in application of financial assistance funds, but the student is given an assignment on a part-time basis, usually as a special assistant to one of the university's administrative officers. The assignment may not necessarily be directly related to the recipient's discipline.

## Residence Hall and Counseling Assistantships

These are frequently assigned to graduate students in psychology, counseling, and social work. Duties can vary from being available in a dean's office for a specific number of hours for consultation with undergraduates to living in campus residences and being responsible for both counseling and administrative tasks or advising student activity groups. Residence hall assistantships sometimes include room and board in addition to tuition and stipends.

# Health Insurance

The availability and affordability of health insurance is an important issue and one that should be considered in an applicant's choice of institution and program. While often included with assistantships and fellowships, this is not always the case and, even if provided, the benefits may be very limited. It is important to note that the U.S. government requires international students to have health insurance.

# The GI Bill

This provides financial assistance for students who are veterans of the United States armed forces. If you are a veteran, contact your local Veterans Administration office to determine your eligibility and to get full details about benefits.

# Federal Work-Study Program (FWS)

Employment is another way some students finance their graduate studies. The federally funded Federal Work-Study Program provides eligible students with employment opportunities, usually in public and private nonprofit organizations. Federal funds pay up to 75 percent of the wages, with the remainder paid by the employing agency. FWS is available to graduate students who demonstrate financial need. Not all schools have these funds, and some only award them to undergraduates. Each school sets its application deadline and work-study earnings limits. Wages vary and are related to the type of work done.

# Loans

Many graduate students borrow to finance their graduate programs when other sources of assistance (which do not have to be repaid) prove insufficient. You should always read and understand the terms of any loan program before submitting your application.

## Federal Loans

**Federal Stafford Loans.** The Federal Stafford Loan Program offers government-sponsored, low-interest loans to students through a private lender such as a bank, credit union, or savings and loan association.

There are two components of the Federal Stafford Loan program. Under the *subsidized* component of the program, the federal government pays the interest accruing on the loan while you are enrolled in graduate school on at least a half-time basis. Under the *unsubsidized* component of the program, you pay the interest on the loan from the day proceeds are issued. Eligibility for the federal subsidy is based on demonstrated financial need as determined by the financial aid office from the information you provide on the Free Application for Federal Student Aid (FAFSA). (See "Applying for Need-Based Financial Aid" for more information on the FAFSA.) A cosigner is not required, since the loan is not based on creditworthiness.

Although *unsubsidized* Federal Stafford Loans may not be as desirable as *subsidized* Federal Stafford Loans from the consumer's perspective, they are a useful source of support for those who may not qualify for the subsidized loans or who need additional financial assistance.

Graduate students may borrow up to $18,500 per year through the Stafford Loan Program, up to a cumulative maximum of $138,500, including undergraduate borrowing. This may include up to $8500 in Subsidized Stafford Loans annually, depending on eligibility, up to a cumulative maximum of $65,500, including undergraduate borrowing. The amount of the loan borrowed through the *unsubsidized* Stafford Program equals the total amount of the loan (as much $18,500) minus your eligibility for a Subsidized Stafford Loan (as much as $8500). You may borrow up to the cost of the school in which you are enrolled or will attend, minus estimated financial assistance from other federal, state, and private sources, up to a maximum of $18,500.

The interest rate for the Federal Stafford Loans varies annually and is set every July. The rate during in-school, grace, and deferment periods is based on the 91-Day U.S. Treasury Bill rate plus 1.7 percent, capped at 8.25 percent. The rate during repayment is based on the 91-Day U.S. Treasury Bill rate plus 2.3 percent, capped at 8.25 percent. The 2002–03 rate is 4.06 percent.

Two fees may be deducted from the loan proceeds upon disbursement: a guarantee fee of up to 1 percent, which is deposited in an insurance pool to ensure repayment to the lender if the borrower defaults, and a federally mandated 3 percent origination fee, which is used to offset the administrative cost of the Federal Stafford Loan Program.

Under the *subsidized* Federal Stafford Loan Program, repayment begins six months after your last enrollment on at least a half-time basis. Under the *unsubsidized* program, repayment of interest begins within thirty days from disbursement of the loan proceeds, and repayment of the principal begins six months after your last enrollment on at least a half-time basis. Some borrowers may choose to defer interest payments while they are in school. The accrued interest is added to the loan balance when the borrower begins repayment. There are several repayment options.

**Federal Direct Loans.** Some schools participate in the Department of Education's Direct Lending Program instead of offering Federal Stafford Loans. The two programs are essentially the same except that with the Direct Loans, schools themselves generate the loans with funds provided from the federal government. Terms and interest rates are virtually the same except that there are a few more repayment options with Federal Direct Loans.

**Federal Perkins Loans.** The Federal Perkins Loan is available to students demonstrating financial need and is administered directly by the school. Not all schools have these funds, and some may award them to undergraduates only. Eligibility is determined from the information you provide on the FAFSA. The school will notify you of your eligibility.

Eligible graduate students may borrow up to $6000 per year, up to a maximum of $40,000, including undergraduate borrowing (even if your previous Perkins Loans have been repaid). The interest rate for Federal Perkins Loans is 5 percent, and no interest accrues while you remain in school at least half-time. There are no guarantee, loan, or disbursement fees. Repayment begins nine months after your last enrollment on at least a half-time basis and may extend over a maximum of ten years with no prepayment penalty.

**Deferring Your Federal Loan Repayments.** If you borrowed under the Federal Stafford Loan Program or the Federal Perkins Loan Program for previous undergraduate or graduate study, your repayments may be deferred when you return to graduate school, depending on when you borrowed and under which program.

There are other deferment options available if you are temporarily unable to repay your loan. Information about these deferments is provided at your entrance and exit interviews. If you believe you are eligible for a deferment of your loan repayments, you must contact your lender to complete a deferment form. The deferment must be filed prior to the time your repayment is due, and it must be refiled when it expires if you remain eligible for deferment at that time.

## Supplemental (Private) Loans

Many lending institutions offer supplemental loan programs and other financing plans, such as the ones described below, to students seeking additional assistance in meeting their educational expenses. Some loan programs target all types of graduate students; others are designed specifically for business, law, or medical students. In addition, you can use private loans not specifically designed for education to help finance your graduate degree.

If you are considering borrowing through a supplemental or private loan program, you should carefully consider the terms and be sure to "read the fine print." Check with the program sponsor for the most current terms that will be applicable to the amounts you intend to borrow for graduate study. Most supplemental loan programs for graduate study offer unsubsidized, credit-based loans. In general, a credit-ready borrower is one who has a satisfactory credit history or no credit history at all. A creditworthy borrower generally must pass a credit test to be eligible to borrow or act as a cosigner for the loan funds.

Many supplemental loan programs have a minimum annual loan limit and a maximum annual loan limit. Some offer amounts equal to the cost of attendance minus any other aid you will receive for graduate study. If you are planning to borrow for several years of graduate study, consider whether there is a cumulative or aggregate limit on the amount you may borrow. Often this cumulative or aggregate limit will include any amounts you borrowed and have not repaid for undergraduate or previous graduate study.

The combination of the annual interest rate, loan fees, and the repayment terms you choose will determine how much you will repay over time. Compare these features in combination before you decide which loan program to use. Some loans offer interest rates that are adjusted monthly, some quarterly, some annually. Some offer interest rates that are lower during the in-school, grace, and deferment periods, and then increase when you

begin repayment. Most programs include a loan "origination" fee, which is usually deducted from the principal amount you receive when the loan is disbursed, and must be repaid along with the interest and other principal when you graduate, withdraw from school, or drop below half-time study. Sometimes the loan fees are reduced if you borrow with a qualified cosigner. Some programs allow you to defer interest and/or principal payments while you are enrolled in graduate school. Many programs allow you to capitalize your interest payments; the interest due on your loan is added to the outstanding balance of your loan, so you don't have to repay immediately, but this increases the amount you owe. Other programs allow you to pay the interest as you go, which will reduce the amount you later have to repay.

Some examples of supplemental programs follow.

**CitiAssist Loans.** Offered by Citibank, these no-fee loans help graduate students fill the gap between the financial aid they receive and the money they need for school. Visit www.studentloan.com for more loan information from Citibank.

**EXCEL Loan.** This program, sponsored by Nellie Mae, is designed for students who are not ready to borrow on their own and wish to borrow with a creditworthy cosigner. Visit www.nelliemae.com for more information.

**Key Alternative Loan.** This loan can bridge the gap between education costs and traditional funding. Visit www.keybank.com for more information.

**Graduate Access Loan.** Sponsored by the Access Group, this is for graduate students enrolled at least half-time. The Web site is www.accessgroup.com.

**Signature Student Loan.** A loan program for students who are enrolled at least half-time, this is sponsored by Sallie Mae. Visit www.salliemae.com for more information.

Remember that these are generalized statements about financial assistance at the graduate level. Because each institution allots its aid differently, you should communicate directly with the school and the specific department of interest to you. It is not unusual, for example, to find that an endowment vested within a specific department supports one or more fellowships. You may fit its requirements and specifications precisely.

# Applying for Need-Based Financial Aid

Schools that award federal and institutional financial assistance based on need will require you to complete the FAFSA and, in some cases, an institutional financial aid application.

If you are applying for federal student assistance, you **must** complete the FAFSA. A service of the U.S. Department of Education, it is free to all applicants. You must send the FAFSA to the address listed in the FAFSA instructions or you can apply online at http://www.fafsa.ed.gov.

After your FAFSA information has been processed, you will receive a Student Aid Report (SAR). If you are an entering student, you may want to make copies of the SAR and send them to the school(s) to which you are applying. If you are a continuing student, you should make a copy of the SAR and forward the original document to the school you are attending.

Follow the instructions on the SAR if your situation changes and you need to correct information reported on your original application.

If you would like more information on federal student financial aid, visit the FAFSA Web site or request *The Student Guide 2003–2004* from the following address: Federal Student Aid Information Center, P.O. Box 84, Washington, DC 20044.

The U.S. Department of Education also has a toll-free number for questions concerning federal student aid programs. The number is 1-800-4-FED AID (1-800-433-3243). If you are hearing impaired, call toll-free, 1-800-730-8913.

# Accreditation
## and Accrediting Agencies

Colleges and universities in the United States, and their individual academic and professional programs, are accredited by nongovernmental agencies concerned with monitoring the quality of education in this country. Agencies with both regional and national jurisdictions grant accreditation to institutions as a whole, while specialized bodies acting on a nationwide basis—often national professional associations—grant accreditation to departments and programs in specific fields.

Institutional and specialized accrediting agencies share the same basic concerns: the purpose an academic unit—whether university or program—has set for itself and how well it fulfills that purpose, the adequacy of its financial and other resources, the quality of its academic offerings, and the level of services it provides. Agencies that grant institutional accreditation take a broader view, of course, and examine university-wide or college-wide services that a specialized agency may not concern itself with.

Both types of agencies follow the same general procedures when considering an application for accreditation. The academic unit prepares a self-evaluation, which focuses on the concerns mentioned above and includes an assessment of both its strengths and weaknesses; a team of representatives of the accrediting body reviews this evaluation, visits the campus, and makes its own report; and finally, the accrediting body makes a decision on the application. Often, even when accreditation is granted, the agency makes a recommendation regarding how the institution or program can improve. All institutions and programs are reviewed every few years to determine whether they continue to meet established standards; if they do not, they may lose their accreditation.

Accrediting agencies themselves are reviewed and evaluated periodically by the U.S. Department of Education and the Council for Higher Education Accreditation (CHEA). Agencies recognized adhere to certain standards and practices, and their authority in matters of accreditation is widely accepted in the educational community.

This does not mean, however, that accreditation is a simple matter, either for schools wishing to become accredited or for students deciding where to apply. Indeed, in certain fields the very meaning and methods of accreditation are the subject of a good deal of debate. **Those who are applying to graduate school should be aware of the safeguards provided by regional accreditation, especially in terms of degree acceptance and institutional longevity. Indeed, many institutions that offer graduate study will accept only those applicants whose undergraduate degree is from a regionally accredited institution.** (NOTE: Most institutions profiled in the *Decision Guides* are regionally accredited.) Beyond this, applicants should understand the role that specialized accreditation plays in their field, as this varies considerably from one discipline to another. In certain professional fields, it is necessary to have graduated from a program that is accredited in order to be eligible for a license to practice, and, in some fields, the federal government also makes this a hiring requirement.

Institutions and programs that present themselves for accreditation are sometimes granted the status of candidate for accreditation, or what is known as "preaccreditation." This may happen, for example, when an academic unit is too new to have met all the requirements for accreditation. Such status signifies initial recognition and indicates that the school or program in question is working to fulfill all requirements; it does not, however, guarantee that accreditation will be granted.

Readers are advised to contact agencies directly for answers to their questions about accreditation. The names and addresses of all agencies recognized by the U.S. Department of Education and the Council for Higher Education Accreditation are listed below.

# Institutional Accrediting Agencies—Regional

## MIDDLE STATES ASSOCIATION OF COLLEGES AND SCHOOLS

Accredits institutions in Delaware, District of Columbia, Maryland, New Jersey, New York, Pennsylvania, Puerto Rico, and the Virgin Islands.

Jean Avnet Morse, Executive Director
Commission on Higher Education
3624 Market Street
Philadelphia, Pennsylvania 19104-2680
Telephone: 215-662-5606
Fax: 215-662-5501
E-mail: jamorse@msache.org
World Wide Web: http://www.msache.org

## NEW ENGLAND ASSOCIATION OF SCHOOLS AND COLLEGES

Accredits institutions in Connecticut, Maine, Massachusetts, New Hampshire, Rhode Island, and Vermont.

Charles M. Cook, Director
Commission on Institutions of Higher
    Education
209 Burlington Road
Bedford, Massachusetts 01730-1433
Telephone: 781-271-0022
Fax: 781-271-0950
E-mail: CIHE@neasc.org
World Wide Web: http://www.neasc.org

## NORTH CENTRAL ASSOCIATION OF COLLEGES AND SCHOOLS

Accredits institutions in Arizona, Arkansas, Colorado, Illinois, Indiana, Iowa, Kansas, Michigan, Minnesota, Missouri, Nebraska, New Mexico, North Dakota, Ohio, Oklahoma, South Dakota, West Virginia, Wisconsin, and Wyoming.

Steven D. Crow, Executive Director
The Higher Learning Commission
30 North LaSalle, Suite 2400
Chicago, Illinois 60602-2504
Telephone: 312-263-0456
Fax: 312-263-7462
E-mail: scrow@hlcommission.org
World Wide Web: http://www.
    ncahigherlearningcommission.org

## NORTHWEST ASSOCIATION OF SCHOOLS AND COLLEGES

Accredits institutions in Alaska, Idaho, Montana, Nevada, Oregon, Utah, and Washington.

Sandra E. Elman, Executive Director
Commission on Colleges and Universities
8060 165th Avenue, NE, Suite 100
Redmond, Washington 98052
Telephone: 425-558-4224
Fax: 425-376-0596
E-mail: pjarnold@nwccu.org
World Wide Web: http://www.nwccu.org

## SOUTHERN ASSOCIATION OF COLLEGES AND SCHOOLS

Accredits institutions in Alabama, Florida, Georgia, Kentucky, Louisiana, Mississippi, North Carolina, South Carolina, Tennessee, Texas, and Virginia.

James T. Rogers, Executive Director
Commission on Colleges
1866 Southern Lane
Decatur, Georgia 30033
Telephone: 404-679-4500
Fax: 404-679-4528
E-mail: jrogers@sacscoc.org
World Wide Web: http://www.sacscoc.org

## WESTERN ASSOCIATION OF SCHOOLS AND COLLEGES

Accredits institutions in California, Guam, and Hawaii.

Ralph A. Wolff, Executive Director
The Senior College Commission
985 Atlantic Avenue, Suite 100
Alameda, California 94501
Telephone: 510-748-9001
Fax: 510-748-9797
E-mail: rwolff@wascsenior.org
World Wide Web: http://www.wascweb.org

# Institutional Accrediting Agencies—Other

## ACCREDITING COUNCIL FOR INDEPENDENT COLLEGES AND SCHOOLS

Dr. Steven A. Eggland, Executive Director
750 First Street, NE, Suite 980
Washington, D.C. 20002-4241
Telephone: 202-336-6780
Fax: 202-842-2593
E-mail: steve@acics.org
World Wide Web: http://www.acics.org

## DISTANCE EDUCATION AND TRAINING COUNCIL

Michael P. Lambert, Executive Secretary
1601 Eighteenth Street, NW
Washington, D.C. 20009
Telephone: 202-234-5100
Fax: 202-332-1386
E-mail: detc@detc.org
World Wide Web: http://www.detc.org

# Specialized Accrediting Agencies

## MARRIAGE AND FAMILY THERAPY

Donald B. Kaveny, Director
Commission on Accreditation
American Association for Marriage and
Family Therapy

112 South Alfred Street
Alexandria, Virginia 22314
Telephone: 703-838-9808
Fax: 703-253-0508
E-mail: dkaveny@aamft.org
World Wide Web: http://www.aamft.org

## PSYCHOLOGY AND COUNSELING

Susan F. Zlotlow, Director
Committee on Accreditation
American Psychological Association
750 First Street, NE
Washington, D.C. 20002
Telephone: 202-336-5979
Fax: 202-336-5978
E-mail: szotlow@apa.org
World Wide Web: http://www.apa.org

Carol L. Bobby, Executive Director
Council for Accreditation of Counseling and
    Related Educational
    Programs
American Counseling Association
5999 Stevenson Avenue
Alexandria, Virginia 22304
Telephone: 703-823-9800
Fax: 703-823-1581
E-mail: cacrep@aol.com
World Wide Web: http://
    www.counseling.org/cacrep

# Graduate Programs in
## Psychology

# Psychology and Counseling

## PSYCHOLOGY— GENERAL

### ■ ABILENE CHRISTIAN UNIVERSITY

Graduate School, College of Arts and Sciences, Department of Psychology, Program in General Psychology, Abilene, TX 79699-9100

AWARDS MS.

**Faculty:** 12 part-time/adjunct (2 women).
**Students:** 5 full-time (3 women); includes 2 minority (both African Americans). 4 applicants, 100% accepted, 3 enrolled. In 2001, 3 degrees awarded.
**Degree requirements:** For master's, comprehensive exam.
**Entrance requirements:** For master's, GRE General Test. *Application deadline:* For fall admission, 4/1 (priority date); for spring admission, 11/1. Applications are processed on a rolling basis. *Application fee:* $25 ($45 for international students).
**Expenses:** Tuition: Full-time $8,904; part-time $371 per hour. Required fees: $520; $17 per hour.
**Financial support:** Federal Work-Study available. Support available to part-time students. Financial award application deadline: 4/1.
Dr. Larry Norsworthy, Graduate Adviser, 915-674-2280, *Fax:* 915-674-6968, *E-mail:* norsworthyl@acu.edu.
**Application contact:** Dr. Roger Gee, Graduate Dean, 915-674-2122, *Fax:* 915-674-2123, *E-mail:* gradinfo@ education.acu.edu.

### ■ ADELPHI UNIVERSITY

Derner Institute of Advanced Psychological Studies, Garden City, NY 11530

AWARDS Clinical psychology (PhD, Post-Doctoral Certificate); general psychology (MA).

**Students:** 123 full-time (100 women), 207 part-time (166 women); includes 47 minority (23 African Americans, 11 Asian Americans or Pacific Islanders, 13 Hispanic Americans), 16 international. Average age 34. 301 applicants, 57% accepted, 72 enrolled. In 2001, 85 master's, 25 doctorates, 4 other advanced degrees awarded.
**Degree requirements:** For master's, thesis; for doctorate, thesis/dissertation, research (second year), 1 year internship.

**Entrance requirements:** For master's, resumé; for doctorate, GRE General Test, GRE Subject Test, interview, resumé; for Post-Doctoral Certificate, doctoral degree in psychology, interview. *Application deadline:* For fall admission, 1/15 (priority date). *Application fee:* $50.
**Expenses:** Contact institution.
**Financial support:** Research assistantships, teaching assistantships, career-related internships or fieldwork, institutionally sponsored loans, and clinical placements available. Financial award application deadline: 2/15; financial award applicants required to submit FAFSA.
**Faculty research:** Psychoanalytic processes, victimization, women's issues, program evaluation, psychotherapy process.
Dr. Louis Primavera, Dean, 516-877-4800.

**Find an in-depth description at www.petersons.com/gradchannel.**

### ■ ADLER SCHOOL OF PROFESSIONAL PSYCHOLOGY

Programs in Psychology, Chicago, IL 60601-7203

AWARDS Art therapy (Certificate); clinical hypnosis (Certificate); clinical psychology (Psy D); counseling psychology (MACP); counseling psychology/art therapy (MACAT); gerontology (MAGP, Certificate); marriage and family counseling (MAMFC); marriage and family therapy (Certificate); organizational psychology (MAO); substance abuse counseling (MASAC, Certificate). Part-time and evening/weekend programs available.

**Faculty:** 19 full-time (9 women), 48 part-time/adjunct (21 women).
**Students:** 124 full-time (78 women), 284 part-time (208 women); includes 77 minority (43 African Americans, 20 Asian Americans or Pacific Islanders, 13 Hispanic Americans, 1 Native American), 8 international. Average age 39. 253 applicants, 59% accepted, 121 enrolled. In 2001, 101 master's, 29 doctorates, 5 other advanced degrees awarded. Terminal master's awarded for partial completion of doctoral program.
**Degree requirements:** For master's, thesis or alternative, oral exam, practicum; for doctorate, thesis/dissertation, clinical exam, internship, oral exam, practicum, written qualifying exam.
**Entrance requirements:** For master's, 12 semester hours in psychology, minimum GPA of 3.0; for doctorate, 18 semester hours in psychology, minimum GPA of 3.25; for Certificate, appropriate master's

or doctoral degree. *Application deadline:* For fall admission, 1/1 (priority date). Applications are processed on a rolling basis. *Application fee:* $50.
**Expenses:** Tuition: Full-time $13,680; part-time $380 per credit. Required fees: $100; $15 per credit.
**Financial support:** In 2001–02, 180 students received support. Career-related internships or fieldwork, Federal Work-Study, scholarships/grants, and tuition waivers (full and partial) available. Support available to part-time students. Financial award application deadline: 5/15; financial award applicants required to submit FAFSA.
Dr. Frank Gruba-McCallister, Dean of Academic Affairs, 312-201-5900, *Fax:* 312-201-5917.
**Application contact:** Erene Soliman, Admissions Counselor, 312-201-5900, *Fax:* 312-201-5917.

**Find an in-depth description at www.petersons.com/gradchannel.**

### ■ ALABAMA AGRICULTURAL AND MECHANICAL UNIVERSITY

School of Graduate Studies, School of Education, Department of Counseling and Special Education, Huntsville, AL 35811

AWARDS Communicative disorders (M Ed, MS); psychology and counseling (MS, Ed S), including clinical psychology (MS), counseling and guidance, counseling psychology (MS), personnel management (MS), psychometry (MS), school psychology (MS); special education (M Ed, MS). Part-time and evening/weekend programs available.

**Faculty:** 38 full-time (20 women).
**Students:** 21 full-time (all women), 119 part-time (90 women); includes 65 minority (64 African Americans, 1 Hispanic American), 2 international. In 2001, 55 master's, 2 other advanced degrees awarded.
**Degree requirements:** For master's, comprehensive exam.
**Entrance requirements:** For master's, GRE General Test. *Application deadline:* For fall admission, 5/1. *Application fee:* $15 ($20 for international students).
**Expenses:** Tuition, state resident: full-time $1,380. Tuition, nonresident: full-time $2,500.
**Financial support:** Career-related internships or fieldwork available. Support available to part-time students. Financial award application deadline: 4/1.

**Faculty research:** Increasing numbers of minorities in special education and speech-language pathology. *Total annual research expenditures:* $300,000.

Dr. Terry L. Douglas, Chair, 256-851-5533.

## ■ ALLIANT INTERNATIONAL UNIVERSITY

**California School of Professional Psychology, San Francisco, CA 94109**

**AWARDS** MA, MS, PhD, Psy D. Programs available at Fresno, Los Angeles, San Diego, and San Francisco.

**Students:** 1,878 (1,449 women); includes 471 minority (106 African Americans, 180 Asian Americans or Pacific Islanders, 162 Hispanic Americans, 23 Native Americans). Average age 32. In 2001, 8 master's, 340 doctorates awarded.

*Application deadline:* For fall admission, 1/2 (priority date).

**Expenses:** Tuition: Part-time $397 per credit hour. Tuition and fees vary according to degree level, campus/location and program.

**Financial support:** Research assistantships, teaching assistantships, career-related internships or fieldwork, Federal Work-Study, institutionally sponsored loans, and scholarships/grants available. Financial award application deadline: 2/15; financial award applicants required to submit FAFSA.

Dr. Adele Rabin, Dean, 858-635-4801, *Fax:* 858-635-4585, *E-mail:* arabin@alliant.edu.

**Application contact:** Patricia J. Mullen, Vice President, Enrollment and Student Services, 800-457-1273 Ext. 303, *Fax:* 415-931-8322, *E-mail:* admissions@alliant.edu. *Web site:* http://www.alliant.edu/

**Find an in-depth description at www.petersons.com/gradchannel.**

## ■ AMERICAN INTERNATIONAL COLLEGE

**School of Continuing Education and Graduate Studies, School of Psychology and Education, Department of Psychology, Springfield, MA 01109-3189**

**AWARDS** Child development (MA, Ed D), including educational psychology; clinical psychology (MS); school psychology (MA, CAGS). Part-time and evening/weekend programs available.

**Degree requirements:** For master's, practicum; for doctorate, thesis/dissertation.

**Entrance requirements:** For master's, minimum C average in undergraduate course work; for doctorate, GRE General Test, interview.

## ■ AMERICAN UNIVERSITY

**College of Arts and Sciences, Department of Psychology, Washington, DC 20016-8001**

**AWARDS** Clinical psychology (PhD); experimental psychology (PhD); general psychology (PhD); psychology (MA), including experimental/biological psychology, general psychology, personality/social psychology. Part-time programs available.

**Faculty:** 15 full-time (4 women), 5 part-time/adjunct (2 women).

**Students:** 54 full-time (44 women), 52 part-time (46 women); includes 19 minority (5 African Americans, 8 Asian Americans or Pacific Islanders, 6 Hispanic Americans), 6 international. Average age 28. 268 applicants, 31% accepted, 33 enrolled. In 2001, 23 master's, 6 doctorates awarded.

**Degree requirements:** For doctorate, thesis/dissertation.

**Entrance requirements:** For master's and doctorate, GRE General Test, GRE Subject Test. *Application fee:* $50.

**Expenses:** Tuition: Full-time $14,274; part-time $793 per credit. Required fees: $290. Tuition and fees vary according to program.

**Financial support:** In 2001–02, 4 fellowships, 6 research assistantships, 10 teaching assistantships were awarded. Career-related internships or fieldwork, Federal Work-Study, institutionally sponsored loans, tuition waivers (full and partial), and unspecified assistantships also available. Support available to part-time students. Financial award application deadline: 2/1.

**Faculty research:** Anxiety disorders, cognitive assessment, neuropsychology, conditioning and learning, psychopharmacology.

Dr. Anthony Riley, Chair, 202-885-1720.

**Application contact:** Sara Holland, Senior Administrative Assistant, 202-885-1717, *Fax:* 202-885-1023.

## ■ ANDREWS UNIVERSITY

**School of Graduate Studies, School of Education, Department of Educational and Counseling Psychology, Berrien Springs, MI 49104**

**AWARDS** Community counseling (MA); counseling psychology (PhD); educational and developmental psychology (MA); educational psychology (Ed D, PhD); school counseling (MA); school psychology (Ed D, Ed S). Part-time programs available.

**Students:** 48 full-time (33 women), 56 part-time (38 women); includes 26 minority (23 African Americans, 1 Asian American or Pacific Islander, 2 Hispanic Americans), 29 international. Average age 35. In 2001, 29 master's, 7 doctorates, 4 other advanced degrees awarded. Terminal

master's awarded for partial completion of doctoral program.

**Degree requirements:** For master's, thesis optional; for doctorate, thesis/dissertation.

**Entrance requirements:** For master's, GRE Subject Test, minimum GPA of 2.6; for doctorate, GRE General Test, MA, minimum GPA of 3.5, sample of research. *Application deadline:* Applications are processed on a rolling basis. *Application fee:* $40.

**Expenses:** Tuition: Full-time $12,600; part-time $525 per semester. Required fees: $268. Tuition and fees vary according to degree level.

**Faculty research:** Testing methods, temperament, African-American studies, counseling process, multicultural issues.

Dr. Jerome D. Thayer, Chair, 616-471-3113.

**Application contact:** Carolyn Hurst, Supervisor of Graduate Admission, 800-253-2874, *Fax:* 616-471-3228, *E-mail:* enroll@andrews.edu.

## ■ ANGELO STATE UNIVERSITY

**Graduate School, College of Liberal and Fine Arts, Department of Psychology and Sociology, San Angelo, TX 76909**

**AWARDS** Psychology (MS), including counseling psychology, general psychology, industrial and organizational psychology. Part-time and evening/weekend programs available.

**Faculty:** 7 full-time (1 woman).

**Students:** 32 full-time (26 women), 25 part-time (21 women); includes 13 minority (2 African Americans, 1 Asian American or Pacific Islander, 9 Hispanic Americans, 1 Native American). Average age 35. 36 applicants, 53% accepted, 13 enrolled. In 2001, 14 degrees awarded.

**Degree requirements:** For master's, thesis, comprehensive exam.

**Entrance requirements:** For master's, GRE General Test, minimum GPA of 2.5. *Application deadline:* For fall admission, 8/7 (priority date); for spring admission, 1/2. Applications are processed on a rolling basis. *Application fee:* $25 ($50 for international students).

**Expenses:** Tuition, area resident: Full-time $960; part-time $40 per credit hour. Tuition, nonresident: full-time $6,120; part-time $255 per credit hour. Required fees: $1,336; $56 per credit hour.

**Financial support:** In 2001–02, 27 students received support, including 20 fellowships, 3 teaching assistantships; career-related internships or fieldwork, Federal Work-Study, tuition waivers (partial), and unspecified assistantships also available. Support available to part-time

*Angelo State University (continued)*
students. Financial award application deadline: 8/1.
Dr. William Davidson, Head, 915-942-2205. *Web site:* http://www.angelo.edu/dept/psychology_sociology/

### ■ ANNA MARIA COLLEGE

**Graduate Division, Program in Psychology, Paxton, MA 01612**

**AWARDS** Counseling psychology (MA, CAGS); psychology (MA, CAGS). Part-time and evening/weekend programs available.

**Faculty:** 1 full-time (0 women), 4 part-time/adjunct (3 women).

**Students:** 16 full-time (12 women), 26 part-time (19 women); includes 1 minority (Hispanic American). Average age 36. In 2001, 10 master's, 2 other advanced degrees awarded.

**Degree requirements:** For master's, practicum.

**Entrance requirements:** For master's, MAT; for CAGS, master's degree in psychology or related field. *Application deadline:* For fall admission, 3/1 (priority date); for spring admission, 11/1 (priority date). Applications are processed on a rolling basis. *Application fee:* $30. Electronic applications accepted.

**Expenses:** Tuition: Part-time $900 per course.

**Financial support:** Institutionally sponsored loans available. Financial award applicants required to submit FAFSA.
Richard L. Connors, Director, 508-849-3413, *Fax:* 508-849-3339, *E-mail:* rconnors@annamaria.edu.

**Application contact:** Eva Eaton, Director of Admissions for Graduate Programs and the Department of Professional Studies, 508-849-3488, *Fax:* 508-849-3362, *E-mail:* eveaton@annamaria.edu. *Web site:* http://www.annamaria.edu/

### ■ ANTIOCH NEW ENGLAND GRADUATE SCHOOL

**Graduate School, Department of Applied Psychology, Keene, NH 03431-3552**

**AWARDS** Counseling psychology (MA), including counseling psychology; dance/movement therapy (M Ed, MA); marriage and family therapy (MA); substance abuse/addictions counseling (M Ed, MA), including substance abuse counseling (M Ed).

**Faculty:** 9 full-time (7 women), 25 part-time/adjunct (15 women).

**Students:** 167 full-time (135 women), 25 part-time (20 women); includes 10 minority (3 African Americans, 2 Asian Americans or Pacific Islanders, 4 Hispanic Americans, 1 Native American), 7 international. Average age 36. 150

applicants, 85% accepted. In 2001, 66 degrees awarded.

**Degree requirements:** For master's, internship, practicum.

**Entrance requirements:** For master's, previous course work and work experience in psychology. *Application deadline:* Applications are processed on a rolling basis. *Application fee:* $40.

**Expenses:** Tuition: Full-time $15,150.

**Financial support:** In 2001–02, 125 students received support, including 6 fellowships (averaging $1,042 per year); Federal Work-Study and scholarships/grants also available. Financial award applicants required to submit FAFSA.

**Faculty research:** Diversity, descendants of survivors of the Holocaust and American slavery.
Dr. Julia Halevy, Chairperson, 603-357-3122 Ext. 225, *Fax:* 603-357-0718, *E-mail:* jhalevy@antiochne.edu.

**Application contact:** Robbie P. Hertneky, Director of Admissions, 603-357-6265, *Fax:* 603-357-0718, *E-mail:* rhertneky@antiochne.edu. *Web site:* http://www.antiochne.edu/

### ■ ANTIOCH UNIVERSITY LOS ANGELES

**Graduate Programs, Program in Psychology, Marina del Rey, CA 90292-7008**

**AWARDS** Clinical psychology (MA); psychology (MA). Part-time programs available.

**Degree requirements:** For master's, thesis (for some programs), internship.

**Entrance requirements:** For master's, TOEFL, interview.

**Faculty research:** Creativity and humor, ethnic humor, adult development, Jungian theory, psychoanalytic theory. *Web site:* http://www.antiochla.edu/

### ■ ANTIOCH UNIVERSITY MCGREGOR

**Graduate Programs, Individualized Liberal and Professional Studies Program, Yellow Springs, OH 45387-1609**

**AWARDS** Liberal and professional studies (MA), including counseling, creative writing, education, film studies, liberal studies, management, modern literature, psychology, theatre, visual arts. Part-time and evening/weekend programs available.
Postbaccalaureate distance learning degree programs offered (minimal on-campus study).

**Faculty:** 4 full-time, 6 part-time/adjunct.

**Students:** 19 applicants, 89% accepted, 16 enrolled. In 2001, 56 degrees awarded.

**Degree requirements:** For master's, thesis or alternative.

*Application deadline:* For fall admission, 8/25; for winter admission, 12/5. Applications are processed on a rolling basis. *Application fee:* $50. Electronic applications accepted.

**Expenses:** Tuition: Part-time $317 per credit hour. Required fees: $75 per quarter.

**Financial support:** Federal Work-Study available. Financial award application deadline: 7/1; financial award applicants required to submit FAFSA.
Dr. Virginia Paget, Director, 937-769-1876, *Fax:* 937-769-1805.

**Application contact:** Karen E. Crist, Enrollment Services Officer, 937-769-1818, *Fax:* 937-769-1804, *E-mail:* kcrist@mcgregor.edu. *Web site:* http://www.mcgregor.edu

**Find an in-depth description at www.petersons.com/gradchannel.**

### ■ ANTIOCH UNIVERSITY SANTA BARBARA

**Psychology Program, Santa Barbara, CA 93101-1581**

**AWARDS** Family and child studies (MA); professional development and career counseling (MA). Part-time and evening/weekend programs available.

**Faculty:** 14 full-time (8 women), 43 part-time/adjunct (29 women).

**Students:** 13 full-time, 8 part-time. In 2001, 12 degrees awarded.

**Entrance requirements:** For master's, TOEFL. *Application deadline:* For fall admission, 8/5 (priority date); for winter admission, 11/11 (priority date). Applications are processed on a rolling basis. *Application fee:* $60.

**Expenses:** Tuition: Part-time $375 per unit. Required fees: $426 per year. $10 per quarter. Tuition and fees vary according to class time and program.

**Financial support:** Federal Work-Study available. Support available to part-time students. Financial award application deadline: 8/5; financial award applicants required to submit FAFSA.
Dr. Catherine Radecki-Bush, Chair, 805-962-8179 Ext. 229, *Fax:* 805-962-4786, *E-mail:* cradecki-bush@antiochsb.edu.

**Application contact:** Carol Flores, Admissions Director, 805-962-8179 Ext. 113, *Fax:* 805-962-4786, *E-mail:* cflores@antiochsb.edu. *Web site:* http://www.antiochsb.edu/

### ■ ANTIOCH UNIVERSITY SEATTLE

**Graduate Programs, Program in Psychology, Seattle, WA 98121-1814**

**AWARDS** MA. Part-time and evening/weekend programs available.

**Faculty:** 11 full-time (6 women), 28 part-time/adjunct (13 women).
**Students:** 63 full-time, 136 part-time. Average age 39. 54 applicants, 74% accepted. In 2001, 70 degrees awarded.
**Degree requirements:** For master's, internship.
*Application deadline:* For fall admission, 4/3; for spring admission, 1/12. Applications are processed on a rolling basis. *Application fee:* $50.
**Expenses:** Tuition: Part-time $395 per credit. Required fees: $45 per year. Tuition and fees vary according to program.
**Financial support:** Federal Work-Study available. Financial award application deadline: 6/15.
**Faculty research:** Trauma and post-traumatic stress disorders, workplace harassment and violence, multicultural issues and diversity.
L. Tien, Director, 206-441-5352.
**Application contact:** Dianne Larsen, Director of Admissions and Enrollment Services, 206-441-5352 Ext. 5200.

### ■ APPALACHIAN STATE UNIVERSITY

**Cratis D. Williams Graduate School, College of Arts and Sciences, Department of Psychology, Boone, NC 28608**

**AWARDS** Clinical psychology (MA); general experimental psychology (MA); health psychology (MA); industrial and organizational psychology (MA); school psychology (MA, CAS). Part-time programs available.

**Faculty:** 24 full-time (8 women).
**Students:** 82 full-time (65 women); includes 4 minority (2 African Americans, 1 Asian American or Pacific Islander, 1 Hispanic American), 1 international. 156 applicants, 41% accepted, 35 enrolled. In 2001, 20 master's, 4 other advanced degrees awarded.
**Degree requirements:** For master's, GRE Subject Test exit exam; for CAS, GRE Subject Test exit exam, thesis optional.
**Entrance requirements:** For master's, GRE General Test, GRE Subject Test.
*Application deadline:* For fall admission, 3/1. Applications are processed on a rolling basis. *Application fee:* $35.
**Expenses:** Tuition, state resident: full-time $1,286. Tuition, nonresident: full-time $9,354. Required fees: $1,116.
**Financial support:** In 2001–02, fellowships (averaging $2,000 per year), 33 research assistantships (averaging $6,250 per year), 10 teaching assistantships (averaging $6,250 per year) were awarded. Career-related internships or fieldwork, Federal Work-Study, scholarships/grants,

and unspecified assistantships also available. Support available to part-time students. Financial award application deadline: 7/1.
**Faculty research:** Eating disorders, school-based consultations, organizational behavior management, brain mechanisms of sound localization, parenting styles.
Dr. Stanley Aeschleman, Chair, 828-262-2272, *Fax:* 828-262-2974, *E-mail:* aeschlemansa@appstate.edu. *Web site:* http://www.acs.appstate.edu/dept/psych/

### ■ ARCADIA UNIVERSITY

**Graduate Studies, Department of Education, Glenside, PA 19038-3295**

**AWARDS** Art education (M Ed, MA Ed); biology education (MA Ed); chemistry education (MA Ed); child development (CAS); computer education (M Ed, CAS); computer education 7–12 (MA Ed); early childhood education (M Ed, CAS), including individualized (M Ed), master teacher (M Ed), research in child development (M Ed); educational leadership (M Ed, CAS); educational psychology (CAS); elementary education (M Ed, CAS); English education (MA Ed); environmental education (MA Ed, CAS); history education (MA Ed); language arts (M Ed, CAS); mathematics education (M Ed, MA Ed, CAS); music education (MA Ed); psychology (MA Ed); pupil personnel services (CAS); reading (M Ed, CAS); school library science (M Ed); science education (M Ed, CAS); secondary education (M Ed, CAS); special education (M Ed, Ed D, CAS); theater arts (MA Ed); written communication (MA Ed). Part-time and evening/weekend programs available.

**Faculty:** 12 full-time (8 women), 38 part-time/adjunct (26 women).
**Students:** 71 full-time (55 women), 506 part-time (398 women); includes 85 minority (75 African Americans, 2 Asian Americans or Pacific Islanders, 5 Hispanic Americans, 3 Native Americans). In 2001, 164 degrees awarded.
*Application deadline:* Applications are processed on a rolling basis. *Application fee:* $35. Electronic applications accepted.
**Expenses:** Tuition: Part-time $420 per credit. Tuition and fees vary according to degree level and program.
**Financial support:** Career-related internships or fieldwork, tuition waivers (partial), and unspecified assistantships available.
Dr. Steven P. Gulkus, Chair, 215-572-2120.
**Application contact:** 215-572-2925, *Fax:* 215-572-2126, *E-mail:* grad@arcadia.edu.

### ■ ARCADIA UNIVERSITY

**Graduate Studies, Department of Psychology, Glenside, PA 19038-3295**

**AWARDS** Counseling (MAC), including community counseling, school counseling. Part-time programs available.

**Faculty:** 4 full-time (2 women), 6 part-time/adjunct (4 women).
**Students:** 18 full-time (all women), 28 part-time (22 women); includes 4 minority (all African Americans), 2 international. In 2001, 14 degrees awarded.
**Degree requirements:** For master's, practicum.
**Entrance requirements:** For master's, GRE General Test or MAT. *Application deadline:* Applications are processed on a rolling basis. *Application fee:* $35.
**Expenses:** Tuition: Part-time $420 per credit. Tuition and fees vary according to degree level and program.
**Financial support:** Research assistantships, career-related internships or fieldwork and unspecified assistantships available. Support available to part-time students. Financial award application deadline: 8/15.
Samuel Cameron, Program Director, 215-572-2181.
**Application contact:** 215-572-2925, *Fax:* 215-572-2126, *E-mail:* grad@arcadia.edu.

### ■ ARGOSY UNIVERSITY-ATLANTA

**Graduate Programs, Atlanta, GA 30328-5505**

**AWARDS** Clinical psychology (MA, Psy D); professional counseling (MA); psychology (MA). Part-time and evening/weekend programs available.

**Faculty:** 11 full-time (6 women), 16 part-time/adjunct (6 women).
**Students:** 398; includes 70 minority (52 African Americans, 8 Asian Americans or Pacific Islanders, 8 Hispanic Americans, 2 Native Americans), 2 international. Average age 26. 272 applicants, 46% accepted. In 2001, 40 degrees awarded. Terminal master's awarded for partial completion of doctoral program.
**Degree requirements:** For master's, comprehensive exam; for doctorate, thesis/dissertation, clinical comprehensive exam, research project, internship.
**Entrance requirements:** For master's and doctorate, GRE General Test or MAT. *Application deadline:* For fall admission, 1/15 (priority date); for spring admission, 10/15 (priority date). Applications are processed on a rolling basis. *Application fee:* $55. Electronic applications accepted.
**Expenses:** Tuition: Part-time $374 per credit.
**Financial support:** In 2001–02, 280 students received support, including 40 teaching assistantships (averaging $700 per year); career-related internships or fieldwork and Federal Work-Study also available. Support available to part-time students. Financial award application deadline: 6/30; financial award applicants required to submit FAFSA.

*Argosy University-Atlanta (continued)*
Dr. Joseph Bascuas, Dean, 770-671-1200, *Fax:* 770-671-0476.
**Application contact:** Nick Colletti, Director of Enrollment Services, 770-671-1200, *Fax:* 770-671-0476, *E-mail:* ncolletti@argosyu.edu.
**Find an in-depth description at www.petersons.com/gradchannel.**

# ■ ARGOSY UNIVERSITY-CHICAGO

**Illinois School of Professional Psychology, Chicago, IL 60603**

**AWARDS** Clinical psychology (MA, Psy D), including child and adolescent psychology (Psy D), ethnic and racial psychology (Psy D), family psychology (Psy D), forensic psychology (Psy D), health psychology (Psy D), maltreatment and trauma (Psy D), psychoanalytic psychotherapy (Psy D), psychology and spirituality (Psy D); clinical respecialization (Certificate); health sciences (MA); professional counseling (MA). Part-time programs available.

**Faculty:** 28 full-time (15 women), 58 part-time/adjunct (35 women).
**Students:** 403 full-time (304 women), 155 part-time (120 women); includes 115 minority (64 African Americans, 28 Asian Americans or Pacific Islanders, 23 Hispanic Americans). Average age 39. 374 applicants, 67% accepted. In 2001, 58 master's, 92 doctorates, 43 other advanced degrees awarded. Terminal master's awarded for partial completion of doctoral program.
**Degree requirements:** For master's, comprehensive exam; for doctorate, thesis/dissertation, internship, research project, clinical competency exam, comprehensive exam.
**Entrance requirements:** For doctorate, minimum GPA of 3.25. *Application deadline:* For fall admission, 5/15; for winter admission, 10/15. *Application fee:* $55. Electronic applications accepted.
**Expenses:** Tuition: Part-time $332 per credit hour. Required fees: $75 per year. $35 per term.
**Financial support:** In 2001–02, 200 students received support, including 25 fellowships with partial tuition reimbursements available (averaging $2,000 per year), 150 teaching assistantships with partial tuition reimbursements available (averaging $600 per year); research assistantships with partial tuition reimbursements available, career-related internships or fieldwork, Federal Work-Study, scholarships/grants, tuition waivers (partial), and unspecified assistantships also available. Support available to part-time students. Financial award application

deadline: 5/29; financial award applicants required to submit FAFSA.
**Faculty research:** Personality disorders, meditation-based stress reduction, cross-cultural mothers and daughters, theory process and schizophrenia, development of clinical competencies. *Total annual research expenditures:* $30,000.
Dr. David Harpool, President, 312-279-3902, *Fax:* 312-201-1907, *E-mail:* dharpool@argosyu.edu.
**Application contact:** Ashley Delaney, Director of Admissions, 312-279-3906, *Fax:* 312-201-1907, *E-mail:* adelaney@argosyu.edu. *Web site:* http://www.argosyu.edu/

# ■ ARGOSY UNIVERSITY-CHICAGO NORTHWEST

**Graduate Programs, Rolling Meadows, IL 60008**

**AWARDS** Clinical psychology (MA, Psy D); professional counseling (MA). Evening/weekend programs available. Terminal master's awarded for partial completion of doctoral program.

**Degree requirements:** For master's, thesis, practicum; for doctorate, thesis/dissertation, internship, qualifying exam.
**Entrance requirements:** For master's, 15 hours in psychology, interview, minimum GPA of 3.0; for doctorate, 15 hours in psychology, interview, minimum GPA of 3.25.
**Find an in-depth description at www.petersons.com/gradchannel.**

# ■ ARGOSY UNIVERSITY-DALLAS

**Program in Clinical Psychology, Dallas, TX 75231**

**AWARDS** Clinical psychology (MA); professional counseling (MA); psychology (Psy D).

**Entrance requirements:** For master's, TOEFL. *Application fee:* $50.
**Expenses:** Tuition: Part-time $345 per credit hour. Required fees: $150 per semester.
Dr. Abby Calish, Head, 214-890-9900, *Fax:* 214-696-3500.
**Application contact:** Dee Pinkston, Director of Admissions, 214-890-9900, *Fax:* 214-696-3500, *E-mail:* dpinkston@argosyu.edu.
**Find an in-depth description at www.petersons.com/gradchannel.**

# ■ ARGOSY UNIVERSITY-HONOLULU

**Graduate Studies, Honolulu, HI 96813**

**AWARDS** Clinical psychology (MA, Psy D); clinical psychopharmacology (Certificate); professional counseling (MA), including marriage and family specialty, professional

counseling. Part-time and evening/weekend programs available.

**Faculty:** 8 full-time, 40 part-time/adjunct.
**Students:** 186 full-time (142 women), 48 part-time (34 women); includes 86 minority (4 African Americans, 77 Asian Americans or Pacific Islanders, 5 Hispanic Americans). Average age 35. 43 applicants, 74% accepted.
*Application fee:* $50. Electronic applications accepted.
**Expenses:** Tuition: Part-time $530 per credit. Tuition and fees vary according to program.
**Financial support:** In 2001–02, 232 students received support, including 9 teaching assistantships; career-related internships or fieldwork, Federal Work-Study, and scholarships/grants also available. Support available to part-time students. Financial award application deadline: 5/1; financial award applicants required to submit FAFSA.
**Faculty research:** Women's issues, diversity, health psychology, family systems, neuropsychological assessment.
Dr. Ray Crossman, President, 808-536-5555, *Fax:* 808-536-5505, *E-mail:* rcrossman@argosyu.edu.
**Application contact:** Eric C. Carlson, Director of Admissions, 808-536-5555, *Fax:* 808-536-5505, *E-mail:* ecarlson@argosyu.edu. *Web site:* http://www.argosyu.edu/
**Find an in-depth description at www.petersons.com/gradchannel.**

# ■ ARGOSY UNIVERSITY-ORANGE COUNTY

**School of Psychology, Orange, CA 92868**

**AWARDS** MA, Ed D, Psy D. Part-time and evening/weekend programs available.

**Faculty:** 3 full-time (1 woman), 11 part-time/adjunct (3 women).
**Students:** 28 full-time (20 women), 10 part-time (7 women); includes 15 minority (6 African Americans, 3 Asian Americans or Pacific Islanders, 5 Hispanic Americans, 1 Native American). Average age 42. 29 applicants, 90% accepted, 15 enrolled. *Application deadline:* Applications are processed on a rolling basis. *Application fee:* $50.
**Expenses:** Tuition: Part-time $437 per credit hour. Required fees: $10 per credit hour. Tuition and fees vary according to degree level and program.
**Financial support:** In 2001–02, 15 students received support. Career-related internships or fieldwork, Federal Work-Study, institutionally sponsored loans, scholarships/grants, traineeships, and

unspecified assistantships available. Support available to part-time students. Financial award applicants required to submit FAFSA.

**Faculty research:** The psychological aspects of infertility medicine, depression, psychoanalytic therapy, experiential approaches to teaching.

Dr. Gary Bruss, Associate Dean, School of Psychology, 714-940-0025 Ext. 110, *Fax:* 714-940-0630, *E-mail:* gbruss@argosyu.edu.

**Application contact:** Joe Buechner, Director of Admissions, 800-716-9598, *Fax:* 714-940-0767, *E-mail:* jbuechner@argosyu.edu. *Web site:* http://www.argosyu.edu

**Find an in-depth description at www.petersons.com/gradchannel.**

### ■ ARGOSY UNIVERSITY-PHOENIX

**Program in Clinical Psychology, Phoenix, AZ 85021**

**AWARDS** MA, Psy D, Post-Doctoral Certificate.

**Faculty:** 10 full-time (5 women), 8 part-time/adjunct (3 women).

**Students:** 124 full-time (98 women), 49 part-time (43 women); includes 29 minority (14 African Americans, 7 Asian Americans or Pacific Islanders, 7 Hispanic Americans, 1 Native American). Average age 30. 150 applicants, 47% accepted, 45 enrolled. In 2001, 46 degrees awarded. Terminal master's awarded for partial completion of doctoral program.

**Degree requirements:** For master's, practicum; for doctorate, thesis/dissertation, internship, practicum, comprehensive exam, registration; for Post-Doctoral Certificate, thesis or alternative, internship, practicum. *Median time to degree:* Master's–2 years full-time, 3 years part-time.

**Entrance requirements:** For master's, minimum undergraduate GPA of 3.0; for doctorate, minimum undergraduate GPA of 3.25. *Application deadline:* For fall admission, 1/15 (priority date); for winter admission, 10/15 (priority date). Applications are processed on a rolling basis. *Application fee:* $50. Electronic applications accepted.

**Expenses:** Tuition: Full-time $16,000; part-time $640 per credit. Required fees: $500; $250 per term. Full-time tuition and fees vary according to program.

**Financial support:** In 2001–02, 36 students received support, including 36 teaching assistantships with partial tuition reimbursements available; career-related internships or fieldwork, Federal Work-Study, and institutionally sponsored loans also available. Support available to part-time students. Financial award application

deadline: 3/20; financial award applicants required to submit FAFSA.

**Faculty research:** Neuropsychology, forensic psychology, health psychology/behavioral medicine, trauma psychology, culturally-responsive models of intervention.

Dr. Philinda Smith Hutchings, Director, 602-216-2600, *Fax:* 602-216-2601, *E-mail:* phutchings@argosyu.edu.

**Application contact:** Gail L. Bartkovich, Director of Admissions, 866-216-2777 Ext. 209, *Fax:* 602-216-2601, *E-mail:* gbartkovich@argosyu.edu. *Web site:* http://www.argosyu.edu/

**Find an in-depth description at www.petersons.com/gradchannel.**

### ■ ARGOSY UNIVERSITY-SAN FRANCISCO BAY AREA

**School of Behavioral Sciences, Point Richmond, CA 94804-3547**

**AWARDS** Clinical psychology (MA, Psy D); counseling psychology (MA). Part-time programs available.

**Faculty:** 8 full-time (3 women), 7 part-time/adjunct (4 women).

**Students:** 94 full-time (71 women), 41 part-time (33 women); includes 38 minority (14 African Americans, 15 Asian Americans or Pacific Islanders, 6 Hispanic Americans, 3 Native Americans). Average age 30. 185 applicants, 37% accepted. In 2001, 2 master's, 1 doctorate awarded.

**Degree requirements:** For master's, registration; for doctorate, thesis/dissertation, comprehensive exam, registration.

**Entrance requirements:** For master's, minimum GPA of 3.0, letters of recommendation; for doctorate, minimum GPA of 3.25, letters of recommendation. *Application deadline:* For fall admission, 1/15 (priority date); for winter admission, 8/15 (priority date). Applications are processed on a rolling basis. *Application fee:* $50. Electronic applications accepted.

**Expenses:** Tuition: Part-time $640 per credit.

**Financial support:** In 2001–02, 36 students received support, including teaching assistantships (averaging $1,200 per year); Federal Work-Study and scholarships/grants also available. Support available to part-time students. Financial award application deadline: 3/1.

**Faculty research:** Consciousness studies, attitudes, non-verbal communication, substance abuse prevention, HIV/AIDS.

Dr. Anarea Morrison, Clinical Psychology Department Head, 510-215-0277, *Fax:* 510-215-0299.

**Application contact:** Cynthia R. Sirkin, Director of Outreach Services, 510-215-0277 Ext. 202, *Fax:* 510-215-0299, *E-mail:* csirkin@argosy.edu.

**Find an in-depth description at www.petersons.com/gradchannel.**

### ■ ARGOSY UNIVERSITY-SARASOTA

**School of Psychology and Behavioral Sciences, Sarasota, FL 34235-8246**

**AWARDS** Counseling psychology (Ed D); guidance counseling (MA); mental health counseling (MA); organizational leadership (Ed D); pastoral community counseling (Ed D); school counseling (Ed S). Part-time and evening/weekend programs available. Postbaccalaureate distance learning degree programs offered (minimal on-campus study).

**Faculty:** 13 full-time (4 women), 19 part-time/adjunct (9 women).

**Students:** 265 full-time (180 women), 220 part-time (149 women); includes 163 minority (138 African Americans, 9 Asian Americans or Pacific Islanders, 12 Hispanic Americans, 4 Native Americans). Average age 45. In 2001, 25 master's, 24 doctorates, 5 other advanced degrees awarded.

**Degree requirements:** For master's, thesis optional; for doctorate, thesis/dissertation, comprehensive exam.

**Entrance requirements:** For master's and doctorate, TOEFL. *Application deadline:* Applications are processed on a rolling basis. *Application fee:* $50.

**Expenses:** Contact institution.

**Financial support:** Federal Work-Study available. Support available to part-time students. Financial award applicants required to submit FAFSA.

Dr. Douglas G. Riedmiller, Dean, 800-331-5995, *Fax:* 941-379-9464, *E-mail:* douglas_griedmiller@embanet.com.

**Application contact:** Admissions Representative, 800-331-5995 Ext. 221, *Fax:* 941-371-8910. *Web site:* http://www.sarasota.edu/

### ■ ARGOSY UNIVERSITY-TAMPA

**Program in Clinical Psychology, Tampa, FL 33619**

**AWARDS** MA, Psy D. Part-time programs available.

**Find an in-depth description at www.petersons.com/gradchannel.**

### ■ ARGOSY UNIVERSITY-TWIN CITIES

**Graduate Programs, Bloomington, MN 55437-9761**

**AWARDS** Clinical psychology (MA, Psy D); education (MA); professional counseling/

*Argosy University-Twin Cities (continued)*
marriage and family therapy (MA). Part-time programs available.

**Faculty:** 13 full-time (6 women), 33 part-time/adjunct (13 women).
**Students:** 233 full-time (192 women), 122 part-time (83 women); includes 9 minority (3 African Americans, 4 Asian Americans or Pacific Islanders, 1 Hispanic American, 1 Native American), 1 international. Average age 31. 224 applicants, 62% accepted, 95 enrolled. In 2001, 27 master's, 41 doctorates awarded. Terminal master's awarded for partial completion of doctoral program.
**Degree requirements:** For master's, thesis (for some programs); for doctorate, thesis/dissertation, internship, research project, comprehensive exam. *Median time to degree:* Master's–2 years full-time, 3 years part-time; doctorate–5 years full-time, 6 years part-time.
**Entrance requirements:** For master's, GRE or MAT, minimum GPA of 3.0 (clinical psychology), 2.8 (professional counseling/marriage and family therapy); interview; for doctorate, GRE or MAT, minimum GPA of 3.25, interview. *Application deadline:* For fall admission, 5/15 (priority date); for winter admission, 1/15 (priority date). Applications are processed on a rolling basis. *Application fee:* $50. Electronic applications accepted.
**Expenses:** Tuition: Part-time $424 per credit hour. Required fees: $31 per year. Tuition and fees vary according to program and student level.
**Financial support:** In 2001–02, 12 fellowships with partial tuition reimbursements, 12 teaching assistantships with partial tuition reimbursements were awarded. Career-related internships or fieldwork and Federal Work-Study also available. Support available to part-time students. Financial award application deadline: 3/14; financial award applicants required to submit FAFSA.
**Faculty research:** Cognitive behavioral therapy, human development, psychological assessment, marriage and family therapy, health psychology, physical/sexual abuse.
Dr. Jack T. O'Regan, Vice President Academic Affairs, 952-252-7575, *Fax:* 952-921-9574, *E-mail:* joregan@argosyu.edu.
**Application contact:** Jennifer Radke, Graduate Admissions Representative, 952-921-9500 Ext. 353, *Fax:* 952-921-9574, *E-mail:* tcadmissions@argosyu.edu. *Web site:* http://www.aspp.edu/
**Find an in-depth description at www.petersons.com/gradchannel.**

■ **ARGOSY UNIVERSITY-WASHINGTON D.C.**
**Professional Programs in Psychology, Arlington, VA 22209**

**AWARDS** Clinical psychology (MA, Psy D, Certificate); counseling psychology (MA); forensic psychology (MA). Part-time and evening/weekend programs available.

**Faculty:** 12 full-time (7 women), 43 part-time/adjunct (26 women).
**Students:** 304 full-time (237 women), 119 part-time (96 women); includes 112 minority (83 African Americans, 15 Asian Americans or Pacific Islanders, 11 Hispanic Americans, 3 Native Americans), 1 international. Average age 33. 341 applicants, 59% accepted. In 2001, 26 master's, 20 doctorates awarded.
**Degree requirements:** For master's, thesis (for some programs), practicum, comprehensive exam (for some programs); for doctorate, thesis/dissertation, internship, comprehensive exam. *Median time to degree:* Master's–2 years full-time, 3 years part-time; doctorate–6 years full-time.
**Entrance requirements:** For master's, clinical experience, minimum GPA of 3.0; for doctorate, clinical experience, minimum GPA of 3.25. *Application deadline:* For fall admission, 1/15 (priority date); for spring admission, 10/15. Applications are processed on a rolling basis. *Application fee:* $55. Electronic applications accepted.
**Expenses:** Tuition: Full-time $6,732; part-time $374 per credit. Required fees: $22; $90 per term. Tuition and fees vary according to course load, degree level and program.
**Financial support:** In 2001–02, 347 students received support, including 2 fellowships with tuition reimbursements available (averaging $3,600 per year), 55 teaching assistantships with full and partial tuition reimbursements available (averaging $1,530 per year); research assistantships, career-related internships or fieldwork, Federal Work-Study, and scholarships/grants also available. Support available to part-time students. Financial award application deadline: 6/30; financial award applicants required to submit FAFSA.
**Faculty research:** Psychotherapy integration, minority mental health, forensic assessment, family violence, child maltreatment. *Total annual research expenditures:* $2,000.
Dr. Cynthia G. Baum, Campus President, 703-243-5300, *Fax:* 703-243-8973, *E-mail:* cbaum@argosyu.edu.
**Application contact:** Debbie Jacobs, Director of Admissions, 703-243-5300 Ext. 118, *Fax:* 703-243-8973, *E-mail:*

ddmjacobs@argosyu.edu. *Web site:* http://www.argosy.edu/
**Find an in-depth description at www.petersons.com/gradchannel.**

■ **ARIZONA STATE UNIVERSITY**
**Graduate College, College of Liberal Arts and Sciences, Department of Psychology, Tempe, AZ 85287**

**AWARDS** Behavioral neuroscience (PhD); clinical psychology (PhD); cognitive/behavioral systems (PhD); developmental psychology (PhD); environmental psychology (PhD); quantitative research methods (PhD); social psychology (PhD).

**Degree requirements:** For doctorate, thesis/dissertation.
**Entrance requirements:** For doctorate, GRE General Test, GRE Subject Test.
**Faculty research:** Reduction of personal stress, cognitive aspects of motor skills training, behavior analysis and treatment of depression.

■ **ASSUMPTION COLLEGE**
**Graduate School, Department of Psychology, Worcester, MA 01609-1296**

**AWARDS** Counseling psychology (MA, CAGS). Part-time and evening/weekend programs available.

**Faculty:** 5 full-time (2 women), 8 part-time/adjunct (3 women).
**Students:** 77 (62 women); includes 1 minority (Asian American or Pacific Islander). 20 applicants, 95% accepted. In 2001, 25 degrees awarded.
**Degree requirements:** For master's, internship, practicum.
**Entrance requirements:** For master's, TOEFL. *Application deadline:* Applications are processed on a rolling basis. *Application fee:* $30.
**Expenses:** Tuition: Part-time $1,005 per credit.
**Financial support:** In 2001–02, 9 fellowships with partial tuition reimbursements (averaging $9,360 per year) were awarded; career-related internships or fieldwork also available. Support available to part-time students. Financial award applicants required to submit FAFSA.
**Faculty research:** Mood disorders, adjustment to life-threatening illness, perception of movement, socio-emotional development of young children, discovery vs. disclosure.
Dr. Leonard A. Doerfler, Chairperson, 508-767-7554, *E-mail:* doerfler@assumption.edu. *Web site:* http://www.assumption.edu/

# ■ AUBURN UNIVERSITY

**Graduate School, College of Liberal Arts, Department of Psychology, Auburn University, AL 36849**

**AWARDS** MS, PhD. Part-time programs available.

**Faculty:** 21 full-time (5 women).
**Students:** 45 full-time (32 women), 26 part-time (18 women); includes 9 minority (5 African Americans, 1 Asian American or Pacific Islander, 1 Hispanic American, 2 Native Americans), 3 international. 151 applicants, 13% accepted. In 2001, 11 master's, 18 doctorates awarded.
**Degree requirements:** For doctorate, thesis/dissertation.
**Entrance requirements:** For master's, GRE General Test, GRE Subject Test, minimum GPA of 3.25 in psychology, 3.0 overall; for doctorate, GRE General Test, GRE Subject Test. *Application deadline:* For fall admission, 7/7; for spring admission, 11/24. Applications are processed on a rolling basis. *Application fee:* $25 ($50 for international students). Electronic applications accepted.
**Financial support:** Research assistantships, teaching assistantships, Federal Work-Study available. Support available to part-time students. Financial award application deadline: 3/15.
**Faculty research:** Clinical psychology, learning, industrial psychology, organizational psychology. *Total annual research expenditures:* $200,000.
Dr. Lewis M. Barker, Chair, 334-844-4412.
**Application contact:** Dr. John F. Pritchett, Dean of the Graduate School, 334-844-4700, *E-mail:* hatchlb@ mail.auburn.edu.

# ■ AUBURN UNIVERSITY MONTGOMERY

**School of Sciences, Department of Psychology, Montgomery, AL 36124-4023**

**AWARDS** MSPG. Part-time and evening/weekend programs available.

**Students:** 12 full-time (5 women), 18 part-time (13 women); includes 9 minority (7 African Americans, 1 Hispanic American, 1 Native American), 1 international. Average age 30. In 2001, 13 degrees awarded.
**Degree requirements:** For master's, thesis optional.
**Entrance requirements:** For master's, GRE General Test or MAT. *Application deadline:* Applications are processed on a rolling basis. *Application fee:* $25. Electronic applications accepted.
**Expenses:** Tuition, state resident: full-time $3,072; part-time $128 per credit hour.

Tuition, nonresident: full-time $9,216; part-time $384 per credit hour.
**Financial support:** In 2001–02, 7 teaching assistantships were awarded; career-related internships or fieldwork and scholarships/grants also available. Support available to part-time students. Financial award application deadline: 3/1; financial award applicants required to submit FAFSA.
**Faculty research:** Community service, diagnosis, behavior modification.
Dr. Allen K. Hess, Head, 334-244-3310, *Fax:* 334-244-3826, *E-mail:* allen@ strudel.aum.edu.

# ■ AUGUSTA STATE UNIVERSITY

**Graduate Studies, College of Arts and Sciences, Department of Psychology, Augusta, GA 30904-2200**

**AWARDS** MS. Part-time programs available.

**Faculty:** 8 full-time (4 women).
**Students:** 24 full-time (21 women); includes 5 minority (4 African Americans, 1 Asian American or Pacific Islander). Average age 27. 32 applicants, 50% accepted, 16 enrolled. In 2001, 6 degrees awarded.
**Degree requirements:** For master's, written/oral exam, thesis optional.
**Entrance requirements:** For master's, GRE General Test, minimum GPA of 2.5, bachelor's degree in psychology or equivalent course work. *Application deadline:* For fall admission, 8/1 (priority date). Applications are processed on a rolling basis. *Application fee:* $20.
**Expenses:** Tuition, area resident: Full-time $2,320; part-time $97 per credit hour. Required fees: $175.
**Financial support:** In 2001–02, 17 research assistantships with partial tuition reimbursements (averaging $2,400 per year) were awarded; career-related internships or fieldwork, Federal Work-Study, and institutionally sponsored loans also available. Financial award application deadline: 4/15; financial award applicants required to submit FAFSA.
**Faculty research:** Developmental, cognitive, gender and aging issues; consumer behavior; conditioned taste aversions; circadian rhythms; use of slang and offensive language; social conformity.
Dr. Deborah S. Richardson, Chair, 706-737-1694.
**Application contact:** Phyllis Boyd, Degree Program Specialist, 706-737-1694, *Fax:* 706-737-1773, *E-mail:* pboyd@aug.edu.

# ■ AUSTIN PEAY STATE UNIVERSITY

**Graduate School, College of Arts and Sciences, Department of Psychology, Clarksville, TN 37044-0001**

**AWARDS** Clinical psychology (MA); guidance and counseling (MS); psychological science (MA); school psychology (MA). Part-time programs available.

**Degree requirements:** For master's, thesis.
**Entrance requirements:** For master's, GRE General Test, minimum GPA of 3.0. *Web site:* http://www.apsu.edu/

# ■ AVILA UNIVERSITY

**Graduate Programs, Department of Education and Psychology, Program in Psychology, Kansas City, MO 64145-1698**

**AWARDS** Counseling psychology (MS). Part-time and evening/weekend programs available.

**Faculty:** 4 full-time (2 women), 4 part-time/adjunct (3 women).
**Students:** 12 full-time (10 women), 35 part-time (27 women); includes 4 minority (1 African American, 1 Asian American or Pacific Islander, 2 Hispanic Americans). Average age 35. 15 applicants, 100% accepted. In 2001, 17 degrees awarded.
**Degree requirements:** For master's, final exam.
**Entrance requirements:** For master's, GRE General Test, TOEFL, minimum GPA of 3.0 in last 60 hours. *Application deadline:* For fall admission, 4/30 (priority date); for spring admission, 11/30. Applications are processed on a rolling basis. *Application fee:* $0. Electronic applications accepted.
**Expenses:** Tuition: Part-time $335 per credit hour. Required fees: $5 per credit hour.
**Financial support:** In 2001–02, 1 research assistantship was awarded; career-related internships or fieldwork also available. Support available to part-time students. Financial award applicants required to submit FAFSA.
**Faculty research:** Preparation for working in mental health services.
Dr. Cathy Bogart, Director, 816-501-3792, *Fax:* 816-501-2455, *E-mail:* bogartcj@ mail.avila.edu.
**Application contact:** Susan Randolph, Admissions Office, 816-501-3792, *Fax:* 816-501-2455, *E-mail:* randolphs@ mail.avila.edu. *Web site:* http:// www.avila.edu/departments/psychology/ mscpweb.htm

## ■ AZUSA PACIFIC UNIVERSITY

**School of Education and Behavioral Studies, Department of Graduate Psychology, Azusa, CA 91702-7000**

**AWARDS** Clinical psychology (MA, Psy D); family therapy (MFT). Part-time and evening/weekend programs available.

**Students:** 87 full-time (65 women), 47 part-time (33 women); includes 43 minority (10 African Americans, 15 Asian Americans or Pacific Islanders, 17 Hispanic Americans, 1 Native American), 7 international.
**Degree requirements:** For master's, 250 hours of clinical experience, individual and group therapy.
**Entrance requirements:** For master's, Minnesota Multiphasic Personality Inventory, interview, minimum GPA of 3.0. *Application deadline:* For fall admission, 6/30 (priority date). Applications are processed on a rolling basis. *Application fee:* $45 ($65 for international students).
**Expenses:** Tuition: Part-time $265 per unit. Required fees: $175 per semester. Tuition and fees vary according to degree level and program.
Dr. Mark Stanton, Chair, 626-815-5008.
**Find an in-depth description at www.petersons.com/gradchannel.**

## ■ BALL STATE UNIVERSITY

**Graduate School, College of Sciences and Humanities, Department of Psychological Science, Muncie, IN 47306-1099**

**AWARDS** Clinical psychology (MA); cognitive and social processes (MA).

**Faculty:** 21.
**Students:** 30 full-time (20 women), 4 part-time (2 women); includes 3 minority (2 African Americans, 1 Asian American or Pacific Islander), 6 international. Average age 23. 66 applicants, 39% accepted. In 2001, 13 degrees awarded.
*Application fee:* $25 ($35 for international students).
**Expenses:** Tuition, state resident: full-time $4,068; part-time $2,542. Tuition, nonresident: full-time $10,944; part-time $6,462. Required fees: $1,000; $500 per term.
**Financial support:** In 2001–02, 17 research assistantships with full tuition reimbursements (averaging $6,733 per year) were awarded. Financial award application deadline: 3/1.
Dr. David Perkins, Chairman, 765-285-1690, *Fax:* 765-285-8980, *E-mail:* dperkins@bsu.edu.

**Application contact:** Dr. Kerri Pickel, Graduate Program Director, 765-285-1690, *Fax:* 765-285-8980, *E-mail:* kpickel@bsu.edu. *Web site:* http://www.bsu.edu/psysc/

## ■ BARRY UNIVERSITY

**School of Arts and Sciences, Department of Psychology, Miami Shores, FL 33161-6695**

**AWARDS** Clinical psychology (MS); school psychology (MS, SSP). Part-time and evening/weekend programs available.
**Faculty:** 9 full-time (5 women).
**Students:** 61. Average age 29. In 2001, 32 master's, 7 other advanced degrees awarded.
**Degree requirements:** For master's, thesis, practicum.
**Entrance requirements:** For master's, GRE General Test, minimum GPA of 3.0, previous course work in psychology. *Application deadline:* Applications are processed on a rolling basis. *Application fee:* $30. Electronic applications accepted.
**Expenses:** Tuition: Full-time $12,480. Tuition and fees vary according to degree level and program.
**Financial support:** In 2001–02, 38 students received support, including 5 research assistantships with partial tuition reimbursements available (averaging $3,000 per year); career-related internships or fieldwork and tuition waivers (partial) also available. Support available to part-time students. Financial award application deadline: 5/1; financial award applicants required to submit FAFSA.
**Faculty research:** Closed head injury, memory and aging, infant/mother interaction, evolutionary aspects of behavior, gender roles.
Dr. Linda Peterson, Chair, 305-899-3274, *Fax:* 305-899-3279, *E-mail:* lpeterson@mail.barry.edu.
**Application contact:** Dave Fletcher, Director of Graduate Admissions, 305-899-3113, *Fax:* 305-899-2971, *E-mail:* dfletcher@mail.barry.edu.

## ■ BAYAMÓN CENTRAL UNIVERSITY

**Graduate Programs, Program in Psychology, Bayamón, PR 00960-1725**
**AWARDS** MA. Part-time and evening/weekend programs available.
**Faculty:** 4 part-time/adjunct (1 woman).
**Students:** 13 full-time (7 women), 10 part-time (8 women); all minorities (all Hispanic Americans). 3 applicants, 100% accepted. In 2001, 4 degrees awarded.
**Entrance requirements:** For master's, PAEG, bachelor's degree in psychology or related field. *Application deadline:* For fall

admission, 10/3; for winter admission, 12/20; for spring admission, 4/3. *Application fee:* $25.
**Expenses:** Tuition: Full-time $5,400; part-time $150 per credit. Required fees: $320.
**Financial support:** Institutionally sponsored loans available.
Dra. María de Lourdes Rivera, Head, 787-786-3030 Ext. 2201.
**Application contact:** Christine Hernández, Director of Admissions, 787-786-3030 Ext. 2100, *Fax:* 787-740-2200, *E-mail:* chernandez@ucb.edu.pr.

## ■ BAYLOR UNIVERSITY

**Graduate School, College of Arts and Sciences, Department of Psychology and Neuroscience, Waco, TX 76798**

**AWARDS** Clinical psychology (MSCP, Psy D); neuroscience (MA, PhD).

**Students:** 49 full-time (36 women), 4 part-time (2 women); includes 6 minority (2 Asian Americans or Pacific Islanders, 4 Hispanic Americans), 2 international. In 2001, 8 master's, 11 doctorates awarded.
**Degree requirements:** For doctorate, comprehensive exam.
**Entrance requirements:** For master's, GRE General Test; for doctorate, GRE General Test, GRE Subject Test (Psy D). *Application deadline:* Applications are processed on a rolling basis. *Application fee:* $25.
**Expenses:** Tuition: Part-time $379 per semester hour. Required fees: $42 per semester hour. $101 per semester. Tuition and fees vary according to program.
**Financial support:** Research assistantships, teaching assistantships, career-related internships or fieldwork, Federal Work-Study, institutionally sponsored loans, tuition waivers (partial), and practicum stipends available. Financial award applicants required to submit FAFSA.
Dr. Jim H. Patton, Chairman, 254-710-2961, *Fax:* 254-710-3033, *E-mail:* jim_patton@baylor.edu.
**Application contact:** Suzanne Keener, Administrative Assistant, 254-710-3588, *Fax:* 254-710-3870, *E-mail:* graduate_school@baylor.edu. *Web site:* http://www.baylor.edu/~Psychology/

## ■ BETHEL COLLEGE

**Center for Graduate and Continuing Studies, Department of Psychology, St. Paul, MN 55112-6999**

**AWARDS** MA. Evening/weekend programs available.

**Faculty:** 7 full-time (4 women), 1 (woman) part-time/adjunct.
**Students:** 26 full-time (24 women), 4 part-time (all women). Average age 30. In 2001, 15 degrees awarded.

**Degree requirements:** For master's, practicum, thesis optional.
**Entrance requirements:** For master's, MAT, interview, minimum GPA of 3.0, previous course work in psychology and statistics. *Application deadline:* For fall admission, 3/1 (priority date). *Application fee:* $25.
**Expenses:** Tuition: Part-time $325 per credit. One-time fee: $125 full-time.
**Financial support:** Institutionally sponsored loans and scholarships/grants available. Financial award applicants required to submit FAFSA.
Dr. James E. Koch, Chair, 651-638-6415, *Fax:* 651-635-1464, *E-mail:* je-koch@bethel.edu.
**Application contact:** Vanessa Beaudry, Senior Admissions Coordinator, 651-635-8000, *Fax:* 651-635-1464, *E-mail:* v_beaudry@bethel.edu. *Web site:* http://www.bethel.edu/cgcs/

## ■ BIOLA UNIVERSITY
**Rosemead School of Psychology, La Mirada, CA 90639-0001**
**AWARDS** MA, PhD, Psy D.
**Faculty:** 14 full-time (5 women), 8 part-time/adjunct (3 women).
**Students:** 130 full-time (77 women); includes 24 minority (1 African American, 19 Asian Americans or Pacific Islanders, 4 Hispanic Americans), 13 international. Average age 29. 116 applicants, 30% accepted, 23 enrolled. In 2001, 17 master's, 30 doctorates awarded. Terminal master's awarded for partial completion of doctoral program.
**Degree requirements:** For master's and doctorate, thesis/dissertation, internship.
**Entrance requirements:** For master's and doctorate, GRE General Test, Minnesota Multiphasic Personality Inventory, interview, 30 undergraduate credits in psychology. *Application deadline:* For fall admission, 1/15. *Application fee:* $45.
**Expenses:** Contact institution.
**Financial support:** Research assistantships, teaching assistantships, career-related internships or fieldwork, institutionally sponsored loans, and scholarships/grants available. Support available to part-time students. Financial award application deadline: 3/2; financial award applicants required to submit FAFSA.
**Faculty research:** Integration of psychology and theology, practice of psychotherapy, therapy process and outcomes.
Dr. Patricia Pike, Administrative Dean, 562-903-4867, *Fax:* 562-903-4864.
**Application contact:** Roy M. Allinson, Director of Graduate Admissions, 562-903-4752, *Fax:* 562-903-4709, *E-mail:*

admissions@biola.edu. *Web site:* http://www.rosemead.edu/

## ■ BOSTON COLLEGE
**Graduate School of Arts and Sciences, Department of Psychology, Chestnut Hill, MA 02467-3800**
**AWARDS** PhD.
**Students:** 5 full-time (all women), 12 part-time (11 women); includes 3 minority (2 Asian Americans or Pacific Islanders, 1 Native American), 3 international. 110 applicants, 11% accepted. In 2001, 3 degrees awarded.
**Degree requirements:** For doctorate, thesis/dissertation, fieldwork.
**Entrance requirements:** For doctorate, GRE General Test, GRE Subject Test. *Application deadline:* For fall admission, 1/2. *Application fee:* $50.
**Expenses:** Tuition: Full-time $17,664; part-time $8,832 per semester.
**Financial support:** Fellowships, research assistantships, teaching assistantships, career-related internships or fieldwork available. Support available to part-time students. Financial award application deadline: 3/1; financial award applicants required to submit FAFSA.
**Faculty research:** Social, cognitive, and biological processes.
Dr. Hiram Brownell, Chairperson, 617-552-4100, *E-mail:* hiram.brownell@bc.edu.
**Application contact:** Dr. Ellen Winner, Graduate Program Director, 617-552-4108, *E-mail:* ellen.winner@bc.edu. *Web site:* http://www.bc.edu/bc_org/avp/cas/psych/psych.html

## ■ BOSTON GRADUATE SCHOOL OF PSYCHOANALYSIS
**Master's, Certificate, and Doctoral Programs, Brookline, MA 02446-4602**
**AWARDS** MA, Psya D, Certificate. Part-time programs available.
**Faculty:** 10 full-time (9 women), 10 part-time/adjunct (4 women).
**Students:** 27 full-time (17 women), 49 part-time (39 women). 19 applicants, 53% accepted. In 2001, 7 master's, 5 other advanced degrees awarded.
**Degree requirements:** For master's and Certificate, thesis.
**Entrance requirements:** For master's, interview; for Certificate, interview, master of arts degree. *Application deadline:* Applications are processed on a rolling basis. *Application fee:* $100. Electronic applications accepted.
**Expenses:** Tuition: Full-time $16,870. Tuition and fees vary according to degree level, program and student level.

**Financial support:** In 2001–02, 6 students received support. Career-related internships or fieldwork and unspecified assistantships available. Financial award applicants required to submit FAFSA.
**Faculty research:** The effect of extra-analytic contact on the analysis, psychoanalytic intervention with schizophrenia, emotional learning in the classroom, psychoanalytic techniques in the geriatric setting, addictions research.
Dr. Jane Snyder, Dean, 617-277-3915, *Fax:* 617-277-0312, *E-mail:* bgsp@bgsp.edu.
**Application contact:** Sherry Ceridan, Registrar, 617-277-3915, *Fax:* 617-277-0312, *E-mail:* bgsp@bgsp.edu.
**Find an in-depth description at www.petersons.com/gradchannel.**

## ■ BOSTON UNIVERSITY
**Graduate School of Arts and Sciences, Department of Psychology, Boston, MA 02215**
**AWARDS** MA, PhD.
**Students:** 132 full-time (108 women), 18 part-time (15 women); includes 23 minority (11 African Americans, 10 Asian Americans or Pacific Islanders, 2 Hispanic Americans), 22 international. Average age 29. 692 applicants, 21% accepted, 48 enrolled. In 2001, 57 master's, 25 doctorates awarded. Terminal master's awarded for partial completion of doctoral program.
**Degree requirements:** For master's, one foreign language, comprehensive exam, registration; for doctorate, one foreign language, thesis/dissertation, comprehensive/qualifying exam.
**Entrance requirements:** For master's and doctorate, GRE General Test, TOEFL. *Application deadline:* For fall admission, 1/15. *Application fee:* $60.
**Expenses:** Tuition: Full-time $25,872; part-time $340 per credit. Required fees: $40 per semester. Part-time tuition and fees vary according to class time, course level and program.
**Financial support:** In 2001–02, 84 students received support, including 4 fellowships (averaging $14,000 per year), 42 research assistantships with full tuition reimbursements available (averaging $12,500 per year), 20 teaching assistantships with full and partial tuition reimbursements available (averaging $12,500 per year); career-related internships or fieldwork, Federal Work-Study, and unspecified assistantships also available. Support available to part-time students. Financial award application deadline: 1/15; financial award applicants required to submit FAFSA.

*Boston University (continued)*
Henry Marcucella, Chairman, 617-353-2571, *Fax:* 617-353-6933, *E-mail:* hm@bu.edu.
**Application contact:** Joanne K. Palfai, Academic Administrator, 617-353-2064, *Fax:* 617-353-6933, *E-mail:* jpalfai@bu.edu. *Web site:* http://www.bu.edu/psych/

■ **BOSTON UNIVERSITY**
**School of Medicine, Division of Graduate Medical Sciences, Program in Mental Health and Behavioral Medicine, Boston, MA 02215**
**AWARDS** MA.

**Faculty:** 18 full-time (8 women).
**Degree requirements:** For master's, qualifying exam.
**Entrance requirements:** For master's, GRE General Test, TOEFL. *Application deadline:* Applications are processed on a rolling basis. *Application fee:* $50.
**Expenses:** Tuition: Full-time $25,872; part-time $340 per credit. Required fees: $40 per semester. Part-time tuition and fees vary according to class time, course level and program.
**Faculty research:** HIV/AIDS, neurosciences, autism, serious mental illness, sports psychology. *Total annual research expenditures:* $3 million.
Dr. Stephen Brady, Director, 617-638-8689, *Fax:* 617-626-8929, *E-mail:* sbrady@bu.edu.
**Application contact:** Information Contact, 617-638-8689, *Fax:* 617-626-8929. *Web site:* http://www.bumc.bu.edu

■ **BOWLING GREEN STATE UNIVERSITY**
**Graduate College, College of Arts and Sciences, Department of Psychology, Bowling Green, OH 43403**
**AWARDS** Clinical psychology (MA, PhD); developmental psychology (MA, PhD); experimental psychology (MA, PhD); industrial/organizational psychology (MA, PhD); quantitative psychology (MA, PhD).
**Faculty:** 31.
**Students:** 89 full-time (57 women), 27 part-time (18 women); includes 14 minority (3 African Americans, 7 Asian Americans or Pacific Islanders, 4 Hispanic Americans), 9 international. Average age 27. 274 applicants, 15% accepted, 24 enrolled. In 2001, 10 master's, 17 doctorates awarded. Terminal master's awarded for partial completion of doctoral program.
**Degree requirements:** For master's and doctorate, thesis/dissertation.
**Entrance requirements:** For master's and doctorate, GRE General Test, TOEFL. *Application deadline:* For fall admission,

1/15. *Application fee:* $30. Electronic applications accepted.
**Expenses:** Tuition, state resident: full-time $7,376; part-time $342 per credit hour. Tuition, nonresident: full-time $13,628; part-time $640 per credit hour.
**Financial support:** In 2001–02, 30 research assistantships with full tuition reimbursements (averaging $9,452 per year), 32 teaching assistantships with full tuition reimbursements (averaging $9,607 per year) were awarded. Career-related internships or fieldwork, Federal Work-Study, institutionally sponsored loans, tuition waivers (full), and unspecified assistantships also available. Financial award applicants required to submit FAFSA.
**Faculty research:** Personnel psychology, developmental-mathematical models, behavioral medication, brain process, child/adolescent social cognition.
Dr. Dale Klopfer, Chair, 419-372-2733.
**Application contact:** Dr. Eric Dubow, Graduate Coordinator, 419-372-2556.

■ **BRANDEIS UNIVERSITY**
**Graduate School of Arts and Sciences, Department of Psychology, Waltham, MA 02454-9110**
**AWARDS** Cognitive neuroscience (PhD); general psychology (MA); social/developmental psychology (PhD). Part-time programs available.
**Faculty:** 18 full-time (4 women), 6 part-time/adjunct (3 women).
**Students:** 25 full-time (18 women); includes 8 minority (1 African American, 5 Asian Americans or Pacific Islanders, 2 Hispanic Americans). Average age 29. 69 applicants, 35% accepted. In 2001, 4 master's, 2 doctorates awarded. Terminal master's awarded for partial completion of doctoral program.
**Degree requirements:** For master's and doctorate, thesis/dissertation.
**Entrance requirements:** For master's, GRE General Test; for doctorate, GRE General Test, GRE Subject Test. *Application deadline:* Applications are processed on a rolling basis. *Application fee:* $60. Electronic applications accepted.
**Expenses:** Tuition: Full-time $27,392. Required fees: $35.
**Financial support:** In 2001–02, 16 students received support, including 12 fellowships with full tuition reimbursements available (averaging $13,600 per year), 4 research assistantships with partial tuition reimbursements available (averaging $2,000 per year); scholarships/grants, traineeships, and tuition waivers (partial) also available. Support available to part-time students. Financial award application

deadline: 5/1; financial award applicants required to submit CSS PROFILE or FAFSA.
**Faculty research:** Development, cognition, social aging, perception. *Total annual research expenditures:* $2.2 million.
Margie Lachman, Director of Graduate Studies, 781-736-3255, *Fax:* 781-736-3291, *E-mail:* lachman@brandeis.edu.
**Application contact:** Janice Steinberg, Graduate Admissions Coordinator, 781-736-3303, *Fax:* 781-736-3291, *E-mail:* steinberg@brandeis.edu. *Web site:* http://www.brandeis.edu/departments/psych/

■ **BRIDGEWATER STATE COLLEGE**
**School of Graduate and Continuing Education, School of Arts and Sciences, Department of Psychology, Bridgewater, MA 02325-0001**
**AWARDS** MA. Part-time and evening/weekend programs available.

**Entrance requirements:** For master's, GRE General Test, GRE Subject Test. *Application deadline:* For fall admission, 3/1 (priority date); for spring admission, 10/1 (priority date). *Application fee:* $50.
**Expenses:** Tuition, state resident: part-time $135 per credit. Tuition, nonresident: part-time $294 per credit. Tuition and fees vary according to class time.

■ **BRIGHAM YOUNG UNIVERSITY**
**Graduate Studies, College of Family, Home, and Social Sciences, Department of Psychology, Provo, UT 84602-1001**
**AWARDS** Clinical psychology (PhD); general psychology (MS); psychology (PhD).
**Faculty:** 31 full-time (6 women), 10 part-time/adjunct (4 women).
**Students:** 92 full-time (45 women), 17 part-time (10 women); includes 5 minority (4 Asian Americans or Pacific Islanders, 1 Hispanic American), 6 international. Average age 30. 113 applicants, 24% accepted. In 2001, 8 master's, 9 doctorates awarded.
**Degree requirements:** For master's, thesis; for doctorate, thesis/dissertation, publishable paper. *Median time to degree:* Master's–2 years full-time; doctorate–5 years full-time.
**Entrance requirements:** For master's and doctorate, GRE General Test, minimum GPA of 3.0 in last 60 hours. *Application deadline:* For fall admission, 1/31. *Application fee:* $50. Electronic applications accepted.
**Expenses:** Tuition: Full-time $3,860; part-time $214 per hour.
**Financial support:** In 2001–02, 65 students received support, including research assistantships with partial tuition

reimbursements available (averaging $3,000 per year), 26 teaching assistantships with partial tuition reimbursements available (averaging $3,000 per year); career-related internships or fieldwork, scholarships/grants, tuition waivers (partial), and unspecified assistantships also available. Financial award application deadline: 1/31.
**Faculty research:** Psychotherapy process, Alzheimer's disease/dementia, psychology and law, health, psychology, magnetic resonance imaging and autism. *Total annual research expenditures:* $800,000.
Dr. Erin D. Bigler, Chair, 801-422-4287, *Fax:* 801-378-7862.
**Application contact:** Karen A. Christensen, Graduate Secretary, 801-422-4560, *Fax:* 801-378-7862, *E-mail:* karen_christensen@byu.edu.

■ **BROOKLYN COLLEGE OF THE CITY UNIVERSITY OF NEW YORK**
**Division of Graduate Studies, Department of Psychology, Brooklyn, NY 11210-2889**
**AWARDS** Experimental psychology (MA); industrial and organizational psychology (MA), including industrial and organizational psychology-human relations, psychology-organizational psychology and behavior; psychology (PhD). Part-time programs available.
**Students:** 7 full-time (4 women), 87 part-time (63 women); includes 40 minority (24 African Americans, 5 Asian Americans or Pacific Islanders, 11 Hispanic Americans), 11 international. 104 applicants, 59% accepted. In 2001, 47 degrees awarded.
**Degree requirements:** For master's, thesis or alternative, comprehensive exam.
**Entrance requirements:** For master's, TOEFL, minimum GPA of 3.0; for doctorate, GRE. *Application deadline:* For fall admission, 3/1 (priority date); for spring admission, 11/1. Applications are processed on a rolling basis. *Application fee:* $40.
**Expenses:** Tuition, state resident: full-time $4,350; part-time $185 per credit. Tuition, nonresident: full-time $7,600; part-time $320 per credit.
**Financial support:** Career-related internships or fieldwork, Federal Work-Study, institutionally sponsored loans, scholarships/grants, and tuition waivers (partial) available. Support available to part-time students. Financial award application deadline: 5/1; financial award applicants required to submit FAFSA.
Dr. Glen Hass, Chairperson, 718-951-5601, *Fax:* 718-951-4814.

**Application contact:** Dr. Benzion Chanowitz, Graduate Deputy, 718-951-5019, *Fax:* 718-951-4814, *E-mail:* psych-ma@brooklyn.cuny.edu. *Web site:* http://academic.brooklyn.cuny.edu/psych

■ **BROWN UNIVERSITY**
**Graduate School, Department of Psychology, Providence, RI 02912**
**AWARDS** AM, Sc M, PhD.
**Degree requirements:** For master's and doctorate, thesis/dissertation.
**Entrance requirements:** For master's and doctorate, GRE General Test, GRE Subject Test.

■ **BRYN MAWR COLLEGE**
**Graduate School of Arts and Sciences, Department of Psychology, Bryn Mawr, PA 19010-2899**
**AWARDS** Clinical developmental psychology (PhD). Part-time programs available.
**Students:** 14 full-time (12 women), 22 part-time (all women); includes 2 minority (both Asian Americans or Pacific Islanders). 57 applicants, 7% accepted. In 2001, 1 doctorate awarded.
**Degree requirements:** For doctorate, one foreign language, thesis/dissertation.
**Entrance requirements:** For doctorate, GRE General Test. *Application deadline:* For fall admission, 2/1. *Application fee:* $25.
**Expenses:** Tuition: Full-time $22,260.
**Financial support:** In 2001–02, 6 teaching assistantships were awarded; fellowships, career-related internships or fieldwork, Federal Work-Study, institutionally sponsored loans, and tuition awards also available. Support available to part-time students. Financial award application deadline: 1/15.
Dr. Leslie Rescorla, Chair, 610-526-5190.
**Application contact:** Graduate School of Arts and Sciences, 610-526-5072.

■ **BUCKNELL UNIVERSITY**
**Graduate Studies, College of Arts and Sciences, Department of Psychology, Lewisburg, PA 17837**
**AWARDS** MA, MS. Part-time programs available.
**Faculty:** 12 full-time (2 women).
**Students:** 3 full-time (2 women).
**Degree requirements:** For master's, thesis.
**Entrance requirements:** For master's, GRE General Test, GRE Subject Test, TOEFL, minimum GPA of 2.8. *Application deadline:* For fall admission, 6/1 (priority date); for spring admission, 12/1 (priority date). Applications are processed on a rolling basis. *Application fee:* $25.
**Expenses:** Tuition: Part-time $2,875 per course.

**Financial support:** Unspecified assistantships available. Financial award application deadline: 3/1.
Kimberly Daubman, Head, 570-577-1200.
*Web site:* http://www.bucknell.edu/

■ **CALIFORNIA INSTITUTE OF INTEGRAL STUDIES**
**Graduate Programs, School of Consciousness and Transformation, San Francisco, CA 94103**
**AWARDS** Cultural anthropology and social transformation (MA); East-West psychology (MA, PhD); philosophy and religion (MA, PhD), including Asian and comparative studies, philosophy, cosmology, and consciousness, women's spirituality; social and cultural anthropology (PhD); transformative learning and change (PhD). Part-time and evening/weekend programs available. Postbaccalaureate distance learning degree programs offered (minimal on-campus study).
**Faculty:** 20 full-time (9 women), 72 part-time/adjunct (35 women).
**Students:** 60 full-time, 143 part-time. 157 applicants, 78% accepted, 85 enrolled. In 2001, 58 master's, 21 doctorates awarded. Terminal master's awarded for partial completion of doctoral program.
**Degree requirements:** For master's, comprehensive exam; for doctorate, thesis/dissertation, comprehensive exam.
**Entrance requirements:** For master's, TOEFL, minimum GPA of 3.0; for doctorate, TOEFL, master's degree. *Application deadline:* For fall admission, 3/15 (priority date); for spring admission, 10/15 (priority date). Applications are processed on a rolling basis. *Application fee:* $65.
**Expenses:** Tuition: Full-time $10,890; part-time $605 per unit. Tuition and fees vary according to degree level.
**Financial support:** Career-related internships or fieldwork, Federal Work-Study, institutionally sponsored loans, and scholarships/grants available. Support available to part-time students. Financial award application deadline: 6/15; financial award applicants required to submit FAFSA.
**Faculty research:** Altered states of consciousness, dreams, cosmology.
Daniel Deslaurier, Director, 415-575-6260, *Fax:* 415-575-1264, *E-mail:* danield@ciis.edu.
**Application contact:** Gregory E. Canada, Director of Admissions, 415-575-6155, *Fax:* 415-575-1268, *E-mail:* gregc@ciis.edu. *Web site:* http://www.ciis.edu/
**Find an in-depth description at www.petersons.com/gradchannel.**

### ■ CALIFORNIA INSTITUTE OF INTEGRAL STUDIES

**Graduate Programs, School of Professional Psychology, San Francisco, CA 94103**

**AWARDS** Drama therapy (MA); expressive arts therapy (MA, Certificate), including consulting and education (Certificate), expressive arts (Certificate), expressive arts therapy (MA); integral counseling psychology (MA); psychology (Psy D), including clinical psychology; somatics (MA, Certificate), including integral health education (Certificate), somatics (MA). Part-time and evening/weekend programs available.

**Students:** 205 full-time, 236 part-time. 298 applicants, 65% accepted, 115 enrolled.
**Degree requirements:** For master's, comprehensive exam; for doctorate, thesis/dissertation, comprehensive exam.
**Entrance requirements:** For master's, TOEFL, minimum GPA of 3.0; for doctorate, TOEFL, field experience, master's degree, minimum GPA of 3.1. *Application deadline:* Applications are processed on a rolling basis. *Application fee:* $65.
**Expenses:** Tuition: Full-time $10,890; part-time $605 per unit. Tuition and fees vary according to degree level.
**Financial support:** Career-related internships or fieldwork, Federal Work-Study, institutionally sponsored loans, and scholarships/grants available. Support available to part-time students. Financial award application deadline: 6/15; financial award applicants required to submit FAFSA.
**Faculty research:** Somatic psychology.
Dr. Harrison Voigt, Head, 415-575-6218.
**Application contact:** David Towner, Admissions Officer, 415-575-6152, *Fax:* 415-575-1268, *E-mail:* dtowner@ciis.edu.

**Find an in-depth description at www.petersons.com/gradchannel.**

### ■ CALIFORNIA LUTHERAN UNIVERSITY

**Graduate Studies, Department of Psychology, Thousand Oaks, CA 91360-2787**

**AWARDS** Clinical psychology (MS); marital and family therapy (MS). Part-time programs available.

**Degree requirements:** For master's, thesis or comprehensive exams.
**Entrance requirements:** For master's, GRE General Test, interview, minimum GPA of 3.0. *Web site:* http://www.clunet.edu/htdocs/ClinicalPsych/ClinicalPsychology.html

### ■ CALIFORNIA POLYTECHNIC STATE UNIVERSITY, SAN LUIS OBISPO

**College of Liberal Arts, Department of Psychology and Human Development, San Luis Obispo, CA 93407**

**AWARDS** Psychology (MS). Part-time programs available.

**Faculty:** 8 full-time (4 women), 3 part-time/adjunct (1 woman).
**Students:** 22 full-time (16 women), 16 part-time (14 women); includes 6 Hispanic Americans. 49 applicants, 41% accepted, 15 enrolled. In 2001, 14 degrees awarded.
**Degree requirements:** For master's, thesis optional.
**Entrance requirements:** For master's, GRE General Test, TOEFL, minimum GPA of 3.0 in last 90 quarter units. *Application deadline:* For fall admission, 2/14 (priority date). *Application fee:* $55. Electronic applications accepted.
**Expenses:** Tuition, nonresident: part-time $164 per unit. One-time fee: $2,153 part-time.
**Financial support:** Career-related internships or fieldwork, Federal Work-Study, and institutionally sponsored loans available. Support available to part-time students. Financial award application deadline: 3/2; financial award applicants required to submit FAFSA.
**Faculty research:** Eating disorders, mood disorders, neuropsychology, forensic psychology, group therapy.
Dr. Shawn Burn, Chair, 805-756-2934, *Fax:* 805-756-1134, *E-mail:* sburn@calpoly.edu.
**Application contact:** Margaret Booker, Administrative Analyst, 805-756-2456, *Fax:* 805-756-1134, *E-mail:* mbooker@calpoly.edu. *Web site:* http://www.calpoly.edu/~psychhd/masters.html

### ■ CALIFORNIA STATE POLYTECHNIC UNIVERSITY, POMONA

**Academic Affairs, College of Letters, Arts, and Social Sciences, Program in Psychology, Pomona, CA 91768-2557**

**AWARDS** MS.

**Students:** 15 full-time (13 women), 1 (woman) part-time; includes 8 minority (1 African American, 4 Asian Americans or Pacific Islanders, 3 Hispanic Americans), 1 international. Average age 27. 24 applicants, 33% accepted. In 2001, 12 degrees awarded.
**Degree requirements:** For master's, thesis or alternative.

*Application deadline:* For fall admission, 4/15. Applications are processed on a rolling basis. *Application fee:* $55. Electronic applications accepted.
**Expenses:** Tuition, nonresident: part-time $164 per unit. Required fees: $1,850.
**Financial support:** Application deadline: 3/2.
Dr. Jeffrey S. Mio, Director, 909-869-3899, *E-mail:* jsmio@csupomona.edu. *Web site:* http://www.csupomona.edu/~bhs/

### ■ CALIFORNIA STATE UNIVERSITY, BAKERSFIELD

**Division of Graduate Studies and Research, School of Humanities and Social Sciences, Program in Psychology, Bakersfield, CA 93311-1099**

**AWARDS** Family and child counseling (MFCC); psychology (MS).

**Degree requirements:** For master's, thesis.
**Entrance requirements:** For master's, GRE Subject Test. *Web site:* http://www.csub.edu/Psychology/Grcourse.htm

### ■ CALIFORNIA STATE UNIVERSITY, CHICO

**Graduate School, College of Behavioral and Social Sciences, Department of Psychology, Chico, CA 95929-0722**

**AWARDS** Counseling (MS); psychology (MA).

**Students:** 60 full-time, 13 part-time; includes 10 minority (1 African American, 3 Asian Americans or Pacific Islanders, 5 Hispanic Americans, 1 Native American). 58 applicants, 84% accepted, 31 enrolled. In 2001, 30 degrees awarded.
**Degree requirements:** For master's, thesis or alternative, oral exam.
**Entrance requirements:** For master's, GRE General Test or MAT, letters of recommendation on departmental form (3). *Application deadline:* For fall admission, 3/1. Applications are processed on a rolling basis. *Application fee:* $55. Electronic applications accepted.
**Expenses:** Tuition, state resident: full-time $2,148. Tuition, nonresident: full-time $6,576.
**Financial support:** Fellowships, teaching assistantships, career-related internships or fieldwork available.
Dr. Paul Spear, Chairman, 530-898-5147.
**Application contact:** Dr. Joseph Russo, Graduate Coordinator, 530-898-5368.

## ■ CALIFORNIA STATE UNIVERSITY, DOMINGUEZ HILLS

**College of Arts and Sciences, Program in Psychology, Carson, CA 90747-0001**

**AWARDS** Clinical psychology (MA); general psychology (MA). Evening/weekend programs available.

**Faculty:** 15 full-time, 5 part-time/adjunct.
**Students:** 19 full-time (15 women), 9 part-time (all women); includes 12 minority (5 African Americans, 1 Asian American or Pacific Islander, 6 Hispanic Americans). Average age 30. 20 applicants, 85% accepted, 4 enrolled. In 2001, 21 degrees awarded.
**Entrance requirements:** For master's, GRE General Test and GRE Subject Test or MAT, interview, minimum GPA of 3.0. *Application deadline:* For fall admission, 6/1. *Application fee:* $55.
**Expenses:** Tuition, nonresident: full-time $1,508; part-time $438 per semester. Required fees: $442; $246 per unit. $227 per semester.
Dr. Ramona Davis, Chair, 310-243-3427, *E-mail:* rdavis@hvx20.csudh.edu.

## ■ CALIFORNIA STATE UNIVERSITY, FRESNO

**Division of Graduate Studies, College of Science and Mathematics, Department of Psychology, Fresno, CA 93740-8027**

**AWARDS** MA, MS.

**Faculty:** 17 full-time (8 women).
**Students:** 24 full-time (19 women), 12 part-time (8 women); includes 11 minority (1 African American, 1 Asian American or Pacific Islander, 8 Hispanic Americans, 1 Native American). Average age 31. 15 applicants, 80% accepted, 10 enrolled. In 2001, 8 degrees awarded.
**Degree requirements:** For master's, thesis. *Median time to degree:* Master's–3 years full-time, 5 years part-time.
**Entrance requirements:** For master's, GRE General Test, GRE Subject Test, TOEFL, minimum GPA of 3.0. *Application deadline:* For fall admission, 3/1 (priority date); for spring admission, 11/1 (priority date). Applications are processed on a rolling basis. *Application fee:* $55. Electronic applications accepted.
**Expenses:** Tuition, nonresident: part-time $246 per unit. Required fees: $605 per semester. Tuition and fees vary according to course load.
**Financial support:** In 2001–02, 11 teaching assistantships were awarded; career-related internships or fieldwork, Federal Work-Study, scholarships/grants, and unspecified assistantships also available. Support available to part-time students.

Financial award application deadline: 3/1; financial award applicants required to submit FAFSA.
**Faculty research:** Oncology prediction, parenting stress, wellness, aging and memory, retrieval inhibition, anger, minority mental health.
Dr. Aroldo Rodriguez, Chair, 559-278-2691, *Fax:* 559-278-7910, *E-mail:* aroldo_rodriguez@csufresno.edu.
**Application contact:** Marilyn Wilson, Graduate Program Coordinator, 559-278-5129, *Fax:* 559-278-7910, *E-mail:* marilyn_wilson@csufresno.edu.

## ■ CALIFORNIA STATE UNIVERSITY, FULLERTON

**Graduate Studies, College of Humanities and Social Sciences, Department of Psychology, Fullerton, CA 92834-9480**

**AWARDS** Clinical/community psychology (MS); psychology (MA). Part-time programs available.

**Faculty:** 24 full-time (11 women), 28 part-time/adjunct.
**Students:** 50 full-time (41 women), 7 part-time (6 women); includes 19 minority (1 African American, 8 Asian Americans or Pacific Islanders, 10 Hispanic Americans), 1 international. Average age 28. 70 applicants, 61% accepted, 33 enrolled. In 2001, 18 degrees awarded.
**Degree requirements:** For master's, thesis.
**Entrance requirements:** For master's, GRE General Test, GRE Subject Test, undergraduate major in psychology or related field. *Application deadline:* For fall admission, 3/15. *Application fee:* $55.
**Expenses:** Tuition, nonresident: part-time $246 per unit. Required fees: $964.
**Financial support:** Teaching assistantships, career-related internships or fieldwork, Federal Work-Study, institutionally sponsored loans, and scholarships/grants available. Support available to part-time students. Financial award application deadline: 3/1.
Dr. David Perkins, Chair, 714-278-3514.

## ■ CALIFORNIA STATE UNIVERSITY, LONG BEACH

**Graduate Studies, College of Liberal Arts, Department of Psychology, Long Beach, CA 90840**

**AWARDS** MA, MS. Part-time and evening/weekend programs available.

**Students:** 20 full-time (18 women), 27 part-time (20 women); includes 13 minority (2 African Americans, 3 Asian Americans or Pacific Islanders, 7 Hispanic Americans, 1 Native American), 1 international. Average age 30. 95

applicants, 32% accepted. In 2001, 26 degrees awarded.
**Degree requirements:** For master's, thesis, comprehensive exam.
**Entrance requirements:** For master's, GRE General Test, GRE Subject Test. *Application deadline:* For fall admission, 3/1. Applications are processed on a rolling basis. *Application fee:* $55. Electronic applications accepted.
**Financial support:** Federal Work-Study, institutionally sponsored loans, and scholarships/grants available. Financial award application deadline: 3/2.
**Faculty research:** Physiological psychology, social and personality psychology, community-clinical psychology, industrial-organizational psychology, developmental psychology.
Dr. Keith Colman, Chair, 562-985-5001, *Fax:* 562-985-8004, *E-mail:* kcolman@csulb.edu.
**Application contact:** Diane Roe, Graduate Adviser, 562-985-5000, *Fax:* 562-985-8004, *E-mail:* droe@csulb.edu.

## ■ CALIFORNIA STATE UNIVERSITY, LOS ANGELES

**Graduate Studies, College of Natural and Social Sciences, Department of Psychology, Los Angeles, CA 90032-8530**

**AWARDS** MA, MS. Part-time and evening/weekend programs available.

**Faculty:** 14 full-time, 11 part-time/adjunct.
**Students:** 46 full-time (32 women), 91 part-time (68 women); includes 87 minority (8 African Americans, 21 Asian Americans or Pacific Islanders, 56 Hispanic Americans, 2 Native Americans), 5 international. In 2001, 20 degrees awarded.
**Degree requirements:** For master's, comprehensive exam or thesis.
**Entrance requirements:** For master's, TOEFL. *Application deadline:* For fall admission, 6/30; for spring admission, 2/1. Applications are processed on a rolling basis. *Application fee:* $55.
**Expenses:** Tuition, nonresident: part-time $164 per unit.
**Financial support:** Career-related internships or fieldwork and Federal Work-Study available. Support available to part-time students. Financial award application deadline: 3/1.
**Faculty research:** Binaural resolution of the size of an acoustic array, response and generalization of matching to sample in children.
Dr. Michael Roffe, Chair, 323-343-2250.

## ■ CALIFORNIA STATE UNIVERSITY, NORTHRIDGE

**Graduate Studies, College of Social and Behavioral Sciences, Department of Psychology, Northridge, CA 91330**

**AWARDS** MA.

**Faculty:** 27 full-time, 24 part-time/adjunct.

**Students:** 40 full-time (28 women), 19 part-time (12 women); includes 16 minority (2 African Americans, 9 Asian Americans or Pacific Islanders, 5 Hispanic Americans), 4 international. Average age 30. 73 applicants, 64% accepted, 18 enrolled. In 2001, 33 degrees awarded.

**Degree requirements:** For master's, thesis.

**Entrance requirements:** For master's, GRE General Test, TOEFL, minimum GPA of 3.0. *Application deadline:* For fall admission, 11/30. *Application fee:* $55.

**Expenses:** Tuition, nonresident: part-time $631 per semester. Required fees: $246 per unit.

**Financial support:** Application deadline: 3/1.

Maura N. Mitrushina, Chair, 818-677-2827.

**Application contact:** Dr. Donald Butler, Graduate Coordinator, 818-677-2225.

## ■ CALIFORNIA STATE UNIVERSITY, SACRAMENTO

**Graduate Studies, College of Social Sciences and Interdisciplinary Studies, Department of Psychology, Sacramento, CA 95819-6048**

**AWARDS** Counseling psychology (MA). Part-time programs available.

**Students:** 36 full-time (28 women), 44 part-time (37 women); includes 19 minority (3 African Americans, 7 Asian Americans or Pacific Islanders, 9 Hispanic Americans), 4 international.

**Degree requirements:** For master's, thesis, writing proficiency exam.

**Entrance requirements:** For master's, GRE Subject Test, TOEFL, minimum GPA of 3.0 during previous 2 years. *Application deadline:* For fall admission, 4/15; for spring admission, 11/1. *Application fee:* $55.

**Expenses:** Tuition, state resident: full-time $1,965; part-time $668 per semester. Tuition, nonresident: part-time $246 per unit.

**Financial support:** Career-related internships or fieldwork and Federal Work-Study available. Support available to part-time students. Financial award application deadline: 3/1.

Dr. Tammy Bourg, Chair, 916-278-6254.

**Application contact:** Dr. Lawrence Meyers, Coordinator, 916-278-6365.

## ■ CALIFORNIA STATE UNIVERSITY, SAN BERNARDINO

**Graduate Studies, College of Social and Behavioral Sciences, Department of Psychology, San Bernardino, CA 92407-2397**

**AWARDS** Child development (MA); clinical/counseling psychology (MS); general/experimental psychology (MA); industrial organizational psychology (MS).

**Faculty:** 26 full-time (13 women).

**Students:** 79 full-time (61 women), 29 part-time (24 women); includes 35 minority (6 African Americans, 8 Asian Americans or Pacific Islanders, 20 Hispanic Americans, 1 Native American), 5 international. Average age 34. 124 applicants, 35% accepted. In 2001, 26 degrees awarded.

**Entrance requirements:** For master's, minimum GPA of 3.0 in major. *Application deadline:* For fall admission, 8/31 (priority date). *Application fee:* $55.

**Expenses:** Tuition, nonresident: full-time $4,428. Required fees: $1,733.

**Financial support:** Fellowships, research assistantships, teaching assistantships, career-related internships or fieldwork, Federal Work-Study, institutionally sponsored loans, and unspecified assistantships available.

**Faculty research:** Perceptual development, human memory, psychopharmacology, psychology of women, language acquisition.

Dr. Stuart R. Ellins, Chair, 909-880-5570, *Fax:* 909-880-7003, *E-mail:* sellins@csusb.edu.

**Application contact:** Luci Van Loon, Graduate Secretary, 909-880-5570, *Fax:* 909-880-7003, *E-mail:* lvanloon@csusb.edu.

## ■ CALIFORNIA STATE UNIVERSITY, SAN MARCOS

**College of Arts and Sciences, Program in Psychology, San Marcos, CA 92096-0001**

**AWARDS** MA.

**Faculty:** 11 full-time (8 women), 2 part-time/adjunct (1 woman).

**Students:** 10 full-time (7 women), 7 part-time (6 women); includes 5 minority (1 Asian American or Pacific Islander, 4 Hispanic Americans), 1 international. Average age 32. 26 applicants, 38% accepted. In 2001, 5 degrees awarded.

**Degree requirements:** For master's, thesis.

**Entrance requirements:** For master's, GRE General Test, GRE Subject Test. *Application deadline:* For fall admission, 2/15 (priority date). *Application fee:* $55.

**Expenses:** Tuition, state resident: part-time $567 per semester. Tuition, nonresident: part-time $813 per semester.

**Financial support:** In 2001–02, 3 research assistantships, 4 teaching assistantships (averaging $1,500 per year) were awarded.

**Faculty research:** Psychopharmacology, recovery from major surgery, computer literacy in children, neuropsychology of hemispheric differences, conservation psychology.

Marie Thomas, Department Chair, 760-750-4157, *Fax:* 760-750-3418, *E-mail:* mthomas@csusm.edu. *Web site:* http://ww2.csusm.edu/psychology-program/

## ■ CALIFORNIA STATE UNIVERSITY, STANISLAUS

**Graduate Programs, College of Arts, Letters, and Sciences, Department of Psychology, Turlock, CA 95382**

**AWARDS** Behavior analysis psychology (MS); counseling psychology (MS); general psychology (MA). Part-time programs available.

**Students:** 42 (33 women); includes 7 minority (3 Asian Americans or Pacific Islanders, 4 Hispanic Americans). 51 applicants, 98% accepted. In 2001, 15 degrees awarded.

**Degree requirements:** For master's, thesis.

**Entrance requirements:** For master's, GRE General Test, minimum GPA of 3.0. *Application deadline:* For fall admission, 2/1. *Application fee:* $55. Electronic applications accepted.

**Expenses:** Tuition, nonresident: part-time $246 per unit. Required fees: $1,919. Tuition and fees vary according to campus/location and program.

**Financial support:** In 2001–02, 1 fellowship (averaging $2,500 per year) was awarded; career-related internships or fieldwork and Federal Work-Study also available. Financial award application deadline: 3/2; financial award applicants required to submit FAFSA.

**Faculty research:** Social roles, counseling problems, psychology of religion, behavior genetics, applied analysis of behavior.

Dr. Bruce Hessee, Chair, 209-667-3386.

**Application contact:** Dr. Gina Pallotta, Director, 209-667-3386, *Fax:* 209-664-7067, *E-mail:* pallotta@toto.csustan.edu.

## ■ CAMERON UNIVERSITY

**School of Graduate Studies, Program in Behavioral Sciences, Lawton, OK 73505-6377**

**AWARDS** MS. Part-time and evening/weekend programs available.

**Faculty:** 9 full-time (2 women), 7 part-time/adjunct (2 women).

**Students:** 41 full-time (31 women), 104 part-time (81 women); includes 43 minority (31 African Americans, 1 Asian American or Pacific Islander, 6 Hispanic Americans, 5 Native Americans), 8 international. Average age 36. In 2001, 45 degrees awarded.

**Degree requirements:** For master's, comprehensive exam or portfolio, thesis optional.

*Application deadline:* For fall admission, 8/9 (priority date); for spring admission, 12/20 (priority date). Applications are processed on a rolling basis. *Application fee:* $15. Electronic applications accepted.

**Expenses:** Tuition, state resident: full-time $1,512; part-time $84 per credit hour. Tuition, nonresident: full-time $3,474; part-time $193 per credit hour. One-time fee: $15 part-time. Tuition and fees vary according to course load.

**Financial support:** In 2001–02, 6 research assistantships (averaging $3,600 per year) were awarded; career-related internships or fieldwork and Federal Work-Study also available. Support available to part-time students. Financial award application deadline: 4/15; financial award applicants required to submit FAFSA.

**Faculty research:** Acoustics, student burnout, attention deficit hyperactivity disorder, communication, group decision making. *Total annual research expenditures:* $10,000.

Dr. Scott Peterson, MS Graduate Coordinator, 580-581-2566, *Fax:* 580-581-2623, *E-mail:* scottp@cameron.edu.

**Application contact:** Suzanne Cartwright, School of Graduate Studies Admissions Coordinator, 580-581-2987, *Fax:* 580-581-5532, *E-mail:* suzannec@cameron.edu. *Web site:* http://www.cameron.edu/

## ■ CAPELLA UNIVERSITY

**Graduate School, School of Psychology, Minneapolis, MN 55402**

**AWARDS** MS, PhD. Part-time and evening/weekend programs available. Postbaccalaureate distance learning degree programs offered (minimal on-campus study).

**Faculty:** 20 full-time, 65 part-time/adjunct.

**Students:** 978. Average age 41. 1,140 applicants, 63% accepted, 621 enrolled. In 2001, 20 master's, 1 doctorate awarded. Terminal master's awarded for partial completion of doctoral program.

**Degree requirements:** For master's, project, thesis optional; for doctorate, thesis/dissertation. *Median time to degree:* Master's–1.5 years full-time, 3 years part-time; doctorate–3 years full-time, 4 years part-time.

**Entrance requirements:** For master's, TOEFL, minimum GPA of 2.7; for

doctorate, TOEFL, minimum GPA of 3.0. *Application deadline:* Applications are processed on a rolling basis. *Application fee:* $50 ($150 for international students). Electronic applications accepted.

**Expenses:** Tuition: Part-time $1,210 per course. Tuition and fees vary according to degree level and program.

**Financial support:** Institutionally sponsored loans and scholarships/grants available. Support available to part-time students. Financial award applicants required to submit FAFSA.

Dr. Karen Viechnicki, Dean, 888-CAPELLA, *E-mail:* kviechnicki@capella.edu.

**Application contact:** Kimberly Hanson, Associate Director of Enrollment Services, 612-278-0495 Ext. 372, *Fax:* 612-337-5396, *E-mail:* info@capella.edu. *Web site:* http://www.capellauniversity.edu/

## ■ CARDINAL STRITCH UNIVERSITY

**College of Arts and Sciences, Department of Psychology, Milwaukee, WI 53217-3985**

**AWARDS** Clinical psychology (MA). Part-time and evening/weekend programs available.

**Faculty:** 2 full-time (1 woman), 3 part-time/adjunct (1 woman).

**Students:** 33 full-time (29 women); includes 7 minority (5 African Americans, 1 Asian American or Pacific Islander, 1 Hispanic American), 1 international. Average age 39. 36 applicants, 56% accepted, 20 enrolled.

**Degree requirements:** For master's, thesis, portfolio, clinical practicum.

**Entrance requirements:** For master's, GRE General Test, GRE psychology subject test, interview, minimum GPA of 3.0, letters of recommendation (3). *Application deadline:* For fall admission, 7/15 (priority date); for spring admission, 12/15 (priority date). Applications are processed on a rolling basis. *Application fee:* $25.

**Expenses:** Tuition: Part-time $390 per credit. Required fees: $150; $75 per semester. One-time fee: $25. Tuition and fees vary according to program.

**Financial support:** In 2001–02, 1 student received support, including 1 research assistantship with partial tuition reimbursement available (averaging $1,500 per year); career-related internships or fieldwork, Federal Work-Study, and scholarships/grants also available. Financial award applicants required to submit FAFSA.

Dr. Asuncion Miteria Austria, Chair, 414-410-4471.

**Application contact:** 800-347-8822 Ext. 4042, *E-mail:* gradadm@stritch.edu. *Web site:* http://www.stritch.edu

## ■ CARLOS ALBIZU UNIVERSITY

**Graduate Programs in Psychology, San Juan, PR 00902-3711**

**AWARDS** Clinical psychology (PhD, Psy D); general psychology (PhD); industrial/organizational psychology (MS, PhD). Part-time and evening/weekend programs available.

**Degree requirements:** For master's, one foreign language, comprehensive exam; for doctorate, one foreign language, thesis/dissertation, written qualifying exams.

**Entrance requirements:** For master's, GRE General Test or PAEG, interview, minimum GPA of 3.0; for doctorate, PAEG, interview, minimum GPA of 3.0.

**Faculty research:** Psychotherapeutic techniques for Hispanics, psychology of the aged, school dropouts, stress, violence.

## ■ CARLOS ALBIZU UNIVERSITY, MIAMI CAMPUS

**Graduate Programs, Miami, FL 33172-2209**

**AWARDS** Clinical psychology (Psy D); industrial/organizational psychology (MS); management (MBA); marriage and family therapy (MS); mental health counseling (MS); psychology (MS); school counseling (MS). Part-time and evening/weekend programs available.

**Faculty:** 19 full-time (9 women), 37 part-time/adjunct (19 women).

**Students:** 432 full-time (322 women), 32 part-time (22 women); includes 328 minority (58 African Americans, 7 Asian Americans or Pacific Islanders, 263 Hispanic Americans), 4 international. Average age 35. 189 applicants, 50% accepted, 69 enrolled. In 2001, 44 master's, 69 doctorates awarded. Terminal master's awarded for partial completion of doctoral program.

**Degree requirements:** For master's, one foreign language, comprehensive exam, integrative project (MBA); for doctorate, one foreign language, thesis/dissertation, written and oral qualifying exam, internship.

**Entrance requirements:** For master's, GMAT (MBA), letters of recommendation (3), interview, minimum GPA of 3.0, resumé; for doctorate, GRE General Test, GRE Subject Test, letters of recommendation (3), minimum GPA of 3.0. *Application deadline:* For fall admission, 8/1 (priority date); for spring admission, 11/30 (priority date). Applications are processed on a rolling basis. *Application fee:* $50.

**Expenses:** Tuition: Part-time $455 per credit. Required fees: $819; $273 per term. Tuition and fees vary according to course load and degree level.

*Carlos Albizu University, Miami Campus (continued)*

**Financial support:** In 2001–02, 22 students received support. Federal Work-Study and scholarships/grants available. Financial award application deadline: 6/1; financial award applicants required to submit FAFSA.

**Faculty research:** Culture, psychodiagnostics, psychotherapy, forensic psychology, neuropsychology; marketing strategy, entrepreneurship.

Dr. Gerardo F. Rodriquez-Menedez, Chancellor, 305-593-1223 Ext. 120, *Fax:* 305-629-8052, *E-mail:* grodriguez@albizu.edu.

**Application contact:** Miriam Matos, Admissions Officer, 305-593-1223 Ext. 134, *Fax:* 305-593-1854, *E-mail:* mmatos@albizu.edu. *Web site:* http://www.albizu.edu/

■ **CARNEGIE MELLON UNIVERSITY**

**College of Humanities and Social Sciences, Department of Psychology, Pittsburgh, PA 15213-3891**

**AWARDS** Cognitive neuropsychology (PhD); cognitive psychology (PhD); developmental psychology (PhD); social/personality psychology (PhD).

**Degree requirements:** For doctorate, thesis/dissertation, comprehensive exam.

**Entrance requirements:** For doctorate, GRE General Test, TOEFL, TSE.

**Faculty research:** Artificial intelligence, stress and the immune system, children's learning strategies, neural basis of cognition. *Web site:* http://www.psy.cmu.edu/

■ **CASE WESTERN RESERVE UNIVERSITY**

**School of Graduate Studies, Department of Psychology, Cleveland, OH 44106**

**AWARDS** Clinical psychology (PhD); experimental psychology (PhD); mental retardation (PhD).

**Degree requirements:** For doctorate, thesis/dissertation, internship.

**Entrance requirements:** For doctorate, GRE General Test, GRE Subject Test, TOEFL.

**Faculty research:** Adolescent suicide, cognitive processing, repressive responses, visual perception, impact of HIV infection, neuropsychology. *Web site:* http://www.cwru.edu/CWRU/Dept/Artsci/pscl/pscl/html

■ **CASTLETON STATE COLLEGE**

**Division of Graduate Studies, Department of Psychology, Castleton, VT 05735**

**AWARDS** Forensic psychology (MA).

**Faculty:** 6 full-time (3 women).

**Students:** 19 full-time (all women), 4 part-time (all women). In 2001, 16 degrees awarded.

**Degree requirements:** For master's, thesis.

**Entrance requirements:** For master's, GRE General Test, minimum undergraduate GPA of 3.5, previous course work in research methodology and statistics. *Application deadline:* For fall admission, 7/1. Applications are processed on a rolling basis. *Application fee:* $30.

**Expenses:** Tuition, state resident: full-time $4,404; part-time $184 per credit. Tuition, nonresident: full-time $10,320; part-time $430 per credit. Required fees: $838; $31 per credit.

**Financial support:** In 2001–02, 8 fellowships (averaging $1,875 per year) were awarded; teaching assistantships, career-related internships or fieldwork and Federal Work-Study also available. Financial award application deadline: 2/15; financial award applicants required to submit FAFSA.

**Faculty research:** Psychology and law, juvenile delinquency, criminal psychology, correctional psychology, police psychology. Dr. Brenda Russell, Program Director, 802-468-1424, *Fax:* 802-468-5237, *E-mail:* brenda.russell@castleton.edu.

**Application contact:** Bill Allen, Dean of Enrollment, 802-468-1213, *Fax:* 802-468-1476, *E-mail:* info@castleton.edu.

■ **THE CATHOLIC UNIVERSITY OF AMERICA**

**School of Arts and Sciences, Department of Psychology, Washington, DC 20064**

**AWARDS** Applied experimental psychology (MA, PhD); clinical psychology (PhD); general psychology (MA); human development (PhD); human factors (MA). Part-time programs available.

**Faculty:** 13 full-time (5 women), 1 part-time/adjunct (0 women).

**Students:** 29 full-time (21 women), 57 part-time (41 women); includes 14 minority (5 African Americans, 5 Asian Americans or Pacific Islanders, 3 Hispanic Americans, 1 Native American), 6 international. Average age 30. 142 applicants, 29% accepted, 15 enrolled. In 2001, 20 master's, 6 doctorates awarded. Terminal master's awarded for partial completion of doctoral program.

**Degree requirements:** For master's, comprehensive exam; for doctorate, thesis/dissertation, comprehensive exam.

**Entrance requirements:** For master's, GRE General Test, TOEFL; for doctorate, GRE General Test, GRE Subject Test. *Application deadline:* Applications are

processed on a rolling basis. *Application fee:* $55. Electronic applications accepted.

**Expenses:** Tuition: Full-time $20,050; part-time $770 per credit. Required fees: $430 per term. Tuition and fees vary according to program.

**Financial support:** Fellowships, research assistantships, teaching assistantships, career-related internships or fieldwork, Federal Work-Study, institutionally sponsored loans, scholarships/grants, and tuition waivers (full and partial) available. Support available to part-time students. Financial award application deadline: 2/1.

**Faculty research:** Social development, family interaction, human perception and cognition, applied cognitive science, individual and group psychotherapy. Dr. Marc M. Sebrechts, Chair, 202-319-5750, *Fax:* 202-319-6263.

**Application contact:** Information Contact, 202-319-5729.

■ **CENTER FOR HUMANISTIC STUDIES**

**Programs in Humanistic, Clinical, and Educational Psychology, Detroit, MI 48202-3802**

**AWARDS** Humanistic and clinical psychology (MA, Psy D).

**Faculty:** 4 full-time (2 women), 12 part-time/adjunct (5 women).

**Students:** 83 full-time (60 women); includes 15 minority (13 African Americans, 2 Asian Americans or Pacific Islanders). Average age 38. 90 applicants, 83% accepted. In 2001, 30 degrees awarded.

**Degree requirements:** For master's, thesis, practicum; for doctorate, thesis/dissertation, internship, practicum.

**Entrance requirements:** For master's, 1 year of work experience, interview, minimum GPA of 3.0; for doctorate, 3 years work experience, 2 interviews, minimum GPA of 3.0 in graduate course work. *Application deadline:* For fall admission, 9/1 (priority date). Applications are processed on a rolling basis. *Application fee:* $75.

**Expenses:** Tuition: Full-time $14,060.

**Financial support:** In 2001–02, 39 students received support. Application deadline: 6/30.

**Faculty research:** Qualitative research, existential-phenomenological psychology, applications to clinical practice.

**Application contact:** Ellen F. Blau, Admissions Adviser, 313-875-7440, *Fax:* 313-875-2610, *E-mail:* eblau@humanpsych.edu.

# ■ CENTRAL CONNECTICUT STATE UNIVERSITY

**School of Graduate Studies, School of Arts and Sciences, Department of Psychology, New Britain, CT 06050-4010**

**AWARDS** Community psychology (MA); psychology (MA). Part-time and evening/weekend programs available.

**Faculty:** 19 full-time (7 women), 15 part-time/adjunct (5 women).
**Students:** 8 full-time (5 women), 12 part-time (9 women); includes 5 minority (4 African Americans, 1 Hispanic American). Average age 30. 9 applicants, 67% accepted. In 2001, 7 degrees awarded.
**Degree requirements:** For master's, thesis, comprehensive exam or special project.
**Entrance requirements:** For master's, TOEFL, minimum GPA of 2.7. *Application deadline:* For fall admission, 8/10 (priority date); for spring admission, 12/10. Applications are processed on a rolling basis. *Application fee:* $40.
**Expenses:** Tuition, state resident: full-time $2,772; part-time $245 per credit. Tuition, nonresident: full-time $7,726; part-time $245 per credit. Required fees: $2,102. Tuition and fees vary according to course level and degree level.
**Financial support:** In 2001–02, 1 research assistantship was awarded; career-related internships or fieldwork and Federal Work-Study also available. Financial award application deadline: 3/15; financial award applicants required to submit FAFSA.
**Faculty research:** Clinical psychology, general psychology, child development, cognitive development, drugs/behavior. Dr. Frank Donis, Chair, 860-832-3100.

# ■ CENTRAL MICHIGAN UNIVERSITY

**College of Graduate Studies, College of Humanities and Social and Behavioral Sciences, Department of Psychology, Mount Pleasant, MI 48859**

**AWARDS** Clinical psychology (Psy D); general, applied, and experimental psychology (MS, PhD), including applied experimental psychology (PhD), general/experimental psychology (MS); industrial/organizational psychology (MA, PhD); school psychology (PhD, S Psy S). Terminal master's awarded for partial completion of doctoral program.

**Degree requirements:** For master's, thesis or alternative; for S Psy S, thesis.
**Entrance requirements:** For doctorate, GRE.
**Expenses:** Tuition, state resident: part-time $182 per unit. Tuition, nonresident: part-time $182 per unit. Required fees:

$208 per semester. Part-time tuition and fees vary according to course load.
**Faculty research:** Occupational stress, hyperamnesia, humor, problem solving, behavioral neuroscience. *Web site:* http://www.cmich.edu/~psy/

# ■ CENTRAL MISSOURI STATE UNIVERSITY

**School of Graduate Studies, College of Education and Human Services, Department of Psychology and Counselor Education, Warrensburg, MO 64093**

**AWARDS** Human services/guidance and counseling (Ed S); psychology (MS); school counseling (MS). Part-time programs available.

**Faculty:** 14 full-time (4 women), 5 part-time/adjunct (3 women).
**Students:** 10 full-time (8 women), 67 part-time (59 women); includes 2 minority (both African Americans), 1 international. Average age 33. 18 applicants, 67% accepted. In 2001, 23 degrees awarded.
**Degree requirements:** For master's, internship, thesis optional; for Ed S, thesis.
**Entrance requirements:** For master's, GRE General Test, GRE Subject Test, minimum GPA of 2.75, Missouri teaching certificate, 2 years of teaching experience (school counseling), previous course work in psychology; for Ed S, MS in counselor education or equivalent. *Application deadline:* For fall admission, 6/1 (priority date); for spring admission, 10/1 (priority date). Applications are processed on a rolling basis. *Application fee:* $25 ($50 for international students).
**Expenses:** Tuition, area resident: Full-time $4,200; part-time $175 per credit hour. Tuition, nonresident: full-time $8,352; part-time $348 per credit hour.
**Financial support:** In 2001–02, 4 research assistantships with full tuition reimbursements (averaging $7,625 per year), 8 teaching assistantships with full tuition reimbursements (averaging $4,578 per year) were awarded. Federal Work-Study, scholarships/grants, unspecified assistantships, and 3 administrative and 2 laboratory assistantships also available. Support available to part-time students. Financial award application deadline: 3/1; financial award applicants required to submit FAFSA.
**Faculty research:** Rapid cholesterol lowering and cognitive function, behavioral intervention for essential tremor, attention deficit and hyperactivity disorder, abstraction memory, neuropsychological assessment. *Total annual research expenditures:* $6,000.
Dr. Joe Ryan, Chair, 660-543-4185, *Fax:* 660-543-8505, *E-mail:* ryan@

cmsu1.cmsu.edu. *Web site:* http://www.cmsu.edu/

# ■ CENTRAL WASHINGTON UNIVERSITY

**Graduate Studies and Research, College of the Sciences, Department of Psychology, Ellensburg, WA 98926-7463**

**AWARDS** Counseling psychology (MS); experimental psychology (MS); guidance and counseling (M Ed); organizational development (MS); school psychology (M Ed). Evening/weekend programs available.

**Faculty:** 23 full-time (9 women).
**Students:** 74 full-time (50 women), 18 part-time (13 women); includes 8 minority (3 African Americans, 1 Asian American or Pacific Islander, 4 Hispanic Americans), 1 international. 93 applicants, 48% accepted, 35 enrolled. In 2001, 34 degrees awarded.
**Degree requirements:** For master's, thesis.
**Entrance requirements:** For master's, GRE General Test, minimum GPA of 3.0. *Application deadline:* For fall admission, 4/1. *Application fee:* $35.
**Expenses:** Tuition, state resident: full-time $4,848; part-time $162 per credit. Tuition, nonresident: full-time $14,772; part-time $492 per credit. Required fees: $324.
**Financial support:** In 2001–02, 20 research assistantships with partial tuition reimbursements (averaging $7,120 per year) were awarded; teaching assistantships, career-related internships or fieldwork and Federal Work-Study also available. Financial award application deadline: 3/1; financial award applicants required to submit FAFSA.
Dr. Philip Tolin, Chair, 509-963-2381.
**Application contact:** Barbara Sisko, Office Assistant, Graduate Studies and Research, 509-963-3103, *Fax:* 509-963-1799, *E-mail:* masters@cwu.edu. *Web site:* http://www.cwu.edu/

# ■ CHAPMAN UNIVERSITY

**Graduate Studies, Division of Psychology, Orange, CA 92866**

**AWARDS** Marriage and family therapy (MA); pre-clinical (MA). Part-time and evening/weekend programs available.

**Faculty:** 11 full-time (5 women).
**Degree requirements:** For master's, comprehensive exam.
**Entrance requirements:** For master's, GRE General Test, MAT, minimum undergraduate GPA of 3.0. *Application deadline:* Applications are processed on a rolling basis. *Application fee:* $40.
**Expenses:** Tuition: Part-time $450 per credit. Tuition and fees vary according to program.

*Chapman University (continued)*
**Financial support:** Application deadline: 3/1.
Dr. Gerhardt Eifert, Chair, 714-997-6776, *E-mail:* eifert@chapman.edu.
**Application contact:** Susan Read-Weil, Coordinator, 714-744-7837, *E-mail:* sreadwei@chapman.edu.

### ■ CHESTNUT HILL COLLEGE
**Graduate Division, Department of Psychology, Philadelphia, PA 19118-2693**

**AWARDS** Clinical psychology (MA, MS, Psy D); counseling psychology and human services (MA, MS). Part-time and evening/weekend programs available.

**Faculty:** 7 full-time (3 women), 29 part-time/adjunct (17 women).
**Students:** 43 full-time (33 women), 183 part-time (135 women); includes 20 minority (14 African Americans, 4 Asian Americans or Pacific Islanders, 2 Hispanic Americans), 6 international. Average age 36. In 2001, 64 degrees awarded. Terminal master's awarded for partial completion of doctoral program.
**Degree requirements:** For master's, thesis (for some programs); for doctorate, thesis/dissertation, internships, practica.
**Entrance requirements:** For master's, GRE General Test or MAT; for doctorate, GRE General Test, master's degree in counseling or related field, 300 hours of clinical experience. *Application deadline:* For fall admission, 7/17 (priority date); for spring admission, 2/15 (priority date). Applications are processed on a rolling basis. *Application fee:* $35.
**Expenses:** Contact institution.
**Financial support:** Career-related internships or fieldwork and unspecified assistantships available. Support available to part-time students. Financial award application deadline: 7/15; financial award applicants required to submit FAFSA.
**Faculty research:** Family therapy/step-parenting, play therapy, adolescent development, object relations, children/pain management/chronic illness.
Dr. Judith Marsh, Chair, 215-248-7070, *Fax:* 215-248-7155, *E-mail:* marshj@chc.edu.
**Application contact:** Sr. Regina Raphael Smith, SSJ, Director of Graduate Admissions, 215-248-7020, *Fax:* 215-248-7161, *E-mail:* graddiv@chc.edu. *Web site:* http://www.chc.edu/

### ■ CHICAGO SCHOOL OF PROFESSIONAL PSYCHOLOGY
**Graduate School, Chicago, IL 60605-2024**

**AWARDS** Clinical psychology (Psy D); forensic psychology (MA); industrial and organizational psychology (MA). Part-time programs available.

**Faculty:** 19 full-time (10 women), 43 part-time/adjunct (25 women).
**Students:** 216 full-time (162 women), 157 part-time (114 women); includes 75 minority (38 African Americans, 16 Asian Americans or Pacific Islanders, 21 Hispanic Americans), 25 international. Average age 25. 215 applicants, 74% accepted, 70 enrolled. In 2001, 48 degrees awarded.
**Degree requirements:** For doctorate, thesis/dissertation, competency exam, internship, practica.
**Entrance requirements:** For master's, 18 undergraduate hours in psychology, course work in statistics; for doctorate, GRE General Test or other graduate entrance exam, 18 hours in psychology (1 course each in statistics, abnormal psychology, and theories of personality). *Application deadline:* For fall admission, 1/15 (priority date); for spring admission, 11/1 (priority date). Applications are processed on a rolling basis. *Application fee:* $50.
**Expenses:** Tuition: Part-time $550 per credit hour. Required fees: $350 per year. Tuition and fees vary according to degree level and program.
**Financial support:** In 2001–02, 16 research assistantships with partial tuition reimbursements, 32 teaching assistantships with partial tuition reimbursements were awarded. Career-related internships or fieldwork, Federal Work-Study, scholarships/grants, and tuition waivers (partial) also available. Support available to part-time students. Financial award application deadline: 5/1; financial award applicants required to submit FAFSA.
**Faculty research:** White racial identity, work with cross-cultural clients, teaching in psychology.
Dr. Michael Horowitz, President, 312-786-9443 Ext. 3033, *Fax:* 312-322-3273, *E-mail:* mhorowitz@csopp.edu.
**Application contact:** Magdelen Kellogg, Director of Admission, 312-786-9443 Ext. 3029, *Fax:* 312-322-3273, *E-mail:* mkellogg@csopp.edu. *Web site:* http://www.csopp.edu/

**Find an in-depth description at www.petersons.com/gradchannel.**

### ■ CHRISTOPHER NEWPORT UNIVERSITY
**Graduate Studies, Department of Psychology, Newport News, VA 23606-2998**

**AWARDS** Applied psychology (MS), including industrial/organizational psychology. Part-time and evening/weekend programs available.
**Faculty:** 6 full-time (3 women).

**Students:** 14 full-time (11 women), 16 part-time (10 women); includes 8 minority (6 African Americans, 1 Asian American or Pacific Islander, 1 Hispanic American). Average age 32. 11 applicants, 100% accepted. In 2001, 8 degrees awarded.
**Degree requirements:** For master's, thesis, comprehensive exam.
**Entrance requirements:** For master's, GRE General Test, GRE Subject Test, minimum GPA of 3.0. *Application deadline:* For fall admission, 7/1 (priority date); for spring admission, 11/15. Applications are processed on a rolling basis. *Application fee:* $40.
**Expenses:** Tuition, state resident: full-time $1,782; part-time $99 per credit. Tuition, nonresident: full-time $6,138; part-time $341 per credit. Required fees: $49 per credit hour. $20 per term.
**Financial support:** In 2001–02, 3 research assistantships with full and partial tuition reimbursements (averaging $1,700 per year) were awarded; career-related internships or fieldwork, Federal Work-Study, institutionally sponsored loans, and scholarships/grants also available. Support available to part-time students. Financial award application deadline: 3/1; financial award applicants required to submit FAFSA.
**Faculty research:** Organizational development, affirmative action attitudes, organizational justice, service organizations, organizational environment, occupational stereotyping.
Dr. Thomas Berry, Coordinator, 757-594-7934, *Fax:* 757-594-7342, *E-mail:* berry@cnu.edu.
**Application contact:** Susan R. Chittenden, Graduate Admissions, 757-594-7359, *Fax:* 757-594-7333, *E-mail:* gradstdy@cnu.edu. *Web site:* http://www.cnu.edu/

### ■ THE CITADEL, THE MILITARY COLLEGE OF SOUTH CAROLINA
**College of Graduate and Professional Studies, Department of Psychology, Charleston, SC 29409**

**AWARDS** MA. Part-time and evening/weekend programs available.

**Faculty:** 8 full-time (3 women), 6 part-time/adjunct (1 woman).
**Students:** 15 full-time (14 women), 62 part-time (55 women); includes 7 minority (4 African Americans, 3 Asian Americans or Pacific Islanders). Average age 31. In 2001, 8 degrees awarded.
**Entrance requirements:** For master's, GRE General Test or MAT. *Application deadline:* For fall admission, 3/15. *Application fee:* $25.
**Expenses:** Tuition, state resident: full-time $1,314; part-time $141 per credit hour.

Tuition, nonresident: full-time $2,619; part-time $285 per credit hour.
**Financial support:** Research assistantships, teaching assistantships, career-related internships or fieldwork and unspecified assistantships available.
**Faculty research:** Childhood depression, victimization, early intervention, mental retardation.
Dr. A. J. Finch, Head, 843-953-5320, *Fax:* 843-953-7084, *E-mail:* finch@citadel.edu.
**Application contact:** Dr. Julie Lipovsky, Coordinator, 843-953-5323, *Fax:* 843-953-7084, *E-mail:* lipouskyj@citadel.edu.

■ **CITY COLLEGE OF THE CITY UNIVERSITY OF NEW YORK**

**Graduate School, College of Liberal Arts and Science, Division of Social Science, Department of Psychology, New York, NY 10031-9198**

**AWARDS** Clinical psychology (PhD); experimental cognition (PhD); general psychology (MA). Part-time programs available.

**Students:** 81. In 2001, 10 degrees awarded.
**Degree requirements:** For master's, one foreign language, thesis, comprehensive exam.
**Entrance requirements:** For master's, TOEFL, minimum undergraduate B average. *Application deadline:* For fall admission, 5/1; for spring admission, 12/1. *Application fee:* $40.
**Expenses:** Tuition, state resident: part-time $185 per credit. Tuition, nonresident: part-time $320 per credit. Required fees: $43 per term.
**Financial support:** Fellowships, teaching assistantships, career-related internships or fieldwork, Federal Work-Study, and tuition waivers (full and partial) available. Support available to part-time students. Financial award application deadline: 5/1.
**Faculty research:** Social/personality psychology, physiological psychology, cognition and development.
Brett Silverstein, Chair, 212-650-5442.
**Application contact:** Dr. William King, Graduate Adviser, 212-650-5723.

■ **CLAREMONT GRADUATE UNIVERSITY**

**Graduate Programs, School of Behavioral and Organizational Sciences, Department of Psychology, Claremont, CA 91711-6160**

**AWARDS** Cognitive psychology (MA, PhD); developmental psychology (MA, PhD); organizational behavior (MA, PhD); program design, management, and evaluation (MA);

social environmental psychology (PhD); social psychology (MA). Part-time programs available.

**Faculty:** 6 full-time (2 women), 7 part-time/adjunct (6 women).
**Students:** 127 full-time (93 women), 23 part-time (19 women); includes 48 minority (8 African Americans, 23 Asian Americans or Pacific Islanders, 15 Hispanic Americans, 2 Native Americans), 9 international. Average age 30. In 2001, 25 master's, 16 doctorates awarded. Terminal master's awarded for partial completion of doctoral program.
**Degree requirements:** For master's, thesis (for some programs); for doctorate, thesis/dissertation, comprehensive exam.
**Entrance requirements:** For master's and doctorate, GRE General Test. *Application deadline:* For fall admission, 2/15 (priority date). Applications are processed on a rolling basis. *Application fee:* $50. Electronic applications accepted.
**Expenses:** Tuition: Full-time $22,984; part-time $1,000 per unit. Required fees: $160; $80 per semester.
**Financial support:** Fellowships, research assistantships, teaching assistantships, career-related internships or fieldwork, Federal Work-Study, institutionally sponsored loans, and tuition waivers (full and partial) available. Support available to part-time students. Financial award application deadline: 2/15; financial award applicants required to submit FAFSA.
**Faculty research:** Social intervention, diversity in organizations, eyewitness memory, aging and cognition, drug policy.
**Application contact:** Jessica Johnson, Program Coordinator, 909-621-8084, *Fax:* 909-621-8905, *E-mail:* jessica.johnson@ cgu.edu. *Web site:* http://www.cgu.edu/sbus
**Find an in-depth description at www.petersons.com/gradchannel.**

■ **CLARK UNIVERSITY**

**Graduate School, Department of Psychology, Worcester, MA 01610-1477**

**AWARDS** Clinical psychology (PhD); developmental psychology (PhD); social-personality psychology (PhD).

**Faculty:** 15 full-time (7 women), 9 part-time/adjunct (3 women).
**Students:** 44 full-time (35 women), 2 part-time (both women); includes 4 minority (1 Asian American or Pacific Islander, 3 Hispanic Americans), 14 international. Average age 29. 179 applicants, 12% accepted, 6 enrolled. In 2001, 13 doctorates awarded.
**Degree requirements:** For doctorate, thesis/dissertation.
**Entrance requirements:** For doctorate, GRE General Test, TOEFL. *Application*

*deadline:* For fall admission, 1/31 (priority date). Applications are processed on a rolling basis. *Application fee:* $40.
**Expenses:** Tuition: Full-time $24,400; part-time $763 per credit. Required fees: $10.
**Financial support:** In 2001–02, 2 fellowships with full tuition reimbursements (averaging $10,900 per year), 11 research assistantships with full tuition reimbursements (averaging $10,900 per year), 19 teaching assistantships with full tuition reimbursements (averaging $10,900 per year) were awarded. Career-related internships or fieldwork and tuition waivers (full and partial) also available.
**Faculty research:** Development of psychological processes in sociocultural context conceptualizing and reasoning, symbolization, psychotherapy, metaphor, emotions and personalities. *Total annual research expenditures:* $599,000.
Dr. Jaan Valsiner, Chair, 508-793-7273.
**Application contact:** Cynthia LaRochelle, Graduate School Secretary, 508-793-7274, *Fax:* 508-793-7265, *E-mail:* clarochelle@ clarku.edu. *Web site:* http://www2.clarku.edu/newsite/graduatefolder/programs/index.shtml

■ **CLEMSON UNIVERSITY**

**Graduate School, College of Business and Behavioral Science, Department of Psychology, Clemson, SC 29634**

**AWARDS** Applied psychology (MS); human factors (MS); industrial/organizational psychology (PhD).

**Students:** 29 full-time (17 women), 8 part-time (4 women); includes 2 minority (1 African American, 1 Asian American or Pacific Islander). 170 applicants, 6% accepted, 9 enrolled. In 2001, 4 degrees awarded.
**Degree requirements:** For master's, thesis, internship; for doctorate, thesis/dissertation.
**Entrance requirements:** For master's, GRE General Test, TOEFL, 18 hours in psychology; for doctorate, GRE General Test, TOEFL. *Application deadline:* For fall admission, 3/15. *Application fee:* $40.
**Expenses:** Tuition, state resident: full-time $5,310. Tuition, nonresident: full-time $11,284.
**Financial support:** Application deadline: 3/15.
Dr. Christopher Pagano, Coordinator, 864-656-4984, *E-mail:* cpagano@ clemson.edu.

## ■ CLEVELAND STATE UNIVERSITY

**College of Graduate Studies, College of Arts and Sciences, Department of Psychology, Cleveland, OH 44115**

**AWARDS** Clinical and counseling psychology (MA); consumer/industrial research (MA); diversity management (MA); research psychology (MA); school psychology (Psy S). Part-time programs available.

**Faculty:** 17 full-time (6 women), 4 part-time/adjunct (1 woman).

**Students:** 48 full-time (34 women), 58 part-time (46 women); includes 15 minority (13 African Americans, 2 Hispanic Americans), 4 international. Average age 29. 152 applicants, 34% accepted. In 2001, 40 degrees awarded.

**Entrance requirements:** For master's, GRE General Test. *Application deadline:* For fall admission, 2/1 (priority date). *Application fee:* $25.

**Expenses:** Tuition, state resident: full-time $6,838; part-time $263 per credit hour. Tuition, nonresident: full-time $13,526; part-time $520 per credit hour.

**Financial support:** In 2001–02, 1 research assistantship was awarded; teaching assistantships with full tuition reimbursements, career-related internships or fieldwork, Federal Work-Study, tuition waivers (full), and unspecified assistantships also available. Financial award application deadline: 5/1. *Total annual research expenditures:* $180,000.

Dr. Mark H. Ashcraft, Chairperson, 216-687-2545, *Fax:* 216-687-9294, *E-mail:* m.ashcraft@csuohio.edu.

**Application contact:** Karen Colston, Administrative Coordinator, 216-687-2552, *E-mail:* k.colston@csuohio.edu. *Web site:* http://www.asic.csuohio.edu/psy/

## ■ COLLEGE OF SAINT ELIZABETH

**Department of Psychology, Morristown, NJ 07960-6989**

**AWARDS** Counseling psychology (MA). Part-time and evening/weekend programs available.

**Faculty:** 5 full-time (4 women), 10 part-time/adjunct (5 women).

**Students:** 10 full-time (8 women), 41 part-time (38 women); includes 11 minority (6 African Americans, 1 Asian American or Pacific Islander, 4 Hispanic Americans), 1 international. Average age 38. 16 applicants, 100% accepted, 10 enrolled. In 2001, 13 degrees awarded.

**Degree requirements:** For master's, thesis or alternative, portfolio. *Median time to degree:* Master's–4 years part-time.

**Entrance requirements:** For master's, minimum GPA of 3.0, BA in psychology

preferred, 12 credits of course work in psychology. *Application deadline:* For fall admission, 4/14 (priority date); for spring admission, 11/15. Applications are processed on a rolling basis. *Application fee:* $35. Electronic applications accepted.

**Expenses:** Tuition: Full-time $8,100; part-time $450 per credit. Required fees: $195. Tuition and fees vary according to course load.

**Financial support:** In 2001–02, 1 student received support. Career-related internships or fieldwork, tuition waivers (partial), and unspecified assistantships available. Support available to part-time students. Financial award application deadline: 3/15; financial award applicants required to submit FAFSA.

**Faculty research:** Family systems, dissociative identity disorder, multicultural counseling, outcomes assessment.

Dr. Valerie Scott, Director of the Graduate Program in Counseling Psychology, 973-290-4102, *Fax:* 973-290-4676, *E-mail:* vscott@cse.edu. *Web site:* http://www.cse.edu/

## ■ COLLEGE OF ST. JOSEPH

**Graduate Program, Division of Psychology and Human Services, Rutland, VT 05701-3899**

**AWARDS** Clinical psychology (MS); community counseling (MS); school guidance counseling (MS). Part-time and evening/weekend programs available.

**Faculty:** 3 full-time (0 women), 6 part-time/adjunct (3 women).

**Students:** 14 full-time, 32 part-time; includes 3 minority (2 African Americans, 1 Asian American or Pacific Islander). Average age 34. In 2001, 7 degrees awarded.

**Degree requirements:** For master's, thesis, comprehensive exam, registration.

**Entrance requirements:** For master's, GRE General Test, interview. *Application deadline:* Applications are processed on a rolling basis. *Application fee:* $35.

**Expenses:** Tuition: Full-time $9,000; part-time $250 per credit. Required fees: $45 per semester. Part-time tuition and fees vary according to course load.

**Financial support:** Career-related internships or fieldwork, Federal Work-Study, and unspecified assistantships available. Support available to part-time students. Financial award application deadline: 3/1.

Dr. Craig Knapp, Chair, 802-773-5900 Ext. 3219, *Fax:* 802-773-5900, *E-mail:* cknapp@csj.edu.

**Application contact:** Steve Soba, Dean of Admissions, 802-773-5900 Ext. 3206, *Fax:* 802-773-5900, *E-mail:* ssoba@csj.edu.

## ■ COLLEGE OF STATEN ISLAND OF THE CITY UNIVERSITY OF NEW YORK

**Graduate Programs, Center for Developmental Neuroscience and Developmental Disabilities, Sub-program in Learning Processes, Staten Island, NY 10314-6600**

**AWARDS** Biopsychology (PhD); clinical psychology (PhD); developmental psychology (PhD); environmental psychology (PhD); experimental cognition (PhD); experimental psychology (PhD); neuropsychology (PhD); psychology (PhD); social-personality psychology (PhD).

**Degree requirements:** For doctorate, one foreign language, thesis/dissertation.

**Entrance requirements:** For doctorate, GRE, TOEFL. *Application deadline:* For fall admission, 3/15 (priority date). Applications are processed on a rolling basis. *Application fee:* $40.

**Expenses:** Tuition, state resident: full-time $4,350; part-time $185 per credit. Tuition, nonresident: full-time $7,600; part-time $320 per credit. Required fees: $53 per semester.

**Financial support:** Fellowships, research assistantships, teaching assistantships, career-related internships or fieldwork and institutionally sponsored loans available. Financial award application deadline: 3/15.

Dr. Nancy Hemmes, Head, 718-997-3561.

## ■ THE COLLEGE OF WILLIAM AND MARY

**Faculty of Arts and Sciences, Department of Psychology, Williamsburg, VA 23187-8795**

**AWARDS** Clinical psychology (Psy D); general experimental psychology (MA). Psy D offered through the Virginia Consortium for Professional Psychology. For information call 757-431-4950.

**Faculty:** 51 full-time (18 women), 26 part-time/adjunct (15 women).

**Students:** 53 full-time (40 women), 9 part-time (all women); includes 12 minority (9 African Americans, 3 Asian Americans or Pacific Islanders).

**Degree requirements:** For master's, thesis, oral exams, comprehensive exam; for doctorate, thesis/dissertation, written, and oral examinations, comprehensive exam.

**Entrance requirements:** For master's, GRE, previous course work in statistics and experimental psychology; for doctorate, GRE General Test, GRE Subject Test, TOEFL. *Application deadline:* For fall admission, 2/15.

**Expenses:** Tuition, state resident: full-time $3,262; part-time $175 per credit hour. Tuition, nonresident: full-time $14,768;

part-time $550 per credit hour. Required fees: $2,478.

**Financial support:** Research assistantships, teaching assistantships, career-related internships or fieldwork, institutionally sponsored loans, scholarships/grants, and tuition waivers available.

**Faculty research:** Personality, developmental, cognition, applied decision theory, social psychology.
Dr. W. Larry Ventis, Chairman, 757-221-3875, *Fax:* 757-221-3896, *E-mail:* wlvent@wm.edu. *Web site:* http://www.wm.edu/psyc/

### ■ COLORADO STATE UNIVERSITY

**Graduate School, College of Natural Sciences, Department of Psychology, Fort Collins, CO 80523-0015**

**AWARDS** Applied social psychology (PhD); behavioral neuroscience (PhD); cognitive psychology (PhD); counseling psychology (PhD); industrial-organizational psychology (PhD).

**Faculty:** 29 full-time (8 women), 13 part-time/adjunct (7 women).
**Students:** 56 full-time (42 women), 37 part-time (29 women). Average age 29. 309 applicants, 12% accepted, 16 enrolled. In 2001, 9 doctorates awarded.
**Degree requirements:** For doctorate, thesis/dissertation.
**Entrance requirements:** For doctorate, GRE General Test, GRE Subject Test, TOEFL, minimum GPA of 3.5. *Application deadline:* For fall admission, 1/15. *Application fee:* $30. Electronic applications accepted.
**Expenses:** Tuition, state resident: full-time $2,880; part-time $160 per credit. Tuition, nonresident: full-time $11,412; part-time $634 per credit. Required fees: $750; $34 per credit.
**Financial support:** In 2001–02, 3 fellowships with full tuition reimbursements (averaging $12,120 per year), 10 research assistantships with full tuition reimbursements (averaging $9,720 per year), 52 teaching assistantships with full tuition reimbursements (averaging $9,720 per year) were awarded. Career-related internships or fieldwork, Federal Work-Study, institutionally sponsored loans, scholarships/grants, and traineeships also available.
**Faculty research:** Environmental psychology, cognitive learning, health psychology, occupations of health. *Total annual research expenditures:* $12.5 million.
Ernest L. Chavez, Chair, 970-491-6363, *Fax:* 970-491-1032, *E-mail:* echavez@lamar.colostate.edu.

**Application contact:** Wendy Standring, Graduate Admissions Coordinator, 970-491-6363, *Fax:* 970-491-1032, *E-mail:* wendyann@lamar.colostate.edu. *Web site:* http://www.colostate.edu/Depts/Psychology/

### ■ COLUMBIA UNIVERSITY

**Graduate School of Arts and Sciences, Division of Natural Sciences, Department of Psychology, New York, NY 10027**

**AWARDS** Experimental psychology (M Phil, MA, PhD); psychobiology (M Phil, MA, PhD); social psychology (M Phil, MA, PhD).

**Faculty:** 23 full-time.
**Students:** 35 full-time (19 women), 2 part-time. Average age 28. 156 applicants, 7% accepted. In 2001, 7 master's, 6 doctorates awarded.
**Degree requirements:** For master's and doctorate, thesis/dissertation.
**Entrance requirements:** For master's and doctorate, GRE General Test, TOEFL. *Application deadline:* For fall admission, 1/3. *Application fee:* $65.
**Expenses:** Tuition: Full-time $27,528. Required fees: $1,638.
**Financial support:** Fellowships, teaching assistantships, Federal Work-Study and institutionally sponsored loans available. Support available to part-time students. Financial award application deadline: 1/5; financial award applicants required to submit FAFSA.
Donald Hood, Chair, 212-854-4587, *Fax:* 212-854-3609.

### ■ CONCORDIA UNIVERSITY

**Graduate Studies, Program in Psychology, River Forest, IL 60305-1499**

**AWARDS** MA, CAS. Part-time and evening/weekend programs available.

**Degree requirements:** For master's, thesis optional; for CAS, thesis, final project.
**Entrance requirements:** For master's, minimum GPA of 2.9; for CAS, master's degree.
**Faculty research:** Lutheran high school counseling research.

### ■ CONNECTICUT COLLEGE

**Graduate School, Department of Psychology, New London, CT 06320-4196**

**AWARDS** MA. Part-time programs available.

**Degree requirements:** For master's, thesis or alternative, comprehensive exam.
**Entrance requirements:** For master's, GRE General Test, GRE Subject Test.

**Faculty research:** Behavioral medicine, personality-social psychology, clinical techniques.

### ■ COPPIN STATE COLLEGE

**Division of Graduate Studies, Division of Arts and Sciences, Department of Applied Psychology and Rehabilitation Counseling, Baltimore, MD 21216-3698**

**AWARDS** Rehabilitation (M Ed). Part-time and evening/weekend programs available.

**Faculty:** 2 full-time (both women), 7 part-time/adjunct (4 women).
**Students:** 7 full-time (5 women), 82 part-time (65 women); includes 85 minority (84 African Americans, 1 Hispanic American), 1 international. 39 applicants, 87% accepted. In 2001, 9 degrees awarded.
**Degree requirements:** For master's, thesis, comprehensive exam.
**Entrance requirements:** For master's, GRE, minimum GPA of 3.0, interview. *Application deadline:* For fall admission, 7/15 (priority date); for spring admission, 12/15 (priority date). Applications are processed on a rolling basis. *Application fee:* $25.
**Expenses:** Tuition, state resident: full-time $3,576; part-time $149 per credit. Tuition, nonresident: full-time $6,360; part-time $265 per credit. Required fees: $589; $589 per year.
**Financial support:** In 2001–02, 10 fellowships (averaging $1,600 per year), 1 research assistantship (averaging $2,000 per year) were awarded. Federal Work-Study, institutionally sponsored loans, scholarships/grants, and traineeships also available. Support available to part-time students. Financial award application deadline: 4/1; financial award applicants required to submit FAFSA.
Dr. Janet Spry, Co-Chairperson, 410-951-3510, *E-mail:* jspry@coppin.edu.
**Application contact:** Vell Lyles, Associate Vice President for Enrollment Management, 410-951-3575, *E-mail:* vlyles@coppin.edu. *Web site:* http://www.coppin.edu/

### ■ COPPIN STATE COLLEGE

**Division of Graduate Studies, Division of Arts and Sciences, Department of Psychology and Rehabilitation Counseling, Baltimore, MD 21216-3698**

**AWARDS** Alcohol and substance abuse (MS).

**Faculty:** 8 part-time/adjunct (4 women).
**Students:** 1 applicant, 0% accepted.
*Application deadline:* For fall admission, 7/15 (priority date); for spring admission, 12/15 (priority date). Applications are processed on a rolling basis. *Application fee:* $25.

*Coppin State College (continued)*

**Expenses:** Tuition, state resident: full-time $3,576; part-time $149 per credit. Tuition, nonresident: full-time $6,360; part-time $265 per credit. Required fees: $589; $589 per year.

Dr. Janet Spry, Co-Chairperson, 410-951-3510, *E-mail:* jspry@coppin.edu.

**Application contact:** Vell Lyles, Associate Vice President for Enrollment Management, 410-951-3575, *E-mail:* vlyles@coppin.edu. *Web site:* http://www.coppin.edu/

## ■ CORNELL UNIVERSITY

**Graduate School, Graduate Fields of Arts and Sciences, Field of Psychology, Ithaca, NY 14853-0001**

**AWARDS** Biopsychology (PhD); general psychology (PhD); human experimental psychology (PhD); personality and social psychology (PhD).

**Faculty:** 36 full-time.
**Students:** 37 full-time (20 women); includes 2 minority (1 Asian American or Pacific Islander, 1 Hispanic American), 10 international. 144 applicants, 8% accepted. In 2001, 2 doctorates awarded.
**Degree requirements:** For doctorate, thesis/dissertation, 2 semesters of teaching experience.
**Entrance requirements:** For doctorate, GRE General Test, TOEFL, 3 letters of recommendation. *Application deadline:* For fall admission, 1/15. *Application fee:* $65. Electronic applications accepted.
**Expenses:** Tuition: Full-time $25,970. Required fees: $50.
**Financial support:** In 2001–02, 36 students received support, including 9 fellowships with full tuition reimbursements available, 27 teaching assistantships with full tuition reimbursements available; research assistantships with full tuition reimbursements available, institutionally sponsored loans, scholarships/grants, tuition waivers (full and partial), and unspecified assistantships also available. Financial award applicants required to submit FAFSA.
**Faculty research:** Sensory and perceptual systems, social cognition, cognitive development, neuroscience, quantitative and computational modeling.
**Application contact:** Graduate Field Assistant, 607-255-6364, *E-mail:* psychapp@cornell.edu. *Web site:* http://www.gradschool.cornell.edu/grad/fields_1/psych.html

## ■ DARTMOUTH COLLEGE

**School of Arts and Sciences, Department of Psychological and Brain Sciences, Hanover, NH 03755**

**AWARDS** Cognitive neuroscience (PhD); psychology (PhD).

**Faculty:** 23 full-time (3 women).
**Students:** 26 full-time (18 women); includes 1 minority (Native American), 4 international. 94 applicants, 16% accepted, 8 enrolled. In 2001, 1 doctorate awarded.
**Degree requirements:** For doctorate, thesis/dissertation.
**Entrance requirements:** For doctorate, GRE General Test, GRE Subject Test. *Application deadline:* For fall admission, 1/15 (priority date). *Application fee:* $40.
**Expenses:** Tuition: Full-time $26,425.
**Financial support:** In 2001–02, 26 students received support, including fellowships with full tuition reimbursements available (averaging $17,380 per year), research assistantships with full tuition reimbursements available (averaging $17,380 per year); Federal Work-Study, institutionally sponsored loans, and tuition waivers (full) also available.
Dr. Howard C. Hughes, Chair, 603-646-3181, *Fax:* 603-646-1419, *E-mail:* howard.hughes@dartmouth.edu.
**Application contact:** Tina Mason, Administrative Assistant, 603-646-3181. *Web site:* http://www.dartmouth.edu/artsci/psych/grad.html

## ■ DEPAUL UNIVERSITY

**College of Liberal Arts and Sciences, Department of Psychology, Chicago, IL 60604-2287**

**AWARDS** Clinical psychology (MA, PhD), including child clinical psychology, community clinical psychology; community psychology (PhD); experimental psychology (MA, PhD); general psychology (MS); industrial/organizational psychology (MA, PhD).

**Faculty:** 28 full-time (16 women), 4 part-time/adjunct (3 women).
**Students:** 56 full-time (37 women), 51 part-time (34 women); includes 17 African Americans, 9 Asian Americans or Pacific Islanders, 4 Hispanic Americans, 3 international. Average age 28. 275 applicants, 8% accepted. In 2001, 11 master's, 15 doctorates awarded.
**Degree requirements:** For master's, thesis, oral exam; for doctorate, thesis/dissertation, oral and written exams, comprehensive exam. *Median time to degree:* Master's–2 years full-time; doctorate–6 years full-time.
**Entrance requirements:** For master's, GRE General Test and subject test, minimum GPA of 3.5; for doctorate, GRE General Test, minimum GPA of 3.5. *Application fee:* $40.
**Expenses:** Tuition: Part-time $362 per credit hour. Tuition and fees vary according to program.
**Financial support:** In 2001–02, 47 students received support, including 30 research assistantships with full and partial tuition reimbursements available (averaging $6,000 per year), 14 teaching assistantships with full and partial tuition reimbursements available (averaging $6,000 per year); career-related internships or fieldwork, scholarships/grants, traineeships, and tuition waivers (full and partial) also available. Financial award application deadline: 1/10.
**Faculty research:** Chronic fatigue study, prevention intervention for high-risk teens, parent trauma, procrastination, self-regulation of affect.
Dr. Ralph Erber, Chairman, 773-325-7887, *E-mail:* reber@condor.depaul.edu.
**Application contact:** Lucinda Rapp, Information Contact, 773-325-7887, *E-mail:* lrapp@depaul.edu. *Web site:* http://www.depaul.edu/~psych/

## ■ DREXEL UNIVERSITY

**Graduate School, College of Arts and Sciences, Department of Psychology, Philadelphia, PA 19104-2875**

**AWARDS** Clinical neuropsychology (PhD).

**Faculty:** 6 full-time (2 women), 12 part-time/adjunct (7 women).
**Students:** 10 full-time (8 women), 12 part-time (11 women); includes 4 minority (2 African Americans, 1 Asian American or Pacific Islander, 1 Hispanic American), 1 international. Average age 27. 78 applicants, 13% accepted, 5 enrolled. In 2001, 8 degrees awarded.
**Degree requirements:** For doctorate, thesis/dissertation, internship.
**Entrance requirements:** For doctorate, GRE General Test, TOEFL. *Application deadline:* For fall admission, 2/1. Applications are processed on a rolling basis. *Application fee:* $50. Electronic applications accepted.
**Expenses:** Contact institution.
**Financial support:** Research assistantships, teaching assistantships, career-related internships or fieldwork, Federal Work-Study, institutionally sponsored loans, tuition waivers (full and partial), unspecified assistantships, and practicum positions available. Financial award application deadline: 2/1.
**Faculty research:** Neurosciences, rehabilitation psychology, cognitive science, neurological assessment.
Dr. Kirk Heilbrun, Head, 215-895-2402, *Fax:* 215-895-1333.

**Application contact:** Director of Graduate Admissions, 215-895-6700, *Fax:* 215-895-5939, *E-mail:* enroll@drexel.edu.

**Find an in-depth description at www.petersons.com/gradchannel.**

■ **DUKE UNIVERSITY**

**Graduate School, Department of Psychology, Durham, NC 27708-0586**

**AWARDS** Biological psychology (PhD); clinical psychology (PhD); cognitive psychology (PhD); developmental psychology (PhD); experimental psychology (PhD); health psychology (PhD); human social development (PhD).

**Faculty:** 52 full-time, 15 part-time/adjunct.

**Students:** 66 full-time (42 women); includes 11 minority (6 African Americans, 2 Asian Americans or Pacific Islanders, 3 Hispanic Americans), 13 international. 386 applicants, 7% accepted, 15 enrolled. In 2001, 8 doctorates awarded.

**Degree requirements:** For doctorate, thesis/dissertation.

**Entrance requirements:** For doctorate, GRE General Test. *Application deadline:* For fall admission, 12/31. *Application fee:* $75.

**Expenses:** Tuition: Full-time $24,600.

**Financial support:** Fellowships, research assistantships, teaching assistantships, career-related internships or fieldwork and Federal Work-Study available. Financial award application deadline: 12/31.
Reiko Mazuka, Co-Director of Graduate Studies, 919-660-5716, *Fax:* 919-660-5726, *E-mail:* bseymore@acpub.duke.edu. *Web site:* http://www.psych.duke.edu/

■ **DUQUESNE UNIVERSITY**

**Graduate School of Liberal Arts, Department of Psychology, Pittsburgh, PA 15282-0001**

**AWARDS** Clinical psychology (PhD); developmental psychology (PhD).

**Faculty:** 15 full-time (5 women), 5 part-time/adjunct (2 women).

**Students:** 83 full-time (42 women), 9 part-time (5 women); includes 6 minority (4 African Americans, 1 Asian American or Pacific Islander, 1 Hispanic American), 4 international. Average age 28. 54 applicants, 56% accepted, 13 enrolled. In 2001, 13 degrees awarded.

**Degree requirements:** For doctorate, 2 foreign languages, thesis/dissertation, comprehensive exam.

**Entrance requirements:** For doctorate, GRE General Test, TOEFL, MA in psychology. *Application deadline:* For fall admission, 2/1. *Application fee:* $50.

**Expenses:** Tuition: Part-time $566 per credit. Required fees: $56 per credit. Part-time tuition and fees vary according to degree level and program.

**Financial support:** In 2001–02, 1 research assistantship with full tuition reimbursement (averaging $11,000 per year), 14 teaching assistantships with full tuition reimbursements (averaging $11,000 per year) were awarded. Fellowships with full tuition reimbursements, career-related internships or fieldwork, scholarships/grants, and tuition waivers (partial) also available. Financial award application deadline: 5/1.

**Faculty research:** Emotion, language motivation, imagination, development.
Dr. Russell Walsh, Chair, 412-396-6520.

■ **EAST CAROLINA UNIVERSITY**

**Graduate School, College of Arts and Sciences, Department of Psychology, Program in General Psychology, Greenville, NC 27858-4353**

**AWARDS** MA.

**Students:** 19 full-time (13 women), 1 (woman) part-time. Average age 23. 52 applicants, 50% accepted. In 2001, 5 degrees awarded.

**Degree requirements:** For master's, one foreign language, thesis, comprehensive exam.

**Entrance requirements:** For master's, GRE General Test, GRE Subject Test, TOEFL. *Application deadline:* Applications are processed on a rolling basis. *Application fee:* $45.

**Expenses:** Tuition, state resident: full-time $2,636. Tuition, nonresident: full-time $11,365.

**Financial support:** Application deadline: 6/1.
Dr. John Cope, Director of Graduate Studies, 252-328-6497, *Fax:* 252-328-6283, *E-mail:* copej@mail.ecu.edu.

**Application contact:** Dr. Paul D. Tschetter, Senior Associate Dean of the Graduate School, 252-328-6012, *Fax:* 252-328-6071, *E-mail:* gradschool@mail.ecu.edu.

■ **EAST CENTRAL UNIVERSITY**

**Graduate School, Department of Psychology, Ada, OK 74820-6899**

**AWARDS** MSPS. Part-time and evening/weekend programs available.

**Entrance requirements:** For master's, GRE General Test, MAT.

**Expenses:** Tuition, state resident: part-time $96 per credit hour. Tuition, nonresident: part-time $225 per credit hour. Full-time tuition and fees vary according to course load.

■ **EASTERN ILLINOIS UNIVERSITY**

**Graduate School, College of Sciences, Department of Psychology, Charleston, IL 61920-3099**

**AWARDS** Clinical psychology (MA); school psychology (SSP).

**Degree requirements:** For master's, comprehensive exam; for SSP, thesis.

**Entrance requirements:** For master's and SSP, GRE General Test.

■ **EASTERN KENTUCKY UNIVERSITY**

**The Graduate School, College of Arts and Sciences, Department of Psychology, Richmond, KY 40475-3102**

**AWARDS** Clinical psychology (MS); industrial/organizational psychology (MS); school psychology (Psy S). Part-time programs available.

**Faculty:** 21 full-time (10 women).

**Students:** 66 full-time (58 women), 4 part-time (2 women); includes 4 minority (3 African Americans, 1 Hispanic American). Average age 24. 303 applicants, 30% accepted. In 2001, 20 degrees awarded.

**Entrance requirements:** For master's and Psy S, GRE General Test, minimum GPA of 2.5. *Application deadline:* For fall admission, 3/15 (priority date). Applications are processed on a rolling basis. *Application fee:* $0.

**Expenses:** Tuition, state resident: full-time $1,468; part-time $165 per credit hour. Tuition, nonresident: full-time $4,034; part-time $450 per credit hour.

**Financial support:** In 2001–02, 30 students received support, including 16 research assistantships, 10 teaching assistantships; career-related internships or fieldwork and Federal Work-Study also available. Support available to part-time students.

**Faculty research:** Cognitive behavior therapy, therapy with the deaf, victims of drunk drivers, autism. *Total annual research expenditures:* $40,000.
Dr. Robert M. Adams, Chair, 859-622-1105, *Fax:* 859-622-5871, *E-mail:* robert.adams@eku.edu. *Web site:* http://www.psychology.eku.edu/

■ **EASTERN MICHIGAN UNIVERSITY**

**Graduate School, College of Arts and Sciences, Department of Psychology, Ypsilanti, MI 48197**

**AWARDS** Clinical psychology (PhD); clinical/behavioral services (MS); psychology (MS), including general psychology. Evening/weekend programs available.

*Eastern Michigan University (continued)*
**Faculty:** 17 full-time (5 women).
**Students:** 53 full-time (42 women), 29 part-time (20 women); includes 13 minority (7 African Americans, 5 Asian Americans or Pacific Islanders, 1 Native American). In 2001, 36 degrees awarded.
**Entrance requirements:** For master's, GRE General Test, TOEFL. *Application deadline:* For fall admission, 5/15; for spring admission, 3/15. Applications are processed on a rolling basis. *Application fee:* $30.
**Expenses:** Tuition, state resident: part-time $285 per credit hour. Tuition, nonresident: part-time $510 per credit hour.
**Financial support:** Fellowships, teaching assistantships available. Support available to part-time students. Financial award application deadline: 3/15; financial award applicants required to submit FAFSA.
Dr. Kenneth Rusiniak, Head, 734-487-1155.

■ **EASTERN NEW MEXICO UNIVERSITY**

**Graduate School, College of Liberal Arts and Sciences, Department of Psychology and Sociology, Portales, NM 88130**

**AWARDS** MA. Part-time programs available.

**Faculty:** 4 full-time (2 women).
**Students:** 3 full-time (2 women), 2 part-time (1 woman); includes 1 minority (Hispanic American). Average age 31. 2 applicants, 100% accepted. In 2001, 2 degrees awarded.
**Degree requirements:** For master's, thesis optional.
**Entrance requirements:** For master's, minimum GPA of 2.75. *Application deadline:* For fall admission, 8/20 (priority date). Applications are processed on a rolling basis. *Application fee:* $10. Electronic applications accepted.
**Expenses:** Tuition, state resident: full-time $1,740; part-time $73 per credit. Tuition, nonresident: full-time $7,296; part-time $304 per credit. Required fees: $588; $25 per credit.
**Financial support:** In 2001–02, 2 research assistantships (averaging $7,700 per year) were awarded; fellowships, teaching assistantships, career-related internships or fieldwork and Federal Work-Study also available. Support available to part-time students. Financial award application deadline: 3/1.
Dr. Leslie Gill, Graduate Coordinator, 505-562-2045.

■ **EASTERN VIRGINIA MEDICAL SCHOOL**

**The Virginia Consortium Program in Clinical Psychology, Norfolk, VA 23501-1980**

**AWARDS** Psy D.
**Students:** 44.
**Entrance requirements:** For doctorate, GRE, BS in behavioral sciences or equivalent. *Application deadline:* For fall admission, 1/5. *Application fee:* $30.
**Expenses:** Contact institution.
Dr. John D. Ball, Director, 757-518-2550, *Fax:* 757-518-2553, *E-mail:* balljd@ evms.edu.
**Application contact:** Eileen O'Neill, Administrative Coordinator, 757-518-2550, *Fax:* 757-518-2553, *E-mail:* exoneill@ odu.edu. *Web site:* http://www.evms.edu/ hlthprof/index/html

■ **EASTERN WASHINGTON UNIVERSITY**

**Graduate School Studies, College of Education and Human Development, Department of Counseling, Educational, and Developmental Psychology, Cheney, WA 99004-2431**

**AWARDS** Developing psychology (MS); school counseling (MS), including counseling psychology, school counseling; school psychology (MS); special education (M Ed).
**Faculty:** 14 full-time (5 women).
**Students:** 62 full-time (53 women), 13 part-time (11 women); includes 3 minority (1 African American, 2 Asian Americans or Pacific Islanders), 3 international. 48 applicants, 67% accepted, 27 enrolled. In 2001, 30 degrees awarded.
**Degree requirements:** For master's, thesis or alternative, comprehensive exam.
**Entrance requirements:** For master's, GRE General Test, minimum GPA of 3.0. *Application deadline:* For fall admission, 2/1. Applications are processed on a rolling basis. *Application fee:* $35.
**Expenses:** Tuition, state resident: full-time $1,586; part-time $159 per credit hour. Tuition, nonresident: full-time $4,677; part-time $468 per credit hour. Required fees: $222; $159 per credit. $74 per quarter.
**Financial support:** In 2001–02, 4 teaching assistantships with partial tuition reimbursements (averaging $7,000 per year) were awarded; career-related internships or fieldwork, Federal Work-Study, institutionally sponsored loans, scholarships/grants, health care benefits, tuition waivers (partial), and unspecified assistantships also available. Support available to part-time students. Financial award application deadline: 2/1; financial award applicants required to submit FAFSA.

Dr. Armin Arndt, Chair, 509-359-2827, *Fax:* 509-359-4366. *Web site:* http:// www.appliedpsyc.ewu.edu

■ **EASTERN WASHINGTON UNIVERSITY**

**Graduate School Studies, College of Social and Behavioral Sciences, Department of Psychology, Cheney, WA 99004-2431**

**AWARDS** Psychology (MS); school psychology (MS).
**Faculty:** 9 full-time (2 women).
**Students:** 27 full-time (18 women), 6 part-time (3 women); includes 2 minority (1 Asian American or Pacific Islander, 1 Native American). 23 applicants, 87% accepted, 14 enrolled. In 2001, 10 degrees awarded.
**Degree requirements:** For master's, thesis or alternative, comprehensive exam.
**Entrance requirements:** For master's, GRE General Test, minimum GPA of 3.0. *Application deadline:* For fall admission, 3/1. Applications are processed on a rolling basis. *Application fee:* $35.
**Expenses:** Tuition, state resident: full-time $1,586; part-time $159 per credit hour. Tuition, nonresident: full-time $4,677; part-time $468 per credit hour. Required fees: $222; $159 per credit. $74 per quarter.
**Financial support:** In 2001–02, 8 teaching assistantships with partial tuition reimbursements (averaging $7,000 per year) were awarded; career-related internships or fieldwork, Federal Work-Study, institutionally sponsored loans, scholarships/grants, health care benefits, tuition waivers (partial), and unspecified assistantships also available. Support available to part-time students. Financial award application deadline: 2/1; financial award applicants required to submit FAFSA.
**Application contact:** Dr. Mahlon Dalley, Chair, 509-359-6174, *Fax:* 509-359-6325.

■ **EAST TENNESSEE STATE UNIVERSITY**

**School of Graduate Studies, College of Arts and Sciences, Department of Psychology, Johnson City, TN 37614**

**AWARDS** Clinical psychology (MA); general psychology (MA).
**Faculty:** 7 full-time (1 woman).
**Students:** 25 full-time (16 women), 11 part-time (5 women); includes 1 minority (African American). Average age 27. In 2001, 13 degrees awarded.
**Degree requirements:** For master's, thesis, oral exams.
**Entrance requirements:** For master's, GRE General Test, GRE Subject Test, TOEFL, minimum GPA of 3.0. *Application*

*deadline:* For fall admission, 7/15 (priority date). Applications are processed on a rolling basis. *Application fee:* $25 ($35 for international students).
**Expenses:** Tuition, state resident: part-time $181 per hour. Tuition, nonresident: part-time $270 per hour. Required fees: $220 per term.
**Financial support:** Research assistantships with full tuition reimbursements, teaching assistantships with full tuition reimbursements, career-related internships or fieldwork, institutionally sponsored loans, and scholarships/grants available.
**Faculty research:** Domestic violence, suicidal behavior, advertising, religious behavior, behavioral medicine. *Total annual research expenditures:* $69,131.
Dr. David J. Marx, Chair, 423-439-6656, *Fax:* 423-439-5695, *E-mail:* marx@etsu.edu. *Web site:* http://www.etsu.edu/

### ■ EDINBORO UNIVERSITY OF PENNSYLVANIA

**Graduate Studies, School of Liberal Arts, Department of Psychology, Edinboro, PA 16444**

**AWARDS** Clinical psychology (MA). Part-time and evening/weekend programs available.

**Faculty:** 4 full-time (3 women).
**Students:** 15 full-time (13 women), 9 part-time (8 women); includes 1 minority (Asian American or Pacific Islander). Average age 32. In 2001, 1 degree awarded.
**Degree requirements:** For master's, thesis or alternative, project, comprehensive exam.
**Entrance requirements:** For master's, GRE or MAT, minimum QPA of 2.5. *Application deadline:* For fall admission, 3/15 (priority date). Applications are processed on a rolling basis. *Application fee:* $25. Electronic applications accepted.
**Expenses:** Tuition, state resident: full-time $4,600; part-time $256 per credit. Tuition, nonresident: full-time $7,554; part-time $420 per credit. Required fees: $68 per credit.
**Financial support:** In 2001–02, 10 students received support. Career-related internships or fieldwork, Federal Work-Study, institutionally sponsored loans, scholarships/grants, and unspecified assistantships available. Support available to part-time students. Financial award application deadline: 5/1; financial award applicants required to submit FAFSA.
Dr. Susan LaBine, Coordinator, 814-732-2774, *E-mail:* slabine@edinboro.edu.
**Application contact:** Dr. Mary Margaret Bevevino, Dean of Graduate Studies, 814-732-2856, *Fax:* 814-732-2611, *E-mail:* mbevevino@edinboro.edu.

### ■ EMORY UNIVERSITY

**Graduate School of Arts and Sciences, Department of Psychology, Atlanta, GA 30322-1100**

**AWARDS** Clinical psychology (PhD); cognition and development (PhD); psychobiology (PhD).

**Faculty:** 26 full-time (6 women), 2 part-time/adjunct (0 women).
**Students:** 73 full-time (55 women); includes 5 minority (1 African American, 2 Asian Americans or Pacific Islanders, 2 Hispanic Americans), 6 international. 272 applicants, 6% accepted, 13 enrolled. In 2001, 10 doctorates awarded.
**Degree requirements:** For doctorate, thesis/dissertation, comprehensive exam, registration.
**Entrance requirements:** For doctorate, GRE General Test, TOEFL, minimum GPA of 3.0. *Application deadline:* For fall admission, 1/15. *Application fee:* $50. Electronic applications accepted.
**Expenses:** Tuition: Full-time $24,770. Required fees: $100. Tuition and fees vary according to program and student level.
**Financial support:** In 2001–02, 56 fellowships were awarded; research assistantships, teaching assistantships, career-related internships or fieldwork, Federal Work-Study, institutionally sponsored loans, scholarships/grants, and tuition waivers (full and partial) also available. Financial award application deadline: 1/20.
**Faculty research:** Neurophysiology, drugs and behavior, hormones and behavior, nonverbal behavior.
Dr. Darryl Neill, Chair, 404-727-7437.
**Application contact:** Dr. Robyn Fivush, Director of Graduate Studies, 404-727-7456, *E-mail:* psyrf@emory.edu.

### ■ EMPORIA STATE UNIVERSITY

**School of Graduate Studies, The Teachers College, Department of Psychology and Special Education, Program in Psychology, Emporia, KS 66801-5087**

**AWARDS** Clinical psychology (MS); general psychology (MS); industrial/organizational psychology (MS).

**Students:** 39 full-time (32 women), 8 part-time (6 women); includes 2 minority (both African Americans), 6 international. 23 applicants, 78% accepted. In 2001, 23 degrees awarded.
**Degree requirements:** For master's, comprehensive exam or thesis.
**Entrance requirements:** For master's, GRE General Test or MAT, TOEFL. *Application deadline:* For fall admission, 6/1 (priority date); for spring admission, 10/1. Applications are processed on a rolling basis. *Application fee:* $30 ($75 for

international students). Electronic applications accepted.
**Expenses:** Tuition, state resident: full-time $2,632; part-time $119 per credit hour. Tuition, nonresident: full-time $6,734; part-time $290 per credit hour.
**Financial support:** Career-related internships or fieldwork, Federal Work-Study, institutionally sponsored loans, health care benefits, and unspecified assistantships available. Financial award application deadline: 3/15; financial award applicants required to submit FAFSA.
**Faculty research:** Driving under the influence (DUI) personality, lifestyles and impostor phenomenon.
Dr. Kenneth A. Weaver, Chair, Department of Psychology and Special Education, 620-341-5317, *E-mail:* weaverke@emporia.edu.

### ■ EVANGEL UNIVERSITY

**Department of Psychology, Springfield, MO 65802-2191**

**AWARDS** Clinical psychology (MS); general psychology (MS); guidance and counseling (MS). Part-time and evening/weekend programs available.

**Faculty:** 4 full-time (1 woman), 4 part-time/adjunct (1 woman).
**Students:** 12 full-time (9 women), 11 part-time (7 women); includes 1 minority (Asian American or Pacific Islander). Average age 29. 10 applicants, 100% accepted. In 2001, 4 degrees awarded.
**Degree requirements:** For master's, thesis, comprehensive exam.
**Entrance requirements:** For master's, GRE General Test, minimum undergraduate GPA of 3.0, undergraduate major or minor in psychology, teaching certificate (guidance and counseling). *Application deadline:* For fall admission, 7/15 (priority date); for spring admission, 11/19 (priority date). Applications are processed on a rolling basis. *Application fee:* $25.
**Expenses:** Tuition: Full-time $3,040; part-time $190 per credit. Required fees: $240. Tuition and fees vary according to program.
**Financial support:** In 2001–02, 6 students received support; research assistantships, teaching assistantships, career-related internships or fieldwork, institutionally sponsored loans, and scholarships/grants available. Financial award application deadline: 5/1; financial award applicants required to submit FAFSA.
Dr. Jeffrey Fulks, Supervisor of Graduate Psychology, 417-865-2815 Ext. 7915.
**Application contact:** Jackie Eutsler, Administrative Assistant of Graduate Studies, 417-865-2815, *Fax:* 417-520-0545, *E-mail:* eutslerj@evangel.edu. *Web site:* http://www.evangel.edu/psycgrad/

## ■ FAIRFIELD UNIVERSITY

**Graduate School of Education and Allied Professions, Department of Psychology and Special Education, Fairfield, CT 06824**

**AWARDS** Applied psychology (MA); school psychology (MA, CAS); special education (MA, CAS). Part-time and evening/weekend programs available.

**Faculty:** 4 full-time (2 women), 9 part-time/adjunct (4 women).
**Students:** 34 full-time (24 women), 103 part-time (88 women); includes 19 minority (4 African Americans, 2 Asian Americans or Pacific Islanders, 13 Hispanic Americans), 3 international. Average age 28. 91 applicants, 69% accepted, 45 enrolled. In 2001, 39 master's, 9 other advanced degrees awarded.
**Degree requirements:** For master's, educational technology course required.
**Entrance requirements:** For master's, PRAXIS I (CBT), TOEFL, minimum QPA of 2.67. *Application deadline:* Applications are processed on a rolling basis. *Application fee:* $55. Electronic applications accepted.
**Expenses:** Tuition: Full-time $9,550; part-time $390 per credit hour. Required fees: $25 per term. Tuition and fees vary according to program.
**Financial support:** Scholarships/grants, tuition waivers (partial), and unspecified assistantships available. Support available to part-time students. Financial award applicants required to submit FAFSA.
**Faculty research:** School university collaboration, special education consultation, child neuropsychology, disabilities, effect of pretreatment orientation on treatment. Dr. Daniel Geller, Chair, 203-254-4000 Ext. 2324, *Fax:* 203-254-4047, *E-mail:* dgeller@fair1.fairfield.edu.
**Application contact:** Karen L Creecy, Assistant Dean, 203-254-4000 Ext. 2414, *Fax:* 203-254-4241, *E-mail:* klcreecy@mail.fairfield.edu. *Web site:* http://www.fairfield.edu/

## ■ FAIRLEIGH DICKINSON UNIVERSITY, COLLEGE AT FLORHAM

**Maxwell Becton College of Arts and Sciences, Department of Psychology, Madison, NJ 07940-1099**

**AWARDS** Applied social and community psychology (MA); clinical /counseling psychology (MA); general experimental psychology (MA); industrial/organizational psychology (MA); organizational behavior (MA).

**Students:** 69 full-time (54 women), 89 part-time (63 women); includes 18 minority (10 African Americans, 4 Asian

Americans or Pacific Islanders, 4 Hispanic Americans), 5 international. Average age 34. 84 applicants, 79% accepted, 40 enrolled. In 2001, 42 degrees awarded.
**Entrance requirements:** For master's, GRE General Test. *Application deadline:* Applications are processed on a rolling basis. *Application fee:* $40.
**Expenses:** Tuition: Full-time $11,484; part-time $638 per credit. Required fees: $420. One-time fee: $97 part-time. Dr. Robert Chell, Chairperson, 973-443-8547, *Fax:* 973-443-8562, *E-mail:* robert_chell@fdu.edu.

## ■ FAIRLEIGH DICKINSON UNIVERSITY, METROPOLITAN CAMPUS

**University College: Arts, Sciences, and Professional Studies, School of Psychology, Teaneck, NJ 07666-1914**

**AWARDS** Clinical psychology (PhD); general-theoretical psychology (MA); school psychology (MA, Psy D).

**Students:** 152 full-time (114 women), 38 part-time (35 women); includes 22 minority (4 African Americans, 5 Asian Americans or Pacific Islanders, 13 Hispanic Americans), 8 international. Average age 30. 93 applicants, 77% accepted, 36 enrolled. In 2001, 35 master's, 13 doctorates awarded.
*Application deadline:* Applications are processed on a rolling basis. *Application fee:* $40.
**Expenses:** Tuition: Full-time $11,484; part-time $638 per credit. Required fees: $420; $97.
Dr. Christopher Capuano, Director, 201-692-2811, *Fax:* 201-692-2304, *E-mail:* capuano@fdu.edu.

## ■ FAYETTEVILLE STATE UNIVERSITY

**Graduate School, Program in Psychology, Fayetteville, NC 28301-4298**

**AWARDS** MA. Part-time and evening/weekend programs available.

**Faculty:** 6 full-time (3 women), 2 part-time/adjunct (0 women).
**Students:** 3 full-time (all women), 13 part-time (10 women); includes 7 minority (all African Americans). Average age 36. 7 applicants, 100% accepted. In 2001, 1 degree awarded.
**Degree requirements:** For master's, internship.
*Application deadline:* For fall admission, 8/1; for spring admission, 12/15. Applications are processed on a rolling basis. *Application fee:* $25.

**Expenses:** Tuition, state resident: full-time $810; part-time $426 per year. Tuition, nonresident: full-time $4,445; part-time $2,223 per year. Tuition and fees vary according to course load.
**Faculty research:** Prostate cancer, hypotension, rape crisis, cross cultural concerns.
Dr. Doreen Hilton, Chairperson, 910-672-1577, *E-mail:* dhilton@uncfsu.edu.

## ■ FIELDING GRADUATE INSTITUTE

**Graduate Programs, Program in Psychology, Santa Barbara, CA 93105-3538**

**AWARDS** Clinical psychology (PhD); psychology (MA). Evening/weekend programs available.

**Faculty:** 34 full-time (15 women), 25 part-time/adjunct (13 women).
**Students:** 452 full-time (317 women); includes 79 minority (36 African Americans, 9 Asian Americans or Pacific Islanders, 27 Hispanic Americans, 7 Native Americans), 12 international. Average age 44. 154 applicants, 30% accepted, 31 enrolled. In 2001, 43 master's, 35 doctorates awarded. Terminal master's awarded for partial completion of doctoral program.
**Degree requirements:** For doctorate, thesis/dissertation. *Median time to degree:* Master's–4.8 years full-time; doctorate–9.7 years full-time.
*Application deadline:* For fall admission, 3/5; for spring admission, 9/5. *Application fee:* $75.
**Expenses:** Tuition: Full-time $14,100.
**Financial support:** In 2001–02, 311 students received support. Career-related internships or fieldwork and diversity scholarships available. Financial award application deadline: 3/1; financial award applicants required to submit FAFSA.
Dr. Ronald Giannetti, Dean, 805-898-2909, *E-mail:* rongian@fielding.edu.
**Application contact:** Marine Dumas, Admissions Manager, 805-898-4039, *Fax:* 805-687-4590, *E-mail:* mdumas@fielding.edu.

## ■ FISK UNIVERSITY

**Graduate Programs, Department of Psychology, Nashville, TN 37208-3051**

**AWARDS** Clinical psychology (MA); psychology (MA).

**Faculty:** 4 full-time (2 women), 1 (woman) part-time/adjunct.
**Students:** 8 full-time (all women); all minorities (all African Americans). Average age 23. 16 applicants, 50% accepted, 3 enrolled. In 2001, 5 degrees awarded.

**Degree requirements:** For master's, thesis. *Median time to degree:* Master's–2 years full-time, 3 years part-time.
**Entrance requirements:** For master's, GRE General Test, GRE Subject Test, minimum GPA of 3.0. *Application deadline:* For fall admission, 4/15 (priority date). Applications are processed on a rolling basis. *Application fee:* $25.
**Expenses:** Tuition: Full-time $9,790.
**Financial support:** In 2001–02, 7 students received support; teaching assistantships with partial tuition reimbursements available available.
**Faculty research:** Ethnic and gender identity, development, female adolescent development, juvenile delinquency prevention. *Total annual research expenditures:* $5,000.
Dr. Sheila Peters, Chair, 615-329-8617, *E-mail:* speters@fisk.edu.
**Application contact:** Director of Admissions, 615-329-8668, *Fax:* 615-329-8774.

■ **FLORIDA AGRICULTURAL AND MECHANICAL UNIVERSITY**
**Division of Graduate Studies, Research, and Continuing Education, College of Arts and Sciences, Department of Psychology, Tallahassee, FL 32307-3200**
**AWARDS** Community psychology (MS); school psychology (MS).
**Degree requirements:** For master's, thesis.
**Entrance requirements:** For master's, GRE General Test, minimum GPA of 3.0.

■ **FLORIDA ATLANTIC UNIVERSITY**
**Charles E. Schmidt College of Science, Department of Psychology, Boca Raton, FL 33431-0991**
**AWARDS** MA, PhD.
**Faculty:** 32 full-time (10 women), 2 part-time/adjunct (both women).
**Students:** 32 full-time (20 women), 14 part-time (10 women); includes 6 minority (2 Asian Americans or Pacific Islanders, 3 Hispanic Americans, 1 Native American), 4 international. Average age 32. 77 applicants, 25% accepted, 15 enrolled. In 2001, 8 master's, 2 doctorates awarded. Terminal master's awarded for partial completion of doctoral program.
**Degree requirements:** For master's, one foreign language, thesis/dissertation, registration; for doctorate, one foreign language, thesis/dissertation, comprehensive exam, registration. *Median time to degree:* Master's–2.5 years full-time; doctorate–5.5 years full-time.
**Entrance requirements:** For master's and doctorate, GRE General Test, minimum

GPA of 3.0 during previous 2 years. *Application deadline:* For fall admission, 1/15. *Application fee:* $20. Electronic applications accepted.
**Expenses:** Tuition, state resident: full-time $3,098; part-time $172 per credit. Tuition, nonresident: full-time $10,427; part-time $579 per credit.
**Financial support:** In 2001–02, 21 students received support, including 2 research assistantships with partial tuition reimbursements available (averaging $12,000 per year), 20 teaching assistantships with partial tuition reimbursements available (averaging $11,200 per year); Federal Work-Study also available. Financial award application deadline: 3/1; financial award applicants required to submit FAFSA.
**Faculty research:** Cognition, psychobiology, developmental psychology, social psychology, neuroscience. *Total annual research expenditures:* $520,000.
Dr. David L. Wolgin, Chair, 561-297-3366, *Fax:* 561-297-2160, *E-mail:* wolgindl@fau.edu.
**Application contact:** Dr. Philip S. Lasiter, Graduate Program Coordinator, 561-297-3368, *Fax:* 561-297-2160, *E-mail:* lasiter@fau.edu. *Web site:* http://www.psy.fau.edu/

■ **FLORIDA INSTITUTE OF TECHNOLOGY**
**Graduate Programs, School of Psychology, Melbourne, FL 32901-6975**
**AWARDS** Applied behavior analysis (MS); clinical psychology (Psy D); industrial/organizational psychology (MS, PhD). Part-time programs available.
**Faculty:** 12 full-time (4 women), 16 part-time/adjunct (1 woman).
**Students:** 117 full-time (87 women), 10 part-time (6 women); includes 14 minority (6 African Americans, 4 Asian Americans or Pacific Islanders, 4 Hispanic Americans), 10 international. Average age 29. 183 applicants, 34% accepted. In 2001, 26 degrees awarded.
**Degree requirements:** For master's, preliminary exam, thesis optional; for doctorate, thesis/dissertation, internship, preliminary exam.
**Entrance requirements:** For master's, GRE General Test, minimum GPA of 3.0; for doctorate, GRE General Test, GRE Subject Test, minimum GPA of 3.2. *Application deadline:* For fall admission, 3/15. Applications are processed on a rolling basis. *Application fee:* $50. Electronic applications accepted.
**Expenses:** Tuition: Part-time $650 per credit.
**Financial support:** In 2001–02, 32 students received support, including 26

research assistantships with full and partial tuition reimbursements available (averaging $3,600 per year), 6 teaching assistantships with partial tuition reimbursements available (averaging $3,600 per year); career-related internships or fieldwork, institutionally sponsored loans, tuition waivers (partial), unspecified assistantships, and tuition remissions also available. Financial award application deadline: 3/1; financial award applicants required to submit FAFSA.
**Faculty research:** Addictions, neuropsychology, child abuse, assessment, psychological trauma. *Total annual research expenditures:* $313,000.
Dr. Mary Beth Kenkel, Dean, 321-674-8142, *Fax:* 321-674-7105.
**Application contact:** Carolyn P. Farrior, Director of Graduate Admissions, 321-674-7118, *Fax:* 321-723-9468, *E-mail:* cfarrior@fit.edu. *Web site:* http://www.fit.edu/

**Find an in-depth description at www.petersons.com/gradchannel.**

■ **FLORIDA INTERNATIONAL UNIVERSITY**
**College of Arts and Sciences, Department of Psychology, Miami, FL 33199**
**AWARDS** Developmental psychology (PhD); general psychology (MS); psychology (MS). Part-time programs available.
**Faculty:** 26 full-time (8 women).
**Students:** 73 full-time (53 women), 35 part-time (26 women); includes 41 minority (4 African Americans, 4 Asian Americans or Pacific Islanders, 33 Hispanic Americans), 13 international. Average age 29. 191 applicants, 29% accepted, 33 enrolled. In 2001, 16 master's, 9 doctorates awarded. Terminal master's awarded for partial completion of doctoral program.
**Degree requirements:** For master's and doctorate, thesis/dissertation.
**Entrance requirements:** For master's and doctorate, GRE General Test, TOEFL. *Application deadline:* For fall admission, 4/1 (priority date); for spring admission, 10/1. Applications are processed on a rolling basis. *Application fee:* $20.
**Expenses:** Tuition, state resident: full-time $2,916; part-time $162 per credit hour. Tuition, nonresident: full-time $10,245; part-time $569 per credit hour. Required fees: $168 per term.
**Financial support:** In 2001–02, 6 fellowships, 2 research assistantships were awarded. Federal Work-Study, institutionally sponsored loans, and tuition waivers (partial) also available. Support available to part-time students. Financial award application deadline: 4/1.

*Florida International University (continued)*
**Faculty research:** Community psychology. Dr. Marvin Dunn, Chairperson, 305-348-3466, *Fax:* 305-348-3879, *E-mail:* dunnm@fiu.edu.

## ■ FLORIDA STATE UNIVERSITY

**Graduate Studies, College of Arts and Sciences, Department of Psychology, Tallahassee, FL 32306**

**AWARDS** Applied behavior analysis (MS); clinical psychology (PhD); cognitive and behavioral science (PhD); neuroscience (PhD).

**Faculty:** 38 full-time (10 women), 1 part-time/adjunct (0 women).
**Students:** 109 full-time (52 women), 5 part-time (4 women); includes 18 minority (9 African Americans, 1 Asian American or Pacific Islander, 7 Hispanic Americans, 1 Native American), 2 international. Average age 26. 300 applicants, 10% accepted, 15 enrolled. In 2001, 18 master's, 15 doctorates awarded. Terminal master's awarded for partial completion of doctoral program.
**Degree requirements:** For master's, comprehensive exam; for doctorate, thesis/dissertation, preliminary exam. *Median time to degree:* Master's–1.66 years full-time; doctorate–3.3 years full-time.
**Entrance requirements:** For master's and doctorate, GRE General Test, minimum GPA of 3.0. *Application deadline:* For fall admission, 12/15. *Application fee:* $20. Electronic applications accepted.
**Expenses:** Tuition, state resident: part-time $163 per credit hour. Tuition, nonresident: part-time $570 per credit hour. Tuition and fees vary according to program.
**Financial support:** In 2001–02, 54 students received support, including 11 fellowships with full tuition reimbursements available (averaging $15,000 per year), 46 research assistantships with full tuition reimbursements available (averaging $12,500 per year), 19 teaching assistantships with full tuition reimbursements available (averaging $12,600 per year); career-related internships or fieldwork, Federal Work-Study, institutionally sponsored loans, traineeships, and unspecified assistantships also available. Financial award applicants required to submit FAFSA. *Total annual research expenditures:* $5 million.
Dr. Janet Kistner, Chairman, 850-644-2040, *Fax:* 850-644-7739.
**Application contact:** Cherie P. Dilworth, Graduate Program Assistant, 850-644-2499, *Fax:* 850-644-7739, *E-mail:* grad-info@psy.fsu.edu.

## ■ FORDHAM UNIVERSITY

**Graduate School of Arts and Sciences, Department of Psychology, New York, NY 10458**

**AWARDS** Clinical psychology (PhD); developmental psychology (PhD); psychometrics (PhD).

**Faculty:** 23 full-time (9 women), 3 part-time/adjunct (2 women).
**Students:** 84 full-time (62 women), 90 part-time (63 women); includes 35 minority (10 African Americans, 6 Asian Americans or Pacific Islanders, 18 Hispanic Americans, 1 Native American), 5 international. 341 applicants, 15% accepted. In 2001, 20 doctorates awarded.
**Degree requirements:** For doctorate, thesis/dissertation, comprehensive exam.
**Entrance requirements:** For doctorate, GRE General Test, GRE Subject Test. *Application deadline:* For fall admission, 1/8. *Application fee:* $65. Electronic applications accepted.
**Expenses:** Tuition: Part-time $720 per credit. Required fees: $135 per semester.
**Financial support:** In 2001–02, 64 students received support, including 1 fellowship with tuition reimbursement available (averaging $15,000 per year), 6 research assistantships with tuition reimbursements available (averaging $12,000 per year), 5 teaching assistantships with tuition reimbursements available (averaging $15,000 per year); career-related internships or fieldwork, institutionally sponsored loans, tuition waivers (full and partial), and unspecified assistantships also available. Financial award application deadline: 1/8.
Dr. Frederick Wertz, Chair, 718-817-3777, *Fax:* 718-817-3785, *E-mail:* wertz@fordham.edu.
**Application contact:** Dr. Craig W. Pilant, Assistant Dean, 718-817-4420, *Fax:* 718-817-3566, *E-mail:* pilant@fordham.edu. *Web site:* http://www.fordham.edu/gsas/

## ■ FOREST INSTITUTE OF PROFESSIONAL PSYCHOLOGY

**Graduate Programs, Springfield, MO 65807**

**AWARDS** Clinical psychology (Psy D); psychology (MA). Part-time programs available. Terminal master's awarded for partial completion of doctoral program.

**Degree requirements:** For master's, thesis or alternative; for doctorate, thesis/dissertation, internship, qualifying exams.
**Entrance requirements:** For master's, GRE General Test, interview, minimum GPA of 3.2, 12 hours in psychology; for doctorate, GRE General Test, interview, minimum GPA of 3.25, 18 hours in psychology. Electronic applications accepted.
**Faculty research:** Closed head injury, pain management, clinical supervision, alternative treatment methods for depression, organizational analysis. *Web site:* http://www.forestinstitute.org/

## ■ FORT HAYS STATE UNIVERSITY

**Graduate School, College of Arts and Sciences, Department of Psychology, Hays, KS 67601-4099**

**AWARDS** Psychology (MS); school psychology (Ed S).

**Faculty:** 7 full-time (1 woman).
**Students:** 19 full-time (14 women), 8 part-time (6 women); includes 3 minority (1 Asian American or Pacific Islander, 2 Hispanic Americans). Average age 31. 30 applicants, 77% accepted. In 2001, 7 master's, 3 other advanced degrees awarded.
**Degree requirements:** For master's, thesis, comprehensive exam; for Ed S, thesis.
**Entrance requirements:** For master's, GRE General Test; for Ed S, GRE Subject Test. *Application deadline:* For fall admission, 3/1 (priority date). Applications are processed on a rolling basis. *Application fee:* $25 ($35 for international students). Electronic applications accepted.
**Expenses:** Tuition, state resident: full-time $927; part-time $103 per credit hour. Tuition, nonresident: full-time $2,466; part-time $247 per credit hour.
**Financial support:** In 2001–02, 12 teaching assistantships were awarded; research assistantships, career-related internships or fieldwork, institutionally sponsored loans, and tuition waivers (full) also available. Support available to part-time students.
**Faculty research:** Memory, learning, motivation, clinical and experimental psychology, history and systems of psychological stressors in rural environments.
Dr. Robert Markley, Chairman, 785-628-4405.

## ■ FRAMINGHAM STATE COLLEGE

**Graduate Programs, Department of Psychology/Philosophy, Framingham, MA 01701-9101**

**AWARDS** Counseling (MA). Part-time and evening/weekend programs available.

**Faculty:** 4 full-time, 3 part-time/adjunct.
**Students:** In 2001, 19 degrees awarded.
Dr. Anthony Dias, Chairman, 508-626-4873.

**Application contact:** Graduate Office, 508-626-4550.

# ■ FRANCIS MARION UNIVERSITY

**Graduate Programs, Department of Psychology, Florence, SC 29501-0547**

**AWARDS** Applied clinical psychology (MS); applied community psychology (MS); school psychology (MS). Part-time and evening/weekend programs available.

**Faculty:** 12 full-time (3 women), 2 part-time/adjunct (1 woman).

**Students:** 57. Average age 36. In 2001, 12 degrees awarded.

**Degree requirements:** For master's, internship.

**Entrance requirements:** For master's, GRE General Test. *Application deadline:* For fall admission, 4/15; for spring admission, 10/15. Applications are processed on a rolling basis. *Application fee:* $30.

**Expenses:** Tuition, state resident: full-time $3,820; part-time $191 per semester hour. Tuition, nonresident: full-time $7,640; part-time $382 per semester hour. Required fees: $170; $4 per semester hour. $30 per semester.

**Financial support:** In 2001–02, fellowships (averaging $6,000 per year); career-related internships or fieldwork and unspecified assistantships also available. Support available to part-time students. Financial award application deadline: 3/1; financial award applicants required to submit FAFSA.

**Faculty research:** Critical thinking, spatial localization, cognition and aging, family psychology.

Dr. John R. Hester, Coordinator, 843-661-1635, *Fax:* 843-661-1628.

**Application contact:** Ginger Ridgill, Administrative Assistant, 843-661-1378, *Fax:* 843-661-1628, *E-mail:* gridgill@fmarion.edu.

# ■ FROSTBURG STATE UNIVERSITY

**Graduate School, College of Liberal Arts and Sciences, Department of Psychology, Frostburg, MD 21532-1099**

**AWARDS** Counseling psychology (MS). Part-time and evening/weekend programs available.

**Faculty:** 8 full-time (6 women), 1 part-time/adjunct (0 women).

**Students:** 26 full-time (21 women), 10 part-time (7 women); includes 2 minority (both Hispanic Americans), 1 international. Average age 30. 24 applicants, 46% accepted. In 2001, 11 degrees awarded.

**Degree requirements:** For master's, internship.

**Entrance requirements:** For master's, GRE General Test or MAT, interview, minimum GPA of 3.0, resumé. *Application deadline:* For fall admission, 2/1. Applications are processed on a rolling basis. *Application fee:* $30. Electronic applications accepted.

**Expenses:** Tuition, area resident: Part-time $187 per credit hour. Tuition, state resident: full-time $3,366; part-time $187 per credit hour. Tuition, nonresident: full-time $3,906; part-time $217 per credit hour. Required fees: $812; $34 per credit hour. One-time fee: $9 full-time.

**Financial support:** In 2001–02, 7 research assistantships with full tuition reimbursements (averaging $5,000 per year) were awarded; career-related internships or fieldwork and Federal Work-Study also available. Financial award application deadline: 4/1; financial award applicants required to submit FAFSA.

Dr. Cindy Herzog, Chair, 301-687-4193.

**Application contact:** Patricia C. Spiker, Director of Graduate Services, 301-687-7053, *Fax:* 301-687-4597, *E-mail:* pspiker@frostburg.edu.

# ■ FULLER THEOLOGICAL SEMINARY

**Graduate School of Psychology, Pasadena, CA 91182**

**AWARDS** MA, MS, PhD, Psy D, MACL/PhD, MACL/Psy D. Terminal master's awarded for partial completion of doctoral program.

**Degree requirements:** For master's, practicum; for doctorate, thesis/dissertation, internships.

**Entrance requirements:** For master's, GRE General Test, TOEFL; for doctorate, GRE General Test GRE Subject Test, TOEFL, interview.

**Faculty research:** Psychology of religion, depression, shame, psychoneuroimmunology, marital intimacy, sex roles, psychoanalytic theory, men's issues, family relations. *Web site:* http://www.fuller.edu/sop/

# ■ GALLAUDET UNIVERSITY

**The Graduate School, College of Arts and Sciences, Department of Psychology, Washington, DC 20002-3625**

**AWARDS** Clinical psychology (PhD); school psychology (MA, Psy S), including developmental psychology (MA), school psychology (Psy S).

**Degree requirements:** For master's, thesis optional; for doctorate, thesis/dissertation.

**Entrance requirements:** For master's, GRE General Test or MAT; for doctorate, GRE General Test or MAT, interview.

# ■ GARDNER-WEBB UNIVERSITY

**Graduate School, Department of Psychology, Boiling Springs, NC 28017**

**AWARDS** Mental health counseling (MA); school counseling (MA). Part-time and evening/weekend programs available.

**Faculty:** 5 full-time (3 women), 2 part-time/adjunct (1 woman).

**Students:** Average age 35. In 2001, 24 degrees awarded.

**Degree requirements:** For master's, comprehensive exam.

**Entrance requirements:** For master's, GRE General Test, MAT, minimum GPA of 2.7. *Application deadline:* For fall admission, 7/1 (priority date). Applications are processed on a rolling basis. *Application fee:* $25. Electronic applications accepted.

**Expenses:** Tuition: Part-time $210 per hour. Part-time tuition and fees vary according to program.

**Financial support:** Unspecified assistantships available.

Dr. David Carscaddon, Chair, 704-406-4437, *Fax:* 704-406-4329, *E-mail:* dcarscaddon@gardner-webb.edu.

# ■ GENEVA COLLEGE

**Program in Counseling, Beaver Falls, PA 15010-3599**

**AWARDS** Marriage and family (MA); mental health (MA); school counseling (MA). Part-time and evening/weekend programs available.

**Faculty:** 5 full-time (2 women), 2 part-time/adjunct (0 women).

**Students:** 16 full-time (14 women), 31 part-time (23 women). Average age 26. In 2001, 4 degrees awarded.

**Degree requirements:** For master's, internship. *Median time to degree:* Master's–2 years full-time, 4.5 years part-time.

**Entrance requirements:** For master's, GRE General Test or MAT, minimum GPA of 3.0, letters of recommendation, faith statement. *Application deadline:* For fall admission, 7/1 (priority date); for spring admission, 11/1 (priority date). Applications are processed on a rolling basis. *Application fee:* $50. Electronic applications accepted.

**Expenses:** Tuition: Part-time $445 per credit hour.

**Financial support:** In 2001–02, 6 teaching assistantships (averaging $2,500 per year) were awarded; career-related internships or fieldwork and unspecified assistantships also available.

Dr. Carol Luce, Director, 724-847-6622, *Fax:* 724-847-6101, *E-mail:* cbluce@geneva.edu.

*Geneva College (continued)*

**Application contact:** Dr. Robin Ware, Director of Graduate Student Services, 724-847-6697, *Fax:* 724-847-6101, *E-mail:* counseling@geneva.edu. *Web site:* http://www.geneva.edu/

**Find an in-depth description at www.petersons.com/gradchannel.**

■ **GEORGE FOX UNIVERSITY**

**Graduate and Professional Studies, Graduate School of Clinical Psychology, Newberg, OR 97132-2697**

AWARDS Clinical psychology (Psy D); psychology (MA).

**Faculty:** 5 full-time (2 women), 3 part-time/adjunct (2 women).

**Students:** 72 full-time (32 women), 12 part-time (6 women); includes 11 minority (2 African Americans, 2 Asian Americans or Pacific Islanders, 3 Hispanic Americans, 4 Native Americans), 3 international. 36 applicants, 75% accepted, 21 enrolled. In 2001, 16 master's, 16 doctorates awarded.

**Degree requirements:** For doctorate, thesis/dissertation, internship.

**Entrance requirements:** For master's, GRE General Test, GRE Subject Test, minimum undergraduate GPA of 3.0 during previous 2 years. *Application deadline:* For fall admission, 1/1. *Application fee:* $40. Electronic applications accepted.

**Expenses:** Contact institution.

**Financial support:** Teaching assistantships, career-related internships or fieldwork available. Financial award applicants required to submit FAFSA.

**Faculty research:** Spiritual well-being, psychosocial development, value and ethics development.

Dr. Wayne Adams, Director, 800-765-4369 Ext. 2760, *E-mail:* wadams@georgefox.edu.

**Application contact:** Dr. Andrea Cook, Vice President for Enrollment Services, 800-631-0921, *Fax:* 503-554-3856, *E-mail:* acook@georgefox.edu. *Web site:* http://www.georgefox.edu/

■ **GEORGE MASON UNIVERSITY**

**College of Arts and Sciences, Department of Psychology, Fairfax, VA 22030-4444**

AWARDS Clinical psychology (PhD); developmental psychology (PhD); experimental neuropsychology (MA); human factors engineering psychology (MA, PhD); industrial/organizational psychology (MA, PhD); life-span development psychology (MA); school psychology (MA).

**Faculty:** 38 full-time (11 women), 36 part-time/adjunct (20 women).

**Students:** 96 full-time (64 women), 103 part-time (76 women); includes 19 minority (6 African Americans, 7 Asian Americans or Pacific Islanders, 6 Hispanic Americans), 7 international. Average age 29. 435 applicants, 33% accepted, 61 enrolled. In 2001, 71 master's, 14 doctorates awarded.

**Degree requirements:** For master's, thesis optional; for doctorate, thesis/dissertation.

**Entrance requirements:** For master's, GRE General Test, minimum GPA of 3.0 in last 60 hours, previous undergraduate course work in psychology; for doctorate, GRE General Test, minimum undergraduate GPA of 3.0, 3.25 in major. *Application fee:* $30. Electronic applications accepted.

**Expenses:** Tuition, state resident: full-time $3,168; part-time $132 per credit hour. Tuition, nonresident: full-time $11,280; part-time $470 per credit hour. Required fees: $1,416; $59 per credit hour.

**Financial support:** Fellowships, research assistantships, teaching assistantships available. Support available to part-time students. Financial award application deadline: 3/1; financial award applicants required to submit FAFSA.

Dr. Robert Smith, Chairperson, 703-993-1342, *Fax:* 703-993-1359, *E-mail:* bsmith@osf1.gmu.edu.

**Application contact:** Dr. James Maddux, Information Contact, 703-993-1342, *E-mail:* psycgrad@gmu.edu. *Web site:* http://www.gmu.edu/departments/psychology/homepage/

■ **GEORGETOWN UNIVERSITY**

**Graduate School of Arts and Sciences, Department of Psychology, Washington, DC 20057**

AWARDS PhD.

**Degree requirements:** For doctorate, thesis/dissertation.

**Entrance requirements:** For doctorate, GRE General Test, GRE Subject Test, TOEFL.

■ **THE GEORGE WASHINGTON UNIVERSITY**

**Columbian College of Arts and Sciences, Department of Psychology, Washington, DC 20052**

AWARDS Applied social psychology (PhD); clinical psychology (PhD, Psy D); cognitive neuropsychology (PhD); industrial-organizational psychology (PhD). Part-time and evening/weekend programs available.

**Faculty:** 15 full-time (8 women), 1 (woman) part-time/adjunct.

**Students:** 133 full-time (106 women), 102 part-time (82 women); includes 50 minority (22 African Americans, 13 Asian Americans or Pacific Islanders, 14 Hispanic Americans, 1 Native American), 15 international. Average age 30. 413 applicants, 18% accepted. In 2001, 32 doctorates awarded.

**Degree requirements:** For doctorate, thesis/dissertation or alternative, general exam.

**Entrance requirements:** For doctorate, GRE General Test, minimum GPA of 3.0. *Application fee:* $55.

**Expenses:** Tuition: Part-time $810 per credit. Required fees: $1 per credit.

**Financial support:** In 2001–02, 27 students received support, including 22 fellowships with tuition reimbursements available (averaging $4,700 per year), 20 teaching assistantships with tuition reimbursements available (averaging $2,900 per year); career-related internships or fieldwork and Federal Work-Study also available. Financial award application deadline: 2/1.

Dr. Rolf Peterson, Chair, 202-994-6544. *Web site:* http://www.gwu.edu/~gradinfo/

■ **GEORGIA COLLEGE & STATE UNIVERSITY**

**Graduate School, College of Arts and Sciences, Department of Psychology, Milledgeville, GA 31061**

AWARDS MS. Part-time programs available.

**Students:** 6 full-time (4 women), 3 part-time (2 women); includes 1 minority (African American). Average age 26. In 2001, 11 degrees awarded.

**Degree requirements:** For master's, thesis optional.

**Entrance requirements:** For master's, GRE General Test, minimum GPA of 2.5. *Application deadline:* For fall admission, 7/15 (priority date). Applications are processed on a rolling basis. *Application fee:* $25. Electronic applications accepted.

**Expenses:** Tuition, state resident: full-time $2,286. Tuition, nonresident: full-time $9,108. Required fees: $500.

**Financial support:** In 2001–02, 6 research assistantships with tuition reimbursements were awarded; career-related internships or fieldwork, Federal Work-Study, and unspecified assistantships also available. Support available to part-time students. Financial award application deadline: 3/1; financial award applicants required to submit FAFSA.

**Faculty research:** Pharmacological intervention of stroke, animal cognition, psychoneuroendocrinology, dissociative disorders, neuropsychology.

Dr. Sheree Barron, Chairperson, 478-445-0860.

**Application contact:** Dr. David Compton, Coordinator, *E-mail:* dcompton@mail.gcsu.edu.

## ■ GEORGIA INSTITUTE OF TECHNOLOGY

**Graduate Studies and Research, College of Sciences, School of Psychology, Atlanta, GA 30332-0001**

**AWARDS** Human computer interaction (MSHCI); psychology (MS, MS Psy, PhD). Terminal master's awarded for partial completion of doctoral program.

**Degree requirements:** For master's and doctorate, thesis/dissertation.

**Entrance requirements:** For master's and doctorate, GRE General Test, GRE Subject Test, TOEFL, minimum GPA of 3.0. Electronic applications accepted.

**Faculty research:** Experimental, industrial-organizational, and engineering psychology; cognitive aging and processes; leadership; human factors. *Web site:* http://www.gatech.edu/psychology/

## ■ GEORGIA SOUTHERN UNIVERSITY

**Jack N. Averitt College of Graduate Studies, College of Liberal Arts and Social Sciences, Department of Psychology, Statesboro, GA 30460**

**AWARDS** MS.

**Faculty:** 15 full-time (6 women).
**Students:** 18 full-time (16 women), 3 part-time (all women); includes 6 minority (5 African Americans, 1 Asian American or Pacific Islander), 1 international. Average age 27. 21 applicants, 71% accepted, 12 enrolled. In 2001, 8 degrees awarded.

**Degree requirements:** For master's, thesis (for some programs), terminal exam.

**Entrance requirements:** For master's, GRE General Test, minimum GPA of 3.0, introductory courses in psychology, statistics. *Application deadline:* For fall admission, 7/1 (priority date). Applications are processed on a rolling basis. *Application fee:* $0. Electronic applications accepted.

**Expenses:** Tuition, state resident: full-time $1,746; part-time $97 per credit hour. Tuition, nonresident: full-time $6,966; part-time $387 per credit hour. Required fees: $294 per semester.

**Financial support:** In 2001–02, 20 students received support, including 8 research assistantships with partial tuition reimbursements available (averaging $5,000 per year); career-related internships or fieldwork, Federal Work-Study, and unspecified assistantships also available. Support available to part-time students. Financial award application deadline: 4/15; financial award applicants required to submit FAFSA.

**Faculty research:** Mother-infant attachment, animal cognition, forward inferences in reading, religiosity, social perception.

Dr. Richard Rogers, Chair, 912-681-5539, *Fax:* 912-681-0751, *E-mail:* rrogers@gasou.edu.
**Application contact:** Dr. John R. Diebolt, Associate Graduate Dean, 912-681-5384, *Fax:* 912-681-0740, *E-mail:* gradschool@gasou.edu. *Web site:* http://www2.gasou.edu/psychology/masters.htm

## ■ GEORGIA STATE UNIVERSITY

**College of Arts and Sciences, Department of Psychology, Atlanta, GA 30303-3083**

**AWARDS** PhD.

**Degree requirements:** For doctorate, thesis/dissertation, exam.

**Entrance requirements:** For doctorate, GRE General Test, TOEFL, departmental supplemental form. Electronic applications accepted.

**Faculty research:** Social psychology, developmental and comparative psychology, neuropsychology, disaster reactions, families of chronically ill children. *Web site:* http://www.gsu.edu/~wwwpsy/

**Find an in-depth description at www.petersons.com/gradchannel.**

## ■ GOLDEN GATE UNIVERSITY

**School of Professional Programs and Undergraduate Studies, Program in Applied Psychology, San Francisco, CA 94105-2968**

**AWARDS** Applied psychology (Certificate); counseling (MA); industrial/organizational psychology (MA); marriage, family and child counseling (MA).

**Entrance requirements:** For master's, TOEFL, minimum GPA of 2.5.

## ■ GOVERNORS STATE UNIVERSITY

**College of Education, Division of Psychology and Counseling, Program in Psychology, University Park, IL 60466-0975**

**AWARDS** MA. Part-time and evening/weekend programs available.

**Faculty:** 9 full-time (4 women), 21 part-time/adjunct (10 women).
**Students:** 13 full-time, 101 part-time. Average age 32. In 2001, 45 degrees awarded.

**Degree requirements:** For master's, thesis or alternative, practicum.

**Entrance requirements:** For master's, GRE or MAT. *Application deadline:* For fall admission, 7/15 (priority date); for spring admission, 11/10. Applications are processed on a rolling basis. *Application fee:* $0.

**Expenses:** Tuition, state resident: part-time $111 per hour. Tuition, nonresident: part-time $333 per hour.

**Financial support:** Career-related internships or fieldwork, Federal Work-Study, institutionally sponsored loans, and tuition waivers (full and partial) available. Support available to part-time students. Financial award application deadline: 5/1.
Dr. Addison Woodward, Chairperson, Division of Psychology and Counseling, 708-534-4840.

## ■ GRADUATE SCHOOL AND UNIVERSITY CENTER OF THE CITY UNIVERSITY OF NEW YORK

**Graduate Studies, Program in Psychology, New York, NY 10016-4039**

**AWARDS** Basic applied neurocognition (PhD); biopsychology (PhD); clinical psychology (PhD); developmental psychology (PhD); environmental psychology (PhD); experimental psychology (PhD); industrial psychology (PhD); learning processes (PhD); neuropsychology (PhD); psychology (PhD); social personality (PhD).

**Faculty:** 119 full-time (40 women).
**Students:** 463 full-time (335 women), 4 part-time (2 women); includes 96 minority (39 African Americans, 20 Asian Americans or Pacific Islanders, 36 Hispanic Americans, 1 Native American), 47 international. Average age 33. 493 applicants, 24% accepted, 65 enrolled. In 2001, 28 degrees awarded.

**Degree requirements:** For doctorate, one foreign language, thesis/dissertation.

**Entrance requirements:** For doctorate, GRE General Test. *Application deadline:* For fall admission, 2/1. *Application fee:* $40.

**Expenses:** Tuition, state resident: part-time $245 per credit. Tuition, nonresident: part-time $425 per credit. Required fees: $72 per semester.

**Financial support:** In 2001–02, 226 students received support, including 141 fellowships, 14 research assistantships, 4 teaching assistantships; career-related internships or fieldwork, Federal Work-Study, institutionally sponsored loans, and tuition waivers (full and partial) also available. Financial award application deadline: 2/1; financial award applicants required to submit FAFSA.
Dr. Joseph Glick, Executive Officer, 212-817-8706, *Fax:* 212-817-1533, *E-mail:* jglick@gc.cuny.edu.

## ■ GRADUATE THEOLOGICAL UNION

**Graduate Programs, Berkeley, CA 94709-1212**

**AWARDS** Arts and religion (MA, Th D); biblical languages (MA); biblical studies (Old and

*Graduate Theological Union (continued)*
New Testament) (MA, PhD, Th D); Buddhist studies (MA); Christian spirituality (MA); cultural and historical studies (MA, PhD); ethics and social theory (PhD); historical studies (MA, PhD, Th D); history of art and religion (PhD); homiletics (MA, PhD, Th D); interdisciplinary studies (PhD, Th D); Jewish studies (MA, PhD, Certificate); liturgical studies (MA, PhD, Th D); Near Eastern religions (PhD); religion and psychology (MA, PhD); religion and society (MA); systematic and philosophical theology (MA, PhD, Th D); ). MA/M Div offered jointly with individual denominations.

**Faculty:** 80 full-time (29 women), 14 part-time/adjunct (3 women).
**Students:** 308 full-time (154 women), 39 part-time (13 women); includes 48 minority (9 African Americans, 28 Asian Americans or Pacific Islanders, 9 Hispanic Americans, 2 Native Americans), 60 international. Average age 42. 193 applicants, 65% accepted, 76 enrolled. In 2001, 28 master's, 20 doctorates awarded. Terminal master's awarded for partial completion of doctoral program.
**Degree requirements:** For master's, one foreign language, thesis/dissertation; for doctorate, one foreign language, thesis/dissertation, comprehensive exam.
**Entrance requirements:** For master's, GRE General Test, TOEFL; for doctorate, GRE General Test, TOEFL, MA or M Div degree. *Application deadline:* For fall admission, 12/15; for winter admission, 2/15; for spring admission, 9/30. *Application fee:* $40. Electronic applications accepted.
**Expenses:** Tuition: Full-time $16,000. Tuition and fees vary according to degree level.
**Financial support:** In 2001–02, 160 students received support, including 15 fellowships (averaging $19,000 per year), 22 research assistantships (averaging $4,000 per year); teaching assistantships, Federal Work-Study, scholarships/grants, and tuition waivers (full and partial) also available. Support available to part-time students. Financial award application deadline: 2/1; financial award applicants required to submit FAFSA.
Dr. Eldon G. Ernst, Interim Dean, 510-649-2440, *Fax:* 510-649-1417, *E-mail:* eernst@gtu.edu.
**Application contact:** Dr. Kathleen Kook, Assistant Dean for Admissions, 800-826-4488, *Fax:* 510-649-1730, *E-mail:* gtuadm@gtu.edu. *Web site:* http://www.gtu.edu/

## ■ HARDIN-SIMMONS UNIVERSITY

**Graduate School, Department of Psychology, Abilene, TX 79698-0001**
**AWARDS** Family psychology (MA). Part-time programs available.
**Faculty:** 6 full-time (2 women).
**Students:** 16 full-time (12 women), 5 part-time (3 women); includes 1 minority (Hispanic American). Average age 28. 13 applicants, 100% accepted, 7 enrolled. In 2001, 15 degrees awarded.
**Degree requirements:** For master's, clinical experience.
**Entrance requirements:** For master's, 21 semester hours in psychology, 18 of those in upper division classes; minimum undergraduate GPA of 3.0 in major, 2.7 overall. *Application deadline:* For fall admission, 8/15 (priority date); for spring admission, 1/5 (priority date). Applications are processed on a rolling basis. *Application fee:* $25 ($100 for international students).
**Expenses:** Tuition: Full-time $6,120; part-time $340 per credit. Required fees: $750.
**Financial support:** In 2001–02, 5 fellowships with partial tuition reimbursements (averaging $1,100 per year) were awarded; career-related internships or fieldwork, Federal Work-Study, scholarships/grants, and tuition waivers (full and partial) also available. Support available to part-time students. Financial award application deadline: 3/15; financial award applicants required to submit FAFSA.
**Faculty research:** Spirituality in marriage, intimacy and sexuality in marriage, sex education in the church, role of faith in marital satisfaction, family stress management.
Dr. Doug Thomas, Director, 915-670-1531, *Fax:* 915-670-1564, *E-mail:* dthomas@hsutx.edu.
**Application contact:** Dr. Gary Stanlake, Dean of Graduate Studies, 915-670-1298, *Fax:* 915-670-1564, *E-mail:* gradoff@hsutx.edu. *Web site:* http://www.hsutx.edu/

## ■ HARVARD UNIVERSITY

**Graduate School of Arts and Sciences, Department of Psychology, Cambridge, MA 02138**
**AWARDS** Psychology (AM, PhD), including behavior and decision analysis, cognition, developmental psychology, experimental psychology, personality, psychobiology, psychopathology; social psychology (AM, PhD).
**Degree requirements:** For doctorate, thesis/dissertation, general exams.
**Entrance requirements:** For master's and doctorate, GRE General Test, TOEFL.
**Expenses:** Tuition: Full-time $23,370. Required fees: $816. Full-time tuition and fees vary according to program and student level.

## ■ HOFSTRA UNIVERSITY

**College of Liberal Arts and Sciences, Division of Social Sciences, Department of Psychology, Hempstead, NY 11549**
**AWARDS** Clinical and school psychology (MA, PhD, Post-Doctoral Certificate); industrial/organizational psychology (MA); school-community psychology (MS, Psy D). Part-time programs available.
**Faculty:** 20 full-time (5 women), 12 part-time/adjunct (6 women).
**Students:** 116 full-time (84 women), 165 part-time (121 women); includes 5 minority (1 African American, 4 Asian Americans or Pacific Islanders). Average age 29. In 2001, 55 master's, 32 doctorates awarded.
**Entrance requirements:** For master's, GRE General Test; for doctorate, GRE General Test, GRE Subject Test, letters of recommendation (3), interview, minimum GPA of 3.0 in psychology. *Application deadline:* Applications are processed on a rolling basis. *Application fee:* $40 ($75 for international students).
**Expenses:** Tuition: Full-time $12,408. Tuition and fees vary according to course load and program.
**Financial support:** In 2001–02, 3 fellowships, 26 research assistantships, 30 teaching assistantships were awarded. Career-related internships or fieldwork, Federal Work-Study, and institutionally sponsored loans also available. Support available to part-time students. Financial award applicants required to submit FAFSA.
**Faculty research:** Anger, applied behavior analysis, behavior modification, parenting of young children, statistics and methodology.
Dr. Howard Kassinove, Chairperson, 516-463-5625, *Fax:* 516-463-6052, *E-mail:* psyhzk@hofstra.edu.
**Application contact:** Mary Beth Carey, Vice President of Enrollment Services, *Fax:* 516-560-7660, *E-mail:* hofstra@hofstra.edu.

## ■ HOOD COLLEGE

**Graduate School, Programs in Human Sciences, Frederick, MD 21701-8575**
**AWARDS** Psychology (MA); thanatology (MA). Part-time and evening/weekend programs available.
**Faculty:** 5 full-time (2 women), 3 part-time/adjunct (1 woman).
**Students:** 6 full-time (4 women), 43 part-time (37 women); includes 4 minority (1 African American, 1 Asian American or Pacific Islander, 2 Native Americans), 1 international. Average age 33. 24 applicants, 79% accepted, 15 enrolled. In 2001, 18 master's awarded.

**Degree requirements:** For master's, thesis or alternative, comprehensive exam, registration.

**Entrance requirements:** For master's, minimum GPA of 2.5. *Application deadline:* Applications are processed on a rolling basis. *Application fee:* $30.

**Expenses:** Tuition: Full-time $5,670; part-time $315 per credit. Required fees: $20 per term.

**Financial support:** Institutionally sponsored loans available. Financial award applicants required to submit FAFSA.

**Faculty research:** Mind-body medicine and multicultural healing, the New Orleans jazz funeral, death practices in African-American culture, bereavement theories and gender differences, Piaget's theory of cognitive development as a formal mathematical model.

Dr. Dana G. Cable, Chairperson, 301-696-3758, *Fax:* 301-696-3597, *E-mail:* cable@hood.edu.

**Application contact:** 301-696-3600, *Fax:* 301-696-3597, *E-mail:* hoodgrad@hood.edu.

## ■ HOPE INTERNATIONAL UNIVERSITY

**School of Graduate Studies, Program in Marriage, Family, and Child Counseling, Fullerton, CA 92831-3138**

**AWARDS** Counseling (MA); marriage and family therapy (MFT); marriage, family, and child counseling (MA); psychology (MA).

**Degree requirements:** For master's, final exam, practicum.

**Entrance requirements:** For master's, minimum GPA of 3.0. Electronic applications accepted.

## ■ HOUSTON BAPTIST UNIVERSITY

**College of Education and Behavioral Sciences, Program in Psychology, Houston, TX 77074-3298**

**AWARDS** MAP. Part-time and evening/weekend programs available.

**Faculty:** 2 full-time (1 woman), 6 part-time/adjunct (2 women).

**Students:** 36 full-time (32 women), 39 part-time (32 women); includes 13 minority (7 African Americans, 1 Asian American or Pacific Islander, 5 Hispanic Americans). 40 applicants, 78% accepted. In 2001, 17 degrees awarded.

**Degree requirements:** For master's, comprehensive exam.

**Entrance requirements:** For master's, GRE General Test, minimum GPA of 3.0. *Application deadline:* For fall admission, 7/1 (priority date); for winter admission, 10/1 (priority date); for spring admission, 1/1 (priority date). Applications are processed

on a rolling basis. *Application fee:* $25 ($100 for international students).

**Expenses:** Tuition: Part-time $990 per course. Required fees: $250 per quarter.

**Financial support:** Federal Work-Study and scholarships/grants available. Support available to part-time students. Financial award application deadline: 4/15; financial award applicants required to submit FAFSA.

Dr. Ann Owen, Behavioral Sciences Department Director, 281-649-3000 Ext. 2436.

**Application contact:** Karen Francies, Program Director, 281-649-3000 Ext. 2392.

## ■ HOWARD UNIVERSITY

**Graduate School of Arts and Sciences, Department of Psychology, Washington, DC 20059-0002**

**AWARDS** Clinical psychology (PhD); developmental psychology (PhD); experimental psychology (PhD); neuropsychology (PhD); personality psychology (PhD); psychology (MS); social psychology (PhD). Part-time programs available.

**Faculty:** 16 full-time (7 women).

**Students:** 70 full-time (51 women), 20 part-time (14 women). Average age 29. 165 applicants, 15% accepted, 20 enrolled. In 2001, 10 master's, 12 doctorates awarded.

**Degree requirements:** For master's, thesis, comprehensive exam; for doctorate, thesis/dissertation, qualifying exam, comprehensive exam. *Median time to degree:* Master's–3 years full-time, 5 years part-time; doctorate–5 years full-time, 9 years part-time.

**Entrance requirements:** For master's, GRE General Test, minimum GPA of 2.5, bachelor's degree in psychology or related field; for doctorate, GRE General Test, minimum GPA of 3.0. *Application deadline:* For fall admission, 4/1; for spring admission, 11/1. Applications are processed on a rolling basis. *Application fee:* $45.

**Financial support:** In 2001–02, 19 students received support, including 3 fellowships with full tuition reimbursements available (averaging $13,500 per year), 2 research assistantships with full tuition reimbursements available (averaging $10,000 per year), 8 teaching assistantships with full tuition reimbursements available (averaging $13,000 per year); career-related internships or fieldwork, institutionally sponsored loans, and scholarships/grants also available. Financial award application deadline: 4/1; financial award applicants required to submit FAFSA.

**Faculty research:** Personality and psychophysiology, educational and social

development of African-American children, child and adult psychopathology.

Dr. Albert Roberts, Chair, 202-806-6805, *Fax:* 202-806-4823, *E-mail:* aroberts@howard.edu.

**Application contact:** Dr. Alfonso Campbell, Chairman, Graduate Admissions Committee, 202-806-6805, *Fax:* 202-806-4873, *E-mail:* acampbell@howard.edu.

## ■ HUMBOLDT STATE UNIVERSITY

**Graduate Studies, College of Natural Resources and Sciences, Department of Psychology, Arcata, CA 95521-8299**

**AWARDS** MA.

**Students:** 57 full-time (44 women), 5 part-time (4 women); includes 8 minority (1 African American, 4 Asian Americans or Pacific Islanders, 1 Hispanic American, 2 Native Americans), 4 international. Average age 29. 65 applicants, 42% accepted, 25 enrolled. In 2001, 19 degrees awarded.

**Degree requirements:** For master's, thesis.

**Entrance requirements:** For master's, TOEFL, appropriate bachelor's degree, minimum GPA of 2.5. *Application deadline:* Applications are processed on a rolling basis. *Application fee:* $55.

**Expenses:** Tuition, state resident: full-time $1,969. Tuition, nonresident: part-time $246 per unit.

**Financial support:** Career-related internships or fieldwork available. Financial award application deadline: 3/1; financial award applicants required to submit FAFSA.

**Faculty research:** School psychology, counseling, eating disorders, mood induction, depression.

Dr. Lou Ann Wieand, Chair, 707-826-3755, *E-mail:* law3@humboldt.edu. *Web site:* http://www.humboldt.edu/~psych

## ■ HUNTER COLLEGE OF THE CITY UNIVERSITY OF NEW YORK

**Graduate School, School of Arts and Sciences, Department of Psychology, New York, NY 10021-5085**

**AWARDS** Applied and evaluative psychology (MA); biopsychology and comparative psychology (MA); social, cognitive, and developmental psychology (MA). Part-time and evening/weekend programs available.

**Faculty:** 21 full-time (10 women), 8 part-time/adjunct (4 women).

**Students:** 3 full-time (2 women), 14 part-time (11 women); includes 5 minority (1 African American, 4 Hispanic Americans), 1 international. Average age 27. 53 applicants, 47% accepted, 5 enrolled. In 2001, 5 degrees awarded.

*Hunter College of the City University of New York (continued)*

**Degree requirements:** For master's, thesis, comprehensive exam. *Median time to degree:* Master's–3.5 years part-time.

**Entrance requirements:** For master's, GRE General Test, TOEFL, minimum 12 credits in psychology, including statistics and experimental psychology. *Application deadline:* For fall admission, 4/1; for spring admission, 11/1. Applications are processed on a rolling basis. *Application fee:* $40.

**Expenses:** Tuition, state resident: full-time $2,175; part-time $185 per credit. Tuition, nonresident: full-time $3,800; part-time $320 per credit.

**Faculty research:** Personality, cognitive and linguistic development, hormonal and neural control of behavior, gender and culture, social cognition of health and attitudes.

Dr. Darlene DeFour, Acting Chairperson. **Application contact:** William Zlata, Director for Graduate Admissions, 212-772-4288, *Fax:* 212-650-3336, *E-mail:* admissions@hunter.cuny.edu. *Web site:* http://maxweber.hunter.cuny.edu/psych/

■ **IDAHO STATE UNIVERSITY**

**Office of Graduate Studies, College of Arts and Sciences, Department of Psychology, Pocatello, ID 83209**

**AWARDS** Clinical psychology (PhD); psychology (MS).

**Faculty:** 9 full-time (4 women).

**Students:** 20 full-time (13 women), 4 part-time (2 women); includes 1 minority (Hispanic American). Average age 30. 75 applicants, 16% accepted. In 2001, 2 master's, 3 doctorates awarded.

**Degree requirements:** For master's and doctorate, thesis/dissertation.

**Entrance requirements:** For master's and doctorate, GRE General Test, GRE Subject Test. *Application deadline:* For fall admission, 7/1; for spring admission, 12/1. Applications are processed on a rolling basis. *Application fee:* $35.

**Expenses:** Tuition, area resident: Full-time $3,432. Tuition, state resident: part-time $172 per credit. Tuition, nonresident: full-time $10,196; part-time $262 per credit. International tuition: $9,672 full-time. Part-time tuition and fees vary according to course load, program and reciprocity agreements.

**Financial support:** In 2001–02, 1 research assistantship with full and partial tuition reimbursement (averaging $12,064 per year), 11 teaching assistantships with full and partial tuition reimbursements (averaging $9,919 per year) were awarded. Career-related internships or fieldwork, Federal Work-Study, and traineeships also

available. Financial award application deadline: 2/15.

**Faculty research:** Decision making, social psychology, personality and affective disorders, marital satisfaction, child pathology. *Total annual research expenditures:* $83,710.

Dr. Victor Joe, Chairman, 208-282-2111. *Web site:* http://www.isu.edu/departments/psych/

■ **ILLINOIS INSTITUTE OF TECHNOLOGY**

**Graduate College, Institute of Psychology, Chicago, IL 60616-3793**

**AWARDS** Clinical psychology (PhD); industrial/organizational psychology (PhD); personnel/human resource development (MS); psychology (MS); rehabilitation counseling (MS); rehabilitation psychology (PhD).

**Faculty:** 17 full-time (7 women), 4 part-time/adjunct (2 women).

**Students:** 84 full-time (56 women), 75 part-time (51 women); includes 32 minority (15 African Americans, 10 Asian Americans or Pacific Islanders, 6 Hispanic Americans, 1 Native American), 15 international. Average age 30. 157 applicants, 49% accepted. In 2001, 21 master's, 15 doctorates awarded. Terminal master's awarded for partial completion of doctoral program.

**Degree requirements:** For master's, thesis (for some programs), comprehensive exam; for doctorate, thesis/dissertation, qualifying exams, comprehensive exam.

**Entrance requirements:** For master's and doctorate, GRE General Test, TOEFL, minimum GPA of 3.0. *Application deadline:* For fall admission, 1/15 (priority date); for spring admission, 11/1. Applications are processed on a rolling basis. *Application fee:* $30. Electronic applications accepted.

**Expenses:** Tuition: Part-time $590 per credit hour.

**Financial support:** In 2001–02, 32 fellowships, 18 teaching assistantships were awarded. Research assistantships, career-related internships or fieldwork, Federal Work-Study, institutionally sponsored loans, scholarships/grants, and unspecified assistantships also available. Financial award application deadline: 3/1; financial award applicants required to submit FAFSA.

**Faculty research:** Leadership, life span developmental processes, rehabilitation engineering technology, behavioral medicine, substance abuse and disability. *Total annual research expenditures:* $494,180.

Dr. M. Ellen Mitchell, Chairman, 312-567-3362, *Fax:* 312-567-3493, *E-mail:* mitchell@itt.edu.

**Application contact:** Dr. Ali Cinar, Dean of Graduate College, 312-567-3637, *Fax:*

312-567-7517, *E-mail:* gradstu@iit.edu. *Web site:* http://www.iit.edu/colleges/psych/

■ **ILLINOIS STATE UNIVERSITY**

**Graduate School, College of Arts and Sciences, Department of Psychology, Normal, IL 61790-2200**

**AWARDS** Psychology (MA, MS), including clinical psychology, counseling psychology, developmental psychology, educational psychology, experimental psychology, measurement-evaluation, organizational-industrial psychology; school psychology (PhD, SSP).

**Faculty:** 30 full-time (10 women), 1 part-time/adjunct (0 women).

**Students:** 59 full-time (48 women), 24 part-time (13 women); includes 7 minority (3 African Americans, 3 Hispanic Americans, 1 Native American), 5 international. 81 applicants, 46% accepted. In 2001, 40 master's, 2 doctorates, 4 other advanced degrees awarded.

**Degree requirements:** For master's, thesis or alternative; for doctorate, variable foreign language requirement, thesis/dissertation, 2 terms of residency, internship, practicum.

**Entrance requirements:** For master's, GRE General Test, GRE Subject Test, minimum GPA of 3.0 in last 60 hours; for doctorate, GRE General Test. *Application deadline:* Applications are processed on a rolling basis. *Application fee:* $30.

**Expenses:** Tuition, state resident: full-time $2,691; part-time $112 per credit hour. Tuition, nonresident: full-time $5,880; part-time $245 per credit hour. Required fees: $1,146; $48 per credit hour.

**Financial support:** In 2001–02, 21 research assistantships (averaging $5,127 per year), 27 teaching assistantships (averaging $4,308 per year) were awarded. Tuition waivers (full) and unspecified assistantships also available. Financial award application deadline: 4/1.

**Faculty research:** Dialogues with children, sexual harassment in the military, mental health consultant. *Total annual research expenditures:* $248,177.

Dr. David Barone, Chairperson, 309-438-8651. *Web site:* http://www.cas.ilstu.edu/psychology/index.html

■ **IMMACULATA UNIVERSITY**

**College of Graduate Studies, Department of Psychology, Immaculata, PA 19345**

**AWARDS** Clinical psychology (Psy D); counseling psychology (MA, Certificate), including school guidance counselor (Certificate), school psychologist (Certificate); school psychology (Psy D). Part-time and evening/weekend programs available.

**Students:** 57 full-time (45 women), 220 part-time (188 women). Average age 34. 88 applicants, 80% accepted, 41 enrolled. In 2001, 36 master's, 9 doctorates awarded.
**Degree requirements:** For master's, thesis optional; for doctorate, thesis/dissertation, comprehensive exam.
**Entrance requirements:** For master's, GRE General Test or MAT, TOEFL, minimum GPA of 3.0; for doctorate, GRE General Test, TOEFL, minimum GPA of 3.5. *Application deadline:* Applications are processed on a rolling basis. *Application fee:* $25.
**Expenses:** Tuition: Part-time $390 per credit.
**Financial support:** Application deadline: 5/1.
**Faculty research:** Supervision ethics, psychology of teaching, gender.
Dr. Jed A. Yalof, Chair, 610-647-4400 Ext. 3503, *E-mail:* jyalof@immaculate.edu.
**Application contact:** Office of Graduate Admission, 610-647-4400 Ext. 3211.

■ **INDIANA STATE UNIVERSITY**

School of Graduate Studies, College of Arts and Sciences, Department of Psychology, Terre Haute, IN 47809-1401

AWARDS Clinical psychology (Psy D); general psychology (MA, MS). Terminal master's awarded for partial completion of doctoral program.

**Degree requirements:** For master's, thesis (for some programs); for doctorate, thesis/dissertation, internship.
**Entrance requirements:** For master's, GRE General Test; for doctorate, GRE General Test, minimum GPA of 3.0. Electronic applications accepted.

■ **INDIANA UNIVERSITY BLOOMINGTON**

Graduate School, College of Arts and Sciences, Department of Psychology, Bloomington, IN 47405

AWARDS Biology and behavior (PhD); clinical science (PhD); cognitive psychology (PhD); developmental psychology (PhD); social psychology (PhD). Offered through the University Graduate School.

**Faculty:** 40 full-time (7 women), 1 (woman) part-time/adjunct.
**Students:** 42 full-time (23 women), 37 part-time (18 women); includes 9 minority (2 African Americans, 5 Asian Americans or Pacific Islanders, 2 Hispanic Americans), 9 international. Average age 28. 222 applicants, 14% accepted. In 2001, 18 doctorates awarded.
**Degree requirements:** For doctorate, thesis/dissertation, 1st- and 2nd-year

projects, 1 year as associate instructor, qualifying exam.
**Entrance requirements:** For doctorate, GRE, TOEFL. *Application deadline:* For fall admission, 12/15. *Application fee:* $45 ($55 for international students). Electronic applications accepted.
**Expenses:** Tuition, state resident: full-time $4,720; part-time $197 per credit. Tuition, nonresident: full-time $13,748; part-time $573 per credit. Required fees: $642.
**Financial support:** In 2001–02, 8 fellowships (averaging $14,000 per year), 24 teaching assistantships (averaging $11,800 per year) were awarded.
Dr. Joseph E. Steinmetz, Chairperson, 812-855-3991, *Fax:* 812-855-4691, *E-mail:* steinmet@indiana.edu.
**Application contact:** Beth Laske-Miller, Graduate Admissions Assistant, 812-855-2014, *Fax:* 812-855-4691, *E-mail:* psychgrd@indiana.edu. *Web site:* http://www.indiana.edu/~psych/

■ **INDIANA UNIVERSITY OF PENNSYLVANIA**

Graduate School and Research, College of Natural Sciences and Mathematics, Department of Psychology, Indiana, PA 15705-1087

AWARDS MA, Psy D. Part-time programs available.

**Faculty:** 20 full-time (10 women).
**Students:** 54 full-time (41 women), 6 part-time (3 women); includes 6 minority (2 African Americans, 3 Asian Americans or Pacific Islanders, 1 Hispanic American), 2 international. Average age 30. 104 applicants, 12% accepted. In 2001, 9 master's, 10 doctorates awarded. Terminal master's awarded for partial completion of doctoral program.
**Degree requirements:** For doctorate, thesis/dissertation, internship, practicum, comprehensive exam.
**Entrance requirements:** For master's, GRE General Test, TOEFL; for doctorate, GRE General Test, TOEFL, minimum GPA of 3.0, interview, letters of recommendation. *Application deadline:* For fall admission, 1/10. Applications are processed on a rolling basis. *Application fee:* $30.
**Expenses:** Tuition, state resident: full-time $4,600; part-time $256 per credit hour. Tuition, nonresident: full-time $7,554; part-time $420 per credit hour. Required fees: $800. Part-time tuition and fees vary according to course load.
**Financial support:** In 2001–02, 3 fellowships (averaging $5,000 per year), 28 research assistantships with full and partial tuition reimbursements (averaging $5,830 per year), 1 teaching assistantship (averaging $17,001 per year) were awarded.

Federal Work-Study and scholarships/grants also available. Financial award application deadline: 3/15; financial award applicants required to submit FAFSA.
Dr. Mary Lou Zanich, Chairperson, 724-357-2426, *E-mail:* mtzanich@iup.edu.
**Application contact:** Dr. Donald Robertson, Graduate Coordinator, 724-357-4522, *E-mail:* durobert@iup.edu.

■ **INDIANA UNIVERSITY–PURDUE UNIVERSITY INDIANAPOLIS**

School of Science, Department of Psychology, Indianapolis, IN 46202-3275

AWARDS Clinical rehabilitation psychology (MS, PhD); industrial/organizational psychology (MS); psychobiology of addictions (PhD). Part-time programs available.

**Students:** 22 full-time (17 women), 14 part-time (12 women); includes 2 minority (1 Asian American or Pacific Islander, 1 Hispanic American), 3 international. Average age 27. In 2001, 12 master's, 3 doctorates awarded. Terminal master's awarded for partial completion of doctoral program.
**Degree requirements:** For master's and doctorate, thesis/dissertation.
**Entrance requirements:** For master's, GRE General Test, minimum undergraduate GPA of 3.0; for doctorate, GRE General Test, GRE Subject Test (clinical rehabilitation psychology), minimum undergraduate GPA of 3.2. *Application deadline:* For fall admission, 2/1 (priority date). *Application fee:* $45 ($55 for international students).
**Expenses:** Tuition, state resident: full-time $4,480; part-time $187 per credit. Tuition, nonresident: full-time $12,926; part-time $539 per credit. Required fees: $177.
**Financial support:** In 2001–02, 21 students received support, including 6 fellowships with partial tuition reimbursements available (averaging $11,000 per year), 15 research assistantships with partial tuition reimbursements available (averaging $9,000 per year), 12 teaching assistantships with partial tuition reimbursements available (averaging $9,000 per year); career-related internships or fieldwork, Federal Work-Study, and institutionally sponsored loans also available. Financial award application deadline: 3/1; financial award applicants required to submit FAFSA.
**Faculty research:** Psychiatric rehabilitation, health psychology, psychopharmacology of drugs of abuse, personnel psychology, organizational decision making.
Dr. J. Gregor Fetterman, Chairman, 317-274-6768, *Fax:* 317-274-6756, *E-mail:* gfetter@iupui.edu.

*Indiana University–Purdue University Indianapolis (continued)*

**Application contact:** Donna Miller, Graduate Program Coordinator, 317-274-6945, *Fax:* 317-274-6756, *E-mail:* dmiller1@iupui.edu. *Web site:* http://www.psynt.iupui.edu/

## ■ INDIANA UNIVERSITY SOUTH BEND

**College of Liberal Arts and Sciences, Program in Applied Psychology, South Bend, IN 46634-7111**

**AWARDS** MA. Part-time and evening/weekend programs available.

**Faculty:** 6 full-time (1 woman).
**Students:** Average age 36. In 2001, 2 degrees awarded.
**Degree requirements:** For master's, thesis.
**Entrance requirements:** For master's, GRE General Test, minimum GPA of 3.0, 18 hours in psychology. *Application deadline:* For fall admission, 4/1 (priority date). Applications are processed on a rolling basis. *Application fee:* $40 ($50 for international students).
**Expenses:** Tuition, state resident: full-time $3,664; part-time $153. Tuition, nonresident: full-time $8,929; part-time $372. Required fees: $390. Tuition and fees vary according to program.
**Financial support:** Career-related internships or fieldwork and Federal Work-Study available. Financial award application deadline: 3/1; financial award applicants required to submit FAFSA.
**Faculty research:** Parenting; social comparison and social well-being; behavioral contagion; temporal pattern perception; community development and social change, social influence, and suicide. Dr. Frank Fujita, Director, Psychology Graduate Programs, 574-237-6593, *Fax:* 574-237-4538, *E-mail:* ffujita@iusb.edu.

## ■ INSTITUTE OF TRANSPERSONAL PSYCHOLOGY

**Global Division, Palo Alto, CA 94303**

**AWARDS** Creative expression (Certificate); spiritual psychology (Certificate); transpersonal psychology (MTP, PhD); transpersonal studies (MA, Certificate); wellness counseling and body-mind consciousness (Certificate); women's spiritual development (Certificate). Postbaccalaureate distance learning degree programs offered (minimal on-campus study).

**Faculty:** 3 full-time (1 woman), 31 part-time/adjunct (25 women).
**Students:** 83 full-time (67 women), 20 part-time (15 women); includes 9 minority (2 African Americans, 1 Asian American or Pacific Islander, 3 Hispanic Americans, 3

Native Americans), 12 international. Average age 43. 80 applicants, 78% accepted. In 2001, 16 degrees awarded.
**Degree requirements:** For master's, thesis (for some programs). *Median time to degree:* Master's–2 years full-time.
**Entrance requirements:** For master's, 8 hours in psychology; for doctorate, bachelor's degree with 18 quarter or 12 semester units in psychology, master's degree in psychology (advanced standing). *Application deadline:* Applications are processed on a rolling basis. *Application fee:* $55.
**Expenses:** Contact institution.
**Financial support:** In 2001–02, 55 students received support. Federal Work-Study available. Support available to part-time students. Financial award application deadline: 6/30; financial award applicants required to submit FAFSA.
Prof. Kurtick Patel, Dean, 650-493-4430, *Fax:* 650-493-6835, *E-mail:* kpatel@itp.edu.
**Application contact:** Edith Parker, Admissions Assistant, 650-493-4430 Ext. 40, *Fax:* 650-493-6593, *E-mail:* itpinfo@itp.edu. *Web site:* http://www.itp.edu/

## ■ INSTITUTE OF TRANSPERSONAL PSYCHOLOGY

**Residential Division, Palo Alto, CA 94303**

**AWARDS** Counseling psychology (MA); transpersonal psychology (MA, PhD). Part-time and evening/weekend programs available.

**Faculty:** 18 full-time (10 women), 22 part-time/adjunct (7 women).
**Students:** 236 full-time (173 women), 12 part-time (10 women); includes 30 minority (7 African Americans, 9 Asian Americans or Pacific Islanders, 11 Hispanic Americans, 3 Native Americans), 13 international. Average age 41. 122 applicants, 78% accepted, 58 enrolled. In 2001, 48 master's, 12 doctorates awarded. Terminal master's awarded for partial completion of doctoral program.
**Degree requirements:** For doctorate, thesis/dissertation.
**Entrance requirements:** For master's, 8 hours in psychology; for doctorate, 12 hours in psychology. *Application deadline:* For fall admission, 4/15 (priority date). Applications are processed on a rolling basis. *Application fee:* $55.
**Expenses:** Tuition: Full-time $17,784. Required fees: $30. Tuition and fees vary according to degree level, campus/location and program.
**Financial support:** In 2001–02, 141 students received support; teaching assistantships, career-related internships or fieldwork and Federal Work-Study available. Support available to part-time

students. Financial award application deadline: 7/1; financial award applicants required to submit FAFSA.
Dr. Paul Roy, Academic Dean, 650-493-4430, *Fax:* 650-493-6835, *E-mail:* proy@itp.edu.
**Application contact:** John Hofmann, Admissions Office, 650-493-4430 Ext. 30, *Fax:* 650-493-6835, *E-mail:* itpinfo@itp.edu. *Web site:* http://www.itp.edu/

## ■ INTER AMERICAN UNIVERSITY OF PUERTO RICO, METROPOLITAN CAMPUS

**Graduate Programs, Division of Behavioral Science and Allied Professions, Program in Psychology, San Juan, PR 00919-1293**

**AWARDS** MA.

**Degree requirements:** For master's, comprehensive exam.
**Entrance requirements:** For master's, GRE or PAEG, interview. Electronic applications accepted.

## ■ INTER AMERICAN UNIVERSITY OF PUERTO RICO, SAN GERMÁN CAMPUS

**Graduate Programs, Department of Social Sciences, San Germán, PR 00683-5008**

**AWARDS** Counseling psychology (PhD); psychology (MA, MS); school psychology (PhD). Part-time and evening/weekend programs available.

**Faculty:** 5 full-time (4 women), 8 part-time/adjunct (4 women).
**Students:** 48 full-time (40 women), 48 part-time (41 women). In 2001, 11 degrees awarded.
**Degree requirements:** For master's and doctorate, thesis/dissertation, comprehensive exam.
**Entrance requirements:** For master's, GRE General Test or PAEG, minimum GPA of 3.0; for doctorate, GRE, PAEG or MAT, minimum GPA of 3.0. *Application deadline:* For fall admission, 4/30 (priority date); for spring admission, 11/15. Applications are processed on a rolling basis. *Application fee:* $31.
**Expenses:** Tuition: Part-time $165 per credit. Required fees: $390; $195 per semester. Tuition and fees vary according to degree level and program.
**Financial support:** Teaching assistantships available.
Carmen Rodriguez, Graduate Coordinator, 787-264-1912 Ext. 7646, *Fax:* 787-892-6350, *E-mail:* carrod@sg.inter.edu.
**Application contact:** Dr. Waldemar Velez, Director of Graduate Program Center,

787-892-4300 Ext. 7358, *Fax:* 787-892-6350, *E-mail:* wvelez@sg.inter.edu.

### ■ IONA COLLEGE

School of Arts and Science, Department of Psychology, New Rochelle, NY 10801-1890

**AWARDS** Psychology (MA); school counseling (MA); school psychologist (MA).

**Faculty:** 7 full-time (4 women).
**Students:** 12 full-time (11 women), 33 part-time (28 women); includes 9 minority (4 African Americans, 1 Asian American or Pacific Islander, 3 Hispanic Americans, 1 Native American). Average age 27. In 2001, 8 degrees awarded.
**Degree requirements:** For master's, thesis.
**Entrance requirements:** For master's, GRE or minimum GPA of 3.0. *Application deadline:* Applications are processed on a rolling basis. *Application fee:* $25.
**Expenses:** Tuition: Part-time $525 per credit.
**Financial support:** Career-related internships or fieldwork, tuition waivers (partial), and unspecified assistantships available. Support available to part-time students. Dr. Paul Greene, Chair, 914-633-2048, *E-mail:* pgreene@iona.edu.
**Application contact:** Alyce Ware, Associate Director of Graduate Recruitment, 914-633-2420, *Fax:* 914-633-2023, *E-mail:* aware@iona.edu. *Web site:* http://www.iona.edu/

### ■ IOWA STATE UNIVERSITY OF SCIENCE AND TECHNOLOGY

Graduate College, College of Liberal Arts and Sciences, Department of Psychology, Ames, IA 50011

**AWARDS** Cognitive psychology (PhD); counseling psychology (PhD); general psychology (MS); social psychology (PhD). Terminal master's awarded for partial completion of doctoral program.

**Degree requirements:** For master's, thesis or alternative; for doctorate, thesis/dissertation.
**Entrance requirements:** For master's and doctorate, GRE General Test, GRE Subject Test (psychology), TOEFL. Electronic applications accepted.
**Expenses:** Tuition, state resident: full-time $1,851. Tuition, nonresident: full-time $5,449. Tuition and fees vary according to program.
**Faculty research:** Counseling psychology, cognitive psychology, social psychology, health psychology, psychology and public policy. *Web site:* http://psych-server.iastate.edu/

### ■ JACKSON STATE UNIVERSITY

Graduate School, School of Liberal Arts, Department of Psychology, Jackson, MS 39217

**AWARDS** Clinical psychology (PhD).

**Degree requirements:** For doctorate, thesis/dissertation, comprehensive exam.
**Entrance requirements:** For doctorate, MAT.

### ■ JACKSONVILLE STATE UNIVERSITY

College of Graduate Studies and Continuing Education, College of Arts and Sciences, Department of Psychology, Jacksonville, AL 36265-1602

**AWARDS** MS.

**Degree requirements:** For master's, thesis optional.
**Entrance requirements:** For master's, GRE General Test or MAT.

### ■ JAMES MADISON UNIVERSITY

College of Graduate and Professional Programs, College of Integrated Science and Technology, Department of Psychology, Harrisonburg, VA 22807

**AWARDS** Counseling psychology (M Ed, MA, Ed S); general psychology (MA, Psy D); school psychology (MA, Ed S). Part-time and evening/weekend programs available.

**Faculty:** 26 full-time (12 women), 6 part-time/adjunct (3 women).
**Students:** 114 full-time (87 women), 43 part-time (29 women); includes 21 minority (14 African Americans, 2 Asian Americans or Pacific Islanders, 5 Hispanic Americans), 2 international. Average age 29. In 2001, 35 master's, 9 doctorates, 18 other advanced degrees awarded.
**Degree requirements:** For doctorate and Ed S, thesis/dissertation.
**Entrance requirements:** For master's, GRE General Test, GRE Subject Test; for doctorate, GRE General Test. *Application deadline:* For fall admission, 7/1 (priority date). Applications are processed on a rolling basis. *Application fee:* $55.
**Expenses:** Tuition, state resident: part-time $143 per credit hour. Tuition, nonresident: part-time $465 per credit hour.
**Financial support:** In 2001–02, 25 teaching assistantships with full tuition reimbursements (averaging $7,170 per year) were awarded; research assistantships, career-related internships or fieldwork, Federal Work-Study, and unspecified assistantships also available. Financial

award application deadline: 3/1; financial award applicants required to submit FAFSA.
Dr. Jane Halonen, Director, 540-568-2555.

### ■ JOHN F. KENNEDY UNIVERSITY

Graduate School of Professional Psychology, Orinda, CA 94563-2603

**AWARDS** MA, Psy D, Certificate. Part-time and evening/weekend programs available.

**Degree requirements:** For master's, thesis or alternative.
**Entrance requirements:** For master's, TOEFL, interview.
**Expenses:** Tuition: Full-time $9,396; part-time $348 per unit. Required fees: $9 per quarter. Tuition and fees vary according to degree level and program.

### ■ JOHNS HOPKINS UNIVERSITY

Zanvyl Krieger School of Arts and Sciences, Department of Psychological and Brain Sciences, Baltimore, MD 21218-2699

**AWARDS** Experimental psychology (PhD); psychology (PhD).

**Faculty:** 9 full-time (3 women).
**Students:** 17 full-time (11 women); includes 1 minority (Asian American or Pacific Islander), 7 international. Average age 24. 84 applicants, 7% accepted, 2 enrolled. In 2001, 4 degrees awarded.
**Degree requirements:** For doctorate, thesis/dissertation, research project, teaching experience.
**Entrance requirements:** For doctorate, GRE General Test, GRE Subject Test. *Application deadline:* For fall admission, 1/15 (priority date). *Application fee:* $55. Electronic applications accepted.
**Expenses:** Tuition: Full-time $27,390.
**Financial support:** In 2001–02, 16 teaching assistantships were awarded; fellowships, research assistantships, Federal Work-Study also available. Financial award application deadline: 4/15; financial award applicants required to submit FAFSA.
**Faculty research:** Biopsychology, cognitive psychology, developmental psychology, quantitative psychology. *Total annual research expenditures:* $4.1 million.
Dr. Michela Gallagher, Chair, 410-516-7057, *Fax:* 410-516-4478, *E-mail:* michela@jhu.edu.
**Application contact:** Joan Krach, Administrative Assistant, 410-516-6175, *Fax:* 410-516-4478, *E-mail:* krach@jhu.edu. *Web site:* http://www.psy.jhu.edu/

## ■ KANSAS STATE UNIVERSITY

**Graduate School, College of Arts and Sciences, Department of Psychology, Manhattan, KS 66506**

**AWARDS** MS, PhD. Part-time programs available.

**Faculty:** 16 full-time (3 women).
**Students:** 42 full-time (23 women), 8 part-time (1 woman); includes 4 minority (1 African American, 3 Asian Americans or Pacific Islanders). Average age 24. 123 applicants, 41% accepted, 19 enrolled. In 2001, 6 master's, 2 doctorates awarded.
**Degree requirements:** For master's, thesis or alternative; for doctorate, thesis/dissertation, preliminary exam.
**Entrance requirements:** For master's, GRE General Test, TOEFL, minimum undergraduate GPA of 3.0; for doctorate, GRE General Test, TOEFL, minimum GPA of 3.0. *Application deadline:* For fall admission, 2/15 (priority date); for spring admission, 10/1. Applications are processed on a rolling basis. *Application fee:* $0 ($25 for international students). Electronic applications accepted.
**Expenses:** Tuition, state resident: part-time $113 per credit hour. Tuition, nonresident: part-time $358 per credit hour.
**Financial support:** In 2001–02, 1 fellowship, 24 research assistantships with partial tuition reimbursements (averaging $9,000 per year), 22 teaching assistantships with full tuition reimbursements (averaging $8,000 per year) were awarded. Career-related internships or fieldwork, institutionally sponsored loans, and scholarships/grants also available. Support available to part-time students. Financial award application deadline: 3/1; financial award applicants required to submit FAFSA.
**Faculty research:** Behavioral neuroscience, human factors, industrial/organizational psychology, social/personality psychology. *Total annual research expenditures:* $660,411.
Stephen W. Kiefer, Head, 785-532-6850, *Fax:* 785-532-5401, *E-mail:* swkiefer@ksu.edu.
**Application contact:** John Uhlarik, Graduate Program Director, 785-532-0620, *Fax:* 785-532-5401, *E-mail:* uhlarik@ksu.edu. *Web site:* http://www.ksu.edu/psych/

## ■ KEAN UNIVERSITY

**College of Arts, Humanities and Social Sciences, Department of Psychology, Union, NJ 07083**

**AWARDS** Behavioral sciences (MA), including business and industry counseling, human behavior and organizational psychology, psychological services; business and industry counseling (PMC); educational psychology (MA); marriage and family therapy (Diploma); school psychology (Diploma). Part-time and evening/weekend programs available.

**Faculty:** 21 full-time (13 women), 25 part-time/adjunct.
**Students:** 25 full-time (16 women), 121 part-time (74 women); includes 38 minority (12 African Americans, 8 Asian Americans or Pacific Islanders, 18 Hispanic Americans), 3 international. Average age 30. 87 applicants, 67% accepted. In 2001, 42 master's, 12 other advanced degrees awarded.
**Degree requirements:** For master's, thesis, comprehensive exam.
**Entrance requirements:** For master's, GRE General Test. *Application deadline:* For fall admission, 6/15; for spring admission, 11/15. *Application fee:* $35.
**Expenses:** Tuition, state resident: full-time $7,372. Tuition, nonresident: full-time $9,004. Required fees: $1,006.
**Financial support:** In 2001–02, 27 research assistantships with full tuition reimbursements (averaging $3,360 per year) were awarded; career-related internships or fieldwork and unspecified assistantships also available.
Dr. Henry L. Kaplowitz, Graduate Coordinator, 908-527-2598.
**Application contact:** Joanne Morris, Director of Graduate Admissions, 908-527-2665, *Fax:* 908-527-2286, *E-mail:* grad_adm@kean.edu.

## ■ KENT STATE UNIVERSITY

**College of Arts and Sciences, Department of Psychology, Kent, OH 44242-0001**

**AWARDS** Clinical psychology (MA, PhD); experimental psychology (MA, PhD).

**Degree requirements:** For master's and doctorate, thesis/dissertation.
**Entrance requirements:** For master's, GRE Subject Test, minimum GPA of 2.75; for doctorate, GRE Subject Test, minimum GPA of 3.0.

## ■ LAMAR UNIVERSITY

**College of Graduate Studies, College of Arts and Sciences, Department of Psychology, Beaumont, TX 77710**

**AWARDS** Community/clinical psychology (MS); industrial/organizational psychology (MS). Part-time programs available.

**Faculty:** 5 full-time (2 women).
**Students:** 15 full-time (8 women), 5 part-time (4 women); includes 4 minority (2 African Americans, 2 Hispanic Americans). Average age 32. 35 applicants, 80% accepted. In 2001, 9 degrees awarded.
**Degree requirements:** For master's, thesis, practicum.

**Entrance requirements:** For master's, GRE General Test, TOEFL, minimum GPA of 2.5 in last 60 hours of undergraduate course work. *Application deadline:* For fall admission, 8/1; for spring admission, 12/1. *Application fee:* $25 ($50 for international students).
**Expenses:** Tuition, state resident: full-time $1,114. Tuition, nonresident: full-time $3,670.
**Financial support:** In 2001–02, 12 students received support, including research assistantships (averaging $6,000 per year), 7 teaching assistantships with tuition reimbursements available (averaging $3,000 per year); fellowships, career-related internships or fieldwork, Federal Work-Study, scholarships/grants, and tuition waivers (partial) also available. Support available to part-time students. Financial award application deadline: 4/1.
**Faculty research:** Counseling psychology, industrial psychology. *Total annual research expenditures:* $17,000.
Dr. Oney D. Fitzpatrick, Chair, 409-880-8285, *Fax:* 409-880-1779, *E-mail:* fitzpatrod@hal.lamar.edu. *Web site:* http://140.158.184.30/

## ■ LA SALLE UNIVERSITY

**School of Arts and Sciences, Program in Psychology, Philadelphia, PA 19141-1199**

**AWARDS** Clinical geropsychology (Psy D); clinical psychology (Psy D); family psychology (Psy D); rehabilitation psychology (Psy D). Part-time and evening/weekend programs available.

**Faculty:** 8 full-time (1 woman), 10 part-time/adjunct (5 women).
**Students:** 40 full-time (25 women), 35 part-time (29 women); includes 7 minority (5 African Americans, 2 Hispanic Americans). Average age 35. 95 applicants, 48% accepted, 25 enrolled. In 2001, 1 degree awarded.
**Entrance requirements:** For doctorate, GRE, minimum GPA of 3.0. *Application deadline:* For fall admission, 3/1. *Application fee:* $30.
**Expenses:** Contact institution.
**Financial support:** Scholarships/grants available.
**Faculty research:** Cognitive therapy, attribution theory, treatment of addiction.
Dr. John A. Smith, Director, 215-951-1350, *Fax:* 215-951-1351, *E-mail:* smithj@lasalle.edu.

## ■ LEHIGH UNIVERSITY

**College of Arts and Sciences, Department of Psychology, Bethlehem, PA 18015-3094**

**AWARDS** Experimental psychology (PhD).

**Faculty:** 9 full-time (4 women), 2 part-time/adjunct (0 women).
**Students:** 14 full-time (10 women); includes 1 minority (Hispanic American), 2 international. Average age 35. 24 applicants, 17% accepted, 1 enrolled.
**Degree requirements:** For doctorate, thesis/dissertation, comprehensive exam.
**Entrance requirements:** For doctorate, GRE General Test, TOEFL. *Application deadline:* For fall admission, 2/1. *Application fee:* $50. Electronic applications accepted.
**Expenses:** Contact institution.
**Financial support:** In 2001–02, 11 students received support, including 1 research assistantship with full tuition reimbursement available (averaging $12,350 per year), 8 teaching assistantships with full tuition reimbursements available (averaging $12,350 per year); scholarships/grants, tuition waivers (full), and unspecified assistantships also available. Financial award application deadline: 1/15.
**Faculty research:** Social-cognitive developmental psychology, cognition and language, social cognition.
Dr. Barbara C. Malt, Chairperson, 610-758-4702, *Fax:* 610-758-6277, *E-mail:* barbara.malt@lehigh.edu.
**Application contact:** Dr. Padraig G. O'Seaghdha, Graduate Coordinator, 610-758-3630, *Fax:* 610-758-6277. *Web site:* http://www.lehigh.edu/~inpsy/inpsy.html
**Find an in-depth description at www.petersons.com/gradchannel.**

■ **LESLEY UNIVERSITY**

**Graduate School of Arts and Social Sciences, Cambridge, MA 02138-2790**
**AWARDS** Clinical mental health counseling (MA), including expressive therapies counseling, holistic counseling, school and community counseling; counseling psychology (MA, CAGS), including school counseling (MA); creative arts in learning (M Ed, CAGS), including individually designed (M Ed, MA), multicultural education (M Ed, MA), storytelling (M Ed), theater studies (M Ed); ecological literacy (MS); environmental education (MS); expressive therapies (MA, PhD, CAGS), including art therapy (MA), dance therapy (MA), individually designed (M Ed, MA), mental health counseling (MA), music therapy (MA); independent studies (M Ed); independent study (MA); intercultural relations (MA, CAGS), including development project administration (MA), individually designed (M Ed, MA), intercultural conflict resolution (MA), intercultural health and human services (MA), intercultural relations (CAGS), intercultural training and consulting (MA), international education exchange (MA), international student advising (MA), managing culturally diverse human resources (MA), multicultural education (M Ed, MA); interdisciplinary studies (MA); visual arts and creative writing (MFA). MS (environmental education) offered jointly with the Audubon Society Expedition Institute. Part-time and evening/weekend programs available. Postbaccalaureate distance learning degree programs offered (minimal on-campus study).

**Faculty:** 73 full-time (58 women), 137 part-time/adjunct (95 women).
**Students:** 108 full-time (97 women), 1,190 part-time (1,084 women); includes 134 minority (81 African Americans, 23 Asian Americans or Pacific Islanders, 26 Hispanic Americans, 4 Native Americans), 16 international. Average age 36. 639 applicants, 91% accepted, 313 enrolled. In 2001, 1106 degrees awarded.
**Degree requirements:** For master's, internship, practicum, thesis (expressive therapies); for doctorate and CAGS, thesis/dissertation, arts apprenticeship, field placement; for CAGS, thesis, internship (counseling psychology, expressive therapies).
**Entrance requirements:** For master's, MAT (counseling psychology), TOEFL, interview; for doctorate, GRE or MAT; for CAGS, interview, master's degree. *Application deadline:* Applications are processed on a rolling basis. *Application fee:* $50.
**Expenses:** Tuition: Part-time $330 per credit. Required fees: $15 per term. Part-time tuition and fees vary according to campus/location and program.
**Financial support:** In 2001–02, 47 students received support; research assistantships, teaching assistantships, career-related internships or fieldwork, Federal Work-Study, and unspecified assistantships available. Support available to part-time students. Financial award application deadline: 4/1; financial award applicants required to submit FAFSA.
**Faculty research:** Developmental psychology, women's issues, health psychology, limited supervision group psychology.
Dr. Martha B. McKenna, Dean, 617-349-8467, *Fax:* 617-349-8366.
**Application contact:** Hugh Norwood, Dean of Admissions and Enrollment Planning, 800-999-1959, *Fax:* 617-349-8366, *E-mail:* hnorwood@mail.lesley.edu. *Web site:* http://www.lesley.edu/gsass.html

■ **LONG ISLAND UNIVERSITY, BROOKLYN CAMPUS**

**Richard L. Conolly College of Liberal Arts and Sciences, Department of Psychology, Brooklyn, NY 11201-8423**
**AWARDS** Clinical psychology (PhD); psychology (MA). Part-time and evening/weekend programs available. Terminal master's awarded for partial completion of doctoral program.

**Degree requirements:** For master's, thesis or alternative; for doctorate, thesis/dissertation.
**Entrance requirements:** For master's and doctorate, GRE Subject Test. Electronic applications accepted.

■ **LONG ISLAND UNIVERSITY, C.W. POST CAMPUS**

**College of Liberal Arts and Sciences, Department of Psychology, Brookville, NY 11548-1300**
**AWARDS** Clinical psychology (Psy D); general experimental psychology (MA). Part-time programs available.

**Faculty:** 13 full-time (5 women), 12 part-time/adjunct (6 women).
**Students:** 47 full-time (39 women), 6 part-time (4 women). Average age 25. 197 applicants, 32% accepted, 18 enrolled. In 2001, 12 master's, 10 doctorates awarded.
**Degree requirements:** For master's, thesis; for doctorate, thesis/dissertation, internship.
**Entrance requirements:** For master's, GRE General Test, GRE Subject Test, minimum GPA of 3.0 in psychology, 2.8 overall; for doctorate, GRE General Test, GRE Subject Test, bachelor's degree in psychology, minimum GPA of 3.25. *Application fee:* $30. Electronic applications accepted.
**Expenses:** Tuition: Full-time $10,296; part-time $572 per credit. Required fees: $380; $190 per semester.
**Financial support:** In 2001–02, 28 students received support, including 10 fellowships with full tuition reimbursements available, 12 research assistantships, 7 teaching assistantships; career-related internships or fieldwork, Federal Work-Study, institutionally sponsored loans, tuition waivers (full and partial), and unspecified assistantships also available. Support available to part-time students. Financial award application deadline: 5/15; financial award applicants required to submit CSS PROFILE or FAFSA.
**Faculty research:** Visual perception, animal learning, attachment neuropsychology, developmental disabilities, severe mental illness.
Dr. Gerald Lachter, Chairperson, 516-299-2184, *E-mail:* glachter@liu.edu.
**Application contact:** Dr. Ethel Matin, Graduate Advisor, 516-299-2063, *E-mail:* ethel.matin@liu.edu. *Web site:* http://www.liu.edu/postlas/

■ **LORAS COLLEGE**

**Graduate Division, Department of Psychology, Dubuque, IA 52004-0178**
**AWARDS** Applied psychology (MA). Part-time programs available.

*Loras College (continued)*
**Faculty:** 7 full-time (3 women).
**Students:** 2 full-time (both women), 12 part-time (7 women). Average age 31. 3 applicants, 67% accepted. In 2001, 7 degrees awarded.
**Degree requirements:** For master's, thesis, comprehensive exam.
**Entrance requirements:** For master's, Ohio State University Psychological Test or GRE General Test. *Application deadline:* Applications are processed on a rolling basis. *Application fee:* $25. Electronic applications accepted.
**Expenses:** Tuition: Part-time $375 per credit hour.
Graduate Coordinator, 563-588-7566.
**Application contact:** Barb Harrington, Graduate Admissions Coordinator, 563-588-4915, *Fax:* 563-588-7119, *E-mail:* bharring@loras.edu.

■ **LOUISIANA STATE UNIVERSITY AND AGRICULTURAL AND MECHANICAL COLLEGE**

**Graduate School, College of Arts and Sciences, Department of Psychology, Baton Rouge, LA 70803**

**AWARDS** Biological psychology (MA, PhD); clinical psychology (MA, PhD); cognitive psychology (MA, PhD); developmental psychology (MA, PhD); industrial/organizational psychology (MA, PhD); school psychology (MA, PhD).

**Faculty:** 25 full-time (7 women).
**Students:** 70 full-time (53 women), 43 part-time (24 women); includes 7 minority (3 African Americans, 2 Asian Americans or Pacific Islanders, 2 Hispanic Americans), 2 international. Average age 30. 179 applicants, 12% accepted, 20 enrolled. In 2001, 19 degrees awarded. Terminal master's awarded for partial completion of doctoral program.
**Degree requirements:** For master's, thesis; for doctorate, thesis/dissertation, 1 year internship.
**Entrance requirements:** For master's and doctorate, GRE General Test, minimum GPA of 3.0. *Application deadline:* For fall admission, 1/25 (priority date). Applications are processed on a rolling basis. *Application fee:* $25.
**Expenses:** Tuition, state resident: full-time $2,551. Tuition, nonresident: full-time $5,551. Required fees: $854. Part-time tuition and fees vary according to course load.
**Financial support:** In 2001–02, 1 fellowship (averaging $14,333 per year), 10 research assistantships with partial tuition reimbursements (averaging $14,200 per year), 33 teaching assistantships with partial tuition reimbursements (averaging

$10,371 per year) were awarded. Career-related internships or fieldwork, institutionally sponsored loans, and contracts also available. Financial award applicants required to submit FAFSA. *Total annual research expenditures:* $242,157.
Dr. Irving Lane, Chair, 225-578-8745, *Fax:* 225-578-4125, *E-mail:* irvlane@unix1.sncc.lsu.edu.
**Application contact:** Dr. Janet McDonald, Coordinator of Graduate Studies, 225-578-4116, *Fax:* 225-578-4125, *E-mail:* psmcdo@lsu.edu. *Web site:* http://www.artsci.lsu.edu/psych

■ **LOUISIANA TECH UNIVERSITY**

**Graduate School, College of Education, Department of Behavioral Sciences, Ruston, LA 71272**

**AWARDS** Counseling (MA, Ed S); counseling psychology (PhD); industrial/organizational psychology (MA); special education (MA). Part-time programs available.

**Degree requirements:** For master's, thesis or alternative; for doctorate, thesis/dissertation.
**Entrance requirements:** For master's and doctorate, GRE General Test.

■ **LOYOLA COLLEGE IN MARYLAND**

**Graduate Programs, College of Arts and Sciences, Department of Psychology, Baltimore, MD 21210-2699**

**AWARDS** Clinical psychology (MA, MS, Psy D, CAS); counseling psychology (MA, MS, CAS), including counseling psychology (MA, MS), employee assistance and substance abuse (CAS); general psychology (MA, CAS). Part-time and evening/weekend programs available.

**Students:** In 2001, 57 master's, 10 doctorates, 1 other advanced degree awarded.
**Entrance requirements:** For master's and doctorate, GRE General Test; for CAS, master's degree. *Application deadline:* For spring admission, 10/1 (priority date). Applications are processed on a rolling basis.
**Expenses:** Tuition: Part-time $244 per unit. Tuition and fees vary according to degree level, program and student level.
**Financial support:** Research assistantships available. Financial award applicants required to submit FAFSA.
Dr. Amanda Thomas, Chairman, 410-617-2342.
**Application contact:** Scott Greatorex, Director, Graduate Admissions, 410-617-5020 Ext. 2407, *Fax:* 410-617-2002, *E-mail:* sgreatorex@loyola.edu.

■ **LOYOLA MARYMOUNT UNIVERSITY**

**Graduate Division, College of Liberal Arts, Department of Psychology, Los Angeles, CA 90045-2659**

**AWARDS** Counseling psychology (MA). Part-time and evening/weekend programs available.

**Faculty:** 14 full-time (7 women), 11 part-time/adjunct (5 women).
**Students:** 4 full-time (all women). In 2001, 17 degrees awarded.
**Degree requirements:** For master's, thesis (for some programs), comprehensive exam.
**Entrance requirements:** For master's, GRE General Test, TOEFL, interview, minimum GPA of 3.0. *Application deadline:* For fall admission, 3/15. *Application fee:* $45. Electronic applications accepted.
**Expenses:** Tuition: Part-time $612 per credit hour. Required fees: $86 per term. Tuition and fees vary according to program.
**Financial support:** Scholarships/grants available. Support available to part-time students. Financial award application deadline: 7/1; financial award applicants required to submit FAFSA.
Dr. Michael O'Sullivan, Director, 310-338-3015, *Fax:* 310-338-7726, *E-mail:* mosulliv@lmu.edu. *Web site:* http://www.lmu.edu/acad/gd/graddiv.htm

■ **LOYOLA UNIVERSITY CHICAGO**

**Graduate School, Department of Psychology, Chicago, IL 60611-2196**

**AWARDS** Applied social psychology (MA, PhD); clinical psychology (PhD); developmental psychology (PhD); perception (PhD).

**Faculty:** 27 full-time (10 women), 2 part-time/adjunct (1 woman).
**Students:** 83 full-time (63 women), 18 part-time (13 women); includes 18 minority (7 African Americans, 7 Asian Americans or Pacific Islanders, 4 Hispanic Americans), 9 international. 301 applicants, 11% accepted. In 2001, 18 master's, 15 doctorates awarded. Terminal master's awarded for partial completion of doctoral program.
**Degree requirements:** For master's and doctorate, thesis/dissertation, comprehensive exam.
**Entrance requirements:** For master's and doctorate, GRE General Test, GRE Subject Test. *Application fee:* $40. Electronic applications accepted.
**Expenses:** Tuition: Part-time $529 per credit hour.

**Financial support:** In 2001–02, 51 students received support, including 9 fellowships with full tuition reimbursements available (averaging $10,000 per year), 38 research assistantships with full tuition reimbursements available, 11 teaching assistantships with full tuition reimbursements available; career-related internships or fieldwork, Federal Work-Study, scholarships/grants, traineeships, and teaching fellowships also available. Financial award applicants required to submit FAFSA.

**Faculty research:** Cognitive development, hearing and vision, attitude and prejudice, child and family, AIDS and health promotion. *Total annual research expenditures:* $2.5 million.

Dr. Isiaah Crawford, Chair, 773-508-3001, *E-mail:* icrawfo@luc.edu. *Web site:* http://www.luc.edu/depts/psychology

**Find an in-depth description at www.petersons.com/gradchannel.**

### ■ MADONNA UNIVERSITY

**Department of Psychology, Livonia, MI 48150-1173**

**AWARDS** Clinical psychology (MS). Part-time and evening/weekend programs available.

**Faculty:** 3 full-time (1 woman), 3 part-time/adjunct (1 woman).

**Students:** 28 applicants, 89% accepted.

**Degree requirements:** For master's, thesis or alternative.

**Entrance requirements:** For master's, GRE General Test. *Application deadline:* For fall admission, 3/1. *Application fee:* $0 ($25 for international students). Electronic applications accepted.

**Expenses:** Tuition: Part-time $325 per credit hour.

**Financial support:** Institutionally sponsored loans available. Support available to part-time students.

Dr. Robert Cohen, Chairperson, 734-432-5736.

**Application contact:** Sandra Kellums, Coordinator of Graduate Admissions, 734-432-5667, *Fax:* 734-432-5862, *E-mail:* kellums@smtp.munet.edu. *Web site:* http://www.munet.edu/gradstdy

### ■ MAHARISHI UNIVERSITY OF MANAGEMENT

**Graduate Studies, Program in Psychology, Fairfield, IA 52557**

**AWARDS** MS, PhD. Program admits applicants every other year. Terminal master's awarded for partial completion of doctoral program.

**Degree requirements:** For master's, thesis or alternative; for doctorate, thesis/dissertation, teaching and research practicum.

**Entrance requirements:** For master's and doctorate, GRE General Test, minimum GPA of 3.0.

**Faculty research:** Development, cognition, perception, psychophysiology, sociology and collective consciousness.

### ■ MARIST COLLEGE

**Graduate Programs, School of Social/Behavioral Sciences, Poughkeepsie, NY 12601-1387**

**AWARDS** Counseling/community psychology (MA); education psychology (MA); school psychology (MA, Adv C). Part-time and evening/weekend programs available.

**Faculty:** 8 full-time (3 women), 20 part-time/adjunct (11 women).

**Students:** 66 full-time (49 women), 149 part-time (113 women); includes 11 minority (5 African Americans, 1 Asian American or Pacific Islander, 4 Hispanic Americans, 1 Native American). Average age 30. 104 applicants, 79% accepted. In 2001, 62 degrees awarded.

**Degree requirements:** For master's, thesis optional.

**Entrance requirements:** For master's, GRE General Test. *Application deadline:* For fall admission, 8/1 (priority date); for spring admission, 12/15. Applications are processed on a rolling basis. *Application fee:* $30.

**Expenses:** Tuition: Full-time $4,320; part-time $480 per credit. Required fees: $30 per semester.

**Financial support:** Career-related internships or fieldwork, Federal Work-Study, and tuition waivers (partial) available. Support available to part-time students. Financial award application deadline: 8/15; financial award applicants required to submit FAFSA.

**Faculty research:** Obsessive-compulsive disorders/eating disorders, AIDS prevention, educational intervention, humanistic counseling research, program evaluation research.

Margaret Calista, Dean, 845-575-3000 Ext. 2960, *E-mail:* margaret.calista@marist.edu.

**Application contact:** Dr. John DeJoy, Acting Dean of Graduate and Continuing Education, 845-575-3530, *Fax:* 845-575-3640, *E-mail:* john.dejoy@marist.edu.

### ■ MARQUETTE UNIVERSITY

**Graduate School, College of Arts and Sciences, Department of Psychology, Milwaukee, WI 53201-1881**

**AWARDS** Clinical psychology (MS); psychology (PhD). Part-time programs available.

**Faculty:** 14 full-time (2 women).

**Students:** 36 full-time (24 women), 14 part-time (12 women); includes 7 minority (3 African Americans, 3 Asian Americans or Pacific Islanders, 1 Hispanic American), 2 international. Average age 38. 25 applicants, 48% accepted. In 2001, 2 master's, 4 doctorates awarded.

**Degree requirements:** For master's, thesis or alternative, comprehensive exam; for doctorate, thesis/dissertation, internship, qualifying exam.

**Entrance requirements:** For master's, GRE General Test, GRE Subject Test, MAT, TOEFL; for doctorate, GRE General Test, MAT, TOEFL, sample of scholarly writing. *Application deadline:* For fall admission, 2/15. *Application fee:* $40.

**Expenses:** Tuition: Full-time $10,170; part-time $445 per credit hour. Tuition and fees vary according to course load.

**Financial support:** In 2001–02, 3 research assistantships, 16 teaching assistantships were awarded. Career-related internships or fieldwork, Federal Work-Study, institutionally sponsored loans, scholarships/grants, and tuition waivers (full and partial) also available. Support available to part-time students. Financial award application deadline: 2/15.

**Faculty research:** Mental imagery, moral development, organizational behavior, depression, psychotherapy outcomes. *Total annual research expenditures:* $111,450.

Dr. Robert Lueger, Chairman, 414-288-7218, *Fax:* 414-288-5333.

### ■ MARSHALL UNIVERSITY

**Graduate College, College of Liberal Arts, Department of Psychology, Huntington, WV 25755**

**AWARDS** Clinical psychology (MA); general psychology (MA); industrial and organizational psychology (MA); psychology (Psy D).

**Faculty:** 15 full-time (6 women), 15 part-time/adjunct (7 women).

**Students:** 78 full-time (59 women), 88 part-time (62 women); includes 5 minority (4 African Americans, 1 Hispanic American), 3 international. In 2001, 65 degrees awarded.

**Degree requirements:** For master's, thesis optional.

**Entrance requirements:** For master's, GRE General Test or MAT. *Application deadline:* For fall admission, 3/1; for spring admission, 11/1.

**Expenses:** Tuition, state resident: part-time $147 per credit. Tuition, nonresident: part-time $468 per credit. Tuition and fees vary according to campus/location and reciprocity agreements.

**Financial support:** Teaching assistantships with tuition reimbursements available.

Dr. Martin Amerikaner, Chairperson, 304-696-6446, *E-mail:* amerikan@marshall.edu.

*Marshall University (continued)*
**Application contact:** Ken O'Neal, Assistant Vice President, Adult Student Services, 304-746-2500 Ext. 1907, *Fax:* 304-746-1902, *E-mail:* oneal@marshall.edu.

### ■ MARTIN UNIVERSITY

**Division of Psychology, Indianapolis, IN 46218-3867**

**AWARDS** Community psychology (MS). Part-time and evening/weekend programs available.

**Faculty:** 4 full-time (1 woman), 2 part-time/adjunct (1 woman).
**Students:** 35 full-time (23 women), 17 part-time (13 women); includes 42 minority (all African Americans), 1 international. Average age 41. In 2001, 11 degrees awarded.
**Degree requirements:** For master's, thesis, comprehensive exam.
**Entrance requirements:** For master's, GRE General Test, GRE Subject Test. *Application deadline:* Applications are processed on a rolling basis. *Application fee:* $55.
**Expenses:** Tuition: Part-time $275 per credit hour.
**Financial support:** In 2001–02, 9 students received support. Applicants required to submit FAFSA.
**Faculty research:** Social and educational issues in minority and low income communities.
Dr. Richard L. Elder, Chairperson, 317-917-3321, *Fax:* 317-543-4790, *E-mail:* relder@martin.edu.
**Application contact:** Brenda Shaheed, Director of Enrollment Management, 317-543-3237, *Fax:* 317-543-4790, *E-mail:* rlelder@iupui.edu.

### ■ MARYMOUNT UNIVERSITY

**School of Education and Human Services, Program in Psychology, Arlington, VA 22207-4299**

**AWARDS** Counseling psychology (MA, Certificate); forensic psychology (MA); school counseling (MA). Part-time and evening/weekend programs available.

**Students:** 80 full-time (71 women), 101 part-time (87 women); includes 28 minority (20 African Americans, 7 Hispanic Americans, 1 Native American), 3 international. Average age 32. 65 applicants, 98% accepted, 44 enrolled. In 2001, 41 degrees awarded.
**Degree requirements:** For master's, thesis or alternative.
**Entrance requirements:** For master's, GRE General Test or MAT, interview; for Certificate, master's degree in counseling. *Application deadline:* Applications are

processed on a rolling basis. *Application fee:* $35. Electronic applications accepted.
**Expenses:** Tuition: Part-time $512 per credit. Required fees: $5 per credit.
**Financial support:** Research assistantships with full tuition reimbursements, career-related internships or fieldwork and scholarships/grants available. Support available to part-time students. Financial award applicants required to submit FAFSA.
Dr. Carolyn Oxenford, Chair, 703-284-1620, *Fax:* 703-284-1631, *E-mail:* carolyn.oxenford@marymount.edu. *Web site:* http://www.marymount.edu/academic/sehs/

### ■ MARYWOOD UNIVERSITY

**Graduate School of Arts and Sciences, Department of Counseling/Psychology, Program in Psychology, Scranton, PA 18509-1598**

**AWARDS** MA. Part-time and evening/weekend programs available.

**Students:** 31 full-time (27 women), 57 part-time (37 women); includes 1 minority (Asian American or Pacific Islander), 1 international. Average age 33. 62 applicants, 66% accepted. In 2001, 24 degrees awarded.
**Degree requirements:** For master's, thesis or alternative, internship/practicum, comprehensive exam.
**Entrance requirements:** For master's, GRE or MAT, TOEFL. *Application deadline:* For fall admission, 4/15; for spring admission, 11/15 (priority date). Applications are processed on a rolling basis. *Application fee:* $20. Electronic applications accepted.
**Financial support:** Research assistantships, career-related internships or fieldwork, scholarships/grants, and tuition waivers (partial) available. Support available to part-time students. Financial award application deadline: 2/15; financial award applicants required to submit FAFSA.
**Faculty research:** Personality disorders, counselor training, preschool development, self-esteem measurement, family dynamics.
**Application contact:** Deborah M. Flynn, Coordinator of Admissions, 570-340-6002, *Fax:* 570-961-4745, *E-mail:* gsas_adm@ac.marywood.edu.

**Find an in-depth description at www.petersons.com/gradchannel.**

### ■ MARYWOOD UNIVERSITY

**Graduate School of Arts and Sciences, Department of Counseling/Psychology, Program in Psychology and Counseling, Scranton, PA 18509-1598**

**AWARDS** Psy D.

*Application deadline:* For fall admission, 1/15. *Application fee:* $20.
**Financial support:** Applicants required to submit FAFSA.
Dr. Brooke Cannon, Clinical Director, 570-348-6211.

### ■ MASSACHUSETTS INSTITUTE OF TECHNOLOGY

**School of Science, Department of Brain and Cognitive Sciences, Cambridge, MA 02139-4307**

**AWARDS** Cellular/molecular neuroscience (PhD); cognitive neuroscience (PhD); cognitive science (PhD); computational cognitive science (PhD); computational neuroscience (PhD); systems neuroscience (PhD).

**Faculty:** 26 full-time (6 women).
**Students:** 58 full-time (15 women); includes 5 minority (1 African American, 4 Asian Americans or Pacific Islanders), 17 international. Average age 26. 257 applicants, 10% accepted, 11 enrolled. In 2001, 5 doctorates awarded.
**Degree requirements:** For doctorate, thesis/dissertation, comprehensive exam.
**Entrance requirements:** For doctorate, GRE General Test, TOEFL. *Application deadline:* For fall admission, 1/1. *Application fee:* $60. Electronic applications accepted.
**Expenses:** Tuition: Full-time $26,960. Full-time tuition and fees vary according to program.
**Financial support:** In 2001–02, 58 students received support, including 43 fellowships (averaging $20,000 per year), 6 research assistantships (averaging $21,600 per year), 20 teaching assistantships (averaging $16,650 per year); Federal Work-Study, institutionally sponsored loans, scholarships/grants, health care benefits, and unspecified assistantships also available. Financial award application deadline: 1/1; financial award applicants required to submit FAFSA.
**Faculty research:** Vision, learning and memory, motor control, plasticity. *Total annual research expenditures:* $12.1 million.
Mriganka Sur, Head, 617-253-8784.
**Application contact:** Denise Heintze, Academic Administrator, 617-253-5742, *Fax:* 617-253-9767, *E-mail:* bcsadmiss@mit.edu. *Web site:* http://web.mit.edu/bcs

**Find an in-depth description at www.petersons.com/gradchannel.**

### ■ MASSACHUSETTS SCHOOL OF PROFESSIONAL PSYCHOLOGY

**Graduate Program, Boston, MA 02132**

**AWARDS** Clinical psychology (Psy D, Certificate); clinical psychopharmacology (Post-Doctoral MS). Part-time programs available.

**Faculty:** 36 part-time/adjunct (13 women).

**Students:** 114 full-time (95 women), 36 part-time (30 women); includes 13 minority (1 African American, 8 Asian Americans or Pacific Islanders, 3 Hispanic Americans, 1 Native American), 17 international. Average age 28. 182 applicants, 43% accepted, 44 enrolled. In 2001, 36 degrees awarded.
**Degree requirements:** For doctorate, thesis/dissertation, registration. *Median time to degree:* Doctorate–4 years full-time.
**Entrance requirements:** For doctorate, GRE General Test, GRE Writing Assessment. *Application deadline:* For fall admission, 1/11. *Application fee:* $50.
**Expenses:** Tuition: Full-time $20,260; part-time $633 per credit.
**Financial support:** In 2001–02, 93 students received support, including 12 teaching assistantships (averaging $2,500 per year); career-related internships or fieldwork, institutionally sponsored loans, and scholarships/grants also available. Financial award application deadline: 2/8; financial award applicants required to submit FAFSA.
Dr. Bruce J. Weiss, President, 617-327-6777, *Fax:* 617-327-4447.
**Application contact:** 617-327-6777, *Fax:* 617-327-4447, *E-mail:* admissions@ mspp.edu. *Web site:* http://www.mspp.edu/
**Find an in-depth description at www.petersons.com/gradchannel.**

■ **MCNEESE STATE UNIVERSITY**
**Graduate School, College of Education, Department of Psychology, Program in Psychology, Lake Charles, LA 70609**
**AWARDS** MA.
**Faculty:** 9 full-time (3 women), 3 part-time/adjunct (all women).
**Students:** 25 full-time (18 women), 36 part-time (29 women); includes 12 minority (10 African Americans, 2 Native Americans), 1 international. In 2001, 10 degrees awarded.
**Degree requirements:** For master's, thesis.
**Entrance requirements:** For master's, GRE General Test, GRE Subject Test, minimum undergraduate GPA of 2.75. *Application deadline:* For fall admission, 7/15 (priority date). Applications are processed on a rolling basis. *Application fee:* $20 ($30 for international students).
**Expenses:** Tuition, state resident: part-time $1,208 per semester. Tuition, nonresident: part-time $4,378 per semester.
**Financial support:** Application deadline: 5/1.
Dr. Jess Feist, Head, Department of Psychology, 337-475-5457, *Fax:* 337-475-5467.

■ **MERCY COLLEGE**
**Division of Social and Behavioral Sciences, Dobbs Ferry, NY 10522-1189**
**AWARDS** Alcohol and substance abuse counseling (AC); family counseling (AC); health services management (MPA, MS); psychology (MS); retirement counseling (AC); school counseling (MS), including bilingual extension; school psychology (MS), including bilingual extension.
**Students:** 51 full-time (41 women), 105 part-time (81 women); includes 104 minority (47 African Americans, 7 Asian Americans or Pacific Islanders, 50 Hispanic Americans), 10 international.
**Entrance requirements:** For master's, 8 years of healthcare management or practitioner (MS in health services management); interview; minimum GPA of 3.0. *Application fee:* $35.
**Expenses:** Tuition: Part-time $450 per credit. Part-time tuition and fees vary according to program.
Dr. Frances T.M. Mahoney, Chairperson, 914-674-7438, *Fax:* 914-674-7542, *E-mail:* fmahoney@mercy.edu.
**Application contact:** Information Contact, 800-MERCY-NY.
**Find an in-depth description at www.petersons.com/gradchannel.**

■ **MIAMI UNIVERSITY**
**Graduate School, College of Arts and Sciences, Department of Psychology, Oxford, OH 45056**
**AWARDS** Clinical psychology (PhD); experimental psychology (PhD); social psychology (PhD).
**Faculty:** 12 full-time (2 women), 9 part-time/adjunct (4 women).
**Students:** 73 full-time (49 women); includes 12 minority (9 African Americans, 3 Asian Americans or Pacific Islanders), 7 international. 128 applicants, 41% accepted, 17 enrolled. In 2001, 12 doctorates awarded.
**Degree requirements:** For doctorate, thesis/dissertation, final exams, comprehensive exam.
**Entrance requirements:** For doctorate, GRE General Test, GRE Subject Test, minimum GPA of 2.75 (undergraduate), 3.0 (graduate). *Application deadline:* For fall admission, 2/1. *Application fee:* $35.
**Expenses:** Tuition, state resident: full-time $7,155; part-time $295 per semester hour. Tuition, nonresident: full-time $14,829; part-time $615 per semester hour. Tuition and fees vary according to degree level and campus/location.
**Financial support:** In 2001–02, 28 fellowships (averaging $9,134 per year), 12 teaching assistantships (averaging $11,337

per year) were awarded. Research assistantships, career-related internships or fieldwork, Federal Work-Study, and tuition waivers (full) also available. Financial award application deadline: 3/1.
Dr. Karen Schilling, Chair, 513-529-2400, *Fax:* 513-529-2420, *E-mail:* psych@ muohio.edu.
**Application contact:** Dr. Phillip Best, Director of Graduate Studies, 513-529-2400, *Fax:* 513-529-2420, *E-mail:* psych@ muohio.edu. *Web site:* http://www.muohio.edu/~psycwis/graduate.html

■ **MICHIGAN STATE UNIVERSITY**
**College of Human Medicine and Graduate School, Graduate Programs in Human Medicine, East Lansing, MI 48824**
**AWARDS** Anatomy (MS); anthropology (MA); biochemistry (MS, PhD), including biochemistry, biochemistry-environmental toxicology (PhD); epidemiology (MS); human pathology (MS, PhD); microbiology (MS, PhD); pharmacology/toxicology (MS, PhD); physiology (MS, PhD); psychology (MA); sociology (MA); surgery (MS); zoology (MS). Part-time programs available.
**Students:** 63 (29 women); includes 7 minority (5 Asian Americans or Pacific Islanders, 2 Hispanic Americans) 7 international. Average age 26. In 2001, 14 master's, 2 doctorates awarded.
**Entrance requirements:** For master's and doctorate, GRE General Test, minimum GPA of 3.0. *Application deadline:* Applications are processed on a rolling basis. *Application fee:* $30 ($40 for international students). Electronic applications accepted.
**Expenses:** Contact institution.
**Financial support:** In 2001–02, 48 research assistantships with tuition reimbursements (averaging $12,058 per year), 1 teaching assistantship with tuition reimbursement (averaging $10,944 per year) were awarded. Fellowships with tuition reimbursements, institutionally sponsored loans also available. Support available to part-time students. Financial award applicants required to submit FAFSA.
Dr. Lynne Farquhar, Director, Medical Science Training Program, 517-353-8858, *Fax:* 517-432-0148, *E-mail:* mdadmissions@msu.edu. *Web site:* http://www.chm.msu.edu/chmhome/gradeducation/GMEWEB/

■ **MICHIGAN STATE UNIVERSITY**
**Graduate School, College of Social Science, Department of Psychology, East Lansing, MI 48824**
**AWARDS** Applied developmental science (MA, PhD); infant studies (MA, PhD);

*Michigan State University (continued)*
neuroscience-psychology (MA, PhD); psychology (MA, PhD); psychology-urban studies (MA, PhD).

**Faculty:** 50.

**Students:** 80 full-time (53 women), 37 part-time (22 women); includes 24 minority (12 African Americans, 8 Asian Americans or Pacific Islanders, 4 Hispanic Americans), 7 international. Average age 28. 312 applicants, 5% accepted. In 2001, 20 master's, 23 doctorates awarded.

**Degree requirements:** For master's, thesis (for some programs); for doctorate, thesis/dissertation.

**Entrance requirements:** For master's, GRE General Test, TOEFL, minimum GPA of 3.25; for doctorate, GRE General Test, TOEFL, minimum GPA of 3.5. *Application deadline:* For fall admission, 1/5. *Application fee:* $30 ($40 for international students). Electronic applications accepted.

**Expenses:** Tuition, state resident: part-time $244 per credit hour. Tuition, nonresident: part-time $494 per credit hour. Required fees: $268 per semester. Tuition and fees vary according to course load, degree level and program.

**Financial support:** In 2001–02, 57 fellowships (averaging $3,788 per year), 51 research assistantships with tuition reimbursements (averaging $12,076 per year), 47 teaching assistantships with tuition reimbursements (averaging $11,555 per year) were awarded. Career-related internships or fieldwork and institutionally sponsored loans also available. Support available to part-time students. Financial award applicants required to submit FAFSA.

**Faculty research:** Hormones and behavior, cognitive processes, personnel selection, social cognition, program evaluation. *Total annual research expenditures:* $4.2 million.

Dr. Neal Schmitt, Chairperson, 517-355-9561, *Fax:* 517-432-2476.

**Application contact:** Graduate Secretary, 517-353-5258, *Fax:* 517-432-2476. *Web site:* http://psychology.msu.edu/

## ■ MIDDLE TENNESSEE STATE UNIVERSITY

**College of Graduate Studies, College of Education and Behavioral Science, Department of Psychology, Murfreesboro, TN 37132**

**AWARDS** Industrial/organizational psychology (MA); psychology (MA); school counseling (M Ed, Ed S); school psychology (Ed S). Part-time and evening/weekend programs available.

**Faculty:** 37 full-time (13 women).

**Students:** 28 full-time, 165 part-time; includes 24 minority (18 African

Americans, 4 Asian Americans or Pacific Islanders, 2 Hispanic Americans). Average age 26. 54 applicants, 67% accepted. In 2001, 46 master's, 12 other advanced degrees awarded.

**Degree requirements:** For master's, one foreign language, thesis, comprehensive exam.

**Entrance requirements:** For master's, GRE. *Application deadline:* For fall admission, 8/1 (priority date). Applications are processed on a rolling basis. *Application fee:* $25. Electronic applications accepted.

**Expenses:** Tuition, state resident: full-time $1,716; part-time $191 per hour. Tuition, nonresident: full-time $4,952; part-time $461 per hour. Required fees: $14 per hour. $58 per semester.

**Financial support:** In 2001–02, 8 teaching assistantships were awarded; research assistantships, career-related internships or fieldwork, institutionally sponsored loans, and scholarships/grants also available. Support available to part-time students. Financial award application deadline: 5/1; financial award applicants required to submit FAFSA.

**Faculty research:** Industrial/organizational, social/personality/sports, counseling/clinical/school, cognitive/language/learning/perception, developmental/aging. *Total annual research expenditures:* $44,089.

Dr. Larry Morris, Chair, 615-898-2706, *Fax:* 615-898-5027, *E-mail:* lmorris@mtsu.edu.

## ■ MIDWESTERN STATE UNIVERSITY

**Graduate Studies, College of Liberal Arts, Psychology Program, Wichita Falls, TX 76308**

**AWARDS** MA.

**Faculty:** 5 full-time (1 woman).

**Students:** 14 full-time (11 women), 3 part-time (all women); includes 3 minority (2 African Americans, 1 Hispanic American). Average age 29. 7 applicants, 100% accepted. In 2001, 4 degrees awarded.

**Degree requirements:** For master's, one foreign language, thesis or alternative.

**Entrance requirements:** For master's, GRE General Test, TOEFL. *Application deadline:* For fall admission, 8/7 (priority date); for spring admission, 12/15. Applications are processed on a rolling basis. *Application fee:* $0 ($50 for international students).

**Expenses:** Tuition, state resident: full-time $936. Tuition, nonresident: full-time $4,734. Required fees: $1,280. One-time fee: $190. Tuition and fees vary according to course load.

**Financial support:** In 2001–02, 6 teaching assistantships with partial tuition

reimbursements were awarded; research assistantships, career-related internships or fieldwork, Federal Work-Study, institutionally sponsored loans, and tuition waivers (partial) also available. Support available to part-time students.

**Faculty research:** Personality disorders, child sexual abuse and sexual coercion, educational psychology.

Dr. Michael Collins, Dean, 940-397-4030, *Fax:* 940-397-4929.

**Application contact:** Dr. George Diekhoff, Chair, 940-397-4348. *Web site:* http://www.mwsu.edu/

## ■ MILLERSVILLE UNIVERSITY OF PENNSYLVANIA

**Graduate School, School of Education, Department of Psychology, Millersville, PA 17551-0302**

**AWARDS** Psychology (MS), including clinical psychology, school psychology; school counseling (M Ed). Part-time and evening/weekend programs available.

**Faculty:** 20 full-time (14 women), 5 part-time/adjunct (3 women).

**Students:** 42 full-time (35 women), 111 part-time (85 women); includes 10 minority (3 African Americans, 4 Asian Americans or Pacific Islanders, 3 Hispanic Americans). Average age 28. 71 applicants, 61% accepted, 39 enrolled. In 2001, 45 degrees awarded.

**Degree requirements:** For master's, departmental exam, thesis optional.

**Entrance requirements:** For master's, GRE General Test, minimum undergraduate GPA of 2.75, 18 undergraduate hours in psychology, interview, letters of recommendation, writing sample. *Application deadline:* For fall admission, 3/31; for spring admission, 11/1. Applications are processed on a rolling basis. *Application fee:* $30.

**Expenses:** Tuition, state resident: part-time $256 per credit. Tuition, nonresident: full-time $7,554; part-time $420 per credit. Required fees: $1,037; $44 per credit.

**Financial support:** In 2001–02, 56 research assistantships with full tuition reimbursements (averaging $4,000 per year) were awarded; career-related internships or fieldwork, Federal Work-Study, institutionally sponsored loans, and unspecified assistantships also available. Support available to part-time students. Financial award application deadline: 3/15; financial award applicants required to submit FAFSA.

Dr. Helena Tuleya-Payne, Chair, 717-872-3925, *Fax:* 717-871-2480, *E-mail:* helena.tuleya-payne@millersville.edu.

**Application contact:** Dr. Duncan M. Perry, Dean of Graduate Studies, Professional Training and Education, 717-872-3030, *E-mail:* duncan.perry@ millersville.edu.

■ **MINNESOTA STATE UNIVERSITY, MANKATO**

**College of Graduate Studies, College of Social and Behavioral Sciences, Department of Psychology, Mankato, MN 56001**

**AWARDS** Clinical psychology (MA); industrial psychology (MA); psychology (MT). Part-time programs available.

**Faculty:** 12 full-time (3 women).
**Students:** 31 full-time (28 women), 8 part-time (3 women). Average age 26. In 2001, 15 degrees awarded.
**Degree requirements:** For master's, one foreign language, thesis (for some programs), comprehensive exam.
**Entrance requirements:** For master's, GRE General Test, GRE Subject Test (clinical psychology), minimum GPA of 3.0 during previous 2 years. *Application deadline:* For fall admission, 3/1; for spring admission, 11/27. Applications are processed on a rolling basis. *Application fee:* $20. Electronic applications accepted.
**Expenses:** Tuition, state resident: full-time $3,253; part-time $157 per credit. Tuition, nonresident: full-time $4,893; part-time $248 per credit. Required fees: $24 per credit. Tuition and fees vary according to reciprocity agreements.
**Financial support:** Research assistantships, teaching assistantships with full tuition reimbursements, career-related internships or fieldwork, Federal Work-Study, and institutionally sponsored loans available. Support available to part-time students. Financial award application deadline: 3/15; financial award applicants required to submit FAFSA.
**Faculty research:** Professional competency in hospitals, mood disturbance, 360-degree feedback, employee selection, planning fallacy. Dr. Michael Fatis, Chairperson, 507-389-1818.
**Application contact:** Joni Roberts, Admissions Coordinator, 507-389-5244, *Fax:* 507-389-5974, *E-mail:* grad@ mankato.msus.edu.

■ **MINNESOTA STATE UNIVERSITY MOORHEAD**

**Graduate Studies, Department of Psychology, Moorhead, MN 56563-0002**

**AWARDS** School psychology (MS, Psy S).
**Faculty:** 8.

**Students:** 17 (11 women). 23 applicants, 52% accepted.
**Degree requirements:** For master's, thesis, final oral and written comprehensive exams.
**Entrance requirements:** For master's, GRE General Test, TOEFL, interview, minimum GPA of 3.0, letters of recommendation (3); for Psy S, MS in school psychology. *Application deadline:* For fall admission, 2/15. *Application fee:* $20 ($35 for international students). Electronic applications accepted.
**Expenses:** Tuition, area resident: Part-time $148 per credit. Tuition, nonresident: part-time $234 per credit.
**Financial support:** Career-related internships or fieldwork, Federal Work-Study, and unspecified assistantships available. Financial award application deadline: 7/15; financial award applicants required to submit FAFSA.
Dr. Gary Nickell, Chairperson, 218-236-4080.
**Application contact:** Margaret Potter, Coordinator, 218-236-2805. *Web site:* http://www.mnstate.edu/gradpsyc/

■ **MISSISSIPPI COLLEGE**

**Graduate School, College of Arts and Sciences, Department of Psychology and Counseling, Program in Psychology, Clinton, MS 39058**

**AWARDS** Counseling psychology (MS).

■ **MISSISSIPPI STATE UNIVERSITY**

**College of Arts and Sciences, Department of Psychology, Mississippi State, MS 39762**

**AWARDS** Clinical psychology (MS); cognitive science (PhD); experimental psychology (MS).

**Faculty:** 16 full-time (6 women).
**Students:** 32 full-time (21 women), 8 part-time (6 women); includes 2 minority (1 African American, 1 Hispanic American), 1 international. Average age 27. 50 applicants, 64% accepted. In 2001, 8 degrees awarded. Terminal master's awarded for partial completion of doctoral program.
**Degree requirements:** For master's, thesis, comprehensive exam; for doctorate, thesis/dissertation, qualifying exam, comprehensive written and oral exam.
**Entrance requirements:** For master's, GRE General Test, TOEFL, minimum GPA of 2.75; for doctorate, GRE General Test, proficiency in at least one computer language. *Application deadline:* For fall admission, 7/1 (priority date); for spring admission, 11/1. Applications are processed on a rolling basis. *Application fee:* $25 for international students.

**Expenses:** Tuition, state resident: full-time $3,586; part-time $150 per credit hour. Tuition, nonresident: full-time $8,128; part-time $339 per credit hour. Tuition and fees vary according to course load and campus/location.
**Financial support:** In 2001–02, 5 research assistantships with full tuition reimbursements (averaging $10,000 per year), 11 teaching assistantships with full tuition reimbursements (averaging $5,940 per year) were awarded. Career-related internships or fieldwork, Federal Work-Study, institutionally sponsored loans, scholarships/grants, and unspecified assistantships also available. Financial award applicants required to submit FAFSA.
**Faculty research:** Personality type, alcoholism, blindness and low vision, mental retardation, language comprehension. *Total annual research expenditures:* $175,000.
Dr. Stephen B. Klein, Head, 662-325-3202, *Fax:* 662-325-7212, *E-mail:* sbkl@ ra.msstate.edu.
**Application contact:** Dr. B. Michael Thorne, Professor and Graduate Coordinator, 662-325-7659, *Fax:* 662-325-7212, *E-mail:* brnt2@ra.msstate.edu. *Web site:* http://www.msstate.edu/dept/ psychology/psych.htm

■ **MONMOUTH UNIVERSITY**

**Graduate School, Department of Psychology, West Long Branch, NJ 07764-1898**

**AWARDS** Professional counseling (PMC); psychological counseling (MA). Part-time and evening/weekend programs available.

**Faculty:** 5 full-time (1 woman), 4 part-time/adjunct (3 women).
**Students:** 22 full-time (19 women), 53 part-time (42 women); includes 7 minority (4 African Americans, 2 Asian Americans or Pacific Islanders, 1 Native American), 1 international. Average age 32. 84 applicants, 55% accepted, 19 enrolled. In 2001, 31 degrees awarded.
**Degree requirements:** For master's, thesis optional.
**Entrance requirements:** For master's, GRE General Test, minimum GPA of 3.0 in major, 24 credits in psychology. *Application deadline:* For fall admission, 8/15 (priority date); for spring admission, 12/15 (priority date). Applications are processed on a rolling basis. *Application fee:* $35. Electronic applications accepted.
**Expenses:** Tuition: Full-time $9,900; part-time $549 per credit. Required fees: $568.
**Financial support:** In 2001–02, 90 fellowships (averaging $1,519 per year), 4 research assistantships (averaging $8,114 per year) were awarded. Career-related

*Monmouth University (continued)*
internships or fieldwork, scholarships/
grants, tuition waivers (partial), and
unspecified assistantships also available.
Support available to part-time students.
Financial award application deadline: 3/1;
financial award applicants required to
submit FAFSA.
**Faculty research:** Systems thinking,
violent crime, single parenting, the
African-American male, counseling older
women.
Dr. Frances K. Trotman, Director, 732-
571-7593, *Fax:* 732-263-5159, *E-mail:*
ftrotman@monmouth.edu.
**Application contact:** Kevin Roane, Director, Office of Graduate Admissions, 732-
571-3452, *Fax:* 732-263-5123, *E-mail:*
gradadm@monmouth.edu. *Web site:* http://
www.monmouth.edu/~psychgr.
**Find an in-depth description at
www.petersons.com/gradchannel.**

### ■ MONTANA STATE UNIVERSITY–BILLINGS

**College of Arts and Sciences,
Department of Psychology, Billings,
MT 59101-0298**

AWARDS MS.

**Expenses:** Tuition, state resident: full-time
$3,560; part-time $1,164 per semester.
Tuition, nonresident: full-time $8,498;
part-time $2,810 per semester.

### ■ MONTANA STATE UNIVERSITY–BOZEMAN

**College of Graduate Studies, College
of Letters and Science, Department of
Psychology, Bozeman, MT 59717**

AWARDS Applied psychology (MS). Part-time
programs available.

**Students:** 6 full-time (4 women), 10 part-
time (5 women); includes 2 minority (1
Asian American or Pacific Islander, 1
Hispanic American). Average age 26. 13
applicants, 62% accepted, 3 enrolled. In
2001, 1 degree awarded.
**Degree requirements:** For master's,
thesis, professional paper or thesis.
**Entrance requirements:** For master's,
GRE General Test, TOEFL, minimum
GPA of 3.0. *Application deadline:* For fall
admission, 2/1; for spring admission, 7/1.
Applications are processed on a rolling
basis. *Application fee:* $50. Electronic
applications accepted.
**Expenses:** Tuition, state resident: full-time
$3,894; part-time $198 per credit. Tuition,
nonresident: full-time $10,661; part-time
$480 per credit. International tuition:
$10,811 full-time. Tuition and fees vary
according to course load and program.

**Financial support:** In 2001–02, 10
students received support, including 10
teaching assistantships with full tuition
reimbursements available (averaging
$5,500 per year). Financial award applica-
tion deadline: 3/1; financial award
applicants required to submit FAFSA.
**Faculty research:** Cerebral ischemia,
workplace romance, sexual harassment,
groups gender bias, performance appraisal.
*Total annual research expenditures:* $5,035.
Dr. Michael Babcock, Head, 406-994-
3801, *Fax:* 406-994-3804, *E-mail:* upymb@
montana.edu. *Web site:* http://
www.montana.edu/wwwpy/

### ■ MONTCLAIR STATE UNIVERSITY

**The School of Graduate, Professional
and Continuing Education, College of
Humanities and Social Sciences,
Department of Psychology, Upper
Montclair, NJ 07043-1624**

AWARDS Child advocacy (Certificate);
educational psychology (MA), including child/
adolescent clinical psychology, clinical
psychology for Spanish/English bilinguals;
psychology (MA), including industrial and
organizational psychology. Part-time and
evening/weekend programs available.

**Degree requirements:** For master's,
comprehensive exam.
**Entrance requirements:** For master's,
GRE General Test, GRE Subject Test,
previous course work in psychology,
interview. Electronic applications accepted.

### ■ MOREHEAD STATE UNIVERSITY

**Graduate Programs, College of
Science and Technology, Department
of Psychology, Morehead, KY 40351**

AWARDS Clinical psychology (MA); counseling psychology (MA); experimental/general
psychology (MA). Part-time programs available.

**Faculty:** 7 full-time (2 women).
**Students:** 30 full-time (19 women), 1
international. Average age 25. 5 applicants,
80% accepted. In 2001, 15 degrees
awarded.
**Entrance requirements:** For master's,
GRE General Test, TOEFL, 18
undergraduate hours in psychology,
minimum GPA of 3.0. *Application deadline:*
For fall admission, 8/1 (priority date); for
spring admission, 12/1. Applications are
processed on a rolling basis. *Application fee:*
$0.
**Expenses:** Tuition, state resident: part-
time $176 per hour. Tuition, nonresident:
full-time $1,584; part-time $472 per hour.
International tuition: $4,247 full-time.

**Financial support:** In 2001–02, 21
research assistantships (averaging $5,000
per year) were awarded; career-related
internships or fieldwork, Federal Work-
Study, and institutionally sponsored loans
also available. Financial award application
deadline: 4/1; financial award applicants
required to submit FAFSA.
**Faculty research:** Mood induction effects,
serotonin receptor activity, stress,
perceptual processes.
Dr. Bruce A. Mattingly, Chair, 606-783-
2891, *Fax:* 606-783-5077, *E-mail:*
b.mattin@moreheadstate.edu.
**Application contact:** Betty R. Cowsert,
Graduate Admissions/Records Manager,
606-783-2039, *Fax:* 606-783-5061, *E-mail:*
b.cowsert@moreheadstate.edu. *Web site:*
http://www.moreheadstate.edu

### ■ MURRAY STATE UNIVERSITY

**College of Humanities and Fine Arts,
Department of Psychology, Murray,
KY 42071-0009**

AWARDS Clinical psychology (MA, MS);
psychology (MA, MS). Part-time programs
available.

**Students:** 17 full-time (12 women), 7 part-
time (4 women); includes 2 minority (1
Asian American or Pacific Islander, 1
Native American), 4 international. 10
applicants, 50% accepted. In 2001, 4
degrees awarded.
**Degree requirements:** For master's, one
foreign language, thesis (for some
programs).
**Entrance requirements:** For master's,
GRE General Test, TOEFL. *Application
deadline:* Applications are processed on a
rolling basis. *Application fee:* $25.
**Expenses:** Tuition, state resident: full-time
$1,440; part-time $169 per hour. Tuition,
nonresident: full-time $4,004; part-time
$450 per hour.
**Financial support:** Research assistantships,
teaching assistantships, Federal Work-
Study available. Financial award application deadline: 4/1.
Dr. Renae Duncan, Chairman, 270-762-
3539, *Fax:* 270-762-2991, *E-mail:*
renae.duncan@murraystate.edu.

### ■ NAROPA UNIVERSITY

**Graduate Programs, Boulder, CO
80302-6697**

AWARDS Body psychotherapy (MA); Buddhist
studies (MA); contemplative education (MA);
creation spirituality (MLA); dance/movement
therapy (MA); divinity (M Div); engaged Buddhism (MA); environmental leadership (MA);
gerontology (MA); Indo-Tibetan Buddhism
(MA); Indo-Tibetan Buddhism with language
(MA); psychology: contemplative
psychotherapy (MA); religious studies (MA);
transpersonal counseling psychology (MA),

including art therapy, music therapy, transpersonal counseling psychology; transpersonal psychology (MA); wilderness therapy (MA); writing and poetics (MFA).

**Faculty:** 34 full-time (14 women), 175 part-time/adjunct (128 women).

**Students:** 404 full-time (277 women), 233 part-time (177 women); includes 51 minority (12 African Americans, 18 Asian Americans or Pacific Islanders, 17 Hispanic Americans, 4 Native Americans), 31 international. Average age 37. 485 applicants, 82% accepted, 242 enrolled. In 2001, 160 degrees awarded.

*Application deadline:* For fall admission, 2/1 (priority date); for spring admission, 11/1 (priority date). Applications are processed on a rolling basis. *Application fee:* $50 ($0 for international students). Electronic applications accepted.

**Expenses:** Tuition: Full-time $10,766; part-time $489 per credit. Required fees: $560; $280 per semester. Tuition and fees vary according to course load and campus/location.

**Financial support:** In 2001–02, 82 students received support. Career-related internships or fieldwork, Federal Work-Study, scholarships/grants, health care benefits, and tuition waivers (partial) available. Support available to part-time students. Financial award application deadline: 3/1; financial award applicants required to submit FAFSA.

John Cobb, President, 303-444-0202.

**Application contact:** Susan Elizabeth Boyle, Director of Admissions, 303-546-3572, *Fax:* 303-546-3583, *E-mail:* sboyle@naropa.edu. *Web site:* http://www.naropa.edu/graduate.html/

**Find an in-depth description at www.petersons.com/gradchannel.**

---

### ■ NATIONAL-LOUIS UNIVERSITY

**College of Arts and Sciences, Division of Liberal Arts and Sciences, Program in Psychology, Chicago, IL 60603**

**AWARDS** Cultural psychology (MA); health psychology (MA); human development (MA); organizational psychology (MA); psychology (Certificate). Part-time and evening/weekend programs available.

**Degree requirements:** For master's, thesis, internship (health psychology).

**Entrance requirements:** For master's, GRE, MAT, or Watson-Glaser Critical Thinking Appraisal, interview, minimum GPA of 3.0; for Certificate, GRE, MAT, or Watson-Glaser Critical Thinking Appraisal, interview, minimum GPA of 3.0, previous undergraduate course work in psychology.

**Expenses:** Tuition: Full-time $13,830; part-time $461 per credit hour.

**Faculty research:** Human development, personality theory, abnormal psychology.

---

### ■ NATIONAL UNIVERSITY

**Academic Affairs, School of Arts and Sciences, Department of Psychology, La Jolla, CA 92037-1011**

**AWARDS** Art therapy (Certificate); counseling psychology (MA); human behavior (MA). Part-time and evening/weekend programs available. Postbaccalaureate distance learning degree programs offered (minimal on-campus study).

**Faculty:** 8 full-time (4 women), 160 part-time/adjunct (90 women).

**Students:** 331 full-time (255 women), 101 part-time (74 women); includes 166 minority (70 African Americans, 26 Asian Americans or Pacific Islanders, 66 Hispanic Americans, 4 Native Americans), 2 international. 117 applicants, 100% accepted. In 2001, 235 degrees awarded.

**Entrance requirements:** For master's, interview, minimum GPA of 2.5. *Application deadline:* Applications are processed on a rolling basis. *Application fee:* $60 ($100 for international students).

**Expenses:** Tuition: Part-time $221 per quarter hour.

**Financial support:** Institutionally sponsored loans, scholarships/grants, and tuition waivers (full and partial) available. Support available to part-time students. Financial award applicants required to submit FAFSA.

Dr. Charles Tatum, Chair, 858-642-8476, *Fax:* 858-642-8715, *E-mail:* ctatum@nu.edu.

**Application contact:** Nancy Rohland, Director of Enrollment Management, 858-642-8180, *Fax:* 858-642-8710, *E-mail:* advisor@nu.edu. *Web site:* http://www.nu.edu/

---

### ■ NEW COLLEGE OF CALIFORNIA

**School of Humanities, Division of Humanities, San Francisco, CA 94102-5206**

**AWARDS** Culture, ecology, and sustainable community (MA); humanities and leadership (MA); media studies (MA); poetics (MA, MFA), including poetics (MA), poetics and writing (MFA); psychology (MA); women's spirituality (MA); writing and consciousness (MA). Part-time and evening/weekend programs available.

**Degree requirements:** For master's, thesis.

---

### ■ NEW COLLEGE OF CALIFORNIA

**School of Psychology, San Francisco, CA 94102-5206**

**AWARDS** Feminist clinical psychology (MA); social-clinical psychology (MA). Evening/weekend programs available.

**Faculty:** 6 full-time (3 women), 10 part-time/adjunct (7 women).

**Students:** 43 full-time (32 women). Average age 28. 60 applicants, 77% accepted, 40 enrolled.

**Degree requirements:** For master's, 3 trimesters of fieldwork.

**Entrance requirements:** For master's, letters of recommendation. *Application deadline:* For fall admission, 4/1 (priority date). Applications are processed on a rolling basis. *Application fee:* $50 ($75 for international students).

**Expenses:** Contact institution.

**Financial support:** In 2001–02, 4 students received support, including 2 teaching assistantships (averaging $900 per year); career-related internships or fieldwork and Federal Work-Study also available. Financial award application deadline: 7/15; financial award applicants required to submit FAFSA.

**Faculty research:** AIDS and therapy, dynamics of unemployment, self-psychology, sexuality and gender issues, multicultural therapy.

Dr. Ali Chavoshian, Dean, 415-437-3435.

**Application contact:** Carmen Gonzalez, Admissions Director, 415-437-3421. *Web site:* http://www.newcollege.edu/psychology/

---

### ■ NEW JERSEY CITY UNIVERSITY

**Graduate Studies, College of Arts and Sciences, Department of Psychology, Jersey City, NJ 07305-1597**

**AWARDS** Counseling (MA); educational psychology (MA, PD); school psychology (PD).

**Students:** 13 full-time (9 women), 133 part-time (107 women). Average age 35. 71 applicants, 66% accepted. In 2001, 36 master's, 4 other advanced degrees awarded.

**Degree requirements:** For PD, summer internship or externship.

**Entrance requirements:** For master's, GRE General Test or MAT, TOEFL; for PD, GRE General Test, TOEFL. *Application deadline:* For fall admission, 8/1 (priority date); for spring admission, 12/1. Applications are processed on a rolling basis. *Application fee:* $0.

**Expenses:** Tuition, state resident: full-time $5,062. Tuition, nonresident: full-time $8,663.

*New Jersey City University (continued)*
**Financial support:** Teaching assistantships, career-related internships or fieldwork available.
Dr. David Hallerman, Chairperson, 201-200-3062.

■ **NEW MEXICO HIGHLANDS UNIVERSITY**

**Graduate Studies, College of Arts and Sciences, Department of Behavioral Sciences, Las Vegas, NM 87701**

**AWARDS** Psychology (MS).

**Faculty:** 8 full-time (4 women).
**Students:** 16 full-time (10 women), 5 part-time (all women); includes 4 minority (1 African American, 3 Hispanic Americans), 1 international. Average age 33. In 2001, 1 degree awarded.
**Degree requirements:** For master's, thesis or alternative.
**Entrance requirements:** For master's, minimum undergraduate GPA of 3.0. *Application deadline:* For fall admission, 8/1 (priority date). Applications are processed on a rolling basis. *Application fee:* $15.
**Expenses:** Tuition, state resident: full-time $2,238. Tuition, nonresident: full-time $9,366.
**Financial support:** Research assistantships with full and partial tuition reimbursements available. Financial award application deadline: 3/1.
Dr. Carlton Cann, Chair, 505-454-3343, *Fax:* 505-454-3331.
**Application contact:** Dr. Linda LaGrange, Associate Dean of Graduate Studies, 505-454-3266, *Fax:* 505-454-3558, *E-mail:* lagrange_l@nmhu.edu.

■ **NEW MEXICO STATE UNIVERSITY**

**Graduate School, College of Arts and Sciences, Department of Psychology, Las Cruces, NM 88003-8001**

**AWARDS** MA, PhD. Part-time programs available.

**Faculty:** 13 full-time (6 women), 2 part-time/adjunct (0 women).
**Students:** 37 full-time (26 women), 17 part-time (7 women); includes 11 minority (3 African Americans, 8 Hispanic Americans). Average age 31. 31 applicants, 77% accepted, 9 enrolled. In 2001, 4 degrees awarded.
**Degree requirements:** For master's, thesis/dissertation; for doctorate, thesis/dissertation, comprehensive exam.
**Entrance requirements:** For master's and doctorate, GRE General Test. *Application deadline:* For fall admission, 3/15 (priority date); for spring admission, 11/1. Applications are processed on a rolling basis.

*Application fee:* $15 ($35 for international students). Electronic applications accepted.
**Expenses:** Tuition, state resident: full-time $3,234; part-time $135 per credit. Tuition, nonresident: full-time $9,420; part-time $428 per credit. Required fees: $858.
**Financial support:** In 2001–02, 20 research assistantships with partial tuition reimbursements, 21 teaching assistantships with partial tuition reimbursements were awarded. Career-related internships or fieldwork and Federal Work-Study also available. Support available to part-time students. Financial award application deadline: 3/1.
**Faculty research:** Engineering, cognitive, and social psychology; human/computer interaction; cognitive science.
Dr. Douglas Gillan, Head, 505-646-2502, *Fax:* 505-646-6218, *E-mail:* gillan@nmsu.edu.
**Application contact:** Dr. Adrienne Y. Lee, Associate Professor and Chair of Graduate Committee, 505-646-6223, *Fax:* 505-646-6218, *E-mail:* alee@crl.nmsu.edu.

■ **NEW SCHOOL UNIVERSITY**

**Graduate Faculty of Political and Social Science, Department of Psychology, New York, NY 10011-8603**

**AWARDS** Clinical psychology (PhD); general psychology (MA, PhD). Part-time and evening/weekend programs available.

**Students:** 190 full-time (132 women), 48 part-time (38 women); includes 34 minority (11 African Americans, 9 Asian Americans or Pacific Islanders, 14 Hispanic Americans), 30 international. Average age 33. 208 applicants, 85% accepted. In 2001, 12 master's, 21 doctorates awarded. Terminal master's awarded for partial completion of doctoral program.
**Degree requirements:** For doctorate, one foreign language, thesis/dissertation, qualifying exam.
**Entrance requirements:** For master's, GRE General Test; for doctorate, GRE General Test, MA. *Application deadline:* For fall admission, 1/15 (priority date). Applications are processed on a rolling basis. *Application fee:* $40.
**Expenses:** Tuition: Full-time $18,720; part-time $1,040 per credit. Required fees: $450; $115 per term. Tuition and fees vary according to program.
**Financial support:** In 2001–02, 94 students received support, including 14 fellowships with full and partial tuition reimbursements available (averaging $1,600 per year), 15 research assistantships with full and partial tuition reimbursements available (averaging $5,000 per year), 17 teaching assistantships with full

and partial tuition reimbursements available (averaging $2,200 per year); career-related internships or fieldwork, Federal Work-Study, scholarships/grants, and tuition waivers (full and partial) also available. Financial award application deadline: 1/15; financial award applicants required to submit FAFSA.
**Faculty research:** Consciousness, memory, language, perceptions, psychopathology.
Dr. Michael Schober, Chair, 212-229-5787.
**Application contact:** Emanuel Lomax, Director of Admissions, 800-523-5411, *Fax:* 212-989-7102, *E-mail:* gfadmit@newschool.edu. *Web site:* http://www.newschool.edu/

**Find an in-depth description at www.petersons.com/gradchannel.**

■ **NEW YORK UNIVERSITY**

**Graduate School of Arts and Science, Department of Psychology, New York, NY 10012-1019**

**AWARDS** Clinical psychology (PhD); cognition and perception (PhD); community psychology (PhD); general psychology (MA); industrial/organizational psychology (MA, PhD); psychoanalysis (Advanced Certificate); social/personality psychology (PhD). Part-time programs available.

**Faculty:** 38 full-time (13 women), 78 part-time/adjunct.
**Students:** 118 full-time (85 women), 304 part-time (235 women); includes 64 minority (14 African Americans, 27 Asian Americans or Pacific Islanders, 22 Hispanic Americans, 1 Native American), 49 international. Average age 28. 586 applicants, 44% accepted, 101 enrolled. In 2001, 67 master's, 22 doctorates awarded. Terminal master's awarded for partial completion of doctoral program.
**Degree requirements:** For master's, thesis or alternative, comprehensive exam; for doctorate, thesis/dissertation.
**Entrance requirements:** For master's, GRE General Test, minimum GPA of 3.0; for doctorate, GRE General Test, GRE Subject Test; for Advanced Certificate, doctoral degree, minimum GPA of 3.0. *Application deadline:* For fall admission, 1/4. *Application fee:* $60.
**Expenses:** Tuition: Full-time $19,536; part-time $814 per credit. Required fees: $1,330; $38 per credit. Tuition and fees vary according to course load and program.
**Financial support:** Fellowships with tuition reimbursements, research assistantships with tuition reimbursements, teaching assistantships with tuition reimbursements, career-related internships or fieldwork, Federal Work-Study, institutionally sponsored loans, and

traineeships available. Financial award application deadline: 1/4; financial award applicants required to submit FAFSA.
**Faculty research:** Vision, memory, social cognition, social and cognitive development, relationships.
Marisa Carrasco, Chair, 212-998-7900.
**Application contact:** Susan Andersen, Director of Graduate Studies, 212-998-7900, *Fax:* 212-995-4018, *E-mail:* psychquery@psych.nyu.edu. *Web site:* http://www.psych.nyu.edu/

■ **NEW YORK UNIVERSITY**
**The Steinhardt School of Education, Department of Applied Psychology, New York, NY 10012-1019**
**AWARDS** Applied psychology (MA, PhD, Psy D, Advanced Certificate), including general educational psychology (MA), professional child/school psychology (Psy D), psychological development (PhD), school psychologist (Advanced Certificate), school psychology (PhD); counselor education (MA, PhD, Advanced Certificate), including counseling and guidance, counseling psychology (PhD); rehabilitation counseling (MA, PhD). Part-time and evening/weekend programs available.
**Faculty:** 24 full-time (14 women), 56 part-time/adjunct (38 women).
**Students:** 193 full-time (162 women), 206 part-time (183 women); includes 126 minority (61 African Americans, 34 Asian Americans or Pacific Islanders, 31 Hispanic Americans). 590 applicants, 27% accepted, 112 enrolled. In 2001, 136 master's, 23 doctorates, 1 other advanced degree awarded. Terminal master's awarded for partial completion of doctoral program.
**Degree requirements:** For master's, thesis (for some programs); for doctorate, thesis/dissertation.
**Entrance requirements:** For master's and Advanced Certificate, TOEFL; for doctorate, GRE General Test, TOEFL, interview. *Application deadline:* For fall admission, 2/1 (priority date); for spring admission, 12/1. Applications are processed on a rolling basis. *Application fee:* $40 ($60 for international students).
**Expenses:** Tuition: Full-time $19,536; part-time $814 per credit. Required fees: $1,330; $38 per credit. Tuition and fees vary according to course load and program.
**Financial support:** Fellowships with full and partial tuition reimbursements, research assistantships with partial tuition reimbursements, teaching assistantships with partial tuition reimbursements, career-related internships or fieldwork, Federal Work-Study, institutionally sponsored loans, scholarships/grants,

tuition waivers (partial), and unspecified assistantships available. Support available to part-time students. Financial award application deadline: 3/1; financial award applicants required to submit FAFSA.
**Faculty research:** Urban adolescents, middle school populations, early childhood, fathers.
Dr. Theresa J. Jordan, Chairperson, 212-998-5360, *Fax:* 212-995-4368.
**Application contact:** 212-998-5030, *Fax:* 212-995-4328, *E-mail:* grad.admissions@nyu.edu. *Web site:* http://www.education.nyu.edu/appsych/

■ **NORFOLK STATE UNIVERSITY**
**School of Graduate Studies, School of Liberal Arts, Department of Psychology, Norfolk, VA 23504**
**AWARDS** Community/clinical psychology (MA); psychology (Psy D). Psy D offered through the Virginia Consortium for Professional Psychology. For information call 757-431-4950. Part-time programs available.
**Students:** 14 applicants, 71% accepted, 10 enrolled.
**Degree requirements:** For master's, thesis or alternative, comprehensive exam; for doctorate, thesis/dissertation, comprehensive exam.
**Entrance requirements:** For master's, minimum GPA of 2.7. *Application deadline:* For fall admission, 3/1; for spring admission, 10/1. *Application fee:* $30.
**Expenses:** Tuition, area resident: Part-time $197 per credit. Tuition, nonresident: part-time $503 per credit.
**Financial support:** Research assistantships, teaching assistantships with partial tuition reimbursements, Federal Work-Study, scholarships/grants, and unspecified assistantships available.
Dr. Delanyard Robinson, Head, 757-823-8573.
**Application contact:** Dr. Darlene Colson, Coordinator, 757-823-9440, *E-mail:* dgcolson@nsu.edu. *Web site:* http://www.nsu.edu/

■ **NORTH CAROLINA CENTRAL UNIVERSITY**
**Division of Academic Affairs, College of Arts and Sciences, Department of Psychology, Durham, NC 27707-3129**
**AWARDS** MA. Part-time and evening/weekend programs available.
**Faculty:** 7 full-time (2 women).
**Students:** 20 full-time (18 women), 48 part-time (34 women); includes 59 minority (57 African Americans, 1 Hispanic American, 1 Native American). Average age 31. 31 applicants, 87% accepted. In 2001, 5 degrees awarded.

**Degree requirements:** For master's, one foreign language, thesis, comprehensive exam.
**Entrance requirements:** For master's, minimum GPA of 3.0 in major, 2.5 overall. *Application deadline:* For fall admission, 8/1. *Application fee:* $30.
**Expenses:** Tuition, state resident: full-time $1,424. Tuition, nonresident: full-time $9,492. Required fees: $1,054.
**Financial support:** Career-related internships or fieldwork, Federal Work-Study, and institutionally sponsored loans available. Support available to part-time students. Financial award application deadline: 5/1.
**Faculty research:** Aggression, hypertension, faces, anger, teaching.
Dr. Les Brinson, Interim Chairperson, 919-560-6368, *Fax:* 919-560-6385, *E-mail:* les@wpo.nccu.edu.
**Application contact:** Dr. Bernice D. Johnson, Dean, College of Arts and Sciences, 919-560-6368, *Fax:* 919-560-5361, *E-mail:* bjohnson@wpo.nccu.edu.

■ **NORTH CAROLINA STATE UNIVERSITY**
**Graduate School, College of Education, Department of Psychology, Raleigh, NC 27695**
**AWARDS** MS, PhD.
**Faculty:** 30 full-time (10 women), 19 part-time/adjunct (5 women).
**Students:** 70 full-time (48 women), 41 part-time (27 women); includes 18 minority (9 African Americans, 5 Asian Americans or Pacific Islanders, 3 Hispanic Americans, 1 Native American), 2 international. Average age 33. 118 applicants, 28% accepted. In 2001, 15 master's, 18 doctorates awarded.
**Degree requirements:** For master's and doctorate, thesis/dissertation, comprehensive exam.
**Entrance requirements:** For master's and doctorate, GRE General Test, GRE Subject Test, minimum GPA of 3.0 in major. *Application deadline:* For fall admission, 2/1. *Application fee:* $45.
**Expenses:** Tuition, state resident: full-time $1,748. Tuition, nonresident: full-time $6,904.
**Financial support:** In 2001–02, 6 fellowships (averaging $5,330 per year), 14 research assistantships (averaging $5,754 per year), 29 teaching assistantships (averaging $5,400 per year) were awarded. Career-related internships or fieldwork also available. Support available to part-time students. Financial award application deadline: 2/1.
**Faculty research:** Cognitive development, human factors, families, the workplace,

*North Carolina State University (continued)*
community issues. *Total annual research expenditures:* $1.9 million.
Dr. David W. Martin, Head, 919-515-2251, *Fax:* 919-515-1716, *E-mail:* martin@poe.coe.ncsu.edu.
**Application contact:** Darnell Johnson, Graduate Secretary, 919-515-1714, *Fax:* 919-515-1716, *E-mail:* psych@ncsu.edu. *Web site:* http://www2.ncsu.edu/ncsu/cep/Psychology/Psychology.html

## ■ NORTH DAKOTA STATE UNIVERSITY

**The Graduate School, College of Science and Mathematics, Department of Psychology, Fargo, ND 58105**
**AWARDS** Clinical psychology (MS, PhD); general psychology (MS); psychology (MS).
**Faculty:** 9 full-time (0 women), 1 (woman) part-time/adjunct.
**Students:** 14 full-time (12 women). Average age 24. 25 applicants, 32% accepted, 8 enrolled. In 2001, 7 master's awarded.
**Degree requirements:** For master's and doctorate, thesis/dissertation, registration. *Median time to degree:* Master's–2 years full-time; doctorate–5 years full-time.
**Entrance requirements:** For master's and doctorate, GRE General Test, GRE Subject Test, TOEFL. *Application deadline:* For fall admission, 3/1. Applications are processed on a rolling basis. *Application fee:* $35.
**Expenses:** Tuition, state resident: part-time $124 per credit. Tuition, nonresident: part-time $325 per credit. Required fees: $22 per credit. Tuition and fees vary according to reciprocity agreements.
**Financial support:** In 2001–02, 7 research assistantships with full tuition reimbursements (averaging $4,200 per year), 7 teaching assistantships with full tuition reimbursements (averaging $4,272 per year) were awarded. Career-related internships or fieldwork, Federal Work-Study, institutionally sponsored loans, traineeships, and tuition waivers (full and partial) also available. Support available to part-time students. Financial award application deadline: 3/1.
**Faculty research:** Cognition science, neuropsychology, group behavior, applied behavior analysis, behavior therapy. *Total annual research expenditures:* $73,950.
Dr. James R. Council, Chair, 701-231-7065, *Fax:* 701-231-8426, *E-mail:* council@badlands.nodak.edu.
**Application contact:** Dr. Raymond G. Miltenberger, Chair, Graduate Recruiting, 701-231-8623, *Fax:* 701-231-8426, *E-mail:* miltenbe@badlands.nodak.edu. *Web site:* http://www.ndsu.nodak.edu/ndsu/psychology/

## ■ NORTHEASTERN ILLINOIS UNIVERSITY

**Graduate College, College of Arts and Sciences, Department of Psychology, Chicago, IL 60625-4699**
**AWARDS** Gerontology (MA). Part-time and evening/weekend programs available.
**Faculty:** 2 full-time (1 woman), 1 (woman) part-time/adjunct.
**Students:** Average age 44. 5 applicants, 100% accepted. In 2001, 2 degrees awarded.
**Degree requirements:** For master's, paper and project or thesis, practicum.
**Entrance requirements:** For master's, 15 hours in social sciences (3 hours in gerontology), 1 course in research methods or statistics, minimum GPA of 2.75. *Application deadline:* For fall admission, 4/1 (priority date); for spring admission, 8/15. Applications are processed on a rolling basis. *Application fee:* $25.
**Expenses:** Tuition, area resident: Full-time $2,882; part-time $107 per semester hour. Tuition, nonresident: part-time $320 per semester hour. International tuition: $8,646 full-time. Required fees: $20 per semester hour.
**Financial support:** In 2001–02, 12 students received support, including 2 research assistantships with full tuition reimbursements available (averaging $6,600 per year); career-related internships or fieldwork, Federal Work-Study, institutionally sponsored loans, and tuition waivers (full and partial) also available. Support available to part-time students. Financial award applicants required to submit FAFSA.
Dr. Saba Aymen-Nolley, Chairperson, 773-442-5844, *Fax:* 773-442-4900, *E-mail:* s-aymennolley@neiu.edu.
**Application contact:** Dr. Mohan K. Sood, Dean of the Graduate College, 773-442-6010, *Fax:* 773-442-6020, *E-mail:* m-sood@neiu.edu.

## ■ NORTHEASTERN STATE UNIVERSITY

**Graduate College, College of Behavioral and Social Sciences, Department of Psychology and Counseling, Tahlequah, OK 74464-2399**
**AWARDS** Counseling psychology (MS). Part-time and evening/weekend programs available.
**Students:** 39 full-time (28 women), 59 part-time (47 women); includes 27 minority (5 African Americans, 22 Native Americans). In 2001, 23 degrees awarded.
**Degree requirements:** For master's, thesis (for some programs), written and oral examinations.

**Entrance requirements:** For master's, minimum GPA of 2.5. *Application deadline:* Applications are processed on a rolling basis. *Application fee:* $0.
**Expenses:** Tuition, area resident: Part-time $87 per credit hour. Tuition, state resident: part-time $206 per credit hour.
**Financial support:** Teaching assistantships, career-related internships or fieldwork and Federal Work-Study available. Financial award application deadline: 3/1.
Dr. Carolyn Hawley, Chair, 918-456-5511 Ext. 3015, *Fax:* 918-458-2397, *E-mail:* hawley@cherokee.nsuok.edu.

## ■ NORTHEASTERN UNIVERSITY

**Bouvé College of Health Sciences Graduate School, Department of Counseling and Applied Educational Psychology, Boston, MA 02115-5096**
**AWARDS** Applied behavior analysis (MS); applied educational psychology (MS), including school counseling, school psychology; college student development and counseling (MS); counseling psychology (MS, PhD, CAGS); rehabilitation counseling (MS); school psychology (PhD, CAGS); special needs and intensive special needs (MS Ed). Part-time and evening/weekend programs available.
**Faculty:** 16 full-time (9 women), 20 part-time/adjunct (10 women).
**Students:** 230 full-time (193 women), 58 part-time (50 women). Average age 27. 398 applicants, 70% accepted. In 2001, 136 master's, 6 doctorates, 11 other advanced degrees awarded.
**Degree requirements:** For doctorate, thesis/dissertation, qualifying exams, comprehensive exam.
**Entrance requirements:** For master's and CAGS, GRE General Test or MAT; for doctorate, GRE General Test. *Application deadline:* Applications are processed on a rolling basis. *Application fee:* $50.
**Expenses:** Tuition: Part-time $535 per credit hour. Required fees: $56. Tuition and fees vary according to program.
**Financial support:** Teaching assistantships with full tuition reimbursements, career-related internships or fieldwork, Federal Work-Study, tuition waivers (partial), and unspecified assistantships available. Support available to part-time students. Financial award application deadline: 3/1; financial award applicants required to submit FAFSA.
**Faculty research:** Early intervention, career development and choice, crisis intervention, family systems, bilingual education in special education.
Dr. Emanuel Mason, Chair, 617-373-3276, *Fax:* 617-373-8892, *E-mail:* e.mason@neu.edu.

**Application contact:** Bill Purnell, Director of Graduate Admissions, 617-373-2708, *Fax:* 617-373-4701, *E-mail:* w.purnell@neu.edu.

**Find an in-depth description at www.petersons.com/gradchannel.**

### ■ NORTHEASTERN UNIVERSITY

**College of Arts and Sciences, Department of Psychology, Boston, MA 02115-5096**

**AWARDS** Experimental psychology (MA, PhD).

**Faculty:** 18 full-time (5 women).
**Students:** 25 full-time (16 women); includes 4 minority (2 African Americans, 1 Asian American or Pacific Islander, 1 Native American), 4 international. Average age 28. 72 applicants, 10% accepted. In 2001, 6 master's, 1 doctorate awarded.
**Degree requirements:** For doctorate, thesis/dissertation.
**Entrance requirements:** For doctorate, GRE General Test, TOEFL. *Application deadline:* For fall admission, 1/15. Applications are processed on a rolling basis. *Application fee:* $50.
**Expenses:** Tuition: Part-time $535 per credit hour. Required fees: $56. Tuition and fees vary according to program.
**Financial support:** In 2001–02, 20 research assistantships with full tuition reimbursements (averaging $14,325 per year) were awarded; fellowships with full tuition reimbursements, teaching assistantships with full tuition reimbursements, career-related internships or fieldwork and traineeships also available. Financial award application deadline: 1/15; financial award applicants required to submit FAFSA.
**Faculty research:** Language/cognition, social/personality, sensation/perception and neuropsychology.
Dr. Stephen Harkins, Chair, 617-373-3076, *Fax:* 617-373-8714, *E-mail:* psychology@neu.edu.
**Application contact:** Dr. Judith Hall, Graduate Coordinator, 617-373-3076, *Fax:* 617-373-8714, *E-mail:* psychology@neu.edu. *Web site:* http://www.psych.neu.edu/

### ■ NORTHERN ARIZONA UNIVERSITY

**Graduate College, College of Social and Behavioral Sciences, Department of Psychology, Flagstaff, AZ 86011**

**AWARDS** Applied health psychology (MA); general (MA). Part-time programs available.

**Students:** 19 full-time (14 women), 12 part-time (10 women); includes 3 minority (2 Hispanic Americans, 1 Native American), 2 international. Average age 26.

41 applicants, 44% accepted, 7 enrolled. In 2001, 10 degrees awarded.
**Degree requirements:** For master's, thesis, oral defense.
**Entrance requirements:** For master's, GRE General Test. *Application deadline:* For fall admission, 2/15 (priority date). Applications are processed on a rolling basis. *Application fee:* $45.
**Expenses:** Tuition, state resident: full-time $2,488. Tuition, nonresident: full-time $10,354.
**Financial support:** In 2001–02, 7 research assistantships, 7 teaching assistantships were awarded. Federal Work-Study, institutionally sponsored loans, and tuition waivers (full and partial) also available. Financial award application deadline: 2/15.
Robert Till, Chair, 928-523-3063.
**Application contact:** Information Contact, 928-523-3063, *E-mail:* psychology.general@nau.edu. *Web site:* http://www.edu/~psych/psyhomepg.html

### ■ NORTHERN ILLINOIS UNIVERSITY

**Graduate School, College of Liberal Arts and Sciences, Department of Psychology, De Kalb, IL 60115-2854**

**AWARDS** MA, PhD.

**Faculty:** 27 full-time (12 women), 3 part-time/adjunct (0 women).
**Students:** 119 full-time (81 women), 19 part-time (15 women); includes 19 minority (6 African Americans, 6 Asian Americans or Pacific Islanders, 7 Hispanic Americans), 8 international. Average age 28. 203 applicants, 33% accepted, 35 enrolled. In 2001, 19 master's, 9 doctorates awarded.
**Degree requirements:** For master's, thesis optional; for doctorate, thesis/dissertation, candidacy exam, dissertation defense.
**Entrance requirements:** For master's, GRE General Test, TOEFL, minimum GPA of 3.0 during previous 2 years; for doctorate, GRE General Test, TOEFL, minimum undergraduate GPA of 2.75, graduate GPA of 3.2; master's degree with research thesis. *Application deadline:* For fall admission, 3/1; for spring admission, 11/1. Applications are processed on a rolling basis. *Application fee:* $30.
**Expenses:** Tuition, state resident: full-time $5,124; part-time $148 per credit hour. Tuition, nonresident: full-time $8,666; part-time $295 per credit hour. Required fees: $51 per term.
**Financial support:** In 2001–02, 5 research assistantships with full tuition reimbursements, 7 teaching assistantships with full tuition reimbursements were awarded. Fellowships with full tuition reimbursements, career-related internships or fieldwork,

Federal Work-Study, tuition waivers (full), and unspecified assistantships also available. Support available to part-time students.
Dr. Charles Miller, Director, Graduate Studies, 815-753-7070.
**Application contact:** Dr. Greg Waas, Director, Graduate Studies, 815-753-7070.

### ■ NORTHERN MICHIGAN UNIVERSITY

**College of Graduate Studies, College of Professional Studies, Department of Psychology, Marquette, MI 49855-5301**

**AWARDS** MS. Part-time and evening/weekend programs available.

**Students:** 1 (woman) full-time, 5 part-time (3 women); includes 1 minority (Asian American or Pacific Islander). In 2001, 1 degree awarded.
**Degree requirements:** For master's, thesis (for some programs).
**Entrance requirements:** For master's, GRE, minimum GPA of 3.0. *Application fee:* $25.
**Expenses:** Tuition, state resident: full-time $158. Tuition, nonresident: full-time $260. Tuition and fees vary according to course load.
**Financial support:** Research assistantships, teaching assistantships, Federal Work-Study, institutionally sponsored loans, scholarships/grants, and unspecified assistantships available. Support available to part-time students.
Dr. Harry Whitaker, Head, 906-227-2935, *Fax:* 906-227-2954.

### ■ NORTHWESTERN OKLAHOMA STATE UNIVERSITY

**School of Education, Psychology, and Health and Physical Education, Program in Behavioral Sciences, Alva, OK 73717-2799**

**AWARDS** MBS. Part-time programs available.

**Entrance requirements:** For master's, GRE General Test or MAT, minimum GPA of 2.75.

### ■ NORTHWESTERN STATE UNIVERSITY OF LOUISIANA

**Graduate Studies and Research and Associate Provost, Department of Psychology, Natchitoches, LA 71497**

**AWARDS** Clinical psychology (MS).

**Faculty:** 5 full-time (3 women), 4 part-time/adjunct (2 women).
**Students:** 24 full-time (20 women), 14 part-time (9 women); includes 2 minority (1 Asian American or Pacific Islander, 1 Hispanic American), 3 international. Average age 26. In 2001, 4 degrees awarded.

*Northwestern State University of Louisiana (continued)*

**Entrance requirements:** For master's, GRE General Test, GRE Subject Test, minimum undergraduate GPA of 2.5. *Application deadline:* For fall admission, 8/1 (priority date); for spring admission, 1/10. Applications are processed on a rolling basis. *Application fee:* $20 ($30 for international students).
**Expenses:** Tuition, state resident: full-time $2,280. Tuition, nonresident: full-time $8,154. Required fees: $134 per semester.
**Financial support:** Application deadline: 7/15.
Dr. Patrice Moulton, Head, 318-357-6594.
**Application contact:** Dr. Anthony J. Scheffler, Dean, Graduate Studies, Research and Information Systems, 318-357-5851, *Fax:* 318-357-5019, *E-mail:* grad_school@alpha.nsula.edu. *Web site:* http://www.nsula.edu/psychology/

■ **NORTHWESTERN UNIVERSITY**

**The Graduate School, Judd A. and Marjorie Weinberg College of Arts and Sciences, Department of Psychology, Evanston, IL 60208**

**AWARDS** Brain, behavior and cognition (PhD); clinical psychology (PhD); cognitive psychology (PhD); personality (PhD); social psychology (PhD). Admissions and degrees offered through The Graduate School. Part-time programs available.

**Faculty:** 22 full-time (6 women).
**Students:** 45 full-time (26 women); includes 4 minority (2 Asian Americans or Pacific Islanders, 2 Hispanic Americans), 14 international. Average age 25. 197 applicants, 14% accepted. In 2001, 5 doctorates awarded.
**Degree requirements:** For doctorate, thesis/dissertation. *Median time to degree:* Doctorate–5 years full-time.
**Entrance requirements:** For doctorate, GRE General Test, GRE Subject Test, TOEFL, TSE. *Application deadline:* For fall admission, 12/31. *Application fee:* $50 ($55 for international students). Electronic applications accepted.
**Expenses:** Tuition: Full-time $26,526.
**Financial support:** In 2001–02, 12 fellowships with full tuition reimbursements (averaging $16,800 per year), 3 research assistantships with partial tuition reimbursements (averaging $13,419 per year), 22 teaching assistantships with full tuition reimbursements (averaging $13,419 per year) were awarded. Career-related internships or fieldwork, Federal Work-Study, institutionally sponsored loans, and tuition waivers (full and partial) also available. Financial award application deadline: 12/31; financial award applicants required to submit FAFSA.

**Faculty research:** Memory and higher order cognition, anxiety and depression, effectiveness of psychotherapy, social cognition, molecular basis of memory.
*Total annual research expenditures:* $2.6 million.
Douglas L. Medin, Chair, 847-491-7406, *Fax:* 847-491-7859, *E-mail:* medin@northwestern.edu.
**Application contact:** Florence S. Sales, Secretary, 847-491-7406, *Fax:* 847-491-7859, *E-mail:* f-sales@northwestern.edu. *Web site:* http://www.psych.northwestern.edu/

■ **NORTHWEST MISSOURI STATE UNIVERSITY**

**Graduate School, College of Education and Human Services, Department of Psychology and Sociology, Maryville, MO 64468-6001**

**AWARDS** Counseling psychology (MS); guidance and counseling (MS Ed). Part-time programs available.

**Faculty:** 10 full-time (5 women).
**Students:** 20 full-time (10 women), 33 part-time (27 women). 20 applicants, 100% accepted, 8 enrolled. In 2001, 15 degrees awarded.
**Degree requirements:** For master's, thesis, comprehensive exam.
**Entrance requirements:** For master's, GRE General Test, GRE Subject Test, TOEFL, minimum undergraduate GPA of 2.5, 3.0 in major; writing sample. *Application deadline:* For fall admission, 3/1. Applications are processed on a rolling basis. *Application fee:* $0 ($50 for international students). Electronic applications accepted.
**Expenses:** Tuition, state resident: full-time $2,777; part-time $154 per hour. Tuition, nonresident: full-time $4,626; part-time $257 per hour. Tuition and fees vary according to course level and course load.
**Financial support:** In 2001–02, 9 research assistantships (averaging $5,250 per year), 1 teaching assistantship (averaging $5,250 per year) were awarded. Unspecified assistantships also available. Financial award application deadline: 3/1.
Dr. John K. Bowers, Chairperson, 660-562-1663.
**Application contact:** Dr. Frances Shipley, Dean of Graduate School, 660-562-1145, *Fax:* 660-562-0000, *E-mail:* gradsch@mail.nwmissouri.edu.

■ **NOTRE DAME DE NAMUR UNIVERSITY**

**Graduate School, School of Sciences, Department of Counseling and Psychology/Gerontology, Belmont, CA 94002-1997**

**AWARDS** Chemical dependency (MACP); counseling psychology (MACP); gerontology (MA, Certificate); marital and family therapy (MACP, MAMFT). Part-time and evening/weekend programs available.

**Faculty:** 3 full-time, 6 part-time/adjunct.
**Students:** 28 full-time (24 women), 85 part-time (71 women); includes 28 minority (8 African Americans, 11 Asian Americans or Pacific Islanders, 9 Hispanic Americans), 1 international. Average age 37. 41 applicants, 76% accepted. In 2001, 36 degrees awarded.
**Entrance requirements:** For master's, TOEFL, interview, minimum GPA of 2.5. *Application deadline:* For fall admission, 8/1 (priority date); for spring admission, 12/1 (priority date). Applications are processed on a rolling basis. *Application fee:* $50 ($500 for international students). Electronic applications accepted.
**Expenses:** Tuition: Full-time $9,450; part-time $525 per unit. Required fees: $35 per term.
**Financial support:** Career-related internships or fieldwork available. Support available to part-time students. Financial award applicants required to submit FAFSA.
Dr. Anna McQuinn, Chair, 650-508-3557.
**Application contact:** Barbara Sterner, Assistant Director of Graduate Admissions, 650-508-3527, *Fax:* 650-508-3662, *E-mail:* grad.admit@ndnu.edu.

■ **NOVA SOUTHEASTERN UNIVERSITY**

**Center for Psychological Studies, Fort Lauderdale, FL 33314-7721**

**AWARDS** MS, PhD, Psy D, SPS, JD/MS. Part-time and evening/weekend programs available.

**Faculty:** 33 full-time (10 women), 37 part-time/adjunct (17 women).
**Students:** 941 full-time (744 women). Average age 34. In 2001, 155 master's, 223 doctorates awarded. Terminal master's awarded for partial completion of doctoral program.
**Degree requirements:** For master's, 3 practica; for doctorate, thesis/dissertation, clinical internship, competency exam; for SPS, internship.
**Entrance requirements:** For doctorate, GRE General Test, GRE Subject Test (recommended), minimum undergraduate GPA of 3.0; for SPS, GRE General Test.

*Application deadline:* Applications are processed on a rolling basis. *Application fee:* $50.

**Expenses:** Contact institution.

**Financial support:** In 2001–02, 4 research assistantships, 17 teaching assistantships (averaging $1,000 per year) were awarded. Career-related internships or fieldwork, Federal Work-Study, and institutionally sponsored loans also available. Support available to part-time students. Financial award application deadline: 4/1.

**Faculty research:** Clinical and child clinical psychology, geriatrics, interpersonal violence.

Dr. Ronald F. Levant, Dean, 954-262-5701, *Fax:* 954-262-3859.

**Application contact:** Nancy L. Smith, Supervisor, 954-262-5760, *Fax:* 954-262-3893, *E-mail:* cpsinfo@cps.nova.edu. *Web site:* http://www.cps.nova.edu/

### ■ THE OHIO STATE UNIVERSITY

**Graduate School, College of Social and Behavioral Sciences, Department of Psychology, Columbus, OH 43210**

**AWARDS** Clinical psychology (PhD); cognitive/experimental psychology (PhD); counseling psychology (PhD); developmental psychology (PhD); mental retardation and developmental disabilities (PhD); psychobiology (PhD); quantitative psychology (PhD); social psychology (PhD).

**Degree requirements:** For doctorate, thesis/dissertation.

**Entrance requirements:** For doctorate, GRE General Test, TOEFL.

### ■ OHIO UNIVERSITY

**Graduate Studies, College of Arts and Sciences, Department of Psychology, Athens, OH 45701-2979**

**AWARDS** Clinical psychology (PhD); experimental psychology (PhD); industrial and organizational psychology (PhD).

**Faculty:** 24 full-time (6 women), 6 part-time/adjunct (2 women).

**Students:** 70 full-time (38 women), 8 part-time (4 women); includes 6 minority (4 Asian Americans or Pacific Islanders, 1 Hispanic American, 1 Native American), 12 international. Average age 28. 184 applicants, 38% accepted, 18 enrolled. In 2001, 13 doctorates awarded.

**Degree requirements:** For doctorate, one foreign language, thesis/dissertation, comprehensive exam.

**Entrance requirements:** For doctorate, GRE General Test, GRE Subject Test. *Application deadline:* For fall admission, 1/15. *Application fee:* $30. Electronic applications accepted.

**Expenses:** Tuition, state resident: full-time $6,585. Tuition, nonresident: full-time $12,254.

**Financial support:** In 2001–02, 67 students received support, including 1 fellowship with full tuition reimbursement available (averaging $11,000 per year), 12 research assistantships with full tuition reimbursements available (averaging $9,497 per year), 21 teaching assistantships with full tuition reimbursements available (averaging $8,076 per year); career-related internships or fieldwork, Federal Work-Study, institutionally sponsored loans, traineeships, tuition waivers (full), and unspecified assistantships also available. Financial award application deadline: 1/15.

**Faculty research:** Health, cognitive, child clinical, and social psychology. *Total annual research expenditures:* $902,000.

Dr. Bruce Carlson, Chair, 740-593-1707, *Fax:* 740-593-0579.

**Application contact:** Administrative Secretary, 740-593-0902, *Fax:* 740-593-0579, *E-mail:* pgraduate1@ohiou.edu. *Web site:* http://www.cats.ohiou.edu/~psydept/

### ■ OKLAHOMA STATE UNIVERSITY

**Graduate College, College of Arts and Sciences, Department of Psychology, Stillwater, OK 74078**

**AWARDS** Clinical psychology (PhD); experimental psychology (PhD); general psychology (MS).

**Faculty:** 16 full-time (5 women), 1 (woman) part-time/adjunct.

**Students:** 32 full-time (24 women), 17 part-time (11 women); includes 13 minority (1 African American, 2 Asian Americans or Pacific Islanders, 4 Hispanic Americans, 6 Native Americans), 1 international. Average age 27. 67 applicants, 24% accepted. In 2001, 5 master's, 10 doctorates awarded.

**Degree requirements:** For doctorate, thesis/dissertation.

**Entrance requirements:** For master's, TOEFL; for doctorate, GRE General Test, TOEFL. *Application deadline:* For fall admission, 2/1 (priority date). *Application fee:* $25.

**Expenses:** Tuition, state resident: part-time $92 per credit hour. Tuition, nonresident: part-time $297 per credit hour. Required fees: $21 per credit hour. $14 per semester. One-time fee: $20. Tuition and fees vary according to course load.

**Financial support:** In 2001–02, 30 students received support, including 12 research assistantships (averaging $12,269 per year), 22 teaching assistantships (averaging $11,551 per year); career-related internships or fieldwork, Federal Work-Study, and tuition waivers (partial) also available. Support available to part-time students. Financial award application deadline: 3/1.

Dr. Maureen A. Sullivan, Head, 405-744-6028.

### ■ OLD DOMINION UNIVERSITY

**College of Sciences, Program in Psychology, Norfolk, VA 23529**

**AWARDS** MS. Part-time programs available.

**Faculty:** 17 full-time (6 women), 1 part-time/adjunct (0 women).

**Students:** 17 full-time (16 women), 14 part-time (11 women); includes 3 minority (1 African American, 1 Hispanic American, 1 Native American), 1 international. Average age 29. 24 applicants, 50% accepted, 10 enrolled. In 2001, 6 degrees awarded.

**Degree requirements:** For master's, thesis optional. *Median time to degree:* Master's–2 years full-time, 4 years part-time.

**Entrance requirements:** For master's, GRE General Test, GRE Subject Test, TOEFL, minimum GPA of 3.0 in major, previous course work in psychology. *Application deadline:* For fall admission, 5/15. Applications are processed on a rolling basis. *Application fee:* $30. Electronic applications accepted.

**Expenses:** Tuition, state resident: part-time $202 per credit. Tuition, nonresident: part-time $534 per credit. Required fees: $76 per semester.

**Financial support:** In 2001–02, 6 students received support, including 1 research assistantship with partial tuition reimbursement available (averaging $7,000 per year), 5 teaching assistantships with partial tuition reimbursements available (averaging $7,000 per year); career-related internships or fieldwork, scholarships/grants, and tuition waivers (partial) also available. Financial award application deadline: 2/15; financial award applicants required to submit FAFSA.

**Faculty research:** Social psychology, developmental psychology, physiopsychology, community psychology, industrial/organizational psychology, psychophysiology.

Dr. Perry Duncan, Graduate Program Director, 757-683-4447, *Fax:* 757-683-5087, *E-mail:* psycgpd@odu.edu. *Web site:* http://www.psychology.odu.edu/psych.html

## ■ OUR LADY OF THE LAKE UNIVERSITY OF SAN ANTONIO

**School of Education and Clinical Studies, Program in Counseling Psychology, San Antonio, TX 78207-4689**

**AWARDS** Counseling psychology (MS, Psy D); psychology (MS, Psy D). Part-time and evening/weekend programs available.

**Degree requirements:** For master's, practicum, thesis optional; for doctorate, thesis/dissertation, internship, qualifying exam.

**Entrance requirements:** For master's and doctorate, GRE General Test or MAT, interview.

**Faculty research:** Marriage and family therapy, supervision, cross-cultural counseling, violence.

## ■ PACE UNIVERSITY

**Dyson College of Arts and Sciences, Department of Psychology, New York, NY 10038**

**AWARDS** Psychology (MA); school-clinical child psychology (Psy D); school-community psychology (MS Ed, Psy D). Part-time and evening/weekend programs available.

**Faculty:** 22 full-time, 51 part-time/adjunct.

**Students:** 80 full-time (69 women), 23 part-time (18 women); includes 17 minority (5 African Americans, 6 Asian Americans or Pacific Islanders, 5 Hispanic Americans, 1 Native American), 2 international. Average age 25. 201 applicants, 43% accepted, 29 enrolled. In 2001, 39 master's, 22 doctorates awarded. Terminal master's awarded for partial completion of doctoral program.

**Degree requirements:** For master's, qualifying exams, internship; for doctorate, qualifying exams, externship, internship, project.

**Entrance requirements:** For master's, interview; for doctorate, GRE General Test, GRE Subject Test, interview. *Application deadline:* Applications are processed on a rolling basis. *Application fee:* $65. Electronic applications accepted.

**Expenses:** Tuition: Part-time $545 per credit.

**Financial support:** Research assistantships, teaching assistantships, career-related internships or fieldwork, Federal Work-Study, tuition waivers (partial), and unspecified assistantships available. Support available to part-time students. Financial award applicants required to submit FAFSA.

Dr. Florence Denmark, Chairperson, 212-346-1506.

**Application contact:** Richard Alvarez, Director of Admissions, 212-346-1531,

*Fax:* 212-346-1585, *E-mail:* gradnyc@pace.edu. *Web site:* http://www.pace.edu/

**Find an in-depth description at www.petersons.com/gradchannel.**

## ■ PACE UNIVERSITY, WHITE PLAINS CAMPUS

**Dyson College of Arts and Sciences, Department of Psychology, White Plains, NY 10603**

**AWARDS** Counseling-substance abuse (MS). Part-time and evening/weekend programs available.

**Faculty:** 7 full-time, 13 part-time/adjunct.

**Students:** 35 full-time (28 women), 29 part-time (27 women); includes 26 minority (19 African Americans, 3 Asian Americans or Pacific Islanders, 4 Hispanic Americans), 5 international. Average age 28. 44 applicants, 84% accepted, 18 enrolled. In 2001, 19 degrees awarded.

**Degree requirements:** For master's, qualifying exams, internship.

**Entrance requirements:** For master's, GRE General and Psychology exams, interview. *Application deadline:* For fall admission, 8/1 (priority date); for spring admission, 12/1 (priority date). Applications are processed on a rolling basis. *Application fee:* $65. Electronic applications accepted.

**Expenses:** Tuition: Part-time $545 per credit.

**Financial support:** Research assistantships, teaching assistantships, career-related internships or fieldwork, Federal Work-Study, tuition waivers (partial), and unspecified assistantships available. Support available to part-time students. Financial award applicants required to submit FAFSA.

Dr. Richard Wessler, Chairperson, 914-773-3786.

**Application contact:** Joanna Broda, Director of Admissions, 914-422-4283, *Fax:* 914-422-4287, *E-mail:* gradwp@pace.edu. *Web site:* http://www.pace.edu/

## ■ PACIFICA GRADUATE INSTITUTE

**Graduate Programs, Carpinteria, CA 93013**

**AWARDS** Clinical psychology (PhD); counseling psychology (MA); depth psychology (PhD); mythological studies (MA, PhD).

**Faculty:** 19 full-time, 50 part-time/adjunct.

**Students:** 545 full-time, 20 part-time. Average age 45. In 2001, 101 master's, 82 doctorates awarded.

**Degree requirements:** For master's, thesis (for some programs), registration; for doctorate, thesis/dissertation, internship, comprehensive exam, registration.

*Median time to degree:* Master's–3 years full-time; doctorate–3 years full-time.
*Application deadline:* For fall admission, 4/30 (priority date). *Application fee:* $60.
**Expenses:** Tuition: Full-time $13,900.
**Financial support:** In 2001–02, 411 students received support. Scholarships/grants available. Financial award application deadline: 6/15; financial award applicants required to submit FAFSA.

**Faculty research:** Imaginal and archetypal theory; post-Colonial psychoanalytic and Jungian theory; myth literature as it applies to the theory and practice of psychology.

Dr. Stephen Aizenstat, President, 805-969-3626 Ext. 102, *Fax:* 805-565-1932, *E-mail:* steve_aizenstat@pacifica.edu.

**Application contact:** Diane Huerta, Admissions Office, 805-969-3626 Ext. 128, *Fax:* 805-565-1932, *E-mail:* diane_huerta@pacifica.edu. *Web site:* http://www.pacifica.edu/

**Find an in-depth description at www.petersons.com/gradchannel.**

## ■ PACIFIC GRADUATE SCHOOL OF PSYCHOLOGY

**Distance Learning Program in Psychology, Palo Alto, CA 94303-4232**

**AWARDS** MS. Postbaccalaureate distance learning degree programs offered (no on-campus study).

## ■ PACIFIC GRADUATE SCHOOL OF PSYCHOLOGY

**Program in Clinical Psychology, Palo Alto, CA 94303-4232**

**AWARDS** PhD, Psy D, JD/PhD, MBA/PhD. Beginning Fall 2002, we have introduced the PGSP-Stanford Psy D Consortium.

**Degree requirements:** For doctorate, thesis/dissertation, 2000 hour clinical internship, oral clinical competency exam.

**Entrance requirements:** For doctorate, GRE General Test, BA or MA in psychology or related area, minimum undergraduate GPA of 3.0, 3.3 graduate.

**Faculty research:** Child/family studies, health psychology, neuropsychology, personality development, assessment. *Web site:* http://www.pgsp.edu/

## ■ PACIFIC UNIVERSITY

**School of Professional Psychology, Forest Grove, OR 97116-1797**

**AWARDS** Clinical psychology (Psy D); counseling psychology (MA). Part-time programs available.

**Faculty:** 13 full-time (7 women), 19 part-time/adjunct (11 women).

**Students:** 166 full-time (125 women), 33 part-time (24 women); includes 24 minority (1 African American, 13 Asian Americans or Pacific Islanders, 9 Hispanic Americans, 1 Native American), 3 international. Average age 31. 175 applicants, 66% accepted, 65 enrolled. In 2001, 41 master's, 19 doctorates awarded. **Degree requirements:** For master's, thesis (for some programs), comprehensive exam (for some programs); for doctorate, thesis/dissertation, comprehensive exam. *Median time to degree:* Master's–2 years full-time, 3 years part-time; doctorate–5 years full-time, 6 years part-time. **Entrance requirements:** For master's, GRE General Test, GRE Subject Test, previous course work in introductory psychology, statistics, and abnormal psychology; minimum GPA of 3.0; for doctorate, GRE General Test, minimum GPA of 3.0, previous undergraduate course work in psychology. *Application deadline:* For fall admission, 1/10 (priority date); for winter admission, 3/15 (priority date). *Application fee:* $40. **Expenses:** Contact institution. **Financial support:** In 2001–02, 21 students received support, including 15 research assistantships (averaging $3,000 per year), 19 teaching assistantships; career-related internships or fieldwork, Federal Work-Study, scholarships/grants, and unspecified assistantships also available. Support available to part-time students. Financial award applicants required to submit FAFSA. **Faculty research:** Single case research, qualitative research, behavioral assessment and treatment of depression and anxiety, behavioral analysis of children and adolescents, psychology of women. Dr. Michel Hersen, Dean, 503-359-2240, *Fax:* 503-359-2314, *E-mail:* spp@pacificu.edu. **Application contact:** 503-359-2900, *Fax:* 503-359-2975, *E-mail:* admissions@pacificu.edu. *Web site:* http://www.spp.pacificu.edu

### ■ THE PENNSYLVANIA STATE UNIVERSITY HARRISBURG CAMPUS OF THE CAPITAL COLLEGE

**Graduate Center, School of Behavioral Sciences and Education, Program in Applied Behavior Analysis, Middletown, PA 17057-4898**

**AWARDS** MA.

**Students:** 3 full-time (all women). **Expenses:** Tuition, state resident: full-time $7,882; part-time $333 per credit. Tuition, nonresident: full-time $14,384; part-time $600 per credit.

Dr. Richard M. Foxx, Coordinator, 717-948-6041.

### ■ THE PENNSYLVANIA STATE UNIVERSITY HARRISBURG CAMPUS OF THE CAPITAL COLLEGE

**Graduate Center, School of Behavioral Sciences and Education, Program in Applied Psychological Research, Middletown, PA 17057-4898**

**AWARDS** MA.

**Expenses:** Tuition, state resident: full-time $7,882; part-time $333 per credit. Tuition, nonresident: full-time $14,384; part-time $600 per credit.

Dr. Thomas G. Bowers, Coordinator, 717-948-6063.

### ■ THE PENNSYLVANIA STATE UNIVERSITY UNIVERSITY PARK CAMPUS

**Graduate School, College of Liberal Arts, Department of Psychology, State College, University Park, PA 16802-1503**

**AWARDS** Clinical psychology (MS, PhD); cognitive psychology (MS, PhD); developmental psychology (MS, PhD); industrial/organizational psychology (MS, PhD); psychobiology (MS, PhD); social psychology (MS, PhD).

**Students:** 126 full-time (83 women), 12 part-time (7 women). In 2001, 15 master's, 14 doctorates awarded. **Degree requirements:** For master's and doctorate, thesis/dissertation. **Entrance requirements:** For master's and doctorate, GRE General Test, GRE Subject Test. *Application fee:* $45. **Expenses:** Tuition, state resident: full-time $7,882; part-time $333 per credit. Tuition, nonresident: full-time $16,142; part-time $673 per credit. Required fees: $124 per semester. **Financial support:** Fellowships, research assistantships, teaching assistantships available. Dr. Keith Crnic, Head, 814-863-1721.

### ■ PEPPERDINE UNIVERSITY

**Graduate School of Education and Psychology, Division of Psychology, Culver City, CA 90230-7615**

**AWARDS** Clinical psychology (MA); psychology (MA, Psy D). Part-time and evening/weekend programs available.

**Faculty:** 31 full-time (13 women), 45 part-time/adjunct (24 women). **Students:** 255 full-time (209 women), 423 part-time (340 women); includes 167 minority (53 African Americans, 42 Asian Americans or Pacific Islanders, 68 Hispanic Americans, 4 Native Americans), 17 international. Average age 33. 428 applicants, 54% accepted. In 2001, 244 master's, 22 doctorates awarded. **Entrance requirements:** For master's, GRE General Test, TOEFL; for doctorate, GRE, TOEFL. *Application deadline:* For fall admission, 2/1. Applications are processed on a rolling basis. *Application fee:* $55. **Expenses:** Contact institution. **Financial support:** Research assistantships, teaching assistantships, career-related internships or fieldwork and scholarships/grants available. Support available to part-time students. Financial award application deadline: 7/1; financial award applicants required to submit FAFSA. Dr. Cary Mitchell, Associate Dean, 310-568-5600 Ext. 5650. **Application contact:** Coordinator, 310-568-5605. *Web site:* http://www.pepperdine.edu/

**Find an in-depth description at www.petersons.com/gradchannel.**

### ■ PHILADELPHIA COLLEGE OF OSTEOPATHIC MEDICINE

**Graduate and Professional Programs, Department of Psychology, Philadelphia, PA 19131-1694**

**AWARDS** Clinical health psychology (MS); clinical psychology (Psy D); organizational leadership and development (MS).

**Faculty:** 6 full-time (3 women), 1 part-time/adjunct (0 women). **Students:** 253 full-time (186 women); includes 35 minority (23 African Americans, 7 Asian Americans or Pacific Islanders, 5 Hispanic Americans). Average age 33. 77 applicants, 86% accepted. In 2001, 1 degree awarded. **Degree requirements:** For master's, thesis; for doctorate, thesis/dissertation, final project, fieldwork, comprehensive exam. **Entrance requirements:** For master's, GRE, minimum GPA of 3.0, previous course work in biology, chemistry, English, physics; for doctorate, MAT. *Application deadline:* For fall admission, 1/17. Applications are processed on a rolling basis. *Application fee:* $50. **Expenses:** Tuition: Part-time $441 per credit. Required fees: $250. Tuition and fees vary according to program. **Faculty research:** Cognitive-behavioral therapy, coping skills. Dr. Arthur Freeman, Chairman, 215-871-6442.

*Philadelphia College of Osteopathic Medicine (continued)*
**Application contact:** Carol A. Fox, Associate Dean for Admissions, 215-871-6700, *Fax:* 215-871-6719, *E-mail:* carolf@pcom.edu.

**Find an in-depth description at www.petersons.com/gradchannel.**

■ **PITTSBURG STATE UNIVERSITY**

**Graduate School, College of Education, Department of Psychology and Counseling, Program in Psychology, Pittsburg, KS 66762**

**AWARDS** MS.

**Degree requirements:** For master's, thesis or alternative.
**Entrance requirements:** For master's, GRE General Test, minimum GPA of 2.8. *Application fee:* $0 ($40 for international students).
**Expenses:** Tuition, state resident: full-time $2,676; part-time $114 per credit hour. Tuition, nonresident: full-time $6,778; part-time $285 per credit hour.
**Financial support:** Teaching assistantships, career-related internships or fieldwork and Federal Work-Study available.
**Application contact:** Marvene Darraugh, Administrative Officer, 620-235-4220, *Fax:* 620-235-4219, *E-mail:* mdarraug@pittstate.edu.

■ **PLATTSBURGH STATE UNIVERSITY OF NEW YORK**

**Faculty of Arts and Science, Department of Psychology, Plattsburgh, NY 12901-2681**

**AWARDS** School psychology (MA, CAS). Part-time programs available.

**Students:** 12 full-time (8 women), 5 part-time (all women); includes 1 minority (Hispanic American).
**Degree requirements:** For master's, thesis, internship.
**Entrance requirements:** For master's, GRE General Test, minimum GPA of 3.0. *Application deadline:* For fall admission, 3/1 (priority date). Applications are processed on a rolling basis. *Application fee:* $50.
**Expenses:** Tuition, state resident: part-time $213 per credit hour. Tuition, nonresident: part-time $351 per credit hour.
**Financial support:** Federal Work-Study available. Support available to part-time students. Financial award application deadline: 4/15; financial award applicants required to submit FAFSA.

**Faculty research:** Alzheimer's disease, adolescent behavior, intellectual assessment, learning disabilities, reading skill acquisition.
Dr. William Gaeddert, Chair, 518-564-3076.
**Application contact:** Dr. Ronald Dumont, Chair, Graduate Admissions Committee.

■ **PONCE SCHOOL OF MEDICINE**

**Program in Clinical Psychology, Ponce, PR 00732-7004**

**AWARDS** Clinical health psychology (Psy D); consultant psychology (Psy D); pediatric psychology (Psy D); psychotherapeutic interventions (Psy D).

**Faculty:** 5 full-time (2 women).
**Students:** 114 full-time (89 women); all minorities (all Hispanic Americans). Average age 30. 63 applicants, 65% accepted, 34 enrolled.
**Degree requirements:** For doctorate, one foreign language, thesis/dissertation, comprehensive exam, registration.
**Entrance requirements:** For doctorate, GRE General Test or PAEG. *Application deadline:* For fall admission, 3/30. Applications are processed on a rolling basis. *Application fee:* $100.
**Expenses:** Tuition: Full-time $17,835. Required fees: $2,340. Full-time tuition and fees vary according to class time, course load, degree level, program and student level.
Dr. José Pons, Head, 787-840-2575, *E-mail:* jponspr@yahoo.com.
**Application contact:** Dr. Carmen Mercado, Assistant Dean of Admissions, 787-840-2575 Ext. 251, *E-mail:* cmercado@psm.edu.

■ **PONTIFICAL CATHOLIC UNIVERSITY OF PUERTO RICO**

**Institute of Graduate Studies in Behavioral Science and Community Affairs, Ponce, PR 00717-0777**

**AWARDS** Clinical psychology (MS); clinical social work (MSW); criminology (MA); industrial psychology (MS); psychology (PhD); public administration (MA). Part-time and evening/weekend programs available.

**Faculty:** 10 full-time (7 women), 17 part-time/adjunct (12 women).
**Students:** 86 full-time (56 women), 394 part-time (266 women); all minorities (all Hispanic Americans). 141 applicants, 83% accepted, 104 enrolled. In 2001, 35 degrees awarded.
**Entrance requirements:** For master's, GRE, 2 recommendation letters, interview, minimum GPA of 2.75. *Application deadline:* For fall admission, 4/30 (priority date). Applications are processed on a rolling

basis. *Application fee:* $50. Electronic applications accepted.
**Expenses:** Tuition: Full-time $2,880; part-time $160 per credit. Required fees: $360. Tuition and fees vary according to degree level and program.
**Financial support:** Federal Work-Study and tuition waivers (partial) available. Support available to part-time students. Financial award application deadline: 7/15.
Dr. Nilde Cordoline, Director, 787-841-2000 Ext. 1024.
**Application contact:** Ana O. Bonilla, Director of Admissions, 787-841-2000 Ext. 1000, *Fax:* 787-840-4295. *Web site:* http://www.pucpr.edu/

■ **PORTLAND STATE UNIVERSITY**

**Graduate Studies, College of Engineering and Computer Science, Systems Science Program, Portland, OR 97207-0751**

**AWARDS** Systems science/anthropology (PhD); systems science/business administration (PhD); systems science/civil engineering (PhD); systems science/economics (PhD); systems science/engineering management (PhD); systems science/general (PhD); systems science/mathematical sciences (PhD); systems science/mechanical engineering (PhD); systems science/psychology (PhD); systems science/sociology (PhD).

**Faculty:** 4 full-time (0 women).
**Students:** 47 full-time (19 women), 32 part-time (10 women); includes 9 minority (4 Asian Americans or Pacific Islanders, 3 Hispanic Americans, 2 Native Americans), 15 international. Average age 36. 52 applicants, 38% accepted. In 2001, 8 degrees awarded.
**Degree requirements:** For doctorate, variable foreign language requirement, thesis/dissertation.
**Entrance requirements:** For doctorate, GMAT, GRE General Test, TOEFL, minimum undergraduate GPA of 3.0. *Application deadline:* For fall admission, 2/1; for spring admission, 11/1. *Application fee:* $50.
**Financial support:** In 2001–02, 1 research assistantship with full tuition reimbursement (averaging $6,839 per year) was awarded; teaching assistantships with full tuition reimbursements, career-related internships or fieldwork, Federal Work-Study, and institutionally sponsored loans also available. Support available to part-time students. Financial award application deadline: 3/1; financial award applicants required to submit FAFSA.
**Faculty research:** Systems theory and methodology, artificial intelligence neural networks, information theory, nonlinear

dynamics/chaos, modeling and simulation. *Total annual research expenditures:* $106,413. Dr. Nancy Perrin, Director, 503-725-4960, *E-mail:* perrinn@pdx.edu.
**Application contact:** Dawn Kuenle, Coordinator, 503-725-4960, *E-mail:* dawn@sysc.pdx.edu. *Web site:* http://www.sysc.pdx.edu/

### ■ PORTLAND STATE UNIVERSITY

**Graduate Studies, College of Liberal Arts and Sciences, Department of Psychology, Portland, OR 97207-0751**
**AWARDS** MA, MS, PhD.
**Faculty:** 12 full-time (5 women), 10 part-time/adjunct (4 women).
**Students:** 15 full-time (13 women), 3 part-time (2 women); includes 3 minority (1 African American, 2 Hispanic Americans). Average age 36. 44 applicants, 11% accepted. In 2001, 4 degrees awarded.
**Degree requirements:** For master's and doctorate, thesis/dissertation.
**Entrance requirements:** For master's, GRE General Test, TOEFL, minimum GPA of 3.0 in upper-division course work or 2.75 overall. *Application deadline:* For fall admission, 2/1. *Application fee:* $50.
**Financial support:** In 2001–02, 6 research assistantships with full tuition reimbursements (averaging $6,401 per year), 22 teaching assistantships with full tuition reimbursements (averaging $7,746 per year) were awarded. Career-related internships or fieldwork, Federal Work-Study, and institutionally sponsored loans also available. Support available to part-time students. Financial award application deadline: 3/1; financial award applicants required to submit FAFSA.
**Faculty research:** Organizational psychology, work and the family, quantitative psychology, decision making, psychosocial factors affecting health. *Total annual research expenditures:* $115,256.
Dr. Keith Kaufman, Head, 503-725-3923, *Fax:* 503-725-3904.
**Application contact:** Pam Livingston, Office Coordinator, 503-725-3923, *Fax:* 503-725-3904. *Web site:* http://www.psy.pdx.edu/

### ■ PRINCETON UNIVERSITY

**Graduate School, Department of Psychology, Princeton, NJ 08544-1019**
**AWARDS** Neuroscience (PhD); psychology (PhD).
**Degree requirements:** For doctorate, thesis/dissertation.
**Entrance requirements:** For doctorate, GRE General Test, GRE Subject Test.

### ■ PURDUE UNIVERSITY

**Graduate School, School of Liberal Arts, Department of Psychological Sciences, West Lafayette, IN 47907**
**AWARDS** PhD.
**Faculty:** 50 full-time (13 women), 7 part-time/adjunct (2 women).
**Students:** 82 full-time (51 women), 17 part-time (13 women); includes 18 minority (3 African Americans, 10 Asian Americans or Pacific Islanders, 4 Hispanic Americans, 1 Native American), 16 international. Average age 29. 384 applicants, 8% accepted. In 2001, 10 doctorates awarded.
**Entrance requirements:** For doctorate, GRE General Test, TOEFL. *Application deadline:* For fall admission, 1/1. *Application fee:* $30. Electronic applications accepted.
**Expenses:** Tuition, state resident: full-time $4,164; part-time $149 per credit hour. Tuition, nonresident: full-time $13,872; part-time $458 per credit hour. Tuition and fees vary according to campus/location and program.
**Financial support:** In 2001–02, 90 students received support, including 5 fellowships with partial tuition reimbursements available (averaging $12,000 per year), 18 research assistantships with partial tuition reimbursements available (averaging $10,400 per year), 72 teaching assistantships with partial tuition reimbursements available (averaging $10,400 per year); career-related internships or fieldwork also available. Support available to part-time students. Financial award applicants required to submit FAFSA.
**Faculty research:** Career development of women in science, development of friendships during childhood and adolescence, social competence, human information processing.
Dr. T. J. Berndt, Head, 765-494-6061, *Fax:* 765-496-1264, *E-mail:* berndt@psych.purdue.edu.
**Application contact:** Marlene Mann, Graduate Admissions Coordinator, 765-494-6067, *Fax:* 765-496-1264, *E-mail:* mann@psych.purdue.edu. *Web site:* http://www.psych.purdue.edu/#Graduate/

### ■ QUEENS COLLEGE OF THE CITY UNIVERSITY OF NEW YORK

**Division of Graduate Studies, Mathematics and Natural Sciences Division, Department of Psychology, Flushing, NY 11367-1597**
**AWARDS** Clinical behavioral applications in mental health settings (MA); psychology (MA). Part-time programs available.
**Faculty:** 22 full-time (8 women).

**Students:** 7 full-time (6 women), 33 part-time (25 women). 76 applicants, 89% accepted. In 2001, 37 degrees awarded.
**Degree requirements:** For master's, thesis or alternative, comprehensive exam.
**Entrance requirements:** For master's, GRE, TOEFL, minimum GPA of 3.0. *Application deadline:* For fall admission, 4/1; for spring admission, 11/1. Applications are processed on a rolling basis. *Application fee:* $40.
**Expenses:** Tuition, state resident: full-time $2,175; part-time $185 per credit. Tuition, nonresident: full-time $3,800; part-time $320 per credit. Required fees: $114; $57 per semester. Tuition and fees vary according to course load.
**Financial support:** Career-related internships or fieldwork, Federal Work-Study, institutionally sponsored loans, and tuition waivers (partial) available. Support available to part-time students. Financial award application deadline: 4/1; financial award applicants required to submit FAFSA. Dr. Richard Bodnar, Chairperson, 718-997-3200.
**Application contact:** Dr. Philip Ramsey, Graduate Adviser, 718-997-3200, *E-mail:* phillip_ramsey@qc.edu.

### ■ RADFORD UNIVERSITY

**Graduate College, College of Arts and Sciences, Department of Psychology, Radford, VA 24142**
**AWARDS** Clinical psychology (MA); counseling psychology (MA); general psychology (MA, MS); industrial-organizational psychology (MA); school psychology (Ed S). Part-time programs available. Postbaccalaureate distance learning degree programs offered (minimal on-campus study).
**Faculty:** 20 full-time (6 women).
**Students:** 65 full-time (46 women), 9 part-time (8 women); includes 6 minority (2 African Americans, 3 Asian Americans or Pacific Islanders, 1 Native American), 1 international. Average age 26. 127 applicants, 83% accepted, 26 enrolled. In 2001, 40 master's, 10 other advanced degrees awarded.
**Degree requirements:** For master's, thesis (for some programs), comprehensive exam.
**Entrance requirements:** For degree, GMAT, GRE General Test, MAT, NTE, TOEFL. *Application deadline:* For fall admission, 2/15 (priority date); for spring admission, 10/15. Applications are processed on a rolling basis. *Application fee:* $25. Electronic applications accepted.
**Expenses:** Tuition, state resident: full-time $2,564; part-time $167 per credit hour. Tuition, nonresident: full-time $6,314; part-time $323 per credit hour. Required fees: $1,440.

*Radford University (continued)*

**Financial support:** In 2001–02, 64 students received support, including 4 fellowships with tuition reimbursements available (averaging $8,060 per year), 46 research assistantships (averaging $4,401 per year), 7 teaching assistantships with tuition reimbursements available (averaging $8,680 per year); career-related internships or fieldwork, Federal Work-Study, institutionally sponsored loans, and scholarships/grants also available. Financial award application deadline: 2/1; financial award applicants required to submit FAFSA.

Dr. Alastair V. Harris, Chair, 540-831-5361, *Fax:* 540-831-6113, *E-mail:* aharris@radford.edu. *Web site:* http://www.radford.edu/

■ **REGIS UNIVERSITY**

**School for Professional Studies, Program in Liberal Studies, Denver, CO 80221-1099**

**AWARDS** Adult learning, training and development (MLS, Certificate); language and communication (MLS); licensed professional counselor (MLS); psychology (MLS); social science (MLS); technical communication (Certificate). Part-time and evening/weekend programs available. Postbaccalaureate distance learning degree programs offered (minimal on-campus study).

**Students:** 400. Average age 35. In 2001, 136 degrees awarded.

**Degree requirements:** For master's and Certificate, thesis or alternative, research project.

**Entrance requirements:** For master's, TOEFL, resumé; for Certificate, GMAT, TOEFL, or university-based test (international applicants), resumé. *Application deadline:* For fall admission, 7/15; for spring admission, 10/15. Applications are processed on a rolling basis. *Application fee:* $75. Electronic applications accepted.

**Expenses:** Contact institution.

**Financial support:** Federal Work-Study available. Support available to part-time students. Financial award application deadline: 3/15; financial award applicants required to submit FAFSA.

**Faculty research:** Independent/nonresidential graduate study: new methods and models, adult learning and the capstone experience.

Dr. David Elliot, Chair, 303-964-5315, *Fax:* 303-964-5538.

**Application contact:** Graduate Admissions, 800-677-9270 Ext. 4080, *Fax:* 303-964-5538, *E-mail:* masters@regis.edu. *Web site:* http://www.regis.edu/spsgraduate/

■ **RENSSELAER POLYTECHNIC INSTITUTE**

**Graduate School, School of Humanities and Social Sciences, Department of Cognitive Science, Program in Psychology, Troy, NY 12180-3590**

**AWARDS** Human factors (MS); industrial-organizational psychology (MS). Part-time programs available.

**Faculty:** 7 full-time (0 women), 4 part-time/adjunct (0 women).

**Students:** 27 full-time (10 women), 3 part-time (1 woman); includes 3 minority (1 African American, 2 Asian Americans or Pacific Islanders), 2 international. Average age 22. 23 applicants, 74% accepted. In 2001, 4 degrees awarded.

**Degree requirements:** For master's, thesis.

**Entrance requirements:** For master's, GRE General Test, GRE Subject Test, TOEFL. *Application deadline:* For fall admission, 1/15 (priority date). Applications are processed on a rolling basis. *Application fee:* $45. Electronic applications accepted.

**Expenses:** Tuition: Full-time $26,400; part-time $1,320 per credit hour. Required fees: $1,437.

**Financial support:** In 2001–02, 1 fellowship with full tuition reimbursement (averaging $10,000 per year), 12 teaching assistantships with partial tuition reimbursements (averaging $4,000 per year) were awarded. Research assistantships, career-related internships or fieldwork, institutionally sponsored loans, scholarships/grants, and tuition waivers (partial) also available. Financial award application deadline: 2/1.

**Faculty research:** Cognitive psychology. *Web site:* http://www.rpi.edu/

**Find an in-depth description at www.petersons.com/gradchannel.**

■ **RHODE ISLAND COLLEGE**

**School of Graduate Studies, Faculty of Arts and Sciences, Department of Psychology, Providence, RI 02908-1991**

**AWARDS** MA. Evening/weekend programs available.

**Faculty:** 18 full-time (8 women).

**Students:** 3 full-time (all women), 8 part-time (5 women). Average age 30. In 2001, 6 degrees awarded.

**Expenses:** Tuition, state resident: full-time $3,060; part-time $170 per credit. Tuition, nonresident: full-time $6,390; part-time $355 per credit.

Dr. Thomas M. Randall, Chair, 401-456-8015, *E-mail:* trandall@ric.edu.

■ **RICE UNIVERSITY**

**Graduate Programs, School of Social Sciences, Department of Psychology, Houston, TX 77251-1892**

**AWARDS** Industrial-organizational/social psychology (MA, PhD); psychology (MA, PhD).

**Faculty:** 21 full-time (4 women), 21 part-time/adjunct (14 women).

**Students:** 35 full-time (27 women); includes 5 minority (1 African American, 2 Asian Americans or Pacific Islanders, 2 Hispanic Americans), 9 international. Average age 29. 91 applicants, 22% accepted, 14 enrolled. In 2001, 3 master's, 9 doctorates awarded. Terminal master's awarded for partial completion of doctoral program.

**Degree requirements:** For master's and doctorate, thesis/dissertation.

**Entrance requirements:** For master's and doctorate, GRE General Test, TOEFL, minimum GPA of 3.0. *Application deadline:* For fall admission, 1/15 (priority date). Applications are processed on a rolling basis. *Application fee:* $25. Electronic applications accepted.

**Expenses:** Tuition: Full-time $17,300. Required fees: $250.

**Financial support:** In 2001–02, 22 fellowships with full tuition reimbursements (averaging $12,500 per year), 2 research assistantships with full tuition reimbursements (averaging $12,500 per year) were awarded. Federal Work-Study and tuition waivers (full) also available. Financial award applicants required to submit FAFSA.

**Faculty research:** Learning and memory, information processing, decision theory.

Robert L. Dipboye, Chairman, 713-348-4764, *Fax:* 713-348-5221, *E-mail:* dpboye@rice.edu.

**Application contact:** Azelia Badruddin, Office Assistant, 713-348-4856, *Fax:* 713-348-5221, *E-mail:* psyc@rice.edu. *Web site:* http://www.ruf.rice.edu/~psyc/

■ **ROOSEVELT UNIVERSITY**

**Graduate Division, College of Arts and Sciences, School of Psychology, Chicago, IL 60605-1394**

**AWARDS** Clinical professional psychology (MA); clinical psychology (MA, Psy D); general psychology (MA); industrial/organizational psychology (MA). Part-time and evening/weekend programs available.

**Faculty:** 12 full-time (3 women), 22 part-time/adjunct (13 women).

**Students:** 97 full-time (64 women), 213 part-time (153 women); includes 39 minority (22 African Americans, 10 Asian Americans or Pacific Islanders, 6 Hispanic Americans, 1 Native American), 10 international.

**Degree requirements:** For master's, thesis or alternative; for doctorate, thesis/ dissertation.

**Entrance requirements:** For master's, 18 undergraduate hours in psychology; for doctorate, GRE, master's degree in psychology. *Application deadline:* For fall admission, 6/1 (priority date). Applications are processed on a rolling basis. *Application fee:* $25 ($35 for international students).

**Expenses:** Tuition: Full-time $9,090; part-time $505 per credit hour. Required fees: $100 per term.

**Financial support:** Application deadline: 2/15.

**Faculty research:** Multicultural issues, psychotherapy research, stress, neuropsychology, psychodiagnostic assessment.

Edward Rossini, Head, 312-341-3760.

**Application contact:** Joanne Canyon-Heller, Coordinator of Graduate Admissions, 312-281-3250, *Fax:* 312-341-3523, *E-mail:* applyru@roosevelt.edu.

## ■ ROWAN UNIVERSITY

**Graduate School, College of Liberal Arts and Sciences, Program in Applied Psychology, Glassboro, NJ 08028-1701**

**AWARDS** MA. Part-time and evening/weekend programs available.

**Students:** 20 full-time (15 women), 12 part-time (11 women); includes 3 minority (all Hispanic Americans). Average age 31. 12 applicants, 67% accepted, 5 enrolled. In 2001, 6 degrees awarded.

*Application deadline:* Applications are processed on a rolling basis. *Application fee:* $50. Electronic applications accepted.

**Expenses:** Tuition, state resident: full-time $7,080; part-time $295 per semester hour. Tuition, nonresident: full-time $11,328; part-time $472 per semester hour. Required fees: $855; $39 per semester hour. Tuition and fees vary according to degree level.

**Financial support:** Career-related internships or fieldwork, Federal Work-Study, and unspecified assistantships available. Support available to part-time students. Dr. Janet Cahill, Adviser, 856-256-4500 Ext. 3520.

## ■ RUTGERS, THE STATE UNIVERSITY OF NEW JERSEY, NEWARK

**Graduate School, Department of Psychology, Newark, NJ 07102**

**AWARDS** Cognitive science (PhD); perception (PhD); psychobiology (PhD); social cognition (PhD). Part-time and evening/weekend programs available.

**Students:** 34 applicants, 59% accepted. In 2001, 2 doctorates awarded.

**Degree requirements:** For doctorate, thesis/dissertation, comprehensive exam.

**Entrance requirements:** For doctorate, GRE Subject Test, minimum undergraduate B average. *Application deadline:* For fall admission, 2/1 (priority date); for spring admission, 11/1. Applications are processed on a rolling basis. *Application fee:* $50. Electronic applications accepted.

**Financial support:** In 2001–02, 12 students received support, including 11 fellowships with full tuition reimbursements available (averaging $13,000 per year), 9 teaching assistantships with full tuition reimbursements available (averaging $13,700 per year); research assistantships, career-related internships or fieldwork, Federal Work-Study, and minority scholarships also available. Support available to part-time students. Financial award application deadline: 3/1.

**Faculty research:** Visual perception (luminance, motion), neuroendocrine mechanisms in behavior (reproduction, pain), attachment theory, connectionist modeling of cognition. *Total annual research expenditures:* $300,000.

Dr. Maggie Shiffrar, Director, 973-353-5971, *Fax:* 973-353-1171, *E-mail:* mag@ psychology.rutgers.edu. *Web site:* http:// www.psych.rutgers.edu/

**Find an in-depth description at www.petersons.com/gradchannel.**

## ■ RUTGERS, THE STATE UNIVERSITY OF NEW JERSEY, NEW BRUNSWICK

**Graduate School of Applied and Professional Psychology, New Brunswick, NJ 08901-1281**

**AWARDS** Psy M, Psy D.

**Degree requirements:** For doctorate, thesis/dissertation, 1 year internship.

**Entrance requirements:** For doctorate, GRE General Test, GRE Subject Test, bachelor's degree in psychology or equivalent. Electronic applications accepted.

**Faculty research:** Organizational psychology, behavior modification, long- and short-term dynamic therapy, school psychology, addictive behaviors, autism. *Web site:* http://www.rci.rutgers.edu/ ~gsapp

## ■ RUTGERS, THE STATE UNIVERSITY OF NEW JERSEY, NEW BRUNSWICK

**Graduate School, Program in Psychology, New Brunswick, NJ 08901-1281**

**AWARDS** Biopsychology and behavioral neuroscience (PhD); clinical psychology (PhD); cognitive psychology (PhD); interdisciplinary developmental psychology (PhD); interdisciplinary health psychology (PhD); social psychology (PhD).

**Students:** Average age 24. 423 applicants, 11% accepted. In 2001, 13 degrees awarded.

**Degree requirements:** For doctorate, thesis/dissertation.

**Entrance requirements:** For doctorate, GRE General Test. *Application deadline:* For fall admission, 12/15. *Application fee:* $50.

**Financial support:** In 2001–02, 68 students received support, including 18 fellowships with full tuition reimbursements available (averaging $15,000 per year), 13 research assistantships with full tuition reimbursements available (averaging $14,000 per year), 43 teaching assistantships with full tuition reimbursements available (averaging $13,800 per year); career-related internships or fieldwork, Federal Work-Study, scholarships/grants, and traineeships also available. Financial award application deadline: 12/15.

Dr. G. Terence Wilson, Director, 732-445-2556, *Fax:* 732-445-2263.

**Application contact:** Joan Olmizzi, Administrative Assistant, 732-445-2555, *Fax:* 732-445-2263, *E-mail:* joan@psych-b.rutgers.edu. *Web site:* http:// psychology.rutgers.edu/

## ■ SAGE GRADUATE SCHOOL

**Graduate School, Division of Psychology, Troy, NY 12180-4115**

**AWARDS** Community psychology (MA), including chemical dependence, child care and children's services, community counseling, community health, general psychology, visual art therapy; forensic psychology (MA). Part-time and evening/weekend programs available.

**Faculty:** 9 full-time (all women), 1 (woman) part-time/adjunct.

**Students:** 19 full-time (17 women), 93 part-time (74 women); includes 8 minority (5 African Americans, 3 Hispanic Americans). Average age 32. 65 applicants, 85% accepted, 30 enrolled. In 2001, 17 degrees awarded.

**Degree requirements:** For master's, thesis or alternative.

*Sage Graduate School (continued)*
**Entrance requirements:** For master's, GRE General Test. *Application fee:* $40.
**Expenses:** Tuition: Full-time $7,600. Required fees: $100.
**Financial support:** Career-related internships or fieldwork, scholarships/grants, and unspecified assistantships available. Support available to part-time students. Financial award application deadline: 3/1; financial award applicants required to submit FAFSA.
**Faculty research:** Effectiveness of arts integration program in elementary/secondary schools, literacy based substance abuse program, outcome evaluation of program to increase college entry among urban youth. *Total annual research expenditures:* $10,000.
Dr. Sam Hill, Director, 518-244-2227, *Fax:* 518-244-4545, *E-mail:* hills@sage.edu.
**Application contact:** Melissa M. Robertson, Associate Director of Admissions, 518-244-6878, *Fax:* 518-244-6880, *E-mail:* sgsadm@sage.edu. *Web site:* http://www.sage.edu/

## ■ ST. CLOUD STATE UNIVERSITY

**School of Graduate Studies, College of Education, Department of Counselor Education and Educational Psychology, St. Cloud, MN 56301-4498**

**AWARDS** College student development (MS); rehabilitation counseling (MS); school counseling (MS), including rehabilitation counseling, school counseling.

**Faculty:** 12 full-time (3 women), 1 (woman) part-time/adjunct.
**Students:** 19 full-time (11 women), 79 part-time (42 women); includes 3 minority (1 Asian American or Pacific Islander, 2 Hispanic Americans). 43 applicants, 98% accepted. In 2001, 23 degrees awarded.
**Degree requirements:** For master's, thesis or alternative.
**Entrance requirements:** For master's, GRE General Test, minimum GPA of 2.75. *Application deadline:* Applications are processed on a rolling basis. *Application fee:* $35.
**Expenses:** Tuition, state resident: part-time $156 per credit. Tuition, nonresident: part-time $244 per credit. Required fees: $20 per credit.
**Financial support:** Career-related internships or fieldwork, Federal Work-Study, and unspecified assistantships available. Financial award application deadline: 3/1.
Dr. Jana Preble, Chairperson, 320-255-3131, *Fax:* 320-255-4082.
**Application contact:** Lindalou Krueger, Graduate Studies Office, 320-255-2113, *Fax:* 320-654-5371, *E-mail:* lekrueger@stcloudstate.edu.

## ■ ST. JOHN'S UNIVERSITY

**St. John's College of Liberal Arts and Sciences, Department of Psychology, Jamaica, NY 11439**

**AWARDS** Clinical psychology (MA, PhD), including clinical psychology-child, clinical psychology-general; general experimental psychology (MA); school psychology (MS, Psy D). Part-time and evening/weekend programs available.
**Faculty:** 28 full-time (9 women), 24 part-time/adjunct (10 women).
**Students:** 159 full-time (129 women), 96 part-time (71 women); includes 45 minority (15 African Americans, 11 Asian Americans or Pacific Islanders, 19 Hispanic Americans), 12 international. Average age 28. 366 applicants, 31% accepted, 60 enrolled. In 2001, 21 master's, 14 doctorates awarded.
**Degree requirements:** For doctorate, thesis/dissertation, internship, comprehensive exam.
**Entrance requirements:** For master's, minimum GPA of 3.0, 2 writing samples; for doctorate, GRE General Test, GRE Subject Test, interview. *Application fee:* $40.
**Expenses:** Tuition: Full-time $14,520; part-time $605 per credit. Required fees: $150; $75 per term. Tuition and fees vary according to class time, course load, degree level, campus/location, program and student level.
**Financial support:** Fellowships with full tuition reimbursements, research assistantships with full tuition reimbursements, career-related internships or fieldwork, scholarships/grants, and unspecified assistantships available. Support available to part-time students. Financial award application deadline: 3/1; financial award applicants required to submit FAFSA.
**Faculty research:** Developmental psychology, health psychology, cross-cultural/multicultural issues and research, evolution of the brain.
Dr. Raymond DiGiuseppe, Chair, 718-990-1546.
**Application contact:** Matthew Whelan, Director, Office of Admission, 718-990-2000, *Fax:* 718-990-2096, *E-mail:* admissions@stjohns.edu. *Web site:* http://www.stjohns.edu/

## ■ SAINT JOSEPH COLLEGE

**Graduate Division, Department of Counseling, West Hartford, CT 06117-2700**

**AWARDS** Community counseling (MA), including child welfare, pastoral counseling; spirituality (Certificate). Part-time and evening/weekend programs available.
**Faculty:** 3 full-time (1 woman), 3 part-time/adjunct (2 women).

**Students:** 11 full-time (all women), 69 part-time (62 women); includes 7 minority (6 African Americans, 1 Hispanic American). Average age 33. In 2001, 24 degrees awarded.
**Degree requirements:** For master's, thesis optional.
**Entrance requirements:** For master's, GRE or MAT. *Application deadline:* Applications are processed on a rolling basis. *Application fee:* $25.
**Expenses:** Tuition: Part-time $475 per credit hour.
**Financial support:** In 2001–02, 2 research assistantships with full tuition reimbursements were awarded; tuition waivers (partial) and unspecified assistantships also available. Financial award application deadline: 7/15; financial award applicants required to submit FAFSA.
Dr. Richard W. Halstead, Chair, 860-231-5213, *E-mail:* rhalstead@sjc.edu. *Web site:* http://www.sjc.edu/

## ■ SAINT JOSEPH'S UNIVERSITY

**College of Arts and Sciences, Program in Psychology, Philadelphia, PA 19131-1395**

**AWARDS** MS.

**Entrance requirements:** For master's, GRE General Test, minimum GPA of 3.0.
**Expenses:** Tuition: Part-time $550 per credit. Tuition and fees vary according to program.

**Find an in-depth description at www.petersons.com/gradchannel.**

## ■ SAINT LOUIS UNIVERSITY

**Graduate School, College of Arts and Sciences, Department of Psychology, St. Louis, MO 63103-2097**

**AWARDS** Applied experimental psychology (MS(R), PhD); clinical psychology (MS(R), PhD).

**Faculty:** 28 full-time (8 women), 16 part-time/adjunct (4 women).
**Students:** 34 full-time (17 women), 65 part-time (38 women); includes 20 minority (15 African Americans, 3 Asian Americans or Pacific Islanders, 2 Hispanic Americans), 1 international. Average age 28. 160 applicants, 27% accepted, 23 enrolled. In 2001, 7 master's, 12 doctorates awarded.
**Degree requirements:** For master's, thesis, comprehensive exam; for doctorate, thesis/dissertation, internship, preliminary exams.
**Entrance requirements:** For master's and doctorate, GRE General Test, interview. *Application deadline:* For fall admission, 1/1; for spring admission, 11/1. *Application fee:* $40.

**Expenses:** Tuition: Part-time $630 per credit hour.

**Financial support:** In 2001–02, 57 students received support, including 6 fellowships with tuition reimbursements available, 4 research assistantships with tuition reimbursements available, 2 teaching assistantships with tuition reimbursements available; career-related internships or fieldwork, tuition waivers (partial), and unspecified assistantships also available. Financial award application deadline: 4/1; financial award applicants required to submit FAFSA.

**Faculty research:** Implicit and explicit memory in older adults, cognitive processes in post-traumatic stress disorder, prejudice and attitude change, locus of control and health psychology, psychometric evaluation of cognitive impairment.

Dr. Ronald T. Kellogg, Chairperson, 314-977-2300, *Fax:* 314-977-3679, *E-mail:* kelloggr@slu.edu.

**Application contact:** Dr. Marcia Buresch, Associate Dean of the Graduate School, 314-977-2240, *Fax:* 314-977-3943, *E-mail:* bureschm@slu.edu.

■ **SAINT MARY COLLEGE**

**Graduate Programs, Program in Psychology, Leavenworth, KS 66048-5082**

**AWARDS** MA.

**Degree requirements:** For master's, thesis.

**Entrance requirements:** For master's, minimum undergraduate GPA of 2.75.

■ **ST. MARY'S UNIVERSITY OF SAN ANTONIO**

**Graduate School, Department of Psychology, San Antonio, TX 78228-8507**

**AWARDS** Clinical psychology (MA, MS); industrial psychology (MA, MS); school psychology (MA). Part-time programs available.

**Faculty:** 5 full-time (4 women), 5 part-time/adjunct.

**Students:** 27 full-time (22 women), 35 part-time (29 women); includes 31 minority (6 African Americans, 1 Asian American or Pacific Islander, 24 Hispanic Americans), 1 international. Average age 24. In 2001, 17 degrees awarded.

**Degree requirements:** For master's, thesis (for some programs), comprehensive exam.

**Entrance requirements:** For master's, GRE General Test. *Application deadline:* Applications are processed on a rolling basis. *Application fee:* $15. Electronic applications accepted.

**Expenses:** Tuition: Full-time $8,190; part-time $455 per credit hour. Required fees: $375.

**Financial support:** Research assistantships, Federal Work-Study and institutionally sponsored loans available. Financial award application deadline: 2/15; financial award applicants required to submit FAFSA.

Dr. Willibrord Silva, Graduate Program Director, 210-436-3314.

■ **SAINT XAVIER UNIVERSITY**

**Graduate Studies, School of Arts and Sciences, Department of Psychology, Chicago, IL 60655-3105**

**AWARDS** Adult counseling (Certificate); child/adolescent counseling (Certificate); core counseling (Certificate); counseling psychology (MA). Part-time and evening/weekend programs available.

**Faculty:** 7.

**Students:** 18 full-time (13 women), 20 part-time (16 women); includes 8 minority (all African Americans). Average age 33. In 2001, 11 degrees awarded.

**Entrance requirements:** For master's, GRE General Test, minimum GPA of 3.0, interview. *Application deadline:* For fall admission, 8/15 (priority date). Applications are processed on a rolling basis. *Application fee:* $35.

**Expenses:** Tuition: Full-time $4,500; part-time $500 per credit. Required fees: $40 per term.

**Financial support:** Career-related internships or fieldwork available. Support available to part-time students. Financial award applicants required to submit FAFSA.

Dr. Anthony Rotatori, Director, 773-298-3477, *Fax:* 773-779-9061.

**Application contact:** Beth Gierach, Managing Director of Admission, 773-298-3053, *Fax:* 773-298-3076, *E-mail:* gierach@sxu.edu.

**Find an in-depth description at www.petersons.com/gradchannel.**

■ **SALEM STATE COLLEGE**

**Graduate School, Department of Psychology, Salem, MA 01970-5353**

**AWARDS** Counseling and psychological services (MS).

**Faculty:** 8 part-time/adjunct (3 women).

**Entrance requirements:** For master's, GRE General Test or MAT. *Application deadline:* Applications are processed on a rolling basis. *Application fee:* $25.

Dr. Patrice Miller, Coordinator, 978-542-6457, *Fax:* 978-542-6596, *E-mail:* patrice.miller@salem.mass.edu.

■ **SAM HOUSTON STATE UNIVERSITY**

**College of Education and Applied Science, Department of Psychology and Philosophy, Huntsville, TX 77341**

**AWARDS** Clinical psychology (MA); counseling (MA); forensic psychology (PhD); psychology (MA); school psychology (MA). Part-time programs available.

**Students:** 44 full-time (36 women), 17 part-time (11 women); includes 6 minority (2 African Americans, 4 Hispanic Americans), 3 international. Average age 29. In 2001, 1 degree awarded.

**Degree requirements:** For master's, thesis.

**Entrance requirements:** For master's, GRE General Test or MAT, minimum GPA of 3.0. *Application deadline:* For fall admission, 8/1; for spring admission, 12/1. Applications are processed on a rolling basis. *Application fee:* $20.

**Expenses:** Tuition, area resident: Part-time $69 per credit. Tuition, state resident: full-time $1,380; part-time $69 per credit. Tuition, nonresident: full-time $5,600; part-time $280 per credit. Required fees: $748. Tuition and fees vary according to course load.

**Financial support:** Research assistantships, teaching assistantships, career-related internships or fieldwork and institutionally sponsored loans available. Support available to part-time students. Financial award application deadline: 5/31; financial award applicants required to submit FAFSA.

**Faculty research:** Recognition memory, embarrassment, divorce, relationship satisfaction, eyewitness testimony. *Total annual research expenditures:* $50,000.

Dr. Donna M. Desforges, Chairperson, 936-294-1174, *Fax:* 936-294-3798.

**Application contact:** Dr. Rowland Miller, Graduate Coordinator, 936-294-1176, *Fax:* 936-294-3798, *E-mail:* psy_rsm@shsu.edu. *Web site:* http://www.shsu.edu/~psy_www/

■ **SAN DIEGO STATE UNIVERSITY**

**Graduate and Research Affairs, College of Sciences, Department of Psychology, San Diego, CA 92182**

**AWARDS** Clinical psychology (MS, PhD); industrial and organizational psychology (MS); program evaluation (MS); psychology (MA). Terminal master's awarded for partial completion of doctoral program.

**Degree requirements:** For master's, thesis, oral exam; for doctorate, thesis/dissertation.

**Entrance requirements:** For master's, GRE General Test, TOEFL; for doctorate, GRE General Test, GRE Subject Test,

*San Diego State University (continued)* minimum GPA of 3.5. *Web site:* http://www.phsychology.sdsu.edu/

# ■ SAN FRANCISCO STATE UNIVERSITY

**Graduate Division, College of Behavioral and Social Sciences, Department of Psychology, San Francisco, CA 94132-1722**

**AWARDS** MA, MS.

**Entrance requirements:** For master's, GRE General Test, minimum GPA of 2.5 in last 60 units.

# ■ SAN JOSE STATE UNIVERSITY

**Graduate Studies, College of Social Sciences, Department of Psychology, San Jose, CA 95192-0001**

**AWARDS** Clinical psychology (MS); counseling (MS); industrial psychology (MS); research psychology (MA).

**Faculty:** 32 full-time (5 women), 13 part-time/adjunct (7 women).
**Students:** 40 full-time (32 women), 20 part-time (12 women); includes 17 minority (2 African Americans, 11 Asian Americans or Pacific Islanders, 4 Hispanic Americans), 6 international. Average age 30. 150 applicants, 32% accepted. In 2001, 25 degrees awarded.
**Degree requirements:** For master's, thesis (for some programs), comprehensive exam.
**Entrance requirements:** For master's, minimum GPA of 3.0. *Application deadline:* For fall admission, 6/29; for spring admission, 11/30. Applications are processed on a rolling basis. *Application fee:* $59. Electronic applications accepted.
**Expenses:** Tuition, nonresident: part-time $246 per unit. Required fees: $678 per semester. Tuition and fees vary according to course load.
**Financial support:** In 2001–02, 15 teaching assistantships were awarded; career-related internships or fieldwork and institutionally sponsored loans also available. Financial award application deadline: 3/1; financial award applicants required to submit FAFSA.
**Faculty research:** Drug and alcohol abuse, neurohormonal mechanisms in motion sickness, behavior modification, sleep research, genetics.
Dr. Robert Pelligrini, Chair, 408-924-5600, *Fax:* 408-924-5605.
**Application contact:** Laree Huntsman, Graduate Adviser, 408-924-5633.

# ■ SAYBROOK GRADUATE SCHOOL AND RESEARCH CENTER

**Program in Psychology, Human Science and Organizational Systems, San Francisco, CA 94133-4640**

**AWARDS** Human science (MA, PhD), including consciousness and spirituality, individualized (PhD), organizational systems, social transformation; organizational systems (MA, PhD), including individualized (PhD), organizational systems; psychology (MA, PhD), including consciousness and spirituality, humanistic and transpersonal, clinical inquiry, and health studies, individualized (PhD), licensure track (MA), organizational systems, social transformation. Postbaccalaureate distance learning degree programs offered (minimal on-campus study).

**Faculty:** 20 full-time (6 women), 83 part-time/adjunct (29 women).
**Students:** 392 full-time (246 women); includes 63 minority (28 African Americans, 16 Asian Americans or Pacific Islanders, 14 Hispanic Americans, 5 Native Americans), 17 international. Average age 42. 280 applicants, 34% accepted. In 2001, 9 master's, 35 doctorates awarded. Terminal master's awarded for partial completion of doctoral program.
**Degree requirements:** For master's, thesis or alternative; for doctorate, thesis/dissertation.
**Entrance requirements:** For master's, TOEFL; for doctorate, TOEFL, master's degree in psychology or related social science. *Application deadline:* For fall admission, 6/1 (priority date); for spring admission, 12/16 (priority date). Electronic applications accepted.
**Expenses:** Tuition: Full-time $13,800. Required fees: $2,000. One-time fee: $600 full-time.
**Financial support:** In 2001–02, 275 students received support. Scholarships/grants available. Financial award applicants required to submit FAFSA.
**Faculty research:** Humanistic theory, health studies, organizational systems, consciousness and spirituality, social transformation. *Total annual research expenditures:* $90,000.
Dr. Maureen O'Hara, President, 800-825-4480, *Fax:* 415-433-9271, *E-mail:* mohara@saybrook.edu.
**Application contact:** Mindy Myers, Vice President for Recruitment and Admissions, 800-825-4480, *Fax:* 415-433-9271, *E-mail:* mmyers@saybrook.edu. *Web site:* http://www.saybrook.edu/

# ■ SEATTLE UNIVERSITY

**College of Arts and Sciences, Department of Psychology, Seattle, WA 98122**

**AWARDS** Existential and phenomenological therapeutic psychology (MA Psych).
**Faculty:** 8 full-time (3 women), 4 part-time/adjunct (3 women).
**Students:** 37 full-time (23 women), 4 part-time (3 women); includes 3 minority (all Asian Americans or Pacific Islanders), 2 international. Average age 35. 51 applicants, 57% accepted, 23 enrolled. In 2001, 15 degrees awarded.
**Degree requirements:** For master's, thesis.
**Entrance requirements:** For master's, interview, minimum GPA of 3.0, previous undergraduate course work in psychology. *Application deadline:* For fall admission, 1/15. *Application fee:* $55.
**Expenses:** Tuition: Full-time $7,740; part-time $430 per credit hour. Tuition and fees vary according to course load, degree level and program.
**Financial support:** Career-related internships or fieldwork and Federal Work-Study available. Support available to part-time students. Financial award applicants required to submit FAFSA.
**Faculty research:** Healing, transformations in relationships, therapy, dialogical research.
Dr. Lane Gerber, Director, 206-296-5400, *Fax:* 206-296-2141.
**Application contact:** Janet Shandley, Associate Dean of Graduate Admissions, 206-296-5900, *Fax:* 206-298-5656, *E-mail:* grad_admissions@seattleu.edu. *Web site:* http://www.seattleu.edu/artsci/departments/psychology/

# ■ SETON HALL UNIVERSITY

**College of Education and Human Services, Department of Professional Psychology and Family Therapy, South Orange, NJ 07079-2697**

**AWARDS** Counseling psychology (PhD); counselor preparation (MA); marriage and family counseling (MS, PhD, Ed S); psychological studies (MA); school psychology (Ed S). Part-time and evening/weekend programs available. Postbaccalaureate distance learning degree programs offered (minimal on-campus study). Terminal master's awarded for partial completion of doctoral program.
**Degree requirements:** For master's, case study; for doctorate, thesis/dissertation, internship, comprehensive exam; for Ed S, internship.
**Entrance requirements:** For master's, GRE or MAT; for doctorate, GRE, interview; for Ed S, GRE or MAT, interview.

**Expenses:** Tuition: Full-time $10,818; part-time $601 per credit. Required fees: $610; $185 per term. Tuition and fees vary according to course load, program and student's religious affiliation.
**Faculty research:** Counseling process, ethics, family systems, child pathology.

## ■ SHIPPENSBURG UNIVERSITY OF PENNSYLVANIA

**School of Graduate Studies and Research, College of Arts and Sciences, Department of Psychology, Shippensburg, PA 17257-2299**

**AWARDS** MS. Part-time and evening/weekend programs available.
**Faculty:** 7 full-time (3 women), 1 part-time/adjunct (0 women).
**Students:** 12 full-time (8 women), 13 part-time (9 women); includes 1 minority (Asian American or Pacific Islander), 1 international. Average age 28. 31 applicants, 52% accepted, 8 enrolled. In 2001, 22 degrees awarded.
**Degree requirements:** For master's, thesis optional. *Median time to degree:* Master's–1.67 years full-time, 3.41 years part-time.
**Entrance requirements:** For master's, minimum GPA of 2.75, 1 course in statistics, 6 undergraduate credit hours in psychology. *Application deadline:* Applications are processed on a rolling basis. *Application fee:* $30. Electronic applications accepted.
**Expenses:** Tuition, state resident: full-time $4,600; part-time $256 per credit hour. Tuition, nonresident: full-time $7,554; part-time $420 per credit hour. Required fees: $290; $145 per semester.
**Financial support:** In 2001–02, 9 research assistantships with full tuition reimbursements were awarded; career-related internships or fieldwork and unspecified assistantships also available. Support available to part-time students. Financial award application deadline: 3/1; financial award applicants required to submit FAFSA.
Dr. Ronald Mehiel, Chairperson, 717-477-1657, *Fax:* 717-477-4057, *E-mail:* rmehie@ship.edu.
**Application contact:** Renee Payne, Associate Dean of Graduate Admissions, 717-477-1231, *Fax:* 717-477-4016, *E-mail:* rmpayn@ship.edu. *Web site:* http://www.ship.edu/academic/artpsy.html

## ■ SOUTHEASTERN BAPTIST THEOLOGICAL SEMINARY

**Graduate and Professional Programs, Wake Forest, NC 27588-1889**

**AWARDS** Advanced biblical studies (M Div); Christian education (M Div, MACE); Christian ethics (PhD); Christian ministry (M Div);

Christian planting (M Div); church music (MACM); counseling (MACO); evangelism (PhD); language (M Div); ministry (D Min); New Testament (PhD); Old Testament (PhD); philosophy (PhD); theology (Th M, PhD); women's studies (M Div).

**Degree requirements:** For M Div, supervised ministry; for master's, thesis (for some programs), oral exam; for doctorate, thesis/dissertation, fieldwork.
**Entrance requirements:** For master's, Cooperative English Test, minimum GPA of 2.0, M Div or equivalent (Th M); for doctorate, GRE General Test or MAT, Cooperative English Test, M Div or equivalent, 3 years of professional experience.

## ■ SOUTHEASTERN LOUISIANA UNIVERSITY

**College of Arts and Sciences, Department of Psychology, Hammond, LA 70402**

**AWARDS** MA. Part-time programs available.
**Faculty:** 11 full-time (5 women), 2 part-time/adjunct (1 woman).
**Students:** 14 full-time (9 women), 8 part-time (all women); includes 5 minority (4 African Americans, 1 Hispanic American). Average age 29. 28 applicants, 68% accepted, 10 enrolled. In 2001, 6 degrees awarded.
**Degree requirements:** For master's, thesis.
**Entrance requirements:** For master's, GRE General Test, minimum GPA of 3.0, previous course work in psychology/educational psychology, letters of reference (3). *Application deadline:* For fall admission, 7/15 (priority date); for spring admission, 12/1 (priority date). Applications are processed on a rolling basis. *Application fee:* $20 ($30 for international students). Electronic applications accepted.
**Expenses:** Tuition, state resident: full-time $2,457. Tuition, nonresident: full-time $6,453. International tuition: $6,573 full-time.
**Financial support:** In 2001–02, 10 research assistantships with full tuition reimbursements (averaging $2,200 per year) were awarded; career-related internships or fieldwork, Federal Work-Study, and unspecified assistantships also available. Support available to part-time students. Financial award application deadline: 5/1; financial award applicants required to submit FAFSA.
**Faculty research:** Police lineup identification, psychology of women criminals, memory for unusual events, body image, social stereotypes. *Total annual research expenditures:* $1,504.

Dr. Alvin Burstein, Department Head, 985-549-2154, *Fax:* 985-549-3892, *E-mail:* aburstein@selu.edu.
**Application contact:** Josie Mercante, Associate Director of Admissions, 985-549-2066, *Fax:* 985-549-5632, *E-mail:* jmercante@selu.edu. *Web site:* http://www.selu.edu/Academics/Depts/Psyc/

## ■ SOUTHERN ADVENTIST UNIVERSITY

**School of Education and Psychology, Collegedale, TN 37315-0370**

**AWARDS** Community counseling (MS); curriculum and instruction (MS Ed); educational administration and supervision (MS Ed); inclusive education (MS Ed); marriage and family therapy (MS); multiage/multigrade teaching (MS Ed); outdoor teacher education (MS Ed); school counseling (MS). Part-time and evening/weekend programs available.
**Faculty:** 11 full-time (7 women), 2 part-time/adjunct (1 woman).
**Students:** 46 full-time (25 women), 70 part-time (48 women); includes 23 minority (11 African Americans, 1 Asian American or Pacific Islander, 10 Hispanic Americans, 1 Native American), 2 international. Average age 36. 22 applicants, 91% accepted. In 2001, 29 degrees awarded.
**Degree requirements:** For master's, position paper (counseling), portfolio (MS Ed in outdoor teacher education).
**Entrance requirements:** For master's, GRE General Test, Minnesota Multiphasic Personality Inventory. *Application deadline:* Applications are processed on a rolling basis. *Application fee:* $25. Electronic applications accepted.
**Expenses:** Tuition: Full-time $5,580; part-time $310 per credit hour.
**Financial support:** In 2001–02, 11 students received support, including 1 research assistantship; career-related internships or fieldwork, scholarships/grants, and tuition waivers (partial) also available. Support available to part-time students. Financial award application deadline: 4/1; financial award applicants required to submit FAFSA.
**Faculty research:** Comparative study of education in North America and Central America, service learning and academic achievement.
Dr. Alberto dos Santos, Dean, 423-238-2779, *Fax:* 423-238-2468, *E-mail:* adossant@southern.edu.
**Application contact:** Cathy Olson, Information Contact, 423-238-2765, *Fax:* 423-238-2468, *E-mail:* cjolson@southern.edu. *Web site:* http://www.southern.edu/edupsy/homepage.html

# ■ SOUTHERN CONNECTICUT STATE UNIVERSITY

**School of Graduate Studies, School of Arts and Sciences, Department of Psychology, New Haven, CT 06515-1355**

**AWARDS** MA. Part-time and evening/weekend programs available.

**Faculty:** 13 full-time (6 women).
**Students:** 15 full-time (11 women), 41 part-time (33 women); includes 6 minority (1 African American, 1 Asian American or Pacific Islander, 4 Hispanic Americans), 1 international. 47 applicants, 30% accepted. In 2001, 19 degrees awarded.
**Degree requirements:** For master's, thesis or alternative.
**Entrance requirements:** For master's, interview, previous course work in psychology. *Application deadline:* For fall admission, 5/15 (priority date). Applications are processed on a rolling basis. *Application fee:* $40.
**Financial support:** Teaching assistantships available. Financial award application deadline: 4/15; financial award applicants required to submit FAFSA.
Dr. Linda Mackey, Chair, 203-392-6868, *Fax:* 203-392-6805, *E-mail:* mackey@southernct.edu.
**Application contact:** Dr. James Mazur, Coordinator, 203-392-6876, *Fax:* 203-392-6805, *E-mail:* mazur@southernct.edu. *Web site:* http://www.southernct.edu/

# ■ SOUTHERN ILLINOIS UNIVERSITY CARBONDALE

**Graduate School, College of Liberal Arts, Department of Psychology, Carbondale, IL 62901-6806**

**AWARDS** Clinical psychology (MA, MS, PhD); counseling psychology (MA, MS, PhD); experimental psychology (MA, MS, PhD).

**Faculty:** 27 full-time (14 women), 1 part-time/adjunct (0 women).
**Students:** 79 full-time (58 women), 42 part-time (29 women); includes 28 minority (16 African Americans, 7 Asian Americans or Pacific Islanders, 4 Hispanic Americans, 1 Native American), 10 international. 128 applicants, 22% accepted. In 2001, 14 master's, 21 doctorates awarded.
**Degree requirements:** For master's and doctorate, thesis/dissertation.
**Entrance requirements:** For master's, GRE General Test, GRE Subject Test, TOEFL, minimum GPA of 2.7; for doctorate, GRE General Test, GRE Subject Test, TOEFL, minimum GPA of 3.25. *Application deadline:* For fall admission, 3/1 (priority date). Applications are processed on a rolling basis. *Application fee:* $20.

**Expenses:** Tuition, state resident: full-time $3,794; part-time $154 per hour. Tuition, nonresident: full-time $6,566; part-time $308 per hour. Required fees: $277 per hour.
**Financial support:** In 2001–02, 82 students received support, including 14 fellowships with full tuition reimbursements available, 23 research assistantships with full tuition reimbursements available, 22 teaching assistantships with full tuition reimbursements available; Federal Work-Study, institutionally sponsored loans, and tuition waivers (full) also available.
**Faculty research:** Developmental neuropsychology; smoking, affect, and cognition; personality measurement; vocational psychology; program evaluation.
Alan Vaux, Chair, 618-453-3529. *Web site:* http://www.siu.edu/departments/cola/psycho/

**Find an in-depth description at www.petersons.com/gradchannel.**

# ■ SOUTHERN ILLINOIS UNIVERSITY EDWARDSVILLE

**Graduate Studies and Research, School of Education, Department of Psychology, Edwardsville, IL 62026-0001**

**AWARDS** Clinical adult (MS); community school (MS); general academic (MA); industrial organizational (MS). Part-time programs available.

**Students:** 33 full-time (26 women), 24 part-time (20 women); includes 6 minority (4 African Americans, 2 Hispanic Americans), 3 international. Average age 33. 64 applicants, 56% accepted, 21 enrolled. In 2001, 29 degrees awarded.
**Degree requirements:** For master's, thesis, final exam.
**Entrance requirements:** For master's, GRE General Test, GRE Subject Test, MAT, TOEFL. *Application deadline:* For fall admission, 7/20; for spring admission, 12/7. *Application fee:* $25.
**Expenses:** Tuition, state resident: full-time $2,712; part-time $113 per credit hour. Tuition, nonresident: full-time $5,424; part-time $226 per credit hour. Required fees: $250; $125 per term. Tuition and fees vary according to course load, campus/location and reciprocity agreements.
**Financial support:** In 2001–02, 3 fellowships with full tuition reimbursements, 4 teaching assistantships with full tuition reimbursements were awarded. Research assistantships, career-related internships or fieldwork, Federal Work-Study, institutionally sponsored loans, traineeships, and unspecified assistantships also available. Support available to part-time students. Financial award application deadline: 3/1;

financial award applicants required to submit FAFSA.
Dr. Bryce Sullivan, Chair, 618-650-2202, *E-mail:* bsulliv@siue.edu.

# ■ SOUTHERN METHODIST UNIVERSITY

**Dedman College, Department of Psychology, Dallas, TX 75275**

**AWARDS** Clinical and counseling psychology (MA); psychology (MA, PhD). Part-time programs available.

**Faculty:** 14 full-time (5 women).
**Students:** 26 full-time (24 women), 19 part-time (13 women); includes 5 minority (2 African Americans, 1 Asian American or Pacific Islander, 2 Hispanic Americans), 1 international. Average age 30. 108 applicants, 18% accepted. In 2001, 1 master's, 6 doctorates awarded.
**Degree requirements:** For master's, thesis, oral exam; for doctorate, thesis/dissertation, oral exam, teaching practicum.
**Entrance requirements:** For master's, GRE General Test, TOEFL, minimum GPA of 3.0; for doctorate, GRE General Test, TOEFL, MA in psychology, minimum GPA of 3.0. *Application deadline:* For fall admission, 2/15 (priority date). *Application fee:* $50.
**Expenses:** Tuition: Part-time $285 per credit hour.
**Financial support:** Research assistantships, teaching assistantships, career-related internships or fieldwork, Federal Work-Study, and institutionally sponsored loans available. Support available to part-time students. Financial award applicants required to submit FAFSA.
**Faculty research:** Experimental, social, developmental, and cognitive psychology.
Dr. Alan Brown, Chair, 214-768-3420.
**Application contact:** Dr. Neil Mulligan, Director, Graduate Studies, 214-768-4385.

# ■ SOUTHERN NAZARENE UNIVERSITY

**Graduate College, School of Psychology, Bethany, OK 73008**

**AWARDS** Counseling psychology (MSCP); marriage and family therapy (MA).

**Degree requirements:** For master's, thesis optional.
**Entrance requirements:** For master's, English proficiency exam, minimum GPA of 3.0 in last 60 hours/major, 2.7 overall.

# SOUTHERN OREGON UNIVERSITY

**Graduate Office, School of Social Science, Health and Physical Education, Department of Psychology, Ashland, OR 97520**

**AWARDS** Applied psychology (MAP); human service-organizational training and development (MA, MS); social science (MA, MS), including professional counseling, psychology. Part-time programs available.

**Faculty:** 10 full-time (5 women), 2 part-time/adjunct (1 woman).
**Students:** 37 full-time (27 women), 3 part-time (1 woman); includes 3 minority (1 Asian American or Pacific Islander, 1 Hispanic American, 1 Native American). Average age 33. 41 applicants, 39% accepted, 13 enrolled. In 2001, 6 degrees awarded.
**Degree requirements:** For master's, thesis, portfolio and oral defense. *Median time to degree:* Master's–2 years full-time.
**Entrance requirements:** For master's, GRE General Test, minimum GPA of 3.0. *Application deadline:* For fall admission, 2/15 (priority date). Applications are processed on a rolling basis. *Application fee:* $50. Electronic applications accepted.
**Expenses:** Tuition, state resident: full-time $5,184; part-time $192 per credit. Tuition, nonresident: full-time $9,828; part-time $364 per credit. Required fees: $927. One-time fee: $75 full-time. Full-time tuition and fees vary according to course load, program and reciprocity agreements.
**Financial support:** Scholarships/grants and unspecified assistantships available. Financial award applicants required to submit FAFSA.
Dr. Josie Wilson, Chair, 541-552-6946, *E-mail:* jwilson@sou.edu.
**Application contact:** Wri Courtney, Graduate Coordinator, 541-552-6947, *E-mail:* map@sou.edu.

# SOUTHERN UNIVERSITY AND AGRICULTURAL AND MECHANICAL COLLEGE

**Graduate School, College of Sciences, Department of Psychology and Rehabilitation Counseling, Baton Rouge, LA 70813**

**AWARDS** Rehabilitation counseling (MS).

**Faculty:** 7 full-time (5 women).
**Students:** 25 full-time (21 women), 5 part-time (4 women); includes 23 minority (all African Americans), 1 international. Average age 32. 51 applicants, 45% accepted. In 2001, 13 degrees awarded.
**Degree requirements:** For master's, thesis optional.

**Entrance requirements:** For master's, GMAT or GRE General Test, TOEFL. *Application deadline:* For fall admission, 6/1 (priority date); for spring admission, 11/1. Applications are processed on a rolling basis. *Application fee:* $25.
**Expenses:** Tuition, state resident: full-time $1,323. Tuition, nonresident: full-time $2,583. International tuition: $2,613 full-time. Tuition and fees vary according to program.
**Financial support:** In 2001–02, 20 research assistantships (averaging $11,500 per year) were awarded; scholarships/grants also available. Financial award application deadline: 4/15.
**Faculty research:** Cultural diversity, professional preparation and participation of minorities, needs and satisfaction of students with disabilities, prediction model for rehabilitation outcome, diabetes.
Dr. Madan Kundu, Coordinator, 225-771-2990, *Fax:* 225-771-2993, *E-mail:* kundusubr@aol.com.

# SOUTHWESTERN COLLEGE

**Program in Psychodrama and Action Methods, Santa Fe, NM 87502-4788**

**AWARDS** Certificate.

**Faculty:** 1 (woman) part-time/adjunct.
**Students:** Average age 41. 12 applicants, 100% accepted, 12 enrolled.
**Entrance requirements:** For degree, letters of reference (3), interview. *Application deadline:* Applications are processed on a rolling basis. *Application fee:* $25.
**Expenses:** Tuition: Full-time $11,760; part-time $245 per unit.
Kate Cook, Director, 877-471-5756, *Fax:* 877-471-4071.
**Application contact:** Kristine Schmidt, Director of Admissions, 877-471-5756, *Fax:* 877-471-4071, *E-mail:* admissions@swc.edu. *Web site:* http://www.swc.edu/

# SOUTHWEST MISSOURI STATE UNIVERSITY

**Graduate College, College of Health and Human Services, Department of Psychology, Springfield, MO 65804-0094**

**AWARDS** MS, MS Ed.

**Faculty:** 20 full-time (4 women).
**Students:** 36 full-time (24 women); includes 3 minority (1 African American, 2 Hispanic Americans), 5 international. Average age 27. In 2001, 17 degrees awarded.
**Degree requirements:** For master's, thesis, comprehensive exam.
**Entrance requirements:** For master's, GRE General Test, GRE Subject Test, minimum GPA of 3.25 in major, 3.0 overall; 20 hours in psychology (experimental and statistics). *Application*

*deadline:* For fall admission, 3/1 (priority date). Applications are processed on a rolling basis. *Application fee:* $25. Electronic applications accepted.
**Expenses:** Tuition, state resident: full-time $2,286; part-time $127 per credit. Tuition, nonresident: full-time $4,572; part-time $254 per credit. Required fees: $151 per semester. Tuition and fees vary according to course level and program.
**Financial support:** In 2001–02, 8 research assistantships with full tuition reimbursements (averaging $6,150 per year), 2 teaching assistantships with full tuition reimbursements (averaging $8,200 per year) were awarded. Career-related internships or fieldwork, Federal Work-Study, scholarships/grants, and unspecified assistantships also available. Support available to part-time students. Financial award application deadline: 3/31.
**Faculty research:** Sports psychology, information processing, motivational processes, interpersonal dynamics, infant visual processing.
Dr. Fred R. Maxwell, Head, 417-836-5797, *Fax:* 417-836-4884, *E-mail:* frm650f@smsu.edu. *Web site:* http://www.smsu.edu/contrib/PSYCH/psychome.html

# SOUTHWEST TEXAS STATE UNIVERSITY

**Graduate School, College of Liberal Arts, Department of Psychology, San Marcos, TX 78666**

**AWARDS** Health psychology (MA).

**Faculty:** 5 full-time (1 woman), 1 (woman) part-time/adjunct.
**Students:** 8 full-time (all women), 11 part-time (8 women); includes 2 minority (both Hispanic Americans). Average age 27. 14 applicants, 64% accepted, 7 enrolled. In 2001, 1 degree awarded.
**Degree requirements:** For master's, thesis, 450 hours of practicum courses.
**Entrance requirements:** For master's, GRE General Test, minimum GPA of 3.0 in last 60 hours, 3.0 in psychology coursework. *Application deadline:* For fall admission, 3/15. Applications are processed on a rolling basis. *Application fee:* $40 ($90 for international students).
**Expenses:** Tuition, state resident: full-time $1,512; part-time $84 per credit hour. Tuition, nonresident: full-time $5,310; part-time $295 per credit hour. Required fees: $864; $29 per credit hour. $195 per term. Full-time tuition and fees vary according to course load.
**Financial support:** In 2001–02, 6 teaching assistantships (averaging $4,656 per year) were awarded

*Southwest Texas State University (continued)*

Dr. Randall E. Osborne, Acting Chair, 512-245-8236, *Fax:* 512-245-3153, *E-mail:* ro10@swt.edu.

**Application contact:** Dr. John Davis, Graduate Advisor, 512-245-3162, *Fax:* 512-245-3153, *E-mail:* jd04@swt.edu.

### ■ SOUTHWEST TEXAS STATE UNIVERSITY

**Graduate School, Interdisciplinary Studies Program in Education Administration and Psychological Services, San Marcos, TX 78666**

AWARDS MAIS.

**Students:** Average age 36.
**Degree requirements:** For master's, comprehensive exam.
*Application deadline:* For fall admission, 6/15 (priority date); for spring admission, 10/15 (priority date). Applications are processed on a rolling basis. *Application fee:* $40 ($90 for international students).
**Expenses:** Tuition, state resident: full-time $1,512; part-time $84 per credit hour. Tuition, nonresident: full-time $5,310; part-time $295 per credit hour. Required fees: $864; $29 per credit hour. $195 per term. Full-time tuition and fees vary according to course load.
**Financial support:** Application deadline: 4/1.
Dr. Sue McCullough, Head, 512-245-3083, *Fax:* 512-245-8872, *E-mail:* cm15@swt.edu.

### ■ SPALDING UNIVERSITY

**Graduate Studies, School of Psychology, Louisville, KY 40203-2188**

AWARDS Clinical psychology (MA, Psy D). Part-time programs available.

**Faculty:** 8 full-time (3 women), 8 part-time/adjunct (3 women).
**Students:** 46 full-time (33 women), 86 part-time (64 women); includes 11 minority (6 African Americans, 2 Asian Americans or Pacific Islanders, 1 Hispanic American, 2 Native Americans), 8 international. 136 applicants, 40% accepted. In 2001, 8 master's, 21 doctorates awarded. Terminal master's awarded for partial completion of doctoral program.
**Degree requirements:** For master's, comprehensive exam; for doctorate, thesis/dissertation.
**Entrance requirements:** For master's, GRE General Test, 18 hours of undergraduate course work in psychology; for doctorate, GRE General Test, interview. *Application deadline:* For fall admission, 1/15. *Application fee:* $30.

**Expenses:** Tuition: Full-time $6,000; part-time $400 per credit hour. Required fees: $96.
**Financial support:** In 2001–02, 28 research assistantships (averaging $4,100 per year) were awarded; career-related internships or fieldwork, Federal Work-Study, and scholarships/grants also available. Financial award application deadline: 3/15.
**Faculty research:** Substance abuse, prayer research, end-of-life issues, complementary and alternative medicine, research methodology and statistical inference. *Total annual research expenditures:* $400,000.
Dr. Barbara Williams, Dean, 502-585-9911.
**Application contact:** 502-585-1705, *Fax:* 502-585-7158, *E-mail:* gradadmissions@spalding.edu.

### ■ STANFORD UNIVERSITY

**School of Humanities and Sciences, Department of Psychology, Stanford, CA 94305-9991**

AWARDS PhD.

**Faculty:** 30 full-time (9 women).
**Students:** 63 full-time (45 women), 11 part-time (7 women); includes 15 minority (4 African Americans, 5 Asian Americans or Pacific Islanders, 5 Hispanic Americans, 1 Native American), 15 international. Average age 26. 172 applicants, 9% accepted. In 2001, 15 doctorates awarded.
**Degree requirements:** For doctorate, thesis/dissertation, oral exam.
**Entrance requirements:** For doctorate, GRE General Test, GRE Subject Test, TOEFL. *Application deadline:* For fall admission, 12/15. *Application fee:* $65 ($80 for international students). Electronic applications accepted.
Mark R. Lepper, Chair, 650-725-2448, *Fax:* 650-725-5699.
**Application contact:** Graduate Admissions Coordinator, 650-725-2403, *Fax:* 650-725-9148. *Web site:* http://www.psych.stanford.edu/

### ■ STATE UNIVERSITY OF NEW YORK AT ALBANY

**College of Arts and Sciences, Department of Psychology, Albany, NY 12222-0001**

AWARDS Biopsychology (PhD); clinical psychology (PhD); general/experimental psychology (PhD); industrial/organizational psychology (PhD); psychology (MA); social/personality psychology (PhD).

**Students:** 69 full-time (45 women), 58 part-time (41 women); includes 12 minority (2 African Americans, 3 Asian Americans or Pacific Islanders, 7 Hispanic Americans), 13 international. Average age 28. 220 applicants, 20% accepted. In 2001, 11 master's, 6 doctorates awarded.
**Degree requirements:** For doctorate, thesis/dissertation.
**Entrance requirements:** For doctorate, GRE General Test, GRE Subject Test. *Application deadline:* For fall admission, 1/15. *Application fee:* $50.
**Expenses:** Tuition, state resident: full-time $2,550; part-time $213 per credit. Tuition, nonresident: full-time $4,208; part-time $351 per credit. Required fees: $470; $470 per year.
**Financial support:** Fellowships, research assistantships, teaching assistantships, career-related internships or fieldwork available. Financial award application deadline: 2/1.
Robert Rosellini, Chair, 518-442-4820.
**Application contact:** Glenn Sanders, Graduate Director, 518-442-4853.

### ■ STATE UNIVERSITY OF NEW YORK AT BINGHAMTON

**Graduate School, School of Arts and Sciences, Department of Psychology, Binghamton, NY 13902-6000**

AWARDS Behavioral neuroscience (MA, PhD); clinical psychology (MA, PhD); cognitive and behavioral science (MA, PhD).

**Faculty:** 27 full-time (11 women), 7 part-time/adjunct (2 women).
**Students:** 79 full-time (51 women), 16 part-time (11 women); includes 13 minority (4 African Americans, 3 Asian Americans or Pacific Islanders, 6 Hispanic Americans), 8 international. Average age 27. 150 applicants, 23% accepted, 20 enrolled. In 2001, 10 master's, 10 doctorates awarded. Terminal master's awarded for partial completion of doctoral program.
**Degree requirements:** For master's, thesis; for doctorate, thesis/dissertation, departmental qualifying exam.
**Entrance requirements:** For master's and doctorate, GRE General Test, GRE Subject Test, TOEFL. *Application deadline:* For fall admission, 4/15 (priority date); for spring admission, 11/1. Applications are processed on a rolling basis. Electronic applications accepted.
**Expenses:** Tuition, state resident: full-time $5,100; part-time $213 per credit. Tuition, nonresident: full-time $8,416; part-time $351 per credit. Required fees: $811.
**Financial support:** In 2001–02, 76 students received support, including 8 fellowships with full tuition reimbursements available (averaging $9,496 per year), 28 research assistantships with full tuition reimbursements available (averaging $10,308 per year), 40 teaching assistantships with full tuition reimbursements available (averaging $10,683 per year); career-related internships or fieldwork,

Federal Work-Study, institutionally sponsored loans, and unspecified assistant-ships also available. Support available to part-time students. Financial award application deadline: 2/15.

Dr. Linda Spear, Chair, 607-777-2449.

## ■ STATE UNIVERSITY OF NEW YORK AT NEW PALTZ

Graduate School, Faculty of Liberal Arts and Sciences, Department of Psychology, New Paltz, NY 12561

**AWARDS** MA.

**Students:** 15 full-time (11 women), 16 part-time (14 women); includes 4 minority (1 African American, 3 Hispanic Americans), 1 international. In 2001, 10 degrees awarded.

**Degree requirements:** For master's, thesis, comprehensive exam.

**Entrance requirements:** For master's, GRE General Test, GRE Subject Test, minimum GPA of 3.0. *Application deadline:* For fall admission, 3/15 (priority date). Applications are processed on a rolling basis. *Application fee:* $50.

**Expenses:** Tuition, state resident: full-time $5,100; part-time $213 per credit. Tuition, nonresident: full-time $8,416; part-time $351 per credit. Required fees: $624; $21 per credit. $60 per semester.

**Financial support:** Research assistantships, teaching assistantships, career-related internships or fieldwork, Federal Work-Study, and institutionally sponsored loans available.

Dr. Ray Schwartz, Acting Chair, 845-257-3470.

**Application contact:** Dr. Phyllis Freeman, Adviser, 845-257-3470.

## ■ STATE UNIVERSITY OF NEW YORK COLLEGE AT BROCKPORT

School of Letters and Sciences, Department of Psychology, Brockport, NY 14420-2997

**AWARDS** MA. Part-time programs available.

**Students:** 10 full-time (8 women), 8 part-time (7 women); includes 1 minority (Asian American or Pacific Islander). 19 applicants, 26% accepted, 5 enrolled. In 2001, 9 degrees awarded.

**Degree requirements:** For master's, thesis optional.

**Entrance requirements:** For master's, GRE General Test. *Application deadline:* For fall admission, 4/15. *Application fee:* $50.

**Expenses:** Tuition, state resident: full-time $5,100; part-time $213 per credit. Tuition,

nonresident: full-time $8,416; part-time $351 per credit. Required fees: $537; $23 per credit.

**Financial support:** In 2001–02, 2 teaching assistantships with tuition reimbursements (averaging $6,000 per year) were awarded; Federal Work-Study also available. Financial award application deadline: 3/15; financial award applicants required to submit FAFSA.

**Faculty research:** Applied behavior analysis, close relationships, emotional development, community psychology, neuropsychology.

Dr. Robert J. Miller, Chairperson, 585-395-2488.

**Application contact:** Dr. Janet Gillespie, Graduate Director, Psychology, 716-395-2433, *E-mail:* jgillesp@brockport.edu. *Web site:* http://www.brockport.edu/~graduate

## ■ STATE UNIVERSITY OF WEST GEORGIA

Graduate School, College of Arts and Sciences, Department of Psychology, Carrollton, GA 30118

**AWARDS** MA. Part-time programs available.

**Faculty:** 13 full-time (3 women).

**Students:** 47 full-time (32 women), 36 part-time (26 women); includes 11 minority (8 African Americans, 3 Hispanic Americans), 4 international. Average age 28. In 2001, 21 degrees awarded.

**Degree requirements:** For master's, one foreign language, comprehensive exam.

**Entrance requirements:** For master's, GRE General Test, interview, minimum GPA of 2.5. *Application deadline:* For fall admission, 3/1 (priority date); for spring admission, 10/1. *Application fee:* $20. Electronic applications accepted.

**Expenses:** Tuition, state resident: full-time $232; part-time $97 per credit hour. Tuition, nonresident: full-time $928; part-time $387 per credit hour. Required fees: $536; $14 per credit. $100 per semester.

**Financial support:** In 2001–02, 12 research assistantships with full tuition reimbursements (averaging $3,000 per year) were awarded; career-related internships or fieldwork, tuition waivers (full), and unspecified assistantships also available. Support available to part-time students. Financial award applicants required to submit FAFSA.

**Faculty research:** Creativity, inspiration and consciousness; symbolism and metaphor in psychotherapy; spirituality of children; feminism and culture; mind/body connection.

Dr. Donadrian L. Rice, Chair, 770-836-6510, *E-mail:* drice@westga.edu.

**Application contact:** Dr. Jack O. Jenkins, Dean, Graduate School, 770-836-6419, *Fax:* 770-836-2301, *E-mail:* jjenkins@

westga.edu. *Web site:* http://www.westga.edu/~psydept/

## ■ STEPHEN F. AUSTIN STATE UNIVERSITY

Graduate School, College of Liberal Arts, Department of Psychology, Nacogdoches, TX 75962

**AWARDS** MA.

**Faculty:** 12 full-time (4 women), 3 part-time/adjunct (0 women).

**Students:** 31 full-time (16 women), 16 part-time (10 women); includes 8 minority (2 African Americans, 2 Asian Americans or Pacific Islanders, 4 Hispanic Americans), 1 international. Average age 27. 20 applicants, 90% accepted. In 2001, 12 degrees awarded.

**Degree requirements:** For master's, thesis, comprehensive exam.

**Entrance requirements:** For master's, GRE General Test, TOEFL. *Application deadline:* For fall admission, 8/1 (priority date); for spring admission, 12/15. Applications are processed on a rolling basis. *Application fee:* $0 ($50 for international students).

**Expenses:** Tuition, state resident: full-time $1,008; part-time $42 per credit. Tuition, nonresident: full-time $6,072; part-time $253 per credit. Required fees: $1,248; $52 per credit. Tuition and fees vary according to course load.

**Financial support:** In 2001–02, research assistantships (averaging $6,633 per year), teaching assistantships (averaging $6,633 per year) were awarded. Career-related internships or fieldwork, Federal Work-Study, health care benefits, and unspecified assistantships also available. Financial award application deadline: 3/1.

Dr. Kandy Stahl, Chair, 936-468-4402.

## ■ STONY BROOK UNIVERSITY, STATE UNIVERSITY OF NEW YORK

Graduate School, College of Arts and Sciences, Department of Psychology, Stony Brook, NY 11794

**AWARDS** Biopsychology (PhD); clinical psychology (PhD); experimental psychology (PhD); psychology (MA); social/health psychology (PhD).

**Faculty:** 31 full-time (13 women).

**Students:** 73 full-time (49 women), 33 part-time (22 women); includes 17 minority (7 African Americans, 3 Asian Americans or Pacific Islanders, 7 Hispanic Americans), 12 international. Average age 29. 331 applicants, 10% accepted. In 2001, 26 master's, 13 doctorates awarded. Terminal master's awarded for partial completion of doctoral program.

*Stony Brook University, State University of New York (continued)*

**Degree requirements:** For master's and doctorate, thesis/dissertation.

**Entrance requirements:** For master's and doctorate, GRE General Test, GRE Subject Test, TOEFL. *Application deadline:* For fall admission, 1/15. *Application fee:* $50.

**Expenses:** Tuition, state resident: full-time $5,100; part-time $213 per credit. Tuition, nonresident: full-time $8,416; part-time $351 per credit. Required fees: $496.

**Financial support:** In 2001–02, 1 fellowship, 8 research assistantships, 57 teaching assistantships were awarded. Career-related internships or fieldwork also available.

**Faculty research:** Behavior therapy, memory and cognition, child and family studies, quantitative methods, health psychology. *Total annual research expenditures:* $2.8 million.

Dr. Nancy Squires, Chair, 631-632-7805.
**Application contact:** Dr. Harriet Waters, Director, 631-632-7855, *Fax:* 631-632-7876, *E-mail:* hwaters@ccvm.sunysb.edu. *Web site:* http://www.psy.sunysb.edu/

Find an in-depth description at www.petersons.com/gradchannel.

■ **SUFFOLK UNIVERSITY**

**College of Arts and Sciences, Department of Psychology, Boston, MA 02108-2770**

**AWARDS** Clinical-developmental psychology (PhD).

**Faculty:** 12 full-time (10 women), 6 part-time/adjunct (4 women).
**Students:** 41 full-time (34 women), 21 part-time (17 women); includes 6 minority (2 African Americans, 3 Asian Americans or Pacific Islanders, 1 Hispanic American), 3 international. Average age 29. 74 applicants, 45% accepted, 15 enrolled. In 2001, 6 degrees awarded.
**Degree requirements:** For doctorate, thesis/dissertation, Practicum.
**Entrance requirements:** For doctorate, GRE General Test or MAT. *Application deadline:* For fall admission, 1/15. Applications are processed on a rolling basis. *Application fee:* $50.
**Expenses:** Contact institution.
**Financial support:** In 2001–02, 50 students received support, including 42 fellowships with full and partial tuition reimbursements available (averaging $10,200 per year); career-related internships or fieldwork, Federal Work-Study, and institutionally sponsored loans also available. Support available to part-time students. Financial award application deadline: 3/15; financial award applicants required to submit FAFSA.

**Faculty research:** Cognitive, emotional, personality, and social development.
Dr. Robert Webb, Chair, 617-573-8293, *Fax:* 617-367-2924, *E-mail:* rwebb@ suffolk.edu.
**Application contact:** Judith Reynolds, Director of Graduate Admissions, 617-573-8302, *Fax:* 617-523-0116, *E-mail:* grad.admission@suffolk.edu. *Web site:* http://www.cas/suffolk.edu/psych/ndonovan/phd.htm

■ **SUL ROSS STATE UNIVERSITY**

**School of Arts and Sciences, Department of Behavioral and Social Sciences, Program in Psychology, Alpine, TX 79832**

**AWARDS** MA.

**Faculty:** 3 full-time (1 woman), 2 part-time/adjunct (both women).
**Students:** 7 full-time (4 women), 3 part-time (2 women); includes 5 minority (2 African Americans, 3 Hispanic Americans). Average age 31.
**Entrance requirements:** For master's, GRE General Test, minimum GPA of 2.5 in last 60 hours of undergraduate work. *Application deadline:* Applications are processed on a rolling basis. *Application fee:* $0 ($50 for international students).
**Expenses:** Tuition, state resident: part-time $64 per semester hour. Tuition, nonresident: part-time $275 per semester hour. Required fees: $71; $32 per semester hour.
**Financial support:** Application deadline: 5/1.
Dr. Jimmy Case, Chairman, Department of Behavioral and Social Sciences, 915-837-8161, *Fax:* 915-837-8046.

■ **SYRACUSE UNIVERSITY**

**Graduate School, College of Arts and Sciences, Department of Psychology, Syracuse, NY 13244-0003**

**AWARDS** Clinical psychology (MA, MS, PhD); experimental psychology (MA, MS, PhD); psychology (MA, MS, PhD); school psychology (PhD); social psychology (PhD). Terminal master's awarded for partial completion of doctoral program.

**Degree requirements:** For master's, thesis (for some programs); for doctorate, thesis/dissertation.
**Entrance requirements:** For master's and doctorate, GRE General Test.
**Expenses:** Tuition: Full-time $15,528; part-time $647 per credit. Required fees: $420; $38 per term. Tuition and fees vary according to program.

■ **TEMPLE UNIVERSITY**

**Graduate School, College of Liberal Arts, Department of Psychology, Philadelphia, PA 19122-6096**

**AWARDS** Clinical psychology (PhD); cognitive psychology (PhD); developmental psychology (PhD); experimental psychology (PhD); social and organizational psychology (PhD).

**Degree requirements:** For doctorate, thesis/dissertation.
**Entrance requirements:** For doctorate, GRE General Test, minimum GPA of 3.0. Electronic applications accepted.
**Expenses:** Tuition, state resident: full-time $8,487; part-time $369 per credit hour. Tuition, nonresident: full-time $12,282; part-time $534 per credit hour. Required fees: $350. Tuition and fees vary according to course load, program and reciprocity agreements.

Find an in-depth description at www.petersons.com/gradchannel.

■ **TENNESSEE STATE UNIVERSITY**

**Graduate School, College of Education, Department of Psychology, Nashville, TN 37209-1561**

**AWARDS** Counseling and guidance (MS), including counseling, elementary school counseling, organizational counseling, secondary school counseling; counseling psychology (PhD); psychology (MS, PhD); school psychology (MS, PhD). Part-time and evening/weekend programs available.

**Faculty:** 13 full-time (6 women), 9 part-time/adjunct (7 women).
**Students:** 43 full-time (34 women), 76 part-time (56 women). Average age 29. 75 applicants, 95% accepted. In 2001, 9 master's, 10 doctorates awarded.
**Degree requirements:** For master's, comprehensive exam or thesis; for doctorate, thesis/dissertation, comprehensive exam.
**Entrance requirements:** For master's, GRE General Test; for doctorate, GRE General Test or MAT, minimum GPA of 3.25, work experience. *Application deadline:* Applications are processed on a rolling basis. *Application fee:* $15.
**Expenses:** Tuition, state resident: full-time $3,884; part-time $247 per hour. Tuition, nonresident: full-time $10,356; part-time $517 per hour.
**Financial support:** In 2001–02, 2 fellowships (averaging $5,924 per year), 3 research assistantships (averaging $5,962 per year), 6 teaching assistantships (averaging $17,432 per year) were awarded. Financial award application deadline: 5/1.
**Faculty research:** Stress reduction, student retention, computer education, marital and family therapy, increasing

faculty effectiveness. *Total annual research expenditures:* $50,000.
Dr. Peter Millet, Head, 615-963-5139, *Fax:* 615-963-5140.
**Application contact:** Dr. Helen Barrett, Dean of the Graduate School, 615-963-5901, *Fax:* 615-963-5963, *E-mail:* hbarrett@picard.tnstate.edu.

### ■ TEXAS A&M INTERNATIONAL UNIVERSITY

**Division of Graduate Studies, College of Arts and Humanities, Department of Psychology and Sociology, Laredo, TX 78041-1900**
**AWARDS** Counseling psychology (MA); sociology (MA).
**Students:** 5 full-time (2 women), 30 part-time (21 women); includes 33 minority (all Hispanic Americans), 1 international. In 2001, 15 degrees awarded.
**Degree requirements:** For master's, thesis (for some programs).
**Entrance requirements:** For master's, GRE General Test. *Application deadline:* For fall admission, 7/15 (priority date); for spring admission, 11/12. Applications are processed on a rolling basis. *Application fee:* $0.
**Expenses:** Tuition, state resident: full-time $1,536; part-time $64 per credit. Tuition, nonresident: full-time $6,600; part-time $275 per credit. Required fees: $594; $9 per credit. $33 per term. One-time fee: $10 part-time.
**Financial support:** Application deadline: 11/1.
Dr. Marion Aguila, Chair, 956-326-2644, *Fax:* 956-326-2459, *E-mail:* maguilar@tamiu.edu.
**Application contact:** Veronica Gonzalez, Director of Enrollment Management and School Relations, 956-326-2270, *Fax:* 956-326-2269, *E-mail:* enroll@tamiu.edu.

### ■ TEXAS A&M UNIVERSITY

**College of Liberal Arts, Department of Psychology, College Station, TX 77843**
**AWARDS** Clinical psychology (MS, PhD); general psychology (MS, PhD); industrial/organizational psychology (MS, PhD).
**Faculty:** 41.
**Students:** 94 (54 women). Average age 28.
**Degree requirements:** For master's and doctorate, thesis/dissertation.
**Entrance requirements:** For master's and doctorate, GRE General Test, TOEFL. *Application deadline:* For fall admission, 1/15. *Application fee:* $50 ($75 for international students). Electronic applications accepted.
**Expenses:** Tuition, state resident: full-time $11,872. Tuition, nonresident: full-time $17,892.

**Financial support:** Fellowships, research assistantships, teaching assistantships, career-related internships or fieldwork and institutionally sponsored loans available. Financial award application deadline: 1/15; financial award applicants required to submit FAFSA.
Dr. Paul Wellman, Head, 979-845-2581.
**Application contact:** Sharon Starr, Graduate Admissions Supervisor, 979-458-1710, *Fax:* 979-845-4727, *E-mail:* gradadv@psyc.tamu.edu. *Web site:* http://psychweb.tamu.edu/

### ■ TEXAS A&M UNIVERSITY–COMMERCE

**Graduate School, College of Education, Department of Psychology and Special Education, Commerce, TX 75429-3011**
**AWARDS** Educational psychology (PhD); psychology (MA, MS); special education (M Ed, MA, MS). Part-time programs available.
**Faculty:** 11 full-time (3 women), 2 part-time/adjunct (1 woman).
**Students:** 25 full-time (21 women), 133 part-time (108 women); includes 40 minority (31 African Americans, 8 Hispanic Americans, 1 Native American), 3 international. 30 applicants, 97% accepted. In 2001, 29 master's, 4 doctorates awarded. Terminal master's awarded for partial completion of doctoral program.
**Degree requirements:** For master's, thesis (for some programs), comprehensive exam; for doctorate, thesis/dissertation, departmental qualifying exam.
**Entrance requirements:** For master's and doctorate, GRE General Test. *Application deadline:* For fall admission, 6/1 (priority date); for spring admission, 11/1 (priority date). Applications are processed on a rolling basis. *Application fee:* $0 ($25 for international students). Electronic applications accepted.
**Expenses:** Tuition, state resident: full-time $2,221. International tuition: $7,285 full-time.
**Financial support:** In 2001–02, research assistantships (averaging $7,875 per year), teaching assistantships (averaging $7,875 per year) were awarded. Career-related internships or fieldwork, Federal Work-Study, institutionally sponsored loans, and scholarships/grants also available. Financial award application deadline: 5/1; financial award applicants required to submit FAFSA.
**Faculty research:** Human learning, study skills, multicultural bilingual, diversity and special education, educationally handicapped. *Total annual research expenditures:* $65,078.

Dr. Paul Zelhart, Head, 903-886-5589, *Fax:* 903-886-5510, *E-mail:* paul_zelhart@tamu-commerce.edu.
**Application contact:** Tammi Higginbotham, Graduate Admissions Adviser, 843-886-5167, *Fax:* 843-886-5165, *E-mail:* tammi_higginbotham@tamu-commerce.edu. *Web site:* http://www.tamu-commerce.edu/coe/psy/etsu.html

### ■ TEXAS A&M UNIVERSITY–CORPUS CHRISTI

**Graduate Programs, College of Arts and Humanities, Program in Psychology, Corpus Christi, TX 78412-5503**
**AWARDS** MA. Part-time and evening/weekend programs available.
**Degree requirements:** For master's, thesis.
**Entrance requirements:** For master's, GRE General Test. Electronic applications accepted.

### ■ TEXAS A&M UNIVERSITY–KINGSVILLE

**College of Graduate Studies, College of Arts and Sciences, Department of Psychology and Sociology, Kingsville, TX 78363**
**AWARDS** Gerontology (MS); psychology (MA, MS); sociology (MA, MS). Part-time and evening/weekend programs available.
**Faculty:** 8 full-time (2 women).
**Students:** 23 full-time (19 women), 40 part-time (33 women); includes 41 minority (3 African Americans, 1 Asian American or Pacific Islander, 37 Hispanic Americans), 2 international. Average age 35. In 2001, 18 degrees awarded.
**Degree requirements:** For master's, thesis or alternative, comprehensive exam.
**Entrance requirements:** For master's, GRE General Test, TOEFL, minimum GPA of 2.5. *Application deadline:* For fall admission, 6/1; for spring admission, 11/15. Applications are processed on a rolling basis. *Application fee:* $15 ($25 for international students).
**Expenses:** Tuition, state resident: part-time $42 per hour. Tuition, nonresident: part-time $253 per hour. Required fees: $56 per hour. One-time fee: $46 part-time. Tuition and fees vary according to program.
**Financial support:** Federal Work-Study and institutionally sponsored loans available. Support available to part-time students. Financial award application deadline: 5/15.
**Faculty research:** Hispanic female voting behavior, attitudes toward criminal justice,

*Texas A&M University–Kingsville (continued)*

immigration of aged into south Texas, folk medicine. *Total annual research expenditures:* $50,000.

Dr. Dorothy Pace, Graduate Coordinator, 361-593-2701, *Fax:* 361-593-3107.

### ■ TEXAS CHRISTIAN UNIVERSITY

**College of Science and Engineering, Department of Psychology, Fort Worth, TX 76129-0002**

**AWARDS** MA, MS, PhD. Part-time and evening/weekend programs available.

**Students:** 19 full-time (15 women), 11 part-time (7 women); includes 5 minority (1 African American, 1 Asian American or Pacific Islander, 2 Hispanic Americans, 1 Native American), 2 international. In 2001, 11 master's, 9 doctorates awarded.
**Degree requirements:** For master's, thesis, foreign language (MA); for doctorate, thesis/dissertation.
**Entrance requirements:** For master's and doctorate, GRE General Test, TOEFL. *Application deadline:* For fall admission, 3/1; for spring admission, 12/1. Applications are processed on a rolling basis. *Application fee:* $0.
**Expenses:** Tuition: Full-time $8,190; part-time $455 per credit hour. Required fees: $1,760.
**Financial support:** Fellowships, teaching assistantships, unspecified assistantships available. Financial award application deadline: 3/1.
Dr. Timothy Barth, Chairperson, 817-257-7410, *E-mail:* t.barth@tcu.edu.
**Application contact:** Dr. Bonnie Melhart, Associate Dean, College of Science and Engineering, *E-mail:* b.melhart@tcu.edu. *Web site:* http://www.graduate.tcu.edu/

### ■ TEXAS TECH UNIVERSITY

**Graduate School, College of Arts and Sciences, Department of Psychology, Lubbock, TX 79409**

**AWARDS** Clinical psychology (PhD); counseling psychology (PhD); general experimental (MA, PhD). Part-time programs available.
**Faculty:** 21 full-time (10 women).
**Students:** 72 full-time (50 women), 19 part-time (10 women); includes 19 minority (1 African American, 3 Asian Americans or Pacific Islanders, 14 Hispanic Americans, 1 Native American). Average age 28. 158 applicants, 20% accepted, 18 enrolled. In 2001, 9 master's, 11 doctorates awarded.
**Degree requirements:** For doctorate, thesis/dissertation.
**Entrance requirements:** For master's and doctorate, GRE General Test, GRE Subject Test. *Application deadline:* Applications are processed on a rolling basis.

*Application fee:* $25 ($50 for international students). Electronic applications accepted.
**Expenses:** Tuition, state resident: full-time $1,926; part-time $107 per credit hour. Tuition, nonresident: full-time $5,724; part-time $318 per credit hour. Required fees: $779; $737 per year. Tuition and fees vary according to course level, course load and program.
**Financial support:** In 2001–02, 71 students received support, including 5 research assistantships with partial tuition reimbursements available (averaging $10,220 per year), 48 teaching assistantships with partial tuition reimbursements available (averaging $10,067 per year); fellowships, career-related internships or fieldwork, Federal Work-Study, and institutionally sponsored loans also available. Support available to part-time students. Financial award application deadline: 5/1; financial award applicants required to submit FAFSA.
**Faculty research:** Failure/success in relationships, peer rejection in school, stress and coping, group processes, use of information technology in education. *Total annual research expenditures:* $95,236.
Dr. Ruth H. Maki, Chair, 806-742-3737, *Fax:* 806-742-0818.
**Application contact:** Graduate Adviser, 806-742-3737, *Fax:* 806-742-0818. *Web site:* http://www.ttu.edu/~psy/

### ■ TEXAS WOMAN'S UNIVERSITY

**Graduate Studies and Research, College of Arts and Sciences, Department of Psychology and Philosophy, Denton, TX 76201**

**AWARDS** Counseling psychology (MA, PhD); school psychology (MA, PhD).
**Faculty:** 10 full-time (6 women), 2 part-time/adjunct (0 women).
**Students:** 51 full-time (all women), 101 part-time (85 women); includes 25 minority (5 African Americans, 7 Asian Americans or Pacific Islanders, 13 Hispanic Americans). Average age 36. 121 applicants, 39% accepted, 40 enrolled. In 2001, 14 master's, 11 doctorates awarded. Terminal master's awarded for partial completion of doctoral program.
**Degree requirements:** For master's, thesis; for doctorate, variable foreign language requirement, thesis/dissertation, internship, residency. *Median time to degree:* Master's–3 years full-time, 4 years part-time; doctorate–5 years full-time, 7 years part-time.
**Entrance requirements:** For master's, GRE General Test, minimum GPA of 3.5 in psychology, 3.0 overall; for doctorate, GRE General Test, minimum graduate GPA of 3.5 in psychology, 3.0 overall, 3

letters of reference. *Application deadline:* For fall admission, 2/1. *Application fee:* $30.
**Expenses:** Tuition, state resident: part-time $90 per semester hour. Tuition, nonresident: part-time $303 per semester hour. Required fees: $24 per credit hour. $79 per semester.
**Financial support:** In 2001–02, 12 teaching assistantships (averaging $8,514 per year) were awarded; research assistantships, career-related internships or fieldwork, Federal Work-Study, and institutionally sponsored loans also available. Support available to part-time students. Financial award application deadline: 4/1.
Dr. Basil Hamilton, Chair, 940-898-2303, *Fax:* 940-898-2301, *E-mail:* bhamilton@twu.edu. *Web site:* http://www.twu.edu/as/psyphil/

### ■ TOWSON UNIVERSITY

**Graduate School, Program in School Psychology, Towson, MD 21252-0001**

**AWARDS** Clinical psychology (MA); counseling psychology (MA); experimental psychology (MA); psychology (MA); school psychology (MA, CAS). Part-time and evening/weekend programs available.

**Faculty:** 13 full-time (5 women), 2 part-time/adjunct (both women).
**Students:** 195. In 2001, 64 master's, 15 other advanced degrees awarded.
**Degree requirements:** For master's, thesis (for some programs), exams.
**Entrance requirements:** For master's, GRE General Test. *Application deadline:* For fall admission, 2/1; for spring admission, 10/1. *Application fee:* $40. Electronic applications accepted.
**Expenses:** Tuition, state resident: part-time $211 per credit. Tuition, nonresident: part-time $435 per credit. Required fees: $52 per credit.
**Financial support:** Fellowships, Federal Work-Study and unspecified assistantships available. Financial award application deadline: 4/1; financial award applicants required to submit FAFSA.
**Faculty research:** Cognitive behavior, issues affecting the aging, relaxation hypnosis and imagery, lesbian and gay issues.
Dr. Susan Bartels, Director, 410-704-3070, *Fax:* 410-704-3800, *E-mail:* sbartels@towson.edu.
**Application contact:** 410-704-2501, *Fax:* 410-704-4675, *E-mail:* grads@towson.edu.

### ■ TUFTS UNIVERSITY

**Division of Graduate and Continuing Studies and Research, Graduate School of Arts and Sciences, Department of Psychology, Medford, MA 02155**

**AWARDS** MS, PhD.

**Faculty:** 17 full-time, 13 part-time/adjunct.
**Students:** 30 (25 women); includes 4 minority (3 Asian Americans or Pacific Islanders, 1 Hispanic American) 5 international. 79 applicants, 10% accepted. In 2001, 2 master's, 4 doctorates awarded. Terminal master's awarded for partial completion of doctoral program.
**Degree requirements:** For master's, thesis; for doctorate, one foreign language, thesis/dissertation.
**Entrance requirements:** For master's and doctorate, GRE General Test, GRE Subject Test, TOEFL. *Application deadline:* For fall admission, 2/15. Applications are processed on a rolling basis. *Application fee:* $50. Electronic applications accepted.
**Expenses:** Tuition: Full-time $26,853. Full-time tuition and fees vary according to program.
**Financial support:** Research assistantships with full and partial tuition reimbursements, teaching assistantships with full and partial tuition reimbursements, Federal Work-Study, scholarships/grants, and tuition waivers (partial) available. Support available to part-time students. Financial award application deadline: 2/15; financial award applicants required to submit FAFSA.
Joseph DeBold, Acting Chair.
**Application contact:** Robert Cook, Head, 617-627-3523, *Fax:* 617-627-3181. *Web site:* http://ase.tufts.edu/psychology

## ■ TULANE UNIVERSITY

**Graduate School, Department of Psychology, New Orleans, LA 70118-5669**

**AWARDS** MS, PhD. Terminal master's awarded for partial completion of doctoral program.

**Degree requirements:** For master's, variable foreign language requirement, thesis; for doctorate, thesis/dissertation.
**Entrance requirements:** For master's, GRE General Test, TSE, minimum B average in undergraduate course work; for doctorate, GRE General Test, TSE.
**Expenses:** Tuition: Full-time $24,675. Required fees: $2,210.
**Faculty research:** Hormones and behavior, aggression, personnel selection, cognitive development, stereotyping, diabetes.

## ■ UNIFORMED SERVICES UNIVERSITY OF THE HEALTH SCIENCES

**School of Medicine, Division of Basic Medical Sciences, Department of Medical and Clinical Psychology, Bethesda, MD 20814-4799**

**AWARDS** Clinical psychology (PhD); medical psychology (PhD). Clinical psychology available to active duty military only.

**Faculty:** 11 full-time (5 women), 35 part-time/adjunct (13 women).
**Students:** 24 full-time (16 women); includes 7 minority (3 African Americans, 2 Asian Americans or Pacific Islanders, 1 Hispanic American, 1 Native American). Average age 29. 35 applicants, 17% accepted, 5 enrolled. In 2001, 4 doctorates awarded.
**Degree requirements:** For doctorate, thesis/dissertation, qualifying exam, comprehensive exam. *Median time to degree:* Doctorate–5 years full-time.
**Entrance requirements:** For doctorate, GRE General Test, TOEFL, minimum GPA of 3.5, U.S. citizenship, active military duty (clinical psychology only). *Application deadline:* For fall admission, 1/15 (priority date). Applications are processed on a rolling basis. *Application fee:* $0.
**Expenses:** Tuition waived.
**Financial support:** In 2001–02, fellowships with full tuition reimbursements (averaging $17,000 per year); tuition waivers (full) also available.
**Faculty research:** Addictive and appetitive behavior, psychopharmacology, stress and eating, obesity, health, social psychology. Dr. David S. Krantz, Chair, 301-295-3270, *Fax:* 301-295-3034, *E-mail:* dkrantz@usuhs.mil.
**Application contact:** Janet M. Anastasi, Graduate Program Coordinator, 301-295-3913, *Fax:* 301-295-6772, *E-mail:* janastasi@usuhs.mil.

## ■ UNION INSTITUTE & UNIVERSITY

**School of Professional Psychology, Cincinnati, OH 45206-1925**

**AWARDS** Clinical psychology (PhD).

**Faculty:** 56 full-time (26 women), 26 part-time/adjunct (9 women).
**Students:** 141 full-time (86 women); includes 24 minority (17 African Americans, 4 Asian Americans or Pacific Islanders, 3 Hispanic Americans), 1 international. Average age 46. In 2001, 26 degrees awarded.
**Degree requirements:** For doctorate, thesis/dissertation, internship, residency.

**Entrance requirements:** For doctorate, master's degree. *Application deadline:* Applications are processed on a rolling basis. *Application fee:* $50.
**Expenses:** Tuition: Full-time $9,392. Full-time tuition and fees vary according to degree level and program.
**Financial support:** In 2001–02, 83 students received support. Federal Work-Study, scholarships/grants, and tuition waivers available. Financial award application deadline: 5/1; financial award applicants required to submit FAFSA. Dr. Richard Green, Vice President and Dean, Graduate Studies, 513-861-6400 Ext. 1133, *E-mail:* rgreen@tui.edu.
**Application contact:** Director of Admissions, 800-486-3116, *Fax:* 513-861-0779, *E-mail:* admissions@tui.edu.

## ■ UNIVERSITY AT BUFFALO, THE STATE UNIVERSITY OF NEW YORK

**Graduate School, College of Arts and Sciences, Department of Psychology, Buffalo, NY 14260**

**AWARDS** Behavioral neuroscience (PhD); clinical psychology (PhD); cognitive psychology (PhD); general psychology (MA); social-personality (PhD). Part-time programs available.

**Faculty:** 28 full-time (13 women), 2 part-time/adjunct (1 woman).
**Students:** 88 full-time (52 women), 13 part-time (8 women); includes 11 minority (5 African Americans, 3 Asian Americans or Pacific Islanders, 3 Hispanic Americans), 12 international. Average age 25. 122 applicants, 31% accepted, 16 enrolled. In 2001, 13 master's, 6 doctorates awarded. Terminal master's awarded for partial completion of doctoral program.
**Degree requirements:** For master's, project; for doctorate, thesis/dissertation.
**Entrance requirements:** For master's and doctorate, GRE General Test, TOEFL. *Application deadline:* For fall admission, 1/5. *Application fee:* $35. Electronic applications accepted.
**Expenses:** Tuition, state resident: full-time $6,118. Tuition, nonresident: full-time $9,434.
**Financial support:** In 2001–02, 37 students received support, including 4 fellowships with full tuition reimbursements available (averaging $14,000 per year), 10 research assistantships with full tuition reimbursements available (averaging $9,512 per year), 37 teaching assistantships with full tuition reimbursements available (averaging $8,400 per year); career-related internships or fieldwork, Federal Work-Study, institutionally sponsored loans, tuition waivers (partial), and minority fellowships also available. Financial award

*University at Buffalo, The State University of New York (continued)*
application deadline: 1/15; financial award applicants required to submit FAFSA.
**Faculty research:** Neural, endocrine, and molecular bases of behavior; adult mood and anxiety disorders; relationship dysfunction; behavioral medicine; attention deficit/hyperactivity disorder. *Total annual research expenditures:* $2.1 million.
Dr. Jack A. Meacham, Chair, 716-645-3650 Ext. 203, *Fax:* 716-645-3801, *E-mail:* meacham@acsu.buffalo.edu.
**Application contact:** Michele Nowacki, Coordinator of Admissions, 716-645-3650 Ext. 209, *Fax:* 716-695-3801, *E-mail:* psych@acsu.buffalo.edu. *Web site:* http://wings.buffalo.edu/psychology/

■ **THE UNIVERSITY OF AKRON**

**Graduate School, Buchtel College of Arts and Sciences, Department of Psychology, Akron, OH 44325-0001**

**AWARDS** Applied cognitive aging (MA, PhD); counseling psychology (MA); industrial/organizational psychology (MA, PhD); psychology (MA, PhD).

**Faculty:** 19 full-time (6 women), 6 part-time/adjunct (3 women).
**Students:** 69 full-time (48 women), 47 part-time (29 women); includes 5 minority (2 African Americans, 1 Asian American or Pacific Islander, 1 Hispanic American, 1 Native American), 10 international. Average age 29. 73 applicants, 29% accepted, 15 enrolled. In 2001, 16 master's, 14 doctorates awarded. Terminal master's awarded for partial completion of doctoral program.
**Degree requirements:** For master's, thesis or specialty exam; for doctorate, one foreign language, thesis/dissertation, comprehensive exam.
**Entrance requirements:** For master's, GRE General Test, GRE Subject Test, minimum GPA of 2.75; for doctorate, GRE General Test, GRE Subject Test. *Application deadline:* For fall admission, 3/1. Applications are processed on a rolling basis. *Application fee:* $40 ($50 for international students).
**Expenses:** Tuition, state resident: full-time $6,562; part-time $219 per credit. Tuition, nonresident: full-time $9,027; part-time $383 per credit. Required fees: $272; $11 per credit. Tuition and fees vary according to course load.
**Financial support:** In 2001–02, 60 students received support, including 47 teaching assistantships with full tuition reimbursements available; fellowships with full tuition reimbursements available, research assistantships with full tuition reimbursements available, career-related internships or fieldwork, Federal Work-Study, institutionally sponsored loans, and tuition waivers (full) also available.
Financial award application deadline: 3/1.
**Faculty research:** Job evaluation, leadership, comparable worth, information processing, memory.
Dr. Linda Subich, Chair, 330-972-5496, *E-mail:* lsubich@uakron.edu. *Web site:* http://www.uakron.edu/artsci/

■ **THE UNIVERSITY OF ALABAMA**

**Graduate School, College of Arts and Sciences, Department of Psychology, Tuscaloosa, AL 35487**

**AWARDS** Clinical psychology (PhD); cognitive psychology (PhD); general psychology (MA).

**Faculty:** 23 full-time (11 women), 2 part-time/adjunct (0 women).
**Students:** 63 full-time (47 women), 11 part-time (8 women); includes 10 minority (8 African Americans, 1 Hispanic American, 1 Native American), 3 international. Average age 27. 182 applicants, 12% accepted, 17 enrolled. In 2001, 8 master's, 12 doctorates awarded.
**Degree requirements:** For doctorate, thesis/dissertation, internship (clinical psychology).
**Entrance requirements:** For doctorate, GRE General Test, minimum GPA of 3.0. *Application deadline:* For fall admission, 1/1. *Application fee:* $25. Electronic applications accepted.
**Expenses:** Tuition, state resident: full-time $3,292; part-time $183 per credit hour. Tuition, nonresident: full-time $8,912; part-time $495 per credit hour. Tuition and fees vary according to course load, campus/location and program.
**Financial support:** In 2001–02, 6 fellowships with full tuition reimbursements (averaging $10,000 per year), 16 research assistantships with full tuition reimbursements (averaging $10,400 per year), 15 teaching assistantships with full tuition reimbursements (averaging $8,433 per year) were awarded. Career-related internships or fieldwork, institutionally sponsored loans, and scholarships/grants also available. Financial award application deadline: 2/1.
**Faculty research:** Health psychology and social behavior, cognitive development/retardation, adult clinical psychology, child clinical/pediatrics, psychology and law.
Dr. Robert Lyman, Chairperson, 205-348-1913, *Fax:* 205-348-8648, *E-mail:* blyman@gp.as.ua.edu.
**Application contact:** Dr. Forrest Scogin, Director of Graduate Studies, 205-348-1924, *Fax:* 205-348-8648, *E-mail:* fscogin@gp.as.ua.edu. *Web site:* http://www.as.ua.edu/psychology/

■ **THE UNIVERSITY OF ALABAMA AT BIRMINGHAM**

**Graduate School, School of Social and Behavioral Sciences, Department of Psychology, Birmingham, AL 35294**

**AWARDS** Behavioral neuroscience (PhD); clinical psychology (PhD); developmental psychology (PhD); medical psychology (PhD); psychology (MA, PhD).

**Students:** 46 full-time (27 women), 5 part-time (3 women); includes 5 minority (4 African Americans, 1 Asian American or Pacific Islander), 1 international. 143 applicants, 17% accepted. In 2001, 6 master's, 9 doctorates awarded.
*Application deadline:* Applications are processed on a rolling basis. *Application fee:* $35 ($60 for international students). Electronic applications accepted.
**Expenses:** Tuition, state resident: full-time $3,058. Tuition, nonresident: full-time $5,746. Tuition and fees vary according to course load, degree level and program.
**Financial support:** Career-related internships or fieldwork available.
**Faculty research:** Biological basis of behavior structure, function of the nervous system.
Dr. Carl E. McFarland, Chairman, 205-934-3850, *E-mail:* cmcfarla@uab.edu. *Web site:* http://www.sbs.uab.edu/psyc.htm/

■ **THE UNIVERSITY OF ALABAMA IN HUNTSVILLE**

**School of Graduate Studies, College of Liberal Arts, Department of Psychology, Huntsville, AL 35899**

**AWARDS** MA. Part-time and evening/weekend programs available.

**Faculty:** 5 full-time (3 women).
**Students:** 6 full-time (5 women), 2 part-time (1 woman); includes 2 minority (both Asian Americans or Pacific Islanders). Average age 28. 8 applicants, 75% accepted, 3 enrolled. In 2001, 3 degrees awarded.
**Degree requirements:** For master's, one foreign language, thesis or alternative, oral and written exams, comprehensive exam, registration.
**Entrance requirements:** For master's, GRE General Test, 15 hours of course work in psychology, minimum GPA of 3.25, sample of written work. *Application deadline:* For fall admission, 7/24 (priority date); for spring admission, 11/15 (priority date). Applications are processed on a rolling basis. *Application fee:* $35.
**Expenses:** Tuition, area resident: Part-time $175 per hour. Tuition, state resident: full-time $4,408. Tuition, nonresident: full-time $9,054; part-time $361 per hour.
**Financial support:** In 2001–02, 5 students received support, including 1 research

assistantship with full and partial tuition reimbursement available (averaging $12,000 per year), 3 teaching assistantships with full and partial tuition reimbursements available (averaging $7,689 per year); fellowships with full and partial tuition reimbursements available, career-related internships or fieldwork, Federal Work-Study, institutionally sponsored loans, scholarships/grants, health care benefits, tuition waivers (full and partial), and unspecified assistantships also available. Support available to part-time students. Financial award application deadline: 4/1; financial award applicants required to submit FAFSA.

**Faculty research:** Human factors, virtual reality, social psychology, hormones and behavior, nonverbal communication. *Total annual research expenditures:* $2,497.
Dr. Sandra L. Carpenter, Chair, 256-824-6191, *Fax:* 256-824-6949, *E-mail:* carpens@email.uah.edu. *Web site:* http://www.uah.edu/colleges/liberal/psychology/

■ **UNIVERSITY OF ALASKA ANCHORAGE**

**College of Arts and Sciences, Department of Psychology, Anchorage, AK 99508-8060**

**AWARDS** Clinical psychology (MS). Part-time programs available.

**Degree requirements:** For master's, thesis.

**Entrance requirements:** For master's, GRE General Test, GRE Subject Test, interview.

**Faculty research:** Substance abuse, childhood autism, biofeedback, psychological assessment, mental health in Native Alaskans.

■ **UNIVERSITY OF ALASKA FAIRBANKS**

**Graduate School, College of Liberal Arts, Department of Psychology, Fairbanks, AK 99775-7480**

**AWARDS** Community psychology (MA). Part-time programs available.

**Faculty:** 6 full-time (2 women), 5 part-time/adjunct (4 women).

**Students:** 17 full-time (12 women), 9 part-time (6 women); includes 7 minority (all Native Americans), 1 international. Average age 37. 26 applicants, 54% accepted, 11 enrolled. In 2001, 2 degrees awarded.

**Degree requirements:** For master's, thesis or alternative, comprehensive exam.

**Entrance requirements:** For master's, GRE General Test, TOEFL. *Application deadline:* For fall admission, 4/1 (priority date); for spring admission, 11/1. *Application fee:* $35. Electronic applications accepted.

**Expenses:** Tuition, state resident: full-time $4,272; part-time $178 per credit. Tuition, nonresident: full-time $8,328; part-time $347 per credit. Required fees: $960; $60 per term. Part-time tuition and fees vary according to course load.

**Financial support:** In 2001–02, fellowships with tuition reimbursements (averaging $10,000 per year); research assistantships with tuition reimbursements, teaching assistantships with tuition reimbursements, Federal Work-Study and scholarships/grants also available.

**Faculty research:** Vocational guidance counseling, entrepreneurship training, adult and youth training, rural community psychology, models of healing.
Dr. Gerald Mohatt, Head, 907-474-7007.

■ **THE UNIVERSITY OF ARIZONA**

**Graduate College, College of Social and Behavioral Sciences, Department of Psychology, Tucson, AZ 85721**

**AWARDS** PhD, JD/PhD.

**Faculty:** 58 full-time (15 women), 9 part-time/adjunct (6 women).

**Students:** 81 full-time (47 women), 23 part-time (17 women); includes 18 minority (3 African Americans, 5 Asian Americans or Pacific Islanders, 7 Hispanic Americans, 3 Native Americans), 7 international. Average age 31. 390 applicants, 5% accepted, 18 enrolled. In 2001, 10 doctorates awarded.

**Degree requirements:** For doctorate, thesis/dissertation.

**Entrance requirements:** For doctorate, GRE General Test, GRE Subject Test, TOEFL. *Application deadline:* For fall admission, 1/1. Applications are processed on a rolling basis. *Application fee:* $45.

**Expenses:** Tuition, state resident: full-time $2,490; part-time $436 per unit. Tuition, nonresident: full-time $10,300; part-time $436 per unit. Full-time tuition and fees vary according to degree level and program.

**Financial support:** In 2001–02, 104 students received support, including 3 fellowships with partial tuition reimbursements available (averaging $1,200 per year), 25 research assistantships with partial tuition reimbursements available (averaging $11,984 per year), 38 teaching assistantships with partial tuition reimbursements available (averaging $11,984 per year); scholarships/grants, health care benefits, and unspecified assistantships also available. Financial award application deadline: 1/1.

**Faculty research:** Cognitive neuroscience, aging, law and psychology, psycholinguistics, family psychology. *Total annual research expenditures:* $3.2 million.
Dr. Lynn Nadel, Head, 520-621-7449.

**Application contact:** Dawn Baugh, Graduate Coordinator, 520-621-7456, *Fax:* 520-621-9306, *E-mail:* dawn@u.arizona.edu. *Web site:* http://www.arizona.edu/~psych/

■ **UNIVERSITY OF ARKANSAS**

**Graduate School, J. William Fulbright College of Arts and Sciences, Department of Psychology, Fayetteville, AR 72701-1201**

**AWARDS** MA, PhD.

**Students:** 30 full-time (20 women), 10 part-time (6 women); includes 4 minority (2 African Americans, 2 Hispanic Americans). 9 applicants, 100% accepted. In 2001, 7 master's, 9 doctorates awarded.

**Degree requirements:** For master's, thesis; for doctorate, variable foreign language requirement, thesis/dissertation.

**Entrance requirements:** For master's and doctorate, GRE General Test, GRE Subject Test. *Application fee:* $40 ($50 for international students).

**Expenses:** Tuition, state resident: full-time $3,553; part-time $197 per credit. Tuition, nonresident: full-time $8,411; part-time $467 per credit. Required fees: $42 per credit. Tuition and fees vary according to course load and program.

**Financial support:** In 2001–02, 10 fellowships, 12 research assistantships, 17 teaching assistantships were awarded. Career-related internships or fieldwork, Federal Work-Study, and traineeships also available. Support available to part-time students. Financial award application deadline: 4/1; financial award applicants required to submit FAFSA.
Dr. David A. Schroeder, Chair, 479-575-4256, *E-mail:* psycapp@comp.uark.edu.

■ **UNIVERSITY OF ARKANSAS AT LITTLE ROCK**

**Graduate School, College of Arts, Humanities, and Social Science, Department of Psychology, Little Rock, AR 72204-1099**

**AWARDS** Applied psychology (MAP). Part-time and evening/weekend programs available.

**Entrance requirements:** For master's, GRE General Test, minimum GPA of 2.7.

**Expenses:** Tuition, state resident: full-time $3,006; part-time $107 per credit. Tuition, nonresident: full-time $6,012; part-time $357 per credit. Required fees: $22 per credit. Tuition and fees vary according to program.

**Faculty research:** Psychological methods and theories in business industry, government, and organizations; personnel

*University of Arkansas at Little Rock (continued)*

program evaluation; training; affirmative action; organizational analysis and development.

# ■ UNIVERSITY OF BALTIMORE

**Graduate School, College of Liberal Arts, Department of Psychology, Baltimore, MD 21201-5779**

**AWARDS** Applied assessment and consulting (Psy D); applied psychology (MS); counseling (MS); industrial and organizational psychology (MS). Part-time and evening/weekend programs available.

**Faculty:** 7 full-time (5 women), 7 part-time/adjunct (2 women).
**Students:** 42 full-time (31 women), 45 part-time (34 women); includes 23 minority (14 African Americans, 5 Asian Americans or Pacific Islanders, 4 Hispanic Americans), 6 international. Average age 27. 102 applicants, 79% accepted. In 2001, 40 degrees awarded.
**Degree requirements:** For master's, thesis optional; for doctorate, thesis/dissertation.
**Entrance requirements:** For master's, GRE, minimum GPA of 3.0; for doctorate, GRE. *Application deadline:* For fall admission, 7/15; for spring admission, 12/15. Applications are processed on a rolling basis. *Application fee:* $30. Electronic applications accepted.
**Expenses:** Contact institution.
**Financial support:** In 2001–02, 5 research assistantships with full and partial tuition reimbursements were awarded; fellowships, career-related internships or fieldwork and Federal Work-Study also available. Support available to part-time students. Financial award application deadline: 4/1; financial award applicants required to submit FAFSA.
**Faculty research:** Participatory decision making, counter productive workplace behavior, organizational consulting, substance abuse treatment, cognitive functioning in head injured. *Total annual research expenditures:* $93,146.
Dr. Paul Mastrangelo, Director, Applied Psychology Program, 410-837-5352, *E-mail:* pmastrangelo@ubalt.edu.
**Application contact:** Jeffrey Zavrotny, Assistant Director of Admissions, 410-837-4777, *Fax:* 410-837-4793, *E-mail:* jzavrotny@ubalt.edu.

**Find an in-depth description at www.petersons.com/gradchannel.**

# ■ UNIVERSITY OF CALIFORNIA, BERKELEY

**Graduate Division, College of Letters and Science, Department of Psychology, Berkeley, CA 94720-1500**
**AWARDS** PhD.
**Students:** 115 full-time (74 women); includes 26 minority (2 African Americans, 15 Asian Americans or Pacific Islanders, 8 Hispanic Americans, 1 Native American), 7 international. 588 applicants, 17 enrolled. In 2001, 15 doctorates awarded.
**Degree requirements:** For doctorate, thesis/dissertation, qualifying exam.
**Entrance requirements:** For doctorate, GRE General Test, GRE Subject Test, minimum GPA of 3.0. *Application deadline:* For fall admission, 12/16. *Application fee:* $60. Electronic applications accepted.
**Expenses:** Tuition, nonresident: full-time $10,704. Required fees: $4,349.
**Financial support:** Application deadline: 12/31.
Karen K. DeValois, Chair, 510-643-8586.
**Application contact:** Jane Tupper, Student Affairs Officer, 510-643-8114, *Fax:* 510-642-5293, *E-mail:* psychapp@socrates.berkeley.edu. *Web site:* http://psychology.berkeley.edu/

# ■ UNIVERSITY OF CALIFORNIA, DAVIS

**Graduate Studies, Program in Psychology, Davis, CA 95616**
**AWARDS** PhD.
**Faculty:** 44 full-time (15 women).
**Students:** 44 full-time (31 women); includes 11 minority (8 Asian Americans or Pacific Islanders, 2 Hispanic Americans, 1 Native American), 1 international. Average age 30. 96 applicants, 30% accepted, 14 enrolled. In 2001, 5 doctorates awarded.
**Degree requirements:** For doctorate, thesis/dissertation.
**Entrance requirements:** For doctorate, GRE General Test, GRE Subject Test, minimum GPA of 3.0. *Application deadline:* For fall admission, 1/15. *Application fee:* $60. Electronic applications accepted.
**Expenses:** Tuition, state resident: full-time $4,831. Tuition, nonresident: full-time $15,725.
**Financial support:** In 2001–02, 42 students received support, including 19 fellowships with full and partial tuition reimbursements available (averaging $6,789 per year), 7 research assistantships with full and partial tuition reimbursements available (averaging $11,148 per year), 27 teaching assistantships with partial tuition reimbursements available (averaging $14,205 per year); Federal

Work-Study, institutionally sponsored loans, scholarships/grants, and tuition waivers (full and partial) also available. Financial award application deadline: 1/15; financial award applicants required to submit FAFSA.
**Faculty research:** Social personality, perception, cognition, psychobiology.
Phillip Shaver, Chair, 530-754-8304, *E-mail:* prshaver@ucdavis.edu.
**Application contact:** Bill Antaramian, Academic Counselor, 530-752-9362, *E-mail:* wrantaramian@ucdavis.edu. *Web site:* http://psychology.ucdavis.edu/default.html

# ■ UNIVERSITY OF CALIFORNIA, IRVINE

**Office of Research and Graduate Studies, School of Social Ecology, Department of Psychology and Social Behavior, Irvine, CA 92697**
**AWARDS** Health psychology (PhD); human development (PhD).
**Faculty:** 18.
**Students:** 39 full-time (30 women), 1 part-time; includes 8 minority (6 Asian Americans or Pacific Islanders, 2 Hispanic Americans). 72 applicants, 25% accepted, 7 enrolled. In 2001, 2 degrees awarded. Terminal master's awarded for partial completion of doctoral program.
**Degree requirements:** For doctorate, thesis/dissertation, research project.
**Entrance requirements:** For doctorate, GRE General Test. *Application deadline:* For fall and spring admission, 1/15 (priority date); for winter admission, 10/15 (priority date). Applications are processed on a rolling basis. *Application fee:* $60. Electronic applications accepted.
**Expenses:** Tuition, nonresident: full-time $10,704. Required fees: $8,396. Tuition and fees vary according to course load, program and student level.
**Financial support:** Fellowships, research assistantships, teaching assistantships, institutionally sponsored loans and tuition waivers (full and partial) available. Financial award application deadline: 3/2; financial award applicants required to submit FAFSA.
**Faculty research:** Psychosocial development in children, adolescents, and adults; gerontology, childhood behavior disorders, and developmental psychopathology; sex differences; attitude change; social psychology.
Chuansheng Chen, Chair, 949-824-4184.
**Application contact:** Jeanne Haynes, Academic Counselor, 949-824-5917, *Fax:* 949-824-2056, *E-mail:* jhaynes@uci.edu. *Web site:* http://www.socecol.uci.edu/~socecol/

# ■ UNIVERSITY OF CALIFORNIA, IRVINE

**Office of Research and Graduate Studies, School of Social Sciences, Department of Cognitive Science, Irvine, CA 92697**

**AWARDS** Psychology (PhD).

**Faculty:** 19.

**Students:** 27 full-time (15 women), 1 (woman) part-time; includes 5 minority (3 Asian Americans or Pacific Islanders, 2 Hispanic Americans), 5 international. 42 applicants, 50% accepted, 7 enrolled. In 2001, 3 doctorates awarded.

**Degree requirements:** For doctorate, one foreign language, thesis/dissertation.

**Entrance requirements:** For doctorate, GRE General Test. *Application deadline:* For fall and spring admission, 1/15 (priority date); for winter admission, 10/15 (priority date). Applications are processed on a rolling basis. *Application fee:* $60. Electronic applications accepted.

**Expenses:** Tuition, nonresident: full-time $10,704. Required fees: $8,396. Tuition and fees vary according to course load, program and student level.

**Financial support:** Fellowships, research assistantships, teaching assistantships, institutionally sponsored loans and tuition waivers (full and partial) available. Financial award application deadline: 3/2; financial award applicants required to submit FAFSA.

**Faculty research:** Mathematical psychology, visual and auditory perception, cognitive development, problem solving, experimental psychology.

Barbara Dosher, Chair, 949-824-7373, *Fax:* 949-824-2307.

**Application contact:** Ivonne Maldonado, Graduate Counselor, 949-824-7352, *Fax:* 949-824-3548, *E-mail:* immaldon@uci.edu. *Web site:* http://www.socsci.uci.edu/cogsci/index.html

# ■ UNIVERSITY OF CALIFORNIA, LOS ANGELES

**Graduate Division, College of Letters and Science, Department of Psychology, Los Angeles, CA 90095**

**AWARDS** MA, PhD.

**Students:** 149 full-time (95 women); includes 26 minority (6 African Americans, 14 Asian Americans or Pacific Islanders, 6 Hispanic Americans), 15 international. 465 applicants, 14% accepted, 35 enrolled. In 2001, 26 master's, 34 doctorates awarded.

**Degree requirements:** For doctorate, thesis/dissertation, oral and written qualifying exams.

**Entrance requirements:** For master's, GRE General Test, GRE Subject Test,

minimum GPA of 3.0; for doctorate, GRE General Test, GRE Subject Test, MAT, TOEFL, minimum undergraduate GPA of 3.0. *Application fee:* $60. Electronic applications accepted.

**Expenses:** Tuition, nonresident: full-time $10,244. Required fees: $3,609. Full-time tuition and fees vary according to program.

**Financial support:** In 2001–02, 113 fellowships, 105 research assistantships, 188 teaching assistantships were awarded. Federal Work-Study, institutionally sponsored loans, scholarships/grants, and tuition waivers (full and partial) also available. Financial award application deadline: 3/1.

Peter Bentler, Chair, 310-825-2617.

**Application contact:** Departmental Office, 310-825-2617, *E-mail:* gradadm@psych.ucla.edu.

# ■ UNIVERSITY OF CALIFORNIA, RIVERSIDE

**Graduate Division, Department of Psychology, Riverside, CA 92521-0102**

**AWARDS** PhD.

**Faculty:** 18 full-time (7 women), 4 part-time/adjunct (2 women).

**Students:** 51 full-time (36 women); includes 13 minority (2 African Americans, 3 Asian Americans or Pacific Islanders, 8 Hispanic Americans), 3 international. Average age 30. 94 applicants, 32% accepted, 12 enrolled. In 2001, 10 doctorates awarded.

**Degree requirements:** For doctorate, thesis/dissertation, 3 quarters of teaching experience, qualifying exams, comprehensive exam. *Median time to degree:* Doctorate–5.3 years full-time.

**Entrance requirements:** For doctorate, GRE General Test, TOEFL, minimum GPA of 3.2. *Application deadline:* For fall admission, 1/2 (priority date). Applications are processed on a rolling basis. *Application fee:* $40. Electronic applications accepted.

**Expenses:** Tuition, state resident: full-time $5,001. Tuition, nonresident: full-time $15,897.

**Financial support:** In 2001–02, 47 students received support, including 8 fellowships with tuition reimbursements available (averaging $12,500 per year), 2 research assistantships with partial tuition reimbursements available (averaging $13,000 per year), 43 teaching assistantships with partial tuition reimbursements available (averaging $13,000 per year); institutionally sponsored loans, health care benefits, and tuition waivers (full and partial) also available. Financial award application deadline: 1/2; financial award applicants required to submit FAFSA.

**Faculty research:** Neuroscience, personality and social psychology, developmental psychology, cognition, health psychology, quantitative psychology. *Total annual research expenditures:* $2.5 million.

Dr. Cart Burgess, Graduate Adviser, 909-787-2392, *Fax:* 909-787-3985, *E-mail:* curt@doumi.ucr.edu.

**Application contact:** Heather Jorgensen, Graduate Student Affairs Officer, 909-787-6306, *Fax:* 909-787-3985, *E-mail:* advisor@cassandra.ucr.edu. *Web site:* http://www.psych.ucr.edu/

# ■ UNIVERSITY OF CALIFORNIA, SAN DIEGO

**Graduate Studies and Research, Department of Psychology, La Jolla, CA 92093**

**AWARDS** PhD.

**Faculty:** 23.

**Students:** 49 (27 women). 125 applicants, 18% accepted, 14 enrolled. In 2001, 10 doctorates awarded.

**Degree requirements:** For doctorate, thesis/dissertation.

**Entrance requirements:** For doctorate, GRE General Test. *Application deadline:* For fall admission, 1/5. *Application fee:* $40. Electronic applications accepted.

**Expenses:** Tuition, nonresident: full-time $10,434. Required fees: $4,883.

James Kulik, Chair.

**Application contact:** Ruby Woods, Graduate Coordinator, 858-534-3002.

# ■ UNIVERSITY OF CALIFORNIA, SAN DIEGO

**Graduate Studies and Research, Interdisciplinary Program in Cognitive Science, La Jolla, CA 92093**

**AWARDS** Cognitive science/anthropology (PhD); cognitive science/communication (PhD); cognitive science/computer science and engineering (PhD); cognitive science/linguistics (PhD); cognitive science/neuroscience (PhD); cognitive science/philosophy (PhD); cognitive science/psychology (PhD); cognitive science/sociology (PhD). Admissions through affiliated departments.

**Faculty:** 57 full-time (12 women).

**Students:** 8 full-time (4 women). Average age 26. 2 applicants. In 2001, 2 degrees awarded.

**Degree requirements:** For doctorate, thesis/dissertation.

**Entrance requirements:** For doctorate, GRE General Test. *Application deadline:* Applications are processed on a rolling basis. *Application fee:* $0.

**Expenses:** Tuition, nonresident: full-time $10,434. Required fees: $4,883.

*University of California, San Diego (continued)*

**Faculty research:** Cognition, neurobiology of cognition, artificial intelligence, neural networks, psycholinguistics. Gary Cottrell, Director, 858-534-7141, *Fax:* 858-534-1128, *E-mail:* gcottrell@ucsd.edu.

**Application contact:** Graduate Coordinator, 858-534-7141, *Fax:* 858-534-1128, *E-mail:* gradinfo@cogsci.ucsd.edu. *Web site:* http://cogsci.ucsd.edu/CURRENT/Cog-interdisciplinary.html

### ■ UNIVERSITY OF CALIFORNIA, SANTA BARBARA

**Graduate Division, College of Letters and Sciences, Division of Mathematics, Life, and Physical Sciences, Department of Psychology, Santa Barbara, CA 93106**

AWARDS MA, PhD. Terminal master's awarded for partial completion of doctoral program.

**Degree requirements:** For master's and doctorate, thesis/dissertation.
**Entrance requirements:** For master's and doctorate, GRE General Test, TOEFL. Electronic applications accepted.
**Faculty research:** Social psychology, developmental and evolutionary psychology, neuroscience and behavior, cognitive and perceptual sciences. *Web site:* http://www.psych.ucsb.edu/

### ■ UNIVERSITY OF CALIFORNIA, SANTA CRUZ

**Division of Graduate Studies, Division of Social Sciences, Program in Psychology, Santa Cruz, CA 95064**

AWARDS Developmental psychology (PhD); experimental psychology (PhD); social psychology (PhD).

**Faculty:** 26 full-time.
**Students:** 52 full-time (39 women); includes 23 minority (1 African American, 10 Asian Americans or Pacific Islanders, 11 Hispanic Americans, 1 Native American), 4 international. 96 applicants, 21% accepted. In 2001, 4 doctorates awarded.
**Degree requirements:** For doctorate, thesis/dissertation, qualifying exam. *Median time to degree:* Doctorate–7 years full-time.
**Entrance requirements:** For doctorate, GRE General Test. *Application deadline:* For fall admission, 1/1. *Application fee:* $40.
**Expenses:** Tuition: Full-time $19,857.
**Financial support:** Fellowships, research assistantships, teaching assistantships, career-related internships or fieldwork, Federal Work-Study, and institutionally sponsored loans available. Financial award application deadline: 1/1.

**Faculty research:** Cognitive psychology, human information processing, sensation perceptions, psychobiology.
Maureen Callanan, Chairperson, 831-459-2153.
**Application contact:** Graduate Admissions, 831-459-2301. *Web site:* http://www.ucsc.edu/

### ■ UNIVERSITY OF CENTRAL ARKANSAS

**Graduate School, College of Education, Department of Counseling and Psychology, Conway, AR 72035-0001**

AWARDS Community service counseling (MS), including community service counseling, student personnel services in higher education; counseling psychology (MS); school counseling (MS), including elementary school counseling, secondary school counseling; school psychology (MS, PhD).

**Faculty:** 18.
**Students:** 52 full-time (45 women), 43 part-time (38 women); includes 16 minority (15 African Americans, 1 Native American), 2 international. In 2001, 29 degrees awarded.
**Degree requirements:** For master's, thesis optional.
**Entrance requirements:** For master's, GRE General Test, minimum GPA of 2.7; for doctorate, GRE General Test. *Application deadline:* For fall admission, 3/1 (priority date); for spring admission, 10/1 (priority date). Applications are processed on a rolling basis. *Application fee:* $25 ($40 for international students).
**Expenses:** Tuition, state resident: full-time $3,303; part-time $184 per hour. Tuition, nonresident: full-time $5,922; part-time $329 per hour. Required fees: $68; $24 per semester.
**Financial support:** In 2001–02, 94 students received support, including 23 research assistantships with partial tuition reimbursements available (averaging $6,000 per year); career-related internships or fieldwork, Federal Work-Study, scholarships/grants, and unspecified assistantships also available. Financial award application deadline: 2/15. *Total annual research expenditures:* $7,028.
Dr. David Skotko, Chairperson, 501-450-3193, *Fax:* 501-450-5424, *E-mail:* davids@mail.uca.edu.
**Application contact:** Jane Douglas, Co-Admissions Secretary, 501-450-5064, *Fax:* 501-450-5066, *E-mail:* janed@ecom.uca.edu.

### ■ UNIVERSITY OF CENTRAL FLORIDA

**College of Arts and Sciences, Department of Psychology, Orlando, FL 32816**

AWARDS Clinical psychology (MA, MS, PhD); human factors psychology (PhD); industrial/organizational psychology (MS, PhD). Part-time and evening/weekend programs available.

**Faculty:** 31 full-time (9 women), 24 part-time/adjunct (12 women).
**Students:** 112 full-time (74 women), 48 part-time (27 women); includes 36 minority (12 African Americans, 2 Asian Americans or Pacific Islanders, 22 Hispanic Americans), 2 international. Average age 29. 285 applicants, 30% accepted, 50 enrolled. In 2001, 8 master's, 5 doctorates awarded.
**Degree requirements:** For doctorate, thesis/dissertation, candidacy exam.
**Entrance requirements:** For master's, GRE General Test, TOEFL, minimum GPA of 3.0 in last 60 hours. *Application deadline:* For fall admission, 2/15. *Application fee:* $20. Electronic applications accepted.
**Expenses:** Tuition, state resident: part-time $162 per hour. Tuition, nonresident: part-time $569 per hour.
**Financial support:** In 2001–02, 55 fellowships with partial tuition reimbursements (averaging $3,618 per year), 122 research assistantships with partial tuition reimbursements (averaging $3,304 per year), 72 teaching assistantships with partial tuition reimbursements (averaging $2,638 per year) were awarded. Career-related internships or fieldwork, Federal Work-Study, institutionally sponsored loans, tuition waivers (partial), and unspecified assistantships also available. Financial award application deadline: 3/1; financial award applicants required to submit FAFSA.
**Faculty research:** Professional ethical decision making, electronic selection systems, psychometrics.
Dr. John M. McGuire, Chair, 407-823-3576, *E-mail:* jmcguire@pegasus.cc.ucf.edu.
**Application contact:** Dr. Eduardo Salas, Coordinator, 407-823-1011, *Fax:* 407-823-5862, *E-mail:* esalas@pegasus.cc.ucf.edu. *Web site:* http://www.ucf.edu/

### ■ UNIVERSITY OF CENTRAL OKLAHOMA

**College of Graduate Studies and Research, College of Education, Department of Psychology, Program in Psychology, Edmond, OK 73034-5209**

AWARDS MA.

**Degree requirements:** For master's, thesis.
**Entrance requirements:** For master's, GRE General Test.

# ■ UNIVERSITY OF CHICAGO

**Division of Social Sciences, Department of Psychology, Chicago, IL 60637-1513**

AWARDS PhD.

Students: 41.
**Degree requirements:** For doctorate, one foreign language, thesis/dissertation, exams.
**Entrance requirements:** For doctorate, GRE General Test, GRE Subject Test, TOEFL. *Application deadline:* For fall admission, 12/28. *Application fee:* $55. Electronic applications accepted.
**Expenses:** Tuition: Full-time $16,548.
**Financial support:** Fellowships, research assistantships, teaching assistantships, Federal Work-Study and institutionally sponsored loans available. Financial award application deadline: 12/28.
Prof. Howard Nusbaum, Chair, 773-702-8861.
**Application contact:** Office of the Dean of Students, 773-702-8415.

# ■ UNIVERSITY OF CINCINNATI

**Division of Research and Advanced Studies, McMicken College of Arts and Sciences, Department of Psychology, Cincinnati, OH 45221**

AWARDS Clinical psychology (PhD); experimental psychology (PhD).

Faculty: 25 full-time.
Students: 69 full-time, 20 part-time; includes 15 minority (12 African Americans, 2 Asian Americans or Pacific Islanders, 1 Hispanic American), 3 international. 210 applicants, 13 enrolled. In 2001, 18 degrees awarded.
**Degree requirements:** For doctorate, thesis/dissertation.
**Entrance requirements:** For doctorate, GRE General Test, GRE Subject Test. *Application deadline:* For fall admission, 1/7. *Application fee:* $35. Electronic applications accepted.
**Expenses:** Tuition, state resident: part-time $2,698 per quarter. Tuition, nonresident: part-time $4,977 per quarter.
**Financial support:** Fellowships with full tuition reimbursements, traineeships, tuition waivers (partial), and unspecified assistantships available. Financial award application deadline: 5/1. *Total annual research expenditures:* $374,651.
Dr. Kevin M. Corcoran, Head, 513-556-5569, *Fax:* 513-556-1904.

**Application contact:** Dr. Paula K. Shear, Graduate Program Director, 513-556-5577, *Fax:* 513-556-1904, *E-mail:* paula.shear@uc.edu. *Web site:* http://asweb.artsci.uc.edu/psychology

# ■ UNIVERSITY OF COLORADO AT BOULDER

**Graduate School, College of Arts and Sciences, Department of Psychology, Boulder, CO 80309**

AWARDS MA, PhD.

Faculty: 46 full-time (13 women).
Students: 63 full-time (41 women), 20 part-time (11 women); includes 9 minority (1 African American, 3 Asian Americans or Pacific Islanders, 5 Hispanic Americans), 7 international. Average age 29. 29 applicants, 52% accepted. In 2001, 14 master's, 14 doctorates awarded.
**Degree requirements:** For master's, comprehensive exam; for doctorate, thesis/dissertation.
**Entrance requirements:** For master's, GRE General Test, minimum undergraduate GPA of 2.75; for doctorate, GRE General Test. *Application deadline:* For fall admission, 1/2. *Application fee:* $50 ($60 for international students).
**Expenses:** Tuition, state resident: full-time $3,474. Tuition, nonresident: full-time $16,624.
**Financial support:** In 2001–02, 14 fellowships (averaging $2,232 per year), 20 research assistantships (averaging $14,721 per year), 36 teaching assistantships (averaging $17,539 per year) were awarded. Tuition waivers (full) also available. Financial award application deadline: 2/1.
**Faculty research:** Clinical, behavioral genetics, behavioral neuroscience, cognitive, social psychology. *Total annual research expenditures:* $13.2 million.
Jerry Rudy, Chair, 303-492-8662, *Fax:* 303-492-2967, *E-mail:* jrudy@clipr.colorado.edu.
**Application contact:** Mary Ann Tucker, Graduate Secretary, 303-492-1553, *Fax:* 303-492-2967. *Web site:* http://psych-www.colorado.edu/

# ■ UNIVERSITY OF COLORADO AT COLORADO SPRINGS

**Graduate School, College of Letters, Arts and Sciences, Department of Psychology, Colorado Springs, CO 80933-7150**

AWARDS MA. Part-time programs available.
Faculty: 12 full-time (5 women).
Students: 34 full-time (28 women), 5 part-time (all women); includes 5 minority (1 African American, 1 Asian American or

Pacific Islander, 2 Hispanic Americans, 1 Native American), 1 international. Average age 28. 78 applicants, 44% accepted. In 2001, 16 degrees awarded.
**Degree requirements:** For master's, thesis.
**Entrance requirements:** For master's, GRE, BA in psychology or equivalent background. *Application deadline:* For fall admission, 2/1. Applications are processed on a rolling basis.
**Expenses:** Tuition, state resident: full-time $2,900; part-time $174 per credit. Tuition, nonresident: full-time $9,961; part-time $591 per credit. Required fees: $14 per credit. $141 per semester. Tuition and fees vary according to course load, program and student level.
**Financial support:** Research assistantships, teaching assistantships, career-related internships or fieldwork and Federal Work-Study available. Support available to part-time students. Financial award applicants required to submit FAFSA.
**Faculty research:** Aging, social psychology, learning and memory, personality disorders, psychology and law.
Dr. Robert L. Durham, Chair, 719-262-4181.
**Application contact:** Dr. Hasker Davis, Graduate Student Adviser, 719-262-4148, *Fax:* 719-262-4166, *E-mail:* hdavis@uccs.edu. *Web site:* http://www.uccs.edu/psychology/

# ■ UNIVERSITY OF COLORADO AT DENVER

**Graduate School, College of Liberal Arts and Sciences, Program in Psychology, Denver, CO 80217-3364**

AWARDS MA. Part-time and evening/weekend programs available.

Faculty: 14 full-time (5 women).
Students: 26 full-time (16 women), 11 part-time (8 women). Average age 26. 35 applicants, 71% accepted, 19 enrolled. In 2001, 14 degrees awarded.
**Degree requirements:** For master's, thesis or alternative.
**Entrance requirements:** For master's, GRE General Test, GRE Subject Test, minimum GPA of 2.75. *Application deadline:* For fall admission, 3/1; for spring admission, 10/1. Applications are processed on a rolling basis. *Application fee:* $50 ($60 for international students). Electronic applications accepted.
**Expenses:** Tuition, state resident: full-time $3,284; part-time $198 per credit hour. Tuition, nonresident: full-time $13,380; part-time $802 per credit hour. Required fees: $444; $222 per semester.
**Financial support:** Research assistantships, teaching assistantships, career-related internships or fieldwork and Federal

*University of Colorado at Denver (continued)*

Work-Study available. Financial award application deadline: 3/1; financial award applicants required to submit FAFSA. *Total annual research expenditures:* $125,822. Elliott Hirshman, Chair, 303-556-8567, *Fax:* 303-556-3520, *E-mail:* elliot.hirshman@cudenver.edu. **Application contact:** Linda Kucia, Program Assistant, 303-556-8565, *Fax:* 303-556-3520, *E-mail:* linda.kucia@cudenver.edu. *Web site:* http://www.cudenver.edu/public/psych/graduate.html

■ **UNIVERSITY OF CONNECTICUT**

**Graduate School, College of Liberal Arts and Sciences, Field of Psychology, Storrs, CT 06269**

**AWARDS** Behavioral neuroscience (PhD); biopsychology (PhD); clinical psychology (PhD); cognition/instruction psychology (PhD); developmental psychology (PhD); ecological psychology (PhD); general experimental psychology (PhD); industrial and organizational psychology (PhD); language psychology (PhD); social psychology (PhD).

**Faculty:** 41 full-time (11 women), 2 part-time/adjunct (both women).
**Students:** 134 full-time (83 women), 17 part-time (9 women); includes 13 minority (9 African Americans, 1 Asian American or Pacific Islander, 3 Hispanic Americans), 17 international. Average age 28. 378 applicants, 14% accepted, 25 enrolled. In 2001, 18 degrees awarded.
**Degree requirements:** For doctorate, thesis/dissertation, internship, comprehensive exam, registration.
**Entrance requirements:** For doctorate, GRE General Test, GRE Subject Test, letters of recommendation. *Application deadline:* For fall admission, 12/31. *Application fee:* $40 ($45 for international students).
**Financial support:** In 2001–02, 45 fellowships (averaging $4,000 per year), 16 research assistantships with full tuition reimbursements (averaging $16,000 per year), 83 teaching assistantships with full tuition reimbursements (averaging $16,000 per year) were awarded. Career-related internships or fieldwork, Federal Work-Study, scholarships/grants, health care benefits, and unspecified assistantships also available. Financial award application deadline: 12/31.
**Faculty research:** Behavioral neuroscience; physiology/chemistry of memory; sensation, motor control/motivation; cognitive, social, personality and language development; infancy/person perceptions and intergroup relations. *Total annual research expenditures:* $8 million.

Charles A. Lowe, Head, *Fax:* 860-486-2760, *E-mail:* charles.lowe@uconn.edu. **Application contact:** Gina Stuart, Graduate Admissions, 860-486-3528, *Fax:* 860-486-2760, *E-mail:* futuregr@psych.psy.uconn.edu. *Web site:* http://psych.uconn.edu/

■ **UNIVERSITY OF DALLAS**

**Braniff Graduate School of Liberal Arts, Program in Psychology, Irving, TX 75062-4736**

**AWARDS** M Psych, MA.
**Faculty:** 4 full-time (1 woman).
**Students:** 5 full-time (4 women), 2 part-time (both women); includes 2 minority (both Hispanic Americans). 7 applicants, 100% accepted, 7 enrolled.
**Degree requirements:** For master's, one foreign language, thesis (for some programs), comprehensive exam.
**Entrance requirements:** For master's, GRE General Test. *Application deadline:* For fall admission, 2/15 (priority date); for spring admission, 11/15. *Application fee:* $40.
**Expenses:** Tuition: Full-time $3,807; part-time $423 per credit.
**Financial support:** Scholarships/grants and tuition waivers available.
Dr. Scott Churchill, Chairman, 972-721-5348, *Fax:* 972-721-4034, *E-mail:* cscott@udallas.edu. **Application contact:** Graduate Coordinator, 972-721-5106, *Fax:* 972-721-5280, *E-mail:* graduate@acad.udallas.edu.

■ **UNIVERSITY OF DAYTON**

**Graduate School, College of Arts and Sciences, Department of Psychology, Dayton, OH 45469-1300**

**AWARDS** Clinical psychology (MA); general psychology (MA); human factors and research (MA). Part-time and evening/weekend programs available.
**Faculty:** 18 full-time (4 women), 2 part-time/adjunct (1 woman).
**Students:** 29 full-time (26 women), 14 part-time (6 women); includes 3 minority (all African Americans), 2 international. 62 applicants, 61% accepted, 17 enrolled. In 2001, 9 degrees awarded.
**Degree requirements:** For master's, thesis.
**Entrance requirements:** For master's, GRE General Test, GRE Subject Test. *Application deadline:* For fall admission, 3/1 (priority date). *Application fee:* $30. Electronic applications accepted.
**Expenses:** Tuition: Full-time $5,436; part-time $453 per credit hour. Required fees: $50; $25 per term.
**Financial support:** In 2001–02, 23 students received support, including 11

research assistantships with full tuition reimbursements available; fellowships, teaching assistantships with full tuition reimbursements available, career-related internships or fieldwork, Federal Work-Study, and traineeships also available. Financial award application deadline: 3/1.
**Faculty research:** Cognitive processes, television and children, interpersonal process, modes and mechanisms of therapy.
Dr. David W. Biers, Chairman, 937-229-2713, *E-mail:* biers@udayton.edu.

■ **UNIVERSITY OF DELAWARE**

**College of Arts and Science, Department of Psychology, Newark, DE 19716**

**AWARDS** Behavioral neuroscience (PhD); clinical psychology (PhD); cognitive psychology (PhD); social psychology (PhD).
**Faculty:** 25 full-time (6 women), 3 part-time/adjunct (0 women).
**Students:** 41 full-time (24 women); includes 3 minority (1 African American, 2 Hispanic Americans). Average age 28. 129 applicants, 13% accepted, 8 enrolled. In 2001, 7 degrees awarded.
**Degree requirements:** For doctorate, thesis/dissertation.
**Entrance requirements:** For doctorate, GRE General Test. *Application deadline:* For fall admission, 1/7 (priority date). *Application fee:* $50. Electronic applications accepted.
**Expenses:** Tuition, state resident: full-time $4,770; part-time $265 per credit. Tuition, nonresident: full-time $13,860; part-time $770 per credit. Required fees: $414.
**Financial support:** In 2001–02, 41 students received support, including 5 fellowships with full tuition reimbursements available (averaging $11,637 per year), 8 research assistantships with full tuition reimbursements available (averaging $11,637 per year), 15 teaching assistantships with full tuition reimbursements available (averaging $11,637 per year); career-related internships or fieldwork, Federal Work-Study, institutionally sponsored loans, scholarships/grants, tuition waivers (full and partial), and minority fellowships also available. Financial award application deadline: 1/7.
**Faculty research:** Emotion development, neural and cognitive aspects of memory, neural control of feeding, intergroup relations, social cognition and communication. *Total annual research expenditures:* $1 million.
Dr. Brian P. Ackerman, Chairperson, 302-831-2271, *Fax:* 302-831-3645, *E-mail:* bpa@udel.edu.

**Application contact:** Information Contact, 302-831-2271, *Fax:* 302-831-3645, *E-mail:* bpa@udel.edu. *Web site:* http://www.udel.edu/catalog/current/as/psyc/grad.html

### ■ UNIVERSITY OF DENVER

**Graduate School of Professional Psychology, Denver, CO 80208**

AWARDS Clinical psychology (Psy D).

**Faculty:** 6 full-time (3 women), 9 part-time/adjunct (4 women).

**Students:** 138 (114 women); includes 24 minority (3 African Americans, 10 Asian Americans or Pacific Islanders, 10 Hispanic Americans, 1 Native American) 1 international. 320 applicants, 31% accepted. In 2001, 31 degrees awarded.

**Degree requirements:** For doctorate, paper, internship.

**Entrance requirements:** For doctorate, GRE General Test, GRE Subject Test, TOEFL. *Application deadline:* For fall admission, 1/6. *Application fee:* $45.

**Expenses:** Tuition: Full-time $21,456.

**Financial support:** In 2001–02, 61 students received support, including 5 fellowships with full and partial tuition reimbursements available, 1 research assistantship with full and partial tuition reimbursement available (averaging $2,322 per year), 5 teaching assistantships with full and partial tuition reimbursements available (averaging $6,957 per year); career-related internships or fieldwork, Federal Work-Study, institutionally sponsored loans, scholarships/grants, and clinical assistantships also available. Support available to part-time students. Financial award application deadline: 3/1; financial award applicants required to submit FAFSA.

Dr. Peter Buirski, Dean, 303-871-2382.

**Application contact:** Samara Ferber, Admissions Coordinator, 303-871-3873, *Fax:* 303-871-4220. *Web site:* http://www.du.edu/gspp/

### ■ UNIVERSITY OF DENVER

**Graduate Studies, Faculty of Arts and Humanities/Social Sciences, Department of Psychology, Denver, CO 80208**

AWARDS PhD, JD/MA, JD/PhD.

**Faculty:** 17 full-time (7 women), 2 part-time/adjunct (1 woman).

**Students:** 37 (30 women); includes 4 minority (2 Asian Americans or Pacific Islanders, 2 Hispanic Americans). 232 applicants, 5% accepted. In 2001, 9 doctorates awarded.

**Degree requirements:** For doctorate, thesis/dissertation.

**Entrance requirements:** For doctorate, GRE General Test, TOEFL. *Application deadline:* For fall admission, 1/1. *Application fee:* $45.

**Expenses:** Tuition: Full-time $21,456.

**Financial support:** In 2001–02, 6 fellowships with full and partial tuition reimbursements, 7 research assistantships with full and partial tuition reimbursements (averaging $9,153 per year), 25 teaching assistantships with full and partial tuition reimbursements (averaging $9,207 per year) were awarded. Career-related internships or fieldwork, Federal Work-Study, institutionally sponsored loans, and scholarships/grants also available. Support available to part-time students. Financial award application deadline: 1/1; financial award applicants required to submit FAFSA.

**Faculty research:** Developmental neuropsychology, self-esteem and peer relationships, child abuse and neglect, marital and family interactions, adolescent peer and romantic relationships. *Total annual research expenditures:* $2.3 million.

Dr. Ralph J. Roberts, Chairperson, 303-871-3792.

**Application contact:** Paula Houghtaling, Graduate Secretary, 303-871-3803. *Web site:* http://www.du.edu/psychology/

### ■ UNIVERSITY OF DETROIT MERCY

**College of Liberal Arts and Education, Department of Psychology, Detroit, MI 48219-0900**

AWARDS Clinical psychology (MA, PhD); industrial/organizational psychology (MA); school psychology (Spec). Evening/weekend programs available.

**Faculty:** 14 full-time (10 women).

**Students:** 46 full-time (35 women), 84 part-time (66 women); includes 22 minority (15 African Americans, 4 Asian Americans or Pacific Islanders, 2 Hispanic Americans, 1 Native American), 6 international. Average age 32. In 2001, 22 master's, 7 doctorates, 10 other advanced degrees awarded.

**Degree requirements:** For doctorate, departmental qualifying exam.

*Application deadline:* For fall admission, 8/1 (priority date). Applications are processed on a rolling basis. *Application fee:* $30 ($50 for international students).

**Expenses:** Tuition: Full-time $10,620; part-time $590 per credit hour. Required fees: $400. Tuition and fees vary according to program.

**Financial support:** Fellowships, career-related internships or fieldwork available.

**Faculty research:** Gerontology.

Dr. Christine Panyard, Chairperson, 313-993-6123, *Fax:* 313-993-6397, *E-mail:* panyarcm@udmercy.edu.

### ■ UNIVERSITY OF FLORIDA

**Graduate School, College of Liberal Arts and Sciences, Department of Psychology, Gainesville, FL 32611**

AWARDS MA, MAT, MS, MST, PhD, JD/PhD. Terminal master's awarded for partial completion of doctoral program.

**Degree requirements:** For master's, thesis or alternative; for doctorate, thesis/dissertation.

**Entrance requirements:** For master's and doctorate, GRE General Test, minimum GPA of 3.0. Electronic applications accepted.

**Expenses:** Tuition, state resident: part-time $164 per hour. Tuition, nonresident: part-time $571 per hour. Tuition and fees vary according to course level and program.

**Faculty research:** Experimental analysis of behavior, psychobiology, cognition and sensory processes, counseling psychology, social psychology, developmental psychology. *Web site:* http://www.psych.ufl.edu/

### ■ UNIVERSITY OF GEORGIA

**Graduate School, College of Arts and Sciences, Department of Psychology, Athens, GA 30602**

AWARDS MS, PhD.

**Faculty:** 40 full-time (15 women).

**Students:** 92 full-time (62 women), 39 part-time (28 women); includes 12 minority (6 African Americans, 4 Asian Americans or Pacific Islanders, 2 Hispanic Americans), 5 international. 382 applicants, 17% accepted. In 2001, 16 master's, 20 doctorates awarded.

**Degree requirements:** For master's, thesis; for doctorate, one foreign language, thesis/dissertation.

**Entrance requirements:** For master's and doctorate, GRE General Test. *Application deadline:* For fall admission, 7/1 (priority date); for spring admission, 11/15. *Application fee:* $30. Electronic applications accepted.

**Expenses:** Tuition, state resident: full-time $2,376; part-time $132 per credit hour. Tuition, nonresident: full-time $9,504; part-time $528 per credit hour. Required fees: $236 per semester.

**Financial support:** Fellowships, research assistantships, teaching assistantships, unspecified assistantships available.

Dr. Garnett Stokes, Head, 706-542-8888, *Fax:* 706-542-3275, *E-mail:* gstokes@uga.edu.

*University of Georgia (continued)*
**Application contact:** Dr. Irwin S. Bernstein, Graduate Coordinator, 706-542-3103, *Fax:* 706-542-3275, *E-mail:* isbern@uga.edu. *Web site:* http://teach.psy.uga.edu/

■ **UNIVERSITY OF HARTFORD**

**College of Arts and Sciences, Department of Psychology, West Hartford, CT 06117-1599**

**AWARDS** Clinical practices (MA); general experimental psychology (MA); school psychology (MS). Part-time programs available.

**Faculty:** 8 full-time (3 women), 9 part-time/adjunct (2 women).
**Students:** 49 full-time (38 women), 25 part-time (21 women), 4 international. Average age 28. 95 applicants, 72% accepted. In 2001, 55 degrees awarded.
**Degree requirements:** For master's, thesis (for some programs), comprehensive exam.
**Entrance requirements:** For master's, GRE General Test, GRE Subject Test, TOEFL, minimum GPA of 3.0. *Application deadline:* For fall admission, 2/15 (priority date). Applications are processed on a rolling basis. *Application fee:* $40 ($55 for international students). Electronic applications accepted.
**Expenses:** Contact institution.
**Financial support:** Fellowships, research assistantships, teaching assistantships, career-related internships or fieldwork and Federal Work-Study available. Support available to part-time students. Financial award application deadline: 6/1; financial award applicants required to submit FAFSA.
Dr. Jack Powell, Chair, 860-768-4720, *E-mail:* jpowell@mail.hartford.edu.
**Application contact:** Kellie Richard Westenfeld, Assistant Director of Graduate Admissions, 860-768-4371, *Fax:* 860-768-5160, *E-mail:* westenfel@mail.hartford.edu. *Web site:* http://www.hartford.edu/

■ **UNIVERSITY OF HAWAII AT MANOA**

**Graduate Division, College of Arts and Sciences, College of Social Sciences, Department of Psychology, Honolulu, HI 96822**

**AWARDS** Clinical psychology (PhD); community and culture (MA, PhD); psychology (MA, PhD).
**Faculty:** 25 full-time (5 women), 15 part-time/adjunct (5 women).
**Students:** 73 full-time (51 women), 28 part-time (19 women); includes 27 Asian Americans or Pacific Islanders, 3 Hispanic Americans. 57 applicants, 68% accepted,

23 enrolled. In 2001, 17 master's, 7 doctorates awarded. Terminal master's awarded for partial completion of doctoral program.
**Degree requirements:** For master's, thesis/dissertation; for doctorate, thesis/dissertation, comprehensive exam. *Median time to degree:* Master's–2 years full-time.
**Entrance requirements:** For master's and doctorate, GRE General Test, GRE Subject Test. *Application deadline:* For fall admission, 1/1. *Application fee:* $25 ($50 for international students).
**Expenses:** Tuition, state resident: full-time $2,160; part-time $1,980 per year. Tuition, nonresident: full-time $5,190; part-time $4,829 per year.
**Financial support:** In 2001–02, 31 research assistantships (averaging $15,881 per year), 7 teaching assistantships (averaging $13,163 per year) were awarded. Career-related internships or fieldwork, institutionally sponsored loans, and tuition waivers (full and partial) also available. Financial award application deadline: 1/1.
**Faculty research:** Cross-cultural psychology, health psychology, marine mammals, child/adult psychopathology.
Dr. Karl A. Minke, Chairperson, 808-956-8414, *Fax:* 808-956-4700, *E-mail:* minke@hawaii.edu.
**Application contact:** Dr. Elaine Heiby, Graduate Field Chairperson, 808-956-8414, *Fax:* 808-956-4700, *E-mail:* heiby@hawaii.edu.

■ **UNIVERSITY OF HOUSTON**

**College of Liberal Arts and Social Sciences, Department of Psychology, Houston, TX 77204**

**AWARDS** Clinical psychology (PhD); industrial/organizational psychology (PhD); social psychology (PhD).
**Faculty:** 22 full-time (9 women), 8 part-time/adjunct (4 women).
**Students:** 82 full-time (57 women), 20 part-time (16 women); includes 12 minority (2 African Americans, 3 Asian Americans or Pacific Islanders, 7 Hispanic Americans), 2 international. Average age 29. 280 applicants, 8% accepted. In 2001, 14 doctorates awarded.
**Degree requirements:** For doctorate, thesis/dissertation.
**Entrance requirements:** For doctorate, GRE General Test, minimum GPA of 3.0. *Application deadline:* For fall admission, 1/1. *Application fee:* $40 ($75 for international students).
**Expenses:** Tuition, state resident: full-time $1,512. Tuition, nonresident: full-time $5,310. Required fees: $1,308. Tuition and fees vary according to program.
**Financial support:** In 2001–02, research assistantships with partial tuition

reimbursements (averaging $12,300 per year), teaching assistantships with partial tuition reimbursements (averaging $10,800 per year) were awarded. Career-related internships or fieldwork, Federal Work-Study, institutionally sponsored loans, and teaching fellowships also available.
**Faculty research:** Health psychology, depression, child/family process, organizational effectiveness, close relationships. *Total annual research expenditures:* $4.5 million.
Dr. John P. Vincent, Chairman, 713-743-8503, *Fax:* 713-743-8588, *E-mail:* jvincent@uh.edu.
**Application contact:** Sherry A. Berun, Coordinator—Academic Affairs, 713-743-8508, *Fax:* 713-743-8588, *E-mail:* sherryr@uh.edu. *Web site:* http://firenza.uh.edu/

■ **UNIVERSITY OF HOUSTON–CLEAR LAKE**

**School of Human Sciences and Humanities, Programs in Human Sciences, Houston, TX 77058-1098**

**AWARDS** Behavioral sciences (MA), including behavioral sciences-general, behavioral sciences-psychology, behavioral sciences-sociology; clinical psychology (MA); cross-cultural studies (MA); family therapy (MA); fitness and human performance (MA); school psychology (MA); studies of the future (MS). Part-time and evening/weekend programs available.

**Students:** 562; includes 183 minority (95 African Americans, 16 Asian Americans or Pacific Islanders, 70 Hispanic Americans, 2 Native Americans), 16 international. Average age 34. In 2001, 152 degrees awarded.
**Degree requirements:** For master's, thesis or alternative.
**Entrance requirements:** For master's, GRE General Test. *Application deadline:* For fall admission, 8/1; for spring admission, 12/1. Applications are processed on a rolling basis. *Application fee:* $30 ($70 for international students). Electronic applications accepted.
**Expenses:** Tuition, state resident: full-time $2,016; part-time $84 per credit hour. Tuition, nonresident: full-time $6,072; part-time $253 per credit hour. Tuition and fees vary according to course load.
**Financial support:** Research assistantships, teaching assistantships, career-related internships or fieldwork, Federal Work-Study, institutionally sponsored loans, and scholarships/grants available. Support available to part-time students. Financial award application deadline: 5/1.
Dr. Hilary Karp, Division Co-Chair, 281-283-3383, *E-mail:* karp@cl.uh.edu.

# UNIVERSITY OF HOUSTON–VICTORIA

**School of Arts and Sciences, Program in Psychology, Victoria, TX 77901-4450**

AWARDS MA. Part-time and evening/weekend programs available. Postbaccalaureate distance learning degree programs offered (no on-campus study).

**Faculty:** 4 full-time (2 women).
**Students:** 15 full-time (12 women), 18 part-time (16 women); includes 9 minority (2 African Americans, 7 Hispanic Americans). Average age 38. In 2001, 7 degrees awarded.
**Degree requirements:** For master's, project or thesis.
**Entrance requirements:** For master's, GRE General Test. *Application deadline:* Applications are processed on a rolling basis. *Application fee:* $0.
**Expenses:** Tuition, state resident: full-time $1,368; part-time $76 per semester. Tuition, nonresident: full-time $4,554. Tuition and fees vary according to course load.
**Financial support:** In 2001–02, research assistantships with partial tuition reimbursements (averaging $2,000 per year), teaching assistantships with partial tuition reimbursements (averaging $2,000 per year) were awarded. Career-related internships or fieldwork and Federal Work-Study also available. Support available to part-time students. Financial award application deadline: 4/15.
Dr. Rick Harrington, Head, 361-570-4205, *Fax:* 361-570-4229, *E-mail:* harringtonr@cobalt.vic.uh.edu.

# UNIVERSITY OF IDAHO

**College of Graduate Studies, College of Letters and Science, Department of Psychology, Moscow, ID 83844-2282**

AWARDS MS.

**Faculty:** 9 full-time (1 woman), 2 part-time/adjunct (1 woman).
**Students:** 10 full-time (5 women), 17 part-time (10 women); includes 1 minority (Asian American or Pacific Islander), 1 international. 32 applicants, 56% accepted. In 2001, 10 degrees awarded.
**Entrance requirements:** For master's, GRE, minimum GPA of 2.8. *Application deadline:* For fall admission, 8/1; for spring admission, 12/15. *Application fee:* $35 ($45 for international students).
**Expenses:** Tuition, state resident: full-time $1,613. Tuition, nonresident: full-time $3,000.
**Financial support:** In 2001–02, 2 research assistantships, 8 teaching assistantships were awarded. Fellowships available. Financial award application deadline: 2/15.

**Faculty research:** Clinical, experimental, and cognitive psychology.
Dr. Richard Reardon, Chair, 208-885-6324.

**Find an in-depth description at www.petersons.com/gradchannel.**

# UNIVERSITY OF ILLINOIS AT CHICAGO

**Graduate College, College of Liberal Arts and Sciences, Department of Psychology, Chicago, IL 60607-7128**

AWARDS PhD.

**Faculty:** 29 full-time (6 women).
**Students:** 94 full-time (67 women), 13 part-time (11 women); includes 18 minority (9 African Americans, 2 Asian Americans or Pacific Islanders, 7 Hispanic Americans), 4 international. Average age 29. 269 applicants, 10% accepted, 26 enrolled. In 2001, 13 doctorates awarded.
**Degree requirements:** For doctorate, thesis/dissertation, departmental qualifying exam.
**Entrance requirements:** For doctorate, GRE General Test, TOEFL, minimum GPA of 3.75 on a 5.0 scale. *Application deadline:* For fall admission, 1/15 (priority date). *Application fee:* $40 ($50 for international students). Electronic applications accepted.
**Expenses:** Tuition, state resident: full-time $3,060. Tuition, nonresident: full-time $6,688.
**Financial support:** In 2001–02, 86 students received support; fellowships with full tuition reimbursements available, research assistantships with full tuition reimbursements available, teaching assistantships with full tuition reimbursements available, career-related internships or fieldwork, Federal Work-Study, institutionally sponsored loans, traineeships, and tuition waivers (full) available. Financial award application deadline: 1/15; financial award applicants required to submit FAFSA.
Leonard Newman, Chairperson, 312-996-1304, *E-mail:* lnewman@uic.edu.
**Application contact:** Admissions Committee, 312-996-2434.

# UNIVERSITY OF ILLINOIS AT URBANA–CHAMPAIGN

**Graduate College, College of Liberal Arts and Sciences, Department of Psychology, Champaign, IL 61820**

AWARDS Applied measurement (MS); biological psychology (AM, PhD); clinical psychology (AM, PhD); cognitive psychology (AM, PhD); developmental psychology (AM, PhD); engineering psychology (MS); personnel psychology (MS); quantitative psychology (AM, PhD); social-personality-organizational

(AM, PhD); visual cognition and human performance (AM, PhD).

**Faculty:** 41 full-time (14 women), 11 part-time/adjunct (3 women).
**Students:** 156 full-time (90 women); includes 23 minority (6 African Americans, 12 Asian Americans or Pacific Islanders, 5 Hispanic Americans), 42 international. 461 applicants, 17% accepted, 27 enrolled. In 2001, 1 master's, 25 doctorates awarded.
**Degree requirements:** For doctorate, thesis/dissertation.
**Entrance requirements:** For master's, GRE General Test, GRE Subject Test (recommended), minimum GPA of 3.0; for doctorate, GRE General Test, GRE Subject Test (recommended). *Application deadline:* For fall admission, 1/1. *Application fee:* $40 ($50 for international students).
**Expenses:** Tuition, state resident: part-time $3,227 per degree program. Tuition, nonresident: part-time $7,169 per degree program. Tuition and fees vary according to program.
**Financial support:** In 2001–02, 31 fellowships with full tuition reimbursements (averaging $15,000 per year), 21 research assistantships with full tuition reimbursements (averaging $13,585 per year), 73 teaching assistantships with full tuition reimbursements (averaging $13,585 per year) were awarded. Career-related internships or fieldwork, traineeships, and tuition waivers (full) also available. Financial award application deadline: 1/1. *Total annual research expenditures:* $4.6 million.
Dr. Edward J. Shoben, Head.
**Application contact:** Cheryl Berger, Assistant Head for Graduate Affairs, 217-333-3429, *Fax:* 217-244-5876, *E-mail:* gradstdy@s.psych.uiuc.edu. *Web site:* http://www.psych.uiuc.edu/

# UNIVERSITY OF INDIANAPOLIS

**Graduate School, School of Psychological Sciences, Indianapolis, IN 46227-3697**

AWARDS MA, Psy D.

**Expenses:** Tuition: Part-time $260 per credit hour. Tuition and fees vary according to degree level.
Dr. John McIlvried, Dean, 317-788-3247, *Fax:* 317-788-3480, *E-mail:* jmcilvried@uindy.edu. *Web site:* http://www.uindy.edu/

# THE UNIVERSITY OF IOWA

**Graduate College, College of Liberal Arts and Sciences, Department of Psychology, Iowa City, IA 52242-1316**

AWARDS Neural and behavioral sciences (PhD); psychology (MA, PhD).
**Faculty:** 29 full-time, 5 part-time/adjunct.
**Students:** 34 full-time (20 women), 39 part-time (26 women); includes 6 minority

*The University of Iowa (continued)*
(1 African American, 5 Asian Americans or Pacific Islanders), 8 international. 201 applicants, 16% accepted, 11 enrolled. In 2001, 4 master's, 9 doctorates awarded.
**Degree requirements:** For master's, exam, thesis optional; for doctorate, thesis/dissertation, comprehensive exam.
**Entrance requirements:** For master's, GRE General Test, TOEFL; for doctorate, GRE General Test, TOEFL, minimum GPA of 3.0. *Application deadline:* For fall admission, 1/1 (priority date). *Application fee:* $30 ($50 for international students). Electronic applications accepted.
**Expenses:** Tuition, state resident: full-time $3,702; part-time $206 per semester hour. Tuition, nonresident: full-time $11,924; part-time $206 per semester hour. Required fees: $101 per semester. Tuition and fees vary according to course load and program.
**Financial support:** In 2001–02, 2 fellowships, 34 research assistantships, 28 teaching assistantships were awarded. Financial award applicants required to submit FAFSA.
Gregg C. Oden, Chair, 319-335-2406, *Fax:* 319-335-0191.

### ■ UNIVERSITY OF JUDAISM

**Graduate School, Fingerhut School of Education, Program in Behavioral Psychology, Bel Air, CA 90077-1599**
AWARDS MA, MS.
**Entrance requirements:** For master's, GRE General Test or GMAT, TOEFL, interview, minimum GPA of 3.25.

### ■ UNIVERSITY OF KANSAS

**Graduate School, College of Liberal Arts and Sciences, Department of Psychology, Lawrence, KS 66045**
AWARDS Clinical child psychology (MA, PhD); psychology (MA, PhD).
**Faculty:** 34.
**Students:** 92 full-time (60 women), 45 part-time (33 women); includes 19 minority (2 African Americans, 8 Asian Americans or Pacific Islanders, 8 Hispanic Americans, 1 Native American), 9 international. Average age 29. 263 applicants, 8% accepted, 21 enrolled. In 2001, 19 master's, 13 doctorates awarded.
**Degree requirements:** For master's, thesis/dissertation; for doctorate, thesis/dissertation, comprehensive exam.
**Entrance requirements:** For doctorate, GRE General Test, GRE Subject Test, TOEFL, minimum GPA of 3.0. *Application deadline:* For fall admission, 1/15. *Application fee:* $35.
**Expenses:** Tuition, state resident: full-time $2,722; part-time $113 per credit. Tuition,

nonresident: full-time $8,586; part-time $358 per credit. Required fees: $551; $46 per credit. Tuition and fees vary according to campus/location, program and reciprocity agreements.
**Financial support:** In 2001–02, 13 research assistantships with partial tuition reimbursements (averaging $10,476 per year), 53 teaching assistantships with full and partial tuition reimbursements (averaging $9,894 per year) were awarded. Fellowships, career-related internships or fieldwork also available. Financial award applicants required to submit FAFSA.
**Faculty research:** Health psychology, cognitive psychology, methodology and statistics.
Greg Simpson, Chair, 785-864-4131, *Fax:* 785-864-5696.
**Application contact:** Graduate Admissions Officer, 785-864-4195, *Fax:* 785-864-5696, *E-mail:* psycgrad@ku.edu. *Web site:* http://www.psych.ku.edu/

### ■ UNIVERSITY OF KENTUCKY

**Graduate School, Graduate School Programs from the College of Arts and Sciences, Program in Psychology, Lexington, KY 40506-0032**
AWARDS MA, PhD.
**Faculty:** 43 full-time (12 women).
**Students:** 75 full-time (47 women), 2 part-time (1 woman); includes 12 minority (7 African Americans, 2 Asian Americans or Pacific Islanders, 2 Hispanic Americans, 1 Native American), 2 international. 159 applicants, 14% accepted. In 2001, 6 master's, 11 doctorates awarded.
**Degree requirements:** For master's and doctorate, thesis/dissertation, comprehensive exam.
**Entrance requirements:** For master's, GRE General Test, minimum undergraduate GPA of 2.5; for doctorate, GRE General Test, minimum graduate GPA of 3.0. *Application deadline:* For fall admission, 2/1. Applications are processed on a rolling basis. *Application fee:* $30 ($35 for international students).
**Expenses:** Tuition, state resident: full-time $4,075; part-time $213 per credit hour. Tuition, nonresident: full-time $11,295; part-time $614 per credit hour.
**Financial support:** In 2001–02, 15 fellowships, 28 research assistantships, 20 teaching assistantships were awarded. Career-related internships or fieldwork, Federal Work-Study, institutionally sponsored loans, and unspecified assistantships also available. Support available to part-time students.
**Faculty research:** Psychopharmacology and teratology, behavioral neuroscience, social psychology, cognitive psychology,

development and developmental psychobiology.
Dr. Michael Bardo, Director of Graduate Studies, 859-257-6456, *Fax:* 859-323-1979, *E-mail:* mbardo@pop.uky.edu.
**Application contact:** Dr. Jeannine Blackwell, Associate Dean, 606-323-4613, *Fax:* 606-323-1928.

### ■ UNIVERSITY OF LA VERNE

**College of Arts and Sciences, Department of Psychology, La Verne, CA 91750-4443**
AWARDS Counseling (MS), including counseling in higher education, general counseling, gerontology, marriage, family and child counseling; psychology (Psy D), including clinical-community psychology. Part-time programs available.
**Faculty:** 9 full-time (5 women), 15 part-time/adjunct (9 women).
**Students:** 56 full-time (49 women), 52 part-time (41 women); includes 53 minority (10 African Americans, 8 Asian Americans or Pacific Islanders, 34 Hispanic Americans, 1 Native American), 1 international. Average age 34. In 2001, 16 degrees awarded.
**Degree requirements:** For master's, competency exam, thesis optional; for doctorate, thesis/dissertation, clinical internship, competency exams, practicum, personal psychotherapy.
**Entrance requirements:** For master's, undergraduate GPA of 3.0; for doctorate, minimum GPA of 3.25 undergraduate, 3.5 graduate. *Application deadline:* Applications are processed on a rolling basis.
**Expenses:** Tuition: Full-time $4,410; part-time $245 per unit. Required fees: $60. Tuition and fees vary according to course load, degree level, campus/location and program.
**Financial support:** In 2001–02, 74 students received support, including 1 fellowship (averaging $4,980 per year), 16 research assistantships (averaging $1,894 per year); career-related internships or fieldwork, institutionally sponsored loans, and scholarships/grants also available. Financial award application deadline: 3/2.
**Faculty research:** Developmental therapy and counseling.
Dr. Roger Russell, Chairperson, 909-593-3511 Ext. 4182, *E-mail:* russellr@ulv.edu.
**Application contact:** Jo Nell Baker, Director, Graduate Admissions and Academic Services, 909-593-3511 Ext. 4504, *Fax:* 909-392-2761, *E-mail:* bakerj@ulv.edu. *Web site:* http://www.ulv.edu/

■ **UNIVERSITY OF LOUISIANA AT LAFAYETTE**

Graduate School, College of Liberal Arts, Department of Psychology, Program in Psychology, Lafayette, LA 70504

AWARDS MS.

Faculty: 9 full-time (4 women).
Students: 13 full-time (8 women), 9 part-time (6 women); includes 2 minority (1 African American, 1 Hispanic American). 27 applicants, 67% accepted, 10 enrolled.
Expenses: Tuition, state resident: full-time $2,317; part-time $79 per credit. Tuition, nonresident: full-time $8,882; part-time $369 per credit. International tuition: $9,018 full-time.
Application contact: Dr. Claude G. Cech, Graduate Coordinator, 337-482-6585, *E-mail:* cech@louisiana.edu.

■ **UNIVERSITY OF LOUISIANA AT MONROE**

Graduate Studies and Research, College of Education and Human Development, Department of Psychology, Monroe, LA 71209-0001

AWARDS Psychology (MS); school psychology (SSP). Part-time and evening/weekend programs available.

Degree requirements: For master's and SSP, thesis.
Entrance requirements: For master's, minimum GPA of 2.5 or GRE General Test; for SSP, GRE General Test, minimum GPA of 2.5.

■ **UNIVERSITY OF LOUISVILLE**

Graduate School, College of Arts and Sciences, Department of Psychology, Louisville, KY 40292-0001

AWARDS Clinical psychology (PhD); experimental psychology (PhD); psychology (MA).

Students: 68 full-time (43 women), 5 part-time (all women); includes 5 minority (3 African Americans, 1 Asian American or Pacific Islander, 1 Hispanic American), 10 international. Average age 31. In 2001, 14 master's, 14 doctorates awarded. Terminal master's awarded for partial completion of doctoral program.
Degree requirements: For master's and doctorate, thesis/dissertation.
Entrance requirements: For master's and doctorate, GRE General Test. *Application deadline:* Applications are processed on a rolling basis. *Application fee:* $25.
Expenses: Tuition, state resident: full-time $4,134. Tuition, nonresident: full-time $11,486.
Financial support: Career-related internships or fieldwork available.

Dr. Dennis L. Molfese, Chair, 502-852-6775, *Fax:* 502-852-8904.

■ **UNIVERSITY OF MAINE**

Graduate School, College of Liberal Arts and Sciences, Department of Psychology, Orono, ME 04469

AWARDS Clinical psychology (PhD); developmental psychology (MA); experimental psychology (MA, PhD); social psychology (MA).

Faculty: 21.
Students: 22 full-time (17 women), 13 part-time (11 women); includes 3 minority (all Native Americans), 2 international. 100 applicants, 14% accepted, 6 enrolled. In 2001, 4 degrees awarded.
Degree requirements: For master's and doctorate, thesis/dissertation.
Entrance requirements: For master's and doctorate, GRE General Test, GRE Subject Test, TOEFL. *Application deadline:* For fall admission, 2/1 (priority date). Applications are processed on a rolling basis. *Application fee:* $50. Electronic applications accepted.
Expenses: Tuition, state resident: full-time $3,780; part-time $210 per credit hour. Tuition, nonresident: full-time $10,782; part-time $599 per credit hour. Required fees: $9.50 per credit hour. $32 per semester. Tuition and fees vary according to reciprocity agreements.
Financial support: In 2001–02, 3 research assistantships with tuition reimbursements (averaging $9,010 per year), 21 teaching assistantships with tuition reimbursements (averaging $9,010 per year) were awarded. Fellowships with tuition reimbursements, Federal Work-Study, institutionally sponsored loans, and tuition waivers (full and partial) also available. Financial award application deadline: 3/1.
Faculty research: Social development, hypertension and aging, attitude change, self-confidence in achievement situations, health psychology.
Dr. Joel Gold, Chair, 207-581-2030, *Fax:* 207-581-6128.
Application contact: Scott G. Delcourt, Director of the Graduate School, 207-581-3218, *Fax:* 207-581-3232, *E-mail:* graduate@maine.edu. *Web site:* http://www.umaine.edu/graduate/

■ **UNIVERSITY OF MARY HARDIN-BAYLOR**

School of Sciences and Humanities, Department of Psychology and Counseling, Program in Psychology, Belton, TX 76513

AWARDS MA. Part-time and evening/weekend programs available.

Faculty: 4 full-time (3 women), 3 part-time/adjunct (1 woman).
Students: 14 full-time (12 women), 12 part-time (10 women); includes 9 minority (4 African Americans, 4 Hispanic Americans, 1 Native American). 10 applicants, 100% accepted, 10 enrolled. In 2001, 10 degrees awarded.
Entrance requirements: For master's, GRE General Test, minimum GPA of 3.0 in last 60 hours or 2.75 overall. *Application deadline:* For fall admission, 6/1 (priority date); for spring admission, 11/1. Applications are processed on a rolling basis. *Application fee:* $35 ($135 for international students).
Expenses: Tuition: Full-time $5,940; part-time $330 per credit hour. Required fees: $554; $28 per credit hour. One-time fee: $40 part-time.
Financial support: In 2001–02, 1 student received support. Career-related internships or fieldwork and scholarship for some active duty military personnel available. Support available to part-time students.
Application contact: Rhonda Neuses, Secretary, 254-295-4555.

■ **UNIVERSITY OF MARYLAND, BALTIMORE COUNTY**

Graduate School, Department of Psychology, Baltimore, MD 21250-5398

AWARDS Applied developmental psychology (PhD); neurosciences and cognitive sciences (MS, PhD); psychology/human services (MA, PhD), including applied behavioral analysis (MA), psychology/human services (PhD).

Degree requirements: For doctorate, thesis/dissertation.
Entrance requirements: For doctorate, GRE General Test, GRE Subject Test, TOEFL.
Faculty research: Health services, interviewing and speech pattern analysis.

■ **UNIVERSITY OF MARYLAND, COLLEGE PARK**

Graduate Studies and Research, College of Behavioral and Social Sciences, Department of Psychology, College Park, MD 20742

AWARDS Clinical psychology (PhD); developmental psychology (PhD); experimental psychology (PhD); industrial psychology (MA, MS, PhD); social psychology (PhD).

Faculty: 52 full-time (17 women), 10 part-time/adjunct (5 women).
Students: 80 full-time (50 women), 22 part-time (15 women); includes 26 minority (14 African Americans, 8 Asian Americans or Pacific Islanders, 3 Hispanic Americans, 1 Native American), 11

*University of Maryland, College Park* *(continued)*
international. 432 applicants, 10% accepted, 18 enrolled. In 2001, 8 master's, 21 doctorates awarded.
**Degree requirements:** For master's, thesis; for doctorate, variable foreign language requirement, thesis/dissertation, comprehensive exam.
**Entrance requirements:** For master's, GRE General Test, GRE Subject Test, minimum GPA of 3.5, research and/or work experience; for doctorate, GRE General Test, GRE Subject Test. *Application deadline:* For fall admission, 12/15. Applications are processed on a rolling basis. *Application fee:* $50 ($70 for international students). Electronic applications accepted.
**Expenses:** Tuition, state resident: part-time $289 per credit hour. Tuition, nonresident: part-time $448 per credit hour. One-time fee: $436 part-time. Full-time tuition and fees vary according to course load, campus/location and program.
**Financial support:** In 2001–02, 15 fellowships with full tuition reimbursements (averaging $11,508 per year), 87 teaching assistantships with tuition reimbursements (averaging $12,153 per year) were awarded. Career-related internships or fieldwork, Federal Work-Study, and scholarships/grants also available. Support available to part-time students. Financial award applicants required to submit FAFSA.
**Faculty research:** Counseling and social psychology.
Dr. William Hall, Chairman, 301-405-5862, *Fax:* 301-314-9566.
**Application contact:** Trudy Lindsey, Director, Graduate Admissions and Records, 301-405-6991, *Fax:* 301-314-9305, *E-mail:* grschool@deans.umd.edu.

■ **UNIVERSITY OF MASSACHUSETTS AMHERST**
**Graduate School, College of Social and Behavioral Sciences, Department of Psychology, Amherst, MA 01003**
**AWARDS** Clinical psychology (MS, PhD).
**Faculty:** 50 full-time (21 women).
**Students:** 68 full-time (45 women), 10 part-time (8 women); includes 13 minority (4 African Americans, 3 Asian Americans or Pacific Islanders, 6 Hispanic Americans), 8 international. Average age 28. 409 applicants, 9% accepted. In 2001, 14 master's, 10 doctorates awarded. Terminal master's awarded for partial completion of doctoral program.
**Degree requirements:** For master's and doctorate, thesis/dissertation.
**Entrance requirements:** For master's and doctorate, GRE General Test. *Application*

*deadline:* For fall admission, 1/2 (priority date). Applications are processed on a rolling basis. *Application fee:* $40 ($50 for international students).
**Expenses:** Tuition, state resident: full-time $1,980; part-time $110 per credit. Tuition, nonresident: full-time $7,456; part-time $414 per credit. Required fees: $4,112. One-time fee: $115 full-time.
**Financial support:** In 2001–02, 23 fellowships with full tuition reimbursements (averaging $8,012 per year), 38 research assistantships with full tuition reimbursements (averaging $10,467 per year), 40 teaching assistantships with full tuition reimbursements (averaging $7,995 per year) were awarded. Career-related internships or fieldwork, Federal Work-Study, scholarships/grants, traineeships, and unspecified assistantships also available. Support available to part-time students. Financial award application deadline: 1/2.
Dr. Melinda Novak, Chair, 413-545-2387, *Fax:* 413-545-0996, *E-mail:* mnovak@psych.umass.edu.
**Application contact:** Graduate Secretary, 413-545-2503.

■ **UNIVERSITY OF MASSACHUSETTS DARTMOUTH**
**Graduate School, College of Arts and Sciences, Department of Psychology, North Dartmouth, MA 02747-2300**
**AWARDS** Clinical psychology (MA); general psychology (MA). Part-time programs available.
**Faculty:** 15 full-time (5 women), 9 part-time/adjunct (2 women).
**Students:** 20 full-time (14 women), 24 part-time (23 women); includes 2 minority (1 Asian American or Pacific Islander, 1 Hispanic American), 1 international. Average age 28. 47 applicants, 55% accepted, 16 enrolled. In 2001, 10 degrees awarded.
**Degree requirements:** For master's, thesis (for some programs).
**Entrance requirements:** For master's, GRE General Test, TOEFL, minimum GPA of 2.75. *Application deadline:* For fall admission, 3/31. *Application fee:* $25 ($45 for international students).
**Expenses:** Tuition, state resident: full-time $2,071; part-time $86 per credit. Tuition, nonresident: full-time $8,099; part-time $337 per credit. Part-time tuition and fees vary according to course load and reciprocity agreements.
**Financial support:** In 2001–02, 2 research assistantships with full tuition reimbursements (averaging $4,500 per year), 6 teaching assistantships with full tuition reimbursements (averaging $4,083 per year) were awarded. Career-related internships or fieldwork, Federal Work-Study,

and unspecified assistantships also available. Support available to part-time students. Financial award application deadline: 3/1; financial award applicants required to submit FAFSA.
**Faculty research:** Nutritional health info for college women, role of gender identity, self-efficacy and academic competence on development of career aspirations. *Total annual research expenditures:* $4,000.
Dr. Paul Donnelly, Director, Clinical Psychology, 508-999-8334, *E-mail:* pdonnelly@umassd.edu.
**Application contact:** Maria E. Lomba, Graduate Admissions Officer, 508-999-8604, *Fax:* 508-999-8183, *E-mail:* graduate@umassd.edu.

■ **UNIVERSITY OF MASSACHUSETTS LOWELL**
**Graduate School, College of Arts and Sciences, Department of Psychology, Lowell, MA 01854-2881**
**AWARDS** Community and social psychology (MA). Part-time programs available.
**Degree requirements:** For master's, thesis optional.
**Entrance requirements:** For master's, GRE General Test or MAT. Electronic applications accepted.
**Faculty research:** Domestic violence, youth sports, teen pregnancy, substance abuse, family and work roles.

■ **THE UNIVERSITY OF MEMPHIS**
**Graduate School, College of Arts and Sciences, Department of Psychology, Memphis, TN 38152**
**AWARDS** Clinical psychology (PhD); experimental psychology (PhD); psychology (MS); school psychology (MA, PhD). Part-time programs available.
**Faculty:** 30 full-time (2 women), 6 part-time/adjunct (3 women).
**Students:** 81 full-time (56 women), 19 part-time (11 women); includes 9 minority (8 African Americans, 1 Native American), 7 international. Average age 28. 188 applicants, 26% accepted. In 2001, 20 master's, 12 doctorates awarded. Terminal master's awarded for partial completion of doctoral program.
**Degree requirements:** For master's, thesis (for some programs), oral exam (MS), comprehensive exam; for doctorate, thesis/dissertation, internship.
**Entrance requirements:** For master's, GRE General Test, 18 undergraduate hours in psychology, minimum GPA of 2.5; for doctorate, GRE General Test, GRE Subject Test. *Application deadline:* For fall admission, 2/1. Applications are processed on a rolling basis. *Application fee:* $35 ($60 for international students).

**Expenses:** Tuition, state resident: full-time $2,026. Tuition, nonresident: full-time $4,528.

**Financial support:** In 2001–02, 2 fellowships with full tuition reimbursements (averaging $13,333 per year), 116 research assistantships with full tuition reimbursements (averaging $5,000 per year), 2 teaching assistantships with full tuition reimbursements (averaging $1,500 per year) were awarded.

**Faculty research:** Psychotherapy and psychopathology, behavioral medicine and community psychology, child and family studies, cognitive and social processes, neuropsychology and behavioral neuroscience. *Total annual research expenditures:* $2.5 million.

Dr. Andrew Meyers, Chairman and Coordinator of Graduate Studies, 901-678-2145.

### ■ UNIVERSITY OF MIAMI

**Graduate School, College of Arts and Sciences, Department of Psychology, Coral Gables, FL 33124**

**AWARDS** Applied developmental psychology (PhD); behavioral neuroscience (PhD); clinical psychology (PhD); health psychology (PhD); psychology (MS).

**Faculty:** 39 full-time (18 women).

**Students:** 70 full-time (51 women); includes 23 minority (6 African Americans, 4 Asian Americans or Pacific Islanders, 13 Hispanic Americans). Average age 25. 200 applicants, 14% accepted, 18 enrolled. In 2001, 12 degrees awarded.

**Degree requirements:** For doctorate, thesis/dissertation, comprehensive exam. *Median time to degree:* Doctorate–5 years full-time.

**Entrance requirements:** For doctorate, GRE General Test, TOEFL, minimum GPA of 3.5. *Application deadline:* For fall admission, 12/1. *Application fee:* $50. Electronic applications accepted.

**Expenses:** Tuition: Part-time $960 per credit hour. Required fees: $85 per semester. Tuition and fees vary according to program.

**Financial support:** In 2001–02, 7 fellowships with full tuition reimbursements (averaging $17,000 per year), 43 research assistantships with full tuition reimbursements (averaging $16,500 per year), 19 teaching assistantships with full tuition reimbursements (averaging $12,300 per year) were awarded. Career-related internships or fieldwork, institutionally sponsored loans, scholarships/grants, and traineeships also available. Financial award applicants required to submit FAFSA.

**Faculty research:** Depression, social and emotional development, stress and coping, AIDS and psychoneuroimmunology,

children's peer relations. *Total annual research expenditures:* $10 million.

Dr. A. Rodney Wellens, Chairman, 305-284-2814, *Fax:* 305-284-3402.

**Application contact:** Patricia L. Perreira, Staff Associate, 305-284-2814, *Fax:* 305-284-3402, *E-mail:* inquire@ mail.psy.miami.edu. *Web site:* http://www.psy.miami.edu/

### ■ UNIVERSITY OF MICHIGAN

**Horace H. Rackham School of Graduate Studies, College of Literature, Science, and the Arts, Department of Psychology, Ann Arbor, MI 48109**

**AWARDS** Biopsychology (PhD); clinical psychology (PhD); cognition and perception (PhD); developmental psychology (PhD); organizational psychology (PhD); personality psychology (PhD); social psychology (PhD).

**Faculty:** 68 full-time, 29 part-time/adjunct.

**Students:** 166 full-time (122 women); includes 57 minority (27 African Americans, 23 Asian Americans or Pacific Islanders, 14 Hispanic Americans, 3 Native Americans), 22 international. Average age 24. 555 applicants, 8% accepted, 27 enrolled. In 2001, 25 degrees awarded.

**Degree requirements:** For doctorate, oral defense of dissertation, preliminary exam.

**Entrance requirements:** For doctorate, GRE General Test, GRE Subject Test, TOEFL. *Application deadline:* For fall admission, 12/15. *Application fee:* $55. Electronic applications accepted.

**Financial support:** Fellowships with full tuition reimbursements, research assistantships with full tuition reimbursements, teaching assistantships with full tuition reimbursements, career-related internships or fieldwork available. Financial award application deadline: 3/15.

Richard Gonzalez, Chair, 734-764-7429.

**Application contact:** 734-764-6316, *Fax:* 734-764-3520. *Web site:* http://www.lsa.umich.edu/psych/

### ■ UNIVERSITY OF MICHIGAN

**Horace H. Rackham School of Graduate Studies, College of Literature, Science, and the Arts, Women's Studies Program, Ann Arbor, MI 48109**

**AWARDS** English and women's studies (PhD); history and women's studies (PhD); psychology and women's studies (PhD); women's studies (Certificate).

**Faculty:** 60 part-time/adjunct (all women).

**Students:** 31 full-time (all women); includes 6 minority (1 African American, 2 Asian Americans or Pacific Islanders, 2 Hispanic Americans, 1 Native American),

2 international. Average age 24. 91 applicants, 8% accepted. In 2001, 1 doctorate, 8 other advanced degrees awarded.

**Degree requirements:** For doctorate, variable foreign language requirement, thesis/dissertation.

**Entrance requirements:** For doctorate, GRE General Test, previous undergraduate course work in women's studies. *Application deadline:* For fall admission, 12/15. *Application fee:* $55.

**Financial support:** In 2001–02, 3 fellowships with full tuition reimbursements (averaging $14,500 per year), 25 teaching assistantships with full and partial tuition reimbursements (averaging $12,984 per year) were awarded.

**Faculty research:** Women and psychology, work and gender, gender issues, English literature, women and science.

Pamela Trotman Reid, Director, 734-763-2047, *Fax:* 734-647-4943, *E-mail:* pamreid@umich.edu.

**Application contact:** Bonnie Miller, Graduate Secretary, 734-763-2047, *Fax:* 734-647-4943, *E-mail:* bonniemj@ umich.edu. *Web site:* http://www.lsa.umich.edu/women/

### ■ UNIVERSITY OF MICHIGAN

**Horace H. Rackham School of Graduate Studies, Combined Program in Education and Psychology, Ann Arbor, MI 48109**

**AWARDS** PhD.

**Faculty:** 16 part-time/adjunct (7 women).

**Students:** 27 full-time (21 women); includes 9 minority (5 African Americans, 2 Asian Americans or Pacific Islanders, 2 Hispanic Americans), 1 international. Average age 29. 76 applicants, 12% accepted, 5 enrolled. In 2001, 1 degree awarded.

**Degree requirements:** For doctorate, thesis/dissertation, oral defense of dissertation, preliminary exam, independent research project. *Median time to degree:* Doctorate–5 years full-time.

**Entrance requirements:** For doctorate, GRE General Test, GRE Subject Test (recommended). *Application deadline:* For fall admission, 1/1. *Application fee:* $55.

**Financial support:** In 2001–02, 17 fellowships with full tuition reimbursements (averaging $18,775 per year), 5 research assistantships with full tuition reimbursements (averaging $14,520 per year), 10 teaching assistantships with full tuition reimbursements (averaging $22,881 per year) were awarded. Institutionally sponsored loans, scholarships/grants, traineeships, and unspecified assistantships also available. Financial award application deadline: 3/15.

*University of Michigan (continued)*
**Faculty research:** Classroom research, instructional psychology.
Paul R. Pintrich, Director, 734-647-0626, *Fax:* 734-615-2164, *E-mail:* pintrich@umich.edu.
**Application contact:** Janie Knieper, Administrative Associate, 734-647-0626, *Fax:* 734-615-2164, *E-mail:* cpep@umich.edu. *Web site:* http://www.soe.umich.edu/programs/comb.html

■ **UNIVERSITY OF MINNESOTA, TWIN CITIES CAMPUS**

**Graduate School, College of Liberal Arts, Department of Psychology, Minneapolis, MN 55455-0213**

**AWARDS** Biological psychopathology (PhD); clinical psychology (PhD); cognitive and biological psychology (PhD); counseling psychology (PhD); differential psychology/behavior genetics (PhD); industrial/organizational psychology (PhD); personality research (PhD); psychometric methods (MA, PhD); school psychology (PhD); social psychology (PhD).

**Faculty:** 37 full-time (8 women), 34 part-time/adjunct (11 women).
**Students:** 141 full-time (82 women); includes 21 minority (5 African Americans, 12 Asian Americans or Pacific Islanders, 4 Hispanic Americans), 12 international. 336 applicants, 15% accepted, 24 enrolled. In 2001, 2 master's, 13 doctorates awarded.
**Degree requirements:** For doctorate, thesis/dissertation, comprehensive exam.
**Entrance requirements:** For master's and doctorate, GRE General Test, GRE Subject Test (recommended), TOEFL, 12 credits of upper-level psychology courses, including a course in statistics or psychological measurement. *Application deadline:* For fall admission, 1/5. *Application fee:* $55 ($75 for international students).
**Expenses:** Tuition, state resident: full-time $2,932; part-time $489 per credit. Tuition, nonresident: full-time $5,758; part-time $960 per credit. Part-time tuition and fees vary according to course load, program and reciprocity agreements.
**Financial support:** In 2001–02, fellowships with full tuition reimbursements (averaging $13,500 per year), research assistantships with full tuition reimbursements (averaging $10,234 per year), teaching assistantships with full tuition reimbursements (averaging $10,234 per year) were awarded. Career-related internships or fieldwork, traineeships, and tuition waivers (partial) also available. Financial award application deadline: 12/1. *Total annual research expenditures:* $3.9 million.
John Campbell, Chairman, 612-625-7873, *Fax:* 612-626-2079.

**Application contact:** Coordinator, 612-624-4181, *Fax:* 612-626-2079, *E-mail:* psyapply@tc.umn.edu. *Web site:* http://www.psych.umn.edu/

■ **UNIVERSITY OF MISSISSIPPI**

**Graduate School, College of Liberal Arts, Department of Psychology, Oxford, University, MS 38677**

**AWARDS** Clinical psychology (PhD); experimental psychology (PhD); psychology (MA).

**Faculty:** 13.
**Students:** 62 full-time (40 women), 12 part-time (4 women); includes 10 minority (6 African Americans, 3 Asian Americans or Pacific Islanders, 1 Hispanic American), 1 international. In 2001, 5 master's, 5 doctorates awarded.
**Degree requirements:** For master's and doctorate, thesis/dissertation.
**Entrance requirements:** For master's, GRE General Test, TOEFL, minimum GPA of 3.0; for doctorate, GRE General Test, TOEFL. *Application deadline:* For fall admission, 8/1. Applications are processed on a rolling basis. *Application fee:* $0 ($25 for international students).
**Expenses:** Tuition, state resident: full-time $3,626; part-time $202 per hour. Tuition, nonresident: full-time $8,172; part-time $454 per hour.
**Financial support:** Application deadline: 3/1.
Dr. David S. Hargrove, Chairman, 662-915-7383, *Fax:* 662-915-5398, *E-mail:* psych@olemiss.edu.

■ **UNIVERSITY OF MISSOURI–COLUMBIA**

**Graduate School, College of Arts and Sciences, Department of Psychological Sciences, Columbia, MO 65211**

**AWARDS** MA, MS, PhD.

**Faculty:** 36 full-time (14 women), 1 (woman) part-time/adjunct.
**Students:** 45 full-time (35 women), 16 part-time (13 women); includes 11 minority (4 African Americans, 2 Asian Americans or Pacific Islanders, 5 Hispanic Americans), 4 international. 36 applicants, 36% accepted. In 2001, 8 master's, 11 doctorates awarded. Terminal master's awarded for partial completion of doctoral program.
**Degree requirements:** For doctorate, thesis/dissertation.
**Entrance requirements:** For master's and doctorate, GRE General Test, minimum GPA of 3.0. *Application deadline:* For fall admission, 2/1 (priority date). Applications are processed on a rolling basis. *Application fee:* $25 ($50 for international students).

**Expenses:** Tuition, state resident: part-time $179 per credit hour. Tuition, nonresident: part-time $539 per credit hour. Required fees: $122 per semester. Tuition and fees vary according to program.
**Financial support:** Research assistantships, teaching assistantships, career-related internships or fieldwork and institutionally sponsored loans available.
Dr. Alan J. Strathman, Director of Graduate Studies, 573-882-1966, *E-mail:* strathmana@missouri.edu. *Web site:* http://web.missouri.edu/~psywww/graduateprograms.htm

■ **UNIVERSITY OF MISSOURI–KANSAS CITY**

**College of Arts and Sciences, Department of Psychology, Doctoral Program in Psychology, Kansas City, MO 64110-2499**

**AWARDS** Community psychology (PhD).

**Students:** Average age 34. 24 applicants, 17% accepted.
**Degree requirements:** For doctorate, thesis/dissertation, comprehensive exam.
**Entrance requirements:** For doctorate, GRE, minimum GPA of 3.25. *Application deadline:* For fall admission, 2/1. *Application fee:* $25.
**Expenses:** Tuition, state resident: part-time $233 per credit hour. Tuition, nonresident: part-time $623 per credit hour. Tuition and fees vary according to course load.
**Financial support:** In 2001–02, 5 fellowships with partial tuition reimbursements, 6 research assistantships, 12 teaching assistantships with partial tuition reimbursements (averaging $9,000 per year) were awarded. Career-related internships or fieldwork, Federal Work-Study, institutionally sponsored loans, scholarships/grants, and tuition waivers (partial) also available.
**Faculty research:** Prevention and health promotion, community organizing and development, program evaluation, child maltreatment, children and youth issues, health psychology.
Dr. Leah K. Gensheimer, Director, 816-235-1067, *Fax:* 816-235-1062.
**Application contact:** 816-235-1111.

■ **UNIVERSITY OF MISSOURI–KANSAS CITY**

**College of Arts and Sciences, Department of Psychology, Master's Program in Psychology, Kansas City, MO 64110-2499**

**AWARDS** MA.

**Students:** Average age 32. 16 applicants, 38% accepted. In 2001, 2 degrees awarded.

**Degree requirements:** For master's, thesis.

**Entrance requirements:** For master's, minimum GPA of 3.5. *Application deadline:* For fall admission, 3/15; for spring admission, 10/1. *Application fee:* $25.

**Expenses:** Tuition, state resident: part-time $233 per credit hour. Tuition, nonresident: part-time $623 per credit hour. Tuition and fees vary according to course load.

**Financial support:** In 2001–02, 4 students received support, including 1 fellowship; career-related internships or fieldwork, Federal Work-Study, and institutionally sponsored loans also available. Support available to part-time students.

**Faculty research:** Health psychology and stress, program evaluation, depression/mood assessment.

Dr. William B. Arndt, Adviser, 816-235-1091, *Fax:* 816-235-1062.

**Application contact:** 816-235-1111.

■ **UNIVERSITY OF MISSOURI–ST. LOUIS**

**Graduate School, College of Arts and Sciences, Department of Psychology, St. Louis, MO 63121-4499**

**AWARDS** Clinical psychology (PhD); clinical psychology respecialization (Certificate); experimental psychology (PhD); general psychology (MA); industrial/organizational (PhD). Evening/weekend programs available.

**Faculty:** 18.

**Students:** 34 full-time (27 women), 38 part-time (25 women); includes 9 minority (6 African Americans, 2 Asian Americans or Pacific Islanders, 1 Hispanic American), 2 international. In 2001, 12 master's, 5 doctorates awarded. Terminal master's awarded for partial completion of doctoral program.

**Degree requirements:** For doctorate, thesis/dissertation.

**Entrance requirements:** For master's and doctorate, GRE General Test, GRE Subject Test. *Application deadline:* For fall admission, 2/1 (priority date). Applications are processed on a rolling basis. *Application fee:* $25 ($40 for international students). Electronic applications accepted.

**Expenses:** Tuition, state resident: part-time $231 per credit hour. Tuition, nonresident: part-time $621 per credit hour.

**Financial support:** In 2001–02, 2 fellowships with full tuition reimbursements (averaging $12,000 per year), 9 research assistantships with full and partial tuition reimbursements (averaging $13,585 per year), 23 teaching assistantships with full and partial tuition reimbursements (averaging $9,096 per year) were awarded.

**Faculty research:** Animal-human learning; physiological, industrial-organizational and cognitive processes; personality-social, clinical and community psychology. *Total annual research expenditures:* $1.1 million.

Dr. Gary Burger, Chair, 314-516-5391, *Fax:* 314-516-5392.

**Application contact:** Graduate Admissions, 314-516-5458, *Fax:* 314-516-5310, *E-mail:* gradadm@umsl.edu.

■ **THE UNIVERSITY OF MONTANA–MISSOULA**

**Graduate School, College of Arts and Sciences, Department of Psychology, Missoula, MT 59812-0002**

**AWARDS** Clinical psychology (PhD); experimental psychology (PhD), including animal behavior, developmental psychology; school psychology (MA, Ed S).

**Faculty:** 19 full-time (9 women), 1 (woman) part-time/adjunct.

**Students:** 36 full-time (28 women), 24 part-time (18 women); includes 7 minority (all Native Americans), 2 international. Average age 30. 70 applicants, 27% accepted, 14 enrolled. In 2001, 13 master's, 7 doctorates, 7 other advanced degrees awarded. Terminal master's awarded for partial completion of doctoral program.

**Degree requirements:** For master's and doctorate, thesis/dissertation.

**Entrance requirements:** For master's, doctorate, and Ed S, GRE General Test. *Application deadline:* For fall admission, 1/15. *Application fee:* $45.

**Expenses:** Tuition, state resident: full-time $2,482; part-time $1,700 per year. Tuition, nonresident: full-time $7,372; part-time $5,000 per year. Required fees: $1,900. Tuition and fees vary according to degree level.

**Financial support:** In 2001–02, 17 teaching assistantships with full tuition reimbursements (averaging $14,000 per year) were awarded; career-related internships or fieldwork, Federal Work-Study, scholarships/grants, traineeships, and unspecified assistantships also available. Financial award application deadline: 3/1; financial award applicants required to submit FAFSA. *Total annual research expenditures:* $1.8 million.

Dr. Nabil Haddad, Chair, 406-243-4521, *Fax:* 406-243-6366, *E-mail:* psycgrad@selway.umt.edu.

**Application contact:** Graduate Secretary, 406-243-4523, *Fax:* 406-243-6366, *E-mail:* psycgrad@selway.umt.edu. *Web site:* http://www.cas.umt.edu/psych/

■ **UNIVERSITY OF NEBRASKA AT OMAHA**

**Graduate Studies and Research, College of Arts and Sciences, Department of Psychology, Omaha, NE 68182**

**AWARDS** Developmental psychobiology (PhD); experimental child psychology (PhD); industrial/organizational psychology (MS, PhD); psychology (MA); school psychology (MS, Ed S). Part-time programs available.

**Faculty:** 17 full-time (7 women).

**Students:** 32 full-time (22 women), 18 part-time (10 women); includes 2 minority (1 African American, 1 Hispanic American). Average age 27. 64 applicants, 44% accepted, 28 enrolled. In 2001, 23 master's, 4 other advanced degrees awarded.

**Degree requirements:** For master's, thesis (for some programs), comprehensive exam; for doctorate, thesis/dissertation.

**Entrance requirements:** For master's, GRE General Test, GRE Subject Test, previous course work in psychology, including statistics and a laboratory course; minimum GPA of 3.0; for doctorate, GRE General Test. *Application deadline:* For fall admission, 2/1. *Application fee:* $35. Electronic applications accepted.

**Expenses:** Tuition, state resident: part-time $116 per credit hour. Tuition, nonresident: part-time $291 per credit hour. Required fees: $13 per credit hour. $4 per semester. One-time fee: $52 part-time.

**Financial support:** In 2001–02, 42 students received support; fellowships, research assistantships, teaching assistantships, career-related internships or fieldwork, Federal Work-Study, institutionally sponsored loans, scholarships/grants, tuition waivers (partial), and unspecified assistantships available. Support available to part-time students. Financial award application deadline: 3/1; financial award applicants required to submit FAFSA.

Dr. Kenneth Deffenbacher, Chairperson, 402-554-2592.

■ **UNIVERSITY OF NEBRASKA–LINCOLN**

**Graduate College, College of Arts and Sciences, Department of Psychology, Lincoln, NE 68588**

**AWARDS** MA, PhD, JD/MA, JD/PhD.

**Faculty:** 28.

**Students:** 106 (71 women); includes 21 minority (3 African Americans, 7 Asian Americans or Pacific Islanders, 9 Hispanic Americans, 2 Native Americans) 10 international. Average age 32. 180 applicants, 9% accepted, 11 enrolled. In 2001, 12 master's, 21 doctorates awarded.

*University of Nebraska–Lincoln (continued)*

**Degree requirements:** For master's, thesis optional; for doctorate, thesis/dissertation, comprehensive exam.
**Entrance requirements:** For master's and doctorate, GRE General Test, GRE Subject Test, TOEFL. *Application deadline:* For fall admission, 1/3. *Application fee:* $35. Electronic applications accepted.
**Expenses:** Tuition, state resident: full-time $2,412; part-time $134 per credit. Tuition, nonresident: full-time $6,223; part-time $346 per credit. Tuition and fees vary according to course load.
**Financial support:** In 2001–02, 3 fellowships, 21 research assistantships, 37 teaching assistantships were awarded. Federal Work-Study, health care benefits, and unspecified assistantships also available. Support available to part-time students. Financial award application deadline: 1/3.
**Faculty research:** Law and psychology, rural mental health, chronic mental illness, neuropsychology, child clinical psychology.
Dr. David Hansen, Chair, 402-472-3721, *Fax:* 402-472-4637. *Web site:* http://www.unl.edu/psypage/

## ■ UNIVERSITY OF NEBRASKA–LINCOLN

**Graduate College, Teachers College, Interdepartmental Area of Psychological and Cultural Studies, Lincoln, NE 68588**

**AWARDS** Ed D, PhD.

**Students:** 115 (75 women); includes 13 minority (6 African Americans, 4 Asian Americans or Pacific Islanders, 3 Hispanic Americans) 12 international. Average age 38. 28 applicants, 54% accepted, 12 enrolled. In 2001, 24 degrees awarded.
**Degree requirements:** For doctorate, thesis/dissertation, comprehensive exam.
**Entrance requirements:** For doctorate, GRE General Test, TOEFL. *Application deadline:* For fall admission, 12/15; for spring admission, 10/1. *Application fee:* $35. Electronic applications accepted.
**Expenses:** Tuition, state resident: full-time $2,412; part-time $134 per credit. Tuition, nonresident: full-time $6,223; part-time $346 per credit. Tuition and fees vary according to course load.
**Financial support:** In 2001–02, 2 fellowships, 16 research assistantships were awarded. Teaching assistantships, Federal Work-Study also available. Support available to part-time students. Financial award application deadline: 2/15.
Dr. E. Charles Healey, Graduate Committee Chair, 402-472-5459, *E-mail:* tcgrad2@unl.edu. *Web site:* http://tc.unl.edu/grad/

## ■ UNIVERSITY OF NEVADA, LAS VEGAS

**Graduate College, College of Liberal Arts, Department of Psychology, Las Vegas, NV 89154-9900**

**AWARDS** Clinical psychology (PhD); experimental psychology (PhD); general psychology (MA). Part-time programs available.

**Faculty:** 21 full-time (7 women).
**Students:** 29 full-time (22 women), 6 part-time (4 women); includes 6 minority (2 Asian Americans or Pacific Islanders, 4 Hispanic Americans). 47 applicants, 28% accepted, 12 enrolled. In 2001, 4 degrees awarded.
**Degree requirements:** For master's and doctorate, thesis/dissertation, oral exam, comprehensive exam.
**Entrance requirements:** For master's, GRE General Test, GRE Subject Test, minimum GPA of 3.2; for doctorate, GRE General Test, GRE Subject Test, minimum GPA of 3.2 in bachelor's and 3.5 in master's. *Application deadline:* For fall admission, 3/1. *Application fee:* $40 ($55 for international students).
**Expenses:** Tuition, state resident: full-time $1,926; part-time $107 per credit. Tuition, nonresident: full-time $9,376; part-time $220 per credit. Tuition and fees vary according to course load.
**Financial support:** In 2001–02, 6 research assistantships with full and partial tuition reimbursements (averaging $11,000 per year), 18 teaching assistantships with partial tuition reimbursements (averaging $11,000 per year) were awarded. Financial award application deadline: 3/1.
Dr. Charles Rasmussen, Chair, 702-895-3305.
**Application contact:** Graduate College Admissions Evaluator, 702-895-3320, *Fax:* 702-895-4180, *E-mail:* gradcollege@ccmail.nevada.edu. *Web site:* http://psychology.unlv.edu/gradinfo.html/

## ■ UNIVERSITY OF NEVADA, RENO

**Graduate School, College of Arts and Science, Department of Psychology, Reno, NV 89557**

**AWARDS** MA, PhD. Postbaccalaureate distance learning degree programs offered.

**Faculty:** 27.
**Students:** 96 full-time (54 women), 54 part-time (44 women); includes 28 minority (2 African Americans, 5 Asian Americans or Pacific Islanders, 20 Hispanic Americans, 1 Native American), 11 international. Average age 29. In 2001, 15 master's, 11 doctorates awarded. Terminal master's awarded for partial completion of doctoral program.
**Degree requirements:** For master's, thesis optional; for doctorate, thesis/dissertation.
**Entrance requirements:** For master's and doctorate, GRE General Test, GRE Subject Test, TOEFL, minimum GPA of 3.0. *Application deadline:* Applications are processed on a rolling basis. *Application fee:* $40.
**Expenses:** Tuition, state resident: full-time $2,067; part-time $108 per credit. Tuition, nonresident: full-time $9,282; part-time $109 per credit. Required fees: $57 per semester. Tuition and fees vary according to course load.
**Financial support:** In 2001–02, 43 research assistantships, 20 teaching assistantships were awarded. Federal Work-Study, institutionally sponsored loans, and unspecified assistantships also available. Financial award application deadline: 3/1.
**Faculty research:** Cognitive psychology, social psychological theory, animal and human intelligence, psychotherapy outcome, perception.
Dr. Steven C. Hayes, Chair, 775-784-6828.

## ■ UNIVERSITY OF NEW HAMPSHIRE

**Graduate School, College of Liberal Arts, Department of Psychology, Durham, NH 03824**

**AWARDS** PhD.

**Faculty:** 20 full-time.
**Students:** 23 full-time (10 women), 10 part-time (5 women); includes 1 minority (African American), 2 international. Average age 27. 27 applicants, 41% accepted, 4 enrolled. In 2001, 2 doctorates awarded.
**Degree requirements:** For doctorate, thesis/dissertation.
**Entrance requirements:** For doctorate, GRE General Test, GRE Subject Test. *Application deadline:* For fall admission, 2/15 (priority date). Applications are processed on a rolling basis. *Application fee:* $50. Electronic applications accepted.
**Expenses:** Tuition, state resident: full-time $6,300; part-time $350 per credit. Tuition, nonresident: full-time $15,720; part-time $643 per credit. Required fees: $560; $280 per term. One-time fee: $15 part-time. Tuition and fees vary according to course load.
**Financial support:** In 2001–02, 2 fellowships, 27 teaching assistantships were awarded. Research assistantships, career-related internships or fieldwork, Federal Work-Study, scholarships/grants, and tuition waivers (full and partial) also available. Support available to part-time students. Financial award application deadline: 2/15.

**Faculty research:** History of psychology; cognition and perception; learning, developmental, physiological, and social psychology.
Dr. Kenneth Fuld, Chairperson, 603-862-3173, *E-mail:* kf@cisunix.unh.edu.
**Application contact:** Dr. Bob Mair, Graduate Coordinator, 603-862-3198. *Web site:* http://www.unh.edu/psychology/

# ■ UNIVERSITY OF NEW MEXICO

**Graduate School, College of Arts and Sciences, Department of Psychology, Albuquerque, NM 87131-2039**

AWARDS MS, PhD.

**Faculty:** 32 full-time (12 women), 8 part-time/adjunct (4 women).
**Students:** 72 full-time (44 women), 6 part-time (3 women); includes 12 minority (1 African American, 1 Asian American or Pacific Islander, 8 Hispanic Americans, 2 Native Americans), 3 international. Average age 33. 123 applicants, 12% accepted, 3 enrolled. In 2001, 8 master's, 17 doctorates awarded.
**Degree requirements:** For master's, thesis/dissertation; for doctorate, thesis/dissertation, comprehensive exam.
**Entrance requirements:** For doctorate, GRE General Test, GRE Subject Test, 1 semester of course work in statistics. *Application deadline:* For fall admission, 1/15 (priority date). *Application fee:* $40.
**Expenses:** Tuition, state resident: full-time $2,771; part-time $115 per credit hour. Tuition, nonresident: full-time $11,207; part-time $467 per credit hour. Required fees: $570; $24 per credit hour. Part-time tuition and fees vary according to course load and program.
**Financial support:** In 2001–02, 59 students received support, including 10 research assistantships with full and partial tuition reimbursements available (averaging $14,000 per year), 30 teaching assistantships with full and partial tuition reimbursements available (averaging $10,064 per year); Federal Work-Study, health care benefits, and unspecified assistantships also available. Financial award application deadline: 3/1; financial award applicants required to submit FAFSA.
**Faculty research:** Addictions; learning, cognition, and memory; neuropsychology; social psychology; quantitative behavioral neuroscience. *Total annual research expenditures:* $881,143.
Dr. Michael J. Dougher, Chair, 505-277-4249, *Fax:* 505-277-1394, *E-mail:* dougher@unm.edu.
**Application contact:** Beth R. Isbell, Program Advisement Coordinator, 505-277-7512, *Fax:* 505-277-1394, *E-mail:* isbell@unm.edu. *Web site:* http://www.unm.edu/~psych/

# ■ UNIVERSITY OF NEW ORLEANS

**Graduate School, College of Sciences, Department of Psychology, New Orleans, LA 70148**

AWARDS Applied psychology (PhD), including applied biopsychology, applied developmental psychology; psychology (MS).

**Faculty:** 6 full-time (3 women).
**Students:** 25 full-time (17 women); includes 1 minority (African American), 1 international. Average age 29. 47 applicants, 23% accepted, 6 enrolled. In 2001, 3 doctorates awarded.
**Degree requirements:** For doctorate, thesis/dissertation.
**Entrance requirements:** For doctorate, GRE General Test, minimum GPA of 3.0, 21 hours of course work in psychology. *Application deadline:* For fall admission, 7/1 (priority date); for spring admission, 11/15 (priority date). Applications are processed on a rolling basis. *Application fee:* $20. Electronic applications accepted.
**Expenses:** Tuition, state resident: full-time $2,748; part-time $435 per credit. Tuition, nonresident: full-time $9,792; part-time $1,773 per credit.
**Financial support:** Fellowships, research assistantships, teaching assistantships, career-related internships or fieldwork and unspecified assistantships available. Financial award application deadline: 2/15; financial award applicants required to submit FAFSA.
**Faculty research:** Biofeedback, visual and auditory perception, psychopharmacology, neuropeptides.
Dr. Matthew Stanford, Graduate Coordinator, 504-280-6185, *Fax:* 504-280-6049, *E-mail:* mstanfor@uno.edu.
**Application contact:** Dr. Paul Frick, Graduate Coordinator, 504-280-6012, *Fax:* 504-280-6049, *E-mail:* pfrick@uno.edu.

# ■ THE UNIVERSITY OF NORTH CAROLINA AT CHAPEL HILL

**Graduate School, College of Arts and Sciences, Department of Psychology, Chapel Hill, NC 27599**

AWARDS Biological psychology (PhD); clinical psychology (PhD); cognitive psychology (PhD); developmental psychology (PhD); quantitative psychology (PhD); social psychology (PhD).

**Faculty:** 46 full-time (25 women), 6 part-time/adjunct (0 women).
**Students:** 116 full-time (63 women). 546 applicants, 7% accepted, 29 enrolled. In 2001, 27 doctorates awarded.

**Degree requirements:** For doctorate, thesis/dissertation, comprehensive exam.
**Entrance requirements:** For doctorate, GRE General Test, minimum GPA of 3.0. *Application deadline:* For fall admission, 12/1. *Application fee:* $55. Electronic applications accepted.
**Expenses:** Tuition, state resident: full-time $2,864. Tuition, nonresident: full-time $12,030.
**Financial support:** In 2001–02, 11 fellowships with tuition reimbursements, 28 research assistantships with tuition reimbursements, 63 teaching assistantships with tuition reimbursements were awarded. Unspecified assistantships also available. Financial award application deadline: 2/1.
**Faculty research:** Expressed emotion, cognitive development, social cognitive neuroscience, human memory personality. *Total annual research expenditures:* $605,806.
Peter A. Ornstein, Chair, 919-962-3088.
**Application contact:** Barbara Atkins, Student Services Manager, 919-962-7149, *Fax:* 919-962-2537, *E-mail:* batkins@email.unc.edu.

# ■ THE UNIVERSITY OF NORTH CAROLINA AT CHARLOTTE

**Graduate School, College of Arts and Sciences, Department of Psychology, Charlotte, NC 28223-0001**

AWARDS Community/clinical psychology (MA); industrial/organizational psychology (MA); psychology (MA). Part-time programs available.

**Faculty:** 25 full-time (9 women), 13 part-time/adjunct (1 woman).
**Students:** 38 full-time (31 women), 21 part-time (17 women); includes 9 minority (6 African Americans, 2 Asian Americans or Pacific Islanders, 1 Native American), 2 international. Average age 27. 123 applicants, 19% accepted, 21 enrolled. In 2001, 13 degrees awarded.
**Degree requirements:** For master's, thesis.
**Entrance requirements:** For master's, GRE General Test, GRE Subject Test, minimum GPA of 3.0 in undergraduate major, 2.8 overall. *Application fee:* $35.
**Expenses:** Tuition, state resident: full-time $1,483; part-time $371 per year. Tuition, nonresident: full-time $9,850; part-time $2,463 per year. Required fees: $1,043; $277 per year. Tuition and fees vary according to course load.
**Financial support:** In 2001–02, 4 research assistantships, 9 teaching assistantships were awarded. Fellowships, career-related internships or fieldwork, Federal Work-Study, institutionally sponsored loans, scholarships/grants, and unspecified assistantships also available. Support available to part-time students. Financial award

*The University of North Carolina at Charlotte (continued)*
application deadline: 4/1; financial award applicants required to submit FAFSA.
**Faculty research:** Psychological reaction to crisis situations; development of at-risk children; bereavements, personality change and growth; total quality management. Dr. Michael S. Doyle, Interim Chair, 704-687-4731, *Fax:* 704-687-3096, *E-mail:* msdoyle@email.uncc.edu.
**Application contact:** Kathy Barringer, Director of Graduate Admissions, 704-687-3366, *Fax:* 704-687-3279, *E-mail:* gradadm@email.uncc.edu. *Web site:* http://www.uncc.edu/gradmiss/

## ■ THE UNIVERSITY OF NORTH CAROLINA AT GREENSBORO

**Graduate School, College of Arts and Sciences, Department of Psychology, Greensboro, NC 27412-5001**

**AWARDS** Clinical psychology (MA, PhD); cognitive psychology (MA, PhD); developmental psychology (MA, PhD); social psychology (MA, PhD).

**Faculty:** 22 full-time (9 women), 1 part-time/adjunct (0 women).
**Students:** 42 full-time (35 women), 20 part-time (13 women); includes 2 African Americans, 2 Asian Americans or Pacific Islanders, 2 Hispanic Americans. In 2001, 13 master's, 5 doctorates awarded. Terminal master's awarded for partial completion of doctoral program.
**Degree requirements:** For master's, thesis, comprehensive exam; for doctorate, one foreign language, thesis/dissertation, preliminary exam.
**Entrance requirements:** For master's, GRE General Test, TOEFL; for doctorate, GRE General Test, GRE Subject Test (recommended), TOEFL. *Application deadline:* For fall admission, 2/1. *Application fee:* $35.
**Expenses:** Tuition, state resident: part-time $344 per course. Tuition, nonresident: part-time $2,457 per course.
**Financial support:** In 2001–02, 3 fellowships with full tuition reimbursements (averaging $10,833 per year), 54 research assistantships with full tuition reimbursements (averaging $8,514 per year), 2 teaching assistantships with full tuition reimbursements (averaging $3,500 per year) were awarded. Unspecified assistantships also available.
**Faculty research:** Sensory and perceptual determinants; evoked potential: disorders, deafness, and development. Dr. Timothy Johnston, Head, 336-334-5013, *Fax:* 336-334-5066, *E-mail:* johnston@uncg.edu.
**Application contact:** Dr. James Lynch, Director of Graduate Recruitment and

Information Services, 336-334-4881, *Fax:* 336-334-4424. *Web site:* http://www.uncg.edu/psy/

## ■ THE UNIVERSITY OF NORTH CAROLINA AT WILMINGTON

**College of Arts and Sciences, Department of Psychology, Wilmington, NC 28403-3297**

**AWARDS** MA. Part-time programs available.

**Faculty:** 11 full-time (5 women).
**Students:** 17 full-time (14 women), 19 part-time (13 women); includes 3 minority (1 African American, 1 Asian American or Pacific Islander, 1 Hispanic American), 3 international. Average age 32. 64 applicants, 23% accepted, 15 enrolled. In 2001, 12 degrees awarded.
**Degree requirements:** For master's, thesis, comprehensive exam.
**Entrance requirements:** For master's, GRE General Test, GRE Subject Test, minimum B average in undergraduate major. *Application deadline:* For fall admission, 2/1. Applications are processed on a rolling basis. *Application fee:* $45.
**Expenses:** Tuition, state resident: full-time $2,675. Tuition, nonresident: full-time $10,936.
**Financial support:** In 2001–02, 15 teaching assistantships were awarded; career-related internships or fieldwork and Federal Work-Study also available. Financial award application deadline: 3/15. Lee A. Jackson, Chairman, 910-962-3370, *Fax:* 910-962-7010.
**Application contact:** Dr. Neil F. Hadley, Dean, Graduate School, 910-962-4117, *Fax:* 910-962-3787, *E-mail:* hadleyn@uncwil.edu.

## ■ UNIVERSITY OF NORTH DAKOTA

**Graduate School, College of Arts and Sciences, Department of Psychology, Grand Forks, ND 58202**

**AWARDS** Clinical psychology (PhD); experimental psychology (PhD); psychology (MA).

**Faculty:** 15 full-time (3 women).
**Students:** 9 full-time (8 women), 37 part-time (20 women). 57 applicants, 23% accepted, 12 enrolled. In 2001, 9 master's, 8 doctorates awarded.
**Degree requirements:** For master's, thesis, final exam; for doctorate, thesis/dissertation, internship, final exam, comprehensive exam.
**Entrance requirements:** For master's, GRE General Test, GRE Subject Test, TOEFL, minimum GPA of 3.0; for doctorate, GRE General Test, GRE Subject Test, TOEFL, minimum GPA of

3.5. *Application deadline:* For fall admission, 2/1. *Application fee:* $30.
**Expenses:** Tuition, state resident: full-time $3,298. Tuition, nonresident: full-time $7,998.
**Financial support:** In 2001–02, 34 students received support, including 2 research assistantships with full tuition reimbursements available (averaging $9,282 per year), 23 teaching assistantships with full tuition reimbursements available (averaging $9,282 per year); fellowships, career-related internships or fieldwork, Federal Work-Study, institutionally sponsored loans, scholarships/grants, tuition waivers (full and partial), and unspecified assistantships also available. Support available to part-time students. Financial award application deadline: 3/15; financial award applicants required to submit FAFSA.
**Faculty research:** Developmental psychology, clinical social psychology, educational psychology, personality disorders. Dr. Mark D. Grabe, Chair, 701-777-3920, *Fax:* 701-777-3454, *E-mail:* mark_grabe@und.nodak.edu. *Web site:* http://www.und.edu/dept/psychol/

## ■ UNIVERSITY OF NORTHERN COLORADO

**Graduate School, College of Arts and Sciences, Department of Psychology, Greeley, CO 80639**

**AWARDS** MA.

**Faculty:** 10 full-time (3 women).
**Students:** 19 full-time (11 women). Average age 25. 23 applicants, 70% accepted. In 2001, 10 degrees awarded.
**Degree requirements:** For master's, thesis or alternative, comprehensive exam.
**Entrance requirements:** For master's, GRE General Test. *Application deadline:* Applications are processed on a rolling basis. *Application fee:* $35.
**Expenses:** Tuition, state resident: full-time $2,549; part-time $546 per credit hour. Tuition, nonresident: full-time $10,459; part-time $581 per credit hour. Required fees: $631; $85 per year. Part-time tuition and fees vary according to course load.
**Financial support:** In 2001–02, 19 students received support, including 2 fellowships (averaging $625 per year), 8 research assistantships (averaging $6,333 per year), 3 teaching assistantships (averaging $7,877 per year); unspecified assistantships also available. Financial award application deadline: 3/1. Mark Alcorn, Chairperson, 970-351-2957.

## ■ UNIVERSITY OF NORTHERN IOWA

**Graduate College, College of Social and Behavioral Sciences, Department of Psychology, Cedar Falls, IA 50614**

AWARDS MA. Part-time programs available.

**Students:** 24 full-time (15 women); includes 5 minority (4 African Americans, 1 Hispanic American), 2 international. 38 applicants, 71% accepted. In 2001, 6 degrees awarded.

**Degree requirements:** For master's, thesis.

*Application deadline:* For fall admission, 8/1 (priority date). Applications are processed on a rolling basis. *Application fee:* $20 ($50 for international students).

**Expenses:** Tuition, state resident: full-time $3,704; part-time $206 per credit hour. Tuition, nonresident: full-time $9,122; part-time $501 per credit hour. Required fees: $324; $108 per semester. Part-time tuition and fees vary according to course load.

**Financial support:** Career-related internships or fieldwork, Federal Work-Study, and tuition waivers (full and partial) available. Support available to part-time students. Financial award application deadline: 3/1.

Dr. Frank X. Barrios, Head, 319-273-2303, *Fax:* 319-273-6188, *E-mail:* frank.barrios@uni.edu. *Web site:* http://www.uni.edu/psych/

## ■ UNIVERSITY OF NORTH FLORIDA

**College of Arts and Sciences, Department of Psychology, Jacksonville, FL 32224-2645**

AWARDS Counseling psychology (MAC); general psychology (MA). Part-time and evening/weekend programs available.

**Faculty:** 17 full-time (7 women).
**Students:** 28 full-time (20 women), 12 part-time (11 women); includes 2 minority (1 African American, 1 Asian American or Pacific Islander). Average age 28. 106 applicants, 29% accepted, 19 enrolled. In 2001, 15 degrees awarded.

**Degree requirements:** For master's, practicum, thesis optional.
**Entrance requirements:** For master's, TOEFL, GRE General Test or minimum GPA of 3.0 in last 60 hours. *Application deadline:* For fall admission, 2/2 (priority date). Applications are processed on a rolling basis. *Application fee:* $20. Electronic applications accepted.

**Expenses:** Tuition, state resident: full-time $2,411; part-time $134 per credit hour. Tuition, nonresident: full-time $9,391; part-time $522 per credit hour. Required fees: $670; $37 per credit hour.

**Financial support:** In 2001–02, 28 students received support. Federal Work-Study and tuition waivers (partial) available. Support available to part-time students. Financial award application deadline: 4/1; financial award applicants required to submit FAFSA.

**Faculty research:** Person by situation interaction, jury decision processes, domestic violence impact on children, head-start and early childhood development, applied behavior analysis. *Total annual research expenditures:* $7,500.

Dr. Minor H. Chamblin, Chair, 904-620-2807, *E-mail:* mchambli@unf.edu.

**Application contact:** Dr. Maury Nation, Coordinator, 904-620-2807, *E-mail:* mnation@unf.edu.

## ■ UNIVERSITY OF NORTH TEXAS

**Robert B. Toulouse School of Graduate Studies, College of Arts and Sciences, Department of Psychology, Denton, TX 76203**

AWARDS Clinical psychology (PhD); counseling psychology (MA, MS, PhD); experimental psychology (MA, MS, PhD); health psychology and behavioral medicine (PhD); industrial psychology (MA, MS); psychology (MA, MS, PhD); school psychology (MA, MS, PhD).

**Faculty:** 29 full-time (5 women), 7 part-time/adjunct (5 women).
**Students:** 129 full-time (96 women), 98 part-time (70 women); includes 23 minority (2 African Americans, 4 Asian Americans or Pacific Islanders, 15 Hispanic Americans, 2 Native Americans), 9 international. Average age 30. In 2001, 24 master's, 17 doctorates awarded. Terminal master's awarded for partial completion of doctoral program.

**Degree requirements:** For master's, thesis or alternative, comprehensive exam; for doctorate, one foreign language, thesis/dissertation, comprehensive exam.

**Entrance requirements:** For master's and doctorate, GRE General Test, GRE Subject Test, interview. *Application deadline:* For fall admission, 2/1. *Application fee:* $25 ($50 for international students).

**Expenses:** Tuition, state resident: part-time $186 per hour. Tuition, nonresident: part-time $319 per hour. Required fees: $88; $21 per hour.

**Financial support:** Fellowships, research assistantships, teaching assistantships, career-related internships or fieldwork, Federal Work-Study, and institutionally sponsored loans available. Financial award application deadline: 8/1.

Dr. Ernest H. Harrell, Chair, 940-565-2671, *Fax:* 940-546-4682, *E-mail:* harrelle@unt.edu.

**Application contact:** Dr. Joseph Critelli, Graduate Adviser, 940-565-2671, *Fax:* 940-565-4682, *E-mail:* critelli@facstaff.cas.unt.edu.

## ■ UNIVERSITY OF NORTH TEXAS

**Robert B. Toulouse School of Graduate Studies, School of Community Service, Department for Behavior Analysis, Denton, TX 76203**

AWARDS MS.

**Faculty:** 7 full-time (3 women).
**Students:** 17 full-time (11 women), 41 part-time (29 women); includes 6 minority (1 African American, 1 Asian American or Pacific Islander, 4 Hispanic Americans), 4 international. Average age 26. In 2001, 10 degrees awarded.

**Degree requirements:** For master's, thesis.

**Entrance requirements:** For master's, GRE General Test. *Application deadline:* For fall admission, 7/17 (priority date). Applications are processed on a rolling basis. *Application fee:* $25 ($50 for international students).

**Expenses:** Tuition, state resident: part-time $186 per hour. Tuition, nonresident: part-time $319 per hour. Required fees: $88; $21 per hour.

**Financial support:** Research assistantships, teaching assistantships, career-related internships or fieldwork, Federal Work-Study, scholarships/grants, and tuition waivers (partial) available. Support available to part-time students. Financial award applicants required to submit FAFSA.

**Faculty research:** Human operant matching, verbal behavior, applied behavior analysis. *Total annual research expenditures:* $45,000.

Dr. Sigrid S. Glenn, Chair, 940-565-2274, *Fax:* 940-565-2467, *E-mail:* glenn@scs.unt.edu.

**Application contact:** Dr. Janet Ellis, Graduate Adviser, 940-565-3318, *Fax:* 940-565-2467, *E-mail:* ellis@scs.cmm.unt.edu.

## ■ UNIVERSITY OF NOTRE DAME

**Graduate School, College of Arts and Letters, Division of Social Science, Department of Psychology, Notre Dame, IN 46556**

AWARDS Cognitive psychology (PhD); counseling psychology (PhD); developmental psychology (PhD); quantitative psychology (PhD).

**Faculty:** 31 full-time (11 women).
**Students:** 60 full-time (42 women); includes 10 minority (3 African Americans, 2 Asian Americans or Pacific Islanders, 5 Hispanic Americans), 5 international. 189 applicants, 12% accepted, 15 enrolled. In 2001, 8 doctorates awarded.

*University of Notre Dame (continued)*
**Degree requirements:** For doctorate, thesis/dissertation, comprehensive exam. *Median time to degree:* Doctorate–5.9 years full-time.
**Entrance requirements:** For doctorate, GRE General Test, GRE Subject Test (strongly recommended), TOEFL. *Application deadline:* For fall admission, 1/2. *Application fee:* $50. Electronic applications accepted.
**Expenses:** Tuition: Full-time $24,220; part-time $1,346 per credit hour. Required fees: $155.
**Financial support:** In 2001–02, 59 students received support, including 31 fellowships with full tuition reimbursements available (averaging $16,000 per year), 10 research assistantships with full tuition reimbursements available (averaging $11,400 per year), 17 teaching assistantships with full tuition reimbursements available (averaging $11,400 per year); career-related internships or fieldwork and tuition waivers (full) also available. Financial award application deadline: 1/2.
**Faculty research:** Cognitive and socioemotional development, marital discord, statistical methods and quantitative models applicable to psychology, interpersonal relations, life span development and developmental delay, childhood depression, structural equation and dynamical systems, modeling, social cognition, ecology, health psychology, aging behavior genetics. *Total annual research expenditures:* $1.8 million.
Dr. Laura Carlson, Director of Graduate Studies, 574-631-6650, *Fax:* 574-631-8883, *E-mail:* lcarlson@nd.edu.
**Application contact:** Dr. Terrence J. Akai, Director of Graduate Admissions, 574-631-7706, *Fax:* 574-631-4183, *E-mail:* gradad@nd.edu. *Web site:* http://www.nd.edu/~psych/

### ■ UNIVERSITY OF OKLAHOMA

**Graduate College, College of Arts and Sciences, Department of Psychology, Norman, OK 73019-0390**
**AWARDS** MS, PhD.
**Faculty:** 18 full-time (8 women), 1 part-time/adjunct (0 women).
**Students:** 37 full-time (21 women), 10 part-time (6 women); includes 4 minority (1 Asian American or Pacific Islander, 2 Hispanic Americans, 1 Native American), 5 international. 61 applicants, 26% accepted, 5 enrolled. In 2001, 8 master's, 3 doctorates awarded. Terminal master's awarded for partial completion of doctoral program.
**Degree requirements:** For master's, thesis or alternative; for doctorate, thesis/dissertation, general exam.

**Entrance requirements:** For master's, GRE General Test, GRE Subject Test, TOEFL, minimum GPA of 3.0, 12 hours of course work in psychology; for doctorate, GRE General Test, GRE Subject Test, TOEFL. *Application deadline:* For fall admission, 2/1 (priority date). Applications are processed on a rolling basis. *Application fee:* $25 ($50 for international students).
**Expenses:** Tuition, state resident: full-time $2,208; part-time $92 per credit hour. Tuition, nonresident: part-time $297 per credit hour. Tuition and fees vary according to course level, course load and program.
**Financial support:** In 2001–02, 24 students received support, including 5 fellowships (averaging $5,000 per year), 8 research assistantships with partial tuition reimbursements available (averaging $10,665 per year), 24 teaching assistantships with partial tuition reimbursements available (averaging $11,590 per year); Federal Work-Study, institutionally sponsored loans, and tuition waivers (partial) also available. Financial award application deadline: 3/1; financial award applicants required to submit FAFSA.
**Faculty research:** Cognitive. *Total annual research expenditures:* $481,201.
Dr. Kirby Gilliland, Chairperson, 405-325-4511, *Fax:* 405-325-4737, *E-mail:* kirby@ou.edu.
**Application contact:** Kathryn Paine, Graduate Admissions Secretary, 405-325-4512, *Fax:* 405-325-4737, *E-mail:* kpaine@ou.edu.

### ■ UNIVERSITY OF OREGON

**Graduate School, College of Arts and Sciences, Department of Psychology, Eugene, OR 97403**
**AWARDS** Clinical psychology (PhD); cognitive psychology (MA, MS, PhD); developmental psychology (MA, MS, PhD); physiological psychology (MA, MS, PhD); psychology (MA, MS, PhD); social/personality psychology (MA, MS, PhD).
**Faculty:** 27 full-time (11 women), 11 part-time/adjunct (8 women).
**Students:** 73 full-time (49 women), 3 part-time (all women); includes 7 minority (3 Asian Americans or Pacific Islanders, 2 Hispanic Americans, 2 Native Americans), 14 international. 176 applicants, 11% accepted. In 2001, 21 master's, 11 doctorates awarded. Terminal master's awarded for partial completion of doctoral program.
**Degree requirements:** For doctorate, thesis/dissertation.
**Entrance requirements:** For master's, GRE General Test, TOEFL, minimum GPA of 3.0; for doctorate, GRE General Test, TOEFL. *Application deadline:* For fall admission, 12/1. *Application fee:* $50.

**Expenses:** Tuition, state resident: full-time $4,968; part-time $501 per credit hour. Tuition, nonresident: full-time $8,400; part-time $691 per credit hour.
**Financial support:** In 2001–02, 48 teaching assistantships were awarded; research assistantships, career-related internships or fieldwork also available.
Marjorie Taylor, Head, 541-346-4921, *Fax:* 541-346-4911.
**Application contact:** Lori Olsen, Admissions Contact, 541-346-5060, *Fax:* 541-346-4911, *E-mail:* gradsec@psych.uoregon.edu. *Web site:* http://psychweb.uoregon.edu/

### ■ UNIVERSITY OF PENNSYLVANIA

**School of Arts and Sciences, Graduate Group in Psychology, Philadelphia, PA 19104**
**AWARDS** PhD.

**Degree requirements:** For doctorate, thesis/dissertation.
**Entrance requirements:** For doctorate, GRE General Test, GRE Subject Test, TOEFL.
**Expenses:** Tuition: Part-time $12,875 per semester.
**Faculty research:** Cognitive psychology, sensation and perception, biological psychology, clinical psychology, social psychology.

### ■ UNIVERSITY OF PHOENIX–HAWAII CAMPUS

**College of Counseling and Human Services, Honolulu, HI 96813-4317**
**AWARDS** Community counseling (MC); marriage and family therapy (MC). Evening/weekend programs available. Postbaccalaureate distance learning degree programs offered (no on-campus study).

**Students:** 77 full-time. Average age 35.
**Degree requirements:** For master's, thesis or alternative.
**Entrance requirements:** For master's, TOEFL, Comprehensive Cognitive Assessment, minimum undergraduate GPA of 2.5, 3 years of work experience. *Application deadline:* Applications are processed on a rolling basis. *Application fee:* $85.
**Expenses:** Tuition: Full-time $8,784; part-time $366 per credit.
**Financial support:** Applicants required to submit FAFSA.
Dr. Patrick Romine, Dean, 480-557-1074, *E-mail:* patrick.romine@phoenix.edu.
**Application contact:** Campus Information Center, 808-536-2686, *Fax:* 808-536-3848.

## ■ UNIVERSITY OF PHOENIX–NEW MEXICO CAMPUS

**College of Counseling and Human Services, Albuquerque, NM 87109-4645**

**AWARDS** Marriage and family therapy (MC); mental health counseling (MC). Evening/weekend programs available. Postbaccalaureate distance learning degree programs offered (no on-campus study).

**Students:** 34 full-time. Average age 34. In 2001, 16 degrees awarded.
**Degree requirements:** For master's, thesis or alternative.
**Entrance requirements:** For master's, TOEFL, Comprehensive Cognitive Assessment, minimum undergraduate GPA of 2.5, 3 years work experience. *Application deadline:* Applications are processed on a rolling basis. *Application fee:* $85.
**Expenses:** Tuition: Full-time $7,336; part-time $306 per credit. Full-time tuition and fees vary according to program.
**Financial support:** Applicants required to submit FAFSA.
Dr. Patrick Romine, Dean, 480-557-1074, *E-mail:* patrick.romine@phoenix.edu. *Web site:* http://www.phoenix.edu/

## ■ UNIVERSITY OF PHOENIX–PUERTO RICO CAMPUS

**College of Counseling and Human Services, Guaynabo, PR 00970-3870**

**AWARDS** MC. Evening/weekend programs available. Postbaccalaureate distance learning degree programs offered (no on-campus study).

**Students:** 227 full-time. Average age 34. In 2001, 19 degrees awarded.
**Degree requirements:** For master's, thesis or alternative.
**Entrance requirements:** For master's, comprehensive cognitive assessment (COCA), minimum undergraduate GPA of 2.5, 3 years work experience. *Application deadline:* Applications are processed on a rolling basis. *Application fee:* $85.
**Expenses:** Tuition: Full-time $4,800; part-time $200 per credit.
**Financial support:** Applicants required to submit FAFSA.
Dr. Patrick Romine, Dean, 480-557-1074, *E-mail:* patrick.romine@phoenix.edu.
**Application contact:** 787-731-5400, *Fax:* 787-731-1510. *Web site:* http://www.phoenix.edu/

## ■ UNIVERSITY OF PHOENIX–SACRAMENTO CAMPUS

**College of Counseling and Human Services, Sacramento, CA 95833-3632**

**AWARDS** Marriage, family and child counseling (MC). Evening/weekend programs available. Postbaccalaureate distance learning degree programs offered (no on-campus study).

**Students:** 109 full-time. Average age 34. In 2001, 46 degrees awarded.
**Degree requirements:** For master's, thesis or alternative.
**Entrance requirements:** For master's, TOEFL, comprehensive cognitive assessment (COCA), minimum undergraduate GPA of 2.5, 3 years work experience. *Application deadline:* Applications are processed on a rolling basis. *Application fee:* $85.
**Expenses:** Tuition: Full-time $9,720; part-time $405 per credit. Full-time tuition and fees vary according to program.
**Financial support:** Applicants required to submit FAFSA.
Dr. Patrick Romine, Dean, 480-557-1074, *E-mail:* patrick.romine@phoenix.edu. *Web site:* http://www.phoenix.edu/

## ■ UNIVERSITY OF PHOENIX–SAN DIEGO CAMPUS

**College of Counseling and Human Services, San Diego, CA 92130-2092**

**AWARDS** Marriage, family and child counseling (MC). Evening/weekend programs available. Postbaccalaureate distance learning degree programs offered (no on-campus study).

**Students:** 133 full-time. Average age 34. In 2001, 30 degrees awarded.
**Degree requirements:** For master's, thesis or alternative.
**Entrance requirements:** For master's, TOEFL, comprehensive cognitive assessment (COCA), minimum undergraduate GPA of 2.5, 3 years work experience. *Application deadline:* Applications are processed on a rolling basis. *Application fee:* $85.
**Expenses:** Tuition: Full-time $8,808; part-time $367 per credit.
**Financial support:** Applicants required to submit FAFSA.
Dr. Patrick Romine, Dean, 480-557-1074, *E-mail:* patrick.romine@phoenix.edu.
**Application contact:** Campus Information Center, 880-UOP-INFO. *Web site:* http://www.phoenix.edu/

## ■ UNIVERSITY OF PHOENIX–SOUTHERN ARIZONA CAMPUS

**College of Counseling and Human Services, Tucson, AZ 85712**

**AWARDS** MC. Evening/weekend programs available. Postbaccalaureate distance learning degree programs offered (no on-campus study).

**Students:** 74 full-time. Average age 34. In 2001, 30 degrees awarded.
**Degree requirements:** For master's, thesis or alternative.
**Entrance requirements:** For master's, TOEFL, comprehensive cognitive assessment (COCA), minimum undergraduate GPA of 2.5, 3 years work experience. *Application deadline:* Applications are processed on a rolling basis. *Application fee:* $85.
**Expenses:** Tuition: Full-time $6,456; part-time $269 per credit.
**Financial support:** Applicants required to submit FAFSA.
Dr. Patrick Romine, Dean, 480-557-1074, *E-mail:* patrick.romine@phoenix.edu.
**Application contact:** 520-881-6512, *Fax:* 520-795-6177. *Web site:* http://www.phoenix.edu/

## ■ UNIVERSITY OF PHOENIX–UTAH CAMPUS

**College of Counseling and Human Services, Salt Lake City, UT 84123-4617**

**AWARDS** MC. Evening/weekend programs available. Postbaccalaureate distance learning degree programs offered (no on-campus study).

**Students:** 176 full-time. Average age 35. In 2001, 50 degrees awarded.
**Degree requirements:** For master's, thesis or alternative.
**Entrance requirements:** For master's, TOEFL, comprehensive cognitive assessment (COCA), minimum undergraduate GPA of 2.5, 3 years work experience. *Application deadline:* Applications are processed on a rolling basis. *Application fee:* $85.
**Expenses:** Tuition: Full-time $7,315; part-time $305 per credit. Full-time tuition and fees vary according to program.
**Financial support:** Applicants required to submit FAFSA.
Dr. Patrick Romine, Dean, 480-557-1074, *E-mail:* patrick.romine@phoenix.edu. *Web site:* http://www.phoenix.edu/

## ■ UNIVERSITY OF PITTSBURGH

**Faculty of Arts and Sciences, Department of Psychology, Pittsburgh, PA 15260**
**AWARDS** MS, PhD.

*University of Pittsburgh (continued)*
**Faculty:** 30 full-time (9 women), 10 part-time/adjunct (5 women).
**Students:** 108 full-time (76 women); includes 11 minority (8 African Americans, 2 Asian Americans or Pacific Islanders, 1 Hispanic American), 6 international. 337 applicants, 8% accepted, 13 enrolled. In 2001, 16 degrees awarded.
**Degree requirements:** For master's and doctorate, thesis/dissertation, comprehensive exam.
**Entrance requirements:** For doctorate, GRE General Test, minimum GPA of 3.5. *Application deadline:* For fall admission, 1/1. *Application fee:* $40. Electronic applications accepted.
**Expenses:** Tuition, state resident: full-time $9,410; part-time $385 per credit. Tuition, nonresident: full-time $19,376; part-time $797 per credit. Required fees: $480; $90 per term. Tuition and fees vary according to program.
**Financial support:** In 2001–02, 6 fellowships with tuition reimbursements (averaging $13,728 per year), 4 research assistantships with full tuition reimbursements (averaging $11,190 per year), 20 teaching assistantships with full tuition reimbursements (averaging $11,980 per year) were awarded. Career-related internships or fieldwork, scholarships/grants, traineeships, health care benefits, tuition waivers (full and partial), and unspecified assistantships also available. Financial award application deadline: 1/1.
**Faculty research:** Behavioral medicine and psychoneuroimmunology learning, reasoning and memory psychopathology and behavioral problems, social cognition, social influence and group processes, social and cognitive development. *Total annual research expenditures:* $13 million.
Dr. Anthony R. Caggiula, Chairman, 412-624-4501, *Fax:* 412-624-4428, *E-mail:* tonypsy@pitt.edu.
**Application contact:** Paula S. Riemer, Graduate Administrative Assistant, 412-624-4502, *Fax:* 412-624-4428, *E-mail:* paular@pitt.edu. *Web site:* http://www.pitt.edu/~psych

### ■ UNIVERSITY OF PUERTO RICO, RÍO PIEDRAS

**College of Social Sciences, Department of Psychology, San Juan, PR 00931**

**AWARDS** MA, PhD. Part-time and evening/weekend programs available.

**Faculty:** 10.
**Students:** 153 full-time (118 women), 124 part-time (94 women); all minorities (all Hispanic Americans). 53 applicants, 91% accepted. In 2001, 7 master's, 17 doctorates awarded.

**Degree requirements:** For master's, thesis, comprehensive exam; for doctorate, thesis/dissertation, internship, comprehensive exam.
**Entrance requirements:** For master's, GRE or PAEG, interview, minimum GPA of 3.0; for doctorate, GRE or PAEG, interview, master's degree, minimum GPA of 3.0. *Application deadline:* For fall admission, 2/1. *Application fee:* $17.
**Expenses:** Students that provide official evidence of private medicine insurance or service are exempt of the payment of $529 per academic year.
**Financial support:** Fellowships, research assistantships, teaching assistantships, career-related internships or fieldwork, Federal Work-Study, institutionally sponsored loans, and tuition waivers (partial) available. Financial award application deadline: 5/31.
**Faculty research:** Learning disabilities and its treatment, mother-child relations evaluation.
Dr. Carmen Colón-Santaella, Chairperson, 787-764-0000 Ext. 4173.
**Application contact:** Ada Pérez, Information Contact, 787-764-0000, *Fax:* 787-763-4599.

### ■ UNIVERSITY OF RHODE ISLAND

**Graduate School, College of Arts and Sciences, Department of Psychology, Kingston, RI 02881**

**AWARDS** Clinical psychology (PhD); experimental psychology (PhD); school psychology (MS).

**Students:** In 2001, 8 master's, 13 doctorates awarded.
*Application fee:* $35.
**Expenses:** Tuition, state resident: full-time $3,756; part-time $209 per credit. Tuition, nonresident: full-time $10,774; part-time $599 per credit. Required fees: $1,586; $76 per credit. One-time fee: $60 full-time.
Dr. Kathryn Quina, Acting Chairperson, 401-874-2193.

### ■ UNIVERSITY OF RICHMOND

**Graduate School, Department of Psychology, Richmond, University of Richmond, VA 23173**

**AWARDS** MA.

**Faculty:** 10 full-time (3 women).
**Students:** 9 full-time (5 women). Average age 23. 29 applicants, 17% accepted, 4 enrolled. In 2001, 1 degree awarded.
**Degree requirements:** For master's, thesis, comprehensive exam.
**Entrance requirements:** For master's, GRE General Test, GRE Subject Test. *Application deadline:* For fall admission, 3/15 (priority date). *Application fee:* $30.

**Expenses:** Tuition: Full-time $22,360; part-time $385 per credit hour.
**Financial support:** In 2001–02, 9 students received support; research assistantships, teaching assistantships, career-related internships or fieldwork, Federal Work-Study, institutionally sponsored loans, unspecified assistantships, and tuition awards available. Financial award application deadline: 3/15; financial award applicants required to submit FAFSA.
**Faculty research:** Aging, memory, and personality; social cognition; binocularity and space perception; brain sexual differentiation; children's social development.
Dr. Craig Kinsley, Coordinator, 804-289-8132.

### ■ UNIVERSITY OF ROCHESTER

**The College, Arts and Sciences, Department of Clinical and Social Sciences in Psychology, Rochester, NY 14627-0250**

**AWARDS** Clinical psychology (PhD); developmental psychology (PhD); psychology (MA); social-personality psychology (PhD).

**Faculty:** 14.
**Students:** 43 full-time (30 women); includes 3 minority (2 African Americans, 1 Native American), 8 international. 166 applicants, 11% accepted, 8 enrolled. In 2001, 4 master's, 7 doctorates awarded. Terminal master's awarded for partial completion of doctoral program.
**Degree requirements:** For doctorate, thesis/dissertation, qualifying exam.
**Entrance requirements:** For doctorate, GRE General Test, TOEFL. *Application deadline:* For fall admission, 2/1 (priority date). *Application fee:* $25.
**Expenses:** Tuition: Part-time $755 per credit hour.
**Financial support:** Fellowships, research assistantships, teaching assistantships, career-related internships or fieldwork and tuition waivers (full and partial) available. Financial award application deadline: 2/1.
Miron Zuckerman, Chair, 585-275-2453.
**Application contact:** Mary Ann Gilbert, Graduate Program Secretary, 585-275-8704.

### ■ UNIVERSITY OF SAINT FRANCIS

**Graduate School, Department of Psychology and Counseling, Fort Wayne, IN 46808-3994**

**AWARDS** General psychology (MS); mental health counseling (MS); school counseling (MS Ed). Part-time and evening/weekend programs available.

**Faculty:** 3 full-time (1 woman).

**Students:** 9 full-time (7 women), 31 part-time (26 women); includes 4 minority (3 African Americans, 1 Asian American or Pacific Islander), 1 international. Average age 34. 16 applicants, 88% accepted. In 2001, 6 degrees awarded.
**Entrance requirements:** For master's, interview, minimum undergraduate GPA of 3.0. *Application deadline:* For fall admission, 7/1; for spring admission, 11/1. Applications are processed on a rolling basis. *Application fee:* $20.
**Expenses:** Tuition: Part-time $430 per hour. Required fees: $10 per hour.
**Financial support:** In 2001–02, 4 students received support. Federal Work-Study, scholarships/grants, and unspecified assistantships available.
Dr. Rolf Daniel, Chair, 260-434-3233, *Fax:* 260-434-7562, *E-mail:* rdaniel@sf.edu.
**Application contact:** David McMahan, Director of Admissions, 260-434-3264, *Fax:* 260-434-7590, *E-mail:* dmcmahan@sf.edu.

■ **UNIVERSITY OF ST. THOMAS**

**Graduate Studies, Graduate School of Professional Psychology, St. Paul, MN 55105-1096**

**AWARDS** Counseling psychology (MA, Psy D); family psychology (Certificate). Part-time and evening/weekend programs available.

**Faculty:** 8 full-time (4 women), 15 part-time/adjunct (8 women).
**Students:** 42 full-time (34 women), 124 part-time (98 women); includes 19 minority (8 African Americans, 6 Asian Americans or Pacific Islanders, 4 Hispanic Americans, 1 Native American). Average age 34. 41 applicants, 76% accepted, 29 enrolled. In 2001, 34 master's, 8 doctorates, 6 other advanced degrees awarded.
**Degree requirements:** For master's, practicum; for doctorate, thesis/dissertation, qualifying exam, practicum, internship, comprehensive exam.
**Entrance requirements:** For master's and doctorate, MAT or GRE, minimum GPA of 2.75. *Application deadline:* For fall admission, 10/1; for winter admission, 2/1; for spring admission, 4/1. *Application fee:* $50.
**Expenses:** Contact institution.
**Financial support:** In 2001–02, 91 students received support; fellowships, research assistantships, institutionally sponsored loans and scholarships/grants available. Support available to part-time students. Financial award application deadline: 4/1.
**Faculty research:** Elderly, eating disorders, anxiety.
Dr. Burton Nolan, Dean, 651-962-4650, *Fax:* 651-962-4651, *E-mail:* bnolan@stthomas.edu.

**Application contact:** Dr. Mary M. Brant, Assistant Professor, 651-962-4641, *Fax:* 651-962-4651, *E-mail:* mmbrant@stthomas.edu.

■ **UNIVERSITY OF SOUTH ALABAMA**

**Graduate School, College of Arts and Sciences, Department of Psychology, Mobile, AL 36688-0002**

**AWARDS** MS. Part-time and evening/weekend programs available.

**Faculty:** 14 full-time (6 women).
**Students:** 17 full-time (9 women), 5 part-time (3 women); includes 1 minority (Hispanic American), 4 international. 36 applicants, 53% accepted. In 2001, 9 degrees awarded.
**Degree requirements:** For master's, thesis optional.
**Entrance requirements:** For master's, GRE General Test, GRE Subject Test, minimum GPA of 3.0, major in psychology or equivalent. *Application deadline:* For fall admission, 9/1 (priority date). Applications are processed on a rolling basis. *Application fee:* $25.
**Expenses:** Tuition, state resident: full-time $3,048. Tuition, nonresident: full-time $6,096. Required fees: $320.
**Financial support:** In 2001–02, 5 research assistantships were awarded; fellowships Support available to part-time students. Financial award application deadline: 4/1.
**Faculty research:** Language acquisition and development.
Dr. Larry Christensen, Chair, 334-460-6321.

■ **UNIVERSITY OF SOUTH CAROLINA**

**The Graduate School, College of Liberal Arts, Department of Psychology, Columbia, SC 29208**

**AWARDS** Clinical/community psychology (PhD); experimental psychology (MA, PhD); school psychology (PhD).

**Faculty:** 29 full-time (8 women), 4 part-time/adjunct (2 women).
**Students:** 124 full-time (96 women), 13 part-time (7 women); includes 20 minority (17 African Americans, 1 Asian American or Pacific Islander, 2 Hispanic Americans), 1 international. Average age 30. 260 applicants, 12% accepted. In 2001, 6 master's, 12 doctorates awarded. Terminal master's awarded for partial completion of doctoral program.
**Degree requirements:** For master's and doctorate, thesis/dissertation.
**Entrance requirements:** For master's and doctorate, GRE General Test. *Application fee:* $35. Electronic applications accepted.

**Expenses:** Tuition, state resident: full-time $4,434. Tuition, nonresident: full-time $9,854. Tuition and fees vary according to program.
**Financial support:** In 2001–02, 9 fellowships with partial tuition reimbursements, 16 research assistantships with partial tuition reimbursements (averaging $9,000 per year), 14 teaching assistantships with partial tuition reimbursements (averaging $9,000 per year) were awarded. Career-related internships or fieldwork, Federal Work-Study, and institutionally sponsored loans also available. Support available to part-time students.
**Faculty research:** Developmental cognitive neuroscience prevention, alcohol and drug addictions, reading and language processing. *Total annual research expenditures:* $3.2 million.
Dr. Jean Ann Linney, Chair, 803-777-4263, *Fax:* 803-777-9558.
**Application contact:** Doris Davis, Graduate Secretary, 803-777-2312, *Fax:* 803-777-9558, *E-mail:* doris@gwm.sc.edu.

■ **THE UNIVERSITY OF SOUTH DAKOTA**

**Graduate School, College of Arts and Sciences, Department of Psychology, Vermillion, SD 57069-2390**

**AWARDS** Clinical psychology (MA, PhD); human factors (MA, PhD).

**Faculty:** 24.
**Students:** 49 full-time (29 women), 2 part-time; includes 11 minority (4 Asian Americans or Pacific Islanders, 6 Hispanic Americans, 1 Native American). 150 applicants, 9% accepted. In 2001, 7 master's, 12 doctorates awarded.
**Degree requirements:** For master's and doctorate, thesis/dissertation.
**Entrance requirements:** For master's, GRE; for doctorate, GRE General Test, GRE Subject Test. *Application deadline:* For fall admission, 2/1. *Application fee:* $35.
**Expenses:** Tuition, state resident: full-time $1,700; part-time $95 per credit hour. Tuition, nonresident: full-time $5,027; part-time $279 per credit hour. Required fees: $1,062; $59 per credit hour.
**Financial support:** Research assistantships, teaching assistantships, unspecified assistantships available. Financial award applicants required to submit FAFSA.
**Faculty research:** Human-computer interactions, perceptual-cognitive processing, medical psychology, depression, moral psychology.
Dr. Randal Quevillon, Chair, 605-677-5351.
**Application contact:** Dr. Barbara Yutrzenka, Graduate Student Adviser.

# ■ UNIVERSITY OF SOUTHERN CALIFORNIA

**Graduate School, College of Letters, Arts and Sciences, Department of Psychology, Los Angeles, CA 90089**

**AWARDS** Clinical psychology (PhD); psychology (MA, PhD).

**Degree requirements:** For doctorate, thesis/dissertation.

**Entrance requirements:** For doctorate, GRE General Test.

**Expenses:** Tuition: Full-time $25,060; part-time $844 per unit. Required fees: $473.

# ■ UNIVERSITY OF SOUTHERN MISSISSIPPI

**Graduate School, College of Education and Psychology, Department of Psychology, Hattiesburg, MS 39406**

**AWARDS** M Ed, MA, MS, PhD, Ed S.

**Faculty:** 33 full-time (8 women), 5 part-time/adjunct (1 woman).

**Students:** 161 full-time (110 women), 58 part-time (45 women); includes 29 minority (18 African Americans, 3 Asian Americans or Pacific Islanders, 7 Hispanic Americans, 1 Native American). Average age 30. 374 applicants, 22% accepted. In 2001, 70 master's, 21 doctorates awarded. Terminal master's awarded for partial completion of doctoral program.

**Degree requirements:** For master's, one foreign language, thesis; for doctorate, 2 foreign languages, thesis/dissertation.

**Entrance requirements:** For master's, GRE General Test, minimum GPA of 3.0; for doctorate, GRE General Test, interview, minimum GPA of 3.0; for Ed S, GRE General Test, minimum GPA of 3.25. *Application deadline:* For fall admission, 2/15 (priority date). Applications are processed on a rolling basis. *Application fee:* $0 ($25 for international students).

**Expenses:** Tuition, state resident: full-time $3,416; part-time $190 per credit hour. Tuition, nonresident: full-time $7,932; part-time $441 per credit hour.

**Financial support:** In 2001–02, 6 research assistantships with full tuition reimbursements (averaging $6,000 per year), 94 teaching assistantships with full tuition reimbursements (averaging $4,800 per year) were awarded. Career-related internships or fieldwork, Federal Work-Study, and institutionally sponsored loans also available. Financial award application deadline: 3/15.

**Faculty research:** Dolphin cognition, sleep, neuropsychology, health-related behaviors, psychopathology. *Total annual research expenditures:* $101,200.

Dr. Stan Kuczaj, Chair, 601-266-4177, *Fax:* 601-266-5580.

# ■ UNIVERSITY OF SOUTH FLORIDA

**College of Graduate Studies, College of Arts and Sciences, Department of Psychology, Tampa, FL 33620-9951**

**AWARDS** Clinical psychology (PhD); experimental psychology (PhD); industrial/organizational psychology (PhD).

**Faculty:** 37 full-time (12 women), 2 part-time/adjunct (0 women).

**Students:** 99 full-time (67 women), 47 part-time (35 women); includes 32 minority (14 African Americans, 5 Asian Americans or Pacific Islanders, 13 Hispanic Americans), 8 international. Average age 30. 367 applicants, 7% accepted, 22 enrolled. In 2001, 5 doctorates awarded.

**Degree requirements:** For doctorate, thesis/dissertation.

**Entrance requirements:** For doctorate, GRE General Test, minimum GPA of 3.0 in last 60 hours. *Application deadline:* For fall admission, 1/15. *Application fee:* $20. Electronic applications accepted.

**Expenses:** Contact institution.

**Financial support:** Fellowships with partial tuition reimbursements, research assistantships with partial tuition reimbursements, teaching assistantships, career-related internships or fieldwork, Federal Work-Study, and institutionally sponsored loans available. Financial award application deadline: 4/15; financial award applicants required to submit FAFSA.

**Faculty research:** Human memory, job analysis, stress, drug and alcohol abuse, neuroscience. *Total annual research expenditures:* $1.4 million.

Emanuel Donchin, Chairperson, 813-974-4066, *Fax:* 813-974-4617, *E-mail:* donchin@luna.cas.usf.edu.

**Application contact:** Michael D. Coovert, Graduate Coordinator, 813-974-0482, *Fax:* 813-974-4617, *E-mail:* coovert@luna.cas.usf.edu. *Web site:* http://www.cas.usf.edu/psychology/

# ■ THE UNIVERSITY OF TENNESSEE

**Graduate School, College of Arts and Sciences, Department of Psychology, Knoxville, TN 37996**

**AWARDS** Clinical psychology (PhD); experimental psychology (MA, PhD); psychology (MA).

**Faculty:** 23 full-time (5 women), 6 part-time/adjunct (1 woman).

**Students:** 70 full-time (40 women), 24 part-time (10 women); includes 14 minority (9 African Americans, 3 Asian

Americans or Pacific Islanders, 2 Native Americans), 10 international. 116 applicants, 12% accepted. In 2001, 9 master's, 18 doctorates awarded. Terminal master's awarded for partial completion of doctoral program.

**Degree requirements:** For master's and doctorate, thesis/dissertation.

**Entrance requirements:** For master's and doctorate, GRE General Test, GRE Subject Test, TOEFL, minimum GPA of 2.7. *Application deadline:* For fall admission, 2/1. *Application fee:* $35. Electronic applications accepted.

**Expenses:** Tuition, state resident: full-time $4,280; part-time $233 per hour. Tuition, nonresident: full-time $12,066; part-time $666 per hour. Tuition and fees vary according to program.

**Financial support:** In 2001–02, 1 fellowship, 10 teaching assistantships were awarded. Research assistantships, Federal Work-Study, institutionally sponsored loans, and unspecified assistantships also available. Financial award application deadline: 2/1; financial award applicants required to submit FAFSA.

Dr. James Lawler, Head, 865-974-3328, *Fax:* 865-974-3330, *E-mail:* jlawler@utk.edu.

# ■ THE UNIVERSITY OF TENNESSEE AT CHATTANOOGA

**Graduate Division, College of Arts and Sciences, Department of Psychology, Chattanooga, TN 37403-2598**

**AWARDS** Industrial/organizational psychology (MS); research psychology (MS); school psychology (MS). Part-time and evening/weekend programs available.

**Faculty:** 9 full-time (3 women).

**Students:** 37 full-time (26 women), 11 part-time (9 women); includes 7 minority (all African Americans). Average age 25. 57 applicants, 82% accepted, 20 enrolled. In 2001, 35 degrees awarded.

**Entrance requirements:** For master's, GRE General Test. *Application deadline:* For fall admission, 8/1 (priority date); for spring admission, 12/1 (priority date). Applications are processed on a rolling basis. *Application fee:* $25.

**Expenses:** Tuition, state resident: full-time $3,752; part-time $228 per hour. Tuition, nonresident: full-time $10,282; part-time $565 per hour.

**Financial support:** Fellowships, research assistantships, Federal Work-Study available. Financial award application deadline: 4/1; financial award applicants required to submit FAFSA.

Dr. David Pittenger, Head, 423-425-4262, *Fax:* 423-425-4279.

**Application contact:** Dr. Deborah E. Arfken, Dean of Graduate Studies, 865-425-1740, *Fax:* 865-425-5223, *E-mail:* deborah-arfken@utc.edu. *Web site:* http://www.utc.edu/

# ■ THE UNIVERSITY OF TEXAS AT ARLINGTON

**Graduate School, College of Science, Department of Psychology, Arlington, TX 76019**

**AWARDS** Experimental psychology (PhD); psychology (MS).

**Faculty:** 13 full-time (3 women), 1 part-time/adjunct (0 women).

**Students:** 33 full-time (25 women), 5 part-time (4 women); includes 9 minority (2 African Americans, 2 Asian Americans or Pacific Islanders, 4 Hispanic Americans, 1 Native American), 5 international. 27 applicants, 74% accepted, 12 enrolled. In 2001, 4 master's, 3 doctorates awarded.

**Degree requirements:** For master's, thesis, comprehensive exam or thesis; for doctorate, one foreign language, thesis/dissertation.

**Entrance requirements:** For master's and doctorate, GRE General Test, TOEFL. *Application deadline:* For fall admission, 6/16. Applications are processed on a rolling basis. *Application fee:* $25 ($50 for international students).

**Expenses:** Tuition, area resident: Full-time $2,268. Tuition, nonresident: full-time $6,264. Required fees: $839. Tuition and fees vary according to course load.

**Financial support:** In 2001–02, 4 fellowships (averaging $1,000 per year), 2 research assistantships (averaging $12,000 per year), 28 teaching assistantships (averaging $12,000 per year) were awarded. Federal Work-Study also available. Financial award application deadline: 6/1; financial award applicants required to submit FAFSA.

Dr. Paul B. Paulus, Chairman, 817-272-2281, *Fax:* 817-272-2364, *E-mail:* paulus@uta.edu.

**Application contact:** Dr. David Gorfein, Graduate Advisor, 817-272-2281, *Fax:* 817-272-2364, *E-mail:* gorfein@uta.edu.

# ■ THE UNIVERSITY OF TEXAS AT AUSTIN

**Graduate School, College of Liberal Arts, Department of Psychology, Austin, TX 78712-1111**

**AWARDS** PhD.

**Degree requirements:** For doctorate, thesis/dissertation.

**Entrance requirements:** For doctorate, GRE General Test. Electronic applications accepted.

**Expenses:** Tuition, state resident: full-time $3,159. Tuition, nonresident: full-time $6,957. Tuition and fees vary according to program.

**Faculty research:** Behavioral neuroscience, sensory neuroscience, evolutionary psychology, cognitive processes in psychopathology, cognitive processes and their development. *Web site:* http://www.psy.utexas.edu/psy/grad-contents.html

# ■ THE UNIVERSITY OF TEXAS AT BROWNSVILLE

**Graduate Studies and Sponsored Programs, College of Liberal Arts, Department of Behavioral Sciences, Brownsville, TX 78520-4991**

**AWARDS** MAIS. Part-time and evening/weekend programs available.

**Degree requirements:** For master's, thesis or satisfactory comprehensive exam.

**Entrance requirements:** For master's, GRE General Test, TOEFL.

**Faculty research:** Memory, socio-political structure of South America, cartography of Mexico and Central America, family economic structure of Spain.

# ■ THE UNIVERSITY OF TEXAS AT EL PASO

**Graduate School, College of Liberal Arts, Department of Psychology, El Paso, TX 79968-0001**

**AWARDS** Clinical psychology (MA); experimental psychology (MA); psychology (PhD). Part-time and evening/weekend programs available.

**Students:** 42 (29 women); includes 21 minority (20 Hispanic Americans, 1 Native American) 2 international. Average age 34. 54 applicants, 98% accepted. In 2001, 2 master's, 2 doctorates awarded.

**Degree requirements:** For master's and doctorate, thesis/dissertation.

**Entrance requirements:** For master's and doctorate, GRE General Test, TOEFL. *Application deadline:* For fall admission, 2/1. Applications are processed on a rolling basis. *Application fee:* $15 ($65 for international students). Electronic applications accepted.

**Expenses:** Tuition, state resident: full-time $2,450. Tuition, nonresident: full-time $6,000.

**Financial support:** In 2001–02, 18 students received support, including research assistantships with partial tuition reimbursements available (averaging $18,625 per year), teaching assistantships with partial tuition reimbursements available (averaging $14,900 per year); fellowships with partial tuition reimbursements available, career-related internships or

fieldwork, Federal Work-Study, institutionally sponsored loans, scholarships/grants, and tuition waivers (partial) also available. Financial award application deadline: 3/15; financial award applicants required to submit FAFSA.

Dr. Judith P. Goggin, Chairperson, 915-747-5551, *Fax:* 915-747-6553, *E-mail:* jgoggin@miners.utep.edu.

**Application contact:** Dr. Charles H. Ambler, Dean of the Graduate School, 915-747-5491 Ext. 7886, *Fax:* 915-747-5788, *E-mail:* cambler@miners.utep.edu.

# ■ THE UNIVERSITY OF TEXAS AT SAN ANTONIO

**College of Liberal and Fine Arts, Department of Psychology, San Antonio, TX 78249-0617**

**AWARDS** MS.

**Faculty:** 7 full-time (3 women).

**Students:** 9 full-time (7 women), 7 part-time (6 women); includes 4 minority (all Hispanic Americans). 11 applicants, 73% accepted, 8 enrolled. In 2001, 5 degrees awarded.

**Degree requirements:** For master's, thesis, comprehensive exam, registration.

**Entrance requirements:** For master's, GRE, minimum GPA of 3.0 in last 60 hours and in all psychology courses.

**Expenses:** Tuition, state resident: full-time $2,268; part-time $126 per credit hour. Tuition, nonresident: full-time $6,066; part-time $337 per credit hour. Required fees: $781. Tuition and fees vary according to course load. *Total annual research expenditures:* $80,884.

Dr. Richard Wenzlaff, Chair, 210-458-7352.

# ■ THE UNIVERSITY OF TEXAS AT TYLER

**Graduate Studies, College of Education and Psychology, Department of Psychology, Tyler, TX 75799-0001**

**AWARDS** Clinical psychology (MS); counseling psychology (MA); interdisciplinary studies (MS, MSIS); school counseling (MA). Part-time and evening/weekend programs available.

**Faculty:** 7 full-time (4 women), 1 (woman) part-time/adjunct.

**Students:** 30 full-time (26 women), 52 part-time (48 women); includes 9 minority (5 African Americans, 1 Asian American or Pacific Islander, 2 Hispanic Americans, 1 Native American), 3 international. Average age 30. 23 applicants, 100% accepted, 16 enrolled. In 2001, 18 degrees awarded.

**Degree requirements:** For master's, comprehensive exam and/or thesis.

*The University of Texas at Tyler*
*(continued)*

**Entrance requirements:** For master's, GRE General Test, GRE Subject Test, minimum GPA of 3.0. *Application deadline:* For fall admission, 2/1; for spring admission, 10/1. *Application fee:* $0 ($50 for international students). Electronic applications accepted.

**Expenses:** Tuition, state resident: part-time $44 per credit hour. Tuition, nonresident: part-time $262 per credit hour. Required fees: $58 per credit hour. $76 per semester.

**Financial support:** Teaching assistantships, career-related internships or fieldwork, Federal Work-Study, and institutionally sponsored loans available. Support available to part-time students. Financial award application deadline: 7/1.

**Faculty research:** Incest, aging, depression, neuropsychology, child psychopathology.

Dr. Henry L. Schreiber, Chairperson, 903-566-7239, *Fax:* 903-565-5656, *E-mail:* hschreiber@mail.uttyl.edu.

**Application contact:** Dr. Robert F. McClure, Graduate Adviser, 903-566-7435, *Fax:* 903-566-7065, *E-mail:* rmcclure@ mail.uttyl.edu. *Web site:* http:// www.uttyl.edu/psychology/grad.htm/

■ **THE UNIVERSITY OF TEXAS OF THE PERMIAN BASIN**

**Graduate School, College of Arts and Sciences, Department of Behavioral Science, Program in Psychology, Odessa, TX 79762-0001**

**AWARDS** Applied behavioral analysis (MA); clinical psychology (MA). Part-time and evening/weekend programs available.

**Degree requirements:** For master's, thesis, practicum.

**Entrance requirements:** For master's, GRE General Test.

**Expenses:** Tuition, state resident: full-time $1,746. Tuition, nonresident: full-time $5,292. Required fees: $523. Tuition and fees vary according to course load.

■ **THE UNIVERSITY OF TEXAS– PAN AMERICAN**

**College of Social and Behavioral Sciences, Department of Psychology and Anthropology, Edinburg, TX 78539-2999**

**AWARDS** Psychology (MA), including clinical psychology, experimental psychology. Part-time and evening/weekend programs available.

**Faculty:** 11 full-time (0 women).

**Students:** 13 full-time (7 women), 29 part-time (20 women); includes 33 minority (1 Asian American or Pacific Islander, 32 Hispanic Americans). Average age 29. 18 applicants, 44% accepted. In 2001, 7 degrees awarded.

**Degree requirements:** For master's, internship, thesis optional.

**Entrance requirements:** For master's, GRE General Test. *Application deadline:* For fall admission, 2/1 (priority date); for winter admission, 10/1 (priority date). Applications are processed on a rolling basis. *Application fee:* $0. Electronic applications accepted.

**Expenses:** Tuition, state resident: part-time $212 per semester hour. Tuition, nonresident: part-time $367 per semester hour.

**Financial support:** In 2001–02, 3 teaching assistantships were awarded; career-related internships or fieldwork, Federal Work-Study, and institutionally sponsored loans also available.

**Faculty research:** Rehabilitation, biofeedback, acculturation, child development, health.

Dr. Mark Winkel, Director, 956-381-3528, *Fax:* 956-381-3333, *E-mail:* winkelm@ panam.edu. *Web site:* http:// www.panam.edu/dept/gsprog/

■ **UNIVERSITY OF THE PACIFIC**

**Graduate School, Department of Psychology, Stockton, CA 95211-0197**

**AWARDS** MA.

**Students:** 1 full-time (0 women), 14 part-time (10 women); includes 6 minority (5 Asian Americans or Pacific Islanders, 1 Hispanic American), 1 international. Average age 28. 15 applicants, 73% accepted, 6 enrolled. In 2001, 10 degrees awarded.

**Degree requirements:** For master's, thesis.

**Entrance requirements:** For master's, GRE General Test. *Application deadline:* For fall admission, 3/1 (priority date). Applications are processed on a rolling basis. *Application fee:* $50.

**Expenses:** Tuition: Full-time $21,150; part-time $661 per unit. Required fees: $375.

**Financial support:** In 2001–02, 17 teaching assistantships were awarded; institutionally sponsored loans also available. Support available to part-time students. Financial award application deadline: 3/1.

Dr. Roseann Hannon, Chairperson, 209-946-2133, *E-mail:* rhannon@uop.edu.

■ **UNIVERSITY OF TOLEDO**

**Graduate School, College of Arts and Sciences, Department of Psychology, Toledo, OH 43606-3398**

**AWARDS** Clinical psychology (PhD); experimental psychology (MA, PhD).

**Faculty:** 20.

**Students:** 51 full-time (43 women). Average age 28. 104 applicants, 21% accepted, 20 enrolled. In 2001, 4 master's, 7 doctorates awarded.

**Degree requirements:** For master's, thesis; for doctorate, one foreign language, thesis/dissertation.

**Entrance requirements:** For master's and doctorate, GRE General Test, GRE Subject Test. *Application deadline:* For fall admission, 1/15. *Application fee:* $30.

**Expenses:** Tuition, state resident: full-time $7,278; part-time $303 per hour. Tuition, nonresident: full-time $15,731; part-time $699 per hour. Required fees: $43 per hour.

**Financial support:** In 2001–02, 41 research assistantships were awarded; career-related internships or fieldwork, Federal Work-Study, and institutionally sponsored loans also available. Support available to part-time students. Financial award application deadline: 1/15; financial award applicants required to submit FAFSA.

**Faculty research:** Neural taste response. Dr. Robert A. Haaf, Chair, 419-530-2717, *Fax:* 419-530-8479, *E-mail:* rhaaf@ uoft02.utoledo.edu. *Web site:* http:// utoledo.edu/www/psychology/ graduate.html

**Find an in-depth description at www.petersons.com/gradchannel.**

■ **UNIVERSITY OF TULSA**

**Graduate School, College of Arts and Sciences, Department of Psychology, Tulsa, OK 74104-3189**

**AWARDS** Clinical psychology (MA, PhD); industrial/organizational psychology (MA, PhD). Part-time programs available.

**Faculty:** 14 full-time (5 women).

**Students:** 63 full-time (37 women), 14 part-time (7 women); includes 4 minority (1 African American, 2 Hispanic Americans, 1 Native American), 6 international. Average age 28. 103 applicants, 49% accepted, 24 enrolled. In 2001, 27 master's, 6 doctorates awarded.

**Degree requirements:** For doctorate, thesis/dissertation, comprehensive exam.

**Entrance requirements:** For master's and doctorate, GRE General Test, TOEFL. *Application deadline:* For fall admission, 2/1 (priority date). Applications are processed on a rolling basis. *Application fee:* $30. Electronic applications accepted.

**Expenses:** Tuition: Full-time $9,540; part-time $530 per credit hour. Required fees: $80. One-time fee: $230 full-time.

**Financial support:** Fellowships with full and partial tuition reimbursements, research assistantships with full and partial tuition reimbursements, teaching assistant-ships with full and partial tuition reimbursements, career-related internships or fieldwork, Federal Work-Study, scholarships/grants, tuition waivers (partial), and unspecified assistantships available. Support available to part-time students. Financial award application deadline: 2/1; financial award applicants required to submit FAFSA.

**Faculty research:** Personality and social psychology, cognitive psychology, biopsychology. *Total annual research expenditures:* $835,245.

Dr. Allan Harkness, Chairperson, 918-631-2543, *Fax:* 918-631-2833, *E-mail:* allan-harkness@utulsa.edu. *Web site:* http://www.cas.utulsa.edu/psych/goverview.html/

### ■ UNIVERSITY OF UTAH

**Graduate School, College of Social and Behavioral Science, Department of Psychology, Salt Lake City, UT 84112-1107**

**AWARDS** M Stat, MA, MS, PhD.

**Faculty:** 9 full-time (1 woman), 5 part-time/adjunct (1 woman).

**Students:** 39 full-time (27 women), 16 part-time (10 women); includes 4 minority (3 Asian Americans or Pacific Islanders, 1 Hispanic American), 4 international. Average age 30. 136 applicants, 15% accepted. In 2001, 5 master's, 4 doctorates awarded.

**Degree requirements:** For master's, one foreign language; for doctorate, thesis/dissertation.

**Entrance requirements:** For master's, GRE General Test, TOEFL; for doctorate, GRE, TOEFL. *Application deadline:* For fall admission, 7/1. *Application fee:* $40 ($60 for international students).

**Expenses:** Tuition, state resident: part-time $320 per semester hour. Tuition, nonresident: part-time $1,135 per semester hour. Required fees: $143 per semester hour. Tuition and fees vary according to course load, degree level and program.

**Financial support:** In 2001–02, 26 teaching assistantships were awarded; fellowships, research assistantships, career-related internships or fieldwork also available.

**Faculty research:** Social perceptions, memory process, clinical counseling, neural systems, motivational processes. Tim Smith, Chair, 801-581-6123, *Fax:* 801-581-5841.

**Application contact:** Jamie Brass, Advisor, 801-585-9095, *Fax:* 801-581-5841, *E-mail:* jamie.brass@psych.utah.edu.

### ■ UNIVERSITY OF VERMONT

**Graduate College, College of Arts and Sciences, Department of Psychology, Burlington, VT 05405**

**AWARDS** Clinical psychology (PhD); psychology (PhD).

**Degree requirements:** For doctorate, thesis/dissertation.

**Entrance requirements:** For doctorate, GRE General Test, GRE Subject Test, TOEFL.

**Expenses:** Tuition, state resident: part-time $335 per credit. Tuition, nonresident: part-time $838 per credit.

**Find an in-depth description at www.petersons.com/gradchannel.**

### ■ UNIVERSITY OF VIRGINIA

**College and Graduate School of Arts and Sciences, Department of Psychology, Charlottesville, VA 22903**

**AWARDS** MA, PhD.

**Faculty:** 37 full-time (13 women), 5 part-time/adjunct (2 women).

**Students:** 87 full-time (60 women), 3 part-time (all women); includes 13 minority (8 African Americans, 3 Asian Americans or Pacific Islanders, 1 Hispanic American, 1 Native American), 9 international. Average age 27. 438 applicants, 8% accepted, 17 enrolled. In 2001, 9 master's, 9 doctorates awarded.

**Degree requirements:** For master's and doctorate, thesis/dissertation.

**Entrance requirements:** For master's and doctorate, GRE General Test, GRE Subject Test. *Application deadline:* For fall admission, 7/15; for spring admission, 12/2. Applications are processed on a rolling basis. *Application fee:* $40. Electronic applications accepted.

**Expenses:** Tuition, state resident: full-time $3,988. Tuition, nonresident: full-time $17,078. Required fees: $1,190.

**Financial support:** Application deadline: 2/1.

Timothy D. Wilson, Chairman, 434-982-4750, *Fax:* 434-982-4766, *E-mail:* psy-dept@virginia.edu.

**Application contact:** Duane J. Osheim, Associate Dean for Graduate Programs, 434-924-7184, *Fax:* 434-924-3084, *E-mail:* grad-a-s@virginia.edu. *Web site:* http://www.virginia.edu/~psych/

### ■ UNIVERSITY OF WASHINGTON

**Graduate School, College of Arts and Sciences, Department of Psychology, Seattle, WA 98195**

**AWARDS** PhD.

**Faculty:** 54 full-time (20 women), 5 part-time/adjunct (4 women).

**Students:** 112 full-time (73 women), 23 part-time (15 women); includes 27 minority (5 African Americans, 12 Asian Americans or Pacific Islanders, 5 Hispanic Americans, 5 Native Americans), 5 international. Average age 28. 419 applicants, 11% accepted, 31 enrolled. In 2001, 16 doctorates awarded.

**Degree requirements:** For doctorate, thesis/dissertation. *Median time to degree:* Doctorate–6 years full-time.

**Entrance requirements:** For doctorate, GRE General Test, TSE, minimum GPA of 3.0. *Application deadline:* For fall admission, 12/15. *Application fee:* $50. Electronic applications accepted.

**Expenses:** Tuition, state resident: full-time $5,539. Tuition, nonresident: full-time $14,376. Required fees: $390. Tuition and fees vary according to course load and program.

**Financial support:** In 2001–02, 119 students received support, including 49 research assistantships with full tuition reimbursements available (averaging $13,950 per year), 51 teaching assistantships with full tuition reimbursements available (averaging $13,950 per year); career-related internships or fieldwork, Federal Work-Study, institutionally sponsored loans, traineeships, and health care benefits also available. Financial award application deadline: 2/1.

**Faculty research:** Addictive behaviors, artificial intelligence, child psychopathology, mechanisms and development of vision, physiology of ingestive behaviors. *Total annual research expenditures:* $7.1 million.

Dr. Michael D. Beecher, Chair, 206-685-9660, *Fax:* 206-685-3157, *E-mail:* beecher@u.washington.edu.

**Application contact:** Graduate Program Office, 206-543-8687, *E-mail:* psygrad@u.washington.edu. *Web site:* http://dept.washington.edu/psych/

### ■ UNIVERSITY OF WEST FLORIDA

**College of Arts and Sciences: Arts, Department of Psychology, Pensacola, FL 32514-5750**

**AWARDS** MA. Part-time and evening/weekend programs available.

**Faculty:** 18 full-time (6 women), 2 part-time/adjunct (1 woman).

**Students:** 68 full-time (52 women), 37 part-time (30 women); includes 15 minority (6 African Americans, 3 Asian Americans or Pacific Islanders, 4 Hispanic Americans, 2 Native Americans), 1 international. Average age 29. 132 applicants, 51% accepted, 24 enrolled. In 2001, 25 degrees awarded.

*University of West Florida (continued)*
**Degree requirements:** For master's, thesis optional.
**Entrance requirements:** For master's, GRE General Test, GRE Subject Test, minimum GPA of 3.0. *Application deadline:* Applications are processed on a rolling basis. *Application fee:* $20.
**Expenses:** Tuition, state resident: full-time $3,995; part-time $166 per credit hour. Tuition, nonresident: full-time $13,766; part-time $574 per credit hour. Tuition and fees vary according to campus/location.
**Financial support:** Fellowships, teaching assistantships, career-related internships or fieldwork and Federal Work-Study available.
**Faculty research:** Prose recall, brain imaging, peak performance, biofeedback and pain control, comparable worth.
Dr. Ronald Belter, Chairperson, 850-474-2363.

■ **UNIVERSITY OF WISCONSIN–EAU CLAIRE**

**College of Arts and Sciences, Department of Psychology, Eau Claire, WI 54702-4004**

**AWARDS** School psychology (MSE, Ed S).
**Faculty:** 18 full-time (7 women).
**Students:** 18 full-time (14 women), 2 part-time (1 woman); includes 1 minority (Asian American or Pacific Islander). Average age 24. 40 applicants, 50% accepted, 18 enrolled. In 2001, 16 degrees awarded.
**Degree requirements:** For master's, thesis, comprehensive exam.
**Entrance requirements:** For master's, GRE. *Application deadline:* For fall admission, 3/1. Applications are processed on a rolling basis. *Application fee:* $45.
**Expenses:** Tuition, state resident: full-time $4,481; part-time $249 per credit. Tuition, nonresident: full-time $14,305; part-time $795 per credit.
**Financial support:** In 2001–02, 8 students received support, including 6 teaching assistantships (averaging $3,600 per year); Federal Work-Study also available. Financial award application deadline: 4/15; financial award applicants required to submit FAFSA.
Dr. Larry Morse, Chair, 715-836-5733, *Fax:* 715-836-2214, *E-mail:* morsela@uwec.edu. *Web site:* http://www.uwec.edu/

■ **UNIVERSITY OF WISCONSIN–LA CROSSE**

**Graduate Studies, College of Liberal Studies, Department of Psychology, La Crosse, WI 54601-3742**

**AWARDS** School psychology (MS Ed, CAGS).

**Degree requirements:** For master's, thesis, seminar, or comprehensive exams.
**Entrance requirements:** For master's, GRE General Test, minimum GPA of 2.85, interview, sample of written work, resumé.

■ **UNIVERSITY OF WISCONSIN–MADISON**

**Graduate School, College of Letters and Science, Department of Psychology, Madison, WI 53706-1380**

**AWARDS** Biological psychology (PhD); clinical psychology (PhD); cognitive and perceptual sciences (PhD); developmental psychology (PhD); psychology (PhD); social and personality psychology (PhD).
**Faculty:** 33 full-time (12 women), 2 part-time/adjunct (1 woman).
**Students:** 75 full-time (43 women); includes 6 minority (3 African Americans, 2 Asian Americans or Pacific Islanders, 1 Hispanic American), 6 international. Average age 23. 257 applicants, 14% accepted, 15 enrolled. In 2001, 7 doctorates awarded.
**Degree requirements:** For doctorate, thesis/dissertation, comprehensive exam, registration. *Median time to degree:* Doctorate–5 years full-time.
**Entrance requirements:** For doctorate, GRE General Test, minimum undergraduate GPA of 3.0. *Application deadline:* For fall admission, 1/5 (priority date). Applications are processed on a rolling basis. *Application fee:* $45. Electronic applications accepted.
**Expenses:** Tuition, state resident: full-time $7,361; part-time $399 per credit. Tuition, nonresident: full-time $20,499; part-time $1,282 per credit. Required fees: $34 per credit. Full-time tuition and fees vary according to course load, program, reciprocity agreements and student level.
**Financial support:** In 2001–02, 52 students received support, including 6 fellowships with full tuition reimbursements available (averaging $13,446 per year), 30 research assistantships with full tuition reimbursements available (averaging $13,814 per year), 17 teaching assistantships with full tuition reimbursements available (averaging $13,814 per year); career-related internships or fieldwork, institutionally sponsored loans, traineeships, health care benefits, and unspecified assistantships also available. Financial award application deadline: 1/5.
Charles T. Snowdon, Chair, 608-262-2079, *Fax:* 608-262-4029, *E-mail:* snowdon@facstaff.wise.edu.
**Application contact:** Jane Fox-Anderson, Secretary, 608-262-2079, *Fax:* 608-262-4029, *E-mail:* jefoxand@facstaff.wisc.edu. *Web site:* http://www.psych.wisc.edu/

■ **UNIVERSITY OF WISCONSIN–MILWAUKEE**

**Graduate School, College of Letters and Sciences, Department of Psychology, Milwaukee, WI 53201-0413**

**AWARDS** Clinical psychology (MS, PhD); psychology (MS, PhD).
**Faculty:** 18 full-time (4 women).
**Students:** 55 full-time (38 women), 10 part-time (6 women); includes 4 minority (1 African American, 2 Asian Americans or Pacific Islanders, 1 Hispanic American), 3 international. 84 applicants, 26% accepted. In 2001, 3 master's, 8 doctorates awarded.
**Degree requirements:** For master's, thesis; for doctorate, variable foreign language requirement, thesis/dissertation.
**Entrance requirements:** For master's and doctorate, GRE General Test, GRE Subject Test. *Application deadline:* For fall admission, 1/1 (priority date); for spring admission, 9/1. Applications are processed on a rolling basis. *Application fee:* $45 ($75 for international students).
**Expenses:** Tuition, state resident: full-time $6,180; part-time $535 per credit. Tuition, nonresident: full-time $19,482; part-time $1,366 per credit. Tuition and fees vary according to course load, program and reciprocity agreements.
**Financial support:** In 2001–02, 7 fellowships, 2 research assistantships, 35 teaching assistantships were awarded. Career-related internships or fieldwork and unspecified assistantships also available. Support available to part-time students. Financial award application deadline: 4/15.
Douglas Woods, Representative, 414-229-4747, *Fax:* 414-229-5219, *E-mail:* dwoods@uwm.edu. *Web site:* http://www.uwm.edu/dept/psychology/

■ **UNIVERSITY OF WISCONSIN–OSHKOSH**

**Graduate School, College of Letters and Science, Department of Psychology, Oshkosh, WI 54901**

**AWARDS** Experimental psychology (MS); industrial/organizational psychology (MS).
**Faculty:** 8 full-time (2 women).
**Students:** 20; includes 2 minority (1 Asian American or Pacific Islander, 1 Hispanic American). Average age 26. In 2001, 7 degrees awarded.
**Degree requirements:** For master's, thesis.
**Entrance requirements:** For master's, GRE, 10 semester hours of undergraduate course work in psychology. *Application deadline:* Applications are processed on a rolling basis. *Application fee:* $45. Electronic applications accepted.

**Expenses:** Tuition, state resident: full-time $2,236; part-time $250 per credit. Tuition, nonresident: full-time $7,148; part-time $795 per credit. Tuition and fees vary according to program.

**Financial support:** Career-related internships or fieldwork, institutionally sponsored loans, and unspecified assistantships available. Financial award application deadline: 3/15; financial award applicants required to submit FAFSA.

**Faculty research:** Performance evaluation, training, biological bases of behavior, tactile perception, aging.

Dr. Susan McFadden, Chair, 920-424-2300.

**Application contact:** 920-424-2300, *E-mail:* psychology@uwosh.edu. *Web site:* http://www.uwosh.edu/departments/psychology/

## ■ UNIVERSITY OF WISCONSIN–STOUT

**Graduate School, College of Human Development, Program in Applied Psychology, Menomonie, WI 54751**

**AWARDS** MS. Part-time programs available.

**Students:** 15 full-time (9 women), 1 part-time. 14 applicants, 93% accepted, 11 enrolled. In 2001, 3 degrees awarded.

**Degree requirements:** For master's, thesis.

**Entrance requirements:** For master's, GRE General Test, GRE Subject Test. *Application fee:* $45.

**Expenses:** Tuition, state resident: full-time $4,915. Tuition, nonresident: full-time $12,553.

**Financial support:** In 2001–02, 13 research assistantships were awarded; teaching assistantships, Federal Work-Study and tuition waivers (full and partial) also available. Support available to part-time students. Financial award application deadline: 4/1; financial award applicants required to submit FAFSA.

Dr. Richard Tafalla, Director, 715-232-1662, *E-mail:* tafallar@uwstout.edu.

**Application contact:** Anne E. Johnson, Graduate Student Evaluator, 715-232-1322, *Fax:* 715-232-2413, *E-mail:* johnsona@uwstout.edu.

## ■ UNIVERSITY OF WISCONSIN–WHITEWATER

**School of Graduate Studies, College of Letters and Sciences, Department of Psychology, Whitewater, WI 53190-1790**

**AWARDS** School psychology (MS Ed). Part-time and evening/weekend programs available.

**Students:** 11 full-time (8 women), 3 part-time (all women); includes 2 minority

(both African Americans). Average age 27. 25 applicants, 88% accepted, 20 enrolled. In 2001, 14 degrees awarded.

**Degree requirements:** For master's, comprehensive exam or thesis.

**Entrance requirements:** For master's, MAT or GRE, interview, minimum GPA of 3.0, 3 letters of recommendation. *Application deadline:* For fall and spring admission, 3/1. Applications are processed on a rolling basis. *Application fee:* $45. Electronic applications accepted.

**Expenses:** Tuition, state resident: full-time $4,511; part-time $251 per credit. Tuition, nonresident: full-time $14,335; part-time $797 per credit. One-time fee: $45. Tuition and fees vary according to course load and program.

**Financial support:** In 2001–02, 6 research assistantships with partial tuition reimbursements (averaging $8,889 per year) were awarded; Federal Work-Study, unspecified assistantships, and out of state fee waiver also available. Support available to part-time students. Financial award application deadline: 3/15; financial award applicants required to submit FAFSA.

**Faculty research:** Neural substrate of reward.

Dr. James Larson, Coordinator, 262-472-5412, *Fax:* 262-472-1863, *E-mail:* larsonj@uww.edu.

**Application contact:** Sally A. Lange, School of Graduate Studies, 262-472-1006, *Fax:* 262-472-5027, *E-mail:* gradschl@uww.edu.

## ■ UNIVERSITY OF WYOMING

**Graduate School, College of Arts and Sciences, Department of Psychology, Laramie, WY 82071**

**AWARDS** MA, MS, PhD.

**Faculty:** 13 full-time (5 women), 3 part-time/adjunct (0 women).

**Students:** 28 full-time (17 women), 13 part-time (11 women); includes 2 minority (both Asian Americans or Pacific Islanders). Average age 31. 8 applicants, 88% accepted. In 2001, 5 master's, 7 doctorates awarded. Terminal master's awarded for partial completion of doctoral program.

**Degree requirements:** For master's, thesis/dissertation; for doctorate, thesis/dissertation, comprehensive exam.

**Entrance requirements:** For master's and doctorate, GRE General Test, GRE Subject Test, minimum GPA of 3.0. *Application deadline:* For fall admission, 1/15. *Application fee:* $40.

**Expenses:** Tuition, state resident: full-time $2,895; part-time $161 per credit hour. Tuition, nonresident: full-time $8,367; part-time $465 per credit hour. Required fees: $491; $10 per credit hour. $2 per

credit hour. Tuition and fees vary according to course load and program.

**Financial support:** In 2001–02, 6 research assistantships with full tuition reimbursements (averaging $10,100 per year), 17 teaching assistantships with full tuition reimbursements (averaging $10,100 per year) were awarded. Career-related internships or fieldwork, Federal Work-Study, and institutionally sponsored loans also available. Financial award application deadline: 3/1.

**Faculty research:** Child development, neuroscience, health psychology, psychology and law, mental retardation. *Total annual research expenditures:* $1.1 million.

Dr. Narina Nunez, Chair, 307-766-6303, *Fax:* 307-766-2926, *E-mail:* narina@uwyo.edu.

**Application contact:** Cheryl Hamilton, Graduate Admission Coordinator, 307-766-6303, *Fax:* 307-766-2926, *E-mail:* psyc-wu@uwyo.edu. *Web site:* http://www.uwyo.edu/psyc/

## ■ UTAH STATE UNIVERSITY

**School of Graduate Studies, College of Education, Department of Psychology, Logan, UT 84322**

**AWARDS** Clinical/counseling/school psychology (PhD); research and evaluation methodology (PhD); school counseling (MS); school psychology (MS). Part-time and evening/weekend programs available. Postbaccalaureate distance learning degree programs offered (no on-campus study).

**Faculty:** 18 full-time (8 women), 40 part-time/adjunct (15 women).

**Students:** 55 full-time (31 women), 80 part-time (62 women); includes 10 minority (3 Asian Americans or Pacific Islanders, 1 Hispanic American, 6 Native Americans), 3 international. Average age 34. 138 applicants, 38% accepted. In 2001, 31 master's, 7 doctorates awarded. Terminal master's awarded for partial completion of doctoral program.

**Degree requirements:** For master's, thesis (for some programs); for doctorate, thesis/dissertation.

**Entrance requirements:** For master's and doctorate, GRE General Test, TOEFL, minimum GPA of 3.5. *Application deadline:* For fall admission, 1/15; for spring admission, 10/15. Applications are processed on a rolling basis. *Application fee:* $40.

**Expenses:** Tuition, state resident: full-time $1,693. Tuition, nonresident: full-time $4,233. Required fees: $501. Tuition and fees vary according to program.

**Financial support:** In 2001–02, 5 fellowships with full and partial tuition reimbursements (averaging $12,000 per year), 25 research assistantships with full

*Utah State University (continued)*
and partial tuition reimbursements (averaging $8,500 per year), 18 teaching assistantships with full and partial tuition reimbursements (averaging $7,000 per year) were awarded. Career-related internships or fieldwork, Federal Work-Study, institutionally sponsored loans, scholarships/grants, tuition waivers (partial), and unspecified assistantships also available. Financial award application deadline: 2/1.
**Faculty research:** Hearing loss detection in infancy, ADHD, eating disorders, domestic violence, neuropsychology.
David M. Stein, Head, 435-797-1460, *Fax:* 435-797-1448, *E-mail:* davids@coe.usu.edu.
**Application contact:** Sheila Jessie, Staff Assistant IV, 435-797-1449, *Fax:* 435-797-1448, *E-mail:* sheilaj@coe.usu.edu. *Web site:* http://www.coe.usu.edu/psyc/ndex.html

■ **VALDOSTA STATE UNIVERSITY**

**Graduate School, College of Education, Department of Psychology and Guidance, Valdosta, GA 31698**
**AWARDS** Clinical/counseling psychology (MS); industrial/organizational psychology (MS); school counseling (M Ed, Ed S); school psychology (M Ed, Ed S). Evening/weekend programs available.

**Faculty:** 13 full-time (2 women).
**Students:** 40 full-time (30 women), 62 part-time (54 women); includes 10 minority (7 African Americans, 1 Asian American or Pacific Islander, 1 Hispanic American, 1 Native American). Average age 26. 67 applicants, 75% accepted. In 2001, 17 degrees awarded.
**Degree requirements:** For master's, thesis or alternative, comprehensive written and/or oral exams; for Ed S, thesis.
**Entrance requirements:** For master's and Ed S, GRE General Test or MAT. *Application deadline:* For fall admission, 7/1; for spring admission, 11/15. Applications are processed on a rolling basis. *Application fee:* $20. Electronic applications accepted.
**Expenses:** Tuition, state resident: full-time $1,746; part-time $97 per hour. Tuition, nonresident: full-time $6,966; part-time $387 per hour. Required fees: $594; $297 per semester.
**Financial support:** In 2001–02, 2 research assistantships with full tuition reimbursements (averaging $2,452 per year) were awarded; institutionally sponsored loans and unspecified assistantships also available. Support available to part-time students. Financial award application deadline: 7/1; financial award applicants required to submit FAFSA.
**Faculty research:** Using Bender-Gestalt to predict graphomotor dimensions of the

draw-a-person test, neurobehavioral hemisphere dominance.
Dr. R. Bauer, Head, 229-333-5930, *Fax:* 229-259-5576, *E-mail:* bbauer@valdosta.edu.

■ **VALPARAISO UNIVERSITY**

**Graduate Division, Department of Psychology, Valparaiso, IN 46383-6493**
**AWARDS** Applied behavioral science (MA); clinical mental health counseling (MA); counseling (MA). Part-time and evening/weekend programs available.

**Students:** 14 full-time (10 women), 14 part-time (10 women); includes 2 minority (1 Asian American or Pacific Islander, 1 Hispanic American), 1 international. Average age 33. In 2001, 8 degrees awarded.
**Degree requirements:** For master's, thesis or alternative, internship.
**Entrance requirements:** For master's, GRE General Test (MA), minimum GPA of 3.0. *Application deadline:* Applications are processed on a rolling basis. *Application fee:* $30.
**Expenses:** Tuition: Full-time $5,400; part-time $300 per credit.
**Financial support:** Career-related internships or fieldwork, Federal Work-Study, and institutionally sponsored loans available. Financial award applicants required to submit FAFSA.
**Faculty research:** Sex roles, environmental psychology, human reproduction, treatment of adolescent assault victims, neuropsychological assessment.
Dr. Jody Esper, Chair, 219-464-5443, *E-mail:* jody.esper@valpo.edu.
**Application contact:** Graduate Division Office, 219-464-5313.

■ **VANDERBILT UNIVERSITY**

**Graduate School, Department of Psychology, Nashville, TN 37240-1001**
**AWARDS** MA, PhD.
**Faculty:** 30 full-time (8 women), 13 part-time/adjunct (7 women).
**Students:** 43 full-time (20 women); includes 4 minority (3 African Americans, 1 Asian American or Pacific Islander), 18 international. Average age 28. 148 applicants, 14% accepted. In 2001, 5 master's, 4 doctorates awarded.
**Degree requirements:** For doctorate, thesis/dissertation, final and qualifying exams.
**Entrance requirements:** For master's, GRE General Test; for doctorate, GRE General Test, GRE Subject Test. *Application deadline:* For fall admission, 1/15. *Application fee:* $40. Electronic applications accepted.
**Expenses:** Tuition: Full-time $28,350.

**Financial support:** In 2001–02, 5 fellowships with full tuition reimbursements (averaging $11,700 per year), 17 teaching assistantships with full tuition reimbursements (averaging $11,700 per year) were awarded. Research assistantships, career-related internships or fieldwork, Federal Work-Study, institutionally sponsored loans, and traineeships also available. Financial award application deadline: 1/15.
**Faculty research:** Clinical, cognitive, developmental, and social psychology; neuroscience; vision; behavior. *Total annual research expenditures:* $3.6 million.
Timothy P. McNamara, Chair, 615-322-2874, *Fax:* 615-343-8449, *E-mail:* t.mcnamara@vanderbilt.edu.
**Application contact:** Andrew Tomerken, Director of Graduate Studies, 615-322-2874, *Fax:* 615-343-8449, *E-mail:* andrew.j.tomerken@vanderbilt.edu. *Web site:* http://www.vanderbilt.edu/AnS/psychology/

■ **VANDERBILT UNIVERSITY**

**Graduate School, Department of Psychology and Human Development, Nashville, TN 37240-1001**
**AWARDS** MS, PhD.
**Faculty:** 23 full-time (12 women), 12 part-time/adjunct (2 women).
**Students:** 42 full-time (30 women), 3 part-time (all women); includes 5 minority (2 African Americans, 2 Asian Americans or Pacific Islanders, 1 Hispanic American), 5 international. Average age 30. 143 applicants, 8% accepted. In 2001, 5 master's, 10 doctorates awarded.
**Degree requirements:** For master's, thesis; for doctorate, thesis/dissertation, final and qualifying exams.
**Entrance requirements:** For master's and doctorate, GRE General Test. *Application deadline:* For fall admission, 1/15. *Application fee:* $40. Electronic applications accepted.
**Expenses:** Tuition: Full-time $28,350.
**Financial support:** In 2001–02, research assistantships with full tuition reimbursements (averaging $9,450 per year), teaching assistantships with full tuition reimbursements (averaging $9,450 per year) were awarded. Fellowships, career-related internships or fieldwork, Federal Work-Study, institutionally sponsored loans, and traineeships also available. Financial award application deadline: 1/15.
**Faculty research:** Applied social, clinical, community, and developmental psychology; children and families; cognition; mental retardation. *Total annual research expenditures:* $41,108.
Kathleen V. Hoover-Dempsey, Chair, 615-322-8141, *Fax:* 615-343-9494, *E-mail:* kathy.hoover-dempsey@vanderbilt.edu.

**Application contact:** David Lubinski, Director of Graduate Studies, 615-322-8141, *Fax:* 615-343-9494, *E-mail:* david.lubinski@vanderbilt.edu. *Web site:* http://peabody.vanderbilt.edu/peabody/psychhum.html

## ■ VILLANOVA UNIVERSITY

**Graduate School of Liberal Arts and Sciences, Department of Psychology, Villanova, PA 19085-1699**

**AWARDS** MS. Part-time and evening/weekend programs available.

**Students:** 19 full-time (15 women), 20 part-time (13 women); includes 3 minority (1 African American, 2 Hispanic Americans), 5 international. Average age 24. 81 applicants, 31% accepted. In 2001, 14 degrees awarded.

**Degree requirements:** For master's, thesis.

**Entrance requirements:** For master's, GRE General Test, minimum GPA of 3.0. *Application deadline:* For fall admission, 8/1 (priority date); for spring admission, 12/1. *Application fee:* $40.

**Expenses:** Tuition: Part-time $340 per credit. One-time fee: $115 full-time. Tuition and fees vary according to program.

**Financial support:** Research assistantships, Federal Work-Study and scholarships/grants available. Financial award application deadline: 4/1; financial award applicants required to submit FAFSA. Dr. Douglas M. Klieger, Chair, 610-519-4720. *Web site:* http://www.psychology.villanova.edu/ms.htm

**Find an in-depth description at www.petersons.com/gradchannel.**

## ■ VIRGINIA COMMONWEALTH UNIVERSITY

**School of Graduate Studies, College of Humanities and Sciences, Department of Psychology, Program in General Psychology, Richmond, VA 23284-9005**

**AWARDS** PhD.

**Students:** 28 full-time, 6 part-time; includes 6 minority (3 African Americans, 1 Asian American or Pacific Islander, 1 Hispanic American, 1 Native American). 34 applicants, 26% accepted. In 2001, 10 doctorates awarded.

**Degree requirements:** For doctorate, thesis/dissertation.

**Entrance requirements:** For doctorate, GRE General Test. *Application deadline:* For fall admission, 2/15. *Application fee:* $30.

**Expenses:** Tuition, state resident: full-time $4,276; part-time $238 per credit. Tuition,

nonresident: full-time $12,672; part-time $704 per credit. Required fees: $1,167; $43 per credit.

**Financial support:** Fellowships, research assistantships, teaching assistantships, Federal Work-Study, institutionally sponsored loans, and scholarships/grants available. Support available to part-time students.

Dr. Barbara J. Myers, Director, 804-828-6752, *Fax:* 804-828-2237, *E-mail:* bmyers@vcu.edu.

**Application contact:** Barbara Hoffman, Department Manager, 804-828-8803, *Fax:* 804-828-2237, *E-mail:* bhoffman@vcu.edu. *Web site:* http://www.vcu.edu/hasweb/psy/psych.html

## ■ VIRGINIA POLYTECHNIC INSTITUTE AND STATE UNIVERSITY

**Graduate School, College of Arts and Sciences, Department of Psychology, Blacksburg, VA 24061**

**AWARDS** Bio-behavioral sciences (PhD); clinical psychology (PhD); developmental psychology (PhD); industrial/organizational psychology (PhD); psychology (MS).

**Faculty:** 22 full-time (4 women), 3 part-time/adjunct (2 women).

**Students:** 68 full-time (45 women), 8 part-time (6 women); includes 13 minority (5 African Americans, 4 Asian Americans or Pacific Islanders, 4 Hispanic Americans). Average age 23. 156 applicants, 21% accepted, 15 enrolled. In 2001, 4 master's, 8 doctorates awarded.

**Degree requirements:** For doctorate, thesis/dissertation.

**Entrance requirements:** For master's and doctorate, GRE General Test, TOEFL. *Application deadline:* For fall admission, 1/15 (priority date); for winter admission, 12/15 (priority date). Applications are processed on a rolling basis. *Application fee:* $45. Electronic applications accepted.

**Expenses:** Tuition, state resident: part-time $241 per hour. Tuition, nonresident: part-time $406 per hour. Tuition and fees vary according to program.

**Financial support:** In 2001–02, 1 fellowship with tuition reimbursement (averaging $12,500 per year), 13 research assistantships with full tuition reimbursements (averaging $11,790 per year), 52 teaching assistantships with full tuition reimbursements (averaging $7,074 per year) were awarded. Unspecified assistantships also available. Financial award application deadline: 4/1.

**Faculty research:** Infant development from electrophysical point of view, work motivation and personnel selection, EEG, ERP and hypnosis with reference to chronic pain, intimate violence.

Dr. Jack W. Finney, Chair, 540-231-6581, *Fax:* 540-231-3652, *E-mail:* finney@vt.edu. *Web site:* http://www.psyc.vt.edu/

## ■ VIRGINIA STATE UNIVERSITY

**School of Graduate Studies, Research, and Outreach, School of Engineering, Science and Technology, Department of Psychology, Petersburg, VA 23806-0001**

**AWARDS** MS.

**Faculty:** 2 full-time (1 woman).

**Students:** In 2001, 4 degrees awarded.

**Degree requirements:** For master's, one foreign language, thesis.

**Entrance requirements:** For master's, GRE General Test. *Application deadline:* For fall admission, 8/15. Applications are processed on a rolling basis. *Application fee:* $25.

**Expenses:** Tuition, area resident: Full-time $2,446; part-time $113 per credit hour. Tuition, state resident: full-time $8,814; part-time $420 per credit hour. Required fees: $1,724; $31 per credit hour.

**Financial support:** Fellowships, career-related internships or fieldwork available. Financial award application deadline: 5/1. Dr. Oliver Hill, Interim Chair, 804-524-5938, *E-mail:* ohill@vsu.edu.

**Application contact:** Dr. Wayne F. Virag, Dean, Graduate Studies, Research, and Outreach, 804-524-5985, *Fax:* 804-524-5104, *E-mail:* wvirag@vsu.edu.

## ■ WAKE FOREST UNIVERSITY

**Graduate School, Department of Psychology, Winston-Salem, NC 27109**

**AWARDS** MA.

**Degree requirements:** For master's, one foreign language, thesis.

**Entrance requirements:** For master's, GRE General Test, GRE Subject Test.

**Faculty research:** Developmental, social, personality, experimental, and physiological psychology.

## ■ WALDEN UNIVERSITY

**Graduate Programs, Program in Professional Psychology, Minneapolis, MN 55401**

**AWARDS** MS, PhD. Part-time and evening/weekend programs available. Postbaccalaureate distance learning degree programs offered (minimal on-campus study).

**Faculty:** 43 part-time/adjunct (17 women).

**Students:** 325 full-time (218 women), 443 part-time (331 women). Average age 45. 72 applicants, 61% accepted. In 2001, 10 master's, 31 doctorates awarded.

**Degree requirements:** For master's, thesis; for doctorate, thesis/dissertation, brief dispersed residency sessions.

*Walden University (continued)*
**Entrance requirements:** For doctorate, 3 years of professional experience, master's degree. *Application deadline:* For fall admission, 7/1; for winter admission, 10/1; for spring admission, 1/1. Applications are processed on a rolling basis. *Application fee:* $50. Electronic applications accepted.
**Expenses:** Tuition: Full-time $8,900. Tuition and fees vary according to degree level and program.
**Financial support:** In 2001–02, 448 students received support, including 2 fellowships with partial tuition reimbursements available (averaging $1,500 per year); tuition waivers (partial) also available. Support available to part-time students. Financial award applicants required to submit FAFSA.
**Faculty research:** Clinical psychology, organizational psychology, forensic psychology, group processes, educational psychology.
Dr. Hilda Glazer, Director, 800-925-3368, *Fax:* 612-338-5092, *E-mail:* hglazer@waldenu.edu.
**Application contact:** 800-444-6795, *Fax:* 941-261-7695, *E-mail:* request@waldenu.edu. *Web site:* http://www.waldenu.edu/

### ■ WASHBURN UNIVERSITY OF TOPEKA

**College of Arts and Sciences, Department of Psychology, Topeka, KS 66621**
**AWARDS** Clinical psychology (MA). Part-time programs available.
**Faculty:** 7 full-time (4 women), 2 part-time/adjunct (1 woman).
**Students:** 16 full-time (15 women), 2 part-time (both women); includes 3 minority (1 African American, 1 Asian American or Pacific Islander, 1 Hispanic American). Average age 25. 21 applicants, 81% accepted, 5 enrolled. In 2001, 3 degrees awarded.
**Degree requirements:** For master's, thesis. *Median time to degree:* Master's–2.5 years full-time, 3.5 years part-time.
**Entrance requirements:** For master's, GRE General Test, 15 hours of course work in psychology. *Application deadline:* For fall admission, 3/15; for spring admission, 12/1. *Application fee:* $0 ($60 for international students). Electronic applications accepted.
**Expenses:** Tuition, state resident: part-time $150 per credit hour. Tuition, nonresident: part-time $307 per credit hour. Required fees: $14 per semester.
**Financial support:** In 2001–02, 16 students received support, including 13 teaching assistantships (averaging $4,500

per year). Financial award application deadline: 3/15.
**Faculty research:** Treatment outcomes, childhood depression, mild depression, brief therapy, rural mental health. *Total annual research expenditures:* $14,000.
Dr. Laura A. Stephenson, Chair, 785-231-1010 Ext. 1564, *Fax:* 785-231-1004, *E-mail:* zzdppy@washburn.edu. *Web site:* http://www.washburn.edu/cas/psychology/

### ■ WASHINGTON COLLEGE

**Graduate Programs, Department of Psychology, Chestertown, MD 21620-1197**
**AWARDS** MA. Part-time and evening/weekend programs available.
**Faculty:** 5 full-time (1 woman), 4 part-time/adjunct (0 women).
**Students:** 3 full-time (all women), 10 part-time (5 women). In 2001, 5 degrees awarded. *Median time to degree:* Master's–5 years part-time.
**Entrance requirements:** For master's, GRE General Test. *Application deadline:* Applications are processed on a rolling basis. *Application fee:* $40.
**Expenses:** Tuition: Full-time $4,380; part-time $730 per course. Required fees: $240; $40 per course. Tuition and fees vary according to course load.
Dr. George Spilich, Chairman, 410-778-7734, *E-mail:* george.spilich@washcoll.edu.
**Application contact:** Todd A. Lineburger, Assistant to the Provost, 800-422-1782 Ext. 7131, *Fax:* 410-778-7850, *E-mail:* todd.lineburger@washcoll.edu.

### ■ WASHINGTON STATE UNIVERSITY

**Graduate School, College of Liberal Arts, Department of Psychology, Pullman, WA 99164**
**AWARDS** Clinical psychology (PhD); psychology (MS, PhD).
**Faculty:** 28 full-time (8 women), 2 part-time/adjunct (1 woman).
**Students:** 42 full-time (24 women), 3 part-time (1 woman); includes 5 minority (1 Asian American or Pacific Islander, 2 Hispanic Americans, 2 Native Americans), 3 international. Average age 28. In 2001, 9 master's, 5 doctorates awarded.
**Degree requirements:** For master's, thesis (for some programs), oral exam; for doctorate, thesis/dissertation, oral exam, written exam.
**Entrance requirements:** For master's and doctorate, GRE General Test, minimum GPA of 3.0. *Application deadline:* For fall admission, 1/1. Applications are processed on a rolling basis. *Application fee:* $35.
**Expenses:** Tuition, state resident: full-time $6,088; part-time $304 per semester.

Tuition, nonresident: full-time $14,918; part-time $746 per semester. Tuition and fees vary according to program.
**Financial support:** In 2001–02, 4 research assistantships with full and partial tuition reimbursements, 39 teaching assistantships with full and partial tuition reimbursements were awarded. Fellowships, career-related internships or fieldwork, Federal Work-Study, institutionally sponsored loans, and unspecified assistantships also available. Financial award application deadline: 4/1; financial award applicants required to submit FAFSA. *Total annual research expenditures:* $303,373.
Dr. Paul Whitney, Chair, 509-335-2631.
**Application contact:** Graduate Admissions Chair, 509-335-2631, *Fax:* 509-335-5043, *E-mail:* psych@wsu.edu. *Web site:* http://www.wsu.edu:8080/~psych/index.html

### ■ WASHINGTON UNIVERSITY IN ST. LOUIS

**Graduate School of Arts and Sciences, Department of Philosophy, Program in Philosophy/Neuroscience/Psychology, St. Louis, MO 63130-4899**
**AWARDS** PhD.
**Degree requirements:** For doctorate, thesis/dissertation.
**Entrance requirements:** For doctorate, GRE General Test, sample of written work. *Application deadline:* For fall admission, 1/15 (priority date). Applications are processed on a rolling basis. *Application fee:* $35. Electronic applications accepted.
**Expenses:** Tuition: Full-time $26,900.
**Financial support:** Fellowships, Federal Work-Study and tuition waivers (full and partial) available. Financial award application deadline: 1/15. *Web site:* http://artsci.wustl.edu/~philos/pnp/home.html

### ■ WASHINGTON UNIVERSITY IN ST. LOUIS

**Graduate School of Arts and Sciences, Department of Psychology, St. Louis, MO 63130-4899**
**AWARDS** Clinical psychology (PhD); general experimental psychology (MA, PhD); social psychology (MA, PhD). Part-time programs available.
**Students:** 55 full-time (35 women); includes 4 minority (3 African Americans, 1 Asian American or Pacific Islander), 4 international. 171 applicants, 18% accepted. In 2001, 7 degrees awarded. Terminal master's awarded for partial completion of doctoral program.
**Degree requirements:** For master's, thesis or alternative; for doctorate, thesis/dissertation.
**Entrance requirements:** For master's and doctorate, GRE General Test. *Application*

*deadline:* For fall admission, 1/15 (priority date). Applications are processed on a rolling basis. *Application fee:* $35. Electronic applications accepted.
**Expenses:** Tuition: Full-time $26,900.
**Financial support:** Fellowships, research assistantships, teaching assistantships, career-related internships or fieldwork, Federal Work-Study, institutionally sponsored loans, and tuition waivers (full and partial) available. Support available to part-time students. Financial award application deadline: 1/15.
Dr. Henry L. Roediger, Chairperson, 314-935-6567. *Web site:* http://artsci.wustl.edu/~psych/

## ■ WAYNE STATE UNIVERSITY

**Graduate School, College of Science, Department of Psychology, Detroit, MI 48202**

**AWARDS** Human development (MA); psychology (MA, PhD), including clinical psychology (PhD), cognitive psychology (PhD), developmental psychology (PhD), industrial/organizational psychology (PhD), psychology, social psychology (PhD).

**Faculty:** 35 full-time.
**Students:** 124. 174 applicants, 21% accepted, 19 enrolled. In 2001, 24 master's, 23 doctorates awarded.
**Degree requirements:** For doctorate, thesis/dissertation.
**Entrance requirements:** For doctorate, GRE General Test, GRE Subject Test. *Application fee:* $20 ($30 for international students). Electronic applications accepted.
**Expenses:** Tuition, state resident: full-time $3,764. Tuition and fees vary according to degree level and program.
**Financial support:** In 2001–02, 8 fellowships, 8 research assistantships, 43 teaching assistantships were awarded. Career-related internships or fieldwork also available. Financial award application deadline: 2/1.
**Faculty research:** Clinical neuropsychology, cognitive neuroscience of aging, industrial/organizational psychology, health psychology, alcohol and drug abuse. *Total annual research expenditures:* $2 million.
Joseph Jacobson, Interim Chairperson, 313-577-2800, *Fax:* 313-577-7636, *E-mail:* joseph.jacobson@wayne.edu.
**Application contact:** Kathryn Urberg, Graduate Director, 313-577-2820, *Fax:* 313-577-7636, *E-mail:* kurberg@sun.science.wayne.edu. *Web site:* http://www.science.wayne.edu/~dleasend/
**Find an in-depth description at www.petersons.com/gradchannel.**

## ■ WESLEYAN UNIVERSITY

**Graduate Programs, Department of Psychology, Middletown, CT 06459-0260**

**AWARDS** MA.

**Faculty:** 12 full-time (4 women), 3 part-time/adjunct (1 woman).
**Students:** 7 full-time (5 women). Average age 23. 25 applicants, 12% accepted. In 2001, 4 degrees awarded.
**Degree requirements:** For master's, thesis.
**Entrance requirements:** For master's, GRE General Test, GRE Subject Test, MAT. *Application deadline:* For fall admission, 3/1. Applications are processed on a rolling basis. *Application fee:* $0.
**Expenses:** Tuition: Full-time $19,716. Required fees: $671. Full-time tuition and fees vary according to program.
**Financial support:** Research assistantships, teaching assistantships available. Financial award application deadline: 3/1.
**Faculty research:** Human perception and cognition; cognitive, social, and moral development; history of psychology; biopsychology; psycholinguistics.
Robert Steele, Chair, 876-685-2328.
**Application contact:** Marina J. Melendez, Director of Graduate Student Services, 860-685-2579, *Fax:* 860-685-2579, *E-mail:* mmelendez@wesleyan.edu.

## ■ WEST CHESTER UNIVERSITY OF PENNSYLVANIA

**Graduate Studies, College of Arts and Sciences, Department of Psychology, West Chester, PA 19383**

**AWARDS** Clinical psychology (MA); general psychology (MA); industrial organizational psychology (MA). Part-time and evening/weekend programs available.

**Faculty:** 11.
**Students:** 44 full-time (36 women), 23 part-time (15 women); includes 3 minority (all African Americans), 2 international. Average age 28. 107 applicants, 71% accepted. In 2001, 26 degrees awarded.
**Degree requirements:** For master's, thesis (for some programs), comprehensive exam.
**Entrance requirements:** For master's, GRE General Test or MAT, interview. *Application deadline:* For fall admission, 4/15 (priority date); for spring admission, 10/15. Applications are processed on a rolling basis. *Application fee:* $25.
**Expenses:** Tuition, state resident: full-time $4,600; part-time $256 per credit. Tuition, nonresident: full-time $7,554; part-time $420 per credit. Required fees: $44 per credit.
**Financial support:** In 2001–02, 10 research assistantships with full tuition

reimbursements (averaging $5,000 per year) were awarded; unspecified assistantships also available. Support available to part-time students. Financial award application deadline: 2/15; financial award applicants required to submit FAFSA.
**Faculty research:** Animal learning and cognition.
Dr. Sandra Kerr, Chair, 610-436-2945.
**Application contact:** Dr. Deanne Bonifazi-Zotter, Graduate Coordinator, 610-436-3143, *E-mail:* dbonifazi@wcupa.edu.

## ■ WESTERN CAROLINA UNIVERSITY

**Graduate School, College of Education and Allied Professions, Department of Psychology, Cullowhee, NC 28723**

**AWARDS** Clinical psychology (MA); school psychology (MA). Part-time and evening/weekend programs available.

**Faculty:** 18 full-time (9 women).
**Students:** 32 full-time (24 women), 3 part-time (all women); includes 1 minority (Hispanic American). 46 applicants, 54% accepted, 15 enrolled. In 2001, 13 degrees awarded.
**Degree requirements:** For master's, thesis, comprehensive exam.
**Entrance requirements:** For master's, GRE General Test. *Application deadline:* For fall admission, 2/1. *Application fee:* $35.
**Expenses:** Tuition, state resident: full-time $1,072. Tuition, nonresident: full-time $8,704. Required fees: $1,171.
**Financial support:** In 2001–02, 20 students received support, including 20 teaching assistantships with full and partial tuition reimbursements available (averaging $4,253 per year); fellowships, research assistantships with full and partial tuition reimbursements available, Federal Work-Study, institutionally sponsored loans, and scholarships/grants also available. Financial award application deadline: 3/15; financial award applicants required to submit FAFSA.
Dr. James Goodwin, Head, 828-227-7361, *E-mail:* jgoodwin@email.wcu.edu.
**Application contact:** Josie Bewsey, Assistant to the Dean, 828-227-7398, *Fax:* 828-227-7480, *E-mail:* jbewsey@email.wcu.edu. *Web site:* http://www.wcu.edu/ceap/psychology/psyhome.htm

## ■ WESTERN ILLINOIS UNIVERSITY

**School of Graduate Studies, College of Arts and Sciences, Department of Psychology, Macomb, IL 61455-1390**

AWARDS Clinical/community mental health (MS); general psychology (MS); psychology (MS, SSP); school psychology (SSP). Part-time programs available.

**Faculty:** 22 full-time (8 women).
**Students:** 45 full-time (34 women), 13 part-time (9 women), 1 international. Average age 33. 54 applicants, 54% accepted. In 2001, 12 master's, 5 other advanced degrees awarded.
**Degree requirements:** For master's, thesis or alternative.
**Entrance requirements:** For master's and SSP, GRE General Test. *Application deadline:* Applications are processed on a rolling basis. *Application fee:* $0 ($25 for international students). Electronic applications accepted.
**Expenses:** Tuition, state resident: part-time $108 per credit hour. Tuition, nonresident: part-time $216 per credit hour. Required fees: $33 per credit hour.
**Financial support:** In 2001–02, 40 students received support, including 40 research assistantships with full tuition reimbursements available (averaging $5,720 per year). Financial award applicants required to submit FAFSA.
**Faculty research:** Geriatric psychology, social psychology, psychology of women, embarrassability.
Dr. James Ackil, Chairperson, 309-298-1593.
**Application contact:** Dr. Barbara Baily, Director of Graduate Studies, 309-298-1806, *Fax:* 309-298-2345, *E-mail:* gradoffice@wiu.edu. *Web site:* http://www.wiu.edu/

## ■ WESTERN KENTUCKY UNIVERSITY

**Graduate Studies, College of Education and Behavioral Sciences, Department of Psychology, Bowling Green, KY 42101-3576**

AWARDS Psychology (MA); school psychology (Ed S).

**Faculty:** 17 full-time (12 women), 1 (woman) part-time/adjunct.
**Students:** In 2001, 15 master's, 6 other advanced degrees awarded.
**Degree requirements:** For master's, thesis (for some programs), comprehensive exam; for Ed S, thesis, oral exam.
**Entrance requirements:** For master's, GRE General Test; for Ed S, GRE General Test, minimum GPA of 3.5.
*Application deadline:* For fall admission, 7/1 (priority date); for spring admission, 11/1

(priority date). Applications are processed on a rolling basis. *Application fee:* $30.
**Expenses:** Tuition, area resident: Part-time $167 per credit. Tuition, state resident: full-time $2,490. Tuition, nonresident: full-time $6,660; part-time $399 per credit. Required fees: $554. Part-time tuition and fees vary according to campus/location and reciprocity agreements.
**Financial support:** Research assistantships with partial tuition reimbursements, teaching assistantships with partial tuition reimbursements, career-related internships or fieldwork, Federal Work-Study, institutionally sponsored loans, and service awards available. Support available to part-time students. Financial award application deadline: 4/1; financial award applicants required to submit FAFSA.
**Faculty research:** Neural regeneration, enhancing mobility in the elderly, improvement in visual processing in older adults, lifespan development. *Total annual research expenditures:* $164,147.
Dr. Steven Haggbloom, Head, 270-745-2696, *Fax:* 270-745-6934, *E-mail:* steven.haggbloom@wku.edu.

## ■ WESTERN MICHIGAN UNIVERSITY

**Graduate College, College of Arts and Sciences, Department of Psychology, Kalamazoo, MI 49008-5202**

AWARDS Applied behavior analysis (MA, PhD); clinical psychology (MA, PhD); experimental analysis of behavior (PhD); experimental psychology (MA); industrial/organizational psychology (MA); school psychology (PhD, Ed S).

**Faculty:** 19 full-time (6 women).
**Students:** 94 full-time (68 women), 41 part-time (26 women); includes 10 minority (1 African American, 3 Asian Americans or Pacific Islanders, 6 Hispanic Americans), 12 international. 192 applicants, 31% accepted, 25 enrolled. In 2001, 21 master's, 6 doctorates, 6 other advanced degrees awarded.
**Degree requirements:** For master's, variable foreign language requirement, thesis, oral exams; for doctorate, 2 foreign languages, thesis/dissertation, oral exams, comprehensive exam; for Ed S, thesis, oral exams.
**Entrance requirements:** For master's, doctorate, and Ed S, GRE General Test. *Application deadline:* For fall admission, 2/15. *Application fee:* $25.
**Expenses:** Tuition, state resident: part-time $186 per credit hour. Tuition, nonresident: part-time $442 per credit hour. Required fees: $602. One-time fee: $132 part-time. Tuition and fees vary according to course load.

**Financial support:** Fellowships, research assistantships, teaching assistantships, Federal Work-Study available. Financial award application deadline: 2/15; financial award applicants required to submit FAFSA.
R. Wayne Fuqua, Chairperson, 616-387-4498.
**Application contact:** Admissions and Orientation, 616-387-2000, *Fax:* 616-387-2355.

## ■ WESTERN WASHINGTON UNIVERSITY

**Graduate School, College of Arts and Sciences, Department of Psychology, Bellingham, WA 98225-5996**

AWARDS Mental health counseling (MS); psychology (MS); school counseling (M Ed).

**Degree requirements:** For master's, thesis (for some programs), comprehensive exam.
**Entrance requirements:** For master's, GRE General Test, TOEFL, minimum GPA of 3.0 in last 60 semester hours or last 90 quarter hours.

## ■ WEST TEXAS A&M UNIVERSITY

**College of Education and Social Sciences, Department of Behavioral Sciences, Canyon, TX 79016-0001**

AWARDS Psychology (MA). Part-time and evening/weekend programs available.

**Faculty:** 3 full-time (0 women), 2 part-time/adjunct (0 women).
**Students:** 4 full-time (all women), 13 part-time (11 women); includes 4 minority (1 African American, 3 Hispanic Americans). Average age 30. 23 applicants, 83% accepted, 17 enrolled. In 2001, 4 degrees awarded.
**Degree requirements:** For master's, thesis optional. *Median time to degree:* Master's–3 years full-time, 6 years part-time.
**Entrance requirements:** For master's, GRE General Test, 3 letters of recommendation; interview; minimum GPA of 3.25 in psychology, 3.0 overall. *Application deadline:* Applications are processed on a rolling basis. *Application fee:* $25 ($75 for international students). Electronic applications accepted.
**Expenses:** Tuition, state resident: part-time $120 per hour. Tuition, nonresident: part-time $253 per hour.
**Financial support:** In 2001–02, research assistantships (averaging $6,500 per year), 6 teaching assistantships with partial tuition reimbursements (averaging $6,700 per year) were awarded. Career-related internships or fieldwork, Federal Work-Study, institutionally sponsored loans,

scholarships/grants, and tuition waivers (partial) also available. Support available to part-time students. Financial award applicants required to submit FAFSA.
**Faculty research:** Application of sociological principles to historical and contemporary analyses of social systems.
Dr. Gary Byrd, Head, 806-651-2590, *Fax:* 806-651-2601, *E-mail:* gbyrd@ mail.wtamu.edu.
**Application contact:** Dr. Richard I. Harland, Graduate Adviser, 806-651-2596, *E-mail:* rharland@mail.wtamu.edu.

### ■ WEST VIRGINIA UNIVERSITY

**Eberly College of Arts and Sciences, Department of Psychology, Morgantown, WV 26506**

**AWARDS** Behavior analysis (PhD); clinical psychology (MA, PhD); development psychology (PhD). Part-time programs available.

**Faculty:** 23 full-time (8 women), 2 part-time/adjunct (both women).
**Students:** 53 full-time (40 women), 17 part-time (9 women); includes 6 minority (3 Asian Americans or Pacific Islanders, 2 Hispanic Americans, 1 Native American), 3 international. Average age 27. 306 applicants, 6% accepted. In 2001, 11 master's, 17 doctorates awarded. Terminal master's awarded for partial completion of doctoral program.
**Degree requirements:** For master's, thesis optional; for doctorate, thesis/ dissertation, comprehensive exam.
**Entrance requirements:** For master's and doctorate, GRE General Test, TOEFL, minimum GPA of 3.0. *Application deadline:* For fall admission, 1/15. *Application fee:* $45.
**Expenses:** Tuition, state resident: full-time $2,791. Tuition, nonresident: full-time $8,659. Required fees: $1,002. Tuition and fees vary according to program.
**Financial support:** In 2001–02, 20 research assistantships, 30 teaching assistantships were awarded. Fellowships, career-related internships or fieldwork, Federal Work-Study, institutionally sponsored loans, and tuition waivers (full and partial) also available. Financial award application deadline: 1/15; financial award applicants required to submit FAFSA.
**Faculty research:** Adult and child clinical psychology, behavioral assessment and therapy, child and adolescent behavior, life span development, experimental and applied behavior analysis. *Total annual research expenditures:* $372,796.
Dr. Michael T. Perone, Chair, 304-293-2001 Ext. 604, *Fax:* 304-293-6606, *E-mail:* michael.perone@mail.wvu.edu.
**Application contact:** Dr. Katherine A. Karraker, Director, Graduate Training,

304-293-2001 Ext. 625, *Fax:* 304-293-6606, *E-mail:* katherine.karraker@ mail.wvu.edu. *Web site:* http:// www.as.wvu.edu/psyc/

### ■ WHEATON COLLEGE

**Graduate School, Department of Psychology, Wheaton, IL 60187-5593**

**AWARDS** Clinical psychology (MA, Psy D).
**Faculty:** 13 full-time (4 women), 4 part-time/adjunct (2 women).
**Students:** 126. 145 applicants, 53% accepted, 52 enrolled. In 2001, 44 master's, 13 doctorates awarded. Terminal master's awarded for partial completion of doctoral program.
**Degree requirements:** For master's, thesis or alternative; for doctorate, thesis/ dissertation, internship.
**Entrance requirements:** For master's, GRE General Test, 18 hours of course work in psychology; for doctorate, GRE General Test.
**Expenses:** Tuition: Part-time $410 per hour.
**Financial support:** In 2001–02, 3 research assistantships (averaging $4,800 per year) were awarded; career-related internships or fieldwork, Federal Work-Study, scholarships/grants, and unspecified assistantships also available. Financial award application deadline: 6/1; financial award applicants required to submit FAFSA.
Dr. Cynthia Neal-Kimball, Chairman, 630-752-5758.
**Application contact:** Julie A. Huebner, Director of Graduate Admissions, 630-752-5195, *Fax:* 630-752-5935, *E-mail:* gradadm@wheaton.edu. *Web site:* http:// www.wheaton.edu/psychology/ psychology.html

### ■ WICHITA STATE UNIVERSITY

**Graduate School, Fairmount College of Liberal Arts and Sciences, Department of Psychology, Wichita, KS 67260**

**AWARDS** Community/clinical psychology (PhD); human factors (PhD); psychology (MA). Part-time programs available.
**Faculty:** 15 full-time (4 women).
**Students:** 44 full-time (35 women), 25 part-time (18 women); includes 6 minority (4 African Americans, 2 Asian Americans or Pacific Islanders), 1 international. Average age 33. 4 applicants, 0% accepted. In 2001, 9 master's, 8 doctorates awarded.
**Degree requirements:** For doctorate, thesis/dissertation.
**Entrance requirements:** For doctorate, GRE, TOEFL. *Application deadline:* For fall admission, 3/1 (priority date); for spring admission, 1/1. Applications are

processed on a rolling basis. *Application fee:* $25 ($40 for international students). Electronic applications accepted.
**Expenses:** Tuition, state resident: full-time $1,888; part-time $105 per credit. Tuition, nonresident: full-time $6,129; part-time $341 per credit. Required fees: $345; $19 per credit. $17 per semester. Tuition and fees vary according to course load and program.
**Financial support:** In 2001–02, 14 research assistantships (averaging $6,202 per year), 53 teaching assistantships with full tuition reimbursements (averaging $4,062 per year) were awarded. Career-related internships or fieldwork, Federal Work-Study, institutionally sponsored loans, and unspecified assistantships also available. Support available to part-time students. Financial award application deadline: 4/1; financial award applicants required to submit FAFSA.
**Faculty research:** Behavioral evolution, women and alcohol, behavioral medicine, delinquency prevention.
Dr. Charles Burdsal, Chairperson, 316-978-3170, *Fax:* 316-978-3006, *E-mail:* charles.burdsal@wichita.edu. *Web site:* http://www.wichita.edu/

### ■ WIDENER UNIVERSITY

**School of Human Service Professions, Institute for Graduate Clinical Psychology, Law-Psychology Program, Chester, PA 19013-5792**

**AWARDS** JD/Psy D.

Electronic applications accepted.
**Expenses:** Tuition: Part-time $500 per credit. Required fees: $25 per semester.
**Find an in-depth description at www.petersons.com/gradchannel.**

### ■ WILLIAM CAREY COLLEGE

**Graduate School, Program in Psychology, Hattiesburg, MS 39401-5499**

**AWARDS** Counseling psychology (MS); industrial and organizational psychology (MS). Part-time programs available.
**Faculty:** 4 full-time (2 women), 5 part-time/adjunct (3 women).
**Students:** 105 full-time (80 women), 37 part-time (31 women); includes 49 minority (46 African Americans, 1 Asian American or Pacific Islander, 2 Hispanic Americans), 1 international. In 2001, 18 degrees awarded.
**Entrance requirements:** For master's, GRE, minimum GPA of 2.5. *Application fee:* $25.
**Expenses:** Contact institution.
**Financial support:** Fellowships with partial tuition reimbursements, Federal

*William Carey College (continued)*
Work-Study available. Support available to part-time students.

**Faculty research:** Counseling, industrial organizations.

Dr. Tommy King, Director, Graduate Psychology, 601-582-6774, *Fax:* 601-582-6454, *E-mail:* tommy.king@wmcarey.edu. *Web site:* http://www.umcarey.edu/

## ■ WILMINGTON COLLEGE

**Division of Behavioral Science, New Castle, DE 19720-6491**

**AWARDS** Community counseling (MS); criminal justice studies (MS); student affairs and college counseling (MS). Part-time and evening/weekend programs available.

**Faculty:** 6 full-time (2 women), 35 part-time/adjunct (15 women).
**Students:** 9 full-time (6 women), 79 part-time (64 women); includes 21 minority (19 African Americans, 2 Hispanic Americans). In 2001, 25 degrees awarded. *Median time to degree:* Master's–3 years full-time, 4 years part-time.
*Application deadline:* For fall admission, 4/15. *Application fee:* $25.
**Expenses:** Tuition: Full-time $4,788; part-time $266 per credit. Required fees: $50; $25 per semester. Tuition and fees vary according to course level, course load, degree level, campus/location and program.
**Financial support:** Applicants required to submit FAFSA.
James Wilson, Chair, 302-328-9401 Ext. 154, *Fax:* 302-328-5164, *E-mail:* jwils@wilmcoll.edu.
**Application contact:** Michael Lee, Director of Admissions and Financial Aid, 302-328-9407 Ext. 102, *Fax:* 302-328-5164, *E-mail:* inquire@wilmcoll.edu.

## ■ WINTHROP UNIVERSITY

**College of Arts and Sciences, Department of Psychology, Rock Hill, SC 29733**

**AWARDS** MS, SSP.

**Faculty:** 6 full-time (2 women).
**Students:** 23 full-time (19 women), 2 part-time (both women); includes 3 minority (all African Americans). Average age 28. In 2001, 5 master's, 9 other advanced degrees awarded.
**Degree requirements:** For master's and SSP, comprehensive exam.
**Entrance requirements:** For master's, GRE General Test, interview, minimum GPA of 3.0. *Application deadline:* For fall admission, 2/15 (priority date). *Application fee:* $35 ($50 for international students). Electronic applications accepted.
**Expenses:** Tuition, state resident: full-time $4,546; part-time $189 per credit hour.

Tuition, nonresident: full-time $8,326; part-time $356 per credit hour. Required fees: $40; $20 per semester.
**Financial support:** In 2001–02, 22 students received support. Career-related internships or fieldwork, Federal Work-Study, scholarships/grants, and unspecified assistantships available. Support available to part-time students. Financial award application deadline: 2/1; financial award applicants required to submit FAFSA.
Dr. Melvin Goldstein, Chair, 803-323-2117, *E-mail:* goldsteinm@winthrop.edu.
**Application contact:** Sharon B. Johnson, Director of Graduate Studies, 800-411-7041, *Fax:* 803-323-2292, *E-mail:* johnsons@winthrop.edu. *Web site:* http://www.winthrop.edu/graduate-studies/school_psychology.htm

## ■ WISCONSIN SCHOOL OF PROFESSIONAL PSYCHOLOGY

**Program in Clinical Psychology, Milwaukee, WI 53225-4960**

**AWARDS** MA, Psy D. Part-time and evening/weekend programs available.

**Faculty:** 3 full-time (all women), 32 part-time/adjunct (13 women).
**Students:** 14 full-time (all women), 31 part-time (27 women); includes 6 minority (3 African Americans, 1 Asian American or Pacific Islander, 2 Hispanic Americans), 1 international. Average age 38. 40 applicants, 23% accepted. In 2001, 6 master's, 8 doctorates awarded. Terminal master's awarded for partial completion of doctoral program.
**Degree requirements:** For master's, candidacy exam, 500 hours of supervised clinical practica; for doctorate, thesis/dissertation, 1 year clinical internship, 2000 hours of supervised clinical practicum experience, candidacy exam, clinical exam. *Median time to degree:* Master's–2 years full-time, 4 years part-time; doctorate–5 years full-time, 8 years part-time.
**Entrance requirements:** For master's, GRE General Test, GRE Subject Test, bachelor's degree in psychology, sample of written work; for doctorate, GRE General Test, GRE Subject Test, master's degree in clinical psychology or equivalent, sample of written work. *Application deadline:* For fall admission, 4/15 (priority date); for spring admission, 10/15 (priority date). Applications are processed on a rolling basis. *Application fee:* $100.
**Expenses:** Tuition: Part-time $550 per credit hour.
**Financial support:** In 2001–02, 6 students received support. Clinical service assistantships, library aid assistantships available. Support available to part-time students.

**Faculty research:** Violence prevention, psychology of women, forensic psychology, custody evaluation, aging, harm reduction in AODA.
**Application contact:** Karen A. Kilman, Assistant to the President, 414-464-9777, *Fax:* 414-358-5590, *E-mail:* karen-wspp@msn.com. *Web site:* http://www.execpe.com/~wspp

## ■ WRIGHT INSTITUTE

**Graduate School of Psychology, Berkeley, CA 94704-1796**

**AWARDS** Psy D.

**Degree requirements:** For doctorate, thesis/dissertation. *Web site:* info@wrightinst.edu

## ■ WRIGHT STATE UNIVERSITY

**School of Graduate Studies, College of Liberal Arts, Program in Applied Behavioral Science, Dayton, OH 45435**

**AWARDS** Criminal justice and social problems (MA); international and comparative politics (MA).

**Students:** 18 full-time (12 women), 14 part-time (11 women); includes 6 minority (5 African Americans, 1 Hispanic American). Average age 32. 20 applicants, 95% accepted. In 2001, 17 degrees awarded.
**Degree requirements:** For master's, thesis optional.
**Entrance requirements:** For master's, TOEFL. *Application fee:* $25.
**Expenses:** Tuition, state resident: full-time $7,161; part-time $225 per quarter hour. Tuition, nonresident: full-time $12,324; part-time $385 per quarter hour. Tuition and fees vary according to course load, degree level and program.
**Financial support:** Fellowships, research assistantships, unspecified assistantships available. Support available to part-time students. Financial award applicants required to submit FAFSA.
**Faculty research:** Training and development, criminal justice and social problems, community systems, human factors, industrial/organizational psychology.
Dr. David M. Orenstein, Director, 937-775-2667, *Fax:* 937-775-4228, *E-mail:* david.orenstein@wright.edu.

## ■ WRIGHT STATE UNIVERSITY

**School of Graduate Studies, College of Science and Mathematics, Department of Psychology, Dayton, OH 45435**

**AWARDS** Human factors and industrial/organizational psychology (MS, PhD).

**Students:** 23 full-time (8 women), 7 part-time (1 woman); includes 2 minority (both

Hispanic Americans), 2 international. Average age 30. 106 applicants, 18% accepted. In 2001, 10 master's, 2 doctorates awarded.

**Degree requirements:** For master's and doctorate, thesis/dissertation.
**Entrance requirements:** For master's, GRE General Test, TOEFL; for doctorate, TOEFL. *Application fee:* $25.
**Expenses:** Tuition, state resident: full-time $7,161; part-time $225 per quarter hour. Tuition, nonresident: full-time $12,324; part-time $385 per quarter hour. Tuition and fees vary according to course load, degree level and program.
**Financial support:** Fellowships, research assistantships, teaching assistantships available. Support available to part-time students. Financial award applicants required to submit FAFSA.
Dr. Wayne L. Shebilske, Chair, 937-775-2391, *Fax:* 937-775-3347, *E-mail:* wayne.shebilske@wright.edu.
**Application contact:** Dr. John M. Flach, Director, 937-775-2391, *Fax:* 937-775-3347, *E-mail:* john.flach@wright.edu.

## ■ WRIGHT STATE UNIVERSITY

**School of Professional Psychology, Dayton, OH 45435**

**AWARDS** Clinical psychology (Psy D).

**Faculty:** 21 full-time (5 women), 2 part-time/adjunct (1 woman).
**Students:** 105 full-time (72 women), 2 part-time (1 woman); includes 30 minority (20 African Americans, 3 Asian Americans or Pacific Islanders, 7 Hispanic Americans), 9 international. Average age 29. In 2001, 20 degrees awarded.
**Degree requirements:** For doctorate, thesis/dissertation.
**Entrance requirements:** For doctorate, GRE General Test, GRE Subject Test, TOEFL. *Application deadline:* 12/15. *Application fee:* $30.
**Expenses:** Contact institution.
**Financial support:** In 2001–02, 30 fellowships with full tuition reimbursements were awarded; teaching assistantships, career-related internships or fieldwork, Federal Work-Study, institutionally sponsored loans, and unspecified assistantships also available. Financial award application deadline: 4/15; financial award applicants required to submit FAFSA.
Dr. John R. Rusisill, Dean, 937-775-3490, *Fax:* 937-775-3434, *E-mail:* john.rudisill@wright.edu.
**Application contact:** Leona L. Gray, Director, Student Services/Admissions, 937-775-3492, *Fax:* 937-775-3493, *E-mail:* leona.gray@wright.edu. *Web site:* http://www.wright.edu/sopp/

## ■ XAVIER UNIVERSITY

**College of Social Sciences, Department of Psychology, Cincinnati, OH 45207**

**AWARDS** Clinical psychology (Psy D); psychology (MA).

**Faculty:** 14 full-time (7 women), 7 part-time/adjunct (4 women).
**Students:** 102 full-time (82 women), 5 part-time (3 women); includes 10 minority (5 African Americans, 2 Asian Americans or Pacific Islanders, 2 Hispanic Americans, 1 Native American). Average age 28. 118 applicants, 53% accepted. In 2001, 33 master's awarded. Terminal master's awarded for partial completion of doctoral program.
**Degree requirements:** For master's, one foreign language, thesis, practicum; for doctorate, one foreign language, thesis/dissertation, internship, practicum. *Median time to degree:* Master's–2 years full-time, 3 years part-time; doctorate–5 years full-time, 7 years part-time.
**Entrance requirements:** For master's, GRE, minimum GPA of 3.3, 18 hours in psychology; for doctorate, GRE, 18 hours in psychology or master's degree in clinical psychology, minimum GPA of 3.5. *Application deadline:* For fall admission, 1/15 (priority date). *Application fee:* $35.
**Expenses:** Contact institution.
**Financial support:** In 2001–02, 34 students received support, including 24 research assistantships with full tuition reimbursements available (averaging $1,500 per year), 16 teaching assistantships with full tuition reimbursements available (averaging $1,500 per year); career-related internships or fieldwork, scholarships/grants, and traineeships also available. Financial award application deadline: 4/1.
**Faculty research:** Cognitive development in children, weight management, psychodiagnostics, psychotherapy.
Dr. Christine M. Dacey, Chair, 513-745-1033, *Fax:* 513-745-3327, *E-mail:* dacey@xu.edu.
**Application contact:** Margaret Maybury, Coordinator, 513-745-1053, *Fax:* 513-745-3327, *E-mail:* maybury@xu.edu. *Web site:* http://www.xu.edu/psychology_grad.index.htm

## ■ YALE UNIVERSITY

**Graduate School of Arts and Sciences, Department of Psychology, New Haven, CT 06520**

**AWARDS** MS, PhD, MD/PhD.

**Degree requirements:** For doctorate, thesis/dissertation.
**Entrance requirements:** For doctorate, GRE General Test.

## ■ YESHIVA UNIVERSITY

**Ferkauf Graduate School of Psychology, New York, NY 10033-3201**
**AWARDS** MA, PhD, Psy D. Part-time programs available.

**Faculty:** 28 full-time (13 women), 73 part-time/adjunct (40 women).
**Students:** 296 full-time (201 women), 64 part-time (44 women); includes 59 minority (16 African Americans, 14 Asian Americans or Pacific Islanders, 29 Hispanic Americans), 38 international. Average age 28. 570 applicants, 13% accepted. In 2001, 13 master's, 83 doctorates awarded. Terminal master's awarded for partial completion of doctoral program.
**Degree requirements:** For doctorate, thesis/dissertation.
**Entrance requirements:** For master's and doctorate, GRE General Test. *Application fee:* $50.
**Financial support:** In 2001–02, 43 fellowships (averaging $5,000 per year), 26 research assistantships (averaging $2,000 per year), 79 teaching assistantships (averaging $2,000 per year) were awarded. Career-related internships or fieldwork, Federal Work-Study, institutionally sponsored loans, and scholarships/grants also available. Support available to part-time students. Financial award application deadline: 4/15.
Dr. Lawrence J. Siegel, Dean, 718-430-3941, *Fax:* 718-430-3960.
**Application contact:** Elaine Schwartz, Assistant Director of Admissions, 718-430-3820, *Fax:* 718-430-3960, *E-mail:* eschart@ymail.yu.edu. *Web site:* http://www.yu.edu/fgs/

# ADDICTIONS/ SUBSTANCE ABUSE COUNSELING

## ■ ADLER SCHOOL OF PROFESSIONAL PSYCHOLOGY

**Programs in Psychology, Chicago, IL 60601-7203**

**AWARDS** Art therapy (Certificate); clinical hypnosis (Certificate); clinical psychology (Psy D); counseling psychology (MACP); counseling psychology/art therapy (MACAT); gerontology (MAGP, Certificate); marriage and family counseling (MAMFC); marriage and family therapy (Certificate); organizational psychology (MAO); substance abuse counseling (MASAC, Certificate). Part-time and evening/weekend programs available.

**Faculty:** 19 full-time (9 women), 48 part-time/adjunct (21 women).

*Adler School of Professional Psychology* (continued)

**Students:** 124 full-time (78 women), 284 part-time (208 women); includes 77 minority (43 African Americans, 20 Asian Americans or Pacific Islanders, 13 Hispanic Americans, 1 Native American), 8 international. Average age 39. 253 applicants, 59% accepted, 121 enrolled. In 2001, 101 master's, 29 doctorates, 5 other advanced degrees awarded. Terminal master's awarded for partial completion of doctoral program.

**Degree requirements:** For master's, thesis or alternative, oral exam, practicum; for doctorate, thesis/dissertation, clinical exam, internship, oral exam, practicum, written qualifying exam.

**Entrance requirements:** For master's, 12 semester hours in psychology, minimum GPA of 3.0; for doctorate, 18 semester hours in psychology, minimum GPA of 3.25; for Certificate, appropriate master's or doctoral degree. *Application deadline:* For fall admission, 1/1 (priority date). Applications are processed on a rolling basis. *Application fee:* $50.

**Expenses:** Tuition: Full-time $13,680; part-time $380 per credit. Required fees: $100; $15 per credit.

**Financial support:** In 2001–02, 180 students received support. Career-related internships or fieldwork, Federal Work-Study, scholarships/grants, and tuition waivers (full and partial) available. Support available to part-time students. Financial award application deadline: 5/15; financial award applicants required to submit FAFSA.

Dr. Frank Gruba-McCallister, Dean of Academic Affairs, 312-201-5900, *Fax:* 312-201-5917.

**Application contact:** Erene Soliman, Admissions Counselor, 312-201-5900, *Fax:* 312-201-5917.

**Find an in-depth description at www.petersons.com/gradchannel.**

■ **ANTIOCH NEW ENGLAND GRADUATE SCHOOL**

**Graduate School, Department of Applied Psychology, Program in Substance Abuse/Addictions Counseling, Keene, NH 03431-3552**

AWARDS Counseling psychology (MA), including substance abuse/addictions counseling; substance abuse counseling (M Ed).

**Faculty:** 9 full-time (7 women), 25 part-time/adjunct (15 women).

**Students:** 12 full-time (11 women), 8 part-time (7 women). Average age 35. 15 applicants, 100% accepted. In 2001, 12 degrees awarded.

**Degree requirements:** For master's, internship, practicum.

**Entrance requirements:** For master's, previous course work and work experience in psychology. *Application deadline:* For fall admission, 8/1; for spring admission, 12/1. Applications are processed on a rolling basis. *Application fee:* $40.

**Expenses:** Tuition: Full-time $15,150.

**Financial support:** In 2001–02, 12 students received support; fellowships, Federal Work-Study available. Financial award applicants required to submit FAFSA.

**Faculty research:** Women and substance abuse, diversity, gambling addictions.

Dr. Diane Kurinsky, Director, 603-357-3122 Ext. 246, *Fax:* 603-357-0718, *E-mail:* dkurinsky@antiochne.edu.

**Application contact:** Robbie P. Hertneky, Director of Admissions, 603-357-6265, *Fax:* 603-357-0718, *E-mail:* rhertneky@antiochne.edu. *Web site:* http://www.antiochne.edu/

■ **THE COLLEGE OF NEW JERSEY**

**Graduate Division, School of Education, Department of Counselor Education, Program in Community Counseling: Substance Abuse and Addiction Specialization, Ewing, NJ 08628**

AWARDS MA, Certificate.

**Students:** 3 full-time (all women), 8 part-time (5 women); includes 1 minority (Native American), 1 international. In 2001, 6 master's, 6 other advanced degrees awarded.

**Degree requirements:** For master's, comprehensive exam.

**Entrance requirements:** For degree, M Ed. *Application deadline:* For fall admission, 4/15; for spring admission, 10/15. Applications are processed on a rolling basis. *Application fee:* $50.

**Expenses:** Tuition, state resident: full-time $6,981; part-time $387 per credit. Tuition, nonresident: full-time $9,772; part-time $542 per credit. Required fees: $1,011.

**Financial support:** Application deadline: 5/1.

Dr. Mark Woodford, Coordinator, 609-771-2478, *Fax:* 609-637-2119, *E-mail:* woodford@tcnj.edu.

**Application contact:** Frank Cooper, Director, Office of Graduate Studies, 609-771-2300, *Fax:* 609-637-5105, *E-mail:* graduate@tcnj.edu.

■ **THE COLLEGE OF WILLIAM AND MARY**

**School of Education, Program in Counselor Education, Williamsburg, VA 23187-8795**

AWARDS Community and addictions counseling (M Ed); community counseling (M Ed); educational counseling (M Ed, Ed D, PhD); family counseling (M Ed); school counseling (M Ed). Part-time and evening/weekend programs available.

**Faculty:** 5 full-time (2 women), 5 part-time/adjunct (3 women).

**Students:** 42 full-time (29 women), 26 part-time (24 women); includes 3 minority (2 African Americans, 1 Hispanic American), 1 international. Average age 32. 103 applicants, 41% accepted, 24 enrolled. In 2001, 14 master's, 1 doctorate awarded.

**Degree requirements:** For doctorate, thesis/dissertation, comprehensive exam.

**Entrance requirements:** For master's, GRE or MAT, minimum GPA of 2.5; for doctorate, GRE or MAT, minimum GPA of 3.5. *Application deadline:* For fall admission, 2/1. *Application fee:* $30.

**Expenses:** Tuition, state resident: full-time $3,262; part-time $175 per credit hour. Tuition, nonresident: full-time $14,768; part-time $550 per credit hour. Required fees: $2,478.

**Financial support:** In 2001–02, 31 research assistantships with full tuition reimbursements (averaging $9,000 per year) were awarded; fellowships with full tuition reimbursements, career-related internships or fieldwork, institutionally sponsored loans, scholarships/grants, and unspecified assistantships also available. Financial award application deadline: 2/1; financial award applicants required to submit FAFSA.

**Faculty research:** Sexuality, multicultural education, substance abuse, transpersonal psychology.

Dr. Sandra Ward, Area Coordinator, 757-221-2326, *E-mail:* scbrub@wm.edu.

**Application contact:** Patricia Burleson, Director of Admissions, 757-221-2317, *E-mail:* paburl@wm.edu. *Web site:* http://www.wm.edu/education/programs/space.html/

■ **COPPIN STATE COLLEGE**

**Division of Graduate Studies, Division of Arts and Sciences, Department of Psychology and Rehabilitation Counseling, Baltimore, MD 21216-3698**

AWARDS Alcohol and substance abuse (MS).

**Faculty:** 8 part-time/adjunct (4 women).

**Students:** 1 applicant, 0% accepted. *Application deadline:* For fall admission, 7/15 (priority date); for spring admission,

12/15 (priority date). Applications are processed on a rolling basis. *Application fee:* $25.

**Expenses:** Tuition, state resident: full-time $3,576; part-time $149 per credit. Tuition, nonresident: full-time $6,360; part-time $265 per credit. Required fees: $589; $589 per year.

Dr. Janet Spry, Co-Chairperson, 410-951-3510, *E-mail:* jspry@coppin.edu.

**Application contact:** Vell Lyles, Associate Vice President for Enrollment Management, 410-951-3575, *E-mail:* vlyles@coppin.edu. *Web site:* http://www.coppin.edu/

## ■ D'YOUVILLE COLLEGE

**Department of Nursing, Buffalo, NY 14201-1084**

**AWARDS** Addictions in the community (Certificate); community health nursing (MSN); family nurse practitioner (Certificate); holistic nursing (Certificate); hospice and palliative care (Certificate); nurse practitioner (MS); nursing and health-related professions (Certificate). Part-time and evening/weekend programs available.

**Faculty:** 15 full-time (14 women), 4 part-time/adjunct (all women).

**Students:** 32 full-time (28 women), 144 part-time (134 women); includes 12 minority (8 African Americans, 3 Hispanic Americans, 1 Native American), 114 international. Average age 34. 83 applicants, 76% accepted, 54 enrolled. In 2001, 22 master's, 2 other advanced degrees awarded.

**Degree requirements:** For master's, membership on board of community agency, publishable paper, thesis optional. *Median time to degree:* Master's–2 years full-time, 6 years part-time; Certificate–4 years part-time.

**Entrance requirements:** For master's, BS in nursing, minimum GPA of 3.0, previous course work in statistics and computers. *Application deadline:* Applications are processed on a rolling basis. *Application fee:* $25. Electronic applications accepted.

**Expenses:** Tuition: Full-time $10,320; part-time $430 per credit hour. Tuition and fees vary according to course load.

**Financial support:** In 2001–02, 1 research assistantship with partial tuition reimbursement (averaging $3,000 per year) was awarded; Federal Work-Study and scholarships/grants also available. Support available to part-time students. Financial award application deadline: 3/1; financial award applicants required to submit FAFSA.

**Faculty research:** Nursing curriculum, nursing theory-testing, wellness research, communication and socialization patterns.

Dr. Verna Kieffer, Chair, 716-881-3200, *Fax:* 716-881-7790.

**Application contact:** Linda Fisher, Graduate Admissions Director, 716-881-7676, *Fax:* 716-881-7790, *E-mail:* graduateadmissions@dyc.edu.

## ■ EAST CAROLINA UNIVERSITY

**Graduate School, School of Allied Health Sciences, Rehabilitation Studies Program, Greenville, NC 27858-4353**

**AWARDS** Rehabilitation studies (MS); substance abuse (MS); vocational evaluation (MS). Part-time and evening/weekend programs available.

**Faculty:** 5 full-time (0 women).

**Students:** 37 full-time (29 women), 29 part-time (20 women); includes 8 minority (4 African Americans, 2 Hispanic Americans, 2 Native Americans). Average age 32. 30 applicants, 63% accepted. In 2001, 34 degrees awarded.

**Degree requirements:** For master's, thesis or alternative, internship, comprehensive exam.

**Entrance requirements:** For master's, GRE General Test or MAT, TOEFL. *Application deadline:* For fall admission, 6/1 (priority date). Applications are processed on a rolling basis. *Application fee:* $45.

**Expenses:** Tuition, state resident: full-time $2,636. Tuition, nonresident: full-time $11,365.

**Financial support:** Research assistantships with partial tuition reimbursements, teaching assistantships with partial tuition reimbursements, Federal Work-Study and scholarships/grants available. Support available to part-time students. Financial award application deadline: 6/1.

Dr. Paul Alston, Director of Graduate Studies, 252-328-4452, *Fax:* 252-328-4470, *E-mail:* alstonp@mail.ecu.edu.

**Application contact:** Dr. Paul D. Tschetter, Senior Associate Dean of the Graduate School, 252-328-6012, *Fax:* 252-328-6071, *E-mail:* gradschool@mail.ecu.edu.

## ■ EASTERN KENTUCKY UNIVERSITY

**The Graduate School, College of Health Sciences, Department of Health Promotion and Administration, Richmond, KY 40475-3102**

**AWARDS** Chemical abuse and dependency (MPH); community health (MPH).

**Expenses:** Tuition, state resident: full-time $1,468; part-time $165 per credit hour. Tuition, nonresident: full-time $4,034; part-time $450 per credit hour.

Dr. Donald Colitri, Chair, 859-622-1142.

## ■ GEORGIAN COURT COLLEGE

**Graduate School, Program in Education, Lakewood, NJ 08701-2697**

**AWARDS** Administration, supervision and curriculum planning (management specialization) (MA); administration, supervision, and curriculum planning (MA); early intervention studies (Certificate); education (MA); instructional technology (MA); reading specialization (MA); special education (MA); substance awareness (Certificate). Part-time and evening/weekend programs available.

**Faculty:** 24 part-time/adjunct (11 women).

**Students:** 16 full-time (13 women), 250 part-time (203 women); includes 14 minority (7 African Americans, 2 Asian Americans or Pacific Islanders, 5 Hispanic Americans). Average age 36. In 2001, 58 degrees awarded.

**Degree requirements:** For master's, projects.

**Entrance requirements:** For master's, GRE, MAT or NTE/Praxis. *Application deadline:* For fall admission, 8/25; for spring admission, 1/15. Applications are processed on a rolling basis. *Application fee:* $40.

**Expenses:** Tuition: Full-time $7,308; part-time $406 per credit. Required fees: $70; $35 per term. Tuition and fees vary according to course load.

**Financial support:** In 2001–02, 47 students received support. Scholarships/grants and unspecified assistantships available. Financial award application deadline: 4/15; financial award applicants required to submit FAFSA.

**Faculty research:** Multiple intelligence, brain-based research, environmental education, leadership, arts in education.

Dr. John Groves, Dean, School of Education, 732-364-2200 Ext. 759, *Fax:* 732-364-4516, *E-mail:* admissions@georgian.edu.

**Application contact:** Michael Backes, Vice President for Enrollment, 732-364-2200 Ext. 760, *Fax:* 732-364-4442, *E-mail:* admissions@georgian.edu.

## ■ GOVERNORS STATE UNIVERSITY

**College of Health Professions, Division of Health Administration and Human Services, Program in Addictions Studies, University Park, IL 60466-0975**

**AWARDS** MHS. Part-time and evening/weekend programs available.

**Faculty:** 2 full-time (1 woman), 4 part-time/adjunct (2 women).

**Students:** 3 full-time, 71 part-time. Average age 39. In 2001, 38 degrees awarded.

*Governors State University (continued)*

**Degree requirements:** For master's, thesis or alternative, internship, comprehensive exam.

**Entrance requirements:** For master's, minimum undergraduate GPA of 2.5, 9 hours in behavioral sciences, 6 hours in biological sciences or chemistry, statistics or research methods course. *Application deadline:* For fall admission, 7/15 (priority date); for spring admission, 11/10. Applications are processed on a rolling basis. *Application fee:* $0.

**Expenses:** Tuition, state resident: part-time $111 per hour. Tuition, nonresident: part-time $333 per hour.

**Financial support:** Research assistantships, career-related internships or fieldwork, Federal Work-Study, institutionally sponsored loans, scholarships/grants, and tuition waivers (full and partial) available. Support available to part-time students. Financial award application deadline: 5/1. Dr. Arthur Durant, Head, 708-534-4918.

## ■ INDIANA WESLEYAN UNIVERSITY

**College of Adult and Professional Studies, Program in Counseling, Marion, IN 46953-4974**

**AWARDS** Community counseling (MA); community/addiction counseling (MA); marriage and family counseling (MA). Part-time programs available.

**Faculty:** 3 full-time (0 women), 7 part-time/adjunct (4 women).

**Students:** 27 full-time (19 women), 30 part-time (24 women); includes 1 minority (African American). Average age 35. In 2001, 5 degrees awarded.

**Degree requirements:** For master's, thesis or alternative.

**Entrance requirements:** For master's, GRE General Test. *Application deadline:* For fall admission, 4/1 (priority date); for spring admission, 10/1 (priority date). *Application fee:* $25. Electronic applications accepted.

**Expenses:** Contact institution.

**Financial support:** In 2001–02, 1 research assistantship with tuition reimbursement, 1 teaching assistantship with partial tuition reimbursement (averaging $1,000 per year) were awarded. Financial award application deadline: 3/1; financial award applicants required to submit FAFSA.

**Faculty research:** Attachment, emotional softening, cultural reentry, third culture kids, sexuality.

Dr. Jerry Davis, Director of Graduate Counseling Studies, 765-677-2995, *Fax:* 765-677-2504, *E-mail:* jdavis@indwes.edu.

**Find an in-depth description at www.petersons.com/gradchannel.**

## ■ JOHNS HOPKINS UNIVERSITY

**School of Professional Studies in Business and Education, Division of Education, Department of Counseling and Human Services, Baltimore, MD 21218-2699**

**AWARDS** Addictions counseling (Post Master's Certificate); career counseling (Post Master's Certificate); clinical community counseling (Post Master's Certificate); counseling (MS, Ed D, CAGS); counseling at-risk students (Post Master's Certificate); organizational counseling (Post Master's Certificate). Part-time and evening/weekend programs available.

**Faculty:** 4 full-time (2 women), 21 part-time/adjunct (12 women).

**Students:** 24 full-time (21 women), 279 part-time (244 women); includes 64 minority (46 African Americans, 6 Asian Americans or Pacific Islanders, 12 Hispanic Americans), 4 international. Average age 34. 126 applicants, 83% accepted, 98 enrolled. In 2001, 76 master's, 53 other advanced degrees awarded.

**Degree requirements:** For master's, registration; for doctorate, thesis/dissertation, comprehensive exam, registration.

**Entrance requirements:** For master's, minimum GPA of 3.0, interview, resumé, letters of recommendation; for doctorate, GRE, MAT, interview, master's degree, minimum GPA of 3.25; for other advanced degree, master's or doctoral degree, interview, resumé. *Application deadline:* Applications are processed on a rolling basis. *Application fee:* $55. Electronic applications accepted.

**Expenses:** Tuition: Full-time $27,390.

**Financial support:** Scholarships/grants available. Support available to part-time students. Financial award application deadline: 6/1.

Mary Guindon, Chair, 301-294-7040.

**Application contact:** Kumari Adams, Admissions Coordinator, 410-872-1234, *Fax:* 410-872-1251, *E-mail:* emsspsbe@jhu.edu.

## ■ KEAN UNIVERSITY

**College of Education, Department of Special Education and Individualized Services, Program in Counselor Education, Union, NJ 07083**

**AWARDS** Alcohol and drug abuse counseling (MA); business and industry counseling (MA, PMC); community/agency counseling (MA); school counseling (MA). Part-time programs available.

**Faculty:** 15 full-time (12 women).

**Students:** 22 full-time (18 women), 133 part-time (103 women); includes 32 minority (23 African Americans, 9 Hispanic Americans), 1 international. Average age 35. 23 applicants, 78% accepted. In 2001, 26 degrees awarded.

**Degree requirements:** For master's, thesis, comprehensive exam.

**Entrance requirements:** For master's, GRE General Test or MAT. *Application deadline:* For fall admission, 6/15; for spring admission, 11/15. *Application fee:* $35.

**Expenses:** Tuition, state resident: full-time $7,372. Tuition, nonresident: full-time $9,004. Required fees: $1,006.

**Financial support:** In 2001–02, 9 research assistantships with full tuition reimbursements (averaging $3,520 per year) were awarded; career-related internships or fieldwork and unspecified assistantships also available.

Dr. Juneau Gary, Coordinator, 908-527-2523.

**Application contact:** Joanne Morris, Director of Graduate Admissions, 908-527-2665, *Fax:* 908-527-2286, *E-mail:* grad_adm@kean.edu.

## ■ LOYOLA COLLEGE IN MARYLAND

**Graduate Programs, College of Arts and Sciences, Department of Psychology, Program in Counseling Psychology, Baltimore, MD 21210-2699**

**AWARDS** Counseling psychology (MA, MS); employee assistance and substance abuse (CAS). Part-time and evening/weekend programs available.

**Students:** 25 full-time (19 women), 21 part-time (19 women). In 2001, 14 degrees awarded.

**Entrance requirements:** For master's, GRE General Test; for CAS, master's degree. *Application deadline:* For spring admission, 10/1 (priority date). Applications are processed on a rolling basis.

**Expenses:** Tuition: Part-time $244 per unit. Tuition and fees vary according to degree level, program and student level.

**Financial support:** Applicants required to submit FAFSA.

**Application contact:** Scott Greatorex, Director, Graduate Admissions, 410-617-5020 Ext. 2407, *Fax:* 410-617-2002, *E-mail:* sgreatorex@loyola.edu.

## ■ MERCY COLLEGE

**Division of Social and Behavioral Sciences, Dobbs Ferry, NY 10522-1189**

**AWARDS** Alcohol and substance abuse counseling (AC); family counseling (AC); health services management (MPA, MS); psychology (MS); retirement counseling (AC); school counseling (MS), including bilingual extension; school psychology (MS), including bilingual extension.

**Students:** 51 full-time (41 women), 105 part-time (81 women); includes 104 minority (47 African Americans, 7 Asian Americans or Pacific Islanders, 50 Hispanic Americans), 10 international.
**Entrance requirements:** For master's, 8 years of healthcare management or practitioner (MS in health services management); interview; minimum GPA of 3.0. *Application fee:* $35.
**Expenses:** Tuition: Part-time $450 per credit. Part-time tuition and fees vary according to program.
Dr. Frances T.M. Mahoney, Chairperson, 914-674-7438, *Fax:* 914-674-7542, *E-mail:* fmahoney@mercy.edu.
**Application contact:** Information Contact, 800-MERCY-NY.

**Find an in-depth description at www.petersons.com/gradchannel.**

### ■ MONMOUTH UNIVERSITY

**Graduate School, The Marjorie K. Unterberg School of Nursing and Health Studies, West Long Branch, NJ 07764-1898**

**AWARDS** Advanced practice nursing (Post-Master's Certificate); nursing (MSN); school nursing (Certificate); substance awareness coordinator (Certificate). Part-time and evening/weekend programs available.

**Faculty:** 5 full-time (all women), 2 part-time/adjunct (1 woman).
**Students:** 11 full-time (all women), 54 part-time (51 women); includes 9 minority (3 African Americans, 6 Asian Americans or Pacific Islanders). Average age 39. 34 applicants, 79% accepted, 21 enrolled. In 2001, 22 degrees awarded.
**Entrance requirements:** For master's, GRE General Test, RN license, 1 year of work experience, minimum undergraduate GPA of 2.75. *Application deadline:* For fall admission, 8/15 (priority date); for spring admission, 12/15 (priority date). Applications are processed on a rolling basis. *Application fee:* $35. Electronic applications accepted.
**Expenses:** Tuition: Full-time $9,900; part-time $549 per credit. Required fees: $568.
**Financial support:** In 2001–02, 53 students received support, including 52 fellowships (averaging $1,756 per year), 3 research assistantships (averaging $3,606 per year); career-related internships or fieldwork, scholarships/grants, tuition waivers (partial), and unspecified assistantships also available. Support available to part-time students. Financial award application deadline: 3/1; financial award applicants required to submit FAFSA.
**Faculty research:** Relationship of undergraduate GPA and GRE to succeed in a graduate nursing program.

Dr. Janet Mahoney, Director, 732-571-3443, *Fax:* 732-263-5131, *E-mail:* jmahoney@monmouth.edu.
**Application contact:** Kevin Roane, Director, Office of Graduate Admissions, 732-571-3452, *Fax:* 732-263-5123, *E-mail:* gradadm@monmouth.edu. *Web site:* http://www.monmouth.edu/~nursing/nursing.html/

**Find an in-depth description at www.petersons.com/gradchannel.**

### ■ NATIONAL-LOUIS UNIVERSITY

**College of Arts and Sciences, Division of Health and Human Services, Chicago, IL 60603**

**AWARDS** Addictions counseling (MS, Certificate); addictions treatment (Certificate); career counseling and development studies (Certificate); community wellness and prevention (MS, Certificate); counseling (MS, Certificate); eating disorders counseling (Certificate); employee assistance programs (MS, Certificate); gerontology administration (Certificate); gerontology counseling (MS, Certificate); human services administration (MS, Certificate); long-term care administration (Certificate). Part-time programs available.

**Degree requirements:** For master's and Certificate, internship.
**Entrance requirements:** For master's and Certificate, GRE, MAT, or Watson-Glaser Critical Thinking Appraisal, interview, minimum GPA of 3.0.
**Expenses:** Tuition: Full-time $13,830; part-time $461 per credit hour.
**Faculty research:** Religion and aging, drug abuse prevention, hunger, homelessness, multicultural diversity.

### ■ NEW YORK UNIVERSITY

**The Steinhardt School of Education, Department of Health Studies, Program in Health Education, New York, NY 10012-1019**

**AWARDS** Community health education (MPH, Ed D, PhD), including alcohol studies (MPH), international community health education; human sexuality education (MA, Ed D, PhD); professional program in health education (Advanced Certificate), including human sexuality education, school and college health education; school and college health education (MA, Ed D, PhD). Part-time and evening/weekend programs available.

**Faculty:** 6 full-time (3 women).
**Students:** 41 full-time (38 women), 27 part-time (25 women); includes 24 minority (17 African Americans, 4 Asian Americans or Pacific Islanders, 2 Hispanic Americans, 1 Native American). 77 applicants, 43% accepted, 14 enrolled. In 2001, 31 master's, 1 doctorate awarded.

Terminal master's awarded for partial completion of doctoral program.
**Degree requirements:** For master's, thesis (for some programs); for doctorate, thesis/dissertation.
**Entrance requirements:** For master's, GRE General Test (MPH), TOEFL; for doctorate, GRE General Test, TOEFL, interview; for Advanced Certificate, TOEFL, master's degree. *Application deadline:* For fall admission, 2/1 (priority date); for spring admission, 12/1. Applications are processed on a rolling basis. *Application fee:* $40 ($60 for international students).
**Expenses:** Tuition: Full-time $19,536; part-time $814 per credit. Required fees: $1,330; $38 per credit. Tuition and fees vary according to course load and program.
**Financial support:** Career-related internships or fieldwork, Federal Work-Study, institutionally sponsored loans, and tuition waivers (partial) available. Support available to part-time students. Financial award application deadline: 3/1; financial award applicants required to submit FAFSA.
**Faculty research:** Poverty and prevention of chronic and infectious diseases, poverty and public health, women's health, sex education for children, health and ethnicity.
Sally Guttmacher, Director, 212-998-5786, *Fax:* 212-995-4192.
**Application contact:** 212-998-5030, *Fax:* 212-995-4328, *E-mail:* grad.admissions@nyu.edu.

**Find an in-depth description at www.petersons.com/gradchannel.**

### ■ NOTRE DAME DE NAMUR UNIVERSITY

**Graduate School, School of Sciences, Department of Counseling and Psychology/Gerontology, Belmont, CA 94002-1997**

**AWARDS** Chemical dependency (MACP); counseling psychology (MACP); gerontology (MA, Certificate); marital and family therapy (MACP, MAMFT). Part-time and evening/weekend programs available.

**Faculty:** 3 full-time, 6 part-time/adjunct.
**Students:** 28 full-time (24 women), 85 part-time (71 women); includes 28 minority (8 African Americans, 11 Asian Americans or Pacific Islanders, 9 Hispanic Americans), 1 international. Average age 37. 41 applicants, 76% accepted. In 2001, 36 degrees awarded.
**Entrance requirements:** For master's, TOEFL, interview, minimum GPA of 2.5. *Application deadline:* For fall admission, 8/1 (priority date); for spring admission, 12/1 (priority date). Applications are processed on a rolling basis. *Application fee:* $50 ($500

*Notre Dame de Namur University* (continued)

for international students). Electronic applications accepted.

**Expenses:** Tuition: Full-time $9,450; part-time $525 per unit. Required fees: $35 per term.

**Financial support:** Career-related internships or fieldwork available. Support available to part-time students. Financial award applicants required to submit FAFSA.

Dr. Anna McQuinn, Chair, 650-508-3557.

**Application contact:** Barbara Sterner, Assistant Director of Graduate Admissions, 650-508-3527, *Fax:* 650-508-3662, *E-mail:* grad.admit@ndnu.edu.

## ■ PACE UNIVERSITY, WHITE PLAINS CAMPUS

**Dyson College of Arts and Sciences, Department of Psychology, Program in Counseling-Substance Abuse, White Plains, NY 10603**

**AWARDS** MS. Part-time and evening/weekend programs available.

**Students:** 35 full-time (28 women), 29 part-time (27 women); includes 26 minority (19 African Americans, 3 Asian Americans or Pacific Islanders, 4 Hispanic Americans), 5 international. Average age 28. 44 applicants, 84% accepted, 18 enrolled. In 2001, 19 degrees awarded.

**Degree requirements:** For master's, qualifying exams, internship.

**Entrance requirements:** For master's, GRE, interview. *Application deadline:* For fall admission, 8/1 (priority date); for spring admission, 12/1 (priority date). Applications are processed on a rolling basis. *Application fee:* $65. Electronic applications accepted.

**Expenses:** Tuition: Part-time $545 per credit.

**Financial support:** Research assistantships, teaching assistantships, career-related internships or fieldwork, Federal Work-Study, and tuition waivers (partial) available. Financial award applicants required to submit FAFSA.

Dr. Ross Robak, Head, 914-773-3673.

**Application contact:** Joanna Broda, Director of Admissions, 914-422-4283, *Fax:* 914-422-4287, *E-mail:* gradwp@pace.edu. *Web site:* http://www.pace.edu/

**Find an in-depth description at www.petersons.com/gradchannel.**

## ■ SAGE GRADUATE SCHOOL

**Graduate School, Division of Psychology, Program in Community Psychology, Troy, NY 12180-4115**

**AWARDS** Chemical dependence (MA); child care and children's services (MA); community

counseling (MA); community health (MA); general psychology (MA); visual art therapy (MA).

**Students:** 10 full-time (9 women), 46 part-time (39 women); includes 2 minority (both African Americans). Average age 32. 20 applicants, 100% accepted, 14 enrolled. In 2001, 15 degrees awarded.

**Degree requirements:** For master's, thesis or alternative.

**Entrance requirements:** For master's, minimum GPA of 2.75. *Application deadline:* Applications are processed on a rolling basis. *Application fee:* $40.

**Expenses:** Tuition: Full-time $7,600. Required fees: $100.

**Financial support:** Application deadline: 3/1.

Dr. Pat O'Connor, Director, 518-244-2221, *E-mail:* oconnp@sage.edu.

**Application contact:** Melissa M. Robertson, Associate Director of Admissions, 518-244-6878, *Fax:* 518-244-6880, *E-mail:* sgsadm@sage.edu.

## ■ ST. MARY'S UNIVERSITY OF SAN ANTONIO

**Graduate School, Department of Counseling and Human Services, San Antonio, TX 78228-8507**

**AWARDS** Community counseling (MA); counseling (PhD, Sp C); marriage and family relations (Certificate); marriage and family therapy (MA, PhD); mental health (MA); mental health and substance abuse counseling (Certificate); substance abuse (MA). Postbaccalaureate distance learning degree programs offered (minimal on-campus study).

**Faculty:** 9 full-time (4 women), 5 part-time/adjunct (3 women).

**Students:** 125 (98 women); includes 48 minority (8 African Americans, 40 Hispanic Americans) 5 international. Average age 28. In 2001, 24 master's, 4 doctorates awarded.

**Degree requirements:** For master's, internship; for doctorate, thesis/dissertation, internship.

**Entrance requirements:** For master's, GRE General Test, MAT; for doctorate, GRE General Test. *Application deadline:* Applications are processed on a rolling basis. *Application fee:* $15. Electronic applications accepted.

**Expenses:** Tuition: Full-time $8,190; part-time $455 per credit hour. Required fees: $375.

**Financial support:** Career-related internships or fieldwork and Federal Work-Study available. Financial award application deadline: 2/15; financial award applicants required to submit FAFSA.

Dr. Dana Comstock, Graduate Program Director, 210-436-3226.

## ■ SPRINGFIELD COLLEGE

**School of Graduate Studies, Programs in Rehabilitation Services, Springfield, MA 01109-3797**

**AWARDS** Alcohol rehabilitation/substance abuse counseling (M Ed, MS, CAS); deaf counseling (M Ed, MS, CAS); developmental disabilities (M Ed, MS, CAS); general counseling and casework (M Ed, MS, CAS); psychiatric rehabilitation/mental health counseling (M Ed, MS, CAS); special services (M Ed, MS, CAS); vocational evaluation and work adjustment (M Ed, MS, CAS). Part-time and evening/weekend programs available.

**Faculty:** 8 full-time (2 women), 1 (woman) part-time/adjunct.

**Students:** 27 full-time, 13 part-time; includes 6 minority (3 African Americans, 1 Asian American or Pacific Islander, 2 Hispanic Americans). Average age 26. 29 applicants, 100% accepted. In 2001, 14 master's awarded.

**Degree requirements:** For master's, thesis (for some programs), comprehensive exam.

**Entrance requirements:** For master's and CAS, interview. *Application deadline:* For spring admission, 12/1. Applications are processed on a rolling basis. *Application fee:* $40.

**Financial support:** In 2001–02, 4 teaching assistantships with partial tuition reimbursements were awarded; fellowships with partial tuition reimbursements, career-related internships or fieldwork, Federal Work-Study, institutionally sponsored loans, traineeships, and tuition waivers (full and partial) also available. Financial award application deadline: 3/1.

**Faculty research:** Mental health, multicultural counseling, alcohol and substance abuse, developmental disabilities, families and disabilities, rehabilitation treatment outcomes.

Thomas J. Ruscio, Director, 413-748-3318.

**Application contact:** Donald James Shaw, Director of Graduate Admissions, 413-748-3225, *Fax:* 413-748-3694, *E-mail:* donald_shaw_jr@spfldcol.edu.

## ■ THOMAS EDISON STATE COLLEGE

**Graduate Studies, Program in Management, Trenton, NJ 08608-1176**

**AWARDS** Insurance (MSM); leadership (MSM); management (MSM); project management (MSM); substance abuse (MSM). Part-time programs available.

**Students:** Average age 42. 90 applicants. In 2001, 39 degrees awarded.

**Degree requirements:** For master's, thesis. *Median time to degree:* Master's–2 years part-time.

**Entrance requirements:** For master's, 3 to 5 years previous working experience. *Application deadline:* For fall admission, 7/1 (priority date); for winter admission, 11/1 (priority date); for spring admission, 3/1 (priority date). Applications are processed on a rolling basis. *Application fee:* $75. Electronic applications accepted.
**Expenses:** Tuition, state resident: part-time $298 per credit. Tuition, nonresident: part-time $298 per credit.
Dr. Esther Taitsman, Director of Graduate Studies/Associate Dean for Graduate Studies, 609-984-1168, *Fax:* 609-633-8593, *E-mail:* graduatestudies@tesc.edu.
**Application contact:** Gregg Dye, Coordinator of Graduate Advising, 800-442-8372, *Fax:* 609-633-8593, *E-mail:* graduatestudies@tesc.edu. *Web site:* http://www.tesc.edu/

■ **UNIVERSITY OF ALASKA ANCHORAGE**

**College of Health, Education, and Social Welfare, Interdisciplinary Program in Substance Abuse Disorders, Anchorage, AK 99508-8060**
**AWARDS** Certificate.

■ **UNIVERSITY OF DETROIT MERCY**

**College of Liberal Arts and Education, Department of Counseling and Addiction Studies, Program in Addiction Studies, Detroit, MI 48219-0900**
**AWARDS** Certificate. Part-time programs available.
**Faculty:** 5 full-time (1 woman).
*Application deadline:* For fall admission, 8/1.
*Application fee:* $30 ($50 for international students).
**Expenses:** Tuition: Full-time $10,620; part-time $590 per credit hour. Required fees: $400. Tuition and fees vary according to program.
Dr. John Franklin, Director, 313-993-6318, *Fax:* 313-993-6303, *E-mail:* frankljt@udmercy.edu.

■ **UNIVERSITY OF GREAT FALLS**

**Graduate Studies Division, Program in Human Services, Great Falls, MT 59405**
**AWARDS** Chemical dependent services (MHSA); family services (MHSA). Part-time and evening/weekend programs available. Postbaccalaureate distance learning degree programs offered (minimal on-campus study).
**Faculty:** 6 full-time (3 women), 10 part-time/adjunct (6 women).
**Students:** 6 full-time (4 women), 6 part-time (5 women); includes 4 minority (all

Native Americans). Average age 41. 20 applicants, 100% accepted. In 2001, 6 degrees awarded. *Median time to degree:* Master's–1 year full-time, 1.5 years part-time.
**Entrance requirements:** For master's, GRE General Test or MAT. *Application deadline:* For fall admission, 8/15 (priority date); for winter admission, 11/15 (priority date); for spring admission, 12/15 (priority date). Applications are processed on a rolling basis. *Application fee:* $35.
**Expenses:** Tuition: Part-time $440 per credit. One-time fee: $35 full-time.
**Financial support:** In 2001–02, 2 research assistantships were awarded; fellowships, career-related internships or fieldwork, Federal Work-Study, and institutionally sponsored loans also available. Support available to part-time students. Financial award application deadline: 3/1.
Dr. Deborah J. Kottel, Dean, 406-791-5339, *Fax:* 406-793-5990, *E-mail:* dkottel@ugf.edu.

■ **UNIVERSITY OF GREAT FALLS**

**Graduate Studies Division, Programs in Addictions Counseling, Great Falls, MT 59405**
**AWARDS** MAC.
**Faculty:** 1 (woman) full-time, 5 part-time/adjunct (3 women).
**Students:** 5 applicants, 5 enrolled.
**Entrance requirements:** For master's, GRE General Test or MAT. *Application deadline:* For fall admission, 8/15 (priority date); for winter admission, 11/15 (priority date); for spring admission, 12/15 (priority date). *Application fee:* $35.
**Expenses:** Tuition: Part-time $440 per credit. One-time fee: $35 full-time.
Dr. Mary Ann Dubay, Head, 406-791-5365, *Fax:* 406-791-5990, *E-mail:* mdubay@ugf.edu.

■ **UNIVERSITY OF ILLINOIS AT SPRINGFIELD**

**Graduate Programs, College of Education and Human Services, Program in Human Services, Springfield, IL 62703-5404**
**AWARDS** Alcoholism and substance abuse (MA); child and family studies (MA); gerontology (MA); social services administration (MA).
**Faculty:** 7 full-time (3 women), 10 part-time/adjunct (7 women).
**Students:** 44 full-time (32 women), 109 part-time (79 women); includes 32 minority (29 African Americans, 1 Asian American or Pacific Islander, 1 Hispanic American, 1 Native American), 2 international. Average age 37. 55

applicants, 85% accepted, 38 enrolled. In 2001, 16 degrees awarded.
**Expenses:** Tuition, state resident: full-time $2,680. Tuition, nonresident: full-time $8,064. Required fees: $626. One-time fee: $626.
**Financial support:** In 2001–02, 71 students received support, including 9 research assistantships (averaging $6,300 per year).
Rachell Anderson, Director, 217-206-7335.

■ **UNIVERSITY OF LOUISIANA AT MONROE**

**Graduate Studies and Research, College of Education and Human Development, Department of Instructional Leadership and Counseling, Program in Substance Abuse Counseling, Monroe, LA 71209-0001**
**AWARDS** MA. Part-time and evening/weekend programs available.
**Degree requirements:** For master's, internship.
**Entrance requirements:** For master's, GRE General Test, minimum GPA of 2.8 in last 60 hours, interview.
**Faculty research:** Addictionology.

■ **UNIVERSITY OF NORTH FLORIDA**

**College of Health, Department of Public Health, Jacksonville, FL 32224-2645**
**AWARDS** Addictions counseling (MSH); aging studies (Certificate); community health (MPH); employee health services (MSH); health administration (MHA); health care administration (MSH); human ecology and nutrition (MSH); human performance (MSH). Part-time and evening/weekend programs available.
**Faculty:** 19 full-time (14 women).
**Students:** 59 full-time (45 women), 60 part-time (40 women); includes 34 minority (19 African Americans, 6 Asian Americans or Pacific Islanders, 7 Hispanic Americans, 2 Native Americans), 1 international. Average age 31. 128 applicants, 49% accepted, 31 enrolled. In 2001, 42 degrees awarded.
**Degree requirements:** For master's, thesis optional.
**Entrance requirements:** For master's, GMAT (MHA), GRE General Test (MSH), TOEFL. *Application deadline:* For fall admission, 7/6 (priority date); for winter admission, 11/2 (priority date); for spring admission, 3/10 (priority date). Applications are processed on a rolling basis. *Application fee:* $20. Electronic applications accepted.

*University of North Florida (continued)*
**Expenses:** Tuition, state resident: full-time $2,411; part-time $134 per credit hour. Tuition, nonresident: full-time $9,391; part-time $522 per credit hour. Required fees: $670; $37 per credit hour.
**Financial support:** In 2001–02, 54 students received support, including 1 research assistantship (averaging $4,205 per year); career-related internships or fieldwork, Federal Work-Study, scholarships/grants, and tuition waivers (partial) also available. Support available to part-time students. Financial award application deadline: 4/1; financial award applicants required to submit FAFSA.
**Faculty research:** Lower extremity biomechanics; alcohol, tobacco, and other drug use prevention; turnover among health professionals; aging; psychosocial aspects of disabilities. *Total annual research expenditures:* $850,234.
Dr. Jeanne Patterson, Chair, 904-620-2840, *E-mail:* jpatters@unf.edu.
**Application contact:** Rachel Broderick, Director of Advising, 904-620-2812, *E-mail:* rbroderi@unf.edu.

### ■ WAYNE STATE UNIVERSITY

**Graduate School, Interdisciplinary Program in Alcohol and Drug Abuse Studies, Detroit, MI 48202**
**AWARDS** Certificate.

**Students:** 1. In 2001, 2 degrees awarded. *Application deadline:* For fall admission, 7/1. *Application fee:* $20 ($30 for international students). Electronic applications accepted.
**Expenses:** Tuition, state resident: full-time $3,764. Tuition and fees vary according to degree level and program.
**Faculty research:** AOD prevention research and evaluation; community empowerment/coalition building; substance abuse treatment research; epidemiology of AOD use. *Total annual research expenditures:* $250,000.
Dr. Eugene Schoener, Director, 313-577-1388, *E-mail:* eschoen@med.wayne.edu.
**Application contact:** Cheryl Madeja, Education Director, 313-577-1388, *Fax:* 313-577-6685.

# CLINICAL PSYCHOLOGY

### ■ ABILENE CHRISTIAN UNIVERSITY

**Graduate School, College of Arts and Sciences, Department of Psychology, Program in Clinical Psychology, Abilene, TX 79699-9100**
**AWARDS** MS. Part-time programs available.

**Faculty:** 12 part-time/adjunct (2 women).
**Students:** 7 full-time (4 women), 5 part-time (3 women); includes 1 minority (African American), 1 international. 12 applicants, 67% accepted, 2 enrolled. In 2001, 5 degrees awarded.
**Degree requirements:** For master's, thesis optional.
**Entrance requirements:** For master's, GRE General Test. *Application deadline:* For fall admission, 4/1 (priority date); for spring admission, 11/1. Applications are processed on a rolling basis. *Application fee:* $25 ($45 for international students).
**Expenses:** Tuition: Full-time $8,904; part-time $371 per hour. Required fees: $520; $17 per hour.
**Financial support:** Career-related internships or fieldwork and Federal Work-Study available. Support available to part-time students. Financial award application deadline: 4/1.
Dr. Larry Norsworthy, Graduate Adviser, 915-674-2280, *Fax:* 915-674-6968, *E-mail:* norsworthyl@acu.edu.
**Application contact:** Dr. Roger Gee, Graduate Dean, 915-674-2122, *Fax:* 915-674-2123, *E-mail:* gradinfo@education.acu.edu.

### ■ ADELPHI UNIVERSITY

**Derner Institute of Advanced Psychological Studies, Program in Clinical Psychology, Garden City, NY 11530**
**AWARDS** PhD.

**Students:** 96 full-time (77 women), 86 part-time (72 women); includes 25 minority (8 African Americans, 9 Asian Americans or Pacific Islanders, 8 Hispanic Americans), 14 international. Average age 34. In 2001, 25 degrees awarded.
**Degree requirements:** For doctorate, thesis/dissertation.
**Entrance requirements:** For doctorate, GRE General Test, GRE Subject Test, interview, resumé. *Application deadline:* For fall admission, 1/15 (priority date). *Application fee:* $50.
**Expenses:** Tuition: Full-time $12,960; part-time $540 per credit. One-time fee: $400 part-time. Tuition and fees vary according to course load, degree level and program.
**Financial support:** Research assistantships, teaching assistantships, career-related internships or fieldwork and institutionally sponsored loans available. Financial award application deadline: 2/15; financial award applicants required to submit FAFSA.
Dr. Louis Primavera, Dean, Derner Institute of Advanced Psychological Studies, 516-877-4800.

### ■ ADELPHI UNIVERSITY

**Derner Institute of Advanced Psychological Studies, Respecialization Program in Clinical Psychology, Garden City, NY 11530**
**AWARDS** Post-Doctoral Certificate.

**Students:** Average age 44. In 2001, 4 degrees awarded.
**Entrance requirements:** For degree, doctoral degree in psychology, interview. *Application deadline:* For fall admission, 1/15 (priority date). Applications are processed on a rolling basis. *Application fee:* $50.
**Expenses:** Tuition: Full-time $12,960; part-time $540 per credit. One-time fee: $400 part-time. Tuition and fees vary according to course load, degree level and program.
**Financial support:** Research assistantships, teaching assistantships, career-related internships or fieldwork and institutionally sponsored loans available. Financial award application deadline: 2/15; financial award applicants required to submit FAFSA.

### ■ ADLER SCHOOL OF PROFESSIONAL PSYCHOLOGY

**Programs in Psychology, Chicago, IL 60601-7203**
**AWARDS** Art therapy (Certificate); clinical hypnosis (Certificate); clinical psychology (Psy D); counseling psychology (MACP); counseling psychology/art therapy (MACAT); gerontology (MAGP, Certificate); marriage and family counseling (MAMFC); marriage and family therapy (Certificate); organizational psychology (MAO); substance abuse counseling (MASAC, Certificate). Part-time and evening/weekend programs available.

**Faculty:** 19 full-time (9 women), 48 part-time/adjunct (21 women).
**Students:** 124 full-time (78 women), 284 part-time (208 women); includes 77 minority (43 African Americans, 20 Asian Americans or Pacific Islanders, 13 Hispanic Americans, 1 Native American), 8 international. Average age 39. 253 applicants, 59% accepted, 121 enrolled. In 2001, 101 master's, 29 doctorates, 5 other advanced degrees awarded. Terminal master's awarded for partial completion of doctoral program.
**Degree requirements:** For master's, thesis or alternative, oral exam, practicum; for doctorate, thesis/dissertation, clinical exam, internship, oral exam, practicum, written qualifying exam.
**Entrance requirements:** For master's, 12 semester hours in psychology, minimum GPA of 3.0; for doctorate, 18 semester hours in psychology, minimum GPA of 3.25; for Certificate, appropriate master's or doctoral degree. *Application deadline:* For

fall admission, 1/1 (priority date). Applications are processed on a rolling basis. *Application fee:* $50.

**Expenses:** Tuition: Full-time $13,680; part-time $380 per credit. Required fees: $100; $15 per credit.

**Financial support:** In 2001–02, 180 students received support. Career-related internships or fieldwork, Federal Work-Study, scholarships/grants, and tuition waivers (full and partial) available. Support available to part-time students. Financial award application deadline: 5/15; financial award applicants required to submit FAFSA.

Dr. Frank Gruba-McCallister, Dean of Academic Affairs, 312-201-5900, *Fax:* 312-201-5917.

**Application contact:** Erene Soliman, Admissions Counselor, 312-201-5900, *Fax:* 312-201-5917.

**Find an in-depth description at www.petersons.com/gradchannel.**

### ■ ALABAMA AGRICULTURAL AND MECHANICAL UNIVERSITY

**School of Graduate Studies, School of Education, Department of Counseling and Special Education, Huntsville, AL 35811**

**AWARDS** Communicative disorders (M Ed, MS); psychology and counseling (MS, Ed S), including clinical psychology (MS), counseling and guidance, counseling psychology (MS), personnel management (MS), psychometry (MS), school psychology (MS); special education (M Ed, MS). Part-time and evening/weekend programs available.

**Faculty:** 38 full-time (20 women).
**Students:** 21 full-time (all women), 119 part-time (90 women); includes 65 minority (64 African Americans, 1 Hispanic American), 2 international. In 2001, 55 master's, 2 other advanced degrees awarded.
**Degree requirements:** For master's, comprehensive exam.
**Entrance requirements:** For master's, GRE General Test. *Application deadline:* For fall admission, 5/1. *Application fee:* $15 ($20 for international students).
**Expenses:** Tuition, state resident: full-time $1,380. Tuition, nonresident: full-time $2,500.
**Financial support:** Career-related internships or fieldwork available. Support available to part-time students. Financial award application deadline: 4/1.
**Faculty research:** Increasing numbers of minorities in special education and speech-language pathology. *Total annual research expenditures:* $300,000.
Dr. Terry L. Douglas, Chair, 256-851-5533.

### ■ ALLIANT INTERNATIONAL UNIVERSITY

**California School of Professional Psychology, PhD Program in Clinical Psychology–Fresno, Fresno, CA 94501**

**AWARDS** PhD.

**Students:** 212 (150 women); includes 61 minority (17 African Americans, 17 Asian Americans or Pacific Islanders, 22 Hispanic Americans, 5 Native Americans). Average age 30. In 2001, 42 degrees awarded.
**Degree requirements:** For doctorate, thesis/dissertation.
**Entrance requirements:** For doctorate, TOEFL, interview, minimum GPA of 3.0 in both psychology and overall. *Application deadline:* For fall admission, 1/2 (priority date). *Application fee:* $65.
**Expenses:** Tuition: Part-time $397 per credit hour. Tuition and fees vary according to degree level, campus/location and program.
**Financial support:** Research assistantships, teaching assistantships, career-related internships or fieldwork, Federal Work-Study, institutionally sponsored loans, and scholarships/grants available. Financial award application deadline: 2/15; financial award applicants required to submit FAFSA.
**Faculty research:** Ecosystematic clinical child psychology, neuropsychology, ethnocultural mental health, health psychology, eating disorders, depth psychology, forensic psychology.
Dr. Barry F. Perlmutter, Director, 559-456-2777, *Fax:* 559-253-2267, *E-mail:* bperlmutter@alliant.edu.
**Application contact:** Patricia J. Mullen, Vice President, Enrollment and Student Services, 800-457-1273 Ext. 303, *Fax:* 415-931-8322, *E-mail:* admissions@alliant.edu. *Web site:* http://www.alliant.edu/

### ■ ALLIANT INTERNATIONAL UNIVERSITY

**California School of Professional Psychology, PhD Program in Clinical Psychology–Los Angeles, Alhambra, CA 91803-1360**

**AWARDS** PhD.

**Students:** 475 (390 women); includes 159 minority (42 African Americans, 57 Asian Americans or Pacific Islanders, 56 Hispanic Americans, 4 Native Americans). Average age 31. In 2001, 106 degrees awarded.
**Degree requirements:** For doctorate, thesis/dissertation.
**Entrance requirements:** For doctorate, TOEFL, interview, minimum GPA of 3.0 in both psychology and overall. *Application*

*deadline:* For fall admission, 1/2 (priority date). *Application fee:* $65.
**Expenses:** Tuition: Part-time $397 per credit hour. Tuition and fees vary according to degree level, campus/location and program.
**Financial support:** Research assistantships, teaching assistantships, career-related internships or fieldwork, Federal Work-Study, institutionally sponsored loans, and scholarships/grants available. Financial award application deadline: 2/15; financial award applicants required to submit FAFSA.
**Faculty research:** Multicultural and community clinical psychology, health psychology, individual and family psychology.
Dr. Ellin L. Bloch, Director, 626-284-2777 Ext. 3009, *Fax:* 626-284-0550, *E-mail:* ebloch@alliant.edu.
**Application contact:** Patricia J. Mullen, Vice President, Enrollment and Student Services, 800-457-1273 Ext. 303, *Fax:* 415-931-8322, *E-mail:* admissions@ mail.cspp.edu. *Web site:* http://www.alliant.edu/

### ■ ALLIANT INTERNATIONAL UNIVERSITY

**California School of Professional Psychology, PhD Program in Clinical Psychology–San Diego, San Diego, CA 92121**

**AWARDS** PhD.

**Students:** 687 (517 women); includes 132 minority (27 African Americans, 39 Asian Americans or Pacific Islanders, 53 Hispanic Americans, 13 Native Americans). Average age 31. In 2001, 110 doctorates awarded.
**Degree requirements:** For doctorate, thesis/dissertation.
**Entrance requirements:** For doctorate, TOEFL, interview, minimum GPA of 3.0 in both psychology and overall. *Application deadline:* For fall admission, 1/2 (priority date). *Application fee:* $50.
**Expenses:** Tuition: Part-time $397 per credit hour. Tuition and fees vary according to degree level, campus/location and program.
**Financial support:** Research assistantships, teaching assistantships, career-related internships or fieldwork, Federal Work-Study, institutionally sponsored loans, and scholarships/grants available. Financial award application deadline: 2/15; financial award applicants required to submit FAFSA.
**Faculty research:** Psychodiagnostic assessment, psychoanalytic psychotherapy, health psychology, industrial-organizational psychology, cultural psychology.

*Alliant International University (continued)*

Dr. Perry Nicassio, Director, 858-635-4837, *Fax:* 858-635-4585, *E-mail:* pnicassio@alliant.edu.

**Application contact:** Patricia J. Mullen, Vice President, Enrollment and Student Services, 800-457-1273 Ext. 303, *Fax:* 415-931-8322, *E-mail:* admissions@mail.cspp.edu. *Web site:* http://www.alliant.edu/

### ■ ALLIANT INTERNATIONAL UNIVERSITY

California School of Professional Psychology, PhD Program in Clinical Psychology–San Francisco Bay, Alameda, CA 94501

AWARDS PhD.

**Students:** 106 full-time (90 women), 109 part-time (80 women); includes 58 minority (11 African Americans, 38 Asian Americans or Pacific Islanders, 8 Hispanic Americans, 1 Native American). Average age 33.

**Degree requirements:** For doctorate, thesis/dissertation.

**Entrance requirements:** For doctorate, TOEFL, interview, minimum GPA of 3.0 in both psychology and overall. *Application deadline:* For fall admission, 1/2 (priority date). *Application fee:* $65.

**Expenses:** Tuition: Part-time $397 per credit hour. Tuition and fees vary according to degree level, campus/location and program.

**Financial support:** Research assistantships, teaching assistantships, career-related internships or fieldwork, Federal Work-Study, institutionally sponsored loans, and scholarships/grants available. Financial award application deadline: 2/15; financial award applicants required to submit FAFSA.

Dr. Rebecca Turner, Director, 510-523-2300 Ext. 114, *Fax:* 510-521-3678, *E-mail:* rturner@alliant.edu.

**Application contact:** Patricia J. Mullen, Vice President, Enrollment and Student Services, 800-457-1273 Ext. 303, *Fax:* 415-931-8322, *E-mail:* admissions@alliant.edu. *Web site:* http://www.alliant.edu/

### ■ ALLIANT INTERNATIONAL UNIVERSITY

California School of Professional Psychology, Program in Clinical Psychology–San Francisco Bay, Alameda, CA 94501

AWARDS Psy D.

**Students:** 213 full-time (162 women), 129 part-time (92 women); includes 94 minority (27 African Americans, 44 Asian Americans or Pacific Islanders, 22

Hispanic Americans, 1 Native American). Average age 32.

**Degree requirements:** For doctorate, thesis/dissertation.

**Entrance requirements:** For doctorate, TOEFL, interview, minimum GPA of 3.0 in both psychology and overall. *Application deadline:* For fall admission, 1/2 (priority date). *Application fee:* $65.

**Expenses:** Tuition: Part-time $397 per credit hour. Tuition and fees vary according to degree level, campus/location and program.

**Financial support:** Research assistantships, teaching assistantships, career-related internships or fieldwork, Federal Work-Study, institutionally sponsored loans, and scholarships/grants available. Financial award application deadline: 2/15; financial award applicants required to submit FAFSA.

**Faculty research:** Health psychology, family and child psychology, postdoctoral training in forensic psychology and psychoanalytic psychotherapy, psychodynamic psychology.

Dr. Diane Adams, Director, 510-523-2300 Ext. 191, *Fax:* 510-521-3678, *E-mail:* dadams@alliant.edu.

**Application contact:** Patricia J. Mullen, Vice President, Enrollment and Student Services, 800-457-1273 Ext. 303, *Fax:* 415-931-8322, *E-mail:* admissions@alliant.edu. *Web site:* http://www.alliant.edu/

### ■ ALLIANT INTERNATIONAL UNIVERSITY

California School of Professional Psychology, Psy D Program in Clinical Psychology–Fresno, Fresno, CA 94501

AWARDS Psy D.

**Students:** 101 full-time (73 women), 30 part-time (19 women); includes 27 minority (7 African Americans, 8 Asian Americans or Pacific Islanders, 8 Hispanic Americans, 4 Native Americans). Average age 30.

**Degree requirements:** For doctorate, thesis/dissertation.

**Entrance requirements:** For doctorate, TOEFL, interview, minimum GPA of 3.0 in both psychology and overall. *Application deadline:* For fall admission, 1/2 (priority date). *Application fee:* $65.

**Expenses:** Tuition: Part-time $397 per credit hour. Tuition and fees vary according to degree level, campus/location and program.

**Financial support:** Research assistantships, teaching assistantships, career-related internships or fieldwork, Federal Work-Study, institutionally sponsored loans, and scholarships/grants available. Financial

award application deadline: 2/15; financial award applicants required to submit FAFSA.

Dr. Kevin O'Connor, Director, 559-456-2777, *Fax:* 559-253-2267, *E-mail:* koconnor@alliant.edu.

**Application contact:** Patricia J. Mullen, Vice President, Enrollment and Student Services, 800-457-1273 Ext. 303, *Fax:* 415-931-8322, *E-mail:* admissions@alliant.edu. *Web site:* http://www.alliant.edu/

### ■ ALLIANT INTERNATIONAL UNIVERSITY

California School of Professional Psychology, Psy D Program in Clinical Psychology–Los Angeles, Alhambra, CA 91803-1360

AWARDS Psy D.

**Students:** 267 full-time (217 women), 17 part-time (14 women); includes 101 minority (27 African Americans, 40 Asian Americans or Pacific Islanders, 32 Hispanic Americans, 2 Native Americans).

**Degree requirements:** For doctorate, thesis/dissertation.

**Entrance requirements:** For doctorate, TOEFL, interview, minimum GPA of 3.0 in both psychology and overall. *Application deadline:* For fall admission, 1/2 (priority date). *Application fee:* $65.

**Expenses:** Tuition: Part-time $397 per credit hour. Tuition and fees vary according to degree level, campus/location and program.

**Financial support:** Research assistantships, teaching assistantships, career-related internships or fieldwork, Federal Work-Study, institutionally sponsored loans, and scholarships/grants available. Financial award application deadline: 2/15; financial award applicants required to submit FAFSA.

Dr. Ken Polite, Director, 626-284-2777 Ext. 3049, *Fax:* 626-284-0550, *E-mail:* kpolite@alliant.edu.

**Application contact:** Patricia J. Mullen, Vice President, Enrollment and Student Services, 800-457-1273 Ext. 303, *Fax:* 415-931-8322, *E-mail:* admissions@alliant.edu.

### ■ ALLIANT INTERNATIONAL UNIVERSITY

California School of Professional Psychology, Psy D Program in Clinical Psychology–San Diego, San Diego, CA 92121

AWARDS Psy D.

**Students:** 120 full-time (95 women), 62 part-time (46 women); includes 39 minority (5 African Americans, 16 Asian Americans or Pacific Islanders, 15 Hispanic Americans, 3 Native Americans). Average age 33.

**Degree requirements:** For doctorate, thesis/dissertation.

**Entrance requirements:** For doctorate, TOEFL, interview, minimum GPA of 3.0 in both psychology and overall. *Application deadline:* For fall admission, 1/2 (priority date). *Application fee:* $65.

**Expenses:** Tuition: Part-time $397 per credit hour. Tuition and fees vary according to degree level, campus/location and program.

**Financial support:** Research assistantships, teaching assistantships, career-related internships or fieldwork, Federal Work-Study, institutionally sponsored loans, and scholarships/grants available. Financial award application deadline: 2/15; financial award applicants required to submit FAFSA.

Dr. Don Viglione, Director, 858-635-4542, *Fax:* 858-635-4585, *E-mail:* dviglione@ alliant.edu.

**Application contact:** Patricia J. Mullen, Vice President, Enrollment and Student Services, 800-457-1273 Ext. 303, *Fax:* 415-931-8322, *E-mail:* admissions@alliant.edu. *Web site:* http://www.alliant.edu/

### ■ AMERICAN INTERNATIONAL COLLEGE

**School of Continuing Education and Graduate Studies, School of Psychology and Education, Department of Psychology, Program in Clinical Psychology, Springfield, MA 01109-3189**

AWARDS MS.

**Degree requirements:** For master's, practicum.

**Entrance requirements:** For master's, minimum C average in undergraduate course work.

### ■ AMERICAN UNIVERSITY

**College of Arts and Sciences, Department of Psychology, Program in Clinical Psychology, Washington, DC 20016-8001**

AWARDS PhD.

**Students:** 11 full-time (8 women), 1 (woman) part-time; includes 1 minority (Asian American or Pacific Islander).

**Degree requirements:** For doctorate, thesis/dissertation.

**Entrance requirements:** For doctorate, GRE General Test, GRE Subject Test. *Application deadline:* For fall admission, 1/15. *Application fee:* $50.

**Expenses:** Tuition: Full-time $14,274; part-time $793 per credit. Required fees: $290. Tuition and fees vary according to program.

**Financial support:** Fellowships, teaching assistantships, career-related internships or

fieldwork, Federal Work-Study, institutionally sponsored loans, tuition waivers (full and partial), and unspecified assistantships available. Support available to part-time students. Financial award application deadline: 2/1.

**Faculty research:** Depression, eating disorders, anxiety disorders, addictions, behavior therapy.

Dr. Carol Weissbrod, Director, Clinical Training, 202-885-1726.

**Application contact:** Sara Holland, Senior Administrative Assistant, 202-885-1717, *Fax:* 202-885-1023.

### ■ ANTIOCH NEW ENGLAND GRADUATE SCHOOL

**Graduate School, Department of Clinical Psychology, Keene, NH 03431-3552**

AWARDS Psy D.

**Faculty:** 9 full-time (4 women), 11 part-time/adjunct (4 women).

**Students:** 169 full-time (117 women), 2 part-time (both women); includes 8 minority (3 African Americans, 1 Asian American or Pacific Islander, 3 Hispanic Americans, 1 Native American), 5 international. Average age 39. 101 applicants, 65% accepted. In 2001, 33 degrees awarded.

**Degree requirements:** For doctorate, thesis/dissertation, internship, practicum.

**Entrance requirements:** For doctorate, GRE General Test, GRE Subject Test, previous course work in psychology. *Application deadline:* For fall admission, 1/12. *Application fee:* $75.

**Expenses:** Contact institution.

**Financial support:** In 2001–02, 108 students received support, including 4 fellowships (averaging $900 per year), 4 research assistantships (averaging $1,350 per year), 4 teaching assistantships (averaging $763 per year); Federal Work-Study also available. Financial award applicants required to submit FAFSA.

**Faculty research:** Psychotherapy outcome and process in private practice, neuropsychiatric evaluations, effects of trauma on adults, supervision, clinical training evaluation.

Dr. Roger L. Peterson, Chairperson, 603-357-3122 Ext. 215, *Fax:* 603-357-1679, *E-mail:* rpeterson@antiochne.edu.

**Application contact:** Robbie P. Hertneky, Director of Admissions, 603-357-6265, *Fax:* 603-357-0718, *E-mail:* rhertneky@ antiochne.edu. *Web site:* http:// www.antiochne.edu/

### ■ ANTIOCH UNIVERSITY LOS ANGELES

**Graduate Programs, Program in Psychology, Marina del Rey, CA 90292-7008**

AWARDS Clinical psychology (MA); psychology (MA). Part-time programs available.

**Degree requirements:** For master's, thesis (for some programs), internship.

**Entrance requirements:** For master's, TOEFL, interview.

**Faculty research:** Creativity and humor, ethnic humor, adult development, Jungian theory, psychoanalytic theory. *Web site:* http://www.antiochla.edu/

### ■ ANTIOCH UNIVERSITY SANTA BARBARA

**Clinical Psychology Program, Santa Barbara, CA 93101-1581**

AWARDS MA. Part-time and evening/weekend programs available.

**Faculty:** 14 full-time (8 women), 43 part-time/adjunct (29 women).

**Students:** 62 full-time, 17 part-time. In 2001, 40 degrees awarded.

**Degree requirements:** For master's, internship.

**Entrance requirements:** For master's, TOEFL. *Application deadline:* For fall admission, 8/5 (priority date); for winter admission, 11/11 (priority date). Applications are processed on a rolling basis. *Application fee:* $60.

**Expenses:** Tuition: Part-time $375 per unit. Required fees: $426 per year. $10 per quarter. Tuition and fees vary according to class time and program.

**Financial support:** Federal Work-Study available. Support available to part-time students. Financial award application deadline: 8/5; financial award applicants required to submit FAFSA.

Dr. Catherine Radecki-Bush, Chair, 805-962-8179 Ext. 229, *Fax:* 805-962-4786, *E-mail:* cradecki-bush@antiochsb.edu.

**Application contact:** Carol Flores, Admissions Director, 805-962-8179 Ext. 113, *Fax:* 805-962-4786, *E-mail:* cflores@ antiochsb.edu. *Web site:* http:// www.antiochsb.edu/

### ■ APPALACHIAN STATE UNIVERSITY

**Cratis D. Williams Graduate School, College of Arts and Sciences, Department of Psychology, Program in Clinical Psychology, Boone, NC 28608**

AWARDS MA.

**Faculty:** 24 full-time (8 women).

**Students:** 27 full-time (24 women); includes 2 minority (both African

*Appalachian State University (continued)*
Americans), 1 international. In 2001, 5 degrees awarded.

**Degree requirements:** For master's, thesis, GRE Subject Test exit exam, comprehensive exam.

**Entrance requirements:** For master's, GRE General Test, GRE Subject Test. *Application deadline:* For fall admission, 3/1. Applications are processed on a rolling basis. *Application fee:* $35.

**Expenses:** Tuition, state resident: full-time $1,286. Tuition, nonresident: full-time $9,354. Required fees: $1,116.

**Financial support:** In 2001–02, research assistantships (averaging $6,250 per year), teaching assistantships (averaging $6,250 per year) were awarded. Fellowships, career-related internships or fieldwork also available. Support available to part-time students. Financial award application deadline: 7/1.

**Faculty research:** Perfectionism, parenting styles, substance abuse treatment, social competence, Attention Deficit/Hyperactivity Disorder.

Dr. Henry Schneider, Director, 828-262-2713, *E-mail:* schniederhg@appstate.edu. *Web site:* http://www.acs.appstate.edu/dept/psych/

## ■ ARGOSY UNIVERSITY-ATLANTA

**Graduate Programs, Atlanta, GA 30328-5505**

**AWARDS** Clinical psychology (MA, Psy D); professional counseling (MA); psychology (MA). Part-time and evening/weekend programs available.

**Faculty:** 11 full-time (6 women), 16 part-time/adjunct (6 women).

**Students:** 398; includes 70 minority (52 African Americans, 8 Asian Americans or Pacific Islanders, 8 Hispanic Americans, 2 Native Americans), 2 international. Average age 26. 272 applicants, 46% accepted. In 2001, 40 degrees awarded. Terminal master's awarded for partial completion of doctoral program.

**Degree requirements:** For master's, comprehensive exam; for doctorate, thesis/dissertation, clinical comprehensive exam, research project, internship.

**Entrance requirements:** For master's and doctorate, GRE General Test or MAT. *Application deadline:* For fall admission, 1/15 (priority date); for spring admission, 10/15 (priority date). Applications are processed on a rolling basis. *Application fee:* $55. Electronic applications accepted.

**Expenses:** Tuition: Part-time $374 per credit.

**Financial support:** In 2001–02, 280 students received support, including 40 teaching assistantships (averaging $700 per

year); career-related internships or fieldwork and Federal Work-Study also available. Support available to part-time students. Financial award application deadline: 6/30; financial award applicants required to submit FAFSA.

Dr. Joseph Bascuas, Dean, 770-671-1200, *Fax:* 770-671-0476.

**Application contact:** Nick Colletti, Director of Enrollment Services, 770-671-1200, *Fax:* 770-671-0476, *E-mail:* ncolletti@argosyu.edu.

**Find an in-depth description at www.petersons.com/gradchannel.**

## ■ ARGOSY UNIVERSITY-CHICAGO

**Illinois School of Professional Psychology, Doctoral Program in Clinical Psychology, Chicago, IL 60603**

**AWARDS** Child and adolescent psychology (Psy D); ethnic and racial psychology (Psy D); family psychology (Psy D); forensic psychology (Psy D); health psychology (Psy D); maltreatment and trauma (Psy D); psychoanalytic psychotherapy (Psy D); psychology and spirituality (Psy D).

**Faculty:** 21 full-time (13 women), 41 part-time/adjunct (18 women).

**Students:** 176 full-time (137 women), 185 part-time (132 women). Average age 31. 293 applicants, 61% accepted. In 2001, 92 degrees awarded.

**Degree requirements:** For doctorate, thesis/dissertation, internship, research project, clinical competency exam, comprehensive exam.

**Entrance requirements:** For doctorate, minimum GPA of 3.25. *Application deadline:* For fall admission, 1/15; for winter admission, 10/15. *Application fee:* $55. Electronic applications accepted.

**Expenses:** Tuition: Part-time $332 per credit hour. Required fees: $75 per year. $35 per term.

**Financial support:** In 2001–02, 200 students received support, including 25 fellowships with partial tuition reimbursements available (averaging $2,000 per year), 150 teaching assistantships with partial tuition reimbursements available (averaging $600 per year); research assistantships with partial tuition reimbursements available, career-related internships or fieldwork, Federal Work-Study, scholarships/grants, tuition waivers (partial), and unspecified assistantships also available. Support available to part-time students. Financial award application deadline: 5/29.

**Faculty research:** Meditation, clinical competency, family cultural patterns, sexual abuse patterns, psychosis and psychotherapy. *Total annual research expenditures:* $30,000.

Dr. Anne Marie Slobig, Director, 312-279-3911, *Fax:* 312-201-1907, *E-mail:* aslobig@argosyu.edu.

**Application contact:** Ashley Delaney, Director of Admissions, 312-279-3906, *Fax:* 312-201-1907, *E-mail:* adelaney@argosyu.edu. *Web site:* http://www.argosy.edu/

**Find an in-depth description at www.petersons.com/gradchannel.**

## ■ ARGOSY UNIVERSITY-CHICAGO

**Illinois School of Professional Psychology, Master's Program in Clinical Psychology, Chicago, IL 60603**

**AWARDS** MA. Part-time programs available.

**Faculty:** 1 (woman) full-time, 25 part-time/adjunct (15 women).

**Students:** 44 full-time (35 women), 38 part-time (29 women); includes 26 minority (12 African Americans, 7 Asian Americans or Pacific Islanders, 7 Hispanic Americans). Average age 29. 50 applicants, 62% accepted. In 2001, 46 degrees awarded.

**Degree requirements:** For master's, thesis or alternative, comprehensive exam.

**Entrance requirements:** For master's, minimum GPA of 3.0. *Application deadline:* For fall admission, 1/15; for winter admission, 10/15. *Application fee:* $55. Electronic applications accepted.

**Expenses:** Tuition: Part-time $332 per credit hour. Required fees: $75 per year. $35 per term.

**Financial support:** Fellowships, research assistantships, teaching assistantships, career-related internships or fieldwork and Federal Work-Study available. Financial award application deadline: 5/29.

Dr. Anne Marie Slobig, Director, 312-279-3911, *Fax:* 312-201-1907, *E-mail:* aslobig@argosyu.edu.

**Application contact:** Ashley Delaney, Director of Admissions, 312-279-3906, *Fax:* 312-201-1907, *E-mail:* adelaney@argosyu.edu.

**Find an in-depth description at www.petersons.com/gradchannel.**

## ■ ARGOSY UNIVERSITY-CHICAGO NORTHWEST

**Graduate Programs, Rolling Meadows, IL 60008**

**AWARDS** Clinical psychology (MA, Psy D); professional counseling (MA). Evening/weekend programs available. Terminal master's awarded for partial completion of doctoral program.

**Degree requirements:** For master's, thesis, practicum; for doctorate, thesis/dissertation, internship, qualifying exam.

**Entrance requirements:** For master's, 15 hours in psychology, interview, minimum GPA of 3.0; for doctorate, 15 hours in psychology, interview, minimum GPA of 3.25.

**Find an in-depth description at www.petersons.com/gradchannel.**

■ **ARGOSY UNIVERSITY-DALLAS**

**Program in Clinical Psychology, Dallas, TX 75231**

**AWARDS** Clinical psychology (MA); professional counseling (MA); psychology (Psy D).

**Entrance requirements:** For master's, TOEFL. *Application fee:* $50.
**Expenses:** Tuition: Part-time $345 per credit hour. Required fees: $150 per semester.
Dr. Abby Calish, Head, 214-890-9900, *Fax:* 214-696-3500.
**Application contact:** Dee Pinkston, Director of Admissions, 214-890-9900, *Fax:* 214-696-3500, *E-mail:* dpinkston@argosyu.edu.

**Find an in-depth description at www.petersons.com/gradchannel.**

■ **ARGOSY UNIVERSITY-HONOLULU**

**Graduate Studies, Postdoctoral Program in Clinical Psychopharmacology, Honolulu, HI 96813**

**AWARDS** Certificate. Evening/weekend programs available.

**Faculty:** 1 full-time (0 women), 10 part-time/adjunct (5 women).
**Students:** 12 full-time (4 women); includes 2 minority (both Asian Americans or Pacific Islanders). Average age 40.
**Entrance requirements:** For degree, doctoral degree, state license. *Application deadline:* Applications are processed on a rolling basis. *Application fee:* $50.
**Expenses:** Tuition: Part-time $530 per credit. Tuition and fees vary according to program.
**Financial support:** Application deadline: 5/1.
Dr. Raymond A. Folen, Coordinator, 808-536-5505, *Fax:* 808-536-5505, *E-mail:* folen@hawaii.edu.
**Application contact:** Eric C. Carlson, Director of Admissions, 808-536-5555, *Fax:* 808-536-5505, *E-mail:* ecarlson@argosyu.edu. *Web site:* http://www.argosyu.edu

**Find an in-depth description at www.petersons.com/gradchannel.**

■ **ARGOSY UNIVERSITY-HONOLULU**

**Graduate Studies, Program in Clinical Psychology, Honolulu, HI 96813**

**AWARDS** Psy D.

**Faculty:** 8 full-time (3 women), 10 part-time/adjunct (4 women).
**Students:** 131 full-time (103 women), 23 part-time (18 women); includes 88 minority (4 African Americans, 76 Asian Americans or Pacific Islanders, 6 Hispanic Americans, 2 Native Americans). Average age 35. 124 applicants, 48% accepted. In 2001, 20 doctorates awarded.
**Degree requirements:** For doctorate, thesis/dissertation, clinical internship, qualifying exam, comprehensive exam. *Median time to degree:* Doctorate–4.5 years full-time, 6 years part-time.
**Entrance requirements:** For doctorate, minimum GPA of 3.25 in last 60 hours. *Application deadline:* For fall admission, 1/15 (priority date); for winter admission, 10/15; for spring admission, 5/15. *Application fee:* $50. Electronic applications accepted.
**Expenses:** Tuition: Part-time $530 per credit. Tuition and fees vary according to program.
**Financial support:** Teaching assistantships, career-related internships or fieldwork, Federal Work-Study, and scholarships/grants available. Support available to part-time students. Financial award application deadline: 5/1; financial award applicants required to submit FAFSA.
Dr. Nancy Sidun, Head of Graduate Psychology Department, 808-536-5555, *Fax:* 808-536-5505, *E-mail:* nsidun@argosyu.edu.
**Application contact:** Eric C. Carlson, Director of Admissions, 808-536-5555, *Fax:* 808-536-5505, *E-mail:* ecarlson@argosyu.edu. *Web site:* http://www.argosyu.edu/

**Find an in-depth description at www.petersons.com/gradchannel.**

■ **ARGOSY UNIVERSITY-ORANGE COUNTY**

**School of Psychology, Program in Clinical Psychology, Orange, CA 92868**

**AWARDS** Psy D.

**Entrance requirements:** For doctorate, TOEFL, minimum GPA of 3.25 overall.
**Expenses:** Tuition: Part-time $437 per credit hour. Required fees: $10 per credit hour. Tuition and fees vary according to degree level and program.
**Application contact:** Joe Buechner, Director of Admissions, 800-716-9598, *Fax:*

714-940-0767, *E-mail:* jbuechner@argosyu.edu.

■ **ARGOSY UNIVERSITY-PHOENIX**

**Program in Clinical Psychology, Phoenix, AZ 85021**

**AWARDS** MA, Psy D, Post-Doctoral Certificate.

**Faculty:** 10 full-time (5 women), 8 part-time/adjunct (3 women).
**Students:** 124 full-time (98 women), 49 part-time (43 women); includes 29 minority (14 African Americans, 7 Asian Americans or Pacific Islanders, 7 Hispanic Americans, 1 Native American). Average age 30. 150 applicants, 47% accepted, 45 enrolled. In 2001, 46 degrees awarded. Terminal master's awarded for partial completion of doctoral program.
**Degree requirements:** For master's, practicum; for doctorate, thesis/dissertation, internship, practicum, comprehensive exam, registration; for Post-Doctoral Certificate, thesis or alternative, internship, practicum. *Median time to degree:* Master's–2 years full-time, 3 years part-time.
**Entrance requirements:** For master's, minimum undergraduate GPA of 3.0; for doctorate, minimum undergraduate GPA of 3.25. *Application deadline:* For fall admission, 1/15 (priority date); for winter admission, 10/15 (priority date). Applications are processed on a rolling basis. *Application fee:* $50. Electronic applications accepted.
**Expenses:** Tuition: Full-time $16,000; part-time $640 per credit. Required fees: $500; $250 per term. Full-time tuition and fees vary according to program.
**Financial support:** In 2001–02, 36 students received support, including 36 teaching assistantships with partial tuition reimbursements available; career-related internships or fieldwork, Federal Work-Study, and institutionally sponsored loans also available. Support available to part-time students. Financial award application deadline: 3/20; financial award applicants required to submit FAFSA.
**Faculty research:** Neuropsychology, forensic psychology, health psychology/behavioral medicine, trauma psychology, culturally-responsive models of intervention.
Dr. Philinda Smith Hutchings, Director, 602-216-2600, *Fax:* 602-216-2601, *E-mail:* phutchings@argosyu.edu.
**Application contact:** Gail L. Bartkovich, Director of Admissions, 866-216-2777 Ext. 209, *Fax:* 602-216-2601, *E-mail:* gbartkovich@argosyu.edu. *Web site:* http://www.argosyu.edu/

**Find an in-depth description at www.petersons.com/gradchannel.**

## ■ ARGOSY UNIVERSITY-PHOENIX

**Program in Sport–Exercise Psychology, Phoenix, AZ 85021**

**AWARDS** Clinical psychology (Psy D); sport–exercise psychology (MA, Post-Doctoral Certificate).

**Faculty:** 3 full-time (0 women), 2 part-time/adjunct (1 woman).

**Students:** 20 full-time (10 women), 1 (woman) part-time. Average age 24. 25 applicants, 60% accepted, 10 enrolled. In 2001, 18 degrees awarded.

**Degree requirements:** For master's, practicum; for doctorate, thesis/dissertation, practicum, internship; for Post-Doctoral Certificate, practicum. *Median time to degree:* Master's–2 years full-time, 3 years part-time.

**Entrance requirements:** For master's, minimum GPA of 3.0; for doctorate, minimum GPA of 3.25; for Post-Doctoral Certificate, doctoral degree in psychology or related profession. *Application deadline:* For fall admission, 1/15 (priority date); for winter admission, 10/15 (priority date). Applications are processed on a rolling basis. *Application fee:* $50. Electronic applications accepted.

**Expenses:** Tuition: Full-time $16,000; part-time $640 per credit. Required fees: $500; $250 per term. Full-time tuition and fees vary according to program.

**Financial support:** Career-related internships or fieldwork, Federal Work-Study, and institutionally sponsored loans available. Support available to part-time students.

**Faculty research:** Sport psychology, personality assessment and psychological correlates of success in professional sports, performance enhancement techniques. Dr. Douglas Jowdy, Director, 602-216-2600, *Fax:* 602-216-2601, *E-mail:* djowdy@argosyu.edu.

**Application contact:** Gail L. Bartkovich, Director of Admissions, 866-216-2777 Ext. 209, *Fax:* 602-216-2601, *E-mail:* gbartkovich@argosyu.edu.

## ■ ARGOSY UNIVERSITY-SAN FRANCISCO BAY AREA

**School of Behavioral Sciences, Point Richmond, CA 94804-3547**

**AWARDS** Clinical psychology (MA, Psy D); counseling psychology (MA). Part-time programs available.

**Faculty:** 8 full-time (3 women), 7 part-time/adjunct (4 women).

**Students:** 94 full-time (71 women), 41 part-time (33 women); includes 38 minority (14 African Americans, 15 Asian Americans or Pacific Islanders, 6 Hispanic Americans, 3 Native Americans). Average age 30. 185 applicants, 37% accepted. In 2001, 2 master's, 1 doctorate awarded.

**Degree requirements:** For master's, registration; for doctorate, thesis/dissertation, comprehensive exam, registration.

**Entrance requirements:** For master's, minimum GPA of 3.0, letters of recommendation; for doctorate, minimum GPA of 3.25, letters of recommendation. *Application deadline:* For fall admission, 1/15 (priority date); for winter admission, 8/15 (priority date). Applications are processed on a rolling basis. *Application fee:* $50. Electronic applications accepted.

**Expenses:** Tuition: Part-time $640 per credit.

**Financial support:** In 2001–02, 36 students received support, including teaching assistantships (averaging $1,200 per year); Federal Work-Study and scholarships/grants also available. Support available to part-time students. Financial award application deadline: 3/1.

**Faculty research:** Consciousness studies, attitudes, non-verbal communication, substance abuse prevention, HIV/AIDS. Dr. Anarea Morrison, Clinical Psychology Department Head, 510-215-0277, *Fax:* 510-215-0299.

**Application contact:** Cynthia R. Sirkin, Director of Outreach Services, 510-215-0277 Ext. 202, *Fax:* 510-215-0299, *E-mail:* csirkin@argosy.edu.

**Find an in-depth description at www.petersons.com/gradchannel.**

## ■ ARGOSY UNIVERSITY-SEATTLE

**Program in Clinical Psychology, Seattle, WA 98109**

**AWARDS** MA, Psy D. Part-time and evening/weekend programs available.

**Faculty:** 6 full-time (4 women), 12 part-time/adjunct (7 women).

**Students:** 58 full-time (38 women), 36 part-time (25 women); includes 5 minority (2 African Americans, 1 Asian American or Pacific Islander, 2 Hispanic Americans). Average age 32. 85 applicants, 75% accepted, 28 enrolled. In 2001, 7 master's, 2 doctorates awarded. Terminal master's awarded for partial completion of doctoral program.

**Degree requirements:** For master's, psychodiagnostic and psychotherapy comprehensive exams; for doctorate, thesis/dissertation, psychotherapy or clinical and psychodiagnostic comprehensive exams, comprehensive exam, registration. *Median time to degree:* Master's–2 years full-time, 3 years part-time; doctorate–4 years full-time.

**Entrance requirements:** For master's, minimum GPA of 3.0, coursework in abnormal psychology and statistics, human services experience; for doctorate, minimum GPA of 3.25, coursework in abnormal psychology and statistics, human services experience. *Application deadline:* For fall admission, 8/11 (priority date). Applications are processed on a rolling basis. *Application fee:* $50. Electronic applications accepted.

**Expenses:** Tuition: Part-time $510 per credit hour. Required fees: $35 per term. Part-time tuition and fees vary according to program.

**Financial support:** In 2001–02, 66 students received support. Federal Work-Study, scholarships/grants, and unspecified assistantships available. Support available to part-time students. Financial award applicants required to submit FAFSA. Dr. F. Jeri Carter, Interim Director of Psychology and Counseling Program, 206-283-4500 Ext. 213, *Fax:* 206-283-5777, *E-mail:* jcarter@argosyu.edu.

**Application contact:** Heather Simpson, Director of Admissions, 206-283-4500 Ext. 206, *Fax:* 206-283-5777, *E-mail:* hsimpson@argosyu.edu. *Web site:* http://www.argosyu.edu/

**Find an in-depth description at www.petersons.com/gradchannel.**

## ■ ARGOSY UNIVERSITY-TAMPA

**Program in Clinical Psychology, Tampa, FL 33619**

**AWARDS** MA, Psy D. Part-time programs available.

**Find an in-depth description at www.petersons.com/gradchannel.**

## ■ ARGOSY UNIVERSITY-TWIN CITIES

**Graduate Programs, Bloomington, MN 55437-9761**

**AWARDS** Clinical psychology (MA, Psy D); education (MA); professional counseling/marriage and family therapy (MA). Part-time programs available.

**Faculty:** 13 full-time (6 women), 33 part-time/adjunct (13 women).

**Students:** 233 full-time (192 women), 122 part-time (83 women); includes 9 minority (3 African Americans, 4 Asian Americans or Pacific Islanders, 1 Hispanic American, 1 Native American), 1 international. Average age 31. 224 applicants, 62% accepted, 95 enrolled. In 2001, 27 master's, 41 doctorates awarded. Terminal master's awarded for partial completion of doctoral program.

**Degree requirements:** For master's, thesis (for some programs); for doctorate, thesis/dissertation, internship, research project, comprehensive exam. *Median time to degree:* Master's–2 years full-time, 3

years part-time; doctorate–5 years full-time, 6 years part-time.
**Entrance requirements:** For master's, GRE or MAT, minimum GPA of 3.0 (clinical psychology), 2.8 (professional counseling/marriage and family therapy); interview; for doctorate, GRE or MAT, minimum GPA of 3.25, interview. *Application deadline:* For fall admission, 5/15 (priority date); for winter admission, 1/15 (priority date). Applications are processed on a rolling basis. *Application fee:* $50. Electronic applications accepted.
**Expenses:** Tuition: Part-time $424 per credit hour. Required fees: $31 per year. Tuition and fees vary according to program and student level.
**Financial support:** In 2001–02, 12 fellowships with partial tuition reimbursements, 12 teaching assistantships with partial tuition reimbursements were awarded. Career-related internships or fieldwork and Federal Work-Study also available. Support available to part-time students. Financial award application deadline: 3/14; financial award applicants required to submit FAFSA.
**Faculty research:** Cognitive behavioral therapy, human development, psychological assessment, marriage and family therapy, health psychology, physical/sexual abuse.
Dr. Jack T. O'Regan, Vice President Academic Affairs, 952-252-7575, *Fax:* 952-921-9574, *E-mail:* joregan@argosyu.edu.
**Application contact:** Jennifer Radke, Graduate Admissions Representative, 952-921-9500 Ext. 353, *Fax:* 952-921-9574, *E-mail:* tcadmissions@argosyu.edu. *Web site:* http://www.aspp.edu/

**Find an in-depth description at www.petersons.com/gradchannel.**

■ **ARGOSY UNIVERSITY-WASHINGTON D.C.**

**Professional Programs in Psychology, Arlington, VA 22209**

**AWARDS** Clinical psychology (MA, Psy D, Certificate); counseling psychology (MA); forensic psychology (MA). Part-time and evening/weekend programs available.

**Faculty:** 12 full-time (7 women), 43 part-time/adjunct (26 women).
**Students:** 304 full-time (237 women), 119 part-time (96 women); includes 112 minority (83 African Americans, 15 Asian Americans or Pacific Islanders, 11 Hispanic Americans, 3 Native Americans), 1 international. Average age 33. 341 applicants, 59% accepted. In 2001, 26 master's, 20 doctorates awarded.
**Degree requirements:** For master's, thesis (for some programs), practicum, comprehensive exam (for some programs);

for doctorate, thesis/dissertation, internship, comprehensive exam. *Median time to degree:* Master's–2 years full-time, 3 years part-time; doctorate–6 years full-time.
**Entrance requirements:** For master's, clinical experience, minimum GPA of 3.0; for doctorate, clinical experience, minimum GPA of 3.25. *Application deadline:* For fall admission, 1/15 (priority date); for spring admission, 10/15. Applications are processed on a rolling basis. *Application fee:* $55. Electronic applications accepted.
**Expenses:** Tuition: Full-time $6,732; part-time $374 per credit. Required fees: $22; $90 per term. Tuition and fees vary according to course load, degree level and program.
**Financial support:** In 2001–02, 347 students received support, including 2 fellowships with tuition reimbursements available (averaging $3,600 per year), 55 teaching assistantships with full and partial tuition reimbursements available (averaging $1,530 per year); research assistantships, career-related internships or fieldwork, Federal Work-Study, and scholarships/grants also available. Support available to part-time students. Financial award application deadline: 6/30; financial award applicants required to submit FAFSA.
**Faculty research:** Psychotherapy integration, minority health, forensic assessment, family violence, child maltreatment. *Total annual research expenditures:* $2,000.
Dr. Cynthia G. Baum, Campus President, 703-243-5300, *Fax:* 703-243-8973, *E-mail:* cbaum@argosyu.edu.
**Application contact:** Debbie Jacobs, Director of Admissions, 703-243-5300 Ext. 118, *Fax:* 703-243-8973, *E-mail:* ddmjacobs@argosyu.edu. *Web site:* http://www.argosy.edu/

**Find an in-depth description at www.petersons.com/gradchannel.**

■ **ARIZONA STATE UNIVERSITY**

**Graduate College, College of Liberal Arts and Sciences, Department of Psychology, Tempe, AZ 85287**

**AWARDS** Behavioral neuroscience (PhD); clinical psychology (PhD); cognitive/behavioral systems (PhD); developmental psychology (PhD); environmental psychology (PhD); quantitative research methods (PhD); social psychology (PhD).

**Degree requirements:** For doctorate, thesis/dissertation.
**Entrance requirements:** For doctorate, GRE General Test, GRE Subject Test.
**Faculty research:** Reduction of personal stress, cognitive aspects of motor skills training, behavior analysis and treatment of depression.

■ **AUSTIN PEAY STATE UNIVERSITY**

**Graduate School, College of Arts and Sciences, Department of Psychology, Clarksville, TN 37044-0001**

**AWARDS** Clinical psychology (MA); guidance and counseling (MS); psychological science (MA); school psychology (MA). Part-time programs available.

**Degree requirements:** For master's, thesis.
**Entrance requirements:** For master's, GRE General Test, minimum GPA of 3.0. *Web site:* http://www.apsu.edu/

■ **AZUSA PACIFIC UNIVERSITY**

**School of Education and Behavioral Studies, Department of Graduate Psychology, Azusa, CA 91702-7000**

**AWARDS** Clinical psychology (MA, Psy D); family therapy (MFT). Part-time and evening/weekend programs available.

**Students:** 87 full-time (65 women), 47 part-time (33 women); includes 43 minority (10 African Americans, 15 Asian Americans or Pacific Islanders, 17 Hispanic Americans, 1 Native American), 7 international.
**Degree requirements:** For master's, 250 hours of clinical experience, individual and group therapy.
**Entrance requirements:** For master's, Minnesota Multiphasic Personality Inventory, interview, minimum GPA of 3.0. *Application deadline:* For fall admission, 6/30 (priority date). Applications are processed on a rolling basis. *Application fee:* $45 ($65 for international students).
**Expenses:** Tuition: Part-time $265 per unit. Required fees: $175 per semester. Tuition and fees vary according to degree level and program.
Dr. Mark Stanton, Chair, 626-815-5008.

**Find an in-depth description at www.petersons.com/gradchannel.**

■ **BALL STATE UNIVERSITY**

**Graduate School, College of Sciences and Humanities, Department of Psychological Science, Program in Clinical Psychology, Muncie, IN 47306-1099**

**AWARDS** MA.

**Faculty:** 5 full-time.
**Students:** 23 full-time (16 women), 1 part-time; includes 3 minority (2 African Americans, 1 Asian American or Pacific Islander), 3 international. Average age 23. 48 applicants, 44% accepted. In 2001, 9 degrees awarded.
**Entrance requirements:** For master's, GRE General Test, interview. *Application fee:* $25 ($35 for international students).

*Ball State University (continued)*

**Expenses:** Tuition, state resident: full-time $4,068; part-time $2,542. Tuition, nonresident: full-time $10,944; part-time $6,462. Required fees: $1,000; $500 per term.
**Financial support:** Research assistantships with full tuition reimbursements available. Financial award application deadline: 3/1. Dr. Kerri Pickel, Graduate Program Director, 765-285-1690, *Fax:* 765-285-8980, *E-mail:* kpickel@bsu.edu. *Web site:* http://www.bsu.edu/psysc/

## ■ BARRY UNIVERSITY

**School of Arts and Sciences, Department of Psychology, Miami Shores, FL 33161-6695**

**AWARDS** Clinical psychology (MS); school psychology (MS, SSP). Part-time and evening/weekend programs available.

**Faculty:** 9 full-time (5 women).
**Students:** 61. Average age 29. In 2001, 32 master's, 7 other advanced degrees awarded.
**Degree requirements:** For master's, thesis, practicum.
**Entrance requirements:** For master's, GRE General Test, minimum GPA of 3.0, previous course work in psychology. *Application deadline:* Applications are processed on a rolling basis. *Application fee:* $30. Electronic applications accepted.
**Expenses:** Tuition: Full-time $12,480. Tuition and fees vary according to degree level and program.
**Financial support:** In 2001–02, 38 students received support, including 5 research assistantships with partial tuition reimbursements available (averaging $3,000 per year); career-related internships or fieldwork and tuition waivers (partial) also available. Support available to part-time students. Financial award application deadline: 5/1; financial award applicants required to submit FAFSA.
**Faculty research:** Closed head injury, memory and aging, infant/mother interaction, evolutionary aspects of behavior, gender roles.
Dr. Linda Peterson, Chair, 305-899-3274, *Fax:* 305-899-3279, *E-mail:* lpeterson@mail.barry.edu.
**Application contact:** Dave Fletcher, Director of Graduate Admissions, 305-899-3113, *Fax:* 305-899-2971, *E-mail:* dfletcher@mail.barry.edu.

## ■ BAYLOR UNIVERSITY

**Graduate School, College of Arts and Sciences, Department of Psychology and Neuroscience, Program in Clinical Psychology, Waco, TX 76798**

**AWARDS** MSCP, Psy D.

**Students:** 43 full-time (32 women), 2 part-time (both women); includes 5 minority (1 Asian American or Pacific Islander, 4 Hispanic Americans), 2 international. In 2001, 8 master's, 10 doctorates awarded.
**Degree requirements:** For doctorate, comprehensive exam.
**Entrance requirements:** For master's, GRE General Test; for doctorate, GRE General Test, GRE Subject Test, minimum GPA of 3.0 in major, 2.7 overall; interview. *Application deadline:* For fall admission, 2/1. Applications are processed on a rolling basis. *Application fee:* $25.
**Expenses:** Tuition: Part-time $379 per semester hour. Required fees: $42 per semester hour. $101 per semester. Tuition and fees vary according to program.
**Financial support:** Research assistantships, teaching assistantships, career-related internships or fieldwork, institutionally sponsored loans, tuition waivers (partial), and practicum stipends available. Financial award applicants required to submit FAFSA.
**Faculty research:** Professional training in clinical psychology, human systems and dynamics, social skills validation, child therapy and assessment.
Dr. David Rudd, Director, 254-710-2961, *Fax:* 254-710-3033, *E-mail:* david_rudd@baylor.edu.
**Application contact:** Bettye Keel, Graduate Coordinator, 254-710-2811, *Fax:* 254-710-3033, *E-mail:* bettye_keel@baylor.edu. *Web site:* http://www.baylor.edu/~Psychology/

## ■ BOWLING GREEN STATE UNIVERSITY

**Graduate College, College of Arts and Sciences, Department of Psychology, Bowling Green, OH 43403**

**AWARDS** Clinical psychology (MA, PhD); developmental psychology (MA, PhD); experimental psychology (MA, PhD); industrial/organizational psychology (MA, PhD); quantitative psychology (MA, PhD).

**Faculty:** 31.
**Students:** 89 full-time (57 women), 27 part-time (18 women); includes 14 minority (3 African Americans, 7 Asian Americans or Pacific Islanders, 4 Hispanic Americans), 9 international. Average age 27. 274 applicants, 15% accepted, 24 enrolled. In 2001, 10 master's, 17 doctorates awarded. Terminal master's awarded for partial completion of doctoral program.
**Degree requirements:** For master's and doctorate, thesis/dissertation.
**Entrance requirements:** For master's and doctorate, GRE General Test, TOEFL. *Application deadline:* For fall admission, 1/15. *Application fee:* $30. Electronic applications accepted.

**Expenses:** Tuition, state resident: full-time $7,376; part-time $342 per credit hour. Tuition, nonresident: full-time $13,628; part-time $640 per credit hour.
**Financial support:** In 2001–02, 30 research assistantships with full tuition reimbursements (averaging $9,452 per year), 32 teaching assistantships with full tuition reimbursements (averaging $9,607 per year) were awarded. Career-related internships or fieldwork, Federal Work-Study, institutionally sponsored loans, tuition waivers (full), and unspecified assistantships also available. Financial award applicants required to submit FAFSA.
**Faculty research:** Personnel psychology, developmental-mathematical models, behavioral medication, brain process, child/adolescent social cognition.
Dr. Dale Klopfer, Chair, 419-372-2733.
**Application contact:** Dr. Eric Dubow, Graduate Coordinator, 419-372-2556.

## ■ BRIGHAM YOUNG UNIVERSITY

**Graduate Studies, College of Family, Home, and Social Sciences, Department of Psychology, Provo, UT 84602-1001**

**AWARDS** Clinical psychology (PhD); general psychology (MS); psychology (PhD).

**Faculty:** 31 full-time (6 women), 10 part-time/adjunct (4 women).
**Students:** 92 full-time (45 women), 17 part-time (10 women); includes 5 minority (4 Asian Americans or Pacific Islanders, 1 Hispanic American), 6 international. Average age 30. 113 applicants, 24% accepted. In 2001, 8 master's, 9 doctorates awarded.
**Degree requirements:** For master's, thesis; for doctorate, thesis/dissertation, publishable paper. *Median time to degree:* Master's–2 years full-time; doctorate–5 years full-time.
**Entrance requirements:** For master's and doctorate, GRE General Test, minimum GPA of 3.0 in last 60 hours. *Application deadline:* For fall admission, 1/31. *Application fee:* $50. Electronic applications accepted.
**Expenses:** Tuition: Full-time $3,860; part-time $214 per hour.
**Financial support:** In 2001–02, 65 students received support, including research assistantships with partial tuition reimbursements available (averaging $3,000 per year), 26 teaching assistantships with partial tuition reimbursements available (averaging $3,000 per year); career-related internships or fieldwork, scholarships/grants, tuition waivers (partial), and unspecified assistantships also available. Financial award application deadline: 1/31.

**Faculty research:** Psychotherapy process, Alzheimer's disease/dementia, psychology and law, health, psychology, magnetic resonance imaging and autism. *Total annual research expenditures:* $800,000.
Dr. Erin D. Bigler, Chair, 801-422-4287, *Fax:* 801-378-7862.
**Application contact:** Karen A. Christensen, Graduate Secretary, 801-422-4560, *Fax:* 801-378-7862, *E-mail:* karen_christensen@byu.edu.

### ■ BRYN MAWR COLLEGE

**Graduate School of Arts and Sciences, Department of Psychology, Bryn Mawr, PA 19010-2899**
**AWARDS** Clinical developmental psychology (PhD). Part-time programs available.
**Students:** 14 full-time (12 women), 22 part-time (all women); includes 2 minority (both Asian Americans or Pacific Islanders). 57 applicants, 7% accepted. In 2001, 1 doctorate awarded.
**Degree requirements:** For doctorate, one foreign language, thesis/dissertation.
**Entrance requirements:** For doctorate, GRE General Test. *Application deadline:* For fall admission, 2/1. *Application fee:* $25.
**Expenses:** Tuition: Full-time $22,260.
**Financial support:** In 2001–02, 6 teaching assistantships were awarded; fellowships, career-related internships or fieldwork, Federal Work-Study, institutionally sponsored loans, and tuition awards also available. Support available to part-time students. Financial award application deadline: 1/15.
Dr. Leslie Rescorla, Chair, 610-526-5190.
**Application contact:** Graduate School of Arts and Sciences, 610-526-5072.

### ■ CALIFORNIA INSTITUTE OF INTEGRAL STUDIES

**Graduate Programs, School of Professional Psychology, San Francisco, CA 94103**
**AWARDS** Drama therapy (MA); expressive arts therapy (MA, Certificate), including consulting and education (Certificate), expressive arts (Certificate), expressive arts therapy (MA); integral counseling psychology (MA); psychology (Psy D), including clinical psychology; somatics (MA, Certificate), including integral health education (Certificate), somatics (MA). Part-time and evening/weekend programs available.
**Students:** 205 full-time, 236 part-time. 298 applicants, 65% accepted, 115 enrolled.
**Degree requirements:** For master's, comprehensive exam; for doctorate, thesis/dissertation, comprehensive exam.
**Entrance requirements:** For master's, TOEFL, minimum GPA of 3.0; for

doctorate, TOEFL, field experience, master's degree, minimum GPA of 3.1. *Application deadline:* Applications are processed on a rolling basis. *Application fee:* $65.
**Expenses:** Tuition: Full-time $10,890; part-time $605 per unit. Tuition and fees vary according to degree level.
**Financial support:** Career-related internships or fieldwork, Federal Work-Study, institutionally sponsored loans, and scholarships/grants available. Support available to part-time students. Financial award application deadline: 6/15; financial award applicants required to submit FAFSA.
**Faculty research:** Somatic psychology.
Dr. Harrison Voigt, Head, 415-575-6218.
**Application contact:** David Towner, Admissions Officer, 415-575-6152, *Fax:* 415-575-1268, *E-mail:* dtowner@ciis.edu.
**Find an in-depth description at www.petersons.com/gradchannel.**

### ■ CALIFORNIA LUTHERAN UNIVERSITY

**Graduate Studies, Department of Psychology, Thousand Oaks, CA 91360-2787**
**AWARDS** Clinical psychology (MS); marital and family therapy (MS). Part-time programs available.
**Degree requirements:** For master's, thesis or comprehensive exams.
**Entrance requirements:** For master's, GRE General Test, interview, minimum GPA of 3.0. *Web site:* http://www.clunet.edu/htdocs/ClinicalPsych/ClinicalPsychology.html

### ■ CALIFORNIA STATE UNIVERSITY, DOMINGUEZ HILLS

**College of Arts and Sciences, Program in Psychology, Carson, CA 90747-0001**
**AWARDS** Clinical psychology (MA); general psychology (MA). Evening/weekend programs available.
**Faculty:** 15 full-time, 5 part-time/adjunct.
**Students:** 19 full-time (15 women), 9 part-time (all women); includes 12 minority (5 African Americans, 1 Asian American or Pacific Islander, 6 Hispanic Americans). Average age 30. 20 applicants, 85% accepted, 4 enrolled. In 2001, 21 degrees awarded.
**Entrance requirements:** For master's, GRE General Test and GRE Subject Test or MAT, interview, minimum GPA of 3.0. *Application deadline:* For fall admission, 6/1. *Application fee:* $55.
**Expenses:** Tuition, nonresident: full-time $1,508; part-time $438 per semester.

Required fees: $442; $246 per unit. $227 per semester.
Dr. Ramona Davis, Chair, 310-243-3427, *E-mail:* rdavis@hvx20.csudh.edu.

### ■ CALIFORNIA STATE UNIVERSITY, FULLERTON

**Graduate Studies, College of Humanities and Social Sciences, Department of Psychology, Fullerton, CA 92834-9480**
**AWARDS** Clinical/community psychology (MS); psychology (MA). Part-time programs available.
**Faculty:** 24 full-time (11 women), 28 part-time/adjunct.
**Students:** 50 full-time (41 women), 7 part-time (6 women); includes 19 minority (1 African American, 8 Asian Americans or Pacific Islanders, 10 Hispanic Americans), 1 international. Average age 28. 70 applicants, 61% accepted, 33 enrolled. In 2001, 18 degrees awarded.
**Degree requirements:** For master's, thesis.
**Entrance requirements:** For master's, GRE General Test, GRE Subject Test, undergraduate major in psychology or related field. *Application deadline:* For fall admission, 3/15. *Application fee:* $55.
**Expenses:** Tuition, nonresident: part-time $246 per unit. Required fees: $964.
**Financial support:** Teaching assistantships, career-related internships or fieldwork, Federal Work-Study, institutionally sponsored loans, and scholarships/grants available. Support available to part-time students. Financial award application deadline: 3/1.
Dr. David Perkins, Chair, 714-278-3514.

### ■ CALIFORNIA STATE UNIVERSITY, SAN BERNARDINO

**Graduate Studies, College of Social and Behavioral Sciences, Department of Psychology, Program in Clinical/Counseling Psychology, San Bernardino, CA 92407-2397**
**AWARDS** MS.
**Faculty:** 10 full-time.
**Students:** 18 full-time (14 women), 4 part-time (3 women); includes 8 minority (1 African American, 1 Asian American or Pacific Islander, 5 Hispanic Americans, 1 Native American). Average age 32. 39 applicants, 21% accepted. In 2001, 8 degrees awarded.
**Degree requirements:** For master's, comprehensive exam or thesis.
**Entrance requirements:** For master's, minimum GPA of 3.0 in major. *Application deadline:* For fall admission, 8/31 (priority date). *Application fee:* $55.

*California State University, San Bernardino (continued)*

**Expenses:** Tuition, nonresident: full-time $4,428. Required fees: $1,733.

**Financial support:** Fellowships, research assistantships, teaching assistantships, career-related internships or fieldwork, Federal Work-Study, and unspecified assistantships available. Financial award application deadline: 3/1.

**Faculty research:** Psychology of women, fathering, depression, families, cross-cultural counseling.

Dr. Faith H. McClure, Head, 909-880-5598, *Fax:* 909-880-7003, *E-mail:* fmcclure@csusb.edu.

**Application contact:** Luci Van Loon, Graduate Secretary, 909-880-5570, *Fax:* 909-880-7003, *E-mail:* lvanloon@csusb.edu.

## ■ CARDINAL STRITCH UNIVERSITY

**College of Arts and Sciences, Department of Psychology, Milwaukee, WI 53217-3985**

**AWARDS** Clinical psychology (MA). Part-time and evening/weekend programs available.

**Faculty:** 2 full-time (1 woman), 3 part-time/adjunct (1 woman).

**Students:** 33 full-time (29 women); includes 7 minority (5 African Americans, 1 Asian American or Pacific Islander, 1 Hispanic American), 1 international. Average age 39. 36 applicants, 56% accepted, 20 enrolled.

**Degree requirements:** For master's, thesis, portfolio, clinical practicum.

**Entrance requirements:** For master's, GRE General Test, GRE psychology subject test, interview, minimum GPA of 3.0, letters of recommendation (3). *Application deadline:* For fall admission, 7/15 (priority date); for spring admission, 12/15 (priority date). Applications are processed on a rolling basis. *Application fee:* $25.

**Expenses:** Tuition: Part-time $390 per credit. Required fees: $150; $75 per semester. One-time fee: $25. Tuition and fees vary according to program.

**Financial support:** In 2001–02, 1 student received support, including 1 research assistantship with partial tuition reimbursement available (averaging $1,500 per year); career-related internships or fieldwork, Federal Work-Study, and scholarships/grants also available. Financial award applicants required to submit FAFSA.

Dr. Asuncion Miteria Austria, Chair, 414-410-4471.

**Application contact:** 800-347-8822 Ext. 4042, *E-mail:* gradadm@stritch.edu. *Web site:* http://www.stritch.edu

## ■ CARLOS ALBIZU UNIVERSITY

**Graduate Programs in Psychology, San Juan, PR 00902-3711**

**AWARDS** Clinical psychology (PhD, Psy D); general psychology (PhD); industrial/organizational psychology (MS, PhD). Part-time and evening/weekend programs available.

**Degree requirements:** For master's, one foreign language, comprehensive exam; for doctorate, one foreign language, thesis/dissertation, written qualifying exams.

**Entrance requirements:** For master's, GRE General Test or PAEG, interview, minimum GPA of 3.0; for doctorate, PAEG, interview, minimum GPA of 3.0.

**Faculty research:** Psychotherapeutic techniques for Hispanics, psychology of the aged, school dropouts, stress, violence.

## ■ CARLOS ALBIZU UNIVERSITY, MIAMI CAMPUS

**Graduate Programs, Miami, FL 33172-2209**

**AWARDS** Clinical psychology (Psy D); industrial/organizational psychology (MS); management (MBA); marriage and family therapy (MS); mental health counseling (MS); psychology (MS); school counseling (MS). Part-time and evening/weekend programs available.

**Faculty:** 19 full-time (9 women), 37 part-time/adjunct (19 women).

**Students:** 432 full-time (322 women), 32 part-time (22 women); includes 328 minority (58 African Americans, 7 Asian Americans or Pacific Islanders, 263 Hispanic Americans), 4 international. Average age 35. 189 applicants, 50% accepted, 69 enrolled. In 2001, 44 master's, 69 doctorates awarded. Terminal master's awarded for partial completion of doctoral program.

**Degree requirements:** For master's, one foreign language, comprehensive exam, integrative project (MBA); for doctorate, one foreign language, thesis/dissertation, written and oral qualifying exam, internship.

**Entrance requirements:** For master's, GMAT (MBA), letters of recommendation (3), interview, minimum GPA of 3.0, resumé; for doctorate, GRE General Test, GRE Subject Test, letters of recommendation (3), minimum GPA of 3.0. *Application deadline:* For fall admission, 8/1 (priority date); for spring admission, 11/30 (priority date). Applications are processed on a rolling basis. *Application fee:* $50.

**Expenses:** Tuition: Part-time $455 per credit. Required fees: $819; $273 per term. Tuition and fees vary according to course load and degree level.

**Financial support:** In 2001–02, 22 students received support. Federal Work-Study and scholarships/grants available. Financial award application deadline: 6/1; financial award applicants required to submit FAFSA.

**Faculty research:** Culture, psychodiagnostics, psychotherapy, forensic psychology, neuropsychology; marketing strategy, entrepreneurship.

Dr. Gerardo F. Rodriquez-Menedez, Chancellor, 305-593-1223 Ext. 120, *Fax:* 305-629-8052, *E-mail:* grodriguez@albizu.edu.

**Application contact:** Miriam Matos, Admissions Officer, 305-593-1223 Ext. 134, *Fax:* 305-593-1854, *E-mail:* mmatos@albizu.edu. *Web site:* http://www.albizu.edu/

## ■ CASE WESTERN RESERVE UNIVERSITY

**School of Graduate Studies, Department of Psychology, Program in Clinical Psychology, Cleveland, OH 44106**

**AWARDS** PhD.

**Degree requirements:** For doctorate, thesis/dissertation, internship.

**Entrance requirements:** For doctorate, GRE General Test, GRE Subject Test, TOEFL.

**Faculty research:** Pediatric psychology, family functioning, depression, geriatric psychopathology, creativity and play.

## ■ THE CATHOLIC UNIVERSITY OF AMERICA

**School of Arts and Sciences, Department of Psychology, Program in Clinical Psychology, Washington, DC 20064**

**AWARDS** PhD.

**Students:** 12 full-time (11 women), 25 part-time (20 women); includes 5 minority (2 Asian Americans or Pacific Islanders, 2 Hispanic Americans, 1 Native American), 2 international. Average age 30. 85 applicants, 12% accepted, 5 enrolled. In 2001, 3 degrees awarded.

**Degree requirements:** For doctorate, thesis/dissertation, comprehensive exam.

**Entrance requirements:** For doctorate, GRE General Test, GRE Subject Test. *Application deadline:* For fall admission, 1/15. Applications are processed on a rolling basis. *Application fee:* $55. Electronic applications accepted.

**Expenses:** Tuition: Full-time $20,050; part-time $770 per credit. Required fees: $430 per term. Tuition and fees vary according to program.

**Financial support:** In 2001–02, 19 students received support; fellowships, research assistantships, teaching assistantships, career-related internships or fieldwork, Federal Work-Study, institutionally sponsored loans, scholarships/grants, and tuition waivers (full and partial) available. Support available to part-time students. Financial award application deadline: 2/1; financial award applicants required to submit FAFSA.

**Faculty research:** Individual and group psychotherapy, marital and family interaction, suicide and depression, anxiety, paraphilias.

Dr. Diane B. Arnkoff, Director, 202-319-5764, *Fax:* 202-319-6263. *Web site:* http://www.cua.edu/www/psy/clprog.htm

## ■ CENTER FOR HUMANISTIC STUDIES

**Programs in Humanistic, Clinical, and Educational Psychology, Detroit, MI 48202-3802**

**AWARDS** Humanistic and clinical psychology (MA, Psy D).

**Faculty:** 4 full-time (2 women), 12 part-time/adjunct (5 women).

**Students:** 83 full-time (60 women); includes 15 minority (13 African Americans, 2 Asian Americans or Pacific Islanders). Average age 38. 90 applicants, 83% accepted. In 2001, 30 degrees awarded.

**Degree requirements:** For master's, thesis, practicum; for doctorate, thesis/dissertation, internship, practicum.

**Entrance requirements:** For master's, 1 year of work experience, interview, minimum GPA of 3.0; for doctorate, 3 years work experience, 2 interviews, minimum GPA of 3.0 in graduate course work. *Application deadline:* For fall admission, 9/1 (priority date). Applications are processed on a rolling basis. *Application fee:* $75.

**Expenses:** Tuition: Full-time $14,060.

**Financial support:** In 2001–02, 39 students received support. Application deadline: 6/30.

**Faculty research:** Qualitative research, existential-phenomenological psychology, applications to clinical practice.

**Application contact:** Ellen F. Blau, Admissions Adviser, 313-875-7440, *Fax:* 313-875-2610, *E-mail:* eblau@humanpsych.edu.

## ■ CENTRAL MICHIGAN UNIVERSITY

**College of Graduate Studies, College of Humanities and Social and Behavioral Sciences, Department of Psychology, Program in Clinical Psychology, Mount Pleasant, MI 48859**

**AWARDS** Psy D.

**Degree requirements:** For doctorate, thesis/dissertation.

**Entrance requirements:** For doctorate, GRE.

**Expenses:** Tuition, state resident: part-time $182 per unit. Tuition, nonresident: part-time $182 per unit. Required fees: $208 per semester. Part-time tuition and fees vary according to course load.

**Faculty research:** Intervention strategies, personal problem solving.

## ■ CHAPMAN UNIVERSITY

**Graduate Studies, Division of Psychology, Orange, CA 92866**

**AWARDS** Marriage and family therapy (MA); pre-clinical (MA). Part-time and evening/weekend programs available.

**Faculty:** 11 full-time (5 women).

**Degree requirements:** For master's, comprehensive exam.

**Entrance requirements:** For master's, GRE General Test, MAT, minimum undergraduate GPA of 3.0. *Application deadline:* Applications are processed on a rolling basis. *Application fee:* $40.

**Expenses:** Tuition: Part-time $450 per credit. Tuition and fees vary according to program.

**Financial support:** Application deadline: 3/1.

Dr. Gerhardt Eifert, Chair, 714-997-6776, *E-mail:* eifert@chapman.edu.

**Application contact:** Susan Read-Weil, Coordinator, 714-744-7837, *E-mail:* sreadwei@chapman.edu.

## ■ CHESTNUT HILL COLLEGE

**Graduate Division, Department of Professional Psychology, Program in Clinical Psychology, Philadelphia, PA 19118-2693**

**AWARDS** Psy D. *Web site:* http://www.chc.edu/graduate/psyd.html

## ■ CHICAGO SCHOOL OF PROFESSIONAL PSYCHOLOGY

**Graduate School, Chicago, IL 60605-2024**

**AWARDS** Clinical psychology (Psy D); forensic psychology (MA); industrial and organizational psychology (MA). Part-time programs available.

**Faculty:** 19 full-time (10 women), 43 part-time/adjunct (25 women).

**Students:** 216 full-time (162 women), 157 part-time (114 women); includes 75 minority (38 African Americans, 16 Asian Americans or Pacific Islanders, 21 Hispanic Americans), 25 international. Average age 25. 215 applicants, 74% accepted, 70 enrolled. In 2001, 48 degrees awarded.

**Degree requirements:** For doctorate, thesis/dissertation, competency exam, internship, practica.

**Entrance requirements:** For master's, 18 undergraduate hours in psychology, course work in statistics; for doctorate, GRE General Test or other graduate entrance exam, 18 hours in psychology (1 course each in statistics, abnormal psychology, and theories of personality). *Application deadline:* For fall admission, 1/15 (priority date); for spring admission, 11/1 (priority date). Applications are processed on a rolling basis. *Application fee:* $50.

**Expenses:** Tuition: Part-time $550 per credit hour. Required fees: $350 per year. Tuition and fees vary according to degree level and program.

**Financial support:** In 2001–02, 16 research assistantships with partial tuition reimbursements, 32 teaching assistantships with partial tuition reimbursements were awarded. Career-related internships or fieldwork, Federal Work-Study, scholarships/grants, and tuition waivers (partial) also available. Support available to part-time students. Financial award application deadline: 5/1; financial award applicants required to submit FAFSA.

**Faculty research:** White racial identity, work with cross-cultural clients, teaching in psychology.

Dr. Michael Horowitz, President, 312-786-9443 Ext. 3033, *Fax:* 312-322-3273, *E-mail:* mhorowitz@csopp.edu.

**Application contact:** Magdelen Kellogg, Director of Admission, 312-786-9443 Ext. 3029, *Fax:* 312-322-3273, *E-mail:* mkellogg@csopp.edu. *Web site:* http://www.csopp.edu/

**Find an in-depth description at www.petersons.com/gradchannel.**

## ■ CITY COLLEGE OF THE CITY UNIVERSITY OF NEW YORK

**Graduate School, College of Liberal Arts and Science, Division of Social Science, Department of Psychology, New York, NY 10031-9198**

**AWARDS** Clinical psychology (PhD); experimental cognition (PhD); general psychology (MA). Part-time programs available.

**Students:** 81. In 2001, 10 degrees awarded.

**Degree requirements:** For master's, one foreign language, thesis, comprehensive exam.

**Entrance requirements:** For master's, TOEFL, minimum undergraduate B average. *Application deadline:* For fall admission, 5/1; for spring admission, 12/1. *Application fee:* $40.

**Expenses:** Tuition, state resident: part-time $185 per credit. Tuition, nonresident:

*City College of the City University of New York (continued)*

part-time $320 per credit. Required fees: $43 per term.

**Financial support:** Fellowships, teaching assistantships, career-related internships or fieldwork, Federal Work-Study, and tuition waivers (full and partial) available. Support available to part-time students. Financial award application deadline: 5/1.

**Faculty research:** Social/personality psychology, physiological psychology, cognition and development.

Brett Silverstein, Chair, 212-650-5442.

**Application contact:** Dr. William King, Graduate Adviser, 212-650-5723.

### ■ CLARK UNIVERSITY

**Graduate School, Department of Psychology, Program in Clinical Psychology, Worcester, MA 01610-1477**

AWARDS PhD.

**Degree requirements:** For doctorate, thesis/dissertation.

**Entrance requirements:** For doctorate, GRE General Test, TOEFL. *Application deadline:* For fall admission, 1/31 (priority date). Applications are processed on a rolling basis. *Application fee:* $40.

**Expenses:** Tuition: Full-time $24,400; part-time $763 per credit. Required fees: $10.

**Financial support:** In 2001–02, fellowships with full tuition reimbursements (averaging $10,900 per year), research assistantships with full tuition reimbursements (averaging $10,900 per year), teaching assistantships with full tuition reimbursements (averaging $10,900 per year) were awarded. Tuition waivers (full) also available.

Dr. Jamie McHale, Director, 508-793-7274.

**Application contact:** Cynthia LaRochelle, Graduate School Secretary, 508-793-7274, *Fax:* 508-793-7265, *E-mail:* clarochelle@clarku.edu. *Web site:* http://www2.clarku.edu/newsite/graduatefolder/programs/index.shtml

### ■ CLEVELAND STATE UNIVERSITY

**College of Graduate Studies, College of Arts and Sciences, Department of Psychology, Professional Program in Clinical and Counseling Psychology, Cleveland, OH 44115**

AWARDS MA.

**Faculty:** 17 full-time (6 women), 4 part-time/adjunct (1 woman).

**Students:** 21 full-time (17 women); includes 1 minority (Hispanic American).

Average age 25. 94 applicants, 22% accepted, 21 enrolled. In 2001, 17 degrees awarded.

**Degree requirements:** For master's, internship, thesis optional. *Median time to degree:* Master's–2 years full-time.

**Entrance requirements:** For master's, GRE General Test, GRE Subject Test, previous course work in psychology, sample of written work. *Application deadline:* For fall admission, 2/1 (priority date). Applications are processed on a rolling basis. *Application fee:* $25 ($50 for international students).

**Expenses:** Tuition, state resident: full-time $6,838; part-time $263 per credit hour. Tuition, nonresident: full-time $13,526; part-time $520 per credit hour.

**Financial support:** In 2001–02, 12 students received support. Career-related internships or fieldwork, Federal Work-Study, and tuition waivers (full) available. Financial award application deadline: 5/1; financial award applicants required to submit FAFSA.

**Faculty research:** Clinical psychopathology, cognitive interventions, personality assessment.

Dr. Steve D. Slane, Director, 216-687-2525, *Fax:* 216-687-9294.

**Application contact:** Karen Colston, Administrative Coordinator, 216-687-2552, *E-mail:* k.colston@csuohio.edu. *Web site:* http://www.asic.csuohio.edu/psy/grad/clin.html

### ■ COLLEGE OF ST. JOSEPH

**Graduate Program, Division of Psychology and Human Services, Program in Clinical Psychology, Rutland, VT 05701-3899**

AWARDS MS.

**Faculty:** 3 full-time (0 women), 6 part-time/adjunct (3 women).

**Students:** 9 full-time, 12 part-time; includes 1 minority (African American). Average age 34.

**Degree requirements:** For master's, thesis optional.

**Entrance requirements:** For master's, GRE General Test, interview. *Application fee:* $35.

**Expenses:** Tuition: Full-time $9,000; part-time $250 per credit. Required fees: $45 per semester. Part-time tuition and fees vary according to course load.

**Financial support:** Unspecified assistantships available. Financial award application deadline: 3/1.

**Application contact:** Steve Soba, Dean of Admissions, 802-773-5900 Ext. 3206, *Fax:* 802-773-5900, *E-mail:* ssoba@csj.edu.

### ■ COLLEGE OF STATEN ISLAND OF THE CITY UNIVERSITY OF NEW YORK

**Graduate Programs, Center for Developmental Neuroscience and Developmental Disabilities, Subprogram in Learning Processes, Staten Island, NY 10314-6600**

AWARDS Biopsychology (PhD); clinical psychology (PhD); developmental psychology (PhD); environmental psychology (PhD); experimental cognition (PhD); experimental psychology (PhD); neuropsychology (PhD); psychology (PhD); social-personality psychology (PhD).

**Degree requirements:** For doctorate, one foreign language, thesis/dissertation.

**Entrance requirements:** For doctorate, GRE, TOEFL. *Application deadline:* For fall admission, 3/15 (priority date). Applications are processed on a rolling basis. *Application fee:* $40.

**Expenses:** Tuition, state resident: full-time $4,350; part-time $185 per credit. Tuition, nonresident: full-time $7,600; part-time $320 per credit. Required fees: $53 per semester.

**Financial support:** Fellowships, research assistantships, teaching assistantships, career-related internships or fieldwork and institutionally sponsored loans available. Financial award application deadline: 3/15.

Dr. Nancy Hemmes, Head, 718-997-3561.

### ■ THE COLLEGE OF WILLIAM AND MARY

**Faculty of Arts and Sciences, Department of Psychology, Virginia Consortium Program in Clinical Psychology, Williamsburg, VA 23187-8795**

AWARDS Psy D. Offered through the Virginia Consortium for Professional Psychology. For information call 757-518-2550.

**Faculty:** 38 full-time (16 women), 26 part-time/adjunct (15 women).

**Students:** 38 full-time (29 women), 9 part-time (all women); includes 12 minority (9 African Americans, 3 Asian Americans or Pacific Islanders). Average age 28. 128 applicants, 16% accepted, 10 enrolled. In 2001, 11 degrees awarded.

**Degree requirements:** For doctorate, thesis/dissertation, written, and oral exams, comprehensive exam.

**Entrance requirements:** For doctorate, GRE General Test, GRE Subject Test. *Application deadline:* For fall admission, 1/5. *Application fee:* $30.

**Expenses:** Tuition, state resident: full-time $3,262; part-time $175 per credit hour. Tuition, nonresident: full-time $14,768; part-time $550 per credit hour. Required fees: $2,478.

**Financial support:** In 2001–02, 26 students received support, including 23 research assistantships with partial tuition reimbursements available (averaging $5,000 per year), 3 teaching assistantships with partial tuition reimbursements available (averaging $5,000 per year); career-related internships or fieldwork and scholarships/grants also available. Financial award application deadline: 2/15; financial award applicants required to submit FAFSA.

Dr. Neill P. Watson, Chair, 757-518-2550, *Fax:* 757-518-2553, *E-mail:* npwats@wm.edu.

**Application contact:** Eileen X. O'Neill, Program Coordinator, 757-518-2550, *Fax:* 757-518-2553, *E-mail:* exoneill@odu.edu. *Web site:* http://www.vcpcp.odu.edu/vcpcp/

## ■ DEPAUL UNIVERSITY

**College of Liberal Arts and Sciences, Department of Psychology, Program in Clinical Psychology, Chicago, IL 60604-2287**

**AWARDS** Child clinical psychology (MA, PhD); community clinical psychology (MA, PhD).

**Faculty:** 17 full-time (10 women), 3 part-time/adjunct (2 women).

**Students:** 24 full-time (17 women), 31 part-time (23 women); includes 14 African Americans, 8 Asian Americans or Pacific Islanders, 4 Hispanic Americans, 1 international. Average age 29. 158 applicants, 5% accepted. In 2001, 5 master's, 10 doctorates awarded.

**Degree requirements:** For master's, thesis, oral exam; for doctorate, thesis/dissertation, internship, oral and written exams, comprehensive exam. *Median time to degree:* Master's–2 years full-time; doctorate–6 years full-time.

**Entrance requirements:** For master's and doctorate, GRE General Test, 32 quarter hours in psychology, minimum GPA of 3.5. *Application deadline:* For fall admission, 1/10. *Application fee:* $40. Electronic applications accepted.

**Expenses:** Tuition: Part-time $362 per credit hour. Tuition and fees vary according to program.

**Financial support:** In 2001–02, 24 students received support, including 20 research assistantships with full and partial tuition reimbursements available (averaging $7,000 per year), 4 teaching assistantships with full and partial tuition reimbursements available (averaging $7,000 per year); career-related internships or fieldwork, scholarships/grants, traineeships, tuition waivers (partial), and unspecified assistantships also available. Financial award application deadline: 1/10.

**Faculty research:** Urban issues, child family issues, diversity, at risk youth, homeless and Latino/a HIV/AIDS.

Dr. Karen Budd, Director of Clinical Training, *E-mail:* rbudd@depaul.edu.

**Application contact:** Lucinda Rapp, Information Contact, 773-325-7887, *E-mail:* lrapp@wppost.depaul.edu. *Web site:* http://condor.depaul.edu/~psych/

## ■ DREXEL UNIVERSITY

**Graduate School, College of Arts and Sciences, Clinical Psychology Program, Philadelphia, PA 19104-2875**

**AWARDS** Clinical psychology (MA, MS); forensic psychology (PhD); health psychology (PhD); neuropsychology (PhD).

**Faculty:** 9 full-time (4 women).

**Students:** 120 full-time (106 women), 3 part-time (2 women); includes 12 minority (7 African Americans, 4 Asian Americans or Pacific Islanders, 1 Hispanic American), 3 international. Average age 27. 82 applicants, 18% accepted, 13 enrolled. In 2001, 22 master's, 11 doctorates awarded. Terminal master's awarded for partial completion of doctoral program.

**Degree requirements:** For master's, thesis, comprehensive exam; for doctorate, thesis/dissertation, qualifying exam. *Median time to degree:* Master's–3 years full-time; doctorate–6 years full-time.

**Entrance requirements:** For master's, GRE General Test, minimum GPA of 3.0; for doctorate, GRE General Test, GRE Subject Test, minimum GPA of 3.0. *Application deadline:* For spring admission, 1/15. *Application fee:* $30. Electronic applications accepted.

**Expenses:** Contact institution.

**Financial support:** Fellowships, research assistantships, teaching assistantships, career-related internships or fieldwork, Federal Work-Study, institutionally sponsored loans, and tuition waivers (partial) available. Support available to part-time students. Financial award application deadline: 5/1; financial award applicants required to submit FAFSA.

**Faculty research:** Cognitive behavioral therapy, stress and coping, eating disorders, substance abuse, developmental disabilities.

Dr. Kirk Heilbrun, Head, 215-895-2402, *Fax:* 215-895-1333.

**Find an in-depth description at www.petersons.com/gradchannel.**

## ■ DREXEL UNIVERSITY

**Graduate School, College of Arts and Sciences, Department of Psychology, Philadelphia, PA 19104-2875**

**AWARDS** Clinical neuropsychology (PhD).

**Faculty:** 6 full-time (2 women), 12 part-time/adjunct (7 women).

**Students:** 10 full-time (8 women), 12 part-time (11 women); includes 4 minority (2 African Americans, 1 Asian American or Pacific Islander, 1 Hispanic American), 1 international. Average age 27. 78 applicants, 13% accepted, 5 enrolled. In 2001, 8 degrees awarded.

**Degree requirements:** For doctorate, thesis/dissertation, internship.

**Entrance requirements:** For doctorate, GRE General Test, TOEFL. *Application deadline:* For fall admission, 2/1. Applications are processed on a rolling basis. *Application fee:* $50. Electronic applications accepted.

**Expenses:** Contact institution.

**Financial support:** Research assistantships, teaching assistantships, career-related internships or fieldwork, Federal Work-Study, institutionally sponsored loans, tuition waivers (full and partial), unspecified assistantships, and practicum positions available. Financial award application deadline: 2/1.

**Faculty research:** Neurosciences, rehabilitation psychology, cognitive science, neurological assessment.

Dr. Kirk Heilbrun, Head, 215-895-2402, *Fax:* 215-895-1333.

**Application contact:** Director of Graduate Admissions, 215-895-6700, *Fax:* 215-895-5939, *E-mail:* enroll@drexel.edu.

**Find an in-depth description at www.petersons.com/gradchannel.**

## ■ DREXEL UNIVERSITY

**Graduate School, College of Arts and Sciences, Program in Law-Psychology, Philadelphia, PA 19104-2875**

**AWARDS** PhD, JD/PhD.

**Students:** 22 full-time (16 women), 9 part-time (8 women); includes 4 minority (2 African Americans, 2 Hispanic Americans), 1 international. Average age 27. 11 applicants, 27% accepted, 3 enrolled. In 2001, 1 degree awarded.

**Degree requirements:** For doctorate, thesis/dissertation, qualifying exam. *Median time to degree:* Doctorate–10 years part-time.

**Entrance requirements:** For doctorate, GRE General Test, GRE Subject Test, minimum GPA of 3.0. *Application deadline:* For fall admission, 2/15. *Application fee:* $50. Electronic applications accepted.

**Expenses:** Contact institution.

**Financial support:** Fellowships, research assistantships, teaching assistantships, career-related internships or fieldwork, Federal Work-Study, and institutionally sponsored loans available. Support available to part-time students. Financial award

*Drexel University (continued)*
application deadline: 5/1; financial award applicants required to submit FAFSA.
**Faculty research:** Mental health law issues, professional ethics, social science applications to law.
Dr. Kirk Heilbrun, Head, 215-895-2402, *Fax:* 215-895-1333.

**Find an in-depth description at www.petersons.com/gradchannel.**

### ■ DUKE UNIVERSITY

**Graduate School, Department of Psychology, Durham, NC 27708-0586**

**AWARDS** Biological psychology (PhD); clinical psychology (PhD); cognitive psychology (PhD); developmental psychology (PhD); experimental psychology (PhD); health psychology (PhD); human social development (PhD).
**Faculty:** 52 full-time, 15 part-time/adjunct.
**Students:** 66 full-time (42 women); includes 11 minority (6 African Americans, 2 Asian Americans or Pacific Islanders, 3 Hispanic Americans, 13 international. 386 applicants, 7% accepted, 15 enrolled. In 2001, 8 doctorates awarded.
**Degree requirements:** For doctorate, thesis/dissertation.
**Entrance requirements:** For doctorate, GRE General Test. *Application deadline:* For fall admission, 12/31. *Application fee:* $75.
**Expenses:** Tuition: Full-time $24,600.
**Financial support:** Fellowships, research assistantships, teaching assistantships, career-related internships or fieldwork and Federal Work-Study available. Financial award application deadline: 12/31.
Reiko Mazuka, Co-Director of Graduate Studies, 919-660-5716, *Fax:* 919-660-5726, *E-mail:* bseymore@acpub.duke.edu. *Web site:* http://www.psych.duke.edu/

### ■ DUQUESNE UNIVERSITY

**Graduate School of Liberal Arts, Department of Psychology, Pittsburgh, PA 15282-0001**

**AWARDS** Clinical psychology (PhD); developmental psychology (PhD).
**Faculty:** 15 full-time (5 women), 5 part-time/adjunct (2 women).
**Students:** 83 full-time (42 women), 9 part-time (5 women); includes 6 minority (4 African Americans, 1 Asian American or Pacific Islander, 1 Hispanic American), 4 international. Average age 28. 54 applicants, 56% accepted, 13 enrolled. In 2001, 13 degrees awarded.
**Degree requirements:** For doctorate, 2 foreign languages, thesis/dissertation, comprehensive exam.

**Entrance requirements:** For doctorate, GRE General Test, TOEFL, MA in psychology. *Application deadline:* For fall admission, 2/1. *Application fee:* $50.
**Expenses:** Tuition: Part-time $566 per credit. Required fees: $56 per credit. Part-time tuition and fees vary according to degree level and program.
**Financial support:** In 2001–02, 1 research assistantship with full tuition reimbursement (averaging $11,000 per year), 14 teaching assistantships with full tuition reimbursements (averaging $11,000 per year) were awarded. Fellowships with full tuition reimbursements, career-related internships or fieldwork, scholarships/grants, and tuition waivers (partial) also available. Financial award application deadline: 5/1.
**Faculty research:** Emotion, language motivation, imagination, development.
Dr. Russell Walsh, Chair, 412-396-6520.

### ■ EAST CAROLINA UNIVERSITY

**Graduate School, College of Arts and Sciences, Department of Psychology, Program in Clinical Psychology, Greenville, NC 27858-4353**

**AWARDS** MA.
**Students:** 16 full-time (10 women), 2 part-time (both women); includes 3 minority (2 African Americans, 1 Asian American or Pacific Islander). Average age 25. 48 applicants, 33% accepted. In 2001, 4 degrees awarded.
**Degree requirements:** For master's, one foreign language, thesis, comprehensive exam.
**Entrance requirements:** For master's, GRE General Test, GRE Subject Test, TOEFL. *Application deadline:* For fall admission, 3/15 (priority date). Applications are processed on a rolling basis. *Application fee:* $45.
**Expenses:** Tuition, state resident: full-time $2,636. Tuition, nonresident: full-time $11,365.
**Financial support:** Research assistantships with partial tuition reimbursements, teaching assistantships with partial tuition reimbursements, traineeships available. Support available to part-time students. Financial award application deadline: 6/1.
Dr. Thomas Durham, Director of Graduate Studies, 252-328-6118, *Fax:* 252-328-6283, *E-mail:* durhamt@mail.ecu.edu.
**Application contact:** Dr. Paul D. Tschetter, Senior Associate Dean of the Graduate School, 252-328-6012, *Fax:* 252-328-6071, *E-mail:* gradschool@mail.ecu.edu.

### ■ EASTERN ILLINOIS UNIVERSITY

**Graduate School, College of Sciences, Department of Psychology, Program in Clinical Psychology, Charleston, IL 61920-3099**

**AWARDS** MA.
**Degree requirements:** For master's, comprehensive exam.
**Entrance requirements:** For master's, GRE General Test.

### ■ EASTERN KENTUCKY UNIVERSITY

**The Graduate School, College of Arts and Sciences, Department of Psychology, Richmond, KY 40475-3102**

**AWARDS** Clinical psychology (MS); industrial/organizational psychology (MS); school psychology (Psy S). Part-time programs available.
**Faculty:** 21 full-time (10 women).
**Students:** 66 full-time (58 women), 4 part-time (2 women); includes 4 minority (3 African Americans, 1 Hispanic American). Average age 24. 303 applicants, 30% accepted. In 2001, 20 degrees awarded.
**Entrance requirements:** For master's and Psy S, GRE General Test, minimum GPA of 2.5. *Application deadline:* For fall admission, 3/15 (priority date). Applications are processed on a rolling basis. *Application fee:* $0.
**Expenses:** Tuition, state resident: full-time $1,468; part-time $165 per credit hour. Tuition, nonresident: full-time $4,034; part-time $450 per credit hour.
**Financial support:** In 2001–02, 30 students received support, including 16 research assistantships, 10 teaching assistantships; career-related internships or fieldwork and Federal Work-Study also available. Support available to part-time students.
**Faculty research:** Cognitive behavior therapy, therapy with the deaf, victims of drunk drivers, autism. *Total annual research expenditures:* $40,000.
Dr. Robert M. Adams, Chair, 859-622-1105, *Fax:* 859-622-5871, *E-mail:* robert.adams@eku.edu. *Web site:* http://www.psychology.eku.edu/

### ■ EASTERN MICHIGAN UNIVERSITY

**Graduate School, College of Arts and Sciences, Department of Psychology, Program in Clinical/Behavioral Services, Ypsilanti, MI 48197**

**AWARDS** MS. Evening/weekend programs available.

**Entrance requirements:** For master's, GRE General Test, TOEFL. *Application deadline:* For fall admission, 5/15; for spring admission, 3/15. Applications are processed on a rolling basis. *Application fee:* $30.

**Expenses:** Tuition, state resident: part-time $285 per credit hour. Tuition, nonresident: part-time $510 per credit hour.

**Financial support:** Fellowships, teaching assistantships available. Support available to part-time students. Financial award application deadline: 3/15; financial award applicants required to submit FAFSA. Dr. Marilyn Bonem, Coordinator.

■ **EAST TENNESSEE STATE UNIVERSITY**

School of Graduate Studies, College of Arts and Sciences, Department of Psychology, Johnson City, TN 37614

AWARDS Clinical psychology (MA); general psychology (MA).

**Faculty:** 7 full-time (1 woman).
**Students:** 25 full-time (16 women), 11 part-time (5 women); includes 1 minority (African American). Average age 27. In 2001, 13 degrees awarded.
**Degree requirements:** For master's, thesis, oral exams.
**Entrance requirements:** For master's, GRE General Test, GRE Subject Test, TOEFL, minimum GPA of 3.0. *Application deadline:* For fall admission, 7/15 (priority date). Applications are processed on a rolling basis. *Application fee:* $25 ($35 for international students).
**Expenses:** Tuition, state resident: part-time $181 per hour. Tuition, nonresident: part-time $270 per hour. Required fees: $220 per term.
**Financial support:** Research assistantships with full tuition reimbursements, teaching assistantships with full tuition reimbursements, career-related internships or fieldwork, institutionally sponsored loans, and scholarships/grants available.
**Faculty research:** Domestic violence, suicidal behavior, advertising, religious behavior, behavioral medicine. *Total annual research expenditures:* $69,131.
Dr. David J. Marx, Chair, 423-439-6656, *Fax:* 423-439-5695, *E-mail:* marx@etsu.edu. *Web site:* http://www.etsu.edu/

■ **EDINBORO UNIVERSITY OF PENNSYLVANIA**

Graduate Studies, School of Liberal Arts, Department of Psychology, Edinboro, PA 16444

AWARDS Clinical psychology (MA). Part-time and evening/weekend programs available.

**Faculty:** 4 full-time (3 women).

**Students:** 15 full-time (13 women), 9 part-time (8 women); includes 1 minority (Asian American or Pacific Islander). Average age 32. In 2001, 1 degree awarded.
**Degree requirements:** For master's, thesis or alternative, project, comprehensive exam.
**Entrance requirements:** For master's, GRE or MAT, minimum QPA of 2.5. *Application deadline:* For fall admission, 3/15 (priority date). Applications are processed on a rolling basis. *Application fee:* $25. Electronic applications accepted.
**Expenses:** Tuition, state resident: full-time $4,600; part-time $256 per credit. Tuition, nonresident: full-time $7,554; part-time $420 per credit. Required fees: $68 per credit.
**Financial support:** In 2001–02, 10 students received support. Career-related internships or fieldwork, Federal Work-Study, institutionally sponsored loans, scholarships/grants, and unspecified assistantships available. Support available to part-time students. Financial award application deadline: 5/1; financial award applicants required to submit FAFSA. Dr. Susan LaBine, Coordinator, 814-732-2774, *E-mail:* slabine@edinboro.edu.
**Application contact:** Dr. Mary Margaret Bevevino, Dean of Graduate Studies, 814-732-2856, *Fax:* 814-732-2611, *E-mail:* mbevevino@edinboro.edu.

■ **EMORY UNIVERSITY**

Graduate School of Arts and Sciences, Department of Psychology, Atlanta, GA 30322-1100

AWARDS Clinical psychology (PhD); cognition and development (PhD); psychobiology (PhD).

**Faculty:** 26 full-time (6 women), 2 part-time/adjunct (0 women).
**Students:** 73 full-time (55 women); includes 5 minority (1 African American, 2 Asian Americans or Pacific Islanders, 2 Hispanic Americans), 6 international. 272 applicants, 6% accepted, 13 enrolled. In 2001, 10 doctorates awarded.
**Degree requirements:** For doctorate, thesis/dissertation, comprehensive exam, registration.
**Entrance requirements:** For doctorate, GRE General Test, TOEFL, minimum GPA of 3.0. *Application deadline:* For fall admission, 1/15. *Application fee:* $50. Electronic applications accepted.
**Expenses:** Tuition: Full-time $24,770. Required fees: $100. Tuition and fees vary according to program and student level.
**Financial support:** In 2001–02, 56 fellowships were awarded; research assistantships, teaching assistantships, career-related internships or fieldwork, Federal Work-Study, institutionally sponsored loans,

scholarships/grants, and tuition waivers (full and partial) also available. Financial award application deadline: 1/20.
**Faculty research:** Neurophysiology, drugs and behavior, hormones and behavior, nonverbal behavior.
Dr. Darryl Neill, Chair, 404-727-7437.
**Application contact:** Dr. Robyn Fivush, Director of Graduate Studies, 404-727-7456, *E-mail:* psyrf@emory.edu.

■ **EMPORIA STATE UNIVERSITY**

School of Graduate Studies, The Teachers College, Department of Psychology and Special Education, Program in Psychology, Emporia, KS 66801-5087

AWARDS Clinical psychology (MS); general psychology (MS); industrial/organizational psychology (MS).

**Students:** 39 full-time (32 women), 8 part-time (6 women); includes 2 minority (both African Americans), 6 international. 23 applicants, 78% accepted. In 2001, 23 degrees awarded.
**Degree requirements:** For master's, comprehensive exam or thesis.
**Entrance requirements:** For master's, GRE General Test or MAT, TOEFL. *Application deadline:* For fall admission, 6/1 (priority date); for spring admission, 10/1. Applications are processed on a rolling basis. *Application fee:* $30 ($75 for international students). Electronic applications accepted.
**Expenses:** Tuition, state resident: full-time $2,632; part-time $119 per credit hour. Tuition, nonresident: full-time $6,734; part-time $290 per credit hour.
**Financial support:** Career-related internships or fieldwork, Federal Work-Study, institutionally sponsored loans, health care benefits, and unspecified assistantships available. Financial award application deadline: 3/15; financial award applicants required to submit FAFSA.
**Faculty research:** Driving under the influence (DUI) personality, lifestyles and imposter phenomenon.
Dr. Kenneth A. Weaver, Chair, Department of Psychology and Special Education, 620-341-5317, *E-mail:* weaverke@emporia.edu.

■ **EVANGEL UNIVERSITY**

Department of Psychology, Springfield, MO 65802-2191

AWARDS Clinical psychology (MS); general psychology (MS); guidance and counseling (MS). Part-time and evening/weekend programs available.

**Faculty:** 4 full-time (1 woman), 4 part-time/adjunct (1 woman).
**Students:** 12 full-time (9 women), 11 part-time (7 women); includes 1 minority

*Evangel University (continued)*
(Asian American or Pacific Islander). Average age 29. 10 applicants, 100% accepted. In 2001, 4 degrees awarded.

**Degree requirements:** For master's, thesis, comprehensive exam.

**Entrance requirements:** For master's, GRE General Test, minimum undergraduate GPA of 3.0, undergraduate major or minor in psychology, teaching certificate (guidance and counseling). *Application deadline:* For fall admission, 7/15 (priority date); for spring admission, 11/19 (priority date). Applications are processed on a rolling basis. *Application fee:* $25.

**Expenses:** Tuition: Full-time $3,040; part-time $190 per credit. Required fees: $240. Tuition and fees vary according to program.

**Financial support:** In 2001–02, 6 students received support; research assistantships, teaching assistantships, career-related internships or fieldwork, institutionally sponsored loans, and scholarships/grants available. Financial award application deadline: 5/1; financial award applicants required to submit FAFSA.

Dr. Jeffrey Fulks, Supervisor of Graduate Psychology, 417-865-2815 Ext. 7915.

**Application contact:** Jackie Eutsler, Administrative Assistant of Graduate Studies, 417-865-2815, *Fax:* 417-520-0545, *E-mail:* eutslerj@evangel.edu. *Web site:* http://www.evangel.edu/psycgrad/

■ **FAIRLEIGH DICKINSON UNIVERSITY, METROPOLITAN CAMPUS**

**University College: Arts, Sciences, and Professional Studies, School of Psychology, Program in Clinical Psychology, Teaneck, NJ 07666-1914**

**AWARDS** PhD.

**Students:** 84 full-time (63 women); includes 10 minority (1 African American, 3 Asian Americans or Pacific Islanders, 6 Hispanic Americans), 5 international. Average age 29. 11 applicants, 100% accepted, 10 enrolled. In 2001, 9 degrees awarded. *Application deadline:* Applications are processed on a rolling basis. *Application fee:* $40.

**Expenses:** Tuition: Full-time $11,484; part-time $638 per credit. Required fees: $420; $97.

**Find an in-depth description at www.petersons.com/gradchannel.**

■ **FIELDING GRADUATE INSTITUTE**

**Graduate Programs, Program in Psychology, Santa Barbara, CA 93105-3538**

**AWARDS** Clinical psychology (PhD); psychology (MA). Evening/weekend programs available.

**Faculty:** 34 full-time (15 women), 25 part-time/adjunct (13 women).

**Students:** 452 full-time (317 women); includes 79 minority (36 African Americans, 9 Asian Americans or Pacific Islanders, 27 Hispanic Americans, 7 Native Americans), 12 international. Average age 44. 154 applicants, 30% accepted, 31 enrolled. In 2001, 43 master's, 35 doctorates awarded. Terminal master's awarded for partial completion of doctoral program.

**Degree requirements:** For doctorate, thesis/dissertation. *Median time to degree:* Master's–4.8 years full-time; doctorate–9.7 years full-time.

*Application deadline:* For fall admission, 3/5; for spring admission, 9/5. *Application fee:* $75.

**Expenses:** Tuition: Full-time $14,100.

**Financial support:** In 2001–02, 311 students received support. Career-related internships or fieldwork and diversity scholarships available. Financial award application deadline: 3/1; financial award applicants required to submit FAFSA.

Dr. Ronald Giannetti, Dean, 805-898-2909, *E-mail:* rongian@fielding.edu.

**Application contact:** Marine Dumas, Admissions Manager, 805-898-4039, *Fax:* 805-687-4590, *E-mail:* mdumas@ fielding.edu.

■ **FINCH UNIVERSITY OF HEALTH SCIENCES/THE CHICAGO MEDICAL SCHOOL**

**School of Graduate and Postdoctoral Studies, Department of Clinical Psychology, North Chicago, IL 60064-3095**

**AWARDS** MS, PhD.

**Faculty:** 8 full-time, 17 part-time/adjunct.

**Students:** 81 full-time (61 women); includes 14 minority (3 African Americans, 5 Asian Americans or Pacific Islanders, 6 Hispanic Americans), 5 international. In 2001, 9 master's, 13 doctorates awarded. Terminal master's awarded for partial completion of doctoral program.

**Degree requirements:** For master's, thesis; for doctorate, thesis/dissertation, 1 year full-time clinical internship,, comprehensive exam.

**Entrance requirements:** For master's, GRE General Test, TOEFL, TWE, TSE; for doctorate, GRE General Test, GRE

Subject Test, TOEFL, TWE, TSE. *Application deadline:* For fall admission, 1/15 (priority date). Applications are processed on a rolling basis. *Application fee:* $25.

**Expenses:** Contact institution.

**Financial support:** Fellowships, research assistantships, teaching assistantships, career-related internships or fieldwork and tuition waivers (full and partial) available. Financial award application deadline: 7/10; financial award applicants required to submit FAFSA.

**Faculty research:** Hormonal influences on human sexually dimorphic behavior, nutrition and mood, aging, anxiety disorders. Dr. Michael Seidenberg, Chairman, 847-578-3305.

**Application contact:** Pat Rigwood, Administrative Secretary, 847-578-3305.

■ **FISK UNIVERSITY**

**Graduate Programs, Department of Psychology, Nashville, TN 37208-3051**

**AWARDS** Clinical psychology (MA); psychology (MA).

**Faculty:** 4 full-time (2 women), 1 (woman) part-time/adjunct.

**Students:** 8 full-time (all women); all minorities (all African Americans). Average age 23. 16 applicants, 50% accepted, 3 enrolled. In 2001, 5 degrees awarded.

**Degree requirements:** For master's, thesis. *Median time to degree:* Master's–2 years full-time, 3 years part-time.

**Entrance requirements:** For master's, GRE General Test, GRE Subject Test, minimum GPA of 3.0. *Application deadline:* For fall admission, 4/15 (priority date). Applications are processed on a rolling basis. *Application fee:* $25.

**Expenses:** Tuition: Full-time $9,790.

**Financial support:** In 2001–02, 7 students received support; teaching assistantships with partial tuition reimbursements available.

**Faculty research:** Ethnic and gender identity, development, female adolescent development, juvenile delinquency prevention. *Total annual research expenditures:* $5,000.

Dr. Sheila Peters, Chair, 615-329-8617, *E-mail:* speters@fisk.edu.

**Application contact:** Director of Admissions, 615-329-8668, *Fax:* 615-329-8774.

■ **FLORIDA INSTITUTE OF TECHNOLOGY**

**Graduate Programs, School of Psychology, Program in Clinical Psychology, Melbourne, FL 32901-6975**

**AWARDS** Psy D.

**Students:** Average age 29.

**Degree requirements:** For doctorate, thesis/dissertation, internship, preliminary exams, CQE exam, comprehensive exam.
**Entrance requirements:** For doctorate, GRE General Test, GRE Subject Test, resume, minimum GPA of 3.2. *Application deadline:* For fall admission, 3/15. Applications are processed on a rolling basis. Electronic applications accepted.
**Expenses:** Tuition: Part-time $650 per credit.
**Financial support:** Research assistantships with partial tuition reimbursements, teaching assistantships with partial tuition reimbursements, career-related internships or fieldwork and tuition waivers (partial) available. Financial award application deadline: 3/1; financial award applicants required to submit FAFSA.
**Faculty research:** Addictions, neuropsychology, child abuse, gender issues, personality assessment, eating disorders, psychological trauma.
Dr. Philip D. Farber, Director of Clinical Training, 321-674-8105, *Fax:* 321-674-7105, *E-mail:* farber@fit.edu.
**Application contact:** Carolyn P. Farrior, Director of Graduate Admissions, 321-674-7118, *Fax:* 321-723-9468, *E-mail:* cfarrior@fit.edu. *Web site:* http://www.fit.edu/
**Find an in-depth description at www.petersons.com/gradchannel.**

■ **FLORIDA STATE UNIVERSITY**

**Graduate Studies, College of Arts and Sciences, Department of Psychology, Program in Clinical Psychology, Tallahassee, FL 32306**

**AWARDS** PhD.

**Faculty:** 16 full-time (6 women), 1 part-time/adjunct (0 women).
**Students:** 53 full-time (36 women); includes 11 minority (6 African Americans, 4 Hispanic Americans, 1 Native American), 1 international. Average age 25. 229 applicants, 6% accepted, 8 enrolled. In 2001, 8 doctorates awarded.
**Degree requirements:** For doctorate, thesis/dissertation, preliminary exam, independent project. *Median time to degree:* Doctorate–3.8 years full-time.
**Entrance requirements:** For doctorate, GRE General Test, minimum GPA of 3.2, research experience, letters of recommendation. *Application deadline:* For fall admission, 12/15. *Application fee:* $20. Electronic applications accepted.
**Expenses:** Tuition, state resident: part-time $163 per credit hour. Tuition, nonresident: part-time $570 per credit hour. Tuition and fees vary according to program.

**Financial support:** In 2001–02, 33 students received support, including 7 fellowships with full tuition reimbursements available (averaging $15,000 per year), 26 research assistantships with full tuition reimbursements available (averaging $12,500 per year), 6 teaching assistantships with full tuition reimbursements available (averaging $12,600 per year); career-related internships or fieldwork, Federal Work-Study, institutionally sponsored loans, traineeships, and unspecified assistantships also available. Financial award applicants required to submit FAFSA.
**Faculty research:** Child clinical psychology, antisocial behavior, depression addictive behavior, emotion. *Total annual research expenditures:* $1.8 million.
Dr. Mark Licht, Director, 850-644-4079, *Fax:* 850-644-7739.
**Application contact:** Cherie P. Dilworth, Graduate Program Assistant, 850-644-2499, *Fax:* 850-644-7739, *E-mail:* gradinfo@psy.fsu.edu.

■ **FORDHAM UNIVERSITY**

**Graduate School of Arts and Sciences, Department of Psychology, Program in Clinical Psychology, New York, NY 10458**

**AWARDS** PhD.

**Students:** 304 applicants, 11% accepted. In 2001, 12 doctorates awarded.
**Degree requirements:** For doctorate, thesis/dissertation, clinical internship, comprehensive exam.
**Entrance requirements:** For doctorate, GRE General Test, GRE Subject Test. *Application deadline:* For fall admission, 1/8. *Application fee:* $65. Electronic applications accepted.
**Expenses:** Tuition: Part-time $720 per credit. Required fees: $135 per semester.
**Financial support:** In 2001–02, 33 students received support, including fellowships with tuition reimbursements available (averaging $15,000 per year), 1 research assistantship with tuition reimbursement available (averaging $12,000 per year), 3 teaching assistantships with tuition reimbursements available (averaging $15,000 per year); career-related internships or fieldwork, institutionally sponsored loans, tuition waivers (full and partial), and unspecified assistantships also available. Financial award application deadline: 1/8.
Dr. Warren Tryon, Director, 718-817-3782, *Fax:* 718-817-3785, *E-mail:* wtryon@fordham.edu.
**Application contact:** Dr. Craig W. Pilant, Assistant Dean, 718-817-4420, *Fax:* 718-817-3566, *E-mail:* pilant@fordham.edu. *Web site:* http://www.fordham.edu/gsas/

■ **FOREST INSTITUTE OF PROFESSIONAL PSYCHOLOGY**

**Graduate Programs, Springfield, MO 65807**

**AWARDS** Clinical psychology (Psy D); psychology (MA). Part-time programs available. Terminal master's awarded for partial completion of doctoral program.

**Degree requirements:** For master's, thesis or alternative; for doctorate, thesis/dissertation, internship, qualifying exams.
**Entrance requirements:** For master's, GRE General Test, interview, minimum GPA of 3.2, 12 hours in psychology; for doctorate, GRE General Test, interview, minimum GPA of 3.25, 18 hours in psychology. Electronic applications accepted.
**Faculty research:** Closed head injury, pain management, clinical supervision, alternative treatment methods for depression, organizational analysis. *Web site:* http://www.forestinstitute.org/

■ **FRANCIS MARION UNIVERSITY**

**Graduate Programs, Department of Psychology, Florence, SC 29501-0547**

**AWARDS** Applied clinical psychology (MS); applied community psychology (MS); school psychology (MS). Part-time and evening/weekend programs available.

**Faculty:** 12 full-time (3 women), 2 part-time/adjunct (1 woman).
**Students:** 57. Average age 36. In 2001, 12 degrees awarded.
**Degree requirements:** For master's, internship.
**Entrance requirements:** For master's, GRE General Test. *Application deadline:* For fall admission, 4/15; for spring admission, 10/15. Applications are processed on a rolling basis. *Application fee:* $30.
**Expenses:** Tuition, state resident: full-time $3,820; part-time $191 per semester hour. Tuition, nonresident: full-time $7,640; part-time $382 per semester hour. Required fees: $170; $4 per semester hour. $30 per semester.
**Financial support:** In 2001–02, fellowships (averaging $6,000 per year); career-related internships or fieldwork and unspecified assistantships also available. Support available to part-time students. Financial award application deadline: 3/1; financial award applicants required to submit FAFSA.
**Faculty research:** Critical thinking, spatial localization, cognition and aging, family psychology.
Dr. John R. Hester, Coordinator, 843-661-1635, *Fax:* 843-661-1628.
**Application contact:** Ginger Ridgill, Administrative Assistant, 843-661-1378,

*Francis Marion University (continued)*
*Fax:* 843-661-1628, *E-mail:* gridgill@fmarion.edu.

### ■ FULLER THEOLOGICAL SEMINARY

**Graduate School of Psychology, Department of Psychology, Pasadena, CA 91182**

AWARDS Clinical psychology (PhD, Psy D); psychology (MA, MS).

**Degree requirements:** For doctorate, thesis/dissertation, internships.
**Entrance requirements:** For doctorate, GRE General Test GRE Subject Test, TOEFL, interview.
**Expenses:** Contact institution.
**Faculty research:** Psychoneuroimmunology, psychology of religion, coping, shame, depression. *Web site:* http://www.fuller.edu/sop/

### ■ GALLAUDET UNIVERSITY

**The Graduate School, College of Arts and Sciences, Department of Psychology, Program in Clinical Psychology, Washington, DC 20002-3625**

AWARDS PhD.

**Degree requirements:** For doctorate, thesis/dissertation.
**Entrance requirements:** For doctorate, GRE General Test or MAT, interview.

### ■ GEORGE FOX UNIVERSITY

**Graduate and Professional Studies, Graduate School of Clinical Psychology, Newberg, OR 97132-2697**

AWARDS Clinical psychology (Psy D); psychology (MA).

**Faculty:** 5 full-time (2 women), 3 part-time/adjunct (2 women).
**Students:** 72 full-time (32 women), 12 part-time (6 women); includes 11 minority (2 African Americans, 2 Asian Americans or Pacific Islanders, 3 Hispanic Americans, 4 Native Americans), 3 international. 36 applicants, 75% accepted, 21 enrolled. In 2001, 16 master's, 16 doctorates awarded.
**Degree requirements:** For doctorate, thesis/dissertation, internship.
**Entrance requirements:** For master's, GRE General Test, GRE Subject Test, minimum undergraduate GPA of 3.0 during previous 2 years. *Application deadline:* For fall admission, 1/1. *Application fee:* $40. Electronic applications accepted.
**Expenses:** Contact institution.
**Financial support:** Teaching assistantships, career-related internships or fieldwork available. Financial award applicants required to submit FAFSA.

**Faculty research:** Spiritual well-being, psychosocial development, value and ethics development.
Dr. Wayne Adams, Director, 800-765-4369 Ext. 2760, *E-mail:* wadams@georgefox.edu.
**Application contact:** Dr. Andrea Cook, Vice President for Enrollment Services, 800-631-0921, *Fax:* 503-554-3856, *E-mail:* acook@georgefox.edu. *Web site:* http://www.georgefox.edu/

### ■ GEORGE MASON UNIVERSITY

**College of Arts and Sciences, Department of Psychology, Program in Clinical Psychology, Fairfax, VA 22030-4444**

AWARDS PhD.

**Degree requirements:** For doctorate, thesis/dissertation, internship.
**Entrance requirements:** For doctorate, GRE General Test, minimum undergraduate GPA of 3.0, 3.25 in major. Electronic applications accepted.
**Expenses:** Tuition, state resident: full-time $3,168; part-time $132 per credit hour. Tuition, nonresident: full-time $11,280; part-time $470 per credit hour. Required fees: $1,416; $59 per credit hour.

### ■ THE GEORGE WASHINGTON UNIVERSITY

**Columbian College of Arts and Sciences, Department of Psychology, Washington, DC 20052**

AWARDS Applied social psychology (PhD); clinical psychology (PhD, Psy D); cognitive neuropsychology (PhD); industrial-organizational psychology (PhD). Part-time and evening/weekend programs available.

**Faculty:** 15 full-time (8 women), 1 (woman) part-time/adjunct.
**Students:** 133 full-time (106 women), 102 part-time (82 women); includes 50 minority (22 African Americans, 13 Asian Americans or Pacific Islanders, 14 Hispanic Americans, 1 Native American), 15 international. Average age 30. 413 applicants, 18% accepted. In 2001, 32 doctorates awarded.
**Degree requirements:** For doctorate, thesis/dissertation or alternative, general exam.
**Entrance requirements:** For doctorate, GRE General Test, minimum GPA of 3.0. *Application fee:* $55.
**Expenses:** Tuition: Part-time $810 per credit. Required fees: $1 per credit.
**Financial support:** In 2001–02, 27 students received support, including 22 fellowships with tuition reimbursements available (averaging $4,700 per year), 20 teaching assistantships with tuition reimbursements available (averaging $2,900 per year); career-related internships

or fieldwork and Federal Work-Study also available. Financial award application deadline: 2/1.
Dr. Rolf Peterson, Chair, 202-994-6544. *Web site:* http://www.gwu.edu/~gradinfo/

### ■ GRADUATE SCHOOL AND UNIVERSITY CENTER OF THE CITY UNIVERSITY OF NEW YORK

**Graduate Studies, Program in Psychology, New York, NY 10016-4039**

AWARDS Basic applied neurocognition (PhD); biopsychology (PhD); clinical psychology (PhD); developmental psychology (PhD); environmental psychology (PhD); experimental psychology (PhD); industrial psychology (PhD); learning processes (PhD); neuropsychology (PhD); psychology (PhD); social personality (PhD).

**Faculty:** 119 full-time (40 women).
**Students:** 463 full-time (335 women), 4 part-time (2 women); includes 96 minority (39 African Americans, 20 Asian Americans or Pacific Islanders, 36 Hispanic Americans, 1 Native American), 47 international. Average age 33. 493 applicants, 24% accepted, 65 enrolled. In 2001, 28 degrees awarded.
**Degree requirements:** For doctorate, one foreign language, thesis/dissertation.
**Entrance requirements:** For doctorate, GRE General Test. *Application deadline:* For fall admission, 2/1. *Application fee:* $40.
**Expenses:** Tuition, state resident: part-time $245 per credit. Tuition, nonresident: part-time $425 per credit. Required fees: $72 per semester.
**Financial support:** In 2001–02, 226 students received support, including 141 fellowships, 14 research assistantships, 4 teaching assistantships; career-related internships or fieldwork, Federal Work-Study, institutionally sponsored loans, and tuition waivers (full and partial) also available. Financial award application deadline: 2/1; financial award applicants required to submit FAFSA.
Dr. Joseph Glick, Executive Officer, 212-817-8706, *Fax:* 212-817-1533, *E-mail:* jglick@gc.cuny.edu.

### ■ HOFSTRA UNIVERSITY

**College of Liberal Arts and Sciences, Division of Social Sciences, Department of Psychology, Program in Clinical and School Psychology, Hempstead, NY 11549**

AWARDS MA, PhD, Post-Doctoral Certificate.

**Faculty:** 26 full-time (5 women), 14 part-time/adjunct (6 women).
**Students:** 59 full-time (48 women), 71 part-time (46 women); includes 4 minority (1 African American, 3 Asian Americans or

Pacific Islanders). Average age 29. In 2001, 20 master's, 23 doctorates awarded.

**Degree requirements:** For doctorate, thesis/dissertation.

**Entrance requirements:** For master's, GRE General Test, GRE Subject Test; for doctorate, GRE General Test, GRE Subject Test, letters of recommendation (3), interview, minimum GPA of 3.0 in psychology. *Application deadline:* For fall admission, 2/1. *Application fee:* $40 ($75 for international students).

**Expenses:** Tuition: Full-time $12,408. Tuition and fees vary according to course load and program.

**Financial support:** Career-related internships or fieldwork available.

Dr. Kurt Salzinger, Director, 516-463-5219, *Fax:* 516-463-6052, *E-mail:* psykzs@hofstra.edu.

**Application contact:** Mary Beth Carey, Vice President of Enrollment Services, *Fax:* 516-560-7660, *E-mail:* hofstra@hofstra.edu.

## ■ HOWARD UNIVERSITY

**Graduate School of Arts and Sciences, Department of Psychology, Washington, DC 20059-0002**

**AWARDS** Clinical psychology (PhD); developmental psychology (PhD); experimental psychology (PhD); neuropsychology (PhD); personality psychology (PhD); psychology (MS); social psychology (PhD). Part-time programs available.

**Faculty:** 16 full-time (7 women).

**Students:** 70 full-time (51 women), 20 part-time (14 women). Average age 29. 165 applicants, 15% accepted, 20 enrolled. In 2001, 10 master's, 12 doctorates awarded.

**Degree requirements:** For master's, thesis, comprehensive exam; for doctorate, thesis/dissertation, qualifying exam, comprehensive exam. *Median time to degree:* Master's–3 years full-time, 5 years part-time; doctorate–5 years full-time, 9 years part-time.

**Entrance requirements:** For master's, GRE General Test, minimum GPA of 2.5, bachelor's degree in psychology or related field; for doctorate, GRE General Test, minimum GPA of 3.0. *Application deadline:* For fall admission, 4/1; for spring admission, 11/1. Applications are processed on a rolling basis. *Application fee:* $45.

**Financial support:** In 2001–02, 19 students received support, including 3 fellowships with full tuition reimbursements available (averaging $13,500 per year), 2 research assistantships with full tuition reimbursements available (averaging $10,000 per year), 8 teaching assistantships with full tuition reimbursements available (averaging $13,000 per year); career-related internships or fieldwork,

institutionally sponsored loans, and scholarships/grants also available. Financial award application deadline: 4/1; financial award applicants required to submit FAFSA.

**Faculty research:** Personality and psychophysiology, educational and social development of African-American children, child and adult psychopathology.

Dr. Albert Roberts, Chair, 202-806-6805, *Fax:* 202-806-4823, *E-mail:* aroberts@howard.edu.

**Application contact:** Dr. Alfonso Campbell, Chairman, Graduate Admissions Committee, 202-806-6805, *Fax:* 202-806-4873, *E-mail:* acampbell@howard.edu.

## ■ IDAHO STATE UNIVERSITY

**Office of Graduate Studies, College of Arts and Sciences, Department of Psychology, Pocatello, ID 83209**

**AWARDS** Clinical psychology (PhD); psychology (MS).

**Faculty:** 9 full-time (4 women).

**Students:** 20 full-time (13 women), 4 part-time (2 women); includes 1 minority (Hispanic American). Average age 30. 75 applicants, 16% accepted. In 2001, 2 master's, 3 doctorates awarded.

**Degree requirements:** For master's and doctorate, thesis/dissertation.

**Entrance requirements:** For master's and doctorate, GRE General Test, GRE Subject Test. *Application deadline:* For fall admission, 7/1; for spring admission, 12/1. Applications are processed on a rolling basis. *Application fee:* $35.

**Expenses:** Tuition, area resident: Full-time $3,432. Tuition, state resident: part-time $172 per credit. Tuition, nonresident: full-time $10,196; part-time $262 per credit. International tuition: $9,672 full-time. Part-time tuition and fees vary according to course load, program and reciprocity agreements.

**Financial support:** In 2001–02, 1 research assistantship with full and partial tuition reimbursement (averaging $12,064 per year), 11 teaching assistantships with full and partial tuition reimbursements (averaging $9,919 per year) were awarded. Career-related internships or fieldwork, Federal Work-Study, and traineeships also available. Financial award application deadline: 2/15.

**Faculty research:** Decision making, social psychology, personality and affective disorders, marital satisfaction, child pathology. *Total annual research expenditures:* $83,710.

Dr. Victor Joe, Chairman, 208-282-2111. *Web site:* http://www.isu.edu/departments/psych/

## ■ ILLINOIS INSTITUTE OF TECHNOLOGY

**Graduate College, Institute of Psychology, Chicago, IL 60616-3793**

**AWARDS** Clinical psychology (PhD); industrial/organizational psychology (PhD); personnel/human resource development (MS); psychology (MS); rehabilitation counseling (MS); rehabilitation psychology (PhD).

**Faculty:** 17 full-time (7 women), 4 part-time/adjunct (2 women).

**Students:** 84 full-time (56 women), 75 part-time (51 women); includes 32 minority (15 African Americans, 10 Asian Americans or Pacific Islanders, 6 Hispanic Americans, 1 Native American), 15 international. Average age 30. 157 applicants, 49% accepted. In 2001, 21 master's, 15 doctorates awarded. Terminal master's awarded for partial completion of doctoral program.

**Degree requirements:** For master's, thesis (for some programs), comprehensive exam; for doctorate, thesis/dissertation, qualifying exams, comprehensive exam.

**Entrance requirements:** For master's and doctorate, GRE General Test, TOEFL, minimum GPA of 3.0. *Application deadline:* For fall admission, 1/15 (priority date); for spring admission, 11/1. Applications are processed on a rolling basis. *Application fee:* $30. Electronic applications accepted.

**Expenses:** Tuition: Part-time $590 per credit hour.

**Financial support:** In 2001–02, 32 fellowships, 18 teaching assistantships were awarded. Research assistantships, career-related internships or fieldwork, Federal Work-Study, institutionally sponsored loans, scholarships/grants, and unspecified assistantships also available. Financial award application deadline: 3/1; financial award applicants required to submit FAFSA.

**Faculty research:** Leadership, life span developmental processes, rehabilitation engineering technology, behavioral medicine, substance abuse and disability. *Total annual research expenditures:* $494,180.

Dr. M. Ellen Mitchell, Chairman, 312-567-3362, *Fax:* 312-567-3493, *E-mail:* mitchell@itt.edu.

**Application contact:** Dr. Ali Cinar, Dean of Graduate College, 312-567-3637, *Fax:* 312-567-7517, *E-mail:* gradstu@iit.edu. *Web site:* http://www.iit.edu/colleges/psych/

## ■ ILLINOIS STATE UNIVERSITY

**Graduate School, College of Arts and Sciences, Department of Psychology, Normal, IL 61790-2200**

**AWARDS** Psychology (MA, MS), including clinical psychology, counseling psychology, developmental psychology, educational

*Illinois State University (continued)* psychology, experimental psychology, measurement-evaluation, organizational-industrial psychology; school psychology (PhD, SSP).

**Faculty:** 30 full-time (10 women), 1 part-time/adjunct (0 women).

**Students:** 59 full-time (48 women), 24 part-time (13 women); includes 7 minority (3 African Americans, 3 Hispanic Americans, 1 Native American), 5 international. 81 applicants, 46% accepted. In 2001, 40 master's, 2 doctorates, 4 other advanced degrees awarded.

**Degree requirements:** For master's, thesis or alternative; for doctorate, variable foreign language requirement, thesis/dissertation, 2 terms of residency, internship, practicum.

**Entrance requirements:** For master's, GRE General Test, GRE Subject Test, minimum GPA of 3.0 in last 60 hours; for doctorate, GRE General Test. *Application deadline:* Applications are processed on a rolling basis. *Application fee:* $30.

**Expenses:** Tuition, state resident: full-time $2,691; part-time $112 per credit hour. Tuition, nonresident: full-time $5,880; part-time $245 per credit hour. Required fees: $1,146; $48 per credit hour.

**Financial support:** In 2001–02, 21 research assistantships (averaging $5,127 per year), 27 teaching assistantships (averaging $4,308 per year) were awarded. Tuition waivers (full) and unspecified assistantships also available. Financial award application deadline: 4/1.

**Faculty research:** Dialogues with children, sexual harassment in the military, mental health consultant. *Total annual research expenditures:* $248,177.

Dr. David Barone, Chairperson, 309-438-8651. *Web site:* http://www.cas.ilstu.edu/psychology/index.html

## ■ IMMACULATA UNIVERSITY

**College of Graduate Studies, Department of Psychology, Immaculata, PA 19345**

**AWARDS** Clinical psychology (Psy D); counseling psychology (MA, Certificate), including school guidance counselor (Certificate), school psychologist (Certificate); school psychology (Psy D). Part-time and evening/weekend programs available.

**Students:** 57 full-time (45 women), 220 part-time (188 women). Average age 34. 88 applicants, 80% accepted, 41 enrolled. In 2001, 36 master's, 9 doctorates awarded.

**Degree requirements:** For master's, thesis optional; for doctorate, thesis/dissertation, comprehensive exam.

**Entrance requirements:** For master's, GRE General Test or MAT, TOEFL, minimum GPA of 3.0; for doctorate, GRE

General Test, TOEFL, minimum GPA of 3.5. *Application deadline:* Applications are processed on a rolling basis. *Application fee:* $25.

**Expenses:** Tuition: Part-time $390 per credit.

**Financial support:** Application deadline: 5/1.

**Faculty research:** Supervision ethics, psychology of teaching, gender. Dr. Jed A. Yalof, Chair, 610-647-4400 Ext. 3503, *E-mail:* jyalof@immaculate.edu.

**Application contact:** Office of Graduate Admission, 610-647-4400 Ext. 3211.

## ■ INDIANA STATE UNIVERSITY

**School of Graduate Studies, College of Arts and Sciences, Department of Psychology, Terre Haute, IN 47809-1401**

**AWARDS** Clinical psychology (Psy D); general psychology (MA, MS). Terminal master's awarded for partial completion of doctoral program.

**Degree requirements:** For master's, thesis (for some programs); for doctorate, thesis/dissertation, internship.

**Entrance requirements:** For master's, GRE General Test; for doctorate, GRE General Test, minimum GPA of 3.0. Electronic applications accepted.

## ■ INDIANA UNIVERSITY OF PENNSYLVANIA

**Graduate School and Research, College of Natural Sciences and Mathematics, Department of Psychology, Program in Clinical Psychology, Indiana, PA 15705-1087**

**AWARDS** Psy D. Part-time programs available.

**Faculty:** 20 full-time (10 women).

**Students:** 54 full-time (41 women), 6 part-time (3 women); includes 6 minority (2 African Americans, 3 Asian Americans or Pacific Islanders, 1 Hispanic American), 2 international. 104 applicants, 12% accepted. In 2001, 10 degrees awarded.

**Degree requirements:** For doctorate, thesis/dissertation, internship, practicum, comprehensive exam.

**Entrance requirements:** For doctorate, GRE General Test, TOEFL, minimum GPA of 3.0, letters of recommendation (3), interview. *Application deadline:* For fall admission, 1/10. *Application fee:* $30.

**Expenses:** Tuition, state resident: full-time $4,600; part-time $256 per credit hour. Tuition, nonresident: full-time $7,554; part-time $420 per credit hour. Required fees: $800. Part-time tuition and fees vary according to course load.

**Financial support:** In 2001–02, 3 fellowships (averaging $5,000 per year), 28

research assistantships with full and partial tuition reimbursements (averaging $5,830 per year), 1 teaching assistantship (averaging $17,001 per year) were awarded. Federal Work-Study and scholarships/grants also available. Financial award application deadline: 3/15; financial award applicants required to submit FAFSA. Dr. Donald Robertson, Graduate Coordinator, 724-357-4522, *E-mail:* durobert@iup.edu.

## ■ INDIANA UNIVERSITY–PURDUE UNIVERSITY INDIANAPOLIS

**School of Science, Department of Psychology, Indianapolis, IN 46202-3275**

**AWARDS** Clinical rehabilitation psychology (MS, PhD); industrial/organizational psychology (MS); psychobiology of addictions (PhD). Part-time programs available.

**Students:** 22 full-time (17 women), 14 part-time (12 women); includes 2 minority (1 Asian American or Pacific Islander, 1 Hispanic American), 3 international. Average age 27. In 2001, 12 master's, 3 doctorates awarded. Terminal master's awarded for partial completion of doctoral program.

**Degree requirements:** For master's and doctorate, thesis/dissertation.

**Entrance requirements:** For master's, GRE General Test, minimum undergraduate GPA of 3.0; for doctorate, GRE General Test, GRE Subject Test (clinical rehabilitation psychology), minimum undergraduate GPA of 3.2. *Application deadline:* For fall admission, 2/1 (priority date). *Application fee:* $45 ($55 for international students).

**Expenses:** Tuition, state resident: full-time $4,480; part-time $187 per credit. Tuition, nonresident: full-time $12,926; part-time $539 per credit. Required fees: $177.

**Financial support:** In 2001–02, 21 students received support, including 6 fellowships with partial tuition reimbursements available (averaging $11,000 per year), 15 research assistantships with partial tuition reimbursements available (averaging $9,000 per year), 12 teaching assistantships with partial tuition reimbursements available (averaging $9,000 per year); career-related internships or fieldwork, Federal Work-Study, and institutionally sponsored loans also available. Financial award application deadline: 3/1; financial award applicants required to submit FAFSA.

**Faculty research:** Psychiatric rehabilitation, health psychology, psychopharmacology of drugs of abuse, personnel psychology, organizational decision making.

Dr. J. Gregor Fetterman, Chairman, 317-274-6768, *Fax:* 317-274-6756, *E-mail:* gfetter@iupui.edu.
**Application contact:** Donna Miller, Graduate Program Coordinator, 317-274-6945, *Fax:* 317-274-6756, *E-mail:* dmiller1@iupui.edu. *Web site:* http://www.psynt.iupui.edu/

### ■ JACKSON STATE UNIVERSITY

**Graduate School, School of Liberal Arts, Department of Psychology, Jackson, MS 39217**

AWARDS Clinical psychology (PhD).

**Degree requirements:** For doctorate, thesis/dissertation, comprehensive exam.
**Entrance requirements:** For doctorate, MAT.

### ■ KENT STATE UNIVERSITY

**College of Arts and Sciences, Department of Psychology, Kent, OH 44242-0001**

AWARDS Clinical psychology (MA, PhD); experimental psychology (MA, PhD).

**Degree requirements:** For master's and doctorate, thesis/dissertation.
**Entrance requirements:** For master's, GRE Subject Test, minimum GPA of 2.75; for doctorate, GRE Subject Test, minimum GPA of 3.0.

### ■ LAMAR UNIVERSITY

**College of Graduate Studies, College of Arts and Sciences, Department of Psychology, Beaumont, TX 77710**

AWARDS Community/clinical psychology (MS); industrial/organizational psychology (MS). Part-time programs available.

**Faculty:** 5 full-time (2 women).
**Students:** 15 full-time (8 women), 5 part-time (4 women); includes 4 minority (2 African Americans, 2 Hispanic Americans). Average age 32. 35 applicants, 80% accepted. In 2001, 9 degrees awarded.
**Degree requirements:** For master's, thesis, practicum.
**Entrance requirements:** For master's, GRE General Test, TOEFL, minimum GPA of 2.5 in last 60 hours of undergraduate course work. *Application deadline:* For fall admission, 8/1; for spring admission, 12/1. *Application fee:* $25 ($50 for international students).
**Expenses:** Tuition, state resident: full-time $1,114. Tuition, nonresident: full-time $3,670.
**Financial support:** In 2001–02, 12 students received support, including research assistantships (averaging $6,000 per year), 7 teaching assistantships with tuition reimbursements available (averaging $3,000 per year); fellowships, career-related internships or fieldwork, Federal

Work-Study, scholarships/grants, and tuition waivers (partial) also available. Support available to part-time students. Financial award application deadline: 4/1.
**Faculty research:** Counseling psychology, industrial psychology. *Total annual research expenditures:* $17,000.
Dr. Oney D. Fitzpatrick, Chair, 409-880-8285, *Fax:* 409-880-1779, *E-mail:* fitzpatrod@hal.lamar.edu. *Web site:* http://140.158.184.30/

### ■ LA SALLE UNIVERSITY

**School of Arts and Sciences, Program in Clinical-Counseling Psychology, Philadelphia, PA 19141-1199**

AWARDS MA. Part-time and evening/weekend programs available.

**Faculty:** 14 full-time (7 women), 18 part-time/adjunct (7 women).
**Students:** 26 full-time (18 women), 133 part-time (102 women). Average age 33. 151 applicants, 58% accepted, 35 enrolled. In 2001, 33 degrees awarded.
**Degree requirements:** For master's, comprehensive exam.
**Entrance requirements:** For master's, GRE or MAT, 15 undergraduate credits in psychology. *Application deadline:* Applications are processed on a rolling basis. *Application fee:* $30.
**Expenses:** Contact institution.
**Financial support:** In 2001–02, 15 students received support; teaching assistantships, career-related internships or fieldwork, institutionally sponsored loans, scholarships/grants, and tuition waivers (partial) available. Support available to part-time students. Financial award application deadline: 8/15.
**Faculty research:** Cognitive therapy, attribution theory, work habits, single parent families, treatment of addictions.
Dr. John Rooney, Director, 215-951-1767, *Fax:* 215-951-1843, *E-mail:* rooney@lasalle.edu.
**Application contact:** Colleen L. Hindman, Administrative Assistant, 215-951-1767, *Fax:* 215-951-1843, *E-mail:* hindman@lasalle.edu. *Web site:* http://www.lasalle.edu/academ/grad/psych/psych.htm

### ■ LA SALLE UNIVERSITY

**School of Arts and Sciences, Program in Psychology, Philadelphia, PA 19141-1199**

AWARDS Clinical geropsychology (Psy D); clinical psychology (Psy D); family psychology (Psy D); rehabilitation psychology (Psy D). Part-time and evening/weekend programs available.

**Faculty:** 8 full-time (1 woman), 10 part-time/adjunct (5 women).

**Students:** 40 full-time (25 women), 35 part-time (29 women); includes 7 minority (5 African Americans, 2 Hispanic Americans). Average age 35. 95 applicants, 48% accepted, 25 enrolled. In 2001, 1 degree awarded.
**Entrance requirements:** For doctorate, GRE, minimum GPA of 3.0. *Application deadline:* For fall admission, 3/1. *Application fee:* $30.
**Expenses:** Contact institution.
**Financial support:** Scholarships/grants available.
**Faculty research:** Cognitive therapy, attribution theory, treatment of addiction.
Dr. John A. Smith, Director, 215-951-1350, *Fax:* 215-951-1351, *E-mail:* smithj@lasalle.edu.

### ■ LESLEY UNIVERSITY

**Graduate School of Arts and Social Sciences, Cambridge, MA 02138-2790**

AWARDS Clinical mental health counseling (MA), including expressive therapies counseling, holistic counseling, school and community counseling; counseling psychology (MA, CAGS), including school counseling (MA); creative arts in learning (M Ed, CAGS), including individually designed (M Ed, MA), multicultural education (M Ed, MA), storytelling (M Ed), theater studies (M Ed); ecological literacy (MS); environmental education (MS); expressive therapies (MA, PhD, CAGS), including art therapy (MA), dance therapy (MA), individually designed (M Ed, MA), mental health counseling (MA), music therapy (MA); independent studies (M Ed); independent study (MA); intercultural relations (MA, CAGS), including development project administration (MA), individually designed (M Ed, MA), intercultural conflict resolution (MA), intercultural health and human services (MA), intercultural relations (CAGS), intercultural training and consulting (MA), international education exchange (MA), international student advising (MA), managing culturally diverse human resources (MA), multicultural education (M Ed, MA); interdisciplinary studies (MA); visual arts and creative writing (MFA). MS (environmental education) offered jointly with the Audubon Society Expedition Institute. Part-time and evening/weekend programs available. Postbaccalaureate distance learning degree programs offered (minimal on-campus study).

**Faculty:** 73 full-time (58 women), 137 part-time/adjunct (95 women).
**Students:** 108 full-time (97 women), 1,190 part-time (1,084 women); includes 134 minority (81 African Americans, 23 Asian Americans or Pacific Islanders, 26 Hispanic Americans, 4 Native Americans), 16 international. Average age 36. 639 applicants, 91% accepted, 313 enrolled. In 2001, 1106 degrees awarded.
**Degree requirements:** For master's, internship, practicum, thesis (expressive

*Lesley University (continued)*
therapies); for doctorate and CAGS, thesis/dissertation, arts apprenticeship, field placement; for CAGS, thesis, internship (counseling psychology, expressive therapies).
**Entrance requirements:** For master's, MAT (counseling psychology), TOEFL, interview; for doctorate, GRE or MAT; for CAGS, interview, master's degree. *Application deadline:* Applications are processed on a rolling basis. *Application fee:* $50.
**Expenses:** Tuition: Part-time $330 per credit. Required fees: $15 per term. Part-time tuition and fees vary according to campus/location and program.
**Financial support:** In 2001–02, 47 students received support; research assistantships, teaching assistantships, career-related internships or fieldwork, Federal Work-Study, and unspecified assistantships available. Support available to part-time students. Financial award application deadline: 4/1; financial award applicants required to submit FAFSA.
**Faculty research:** Developmental psychology, women's issues, health psychology, limited supervision group psychology.
Dr. Martha B. McKenna, Dean, 617-349-8467, *Fax:* 617-349-8366.
**Application contact:** Hugh Norwood, Dean of Admissions and Enrollment Planning, 800-999-1959, *Fax:* 617-349-8366, *E-mail:* hnorwood@mail.lesley.edu. *Web site:* http://www.lesley.edu/gsass.html

### ■ LOMA LINDA UNIVERSITY

**Graduate School, Department of Clinical Psychology, Loma Linda, CA 92350**
**AWARDS** PhD, Psy D.
**Faculty:** 9 full-time (2 women), 49 part-time/adjunct (17 women).
**Students:** 105 full-time (76 women), 28 part-time (15 women).
**Entrance requirements:** For doctorate, GRE General Test. *Application fee:* $40.
**Expenses:** Tuition: Part-time $420 per unit.
Dr. Louis E. Jenkins, Chair, 909-824-8577.

### ■ LONG ISLAND UNIVERSITY, BROOKLYN CAMPUS

**Richard L. Conolly College of Liberal Arts and Sciences, Department of Psychology, Program in Clinical Psychology, Brooklyn, NY 11201-8423**
**AWARDS** PhD.
**Degree requirements:** For doctorate, thesis/dissertation.
**Entrance requirements:** For doctorate, GRE Subject Test. Electronic applications accepted.

**Faculty research:** Ethnicity and human development.

### ■ LONG ISLAND UNIVERSITY, C.W. POST CAMPUS

**College of Liberal Arts and Sciences, Department of Psychology, Program in Clinical Psychology, Brookville, NY 11548-1300**
**AWARDS** Psy D.
**Faculty:** 6 full-time (2 women), 15 part-time/adjunct (6 women).
**Students:** 36 full-time (30 women), 1 part-time. 175 applicants, 30% accepted, 16 enrolled. In 2001, 10 degrees awarded.
**Degree requirements:** For doctorate, thesis/dissertation, internship.
**Entrance requirements:** For doctorate, GRE General Test, GRE Subject Test, bachelor's degree in psychology, minimum GPA of 3.25. *Application deadline:* For fall admission, 1/31. *Application fee:* $30.
**Expenses:** Contact institution.
**Financial support:** In 2001–02, 10 fellowships with full tuition reimbursements (averaging $12,000 per year), 11 research assistantships, 4 teaching assistantships (averaging $21,600 per year) were awarded. Career-related internships or fieldwork also available. Financial award application deadline: 5/15; financial award applicants required to submit CSS PROFILE or FAFSA.
**Faculty research:** Family violence, schizophrenia, developmental disabilities, psychotherapy.
Dr. Robert Keisner, Director, 516-299-2090, *Fax:* 516-299-2738, *E-mail:* rkeisner@aol.com. *Web site:* http://www.liu.edu/postlas/

### ■ LOUISIANA STATE UNIVERSITY AND AGRICULTURAL AND MECHANICAL COLLEGE

**Graduate School, College of Arts and Sciences, Department of Psychology, Baton Rouge, LA 70803**
**AWARDS** Biological psychology (MA, PhD); clinical psychology (MA, PhD); cognitive psychology (MA, PhD); developmental psychology (MA, PhD); industrial/organizational psychology (MA, PhD); school psychology (MA, PhD).
**Faculty:** 25 full-time (7 women).
**Students:** 70 full-time (53 women), 43 part-time (24 women); includes 7 minority (3 African Americans, 2 Asian Americans or Pacific Islanders, 2 Hispanic Americans), 2 international. Average age 30. 179 applicants, 12% accepted, 20 enrolled. In 2001, 19 degrees awarded. Terminal master's awarded for partial completion of doctoral program.

**Degree requirements:** For master's, thesis; for doctorate, thesis/dissertation, 1 year internship.
**Entrance requirements:** For master's and doctorate, GRE General Test, minimum GPA of 3.0. *Application deadline:* For fall admission, 1/25 (priority date). Applications are processed on a rolling basis. *Application fee:* $25.
**Expenses:** Tuition, state resident: full-time $2,551. Tuition, nonresident: full-time $5,551. Required fees: $854. Part-time tuition and fees vary according to course load.
**Financial support:** In 2001–02, 1 fellowship (averaging $14,333 per year), 10 research assistantships with partial tuition reimbursements (averaging $14,200 per year), 33 teaching assistantships with partial tuition reimbursements (averaging $10,371 per year) were awarded. Career-related internships or fieldwork, institutionally sponsored loans, and contracts also available. Financial award applicants required to submit FAFSA. *Total annual research expenditures:* $242,157.
Dr. Irving Lane, Chair, 225-578-8745, *Fax:* 225-578-4125, *E-mail:* irvlane@unix1.sncc.lsu.edu.
**Application contact:** Dr. Janet McDonald, Coordinator of Graduate Studies, 225-578-4116, *Fax:* 225-578-4125, *E-mail:* psmcdo@lsu.edu. *Web site:* http://www.artsci.lsu.edu/psych

### ■ LOYOLA COLLEGE IN MARYLAND

**Graduate Programs, College of Arts and Sciences, Department of Psychology, Program in Clinical Psychology, Baltimore, MD 21210-2699**
**AWARDS** MA, MS, Psy D, CAS. Part-time and evening/weekend programs available.
**Students:** 94 full-time (74 women), 51 part-time (40 women). In 2001, 43 master's, 10 doctorates awarded.
**Entrance requirements:** For master's and doctorate, GRE General Test; for CAS, master's degree. *Application deadline:* For spring admission, 10/1 (priority date). Applications are processed on a rolling basis.
**Expenses:** Tuition: Part-time $244 per unit. Tuition and fees vary according to degree level, program and student level.
**Financial support:** Applicants required to submit FAFSA.

### ■ LOYOLA UNIVERSITY CHICAGO

**Graduate School, Department of Psychology, Program in Clinical Psychology, Chicago, IL 60611-2196**
**AWARDS** MA, PhD.

**Faculty:** 10 full-time (4 women), 3 part-time/adjunct (0 women).

**Students:** 41 full-time (30 women), 5 part-time (all women); includes 12 minority (5 African Americans, 5 Asian Americans or Pacific Islanders, 2 Hispanic Americans), 1 international. Average age 26. 237 applicants, 3% accepted. In 2001, 8 master's, 8 doctorates awarded. Terminal master's awarded for partial completion of doctoral program.

**Degree requirements:** For master's, thesis/dissertation; for doctorate, thesis/dissertation, comprehensive exam.

**Entrance requirements:** For doctorate, GRE General Test, GRE Subject Test. *Application deadline:* For fall admission, 12/15. *Application fee:* $40. Electronic applications accepted.

**Expenses:** Tuition: Part-time $529 per credit hour.

**Financial support:** In 2001–02, 30 students received support, including 4 fellowships with full tuition reimbursements available (averaging $10,400 per year), 21 research assistantships with full tuition reimbursements available (averaging $10,000 per year), 5 teaching assistantships with tuition reimbursements available (averaging $10,400 per year); career-related internships or fieldwork, Federal Work-Study, scholarships/grants, traineeships, and teaching fellowships also available. Financial award application deadline: 12/15; financial award applicants required to submit FAFSA.

**Faculty research:** Child and family, AIDS, ethics and professional practice, psychotherapy, social anxiety, health behavior and illness, adolescent development.

Dr. Joseph A. Durlak, Director, 773-508-2969, *Fax:* 773-508-8713, *E-mail:* jdurlak@luc.edu.

**Application contact:** Jacquie Hamilton, Secretary, 773-508-6018, *Fax:* 773-508-8713, *E-mail:* jhamilt@luc.edu. *Web site:* http://www.luc.edu/depts/psychology/grad/clinical/hometext.htm

### ■ MADONNA UNIVERSITY

**Department of Psychology, Livonia, MI 48150-1173**

**AWARDS** Clinical psychology (MS). Part-time and evening/weekend programs available.

**Faculty:** 3 full-time (1 woman), 3 part-time/adjunct (1 woman).

**Students:** 28 applicants, 89% accepted.

**Degree requirements:** For master's, thesis or alternative.

**Entrance requirements:** For master's, GRE General Test. *Application deadline:* For fall admission, 3/1. *Application fee:* $0 ($25 for international students). Electronic applications accepted.

**Expenses:** Tuition: Part-time $325 per credit hour.

**Financial support:** Institutionally sponsored loans available. Support available to part-time students.

Dr. Robert Cohen, Chairperson, 734-432-5736.

**Application contact:** Sandra Kellums, Coordinator of Graduate Admissions, 734-432-5667, *Fax:* 734-432-5862, *E-mail:* kellums@smtp.munet.edu. *Web site:* http://www.munet.edu/gradstdy

### ■ MARQUETTE UNIVERSITY

**Graduate School, College of Arts and Sciences, Department of Psychology, Milwaukee, WI 53201-1881**

**AWARDS** Clinical psychology (MS); psychology (PhD). Part-time programs available.

**Faculty:** 14 full-time (2 women).

**Students:** 36 full-time (24 women), 14 part-time (12 women); includes 7 minority (3 African Americans, 3 Asian Americans or Pacific Islanders, 1 Hispanic American), 2 international. Average age 38. 25 applicants, 48% accepted. In 2001, 2 master's, 4 doctorates awarded.

**Degree requirements:** For master's, thesis or alternative, comprehensive exam; for doctorate, thesis/dissertation, internship, qualifying exam.

**Entrance requirements:** For master's, GRE General Test, GRE Subject Test, MAT, TOEFL; for doctorate, GRE General Test, MAT, TOEFL, sample of scholarly writing. *Application deadline:* For fall admission, 2/15. *Application fee:* $40.

**Expenses:** Tuition: Full-time $10,170; part-time $445 per credit hour. Tuition and fees vary according to course load.

**Financial support:** In 2001–02, 3 research assistantships, 16 teaching assistantships were awarded. Career-related internships or fieldwork, Federal Work-Study, institutionally sponsored loans, scholarships/grants, and tuition waivers (full and partial) also available. Support available to part-time students. Financial award application deadline: 2/15.

**Faculty research:** Mental imagery, moral development, organizational behavior, depression, psychotherapy outcomes. *Total annual research expenditures:* $111,450.

Dr. Robert Lueger, Chairman, 414-288-7218, *Fax:* 414-288-5333.

### ■ MARSHALL UNIVERSITY

**Graduate College, College of Liberal Arts, Department of Psychology, Huntington, WV 25755**

**AWARDS** Clinical psychology (MA); general psychology (MA); industrial and organizational psychology (MA); psychology (Psy D).

**Faculty:** 15 full-time (6 women), 15 part-time/adjunct (7 women).

**Students:** 78 full-time (59 women), 88 part-time (62 women); includes 5 minority (4 African Americans, 1 Hispanic American), 3 international. In 2001, 65 degrees awarded.

**Degree requirements:** For master's, thesis optional.

**Entrance requirements:** For master's, GRE General Test or MAT. *Application deadline:* For fall admission, 3/1; for spring admission, 11/1.

**Expenses:** Tuition, state resident: part-time $147 per credit. Tuition, nonresident: part-time $468 per credit. Tuition and fees vary according to campus/location and reciprocity agreements.

**Financial support:** Teaching assistantships with tuition reimbursements available.

Dr. Martin Amerikaner, Chairperson, 304-696-6446, *E-mail:* amerikan@marshall.edu.

**Application contact:** Ken O'Neal, Assistant Vice President, Adult Student Services, 304-746-2500 Ext. 1907, *Fax:* 304-746-1902, *E-mail:* oneal@marshall.edu.

### ■ MASSACHUSETTS SCHOOL OF PROFESSIONAL PSYCHOLOGY

**Graduate Program, Boston, MA 02132**

**AWARDS** Clinical psychology (Psy D, Certificate); clinical psychopharmacology (Post-Doctoral MS). Part-time programs available.

**Faculty:** 36 part-time/adjunct (13 women).

**Students:** 114 full-time (95 women), 36 part-time (30 women); includes 13 minority (1 African American, 8 Asian Americans or Pacific Islanders, 3 Hispanic Americans, 1 Native American), 17 international. Average age 28. 182 applicants, 43% accepted, 44 enrolled. In 2001, 36 degrees awarded.

**Degree requirements:** For doctorate, thesis/dissertation, registration. *Median time to degree:* Doctorate–4 years full-time.

**Entrance requirements:** For doctorate, GRE General Test, GRE Writing Assessment. *Application deadline:* For fall admission, 1/11. *Application fee:* $50.

**Expenses:** Tuition: Full-time $20,260; part-time $633 per credit.

**Financial support:** In 2001–02, 93 students received support, including 12 teaching assistantships (averaging $2,500 per year); career-related internships or fieldwork, institutionally sponsored loans, and scholarships/grants also available. Financial award application deadline: 2/8; financial award applicants required to submit FAFSA.

Dr. Bruce J. Weiss, President, 617-327-6777, *Fax:* 617-327-4447.

*Massachusetts School of Professional Psychology (continued)*
**Application contact:** 617-327-6777, *Fax:* 617-327-4447, *E-mail:* admissions@ mspp.edu. *Web site:* http://www.mspp.edu/

**Find an in-depth description at www.petersons.com/gradchannel.**

■ **MIAMI UNIVERSITY**

**Graduate School, College of Arts and Sciences, Department of Psychology, Oxford, OH 45056**

**AWARDS** Clinical psychology (PhD); experimental psychology (PhD); social psychology (PhD).

**Faculty:** 12 full-time (2 women), 9 part-time/adjunct (5 women).
**Students:** 73 full-time (49 women); includes 12 minority (9 African Americans, 3 Asian Americans or Pacific Islanders), 7 international. 128 applicants, 41% accepted, 17 enrolled. In 2001, 12 doctorates awarded.
**Degree requirements:** For doctorate, thesis/dissertation, final exams, comprehensive exam.
**Entrance requirements:** For doctorate, GRE General Test, GRE Subject Test, minimum GPA of 2.75 (undergraduate), 3.0 (graduate). *Application deadline:* For fall admission, 2/1. *Application fee:* $35.
**Expenses:** Tuition, state resident: full-time $7,155; part-time $295 per semester hour. Tuition, nonresident: full-time $14,829; part-time $615 per semester hour. Tuition and fees vary according to degree level and campus/location.
**Financial support:** In 2001–02, 28 fellowships (averaging $9,134 per year), 12 teaching assistantships (averaging $11,337 per year) were awarded. Research assistantships, career-related internships or fieldwork, Federal Work-Study, and tuition waivers (full) also available. Financial award application deadline: 3/1.
Dr. Karen Schilling, Chair, 513-529-2400, *Fax:* 513-529-2420, *E-mail:* psych@ muohio.edu.
**Application contact:** Dr. Phillip Best, Director of Graduate Studies, 513-529-2400, *Fax:* 513-529-2420, *E-mail:* psych@ muohio.edu. *Web site:* http:// www.muohio.edu/~psycwis/graduate.html

■ **MILLERSVILLE UNIVERSITY OF PENNSYLVANIA**

**Graduate School, School of Education, Department of Psychology, Program in Psychology, Millersville, PA 17551-0302**

**AWARDS** Clinical psychology (MS); school psychology (MS). Part-time and evening/ weekend programs available.

**Faculty:** 20 full-time (14 women), 5 part-time/adjunct (3 women).
**Students:** 37 full-time (31 women), 58 part-time (49 women); includes 7 minority (3 African Americans, 2 Asian Americans or Pacific Islanders, 2 Hispanic Americans). Average age 28. 54 applicants, 65% accepted, 32 enrolled. In 2001, 30 degrees awarded.
**Degree requirements:** For master's, departmental exam, thesis optional.
**Entrance requirements:** For master's, GRE General Test, minimum undergraduate GPA of 2.75, 18 undergraduate hours in psychology, group interview, letters of recommendation, writing sample. *Application deadline:* For fall admission, 3/31; for spring admission, 11/1. Applications are processed on a rolling basis. *Application fee:* $30.
**Expenses:** Tuition, state resident: part-time $256 per credit. Tuition, nonresident: full-time $7,554; part-time $420 per credit. Required fees: $1,037; $44 per credit.
**Financial support:** In 2001–02, 44 research assistantships with full tuition reimbursements (averaging $4,250 per year) were awarded; career-related internships or fieldwork, Federal Work-Study, institutionally sponsored loans, and unspecified assistantships also available. Support available to part-time students. Financial award application deadline: 3/15; financial award applicants required to submit FAFSA.
Dr. Helena Tuleya-Payne, Chair, 717-872-3925, *Fax:* 717-871-2480, *E-mail:* helena.tuleya-payne@millersville.edu.
**Application contact:** Dr. Duncan M. Perry, Dean of Graduate Studies, Professional Training and Education, 717-872-3030, *E-mail:* duncan.perry@ millersville.edu.

■ **MINNESOTA STATE UNIVERSITY, MANKATO**

**College of Graduate Studies, College of Social and Behavioral Sciences, Department of Psychology, Mankato, MN 56001**

**AWARDS** Clinical psychology (MA); industrial psychology (MA); psychology (MT). Part-time programs available.

**Faculty:** 12 full-time (3 women).
**Students:** 31 full-time (28 women), 8 part-time (3 women). Average age 26. In 2001, 15 degrees awarded.
**Degree requirements:** For master's, one foreign language, thesis (for some programs), comprehensive exam.
**Entrance requirements:** For master's, GRE General Test, GRE Subject Test (clinical psychology), minimum GPA of 3.0 during previous 2 years. *Application deadline:* For fall admission, 3/1; for spring

admission, 11/27. Applications are processed on a rolling basis. *Application fee:* $20. Electronic applications accepted.
**Expenses:** Tuition, state resident: full-time $3,253; part-time $157 per credit. Tuition, nonresident: full-time $4,893; part-time $248 per credit. Required fees: $24 per credit. Tuition and fees vary according to reciprocity agreements.
**Financial support:** Research assistantships, teaching assistantships with full tuition reimbursements, career-related internships or fieldwork, Federal Work-Study, and institutionally sponsored loans available. Support available to part-time students. Financial award application deadline: 3/15; financial award applicants required to submit FAFSA.
**Faculty research:** Professional competency in hospitals, mood disturbance, 360-degree feedback, employee selection, planning fallacy.
Dr. Michael Fatis, Chairperson, 507-389-1818.
**Application contact:** Joni Roberts, Admissions Coordinator, 507-389-5244, *Fax:* 507-389-5974, *E-mail:* grad@ mankato.msus.edu.

■ **MONTCLAIR STATE UNIVERSITY**

**The School of Graduate, Professional and Continuing Education, College of Humanities and Social Sciences, Department of Psychology, Program in Educational Psychology, Upper Montclair, NJ 07043-1624**

**AWARDS** Child/adolescent clinical psychology (MA); clinical psychology for Spanish/English bilinguals (MA). Part-time and evening/ weekend programs available.

**Degree requirements:** For master's, thesis optional.
**Entrance requirements:** For master's, GRE General Test, GRE Subject Test, previous course work in psychology. Electronic applications accepted.

■ **MOREHEAD STATE UNIVERSITY**

**Graduate Programs, College of Science and Technology, Department of Psychology, Morehead, KY 40351**

**AWARDS** Clinical psychology (MA); counseling psychology (MA); experimental/general psychology (MA). Part-time programs available.

**Faculty:** 7 full-time (2 women).
**Students:** 30 full-time (19 women), 1 international. Average age 25. 5 applicants, 80% accepted. In 2001, 15 degrees awarded.
**Entrance requirements:** For master's, GRE General Test, TOEFL, 18

undergraduate hours in psychology, minimum GPA of 3.0. *Application deadline:* For fall admission, 8/1 (priority date); for spring admission, 12/1. Applications are processed on a rolling basis. *Application fee:* $0.

**Expenses:** Tuition, state resident: part-time $176 per hour. Tuition, nonresident: full-time $1,584; part-time $472 per hour. International tuition: $4,247 full-time.

**Financial support:** In 2001–02, 21 research assistantships (averaging $5,000 per year) were awarded; career-related internships or fieldwork, Federal Work-Study, and institutionally sponsored loans also available. Financial award application deadline: 4/1; financial award applicants required to submit FAFSA.

**Faculty research:** Mood induction effects, serotonin receptor activity, stress, perceptual processes.

Dr. Bruce A. Mattingly, Chair, 606-783-2891, *Fax:* 606-783-5077, *E-mail:* b.mattin@moreheadstate.edu.

**Application contact:** Betty R. Cowsert, Graduate Admissions/Records Manager, 606-783-2039, *Fax:* 606-783-5061, *E-mail:* b.cowsert@moreheadstate.edu. *Web site:* http://www.moreheadstate.edu

### ■ MURRAY STATE UNIVERSITY

**College of Humanities and Fine Arts, Department of Psychology, Murray, KY 42071-0009**

**AWARDS** Clinical psychology (MA, MS); psychology (MA, MS). Part-time programs available.

**Students:** 17 full-time (12 women), 7 part-time (4 women); includes 2 minority (1 Asian American or Pacific Islander, 1 Native American), 4 international. 10 applicants, 50% accepted. In 2001, 4 degrees awarded.

**Degree requirements:** For master's, one foreign language, thesis (for some programs).

**Entrance requirements:** For master's, GRE General Test, TOEFL. *Application deadline:* Applications are processed on a rolling basis. *Application fee:* $25.

**Expenses:** Tuition, state resident: full-time $1,440; part-time $169 per hour. Tuition, nonresident: full-time $4,004; part-time $450 per hour.

**Financial support:** Research assistantships, teaching assistantships, Federal Work-Study available. Financial award application deadline: 4/1.

Dr. Renae Duncan, Chairman, 270-762-3539, *Fax:* 270-762-2991, *E-mail:* renae.duncan@murraystate.edu.

### ■ NEW COLLEGE OF CALIFORNIA

**School of Psychology, San Francisco, CA 94102-5206**

**AWARDS** Feminist clinical psychology (MA); social-clinical psychology (MA). Evening/weekend programs available.

**Faculty:** 6 full-time (3 women), 10 part-time/adjunct (7 women).

**Students:** 43 full-time (32 women). Average age 28. 60 applicants, 77% accepted, 40 enrolled.

**Degree requirements:** For master's, 3 trimesters of fieldwork.

**Entrance requirements:** For master's, letters of recommendation. *Application deadline:* For fall admission, 4/1 (priority date). Applications are processed on a rolling basis. *Application fee:* $50 ($75 for international students).

**Expenses:** Contact institution.

**Financial support:** In 2001–02, 4 students received support, including 2 teaching assistantships (averaging $900 per year); career-related internships or fieldwork and Federal Work-Study also available. Financial award application deadline: 7/15; financial award applicants required to submit FAFSA.

**Faculty research:** AIDS and therapy, dynamics of unemployment, self-psychology, sexuality and gender issues, multicultural therapy.

Dr. Ali Chavoshian, Dean, 415-437-3435.

**Application contact:** Carmen Gonzalez, Admissions Director, 415-437-3421. *Web site:* http://www.newcollege.edu/psychology/

### ■ NEW SCHOOL UNIVERSITY

**Graduate Faculty of Political and Social Science, Department of Psychology, New York, NY 10011-8603**

**AWARDS** Clinical psychology (PhD); general psychology (MA, PhD). Part-time and evening/weekend programs available.

**Students:** 190 full-time (132 women), 48 part-time (38 women); includes 34 minority (11 African Americans, 9 Asian Americans or Pacific Islanders, 14 Hispanic Americans), 30 international. Average age 33. 208 applicants, 85% accepted. In 2001, 12 master's, 21 doctorates awarded. Terminal master's awarded for partial completion of doctoral program.

**Degree requirements:** For doctorate, one foreign language, thesis/dissertation, qualifying exam.

**Entrance requirements:** For master's, GRE General Test; for doctorate, GRE General Test, MA. *Application deadline:* For fall admission, 1/15 (priority date). Applications are processed on a rolling basis. *Application fee:* $40.

**Expenses:** Tuition: Full-time $18,720; part-time $1,040 per credit. Required fees: $450; $115 per term. Tuition and fees vary according to program.

**Financial support:** In 2001–02, 94 students received support, including 14 fellowships with full and partial tuition reimbursements available (averaging $1,600 per year), 15 research assistantships with full and partial tuition reimbursements available (averaging $5,000 per year), 17 teaching assistantships with full and partial tuition reimbursements available (averaging $2,200 per year); career-related internships or fieldwork, Federal Work-Study, scholarships/grants, and tuition waivers (full and partial) also available. Financial award application deadline: 1/15; financial award applicants required to submit FAFSA.

**Faculty research:** Consciousness, memory, language, perceptions, psychopathology.

Dr. Michael Schober, Chair, 212-229-5787.

**Application contact:** Emanuel Lomax, Director of Admissions, 800-523-5411, *Fax:* 212-989-7102, *E-mail:* gfadmit@newschool.edu. *Web site:* http://www.newschool.edu/

**Find an in-depth description at www.petersons.com/gradchannel.**

### ■ NEW YORK UNIVERSITY

**Graduate School of Arts and Science, Department of Psychology, New York, NY 10012-1019**

**AWARDS** Clinical psychology (PhD); cognition and perception (PhD); community psychology (PhD); general psychology (MA); industrial/organizational psychology (MA, PhD); psychoanalysis (Advanced Certificate); social/personality psychology (PhD). Part-time programs available.

**Faculty:** 38 full-time (13 women), 78 part-time/adjunct.

**Students:** 118 full-time (85 women), 304 part-time (235 women); includes 64 minority (14 African Americans, 27 Asian Americans or Pacific Islanders, 22 Hispanic Americans, 1 Native American), 49 international. Average age 28. 586 applicants, 44% accepted, 101 enrolled. In 2001, 67 master's, 22 doctorates awarded. Terminal master's awarded for partial completion of doctoral program.

**Degree requirements:** For master's, thesis or alternative, comprehensive exam; for doctorate, thesis/dissertation.

**Entrance requirements:** For master's, GRE General Test, minimum GPA of 3.0; for doctorate, GRE General Test, GRE Subject Test; for Advanced Certificate, doctoral degree, minimum GPA of 3.0. *Application deadline:* For fall admission, 1/4. *Application fee:* $60.

*New York University (continued)*
**Expenses:** Tuition: Full-time $19,536; part-time $814 per credit. Required fees: $1,330; $38 per credit. Tuition and fees vary according to course load and program.
**Financial support:** Fellowships with tuition reimbursements, research assistantships with tuition reimbursements, teaching assistantships with tuition reimbursements, career-related internships or fieldwork, Federal Work-Study, institutionally sponsored loans, and traineeships available. Financial award application deadline: 1/4; financial award applicants required to submit FAFSA.
**Faculty research:** Vision, memory, social cognition, social and cognitive development, relationships.
Marisa Carrasco, Chair, 212-998-7900.
**Application contact:** Susan Andersen, Director of Graduate Studies, 212-998-7900, *Fax:* 212-995-4018, *E-mail:* psychquery@psych.nyu.edu. *Web site:* http://www.psych.nyu.edu/

■ **NORFOLK STATE UNIVERSITY**
**School of Graduate Studies, School of Liberal Arts, Department of Psychology, Program in Community/Clinical Psychology, Norfolk, VA 23504**
AWARDS MA.
**Entrance requirements:** For master's, minimum GPA of 2.7.
**Expenses:** Tuition, area resident: Part-time $197 per credit. Tuition, nonresident: part-time $503 per credit.

■ **NORTH DAKOTA STATE UNIVERSITY**
**The Graduate School, College of Science and Mathematics, Department of Psychology, Fargo, ND 58105**
AWARDS Clinical psychology (MS, PhD); general psychology (MS); psychology (MS).
**Faculty:** 9 full-time (0 women), 1 (woman) part-time/adjunct.
**Students:** 14 full-time (12 women). Average age 24. 25 applicants, 32% accepted, 8 enrolled. In 2001, 7 master's awarded.
**Degree requirements:** For master's and doctorate, thesis/dissertation, registration. *Median time to degree:* Master's–2 years full-time; doctorate–5 years full-time.
**Entrance requirements:** For master's and doctorate, GRE General Test, GRE Subject Test, TOEFL. *Application deadline:* For fall admission, 3/1. Applications are processed on a rolling basis. *Application fee:* $35.
**Expenses:** Tuition, state resident: part-time $124 per credit. Tuition, nonresident: part-time $325 per credit. Required fees:

$22 per credit. Tuition and fees vary according to reciprocity agreements.
**Financial support:** In 2001–02, 7 research assistantships with full tuition reimbursements (averaging $4,200 per year), 7 teaching assistantships with full tuition reimbursements (averaging $4,272 per year) were awarded. Career-related internships or fieldwork, Federal Work-Study, institutionally sponsored loans, traineeships, and tuition waivers (full and partial) also available. Support available to part-time students. Financial award application deadline: 3/1.
**Faculty research:** Cognition science, neuropsychology, group behavior, applied behavior analysis, behavior therapy. *Total annual research expenditures:* $73,950.
Dr. James R. Council, Chair, 701-231-7065, *Fax:* 701-231-8426, *E-mail:* council@badlands.nodak.edu.
**Application contact:** Dr. Raymond G. Miltenberger, Chair, Graduate Recruiting, 701-231-8623, *Fax:* 701-231-8426, *E-mail:* miltenbe@badlands.nodak.edu. *Web site:* http://www.ndsu.nodak.edu/ndsu/psychology/

■ **NORTHWESTERN STATE UNIVERSITY OF LOUISIANA**
**Graduate Studies and Research and Associate Provost, Department of Psychology, Natchitoches, LA 71497**
AWARDS Clinical psychology (MS).
**Faculty:** 5 full-time (3 women), 4 part-time/adjunct (2 women).
**Students:** 24 full-time (20 women), 14 part-time (9 women); includes 2 minority (1 Asian American or Pacific Islander, 1 Hispanic American), 3 international. Average age 26. In 2001, 4 degrees awarded.
**Entrance requirements:** For master's, GRE General Test, GRE Subject Test, minimum undergraduate GPA of 2.5. *Application deadline:* For fall admission, 8/1 (priority date); for spring admission, 1/10. Applications are processed on a rolling basis. *Application fee:* $20 ($30 for international students).
**Expenses:** Tuition, state resident: full-time $2,280. Tuition, nonresident: full-time $8,154. Required fees: $134 per semester.
**Financial support:** Application deadline: 7/15.
Dr. Patrice Moulton, Head, 318-357-6594.
**Application contact:** Dr. Anthony J. Scheffler, Dean, Graduate Studies, Research and Information Systems, 318-357-5851, *Fax:* 318-357-5019, *E-mail:* grad_school@alpha.nsula.edu. *Web site:* http://www.nsula.edu/psychology/

■ **NORTHWESTERN UNIVERSITY**
**The Graduate School, Judd A. and Marjorie Weinberg College of Arts and Sciences, Department of Psychology, Evanston, IL 60208**
AWARDS Brain, behavior and cognition (PhD); clinical psychology (PhD); cognitive psychology (PhD); personality (PhD); social psychology (PhD). Admissions and degrees offered through The Graduate School. Part-time programs available.
**Faculty:** 22 full-time (6 women).
**Students:** 45 full-time (26 women); includes 4 minority (2 Asian Americans or Pacific Islanders, 2 Hispanic Americans), 14 international. Average age 25. 197 applicants, 14% accepted. In 2001, 5 doctorates awarded.
**Degree requirements:** For doctorate, thesis/dissertation. *Median time to degree:* Doctorate–5 years full-time.
**Entrance requirements:** For doctorate, GRE General Test, GRE Subject Test, TOEFL, TSE. *Application deadline:* For fall admission, 12/31. *Application fee:* $50 ($55 for international students). Electronic applications accepted.
**Expenses:** Tuition: Full-time $26,526.
**Financial support:** In 2001–02, 12 fellowships with full tuition reimbursements (averaging $16,800 per year), 3 research assistantships with partial tuition reimbursements (averaging $13,419 per year), 22 teaching assistantships with full tuition reimbursements (averaging $13,419 per year) were awarded. Career-related internships or fieldwork, Federal Work-Study, institutionally sponsored loans, and tuition waivers (full and partial) also available. Financial award application deadline: 12/31; financial award applicants required to submit FAFSA.
**Faculty research:** Memory and higher order cognition, anxiety and depression, effectiveness of psychotherapy, social cognition, molecular basis of memory. *Total annual research expenditures:* $2.6 million.
Douglas L. Medin, Chair, 847-491-7406, *Fax:* 847-491-7859, *E-mail:* medin@northwestern.edu.
**Application contact:** Florence S. Sales, Secretary, 847-491-7406, *Fax:* 847-491-7859, *E-mail:* f-sales@northwestern.edu. *Web site:* http://www.psych.northwestern.edu/

■ **NORTHWESTERN UNIVERSITY**
**The Graduate School and Medical School, Program in Clinical Psychology, Evanston, IL 60208**
AWARDS Clinical psychology (PhD), including clinical neuropsychology, general clinical. PhD admissions and degree offered through The Graduate School.

**Faculty:** 16 full-time (9 women), 61 part-time/adjunct (35 women).
**Students:** 31 full-time (25 women); includes 4 minority (2 African Americans, 1 Asian American or Pacific Islander, 1 Native American). Average age 29. 140 applicants, 4% accepted. In 2001, 5 degrees awarded.
**Degree requirements:** For doctorate, thesis/dissertation, clinical internship. *Median time to degree:* Doctorate–6 years full-time.
**Entrance requirements:** For doctorate, GRE General Test, GRE Subject Test; TOEFL, minimum GPA of 3.2, previous course work in psychology. *Application deadline:* For fall admission, 1/12. *Application fee:* $50 ($55 for international students).
**Expenses:** Tuition: Full-time $26,526.
**Financial support:** In 2001–02, 1 fellowship with full and partial tuition reimbursement (averaging $11,673 per year), 6 research assistantships with partial tuition reimbursements (averaging $16,285 per year) were awarded. Career-related internships or fieldwork, institutionally sponsored loans, scholarships/grants, and tuition waivers (full) also available. Financial award application deadline: 1/12; financial award applicants required to submit FAFSA.
**Faculty research:** Cancer and cardiovascular risk reduction, evaluation of mental health services and policy, neuropsychological assessment, outcome of psychotherapy, cognitive therapy, pediatric and clinical child psychology.
Dr. Mark J. Reinecke, Chief, 312-908-1465, *Fax:* 312-908-5070, *E-mail:* m-reinecke@northwestern.edu.
**Application contact:** Padraic Connolly, Admissions Assistant, 312-908-8262, *Fax:* 312-908-5070, *E-mail:* j-johnson@northwestern.edu. *Web site:* http://www.clinpsych.northwestern.edu/

### ■ NOVA SOUTHEASTERN UNIVERSITY

**Center for Psychological Studies, Program in Clinical Psychology, Fort Lauderdale, FL 33314-7721**
**AWARDS** PhD, Psy D, SPS.
**Faculty:** 33 full-time (10 women), 27 part-time/adjunct (13 women).
**Students:** 432 full-time (331 women). In 2001, 223 degrees awarded.
**Degree requirements:** For doctorate, thesis/dissertation, clinical internship, competency exam; for SPS, internship.
**Entrance requirements:** For doctorate, GRE General Test, GRE Subject Test (recommended), 18 credits in psychology including one hour of experimental psychology and three hours of statistics;

minimum undergraduate GPA of 3.0; for SPS, GRE General Test. *Application deadline:* For fall admission, 1/15. Applications are processed on a rolling basis. *Application fee:* $50.
**Expenses:** Contact institution.
**Financial support:** In 2001–02, 4 research assistantships, 17 teaching assistantships (averaging $1,000 per year) were awarded. Career-related internships or fieldwork and Federal Work-Study also available. Support available to part-time students. Financial award application deadline: 4/1.
**Faculty research:** Eating disorders, neuropsychology, family violence, sports psychology, child-pediatric psychology.
**Application contact:** Nancy L. Smith, Supervisor, 954-262-5760, *Fax:* 954-262-3893, *E-mail:* cpsinfo@cps.nova.edu. *Web site:* http://www.cps.nova.edu/

### ■ THE OHIO STATE UNIVERSITY

**Graduate School, College of Social and Behavioral Sciences, Department of Psychology, Columbus, OH 43210**
**AWARDS** Clinical psychology (PhD); cognitive/experimental psychology (PhD); counseling psychology (PhD); developmental psychology (PhD); mental retardation and developmental disabilities (PhD); psychobiology (PhD); quantitative psychology (PhD); social psychology (PhD).
**Degree requirements:** For doctorate, thesis/dissertation.
**Entrance requirements:** For doctorate, GRE General Test, TOEFL.

### ■ OHIO UNIVERSITY

**Graduate Studies, College of Arts and Sciences, Department of Psychology, Program in Clinical Psychology, Athens, OH 45701-2979**
**AWARDS** PhD.
**Faculty:** 15 full-time (3 women), 3 part-time/adjunct (1 woman).
**Students:** 49 full-time (31 women), 4 part-time (3 women); includes 6 minority (4 Asian Americans or Pacific Islanders, 1 Hispanic American, 1 Native American), 7 international. Average age 28. 132 applicants, 9% accepted.
**Degree requirements:** For doctorate, one foreign language, thesis/dissertation, comprehensive exam.
**Entrance requirements:** For doctorate, GRE General Test, GRE Subject Test, minimum graduate GPA of 3.4. *Application deadline:* For fall admission, 1/15. *Application fee:* $30. Electronic applications accepted.
**Expenses:** Tuition, state resident: full-time $6,585. Tuition, nonresident: full-time $12,254.

**Financial support:** In 2001–02, 41 students received support, including fellowships with full tuition reimbursements available (averaging $11,333 per year), 8 research assistantships (averaging $9,124 per year), 11 teaching assistantships (averaging $8,203 per year); career-related internships or fieldwork, Federal Work-Study, institutionally sponsored loans, traineeships, tuition waivers (full), and unspecified assistantships also available. Financial award application deadline: 1/15.
**Faculty research:** Health psychology, child clinical psychology, psychotherapy outcome.
Ben M. Ogles, Director of Clinical Training, 740-593-1077, *Fax:* 740-593-0579.
**Application contact:** Admissions Secretary, 740-593-0902, *Fax:* 740-593-0579, *E-mail:* pgraduate1@ohiou.edu. *Web site:* http://www.cats.ohiou.edu/~psydept/

### ■ OKLAHOMA STATE UNIVERSITY

**Graduate College, College of Arts and Sciences, Department of Psychology, Stillwater, OK 74078**
**AWARDS** Clinical psychology (PhD); experimental psychology (PhD); general psychology (MS).
**Faculty:** 16 full-time (5 women), 1 (woman) part-time/adjunct.
**Students:** 32 full-time (24 women), 17 part-time (11 women); includes 13 minority (1 African American, 2 Asian Americans or Pacific Islanders, 4 Hispanic Americans, 6 Native Americans), 1 international. Average age 27. 67 applicants, 24% accepted. In 2001, 5 master's, 10 doctorates awarded.
**Degree requirements:** For doctorate, thesis/dissertation.
**Entrance requirements:** For master's, TOEFL; for doctorate, GRE General Test, TOEFL. *Application deadline:* For fall admission, 2/1 (priority date). *Application fee:* $25.
**Expenses:** Tuition, state resident: part-time $92 per credit hour. Tuition, nonresident: part-time $297 per credit hour. Required fees: $21 per credit hour. $14 per semester. One-time fee: $20. Tuition and fees vary according to course load.
**Financial support:** In 2001–02, 30 students received support, including 12 research assistantships (averaging $12,269 per year), 22 teaching assistantships (averaging $11,551 per year); career-related internships or fieldwork, Federal Work-Study, and tuition waivers (partial) also available. Support available to part-time students. Financial award application deadline: 3/1.

*Oklahoma State University (continued)*
Dr. Maureen A. Sullivan, Head, 405-744-6028.

## ■ OLD DOMINION UNIVERSITY

**College of Sciences, Program in Clinical Psychology, Norfolk, VA 23529**

**AWARDS** Psy D.

**Students:** 27 full-time (20 women), 19 part-time (17 women); includes 10 minority (8 African Americans, 2 Asian Americans or Pacific Islanders), 1 international. Average age 28. 97 applicants, 8% accepted. In 2001, 4 degrees awarded.
**Degree requirements:** For doctorate, thesis/dissertation, internship, written and oral exam.
**Entrance requirements:** For doctorate, GRE General Test, GRE Subject Test. *Application deadline:* For fall admission, 1/5. *Application fee:* $30.
**Expenses:** Contact institution.
**Financial support:** In 2001–02, 28 students received support, including 25 research assistantships with partial tuition reimbursements available (averaging $4,500 per year), 3 teaching assistantships with partial tuition reimbursements available (averaging $5,000 per year); career-related internships or fieldwork, scholarships/grants, and tuition waivers (partial) also available. Financial award application deadline: 2/15; financial award applicants required to submit FAFSA.
**Faculty research:** Body image, depression, coping with stress, minority and women's issues, family therapy, neuropsychology.
Dr. Robin J. Lewis, Graduate Program Director, 757-683-4210, *Fax:* 757-683-5087, *E-mail:* psydgpd@odu.edu.
**Application contact:** Eileen X. O'Neill, Program Coordinator, 757-518-2550, *Fax:* 757-518-2553, *E-mail:* exoneill@odu.edu. *Web site:* http://www.vcpcp.odu.edu/vcpcp/

## ■ PACE UNIVERSITY

**Dyson College of Arts and Sciences, Department of Psychology, New York, NY 10038**

**AWARDS** Psychology (MA); school-clinical child psychology (Psy D); school-community psychology (MS Ed, Psy D). Part-time and evening/weekend programs available.

**Faculty:** 22 full-time, 51 part-time/adjunct.
**Students:** 80 full-time (69 women), 23 part-time (18 women); includes 17 minority (5 African Americans, 6 Asian Americans or Pacific Islanders, 5 Hispanic Americans, 1 Native American), 2 international. Average age 25. 201 applicants, 43% accepted, 29 enrolled. In

2001, 39 master's, 22 doctorates awarded. Terminal master's awarded for partial completion of doctoral program.
**Degree requirements:** For master's, qualifying exams, internship; for doctorate, qualifying exams, externship, internship, project.
**Entrance requirements:** For master's, interview; for doctorate, GRE General Test, GRE Subject Test, interview. *Application deadline:* Applications are processed on a rolling basis. *Application fee:* $65. Electronic applications accepted.
**Expenses:** Tuition: Part-time $545 per credit.
**Financial support:** Research assistantships, teaching assistantships, career-related internships or fieldwork, Federal Work-Study, tuition waivers (partial), and unspecified assistantships available. Support available to part-time students. Financial award applicants required to submit FAFSA.
Dr. Florence Denmark, Chairperson, 212-346-1506.
**Application contact:** Richard Alvarez, Director of Admissions, 212-346-1531, *Fax:* 212-346-1585, *E-mail:* gradnyc@pace.edu. *Web site:* http://www.pace.edu/

**Find an in-depth description at www.petersons.com/gradchannel.**

## ■ PACIFICA GRADUATE INSTITUTE

**Graduate Programs, Carpinteria, CA 93013**

**AWARDS** Clinical psychology (PhD); counseling psychology (MA); depth psychology (PhD); mythological studies (MA, PhD).

**Faculty:** 19 full-time, 50 part-time/adjunct.
**Students:** 545 full-time, 20 part-time. Average age 45. In 2001, 101 master's, 82 doctorates awarded.
**Degree requirements:** For master's, thesis (for some programs), registration; for doctorate, thesis/dissertation, internship, comprehensive exam, registration. *Median time to degree:* Master's–3 years full-time; doctorate–3 years full-time. *Application deadline:* For fall admission, 4/30 (priority date). *Application fee:* $60.
**Expenses:** Tuition: Full-time $13,900.
**Financial support:** In 2001–02, 411 students received support. Scholarships/grants available. Financial award application deadline: 6/15; financial award applicants required to submit FAFSA.
**Faculty research:** Imaginal and archetypal theory; post-Colonial psychoanalytic and Jungian theory; myth literature as it applies to the theory and practice of psychology.

Dr. Stephen Aizenstat, President, 805-969-3626 Ext. 102, *Fax:* 805-565-1932, *E-mail:* steve_aizenstat@pacifica.edu.
**Application contact:** Diane Huerta, Admissions Office, 805-969-3626 Ext. 128, *Fax:* 805-565-1932, *E-mail:* diane_huerta@pacifica.edu. *Web site:* http://www.pacifica.edu/

**Find an in-depth description at www.petersons.com/gradchannel.**

## ■ PACIFIC GRADUATE SCHOOL OF PSYCHOLOGY

**Program in Clinical Psychology, Palo Alto, CA 94303-4232**

**AWARDS** PhD, Psy D, JD/PhD, MBA/PhD. Beginning Fall 2002, we have introduced the PGSP-Stanford Psy D Consortium.

**Degree requirements:** For doctorate, thesis/dissertation, 2000 hour clinical internship, oral clinical competency exam.
**Entrance requirements:** For doctorate, GRE General Test, BA or MA in psychology or related area, minimum undergraduate GPA of 3.0, 3.3 graduate.
**Faculty research:** Child/family studies, health psychology, neuropsychology, personality development, assessment. *Web site:* http://www.pgsp.edu/

## ■ THE PENNSYLVANIA STATE UNIVERSITY HARRISBURG CAMPUS OF THE CAPITAL COLLEGE

**Graduate Center, School of Behavioral Sciences and Education, Program in Applied Clinical Psychology, Middletown, PA 17057-4898**

**AWARDS** MA.

**Expenses:** Tuition, state resident: full-time $7,882; part-time $333 per credit. Tuition, nonresident: full-time $14,384; part-time $600 per credit.

## ■ THE PENNSYLVANIA STATE UNIVERSITY UNIVERSITY PARK CAMPUS

**Graduate School, College of Liberal Arts, Department of Psychology, State College, University Park, PA 16802-1503**

**AWARDS** Clinical psychology (MS, PhD); cognitive psychology (MS, PhD); developmental psychology (MS, PhD); industrial/organizational psychology (MS, PhD); psychobiology (MS, PhD); social psychology (MS, PhD).

**Students:** 126 full-time (83 women), 12 part-time (7 women). In 2001, 15 master's, 14 doctorates awarded.

**Degree requirements:** For master's and doctorate, thesis/dissertation.

**Entrance requirements:** For master's and doctorate, GRE General Test, GRE Subject Test. *Application fee:* $45.

**Expenses:** Tuition, state resident: full-time $7,882; part-time $333 per credit. Tuition, nonresident: full-time $16,142; part-time $673 per credit. Required fees: $124 per semester.

**Financial support:** Fellowships, research assistantships, teaching assistantships available.

Dr. Keith Crnic, Head, 814-863-1721.

## ■ PEPPERDINE UNIVERSITY

**Graduate School of Education and Psychology, Division of Psychology, Program in Clinical Psychology, Culver City, CA 90230-7615**

**AWARDS** MA. Part-time and evening/weekend programs available.

**Students:** 143 full-time (126 women), 242 part-time (201 women); includes 96 minority (29 African Americans, 23 Asian Americans or Pacific Islanders, 40 Hispanic Americans, 4 Native Americans), 10 international. Average age 32. 283 applicants, 58% accepted. In 2001, 126 degrees awarded.

**Entrance requirements:** For master's, GRE General Test, TOEFL, bachelor's degree in psychology or related field. *Application deadline:* For fall admission, 2/1. Applications are processed on a rolling basis. *Application fee:* $55.

**Expenses:** Tuition: Full-time $15,700; part-time $785 per unit. Tuition and fees vary according to degree level and program.

**Financial support:** Research assistantships, teaching assistantships available. Financial award application deadline: 7/1; financial award applicants required to submit FAFSA.

**Application contact:** Program Administrator, 310-568-5605. *Web site:* http://www.pepperdine.edu/

**Find an in-depth description at www.petersons.com/gradchannel.**

## ■ PHILADELPHIA COLLEGE OF OSTEOPATHIC MEDICINE

**Graduate and Professional Programs, Department of Psychology, Philadelphia, PA 19131-1694**

**AWARDS** Clinical health psychology (MS); clinical psychology (Psy D); organizational leadership and development (MS).

**Faculty:** 6 full-time (3 women), 1 part-time/adjunct (0 women).

**Students:** 253 full-time (186 women); includes 35 minority (23 African Americans, 7 Asian Americans or Pacific

Islanders, 5 Hispanic Americans). Average age 33. 77 applicants, 86% accepted. In 2001, 1 degree awarded.

**Degree requirements:** For master's, thesis; for doctorate, thesis/dissertation, final project, fieldwork, comprehensive exam.

**Entrance requirements:** For master's, GRE, minimum GPA of 3.0, previous course work in biology, chemistry, English, physics; for doctorate, MAT. *Application deadline:* For fall admission, 1/17. Applications are processed on a rolling basis. *Application fee:* $50.

**Expenses:** Tuition: Part-time $441 per credit. Required fees: $250. Tuition and fees vary according to program.

**Faculty research:** Cognitive-behavioral therapy, coping skills.

Dr. Arthur Freeman, Chairman, 215-871-6442.

**Application contact:** Carol A. Fox, Associate Dean for Admissions, 215-871-6700, *Fax:* 215-871-6719, *E-mail:* carolf@pcom.edu.

**Find an in-depth description at www.petersons.com/gradchannel.**

## ■ PONCE SCHOOL OF MEDICINE

**Program in Clinical Psychology, Ponce, PR 00732-7004**

**AWARDS** Clinical health psychology (Psy D); consultant psychology (Psy D); pediatric psychology (Psy D); psychotherapeutic interventions (Psy D).

**Faculty:** 5 full-time (2 women).

**Students:** 114 full-time (89 women); all minorities (all Hispanic Americans). Average age 30. 63 applicants, 65% accepted, 34 enrolled.

**Degree requirements:** For doctorate, one foreign language, thesis/dissertation, comprehensive exam, registration.

**Entrance requirements:** For doctorate, GRE General Test or PAEG. *Application deadline:* For fall admission, 3/30. Applications are processed on a rolling basis. *Application fee:* $100.

**Expenses:** Tuition: Full-time $17,835. Required fees: $2,340. Full-time tuition and fees vary according to class time, course load, degree level, program and student level.

Dr. José Pons, Head, 787-840-2575, *E-mail:* jponspr@yahoo.com.

**Application contact:** Dr. Carmen Mercado, Assistant Dean of Admissions, 787-840-2575 Ext. 251, *E-mail:* cmercado@psm.edu.

## ■ PONTIFICAL CATHOLIC UNIVERSITY OF PUERTO RICO

**Institute of Graduate Studies in Behavioral Science and Community Affairs, Ponce, PR 00717-0777**

**AWARDS** Clinical psychology (MS); clinical social work (MSW); criminology (MA); industrial psychology (MS); psychology (PhD); public administration (MA). Part-time and evening/weekend programs available.

**Faculty:** 10 full-time (7 women), 17 part-time/adjunct (12 women).

**Students:** 86 full-time (56 women), 394 part-time (266 women); all minorities (all Hispanic Americans). 141 applicants, 83% accepted, 104 enrolled. In 2001, 35 degrees awarded.

**Entrance requirements:** For master's, GRE, 2 recommendation letters, interview, minimum GPA of 2.75. *Application deadline:* For fall admission, 4/30 (priority date). Applications are processed on a rolling basis. *Application fee:* $50. Electronic applications accepted.

**Expenses:** Tuition: Full-time $2,880; part-time $160 per credit. Required fees: $360. Tuition and fees vary according to degree level and program.

**Financial support:** Federal Work-Study and tuition waivers (partial) available. Support available to part-time students. Financial award application deadline: 7/15.

Dr. Nilde Cordoline, Director, 787-841-2000 Ext. 1024.

**Application contact:** Ana O. Bonilla, Director of Admissions, 787-841-2000 Ext. 1000, *Fax:* 787-840-4295. *Web site:* http://www.pucpr.edu/

## ■ QUEENS COLLEGE OF THE CITY UNIVERSITY OF NEW YORK

**Division of Graduate Studies, Mathematics and Natural Sciences Division, Department of Psychology, Flushing, NY 11367-1597**

**AWARDS** Clinical behavioral applications in mental health settings (MA); psychology (MA). Part-time programs available.

**Faculty:** 22 full-time (8 women).

**Students:** 7 full-time (6 women), 33 part-time (25 women). 76 applicants, 89% accepted. In 2001, 37 degrees awarded.

**Degree requirements:** For master's, thesis or alternative, comprehensive exam.

**Entrance requirements:** For master's, GRE, TOEFL, minimum GPA of 3.0. *Application deadline:* For fall admission, 4/1; for spring admission, 11/1. Applications are processed on a rolling basis. *Application fee:* $40.

**Expenses:** Tuition, state resident: full-time $2,175; part-time $185 per credit. Tuition, nonresident: full-time $3,800; part-time $320 per credit. Required fees: $114; $57

*Queens College of the City University of New York (continued)*
per semester. Tuition and fees vary according to course load.

**Financial support:** Career-related internships or fieldwork, Federal Work-Study, institutionally sponsored loans, and tuition waivers (partial) available. Support available to part-time students. Financial award application deadline: 4/1; financial award applicants required to submit FAFSA. Dr. Richard Bodnar, Chairperson, 718-997-3200.

**Application contact:** Dr. Philip Ramsey, Graduate Adviser, 718-997-3200, *E-mail:* phillip_ramsey@qc.edu.

## ■ RADFORD UNIVERSITY

**Graduate College, College of Arts and Sciences, Department of Psychology, Radford, VA 24142**

**AWARDS** Clinical psychology (MA); counseling psychology (MA); general psychology (MA, MS); industrial-organizational psychology (MA); school psychology (Ed S). Part-time programs available. Postbaccalaureate distance learning degree programs offered (minimal on-campus study).

**Faculty:** 20 full-time (6 women).
**Students:** 65 full-time (46 women), 9 part-time (8 women); includes 6 minority (2 African Americans, 3 Asian Americans or Pacific Islanders, 1 Native American), 1 international. Average age 26. 127 applicants, 83% accepted, 26 enrolled. In 2001, 40 master's, 10 other advanced degrees awarded.
**Degree requirements:** For master's, thesis (for some programs), comprehensive exam.
**Entrance requirements:** For degree, GMAT, GRE General Test, MAT, NTE, TOEFL. *Application deadline:* For fall admission, 2/15 (priority date); for spring admission, 10/15. Applications are processed on a rolling basis. *Application fee:* $25. Electronic applications accepted.
**Expenses:** Tuition, state resident: full-time $2,564; part-time $167 per credit hour. Tuition, nonresident: full-time $6,314; part-time $323 per credit hour. Required fees: $1,440.
**Financial support:** In 2001–02, 64 students received support, including 4 fellowships with tuition reimbursements available (averaging $8,060 per year), 46 research assistantships (averaging $4,401 per year), 7 teaching assistantships with tuition reimbursements available (averaging $8,680 per year); career-related internships or fieldwork, Federal Work-Study, institutionally sponsored loans, and scholarships/grants also available. Financial

award application deadline: 2/1; financial award applicants required to submit FAFSA.
Dr. Alastair V. Harris, Chair, 540-831-5361, *Fax:* 540-831-6113, *E-mail:* aharris@radford.edu. *Web site:* http://www.radford.edu/

## ■ ROOSEVELT UNIVERSITY

**Graduate Division, College of Arts and Sciences, School of Psychology, Chicago, IL 60605-1394**

**AWARDS** Clinical professional psychology (MA); clinical psychology (MA, Psy D); general psychology (MA); industrial/organizational psychology (MA). Part-time and evening/weekend programs available.
**Faculty:** 12 full-time (3 women), 22 part-time/adjunct (13 women).
**Students:** 97 full-time (64 women), 213 part-time (153 women); includes 39 minority (22 African Americans, 10 Asian Americans or Pacific Islanders, 6 Hispanic Americans, 1 Native American), 10 international.
**Degree requirements:** For master's, thesis or alternative; for doctorate, thesis/dissertation.
**Entrance requirements:** For master's, 18 undergraduate hours in psychology; for doctorate, GRE, master's degree in psychology. *Application deadline:* For fall admission, 6/1 (priority date). Applications are processed on a rolling basis. *Application fee:* $25 ($35 for international students).
**Expenses:** Tuition: Full-time $9,090; part-time $505 per credit hour. Required fees: $100 per term.
**Financial support:** Application deadline: 2/15.
**Faculty research:** Multicultural issues, psychotherapy research, stress, neuropsychology, psychodiagnostic assessment.
Edward Rossini, Head, 312-341-3760.
**Application contact:** Joanne Canyon-Heller, Coordinator of Graduate Admissions, 312-281-3250, *Fax:* 312-341-3523, *E-mail:* applyru@roosevelt.edu.

## ■ RUTGERS, THE STATE UNIVERSITY OF NEW JERSEY, NEW BRUNSWICK

**Graduate School of Applied and Professional Psychology, Department of Clinical Psychology, New Brunswick, NJ 08901-1281**
**AWARDS** Psy M, Psy D.
**Degree requirements:** For doctorate, thesis/dissertation, 1 year internship.
**Entrance requirements:** For doctorate, GRE General Test, GRE Subject Test,

bachelor's degree in psychology or equivalent. Electronic applications accepted.
**Faculty research:** Long- and short-term dynamic therapy, community psychology, cognitive-behavioral therapy: anxiety and depressive disorders, addictive behaviors: eating disorders and alcoholism. *Web site:* http://www.rci.rutgers.edu/~gsapp

## ■ RUTGERS, THE STATE UNIVERSITY OF NEW JERSEY, NEW BRUNSWICK

**Graduate School, Program in Psychology, New Brunswick, NJ 08901-1281**

**AWARDS** Biopsychology and behavioral neuroscience (PhD); clinical psychology (PhD); cognitive psychology (PhD); interdisciplinary developmental psychology (PhD); interdisciplinary health psychology (PhD); social psychology (PhD).
**Students:** Average age 24. 423 applicants, 11% accepted. In 2001, 13 degrees awarded.
**Degree requirements:** For doctorate, thesis/dissertation.
**Entrance requirements:** For doctorate, GRE General Test. *Application deadline:* For fall admission, 12/15. *Application fee:* $50.
**Financial support:** In 2001–02, 68 students received support, including 18 fellowships with full tuition reimbursements available (averaging $15,000 per year), 13 research assistantships with full tuition reimbursements available (averaging $14,000 per year), 43 teaching assistantships with full tuition reimbursements available (averaging $13,800 per year); career-related internships or fieldwork, Federal Work-Study, scholarships/grants, and traineeships also available. Financial award application deadline: 12/15.
Dr. G. Terence Wilson, Director, 732-445-2556, *Fax:* 732-445-2263.
**Application contact:** Joan Olmizzi, Administrative Assistant, 732-445-2555, *Fax:* 732-445-2263, *E-mail:* joan@psych-b.rutgers.edu. *Web site:* http://psychology.rutgers.edu/

## ■ ST. JOHN'S UNIVERSITY

**St. John's College of Liberal Arts and Sciences, Department of Psychology, Program in Clinical Psychology, Jamaica, NY 11439**

**AWARDS** Clinical psychology-child (MA, PhD); clinical psychology-general (MA, PhD).
**Students:** 73 full-time (59 women), 28 part-time (20 women); includes 21 minority (9 African Americans, 7 Asian Americans or Pacific Islanders, 5 Hispanic

Americans), 4 international. Average age 29. 210 applicants, 14% accepted, 12 enrolled. In 2001, 13 degrees awarded.
**Degree requirements:** For doctorate, one foreign language, thesis/dissertation, internship, externship, comprehensive exam.
**Entrance requirements:** For doctorate, GRE General Test, GRE Subject Test, 24 undergraduate credits in psychology, 2 writing samples. *Application deadline:* For fall admission, 2/1. Applications are processed on a rolling basis. *Application fee:* $40.
**Expenses:** Contact institution.
**Financial support:** Fellowships with full tuition reimbursements, research assistantships, career-related internships or fieldwork and scholarships/grants available. Support available to part-time students. Financial award application deadline: 3/1; financial award applicants required to submit FAFSA.
**Faculty research:** Health psychology, psychopathology, therapy process, multicultural issues, cross-cultural psychology.
Dr. Jeffery S. Nevid, Director, 718-990-1545, *E-mail:* nevidj@stjohns.edu.
**Application contact:** Matthew Whelan, Director, Office of Admission, 718-990-2000, *Fax:* 718-990-2096, *E-mail:* admissions@stjohns.edu. *Web site:* http://www.stjohns.edu/

### ■ SAINT LOUIS UNIVERSITY

**Graduate School, College of Arts and Sciences, Department of Psychology, St. Louis, MO 63103-2097**

**AWARDS** Applied experimental psychology (MS(R), PhD); clinical psychology (MS(R), PhD).

**Faculty:** 28 full-time (8 women), 16 part-time/adjunct (4 women).
**Students:** 34 full-time (17 women), 65 part-time (38 women); includes 20 minority (15 African Americans, 3 Asian Americans or Pacific Islanders, 2 Hispanic Americans), 1 international. Average age 28. 160 applicants, 27% accepted, 23 enrolled. In 2001, 7 master's, 12 doctorates awarded.
**Degree requirements:** For master's, thesis, comprehensive exam; for doctorate, thesis/dissertation, internship, preliminary exams.
**Entrance requirements:** For master's and doctorate, GRE General Test, interview. *Application deadline:* For fall admission, 1/1; for spring admission, 11/1. *Application fee:* $40.
**Expenses:** Tuition: Part-time $630 per credit hour.

**Financial support:** In 2001–02, 57 students received support, including 6 fellowships with tuition reimbursements available, 4 research assistantships with tuition reimbursements available, 2 teaching assistantships with tuition reimbursements available; career-related internships or fieldwork, tuition waivers (partial), and unspecified assistantships also available. Financial award application deadline: 4/1; financial award applicants required to submit FAFSA.
**Faculty research:** Implicit and explicit memory in older adults, cognitive processes in post-traumatic stress disorder, prejudice and attitude change, locus of control and health psychology, psychometric evaluation of cognitive impairment.
Dr. Ronald T. Kellogg, Chairperson, 314-977-2300, *Fax:* 314-977-3679, *E-mail:* kelloggr@slu.edu.
**Application contact:** Dr. Marcia Buresch, Associate Dean of the Graduate School, 314-977-2240, *Fax:* 314-977-3943, *E-mail:* bureschm@slu.edu.

### ■ ST. MARY'S UNIVERSITY OF SAN ANTONIO

**Graduate School, Department of Psychology, San Antonio, TX 78228-8507**

**AWARDS** Clinical psychology (MA, MS); industrial psychology (MA, MS); school psychology (MA). Part-time programs available.

**Faculty:** 5 full-time (4 women), 5 part-time/adjunct.
**Students:** 27 full-time (22 women), 35 part-time (29 women); includes 31 minority (6 African Americans, 1 Asian American or Pacific Islander, 24 Hispanic Americans), 1 international. Average age 24. In 2001, 17 degrees awarded.
**Degree requirements:** For master's, thesis (for some programs), comprehensive exam.
**Entrance requirements:** For master's, GRE General Test. *Application deadline:* Applications are processed on a rolling basis. *Application fee:* $15. Electronic applications accepted.
**Expenses:** Tuition: Full-time $8,190; part-time $455 per credit hour. Required fees: $375.
**Financial support:** Research assistantships, Federal Work-Study and institutionally sponsored loans available. Financial award application deadline: 2/15; financial award applicants required to submit FAFSA.
Dr. Willibrord Silva, Graduate Program Director, 210-436-3314.

### ■ SAINT MICHAEL'S COLLEGE

**Graduate Programs, Program in Clinical Psychology, Colchester, VT 05439**

**AWARDS** MA. Part-time and evening/weekend programs available.

**Degree requirements:** For master's, thesis or alternative, internship, practicum, research seminar.
**Entrance requirements:** For master's, GRE General Test, GRE Subject Test, undergraduate major in psychology or related area, minimum 12 credits in psychology.
**Expenses:** Tuition: Full-time $8,280; part-time $345 per credit.
**Faculty research:** Psychodynamic psychotherapy, family therapy, philosophical foundations of clinical psychology. *Web site:* http://www.smcvt.edu/gradprograms/

### ■ SAM HOUSTON STATE UNIVERSITY

**College of Education and Applied Science, Department of Psychology and Philosophy, Program in Clinical Psychology, Huntsville, TX 77341**

**AWARDS** MA.

**Students:** 8 full-time (6 women), 5 part-time (all women); includes 1 minority (African American). Average age 31. In 2001, 15 degrees awarded.
*Application deadline:* For fall admission, 8/1; for spring admission, 12/1. *Application fee:* $20.
**Expenses:** Tuition, area resident: Part-time $69 per credit. Tuition, state resident: full-time $1,380; part-time $69 per credit. Tuition, nonresident: full-time $5,600; part-time $280 per credit. Required fees: $748. Tuition and fees vary according to course load.
**Financial support:** Application deadline: 5/31.
**Application contact:** Dr. Rowland Miller, Graduate Coordinator, 936-294-1176, *Fax:* 936-294-3798, *E-mail:* psy_rsm@shsu.edu. *Web site:* http://www.shsu.edu/~psy_www/clinical/

### ■ SAN DIEGO STATE UNIVERSITY

**Graduate and Research Affairs, College of Sciences, Department of Psychology, San Diego, CA 92182**

**AWARDS** Clinical psychology (MS, PhD); industrial and organizational psychology (MS); program evaluation (MS); psychology (MA). Terminal master's awarded for partial completion of doctoral program.

**Degree requirements:** For master's, thesis, oral exam; for doctorate, thesis/dissertation.

*San Diego State University (continued)*

**Entrance requirements:** For master's, GRE General Test, TOEFL; for doctorate, GRE General Test, GRE Subject Test, minimum GPA of 3.5. *Web site:* http://www.phsychology.sdsu.edu/

### ■ SAN JOSE STATE UNIVERSITY

**Graduate Studies, College of Social Sciences, Department of Psychology, San Jose, CA 95192-0001**

**AWARDS** Clinical psychology (MS); counseling (MS); industrial psychology (MS); research psychology (MA).

**Faculty:** 32 full-time (5 women), 13 part-time/adjunct (7 women).

**Students:** 40 full-time (32 women), 20 part-time (12 women); includes 17 minority (2 African Americans, 11 Asian Americans or Pacific Islanders, 4 Hispanic Americans), 6 international. Average age 30. 150 applicants, 32% accepted. In 2001, 25 degrees awarded.

**Degree requirements:** For master's, thesis (for some programs), comprehensive exam.

**Entrance requirements:** For master's, minimum GPA of 3.0. *Application deadline:* For fall admission, 6/29; for spring admission, 11/30. Applications are processed on a rolling basis. *Application fee:* $59. Electronic applications accepted.

**Expenses:** Tuition, nonresident: part-time $246 per unit. Required fees: $678 per semester. Tuition and fees vary according to course load.

**Financial support:** In 2001–02, 15 teaching assistantships were awarded; career-related internships or fieldwork and institutionally sponsored loans also available. Financial award application deadline: 3/1; financial award applicants required to submit FAFSA.

**Faculty research:** Drug and alcohol abuse, neurohormonal mechanisms in motion sickness, behavior modification, sleep research, genetics.

Dr. Robert Pelligrini, Chair, 408-924-5600, *Fax:* 408-924-5605.

**Application contact:** Laree Huntsman, Graduate Adviser, 408-924-5633.

### ■ SEATTLE PACIFIC UNIVERSITY

**Graduate School, School of Psychology, Family and Community, Program in Clinical Psychology, Seattle, WA 98119-1997**

**AWARDS** PhD.

**Students:** 105 (80 women); includes 15 minority (5 African Americans, 3 Asian Americans or Pacific Islanders, 6 Hispanic Americans, 1 Native American) 3 international. In 2001, 10 degrees awarded.

**Degree requirements:** For doctorate, thesis/dissertation, clinical internship, practicum.

**Entrance requirements:** For doctorate, GRE General Test or MAT. *Application deadline:* For fall admission, 2/1.

**Expenses:** Tuition: Part-time $300 per credit hour. Tuition and fees vary according to program.

**Financial support:** In 2001–02, 2 research assistantships (averaging $6,000 per year) were awarded; career-related internships or fieldwork and unspecified assistantships also available. Financial award applicants required to submit FAFSA.

**Faculty research:** Social network support, attachment, integration of faith and family psychology, developmental psychology. *Total annual research expenditures:* $10,000. Dr. Leonardo Mármol, Chair, 706-281-2660.

**Application contact:** Kelley Unger, Program Manager, 206-281-2759, *Fax:* 206-281-2695, *E-mail:* kunger@spu.edu. *Web site:* http://www.spu.edu/depts/grad-psych/

### ■ SOUTHERN ILLINOIS UNIVERSITY CARBONDALE

**Graduate School, College of Liberal Arts, Department of Psychology, Carbondale, IL 62901-6806**

**AWARDS** Clinical psychology (MA, MS, PhD); counseling psychology (MA, MS, PhD); experimental psychology (MA, MS, PhD).

**Faculty:** 27 full-time (14 women), 1 part-time/adjunct (0 women).

**Students:** 79 full-time (58 women), 42 part-time (29 women); includes 28 minority (16 African Americans, 7 Asian Americans or Pacific Islanders, 4 Hispanic Americans, 1 Native American), 10 international. 128 applicants, 22% accepted. In 2001, 14 master's, 21 doctorates awarded.

**Degree requirements:** For master's and doctorate, thesis/dissertation.

**Entrance requirements:** For master's, GRE General Test, GRE Subject Test, TOEFL, minimum GPA of 2.7; for doctorate, GRE General Test, GRE Subject Test, TOEFL, minimum GPA of 3.25. *Application deadline:* For fall admission, 3/1 (priority date). Applications are processed on a rolling basis. *Application fee:* $20.

**Expenses:** Tuition, state resident: full-time $3,794; part-time $154 per hour. Tuition, nonresident: full-time $6,566; part-time $308 per hour. Required fees: $277 per hour.

**Financial support:** In 2001–02, 82 students received support, including 14 fellowships with full tuition reimbursements available, 23 research assistantships with full tuition reimbursements available, 22 teaching assistantships with full tuition reimbursements available; Federal Work-Study, institutionally sponsored loans, and tuition waivers (full) also available.

**Faculty research:** Developmental neuropsychology; smoking, affect, and cognition; personality measurement; vocational psychology; program evaluation. Alan Vaux, Chair, 618-453-3529. *Web site:* http://www.siu.edu/departments/cola/psycho/

**Find an in-depth description at www.petersons.com/gradchannel.**

### ■ SOUTHERN ILLINOIS UNIVERSITY EDWARDSVILLE

**Graduate Studies and Research, School of Education, Department of Psychology, Edwardsville, IL 62026-0001**

**AWARDS** Clinical adult (MS); community school (MS); general academic (MA); industrial organizational (MS). Part-time programs available.

**Students:** 33 full-time (26 women), 24 part-time (20 women); includes 6 minority (4 African Americans, 2 Hispanic Americans), 3 international. Average age 33. 64 applicants, 56% accepted, 21 enrolled. In 2001, 29 degrees awarded.

**Degree requirements:** For master's, thesis, final exam.

**Entrance requirements:** For master's, GRE General Test, GRE Subject Test, MAT, TOEFL. *Application deadline:* For fall admission, 7/20; for spring admission, 12/7. *Application fee:* $25.

**Expenses:** Tuition, state resident: full-time $2,712; part-time $113 per credit hour. Tuition, nonresident: full-time $5,424; part-time $226 per credit hour. Required fees: $250; $125 per term. Tuition and fees vary according to course load, campus/location and reciprocity agreements.

**Financial support:** In 2001–02, 3 fellowships with full tuition reimbursements, 4 teaching assistantships with full tuition reimbursements were awarded. Research assistantships, career-related internships or fieldwork, Federal Work-Study, institutionally sponsored loans, traineeships, and unspecified assistantships also available. Support available to part-time students. Financial award application deadline: 3/1; financial award applicants required to submit FAFSA.

Dr. Bryce Sullivan, Chair, 618-650-2202, *E-mail:* bsulliv@siue.edu.

## ■ SOUTHERN METHODIST UNIVERSITY

**Dedman College, Department of Psychology, Program in Clinical and Counseling Psychology, Dallas, TX 75275**

**AWARDS** MA. Part-time programs available.

**Students:** 19 full-time (17 women), 6 part-time (5 women); includes 2 minority (1 African American, 1 Asian American or Pacific Islander), 1 international. Average age 28. In 2001, 12 degrees awarded.
**Degree requirements:** For master's, thesis, oral exam.
**Entrance requirements:** For master's, minimum GPA of 3.0. *Application deadline:* For fall admission, 2/15. *Application fee:* $50.
**Expenses:** Tuition: Part-time $285 per credit hour.
**Financial support:** Research assistantships, teaching assistantships, career-related internships or fieldwork, Federal Work-Study, and institutionally sponsored loans available. Support available to part-time students. Financial award application deadline: 3/1; financial award applicants required to submit FAFSA.
**Faculty research:** Family assessment, personality disorders, development of self-concept, learning disabilities, mood and emotion.
**Application contact:** Dr. Neil Mulligan, Director, Graduate Studies, 214-768-4385.

## ■ SPALDING UNIVERSITY

**Graduate Studies, School of Psychology, Louisville, KY 40203-2188**

**AWARDS** Clinical psychology (MA, Psy D). Part-time programs available.

**Faculty:** 8 full-time (3 women), 8 part-time/adjunct (3 women).
**Students:** 46 full-time (33 women), 86 part-time (64 women); includes 11 minority (6 African Americans, 2 Asian Americans or Pacific Islanders, 1 Hispanic American, 2 Native Americans), 8 international. 136 applicants, 40% accepted. In 2001, 8 master's, 21 doctorates awarded. Terminal master's awarded for partial completion of doctoral program.
**Degree requirements:** For master's, comprehensive exam; for doctorate, thesis/dissertation.
**Entrance requirements:** For master's, GRE General Test, 18 hours of undergraduate course work in psychology; for doctorate, GRE General Test, interview. *Application deadline:* For fall admission, 1/15. *Application fee:* $30.
**Expenses:** Tuition: Full-time $6,000; part-time $400 per credit hour. Required fees: $96.

**Financial support:** In 2001–02, 28 research assistantships (averaging $4,100 per year) were awarded; career-related internships or fieldwork, Federal Work-Study, and scholarships/grants also available. Financial award application deadline: 3/15.
**Faculty research:** Substance abuse, prayer research, end-of-life issues, complementary and alternative medicine, research methodology and statistical inference. *Total annual research expenditures:* $400,000.
Dr. Barbara Williams, Dean, 502-585-9911.
**Application contact:** 502-585-1705, *Fax:* 502-585-7158, *E-mail:* gradadmissions@spalding.edu.

## ■ STATE UNIVERSITY OF NEW YORK AT ALBANY

**College of Arts and Sciences, Department of Psychology, Albany, NY 12222-0001**

**AWARDS** Biopsychology (PhD); clinical psychology (PhD); general/experimental psychology (PhD); industrial/organizational psychology (PhD); psychology (MA); social/personality psychology (PhD).

**Students:** 69 full-time (45 women), 58 part-time (41 women); includes 12 minority (2 African Americans, 3 Asian Americans or Pacific Islanders, 7 Hispanic Americans), 13 international. Average age 28. 220 applicants, 20% accepted. In 2001, 11 master's, 6 doctorates awarded.
**Degree requirements:** For doctorate, thesis/dissertation.
**Entrance requirements:** For doctorate, GRE General Test, GRE Subject Test. *Application deadline:* For fall admission, 1/15. *Application fee:* $50.
**Expenses:** Tuition, state resident: full-time $2,550; part-time $213 per credit. Tuition, nonresident: full-time $4,208; part-time $351 per credit. Required fees: $470; $470 per year.
**Financial support:** Fellowships, research assistantships, teaching assistantships, career-related internships or fieldwork available. Financial award application deadline: 2/1.
Robert Rosellini, Chair, 518-442-4820.
**Application contact:** Glenn Sanders, Graduate Director, 518-442-4853.

## ■ STATE UNIVERSITY OF NEW YORK AT BINGHAMTON

**Graduate School, School of Arts and Sciences, Department of Psychology, Specialization in Clinical Psychology, Binghamton, NY 13902-6000**

**AWARDS** MA, PhD.

**Students:** 44 full-time (31 women), 9 part-time (8 women); includes 9 minority (4

African Americans, 2 Asian Americans or Pacific Islanders, 3 Hispanic Americans), 3 international. Average age 28. 102 applicants, 13% accepted, 9 enrolled. In 2001, 4 master's, 3 doctorates awarded.
**Degree requirements:** For master's, thesis; for doctorate, thesis/dissertation, departmental qualifying exam.
**Entrance requirements:** For master's and doctorate, GRE General Test, GRE Subject Test, TOEFL. *Application deadline:* For fall admission, 4/15 (priority date); for spring admission, 11/1. Applications are processed on a rolling basis. Electronic applications accepted.
**Expenses:** Tuition, state resident: full-time $5,100; part-time $213 per credit. Tuition, nonresident: full-time $8,416; part-time $351 per credit. Required fees: $811.
**Financial support:** In 2001–02, 40 students received support, including 5 fellowships with full tuition reimbursements available (averaging $8,951 per year), 19 research assistantships with full tuition reimbursements available (averaging $10,041 per year), 16 teaching assistantships with full tuition reimbursements available (averaging $10,695 per year); career-related internships or fieldwork, Federal Work-Study, institutionally sponsored loans, and unspecified assistantships also available. Support available to part-time students. Financial award application deadline: 2/15.
Dr. Alice Friedman, Graduate Coordinator, 607-777-4570.

## ■ STONY BROOK UNIVERSITY, STATE UNIVERSITY OF NEW YORK

**Graduate School, College of Arts and Sciences, Department of Psychology, Program in Clinical Psychology, Stony Brook, NY 11794**

**AWARDS** PhD.

**Students:** 34 full-time (25 women), 11 part-time (9 women); includes 4 minority (all Hispanic Americans), 2 international. Average age 29. 221 applicants, 6% accepted. In 2001, 5 degrees awarded.
**Degree requirements:** For doctorate, thesis/dissertation.
**Entrance requirements:** For doctorate, GRE General Test, GRE Subject Test, TOEFL. *Application deadline:* For fall admission, 1/15. *Application fee:* $50.
**Expenses:** Tuition, state resident: full-time $5,100; part-time $213 per credit. Tuition, nonresident: full-time $8,416; part-time $351 per credit. Required fees: $496.
**Application contact:** Dr. Harriet Waters, Director, 631-632-7855, *Fax:* 631-632-7876, *E-mail:* hwaters@ccvm.sunysb.edu.

# ■ SUFFOLK UNIVERSITY

College of Arts and Sciences, Department of Psychology, Boston, MA 02108-2770

**AWARDS** Clinical-developmental psychology (PhD).

**Faculty:** 12 full-time (10 women), 6 part-time/adjunct (4 women).
**Students:** 41 full-time (34 women), 21 part-time (17 women); includes 6 minority (2 African Americans, 3 Asian Americans or Pacific Islanders, 1 Hispanic American), 3 international. Average age 29. 74 applicants, 45% accepted, 15 enrolled. In 2001, 6 degrees awarded.
**Degree requirements:** For doctorate, thesis/dissertation, Practicum.
**Entrance requirements:** For doctorate, GRE General Test or MAT. *Application deadline:* For fall admission, 1/15. Applications are processed on a rolling basis. *Application fee:* $50.
**Expenses:** Contact institution.
**Financial support:** In 2001–02, 50 students received support, including 42 fellowships with full and partial tuition reimbursements available (averaging $10,200 per year); career-related internships or fieldwork, Federal Work-Study, and institutionally sponsored loans also available. Support available to part-time students. Financial award application deadline: 3/15; financial award applicants required to submit FAFSA.
**Faculty research:** Cognitive, emotional, personality, and social development.
Dr. Robert Webb, Chair, 617-573-8293, *Fax:* 617-367-2924, *E-mail:* rwebb@suffolk.edu.
**Application contact:** Judith Reynolds, Director of Graduate Admissions, 617-573-8302, *Fax:* 617-523-0116, *E-mail:* grad.admission@suffolk.edu. *Web site:* http://www/cas/suffolk.edu/psych/ndonovan/phd.htm

# ■ SYRACUSE UNIVERSITY

Graduate School, College of Arts and Sciences, Department of Psychology, Program in Clinical Psychology, Syracuse, NY 13244-0003

**AWARDS** MA, MS, PhD.

**Degree requirements:** For master's, thesis (for some programs); for doctorate, thesis/dissertation.
**Entrance requirements:** For master's and doctorate, GRE General Test.
**Expenses:** Tuition: Full-time $15,528; part-time $647 per credit. Required fees: $420; $38 per term. Tuition and fees vary according to program.

# ■ TEACHERS COLLEGE COLUMBIA UNIVERSITY

Graduate Faculty of Education, Department of Counseling and Clinical Psychology, Program in Clinical Psychology, New York, NY 10027-6696

**AWARDS** MA, PhD.

**Expenses:** Tuition: Full-time $19,080; part-time $780 per unit. Required fees: $170 per semester.
**Faculty research:** Psychotherapy education, trauma, stress, psychopathology, life span and aging issues.

# ■ TEMPLE UNIVERSITY

Graduate School, College of Liberal Arts, Department of Psychology, Program in Clinical Psychology, Philadelphia, PA 19122-6096

**AWARDS** PhD.

**Degree requirements:** For doctorate, thesis/dissertation.
**Entrance requirements:** For doctorate, GRE General Test, minimum GPA of 3.0. Electronic applications accepted.
**Expenses:** Tuition, state resident: full-time $8,487; part-time $369 per credit hour. Tuition, nonresident: full-time $12,282; part-time $534 per credit hour. Required fees: $350. Tuition and fees vary according to course load, program and reciprocity agreements.
**Faculty research:** Depression, addictive disorders, parenting and families, social phobia, child and adolescent treatment research.

**Find an in-depth description at www.petersons.com/gradchannel.**

# ■ TEXAS A&M UNIVERSITY

College of Liberal Arts, Department of Psychology, Program in Clinical Psychology, College Station, TX 77843

**AWARDS** MS, PhD.

**Degree requirements:** For master's and doctorate, thesis/dissertation.
**Entrance requirements:** For master's and doctorate, GRE General Test, TOEFL. *Application deadline:* For fall admission, 1/15. *Application fee:* $50 ($75 for international students). Electronic applications accepted.
**Expenses:** Tuition, state resident: full-time $11,872. Tuition, nonresident: full-time $17,892.
**Financial support:** Fellowships, research assistantships, teaching assistantships, career-related internships or fieldwork and institutionally sponsored loans available. Financial award application deadline: 1/15; financial award applicants required to submit FAFSA.

Dr. Douglas Snyder, Head, 979-845-2539, *E-mail:* dks@psyc.tamu.edu.
**Application contact:** Sharon Starr, Graduate Admissions Supervisor, 979-458-1710, *Fax:* 979-845-4727, *E-mail:* gradadv@psyc.tamu.edu. *Web site:* http://psychweb.tamu.edu/

# ■ TEXAS TECH UNIVERSITY

Graduate School, College of Arts and Sciences, Department of Psychology, Lubbock, TX 79409

**AWARDS** Clinical psychology (PhD); counseling psychology (PhD); general experimental (MA, PhD). Part-time programs available.

**Faculty:** 21 full-time (10 women).
**Students:** 72 full-time (50 women), 19 part-time (10 women); includes 19 minority (1 African American, 3 Asian Americans or Pacific Islanders, 14 Hispanic Americans, 1 Native American). Average age 28. 158 applicants, 20% accepted, 18 enrolled. In 2001, 9 master's, 11 doctorates awarded.
**Degree requirements:** For doctorate, thesis/dissertation.
**Entrance requirements:** For master's and doctorate, GRE General Test, GRE Subject Test. *Application deadline:* Applications are processed on a rolling basis. *Application fee:* $25 ($50 for international students). Electronic applications accepted.
**Expenses:** Tuition, state resident: full-time $1,926; part-time $107 per credit hour. Tuition, nonresident: full-time $5,724; part-time $318 per credit hour. Required fees: $779; $737 per year. Tuition and fees vary according to course level, course load and program.
**Financial support:** In 2001–02, 71 students received support, including 5 research assistantships with partial tuition reimbursements available (averaging $10,220 per year), 48 teaching assistantships with partial tuition reimbursements available (averaging $10,067 per year); fellowships, career-related internships or fieldwork, Federal Work-Study, and institutionally sponsored loans also available. Support available to part-time students. Financial award application deadline: 5/1; financial award applicants required to submit FAFSA.
**Faculty research:** Failure/success in relationships, peer rejection in school, stress and coping, group processes, use of information technology in education. *Total annual research expenditures:* $95,236.
Dr. Ruth H. Maki, Chair, 806-742-3737, *Fax:* 806-742-0818.
**Application contact:** Graduate Adviser, 806-742-3737, *Fax:* 806-742-0818. *Web site:* http://www.ttu.edu/~psy/

## ■ TOWSON UNIVERSITY

**Graduate School, Program in School Psychology, Towson, MD 21252-0001**

**AWARDS** Clinical psychology (MA); counseling psychology (MA); experimental psychology (MA); psychology (MA); school psychology (MA, CAS). Part-time and evening/weekend programs available.

**Faculty:** 13 full-time (5 women), 2 part-time/adjunct (both women).
**Students:** 195. In 2001, 64 master's, 15 other advanced degrees awarded.
**Degree requirements:** For master's, thesis (for some programs), exams.
**Entrance requirements:** For master's, GRE General Test. *Application deadline:* For fall admission, 2/1; for spring admission, 10/1. *Application fee:* $40. Electronic applications accepted.
**Expenses:** Tuition, state resident: part-time $211 per credit. Tuition, nonresident: part-time $435 per credit. Required fees: $52 per credit.
**Financial support:** Fellowships, Federal Work-Study and unspecified assistantships available. Financial award application deadline: 4/1; financial award applicants required to submit FAFSA.
**Faculty research:** Cognitive behavior, issues affecting the aging, relaxation hypnosis and imagery, lesbian and gay issues.
Dr. Susan Bartels, Director, 410-704-3070, *Fax:* 410-704-3800, *E-mail:* sbartels@towson.edu.
**Application contact:** 410-704-2501, *Fax:* 410-704-4675, *E-mail:* grads@towson.edu.

## ■ UNIFORMED SERVICES UNIVERSITY OF THE HEALTH SCIENCES

**School of Medicine, Division of Basic Medical Sciences, Department of Medical and Clinical Psychology, Bethesda, MD 20814-4799**

**AWARDS** Clinical psychology (PhD); medical psychology (PhD). Clinical psychology available to active duty military only.

**Faculty:** 11 full-time (5 women), 35 part-time/adjunct (13 women).
**Students:** 24 full-time (16 women); includes 7 minority (3 African Americans, 2 Asian Americans or Pacific Islanders, 1 Hispanic American, 1 Native American). Average age 29. 35 applicants, 17% accepted, 5 enrolled. In 2001, 4 doctorates awarded.
**Degree requirements:** For doctorate, thesis/dissertation, qualifying exam, comprehensive exam. *Median time to degree:* Doctorate–5 years full-time.
**Entrance requirements:** For doctorate, GRE General Test, TOEFL, minimum GPA of 3.5, U.S. citizenship, active

military duty (clinical psychology only). *Application deadline:* For fall admission, 1/15 (priority date). Applications are processed on a rolling basis. *Application fee:* $0.
**Expenses:** Tuition waived.
**Financial support:** In 2001–02, fellowships with full tuition reimbursements (averaging $17,000 per year); tuition waivers (full) also available.
**Faculty research:** Addictive and appetitive behavior, psychopharmacology, stress and eating, obesity, health, social psychology.
Dr. David S. Krantz, Chair, 301-295-3270, *Fax:* 301-295-3034, *E-mail:* dkrantz@usuhs.mil.
**Application contact:** Janet M. Anastasi, Graduate Program Coordinator, 301-295-3913, *Fax:* 301-295-6772, *E-mail:* janastasi@usuhs.mil.

## ■ UNION INSTITUTE & UNIVERSITY

**School of Professional Psychology, Cincinnati, OH 45206-1925**

**AWARDS** Clinical psychology (PhD).

**Faculty:** 56 full-time (26 women), 26 part-time/adjunct (9 women).
**Students:** 141 full-time (86 women); includes 24 minority (17 African Americans, 4 Asian Americans or Pacific Islanders, 3 Hispanic Americans), 1 international. Average age 46. In 2001, 26 degrees awarded.
**Degree requirements:** For doctorate, thesis/dissertation, internship, residency.
**Entrance requirements:** For doctorate, master's degree. *Application deadline:* Applications are processed on a rolling basis. *Application fee:* $50.
**Expenses:** Tuition: Full-time $9,392. Full-time tuition and fees vary according to degree level and program.
**Financial support:** In 2001–02, 83 students received support. Federal Work-Study, scholarships/grants, and tuition waivers available. Financial award application deadline: 5/1; financial award applicants required to submit FAFSA.
Dr. Richard Green, Vice President and Dean, Graduate Studies, 513-861-6400 Ext. 1133, *E-mail:* rgreen@tui.edu.
**Application contact:** Director of Admissions, 800-486-3116, *Fax:* 513-861-0779, *E-mail:* admissions@tui.edu.

## ■ UNIVERSITY AT BUFFALO, THE STATE UNIVERSITY OF NEW YORK

**Graduate School, College of Arts and Sciences, Department of Psychology, Buffalo, NY 14260**

**AWARDS** Behavioral neuroscience (PhD); clinical psychology (PhD); cognitive psychology (PhD); general psychology (MA); social-personality (PhD). Part-time programs available.

**Faculty:** 28 full-time (13 women), 2 part-time/adjunct (1 woman).
**Students:** 88 full-time (52 women), 13 part-time (8 women); includes 11 minority (5 African Americans, 3 Asian Americans or Pacific Islanders, 3 Hispanic Americans), 12 international. Average age 25. 122 applicants, 31% accepted, 16 enrolled. In 2001, 13 master's, 6 doctorates awarded. Terminal master's awarded for partial completion of doctoral program.
**Degree requirements:** For master's, project; for doctorate, thesis/dissertation.
**Entrance requirements:** For master's and doctorate, GRE General Test, TOEFL. *Application deadline:* For fall admission, 1/5. *Application fee:* $35. Electronic applications accepted.
**Expenses:** Tuition, state resident: full-time $6,118. Tuition, nonresident: full-time $9,434.
**Financial support:** In 2001–02, 37 students received support, including 4 fellowships with full tuition reimbursements available (averaging $14,000 per year), 10 research assistantships with full tuition reimbursements available (averaging $9,512 per year), 37 teaching assistantships with full tuition reimbursements available (averaging $8,400 per year); career-related internships or fieldwork, Federal Work-Study, institutionally sponsored loans, tuition waivers (partial), and minority fellowships also available. Financial award application deadline: 1/15; financial award applicants required to submit FAFSA.
**Faculty research:** Neural, endocrine, and molecular bases of behavior; adult mood and anxiety disorders; relationship dysfunction; behavioral medicine; attention deficit/hyperactivity disorder. *Total annual research expenditures:* $2.1 million.
Dr. Jack A. Meacham, Chair, 716-645-3650 Ext. 203, *Fax:* 716-645-3801, *E-mail:* meacham@acsu.buffalo.edu.
**Application contact:** Michele Nowacki, Coordinator of Admissions, 716-645-3650 Ext. 209, *Fax:* 716-695-3801, *E-mail:* psych@acsu.buffalo.edu. *Web site:* http://wings.buffalo.edu/psychology/

## ■ THE UNIVERSITY OF ALABAMA

**Graduate School, College of Arts and Sciences, Department of Psychology, Tuscaloosa, AL 35487**

**AWARDS** Clinical psychology (PhD); cognitive psychology (PhD); general psychology (MA).

**Faculty:** 23 full-time (11 women), 2 part-time/adjunct (0 women).
**Students:** 63 full-time (47 women), 11 part-time (8 women); includes 10 minority (8 African Americans, 1 Hispanic American, 1 Native American), 3 international. Average age 27. 182 applicants, 12% accepted, 17 enrolled. In 2001, 8 master's, 12 doctorates awarded.
**Degree requirements:** For doctorate, thesis/dissertation, internship (clinical psychology).
**Entrance requirements:** For doctorate, GRE General Test, minimum GPA of 3.0. *Application deadline:* For fall admission, 1/1. *Application fee:* $25. Electronic applications accepted.
**Expenses:** Tuition, state resident: full-time $3,292; part-time $183 per credit hour. Tuition, nonresident: full-time $8,912; part-time $495 per credit hour. Tuition and fees vary according to course load, campus/location and program.
**Financial support:** In 2001–02, 6 fellowships with full tuition reimbursements (averaging $10,000 per year), 16 research assistantships with full tuition reimbursements (averaging $10,400 per year), 15 teaching assistantships with full tuition reimbursements (averaging $8,433 per year) were awarded. Career-related internships or fieldwork, institutionally sponsored loans, and scholarships/grants also available. Financial award application deadline: 2/1.
**Faculty research:** Health psychology and social behavior, cognitive development/retardation, adult clinical psychology, child clinical/pediatrics, psychology and law.
Dr. Robert Lyman, Chairperson, 205-348-1913, *Fax:* 205-348-8648, *E-mail:* blyman@gp.as.ua.edu.
**Application contact:** Dr. Forrest Scogin, Director of Graduate Studies, 205-348-1924, *Fax:* 205-348-8648, *E-mail:* fscogin@gp.as.ua.edu. *Web site:* http://www.as.ua.edu/psychology/

## ■ THE UNIVERSITY OF ALABAMA AT BIRMINGHAM

**Graduate School, School of Social and Behavioral Sciences, Department of Psychology, Birmingham, AL 35294**

**AWARDS** Behavioral neuroscience (PhD); clinical psychology (PhD); developmental psychology (PhD); medical psychology (PhD); psychology (MA, PhD).

**Students:** 46 full-time (27 women), 5 part-time (3 women); includes 5 minority (4 African Americans, 1 Asian American or Pacific Islander), 1 international. 143 applicants, 17% accepted. In 2001, 6 master's, 9 doctorates awarded.
*Application deadline:* Applications are processed on a rolling basis. *Application fee:* $35 ($60 for international students). Electronic applications accepted.
**Expenses:** Tuition, state resident: full-time $3,058. Tuition, nonresident: full-time $5,746. Tuition and fees vary according to course load, degree level and program.
**Financial support:** Career-related internships or fieldwork available.
**Faculty research:** Biological basis of behavior structure, function of the nervous system.
Dr. Carl E. McFarland, Chairman, 205-934-3850, *E-mail:* cmcfarla@uab.edu. *Web site:* http://www.sbs.uab.edu/psyc.htm/

## ■ UNIVERSITY OF ALASKA ANCHORAGE

**College of Arts and Sciences, Department of Psychology, Anchorage, AK 99508-8060**

**AWARDS** Clinical psychology (MS). Part-time programs available.

**Degree requirements:** For master's, thesis.
**Entrance requirements:** For master's, GRE General Test, GRE Subject Test, interview.
**Faculty research:** Substance abuse, childhood autism, biofeedback, psychological assessment, mental health in Native Alaskans.

## ■ UNIVERSITY OF CALIFORNIA, SAN DIEGO

**Graduate Studies and Research, Group in Clinical Psychology, La Jolla, CA 92093**

**AWARDS** PhD.

**Students:** 54 (38 women). In 2001, 11 degrees awarded.
*Application fee:* $40. Electronic applications accepted.
**Expenses:** Tuition, nonresident: full-time $10,434. Required fees: $4,883.
Robert Heaton, Chair.
**Application contact:** Carol Demong, Coordinator, 858-497-6659.

## ■ UNIVERSITY OF CALIFORNIA, SANTA BARBARA

**Graduate Division, Graduate School of Education, Program in Clinical/School/Counseling Psychology, Santa Barbara, CA 93106**

**AWARDS** Clinical/school/counseling psychology (PhD); school psychology (M Ed).

**Degree requirements:** For master's, thesis or alternative; for doctorate, thesis/dissertation.
**Entrance requirements:** For master's and doctorate, GRE General Test or MAT, TOEFL, background questionnaire, minimum GPA of 3.0. Electronic applications accepted.

## ■ UNIVERSITY OF CENTRAL FLORIDA

**College of Arts and Sciences, Department of Psychology, Program in Clinical Psychology, Orlando, FL 32816**

**AWARDS** MA, MS, PhD. Part-time and evening/weekend programs available.

**Faculty:** 31 full-time (9 women), 24 part-time/adjunct (12 women).
**Students:** 57 full-time (43 women), 5 part-time (4 women); includes 13 minority (3 African Americans, 1 Asian American or Pacific Islander, 9 Hispanic Americans), 1 international. Average age 27. 139 applicants, 24% accepted, 20 enrolled. In 2001, 7 degrees awarded.
**Degree requirements:** For master's, thesis or alternative, clinical internship; for doctorate, thesis/dissertation, candidacy exam, internship.
**Entrance requirements:** For master's and doctorate, GRE General Test, TOEFL, minimum GPA of 3.0 in last 60 hours, resumé. *Application deadline:* For fall admission, 2/15. *Application fee:* $20. Electronic applications accepted.
**Expenses:** Tuition, state resident: part-time $162 per hour. Tuition, nonresident: part-time $569 per hour.
**Financial support:** In 2001–02, 22 fellowships with partial tuition reimbursements (averaging $3,624 per year), 65 research assistantships with partial tuition reimbursements (averaging $2,072 per year), 42 teaching assistantships with partial tuition reimbursements (averaging $2,623 per year) were awarded. Career-related internships or fieldwork, Federal Work-Study, institutionally sponsored loans, tuition waivers (partial), and unspecified assistantships also available. Financial award application deadline: 3/1; financial award applicants required to submit FAFSA.
**Faculty research:** Professional ethical decision making, computer experience and

anxiety, effects of expert testimony on decision making in a rape trial, religiosity, relationship beliefs and marital adjustment. Dr. Bernard J. Jensen, Coordinator, 407-823-2974, *Fax:* 407-823-5862, *E-mail:* b.jensen@pegasus.cc.ucf.edu. *Web site:* http://www.ucf.edu/

### ■ UNIVERSITY OF CINCINNATI

**Division of Research and Advanced Studies, McMicken College of Arts and Sciences, Department of Psychology, Cincinnati, OH 45221**

**AWARDS** Clinical psychology (PhD); experimental psychology (PhD).

**Faculty:** 25 full-time.
**Students:** 69 full-time, 20 part-time; includes 15 minority (12 African Americans, 2 Asian Americans or Pacific Islanders, 1 Hispanic American), 3 international. 210 applicants, 13 enrolled. In 2001, 18 degrees awarded.
**Degree requirements:** For doctorate, thesis/dissertation.
**Entrance requirements:** For doctorate, GRE General Test, GRE Subject Test. *Application deadline:* For fall admission, 1/7. *Application fee:* $35. Electronic applications accepted.
**Expenses:** Tuition, state resident: part-time $2,698 per quarter. Tuition, nonresident: part-time $4,977 per quarter.
**Financial support:** Fellowships with full tuition reimbursements, traineeships, tuition waivers (partial), and unspecified assistantships available. Financial award application deadline: 5/1. *Total annual research expenditures:* $374,651.
Dr. Kevin M. Corcoran, Head, 513-556-5569, *Fax:* 513-556-1904.
**Application contact:** Dr. Paula K. Shear, Graduate Program Director, 513-556-5577, *Fax:* 513-556-1904, *E-mail:* paula.shear@uc.edu. *Web site:* http://asweb.artsci.uc.edu/psychology

### ■ UNIVERSITY OF CONNECTICUT

**Graduate School, College of Liberal Arts and Sciences, Field of Psychology, Storrs, CT 06269**

**AWARDS** Behavioral neuroscience (PhD); biopsychology (PhD); clinical psychology (PhD); cognition/instruction psychology (PhD); developmental psychology (PhD); ecological psychology (PhD); general experimental psychology (PhD); industrial and organizational psychology (PhD); language psychology (PhD); social psychology (PhD).

**Faculty:** 41 full-time (11 women), 2 part-time/adjunct (both women).
**Students:** 134 full-time (83 women), 17 part-time (9 women); includes 13 minority (9 African Americans, 1 Asian American or Pacific Islander, 3 Hispanic Americans), 17 international. Average age 28. 378

applicants, 14% accepted, 25 enrolled. In 2001, 18 degrees awarded.
**Degree requirements:** For doctorate, thesis/dissertation, internship, comprehensive exam, registration.
**Entrance requirements:** For doctorate, GRE General Test, GRE Subject Test, letters of recommendation. *Application deadline:* For fall admission, 12/31. *Application fee:* $40 ($45 for international students).
**Financial support:** In 2001–02, 45 fellowships (averaging $4,000 per year), 16 research assistantships with full tuition reimbursements (averaging $16,000 per year), 83 teaching assistantships with full tuition reimbursements (averaging $16,000 per year) were awarded. Career-related internships or fieldwork, Federal Work-Study, scholarships/grants, health care benefits, and unspecified assistantships also available. Financial award application deadline: 12/31.
**Faculty research:** Behavioral neuroscience; physiology/chemistry of memory; sensation, motor control/motivation; cognitive, social, personality and language development; infancy/person perceptions and intergroup relations. *Total annual research expenditures:* $8 million.
Charles A. Lowe, Head, *Fax:* 860-486-2760, *E-mail:* charles.lowe@uconn.edu.
**Application contact:** Gina Stuart, Graduate Admissions, 860-486-3528, *Fax:* 860-486-2760, *E-mail:* futuregr@psych.psy.uconn.edu. *Web site:* http://psych.uconn.edu/

### ■ UNIVERSITY OF DAYTON

**Graduate School, College of Arts and Sciences, Department of Psychology, Program in Clinical Psychology, Dayton, OH 45469-1300**

**AWARDS** MA. Part-time programs available.

**Faculty:** 6 full-time (3 women), 2 part-time/adjunct (1 woman).
**Students:** 23 full-time (20 women), 1 (woman) part-time; includes 2 minority (both African Americans), 2 international. Average age 24. 43 applicants, 56% accepted, 12 enrolled. In 2001, 5 degrees awarded.
**Degree requirements:** For master's, thesis.
**Entrance requirements:** For master's, GRE General Test, GRE Subject Test, minimum undergraduate GPA of 3.0 or 3.3 during final 2 years. *Application deadline:* For fall admission, 3/1 (priority date). *Application fee:* $30. Electronic applications accepted.
**Expenses:** Tuition: Full-time $5,436; part-time $453 per credit hour. Required fees: $50; $25 per term.

**Financial support:** In 2001–02, 5 research assistantships with full tuition reimbursements were awarded; teaching assistantships, career-related internships or fieldwork, Federal Work-Study, and traineeships also available. Financial award application deadline: 3/1.
**Faculty research:** Family issues, modes and mechanisms of therapy, gender issues, personality disorders, stress and coping.
Dr. John Korte, Director, 937-229-2169, *Fax:* 937-229-3900, *E-mail:* korte@notes.udayton.edu. *Web site:* http://www.udayton.edu/~psych/

### ■ UNIVERSITY OF DELAWARE

**College of Arts and Science, Department of Psychology, Newark, DE 19716**

**AWARDS** Behavioral neuroscience (PhD); clinical psychology (PhD); cognitive psychology (PhD); social psychology (PhD).

**Faculty:** 25 full-time (6 women), 3 part-time/adjunct (0 women).
**Students:** 41 full-time (24 women); includes 3 minority (1 African American, 2 Hispanic Americans). Average age 28. 129 applicants, 13% accepted, 8 enrolled. In 2001, 7 degrees awarded.
**Degree requirements:** For doctorate, thesis/dissertation.
**Entrance requirements:** For doctorate, GRE General Test. *Application deadline:* For fall admission, 1/7 (priority date). *Application fee:* $50. Electronic applications accepted.
**Expenses:** Tuition, state resident: full-time $4,770; part-time $265 per credit. Tuition, nonresident: full-time $13,860; part-time $770 per credit. Required fees: $414.
**Financial support:** In 2001–02, 41 students received support, including 5 fellowships with full tuition reimbursements available (averaging $11,637 per year), 8 research assistantships with full tuition reimbursements available (averaging $11,637 per year), 15 teaching assistantships with full tuition reimbursements available (averaging $11,637 per year); career-related internships or fieldwork, Federal Work-Study, institutionally sponsored loans, scholarships/grants, tuition waivers (full and partial), and minority fellowships also available. Financial award application deadline: 1/7.
**Faculty research:** Emotion development, neural and cognitive aspects of memory, neural control of feeding, intergroup relations, social cognition and communication. *Total annual research expenditures:* $1 million.
Dr. Brian P. Ackerman, Chairperson, 302-831-2271, *Fax:* 302-831-3645, *E-mail:* bpa@udel.edu.

*University of Delaware (continued)*
**Application contact:** Information Contact, 302-831-2271, *Fax:* 302-831-3645, *E-mail:* bpa@udel.edu. *Web site:* http://www.udel.edu/catalog/current/as/psyc/grad.html

### ■ UNIVERSITY OF DENVER

**Graduate School of Professional Psychology, Denver, CO 80208**
**AWARDS** Clinical psychology (Psy D).
**Faculty:** 6 full-time (3 women), 9 part-time/adjunct (4 women).
**Students:** 138 (114 women); includes 24 minority (3 African Americans, 10 Asian Americans or Pacific Islanders, 10 Hispanic Americans, 1 Native American) 1 international. 320 applicants, 31% accepted. In 2001, 31 degrees awarded.
**Degree requirements:** For doctorate, paper, internship.
**Entrance requirements:** For doctorate, GRE General Test, GRE Subject Test, TOEFL. *Application deadline:* For fall admission, 1/6. *Application fee:* $45.
**Expenses:** Tuition: Full-time $21,456.
**Financial support:** In 2001–02, 61 students received support, including 5 fellowships with full and partial tuition reimbursements available, 1 research assistantship with full and partial tuition reimbursement available (averaging $2,322 per year), 5 teaching assistantships with full and partial tuition reimbursements available (averaging $6,957 per year); career-related internships or fieldwork, Federal Work-Study, institutionally sponsored loans, scholarships/grants, and clinical assistantships also available. Support available to part-time students. Financial award application deadline: 3/1; financial award applicants required to submit FAFSA.
Dr. Peter Buirski, Dean, 303-871-2382.
**Application contact:** Samara Ferber, Admissions Coordinator, 303-871-3873, *Fax:* 303-871-4220. *Web site:* http://www.du.edu/gspp/

### ■ UNIVERSITY OF DETROIT MERCY

**College of Liberal Arts and Education, Department of Psychology, Program in Clinical Psychology, Detroit, MI 48219-0900**
**AWARDS** MA, PhD.
**Faculty:** 14 full-time (10 women).
**Students:** 28 full-time (19 women), 51 part-time (35 women); includes 11 minority (6 African Americans, 4 Asian Americans or Pacific Islanders, 1 Hispanic American), 6 international. Average age 32. In 2001, 13 master's, 7 doctorates awarded.

**Degree requirements:** For doctorate, departmental qualifying exam.
*Application deadline:* For fall admission, 8/1 (priority date). Applications are processed on a rolling basis. *Application fee:* $30 ($50 for international students).
**Expenses:** Tuition: Full-time $10,620; part-time $590 per credit hour. Required fees: $400. Tuition and fees vary according to program.
**Financial support:** Fellowships, career-related internships or fieldwork available.
Dr. Margaret Stack, Coordinator, 313-993-6193, *Fax:* 313-993-6397, *E-mail:* stackma@udmercy.edu.

### ■ UNIVERSITY OF FLORIDA

**Graduate School, College of Health Professions, Department of Clinical and Health Psychology, Gainesville, FL 32611**
**AWARDS** PhD.
**Degree requirements:** For doctorate, thesis/dissertation.
**Entrance requirements:** For doctorate, GRE General Test, minimum GPA of 3.0. Electronic applications accepted.
**Expenses:** Tuition, state resident: part-time $164 per hour. Tuition, nonresident: part-time $571 per hour. Tuition and fees vary according to course level and program.
**Faculty research:** Child psychology, pediatric psychology, health/medical psychology, neuropsychology. *Web site:* http://www.hp.ufl.edu/chp

### ■ UNIVERSITY OF HARTFORD

**College of Arts and Sciences, Department of Psychology, Program in Clinical Practices, West Hartford, CT 06117-1599**
**AWARDS** MA.
**Faculty:** 7 full-time (3 women), 8 part-time/adjunct (2 women).
**Students:** 27 full-time (20 women), 3 part-time (all women), 3 international. Average age 28. 46 applicants, 70% accepted. In 2001, 42 degrees awarded.
**Degree requirements:** For master's, thesis optional.
**Entrance requirements:** For master's, GRE General Test, GRE Subject Test, TOEFL, minimum GPA of 3.0. *Application deadline:* For fall admission, 2/15 (priority date). Applications are processed on a rolling basis. *Application fee:* $40 ($55 for international students). Electronic applications accepted.
**Expenses:** Tuition: Part-time $300 per credit hour.
**Financial support:** In 2001–02, 7 research assistantships (averaging $2,000 per year), 8 teaching assistantships (averaging $2,550

per year) were awarded. Financial award application deadline: 6/1; financial award applicants required to submit FAFSA.
**Faculty research:** Attachment issues, child abuse prevention, master's psychologist issues, neuropsychology.
Dr. Mary E. Steir, Director, 860-768-5104, *E-mail:* steir@mail.hartford.edu.
**Application contact:** Kellie Richard Westenfeld, Assistant Director of Graduate Admissions, 860-768-4371, *Fax:* 860-768-5160, *E-mail:* westenfel@mail.hartford.edu. *Web site:* http://www.hartford.edu/

### ■ UNIVERSITY OF HARTFORD

**College of Arts and Sciences, Graduate Institute of Professional Psychology, West Hartford, CT 06117-1599**
**AWARDS** Clinical psychology (Psy D).
**Faculty:** 4 full-time (1 woman), 12 part-time/adjunct (8 women).
**Students:** 89 full-time (72 women), 75 part-time (58 women); includes 15 minority (5 African Americans, 7 Asian Americans or Pacific Islanders, 3 Hispanic Americans), 4 international. Average age 30. 130 applicants, 53% accepted. In 2001, 24 degrees awarded.
**Degree requirements:** For doctorate, thesis/dissertation, qualifying exam.
**Entrance requirements:** For doctorate, GRE General Test, GRE Subject Test, minimum GPA of 3.2. *Application deadline:* For fall admission, 1/15 (priority date). Applications are processed on a rolling basis. *Application fee:* $40 ($55 for international students). Electronic applications accepted.
**Expenses:** Contact institution.
**Financial support:** In 2001–02, 35 students received support, including 16 fellowships (averaging $2,000 per year), 3 research assistantships (averaging $3,100 per year), 16 teaching assistantships (averaging $3,100 per year); career-related internships or fieldwork and Federal Work-Study also available. Support available to part-time students. Financial award application deadline: 6/1; financial award applicants required to submit FAFSA.
**Faculty research:** Outcome evaluation of community outreach programs, women's issues, outcome evaluation of clinical training programs, sleep and dream research, child interventions.
Dr. David L. Singer, Director, 860-520-1151, *Fax:* 860-520-1156, *E-mail:* dasinger@mail.hartford.edu.
**Application contact:** Robert D'Angelo, Program Administrator, 860-520-1151, *Fax:* 860-520-1156, *E-mail:* dangelo@mail.hartford.edu. *Web site:* http://www.hartford.edu/

# ■ UNIVERSITY OF HAWAII AT MANOA

**Graduate Division, College of Arts and Sciences, College of Social Sciences, Department of Psychology, Honolulu, HI 96822**

**AWARDS** Clinical psychology (PhD); community and culture (MA, PhD); psychology (MA, PhD).

**Faculty:** 25 full-time (5 women), 15 part-time/adjunct (5 women).

**Students:** 73 full-time (51 women), 28 part-time (19 women); includes 27 Asian Americans or Pacific Islanders, 3 Hispanic Americans. 57 applicants, 68% accepted, 23 enrolled. In 2001, 17 master's, 7 doctorates awarded. Terminal master's awarded for partial completion of doctoral program.

**Degree requirements:** For master's, thesis/dissertation; for doctorate, thesis/dissertation, comprehensive exam. *Median time to degree:* Master's–2 years full-time.

**Entrance requirements:** For master's and doctorate, GRE General Test, GRE Subject Test. *Application deadline:* For fall admission, 1/1. *Application fee:* $25 ($50 for international students).

**Expenses:** Tuition, state resident: full-time $2,160; part-time $1,980 per year. Tuition, nonresident: full-time $5,190; part-time $4,829 per year.

**Financial support:** In 2001–02, 31 research assistantships (averaging $15,881 per year), 7 teaching assistantships (averaging $13,163 per year) were awarded. Career-related internships or fieldwork, institutionally sponsored loans, and tuition waivers (full and partial) also available. Financial award application deadline: 1/1.

**Faculty research:** Cross-cultural psychology, health psychology, marine mammals, child/adult psychopathology.

Dr. Karl A. Minke, Chairperson, 808-956-8414, *Fax:* 808-956-4700, *E-mail:* minke@hawaii.edu.

**Application contact:** Dr. Elaine Heiby, Graduate Field Chairperson, 808-956-8414, *Fax:* 808-956-4700, *E-mail:* heiby@hawaii.edu.

# ■ UNIVERSITY OF HOUSTON

**College of Liberal Arts and Social Sciences, Department of Psychology, Houston, TX 77204**

**AWARDS** Clinical psychology (PhD); industrial/organizational psychology (PhD); social psychology (PhD).

**Faculty:** 22 full-time (9 women), 8 part-time/adjunct (4 women).

**Students:** 82 full-time (57 women), 20 part-time (16 women); includes 12 minority (2 African Americans, 3 Asian Americans or Pacific Islanders, 7 Hispanic Americans), 2 international. Average age 29. 280 applicants, 8% accepted. In 2001, 14 doctorates awarded.

**Degree requirements:** For doctorate, thesis/dissertation.

**Entrance requirements:** For doctorate, GRE General Test, minimum GPA of 3.0. *Application deadline:* For fall admission, 1/1. *Application fee:* $40 ($75 for international students).

**Expenses:** Tuition, state resident: full-time $1,512. Tuition, nonresident: full-time $5,310. Required fees: $1,308. Tuition and fees vary according to program.

**Financial support:** In 2001–02, research assistantships with partial tuition reimbursements (averaging $12,300 per year), teaching assistantships with partial tuition reimbursements (averaging $10,800 per year) were awarded. Career-related internships or fieldwork, Federal Work-Study, institutionally sponsored loans, and teaching fellowships also available.

**Faculty research:** Health psychology, depression, child/family process, organizational effectiveness, close relationships. *Total annual research expenditures:* $4.5 million.

Dr. John P. Vincent, Chairman, 713-743-8503, *Fax:* 713-743-8588, *E-mail:* jvincent@uh.edu.

**Application contact:** Sherry A. Berun, Coordinator—Academic Affairs, 713-743-8508, *Fax:* 713-743-8588, *E-mail:* sherryr@uh.edu. *Web site:* http://firenza.uh.edu/

# ■ UNIVERSITY OF HOUSTON–CLEAR LAKE

**School of Human Sciences and Humanities, Programs in Human Sciences, Houston, TX 77058-1098**

**AWARDS** Behavioral sciences (MA), including behavioral sciences-general, behavioral sciences-psychology, behavioral sciences-sociology; clinical psychology (MA); cross-cultural studies (MA); family therapy (MA); fitness and human performance (MA); school psychology (MA); studies of the future (MS). Part-time and evening/weekend programs available.

**Students:** 562; includes 183 minority (95 African Americans, 16 Asian Americans or Pacific Islanders, 70 Hispanic Americans, 2 Native Americans), 16 international. Average age 34. In 2001, 152 degrees awarded.

**Degree requirements:** For master's, thesis or alternative.

**Entrance requirements:** For master's, GRE General Test. *Application deadline:* For fall admission, 8/1; for spring admission, 12/1. Applications are processed on a rolling basis. *Application fee:* $30 ($70 for international students). Electronic applications accepted.

**Expenses:** Tuition, state resident: full-time $2,016; part-time $84 per credit hour. Tuition, nonresident: full-time $6,072; part-time $253 per credit hour. Tuition and fees vary according to course load.

**Financial support:** Research assistantships, teaching assistantships, career-related internships or fieldwork, Federal Work-Study, institutionally sponsored loans, and scholarships/grants available. Support available to part-time students. Financial award application deadline: 5/1.

Dr. Hilary Karp, Division Co-Chair, 281-283-3383, *E-mail:* karp@cl.uh.edu.

# ■ UNIVERSITY OF ILLINOIS AT URBANA–CHAMPAIGN

**Graduate College, College of Liberal Arts and Sciences, Department of Psychology, Champaign, IL 61820**

**AWARDS** Applied measurement (MS); biological psychology (AM, PhD); clinical psychology (AM, PhD); cognitive psychology (AM, PhD); developmental psychology (AM, PhD); engineering psychology (MS); personnel psychology (MS); quantitative psychology (AM, PhD); social-personality-organizational (AM, PhD); visual cognition and human performance (AM, PhD).

**Faculty:** 41 full-time (14 women), 11 part-time/adjunct (3 women).

**Students:** 156 full-time (90 women); includes 23 minority (6 African Americans, 12 Asian Americans or Pacific Islanders, 5 Hispanic Americans), 42 international. 461 applicants, 17% accepted, 27 enrolled. In 2001, 1 master's, 25 doctorates awarded.

**Degree requirements:** For doctorate, thesis/dissertation.

**Entrance requirements:** For master's, GRE General Test, GRE Subject Test (recommended), minimum GPA of 3.0; for doctorate, GRE General Test, GRE Subject Test (recommended). *Application deadline:* For fall admission, 1/1. *Application fee:* $40 ($50 for international students).

**Expenses:** Tuition, state resident: part-time $3,227 per degree program. Tuition, nonresident: part-time $7,169 per degree program. Tuition and fees vary according to program.

**Financial support:** In 2001–02, 31 fellowships with full tuition reimbursements (averaging $15,000 per year), 21 research assistantships with full tuition reimbursements (averaging $13,585 per year), 73 teaching assistantships with full tuition reimbursements (averaging $13,585 per year) were awarded. Career-related internships or fieldwork, traineeships, and tuition waivers (full) also available. Financial award application deadline: 1/1. *Total annual research expenditures:* $4.6 million.

Dr. Edward J. Shoben, Head.

*University of Illinois at Urbana–Champaign (continued)*

**Application contact:** Cheryl Berger, Assistant Head for Graduate Affairs, 217-333-3429, *Fax:* 217-244-5876, *E-mail:* gradstdy@s.psych.uiuc.edu. *Web site:* http://www.psych.uiuc.edu/

# ■ UNIVERSITY OF KANSAS

**Graduate School, College of Liberal Arts and Sciences, Department of Psychology, Program in Clinical Child Psychology, Lawrence, KS 66045**

AWARDS PhD.

**Students:** 22 full-time (14 women), 13 part-time (9 women); includes 6 minority (1 Asian American or Pacific Islander, 4 Hispanic Americans, 1 Native American). Average age 27. 84 applicants, 7% accepted, 6 enrolled. In 2001, 3 degrees awarded.

**Degree requirements:** For doctorate, thesis/dissertation, comprehensive exam.

**Entrance requirements:** For doctorate, GRE General Test, GRE Subject Test, TOEFL, minimum GPA of 3.5. *Application deadline:* For fall admission, 1/15. *Application fee:* $35.

**Expenses:** Tuition, state resident: full-time $2,722; part-time $113 per credit. Tuition, nonresident: full-time $8,586; part-time $358 per credit. Required fees: $551; $46 per credit. Tuition and fees vary according to campus/location, program and reciprocity agreements.

**Financial support:** Fellowships, research assistantships, teaching assistantships available.

**Faculty research:** Pediatric psychology, stress and coping, children's services. Michael Roberts, Director, 785-864-4226, *Fax:* 785-864-5024.

**Application contact:** Graduate Admissions, 785-864-4131, *Fax:* 785-864-5696, *E-mail:* psycgrad@ku.edu. *Web site:* http://www.ku.edu/~clchild/

# ■ UNIVERSITY OF LOUISVILLE

**Graduate School, College of Arts and Sciences, Department of Psychology, Program in Clinical Psychology, Louisville, KY 40292-0001**

AWARDS PhD.

**Students:** 41 full-time (29 women); includes 2 minority (both African Americans), 4 international. Average age 30. In 2001, 8 degrees awarded.

**Degree requirements:** For doctorate, thesis/dissertation.

**Entrance requirements:** For doctorate, GRE General Test. *Application deadline:* Applications are processed on a rolling basis. *Application fee:* $25.

**Expenses:** Tuition, state resident: full-time $4,134. Tuition, nonresident: full-time $11,486.

**Financial support:** Career-related internships or fieldwork available. Dr. Janet Woodruff-Borden, Director, 502-852-6775, *E-mail:* jwbord01@louisville.edu.

# ■ UNIVERSITY OF MAINE

**Graduate School, College of Liberal Arts and Sciences, Department of Psychology, Orono, ME 04469**

AWARDS Clinical psychology (PhD); developmental psychology (MA); experimental psychology (MA, PhD); social psychology (MA).

**Faculty:** 21.

**Students:** 22 full-time (17 women), 13 part-time (11 women); includes 3 minority (all Native Americans), 2 international. 100 applicants, 14% accepted, 6 enrolled. In 2001, 4 degrees awarded.

**Degree requirements:** For master's and doctorate, thesis/dissertation.

**Entrance requirements:** For master's and doctorate, GRE General Test, GRE Subject Test, TOEFL. *Application deadline:* For fall admission, 2/1 (priority date). Applications are processed on a rolling basis. *Application fee:* $50. Electronic applications accepted.

**Expenses:** Tuition, state resident: full-time $3,780; part-time $210 per credit hour. Tuition, nonresident: full-time $10,782; part-time $599 per credit hour. Required fees: $9.50 per credit hour. $32 per semester. Tuition and fees vary according to reciprocity agreements.

**Financial support:** In 2001–02, 3 research assistantships with tuition reimbursements (averaging $9,010 per year), 21 teaching assistantships with tuition reimbursements (averaging $9,010 per year) were awarded. Fellowships with tuition reimbursements, Federal Work-Study, institutionally sponsored loans, and tuition waivers (full and partial) also available. Financial award application deadline: 3/1.

**Faculty research:** Social development, hypertension and aging, attitude change, self-confidence in achievement situations, health psychology. Dr. Joel Gold, Chair, 207-581-2030, *Fax:* 207-581-6128.

**Application contact:** Scott G. Delcourt, Director of the Graduate School, 207-581-3218, *Fax:* 207-581-3232, *E-mail:* graduate@maine.edu. *Web site:* http://www.umaine.edu/graduate/

# ■ UNIVERSITY OF MARYLAND, COLLEGE PARK

**Graduate Studies and Research, College of Behavioral and Social Sciences, Department of Psychology, College Park, MD 20742**

AWARDS Clinical psychology (PhD); developmental psychology (PhD); experimental psychology (PhD); industrial psychology (MA, MS, PhD); social psychology (PhD).

**Faculty:** 52 full-time (17 women), 10 part-time/adjunct (5 women).

**Students:** 80 full-time (50 women), 22 part-time (15 women); includes 26 minority (14 African Americans, 8 Asian Americans or Pacific Islanders, 3 Hispanic Americans, 1 Native American), 11 international. 432 applicants, 10% accepted, 18 enrolled. In 2001, 8 master's, 21 doctorates awarded.

**Degree requirements:** For master's, thesis; for doctorate, variable foreign language requirement, thesis/dissertation, comprehensive exam.

**Entrance requirements:** For master's, GRE General Test, GRE Subject Test, minimum GPA of 3.5, research and/or work experience; for doctorate, GRE General Test, GRE Subject Test. *Application deadline:* For fall admission, 12/15. Applications are processed on a rolling basis. *Application fee:* $50 ($70 for international students). Electronic applications accepted.

**Expenses:** Tuition, state resident: part-time $289 per credit hour. Tuition, nonresident: part-time $448 per credit hour. One-time fee: $436 part-time. Full-time tuition and fees vary according to course load, campus/location and program.

**Financial support:** In 2001–02, 15 fellowships with full tuition reimbursements (averaging $11,508 per year), 87 teaching assistantships with tuition reimbursements (averaging $12,153 per year) were awarded. Career-related internships or fieldwork, Federal Work-Study, and scholarships/grants also available. Support available to part-time students. Financial award applicants required to submit FAFSA.

**Faculty research:** Counseling and social psychology. Dr. William Hall, Chairman, 301-405-5862, *Fax:* 301-314-9566.

**Application contact:** Trudy Lindsey, Director, Graduate Admissions and Records, 301-405-6991, *Fax:* 301-314-9305, *E-mail:* grschool@deans.umd.edu.

# ■ UNIVERSITY OF MASSACHUSETTS AMHERST

**Graduate School, College of Social and Behavioral Sciences, Department of Psychology, Amherst, MA 01003**

**AWARDS** Clinical psychology (MS, PhD).

**Faculty:** 50 full-time (21 women).
**Students:** 68 full-time (45 women), 10 part-time (8 women); includes 13 minority (4 African Americans, 3 Asian Americans or Pacific Islanders, 6 Hispanic Americans), 8 international. Average age 28. 409 applicants, 9% accepted. In 2001, 14 master's, 10 doctorates awarded. Terminal master's awarded for partial completion of doctoral program.
**Degree requirements:** For master's and doctorate, thesis/dissertation.
**Entrance requirements:** For master's and doctorate, GRE General Test. *Application deadline:* For fall admission, 1/2 (priority date). Applications are processed on a rolling basis. *Application fee:* $40 ($50 for international students).
**Expenses:** Tuition, state resident: full-time $1,980; part-time $110 per credit. Tuition, nonresident: full-time $7,456; part-time $414 per credit. Required fees: $4,112. One-time fee: $115 full-time.
**Financial support:** In 2001–02, 23 fellowships with full tuition reimbursements (averaging $8,012 per year), 38 research assistantships with full tuition reimbursements (averaging $10,467 per year), 40 teaching assistantships with full tuition reimbursements (averaging $7,995 per year) were awarded. Career-related internships or fieldwork, Federal Work-Study, scholarships/grants, traineeships, and unspecified assistantships also available. Support available to part-time students. Financial award application deadline: 1/2.
Dr. Melinda Novak, Chair, 413-545-2387, *Fax:* 413-545-0996, *E-mail:* mnovak@ psych.umass.edu.
**Application contact:** Graduate Secretary, 413-545-2503.

# ■ UNIVERSITY OF MASSACHUSETTS BOSTON

**Office of Graduate Studies and Research, College of Arts and Sciences, Faculty of Arts, Program in Clinical Psychology, Boston, MA 02125-3393**

**AWARDS** PhD. Part-time and evening/ weekend programs available.

**Degree requirements:** For doctorate, thesis/dissertation, oral exams, practicum, comprehensive exam.
**Entrance requirements:** For doctorate, GRE General Test, GRE Subject Test, minimum GPA of 2.75.

**Faculty research:** Community psychology, psychology, racism and mental health, gender and culture, posttraumatic stress disorder.

# ■ UNIVERSITY OF MASSACHUSETTS DARTMOUTH

**Graduate School, College of Arts and Sciences, Department of Psychology, North Dartmouth, MA 02747-2300**

**AWARDS** Clinical psychology (MA); general psychology (MA). Part-time programs available.

**Faculty:** 15 full-time (5 women), 9 part-time/adjunct (2 women).
**Students:** 20 full-time (14 women), 24 part-time (23 women); includes 2 minority (1 Asian American or Pacific Islander, 1 Hispanic American), 1 international. Average age 28. 47 applicants, 55% accepted, 16 enrolled. In 2001, 10 degrees awarded.
**Degree requirements:** For master's, thesis (for some programs).
**Entrance requirements:** For master's, GRE General Test, TOEFL, minimum GPA of 2.75. *Application deadline:* For fall admission, 3/31. *Application fee:* $25 ($45 for international students).
**Expenses:** Tuition, state resident: full-time $2,071; part-time $86 per credit. Tuition, nonresident: full-time $8,099; part-time $337 per credit. Part-time tuition and fees vary according to course load and reciprocity agreements.
**Financial support:** In 2001–02, 2 research assistantships with full tuition reimbursements (averaging $4,500 per year), 6 teaching assistantships with full tuition reimbursements (averaging $4,083 per year) were awarded. Career-related internships or fieldwork, Federal Work-Study, and unspecified assistantships also available. Support available to part-time students. Financial award application deadline: 3/1; financial award applicants required to submit FAFSA.
**Faculty research:** Nutritional health info for college women, role of gender identity, self-efficacy and academic competence on development of career aspirations. *Total annual research expenditures:* $4,000.
Dr. Paul Donnelly, Director, Clinical Psychology, 508-999-8334, *E-mail:* pdonnelly@umassd.edu.
**Application contact:** Maria E. Lomba, Graduate Admissions Officer, 508-999-8604, *Fax:* 508-999-8183, *E-mail:* graduate@umassd.edu.

# ■ THE UNIVERSITY OF MEMPHIS

**Graduate School, College of Arts and Sciences, Department of Psychology, Memphis, TN 38152**

**AWARDS** Clinical psychology (PhD); experimental psychology (PhD); psychology

(MS); school psychology (MA, PhD). Part-time programs available.

**Faculty:** 30 full-time (2 women), 6 part-time/adjunct (3 women).
**Students:** 81 full-time (56 women), 19 part-time (11 women); includes 9 minority (8 African Americans, 1 Native American), 7 international. Average age 28. 188 applicants, 26% accepted. In 2001, 20 master's, 12 doctorates awarded. Terminal master's awarded for partial completion of doctoral program.
**Degree requirements:** For master's, thesis (for some programs), oral exam (MS), comprehensive exam; for doctorate, thesis/dissertation, internship.
**Entrance requirements:** For master's, GRE General Test, 18 undergraduate hours in psychology, minimum GPA of 2.5; for doctorate, GRE General Test, GRE Subject Test. *Application deadline:* For fall admission, 2/1. Applications are processed on a rolling basis. *Application fee:* $35 ($60 for international students).
**Expenses:** Tuition, state resident: full-time $2,026. Tuition, nonresident: full-time $4,528.
**Financial support:** In 2001–02, 2 fellowships with full tuition reimbursements (averaging $13,333 per year), 116 research assistantships with full tuition reimbursements (averaging $5,000 per year), 2 teaching assistantships with full tuition reimbursements (averaging $1,500 per year) were awarded.
**Faculty research:** Psychotherapy and psychopathology, behavioral medicine and community psychology, child and family studies, cognitive and social processes, neuropsychology and behavioral neuroscience. *Total annual research expenditures:* $2.5 million.
Dr. Andrew Meyers, Chairman and Coordinator of Graduate Studies, 901-678-2145.

# ■ UNIVERSITY OF MIAMI

**Graduate School, College of Arts and Sciences, Department of Psychology, Coral Gables, FL 33124**

**AWARDS** Applied developmental psychology (PhD); behavioral neuroscience (PhD); clinical psychology (PhD); health psychology (PhD); psychology (MS).

**Faculty:** 39 full-time (18 women).
**Students:** 70 full-time (51 women); includes 23 minority (6 African Americans, 4 Asian Americans or Pacific Islanders, 13 Hispanic Americans). Average age 25. 200 applicants, 14% accepted, 18 enrolled. In 2001, 12 degrees awarded.
**Degree requirements:** For doctorate, thesis/dissertation, comprehensive exam. *Median time to degree:* Doctorate–5 years full-time.

*University of Miami (continued)*

**Entrance requirements:** For doctorate, GRE General Test, TOEFL, minimum GPA of 3.5. *Application deadline:* For fall admission, 12/1. *Application fee:* $50. Electronic applications accepted.

**Expenses:** Tuition: Part-time $960 per credit hour. Required fees: $85 per semester. Tuition and fees vary according to program.

**Financial support:** In 2001–02, 7 fellowships with full tuition reimbursements (averaging $17,000 per year), 43 research assistantships with full tuition reimbursements (averaging $16,500 per year), 19 teaching assistantships with full tuition reimbursements (averaging $12,300 per year) were awarded. Career-related internships or fieldwork, institutionally sponsored loans, scholarships/grants, and traineeships also available. Financial award applicants required to submit FAFSA.

**Faculty research:** Depression, social and emotional development, stress and coping, AIDS and psychoneuroimmunology, children's peer relations. *Total annual research expenditures:* $10 million.

Dr. A. Rodney Wellens, Chairman, 305-284-2814, *Fax:* 305-284-3402.

**Application contact:** Patricia L. Perreira, Staff Associate, 305-284-2814, *Fax:* 305-284-3402, *E-mail:* inquire@mail.psy.miami.edu. *Web site:* http://www.psy.miami.edu/

■ **UNIVERSITY OF MICHIGAN**

**Horace H. Rackham School of Graduate Studies, College of Literature, Science, and the Arts, Department of Psychology, Ann Arbor, MI 48109**

**AWARDS** Biopsychology (PhD); clinical psychology (PhD); cognition and perception (PhD); developmental psychology (PhD); organizational psychology (PhD); personality psychology (PhD); social psychology (PhD).

**Faculty:** 68 full-time, 29 part-time/adjunct.

**Students:** 166 full-time (122 women); includes 57 minority (27 African Americans, 13 Asian Americans or Pacific Islanders, 14 Hispanic Americans, 3 Native Americans), 22 international. Average age 24. 555 applicants, 8% accepted, 27 enrolled. In 2001, 25 degrees awarded.

**Degree requirements:** For doctorate, oral defense of dissertation, preliminary exam.

**Entrance requirements:** For doctorate, GRE General Test, GRE Subject Test, TOEFL. *Application deadline:* For fall admission, 12/15. *Application fee:* $55. Electronic applications accepted.

**Financial support:** Fellowships with full tuition reimbursements, research assistantships with full tuition reimbursements, teaching assistantships with full tuition reimbursements, career-related internships or fieldwork available. Financial award application deadline: 3/15.

Richard Gonzalez, Chair, 734-764-7429.

**Application contact:** 734-764-6316, *Fax:* 734-764-3520. *Web site:* http://www.lsa.umich.edu/psych/

■ **UNIVERSITY OF MINNESOTA, TWIN CITIES CAMPUS**

**Graduate School, College of Liberal Arts, Department of Psychology, Program in Clinical Psychology, Minneapolis, MN 55455-0213**

**AWARDS** PhD.

**Students:** 22 full-time (15 women); includes 2 minority (1 Asian American or Pacific Islander, 1 Hispanic American), 1 international. 89 applicants, 9% accepted, 4 enrolled. In 2001, 1 degree awarded.

**Degree requirements:** For doctorate, thesis/dissertation, internship, comprehensive exam.

**Entrance requirements:** For doctorate, GRE General Test, TOEFL, minimum GPA of 3.5; 12 credits of upper-level psychology courses, including statistics or psychological measurement, previous course work in abnormal psychology. *Application deadline:* For fall admission, 1/5. *Application fee:* $55 ($75 for international students).

**Expenses:** Tuition, state resident: full-time $2,932; part-time $489 per credit. Tuition, nonresident: full-time $5,758; part-time $960 per credit. Part-time tuition and fees vary according to course load, program and reciprocity agreements.

**Financial support:** Fellowships, research assistantships, teaching assistantships, career-related internships or fieldwork, traineeships, and tuition waivers (partial) available. Financial award application deadline: 12/1.

**Application contact:** Coordinator, 612-624-4181, *Fax:* 612-626-2079, *E-mail:* psyapply@tc.umn.edu.

■ **UNIVERSITY OF MISSISSIPPI**

**Graduate School, College of Liberal Arts, Department of Psychology, Oxford, University, MS 38677**

**AWARDS** Clinical psychology (PhD); experimental psychology (PhD); psychology (MA).

**Faculty:** 13.

**Students:** 62 full-time (40 women), 12 part-time (4 women); includes 10 minority (6 African Americans, 3 Asian Americans or Pacific Islanders, 1 Hispanic American), 1 international. In 2001, 5 master's, 5 doctorates awarded.

**Degree requirements:** For master's and doctorate, thesis/dissertation.

**Entrance requirements:** For master's, GRE General Test, TOEFL, minimum GPA of 3.0; for doctorate, GRE General Test, TOEFL. *Application deadline:* For fall admission, 8/1. Applications are processed on a rolling basis. *Application fee:* $0 ($25 for international students).

**Expenses:** Tuition, state resident: full-time $3,626; part-time $202 per hour. Tuition, nonresident: full-time $8,172; part-time $454 per hour.

**Financial support:** Application deadline: 3/1.

Dr. David S. Hargrove, Chairman, 662-915-7383, *Fax:* 662-915-5398, *E-mail:* psych@olemiss.edu.

■ **UNIVERSITY OF MISSOURI–ST. LOUIS**

**Graduate School, College of Arts and Sciences, Department of Psychology, St. Louis, MO 63121-4499**

**AWARDS** Clinical psychology (PhD); clinical psychology respecialization (Certificate); experimental psychology (PhD); general psychology (MA); industrial/organizational (PhD). Evening/weekend programs available.

**Faculty:** 18.

**Students:** 34 full-time (27 women), 38 part-time (25 women); includes 9 minority (6 African Americans, 2 Asian Americans or Pacific Islanders, 1 Hispanic American), 2 international. In 2001, 12 master's, 5 doctorates awarded. Terminal master's awarded for partial completion of doctoral program.

**Degree requirements:** For doctorate, thesis/dissertation.

**Entrance requirements:** For master's and doctorate, GRE General Test, GRE Subject Test. *Application deadline:* For fall admission, 2/1 (priority date). Applications are processed on a rolling basis. *Application fee:* $25 ($40 for international students). Electronic applications accepted.

**Expenses:** Tuition, state resident: part-time $231 per credit hour. Tuition, nonresident: part-time $621 per credit hour.

**Financial support:** In 2001–02, 2 fellowships with full tuition reimbursements (averaging $12,000 per year), 9 research assistantships with full and partial tuition reimbursements (averaging $13,585 per year), 23 teaching assistantships with full and partial tuition reimbursements (averaging $9,096 per year) were awarded.

**Faculty research:** Animal-human learning; physiological, industrial-organizational and cognitive processes; personality-social, clinical and community psychology. *Total annual research expenditures:* $1.1 million.

Dr. Gary Burger, Chair, 314-516-5391, *Fax:* 314-516-5392.
**Application contact:** Graduate Admissions, 314-516-5458, *Fax:* 314-516-5310, *E-mail:* gradadm@umsl.edu.

## ■ THE UNIVERSITY OF MONTANA–MISSOULA

**Graduate School, College of Arts and Sciences, Department of Psychology, Program in Clinical Psychology, Missoula, MT 59812-0002**

**AWARDS** PhD.

**Degree requirements:** For doctorate, thesis/dissertation, oral exam.
**Entrance requirements:** For doctorate, GRE General Test, GRE Subject Test. *Application deadline:* For fall admission, 1/15. *Application fee:* $45.
**Expenses:** Tuition, state resident: full-time $2,482; part-time $1,700 per year. Tuition, nonresident: full-time $7,372; part-time $5,000 per year. Required fees: $1,900. Tuition and fees vary according to degree level.
**Financial support:** In 2001–02, teaching assistantships with full tuition reimbursements (averaging $8,065 per year); career-related internships or fieldwork, Federal Work-Study, and institutionally sponsored loans also available. Financial award application deadline: 3/1; financial award applicants required to submit FAFSA.
**Application contact:** Graduate Secretary, 406-243-4523, *Fax:* 406-243-6366, *E-mail:* psycgrad@selway.umt.edu. *Web site:* http://www.cas.umt.edu/psych/

## ■ UNIVERSITY OF NEVADA, LAS VEGAS

**Graduate College, College of Liberal Arts, Department of Psychology, Las Vegas, NV 89154-9900**

**AWARDS** Clinical psychology (PhD); experimental psychology (PhD); general psychology (MA). Part-time programs available.

**Faculty:** 21 full-time (7 women).
**Students:** 29 full-time (22 women), 6 part-time (4 women); includes 6 minority (2 Asian Americans or Pacific Islanders, 4 Hispanic Americans). 47 applicants, 28% accepted, 12 enrolled. In 2001, 4 degrees awarded.
**Degree requirements:** For master's and doctorate, thesis/dissertation, oral exam, comprehensive exam.
**Entrance requirements:** For master's, GRE General Test, GRE Subject Test, minimum GPA of 3.2; for doctorate, GRE General Test, GRE Subject Test, minimum GPA of 3.2 in bachelor's and 3.5 in master's. *Application deadline:* For fall

admission, 3/1. *Application fee:* $40 ($55 for international students).
**Expenses:** Tuition, state resident: full-time $1,926; part-time $107 per credit. Tuition, nonresident: full-time $9,376; part-time $220 per credit. Tuition and fees vary according to course load.
**Financial support:** In 2001–02, 6 research assistantships with full and partial tuition reimbursements (averaging $11,000 per year), 18 teaching assistantships with partial tuition reimbursements (averaging $11,000 per year) were awarded. Financial award application deadline: 3/1.
Dr. Charles Rusmussen, Chair, 702-895-3305.
**Application contact:** Graduate College Admissions Evaluator, 702-895-3320, *Fax:* 702-895-4180, *E-mail:* gradcollege@ccmail.nevada.edu. *Web site:* http://psychology.unlv.edu/gradinfo.html/

## ■ UNIVERSITY OF NEW MEXICO

**Graduate School, College of Arts and Sciences, Department of Psychology, Program in Clinical Psychology, Albuquerque, NM 87131-2039**

**AWARDS** MS, PhD.

**Students:** 39 full-time (27 women), 3 part-time; includes 10 minority (1 African American, 7 Hispanic Americans, 2 Native Americans), 2 international. Average age 35. In 2001, 4 master's, 11 doctorates awarded.
**Degree requirements:** For master's, thesis/dissertation; for doctorate, thesis/dissertation, comprehensive exam.
**Entrance requirements:** For doctorate, GRE General Test, GRE Subject Test, 1 semester in statistics. *Application deadline:* For fall admission, 1/15 (priority date). *Application fee:* $40.
**Expenses:** Tuition, state resident: full-time $2,771; part-time $115 per credit hour. Tuition, nonresident: full-time $11,207; part-time $467 per credit hour. Required fees: $570; $24 per credit hour. Part-time tuition and fees vary according to course load and program.
**Financial support:** In 2001–02, 32 students received support. Application deadline: 3/1.
**Application contact:** Beth R. Isbell, Program Advisement Coordinator, 505-277-7512, *Fax:* 505-277-1394, *E-mail:* isbell@unm.edu. *Web site:* http://www.unm.edu/~psych

## ■ THE UNIVERSITY OF NORTH CAROLINA AT CHAPEL HILL

**Graduate School, College of Arts and Sciences, Department of Psychology, Chapel Hill, NC 27599**

**AWARDS** Biological psychology (PhD); clinical psychology (PhD); cognitive psychology (PhD); developmental psychology (PhD); quantitative psychology (PhD); social psychology (PhD).

**Faculty:** 46 full-time (25 women), 6 part-time/adjunct (0 women).
**Students:** 116 full-time (63 women). 546 applicants, 7% accepted, 29 enrolled. In 2001, 27 doctorates awarded.
**Degree requirements:** For doctorate, thesis/dissertation, comprehensive exam.
**Entrance requirements:** For doctorate, GRE General Test, minimum GPA of 3.0. *Application deadline:* For fall admission, 12/1. *Application fee:* $55. Electronic applications accepted.
**Expenses:** Tuition, state resident: full-time $2,864. Tuition, nonresident: full-time $12,030.
**Financial support:** In 2001–02, 11 fellowships with tuition reimbursements, 28 research assistantships with tuition reimbursements, 63 teaching assistantships with tuition reimbursements were awarded. Unspecified assistantships also available. Financial award application deadline: 2/1.
**Faculty research:** Expressed emotion, cognitive development, social cognitive neuroscience, human memory personality. *Total annual research expenditures:* $605,806.
Peter A. Ornstein, Chair, 919-962-3088.
**Application contact:** Barbara Atkins, Student Services Manager, 919-962-7149, *Fax:* 919-962-2537, *E-mail:* batkins@email.unc.edu.

## ■ THE UNIVERSITY OF NORTH CAROLINA AT CHARLOTTE

**Graduate School, College of Arts and Sciences, Department of Psychology, Concentration in Community/Clinical Psychology, Charlotte, NC 28223-0001**

**AWARDS** MA.

**Students:** 14 full-time (all women), 12 part-time (11 women); includes 3 minority (all African Americans). Average age 28. 55 applicants, 20% accepted, 10 enrolled. In 2001, 5 degrees awarded.
**Degree requirements:** For master's, thesis, comprehensive exam.
**Entrance requirements:** For master's, GRE General Test, GRE Subject Test, minimum GPA of 3.0 in undergraduate major, 2.8 overall. *Application deadline:* For fall admission, 3/1. *Application fee:* $35. Electronic applications accepted.
**Expenses:** Tuition, state resident: full-time $1,483; part-time $371 per year. Tuition,

*The University of North Carolina at Charlotte (continued)*

nonresident: full-time $9,850; part-time $2,463 per year. Required fees: $1,043; $277 per year. Tuition and fees vary according to course load.

**Financial support:** In 2001–02, 2 research assistantships, 5 teaching assistantships were awarded. Fellowships, career-related internships or fieldwork, Federal Work-Study, institutionally sponsored loans, scholarships/grants, and unspecified assistantships also available. Support available to part-time students. Financial award application deadline: 4/1; financial award applicants required to submit FAFSA.
Dr. William Scott Terry, Coordinator, 704-687-4751, *Fax:* 704-687-3096, *E-mail:* wsterry@email.wcc.edu.

**Application contact:** Kathy Barringer, Director of Graduate Admissions, 704-687-3366, *Fax:* 704-687-3279, *E-mail:* gradadm@email.uncc.edu.

### ■ THE UNIVERSITY OF NORTH CAROLINA AT GREENSBORO

**Graduate School, College of Arts and Sciences, Department of Psychology, Greensboro, NC 27412-5001**

**AWARDS** Clinical psychology (MA, PhD); cognitive psychology (MA, PhD); developmental psychology (MA, PhD); social psychology (MA, PhD).

**Faculty:** 22 full-time (9 women), 1 part-time/adjunct (0 women).
**Students:** 42 full-time (35 women), 20 part-time (13 women); includes 2 African Americans, 2 Asian Americans or Pacific Islanders, 2 Hispanic Americans. In 2001, 13 master's, 5 doctorates awarded. Terminal master's awarded for partial completion of doctoral program.
**Degree requirements:** For master's, thesis, comprehensive exam; for doctorate, one foreign language, thesis/dissertation, preliminary exam.
**Entrance requirements:** For master's, GRE General Test, TOEFL; for doctorate, GRE General Test, GRE Subject Test (recommended), TOEFL. *Application deadline:* For fall admission, 2/1. *Application fee:* $35.
**Expenses:** Tuition, state resident: part-time $344 per course. Tuition, nonresident: part-time $2,457 per course.
**Financial support:** In 2001–02, 3 fellowships with full tuition reimbursements (averaging $10,833 per year), 54 research assistantships with full tuition reimbursements (averaging $8,514 per year), 2 teaching assistantships with full tuition reimbursements (averaging $3,500 per year) were awarded. Unspecified assistantships also available.

**Faculty research:** Sensory and perceptual determinants; evoked potential: disorders, deafness, and development.
Dr. Timothy Johnston, Head, 336-334-5013, *Fax:* 336-334-5066, *E-mail:* johnston@uncg.edu.

**Application contact:** Dr. James Lynch, Director of Graduate Recruitment and Information Services, 336-334-4881, *Fax:* 336-334-4424. *Web site:* http://www.uncg.edu/psy/

### ■ UNIVERSITY OF NORTH DAKOTA

**Graduate School, College of Arts and Sciences, Department of Psychology, Program in Clinical Psychology, Grand Forks, ND 58202**

**AWARDS** PhD.

**Degree requirements:** For doctorate, thesis/dissertation, internship, comprehensive exam.
**Entrance requirements:** For doctorate, GRE General Test, GRE Subject Test, TOEFL, minimum GPA of 3.5. *Application deadline:* For fall admission, 2/1. *Application fee:* $30.
**Expenses:** Tuition, state resident: full-time $3,298. Tuition, nonresident: full-time $7,998.
**Financial support:** Fellowships, research assistantships, teaching assistantships, career-related internships or fieldwork and tuition waivers (partial) available. Financial award application deadline: 3/15; financial award applicants required to submit FAFSA.
Dr. Alan R. King, Director, Clinical Psychology, 701-777-3644, *Fax:* 701-777-3454, *E-mail:* alan_king@und.nodak.edu. *Web site:* http://www.und.edu/dept/psychol/

### ■ UNIVERSITY OF NORTH TEXAS

**Robert B. Toulouse School of Graduate Studies, College of Arts and Sciences, Department of Psychology, Denton, TX 76203**

**AWARDS** Clinical psychology (PhD); counseling psychology (MA, MS, PhD); experimental psychology (MA, MS, PhD); health psychology and behavioral medicine (PhD); industrial psychology (MA, MS); psychology (MA, MS, PhD); school psychology (MA, MS, PhD).

**Faculty:** 29 full-time (5 women), 7 part-time/adjunct (5 women).
**Students:** 129 full-time (96 women), 98 part-time (70 women); includes 23 minority (2 African Americans, 4 Asian Americans or Pacific Islanders, 15 Hispanic Americans, 2 Native Americans), 9 international. Average age 30. In 2001, 24 master's, 17 doctorates awarded. Terminal master's awarded for partial completion of doctoral program.

**Degree requirements:** For master's, thesis or alternative, comprehensive exam; for doctorate, one foreign language, thesis/dissertation, comprehensive exam.
**Entrance requirements:** For master's and doctorate, GRE General Test, GRE Subject Test, interview. *Application deadline:* For fall admission, 2/1. *Application fee:* $25 ($50 for international students).
**Expenses:** Tuition, state resident: part-time $186 per hour. Tuition, nonresident: part-time $319 per hour. Required fees: $88; $21 per hour.
**Financial support:** Fellowships, research assistantships, teaching assistantships, career-related internships or fieldwork, Federal Work-Study, and institutionally sponsored loans available. Financial award application deadline: 8/1.
Dr. Ernest H. Harrell, Chair, 940-565-2671, *Fax:* 940-546-4682, *E-mail:* harrelle@unt.edu.

**Application contact:** Dr. Joseph Critelli, Graduate Adviser, 940-565-2671, *Fax:* 940-565-4682, *E-mail:* critelli@facstaff.cas.unt.edu.

### ■ UNIVERSITY OF OREGON

**Graduate School, College of Arts and Sciences, Department of Psychology, Program in Clinical Psychology, Eugene, OR 97403**

**AWARDS** PhD.

**Students:** 169 applicants, 2% accepted. In 2001, 6 degrees awarded.
**Degree requirements:** For doctorate, thesis/dissertation.
**Entrance requirements:** For doctorate, GRE General Test, TOEFL. *Application deadline:* For fall admission, 12/1. *Application fee:* $50.
**Expenses:** Tuition, state resident: full-time $4,968; part-time $501 per credit hour. Tuition, nonresident: full-time $8,400; part-time $691 per credit hour.
**Financial support:** Research assistantships, teaching assistantships, career-related internships or fieldwork available.
Scott Monroe, Director, 541-346-5561.

**Application contact:** Lori Olsen, Admissions Contact, 541-346-5060, *Fax:* 541-346-4911, *E-mail:* gradsec@psych.uoregon.edu. *Web site:* http://psychweb.uoregon.edu/

### ■ UNIVERSITY OF PENNSYLVANIA

**Graduate School of Education, Division of Psychology in Education, Program in School, Community, and Clinical Child Psychology, Philadelphia, PA 19104**

**AWARDS** PhD.

**Degree requirements:** For doctorate, thesis/dissertation, exams.
**Entrance requirements:** For doctorate, GRE General Test, GRE Subject Test. Electronic applications accepted.
**Expenses:** Tuition: Part-time $12,875 per semester.
**Faculty research:** Therapeutic interventions at a preschool level, childhood stress, college psychology, school and community psychology.

### ■ UNIVERSITY OF RHODE ISLAND

Graduate School, College of Arts and Sciences, Department of Psychology, Program in Clinical Psychology, Kingston, RI 02881

**AWARDS** PhD.

**Students:** In 2001, 5 doctorates awarded. *Application deadline:* For fall admission, 1/1. *Application fee:* $35.
**Expenses:** Tuition, state resident: full-time $3,756; part-time $209 per credit. Tuition, nonresident: full-time $10,774; part-time $599 per credit. Required fees: $1,586; $76 per credit. One-time fee: $60 full-time. Patricia Morokoff, Director, 401-874-2193.

### ■ UNIVERSITY OF ROCHESTER

The College, Arts and Sciences, Department of Clinical and Social Sciences in Psychology, Rochester, NY 14627-0250

**AWARDS** Clinical psychology (PhD); developmental psychology (PhD); psychology (MA); social-personality psychology (PhD).
**Faculty:** 14.
**Students:** 43 full-time (30 women); includes 3 minority (2 African Americans, 1 Native American), 8 international. 166 applicants, 11% accepted, 8 enrolled. In 2001, 4 master's, 7 doctorates awarded. Terminal master's awarded for partial completion of doctoral program.
**Degree requirements:** For doctorate, thesis/dissertation, qualifying exam.
**Entrance requirements:** For doctorate, GRE General Test, TOEFL. *Application deadline:* For fall admission, 2/1 (priority date). *Application fee:* $25.
**Expenses:** Tuition: Part-time $755 per credit hour.
**Financial support:** Fellowships, research assistantships, teaching assistantships, career-related internships or fieldwork and tuition waivers (full and partial) available. Financial award application deadline: 2/1. Miron Zuckerman, Chair, 585-275-2453.
**Application contact:** Mary Ann Gilbert, Graduate Program Secretary, 585-275-8704.

### ■ UNIVERSITY OF SOUTH CAROLINA

The Graduate School, College of Liberal Arts, Department of Psychology, Program in Clinical/Community Psychology, Columbia, SC 29208

**AWARDS** PhD.

**Faculty:** 14 full-time (3 women), 1 (woman) part-time/adjunct.
**Students:** 71 full-time (55 women), 7 part-time (1 woman); includes 15 minority (12 African Americans, 1 Asian American or Pacific Islander, 2 Hispanic Americans). Average age 31. In 2001, 6 degrees awarded.
**Degree requirements:** For doctorate, thesis/dissertation.
**Entrance requirements:** For doctorate, GRE General Test, minimum GPA of 3.2. *Application deadline:* For fall admission, 1/4 (priority date). Applications are processed on a rolling basis. *Application fee:* $35. Electronic applications accepted.
**Expenses:** Tuition, state resident: full-time $4,434. Tuition, nonresident: full-time $9,854. Tuition and fees vary according to program.
**Financial support:** In 2001–02, 3 fellowships, 6 research assistantships, 6 teaching assistantships were awarded. Career-related internships or fieldwork, Federal Work-Study, and institutionally sponsored loans also available. Support available to part-time students.
Diane Follingstad, Director, 803-777-2836, *Fax:* 803-777-9558.
**Application contact:** Doris Davis, Graduate Secretary, 803-777-2312, *Fax:* 803-777-9558, *E-mail:* doris@gwm.sc.edu.

### ■ UNIVERSITY OF SOUTH CAROLINA AIKEN

Program in Applied Clinical Psychology, Aiken, SC 29801-6309

**AWARDS** MS.

**Students:** 9 full-time (7 women), 7 part-time (all women).
**Degree requirements:** For master's, thesis.
**Entrance requirements:** For master's, GRE General Test, GRE Psychology test. *Application deadline:* Applications are processed on a rolling basis. *Application fee:* $35. Electronic applications accepted.
**Expenses:** Tuition, state resident: part-time $220 per semester hour. Tuition, nonresident: part-time $466 per semester hour.
Dr. Edward Callen, Chair, 803-641-3446, *Fax:* 803-641-3726, *E-mail:* edc@usca.edu.
**Application contact:** Karen Morris, Graduate Studies Coordinator, 803-641-3489, *E-mail:* karenm@usca.edu.

### ■ THE UNIVERSITY OF SOUTH DAKOTA

Graduate School, College of Arts and Sciences, Department of Psychology, Vermillion, SD 57069-2390

**AWARDS** Clinical psychology (MA, PhD); human factors (MA, PhD).
**Faculty:** 24.
**Students:** 49 full-time (29 women), 2 part-time; includes 11 minority (4 Asian Americans or Pacific Islanders, 6 Hispanic Americans, 1 Native American). 150 applicants, 9% accepted. In 2001, 7 master's, 12 doctorates awarded.
**Degree requirements:** For master's and doctorate, thesis/dissertation.
**Entrance requirements:** For master's, GRE; for doctorate, GRE General Test, GRE Subject Test. *Application deadline:* For fall admission, 2/1. *Application fee:* $35.
**Expenses:** Tuition, state resident: full-time $1,700; part-time $95 per credit hour. Tuition, nonresident: full-time $5,027; part-time $279 per credit hour. Required fees: $1,062; $59 per credit hour.
**Financial support:** Research assistantships, teaching assistantships, unspecified assistantships available. Financial award applicants required to submit FAFSA.
**Faculty research:** Human-computer interactions, perceptual-cognitive processing, medical psychology, depression, moral psychology.
Dr. Randal Quevillon, Chair, 605-677-5351.
**Application contact:** Dr. Barbara Yutrzenka, Graduate Student Adviser.

### ■ UNIVERSITY OF SOUTHERN CALIFORNIA

Graduate School, College of Letters, Arts and Sciences, Department of Psychology, Los Angeles, CA 90089

**AWARDS** Clinical psychology (PhD); psychology (MA, PhD).
**Degree requirements:** For doctorate, thesis/dissertation.
**Entrance requirements:** For doctorate, GRE General Test.
**Expenses:** Tuition: Full-time $25,060; part-time $844 per unit. Required fees: $473.

### ■ UNIVERSITY OF SOUTH FLORIDA

College of Graduate Studies, College of Arts and Sciences, Department of Psychology, Tampa, FL 33620-9951

**AWARDS** Clinical psychology (PhD); experimental psychology (PhD); industrial/organizational psychology (PhD).
**Faculty:** 37 full-time (12 women), 2 part-time/adjunct (0 women).

*University of South Florida (continued)*
**Students:** 99 full-time (67 women), 47 part-time (35 women); includes 32 minority (14 African Americans, 5 Asian Americans or Pacific Islanders, 13 Hispanic Americans), 8 international. Average age 30. 367 applicants, 7% accepted, 22 enrolled. In 2001, 5 doctorates awarded.
**Degree requirements:** For doctorate, thesis/dissertation.
**Entrance requirements:** For doctorate, GRE General Test, minimum GPA of 3.0 in last 60 hours. *Application deadline:* For fall admission, 1/15. *Application fee:* $20. Electronic applications accepted.
**Expenses:** Contact institution.
**Financial support:** Fellowships with partial tuition reimbursements, research assistantships with partial tuition reimbursements, teaching assistantships, career-related internships or fieldwork, Federal Work-Study, and institutionally sponsored loans available. Financial award application deadline: 4/15; financial award applicants required to submit FAFSA.
**Faculty research:** Human memory, job analysis, stress, drug and alcohol abuse, neuroscience. *Total annual research expenditures:* $1.4 million.
Emanuel Donchin, Chairperson, 813-974-4066, *Fax:* 813-974-4617, *E-mail:* donchin@luna.cas.usf.edu.
**Application contact:** Michael D. Coovert, Graduate Coordinator, 813-974-0482, *Fax:* 813-974-4617, *E-mail:* coovert@luna.cas.usf.edu. *Web site:* http://www.cas.usf.edu/psychology/

■ **THE UNIVERSITY OF TENNESSEE**

**Graduate School, College of Arts and Sciences, Department of Psychology, Knoxville, TN 37996**

**AWARDS** Clinical psychology (PhD); experimental psychology (MA, PhD); psychology (MA).
**Faculty:** 23 full-time (5 women), 6 part-time/adjunct (1 woman).
**Students:** 70 full-time (40 women), 24 part-time (10 women); includes 14 minority (9 African Americans, 3 Asian Americans or Pacific Islanders, 2 Native Americans), 10 international. 116 applicants, 12% accepted. In 2001, 9 master's, 18 doctorates awarded. Terminal master's awarded for partial completion of doctoral program.
**Degree requirements:** For master's and doctorate, thesis/dissertation.
**Entrance requirements:** For master's and doctorate, GRE General Test, GRE Subject Test, TOEFL, minimum GPA of 2.7. *Application deadline:* For fall admission,

2/1. *Application fee:* $35. Electronic applications accepted.
**Expenses:** Tuition, state resident: full-time $4,280; part-time $233 per hour. Tuition, nonresident: full-time $12,066; part-time $666 per hour. Tuition and fees vary according to program.
**Financial support:** In 2001–02, 1 fellowship, 10 teaching assistantships were awarded. Research assistantships, Federal Work-Study, institutionally sponsored loans, and unspecified assistantships also available. Financial award application deadline: 2/1; financial award applicants required to submit FAFSA.
Dr. James Lawler, Head, 865-974-3328, *Fax:* 865-974-3330, *E-mail:* jlawler@utk.edu.

■ **THE UNIVERSITY OF TEXAS AT EL PASO**

**Graduate School, College of Liberal Arts, Department of Psychology, El Paso, TX 79968-0001**

**AWARDS** Clinical psychology (MA); experimental psychology (MA); psychology (PhD). Part-time and evening/weekend programs available.

**Students:** 42 (29 women); includes 21 minority (20 Hispanic Americans, 1 Native American) 2 international. Average age 34. 54 applicants, 98% accepted. In 2001, 2 master's, 2 doctorates awarded.
**Degree requirements:** For master's and doctorate, thesis/dissertation.
**Entrance requirements:** For master's and doctorate, GRE General Test, TOEFL. *Application deadline:* For fall admission, 2/1. Applications are processed on a rolling basis. *Application fee:* $15 ($65 for international students). Electronic applications accepted.
**Expenses:** Tuition, state resident: full-time $2,450. Tuition, nonresident: full-time $6,000.
**Financial support:** In 2001–02, 18 students received support, including research assistantships with partial tuition reimbursements available (averaging $18,625 per year), teaching assistantships with partial tuition reimbursements available (averaging $14,900 per year); fellowships with partial tuition reimbursements available, career-related internships or fieldwork, Federal Work-Study, institutionally sponsored loans, scholarships/grants, and tuition waivers (partial) also available. Financial award application deadline: 3/15; financial award applicants required to submit FAFSA.
Dr. Judith P. Goggin, Chairperson, 915-747-5551, *Fax:* 915-747-6553, *E-mail:* jgoggin@miners@utep.edu.
**Application contact:** Dr. Charles H. Ambler, Dean of the Graduate School,

915-747-5491 Ext. 7886, *Fax:* 915-747-5788, *E-mail:* cambler@miners.utep.edu.

■ **THE UNIVERSITY OF TEXAS AT TYLER**

**Graduate Studies, College of Education and Psychology, Department of Psychology, Tyler, TX 75799-0001**

**AWARDS** Clinical psychology (MS); counseling psychology (MA); interdisciplinary studies (MS, MSIS); school counseling (MA). Part-time and evening/weekend programs available.

**Faculty:** 7 full-time (4 women), 1 (woman) part-time/adjunct.
**Students:** 30 full-time (26 women), 52 part-time (48 women); includes 9 minority (5 African Americans, 1 Asian American or Pacific Islander, 2 Hispanic Americans, 1 Native American), 3 international. Average age 30. 23 applicants, 100% accepted, 16 enrolled. In 2001, 18 degrees awarded.
**Degree requirements:** For master's, comprehensive exam and/or thesis.
**Entrance requirements:** For master's, GRE General Test, GRE Subject Test, minimum GPA of 3.0. *Application deadline:* For fall admission, 2/1; for spring admission, 10/1. *Application fee:* $0 ($50 for international students). Electronic applications accepted.
**Expenses:** Tuition, state resident: part-time $44 per credit hour. Tuition, nonresident: part-time $262 per credit hour. Required fees: $58 per credit hour. $76 per semester.
**Financial support:** Teaching assistantships, career-related internships or fieldwork, Federal Work-Study, and institutionally sponsored loans available. Support available to part-time students. Financial award application deadline: 7/1.
**Faculty research:** Incest, aging, depression, neuropsychology, child psychopathology.
Dr. Henry L. Schreiber, Chairperson, 903-566-7239, *Fax:* 903-565-5656, *E-mail:* hschreiber@mail.uttyl.edu.
**Application contact:** Dr. Robert F. McClure, Graduate Adviser, 903-566-7435, *Fax:* 903-566-7065, *E-mail:* rmcclure@mail.uttyl.edu. *Web site:* http://www.uttyl.edu/psychology/grad.htm/

■ **THE UNIVERSITY OF TEXAS OF THE PERMIAN BASIN**

**Graduate School, College of Arts and Sciences, Department of Behavioral Science, Program in Psychology, Odessa, TX 79762-0001**

**AWARDS** Applied behavioral analysis (MA); clinical psychology (MA). Part-time and evening/weekend programs available.

**Degree requirements:** For master's, thesis, practicum.
**Entrance requirements:** For master's, GRE General Test.
**Expenses:** Tuition, state resident: full-time $1,746. Tuition, nonresident: full-time $5,292. Required fees: $523. Tuition and fees vary according to course load.

## ■ THE UNIVERSITY OF TEXAS– PAN AMERICAN

### College of Social and Behavioral Sciences, Department of Psychology and Anthropology, Edinburg, TX 78539-2999

**AWARDS** Psychology (MA), including clinical psychology, experimental psychology. Part-time and evening/weekend programs available.

**Faculty:** 11 full-time (0 women).
**Students:** 13 full-time (7 women), 29 part-time (20 women); includes 33 minority (1 Asian American or Pacific Islander, 32 Hispanic Americans). Average age 29. 18 applicants, 44% accepted. In 2001, 7 degrees awarded.
**Degree requirements:** For master's, internship, thesis optional.
**Entrance requirements:** For master's, GRE General Test. *Application deadline:* For fall admission, 2/1 (priority date); for winter admission, 10/1 (priority date). Applications are processed on a rolling basis. *Application fee:* $0. Electronic applications accepted.
**Expenses:** Tuition, state resident: part-time $212 per semester hour. Tuition, nonresident: part-time $367 per semester hour.
**Financial support:** In 2001–02, 3 teaching assistantships were awarded; career-related internships or fieldwork, Federal Work-Study, and institutionally sponsored loans also available.
**Faculty research:** Rehabilitation, biofeedback, acculturation, child development, health.
Dr. Mark Winkel, Director, 956-381-3528, *Fax:* 956-381-3333, *E-mail:* winkelm@panam.edu. *Web site:* http://www.panam.edu/dept/gsprog/

## ■ THE UNIVERSITY OF TEXAS SOUTHWESTERN MEDICAL CENTER AT DALLAS

### Southwestern Graduate School of Biomedical Sciences, Clinical Psychology Program, Dallas, TX 75390

**AWARDS** PhD.

**Faculty:** 28 full-time (9 women), 5 part-time/adjunct (all women).
**Students:** 51 full-time (36 women); includes 7 minority (1 Asian American or Pacific Islander, 6 Hispanic Americans). Average age 27. 126 applicants, 10% accepted. In 2001, 12 degrees awarded.
**Degree requirements:** For doctorate, thesis/dissertation, clinical and qualifying exams.
**Entrance requirements:** For doctorate, GRE General Test, minimum undergraduate GPA of 3.0. *Application deadline:* For fall admission, 1/1. *Application fee:* $0.
**Expenses:** Tuition, state resident: full-time $990. Tuition, nonresident: full-time $6,062. Required fees: $843.
**Financial support:** In 2001–02, 30 research assistantships were awarded; career-related internships or fieldwork and institutionally sponsored loans also available. Financial award application deadline: 3/15; financial award applicants required to submit FAFSA.
**Faculty research:** Health psychology, depression, cross-cultural research, neuropsychology, sequelae children's illness.
Dr. Maurice Korman, Chair, 214-648-5277, *Fax:* 214-648-5297, *E-mail:* mkorma@mednet.swmed.edu.
**Application contact:** Dr. Betsy Kennard, Chair, Admissions Committee, 214-648-5263, *Fax:* 214-648-5297, *E-mail:* beth.kennard@email.swmed.edu. *Web site:* http://www.swmed.edu/home_pages/clpsych/

## ■ UNIVERSITY OF THE DISTRICT OF COLUMBIA

### College of Arts and Sciences, Division of Urban Affairs, Social, and Behavioral Sciences, Department of Psychology and Counseling, Washington, DC 20008-1175

**AWARDS** Clinical psychology (MS); counseling (MS).

**Students:** 10 full-time (5 women), 40 part-time (27 women); includes 48 minority (44 African Americans, 4 Hispanic Americans), 1 international. Average age 35. 33 applicants, 91% accepted, 26 enrolled. In 2001, 11 degrees awarded.
**Degree requirements:** For master's, seminar paper, thesis optional.
**Entrance requirements:** For master's, GRE General Test, writing proficiency exam. *Application deadline:* For fall admission, 6/15 (priority date); for spring admission, 11/1. Applications are processed on a rolling basis. *Application fee:* $20.
**Expenses:** Tuition, state resident: full-time $3,564; part-time $198 per credit hour. Tuition, nonresident: full-time $5,922; part-time $329 per credit hour. Required fees: $270; $135 per term.
Dr. Kathleen Dockett, Chairperson, 202-274-7406.

**Application contact:** LaVerne Hill Flannigan, Director of Admission, 202-274-6069.

## ■ UNIVERSITY OF TOLEDO

### Graduate School, College of Arts and Sciences, Department of Psychology, Toledo, OH 43606-3398

**AWARDS** Clinical psychology (PhD); experimental psychology (MA, PhD).
**Faculty:** 20.
**Students:** 51 full-time (43 women). Average age 28. 104 applicants, 21% accepted, 20 enrolled. In 2001, 4 master's, 7 doctorates awarded.
**Degree requirements:** For master's, thesis; for doctorate, one foreign language, thesis/dissertation.
**Entrance requirements:** For master's and doctorate, GRE General Test, GRE Subject Test. *Application deadline:* For fall admission, 1/15. *Application fee:* $30.
**Expenses:** Tuition, state resident: full-time $7,278; part-time $303 per hour. Tuition, nonresident: full-time $15,731; part-time $699 per hour. Required fees: $43 per hour.
**Financial support:** In 2001–02, 41 research assistantships were awarded; career-related internships or fieldwork, Federal Work-Study, and institutionally sponsored loans also available. Support available to part-time students. Financial award application deadline: 1/15; financial award applicants required to submit FAFSA.
**Faculty research:** Neural taste response.
Dr. Robert A. Haaf, Chair, 419-530-2717, *Fax:* 419-530-8479, *E-mail:* rhaaf@uoft02.utoledo.edu. *Web site:* http://utoledo.edu/www/psychology/graduate.html
**Find an in-depth description at www.petersons.com/gradchannel.**

## ■ UNIVERSITY OF TULSA

### Graduate School, College of Arts and Sciences, Department of Psychology, Program in Clinical Psychology, Tulsa, OK 74104-3189

**AWARDS** MA, PhD. Part-time programs available.

**Faculty:** 9 full-time (3 women).
**Students:** 32 full-time (24 women), 7 part-time (3 women), 4 international. Average age 29. 51 applicants, 57% accepted, 12 enrolled. In 2001, 6 master's, 2 doctorates awarded. Terminal master's awarded for partial completion of doctoral program.
**Degree requirements:** For master's, 6 hours of practicum training; for doctorate, thesis/dissertation, comprehensive exam.
**Entrance requirements:** For master's and doctorate, GRE General Test, TOEFL.

*University of Tulsa (continued)*
*Application deadline:* For fall admission, 2/1 (priority date). Applications are processed on a rolling basis. *Application fee:* $30. Electronic applications accepted.
**Expenses:** Tuition: Full-time $9,540; part-time $530 per credit hour. Required fees: $80. One-time fee: $230 full-time.
**Financial support:** In 2001–02, 2 fellowships with full and partial tuition reimbursements (averaging $9,000 per year), 2 research assistantships with full and partial tuition reimbursements (averaging $8,000 per year), 13 teaching assistantships with full and partial tuition reimbursements (averaging $6,700 per year) were awarded. Career-related internships or fieldwork, Federal Work-Study, and tuition waivers (partial) also available. Support available to part-time students. Financial award application deadline: 2/1; financial award applicants required to submit FAFSA.
**Faculty research:** Psychopathology, personality disorders, assessment/psychometrics, stress and coping.
Dr. Tom Brian, Director, 918-631-2200, *Fax:* 918-631-2833, *E-mail:* thomas-brian@utulsa.edu. *Web site:* http://www.cas.utulsa.edu/psych/clinical_index.html/

■ **UNIVERSITY OF VERMONT**
**Graduate College, College of Arts and Sciences, Department of Psychology, Burlington, VT 05405**
**AWARDS** Clinical psychology (PhD); psychology (PhD).
**Degree requirements:** For doctorate, thesis/dissertation.
**Entrance requirements:** For doctorate, GRE General Test, GRE Subject Test, TOEFL.
**Expenses:** Tuition, state resident: part-time $335 per credit. Tuition, nonresident: part-time $838 per credit.
**Find an in-depth description at www.petersons.com/gradchannel.**

■ **UNIVERSITY OF VIRGINIA**
**College and Graduate School of Arts and Sciences and Curry School of Education, Program in Clinical Psychology, Charlottesville, VA 22903**
**AWARDS** PhD.
**Students:** 34 full-time (27 women); includes 12 minority (7 African Americans, 3 Asian Americans or Pacific Islanders, 2 Hispanic Americans). Average age 27. 39 applicants, 23% accepted, 9 enrolled. In 2001, 9 degrees awarded.
**Degree requirements:** For doctorate, thesis/dissertation.

**Entrance requirements:** For doctorate, GRE General Test. *Application deadline:* For fall admission, 1/15. *Application fee:* $40. Electronic applications accepted.
**Expenses:** Tuition, state resident: full-time $3,988. Tuition, nonresident: full-time $17,078. Required fees: $1,190.
**Financial support:** Applicants required to submit FAFSA.
Ronald E. Reeve, Director, 434-924-7472.
**Application contact:** Duane J. Osheim, Associate Dean for Graduate Programs, 434-924-7184, *Fax:* 434-924-3084, *E-mail:* grad-a-s@virginia.edu.

■ **UNIVERSITY OF WASHINGTON**
**Graduate School, College of Arts and Sciences, Department of Psychology, Seattle, WA 98195**
**AWARDS** PhD.
**Faculty:** 54 full-time (20 women), 5 part-time/adjunct (4 women).
**Students:** 112 full-time (73 women), 23 part-time (15 women); includes 27 minority (5 African Americans, 12 Asian Americans or Pacific Islanders, 5 Hispanic Americans, 5 Native Americans), 5 international. Average age 28. 419 applicants, 11% accepted, 31 enrolled. In 2001, 16 doctorates awarded.
**Degree requirements:** For doctorate, thesis/dissertation. *Median time to degree:* Doctorate–6 years full-time.
**Entrance requirements:** For doctorate, GRE General Test, TSE, minimum GPA of 3.0. *Application deadline:* For fall admission, 12/15. *Application fee:* $50. Electronic applications accepted.
**Expenses:** Tuition, state resident: full-time $5,539. Tuition, nonresident: full-time $14,376. Required fees: $390. Tuition and fees vary according to course load and program.
**Financial support:** In 2001–02, 119 students received support, including 49 research assistantships with full tuition reimbursements available (averaging $13,950 per year), 51 teaching assistantships with full tuition reimbursements available (averaging $13,950 per year); career-related internships or fieldwork, Federal Work-Study, institutionally sponsored loans, traineeships, and health care benefits also available. Financial award application deadline: 2/1.
**Faculty research:** Addictive behaviors, artificial intelligence, child psychopathology, mechanisms and development of vision, physiology of ingestive behaviors. *Total annual research expenditures:* $7.1 million.
Dr. Michael D. Beecher, Chair, 206-685-9660, *Fax:* 206-685-3157, *E-mail:* beecher@u.washington.edu.

**Application contact:** Graduate Program Office, 206-543-8687, *E-mail:* psygrad@u.washington.edu. *Web site:* http://dept.washington.edu/psych/

■ **UNIVERSITY OF WASHINGTON**
**Graduate School, College of Engineering, Department of Materials Science and Engineering, Seattle, WA 98195-2120**
**AWARDS** Inter-engineering specialization in materials science and engineering (MS); materials science and engineering (MS, PhD); materials science and engineering nanotechnology (PhD). Part-time programs available. Postbaccalaureate distance learning degree programs offered (no on-campus study).
**Faculty:** 15 full-time (2 women), 8 part-time/adjunct (0 women).
**Students:** 40 full-time (14 women), 19 part-time (13 women); includes 10 minority (2 African Americans, 6 Asian Americans or Pacific Islanders, 2 Hispanic Americans), 18 international. 54 applicants, 33% accepted, 7 enrolled. In 2001, 9 master's, 3 doctorates awarded.
**Degree requirements:** For master's and doctorate, thesis/dissertation, comprehensive exam, registration. *Median time to degree:* Master's–2.4 years full-time, 5.25 years part-time; doctorate–3.5 years full-time, 8 years part-time.
**Entrance requirements:** For master's and doctorate, GRE General Test, TOEFL, minimum GPA of 3.0. *Application deadline:* For fall admission, 1/15 (priority date); for winter admission, 9/30 (priority date); for spring admission, 12/30 (priority date). Applications are processed on a rolling basis. *Application fee:* $50. Electronic applications accepted.
**Expenses:** Tuition, state resident: full-time $5,539. Tuition, nonresident: full-time $14,376. Required fees: $390. Tuition and fees vary according to course load and program.
**Financial support:** In 2001–02, 42 students received support, including 4 fellowships with full tuition reimbursements available (averaging $8,375 per year), 24 research assistantships with full tuition reimbursements available (averaging $13,465 per year), 11 teaching assistantships with full tuition reimbursements available (averaging $13,275 per year); career-related internships or fieldwork, Federal Work-Study, institutionally sponsored loans, scholarships/grants, unspecified assistantships, and stipend supplements also available. Financial award application deadline: 1/15.
**Faculty research:** Processing, characterization and properties of all classes of materials, research on ceramics,

composites, metals, polymers and semiconductors. *Total annual research expenditures:* $1.2 million.
Dr. Rajendra K. Bordia, Chair, 206-543-2600, *Fax:* 206-543-3100, *E-mail:* bordia@u.washington.edu.
**Application contact:** Lara A. Davis, Academic Counselor, 206-616-6581, *Fax:* 206-543-3100, *E-mail:* mse@u.washington.edu. *Web site:* http://depts.washington.edu/mse/

## ■ UNIVERSITY OF WISCONSIN–MADISON

**Graduate School, College of Letters and Science, Department of Psychology, Program in Clinical Psychology, Madison, WI 53706-1380**

AWARDS PhD.

**Faculty:** 8 full-time (3 women).
**Students:** 26 full-time (18 women); includes 1 minority (African American), 2 international. Average age 23. 102 applicants, 6% accepted, 2 enrolled. In 2001, 3 doctorates awarded.
**Degree requirements:** For doctorate, thesis/dissertation, comprehensive exam, registration. *Median time to degree:* Doctorate–6 years full-time.
**Entrance requirements:** For doctorate, GRE General Test, minimum undergraduate GPA of 3.0. *Application deadline:* For fall admission, 1/5 (priority date). Applications are processed on a rolling basis. *Application fee:* $45. Electronic applications accepted.
**Expenses:** Tuition, state resident: full-time $7,361; part-time $399 per credit. Tuition, nonresident: full-time $20,499; part-time $1,282 per credit. Required fees: $34 per credit. Full-time tuition and fees vary according to course load, program, reciprocity agreements and student level.
**Financial support:** In 2001–02, 19 students received support, including 1 fellowship with full tuition reimbursement available (averaging $13,446 per year), 1 research assistantship with full tuition reimbursement available (averaging $13,814 per year), 4 teaching assistantships with full tuition reimbursements available (averaging $13,814 per year); career-related internships or fieldwork, institutionally sponsored loans, traineeships, health care benefits, and unspecified assistantships also available. Financial award application deadline: 1/5.
Joseph Newman, Chair, 608-262-3810, *Fax:* 608-262-2049, *E-mail:* jpnewman@facstaff.wisc.edu.
**Application contact:** Jane Fox-Anderson, Secretary, 608-262-2079, *Fax:* 608-262-4029, *E-mail:* jefoxand@facstaff.wisc.edu.

## ■ UNIVERSITY OF WISCONSIN–MILWAUKEE

**Graduate School, College of Letters and Sciences, Department of Psychology, Milwaukee, WI 53201-0413**

AWARDS Clinical psychology (MS, PhD); psychology (MS, PhD).

**Faculty:** 18 full-time (4 women).
**Students:** 55 full-time (38 women), 10 part-time (6 women); includes 4 minority (1 African American, 2 Asian Americans or Pacific Islanders, 1 Hispanic American), 3 international. 84 applicants, 26% accepted. In 2001, 3 master's, 8 doctorates awarded.
**Degree requirements:** For master's, thesis; for doctorate, variable foreign language requirement, thesis/dissertation.
**Entrance requirements:** For master's and doctorate, GRE General Test, GRE Subject Test. *Application deadline:* For fall admission, 1/1 (priority date); for spring admission, 9/1. Applications are processed on a rolling basis. *Application fee:* $45 ($75 for international students).
**Expenses:** Tuition, state resident: full-time $6,180; part-time $535 per credit. Tuition, nonresident: full-time $19,482; part-time $1,366 per credit. Tuition and fees vary according to course load, program and reciprocity agreements.
**Financial support:** In 2001–02, 7 fellowships, 2 research assistantships, 35 teaching assistantships were awarded. Career-related internships or fieldwork and unspecified assistantships also available. Support available to part-time students. Financial award application deadline: 4/15.
Douglas Woods, Representative, 414-229-4747, *Fax:* 414-229-5219, *E-mail:* dwoods@uwm.edu. *Web site:* http://www.uwm.edu/dept/psychology/

## ■ UTAH STATE UNIVERSITY

**School of Graduate Studies, College of Education, Department of Psychology, Logan, UT 84322**

AWARDS Clinical/counseling/school psychology (PhD); research and evaluation methodology (PhD); school counseling (MS); school psychology (MS). Part-time and evening/weekend programs available.
Postbaccalaureate distance learning degree programs offered (no on-campus study).

**Faculty:** 18 full-time (8 women), 40 part-time/adjunct (15 women).
**Students:** 55 full-time (31 women), 80 part-time (62 women); includes 10 minority (3 Asian Americans or Pacific Islanders, 1 Hispanic American, 6 Native Americans), 3 international. Average age 34. 138 applicants, 38% accepted. In 2001, 31 master's, 7 doctorates awarded.

Terminal master's awarded for partial completion of doctoral program.
**Degree requirements:** For master's, thesis (for some programs); for doctorate, thesis/dissertation.
**Entrance requirements:** For master's and doctorate, GRE General Test, TOEFL, minimum GPA of 3.5. *Application deadline:* For fall admission, 1/15; for spring admission, 10/15. Applications are processed on a rolling basis. *Application fee:* $40.
**Expenses:** Tuition, state resident: full-time $1,693. Tuition, nonresident: full-time $4,233. Required fees: $501. Tuition and fees vary according to program.
**Financial support:** In 2001–02, 5 fellowships with full and partial tuition reimbursements (averaging $12,000 per year), 25 research assistantships with full and partial tuition reimbursements (averaging $8,500 per year), 18 teaching assistantships with full and partial tuition reimbursements (averaging $7,000 per year) were awarded. Career-related internships or fieldwork, Federal Work-Study, institutionally sponsored loans, scholarships/grants, tuition waivers (partial), and unspecified assistantships also available. Financial award application deadline: 2/1.
**Faculty research:** Hearing loss detection in infancy, ADHD, eating disorders, domestic violence, neuropsychology.
David M. Stein, Head, 435-797-1460, *Fax:* 435-797-1448, *E-mail:* davids@coe.usu.edu.
**Application contact:** Sheila Jessie, Staff Assistant IV, 435-797-1449, *Fax:* 435-797-1448, *E-mail:* sheilaj@coe.usu.edu. *Web site:* http://www.coe.usu.edu/psyc/ndex.html

## ■ VALDOSTA STATE UNIVERSITY

**Graduate School, College of Education, Department of Psychology and Guidance, Valdosta, GA 31698**

AWARDS Clinical/counseling psychology (MS); industrial/organizational psychology (MS); school counseling (M Ed, Ed S); school psychology (M Ed, Ed S). Evening/weekend programs available.

**Faculty:** 13 full-time (2 women).
**Students:** 40 full-time (30 women), 62 part-time (54 women); includes 10 minority (7 African Americans, 1 Asian American or Pacific Islander, 1 Hispanic American, 1 Native American). Average age 26. 67 applicants, 75% accepted. In 2001, 17 degrees awarded.
**Degree requirements:** For master's, thesis or alternative, comprehensive written and/or oral exams; for Ed S, thesis.
**Entrance requirements:** For master's and Ed S, GRE General Test or MAT. *Application deadline:* For fall admission, 7/1; for spring admission, 11/15. Applications are

*Valdosta State University (continued)*
processed on a rolling basis. *Application fee:* $20. Electronic applications accepted.

**Expenses:** Tuition, state resident: full-time $1,746; part-time $97 per hour. Tuition, nonresident: full-time $6,966; part-time $387 per hour. Required fees: $594; $297 per semester.

**Financial support:** In 2001–02, 2 research assistantships with full tuition reimbursements (averaging $2,452 per year) were awarded; institutionally sponsored loans and unspecified assistantships also available. Support available to part-time students. Financial award application deadline: 7/1; financial award applicants required to submit FAFSA.

**Faculty research:** Using Bender-Gestalt to predict graphomotor dimensions of the draw-a-person test, neurobehavioral hemispheric dominance.

Dr. R. Bauer, Head, 229-333-5930, *Fax:* 229-259-5576, *E-mail:* bbauer@valdosta.edu.

---

■ **VALPARAISO UNIVERSITY**

**Graduate Division, Department of Psychology, Valparaiso, IN 46383-6493**

**AWARDS** Applied behavioral science (MA); clinical mental health counseling (MA); counseling (MA). Part-time and evening/weekend programs available.

**Students:** 14 full-time (10 women), 14 part-time (10 women); includes 2 minority (1 Asian American or Pacific Islander, 1 Hispanic American), 1 international. Average age 33. In 2001, 8 degrees awarded.

**Degree requirements:** For master's, thesis or alternative, internship.

**Entrance requirements:** For master's, GRE General Test (MA), minimum GPA of 3.0. *Application deadline:* Applications are processed on a rolling basis. *Application fee:* $30.

**Expenses:** Tuition: Full-time $5,400; part-time $300 per credit.

**Financial support:** Career-related internships or fieldwork, Federal Work-Study, and institutionally sponsored loans available. Financial award applicants required to submit FAFSA.

**Faculty research:** Sex roles, environmental psychology, human reproduction, treatment of adolescent assault victims, neuropsychological assessment.

Dr. Jody Esper, Chair, 219-464-5443, *E-mail:* jody.esper@valpo.edu.

**Application contact:** Graduate Division Office, 219-464-5313.

---

■ **VANGUARD UNIVERSITY OF SOUTHERN CALIFORNIA**

**Program in Clinical Psychology, Costa Mesa, CA 92626-6597**

**AWARDS** MS. Part-time and evening/weekend programs available.

**Faculty:** 2 full-time (1 woman), 2 part-time/adjunct (1 woman).

**Students:** 49 full-time (38 women), 17 part-time (11 women); includes 21 minority (4 African Americans, 3 Asian Americans or Pacific Islanders, 13 Hispanic Americans, 1 Native American), 1 international. Average age 29. 40 applicants, 95% accepted, 30 enrolled. In 2001, 10 degrees awarded.

**Degree requirements:** For master's, thesis or alternative. *Median time to degree:* Master's–2 years full-time.

**Entrance requirements:** For master's, minimum GPA of 3.0. *Application deadline:* For fall admission, 4/1 (priority date). *Application fee:* $30.

**Expenses:** Contact institution.

**Financial support:** In 2001–02, 63 students received support, including 22 research assistantships (averaging $3,000 per year), 22 teaching assistantships (averaging $3,000 per year); scholarships/grants and tuition waivers (full) also available. Financial award application deadline: 4/15; financial award applicants required to submit FAFSA.

**Faculty research:** Multiculturalism, Christian counseling, ethical issues, conflict resolution.

Dr. Martin Harris, Director, 714-556-3610 Ext. 409, *Fax:* 714-662-5226, *E-mail:* mharris@vanguard.edu.

**Application contact:** Tim Sorrick, Program Coordinator, 714-556-3610 Ext. 350, *Fax:* 714-662-5226, *E-mail:* gradpsychinfo@vanguard.edu. *Web site:* http://www.vanguard.edu/gradpsych/

---

■ **VIRGINIA COMMONWEALTH UNIVERSITY**

**School of Graduate Studies, College of Humanities and Sciences, Department of Psychology, Program in Clinical Psychology, Richmond, VA 23284-9005**

**AWARDS** PhD.

**Students:** 27 full-time, 14 part-time; includes 9 minority (3 African Americans, 3 Asian Americans or Pacific Islanders, 3 Hispanic Americans). 131 applicants, 8% accepted. In 2001, 5 doctorates awarded.

**Degree requirements:** For doctorate, thesis/dissertation.

**Entrance requirements:** For doctorate, GRE General Test. *Application deadline:* For fall admission, 1/15. *Application fee:* $30.

**Expenses:** Tuition, state resident: full-time $4,276; part-time $238 per credit. Tuition, nonresident: full-time $12,672; part-time $704 per credit. Required fees: $1,167; $43 per credit.

**Financial support:** Fellowships, research assistantships, teaching assistantships, Federal Work-Study, institutionally sponsored loans, and scholarships/grants available. Support available to part-time students.

Dr. Scott R. Vrana, Director, 804-828-8792, *Fax:* 804-828-2273.

**Application contact:** Clinical Program Assistant, 804-828-1158, *Fax:* 804-828-2237. *Web site:* http://www.vcu.edu/hasweb/psy/psych.html

---

■ **VIRGINIA POLYTECHNIC INSTITUTE AND STATE UNIVERSITY**

**Graduate School, College of Arts and Sciences, Department of Psychology, Blacksburg, VA 24061**

**AWARDS** Bio-behavioral sciences (PhD); clinical psychology (PhD); developmental psychology (PhD); industrial/organizational psychology (PhD); psychology (MS).

**Faculty:** 22 full-time (4 women), 3 part-time/adjunct (2 women).

**Students:** 68 full-time (45 women), 8 part-time (6 women); includes 13 minority (5 African Americans, 4 Asian Americans or Pacific Islanders, 4 Hispanic Americans). Average age 23. 156 applicants, 21% accepted, 15 enrolled. In 2001, 4 master's, 8 doctorates awarded.

**Degree requirements:** For doctorate, thesis/dissertation.

**Entrance requirements:** For master's and doctorate, GRE General Test, TOEFL. *Application deadline:* For fall admission, 1/15 (priority date); for winter admission, 12/15 (priority date). Applications are processed on a rolling basis. *Application fee:* $45. Electronic applications accepted.

**Expenses:** Tuition, state resident: part-time $241 per hour. Tuition, nonresident: part-time $406 per hour. Tuition and fees vary according to program.

**Financial support:** In 2001–02, 1 fellowship with tuition reimbursement (averaging $12,500 per year), 13 research assistantships with full tuition reimbursements (averaging $11,790 per year), 52 teaching assistantships with full tuition reimbursements (averaging $7,074 per year) were awarded. Unspecified assistantships also available. Financial award application deadline: 4/1.

**Faculty research:** Infant development from electrophysical point of view, work motivation and personnel selection, EEG, ERP and hypnosis with reference to chronic pain, intimate violence.

Dr. Jack W. Finney, Chair, 540-231-6581, *Fax:* 540-231-3652, *E-mail:* finney@vt.edu. *Web site:* http://www.psyc.vt.edu/

## ■ WASHBURN UNIVERSITY OF TOPEKA

College of Arts and Sciences, Department of Psychology, Topeka, KS 66621

**AWARDS** Clinical psychology (MA). Part-time programs available.

**Faculty:** 7 full-time (4 women), 2 part-time/adjunct (1 woman).

**Students:** 16 full-time (15 women), 2 part-time (both women); includes 3 minority (1 African American, 1 Asian American or Pacific Islander, 1 Hispanic American). Average age 25. 21 applicants, 81% accepted, 5 enrolled. In 2001, 3 degrees awarded.

**Degree requirements:** For master's, thesis. *Median time to degree:* Master's–2.5 years full-time, 3.5 years part-time.

**Entrance requirements:** For master's, GRE General Test, 15 hours of course work in psychology. *Application deadline:* For fall admission, 3/15; for spring admission, 12/1. *Application fee:* $0 ($60 for international students). Electronic applications accepted.

**Expenses:** Tuition, state resident: part-time $150 per credit hour. Tuition, nonresident: part-time $307 per credit hour. Required fees: $14 per semester.

**Financial support:** In 2001–02, 16 students received support, including 13 teaching assistantships (averaging $4,500 per year). Financial award application deadline: 3/15.

**Faculty research:** Treatment outcomes, childhood depression, mild depression, brief therapy, rural mental health. *Total annual research expenditures:* $14,000. Dr. Laura A. Stephenson, Chair, 785-231-1010 Ext. 1564, *Fax:* 785-231-1004, *E-mail:* zzdppy@washburn.edu. *Web site:* http://www.washburn.edu/cas/psychology/

## ■ WASHINGTON STATE UNIVERSITY

Graduate School, College of Liberal Arts, Department of Psychology, Pullman, WA 99164

**AWARDS** Clinical psychology (PhD); psychology (MS, PhD).

**Faculty:** 28 full-time (8 women), 2 part-time/adjunct (1 woman).

**Students:** 42 full-time (24 women), 3 part-time (1 woman); includes 5 minority (1 Asian American or Pacific Islander, 2 Hispanic Americans, 2 Native Americans), 3 international. Average age 28. In 2001, 9 master's, 5 doctorates awarded.

**Degree requirements:** For master's, thesis (for some programs), oral exam; for doctorate, thesis/dissertation, oral exam, written exam.

**Entrance requirements:** For master's and doctorate, GRE General Test, minimum GPA of 3.0. *Application deadline:* For fall admission, 1/1. Applications are processed on a rolling basis. *Application fee:* $35.

**Expenses:** Tuition, state resident: full-time $6,088; part-time $304 per semester. Tuition, nonresident: full-time $14,918; part-time $746 per semester. Tuition and fees vary according to program.

**Financial support:** In 2001–02, 4 research assistantships with full and partial tuition reimbursements, 39 teaching assistantships with full and partial tuition reimbursements were awarded. Fellowships, career-related internships or fieldwork, Federal Work-Study, institutionally sponsored loans, and unspecified assistantships also available. Financial award application deadline: 4/1; financial award applicants required to submit FAFSA. *Total annual research expenditures:* $303,373. Dr. Paul Whitney, Chair, 509-335-2631. **Application contact:** Graduate Admissions Chair, 509-335-2631, *Fax:* 509-335-5043, *E-mail:* psych@wsu.edu. *Web site:* http://www.wsu.edu:8080/~psych/index.html

## ■ WASHINGTON UNIVERSITY IN ST. LOUIS

Graduate School of Arts and Sciences, Department of Psychology, St. Louis, MO 63130-4899

**AWARDS** Clinical psychology (PhD); general experimental psychology (MA, PhD); social psychology (MA, PhD). Part-time programs available.

**Students:** 55 full-time (35 women); includes 4 minority (3 African Americans, 1 Asian American or Pacific Islander), 4 international. 171 applicants, 18% accepted. In 2001, 7 degrees awarded. Terminal master's awarded for partial completion of doctoral program.

**Degree requirements:** For master's, thesis or alternative; for doctorate, thesis/dissertation.

**Entrance requirements:** For master's and doctorate, GRE General Test. *Application deadline:* For fall admission, 1/15 (priority date). Applications are processed on a rolling basis. *Application fee:* $35. Electronic applications accepted.

**Expenses:** Tuition: Full-time $26,900.

**Financial support:** Fellowships, research assistantships, teaching assistantships, career-related internships or fieldwork, Federal Work-Study, institutionally sponsored loans, and tuition waivers (full and partial) available. Support available to part-time students. Financial award application deadline: 1/15. Dr. Henry L. Roediger, Chairperson, 314-935-6567. *Web site:* http://artsci.wustl.edu/~psych/

## ■ WAYNE STATE UNIVERSITY

Graduate School, College of Science, Department of Psychology, Program in Psychology, Detroit, MI 48202

**AWARDS** Clinical psychology (PhD); cognitive psychology (PhD); developmental psychology (PhD); industrial/organizational psychology (PhD); psychology (MA, PhD); social psychology (PhD).

**Students:** 114. In 2001, 22 master's, 23 doctorates awarded.

**Degree requirements:** For doctorate, thesis/dissertation.

**Entrance requirements:** For doctorate, GRE General Test, GRE Subject Test. *Application deadline:* For fall admission, 2/1. *Application fee:* $20 ($30 for international students). Electronic applications accepted.

**Expenses:** Tuition, state resident: full-time $3,764. Tuition and fees vary according to degree level and program.

**Financial support:** Application deadline: 2/1.

**Application contact:** Kathryn Urberg, Graduate Director, 313-577-2820, *Fax:* 313-577-7636, *E-mail:* kurberg@sun.science.wayne.edu.

## ■ WEST CHESTER UNIVERSITY OF PENNSYLVANIA

Graduate Studies, College of Arts and Sciences, Department of Psychology, West Chester, PA 19383

**AWARDS** Clinical psychology (MA); general psychology (MA); industrial organizational psychology (MA). Part-time and evening/weekend programs available.

**Faculty:** 11.

**Students:** 44 full-time (36 women), 23 part-time (15 women); includes 3 minority (all African Americans), 2 international. Average age 28. 107 applicants, 71% accepted. In 2001, 26 degrees awarded.

**Degree requirements:** For master's, thesis (for some programs), comprehensive exam.

**Entrance requirements:** For master's, GRE General Test or MAT, interview. *Application deadline:* For fall admission, 4/15 (priority date); for spring admission, 10/15. Applications are processed on a rolling basis. *Application fee:* $25.

**Expenses:** Tuition, state resident: full-time $4,600; part-time $256 per credit. Tuition, nonresident: full-time $7,554; part-time $420 per credit. Required fees: $44 per credit.

*West Chester University of Pennsylvania (continued)*

**Financial support:** In 2001–02, 10 research assistantships with full tuition reimbursements (averaging $5,000 per year) were awarded; unspecified assistantships also available. Support available to part-time students. Financial award application deadline: 2/15; financial award applicants required to submit FAFSA.

**Faculty research:** Animal learning and cognition.

Dr. Sandra Kerr, Chair, 610-436-2945.

**Application contact:** Dr. Deanne Bonifazi-Zotter, Graduate Coordinator, 610-436-3143, *E-mail:* dbonifazi@wcupa.edu.

### ■ WESTERN CAROLINA UNIVERSITY

**Graduate School, College of Education and Allied Professions, Department of Psychology, Program in Clinical Psychology, Cullowhee, NC 28723**

**AWARDS** MA. Part-time and evening/weekend programs available.

**Faculty:** 18 full-time (9 women).
**Students:** 16 full-time (14 women). 31 applicants, 35% accepted, 7 enrolled. In 2001, 8 degrees awarded.
**Degree requirements:** For master's, thesis, comprehensive exam.
**Entrance requirements:** For master's, GRE General Test. *Application deadline:* For fall admission, 2/1. *Application fee:* $35.
**Expenses:** Tuition, state resident: full-time $1,072. Tuition, nonresident: full-time $8,704. Required fees: $1,171.
**Financial support:** In 2001–02, 12 students received support, including 12 teaching assistantships with full and partial tuition reimbursements available (averaging $3,961 per year); fellowships, research assistantships with full and partial tuition reimbursements available, Federal Work-Study, institutionally sponsored loans, and scholarships/grants also available. Financial award application deadline: 3/15.
**Application contact:** Josie Bewsey, Assistant to the Dean, 828-227-7398, *Fax:* 828-227-7480, *E-mail:* jbewsey@email.wcu.edu. *Web site:* http://www.wcu.edu/ceap/psychology/psyhome.htm

### ■ WESTERN ILLINOIS UNIVERSITY

**School of Graduate Studies, College of Arts and Sciences, Department of Psychology, Macomb, IL 61455-1390**

**AWARDS** Clinical/community mental health (MS); general psychology (MS); psychology (MS, SSP); school psychology (SSP). Part-time programs available.

**Faculty:** 22 full-time (8 women).
**Students:** 45 full-time (34 women), 13 part-time (9 women), 1 international. Average age 33. 54 applicants, 54% accepted. In 2001, 12 master's, 5 other advanced degrees awarded.
**Degree requirements:** For master's, thesis or alternative.
**Entrance requirements:** For master's and SSP, GRE General Test. *Application deadline:* Applications are processed on a rolling basis. *Application fee:* $0 ($25 for international students). Electronic applications accepted.
**Expenses:** Tuition, state resident: part-time $108 per credit hour. Tuition, nonresident: part-time $216 per credit hour. Required fees: $33 per credit hour.
**Financial support:** In 2001–02, 40 students received support, including 40 research assistantships with full tuition reimbursements available (averaging $5,720 per year). Financial award applicants required to submit FAFSA.
**Faculty research:** Geriatric psychology, social psychology, psychology of women, embarrassability.
Dr. James Ackil, Chairperson, 309-298-1593.
**Application contact:** Dr. Barbara Baily, Director of Graduate Studies, 309-298-1806, *Fax:* 309-298-2345, *E-mail:* gradoffice@wiu.edu. *Web site:* http://www.wiu.edu/

### ■ WESTERN MICHIGAN UNIVERSITY

**Graduate College, College of Arts and Sciences, Department of Psychology, Kalamazoo, MI 49008-5202**

**AWARDS** Applied behavior analysis (MA, PhD); clinical psychology (MA, PhD); experimental analysis of behavior (PhD); experimental psychology (MA); industrial/organizational psychology (MA); school psychology (PhD, Ed S).

**Faculty:** 19 full-time (6 women).
**Students:** 94 full-time (68 women), 41 part-time (26 women); includes 10 minority (1 African American, 3 Asian Americans or Pacific Islanders, 6 Hispanic Americans), 12 international. 192 applicants, 31% accepted, 25 enrolled. In 2001, 21 master's, 6 doctorates, 6 other advanced degrees awarded.
**Degree requirements:** For master's, variable foreign language requirement, thesis, oral exams; for doctorate, 2 foreign languages, thesis/dissertation, oral exams, comprehensive exam; for Ed S, thesis, oral exams.
**Entrance requirements:** For master's, doctorate, and Ed S, GRE General Test.

*Application deadline:* For fall admission, 2/15. *Application fee:* $25.
**Expenses:** Tuition, state resident: part-time $186 per credit hour. Tuition, nonresident: part-time $442 per credit hour. Required fees: $602. One-time fee: $132 part-time. Tuition and fees vary according to course load.
**Financial support:** Fellowships, research assistantships, teaching assistantships, Federal Work-Study available. Financial award application deadline: 2/15; financial award applicants required to submit FAFSA.
R. Wayne Fuqua, Chairperson, 616-387-4498.
**Application contact:** Admissions and Orientation, 616-387-2000, *Fax:* 616-387-2355.

### ■ WESTFIELD STATE COLLEGE

**Division of Graduate Studies and Continuing Education, Program in Counseling/Clinical Psychology, Westfield, MA 01086**

**AWARDS** MA. Part-time and evening/weekend programs available.

**Faculty:** 9 part-time/adjunct (6 women).
**Students:** 22 full-time (20 women), 30 part-time (19 women). Average age 32. In 2001, 13 degrees awarded.
**Degree requirements:** For master's, comprehensive exam.
**Entrance requirements:** For master's, GRE General Test, MAT, minimum undergraduate GPA of 2.7. *Application deadline:* Applications are processed on a rolling basis. *Application fee:* $30.
**Expenses:** Tuition, state resident: part-time $155 per credit. Tuition, nonresident: part-time $165 per credit.
**Financial support:** In 2001–02, 5 research assistantships (averaging $1,600 per year) were awarded; teaching assistantships, career-related internships or fieldwork, Federal Work-Study, and tuition waivers (full and partial) also available. Support available to part-time students. Financial award application deadline: 4/1; financial award applicants required to submit CSS PROFILE.
Dr. Ricki Kantrowitz, Co-Director, 413-572-5376.
**Application contact:** Russ Leary, Admissions Clerk, 413-572-8022, *Fax:* 413-572-5227, *E-mail:* rleary@wisdom.wsc.mass.edu.

### ■ WEST VIRGINIA UNIVERSITY

**Eberly College of Arts and Sciences, Department of Psychology, Morgantown, WV 26506**

**AWARDS** Behavior analysis (PhD); clinical psychology (MA, PhD); development psychology (PhD). Part-time programs available.

**Faculty:** 23 full-time (8 women), 2 part-time/adjunct (both women).
**Students:** 53 full-time (40 women), 17 part-time (9 women); includes 6 minority (3 Asian Americans or Pacific Islanders, 2 Hispanic Americans, 1 Native American), 3 international. Average age 27. 306 applicants, 6% accepted. In 2001, 11 master's, 17 doctorates awarded. Terminal master's awarded for partial completion of doctoral program.
**Degree requirements:** For master's, thesis optional; for doctorate, thesis/dissertation, comprehensive exam.
**Entrance requirements:** For master's and doctorate, GRE General Test, TOEFL, minimum GPA of 3.0. *Application deadline:* For fall admission, 1/15. *Application fee:* $45.
**Expenses:** Tuition, state resident: full-time $2,791. Tuition, nonresident: full-time $8,659. Required fees: $1,002. Tuition and fees vary according to program.
**Financial support:** In 2001–02, 20 research assistantships, 30 teaching assistantships were awarded. Fellowships, career-related internships or fieldwork, Federal Work-Study, institutionally sponsored loans, and tuition waivers (full and partial) also available. Financial award application deadline: 1/15; financial award applicants required to submit FAFSA.
**Faculty research:** Adult and child clinical psychology, behavioral assessment and therapy, child and adolescent behavior, life span development, experimental and applied behavior analysis. *Total annual research expenditures:* $372,796.
Dr. Michael T. Perone, Chair, 304-293-2001 Ext. 604, *Fax:* 304-293-6606, *E-mail:* michael.perone@mail.wvu.edu.
**Application contact:** Dr. Katherine A. Karraker, Director, Graduate Training, 304-293-2001 Ext. 625, *Fax:* 304-293-6606, *E-mail:* katherine.karraker@mail.wvu.edu. *Web site:* http://www.as.wvu.edu/psyc/

### ■ WHEATON COLLEGE

**Graduate School, Department of Psychology, Wheaton, IL 60187-5593**
**AWARDS** Clinical psychology (MA, Psy D).

**Faculty:** 13 full-time (4 women), 4 part-time/adjunct (2 women).
**Students:** 126. 145 applicants, 53% accepted, 52 enrolled. In 2001, 44 master's, 13 doctorates awarded. Terminal master's awarded for partial completion of doctoral program.
**Degree requirements:** For master's, thesis or alternative; for doctorate, thesis/dissertation, internship.
**Entrance requirements:** For master's, GRE General Test, 18 hours of course work in psychology; for doctorate, GRE General Test.
**Expenses:** Tuition: Part-time $410 per hour.
**Financial support:** In 2001–02, 3 research assistantships (averaging $4,800 per year) were awarded; career-related internships or fieldwork, Federal Work-Study, scholarships/grants, and unspecified assistantships also available. Financial award application deadline: 6/1; financial award applicants required to submit FAFSA.
Dr. Cynthia Neal-Kimball, Chairman, 630-752-5758.
**Application contact:** Julie A. Huebner, Director of Graduate Admissions, 630-752-5195, *Fax:* 630-752-5935, *E-mail:* gradadm@wheaton.edu. *Web site:* http://www.wheaton.edu/psychology/psychology.html

### ■ WICHITA STATE UNIVERSITY

**Graduate School, Fairmount College of Liberal Arts and Sciences, Department of Psychology, Wichita, KS 67260**
**AWARDS** Community/clinical psychology (PhD); human factors (PhD); psychology (MA). Part-time programs available.

**Faculty:** 15 full-time (4 women).
**Students:** 44 full-time (35 women), 25 part-time (18 women); includes 6 minority (4 African Americans, 2 Asian Americans or Pacific Islanders), 1 international. Average age 33. 4 applicants, 0% accepted. In 2001, 9 master's, 8 doctorates awarded.
**Degree requirements:** For doctorate, thesis/dissertation.
**Entrance requirements:** For doctorate, GRE, TOEFL. *Application deadline:* For fall admission, 3/1 (priority date); for spring admission, 1/1. Applications are processed on a rolling basis. *Application fee:* $25 ($40 for international students). Electronic applications accepted.
**Expenses:** Tuition, state resident: full-time $1,888; part-time $105 per credit. Tuition, nonresident: full-time $6,129; part-time $341 per credit. Required fees: $345; $19 per credit. $17 per semester. Tuition and fees vary according to course load and program.
**Financial support:** In 2001–02, 14 research assistantships (averaging $6,202 per year), 53 teaching assistantships with full tuition reimbursements (averaging $4,062 per year) were awarded. Career-related internships or fieldwork, Federal Work-Study, institutionally sponsored loans, and unspecified assistantships also available. Support available to part-time students. Financial award application deadline: 4/1; financial award applicants required to submit FAFSA.

**Faculty research:** Behavioral evolution, women and alcohol, behavioral medicine, delinquency prevention.
Dr. Charles Burdsal, Chairperson, 316-978-3170, *Fax:* 316-978-3006, *E-mail:* charles.burdsal@wichita.edu. *Web site:* http://www.wichita.edu/

### ■ WIDENER UNIVERSITY

**School of Human Service Professions, Institute for Graduate Clinical Psychology, Program in Clinical Psychology, Chester, PA 19013-5792**
**AWARDS** Psy D, Psy D/M Ed, Psy D/MA, Psy D/MBA, Psy D/MHA, Psy D/MPA, Psy D/MSHR.

**Faculty:** 14 full-time (6 women), 24 part-time/adjunct (9 women).
**Students:** 193 full-time (153 women); includes 26 minority (12 African Americans, 9 Asian Americans or Pacific Islanders, 4 Hispanic Americans, 1 Native American). Average age 24. 233 applicants, 29% accepted, 32 enrolled. In 2001, 30 degrees awarded.
**Degree requirements:** For doctorate, thesis/dissertation, final oral and written qualifying exams. *Median time to degree:* Doctorate–5 years full-time.
**Entrance requirements:** For doctorate, GRE General Test or MAT. *Application deadline:* For fall admission, 12/31. *Application fee:* $75. Electronic applications accepted.
**Expenses:** Contact institution.
**Financial support:** In 2001–02, 185 students received support. Career-related internships or fieldwork, Federal Work-Study, institutionally sponsored loans, scholarships/grants, and stipends available. Financial award application deadline: 4/15.
**Faculty research:** Cognitive and personality diagnostic testing, depression, child and adolescent competencies, learning disabilities, family therapy.
Dr. Virginia Brabender, Associate Dean/Director, 610-499-1208, *Fax:* 610-499-4625, *E-mail:* graduate.psychology@widener.edu.
**Application contact:** Maureen A. Brennan, Admissions Coordinator, 610-499-1206, *Fax:* 610-499-4625, *E-mail:* maureen.a.brennan@widener.edu. *Web site:* http://muse.widener.edu/graduate/

**Find an in-depth description at www.petersons.com/gradchannel.**

### ■ WIDENER UNIVERSITY

**School of Human Service Professions, Institute for Graduate Clinical Psychology, Program in Clinical Psychology and Health and Medical Services Administration, Chester, PA 19013-5792**
**AWARDS** Psy D/MBA, Psy D/MHA.

*Widener University (continued)*
Electronic applications accepted.
**Expenses:** Tuition: Part-time $500 per credit. Required fees: $25 per semester.
**Faculty research:** Psychosocial competence, family systems, medical care systems and financing.
**Find an in-depth description at www.petersons.com/gradchannel.**

### ■ WILLIAM PATERSON UNIVERSITY OF NEW JERSEY

**College of the Humanities and Social Sciences, Program in Applied Clinical Psychology, Wayne, NJ 07470-8420**
**AWARDS** MA.

**Students:** 18 full-time (14 women), 7 part-time (5 women); includes 6 minority (2 Asian Americans or Pacific Islanders, 4 Hispanic Americans). 47 applicants, 43% accepted, 14 enrolled. In 2001, 2 degrees awarded.
**Entrance requirements:** For master's, GRE General Test. *Application deadline:* For fall admission, 3/1. Applications are processed on a rolling basis. *Application fee:* $35. Electronic applications accepted.
**Expenses:** Tuition, state resident: part-time $322 per credit. Tuition, nonresident: part-time $468 per credit.
**Financial support:** Research assistantships with full tuition reimbursements available. Financial award application deadline: 4/1; financial award applicants required to submit FAFSA.
Dr. Bernaz Pakizegi, Program Director, 973-720-2643.
**Application contact:** Danielle Liautaud, Graduate Admissions Counselor, 973-720-3579, *Fax:* 973-720-2035, *E-mail:* liautaudd@wpunj.edu. *Web site:* http://www.wpunj.edu/

### ■ WISCONSIN SCHOOL OF PROFESSIONAL PSYCHOLOGY

**Program in Clinical Psychology, Milwaukee, WI 53225-4960**
**AWARDS** MA, Psy D. Part-time and evening/weekend programs available.

**Faculty:** 3 full-time (all women), 32 part-time/adjunct (13 women).
**Students:** 14 full-time (all women), 31 part-time (27 women); includes 6 minority (3 African Americans, 1 Asian American or Pacific Islander, 2 Hispanic Americans), 1 international. Average age 38. 40 applicants, 23% accepted. In 2001, 6 master's, 8 doctorates awarded. Terminal master's awarded for partial completion of doctoral program.
**Degree requirements:** For master's, candidacy exam, 500 hours of supervised clinical practica; for doctorate, thesis/

dissertation, 1 year clinical internship, 2000 hours of supervised clinical practicum experience, candidacy exam, clinical exam. *Median time to degree:* Master's–2 years full-time, 4 years part-time; doctorate–5 years full-time, 8 years part-time.
**Entrance requirements:** For master's, GRE General Test, GRE Subject Test, bachelor's degree in psychology, sample of written work; for doctorate, GRE General Test, GRE Subject Test, master's degree in clinical psychology or equivalent, sample of written work. *Application deadline:* For fall admission, 4/15 (priority date); for spring admission, 10/15 (priority date). Applications are processed on a rolling basis. *Application fee:* $100.
**Expenses:** Tuition: Part-time $550 per credit hour.
**Financial support:** In 2001–02, 6 students received support. Clinical service assistantships, library aid assistantships available. Support available to part-time students.
**Faculty research:** Violence prevention, psychology of women, forensic psychology, custody evaluation, aging, harm reduction in AODA.
**Application contact:** Karen A. Kilman, Assistant to the President, 414-464-9777, *Fax:* 414-358-5590, *E-mail:* karen-wspp@msn.com. *Web site:* http://www.execpe.com/~wspp

### ■ WRIGHT STATE UNIVERSITY

**School of Professional Psychology, Dayton, OH 45435**
**AWARDS** Clinical psychology (Psy D).

**Faculty:** 21 full-time (5 women), 2 part-time/adjunct (1 woman).
**Students:** 105 full-time (72 women), 2 part-time (1 woman); includes 30 minority (20 African Americans, 3 Asian Americans or Pacific Islanders, 7 Hispanic Americans), 9 international. Average age 29. In 2001, 20 degrees awarded.
**Degree requirements:** For doctorate, thesis/dissertation.
**Entrance requirements:** For doctorate, GRE General Test, GRE Subject Test, TOEFL. *Application deadline:* For fall admission, 12/15. *Application fee:* $30.
**Expenses:** Contact institution.
**Financial support:** In 2001–02, 30 fellowships with full tuition reimbursements were awarded; teaching assistantships, career-related internships or fieldwork, Federal Work-Study, institutionally sponsored loans, and unspecified assistantships also available. Financial award application deadline: 4/15; financial award applicants required to submit FAFSA.
Dr. John R. Rusisill, Dean, 937-775-3490, *Fax:* 937-775-3434, *E-mail:* john.rudisill@wright.edu.

**Application contact:** Leona L. Gray, Director, Student Services/Admissions, 937-775-3492, *Fax:* 937-775-3493, *E-mail:* leona.gray@wright.edu. *Web site:* http://www.wright.edu/sopp/

### ■ XAVIER UNIVERSITY

**College of Social Sciences, Department of Psychology, Cincinnati, OH 45207**
**AWARDS** Clinical psychology (Psy D); psychology (MA).

**Faculty:** 14 full-time (7 women), 7 part-time/adjunct (4 women).
**Students:** 102 full-time (82 women), 5 part-time (3 women); includes 10 minority (5 African Americans, 2 Asian Americans or Pacific Islanders, 2 Hispanic Americans, 1 Native American). Average age 28. 118 applicants, 53% accepted. In 2001, 33 master's awarded. Terminal master's awarded for partial completion of doctoral program.
**Degree requirements:** For master's, one foreign language, thesis, practicum; for doctorate, one foreign language, thesis/dissertation, internship, practicum. *Median time to degree:* Master's–2 years full-time, 3 years part-time; doctorate–5 years full-time, 7 years part-time.
**Entrance requirements:** For master's, GRE, minimum GPA of 3.3, 18 hours in psychology; for doctorate, GRE, 18 hours in psychology or master's degree in clinical psychology, minimum GPA of 3.5. *Application deadline:* For fall admission, 1/15 (priority date). *Application fee:* $35.
**Expenses:** Contact institution.
**Financial support:** In 2001–02, 34 students received support, including 24 research assistantships with full tuition reimbursements available (averaging $1,500 per year), 16 teaching assistantships with full tuition reimbursements available (averaging $1,500 per year); career-related internships or fieldwork, scholarships/grants, and traineeships also available. Financial award application deadline: 4/1.
**Faculty research:** Cognitive development in children, weight management, psychodiagnostics, psychotherapy.
Dr. Christine M. Dacey, Chair, 513-745-1033, *Fax:* 513-745-3327, *E-mail:* dacey@xu.edu.
**Application contact:** Margaret Maybury, Coordinator, 513-745-1053, *Fax:* 513-745-3327, *E-mail:* maybury@xu.edu. *Web site:* http://www.xu.edu/psychology_grad.index.htm

*Bronx @ 1300 Morris Park Ave.*

## ■ YESHIVA UNIVERSITY

**Ferkauf Graduate School of Psychology, Program in Clinical Psychology, New York, NY 10033-3201**

**AWARDS** Psy D. Part-time programs available.

**Faculty:** 12 full-time (6 women), 22 part-time/adjunct (15 women).
**Students:** 125 full-time (89 women), 18 part-time (13 women); includes 17 minority (2 African Americans, 3 Asian Americans or Pacific Islanders, 12 Hispanic Americans), 13 international. Average age 26. 325 applicants, 7% accepted. In 2001, 29 degrees awarded.
**Degree requirements:** For doctorate, thesis/dissertation.
**Entrance requirements:** For doctorate, GRE General Test. *Application deadline:* For fall admission, 1/15. *Application fee:* $50.
**Financial support:** In 2001–02, 18 fellowships (averaging $5,000 per year), 8 research assistantships (averaging $2,000 per year), 40 teaching assistantships (averaging $2,000 per year) were awarded. Career-related internships or fieldwork, Federal Work-Study, institutionally sponsored loans, and scholarships/grants also available. Support available to part-time students. Financial award application deadline: 4/15.
**Faculty research:** Psychotherapy, family therapy, psychoanalysis, cognitive behavior therapy.
Dr. Lawrence J. Siegel, Acting Director, 718-430-3941, *E-mail:* lsiegel@aecom.yu.edu.
**Application contact:** Elaine Schwartz, Assistant Director of Admissions, 718-430-3820, *Fax:* 718-430-3960, *E-mail:* eschart@ymail.yu.edu. *Web site:* http://www.yu.edu/fgs/

## ■ YESHIVA UNIVERSITY

**Ferkauf Graduate School of Psychology, Program in School/Clinical-Child Psychology, New York, NY 10033-3201**

**AWARDS** Psy D. Part-time programs available.

**Faculty:** 8 full-time (6 women), 13 part-time/adjunct (7 women).
**Students:** 93 full-time (62 women), 32 part-time (19 women); includes 23 minority (8 African Americans, 3 Asian Americans or Pacific Islanders, 12 Hispanic Americans), 9 international. Average age 27. 135 applicants, 24% accepted. In 2001, 34 degrees awarded.
**Degree requirements:** For doctorate, thesis/dissertation.

**Entrance requirements:** For doctorate, GRE General Test. *Application deadline:* For fall admission, 1/15. *Application fee:* $50.
**Financial support:** In 2001–02, 85 students received support, including 15 fellowships (averaging $5,000 per year), research assistantships (averaging $2,000 per year), 25 teaching assistantships (averaging $2,000 per year); career-related internships or fieldwork, Federal Work-Study, institutionally sponsored loans, and scholarships/grants also available. Support available to part-time students. Financial award application deadline: 4/15.
**Faculty research:** Testing, early childhood intervention, child and adolescent psychotherapy, clinical child psychology. Dr. Abraham Givner, Director, 718-430-3945, *E-mail:* givner@aecom.yu.edu.
**Application contact:** Elaine Schwartz, Assistant Director of Admissions, 718-430-3820, *Fax:* 718-430-3960, *E-mail:* eschart@ymail.yu.edu. *Web site:* http://www.yu.edu/fgs/

# COGNITIVE SCIENCES

## ■ ARIZONA STATE UNIVERSITY

**Graduate College, College of Liberal Arts and Sciences, Department of Psychology, Tempe, AZ 85287**

**AWARDS** Behavioral neuroscience (PhD); clinical psychology (PhD); cognitive/behavioral systems (PhD); developmental psychology (PhD); environmental psychology (PhD); quantitative research methods (PhD); social psychology (PhD).

**Degree requirements:** For doctorate, thesis/dissertation.
**Entrance requirements:** For doctorate, GRE General Test, GRE Subject Test.
**Faculty research:** Reduction of personal stress, cognitive aspects of motor skills training, behavior analysis and treatment of depression.

## ■ BALL STATE UNIVERSITY

**Graduate School, College of Sciences and Humanities, Department of Psychological Science, Program in Cognitive and Social Processes, Muncie, IN 47306-1099**

**AWARDS** MA.

**Students:** 7 full-time (4 women), 3 part-time (2 women). In 2001, 3 degrees awarded.
**Expenses:** Tuition, state resident: full-time $4,068; part-time $2,542. Tuition, nonresident: full-time $10,944; part-time $6,462. Required fees: $1,000; $500 per term.

Dr. Kerri Pickel, Graduate Program Director, 765-285-1690, *Fax:* 765-285-8980, *E-mail:* kpickel@bsu.edu.

## ■ BOSTON UNIVERSITY

**Graduate School of Arts and Sciences, Department of Cognitive and Neural Systems, Boston, MA 02215**

**AWARDS** MA, PhD.

**Students:** 47 full-time (6 women), 8 part-time (2 women); includes 1 minority (Asian American or Pacific Islander), 29 international. Average age 30. 56 applicants, 57% accepted, 14 enrolled. Terminal master's awarded for partial completion of doctoral program.
**Degree requirements:** For master's, one foreign language, registration; for doctorate, one foreign language, thesis/dissertation, qualifying exam.
**Entrance requirements:** For master's and doctorate, GRE General Test, GRE Subject Test (recommended), TOEFL, 3 letters of recommendation. *Application deadline:* For fall admission, 5/1; for spring admission, 11/15. *Application fee:* $60.
**Expenses:** Tuition: Full-time $25,872; part-time $340 per credit. Required fees: $40 per semester. Part-time tuition and fees vary according to class time, course level and program.
**Financial support:** In 2001–02, 34 students received support, including 3 fellowships with full tuition reimbursements available (averaging $14,000 per year), 29 research assistantships with full tuition reimbursements available, 2 teaching assistantships with full tuition reimbursements available; Federal Work-Study and unspecified assistantships also available. Support available to part-time students. Financial award application deadline: 1/15; financial award applicants required to submit FAFSA.
Stephen Grossberg, Chairman, 617-353-7858, *Fax:* 617-353-7755, *E-mail:* steve@bu.edu.
**Application contact:** Carol Y. Jefferson, Administrative Assistant, 617-353-9481, *Fax:* 617-353-7755, *E-mail:* caroly@bu.edu. *Web site:* http://cns-web.bu.edu/

## ■ BRANDEIS UNIVERSITY

**Graduate School of Arts and Sciences, Department of Psychology, Waltham, MA 02454-9110**

**AWARDS** Cognitive neuroscience (PhD); general psychology (MA); social/developmental psychology (PhD). Part-time programs available.

**Faculty:** 18 full-time (4 women), 6 part-time/adjunct (3 women).

*Brandeis University (continued)*
**Students:** 25 full-time (18 women); includes 8 minority (1 African American, 5 Asian Americans or Pacific Islanders, 2 Hispanic Americans). Average age 29. 69 applicants, 35% accepted. In 2001, 4 master's, 2 doctorates awarded. Terminal master's awarded for partial completion of doctoral program.
**Degree requirements:** For master's and doctorate, thesis/dissertation.
**Entrance requirements:** For master's, GRE General Test; for doctorate, GRE General Test, GRE Subject Test. *Application deadline:* Applications are processed on a rolling basis. *Application fee:* $60. Electronic applications accepted.
**Expenses:** Tuition: Full-time $27,392. Required fees: $35.
**Financial support:** In 2001–02, 16 students received support, including 12 fellowships with full tuition reimbursements available (averaging $13,600 per year), 4 research assistantships with partial tuition reimbursements available (averaging $2,000 per year); scholarships/grants, traineeships, and tuition waivers (partial) also available. Support available to part-time students. Financial award application deadline: 5/1; financial award applicants required to submit CSS PROFILE or FAFSA.
**Faculty research:** Development, cognition, social aging, perception. *Total annual research expenditures:* $2.2 million. Margie Lachman, Director of Graduate Studies, 781-736-3255, *Fax:* 781-736-3291, *E-mail:* lachman@brandeis.edu.
**Application contact:** Janice Steinberg, Graduate Admissions Coordinator, 781-736-3303, *Fax:* 781-736-3291, *E-mail:* steinberg@brandeis.edu. *Web site:* http://www.brandeis.edu/departments/psych/

■ **BROWN UNIVERSITY**
**Graduate School, Department of Cognitive and Linguistic Sciences, Providence, RI 02912**
**AWARDS** Cognitive science (Sc M, PhD); linguistics (AM, PhD).
**Degree requirements:** For master's, one foreign language, thesis or alternative; for doctorate, 2 foreign languages, thesis/dissertation.

■ **CARNEGIE MELLON UNIVERSITY**
**College of Humanities and Social Sciences, Department of Psychology, Area of Cognitive Neuropsychology, Pittsburgh, PA 15213-3891**
**AWARDS** PhD.
**Degree requirements:** For doctorate, thesis/dissertation, comprehensive exam.

**Entrance requirements:** For doctorate, GRE General Test, TOEFL, TSE.

■ **CARNEGIE MELLON UNIVERSITY**
**College of Humanities and Social Sciences, Department of Psychology, Area of Cognitive Psychology, Pittsburgh, PA 15213-3891**
**AWARDS** PhD.
**Degree requirements:** For doctorate, thesis/dissertation, comprehensive exam.
**Entrance requirements:** For doctorate, GRE General Test, TOEFL, TSE.

■ **CLAREMONT GRADUATE UNIVERSITY**
**Graduate Programs, School of Behavioral and Organizational Sciences, Department of Psychology, Claremont, CA 91711-6160**
**AWARDS** Cognitive psychology (MA, PhD); developmental psychology (MA, PhD); organizational behavior (MA, PhD); program design, management, and evaluation (MA); social environmental psychology (PhD); social psychology (MA). Part-time programs available.
**Faculty:** 6 full-time (2 women), 7 part-time/adjunct (6 women).
**Students:** 127 full-time (93 women), 23 part-time (19 women); includes 48 minority (8 African Americans, 23 Asian Americans or Pacific Islanders, 15 Hispanic Americans, 2 Native Americans), 9 international. Average age 30. In 2001, 25 master's, 16 doctorates awarded. Terminal master's awarded for partial completion of doctoral program.
**Degree requirements:** For master's, thesis (for some programs); for doctorate, thesis/dissertation, comprehensive exam.
**Entrance requirements:** For master's and doctorate, GRE General Test. *Application deadline:* For fall admission, 2/15 (priority date). Applications are processed on a rolling basis. *Application fee:* $50. Electronic applications accepted.
**Expenses:** Tuition: Full-time $22,984; part-time $1,000 per unit. Required fees: $160; $80 per semester.
**Financial support:** Fellowships, research assistantships, teaching assistantships, career-related internships or fieldwork, Federal Work-Study, institutionally sponsored loans, and tuition waivers (full and partial) available. Support available to part-time students. Financial award application deadline: 2/15; financial award applicants required to submit FAFSA.
**Faculty research:** Social intervention, diversity in organizations, eyewitness memory, aging and cognition, drug policy.

**Application contact:** Jessica Johnson, Program Coordinator, 909-621-8084, *Fax:* 909-621-8905, *E-mail:* jessica.johnson@cgu.edu. *Web site:* http://www.cgu.edu/sbus
**Find an in-depth description at www.petersons.com/gradchannel.**

■ **COLLEGE OF STATEN ISLAND OF THE CITY UNIVERSITY OF NEW YORK**
**Graduate Programs, Center for Developmental Neuroscience and Developmental Disabilities, Subprogram in Learning Processes, Staten Island, NY 10314-6600**
**AWARDS** Biopsychology (PhD); clinical psychology (PhD); developmental psychology (PhD); environmental psychology (PhD); experimental cognition (PhD); experimental psychology (PhD); neuropsychology (PhD); psychology (PhD); social-personality psychology (PhD).
**Degree requirements:** For doctorate, one foreign language, thesis/dissertation.
**Entrance requirements:** For doctorate, GRE, TOEFL. *Application deadline:* For fall admission, 3/15 (priority date). Applications are processed on a rolling basis. *Application fee:* $40.
**Expenses:** Tuition, state resident: full-time $4,350; part-time $185 per credit. Tuition, nonresident: full-time $7,600; part-time $320 per credit. Required fees: $53 per semester.
**Financial support:** Fellowships, research assistantships, teaching assistantships, career-related internships or fieldwork and institutionally sponsored loans available. Financial award application deadline: 3/15. Dr. Nancy Hemmes, Head, 718-997-3561.

■ **COLORADO STATE UNIVERSITY**
**Graduate School, College of Natural Sciences, Department of Psychology, Fort Collins, CO 80523-0015**
**AWARDS** Applied social psychology (PhD); behavioral neuroscience (PhD); cognitive psychology (PhD); counseling psychology (PhD); industrial-organizational psychology (PhD).
**Faculty:** 29 full-time (8 women), 13 part-time/adjunct (7 women).
**Students:** 56 full-time (42 women), 37 part-time (29 women). Average age 29. 309 applicants, 12% accepted, 16 enrolled. In 2001, 9 doctorates awarded.
**Degree requirements:** For doctorate, thesis/dissertation.
**Entrance requirements:** For doctorate, GRE General Test, GRE Subject Test, TOEFL, minimum GPA of 3.5. *Application*

*deadline:* For fall admission, 1/15. *Application fee:* $30. Electronic applications accepted.
**Expenses:** Tuition, state resident: full-time $2,880; part-time $160 per credit. Tuition, nonresident: full-time $11,412; part-time $634 per credit. Required fees: $750; $34 per credit.
**Financial support:** In 2001–02, 3 fellowships with full tuition reimbursements (averaging $12,120 per year), 10 research assistantships with full tuition reimbursements (averaging $9,720 per year), 52 teaching assistantships with full tuition reimbursements (averaging $9,720 per year) were awarded. Career-related internships or fieldwork, Federal Work-Study, institutionally sponsored loans, scholarships/grants, and traineeships also available.
**Faculty research:** Environmental psychology, cognitive learning, health psychology, occupations of health. *Total annual research expenditures:* $12.5 million.
Ernest L. Chavez, Chair, 970-491-6363, *Fax:* 970-491-1032, *E-mail:* echavez@lamar.colostate.edu.
**Application contact:** Wendy Standring, Graduate Admissions Coordinator, 970-491-6363, *Fax:* 970-491-1032, *E-mail:* wendyann@lamar.colostate.edu. *Web site:* http://www.colostate.edu/Depts/Psychology/

### ■ DARTMOUTH COLLEGE

**School of Arts and Sciences, Department of Psychological and Brain Sciences, Hanover, NH 03755**
**AWARDS** Cognitive neuroscience (PhD); psychology (PhD).
**Faculty:** 23 full-time (3 women).
**Students:** 26 full-time (18 women); includes 1 minority (Native American), 4 international. 94 applicants, 16% accepted, 8 enrolled. In 2001, 1 doctorate awarded.
**Degree requirements:** For doctorate, thesis/dissertation.
**Entrance requirements:** For doctorate, GRE General Test, GRE Subject Test. *Application deadline:* For fall admission, 1/15 (priority date). *Application fee:* $40.
**Expenses:** Tuition: Full-time $26,425.
**Financial support:** In 2001–02, 26 students received support, including fellowships with full tuition reimbursements available (averaging $17,380 per year), research assistantships with full tuition reimbursements available (averaging $17,380 per year); Federal Work-Study, institutionally sponsored loans, and tuition waivers (full) also available.
Dr. Howard C. Hughes, Chair, 603-646-3181, *Fax:* 603-646-1419, *E-mail:* howard.hughes@dartmouth.edu.

**Application contact:** Tina Mason, Administrative Assistant, 603-646-3181. *Web site:* http://www.dartmouth.edu/artsci/psych/grad.html

### ■ DUKE UNIVERSITY

**Graduate School, Department of Psychology, Durham, NC 27708-0586**
**AWARDS** Biological psychology (PhD); clinical psychology (PhD); cognitive psychology (PhD); developmental psychology (PhD); experimental psychology (PhD); health psychology (PhD); human social development (PhD).
**Faculty:** 52 full-time, 15 part-time/adjunct.
**Students:** 66 full-time (42 women); includes 11 minority (6 African Americans, 2 Asian Americans or Pacific Islanders, 3 Hispanic Americans), 13 international. 386 applicants, 7% accepted, 15 enrolled. In 2001, 8 doctorates awarded.
**Degree requirements:** For doctorate, thesis/dissertation.
**Entrance requirements:** For doctorate, GRE General Test. *Application deadline:* For fall admission, 12/31. *Application fee:* $75.
**Expenses:** Tuition: Full-time $24,600.
**Financial support:** Fellowships, research assistantships, teaching assistantships, career-related internships or fieldwork and Federal Work-Study available. Financial award application deadline: 12/31.
Reiko Mazuka, Co-Director of Graduate Studies, 919-660-5716, *Fax:* 919-660-5726, *E-mail:* bseymore@acpub.duke.edu. *Web site:* http://www.psych.duke.edu/

### ■ EMORY UNIVERSITY

**Graduate School of Arts and Sciences, Department of Psychology, Atlanta, GA 30322-1100**
**AWARDS** Clinical psychology (PhD); cognition and development (PhD); psychobiology (PhD).
**Faculty:** 26 full-time (6 women), 2 part-time/adjunct (0 women).
**Students:** 73 full-time (55 women); includes 5 minority (1 African American, 2 Asian Americans or Pacific Islanders, 2 Hispanic Americans), 6 international. 272 applicants, 6% accepted, 13 enrolled. In 2001, 10 doctorates awarded.
**Degree requirements:** For doctorate, thesis/dissertation, comprehensive exam, registration.
**Entrance requirements:** For doctorate, GRE General Test, TOEFL, minimum GPA of 3.0. *Application deadline:* For fall admission, 1/15. *Application fee:* $50. Electronic applications accepted.
**Expenses:** Tuition: Full-time $24,770. Required fees: $100. Tuition and fees vary according to program and student level.

**Financial support:** In 2001–02, 56 fellowships were awarded; research assistantships, teaching assistantships, career-related internships or fieldwork, Federal Work-Study, institutionally sponsored loans, scholarships/grants, and tuition waivers (full and partial) also available. Financial award application deadline: 1/20.
**Faculty research:** Neurophysiology, drugs and behavior, hormones and behavior, nonverbal behavior.
Dr. Darryl Neill, Chair, 404-727-7437.
**Application contact:** Dr. Robyn Fivush, Director of Graduate Studies, 404-727-7456, *E-mail:* psyrf@emory.edu.

### ■ FLORIDA STATE UNIVERSITY

**Graduate Studies, College of Arts and Sciences, Department of Psychology, Program in Cognitive and Behavioral Science, Tallahassee, FL 32306**
**AWARDS** PhD.
**Faculty:** 11 full-time (2 women).
**Students:** 26 full-time (15 women); includes 1 minority (Hispanic American), 1 international. Average age 26. 40 applicants, 25% accepted, 2 enrolled. In 2001, 3 doctorates awarded.
**Degree requirements:** For doctorate, thesis/dissertation, preliminary exam. *Median time to degree:* Doctorate–2.3 years full-time.
**Entrance requirements:** For doctorate, GRE General Test, minimum GPA of 3.0, research experience, letters of recommendation. *Application deadline:* For fall admission, 12/15. *Application fee:* $20. Electronic applications accepted.
**Expenses:** Tuition, state resident: part-time $163 per credit hour. Tuition, nonresident: part-time $570 per credit hour. Tuition and fees vary according to program.
**Financial support:** In 2001–02, 16 students received support, including fellowships with full tuition reimbursements available (averaging $15,000 per year), 12 research assistantships with full tuition reimbursements available (averaging $12,500 per year), 11 teaching assistantships with full tuition reimbursements available (averaging $12,600 per year); institutionally sponsored loans, traineeships, and unspecified assistantships also available. Financial award applicants required to submit FAFSA.
**Faculty research:** Memory, learning and reading disabilities, social influences on behavior, applied behavior analysis, expert performance. *Total annual research expenditures:* $1.9 million.
Dr. Rolf Zwaan, Director, 850-644-2768, *Fax:* 850-644-7739, *E-mail:* zwaan@psy.fsu.edu.

*Florida State University (continued)*
**Application contact:** Cherie P. Dilworth, Graduate Secretary, 850-644-2499, *Fax:* 850-644-7739, *E-mail:* grad-info@psy.fsu.edu.

## ■ THE GEORGE WASHINGTON UNIVERSITY

**Columbian College of Arts and Sciences, Department of Psychology, Washington, DC 20052**

**AWARDS** Applied social psychology (PhD); clinical psychology (PhD, Psy D); cognitive neuropsychology (PhD); industrial-organizational psychology (PhD). Part-time and evening/weekend programs available.

**Faculty:** 15 full-time (8 women), 1 (woman) part-time/adjunct.
**Students:** 133 full-time (106 women), 102 part-time (82 women); includes 50 minority (22 African Americans, 13 Asian Americans or Pacific Islanders, 14 Hispanic Americans, 1 Native American), 15 international. Average age 30. 413 applicants, 18% accepted. In 2001, 32 doctorates awarded.
**Degree requirements:** For doctorate, thesis/dissertation or alternative, general exam.
**Entrance requirements:** For doctorate, GRE General Test, minimum GPA of 3.0. *Application fee:* $55.
**Expenses:** Tuition: Part-time $810 per credit. Required fees: $1 per credit.
**Financial support:** In 2001–02, 27 students received support, including 22 fellowships with tuition reimbursements available (averaging $4,700 per year), 20 teaching assistantships with tuition reimbursements available (averaging $2,900 per year); career-related internships or fieldwork and Federal Work-Study also available. Financial award application deadline: 2/1.
Dr. Rolf Peterson, Chair, 202-994-6544. *Web site:* http://www.gwu.edu/~gradinfo/

## ■ GEORGIA INSTITUTE OF TECHNOLOGY

**Graduate Studies and Research, Ivan Allen College of Policy and International Affairs, Multidisciplinary Program in Human Computer Interaction, Atlanta, GA 30332-0001**

**AWARDS** MSHCI.

**Entrance requirements:** For master's, TOEFL.

## ■ GRADUATE SCHOOL AND UNIVERSITY CENTER OF THE CITY UNIVERSITY OF NEW YORK

**Graduate Studies, Program in Psychology, New York, NY 10016-4039**

**AWARDS** Basic applied neurocognition (PhD); biopsychology (PhD); clinical psychology (PhD); developmental psychology (PhD); environmental psychology (PhD); experimental psychology (PhD); industrial psychology (PhD); learning processes (PhD); neuropsychology (PhD); psychology (PhD); social personality (PhD).

**Faculty:** 119 full-time (40 women).
**Students:** 463 full-time (335 women), 4 part-time (2 women); includes 96 minority (39 African Americans, 20 Asian Americans or Pacific Islanders, 36 Hispanic Americans, 1 Native American), 47 international. Average age 33. 493 applicants, 24% accepted, 65 enrolled. In 2001, 28 degrees awarded.
**Degree requirements:** For doctorate, one foreign language, thesis/dissertation.
**Entrance requirements:** For doctorate, GRE General Test. *Application deadline:* For fall admission, 2/1. *Application fee:* $40.
**Expenses:** Tuition, state resident: part-time $245 per credit. Tuition, nonresident: part-time $425 per credit. Required fees: $72 per semester.
**Financial support:** In 2001–02, 226 students received support, including 141 fellowships, 14 research assistantships, 4 teaching assistantships; career-related internships or fieldwork, Federal Work-Study, institutionally sponsored loans, and tuition waivers (full and partial) also available. Financial award application deadline: 2/1; financial award applicants required to submit FAFSA.
Dr. Joseph Glick, Executive Officer, 212-817-8706, *Fax:* 212-817-1533, *E-mail:* jglick@gc.cuny.edu.

## ■ HARVARD UNIVERSITY

**Graduate School of Arts and Sciences, Department of Psychology, Cambridge, MA 02138**

**AWARDS** Psychology (AM, PhD), including behavior and decision analysis, cognition, developmental psychology, experimental psychology, personality, psychobiology, psychopathology; social psychology (AM, PhD).

**Degree requirements:** For doctorate, thesis/dissertation, general exams.
**Entrance requirements:** For master's and doctorate, GRE General Test, TOEFL.
**Expenses:** Tuition: Full-time $23,370. Required fees: $816. Full-time tuition and fees vary according to program and student level.

## ■ HARVARD UNIVERSITY

**Graduate School of Education, Area of Human Development and Psychology, Cambridge, MA 02138**

**AWARDS** Gender studies (Ed M); human development and psychology (Ed M, Ed D, CAS); individualized program (Ed M); language and literacy (Ed M, Ed D, CAS); mind brain and education (Ed M); risk and prevention (Ed M, CAS). Part-time programs available.

**Faculty:** 13 full-time (7 women), 33 part-time/adjunct (12 women).
**Students:** 243 full-time (204 women), 37 part-time (31 women); includes 59 minority (21 African Americans, 16 Asian Americans or Pacific Islanders, 18 Hispanic Americans, 4 Native Americans), 35 international. Average age 32. 162 applicants, 21% accepted. In 2001, 118 master's, 18 doctorates, 2 other advanced degrees awarded. Terminal master's awarded for partial completion of doctoral program.
**Degree requirements:** For doctorate, thesis/dissertation.
**Entrance requirements:** For master's, GRE General Test or MAT, TOEFL, TWE; for doctorate and CAS, GRE General Test, TOEFL, TWE. *Application deadline:* For fall admission, 1/2. *Application fee:* $65.
**Financial support:** In 2001–02, 146 students received support, including 22 fellowships (averaging $19,708 per year), 5 research assistantships, 106 teaching assistantships (averaging $3,733 per year); career-related internships or fieldwork, Federal Work-Study, and scholarships/grants also available. Support available to part-time students. Financial award application deadline: 2/3; financial award applicants required to submit FAFSA.
**Faculty research:** Educational technologies; reading, writing, and language; risk and prevention of developmental and educational problems; bilingualism and multicultural education; gender difference in development.
Dr. Robert L. Selman, Chair, 617-495-3414.
**Application contact:** Roland A. Hence, Director of Admissions, 617-495-3414, *Fax:* 617-496-3577, *E-mail:* gseadmissions@harvard.edu. *Web site:* http://gse.harvard.edu/

## ■ HUNTER COLLEGE OF THE CITY UNIVERSITY OF NEW YORK

**Graduate School, School of Arts and Sciences, Department of Psychology, New York, NY 10021-5085**

**AWARDS** Applied and evaluative psychology (MA); biopsychology and comparative psychology (MA); social, cognitive, and developmental psychology (MA). Part-time and evening/weekend programs available.

**Faculty:** 21 full-time (10 women), 8 part-time/adjunct (4 women).

**Students:** 3 full-time (2 women), 14 part-time (11 women); includes 5 minority (1 African American, 4 Hispanic Americans), 1 international. Average age 27. 53 applicants, 47% accepted, 5 enrolled. In 2001, 5 degrees awarded.

**Degree requirements:** For master's, thesis, comprehensive exam. *Median time to degree:* Master's–3.5 years part-time.

**Entrance requirements:** For master's, GRE General Test, TOEFL, minimum 12 credits in psychology, including statistics and experimental psychology. *Application deadline:* For fall admission, 4/1; for spring admission, 11/1. Applications are processed on a rolling basis. *Application fee:* $40.

**Expenses:** Tuition, state resident: full-time $2,175; part-time $185 per credit. Tuition, nonresident: full-time $3,800; part-time $320 per credit.

**Faculty research:** Personality, cognitive and linguistic development, hormonal and neural control of behavior, gender and culture, social cognition of health and attitudes.

Dr. Darlene DeFour, Acting Chairperson.
**Application contact:** William Zlata, Director for Graduate Admissions, 212-772-4288, *Fax:* 212-650-3336, *E-mail:* admissions@hunter.cuny.edu. *Web site:* http://maxweber.hunter.cuny.edu/psych/

## ■ INDIANA UNIVERSITY BLOOMINGTON

**Graduate School, College of Arts and Sciences, Department of Psychology, Bloomington, IN 47405**

**AWARDS** Biology and behavior (PhD); clinical science (PhD); cognitive psychology (PhD); developmental psychology (PhD); social psychology (PhD). Offered through the University Graduate School.

**Faculty:** 40 full-time (7 women), 1 (woman) part-time/adjunct.

**Students:** 42 full-time (23 women), 37 part-time (18 women); includes 9 minority (2 African Americans, 5 Asian Americans or Pacific Islanders, 2 Hispanic Americans), 9 international. Average age 28. 222 applicants, 14% accepted. In 2001, 18 doctorates awarded.

**Degree requirements:** For doctorate, thesis/dissertation, 1st- and 2nd-year projects, 1 year as associate instructor, qualifying exam.

**Entrance requirements:** For doctorate, GRE, TOEFL. *Application deadline:* For fall admission, 12/15. *Application fee:* $45 ($55 for international students). Electronic applications accepted.

**Expenses:** Tuition, state resident: full-time $4,720; part-time $197 per credit. Tuition, nonresident: full-time $13,748; part-time $573 per credit. Required fees: $642.
**Financial support:** In 2001–02, 8 fellowships (averaging $14,000 per year), 24 teaching assistantships (averaging $11,800 per year) were awarded.
Dr. Joseph E. Steinmetz, Chairperson, 812-855-3991, *Fax:* 812-855-4691, *E-mail:* steinmet@indiana.edu.
**Application contact:** Beth Laske-Miller, Graduate Admissions Assistant, 812-855-2014, *Fax:* 812-855-4691, *E-mail:* psychgrd@indiana.edu. *Web site:* http://www.indiana.edu/~psych/

## ■ IOWA STATE UNIVERSITY OF SCIENCE AND TECHNOLOGY

**Graduate College, College of Liberal Arts and Sciences, Department of Psychology, Ames, IA 50011**

**AWARDS** Cognitive psychology (PhD); counseling psychology (PhD); general psychology (MS); social psychology (PhD). Terminal master's awarded for partial completion of doctoral program.

**Degree requirements:** For master's, thesis or alternative; for doctorate, thesis/dissertation.

**Entrance requirements:** For master's and doctorate, GRE General Test, GRE Subject Test (psychology), TOEFL. Electronic applications accepted.

**Expenses:** Tuition, state resident: full-time $1,851. Tuition, nonresident: full-time $5,449. Tuition and fees vary according to program.

**Faculty research:** Counseling psychology, cognitive psychology, social psychology, health psychology, psychology and public policy. *Web site:* http://psych-server.iastate.edu/

## ■ JOHNS HOPKINS UNIVERSITY

**Zanvyl Krieger School of Arts and Sciences, Department of Cognitive Science, Baltimore, MD 21218-2699**

**AWARDS** PhD.

**Faculty:** 8 full-time (3 women).
**Students:** 17 full-time (10 women); includes 4 minority (3 Asian Americans or Pacific Islanders, 1 Hispanic American), 3 international. Average age 25. 72 applicants, 18% accepted, 5 enrolled. In 2001, 2 doctorates awarded.

**Degree requirements:** For doctorate, one foreign language, thesis/dissertation, registration.

**Entrance requirements:** For doctorate, GRE General Test, TOEFL. *Application deadline:* For fall admission, 1/15. *Application fee:* $55. Electronic applications accepted.

**Expenses:** Tuition: Full-time $27,390.
**Financial support:** In 2001–02, 3 fellowships, 14 research assistantships, 3 teaching assistantships were awarded. Federal Work-Study and institutionally sponsored loans also available. Financial award application deadline: 4/15; financial award applicants required to submit FAFSA.
**Faculty research:** Cognitive neuropsychology, neuroscience, linguistics computation, language acquisition and psycholinguistics, perception and attention, theoretical linguistics (syntax and phonology). *Total annual research expenditures:* $646,991.
Dr. Luigi Burzio, Chair, 410-516-7214, *Fax:* 410-516-4896, *E-mail:* burzio@cogsci.jhu.edu.
**Application contact:** Barbara Fisher, Secretary, 410-516-5250, *Fax:* 410-516-8020, *E-mail:* inquire@mail.cog.jhu.edu. *Web site:* http://www.hebb.coq.jhu.edu/

## ■ LOUISIANA STATE UNIVERSITY AND AGRICULTURAL AND MECHANICAL COLLEGE

**Graduate School, College of Arts and Sciences, Department of Psychology, Baton Rouge, LA 70803**

**AWARDS** Biological psychology (MA, PhD); clinical psychology (MA, PhD); cognitive psychology (MA, PhD); developmental psychology (MA, PhD); industrial/organizational psychology (MA, PhD); school psychology (MA, PhD).

**Faculty:** 25 full-time (7 women).
**Students:** 70 full-time (53 women), 43 part-time (24 women); includes 7 minority (3 African Americans, 2 Asian Americans or Pacific Islanders, 2 Hispanic Americans), 2 international. Average age 30. 179 applicants, 12% accepted, 20 enrolled. In 2001, 19 degrees awarded. Terminal master's awarded for partial completion of doctoral program.
**Degree requirements:** For master's, thesis; for doctorate, thesis/dissertation, 1 year internship.
**Entrance requirements:** For master's and doctorate, GRE General Test, minimum GPA of 3.0. *Application deadline:* For fall admission, 1/25 (priority date). Applications are processed on a rolling basis. *Application fee:* $25.
**Expenses:** Tuition, state resident: full-time $2,551. Tuition, nonresident: full-time $5,551. Required fees: $854. Part-time tuition and fees vary according to course load.
**Financial support:** In 2001–02, 1 fellowship (averaging $14,333 per year), 10 research assistantships with partial tuition reimbursements (averaging $14,200 per year), 33 teaching assistantships with

*Louisiana State University and Agricultural and Mechanical College (continued)*
partial tuition reimbursements (averaging $10,371 per year) were awarded. Career-related internships or fieldwork, institutionally sponsored loans, and contracts also available. Financial award applicants required to submit FAFSA. *Total annual research expenditures:* $242,157.
Dr. Irving Lane, Chair, 225-578-8745, *Fax:* 225-578-4125, *E-mail:* irvlane@unix1.sncc.lsu.edu.
**Application contact:** Dr. Janet McDonald, Coordinator of Graduate Studies, 225-578-4116, *Fax:* 225-578-4125, *E-mail:* psmcdo@lsu.edu. *Web site:* http://www.artsci.lsu.edu/psych

## ■ MASSACHUSETTS INSTITUTE OF TECHNOLOGY

**School of Science, Department of Brain and Cognitive Sciences, Cambridge, MA 02139-4307**

**AWARDS** Cellular/molecular neuroscience (PhD); cognitive neuroscience (PhD); cognitive science (PhD); computational cognitive science (PhD); computational neuroscience (PhD); systems neuroscience (PhD).

**Faculty:** 26 full-time (6 women).
**Students:** 58 full-time (15 women); includes 5 minority (1 African American, 4 Asian Americans or Pacific Islanders), 17 international. Average age 26. 257 applicants, 10% accepted, 11 enrolled. In 2001, 5 doctorates awarded.
**Degree requirements:** For doctorate, thesis/dissertation, comprehensive exam.
**Entrance requirements:** For doctorate, GRE General Test, TOEFL. *Application deadline:* For fall admission, 1/1. *Application fee:* $60. Electronic applications accepted.
**Expenses:** Tuition: Full-time $26,960. Full-time tuition and fees vary according to program.
**Financial support:** In 2001–02, 58 students received support, including 43 fellowships (averaging $20,000 per year), 6 research assistantships (averaging $21,600 per year), 20 teaching assistantships (averaging $16,650 per year); Federal Work-Study, institutionally sponsored loans, scholarships/grants, health care benefits, and unspecified assistantships also available. Financial award application deadline: 1/1; financial award applicants required to submit FAFSA.
**Faculty research:** Vision, learning and memory, motor control, plasticity. *Total annual research expenditures:* $12.1 million.
Mriganka Sur, Head, 617-253-8784.
**Application contact:** Denise Heintze, Academic Administrator, 617-253-5742,

*Fax:* 617-253-9767, *E-mail:* bcsadmiss@mit.edu. *Web site:* http://web.mit.edu/bcs
**Find an in-depth description at www.petersons.com/gradchannel.**

## ■ NEW MEXICO HIGHLANDS UNIVERSITY

**Graduate Studies, College of Arts and Sciences, Program in Media Arts and Computer Science, Las Vegas, NM 87701**

**AWARDS** Cognitive science (MA, MS); computer graphics (MA, MS); design studies (MA); digital audio and video production (MA); multimedia systems (MS); networking technology (MA, MS).

**Faculty:** 13 full-time (2 women).
**Students:** 10 full-time (4 women), 8 part-time (6 women); includes 5 minority (all Hispanic Americans), 6 international. Average age 34. In 2001, 2 degrees awarded.
**Expenses:** Tuition, state resident: full-time $2,238. Tuition, nonresident: full-time $9,366.
**Financial support:** Research assistantships with full and partial tuition reimbursements available.
Dr. Tomas Salazar, Dean, 505-454-3080, *Fax:* 505-454-3389, *E-mail:* salazar_t@nmhu.edu.
**Application contact:** Dr. Linda LaGrange, Associate Dean of Graduate Studies, 505-454-3266, *Fax:* 505-454-3558, *E-mail:* lagrange_l@nmhu.edu.

## ■ NEW YORK UNIVERSITY

**Graduate School of Arts and Science, Department of Psychology, New York, NY 10012-1019**

**AWARDS** Clinical psychology (PhD); cognition and perception (PhD); community psychology (PhD); general psychology (MA); industrial/organizational psychology (MA, MA); psychoanalysis (Advanced Certificate); social/personality psychology (PhD). Part-time programs available.

**Faculty:** 38 full-time (13 women), 78 part/adjunct.
**Students:** 118 full-time (85 women), 304 part-time (235 women); includes 64 minority (14 African Americans, 27 Asian Americans or Pacific Islanders, 22 Hispanic Americans, 1 Native American), 49 international. Average age 28. 586 applicants, 44% accepted, 101 enrolled. In 2001, 67 master's, 22 doctorates awarded. Terminal master's awarded for partial completion of doctoral program.
**Degree requirements:** For master's, thesis or alternative, comprehensive exam; for doctorate, thesis/dissertation.
**Entrance requirements:** For master's, GRE General Test, minimum GPA of 3.0; for doctorate, GRE General Test, GRE

Subject Test; for Advanced Certificate, doctoral degree, minimum GPA of 3.0. *Application deadline:* For fall admission, 1/4. *Application fee:* $60.
**Expenses:** Tuition: Full-time $19,536; part-time $814 per credit. Required fees: $1,330; $38 per credit. Tuition and fees vary according to course load and program.
**Financial support:** Fellowships with tuition reimbursements, research assistantships with tuition reimbursements, teaching assistantships with tuition reimbursements, career-related internships or fieldwork, Federal Work-Study, institutionally sponsored loans, and traineeships available. Financial award application deadline: 1/4; financial award applicants required to submit FAFSA.
**Faculty research:** Vision, memory, social cognition, social and cognitive development, relationships.
Marisa Carrasco, Chair, 212-998-7900.
**Application contact:** Susan Andersen, Director of Graduate Studies, 212-998-7900, *Fax:* 212-995-4018, *E-mail:* psychquery@psych.nyu.edu. *Web site:* http://www.psych.nyu.edu/

## ■ NORTHWESTERN UNIVERSITY

**The Graduate School, Judd A. and Marjorie Weinberg College of Arts and Sciences, Department of Psychology, Evanston, IL 60208**

**AWARDS** Brain, behavior and cognition (PhD); clinical psychology (PhD); cognitive psychology (PhD); personality (PhD); social psychology (PhD). Admissions and degrees offered through The Graduate School. Part-time programs available.

**Faculty:** 22 full-time (6 women).
**Students:** 45 full-time (26 women); includes 4 minority (2 Asian Americans or Pacific Islanders, 2 Hispanic Americans), 14 international. Average age 25. 197 applicants, 14% accepted. In 2001, 5 doctorates awarded.
**Degree requirements:** For doctorate, thesis/dissertation. *Median time to degree:* Doctorate–5 years full-time.
**Entrance requirements:** For doctorate, GRE General Test, GRE Subject Test, TOEFL, TSE. *Application deadline:* For fall admission, 12/31. *Application fee:* $50 ($55 for international students). Electronic applications accepted.
**Expenses:** Tuition: Full-time $26,526.
**Financial support:** In 2001–02, 12 fellowships with full tuition reimbursements (averaging $16,800 per year), 3 research assistantships with partial tuition reimbursements (averaging $13,419 per year), 22 teaching assistantships with full tuition reimbursements (averaging $13,419 per year) were awarded. Career-related

internships or fieldwork, Federal Work-Study, institutionally sponsored loans, and tuition waivers (full and partial) also available. Financial award application deadline: 12/31; financial award applicants required to submit FAFSA.

**Faculty research:** Memory and higher order cognition, anxiety and depression, effectiveness of psychotherapy, social cognition, molecular basis of memory. *Total annual research expenditures:* $2.6 million.

Douglas L. Medin, Chair, 847-491-7406, *Fax:* 847-491-7859, *E-mail:* medin@ northwestern.edu.

**Application contact:** Florence S. Sales, Secretary, 847-491-7406, *Fax:* 847-491-7859, *E-mail:* f-sales@northwestern.edu. *Web site:* http:// www.psych.northwestern.edu/

### ■ THE OHIO STATE UNIVERSITY

**Graduate School, College of Social and Behavioral Sciences, Department of Psychology, Columbus, OH 43210**

**AWARDS** Clinical psychology (PhD); cognitive/experimental psychology (PhD); counseling psychology (PhD); developmental psychology (PhD); mental retardation and developmental disabilities (PhD); psychobiology (PhD); quantitative psychology (PhD); social psychology (PhD).

**Degree requirements:** For doctorate, thesis/dissertation.

**Entrance requirements:** For doctorate, GRE General Test, TOEFL.

### ■ THE PENNSYLVANIA STATE UNIVERSITY UNIVERSITY PARK CAMPUS

**Graduate School, College of Liberal Arts, Department of Psychology, State College, University Park, PA 16802-1503**

**AWARDS** Clinical psychology (MS, PhD); cognitive psychology (MS, PhD); developmental psychology (MS, PhD); industrial/organizational psychology (MS, PhD); psychobiology (MS, PhD); social psychology (MS, PhD).

**Students:** 126 full-time (83 women), 12 part-time (7 women). In 2001, 15 master's, 14 doctorates awarded.

**Degree requirements:** For master's and doctorate, thesis/dissertation.

**Entrance requirements:** For master's and doctorate, GRE General Test, GRE Subject Test. *Application fee:* $45.

**Expenses:** Tuition, state resident: full-time $7,882; part-time $333 per credit. Tuition, nonresident: full-time $16,142; part-time $673 per credit. Required fees: $124 per semester.

**Financial support:** Fellowships, research assistantships, teaching assistantships available.

Dr. Keith Crnic, Head, 814-863-1721.

### ■ RUTGERS, THE STATE UNIVERSITY OF NEW JERSEY, NEWARK

**Graduate School, Department of Psychology, Newark, NJ 07102**

**AWARDS** Cognitive science (PhD); perception (PhD); psychobiology (PhD); social cognition (PhD). Part-time and evening/weekend programs available.

**Students:** 34 applicants, 59% accepted. In 2001, 2 doctorates awarded.

**Degree requirements:** For doctorate, thesis/dissertation, comprehensive exam.

**Entrance requirements:** For doctorate, GRE Subject Test, minimum undergraduate B average. *Application deadline:* For fall admission, 2/1 (priority date); for spring admission, 11/1. Applications are processed on a rolling basis. *Application fee:* $50. Electronic applications accepted.

**Financial support:** In 2001–02, 12 students received support, including 11 fellowships with full tuition reimbursements available (averaging $13,000 per year), 9 teaching assistantships with full tuition reimbursements available (averaging $13,700 per year); research assistantships, career-related internships or fieldwork, Federal Work-Study, and minority scholarships also available. Support available to part-time students. Financial award application deadline: 3/1.

**Faculty research:** Visual perception (luminance, motion), neuroendocrine mechanisms in behavior (reproduction, pain), attachment theory, connectionist modeling of cognition. *Total annual research expenditures:* $300,000.

Dr. Maggie Shiffrar, Director, 973-353-5971, *Fax:* 973-353-1171, *E-mail:* mag@ psychology.rutgers.edu. *Web site:* http:// www.psych.rutgers.edu/

**Find an in-depth description at www.petersons.com/gradchannel.**

### ■ RUTGERS, THE STATE UNIVERSITY OF NEW JERSEY, NEW BRUNSWICK

**Graduate School, Program in Psychology, New Brunswick, NJ 08901-1281**

**AWARDS** Biopsychology and behavioral neuroscience (PhD); clinical psychology (PhD); cognitive psychology (PhD); interdisciplinary developmental psychology (PhD); interdisciplinary health psychology (PhD); social psychology (PhD).

**Students:** Average age 24. 423 applicants, 11% accepted. In 2001, 13 degrees awarded.

**Degree requirements:** For doctorate, thesis/dissertation.

**Entrance requirements:** For doctorate, GRE General Test. *Application deadline:* For fall admission, 12/15. *Application fee:* $50.

**Financial support:** In 2001–02, 68 students received support, including 18 fellowships with full tuition reimbursements available (averaging $15,000 per year), 13 research assistantships with full tuition reimbursements available (averaging $14,000 per year), 43 teaching assistantships with full tuition reimbursements available (averaging $13,800 per year); career-related internships or fieldwork, Federal Work-Study, scholarships/grants, and traineeships also available. Financial award application deadline: 12/15.

Dr. G. Terence Wilson, Director, 732-445-2556, *Fax:* 732-445-2263.

**Application contact:** Joan Olmizzi, Administrative Assistant, 732-445-2555, *Fax:* 732-445-2263, *E-mail:* joan@psych-b.rutgers.edu. *Web site:* http:// psychology.rutgers.edu/

### ■ STATE UNIVERSITY OF NEW YORK AT BINGHAMTON

**Graduate School, School of Arts and Sciences, Department of Psychology, Specialization in Cognitive and Behavioral Science, Binghamton, NY 13902-6000**

**AWARDS** MA, PhD.

**Students:** 19 full-time (10 women), 4 part-time (1 woman); includes 3 minority (1 Asian American or Pacific Islander, 2 Hispanic Americans), 2 international. Average age 26. 22 applicants, 36% accepted, 4 enrolled. In 2001, 3 master's, 1 doctorate awarded.

**Degree requirements:** For master's, thesis; for doctorate, thesis/dissertation, departmental qualifying exam.

**Entrance requirements:** For master's and doctorate, GRE General Test, GRE Subject Test, TOEFL. *Application deadline:* For fall admission, 4/15 (priority date); for spring admission, 11/1. Applications are processed on a rolling basis. Electronic applications accepted.

**Expenses:** Tuition, state resident: full-time $5,100; part-time $213 per credit. Tuition, nonresident: full-time $8,416; part-time $351 per credit. Required fees: $811.

**Financial support:** In 2001–02, 19 students received support, including 2 fellowships with full tuition reimbursements available (averaging $9,425 per year), 5 research assistantships (averaging $12,520

*State University of New York at Binghamton (continued)*

per year), 12 teaching assistantships with full tuition reimbursements available (averaging $10,980 per year); career-related internships or fieldwork, Federal Work-Study, institutionally sponsored loans, and unspecified assistantships also available. Support available to part-time students. Financial award application deadline: 2/15.

Dr. Cynthia Connine, Graduate Coordinator, 607-777-2286.

■ **TEMPLE UNIVERSITY**

**Graduate School, College of Liberal Arts, Department of Psychology, Program in Cognitive Psychology, Philadelphia, PA 19122-6096**

**AWARDS** PhD.

**Degree requirements:** For doctorate, thesis/dissertation.

**Entrance requirements:** For doctorate, GRE General Test, minimum GPA of 3.0. Electronic applications accepted.

**Expenses:** Tuition, state resident: full-time $8,487; part-time $369 per credit hour. Tuition, nonresident: full-time $12,282; part-time $534 per credit hour. Required fees: $350. Tuition and fees vary according to course load, program and reciprocity agreements.

**Faculty research:** Language development, creativity, childhood memory, visual perception, aging.

**Find an in-depth description at www.petersons.com/gradchannel.**

■ **UNIVERSITY AT BUFFALO, THE STATE UNIVERSITY OF NEW YORK**

**Graduate School, College of Arts and Sciences, Department of Psychology, Buffalo, NY 14260**

**AWARDS** Behavioral neuroscience (PhD); clinical psychology (PhD); cognitive psychology (PhD); general psychology (MA); social-personality (PhD). Part-time programs available.

**Faculty:** 28 full-time (13 women), 2 part-time/adjunct (1 woman).

**Students:** 88 full-time (52 women), 13 part-time (8 women); includes 11 minority (5 African Americans, 3 Asian Americans or Pacific Islanders, 3 Hispanic Americans), 12 international. Average age 25. 122 applicants, 31% accepted, 16 enrolled. In 2001, 13 master's, 6 doctorates awarded. Terminal master's awarded for partial completion of doctoral program. **Degree requirements:** For master's, project; for doctorate, thesis/dissertation. **Entrance requirements:** For master's and doctorate, GRE General Test, TOEFL.

*Application deadline:* For fall admission, 1/5. *Application fee:* $35. Electronic applications accepted.

**Expenses:** Tuition, state resident: full-time $6,118. Tuition, nonresident: full-time $9,434.

**Financial support:** In 2001–02, 37 students received support, including 4 fellowships with full tuition reimbursements available (averaging $14,000 per year), 10 research assistantships with full tuition reimbursements available (averaging $9,512 per year), 37 teaching assistantships with full tuition reimbursements available (averaging $8,400 per year); career-related internships or fieldwork, Federal Work-Study, institutionally sponsored loans, tuition waivers (partial), and minority fellowships also available. Financial award application deadline: 1/15; financial award applicants required to submit FAFSA.

**Faculty research:** Neural, endocrine, and molecular bases of behavior; adult mood and anxiety disorders; relationship dysfunction; behavioral medicine; attention deficit/hyperactivity disorder. *Total annual research expenditures:* $2.1 million.

Dr. Jack A. Meacham, Chair, 716-645-3650 Ext. 203, *Fax:* 716-645-3801, *E-mail:* meacham@acsu.buffalo.edu.

**Application contact:** Michele Nowacki, Coordinator of Admissions, 716-645-3650 Ext. 209, *Fax:* 716-695-3801, *E-mail:* psych@acsu.buffalo.edu. *Web site:* http://wings.buffalo.edu/psychology/

■ **THE UNIVERSITY OF AKRON**

**Graduate School, Buchtel College of Arts and Sciences, Department of Psychology, Program in Applied Cognitive Aging, Akron, OH 44325-0001**

**AWARDS** MA, PhD.

**Students:** 12 full-time (10 women), 2 part-time (1 woman); includes 1 minority (Native American). Average age 30. 6 applicants, 50% accepted, 3 enrolled. In 2001, 2 degrees awarded.

**Degree requirements:** For master's, thesis or specialty exam; for doctorate, one foreign language, thesis/dissertation, comprehensive exam.

**Entrance requirements:** For master's, GRE General Test, GRE Subject Test, minimum GPA of 2.75; for doctorate, GRE General Test, GRE Subject Test. *Application deadline:* For fall admission, 3/1. Applications are processed on a rolling basis. *Application fee:* $40 ($50 for international students).

**Expenses:** Tuition, state resident: full-time $6,562; part-time $219 per credit. Tuition, nonresident: full-time $9,027; part-time $383 per credit. Required fees: $272; $11

per credit. Tuition and fees vary according to course load.

**Financial support:** Fellowships with full tuition reimbursements, research assistantships with full tuition reimbursements, teaching assistantships with full tuition reimbursements available. Financial award application deadline: 3/1.

**Faculty research:** Changes in memory and cognition with age, automaticity and effects of training, use of direct measures to assess strategy and knowledge.

Dr. Martin D. Murphy, Chair, 330-972-8374, *E-mail:* mmurphy@uakron.edu.

**Application contact:** Dr. Raymond E. Sanders, Head, 330-972-8376, *E-mail:* rsanders@uakron.edu.

■ **THE UNIVERSITY OF ALABAMA**

**Graduate School, College of Arts and Sciences, Department of Psychology, Tuscaloosa, AL 35487**

**AWARDS** Clinical psychology (PhD); cognitive psychology (PhD); general psychology (MA).

**Faculty:** 23 full-time (11 women), 2 part-time/adjunct (0 women).

**Students:** 63 full-time (47 women), 11 part-time (8 women); includes 10 minority (8 African Americans, 1 Hispanic American, 1 Native American), 3 international. Average age 27. 182 applicants, 12% accepted, 17 enrolled. In 2001, 8 master's, 12 doctorates awarded.

**Degree requirements:** For doctorate, thesis/dissertation, internship (clinical psychology).

**Entrance requirements:** For doctorate, GRE General Test, minimum GPA of 3.0. *Application deadline:* For fall admission, 1/1. *Application fee:* $25. Electronic applications accepted.

**Expenses:** Tuition, state resident: full-time $3,292; part-time $183 per credit hour. Tuition, nonresident: full-time $8,912; part-time $495 per credit hour. Tuition and fees vary according to course load, campus/location and program.

**Financial support:** In 2001–02, 6 fellowships with full tuition reimbursements (averaging $10,000 per year), 16 research assistantships with full tuition reimbursements (averaging $10,400 per year), 15 teaching assistantships with full tuition reimbursements (averaging $8,433 per year) were awarded. Career-related internships or fieldwork, institutionally sponsored loans, and scholarships/grants also available. Financial award application deadline: 2/1.

**Faculty research:** Health psychology and social behavior, cognitive development/retardation, adult clinical psychology, child clinical/pediatrics, psychology and law.

Dr. Robert Lyman, Chairperson, 205-348-1913, *Fax:* 205-348-8648, *E-mail:* blyman@gp.as.ua.edu.
**Application contact:** Dr. Forrest Scogin, Director of Graduate Studies, 205-348-1924, *Fax:* 205-348-8648, *E-mail:* fscogin@gp.as.ua.edu. *Web site:* http://www.as.ua.edu/psychology/

### ■ UNIVERSITY OF CALIFORNIA, SAN DIEGO

**Graduate Studies and Research, Department of Cognitive Science, La Jolla, CA 92093**

**AWARDS** PhD.

**Faculty:** 19 full-time (6 women), 4 part-time/adjunct (2 women).
**Students:** 33 full-time (13 women), 1 part-time; includes 9 minority (5 Asian Americans or Pacific Islanders, 4 Hispanic Americans). Average age 24. 102 applicants, 18% accepted, 9 enrolled. In 2001, 1 doctorate awarded.
**Degree requirements:** For doctorate, one foreign language, thesis/dissertation.
**Entrance requirements:** For doctorate, GRE General Test. *Application deadline:* For fall admission, 1/10 (priority date). Applications are processed on a rolling basis. *Application fee:* $40. Electronic applications accepted.
**Expenses:** Tuition, nonresident: full-time $10,434. Required fees: $4,883.
**Financial support:** In 2001–02, 31 students received support, including 10 fellowships with full and partial tuition reimbursements available (averaging $19,651 per year), 7 research assistantships with full tuition reimbursements available (averaging $14,926 per year), 7 teaching assistantships with partial tuition reimbursements available (averaging $13,596 per year). Financial award applicants required to submit FAFSA.
**Faculty research:** Cognition, neurobiology of cognition, cognitive modeling, distributed cognition, psycholinguistics.
Edwin Hutchins, Chair, 858-534-7141, *Fax:* 858-534-1128, *E-mail:* gradinfo@cogsci.ucsd.edu.
**Application contact:** Becky Burrola, Graduate Coordinator, 858-534-7141, *Fax:* 858-534-1128, *E-mail:* gradinfo@cogsci.ucsd.edu. *Web site:* http://cogsci.ucsd.edu/

### ■ UNIVERSITY OF CALIFORNIA, SAN DIEGO

**Graduate Studies and Research, Interdisciplinary Program in Cognitive Science, La Jolla, CA 92093**

**AWARDS** Cognitive science/anthropology (PhD); cognitive science/communication (PhD); cognitive science/computer science and engineering (PhD); cognitive science/linguistics (PhD); cognitive science/neuroscience (PhD); cognitive science/philosophy (PhD); cognitive science/psychology (PhD); cognitive science/sociology (PhD). Admissions through affiliated departments.

**Faculty:** 57 full-time (12 women).
**Students:** 8 full-time (4 women). Average age 26. 2 applicants. In 2001, 2 degrees awarded.
**Degree requirements:** For doctorate, thesis/dissertation.
**Entrance requirements:** For doctorate, GRE General Test. *Application deadline:* Applications are processed on a rolling basis. *Application fee:* $0.
**Expenses:** Tuition, nonresident: full-time $10,434. Required fees: $4,883.
**Faculty research:** Cognition, neurobiology of cognition, artificial intelligence, neural networks, psycholinguistics.
Gary Cottrell, Director, 858-534-7141, *Fax:* 858-534-1128, *E-mail:* gcottrell@ucsd.edu.
**Application contact:** Graduate Coordinator, 858-534-7141, *Fax:* 858-534-1128, *E-mail:* gradinfo@cogsci.ucsd.edu. *Web site:* http://cogsci.ucsd.edu/CURRENT/Cog-interdisciplinary.html

### ■ UNIVERSITY OF CONNECTICUT

**Graduate School, College of Liberal Arts and Sciences, Field of Psychology, Storrs, CT 06269**

**AWARDS** Behavioral neuroscience (PhD); biopsychology (PhD); clinical psychology (PhD); cognition/instruction psychology (PhD); developmental psychology (PhD); ecological psychology (PhD); general experimental psychology (PhD); industrial and organizational psychology (PhD); language psychology (PhD); social psychology (PhD).

**Faculty:** 41 full-time (11 women), 2 part-time/adjunct (both women).
**Students:** 134 full-time (83 women), 17 part-time (9 women); includes 13 minority (9 African Americans, 1 Asian American or Pacific Islander, 3 Hispanic Americans), 17 international. Average age 28. 378 applicants, 14% accepted, 25 enrolled. In 2001, 18 degrees awarded.
**Degree requirements:** For doctorate, thesis/dissertation, internship, comprehensive exam, registration.
**Entrance requirements:** For doctorate, GRE General Test, GRE Subject Test, letters of recommendation. *Application deadline:* For fall admission, 12/31. *Application fee:* $40 ($45 for international students).
**Financial support:** In 2001–02, 45 fellowships (averaging $4,000 per year), 16 research assistantships with full tuition reimbursements (averaging $16,000 per year), 83 teaching assistantships with full tuition reimbursements (averaging $16,000 per year) were awarded. Career-related internships or fieldwork, Federal Work-Study, scholarships/grants, health care benefits, and unspecified assistantships also available. Financial award application deadline: 12/31.
**Faculty research:** Behavioral neuroscience; physiology/chemistry of memory; sensation, motor control/motivation; cognitive, social, personality and language development; infancy/person perceptions and intergroup relations. *Total annual research expenditures:* $8 million.
Charles A. Lowe, Head, *Fax:* 860-486-2760, *E-mail:* charles.lowe@uconn.edu.
**Application contact:** Gina Stuart, Graduate Admissions, 860-486-3528, *Fax:* 860-486-2760, *E-mail:* futuregr@psych.psy.uconn.edu. *Web site:* http://psych.uconn.edu/

### ■ UNIVERSITY OF DELAWARE

**College of Arts and Science, Department of Psychology, Newark, DE 19716**

**AWARDS** Behavioral neuroscience (PhD); clinical psychology (PhD); cognitive psychology (PhD); social psychology (PhD).

**Faculty:** 25 full-time (6 women), 3 part-time/adjunct (0 women).
**Students:** 41 full-time (24 women); includes 3 minority (1 African American, 2 Hispanic Americans). Average age 28. 129 applicants, 13% accepted, 8 enrolled. In 2001, 7 degrees awarded.
**Degree requirements:** For doctorate, thesis/dissertation.
**Entrance requirements:** For doctorate, GRE General Test. *Application deadline:* For fall admission, 1/7 (priority date). *Application fee:* $50. Electronic applications accepted.
**Expenses:** Tuition, state resident: full-time $4,770; part-time $265 per credit. Tuition, nonresident: full-time $13,860; part-time $770 per credit. Required fees: $414.
**Financial support:** In 2001–02, 41 students received support, including 5 fellowships with full tuition reimbursements available (averaging $11,637 per year), 8 research assistantships with full tuition reimbursements available (averaging $11,637 per year), 15 teaching assistantships with full tuition reimbursements available (averaging $11,637 per year); career-related internships or fieldwork, Federal Work-Study, institutionally sponsored loans, scholarships/grants, tuition waivers (full and partial), and minority fellowships also available. Financial award application deadline: 1/7.

University of Delaware (continued)
**Faculty research:** Emotion development, neural and cognitive aspects of memory, neural control of feeding, intergroup relations, social cognition and communication. *Total annual research expenditures:* $1 million.
Dr. Brian P. Ackerman, Chairperson, 302-831-2271, *Fax:* 302-831-3645, *E-mail:* bpa@udel.edu.
**Application contact:** Information Contact, 302-831-2271, *Fax:* 302-831-3645, *E-mail:* bpa@udel.edu. *Web site:* http://www.udel.edu/catalog/current/as/psyc/grad.html

■ **UNIVERSITY OF ILLINOIS AT URBANA–CHAMPAIGN**
**Graduate College, College of Liberal Arts and Sciences, Department of Psychology, Champaign, IL 61820**
**AWARDS** Applied measurement (MS); biological psychology (AM, PhD); clinical psychology (AM, PhD); cognitive psychology (AM, PhD); developmental psychology (AM, PhD); engineering psychology (MS); personnel psychology (MS); quantitative psychology (AM, PhD); social-personality-organizational (AM, PhD); visual cognition and human performance (AM, PhD).
**Faculty:** 41 full-time (14 women), 11 part-time/adjunct (3 women).
**Students:** 156 full-time (90 women); includes 23 minority (6 African Americans, 12 Asian Americans or Pacific Islanders, 5 Hispanic Americans), 42 international. 461 applicants, 17% accepted, 27 enrolled. In 2001, 1 master's, 25 doctorates awarded.
**Degree requirements:** For doctorate, thesis/dissertation.
**Entrance requirements:** For master's, GRE General Test, GRE Subject Test (recommended), minimum GPA of 3.0; for doctorate, GRE General Test, GRE Subject Test (recommended). *Application deadline:* For fall admission, 1/1. *Application fee:* $40 ($50 for international students).
**Expenses:** Tuition, state resident: part-time $3,227 per degree program. Tuition, nonresident: part-time $7,169 per degree program. Tuition and fees vary according to program.
**Financial support:** In 2001–02, 31 fellowships with full tuition reimbursements (averaging $15,000 per year), 21 research assistantships with full tuition reimbursements (averaging $13,585 per year), 73 teaching assistantships with full tuition reimbursements (averaging $13,585 per year) were awarded. Career-related internships or fieldwork, traineeships, and tuition waivers (full) also available. Financial award application deadline: 1/1. *Total annual research expenditures:* $4.6 million.
Dr. Edward J. Shoben, Head.

**Application contact:** Cheryl Berger, Assistant Head for Graduate Affairs, 217-333-3429, *Fax:* 217-244-5876, *E-mail:* gradstdy@s.psych.uiuc.edu. *Web site:* http://www.psych.uiuc.edu/

■ **UNIVERSITY OF LOUISIANA AT LAFAYETTE**
**Graduate School, College of Sciences, Institute of Cognitive Science, Lafayette, LA 70504**
**AWARDS** PhD.
**Faculty:** 10 full-time (3 women).
**Students:** 6 full-time (3 women), 1 international. Average age 24. 13 applicants, 62% accepted, 3 enrolled.
**Degree requirements:** For doctorate, 2 foreign languages, thesis/dissertation.
**Entrance requirements:** For doctorate, GRE General Test, minimum GPA of 3.0. *Application deadline:* For fall admission, 2/1 (priority date); for spring admission, 10/15 (priority date). Applications are processed on a rolling basis. *Application fee:* $20 ($30 for international students).
**Expenses:** Tuition, state resident: full-time $2,317; part-time $79 per credit. Tuition, nonresident: full-time $8,882; part-time $369 per credit. International tuition: $9,018 full-time.
**Financial support:** In 2001–02, 6 students received support, including 1 fellowship with full tuition reimbursement available (averaging $12,000 per year), 4 research assistantships with full tuition reimbursements available (averaging $10,000 per year); career-related internships or fieldwork also available. Financial award application deadline: 5/1.
**Faculty research:** Computational models of cognition, comparative cognition, cognitive development, cognitive neuroscience, memory.
Dr. Subrata Dasgupta, Director, 337-482-1130, *E-mail:* subrata@louisiana.edu.
**Application contact:** Dr. Claude G. Cech, Graduate Coordinator, 337-482-6585, *E-mail:* cech@louisiana.edu. *Web site:* http://www.louisiana.edu/Research/ICS/

■ **UNIVERSITY OF MARYLAND**
**Graduate School, Graduate Programs in Medicine, Program in Neuroscience and Cognitive Sciences, Baltimore, MD 21201-1627**
**AWARDS** MS, PhD, MD/PhD. Part-time programs available.
**Faculty:** 55 full-time.
**Students:** 20 full-time, 2 part-time; includes 3 minority (1 African American, 2 Asian Americans or Pacific Islanders), 3 international. 28 applicants, 43% accepted, 5 enrolled. Terminal master's awarded for partial completion of doctoral program.

**Degree requirements:** For master's and doctorate, thesis/dissertation.
**Entrance requirements:** For master's and doctorate, GRE General Test, TOEFL or IELTS, minimum GPA of 3.0. *Application deadline:* For fall admission, 7/1. *Application fee:* $50.
**Expenses:** Tuition, state resident: part-time $281 per credit. Tuition, nonresident: part-time $503 per credit. Tuition and fees vary according to class time, course load, degree level and program.
**Financial support:** Fellowships, research assistantships available. Financial award application deadline: 2/15.
**Faculty research:** Molecular, biochemical, and cellular pharmacology; membrane biophysics; synaptology; developmental neurobiology.
Dr. Michael Shipley, Director, 410-706-3590, *Fax:* 410-706-2512, *E-mail:* msnipley@umaryland.edu.
**Application contact:** Dr. Asaf Keller, Program Director, 410-706-8912, *E-mail:* akeller@umaryland.edu.

■ **UNIVERSITY OF MARYLAND, BALTIMORE COUNTY**
**Graduate School, Department of Biological Sciences and Department of Psychology, Program in Neurosciences and Cognitive Sciences, Baltimore, MD 21250-5398**
**AWARDS** PhD.
**Degree requirements:** For doctorate, thesis/dissertation.
**Entrance requirements:** For doctorate, GRE General Test, TOEFL, minimum GPA of 3.0.
**Find an in-depth description at www.petersons.com/gradchannel.**

■ **UNIVERSITY OF MARYLAND, BALTIMORE COUNTY**
**Graduate School, Department of Psychology, Baltimore, MD 21250-5398**
**AWARDS** Applied developmental psychology (PhD); neurosciences and cognitive sciences (MS, PhD); psychology/human services (MA, PhD), including applied behavioral analysis (MA), psychology/human services (PhD).
**Degree requirements:** For doctorate, thesis/dissertation.
**Entrance requirements:** For doctorate, GRE General Test, GRE Subject Test, TOEFL.
**Faculty research:** Health services, interviewing and speech pattern analysis.

## ■ UNIVERSITY OF MARYLAND, COLLEGE PARK

**Graduate Studies and Research, Interdepartmental Programs, Program in Neurosciences and Cognitive Sciences, College Park, MD 20742**

**AWARDS** PhD.

**Students:** 23 full-time (9 women), 5 part-time (3 women); includes 4 minority (1 African American, 3 Asian Americans or Pacific Islanders), 10 international. 46 applicants, 26% accepted, 7 enrolled. In 2001, 1 degree awarded.

**Degree requirements:** For doctorate, thesis/dissertation, comprehensive exam.

**Entrance requirements:** For doctorate, GRE General Test. *Application deadline:* For fall admission, 1/7. Applications are processed on a rolling basis. *Application fee:* $50 ($70 for international students). Electronic applications accepted.

**Expenses:** Tuition, state resident: part-time $289 per credit hour. Tuition, nonresident: part-time $448 per credit hour. One-time fee: $436 part-time. Full-time tuition and fees vary according to course load, campus/location and program.

**Financial support:** Fellowships, teaching assistantships, Federal Work-Study and scholarships/grants available. Support available to part-time students. Financial award applicants required to submit FAFSA.

**Faculty research:** Molecular neurobiology, cognition, neural and behavioral systems language.

Dr. Arthur Popper, Director, 301-405-8910, *Fax:* 301-314-9358.

## ■ UNIVERSITY OF MINNESOTA, TWIN CITIES CAMPUS

**Graduate School, College of Liberal Arts, Department of Psychology, Program in Cognitive and Biological Psychology, Minneapolis, MN 55455-0213**

**AWARDS** PhD.

**Students:** 27 full-time (9 women); includes 5 minority (1 African American, 3 Asian Americans or Pacific Islanders, 1 Hispanic American), 4 international. 27 applicants, 33% accepted, 5 enrolled. In 2001, 3 degrees awarded.

**Degree requirements:** For doctorate, thesis/dissertation, comprehensive exam.

**Entrance requirements:** For doctorate, GRE General Test, GRE Subject Test (recommended), TOEFL, 12 credits of upper-level psychology courses, including a course in statistics or psychological measurement. *Application deadline:* For fall admission, 1/5. *Application fee:* $55 ($75 for international students).

**Expenses:** Tuition, state resident: full-time $2,932; part-time $489 per credit. Tuition, nonresident: full-time $5,758; part-time $960 per credit. Part-time tuition and fees vary according to course load, program and reciprocity agreements.

**Financial support:** Fellowships, research assistantships, teaching assistantships, career-related internships or fieldwork, traineeships, and tuition waivers (partial) available. Financial award application deadline: 12/1.

**Application contact:** Coordinator, 612-624-4181, *Fax:* 612-626-2079, *E-mail:* psyapply@tc.umn.edu.

## ■ THE UNIVERSITY OF NORTH CAROLINA AT GREENSBORO

**Graduate School, College of Arts and Sciences, Department of Psychology, Greensboro, NC 27412-5001**

**AWARDS** Clinical psychology (MA, PhD); cognitive psychology (MA, PhD); developmental psychology (MA, PhD); social psychology (MA, PhD).

**Faculty:** 22 full-time (9 women), 1 part-time/adjunct (0 women).

**Students:** 42 full-time (35 women), 20 part-time (13 women); includes 2 African Americans, 2 Asian Americans or Pacific Islanders, 2 Hispanic Americans. In 2001, 13 master's, 5 doctorates awarded. Terminal master's awarded for partial completion of doctoral program.

**Degree requirements:** For master's, thesis, comprehensive exam; for doctorate, one foreign language, thesis/dissertation, preliminary exam.

**Entrance requirements:** For master's, GRE General Test, TOEFL; for doctorate, GRE General Test, GRE Subject Test (recommended), TOEFL. *Application deadline:* For fall admission, 2/1. *Application fee:* $35.

**Expenses:** Tuition, state resident: part-time $344 per course. Tuition, nonresident: part-time $2,457 per course.

**Financial support:** In 2001–02, 3 fellowships with full tuition reimbursements (averaging $10,833 per year), 54 research assistantships with full tuition reimbursements (averaging $8,514 per year), 2 teaching assistantships with full tuition reimbursements (averaging $3,500 per year) were awarded. Unspecified assistantships also available.

**Faculty research:** Sensory and perceptual determinants; evoked potential: disorders, deafness, and development.

Dr. Timothy Johnston, Head, 336-334-5013, *Fax:* 336-334-5066, *E-mail:* johnston@uncg.edu.

**Application contact:** Dr. James Lynch, Director of Graduate Recruitment and Information Services, 336-334-4881, *Fax:* 336-334-4424. *Web site:* http://www.uncg.edu/psy/

## ■ UNIVERSITY OF NOTRE DAME

**Graduate School, College of Arts and Letters, Division of Social Science, Department of Psychology, Notre Dame, IN 46556**

**AWARDS** Cognitive psychology (PhD); counseling psychology (PhD); developmental psychology (PhD); quantitative psychology (PhD).

**Faculty:** 31 full-time (11 women).

**Students:** 60 full-time (42 women); includes 10 minority (3 African Americans, 2 Asian Americans or Pacific Islanders, 5 Hispanic Americans), 5 international. 189 applicants, 12% accepted, 15 enrolled. In 2001, 8 doctorates awarded.

**Degree requirements:** For doctorate, thesis/dissertation, comprehensive exam. *Median time to degree:* Doctorate–5.9 years full-time.

**Entrance requirements:** For doctorate, GRE General Test, GRE Subject Test (strongly recommended), TOEFL. *Application deadline:* For fall admission, 1/2. *Application fee:* $50. Electronic applications accepted.

**Expenses:** Tuition: Full-time $24,220; part-time $1,346 per credit hour. Required fees: $155.

**Financial support:** In 2001–02, 59 students received support, including 31 fellowships with full tuition reimbursements available (averaging $16,000 per year), 10 research assistantships with full tuition reimbursements available (averaging $11,400 per year), 17 teaching assistantships with full tuition reimbursements available (averaging $11,400 per year); career-related internships or fieldwork and tuition waivers (full) also available. Financial award application deadline: 1/2.

**Faculty research:** Cognitive and socio-emotional development, marital discord, statistical methods and quantitative models applicable to psychology, interpersonal relations, life span development and developmental delay, childhood depression, structural equation and dynamical systems, modeling, social cognition, ecology, health psychology, aging behavior genetics. *Total annual research expenditures:* $1.8 million.

Dr. Laura Carlson, Director of Graduate Studies, 574-631-6650, *Fax:* 574-631-8883, *E-mail:* lcarlson@nd.edu.

**Application contact:** Dr. Terrence J. Akai, Director of Graduate Admissions, 574-631-7706, *Fax:* 574-631-4183, *E-mail:* gradad@nd.edu. *Web site:* http://www.nd.edu/~psych/

# ■ UNIVERSITY OF OREGON

**Graduate School, College of Arts and Sciences, Department of Psychology, Eugene, OR 97403**

**AWARDS** Clinical psychology (PhD); cognitive psychology (MA, MS, PhD); developmental psychology (MA, MS, PhD); physiological psychology (MA, MS, PhD); psychology (MA, MS, PhD); social/personality psychology (MA, MS, PhD).

**Faculty:** 27 full-time (11 women), 11 part-time/adjunct (8 women).

**Students:** 73 full-time (49 women), 3 part-time (all women); includes 7 minority (3 Asian Americans or Pacific Islanders, 2 Hispanic Americans, 2 Native Americans), 14 international. 176 applicants, 11% accepted. In 2001, 21 master's, 11 doctorates awarded. Terminal master's awarded for partial completion of doctoral program.

**Degree requirements:** For doctorate, thesis/dissertation.

**Entrance requirements:** For master's, GRE General Test, TOEFL, minimum GPA of 3.0; for doctorate, GRE General Test, TOEFL. *Application deadline:* For fall admission, 12/1. *Application fee:* $50.

**Expenses:** Tuition, state resident: full-time $4,968; part-time $501 per credit hour. Tuition, nonresident: full-time $8,400; part-time $691 per credit hour.

**Financial support:** In 2001–02, 48 teaching assistantships were awarded; research assistantships, career-related internships or fieldwork also available. Marjorie Taylor, Head, 541-346-4921, *Fax:* 541-346-4911.

**Application contact:** Lori Olsen, Admissions Contact, 541-346-5060, *Fax:* 541-346-4911, *E-mail:* gradsec@psych.uoregon.edu. *Web site:* http://psychweb.uoregon.edu/

# ■ UNIVERSITY OF PITTSBURGH

**School of Education, Department of Instruction and Learning, Program in Cognitive Studies, Pittsburgh, PA 15260**

**AWARDS** PhD.

**Students:** 6 full-time (5 women), 2 international. 7 applicants, 29% accepted, 1 enrolled. In 2001, 2 degrees awarded.

**Degree requirements:** For doctorate, thesis/dissertation.

**Entrance requirements:** For doctorate, GRE General Test, TOEFL. *Application deadline:* For fall admission, 2/1. *Application fee:* $40. Electronic applications accepted.

**Expenses:** Tuition, state resident: full-time $9,410; part-time $385 per credit. Tuition, nonresident: full-time $19,376; part-time $797 per credit. Required fees: $480; $90 per term. Tuition and fees vary according to program.

**Financial support:** In 2001–02, research assistantships (averaging $8,000 per year). Financial award application deadline: 3/15; financial award applicants required to submit FAFSA.

**Application contact:** Jackie Harden, Manager, 412-648-2230, *Fax:* 412-648-1899, *E-mail:* soeinfo@pitt.edu. *Web site:* http://www.education.pitt.edu/

# ■ UNIVERSITY OF ROCHESTER

**The College, Arts and Sciences, Department of Brain and Cognitive Sciences, Rochester, NY 14627-0250**

**AWARDS** MS, PhD.

**Faculty:** 15.

**Students:** 27 full-time (13 women); includes 3 minority (1 African American, 1 Asian American or Pacific Islander, 1 Native American), 9 international. 96 applicants, 14% accepted, 6 enrolled. In 2001, 3 master's, 3 doctorates awarded. Terminal master's awarded for partial completion of doctoral program.

**Degree requirements:** For doctorate, thesis/dissertation, qualifying exam.

**Entrance requirements:** For master's, GRE General Test; for doctorate, GRE General Test, TOEFL. *Application deadline:* For fall admission, 2/1 (priority date). *Application fee:* $25. Electronic applications accepted.

**Expenses:** Tuition: Part-time $755 per credit hour.

**Financial support:** Fellowships, research assistantships, teaching assistantships, tuition waivers (full and partial) available. Financial award application deadline: 2/1. Elissa Newport, Chair, 585-275-8689.

**Application contact:** Bette McCormick, Graduate Program Secretary, 585-275-7115.

# ■ THE UNIVERSITY OF TEXAS AT AUSTIN

**Graduate School, College of Education, Department of Educational Psychology, Austin, TX 78712-1111**

**AWARDS** Academic educational psychology (M Ed, MA); counseling education (M Ed); counseling psychology (PhD); human development and education (PhD); learning cognition and instruction (PhD); quantitative methods (PhD); school psychology (PhD).

**Faculty:** 30 full-time (16 women), 17 part-time/adjunct (8 women).

**Students:** 233 full-time (191 women), 55 part-time (44 women); includes 52 minority (13 African Americans, 8 Asian Americans or Pacific Islanders, 29 Hispanic Americans, 2 Native Americans), 36 international. Average age 29. 292 applicants, 47% accepted, 70 enrolled. In 2001, 20 master's, 38 doctorates awarded.

**Degree requirements:** For master's, thesis optional; for doctorate, thesis/dissertation.

**Entrance requirements:** For master's and doctorate, GRE General Test, 3 letters of recommendation. *Application deadline:* For fall admission, 1/15 (priority date); for winter admission, 3/1 (priority date); for spring admission, 10/1 (priority date). Applications are processed on a rolling basis. *Application fee:* $50 ($75 for international students).

**Expenses:** Tuition, state resident: full-time $3,159. Tuition, nonresident: full-time $6,957. Tuition and fees vary according to program.

**Financial support:** In 2001–02, 21 fellowships with full and partial tuition reimbursements (averaging $1,700 per year), 33 research assistantships (averaging $4,500 per year), 116 teaching assistantships (averaging $4,250 per year) were awarded. Career-related internships or fieldwork, Federal Work-Study, institutionally sponsored loans, scholarships/grants, tuition waivers (full and partial), and unspecified assistantships also available. Financial award application deadline: 1/15. Dr. Edmund T. Emmer, Department Chair, 512-471-4155 Ext. 22, *Fax:* 512-471-1288, *E-mail:* emmer@mail.utexas.edu.

**Application contact:** Dr. Cindy I. Carlson, Graduate Adviser, 512-471-4155 Ext. 24, *Fax:* 512-471-1288, *E-mail:* cindy.carlson@mail.utexas.edu. *Web site:* http://www.edb.utexas.edu/coe/depts/edp/edp.html

# ■ THE UNIVERSITY OF TEXAS AT DALLAS

**School of Human Development, Program in Applied Cognition and Neuroscience, Richardson, TX 75083-0688**

**AWARDS** MS. Part-time and evening/weekend programs available.

**Faculty:** 11 full-time (1 woman).

**Students:** 12 full-time (9 women), 8 part-time (4 women); includes 6 minority (1 African American, 5 Asian Americans or Pacific Islanders), 4 international. Average age 31. In 2001, 6 degrees awarded.

**Degree requirements:** For master's, internship.

**Entrance requirements:** For master's, GRE General Test, TOEFL, minimum GPA of 3.0 in upper-level coursework in field. *Application deadline:* For fall admission, 7/15; for spring admission, 11/15. Applications are processed on a rolling basis. *Application fee:* $25 ($75 for international students). Electronic applications accepted.

**Expenses:** Tuition, state resident: full-time $1,440; part-time $84 per credit. Tuition, nonresident: full-time $5,310; part-time $295 per credit. Required fees: $1,835; $87 per credit. $138 per term.

**Financial support:** Fellowships, research assistantships, teaching assistantships, Federal Work-Study available. Support available to part-time students. Financial award application deadline: 4/30; financial award applicants required to submit FAFSA.

**Faculty research:** Combination of biological, behavioral, and computational approaches for evaluating biological and artificial information processing systems. Dr. W. Jay Dowling, Head, 972-883-2050, *Fax:* 972-883-2491, *E-mail:* jdowling@ utdallas.edu.

**Application contact:** Dr. Robert D. Stillman, Head, 972-883-3106, *Fax:* 972-883-3022, *E-mail:* stillman@utdallas.edu. *Web site:* http://utdallas.edu/dept/hd/

### ■ UNIVERSITY OF WISCONSIN–MADISON

**Graduate School, College of Letters and Science, Department of Psychology, Program in Cognitive and Perceptual Sciences, Madison, WI 53706-1380**

**AWARDS** PhD.

**Faculty:** 9 full-time (3 women).
**Students:** 10 full-time (5 women); includes 2 minority (1 African American, 1 Asian American or Pacific Islander), 1 international. Average age 23. 39 applicants, 31% accepted, 6 enrolled.
**Degree requirements:** For doctorate, thesis/dissertation, comprehensive exam, registration.
**Entrance requirements:** For doctorate, GRE General Test, minimum undergraduate GPA of 3.0. *Application deadline:* For fall admission, 1/5 (priority date). Applications are processed on a rolling basis. *Application fee:* $45. Electronic applications accepted.
**Expenses:** Tuition, state resident: full-time $7,361; part-time $399 per credit. Tuition, nonresident: full-time $20,499; part-time $1,282 per credit. Required fees: $34 per credit. Full-time tuition and fees vary according to course load, program, reciprocity agreements and student level.
**Financial support:** In 2001–02, 10 students received support, including 2 fellowships with full tuition reimbursements available (averaging $13,446 per year), 7 research assistantships with full tuition reimbursements available (averaging $13,814 per year), 1 teaching assistantship with full tuition reimbursement available (averaging $13,814 per year); institutionally sponsored loans, traineeships, health care benefits, and unspecified assistantships

also available. Financial award application deadline: 1/5.
Arthur Glenberg, Chair, 608-262-8792, *Fax:* 608-262-2049, *E-mail:* glenberg@ facstaff.wisc.edu.
**Application contact:** Jane Fox-Anderson, Graduate Admissions Secretary, 608-262-2079, *Fax:* 608-262-4029, *E-mail:* jefoxand@facstaff.wisc.edu.

### ■ WAYNE STATE UNIVERSITY

**Graduate School, College of Science, Department of Psychology, Program in Psychology, Detroit, MI 48202**

**AWARDS** Clinical psychology (PhD); cognitive psychology (PhD); developmental psychology (PhD); industrial/organizational psychology (PhD); psychology (MA, PhD); social psychology (PhD).

**Students:** 114. In 2001, 22 master's, 23 doctorates awarded.
**Degree requirements:** For doctorate, thesis/dissertation.
**Entrance requirements:** For doctorate, GRE General Test, GRE Subject Test. *Application deadline:* For fall admission, 2/1. *Application fee:* $20 ($30 for international students). Electronic applications accepted.
**Expenses:** Tuition, state resident: full-time $3,764. Tuition and fees vary according to degree level and program.
**Financial support:** Application deadline: 2/1.
**Application contact:** Kathryn Urberg, Graduate Director, 313-577-2820, *Fax:* 313-577-7636, *E-mail:* kurberg@ sun.science.wayne.edu.

## COUNSELING PSYCHOLOGY

### ■ ABILENE CHRISTIAN UNIVERSITY

**Graduate School, College of Arts and Sciences, Department of Psychology, Program in Counseling Psychology, Abilene, TX 79699-9100**

**AWARDS** MS.

**Faculty:** 12 part-time/adjunct (2 women).
**Students:** 2 full-time (1 woman), 4 part-time (2 women), 1 international. 8 applicants, 75% accepted, 5 enrolled. In 2001, 17 degrees awarded.
**Degree requirements:** For master's, comprehensive exam.
**Entrance requirements:** For master's, GRE General Test. *Application deadline:* For fall admission, 4/1 (priority date); for spring admission, 11/1. Applications are processed on a rolling basis. *Application fee:* $25 ($45 for international students).

**Expenses:** Tuition: Full-time $8,904; part-time $371 per hour. Required fees: $520; $17 per hour.
Dr. Larry Norsworthy, Graduate Adviser, 915-674-2280, *Fax:* 915-674-6968, *E-mail:* norsworthyl@acu.edu.
**Application contact:** Dr. Roger Gee, Graduate Dean, 915-674-2122, *Fax:* 915-674-2123, *E-mail:* gradinfo@ education.acu.edu.

### ■ ADLER SCHOOL OF PROFESSIONAL PSYCHOLOGY

**Programs in Psychology, Chicago, IL 60601-7203**

**AWARDS** Art therapy (Certificate); clinical hypnosis (Certificate); clinical psychology (Psy D); counseling psychology (MACP); counseling psychology/art therapy (MACAT); gerontology (MAGP, Certificate); marriage and family counseling (MAMFC); marriage and family therapy (Certificate); organizational psychology (MAO); substance abuse counseling (MASAC, Certificate). Part-time and evening/weekend programs available.

**Faculty:** 19 full-time (9 women), 48 part-time/adjunct (21 women).
**Students:** 124 full-time (78 women), 284 part-time (208 women); includes 77 minority (43 African Americans, 20 Asian Americans or Pacific Islanders, 13 Hispanic Americans, 1 Native American), 8 international. Average age 39. 253 applicants, 59% accepted, 121 enrolled. In 2001, 101 master's, 29 doctorates, 5 other advanced degrees awarded. Terminal master's awarded for partial completion of doctoral program.
**Degree requirements:** For master's, thesis or alternative, oral exam, practicum; for doctorate, thesis/dissertation, clinical exam, internship, oral exam, practicum, written qualifying exam.
**Entrance requirements:** For master's, 12 semester hours in psychology, minimum GPA of 3.0; for doctorate, 18 semester hours in psychology, minimum GPA of 3.25; for Certificate, appropriate master's or doctoral degree. *Application deadline:* For fall admission, 1/1 (priority date). Applications are processed on a rolling basis. *Application fee:* $50.
**Expenses:** Tuition: Full-time $13,680; part-time $380 per credit. Required fees: $100; $15 per credit.
**Financial support:** In 2001–02, 180 students received support. Career-related internships or fieldwork, Federal Work-Study, scholarships/grants, and tuition waivers (full and partial) available. Support available to part-time students. Financial award application deadline: 5/15; financial award applicants required to submit FAFSA.

*Adler School of Professional Psychology (continued)*
Dr. Frank Gruba-McCallister, Dean of Academic Affairs, 312-201-5900, *Fax:* 312-201-5917.
**Application contact:** Erene Soliman, Admissions Counselor, 312-201-5900, *Fax:* 312-201-5917.

**Find an in-depth description at www.petersons.com/gradchannel.**

■ **ALABAMA AGRICULTURAL AND MECHANICAL UNIVERSITY**
**School of Graduate Studies, School of Education, Department of Counseling and Special Education, Huntsville, AL 35811**
**AWARDS** Communicative disorders (M Ed, MS); psychology and counseling (MS, Ed S), including clinical psychology (MS), counseling and guidance, counseling psychology (MS), personnel management (MS), psychometry (MS), school psychology (MS); special education (M Ed, MS). Part-time and evening/weekend programs available.
**Faculty:** 38 full-time (20 women).
**Students:** 21 full-time (all women), 119 part-time (90 women); includes 65 minority (64 African Americans, 1 Hispanic American), 2 international. In 2001, 55 master's, 2 other advanced degrees awarded.
**Degree requirements:** For master's, comprehensive exam.
**Entrance requirements:** For master's, GRE General Test. *Application deadline:* For fall admission, 5/1. *Application fee:* $15 ($20 for international students).
**Expenses:** Tuition, state resident: full-time $1,380. Tuition, nonresident: full-time $2,500.
**Financial support:** Career-related internships or fieldwork available. Support available to part-time students. Financial award application deadline: 4/1.
**Faculty research:** Increasing numbers of minorities in special education and speech-language pathology. *Total annual research expenditures:* $300,000.
Dr. Terry L. Douglas, Chair, 256-851-5533.

■ **ALASKA PACIFIC UNIVERSITY**
**Graduate Programs, Department of Counseling and Psychological Studies, Anchorage, AK 99508-4672**
**AWARDS** MSCP. Part-time programs available.
**Faculty:** 3 full-time (2 women), 2 part-time/adjunct (both women).
**Students:** 34 full-time (23 women), 8 part-time (7 women); includes 7 minority (3 African Americans, 1 Asian American or Pacific Islander, 1 Hispanic American, 2

Native Americans). Average age 35. In 2001, 23 degrees awarded.
**Degree requirements:** For master's, professional seminar, internship, thesis optional.
**Entrance requirements:** For master's, MAT, interview, minimum GPA of 3.0. *Application deadline:* For fall admission, 4/1. *Application fee:* $25.
**Expenses:** Tuition: Full-time $9,600; part-time $400 per semester hour. Required fees: $80; $40 per semester. Tuition and fees vary according to program.
**Financial support:** In 2001–02, 4 research assistantships were awarded; career-related internships or fieldwork, Federal Work-Study, and scholarships/grants also available. Support available to part-time students. Financial award application deadline: 3/15; financial award applicants required to submit FAFSA.
Dr. Ellen Cole, Director, 907-564-8216, *Fax:* 907-562-4276, *E-mail:* ecole@alaskapacific.edu.
**Application contact:** Ernie Norton, Director of Admissions, 907-564-8248, *Fax:* 907-564-8317, *E-mail:* ernien@alaskapacific.edu. *Web site:* http://www.alaskapacific.edu/

■ **ALFRED ADLER GRADUATE SCHOOL**
**Program in Counseling and Psychotherapy, Hopkins, MN 55305**
**AWARDS** Adlerian psychotherapy (Diploma); counseling and psychotherapy (MA). Part-time and evening/weekend programs available.
**Faculty:** 1 full-time (0 women), 30 part-time/adjunct (18 women).
**Students:** Average age 37. 30 applicants, 90% accepted. In 2001, 32 degrees awarded.
**Degree requirements:** For master's, thesis or alternative. *Median time to degree:* Master's–2.5 years part-time.
**Entrance requirements:** For master's, minimum undergraduate GPA of 3.0, 12 credits in psychology. *Application deadline:* For fall admission, 10/1 (priority date); for winter admission, 1/1 (priority date); for spring admission, 4/1 (priority date). Applications are processed on a rolling basis. *Application fee:* $50.
**Expenses:** Tuition: Full-time $10,620; part-time $295 per credit. Required fees: $40 per quarter. Tuition and fees vary according to course load.
**Financial support:** Career-related internships or fieldwork and tuition waivers (partial) available. Support available to part-time students. Financial award applicants required to submit FAFSA.

Dennis Rislove, President, 952-988-4185, *Fax:* 952-988-4171, *E-mail:* rislove@alfredadler.edu.
**Application contact:** Evelyn B. Haas, Director of Academic Affairs, 952-988-4327 Ext. 5723, *Fax:* 952-988-4171, *E-mail:* ev@alfredadler.edu. *Web site:* http://www.alfredadler.edu/

■ **ALLIANT INTERNATIONAL UNIVERSITY**
**California School of Professional Psychology, Program in Counseling Psychology–San Diego, San Diego, CA 92121**
**AWARDS** Indian family and child mental health (MA).
**Students:** 16 full-time (11 women); all minorities (all Native Americans). Average age 44.
**Entrance requirements:** For master's, TOEFL, minimum GPA of 3.0 in both psychology and overall. *Application deadline:* For fall admission, 4/1. *Application fee:* $50.
**Expenses:** Tuition: Part-time $397 per credit hour. Tuition and fees vary according to degree level, campus/location and program.
Director.
**Application contact:** Patricia J. Mullen, Vice President, Enrollment and Student Services, 800-457-1273 Ext. 303, *Fax:* 415-931-8322, *E-mail:* admissions@mail.cspp.edu. *Web site:* http://www.alliant.edu/

■ **AMBERTON UNIVERSITY**
**Graduate School, Program in Counseling, Garland, TX 75041-5595**
**AWARDS** MA.
**Entrance requirements:** For master's, minimum GPA of 3.0.

■ **ANDREWS UNIVERSITY**
**School of Graduate Studies, School of Education, Department of Educational and Counseling Psychology, Program in Counseling Psychology, Berrien Springs, MI 49104**
**AWARDS** PhD.
**Students:** 10 full-time (6 women), 19 part-time (14 women); includes 10 minority (3 African Americans, 7 Hispanic Americans), 2 international. Average age 36. In 2001, 4 degrees awarded.
**Degree requirements:** For doctorate, thesis/dissertation.
*Application fee:* $40.
**Expenses:** Tuition: Full-time $12,600; part-time $525 per semester. Required fees: $268. Tuition and fees vary according to degree level.

Dr. Dennis E. White, Program Coordinator, 616-471-3133.
**Application contact:** Carolyn Hurst, Supervisor of Graduate Admission, 800-253-2874, *Fax:* 616-471-3228, *E-mail:* enroll@andrews.edu.

## ■ ANGELO STATE UNIVERSITY

**Graduate School, College of Liberal and Fine Arts, Department of Psychology and Sociology, San Angelo, TX 76909**

**AWARDS** Psychology (MS), including counseling psychology, general psychology, industrial and organizational psychology. Part-time and evening/weekend programs available.

**Faculty:** 7 full-time (1 woman).
**Students:** 32 full-time (26 women), 25 part-time (21 women); includes 13 minority (2 African Americans, 1 Asian American or Pacific Islander, 9 Hispanic Americans, 1 Native American). Average age 35. 36 applicants, 53% accepted, 13 enrolled. In 2001, 14 degrees awarded.
**Degree requirements:** For master's, thesis, comprehensive exam.
**Entrance requirements:** For master's, GRE General Test, minimum GPA of 2.5. *Application deadline:* For fall admission, 8/7 (priority date); for spring admission, 1/2. Applications are processed on a rolling basis. *Application fee:* $25 ($50 for international students).
**Expenses:** Tuition, area resident: Full-time $960; part-time $40 per credit hour. Tuition, nonresident: full-time $6,120; part-time $255 per credit hour. Required fees: $1,336; $56 per credit hour.
**Financial support:** In 2001–02, 27 students received support, including 20 fellowships, 3 teaching assistantships; career-related internships or fieldwork, Federal Work-Study, tuition waivers (partial), and unspecified assistantships also available. Support available to part-time students. Financial award application deadline: 8/1.
Dr. William Davidson, Head, 915-942-2205. *Web site:* http://www.angelo.edu/dept/psychology_sociology/

## ■ ANNA MARIA COLLEGE

**Graduate Division, Program in Psychology, Paxton, MA 01612**

**AWARDS** Counseling psychology (MA, CAGS); psychology (MA, CAGS). Part-time and evening/weekend programs available.

**Faculty:** 1 full-time (0 women), 4 part-time/adjunct (3 women).
**Students:** 16 full-time (12 women), 26 part-time (19 women); includes 1 minority (Hispanic American). Average age 36. In 2001, 10 master's, 2 other advanced degrees awarded.

**Degree requirements:** For master's, practicum.
**Entrance requirements:** For master's, MAT; for CAGS, master's degree in psychology or related field. *Application deadline:* For fall admission, 3/1 (priority date); for spring admission, 11/1 (priority date). Applications are processed on a rolling basis. *Application fee:* $30. Electronic applications accepted.
**Expenses:** Tuition: Part-time $900 per course.
**Financial support:** Institutionally sponsored loans available. Financial award applicants required to submit FAFSA.
Richard L. Connors, Director, 508-849-3413, *Fax:* 508-849-3339, *E-mail:* rconnors@annamaria.edu.
**Application contact:** Eva Eaton, Director of Admissions for Graduate Programs and the Department of Professional Studies, 508-849-3488, *Fax:* 508-849-3362, *E-mail:* eveaton@annamaria.edu. *Web site:* http://www.annamaria.edu/

## ■ ANTIOCH NEW ENGLAND GRADUATE SCHOOL

**Graduate School, Department of Applied Psychology, Program in Counseling Psychology, Keene, NH 03431-3552**
**AWARDS** MA.
**Faculty:** 9 full-time (7 women), 25 part-time/adjunct (15 women).
**Students:** 87 full-time (60 women), 13 part-time (10 women); includes 3 minority (2 African Americans, 1 Native American), 5 international. Average age 35. 72 applicants, 88% accepted. In 2001, 42 degrees awarded.
**Degree requirements:** For master's, internship, practicum.
**Entrance requirements:** For master's, previous course work and work experience in psychology. *Application deadline:* For fall admission, 8/1; for spring admission, 12/1. Applications are processed on a rolling basis. *Application fee:* $40.
**Expenses:** Tuition: Full-time $15,150.
**Financial support:** In 2001–02, 66 students received support, including 2 fellowships (averaging $1,500 per year); career-related internships or fieldwork and Federal Work-Study also available. Financial award applicants required to submit FAFSA.
**Faculty research:** Multicultural issues in field supervision.
Dr. Diane Kurinsky, Director, 603-357-3122 Ext. 246, *Fax:* 603-357-0718, *E-mail:* dkurinsky@antiochne.edu.
**Application contact:** Robbie P. Hertneky, Director of Admissions, 603-357-6265, *Fax:* 603-357-0718, *E-mail:* rhertneky@

antiochne.edu. *Web site:* http://www.antiochne.edu/

## ■ ANTIOCH UNIVERSITY MCGREGOR

**Graduate Programs, Individualized Liberal and Professional Studies Program, Yellow Springs, OH 45387-1609**

**AWARDS** Liberal and professional studies (MA), including counseling, creative writing, education, film studies, liberal studies, management, modern literature, psychology, theatre, visual arts. Part-time and evening/weekend programs available. Postbaccalaureate distance learning degree programs offered (minimal on-campus study).

**Faculty:** 4 full-time, 6 part-time/adjunct.
**Students:** 19 applicants, 89% accepted, 16 enrolled. In 2001, 56 degrees awarded.
**Degree requirements:** For master's, thesis or alternative.
*Application deadline:* For fall admission, 8/25; for winter admission, 12/5. Applications are processed on a rolling basis. *Application fee:* $50. Electronic applications accepted.
**Expenses:** Tuition: Part-time $317 per credit hour. Required fees: $75 per quarter.
**Financial support:** Federal Work-Study available. Financial award application deadline: 7/1; financial award applicants required to submit FAFSA.
Dr. Virginia Paget, Director, 937-769-1876, *Fax:* 937-769-1805.
**Application contact:** Karen E. Crist, Enrollment Services Officer, 937-769-1818, *Fax:* 937-769-1804, *E-mail:* kcrist@mcgregor.edu. *Web site:* http://www.mcgregor.edu

**Find an in-depth description at www.petersons.com/gradchannel.**

## ■ ANTIOCH UNIVERSITY SANTA BARBARA

**Psychology Program, Santa Barbara, CA 93101-1581**

**AWARDS** Family and child studies (MA); professional development and career counseling (MA). Part-time and evening/weekend programs available.

**Faculty:** 14 full-time (8 women), 43 part-time/adjunct (29 women).
**Students:** 13 full-time, 8 part-time. In 2001, 12 degrees awarded.
**Entrance requirements:** For master's, TOEFL. *Application deadline:* For fall admission, 8/5 (priority date); for winter admission, 11/11 (priority date). Applications are processed on a rolling basis. *Application fee:* $60.
**Expenses:** Tuition: Part-time $375 per unit. Required fees: $426 per year. $10 per

*Antioch University Santa Barbara (continued)*

quarter. Tuition and fees vary according to class time and program.

**Financial support:** Federal Work-Study available. Support available to part-time students. Financial award application deadline: 8/5; financial award applicants required to submit FAFSA.

Dr. Catherine Radecki-Bush, Chair, 805-962-8179 Ext. 229, *Fax:* 805-962-4786, *E-mail:* cradecki-bush@antiochsb.edu.

**Application contact:** Carol Flores, Admissions Director, 805-962-8179 Ext. 113, *Fax:* 805-962-4786, *E-mail:* cflores@antiochsb.edu. *Web site:* http://www.antiochsb.edu/

■ **ARCADIA UNIVERSITY**

**Graduate Studies, Department of Psychology, Glenside, PA 19038-3295**

**AWARDS** Counseling (MAC), including community counseling, school counseling. Part-time programs available.

**Faculty:** 4 full-time (2 women), 6 part-time/adjunct (4 women).

**Students:** 18 full-time (all women), 28 part-time (22 women); includes 4 minority (all African Americans), 2 international. In 2001, 14 degrees awarded.

**Degree requirements:** For master's, practicum.

**Entrance requirements:** For master's, GRE General Test or MAT. *Application deadline:* Applications are processed on a rolling basis. *Application fee:* $35.

**Expenses:** Tuition: Part-time $420 per credit. Tuition and fees vary according to degree level and program.

**Financial support:** Research assistantships, career-related internships or fieldwork and unspecified assistantships available. Support available to part-time students. Financial award application deadline: 8/15. Samuel Cameron, Program Director, 215-572-2181.

**Application contact:** 215-572-2925, *Fax:* 215-572-2126, *E-mail:* grad@arcadia.edu.

■ **ARGOSY UNIVERSITY-ATLANTA**

**Graduate Programs, Atlanta, GA 30328-5505**

**AWARDS** Clinical psychology (MA, Psy D); professional counseling (MA); psychology (MA). Part-time and evening/weekend programs available.

**Faculty:** 11 full-time (6 women), 16 part-time/adjunct (6 women).

**Students:** 398; includes 70 minority (52 African Americans, 8 Asian Americans or Pacific Islanders, 8 Hispanic Americans, 2 Native Americans), 2 international. Average age 26. 272 applicants, 46% accepted.

In 2001, 40 degrees awarded. Terminal master's awarded for partial completion of doctoral program.

**Degree requirements:** For master's, comprehensive exam; for doctorate, thesis/dissertation, clinical comprehensive exam, research project, internship.

**Entrance requirements:** For master's and doctorate, GRE General Test or MAT. *Application deadline:* For fall admission, 1/15 (priority date); for spring admission, 10/15 (priority date). Applications are processed on a rolling basis. *Application fee:* $55. Electronic applications accepted.

**Expenses:** Tuition: Part-time $374 per credit.

**Financial support:** In 2001–02, 280 students received support, including 40 teaching assistantships (averaging $700 per year); career-related internships or fieldwork and Federal Work-Study also available. Support available to part-time students. Financial award application deadline: 6/30; financial award applicants required to submit FAFSA.

Dr. Joseph Bascuas, Dean, 770-671-1200, *Fax:* 770-671-0476.

**Application contact:** Nick Colletti, Director of Enrollment Services, 770-671-1200, *Fax:* 770-671-0476, *E-mail:* ncolletti@argosyu.edu.

**Find an in-depth description at www.petersons.com/gradchannel.**

■ **ARGOSY UNIVERSITY-CHICAGO**

**Illinois School of Professional Psychology, Program in Professional Counseling, Chicago, IL 60603**

**AWARDS** MA. Part-time programs available.

**Faculty:** 2 full-time (1 woman), 17 part-time/adjunct (10 women).

**Students:** 64 full-time (53 women), 10 part-time (6 women); includes 28 minority (26 African Americans, 1 Asian American or Pacific Islander, 1 Hispanic American). Average age 33. 31 applicants, 61% accepted. In 2001, 8 degrees awarded.

**Degree requirements:** For master's, comprehensive exam.

*Application deadline:* For fall admission, 6/30; for winter admission, 10/30; for spring admission, 2/28. Applications are processed on a rolling basis. *Application fee:* $55.

**Expenses:** Tuition: Part-time $332 per credit hour. Required fees: $75 per year. $35 per term.

**Financial support:** Teaching assistantships, career-related internships or fieldwork and Federal Work-Study available. Financial award application deadline: 5/29.

Dr. Thomas Pourchot, Department Head, 312-279-3936, *Fax:* 312-201-1907.

**Application contact:** Ashley Delaney, Director of Admissions, 312-279-3906, *Fax:* 312-201-1907, *E-mail:* adelaney@argosyu.edu.

■ **ARGOSY UNIVERSITY-CHICAGO NORTHWEST**

**Graduate Programs, Rolling Meadows, IL 60008**

**AWARDS** Clinical psychology (MA, Psy D); professional counseling (MA). Evening/weekend programs available. Terminal master's awarded for partial completion of doctoral program.

**Degree requirements:** For master's, thesis, practicum; for doctorate, thesis/dissertation, internship, qualifying exam.

**Entrance requirements:** For master's, 15 hours in psychology, interview, minimum GPA of 3.0; for doctorate, 15 hours in psychology, interview, minimum GPA of 3.25.

**Find an in-depth description at www.petersons.com/gradchannel.**

■ **ARGOSY UNIVERSITY-DALLAS**

**Program in Clinical Psychology, Dallas, TX 75231**

**AWARDS** Clinical psychology (MA); professional counseling (MA); psychology (Psy D).

**Entrance requirements:** For master's, TOEFL. *Application fee:* $50.

**Expenses:** Tuition: Part-time $345 per credit hour. Required fees: $150 per semester.

Dr. Abby Calish, Head, 214-890-9900, *Fax:* 214-696-3500.

**Application contact:** Dee Pinkston, Director of Admissions, 214-890-9900, *Fax:* 214-696-3500, *E-mail:* dpinkston@argosyu.edu.

**Find an in-depth description at www.petersons.com/gradchannel.**

■ **ARGOSY UNIVERSITY-HONOLULU**

**Graduate Studies, Program in Professional Counseling, Honolulu, HI 96813**

**AWARDS** Marriage and family specialty (MA); professional counseling (MA). Part-time and evening/weekend programs available.

**Faculty:** 20 part-time/adjunct (13 women).

**Students:** 70 full-time (50 women), 3 part-time (2 women); includes 36 minority (1 African American, 30 Asian Americans or Pacific Islanders, 2 Hispanic Americans, 3 Native Americans). Average age 32. 55 applicants, 100% accepted. In 2001, 45 degrees awarded.

**Degree requirements:** For master's, practica. *Median time to degree:* Master's–2 years full-time, 3 years part-time.

**Entrance requirements:** For master's, minimum GPA of 3.0 in last 60 hours. *Application deadline:* For fall admission, 6/1; for winter admission, 11/1; for spring admission, 5/1. Applications are processed on a rolling basis. *Application fee:* $50. Electronic applications accepted.
**Expenses:** Contact institution.
**Financial support:** In 2001–02, 9 students received support. Career-related internships or fieldwork and Federal Work-Study available. Support available to part-time students. Financial award application deadline: 5/1; financial award applicants required to submit FAFSA.
Addie Jackson, Coordinator, 808-536-5555, *Fax:* 808-536-5505.
**Application contact:** Eric C. Carlson, Director of Admissions, 808-536-5555, *Fax:* 808-536-5505, *E-mail:* ecarlson@argosyu.edu. *Web site:* http://www.argosyu.edu/

**Find an in-depth description at www.petersons.com/gradchannel.**

■ **ARGOSY UNIVERSITY-ORANGE COUNTY**

**School of Psychology, Program in Counseling Psychology, Orange, CA 92868**
**AWARDS** Counseling psychology (Ed D); counseling psychology with MFT licensure (MA).

**Entrance requirements:** For master's, TOEFL, minimum GPA of 3.0 in final two years; for doctorate, TOEFL, minimum GPA of 3.0 in graduate study.
**Expenses:** Tuition: Part-time $437 per credit hour. Required fees: $10 per credit hour. Tuition and fees vary according to degree level and program.
**Application contact:** Joe Buechner, Director of Admissions, 800-716-9598, *Fax:* 714-940-0767, *E-mail:* jbuechner@argosyu.edu.

■ **ARGOSY UNIVERSITY-PHOENIX**

**Program in Professional Counseling, Phoenix, AZ 85021**
**AWARDS** MA. Part-time and evening/weekend programs available.

**Faculty:** 12 part-time/adjunct (6 women).
**Students:** Average age 33. 25 applicants, 60% accepted, 12 enrolled. In 2001, 6 degrees awarded.
**Degree requirements:** For master's, practicum. *Median time to degree:* Master's–2 years full-time, 3 years part-time.
*Application deadline:* For fall admission, 7/15 (priority date); for spring admission, 11/15 (priority date). Applications are

processed on a rolling basis. *Application fee:* $50. Electronic applications accepted.
**Expenses:** Tuition: Full-time $16,000; part-time $640 per credit. Required fees: $500; $250 per term. Full-time tuition and fees vary according to program.
Dr. Bart Lerner, Director, 602-216-2600, *Fax:* 602-216-2601, *E-mail:* blerner@argosyu.edu.
**Application contact:** Gail L. Bartkovich, Director of Admissions, 866-216-2777 Ext. 209, *Fax:* 602-216-2601, *E-mail:* gbartkovich@argosyu.edu.

■ **ARGOSY UNIVERSITY-SAN FRANCISCO BAY AREA**

**School of Behavioral Sciences, Point Richmond, CA 94804-3547**
**AWARDS** Clinical psychology (MA, Psy D); counseling psychology (MA). Part-time programs available.

**Faculty:** 8 full-time (3 women), 7 part-time/adjunct (4 women).
**Students:** 94 full-time (71 women), 41 part-time (33 women); includes 38 minority (14 African Americans, 15 Asian Americans or Pacific Islanders, 6 Hispanic Americans, 3 Native Americans). Average age 30. 185 applicants, 37% accepted. In 2001, 2 master's, 1 doctorate awarded.
**Degree requirements:** For master's, registration; for doctorate, thesis/dissertation, comprehensive exam, registration.
**Entrance requirements:** For master's, minimum GPA of 3.0, letters of recommendation; for doctorate, minimum GPA of 3.25, letters of recommendation.
*Application deadline:* For fall admission, 1/15 (priority date); for winter admission, 8/15 (priority date). Applications are processed on a rolling basis. *Application fee:* $50. Electronic applications accepted.
**Expenses:** Tuition: Part-time $640 per credit.
**Financial support:** In 2001–02, 36 students received support, including teaching assistantships (averaging $1,200 per year); Federal Work-Study and scholarships/grants also available. Support available to part-time students. Financial award application deadline: 3/1.
**Faculty research:** Consciousness studies, attitudes, non-verbal communication, substance abuse prevention, HIV/AIDS.
Dr. Anarea Morrison, Clinical Psychology Department Head, 510-215-0277, *Fax:* 510-215-0299.
**Application contact:** Cynthia R. Sirkin, Director of Outreach Services, 510-215-0277 Ext. 202, *Fax:* 510-215-0299, *E-mail:* csirkin@argosy.edu.

**Find an in-depth description at www.petersons.com/gradchannel.**

■ **ARGOSY UNIVERSITY-SARASOTA**

**School of Psychology and Behavioral Sciences, Sarasota, FL 34235-8246**
**AWARDS** Counseling psychology (Ed D); guidance counseling (MA); mental health counseling (MA); organizational leadership (Ed D); pastoral community counseling (Ed D); school counseling (Ed S). Part-time and evening/weekend programs available. Postbaccalaureate distance learning degree programs offered (minimal on-campus study).

**Faculty:** 13 full-time (4 women), 19 part-time/adjunct (9 women).
**Students:** 265 full-time (180 women), 220 part-time (149 women); includes 163 minority (138 African Americans, 9 Asian Americans or Pacific Islanders, 12 Hispanic Americans, 4 Native Americans). Average age 45. In 2001, 25 master's, 24 doctorates, 5 other advanced degrees awarded.
**Degree requirements:** For master's, thesis optional; for doctorate, thesis/dissertation, comprehensive exam.
**Entrance requirements:** For master's and doctorate, TOEFL. *Application deadline:* Applications are processed on a rolling basis. *Application fee:* $50.
**Expenses:** Contact institution.
**Financial support:** Federal Work-Study available. Support available to part-time students. Financial award applicants required to submit FAFSA.
Dr. Douglas G. Riedmiller, Dean, 800-331-5995, *Fax:* 941-379-9464, *E-mail:* douglas_griedmiller@embanet.com.
**Application contact:** Admissions Representative, 800-331-5995 Ext. 221, *Fax:* 941-371-8910. *Web site:* http://www.sarasota.edu/

■ **ARGOSY UNIVERSITY-SEATTLE**

**Program in Mental Health Counseling, Seattle, WA 98109**
**AWARDS** MA. Part-time and evening/weekend programs available. Postbaccalaureate distance learning degree programs offered (minimal on-campus study).

**Faculty:** 1 full-time (0 women), 3 part-time/adjunct (all women).
**Students:** 23 full-time (18 women), 4 part-time (2 women); includes 3 minority (1 African American, 1 Asian American or Pacific Islander, 1 Native American). Average age 28. 21 applicants, 90% accepted, 19 enrolled.
**Degree requirements:** For master's, registration.
**Entrance requirements:** For master's, minimum GPA of 3.0 (recommended). *Application deadline:* Applications are

*Argosy University-Seattle (continued)* processed on a rolling basis. *Application fee:* $50. Electronic applications accepted. **Expenses:** Contact institution. **Financial support:** In 2001–02, 24 students received support. Federal Work-Study and unspecified assistantships available. Support available to part-time students. Financial award applicants required to submit FAFSA.

Dr. F. Jeri Carter, Interim Director of Psychology and Counseling Program, 206-283-4500 Ext. 213, *Fax:* 206-283-5777, *E-mail:* jcarter@argosyu.edu.

**Application contact:** Heather Simpson, Director of Admissions, 206-283-4500 Ext. 206, *Fax:* 206-283-5777, *E-mail:* hsimpson@argosyu.edu. *Web site:* http://www.argosyu.edu/

## ■ ARGOSY UNIVERSITY-TWIN CITIES

**Graduate Programs, Bloomington, MN 55437-9761**

**AWARDS** Clinical psychology (MA, Psy D); education (MA); professional counseling/marriage and family therapy (MA). Part-time programs available.

**Faculty:** 13 full-time (6 women), 33 part-time/adjunct (13 women).

**Students:** 233 full-time (192 women), 122 part-time (83 women); includes 9 minority (3 African Americans, 4 Asian Americans or Pacific Islanders, 1 Hispanic American, 1 Native American, 1 international. Average age 31. 224 applicants, 62% accepted, 95 enrolled. In 2001, 27 master's, 41 doctorates awarded. Terminal master's awarded for partial completion of doctoral program.

**Degree requirements:** For master's, thesis (for some programs); for doctorate, thesis/dissertation, internship, research project, comprehensive exam. *Median time to degree:* Master's–2 years full-time, 3 years part-time; doctorate–5 years full-time, 6 years part-time.

**Entrance requirements:** For master's, GRE or MAT, minimum GPA of 3.0 (clinical psychology), 2.8 (professional counseling/marriage and family therapy); interview; for doctorate, GRE or MAT, minimum GPA of 3.25, interview. *Application deadline:* For fall admission, 5/15 (priority date); for winter admission, 1/15 (priority date). Applications are processed on a rolling basis. *Application fee:* $50. Electronic applications accepted.

**Expenses:** Tuition: Part-time $424 per credit hour. Required fees: $31 per year. Tuition and fees vary according to program and student level.

**Financial support:** In 2001–02, 12 fellowships with partial tuition reimbursements, 12 teaching assistantships with partial

tuition reimbursements were awarded. Career-related internships or fieldwork and Federal Work-Study also available. Support available to part-time students. Financial award application deadline: 3/14; financial award applicants required to submit FAFSA.

**Faculty research:** Cognitive behavioral therapy, human development, psychological assessment, marriage and family therapy, health psychology, physical/sexual abuse.

Dr. Jack T. O'Regan, Vice President Academic Affairs, 952-252-7575, *Fax:* 952-921-9574, *E-mail:* joregan@argosyu.edu.

**Application contact:** Jennifer Radke, Graduate Admissions Representative, 952-921-9500 Ext. 353, *Fax:* 952-921-9574, *E-mail:* tcadmissions@argosyu.edu. *Web site:* http://www.aspp.edu/

**Find an in-depth description at www.petersons.com/gradchannel.**

## ■ ARGOSY UNIVERSITY-WASHINGTON D.C.

**Professional Programs in Psychology, Arlington, VA 22209**

**AWARDS** Clinical psychology (MA, Psy D, Certificate); counseling psychology (MA); forensic psychology (MA). Part-time and evening/weekend programs available.

**Faculty:** 12 full-time (7 women), 43 part-time/adjunct (26 women).

**Students:** 304 full-time (237 women), 119 part-time (96 women); includes 112 minority (83 African Americans, 15 Asian Americans or Pacific Islanders, 11 Hispanic Americans, 3 Native Americans), 1 international. Average age 33. 341 applicants, 59% accepted. In 2001, 26 master's, 20 doctorates awarded.

**Degree requirements:** For master's, thesis (for some programs), practicum, comprehensive exam (for some programs); for doctorate, thesis/dissertation, internship, comprehensive exam. *Median time to degree:* Master's–2 years full-time, 3 years part-time; doctorate–6 years full-time.

**Entrance requirements:** For master's, clinical experience, minimum GPA of 3.0; for doctorate, clinical experience, minimum GPA of 3.25. *Application deadline:* For fall admission, 1/15 (priority date); for spring admission, 10/15. Applications are processed on a rolling basis. *Application fee:* $55. Electronic applications accepted.

**Expenses:** Tuition: Full-time $6,732; part-time $374 per credit. Required fees: $22; $90 per term. Tuition and fees vary according to course load, degree level and program.

**Financial support:** In 2001–02, 347 students received support, including 2 fellowships with tuition reimbursements available (averaging $3,600 per year), 55

teaching assistantships with full and partial tuition reimbursements available (averaging $1,530 per year); research assistantships, career-related internships or fieldwork, Federal Work-Study, and scholarships/grants also available. Support available to part-time students. Financial award application deadline: 6/30; financial award applicants required to submit FAFSA.

**Faculty research:** Psychotherapy integration, minority health, forensic assessment, family violence, child maltreatment. *Total annual research expenditures:* $2,000.

Dr. Cynthia G. Baum, Campus President, 703-243-5300, *Fax:* 703-243-8973, *E-mail:* cbaum@argosyu.edu.

**Application contact:** Debbie Jacobs, Director of Admissions, 703-243-5300 Ext. 118, *Fax:* 703-243-8973, *E-mail:* ddmjacobs@argosyu.edu. *Web site:* http://www.argosy.edu/

**Find an in-depth description at www.petersons.com/gradchannel.**

## ■ ARIZONA STATE UNIVERSITY

**Graduate College, College of Education, Division of Psychology in Education, Academic Program in Counseling Psychology, Tempe, AZ 85287**

**AWARDS** PhD.

**Degree requirements:** For doctorate, thesis/dissertation.

**Entrance requirements:** For doctorate, GRE General Test or MAT.

**Faculty research:** Career development; self-efficacy; school based drug abuse prevention; adolescent suicide prevention, consultation.

## ■ ASSUMPTION COLLEGE

**Graduate School, Department of Psychology, Worcester, MA 01609-1296**

**AWARDS** Counseling psychology (MA, CAGS). Part-time and evening/weekend programs available.

**Faculty:** 5 full-time (2 women), 8 part-time/adjunct (3 women).

**Students:** 77 (62 women); includes 1 minority (Asian American or Pacific Islander). 20 applicants, 95% accepted. In 2001, 25 degrees awarded.

**Degree requirements:** For master's, internship, practicum.

**Entrance requirements:** For master's, TOEFL. *Application deadline:* Applications are processed on a rolling basis. *Application fee:* $30.

**Expenses:** Tuition: Part-time $1,005 per credit.

**Financial support:** In 2001–02, 9 fellowships with partial tuition reimbursements (averaging $9,360 per year) were awarded; career-related internships or fieldwork also available. Support available to part-time students. Financial award applicants required to submit FAFSA.

**Faculty research:** Mood disorders, adjustment to life-threatening illness, perception of movement, socio-emotional development of young children, discovery vs. disclosure.

Dr. Leonard A. Doerfler, Chairperson, 508-767-7554, *E-mail:* doerfler@ assumption.edu. *Web site:* http:// www.assumption.edu/

## ■ AUBURN UNIVERSITY

**Graduate School, College of Education, Department of Counseling and Counseling Psychology, Auburn University, AL 36849**

**AWARDS** Community agency counseling (M Ed, MS, Ed D, PhD, Ed S); counseling psychology (PhD); counselor education (Ed D, PhD); school counseling (M Ed, MS, Ed D, PhD, Ed S); school psychometry (M Ed, MS, Ed D, PhD, Ed S). Part-time programs available.

**Faculty:** 9 full-time (5 women).
**Students:** 57 full-time (51 women), 53 part-time (37 women); includes 32 minority (28 African Americans, 1 Asian American or Pacific Islander, 2 Hispanic Americans, 1 Native American), 4 international. 105 applicants, 57% accepted. In 2001, 19 master's, 8 doctorates awarded.
**Degree requirements:** For master's, thesis (for some programs); for doctorate, thesis/dissertation; for Ed S, thesis or alternative.
**Entrance requirements:** For master's and Ed S, GRE General Test; for doctorate, GRE General Test, GRE Subject Test. *Application deadline:* For fall admission, 5/15. *Application fee:* $25 ($50 for international students). Electronic applications accepted.
**Financial support:** Research assistantships, Federal Work-Study and traineeships available. Support available to part-time students. Financial award application deadline: 3/15.
**Faculty research:** At-risk students, substance abuse, gender roles, AIDS, professional ethics.
Dr. Holly Stadler, Head, 334-844-5160.
**Application contact:** Dr. John F. Pritchett, Dean of the Graduate School, 334-844-4700, *E-mail:* hatchlb@ mail.auburn.edu. *Web site:* http:// www.auburn.edu/academic/education/ccp/ an_ccp.html

## ■ AVILA UNIVERSITY

**Graduate Programs, Department of Education and Psychology, Program in Psychology, Kansas City, MO 64145-1698**

**AWARDS** Counseling psychology (MS). Part-time and evening/weekend programs available.

**Faculty:** 4 full-time (2 women), 4 part-time/adjunct (3 women).
**Students:** 12 full-time (10 women), 35 part-time (27 women); includes 4 minority (1 African American, 1 Asian American or Pacific Islander, 2 Hispanic Americans). Average age 35. 15 applicants, 100% accepted. In 2001, 17 degrees awarded.
**Degree requirements:** For master's, final exam.
**Entrance requirements:** For master's, GRE General Test, TOEFL, minimum GPA of 3.0 in last 60 hours. *Application deadline:* For fall admission, 4/30 (priority date); for spring admission, 11/30. Applications are processed on a rolling basis. *Application fee:* $0. Electronic applications accepted.
**Expenses:** Tuition: Part-time $335 per credit hour. Required fees: $5 per credit hour.
**Financial support:** In 2001–02, 1 research assistantship was awarded; career-related internships or fieldwork also available. Support available to part-time students. Financial award applicants required to submit FAFSA.
**Faculty research:** Preparation for working in mental health services.
Dr. Cathy Bogart, Director, 816-501-3792, *Fax:* 816-501-2455, *E-mail:* bogartcj@ mail.avila.edu.
**Application contact:** Susan Randolph, Admissions Office, 816-501-3792, *Fax:* 816-501-2455, *E-mail:* randolphs@ mail.avila.edu. *Web site:* http:// www.avila.edu/departments/psychology/ mscpweb.htm

## ■ BALL STATE UNIVERSITY

**Graduate School, Teachers College, Department of Counseling Psychology and Guidance Services, Program in Counseling Psychology, Muncie, IN 47306-1099**

**AWARDS** MA, PhD.

**Students:** 83 full-time (61 women), 76 part-time (56 women). Average age 30. 180 applicants, 62% accepted. In 2001, 32 master's, 6 doctorates awarded.
**Degree requirements:** For doctorate, thesis/dissertation.
**Entrance requirements:** For doctorate, GRE General Test, GRE General Test, interview, minimum graduate GPA of 3.2,

resumé. *Application fee:* $25 ($35 for international students).
**Expenses:** Tuition, state resident: full-time $4,068; part-time $2,542. Tuition, nonresident: full-time $10,944; part-time $6,462. Required fees: $1,000; $500 per term.
**Financial support:** Research assistantships with full tuition reimbursements available. Financial award application deadline: 3/1.
Dr. Phyllis Gordon, Head, 765-285-8040. *Web site:* http://www.bsu.edu/teachers/ counseling/cpsy/

## ■ BENEDICTINE UNIVERSITY

**Graduate Programs, Program in Counseling Psychology, Lisle, IL 60532-0900**

**AWARDS** MS. Part-time programs available.

**Degree requirements:** For master's, internship.
**Entrance requirements:** For master's, MAT. *Web site:* http://www.ben.edu/

## ■ BETHEL COLLEGE

**Division of Graduate Studies, Program in Counseling, Mishawaka, IN 46545-5591**

**AWARDS** Marriage and family counseling/ therapy (MA); mental health counseling (MA).

**Faculty:** 6 part-time/adjunct (2 women).
**Students:** In 2001, 1 degree awarded.
**Entrance requirements:** For master's, GRE, interview, previous undergraduate course work in psychology and religion. *Application deadline:* For fall admission, 7/1 (priority date); for winter admission, 11/1 (priority date); for spring admission, 3/15 (priority date). Applications are processed on a rolling basis. *Application fee:* $25. Electronic applications accepted.
**Expenses:** Tuition: Full-time $5,940; part-time $330 per semester hour.
**Financial support:** Unspecified assistantships available. Financial award applicants required to submit FAFSA.
**Faculty research:** Counseling and religiosity, aging and hearing, cognitive schema.
Dr. Mark J. Gerig, Director, 219-257-2595, *Fax:* 219-257-3357, *E-mail:* gerigm1@bethel-in.edu.
**Application contact:** Elizabeth W. McLaughlin, Assistant Director of Graduate Admissions, 219-257-3360, *Fax:* 219-257-3357, *E-mail:* mclaughb2@bethel-in.edu.

## ■ BOSTON COLLEGE

**Lynch Graduate School of Education, Department of Counseling Psychology, Developmental and Educational Psychology, Program in Counseling Psychology, Chestnut Hill, MA 02467-3800**

**AWARDS** MA, PhD, MA/MA.

**Students:** 85 full-time (66 women), 110 part-time (85 women); includes 40 minority (12 African Americans, 13 Asian Americans or Pacific Islanders, 14 Hispanic Americans, 1 Native American), 16 international. 416 applicants, 56% accepted. In 2001, 85 master's, 3 doctorates awarded. Terminal master's awarded for partial completion of doctoral program.
**Degree requirements:** For master's, comprehensive exam; for doctorate, thesis/dissertation, comprehensive exam.
**Entrance requirements:** For master's and doctorate, GRE General Test. *Application fee:* $40.
**Expenses:** Tuition: Full-time $17,664; part-time $8,832 per semester.
**Financial support:** Fellowships with full and partial tuition reimbursements, research assistantships with full and partial tuition reimbursements, teaching assistantships with full and partial tuition reimbursements, career-related internships or fieldwork, Federal Work-Study, scholarships/grants, traineeships, tuition waivers (full and partial), and unspecified assistantships available. Support available to part-time students. Financial award applicants required to submit FAFSA.
**Faculty research:** Juvenile delinquency, ethics, intellectual and ethical development, family functioning, effect of urban violence on children.
**Application contact:** Arline Riordan, Graduate Admissions Director, 617-552-4214, *Fax:* 617-552-0812, *E-mail:* grad.ed.info@bc.edu. *Web site:* http://www.bc.edu/education

## ■ BOSTON UNIVERSITY

**School of Education, Department of Developmental Studies and Counseling, Program in Counseling Psychology, Boston, MA 02215**

**AWARDS** Ed D.

**Degree requirements:** For doctorate, thesis/dissertation, comprehensive exam.
**Entrance requirements:** For doctorate, GRE General Test or MAT, TOEFL. Electronic applications accepted.
**Expenses:** Tuition: Full-time $25,872; part-time $340 per credit. Required fees: $40 per semester. Part-time tuition and fees vary according to class time, course level and program.

**Faculty research:** Cross-cultural counseling, parenting, women's development, mental health.

## ■ BOSTON UNIVERSITY

**School of Medicine, Division of Graduate Medical Sciences, Program in Mental Health and Behavioral Medicine, Boston, MA 02215**

**AWARDS** MA.

**Faculty:** 18 full-time (8 women).
**Degree requirements:** For master's, qualifying exam.
**Entrance requirements:** For master's, GRE General Test, TOEFL. *Application deadline:* Applications are processed on a rolling basis. *Application fee:* $50.
**Expenses:** Tuition: Full-time $25,872; part-time $340 per credit. Required fees: $40 per semester. Part-time tuition and fees vary according to class time, course level and program.
**Faculty research:** HIV/AIDS, neurosciences, autism, serious mental illness, sports psychology. *Total annual research expenditures:* $3 million.
Dr. Stephen Brady, Director, 617-638-8689, *Fax:* 617-626-8929, *E-mail:* sbrady@bu.edu.
**Application contact:** Information Contact, 617-638-8689, *Fax:* 617-626-8929. *Web site:* http://www.bumc.bu.edu

## ■ BOWIE STATE UNIVERSITY

**Graduate Programs, Program in Counseling Psychology, Bowie, MD 20715-9465**

**AWARDS** MA. Evening/weekend programs available.

**Degree requirements:** For master's, research paper, thesis optional.

## ■ BRIGHAM YOUNG UNIVERSITY

**Graduate Studies, David O. McKay School of Education, Department of Counseling Psychology and Special Education, Provo, UT 84602-1001**

**AWARDS** Counseling and school psychology (MS); counseling psychology (PhD); special education (MS).

**Faculty:** 15 full-time (8 women), 7 part-time/adjunct (2 women).
**Students:** 57 full-time (37 women), 14 part-time (9 women); includes 5 minority (1 African American, 3 Asian Americans or Pacific Islanders, 1 Hispanic American), 4 international. Average age 31. 77 applicants, 31% accepted, 24 enrolled. In 2001, 14 master's, 3 doctorates awarded.
**Degree requirements:** For master's, thesis optional; for doctorate, thesis/dissertation, comprehensive exam. *Median time to degree:* Master's–2.3 years full-time; doctorate–4.8 years full-time.

**Entrance requirements:** For master's, GRE General Test or MAT, minimum GPA of 3.0 in last 60 hours; for doctorate, GRE General Test, minimum GPA of 3.4 in last 60 hours. *Application deadline:* For fall admission, 2/1. *Application fee:* $50. Electronic applications accepted.
**Expenses:** Tuition: Full-time $3,860; part-time $214 per hour.
**Financial support:** In 2001–02, 42 students received support, including 20 research assistantships with partial tuition reimbursements available (averaging $5,500 per year), 3 teaching assistantships with partial tuition reimbursements available (averaging $5,500 per year); career-related internships or fieldwork, institutionally sponsored loans, and tuition waivers (partial) also available.
**Faculty research:** Values and mental health, distance education, career counselors, special education.
Dr. Ronald D. Bingham, Chair, 801-422-3857, *Fax:* 801-422-0198, *E-mail:* ron_bingham@byu.edu.
**Application contact:** Diane E. Hancock, Executive Secretary, 801-422-3859, *Fax:* 801-422-0198, *E-mail:* diane_hancock@byu.edu. *Web site:* http://www.byu.edu/cse/

## ■ CALDWELL COLLEGE

**Graduate Studies, Program in Counseling Psychology, Caldwell, NJ 07006-6195**

**AWARDS** Art therapy (MA); counseling psychology (MA). Part-time and evening/weekend programs available.

**Faculty:** 3 full-time (1 woman), 1 part-time/adjunct (0 women).
**Students:** 4 full-time (all women), 23 part-time (19 women); includes 3 minority (2 African Americans, 1 Hispanic American). Average age 35. 8 applicants, 75% accepted, 5 enrolled. In 2001, 7 degrees awarded.
**Degree requirements:** For master's, thesis, practicum, research paper, comprehensive exam.
**Entrance requirements:** For master's, GRE, 15 undergraduate credits in psychology, interview, minimum GPA of 3.0. *Application deadline:* Applications are processed on a rolling basis. *Application fee:* $40.
**Expenses:** Tuition: Part-time $437 per credit.
**Financial support:** Applicants required to submit FAFSA.
Sr. Catherine Waters, Coordinator, 973-618-3658, *Fax:* 973-618-3640, *E-mail:* watersca@caldwell.edu.
**Application contact:** Bette Jo Ho'Aire, Administrative Assistant, 973-618-3408, *Fax:* 973-618-3640, *E-mail:* ehoaire@

caldwell.edu. *Web site:* http://www.caldwell.edu/graduate/

### ■ CALDWELL COLLEGE

**Graduate Studies, Program in Counseling Psychology with Art Therapy Specialization, Caldwell, NJ 07006-6195**

**AWARDS** Art therapy (MA). Part-time and evening/weekend programs available.

**Faculty:** 3 full-time (1 woman), 1 part-time/adjunct (0 women).
**Students:** 4 full-time (all women), 5 part-time (all women), 1 international. Average age 31. 4 applicants, 100% accepted, 1 enrolled.
**Entrance requirements:** For master's, GRE, minimum GPA of 3.0, 15 credits in studio arts, portfolio. *Application fee:* $40.
**Expenses:** Tuition: Part-time $437 per credit.
Prof. Marie Wilson, Coordinator, 973-618-3511, *Fax:* 973-618-3915, *E-mail:* mwilson@caldwell.edu.
**Application contact:** Bette Jo Ho'Aire, Administrative Assistant, 973-618-3408, *Fax:* 973-618-3640, *E-mail:* ehoaire@caldwell.edu.

### ■ CALIFORNIA BAPTIST UNIVERSITY

**Graduate Program in Marriage and Family Therapy, Riverside, CA 92504-3206**

**AWARDS** Counseling psychology (MS). Part-time programs available.

**Faculty:** 4 full-time (1 woman), 3 part-time/adjunct (1 woman).
**Students:** 75. 40 applicants, 78% accepted, 23 enrolled. In 2001, 18 degrees awarded.
**Degree requirements:** For master's, thesis or alternative, 24 hours (individual) or 50 hours (group) psychotherapy, comprehensive exam.
**Entrance requirements:** For master's, Minnesota Multiphasic Personality Inventory and Myers-Briggs Personality Inventory, previous course work in developmental psychology, theories of personality, and statistics, minimum undergraduate GPA of 3.0. *Application deadline:* For fall admission, 7/15; for spring admission, 11/1. Applications are processed on a rolling basis. *Application fee:* $45.
**Expenses:** Contact institution.
**Financial support:** In 2001–02, 59 students received support. Career-related internships or fieldwork and Federal Work-Study available. Support available to part-time students. Financial award applicants required to submit FAFSA.

Dr. Gary Collins, Director, 909-343-4304, *Fax:* 909-343-4569, *E-mail:* gcollins@calbaptist.edu.
**Application contact:** Gail Ronveaux, Associate Dean, Enrollment Services, 909-343-5045, *Fax:* 909-343-5095, *E-mail:* gradservices@calbaptist.edu. *Web site:* http://www.calbaptist.edu/

### ■ CALIFORNIA INSTITUTE OF INTEGRAL STUDIES

**Graduate Programs, School of Professional Psychology, San Francisco, CA 94103**

**AWARDS** Drama therapy (MA); expressive arts therapy (MA, Certificate), including consulting and education (Certificate), expressive arts (Certificate), expressive arts therapy (MA); integral counseling psychology (MA); psychology (Psy D), including clinical psychology; somatics (MA, Certificate), including integral health education (Certificate), somatics (MA). Part-time and evening/weekend programs available.

**Students:** 205 full-time, 236 part-time. 298 applicants, 65% accepted, 115 enrolled.
**Degree requirements:** For master's, comprehensive exam; for doctorate, thesis/dissertation, comprehensive exam.
**Entrance requirements:** For master's, TOEFL, minimum GPA of 3.0; for doctorate, TOEFL, field experience, master's degree, minimum GPA of 3.1. *Application deadline:* Applications are processed on a rolling basis. *Application fee:* $65.
**Expenses:** Tuition: Full-time $10,890; part-time $605 per unit. Tuition and fees vary according to degree level.
**Financial support:** Career-related internships or fieldwork, Federal Work-Study, institutionally sponsored loans, and scholarships/grants available. Support available to part-time students. Financial award application deadline: 6/15; financial award applicants required to submit FAFSA.
**Faculty research:** Somatic psychology.
Dr. Harrison Voigt, Head, 415-575-6218.
**Application contact:** David Towner, Admissions Officer, 415-575-6152, *Fax:* 415-575-1268, *E-mail:* dtowner@ciis.edu.

**Find an in-depth description at www.petersons.com/gradchannel.**

### ■ CALIFORNIA STATE UNIVERSITY, BAKERSFIELD

**Division of Graduate Studies and Research, Program in Counseling Psychology, Bakersfield, CA 93311-1099**

**AWARDS** MS. *Web site:* http://www.csub.edu/cpsy

### ■ CALIFORNIA STATE UNIVERSITY, CHICO

**Graduate School, College of Behavioral and Social Sciences, Department of Psychology, Chico, CA 95929-0722**

**AWARDS** Counseling (MS); psychology (MA).

**Students:** 60 full-time, 13 part-time; includes 10 minority (1 African American, 3 Asian Americans or Pacific Islanders, 5 Hispanic Americans, 1 Native American). 58 applicants, 84% accepted, 31 enrolled. In 2001, 30 degrees awarded.
**Degree requirements:** For master's, thesis or alternative, oral exam.
**Entrance requirements:** For master's, GRE General Test or MAT, letters of recommendation on departmental form (3). *Application deadline:* For fall admission, 3/1. Applications are processed on a rolling basis. *Application fee:* $55. Electronic applications accepted.
**Expenses:** Tuition, state resident: full-time $2,148. Tuition, nonresident: full-time $6,576.
**Financial support:** Fellowships, teaching assistantships, career-related internships or fieldwork available.
Dr. Paul Spear, Chairman, 530-898-5147.
**Application contact:** Dr. Joseph Russo, Graduate Coordinator, 530-898-5368.

### ■ CALIFORNIA STATE UNIVERSITY, SACRAMENTO

**Graduate Studies, College of Social Sciences and Interdisciplinary Studies, Department of Psychology, Sacramento, CA 95819-6048**

**AWARDS** Counseling psychology (MA). Part-time programs available.

**Students:** 36 full-time (28 women), 44 part-time (37 women); includes 19 minority (3 African Americans, 7 Asian Americans or Pacific Islanders, 9 Hispanic Americans), 4 international.
**Degree requirements:** For master's, thesis, writing proficiency exam.
**Entrance requirements:** For master's, GRE Subject Test, TOEFL, minimum GPA of 3.0 during previous 2 years. *Application deadline:* For fall admission, 4/15; for spring admission, 11/1. *Application fee:* $55.
**Expenses:** Tuition, state resident: full-time $1,965; part-time $668 per semester. Tuition, nonresident: part-time $246 per unit.
**Financial support:** Career-related internships or fieldwork and Federal Work-Study available. Support available to part-time students. Financial award application deadline: 3/1.
Dr. Tammy Bourg, Chair, 916-278-6254.

*California State University, Sacramento (continued)*

**Application contact:** Dr. Lawrence Meyers, Coordinator, 916-278-6365.

## ■ CALIFORNIA STATE UNIVERSITY, SAN BERNARDINO

**Graduate Studies, College of Social and Behavioral Sciences, Department of Psychology, Program in Clinical/Counseling Psychology, San Bernardino, CA 92407-2397**

**AWARDS** MS.

**Faculty:** 10 full-time.

**Students:** 18 full-time (14 women), 4 part-time (3 women); includes 8 minority (1 African American, 1 Asian American or Pacific Islander, 5 Hispanic Americans, 1 Native American). Average age 32. 39 applicants, 21% accepted. In 2001, 8 degrees awarded.

**Degree requirements:** For master's, comprehensive exam or thesis.

**Entrance requirements:** For master's, minimum GPA of 3.0 in major. *Application deadline:* For fall admission, 8/31 (priority date). *Application fee:* $55.

**Expenses:** Tuition, nonresident: full-time $4,428. Required fees: $1,733.

**Financial support:** Fellowships, research assistantships, teaching assistantships, career-related internships or fieldwork, Federal Work-Study, and unspecified assistantships available. Financial award application deadline: 3/1.

**Faculty research:** Psychology of women, fathering, depression, families, cross-cultural counseling.

Dr. Faith H. McClure, Head, 909-880-5598, *Fax:* 909-880-7003, *E-mail:* fmcclure@csusb.edu.

**Application contact:** Luci Van Loon, Graduate Secretary, 909-880-5570, *Fax:* 909-880-7003, *E-mail:* lvanloon@csusb.edu.

## ■ CALIFORNIA STATE UNIVERSITY, STANISLAUS

**Graduate Programs, College of Arts, Letters, and Sciences, Department of Psychology, Turlock, CA 95382**

**AWARDS** Behavior analysis psychology (MS); counseling psychology (MS); general psychology (MA). Part-time programs available.

**Students:** 42 (33 women); includes 7 minority (3 Asian Americans or Pacific Islanders, 4 Hispanic Americans). 51 applicants, 98% accepted. In 2001, 15 degrees awarded.

**Degree requirements:** For master's, thesis.

**Entrance requirements:** For master's, GRE General Test, minimum GPA of 3.0.

*Application deadline:* For fall admission, 2/1. *Application fee:* $55. Electronic applications accepted.

**Expenses:** Tuition, nonresident: part-time $246 per unit. Required fees: $1,919. Tuition and fees vary according to campus/location and program.

**Financial support:** In 2001–02, 1 fellowship (averaging $2,500 per year) was awarded; career-related internships or fieldwork and Federal Work-Study also available. Financial award application deadline: 3/2; financial award applicants required to submit FAFSA.

**Faculty research:** Social roles, counseling problems, psychology of religion, behavior genetics, applied analysis of behavior.

Dr. Bruce Hessee, Chair, 209-667-3386.

**Application contact:** Dr. Gina Pallotta, Director, 209-667-3386, *Fax:* 209-664-7067, *E-mail:* pallotta@toto.csustan.edu.

## ■ CAMBRIDGE COLLEGE

**Graduate Studies, Program in Counseling Psychology, Cambridge, MA 02138-5304**

**AWARDS** M Ed. Part-time and evening/weekend programs available.

**Degree requirements:** For master's, thesis, internship/practicum.

**Entrance requirements:** For master's, TOEFL.

## ■ CARLOS ALBIZU UNIVERSITY, MIAMI CAMPUS

**Graduate Programs, Miami, FL 33172-2209**

**AWARDS** Clinical psychology (Psy D); industrial/organizational psychology (MS); management (MBA); marriage and family therapy (MS); mental health counseling (MS); psychology (MS); school counseling (MS). Part-time and evening/weekend programs available.

**Faculty:** 19 full-time (9 women), 37 part-time/adjunct (19 women).

**Students:** 432 full-time (322 women), 32 part-time (22 women); includes 328 minority (58 African Americans, 7 Asian Americans or Pacific Islanders, 263 Hispanic Americans), 4 international. Average age 35. 189 applicants, 50% accepted, 69 enrolled. In 2001, 44 master's, 69 doctorates awarded. Terminal master's awarded for partial completion of doctoral program.

**Degree requirements:** For master's, one foreign language, comprehensive exam, integrative project (MBA); for doctorate, one foreign language, thesis/dissertation, written and oral qualifying exam, internship.

**Entrance requirements:** For master's, GMAT (MBA), letters of recommendation

(3), interview, minimum GPA of 3.0, resumé; for doctorate, GRE General Test, GRE Subject Test, letters of recommendation (3), minimum GPA of 3.0. *Application deadline:* For fall admission, 8/1 (priority date); for spring admission, 11/30 (priority date). Applications are processed on a rolling basis. *Application fee:* $50.

**Expenses:** Tuition: Part-time $455 per credit. Required fees: $819; $273 per term. Tuition and fees vary according to course load and degree level.

**Financial support:** In 2001–02, 22 students received support. Federal Work-Study and scholarships/grants available. Financial award application deadline: 6/1; financial award applicants required to submit FAFSA.

**Faculty research:** Culture, psychodiagnostics, psychotherapy, forensic psychology, neuropsychology; marketing strategy, entrepreneurship.

Dr. Gerardo F. Rodriquez-Menedez, Chancellor, 305-593-1223 Ext. 120, *Fax:* 305-629-8052, *E-mail:* grodriguez@albizu.edu.

**Application contact:** Miriam Matos, Admissions Officer, 305-593-1223 Ext. 134, *Fax:* 305-593-1854, *E-mail:* mmatos@albizu.edu. *Web site:* http://www.albizu.edu/

## ■ CENTENARY COLLEGE

**Program in Counseling Psychology, Hackettstown, NJ 07840-2100**

**AWARDS** Counseling (MA); counseling psychology (MA). Part-time and evening/weekend programs available. Postbaccalaureate distance learning degree programs offered (minimal on-campus study).

**Degree requirements:** For master's, thesis, fieldwork.

**Expenses:** Tuition: Full-time $10,320; part-time $430 per credit.

## ■ CENTRAL WASHINGTON UNIVERSITY

**Graduate Studies and Research, College of the Sciences, Department of Psychology, Program in Counseling Psychology, Ellensburg, WA 98926-7463**

**AWARDS** MS.

**Faculty:** 23 full-time (9 women).

**Students:** 20 full-time (14 women), 9 part-time (7 women); includes 3 minority (1 Asian American or Pacific Islander, 2 Hispanic Americans), 1 international. 27 applicants, 44% accepted, 7 enrolled. In 2001, 13 degrees awarded.

**Degree requirements:** For master's, thesis, internship.

**Entrance requirements:** For master's, GRE General Test, minimum GPA of 3.0.

*Application deadline:* For fall admission, 4/1. *Application fee:* $35.

**Expenses:** Tuition, state resident: full-time $4,848; part-time $162 per credit. Tuition, nonresident: full-time $14,772; part-time $492 per credit. Required fees: $324.

**Financial support:** In 2001–02, 9 research assistantships with partial tuition reimbursements (averaging $7,120 per year) were awarded; teaching assistantships, career-related internships or fieldwork and Federal Work-Study also available. Financial award application deadline: 3/1; financial award applicants required to submit FAFSA.

**Application contact:** Barbara Sisko, Office Assistant, Graduate Studies and Research, 509-963-3103, *Fax:* 509-963-1799, *E-mail:* masters@cwu.edu. *Web site:* http://www.cwu.edu/

### ■ CHAMINADE UNIVERSITY OF HONOLULU

**Graduate Programs, Program in Counseling Psychology, Honolulu, HI 96816-1578**

**AWARDS** MSCP. Part-time and evening/weekend programs available.

**Faculty:** 6 full-time (2 women), 21 part-time/adjunct (12 women).

**Students:** 153 full-time (118 women), 54 part-time (39 women); includes 156 minority (14 African Americans, 132 Asian Americans or Pacific Islanders, 9 Hispanic Americans, 1 Native American), 5 international. Average age 33. 82 applicants, 83% accepted. In 2001, 65 degrees awarded.

**Degree requirements:** For master's, comprehensive exam.

**Entrance requirements:** For master's, TOEFL, minimum undergraduate GPA of 3.0. *Application deadline:* For fall admission, 9/1 (priority date); for winter admission, 11/15; for spring admission, 3/1. Applications are processed on a rolling basis. *Application fee:* $50.

**Financial support:** In 2001–02, 132 students received support. Career-related internships or fieldwork, Federal Work-Study, and institutionally sponsored loans available. Support available to part-time students. Financial award application deadline: 3/1.

**Faculty research:** Taoist/Buddhist psychology, psychology of T'ai Chi Ch'uan, sleep disorders, drug/alcohol prevention with adolescent girls, anger/aggression with kids.

Dr. Robert G. Santee, Director, 808-735-4720, *Fax:* 808-739-4670, *E-mail:* rsantee@chaminade.edu.

**Application contact:** Janet C. Martin, Secretary, 808-735-4751, *Fax:* 808-739-4670, *E-mail:* jmartin@chaminade.edu.

### ■ CHATHAM COLLEGE

**Graduate and Professional Studies, Program in Counseling Psychology, Pittsburgh, PA 15232-2826**

**AWARDS** MS. Part-time and evening/weekend programs available.

**Faculty:** 4 full-time (3 women), 7 part-time/adjunct (3 women).

**Students:** 19 full-time (16 women), 64 part-time (58 women); includes 6 minority (5 African Americans, 1 Asian American or Pacific Islander), 1 international. Average age 33. 54 applicants, 72% accepted, 31 enrolled. In 2001, 7 degrees awarded.

**Degree requirements:** For master's, supervised internship, optional advanced research project, thesis optional.

**Entrance requirements:** For master's, interview, minimum GPA of 3.0. *Application deadline:* Applications are processed on a rolling basis. *Application fee:* $35. Electronic applications accepted.

**Expenses:** Tuition: Full-time $17,764; part-time $458 per credit. Tuition and fees vary according to program.

**Financial support:** In 2001–02, 50 students received support, including 15 research assistantships (averaging $6,000 per year); career-related internships or fieldwork and institutionally sponsored loans also available. Support available to part-time students. Financial award applicants required to submit FAFSA.

**Faculty research:** Trauma and recovery, hypnosis, psychospiritual dimensions of healing, psychotherapy of schizophrenia. Dr. Gloria Novel, Director, 412-365-2766, *Fax:* 412-365-1505.

**Application contact:** Office of Graduate Admissions, 412-365-1290, *Fax:* 412-365-1609, *E-mail:* admissions@chatham.edu. *Web site:* http://www.chatham.edu/

### ■ CHESTNUT HILL COLLEGE

**Graduate Division, Department of Professional Psychology, Program in Counseling Psychology and Human Services, Philadelphia, PA 19118-2693**

**AWARDS** MA, MS, CAS.

**Degree requirements:** For master's, thesis.

**Entrance requirements:** For master's, GRE or MAT, TOEFL, TSE, and TWE; for CAS, Master's degree in counseling or a related discipline. *Web site:* http://www.chc.edu/graduate/Gpsych.html

### ■ CITY UNIVERSITY

**Graduate Division, School of Human Services and Applied Behavioral Sciences, Bellevue, WA 98005**

**AWARDS** Counseling psychology (MA). Part-time and evening/weekend programs available. Postbaccalaureate distance learning degree programs offered (no on-campus study).

**Faculty:** 5 full-time (4 women), 58 part-time/adjunct (37 women).

**Students:** 105 full-time, 243 part-time; includes 40 minority (23 African Americans, 8 Asian Americans or Pacific Islanders, 7 Hispanic Americans, 2 Native Americans), 2 international. Average age 36. 60 applicants, 100% accepted, 7 enrolled. In 2001, 41 degrees awarded. *Application deadline:* Applications are processed on a rolling basis. *Application fee:* $75 ($175 for international students). Electronic applications accepted.

**Expenses:** Tuition: Part-time $324 per credit.

**Financial support:** In 2001–02, 31 students received support. Federal Work-Study available. Support available to part-time students. Financial award applicants required to submit FAFSA.

**Application contact:** 800-426-5596, *Fax:* 425-709-5361, *E-mail:* info@citryu.edu. *Web site:* http://www.cityu.edu/

### ■ CLEVELAND STATE UNIVERSITY

**College of Graduate Studies, College of Arts and Sciences, Department of Psychology, Professional Program in Clinical and Counseling Psychology, Cleveland, OH 44115**

**AWARDS** MA.

**Faculty:** 17 full-time (6 women), 4 part-time/adjunct (1 woman).

**Students:** 21 full-time (17 women); includes 1 minority (Hispanic American). Average age 25. 94 applicants, 22% accepted, 21 enrolled. In 2001, 17 degrees awarded.

**Degree requirements:** For master's, internship, thesis optional. *Median time to degree:* Master's–2 years full-time.

**Entrance requirements:** For master's, GRE General Test, GRE Subject Test, previous course work in psychology, sample of written work. *Application deadline:* For fall admission, 2/1 (priority date). Applications are processed on a rolling basis. *Application fee:* $25 ($50 for international students).

**Expenses:** Tuition, state resident: full-time $6,838; part-time $263 per credit hour. Tuition, nonresident: full-time $13,526; part-time $520 per credit hour.

*Cleveland State University (continued)*
**Financial support:** In 2001–02, 12 students received support. Career-related internships or fieldwork, Federal Work-Study, and tuition waivers (full) available. Financial award application deadline: 5/1; financial award applicants required to submit FAFSA.
**Faculty research:** Clinical psychopathology, cognitive interventions, personality assessment.
Dr. Steve D. Slane, Director, 216-687-2525, *Fax:* 216-687-9294.
**Application contact:** Karen Colston, Administrative Coordinator, 216-687-2552, *E-mail:* k.colston@csuohio.edu. *Web site:* http://www.asic.csuohio.edu/psy/grad/clin.html

### ■ COLLEGE OF MOUNT SAINT VINCENT

**Program in Allied Health Studies, Riverdale, NY 10471-1093**
**AWARDS** Allied health studies (MS), including child and family health, counseling, health care management, health care systems and policies; counseling (Certificate); health care management (Certificate); health care systems and policies (Certificate). Part-time and evening/weekend programs available.
**Faculty:** 7 full-time (4 women), 4 part-time/adjunct (1 woman).
**Students:** 7 full-time (all women), 43 part-time (35 women); includes 33 minority (19 African Americans, 1 Asian American or Pacific Islander, 13 Hispanic Americans). Average age 36. In 2001, 14 master's, 2 other advanced degrees awarded.
**Degree requirements:** For master's, thesis or alternative, project, 250 hours of field work. *Median time to degree:* Master's–2 years part-time; Certificate–1 year part-time.
**Entrance requirements:** For master's and Certificate, interview, writing sample. *Application deadline:* For fall admission, 8/1 (priority date); for winter admission, 11/1 (priority date); for spring admission, 1/1 (priority date). Applications are processed on a rolling basis. *Application fee:* $50.
**Expenses:** Tuition: Part-time $496 per credit.
**Financial support:** Career-related internships or fieldwork available. Support available to part-time students. Financial award applicants required to submit FAFSA.
**Faculty research:** Work and family stress and health outcomes, siblings, women's health issues, children's stress, international health, legal issues.
Dr. Rita Scher Dytell, Director, 718-405-3788, *Fax:* 718-405-3734, *E-mail:* rdytell@cmsv.edu.
**Application contact:** Director of Transfer and Graduate Admissions, 718-405-3267,

*Fax:* 718-549-7945, *E-mail:* admissns@cmsv.edu. *Web site:* http://www.cmsv.edu/

### ■ THE COLLEGE OF NEW ROCHELLE

**Graduate School, Division of Human Services, Program in Guidance and Counseling, New Rochelle, NY 10805-2308**
**AWARDS** MS. Part-time programs available.
**Degree requirements:** For master's, internship.
**Entrance requirements:** For master's, interview, minimum GPA of 3.0.

### ■ COLLEGE OF SAINT ELIZABETH

**Department of Psychology, Morristown, NJ 07960-6989**
**AWARDS** Counseling psychology (MA). Part-time and evening/weekend programs available.
**Faculty:** 5 full-time (4 women), 10 part-time/adjunct (5 women).
**Students:** 10 full-time (8 women), 41 part-time (38 women); includes 11 minority (6 African Americans, 1 Asian American or Pacific Islander, 4 Hispanic Americans), 1 international. Average age 38. 16 applicants, 100% accepted, 10 enrolled. In 2001, 13 degrees awarded.
**Degree requirements:** For master's, thesis or alternative, portfolio. *Median time to degree:* Master's–4 years part-time.
**Entrance requirements:** For master's, minimum GPA of 3.0, BA in psychology preferred, 12 credits of course work in psychology. *Application deadline:* For fall admission, 4/14 (priority date); for spring admission, 11/15. Applications are processed on a rolling basis. *Application fee:* $35. Electronic applications accepted.
**Expenses:** Tuition: Full-time $8,100; part-time $450 per credit. Required fees: $195. Tuition and fees vary according to course load.
**Financial support:** In 2001–02, 1 student received support. Career-related internships or fieldwork, tuition waivers (partial), and unspecified assistantships available. Support available to part-time students. Financial award application deadline: 3/15; financial award applicants required to submit FAFSA.
**Faculty research:** Family systems, dissociative identity disorder, multicultural counseling, outcomes assessment.
Dr. Valerie Scott, Director of the Graduate Program in Counseling Psychology, 973-290-4102, *Fax:* 973-290-4676, *E-mail:* vscott@cse.edu. *Web site:* http://www.cse.edu/

### ■ COLLEGE OF ST. JOSEPH

**Graduate Program, Division of Psychology and Human Services, Program in Community Counseling, Rutland, VT 05701-3899**
**AWARDS** MS.
**Faculty:** 3 full-time (0 women), 6 part-time/adjunct (3 women).
**Students:** 1 full-time, 12 part-time; all minorities (all Hispanic Americans). Average age 34. In 2001, 1 degree awarded.
**Degree requirements:** For master's, thesis optional.
**Entrance requirements:** For master's, GRE General Test, interview. *Application fee:* $35.
**Expenses:** Tuition: Full-time $9,000; part-time $250 per credit. Required fees: $45 per semester. Part-time tuition and fees vary according to course load.
**Financial support:** Career-related internships or fieldwork, Federal Work-Study, and unspecified assistantships available. Support available to part-time students. Financial award application deadline: 3/1.
**Application contact:** Steve Soba, Dean of Admissions, 802-773-5900 Ext. 3206, *Fax:* 802-773-5900, *E-mail:* ssoba@csj.edu.

### ■ COLORADO STATE UNIVERSITY

**Graduate School, College of Natural Sciences, Department of Psychology, Fort Collins, CO 80523-0015**
**AWARDS** Applied social psychology (PhD); behavioral neuroscience (PhD); cognitive psychology (PhD); counseling psychology (PhD); industrial-organizational psychology (PhD).
**Faculty:** 29 full-time (8 women), 13 part-time/adjunct (7 women).
**Students:** 56 full-time (42 women), 37 part-time (29 women). Average age 29. 309 applicants, 12% accepted, 16 enrolled. In 2001, 9 doctorates awarded.
**Degree requirements:** For doctorate, thesis/dissertation.
**Entrance requirements:** For doctorate, GRE General Test, GRE Subject Test, TOEFL, minimum GPA of 3.5. *Application deadline:* For fall admission, 1/15. *Application fee:* $30. Electronic applications accepted.
**Expenses:** Tuition, state resident: full-time $2,880; part-time $160 per credit. Tuition, nonresident: full-time $11,412; part-time $634 per credit. Required fees: $750; $34 per credit.
**Financial support:** In 2001–02, 3 fellowships with full tuition reimbursements (averaging $12,120 per year), 10 research assistantships with full tuition reimbursements (averaging $9,720 per year), 52 teaching assistantships with full tuition

reimbursements (averaging $9,720 per year) were awarded. Career-related internships or fieldwork, Federal Work-Study, institutionally sponsored loans, scholarships/grants, and traineeships also available.

**Faculty research:** Environmental psychology, cognitive learning, health psychology, occupations of health. *Total annual research expenditures:* $12.5 million.

Ernest L. Chavez, Chair, 970-491-6363, *Fax:* 970-491-1032, *E-mail:* echavez@ lamar.colostate.edu.

**Application contact:** Wendy Standring, Graduate Admissions Coordinator, 970-491-6363, *Fax:* 970-491-1032, *E-mail:* wendyann@lamar.colostate.edu. *Web site:* http://www.colostate.edu/Depts/ Psychology/

## ■ COLUMBUS STATE UNIVERSITY

**Graduate Studies, College of Education, Department of Counseling and Educational Leadership, Columbus, GA 31907-5645**

**AWARDS** Community counseling (MS); educational leadership (M Ed, Ed S); school counseling (M Ed, Ed S). Part-time and evening/weekend programs available. Postbaccalaureate distance learning degree programs offered (minimal on-campus study).

**Faculty:** 11 full-time (7 women).

**Students:** 44 full-time (33 women), 156 part-time (114 women); includes 60 minority (56 African Americans, 3 Hispanic Americans, 1 Native American). Average age 37. 72 applicants, 53% accepted. In 2001, 40 master's, 20 other advanced degrees awarded.

**Degree requirements:** For master's, exit exam; for Ed S, thesis or alternative.

**Entrance requirements:** For master's, GRE General Test, MAT, minimum GPA of 2.75; for Ed S, GRE General Test, MAT. *Application deadline:* For fall admission, 7/6 (priority date); for spring admission, 12/14. Applications are processed on a rolling basis. *Application fee:* $25.

**Expenses:** Tuition, state resident: full-time $1,166. Tuition, nonresident: full-time $7,386.

**Financial support:** In 2001–02, 126 students received support, including 5 research assistantships with partial tuition reimbursements available (averaging $3,000 per year); career-related internships or fieldwork, Federal Work-Study, institutionally sponsored loans, scholarships/grants, tuition waivers (partial), and unspecified assistantships also available. Support available to part-time students. Financial award application deadline: 5/1; financial award applicants required to submit FAFSA.

Dr. Joyce Hickson, Chair, 706-568-2222, *Fax:* 706-569-3134, *E-mail:* hickson_ joyce@colstate.edu.

**Application contact:** Katie Thornton, Graduate Admissions Specialist, 706-568-2279, *Fax:* 706-568-2462, *E-mail:* thornton_katie@colstate.edu. *Web site:* http://www.cel.colstate.edu/

## ■ CONCORDIA UNIVERSITY

**Graduate Studies, Program in Professional Counseling, River Forest, IL 60305-1499**

**AWARDS** MA, CAS.

**Students:** 37 (29 women); includes 7 minority (2 African Americans, 3 Asian Americans or Pacific Islanders, 2 Hispanic Americans) 1 international.

**Degree requirements:** For master's, final project; for CAS, thesis, final project.

**Entrance requirements:** For master's, minimum GPA of 2.9; for CAS, master's degree. *Application deadline:* Applications are processed on a rolling basis. *Application fee:* $0.

**Financial support:** In 2001–02, 3 students received support, including 3 research assistantships; institutionally sponsored loans also available. Support available to part-time students.

Dr. Michael Smith, Coordinator, 708-209-3448, *Fax:* 708-209-3454.

**Application contact:** Jean Hubbard, Coordinator of Graduate Admissions, 708-209-4093, *Fax:* 708-209-3454, *E-mail:* curfdngrad@curf.edu.

## ■ DOMINICAN UNIVERSITY OF CALIFORNIA

**Graduate Programs, School of Arts and Sciences, Department of Counseling Psychology, San Rafael, CA 94901-2298**

**AWARDS** MS. Part-time programs available.

**Faculty:** 2 full-time (1 woman), 6 part-time/adjunct (4 women).

**Students:** 32 full-time (26 women), 38 part-time (32 women); includes 6 minority (3 African Americans, 3 Hispanic Americans), 1 international. Average age 34. 42 applicants, 67% accepted, 21 enrolled. In 2001, 17 degrees awarded.

**Degree requirements:** For master's, fieldwork.

**Entrance requirements:** For master's, TOEFL, interview, minimum GPA of 3.0. *Application deadline:* For fall admission, 5/1; for spring admission, 11/1. *Application fee:* $40.

**Expenses:** Tuition: Full-time $14,040; part-time $585 per unit. One-time fee: $335. Full-time tuition and fees vary according to program.

**Financial support:** In 2001–02, 28 students received support, including 28 fellowships (averaging $2,848 per year); career-related internships or fieldwork, Federal Work-Study, institutionally sponsored loans, scholarships/grants, and tuition discounts also available. Support available to part-time students. Financial award application deadline: 3/15; financial award applicants required to submit FAFSA.

Dr. Charles R. Billings, Chair, 415-485-3263, *Fax:* 415-458-3700, *E-mail:* billings@ dominican.edu.

**Application contact:** Lorrie Crivello, Associate Director of Graduate Admissions, 415-485-3754, *Fax:* 415-485-3293, *E-mail:* crivello@dominican.edu. *Web site:* http://www.dominican.edu/counpsych/ index.html

## ■ EASTERN NAZARENE COLLEGE

**Graduate Studies, Program in Family Counseling, Quincy, MA 02170-2999**

**AWARDS** MS. Part-time and evening/weekend programs available.

**Faculty:** 4 full-time (1 woman), 2 part-time/adjunct (1 woman).

**Students:** 35; includes 4 minority (3 African Americans, 1 Native American), 1 international. Average age 35. 5 applicants, 100% accepted. In 2001, 24 degrees awarded.

**Entrance requirements:** For master's, TOEFL. *Application deadline:* Applications are processed on a rolling basis. *Application fee:* $35.

**Expenses:** Tuition: Part-time $360 per credit hour. Required fees: $50 per semester.

**Financial support:** Career-related internships or fieldwork and scholarships/grants available. Support available to part-time students. Financial award applicants required to submit FAFSA.

Dr. Mark Bromley, Graduate Coordinator, 617-745-3562.

**Application contact:** Cleo P. Cakridas, Assistant Director of Graduate Studies, 617-745-3870, *Fax:* 617-774-6800, *E-mail:* cakridac@enc.edu.

## ■ EASTERN UNIVERSITY

**Programs in Counseling, St. Davids, PA 19087-3696**

**AWARDS** Community/clinical counseling (MA); educational counseling (MA, MS), including school counseling (MA), school psychology (MS); marriage and family (MA); student development (MA).

**Degree requirements:** For master's, internship.

*Eastern University (continued)*
**Entrance requirements:** For master's, TOEFL, minimum GPA of 2.5.

**Find an in-depth description at www.petersons.com/gradchannel.**

# ■ EASTERN WASHINGTON UNIVERSITY

**Graduate School Studies, College of Education and Human Development, Department of Counseling, Educational, and Developmental Psychology, Program in School Counseling, Cheney, WA 99004-2431**

AWARDS Counseling psychology (MS); school counseling (MS).

**Students:** 36 full-time (33 women), 2 part-time (1 woman), 1 international. 20 applicants, 85% accepted, 17 enrolled. In 2001, 15 degrees awarded.
**Degree requirements:** For master's, thesis or alternative, comprehensive exam.
**Entrance requirements:** For master's, GRE General Test, minimum GPA of 3.0. *Application deadline:* For fall admission, 2/1. Applications are processed on a rolling basis. *Application fee:* $35.
**Expenses:** Tuition, state resident: full-time $1,586; part-time $159 per credit hour. Tuition, nonresident: full-time $4,677; part-time $468 per credit hour. Required fees: $222; $159 per credit. $74 per quarter.
**Financial support:** In 2001–02, teaching assistantships with partial tuition reimbursements (averaging $7,000 per year); career-related internships or fieldwork, Federal Work-Study, institutionally sponsored loans, scholarships/grants, health care benefits, tuition waivers (partial), and unspecified assistantships also available. Support available to part-time students. Financial award application deadline: 2/1; financial award applicants required to submit FAFSA.
Dr. Sarah Leverett-Main, Director, 509-359-6195, *Fax:* 509-359-4366. *Web site:* http://www.appliedpsyc.ewu.edu/

# ■ FITCHBURG STATE COLLEGE

**Division of Graduate and Continuing Education, Programs in Counseling, Fitchburg, MA 01420-2697**

AWARDS Adolescent and family therapy (Certificate); child protective services (Certificate); elementary school guidance counseling (MS); forensic case work (Certificate); mental health counseling (MS); school guidance counselor (Certificate); secondary school guidance counseling (MS). Part-time and evening/weekend programs available.

**Students:** 30 full-time (24 women), 52 part-time (48 women); includes 4 minority

(1 African American, 1 Asian American or Pacific Islander, 2 Hispanic Americans), 3 international. In 2001, 27 degrees awarded.
**Entrance requirements:** For master's, GRE General Test or MAT, interview, previous course work in psychology; for Certificate, master's degree. *Application deadline:* Applications are processed on a rolling basis. *Application fee:* $10.
**Expenses:** Tuition, state resident: part-time $150 per credit. Required fees: $7 per credit. $65 per term. Tuition and fees vary according to course load.
**Financial support:** In 2001–02, research assistantships with partial tuition reimbursements (averaging $5,500 per year), teaching assistantships with partial tuition reimbursements (averaging $5,500 per year) were awarded. Federal Work-Study and unspecified assistantships also available. Support available to part-time students. Financial award application deadline: 3/1; financial award applicants required to submit FAFSA.
Dr. Richard Spencer, Co-Chair, 978-665-3349, *Fax:* 978-665-3658, *E-mail:* gce@fsc.edu.

**Application contact:** Director of Admissions, 978-665-3144, *Fax:* 978-665-4540, *E-mail:* admissions@fsc.edu. *Web site:* http://www.fsc.edu/

# ■ FLORIDA STATE UNIVERSITY

**Graduate Studies, College of Education, Department of Educational Psychology and Learning Systems, Program in Counseling Psychology, Tallahassee, FL 32306**

AWARDS PhD.

**Faculty:** 2 full-time (0 women).
**Students:** 21 full-time (13 women), 23 part-time (13 women); includes 11 minority (7 African Americans, 2 Asian Americans or Pacific Islanders, 2 Hispanic Americans), 2 international. 57 applicants, 16% accepted. In 2001, 6 degrees awarded.
**Degree requirements:** For doctorate, thesis/dissertation, comprehensive exam.
**Entrance requirements:** For doctorate, GRE General Test, minimum GPA of 3.0. *Application deadline:* For fall admission, 7/1 (priority date); for spring admission, 11/1. Applications are processed on a rolling basis. *Application fee:* $20.
**Expenses:** Tuition, state resident: part-time $163 per credit hour. Tuition, nonresident: part-time $570 per credit hour. Tuition and fees vary according to program.
**Financial support:** In 2001–02, 5 fellowships were awarded; research assistantships, teaching assistantships, career-related internships or fieldwork also available. Financial award applicants required to submit FAFSA.

# ■ FORDHAM UNIVERSITY

**Graduate School of Education, Division of Psychological and Educational Services, New York, NY 10023**

AWARDS Counseling and personnel services (MSE, Adv C); counseling psychology (PhD); educational psychology (MSE, PhD); school psychology (PhD); urban and urban bilingual school psychology (Adv C).

**Students:** 89 full-time (76 women), 307 part-time (257 women); includes 114 minority (41 African Americans, 20 Asian Americans or Pacific Islanders, 52 Hispanic Americans, 1 Native American). Average age 30. 506 applicants, 56% accepted, 111 enrolled. In 2001, 73 master's, 14 doctorates, 24 other advanced degrees awarded.
**Degree requirements:** For doctorate, thesis/dissertation.
**Entrance requirements:** For doctorate, GRE General Test. *Application fee:* $65.
**Financial support:** Applicants required to submit FAFSA.
Dr. Giselle Esquivel, Chairman, 212-636-6460.

# ■ FORT VALLEY STATE UNIVERSITY

**Graduate Division, Department of Counseling Psychology, Program in Mental Health Counseling, Fort Valley, GA 31030-4313**

AWARDS MS. Part-time programs available.

**Degree requirements:** For master's, thesis optional.
**Entrance requirements:** For master's, GRE General Test or MAT.

# ■ FRAMINGHAM STATE COLLEGE

**Graduate Programs, Department of Psychology/Philosophy, Framingham, MA 01701-9101**

AWARDS Counseling (MA). Part-time and evening/weekend programs available.

**Faculty:** 4 full-time, 3 part-time/adjunct.
**Students:** In 2001, 19 degrees awarded.
Dr. Anthony Dias, Chairman, 508-626-4873.
**Application contact:** Graduate Office, 508-626-4550.

# ■ FRANCISCAN UNIVERSITY OF STEUBENVILLE

**Graduate Programs, Department of Counseling, Steubenville, OH 43952-1763**

AWARDS MA. Part-time programs available.
**Faculty:** 3 full-time (1 woman), 3 part-time/adjunct (1 woman).

**Students:** 38 full-time (28 women), 22 part-time (15 women); includes 2 minority (1 African American, 1 Hispanic American), 5 international. Average age 32. 44 applicants, 86% accepted. In 2001, 11 degrees awarded.
**Degree requirements:** For master's, case presentation, integrative paper.
**Entrance requirements:** For master's, GRE General Test or MAT, minimum undergraduate GPA of 3.0. *Application deadline:* For fall admission, 7/1; for spring admission, 12/15. Applications are processed on a rolling basis. *Application fee:* $20.
**Expenses:** Tuition: Part-time $470 per credit hour. Required fees: $10 per credit. Part-time tuition and fees vary according to course level and program.
**Financial support:** Career-related internships or fieldwork, Federal Work-Study, and scholarships/grants available. Support available to part-time students. Financial award application deadline: 7/1; financial award applicants required to submit FAFSA.
Dr. Andrew Hrezo, Program Director, 740-284-7220.
**Application contact:** Mark McGuire, Director of Graduate Enrollment, 800-783-6220, *Fax:* 740-284-5456, *E-mail:* mmcguire@franuniv.edu.

### ■ FROSTBURG STATE UNIVERSITY

**Graduate School, College of Liberal Arts and Sciences, Department of Psychology, Program in Counseling Psychology, Frostburg, MD 21532-1099**

**AWARDS** MS. Part-time and evening/weekend programs available.
**Faculty:** 8 full-time (6 women), 1 part-time/adjunct (0 women).
**Students:** 26 full-time (21 women), 10 part-time (7 women); includes 2 minority (both Hispanic Americans), 1 international. Average age 30. 24 applicants, 46% accepted. In 2001, 11 degrees awarded.
**Degree requirements:** For master's, internship.
**Entrance requirements:** For master's, GRE General Test or MAT, interview, minimum GPA of 3.0, resumé. *Application deadline:* For fall admission, 2/1. Applications are processed on a rolling basis. *Application fee:* $30. Electronic applications accepted.
**Expenses:** Tuition, area resident: Part-time $187 per credit hour. Tuition, state resident: full-time $3,366; part-time $187 per credit hour. Tuition, nonresident: full-time $3,906; part-time $217 per credit hour. Required fees: $812; $34 per credit hour. One-time fee: $9 full-time.

**Financial support:** In 2001–02, 7 research assistantships with full tuition reimbursements (averaging $5,000 per year) were awarded; career-related internships or fieldwork and Federal Work-Study also available. Financial award application deadline: 4/1; financial award applicants required to submit FAFSA.
Dr. Ann Bristow, Coordinator, 301-687-4193.
**Application contact:** Patricia C. Spiker, Director of Graduate Services, 301-687-7053, *Fax:* 301-687-4597, *E-mail:* pspiker@frostburg.edu.

### ■ GALLAUDET UNIVERSITY

**The Graduate School, School of Education and Human Services, Department of Counseling, Washington, DC 20002-3625**

**AWARDS** Community counseling (MA); mental health counseling (MA); school counseling (MA).
**Degree requirements:** For master's, thesis optional.
**Entrance requirements:** For master's, GRE General Test or MAT.

### ■ GANNON UNIVERSITY

**School of Graduate Studies, College of Humanities, Business, and Education, School of Humanities, Doctoral Program in Counseling Psychology, Erie, PA 16541-0001**

**AWARDS** PhD. Part-time and evening/weekend programs available.
**Degree requirements:** For doctorate, thesis/dissertation, internship.
**Entrance requirements:** For doctorate, GRE General Test, minimum GPA of 3.25, master's degree.

### ■ GANNON UNIVERSITY

**School of Graduate Studies, College of Humanities, Business, and Education, School of Humanities, Master's Program in Counseling Psychology, Erie, PA 16541-0001**

**AWARDS** MS. Part-time and evening/weekend programs available.
**Degree requirements:** For master's, thesis, comprehensive exam.
**Entrance requirements:** For master's, MAT, interview. *Web site:* http://www.gannon.edu/

### ■ GARDNER-WEBB UNIVERSITY

**Graduate School, Department of Psychology, Program in Mental Health Counseling, Boiling Springs, NC 28017**

**AWARDS** MA. Part-time and evening/weekend programs available.

**Faculty:** 5 full-time (3 women), 2 part-time/adjunct (1 woman).
**Students:** Average age 34. In 2001, 10 degrees awarded.
**Degree requirements:** For master's, comprehensive exam.
**Entrance requirements:** For master's, GRE General Test, MAT, minimum GPA of 2.7. *Application deadline:* For fall admission, 7/1 (priority date). Applications are processed on a rolling basis. *Application fee:* $25. Electronic applications accepted.
**Expenses:** Tuition: Part-time $210 per hour. Part-time tuition and fees vary according to program.
**Financial support:** Unspecified assistantships available.
Dr. Frieda Brown, Coordinator, 704-406-4436, *Fax:* 704-406-4329, *E-mail:* fbrown@gardner-webb.edu.

### ■ GENEVA COLLEGE

**Program in Counseling, Beaver Falls, PA 15010-3599**

**AWARDS** Marriage and family (MA); mental health (MA); school counseling (MA). Part-time and evening/weekend programs available.

**Faculty:** 5 full-time (2 women), 2 part-time/adjunct (0 women).
**Students:** 16 full-time (14 women), 31 part-time (23 women). Average age 26. In 2001, 4 degrees awarded.
**Degree requirements:** For master's, internship. *Median time to degree:* Master's–2 years full-time, 4.5 years part-time.
**Entrance requirements:** For master's, GRE General Test or MAT, minimum GPA of 3.0, letters of recommendation, faith statement. *Application deadline:* For fall admission, 7/1 (priority date); for spring admission, 11/1 (priority date). Applications are processed on a rolling basis. *Application fee:* $50. Electronic applications accepted.
**Expenses:** Tuition: Part-time $445 per credit hour.
**Financial support:** In 2001–02, 6 teaching assistantships (averaging $2,500 per year) were awarded; career-related internships or fieldwork and unspecified assistantships also available.
Dr. Carol Luce, Director, 724-847-6622, *Fax:* 724-847-6101, *E-mail:* cbluce@geneva.edu.
**Application contact:** Dr. Robin Ware, Director of Graduate Student Services, 724-847-6697, *Fax:* 724-847-6101, *E-mail:* counseling@geneva.edu. *Web site:* http://www.geneva.edu/

**Find an in-depth description at www.petersons.com/gradchannel.**

## ■ GEORGE FOX UNIVERSITY

**Graduate and Professional Studies, Graduate Department of Counseling, Newberg, OR 97132-2697**

**AWARDS** Counseling (MA); marriage and family therapy (MA). Part-time programs available.

**Faculty:** 7 full-time (3 women), 4 part-time/adjunct (3 women).
**Students:** 117 full-time (95 women), 86 part-time (71 women); includes 17 minority (2 African Americans, 7 Asian Americans or Pacific Islanders, 5 Hispanic Americans, 3 Native Americans), 3 international. 88 applicants, 69% accepted, 53 enrolled. In 2001, 25 degrees awarded.
**Degree requirements:** For master's, thesis optional.
*Application deadline:* For fall admission, 7/1; for spring admission, 10/15. Applications are processed on a rolling basis. *Application fee:* $40. Electronic applications accepted.
**Expenses:** Contact institution.
**Financial support:** Career-related internships or fieldwork available.
Dr. Karin Jordan, Director, 503-554-6141, *E-mail:* kjordan@georgefox.edu.
**Application contact:** Dr. Andrea Cook, Vice President for Enrollment Services, 800-631-0921, *Fax:* 503-554-3856, *E-mail:* acook@georgefox.edu. *Web site:* http://www.georgefox.edu

## ■ GEORGIAN COURT COLLEGE

**Graduate School, Program in Counseling Psychology, Lakewood, NJ 08701-2697**

**AWARDS** MA. Part-time and evening/weekend programs available.

**Faculty:** 2 part-time/adjunct (both women).
**Students:** 18 full-time (all women), 43 part-time (40 women); includes 4 minority (1 African American, 1 Asian American or Pacific Islander, 2 Hispanic Americans). Average age 32. In 2001, 8 degrees awarded.
**Degree requirements:** For master's, thesis, comprehensive exam.
**Entrance requirements:** For master's, GRE General Test, GRE Subject Test (psychology). *Application deadline:* For fall admission, 8/25; for spring admission, 1/15. Applications are processed on a rolling basis. *Application fee:* $40.
**Expenses:** Tuition: Full-time $7,308; part-time $406 per credit. Required fees: $70; $35 per term. Tuition and fees vary according to course load.
**Financial support:** In 2001–02, 35 students received support. Scholarships/grants and unspecified assistantships available. Financial award application deadline:

4/15; financial award applicants required to submit FAFSA.
**Faculty research:** Academic couples; academic dishonesty and plagiarism; oppositional defiant disorder, ADHD, and self-esteem; writing in response to trauma.
Dr. Linda James, Chairperson, Psychology Department, 732-364-2200 Ext. 636, *Fax:* 732-367-7301, *E-mail:* james@georgian.edu.
**Application contact:** Michael Backes, Vice President for Enrollment, 732-364-2200 Ext. 760, *Fax:* 732-364-4442, *E-mail:* admissions@georgian.edu.

## ■ GEORGIA STATE UNIVERSITY

**College of Education, Department of Counseling and Psychological Services, Program in Professional Counseling, Atlanta, GA 30303-3083**

**AWARDS** Counseling (PhD); counseling psychology (PhD); professional counseling (MS, Ed S).

**Students:** 148 full-time (132 women), 128 part-time (105 women); includes 66 minority (52 African Americans, 6 Asian Americans or Pacific Islanders, 4 Hispanic Americans, 4 Native Americans), 10 international. Average age 32. 147 applicants, 67% accepted. In 2001, 63 master's, 9 doctorates, 8 other advanced degrees awarded.
**Degree requirements:** For master's, comprehensive exam; for doctorate, thesis/dissertation, comprehensive exam.
**Entrance requirements:** For master's, GRE General Test, minimum GPA of 2.5; for doctorate, GRE General Test, minimum GPA of 3.3; for Ed S, GRE General Test, minimum graduate GPA of 3.25. *Application fee:* $25.
**Financial support:** Scholarships/grants available. Financial award application deadline: 4/1.
**Faculty research:** Dropout prevention, school reform, school violence, lifestyle correlates, stress management.
Dr. Joanna White, Chairperson, Department of Counseling and Psychological Services, 404-651-2550.

## ■ GODDARD COLLEGE

**Graduate Programs, Program in Psychology and Counseling, Plainfield, VT 05667-9432**

**AWARDS** Organizational development (MA); psychology and counseling (MA). Postbaccalaureate distance learning degree programs offered (minimal on-campus study).

**Degree requirements:** For master's, thesis.
Electronic applications accepted. *Web site:* http://www.goddard.edu/

## ■ GOLDEN GATE UNIVERSITY

**School of Professional Programs and Undergraduate Studies, Program in Applied Psychology, San Francisco, CA 94105-2968**

**AWARDS** Applied psychology (Certificate); counseling (MA); industrial/organizational psychology (MA); marriage, family and child counseling (MA).

**Entrance requirements:** For master's, TOEFL, minimum GPA of 2.5.

## ■ GONZAGA UNIVERSITY

**Graduate School, School of Education, Program in Counseling Psychology, Spokane, WA 99258**

**AWARDS** MAC, MAP.

**Faculty:** 3 full-time (1 woman), 4 part-time/adjunct (1 woman).
**Students:** 136 full-time (117 women); includes 3 minority (all Hispanic Americans), 73 international. Average age 36. 105 applicants, 58% accepted. In 2001, 72 degrees awarded.
**Degree requirements:** For master's, comprehensive exam.
**Entrance requirements:** For master's, GRE General Test or MAT, TOEFL, minimum B average in undergraduate course work. *Application deadline:* For fall admission, 3/1. *Application fee:* $40.
**Financial support:** Teaching assistantships available. Support available to part-time students. Financial award application deadline: 3/1.
Dr. Lisa Bennett, Director, 509-328-4220 Ext. 3512.

## ■ GRACE COLLEGE

**Program in Counseling, Winona Lake, IN 46590-1294**

**AWARDS** Clinical counseling (MA); ministry (MA). Part-time and evening/weekend programs available.

**Faculty:** 3 full-time (1 woman), 2 part-time/adjunct (0 women).
**Students:** 6 full-time (3 women), 38 part-time (22 women). 15 applicants, 100% accepted. In 2001, 4 degrees awarded.
*Median time to degree:* Master's–1.75 years full-time, 3.5 years part-time.
**Entrance requirements:** For master's, GRE. *Application deadline:* For fall admission, 7/1 (priority date). Applications are processed on a rolling basis. *Application fee:* $25.
**Expenses:** Tuition: Part-time $335 per credit hour. Required fees: $30 per semester.
**Financial support:** In 2001–02, 2 teaching assistantships (averaging $2,000 per year) were awarded

Dr. Thomas J. Edgington, Head, 800-54-GRACE Ext. 6052, *Fax:* 574-372-5143, *E-mail:* edgingtj@grace.edu.
**Application contact:** Shilo A. Maack, Admissions Counselor, 800-54 GRACE Ext. 6001, *Fax:* 574-372-5120, *E-mail:* macslg@grace.edu. *Web site:* http://www.grace.edu/

### ■ GRACE UNIVERSITY

**College of Graduate Studies, Counseling Program, Omaha, NE 68108**
**AWARDS** MA.
**Faculty:** 2 full-time (1 woman), 1 part-time/adjunct (0 women).
**Students:** 23 full-time (14 women), 14 part-time (10 women); includes 3 minority (2 African Americans, 1 Native American), 1 international. Average age 35. In 2001, 8 degrees awarded.
**Entrance requirements:** For master's, minimum undergraduate GPA of 3.0. *Application deadline:* For fall admission, 8/15 (priority date); for spring admission, 1/1. Applications are processed on a rolling basis. *Application fee:* $50.
**Expenses:** Tuition: Part-time $330 per credit hour. Required fees: $200; $200 per year.
Dr. Norman Thiesen, Head, 402-449-2805, *Fax:* 402-449-2803, *E-mail:* academics@graceu.edu.
**Application contact:** Jen Mulder, Graduate Admissions Counselor, 402-449-2817, *Fax:* 402-341-9587, *E-mail:* admissions@graceu.edu. *Web site:* http://www.graceu.edu/

### ■ HOLY FAMILY COLLEGE

**Graduate Studies, School of Social and Behavioral Sciences, Philadelphia, PA 19114-2094**
**AWARDS** Counseling psychology (MS). Part-time and evening/weekend programs available.
**Faculty:** 1 (woman) full-time, 4 part-time/adjunct (2 women).
**Students:** 3 full-time (all women), 33 part-time (26 women); includes 1 minority (Asian American or Pacific Islander). Average age 29. 17 applicants, 100% accepted. In 2001, 9 degrees awarded.
**Degree requirements:** For master's, thesis optional.
**Entrance requirements:** For master's, MAT, interview, minimum GPA of 3.0. *Application deadline:* For fall admission, 4/15 (priority date). Applications are processed on a rolling basis. *Application fee:* $25.
**Expenses:** Tuition: Full-time $7,650; part-time $425 per credit. Required fees: $340; $170 per term.

**Financial support:** Research assistantships with full and partial tuition reimbursements, Federal Work-Study available. Support available to part-time students. Financial award application deadline: 2/15; financial award applicants required to submit FAFSA.
Dr. Jane McGarrahan, Graduate Coordinator, 215-504-2000, *Fax:* 215-504-2050, *E-mail:* jmc.garrahan@hfc.edu.
**Application contact:** Joseph Canaday, Director of Graduate Admissions, 215-637-7203, *Fax:* 215-637-1478, *E-mail:* jcanaday@hfc.edu.

### ■ HOLY NAMES COLLEGE

**Graduate Division, Department of Counseling Psychology, Oakland, CA 94619-1699**
**AWARDS** Counseling psychology with emphasis in pastoral counseling (MA); pastoral counseling (MA, Certificate). Part-time and evening/weekend programs available.
**Faculty:** 2 full-time (both women), 4 part-time/adjunct (2 women).
**Students:** 6 full-time (5 women), 20 part-time (15 women); includes 11 minority (7 African Americans, 1 Asian American or Pacific Islander, 3 Hispanic Americans), 1 international. Average age 41. 10 applicants, 30% accepted. In 2001, 4 master's, 1 other advanced degree awarded.
**Degree requirements:** For master's, comprehensive paper, seminars.
**Entrance requirements:** For master's, TOEFL, minimum undergraduate GPA of 2.6 overall, 3.0 in major. *Application deadline:* For fall admission, 8/1 (priority date); for spring admission, 12/1 (priority date). Applications are processed on a rolling basis. *Application fee:* $50.
**Expenses:** Tuition: Part-time $460 per unit. Required fees: $120.
**Financial support:** In 2001–02, 16 students received support. Available to part-time students. Application deadline: 3/2.
Cari Lenahan, Co-Director, 510-436-1235.
**Application contact:** 800-430-1321, *Fax:* 510-436-1317, *E-mail:* hall@hnc.edu.

### ■ HOPE INTERNATIONAL UNIVERSITY

**School of Graduate Studies, Program in Marriage, Family, and Child Counseling, Fullerton, CA 92831-3138**
**AWARDS** Counseling (MA); marriage and family therapy (MFT); marriage, family, and child counseling (MA); psychology (MA).
**Degree requirements:** For master's, final exam, practicum.

**Entrance requirements:** For master's, minimum GPA of 3.0. Electronic applications accepted.

### ■ HOUSTON BAPTIST UNIVERSITY

**College of Education and Behavioral Sciences, Master of Science in Christian Counseling, Houston, TX 77074-3298**
**AWARDS** MAPCP.
**Students:** 2 applicants, 100% accepted. *Application fee:* $25 ($100 for international students).
**Expenses:** Tuition: Part-time $990 per course. Required fees: $250 per quarter.
Dr. Ann Owen, Behavioral Sciences Department Director, 281-649-3000 Ext. 2436.
**Application contact:** Judy Ferguson, Program Secretary, 281-649-3000 Ext. 3241.

### ■ HOWARD UNIVERSITY

**School of Education, Department of Human Development and Psychoeducational Studies, Program in Counseling Psychology, Washington, DC 20059-0002**
**AWARDS** M Ed, MA, Ed D, PhD, CAGS.
**Degree requirements:** For master's, thesis (for some programs), expository writing exam, comprehensive exam; for doctorate, one foreign language, thesis/dissertation, expository writing exam, internship, comprehensive exam.
**Entrance requirements:** For master's, GRE General Test (MA), minimum GPA of 2.7; for doctorate, GRE General Test, minimum GPA of 3.4; for CAGS, GRE General Test, minimum graduate GPA of 3.0.

### ■ IDAHO STATE UNIVERSITY

**Office of Graduate Studies, College of Health Professions, Department of Counseling, Department of Counseling, Pocatello, ID 83209**
**AWARDS** Counseling (Ed S); marriage and family counseling (M Coun); mental health counseling (M Coun); school counseling (M Coun); student affairs and college counseling (M Coun).
**Students:** In 2001, 13 master's, 2 other advanced degrees awarded.
**Degree requirements:** For Ed S, thesis.
**Entrance requirements:** For master's, GRE General Test, MAT, minimum GPA of 2.75; for Ed S, GRE General Test, minimum graduate GPA of 3.0. *Application deadline:* For fall admission, 2/15 (priority date). Applications are processed on a rolling basis. *Application fee:* $55.

*Idaho State University (continued)*

**Expenses:** Tuition, area resident: Full-time $3,432. Tuition, state resident: part-time $172 per credit. Tuition, nonresident: full-time $10,196; part-time $262 per credit. International tuition: $9,672 full-time. Part-time tuition and fees vary according to course load, program and reciprocity agreements.

**Financial support:** In 2001–02, 15 teaching assistantships with full and partial tuition reimbursements (averaging $10,099 per year) were awarded. Financial award application deadline: 3/15.

Dr. Steve Feit, Chair, Department of Counseling, 208-282-3156.

### ■ ILLINOIS STATE UNIVERSITY

**Graduate School, College of Arts and Sciences, Department of Psychology, Normal, IL 61790-2200**

**AWARDS** Psychology (MA, MS), including clinical psychology, counseling psychology, developmental psychology, educational psychology, experimental psychology, measurement-evaluation, organizational-industrial psychology; school psychology (PhD, SSP).

**Faculty:** 30 full-time (10 women), 1 part-time/adjunct (0 women).

**Students:** 59 full-time (48 women), 24 part-time (13 women); includes 7 minority (3 African Americans, 3 Hispanic Americans, 1 Native American), 5 international. 81 applicants, 46% accepted. In 2001, 40 master's, 2 doctorates, 4 other advanced degrees awarded.

**Degree requirements:** For master's, thesis or alternative; for doctorate, variable foreign language requirement, thesis/dissertation, 2 terms of residency, internship, practicum.

**Entrance requirements:** For master's, GRE General Test, GRE Subject Test, minimum GPA of 3.0 in last 60 hours; for doctorate, GRE General Test. *Application deadline:* Applications are processed on a rolling basis. *Application fee:* $30.

**Expenses:** Tuition, state resident: full-time $2,691; part-time $112 per credit hour. Tuition, nonresident: full-time $5,880; part-time $245 per credit hour. Required fees: $1,146; $48 per credit hour.

**Financial support:** In 2001–02, 21 research assistantships (averaging $5,127 per year), 27 teaching assistantships (averaging $4,308 per year) were awarded. Tuition waivers (full) and unspecified assistantships also available. Financial award application deadline: 4/1.

**Faculty research:** Dialogues with children, sexual harassment in the military, mental health consultant. *Total annual research expenditures:* $248,177.

Dr. David Barone, Chairperson, 309-438-8651. *Web site:* http://www.cas.ilstu.edu/psychology/index.html

### ■ IMMACULATA UNIVERSITY

**College of Graduate Studies, Department of Psychology, Immaculata, PA 19345**

**AWARDS** Clinical psychology (Psy D); counseling psychology (MA, Certificate), including school guidance counselor (Certificate), school psychologist (Certificate); school psychology (Psy D). Part-time and evening/weekend programs available.

**Students:** 57 full-time (45 women), 220 part-time (188 women). Average age 34. 88 applicants, 80% accepted, 41 enrolled. In 2001, 36 master's, 9 doctorates awarded.

**Degree requirements:** For master's, thesis optional; for doctorate, thesis/dissertation, comprehensive exam.

**Entrance requirements:** For master's, GRE General Test or MAT, TOEFL, minimum GPA of 3.0; for doctorate, GRE General Test, TOEFL, minimum GPA of 3.5. *Application deadline:* Applications are processed on a rolling basis. *Application fee:* $25.

**Expenses:** Tuition: Part-time $390 per credit.

**Financial support:** Application deadline: 5/1.

**Faculty research:** Supervision ethics, psychology of teaching, gender.

Dr. Jed A. Yalof, Chair, 610-647-4400 Ext. 3503, *E-mail:* jyalof@immaculate.edu.

**Application contact:** Office of Graduate Admission, 610-647-4400 Ext. 3211.

### ■ INDIANA STATE UNIVERSITY

**School of Graduate Studies, School of Education, Department of Counseling, Terre Haute, IN 47809-1401**

**AWARDS** Counseling psychology (PhD); counselor education (PhD); guidance (PhD, Ed S); higher education (MA, MS); marriage and family counseling (MA, MS); school counseling (M Ed). Part-time and evening/weekend programs available.

**Degree requirements:** For doctorate, 2 foreign languages, thesis/dissertation.

**Entrance requirements:** For master's, minimum undergraduate GPA of 2.5; for doctorate, GRE General Test, master's degree, minimum undergraduate GPA of 3.5; for Ed S, GRE General Test, minimum graduate GPA of 3.25. Electronic applications accepted.

**Faculty research:** Vocational development supervision.

### ■ INSTITUTE OF TRANSPERSONAL PSYCHOLOGY

**Residential Division, Palo Alto, CA 94303**

**AWARDS** Counseling psychology (MA); transpersonal psychology (MA, PhD). Part-time and evening/weekend programs available.

**Faculty:** 18 full-time (10 women), 22 part-time/adjunct (7 women).

**Students:** 236 full-time (173 women), 12 part-time (10 women); includes 30 minority (7 African Americans, 9 Asian Americans or Pacific Islanders, 11 Hispanic Americans, 3 Native Americans), 13 international. Average age 41. 122 applicants, 78% accepted, 58 enrolled. In 2001, 48 master's, 12 doctorates awarded. Terminal master's awarded for partial completion of doctoral program.

**Degree requirements:** For doctorate, thesis/dissertation.

**Entrance requirements:** For master's, 8 hours in psychology; for doctorate, 12 hours in psychology. *Application deadline:* For fall admission, 4/15 (priority date). Applications are processed on a rolling basis. *Application fee:* $55.

**Expenses:** Tuition: Full-time $17,784. Required fees: $30. Tuition and fees vary according to degree level, campus/location and program.

**Financial support:** In 2001–02, 141 students received support; teaching assistantships, career-related internships or fieldwork and Federal Work-Study available. Support available to part-time students. Financial award application deadline: 7/1; financial award applicants required to submit FAFSA.

Dr. Paul Roy, Academic Dean, 650-493-4430, *Fax:* 650-493-6835, *E-mail:* proy@itp.edu.

**Application contact:** John Hofmann, Admissions Office, 650-493-4430 Ext. 30, *Fax:* 650-493-6835, *E-mail:* itpinfo@itp.edu. *Web site:* http://www.itp.edu/

### ■ INTER AMERICAN UNIVERSITY OF PUERTO RICO, SAN GERMÁN CAMPUS

**Graduate Programs, Department of Social Sciences, San Germán, PR 00683-5008**

**AWARDS** Counseling psychology (PhD); psychology (MA, MS); school psychology (PhD). Part-time and evening/weekend programs available.

**Faculty:** 5 full-time (4 women), 8 part-time/adjunct (4 women).

**Students:** 48 full-time (40 women), 48 part-time (41 women). In 2001, 11 degrees awarded.

**Degree requirements:** For master's and doctorate, thesis/dissertation, comprehensive exam.

**Entrance requirements:** For master's, GRE General Test or PAEG, minimum GPA of 3.0; for doctorate, GRE, PAEG or MAT, minimum GPA of 3.0. *Application deadline:* For fall admission, 4/30 (priority date); for spring admission, 11/15. Applications are processed on a rolling basis. *Application fee:* $31.

**Expenses:** Tuition: Part-time $165 per credit. Required fees: $390; $195 per semester. Tuition and fees vary according to degree level and program.

**Financial support:** Teaching assistantships available.

Carmen Rodriguez, Graduate Coordinator, 787-264-1912 Ext. 7646, *Fax:* 787-892-6350, *E-mail:* carrod@sg.inter.edu.

**Application contact:** Dr. Waldemar Velez, Director of Graduate Program Center, 787-892-4300 Ext. 7358, *Fax:* 787-892-6350, *E-mail:* wvelez@sg.inter.edu.

■ **IOWA STATE UNIVERSITY OF SCIENCE AND TECHNOLOGY**

**Graduate College, College of Liberal Arts and Sciences, Department of Psychology, Ames, IA 50011**

**AWARDS** Cognitive psychology (PhD); counseling psychology (PhD); general psychology (MS); social psychology (PhD). Terminal master's awarded for partial completion of doctoral program.

**Degree requirements:** For master's, thesis or alternative; for doctorate, thesis/dissertation.

**Entrance requirements:** For master's and doctorate, GRE General Test, GRE Subject Test (psychology), TOEFL. Electronic applications accepted.

**Expenses:** Tuition, state resident: full-time $1,851. Tuition, nonresident: full-time $5,449. Tuition and fees vary according to program.

**Faculty research:** Counseling psychology, cognitive psychology, social psychology, health psychology, psychology and public policy. *Web site:* http://psych-server.iastate.edu/

■ **JAMES MADISON UNIVERSITY**

**College of Graduate and Professional Programs, College of Integrated Science and Technology, Department of Psychology, Program in Counseling Psychology, Harrisonburg, VA 22807**

**AWARDS** M Ed, MA, Ed S. Part-time and evening/weekend programs available.

**Students:** 56 full-time (48 women), 27 part-time (20 women); includes 12 minority (8 African Americans, 1 Asian American or Pacific Islander, 3 Hispanic Americans),

1 international. Average age 29. In 2001, 25 master's, 11 other advanced degrees awarded.

**Degree requirements:** For Ed S, thesis.

**Entrance requirements:** For master's, GRE General Test. *Application deadline:* For fall admission, 7/1 (priority date). Applications are processed on a rolling basis. *Application fee:* $55.

**Expenses:** Tuition, state resident: part-time $143 per credit hour. Tuition, nonresident: part-time $465 per credit hour.

**Financial support:** In 2001–02, 1 teaching assistantship with full tuition reimbursement (averaging $7,170 per year) was awarded; research assistantships with full tuition reimbursements, career-related internships or fieldwork, Federal Work-Study, and unspecified assistantships also available. Financial award application deadline: 3/1; financial award applicants required to submit FAFSA.

Dr. Jane Halonen, Director, Department of Psychology, 540-568-2555.

■ **JOHN CARROLL UNIVERSITY**

**Graduate School, Program in Community Counseling, University Heights, OH 44118-4581**

**AWARDS** Clinical counseling (Certificate); community counseling (MA). Part-time and evening/weekend programs available.

**Faculty:** 7 full-time (4 women), 15 part-time/adjunct (10 women).

**Students:** 51 full-time (43 women), 49 part-time (39 women); includes 12 minority (11 African Americans, 1 Asian American or Pacific Islander). Average age 34. 18 applicants, 94% accepted. In 2001, 22 degrees awarded.

**Degree requirements:** For master's, internship, practicum.

**Entrance requirements:** For master's, MAT or GRE, minimum GPA of 2.75, statement of volunteer experience, interview. *Application deadline:* For fall admission, 8/15 (priority date); for spring admission, 1/3. Applications are processed on a rolling basis. *Application fee:* $25 ($35 for international students).

**Expenses:** Tuition: Full-time $9,900; part-time $550 per credit hour. Required fees: $10 per credit hour. Tuition and fees vary according to program.

**Financial support:** In 2001–02, 75 students received support, including 1 research assistantship with full tuition reimbursement available (averaging $8,000 per year); career-related internships or fieldwork, institutionally sponsored loans, and unspecified assistantships also available. Financial award application deadline: 3/1; financial award applicants required to submit FAFSA.

**Faculty research:** Child and adolescent development, HIV, hypnosis, wellness, women's issues, spirituality.

Dr. Christopher M. Faiver, Coordinator, 216-397-3001, *Fax:* 216-397-3045, *E-mail:* faiver@jcu.edu.

■ **JOHN F. KENNEDY UNIVERSITY**

**Graduate School for Holistic Studies, Program in Transpersonal Counseling Psychology, Orinda, CA 94563-2603**

**AWARDS** MA. Part-time and evening/weekend programs available.

**Degree requirements:** For master's, thesis or alternative.

**Entrance requirements:** For master's, TOEFL, interview.

**Expenses:** Tuition: Full-time $9,396; part-time $348 per unit. Required fees: $9 per quarter. Tuition and fees vary according to degree level and program.

■ **JOHN F. KENNEDY UNIVERSITY**

**Graduate School of Professional Psychology, Program in Counseling Psychology, Orinda, CA 94563-2603**

**AWARDS** MA. Part-time and evening/weekend programs available.

**Degree requirements:** For master's, thesis or alternative.

**Entrance requirements:** For master's, TOEFL, interview.

**Expenses:** Tuition: Full-time $9,396; part-time $348 per unit. Required fees: $9 per quarter. Tuition and fees vary according to degree level and program.

■ **KUTZTOWN UNIVERSITY OF PENNSYLVANIA**

**College of Graduate Studies and Extended Learning, Program in Counseling Psychology, Kutztown, PA 19530-0730**

**AWARDS** Agency counseling (MA); marital and family therapy (MA). Part-time and evening/weekend programs available.

**Faculty:** 7 full-time (6 women).

**Students:** 10 full-time (8 women), 49 part-time (37 women); includes 1 minority (Asian American or Pacific Islander), 1 international. Average age 33. In 2001, 16 degrees awarded.

**Degree requirements:** For master's, thesis optional.

**Entrance requirements:** For master's, GRE General Test, TOEFL, TSE, interview. *Application deadline:* For fall admission, 3/1; for spring admission, 8/11. *Application fee:* $35.

**Expenses:** Tuition, state resident: full-time $4,600; part-time $256 per credit. Tuition,

*Kutztown University of Pennsylvania (continued)*
nonresident: full-time $7,554; part-time $420 per credit. Required fees: $835.
**Financial support:** Career-related internships or fieldwork, Federal Work-Study, and unspecified assistantships available. Financial award application deadline: 3/15; financial award applicants required to submit FAFSA.
**Faculty research:** Addicted families.
Dr. Margaret A. Herrick, Chairperson, 610-683-4204, *Fax:* 610-683-1585, *E-mail:* herrick@kutztown.edu. *Web site:* http:// www.kutztown.edu/acad/

### ■ LA SALLE UNIVERSITY

**School of Arts and Sciences, Program in Clinical-Counseling Psychology, Philadelphia, PA 19141-1199**
**AWARDS** MA. Part-time and evening/weekend programs available.
**Faculty:** 14 full-time (7 women), 18 part-time/adjunct (7 women).
**Students:** 26 full-time (18 women), 133 part-time (102 women). Average age 33. 151 applicants, 58% accepted, 35 enrolled. In 2001, 33 degrees awarded.
**Degree requirements:** For master's, comprehensive exam.
**Entrance requirements:** For master's, GRE or MAT, 15 undergraduate credits in psychology. *Application deadline:* Applications are processed on a rolling basis. *Application fee:* $30.
**Expenses:** Contact institution.
**Financial support:** In 2001–02, 15 students received support; teaching assistantships, career-related internships or fieldwork, institutionally sponsored loans, scholarships/grants, and tuition waivers (partial) available. Support available to part-time students. Financial award application deadline: 8/15.
**Faculty research:** Cognitive therapy, attribution theory, work habits, single parent families, treatment of addictions.
Dr. John Rooney, Director, 215-951-1767, *Fax:* 215-951-1843, *E-mail:* rooney@lasalle.edu.
**Application contact:** Colleen L. Hindman, Administrative Assistant, 215-951-1767, *Fax:* 215-951-1843, *E-mail:* hindman@lasalle.edu. *Web site:* http:// www.lasalle.edu/academ/grad/psych/psych.htm

### ■ LEE UNIVERSITY

**Department of Behavioral Sciences, Cleveland, TN 37320-3450**
**AWARDS** Counseling psychology (MS).
**Degree requirements:** For master's, internship.

**Entrance requirements:** For master's, GRE General Test, minimum undergraduate GPA of 3.0. *Web site:* http:// www.leeuniversity.edu/

### ■ LEHIGH UNIVERSITY

**College of Education, Department of Education and Human Services, Program in Counseling Psychology, Bethlehem, PA 18015-3094**
**AWARDS** Counseling and human services (M Ed); counseling psychology (PhD); school counseling (M Ed, Certificate). Part-time and evening/weekend programs available.
**Faculty:** 4 full-time (2 women), 3 part-time/adjunct (1 woman).
**Students:** 34 full-time (27 women), 37 part-time (27 women). 132 applicants, 34% accepted, 13 enrolled. In 2001, 24 master's, 6 doctorates awarded.
**Degree requirements:** For doctorate, thesis/dissertation.
**Entrance requirements:** For master's, GRE General Test or MAT, TOEFL, minimum GPA of 2.75; for doctorate, GRE General Test or MAT, TOEFL; for Certificate, TOEFL. *Application deadline:* For fall admission, 2/1. *Application fee:* $50. Electronic applications accepted.
**Expenses:** Tuition: Part-time $468 per credit hour. Required fees: $200; $100 per semester. Tuition and fees vary according to program.
**Financial support:** Fellowships with full and partial tuition reimbursements, research assistantships with full and partial tuition reimbursements, career-related internships or fieldwork, Federal Work-Study, institutionally sponsored loans, scholarships/grants, and tuition waivers (full and partial) available. Financial award application deadline: 1/31.
**Faculty research:** Multicultural counseling, career development, family systems.
Dr. Nicholas Ladany, Coordinator, 610-758-3250, *Fax:* 610-758-3227, *E-mail:* nil3@lehigh.edu.

### ■ LESLEY UNIVERSITY

**Graduate School of Arts and Social Sciences, Cambridge, MA 02138-2790**
**AWARDS** Clinical mental health counseling (MA), including expressive therapies counseling, holistic counseling, school and community counseling; counseling psychology (MA, CAGS), including school counseling (MA); creative arts in learning (M Ed, CAGS), including individually designed (M Ed, MA), multicultural education (M Ed, MA), storytelling (M Ed), theater studies (M Ed); ecological literacy (MS); environmental education (MS); expressive therapies (MA, PhD, CAGS), including art therapy (MA), dance therapy (MA), individually designed (M Ed, MA), mental health counseling (MA), music

therapy (MA); independent studies (M Ed); independent study (MA); intercultural relations (MA, CAGS), including development project administration (MA), individually designed (M Ed, MA), intercultural conflict resolution (MA), intercultural health and human services (MA), intercultural relations (CAGS), intercultural training and consulting (MA), international education exchange (MA), international student advising (MA), managing culturally diverse human resources (MA), multicultural education (M Ed, MA); interdisciplinary studies (MA); visual arts and creative writing (MFA). MS (environmental education) offered jointly with the Audubon Society Expedition Institute. Part-time and evening/weekend programs available. Postbaccalaureate distance learning degree programs offered (minimal on-campus study).
**Faculty:** 73 full-time (58 women), 137 part-time/adjunct (95 women).
**Students:** 108 full-time (97 women), 1,190 part-time (1,084 women); includes 134 minority (81 African Americans, 23 Asian Americans or Pacific Islanders, 26 Hispanic Americans, 4 Native Americans), 16 international. Average age 36. 639 applicants, 91% accepted, 313 enrolled. In 2001, 1106 degrees awarded.
**Degree requirements:** For master's, internship, practicum, thesis (expressive therapies); for doctorate and CAGS, thesis/dissertation, arts apprenticeship, field placement; for CAGS, thesis, internship (counseling psychology, expressive therapies).
**Entrance requirements:** For master's, MAT (counseling psychology), TOEFL, interview; for doctorate, GRE or MAT; for CAGS, interview, master's degree. *Application deadline:* Applications are processed on a rolling basis. *Application fee:* $50.
**Expenses:** Tuition: Part-time $330 per credit. Required fees: $15 per term. Part-time tuition and fees vary according to campus/location and program.
**Financial support:** In 2001–02, 47 students received support; research assistantships, teaching assistantships, career-related internships or fieldwork, Federal Work-Study, and unspecified assistantships available. Support available to part-time students. Financial award application deadline: 4/1; financial award applicants required to submit FAFSA.
**Faculty research:** Developmental psychology, women's issues, health psychology, limited supervision group psychology.
Dr. Martha B. McKenna, Dean, 617-349-8467, *Fax:* 617-349-8366.
**Application contact:** Hugh Norwood, Dean of Admissions and Enrollment Planning, 800-999-1959, *Fax:* 617-349-8366, *E-mail:* hnorwood@mail.lesley.edu. *Web site:* http://www.lesley.edu/gsass.html

## ■ LEWIS & CLARK COLLEGE

**Graduate School of Professional Studies, Department of Counseling Psychology, Portland, OR 97219-7899**

**AWARDS** Counseling psychology (MA, MS); counseling psychology/school counseling (MA); school psychology (MS). Part-time and evening/weekend programs available.

**Degree requirements:** For master's, thesis (MS).
**Entrance requirements:** For master's, GRE General Test.
**Faculty research:** Treatment of depression, substance abuse, child-family problems, health psychology, marital relations.

## ■ LEWIS UNIVERSITY

**College of Arts and Sciences, Program in Counseling Psychology, Romeoville, IL 60446**

**AWARDS** Counseling psychology (MA); school counseling and guidance (MA). Part-time and evening/weekend programs available.

**Faculty:** 6 full-time (2 women).
**Students:** 31 full-time (23 women), 84 part-time (62 women); includes 17 minority (14 African Americans, 3 Hispanic Americans), 2 international. Average age 31. In 2001, 25 degrees awarded.
**Degree requirements:** For master's, thesis optional.
**Entrance requirements:** For master's, 15 hours of psychology, including statistics or research; 2 letters of recommendation; writing assessment; minimum GPA of 3.0 in last 60 hours. *Application deadline:* For fall admission, 9/1. Applications are processed on a rolling basis. *Application fee:* $35.
**Expenses:** Tuition: Part-time $425. Tuition and fees vary according to program.
**Financial support:** In 2001–02, 2 research assistantships with full tuition reimbursements (averaging $10,848 per year) were awarded; career-related internships or fieldwork, institutionally sponsored loans, and scholarships/grants also available. Financial award application deadline: 4/1; financial award applicants required to submit FAFSA.
**Faculty research:** Cognitive development, attitude formation, juvenile delinquency, gender issues, work-family conflict.
Dr. Edmund Kearney, Director, 815-838-0500 Ext. 5366, *Fax:* 815-836-5032, *E-mail:* kearneed@lewisu.edu. *Web site:* http://www.lewisu/edu/academics/grad.htm/

## ■ LIBERTY UNIVERSITY

**College of Arts and Science, Lynchburg, VA 24502**

**AWARDS** Counseling (MA); nursing (MSN). Part-time programs available. Postbaccalaureate distance learning degree programs offered (minimal on-campus study).
**Faculty:** 9 full-time (4 women), 2 part-time/adjunct (0 women).
**Students:** 68 full-time (42 women), 203 part-time (134 women).
**Degree requirements:** For master's, comprehensive exam.
**Entrance requirements:** For master's, GRE General Test, TOEFL. *Application deadline:* For fall admission, 6/1 (priority date); for spring admission, 11/1. Applications are processed on a rolling basis. *Application fee:* $35.
**Expenses:** Tuition: Full-time $5,130; part-time $285 per credit. Required fees: $500. Tuition and fees vary according to degree level and program.
**Financial support:** Federal Work-Study available. Financial award application deadline: 4/15; financial award applicants required to submit FAFSA.
Dr. Ronald E. Hawkins, Dean, 434-582-2490, *Fax:* 434-582-2468, *E-mail:* rehawkin@liberty.edu.
**Application contact:** Dr. William E. Wegert, Coordinator of Graduate Admissions, 434-582-2175, *Fax:* 434-582-2421, *E-mail:* wewegert@liberty.edu. *Web site:* http://www.liberty.edu/academics/artsci/index/

## ■ LINDENWOOD UNIVERSITY

**Graduate Programs, Programs in Individualized Education, St. Charles, MO 63301-1695**

**AWARDS** Administration (MSA); business administration (MBA); corporate communication (MS); counseling psychology (MA); gerontology (MA); health management (MS); human resource management (MS); human service agency management (MS); management (MSA); marketing (MSA); mass communication (MS). Part-time and evening/weekend programs available.

**Faculty:** 11 full-time (6 women), 23 part-time/adjunct (6 women).
**Students:** 515 full-time (340 women), 266 part-time (232 women); includes 117 minority (107 African Americans, 1 Asian American or Pacific Islander, 5 Hispanic Americans, 4 Native Americans), 11 international. Average age 35. In 2001, 298 degrees awarded.
**Degree requirements:** For master's, thesis. *Median time to degree:* Master's–1.25 years full-time.
**Entrance requirements:** For master's, interview, minimum GPA of 3.0. *Application deadline:* For fall admission, 6/30

(priority date); for spring admission, 12/1. Applications are processed on a rolling basis. *Application fee:* $25.
**Expenses:** Tuition: Full-time $10,800; part-time $300 per hour. Tuition and fees vary according to course load and program.
**Financial support:** Career-related internships or fieldwork, institutionally sponsored loans, tuition waivers (partial), and unspecified assistantships available. Financial award application deadline: 6/30. Dan Kemper, Director, 636-916-9125, *E-mail:* dkemper@lindenwood.edu.
**Application contact:** John Guffey, Dean of Admissions, 636-949-4934, *Fax:* 636-949-4910, *E-mail:* jguffey@lindenwood.edu.

## ■ LOUISIANA TECH UNIVERSITY

**Graduate School, College of Education, Department of Behavioral Sciences, Ruston, LA 71272**

**AWARDS** Counseling (MA, Ed S); counseling psychology (PhD); industrial/organizational psychology (MA); special education (MA). Part-time programs available.

**Degree requirements:** For master's, thesis or alternative; for doctorate, thesis/dissertation.
**Entrance requirements:** For master's and doctorate, GRE General Test.

## ■ LOYOLA COLLEGE IN MARYLAND

**Graduate Programs, College of Arts and Sciences, Department of Psychology, Program in Counseling Psychology, Baltimore, MD 21210-2699**

**AWARDS** Counseling psychology (MA, MS); employee assistance and substance abuse (CAS). Part-time and evening/weekend programs available.

**Students:** 25 full-time (19 women), 21 part-time (19 women). In 2001, 14 degrees awarded.
**Entrance requirements:** For master's, GRE General Test; for CAS, master's degree. *Application deadline:* For spring admission, 10/1 (priority date). Applications are processed on a rolling basis.
**Expenses:** Tuition: Part-time $244 per unit. Tuition and fees vary according to degree level, program and student level.
**Financial support:** Applicants required to submit FAFSA.
**Application contact:** Scott Greatorex, Director, Graduate Admissions, 410-617-5020 Ext. 2407, *Fax:* 410-617-2002, *E-mail:* sgreatorex@loyola.edu.

# ■ LOYOLA MARYMOUNT UNIVERSITY

**Graduate Division, College of Liberal Arts, Department of Psychology, Los Angeles, CA 90045-2659**

**AWARDS** Counseling psychology (MA). Part-time and evening/weekend programs available.

**Faculty:** 14 full-time (7 women), 11 part-time/adjunct (5 women).

**Students:** 4 full-time (all women). In 2001, 17 degrees awarded.

**Degree requirements:** For master's, thesis (for some programs), comprehensive exam.

**Entrance requirements:** For master's, GRE General Test, TOEFL, interview, minimum GPA of 3.0. *Application deadline:* For fall admission, 3/15. *Application fee:* $45. Electronic applications accepted.

**Expenses:** Tuition: Part-time $612 per credit hour. Required fees: $86 per term. Tuition and fees vary according to program.

**Financial support:** Scholarships/grants available. Support available to part-time students. Financial award application deadline: 7/1; financial award applicants required to submit FAFSA.

Dr. Michael O'Sullivan, Director, 310-338-3015, *Fax:* 310-338-7726, *E-mail:* mosulliv@lmu.edu. *Web site:* http://www.lmu.edu/acad/gd/graddiv.htm

# ■ LOYOLA UNIVERSITY CHICAGO

**School of Education, Department of Leadership, Foundations, and Counseling Psychology, Program in Counseling Psychology, Chicago, IL 60611-2196**

**AWARDS** PhD. Offered through the Graduate School.

**Faculty:** 5 full-time (3 women), 1 (woman) part-time/adjunct.

**Students:** 41 full-time (24 women); includes 16 minority (8 African Americans, 6 Asian Americans or Pacific Islanders, 2 Hispanic Americans). Average age 26. 49 applicants, 27% accepted, 9 enrolled. In 2001, 4 degrees awarded.

**Degree requirements:** For doctorate, thesis/dissertation, comprehensive exam. *Median time to degree:* Doctorate–6 years full-time.

**Entrance requirements:** For doctorate, GRE General Test, GRE Subject Test, interview. *Application deadline:* For fall admission, 1/1. *Application fee:* $40.

**Expenses:** Tuition: Part-time $529 per credit hour.

**Financial support:** In 2001–02, 23 students received support, including 7 fellowships with full tuition reimbursements

available (averaging $10,000 per year), 7 research assistantships with full tuition reimbursements available (averaging $10,000 per year), 7 teaching assistantships with full tuition reimbursements available (averaging $10,000 per year); career-related internships or fieldwork, Federal Work-Study, traineeships, and unspecified assistantships also available. Financial award application deadline: 2/1; financial award applicants required to submit FAFSA.

**Faculty research:** Career choice and development, multicultural counseling, counseling process, psychological measurement, prevention and intervention. *Total annual research expenditures:* $200,000.

Dr. Elizabeth M. Vera, Director, 312-915-6958, *E-mail:* evera@luc.edu.

**Application contact:** Marie Rosin-Dittmar, Information Contact, 312-915-6722, *E-mail:* schleduc@luc.edu.

# ■ MARIST COLLEGE

**Graduate Programs, School of Social/Behavioral Sciences, Poughkeepsie, NY 12601-1387**

**AWARDS** Counseling/community psychology (MA); education psychology (MA); school psychology (MA, Adv C). Part-time and evening/weekend programs available.

**Faculty:** 8 full-time (3 women), 20 part-time/adjunct (11 women).

**Students:** 66 full-time (49 women), 149 part-time (113 women); includes 11 minority (5 African Americans, 1 Asian American or Pacific Islander, 4 Hispanic Americans, 1 Native American). Average age 30. 104 applicants, 79% accepted. In 2001, 62 degrees awarded.

**Degree requirements:** For master's, thesis optional.

**Entrance requirements:** For master's, GRE General Test. *Application deadline:* For fall admission, 8/1 (priority date); for spring admission, 12/15. Applications are processed on a rolling basis. *Application fee:* $30.

**Expenses:** Tuition: Full-time $4,320; part-time $480 per credit. Required fees: $30 per semester.

**Financial support:** Career-related internships or fieldwork, Federal Work-Study, and tuition waivers (partial) available. Support available to part-time students. Financial award application deadline: 8/15; financial award applicants required to submit FAFSA.

**Faculty research:** Obsessive-compulsive disorders/eating disorders, AIDS prevention, educational intervention, humanistic counseling research, program evaluation research.

Margaret Calista, Dean, 845-575-3000 Ext. 2960, *E-mail:* margaret.calista@marist.edu.

**Application contact:** Dr. John DeJoy, Acting Dean of Graduate and Continuing Education, 845-575-3530, *Fax:* 845-575-3640, *E-mail:* john.dejoy@marist.edu.

# ■ MARYMOUNT UNIVERSITY

**School of Education and Human Services, Program in Psychology, Arlington, VA 22207-4299**

**AWARDS** Counseling psychology (MA, Certificate); forensic psychology (MA); school counseling (MA). Part-time and evening/weekend programs available.

**Students:** 80 full-time (71 women), 101 part-time (87 women); includes 28 minority (20 African Americans, 7 Hispanic Americans, 1 Native American), 3 international. Average age 32. 65 applicants, 98% accepted, 44 enrolled. In 2001, 41 degrees awarded.

**Degree requirements:** For master's, thesis or alternative.

**Entrance requirements:** For master's, GRE General Test or MAT, interview; for Certificate, master's degree in counseling. *Application deadline:* Applications are processed on a rolling basis. *Application fee:* $35. Electronic applications accepted.

**Expenses:** Tuition: Part-time $512 per credit. Required fees: $5 per credit.

**Financial support:** Research assistantships with full tuition reimbursements, career-related internships or fieldwork and scholarships/grants available. Support available to part-time students. Financial award applicants required to submit FAFSA.

Dr. Carolyn Oxenford, Chair, 703-284-1620, *Fax:* 703-284-1631, *E-mail:* carolyn.oxenford@marymount.edu. *Web site:* http://www.marymount.edu/academic/sehs/

# ■ MARYWOOD UNIVERSITY

**Graduate School of Arts and Sciences, Department of Counseling/Psychology, Program in Counseling, Scranton, PA 18509-1598**

**AWARDS** MA.

**Students:** 13 full-time (12 women), 18 part-time (11 women); includes 1 minority (Asian American or Pacific Islander). Average age 34. 15 applicants, 67% accepted.

**Degree requirements:** For master's, internship/practicum.

**Entrance requirements:** For master's, GRE or MAT, TOEFL. *Application deadline:* For fall admission, 4/15; for spring admission, 11/15 (priority date). Applications are processed on a rolling basis. *Application fee:* $20. Electronic applications accepted.

**Financial support:** Research assistantships, career-related internships or fieldwork, scholarships/grants, and tuition waivers (partial) available. Support available to part-time students. Financial award application deadline: 2/15; financial award applicants required to submit FAFSA.

**Application contact:** Deborah M. Flynn, Coordinator of Admissions, 570-340-6002, *Fax:* 570-961-4745, *E-mail:* gsas_adm@ ac.marywood.edu.

■ **MARYWOOD UNIVERSITY**

**Graduate School of Arts and Sciences, Department of Counseling/ Psychology, Program in Psychology and Counseling, Scranton, PA 18509-1598**

**AWARDS** Psy D.

*Application deadline:* For fall admission, 1/15. *Application fee:* $20.

**Financial support:** Applicants required to submit FAFSA.

Dr. Brooke Cannon, Clinical Director, 570-348-6211.

■ **MICHIGAN STATE UNIVERSITY**

**Graduate School, College of Education, Department of Counseling, Educational Psychology and Special Education, East Lansing, MI 48824**

**AWARDS** Counseling (MA, Ed D, Ed S); counseling psychology (MA, PhD); counselor education (PhD); educational psychology (MA, Ed D, PhD, Ed S); educational system design (Ed S); educational system development (MA, Ed D); educational technology and instructional design (MA); educational technology and system design (MA); measurement and quantitative methods (MA, PhD); measurement, evaluation and research design (Ed D, PhD); rehabilitation counseling (MA); rehabilitation counseling and school counseling (PhD); school psychology (PhD, Ed S); special education (MA, Ed D, PhD, Ed S). Part-time programs available.

**Faculty:** 37.

**Students:** 174 full-time (134 women), 145 part-time (104 women); includes 38 minority (24 African Americans, 11 Asian Americans or Pacific Islanders, 3 Hispanic Americans), 47 international. Average age 32. 359 applicants, 38% accepted. In 2001, 99 master's, 28 doctorates, 7 other advanced degrees awarded.

**Degree requirements:** For doctorate, thesis/dissertation.

**Entrance requirements:** For master's and doctorate, GRE General Test. *Application deadline:* For fall admission, 2/15 (priority date). Applications are processed on a rolling basis. *Application fee:* $30 ($40 for

international students). Electronic applications accepted.

**Expenses:** Tuition, state resident: part-time $244 per credit hour. Tuition, nonresident: part-time $494 per credit hour. Required fees: $268 per semester. Tuition and fees vary according to course load, degree level and program.

**Financial support:** In 2001–02, 104 fellowships (averaging $3,880 per year), 26 research assistantships with tuition reimbursements (averaging $12,108 per year), 36 teaching assistantships with tuition reimbursements (averaging $11,963 per year) were awarded. Career-related internships or fieldwork and Federal Work-Study also available. Financial award applicants required to submit FAFSA.

**Faculty research:** Longitudinal and multilevel research, international mathematics and science curriculum, early intervention for non readers/writers, predictions and consequences of exposure to violence. *Total annual research expenditures:* $2.7 million.

Dr. Richard Prawat, Chairperson, 517-353-7863.

**Application contact:** Graduate Admissions, 517-355-6683, *Fax:* 517-353-6393. *Web site:* http://ed-web3.educ.msu.edu/ CEPSE/

■ **MICHIGAN THEOLOGICAL SEMINARY**

**Graduate Programs, Plymouth, MI 48170**

**AWARDS** Christian education (MA); counseling psychology (MA); divinity (M Div); expository communication (D Min); theological studies (MA). Part-time and evening/weekend programs available.

**Degree requirements:** For M Div, 2 foreign languages; for master's, one foreign language, thesis; for doctorate, 2 foreign languages, thesis/dissertation.

**Faculty research:** Judaism, cults, world religions. *Web site:* http://www.mts.edu/

■ **MIDAMERICA NAZARENE UNIVERSITY**

**Graduate Studies in Counseling, Olathe, KS 66062-1899**

**AWARDS** MAC.

**Faculty:** 3 full-time (0 women), 8 part-time/adjunct (2 women).

**Students:** 31 full-time (22 women), 8 part-time (6 women); includes 1 minority (African American). 30 applicants, 67% accepted.

**Entrance requirements:** For master's, GRE, Minnesota Multiphasic Personality Inventory, minimum GPA of 3.0. *Application deadline:* For fall admission, 6/15. *Application fee:* $75.

**Expenses:** Contact institution.

Roy Rotz, Director, 913-791-3449, *Fax:* 913-791-3402, *E-mail:* rrotz@mnu.edu.

**Application contact:** Aileen Douglas, Secretary, 913-791-3449, *Fax:* 913-791-3402, *E-mail:* adouglas@mnu.edu. *Web site:* http://www.mnu.edu/

■ **MISSISSIPPI COLLEGE**

**Graduate School, College of Arts and Sciences, Department of Psychology and Counseling, Program in Psychology, Clinton, MS 39058**

**AWARDS** Counseling psychology (MS).

■ **MISSISSIPPI COLLEGE**

**Graduate School, School of Education, Programs in Guidance and Counseling, Clinton, MS 39058**

**AWARDS** Counseling psychology (MCP); guidance and counseling (M Ed, Ed S). Evening/weekend programs available.

**Degree requirements:** For master's, comprehensive exam.

**Entrance requirements:** For master's, GRE or NTE, minimum GPA of 2.5, Class A Certificate; for Ed S, NTE, minimum GPA of 3.0.

■ **MONMOUTH UNIVERSITY**

**Graduate School, Department of Psychology, West Long Branch, NJ 07764-1898**

**AWARDS** Professional counseling (PMC); psychological counseling (MA). Part-time and evening/weekend programs available.

**Faculty:** 5 full-time (1 woman), 4 part-time/adjunct (3 women).

**Students:** 22 full-time (19 women), 53 part-time (42 women); includes 7 minority (4 African Americans, 2 Asian Americans or Pacific Islanders, 1 Native American), 1 international. Average age 32. 84 applicants, 55% accepted, 19 enrolled. In 2001, 31 degrees awarded.

**Degree requirements:** For master's, thesis optional.

**Entrance requirements:** For master's, GRE General Test, minimum GPA of 3.0 in major, 24 credits in psychology. *Application deadline:* For fall admission, 8/15 (priority date); for spring admission, 12/15 (priority date). Applications are processed on a rolling basis. *Application fee:* $35. Electronic applications accepted.

**Expenses:** Tuition: Full-time $9,900; part-time $549 per credit. Required fees: $568.

**Financial support:** In 2001–02, 90 fellowships (averaging $1,519 per year), 4 research assistantships (averaging $8,114 per year) were awarded. Career-related internships or fieldwork, scholarships/ grants, tuition waivers (partial), and unspecified assistantships also available.

*Monmouth University (continued)*
Support available to part-time students. Financial award application deadline: 3/1; financial award applicants required to submit FAFSA.

**Faculty research:** Systems thinking, violent crime, single parenting, the African-American male, counseling older women.
Dr. Frances K. Trotman, Director, 732-571-7593, *Fax:* 732-263-5159, *E-mail:* ftrotman@monmouth.edu.

**Application contact:** Kevin Roane, Director, Office of Graduate Admissions, 732-571-3452, *Fax:* 732-263-5123, *E-mail:* gradadm@monmouth.edu. *Web site:* http://www.monmouth.edu/~psychgr/

**Find an in-depth description at www.petersons.com/gradchannel.**

■ **MOREHEAD STATE UNIVERSITY**

**Graduate Programs, College of Science and Technology, Department of Psychology, Morehead, KY 40351**

**AWARDS** Clinical psychology (MA); counseling psychology (MA); experimental/general psychology (MA). Part-time programs available.

**Faculty:** 7 full-time (2 women).
**Students:** 30 full-time (19 women), 1 international. Average age 25. 5 applicants, 80% accepted. In 2001, 15 degrees awarded.
**Entrance requirements:** For master's, GRE General Test, TOEFL, 18 undergraduate hours in psychology, minimum GPA of 3.0. *Application deadline:* For fall admission, 8/1 (priority date); for spring admission, 12/1. Applications are processed on a rolling basis. *Application fee:* $0.
**Expenses:** Tuition, state resident: part-time $176 per hour. Tuition, nonresident: full-time $1,584; part-time $472 per hour. International tuition: $4,247 full-time.
**Financial support:** In 2001–02, 21 research assistantships (averaging $5,000 per year) were awarded; career-related internships or fieldwork, Federal Work-Study, and institutionally sponsored loans also available. Financial award application deadline: 4/1; financial award applicants required to submit FAFSA.
**Faculty research:** Mood induction effects, serotonin receptor activity, stress, perceptual processes.
Dr. Bruce A. Mattingly, Chair, 606-783-2891, *Fax:* 606-783-5077, *E-mail:* b.mattin@moreheadstate.edu.

**Application contact:** Betty R. Cowsert, Graduate Admissions/Records Manager, 606-783-2039, *Fax:* 606-783-5061, *E-mail:* b.cowsert@moreheadstate.edu. *Web site:* http://www.moreheadstate.edu

■ **MOUNT ST. MARY'S COLLEGE**

**Graduate Division, Program in Counseling Psychology, Los Angeles, CA 90049-1599**

**AWARDS** MS. Part-time and evening/weekend programs available.

**Degree requirements:** For master's, research project.
**Entrance requirements:** For master's, MAT, minimum GPA of 2.75.

■ **NATIONAL UNIVERSITY**

**Academic Affairs, School of Arts and Sciences, Department of Psychology, La Jolla, CA 92037-1011**

**AWARDS** Art therapy (Certificate); counseling psychology (MA); human behavior (MA). Part-time and evening/weekend programs available. Postbaccalaureate distance learning degree programs offered (minimal on-campus study).

**Faculty:** 8 full-time (4 women), 160 part-time/adjunct (90 women).
**Students:** 331 full-time (255 women), 101 part-time (74 women); includes 166 minority (70 African Americans, 26 Asian Americans or Pacific Islanders, 66 Hispanic Americans, 4 Native Americans), 2 international. 117 applicants, 100% accepted. In 2001, 235 degrees awarded.
**Entrance requirements:** For master's, interview, minimum GPA of 2.5. *Application deadline:* Applications are processed on a rolling basis. *Application fee:* $60 ($100 for international students).
**Expenses:** Tuition: Part-time $221 per quarter hour.
**Financial support:** Institutionally sponsored loans, scholarships/grants, and tuition waivers (full and partial) available. Support available to part-time students. Financial award applicants required to submit FAFSA.
Dr. Charles Tatum, Chair, 858-642-8476, *Fax:* 858-642-8715, *E-mail:* ctatum@nu.edu.

**Application contact:** Nancy Rohland, Director of Enrollment Management, 858-642-8180, *Fax:* 858-642-8710, *E-mail:* advisor@nu.edu. *Web site:* http://www.nu.edu/

■ **NEW JERSEY CITY UNIVERSITY**

**Graduate Studies, College of Arts and Sciences, Department of Psychology, Program in Counseling, Jersey City, NJ 07305-1597**

**AWARDS** MA.

**Faculty:** 3 full-time, 2 part-time/adjunct (1 woman).

**Students:** 10 full-time (7 women), 106 part-time (81 women); includes 35 minority (14 African Americans, 2 Asian Americans or Pacific Islanders, 19 Hispanic Americans). Average age 35. 45 applicants, 69% accepted. In 2001, 23 degrees awarded.
**Degree requirements:** For master's, practicum.
**Entrance requirements:** For master's, GRE General Test or MAT, TOEFL, interview. *Application deadline:* For fall admission, 8/1 (priority date); for spring admission, 12/1. Applications are processed on a rolling basis. *Application fee:* $0.
**Expenses:** Tuition, state resident: full-time $5,062. Tuition, nonresident: full-time $8,663.
**Financial support:** Teaching assistantships, career-related internships or fieldwork available.
Dr. David Hallerman, Chairperson, Department of Psychology, 201-200-3062.

■ **NEW MEXICO STATE UNIVERSITY**

**Graduate School, College of Education, Department of Counseling and Educational Psychology, Las Cruces, NM 88003-8001**

**AWARDS** Counseling and guidance (MA, Ed S); counseling psychology (PhD). Part-time programs available.

**Faculty:** 9 full-time (3 women), 3 part-time/adjunct (1 woman).
**Students:** 42 full-time (30 women), 21 part-time (16 women); includes 17 minority (2 African Americans, 1 Asian American or Pacific Islander, 13 Hispanic Americans, 1 Native American), 1 international. Average age 34. 26 applicants, 38% accepted, 6 enrolled. In 2001, 6 master's, 3 doctorates, 2 other advanced degrees awarded.
**Degree requirements:** For master's, internship, thesis optional; for doctorate, thesis/dissertation, internship; for Ed S, thesis or alternative, internship.
**Entrance requirements:** For master's, GRE General Test; for doctorate, GRE General Test, master's degree in counseling; for Ed S, GRE General Test, master's degree. *Application fee:* $15 ($35 for international students). Electronic applications accepted.
**Expenses:** Tuition, state resident: full-time $3,234; part-time $135 per credit. Tuition, nonresident: full-time $9,420; part-time $428 per credit. Required fees: $858.
**Financial support:** In 2001–02, 15 teaching assistantships were awarded; fellowships, career-related internships or fieldwork and Federal Work-Study also available. Support available to part-time students. Financial award application deadline: 3/1.

**Faculty research:** Cultural diversity, family counseling, group counseling, supervision, professional issues.
Dr. Luis Vazquez, Head, 505-646-2121, *Fax:* 505-646-8035, *E-mail:* lvazquez@nmsu.edu. *Web site:* http://www.nmsu.edu/~colgeduc/Dept_Fac/Con_Psy/Counsel.html

### ■ NEW YORK INSTITUTE OF TECHNOLOGY

**Graduate Division, School of Education and Professional Services, Program in Mental Health Counseling & School Counseling, Old Westbury, NY 11568-8000**

**AWARDS** MS.

**Students:** 1 (woman) full-time, 7 part-time (6 women); includes 1 minority (African American). Average age 31. 6 applicants, 67% accepted, 4 enrolled.
**Degree requirements:** For master's, thesis.
**Entrance requirements:** For master's, minimum GPA of 2.85, interview, letters of references (3). *Application deadline:* For fall admission, 7/1 (priority date); for spring admission, 12/1 (priority date). *Application fee:* $50.
**Expenses:** Tuition: Part-time $545 per credit. Tuition and fees vary according to course load, degree level, program and student level.
**Financial support:** Research assistantships with partial tuition reimbursements, career-related internships or fieldwork, institutionally sponsored loans, and unspecified assistantships available. Support available to part-time students. Financial award applicants required to submit FAFSA.
Dr. Carol Dahir, Coordinator, 516-686-7616, *Fax:* 516-686-7655, *E-mail:* cdahir@nyit.edu.
**Application contact:** Jacquelyn Nealon, Dean of Admissions and Financial Aid, 516-686-7925, *Fax:* 516-686-7613, *E-mail:* jnealon@nyit.edu.

### ■ NEW YORK UNIVERSITY

**The Steinhardt School of Education, Department of Applied Psychology, Program in Counselor Education, New York, NY 10012-1019**

**AWARDS** Counseling and guidance (MA, PhD, Advanced Certificate), including bilingual school counseling (MA); counseling psychology (PhD). Part-time and evening/weekend programs available.

**Faculty:** 8 full-time (4 women).
**Students:** 94 full-time (84 women), 86 part-time (73 women); includes 56 minority (20 African Americans, 17 Asian Americans or Pacific Islanders, 19

Hispanic Americans). 308 applicants, 27% accepted, 52 enrolled. In 2001, 68 master's, 6 doctorates awarded. Terminal master's awarded for partial completion of doctoral program.
**Degree requirements:** For master's, thesis (for some programs); for doctorate, thesis/dissertation.
**Entrance requirements:** For master's and Advanced Certificate, TOEFL; for doctorate, GRE General Test, TOEFL, interview. *Application deadline:* For fall admission, 2/1 (priority date); for spring admission, 12/1. Applications are processed on a rolling basis. *Application fee:* $40 ($60 for international students).
**Expenses:** Tuition: Full-time $19,536; part-time $814 per credit. Required fees: $1,330; $38 per credit. Tuition and fees vary according to course load and program.
**Financial support:** Fellowships with full and partial tuition reimbursements, teaching assistantships with partial tuition reimbursements, career-related internships or fieldwork, Federal Work-Study, institutionally sponsored loans, scholarships/grants, tuition waivers (partial), and unspecified assistantships available. Support available to part-time students. Financial award application deadline: 3/1; financial award applicants required to submit FAFSA.
**Faculty research:** Cross-cultural counseling, thanatology, group dynamics, sex and race discrimination, substance abuse.
Dr. Samuel Juni, Co-Director, 212-998-5548, *Fax:* 212-995-4368.
**Application contact:** 212-998-5030, *Fax:* 212-995-4328, *E-mail:* grad.admissions@nyu.edu.

### ■ NICHOLLS STATE UNIVERSITY

**Graduate Studies, College of Education, Department of Psychology and Counselor Education, Thibodaux, LA 70310**

**AWARDS** Counselor education (M Ed); psychological counseling (MA); school psychology (SSP). Part-time and evening/weekend programs available.

**Faculty:** 8 full-time (2 women).
**Students:** 26 full-time (23 women), 63 part-time (56 women); includes 14 minority (13 African Americans, 1 Asian American or Pacific Islander). In 2001, 15 master's, 3 other advanced degrees awarded.
**Degree requirements:** For master's, comprehensive exam.
**Entrance requirements:** For master's, GRE General Test. *Application deadline:* For fall admission, 6/17 (priority date); for spring admission, 11/15 (priority date). Applications are processed on a rolling

basis. *Application fee:* $20 ($30 for international students). Electronic applications accepted.
**Financial support:** In 2001–02, research assistantships with tuition reimbursements (averaging $4,000 per year), teaching assistantships with tuition reimbursements (averaging $6,000 per year) were awarded. Financial award application deadline: 6/17.
Dr. J. Steven Welsh, Head, 985-448-4371, *E-mail:* gred-jtb@mail.nich.edu.

### ■ NORTHEASTERN STATE UNIVERSITY

**Graduate College, College of Behavioral and Social Sciences, Department of Psychology and Counseling, Program in Counseling Psychology, Tahlequah, OK 74464-2399**

**AWARDS** MS. Evening/weekend programs available.

**Students:** 39 full-time (28 women), 59 part-time (47 women); includes 27 minority (5 African Americans, 22 Native Americans). Average age 31. In 2001, 23 degrees awarded.
**Degree requirements:** For master's, thesis, internship, practicum.
**Entrance requirements:** For master's, minimum GPA of 2.5. *Application deadline:* For fall admission, 3/1 (priority date); for spring admission, 10/1. Applications are processed on a rolling basis. *Application fee:* $0.
**Expenses:** Tuition, area resident: Part-time $87 per credit hour. Tuition, state resident: part-time $206 per credit hour.
**Financial support:** Teaching assistantships, career-related internships or fieldwork and Federal Work-Study available. Financial award application deadline: 3/1.
Dr. Mary Sweet-Darter, Chair, 918-456-5511 Ext. 3015, *Fax:* 918-458-2397, *E-mail:* schiller@cherokee.nsuok.edu.

### ■ NORTHEASTERN UNIVERSITY

**Bouvé College of Health Sciences Graduate School, Department of Counseling and Applied Educational Psychology, Program in Counseling Psychology, Boston, MA 02115-5096**

**AWARDS** MS, PhD, CAGS. Part-time programs available.

**Faculty:** 7 full-time (4 women), 4 part-time/adjunct (2 women).
**Students:** 79 full-time (63 women), 3 part-time (1 woman). Average age 28. 208 applicants, 43% accepted. In 2001, 18 master's, 4 doctorates awarded.
**Degree requirements:** For doctorate, thesis/dissertation, qualifying exams, comprehensive exam.

*Northeastern University (continued)*

**Entrance requirements:** For master's and CAGS, GRE General Test or MAT; for doctorate, GRE General Test. *Application deadline:* For fall admission, 2/1. Applications are processed on a rolling basis. *Application fee:* $50.

**Expenses:** Tuition: Part-time $535 per credit hour. Required fees: $56. Tuition and fees vary according to program.

**Financial support:** In 2001–02, 1 teaching assistantship with full tuition reimbursement (averaging $11,250 per year) was awarded; career-related internships or fieldwork, Federal Work-Study, tuition waivers (partial), and unspecified assistantships also available. Support available to part-time students. Financial award application deadline: 3/1; financial award applicants required to submit FAFSA.

**Faculty research:** Crisis intervention, family systems.

Dr. Mary B. Ballou, Director, 617-373-5937, *Fax:* 617-373-8892, *E-mail:* m.ballou@neu.edu.

**Application contact:** Bill Purnell, Director of Graduate Admissions, 617-373-2708, *Fax:* 617-373-4701, *E-mail:* w.purnell@neu.edu.

**Find an in-depth description at www.petersons.com/gradchannel.**

### ■ NORTHERN ARIZONA UNIVERSITY

**Graduate College, Center for Excellence in Education, Program in Educational Psychology, Flagstaff, AZ 86011**

**AWARDS** Counseling psychology (Ed D); learning and instruction (Ed D); school psychology (Ed D).

**Students:** 33 full-time (26 women), 28 part-time (19 women); includes 10 minority (5 African Americans, 1 Asian American or Pacific Islander, 3 Hispanic Americans, 1 Native American), 2 international. Average age 35. 13 applicants, 69% accepted, 7 enrolled. In 2001, 1 degree awarded.

**Degree requirements:** For doctorate, thesis/dissertation, internship, comprehensive exam.

**Entrance requirements:** For doctorate, GRE General Test. *Application deadline:* For fall admission, 1/15. *Application fee:* $45.

**Expenses:** Tuition, state resident: full-time $2,488. Tuition, nonresident: full-time $10,354.

Dr. Ramona Mellott, Chair, 928-523-7103, *E-mail:* ramona.mellott@nau.edu.

**Application contact:** Marcia Couch, Secretary, 928-523-7103. *Web site:* http://www.nau.edu/~cee/academics/

### ■ NORTHWESTERN UNIVERSITY

**The Graduate School, Interdepartmental Degree Programs, Education and Social Policy-Counseling Psychology, Evanston, IL 60208**

**AWARDS** MA. Admissions and degrees offered through The Graduate School. Part-time programs available.

**Faculty:** 5 full-time (2 women), 10 part-time/adjunct (6 women).

**Students:** 36 full-time (28 women), 9 part-time (6 women); includes 7 minority (2 African Americans, 5 Asian Americans or Pacific Islanders), 3 international. Average age 31. 88 applicants, 40% accepted. In 2001, 17 degrees awarded.

**Degree requirements:** For master's, comprehensive exam.

**Entrance requirements:** For master's, GRE General Test, 4 specific essay questions. *Application deadline:* Applications are processed on a rolling basis. *Application fee:* $50 ($55 for international students). Electronic applications accepted.

**Expenses:** Tuition: Full-time $26,526.

**Financial support:** In 2001–02, 30 students received support. Institutionally sponsored loans and unspecified assistantships available. Financial award application deadline: 5/15.

**Faculty research:** Family psychology, adult development and pathology, minority counseling, groups and systems, clinical training, stress and coping, health psychology.

Dr. Solomon Cytrynbaum, Director, 847-491-5754.

**Application contact:** Dr. Ava Carn-Watkins, Assistant Director, 847-491-3265, *Fax:* 847-467-8999, *E-mail:* cspy-inquiries@northwestern.edu. *Web site:* http://www.northwestern.edu/graduate/cpsy

**Find an in-depth description at www.petersons.com/gradchannel.**

### ■ NORTHWEST MISSOURI STATE UNIVERSITY

**Graduate School, College of Education and Human Services, Department of Psychology and Sociology, Program in Counseling Psychology, Maryville, MO 64468-6001**

**AWARDS** MS.

**Faculty:** 10 full-time (5 women).

**Students:** 20 full-time (10 women), 7 part-time (6 women). 18 applicants, 100% accepted, 8 enrolled. In 2001, 4 degrees awarded.

**Degree requirements:** For master's, thesis, comprehensive exam.

**Entrance requirements:** For master's, GRE General Test, GRE Subject Test, TOEFL, minimum undergraduate GPA of 2.5, 3.0 in major; writing sample. *Application deadline:* For fall admission, 3/1. *Application fee:* $0 ($50 for international students). Electronic applications accepted.

**Expenses:** Tuition, state resident: full-time $2,777; part-time $154 per hour. Tuition, nonresident: full-time $4,626; part-time $257 per hour. Tuition and fees vary according to course level and course load.

**Financial support:** In 2001–02, 6 research assistantships (averaging $5,250 per year) were awarded; unspecified assistantships also available. Financial award application deadline: 3/1.

Dr. John K. Bowers, Director, 660-562-1260.

**Application contact:** Dr. Frances Shipley, Dean of Graduate School, 660-562-1145, *Fax:* 660-562-0000, *E-mail:* gradsch@mail.nwmissouri.edu. *Web site:* http://www.acad.nwmissouri.edu/

### ■ NOTRE DAME DE NAMUR UNIVERSITY

**Graduate School, School of Sciences, Department of Counseling and Psychology/Gerontology, Belmont, CA 94002-1997**

**AWARDS** Chemical dependency (MACP); counseling psychology (MACP); gerontology (MA, Certificate); marital and family therapy (MACP, MAMFT). Part-time and evening/weekend programs available.

**Faculty:** 3 full-time, 6 part-time/adjunct.

**Students:** 28 full-time (24 women), 85 part-time (71 women); includes 28 minority (8 African Americans, 11 Asian Americans or Pacific Islanders, 9 Hispanic Americans), 1 international. Average age 37. 41 applicants, 76% accepted. In 2001, 36 degrees awarded.

**Entrance requirements:** For master's, TOEFL, interview, minimum GPA of 2.5. *Application deadline:* For fall admission, 8/1 (priority date); for spring admission, 12/1 (priority date). Applications are processed on a rolling basis. *Application fee:* $50 ($500 for international students). Electronic applications accepted.

**Expenses:** Tuition: Full-time $9,450; part-time $525 per unit. Required fees: $35 per term.

**Financial support:** Career-related internships or fieldwork available. Support available to part-time students. Financial award applicants required to submit FAFSA.

Dr. Anna McQuinn, Chair, 650-508-3557.

**Application contact:** Barbara Sterner, Assistant Director of Graduate Admissions, 650-508-3527, *Fax:* 650-508-3662, *E-mail:* grad.admit@ndnu.edu.

## ■ NOVA SOUTHEASTERN UNIVERSITY

**Center for Psychological Studies, Master's Program in Counseling, Mental Health, and School Guidance, Fort Lauderdale, FL 33314-7721**

**AWARDS** Mental health counseling (MS); school guidance and counseling (MS). Part-time and evening/weekend programs available.

**Faculty:** 33 full-time (10 women), 19 part-time/adjunct (10 women).
**Students:** 468 full-time (410 women). In 2001, 155 degrees awarded.
**Degree requirements:** For master's, 3 practica.
*Application deadline:* For fall admission, 6/11; for spring admission, 10/19. Applications are processed on a rolling basis. *Application fee:* $50.
**Expenses:** Tuition: Full-time $7,380; part-time $432 per credit. Required fees: $200. Tuition and fees vary according to campus/location and program.
**Financial support:** Career-related internships or fieldwork, Federal Work-Study, and institutionally sponsored loans available. Financial award application deadline: 4/1.
**Faculty research:** Clinical and child clinical psychology, geriatrics, interpersonal violence.
**Application contact:** Nancy L. Smith, Supervisor, 954-262-5760, *Fax:* 954-262-3893, *E-mail:* cpsinfo@cps.nova.edu. *Web site:* http://www.cps.nova.edu/

## ■ THE OHIO STATE UNIVERSITY

**Graduate School, College of Social and Behavioral Sciences, Department of Psychology, Columbus, OH 43210**

**AWARDS** Clinical psychology (PhD); cognitive/experimental psychology (PhD); counseling psychology (PhD); developmental psychology (PhD); mental retardation and developmental disabilities (PhD); psychobiology (PhD); quantitative psychology (PhD); social psychology (PhD).

**Degree requirements:** For doctorate, thesis/dissertation.
**Entrance requirements:** For doctorate, GRE General Test, TOEFL.

## ■ OTTAWA UNIVERSITY

**Graduate Studies-Phoenix, Major in Professional Counseling, Ottawa, KS 66067-3399**

**AWARDS** MA. Part-time programs available.

**Faculty:** 2 full-time (1 woman).
**Students:** 32 (27 women). In 2001, 42 degrees awarded.
**Degree requirements:** For master's, thesis or alternative, field experience, practicum.

*Application deadline:* For fall admission, 7/1 (priority date); for spring admission, 11/1. Applications are processed on a rolling basis. *Application fee:* $40.
**Financial support:** Available to part-time students. Applicants required to submit FAFSA.
Dr. Ron Frost, Director, 602-371-0993.
**Application contact:** Jean Gray, Advisement Coordinator, 602-749-5151, *Fax:* 602-371-0035, *E-mail:* grayj@ottawa.edu.

## ■ OUR LADY OF THE LAKE UNIVERSITY OF SAN ANTONIO

**School of Education and Clinical Studies, Program in Counseling Psychology, San Antonio, TX 78207-4689**

**AWARDS** Counseling psychology (MS, Psy D); psychology (MS, Psy D). Part-time and evening/weekend programs available.

**Degree requirements:** For master's, practicum, thesis optional; for doctorate, thesis/dissertation, internship, qualifying exam.
**Entrance requirements:** For master's and doctorate, GRE General Test or MAT, interview.
**Faculty research:** Marriage and family therapy, supervision, cross-cultural counseling, violence.

## ■ PACIFICA GRADUATE INSTITUTE

**Graduate Programs, Carpinteria, CA 93013**

**AWARDS** Clinical psychology (PhD); counseling psychology (MA); depth psychology (PhD); mythological studies (MA, PhD).

**Faculty:** 19 full-time, 50 part-time/adjunct.
**Students:** 545 full-time, 20 part-time. Average age 45. In 2001, 101 master's, 82 doctorates awarded.
**Degree requirements:** For master's, thesis (for some programs), registration; for doctorate, thesis/dissertation, internship, comprehensive exam, registration.
*Median time to degree:* Master's–3 years full-time; doctorate–3 years full-time.
*Application deadline:* For fall admission, 4/30 (priority date). *Application fee:* $60.
**Expenses:** Tuition: Full-time $13,900.
**Financial support:** In 2001–02, 411 students received support. Scholarships/grants available. Financial award application deadline: 6/15; financial award applicants required to submit FAFSA.
**Faculty research:** Imaginal and archetypal theory; post-Colonial psychoanalytic and Jungian theory; myth literature as it applies to the theory and practice of psychology.

Dr. Stephen Aizenstat, President, 805-969-3626 Ext. 102, *Fax:* 805-565-1932, *E-mail:* steve_aizenstat@pacifica.edu.
**Application contact:** Diane Huerta, Admissions Office, 805-969-3626 Ext. 128, *Fax:* 805-565-1932, *E-mail:* diane_huerta@pacifica.edu. *Web site:* http://www.pacifica.edu/

**Find an in-depth description at www.petersons.com/gradchannel.**

## ■ PALM BEACH ATLANTIC UNIVERSITY

**School of Education and Behavioral Studies, West Palm Beach, FL 33416-4708**

**AWARDS** Counseling psychology (MSCP), including marriage and family therapy, mental health counseling, school guidance counseling; elementary education (M Ed).

**Faculty:** 4 full-time (2 women), 7 part-time/adjunct (6 women).
**Students:** 129 full-time (102 women), 64 part-time (52 women); includes 46 minority (29 African Americans, 2 Asian Americans or Pacific Islanders, 14 Hispanic Americans, 1 Native American), 6 international. Average age 34. 118 applicants, 69% accepted, 65 enrolled. In 2001, 55 degrees awarded.
**Entrance requirements:** For master's, GRE General Test, minimum GPA of 3.0 in last 60 hours. *Application deadline:* For fall admission, 7/15 (priority date); for spring admission, 11/15 (priority date). Applications are processed on a rolling basis. *Application fee:* $35. Electronic applications accepted.
**Expenses:** Tuition: Part-time $290 per credit hour.
**Financial support:** Available to part-time students. Applicants required to submit FAFSA.
Dr. Dona Thornton, Dean, 561-803-2350, *Fax:* 561-803-2186, *E-mail:* thorntond@pbac.edu.
**Application contact:** Carolanne M. Brown, Director of Graduate Admissions, 800-281-3466, *Fax:* 561-803-2115, *E-mail:* grad@pbac.edu. *Web site:* http://www.pbac.edu/

## ■ THE PENNSYLVANIA STATE UNIVERSITY UNIVERSITY PARK CAMPUS

**Graduate School, College of Education, Department of Counselor Education, Counseling Psychology and Rehabilitation Services, Program in Counseling Psychology, State College, University Park, PA 16802-1503**

**AWARDS** PhD.

*The Pennsylvania State University University Park Campus (continued)*
**Students:** 27 full-time (18 women), 11 part-time (8 women). In 2001, 6 degrees awarded.
**Entrance requirements:** For doctorate, GRE General Test. *Application fee:* $45.
**Expenses:** Tuition, state resident: full-time $7,882; part-time $333 per credit. Tuition, nonresident: full-time $16,142; part-time $673 per credit. Required fees: $124 per semester.
Dr. Jeffrey Hayes, Professor in Charge, 814-863-3799.

### ■ PRESCOTT COLLEGE

**Graduate Programs, Program in Counseling and Psychology, Prescott, AZ 86301-2990**
**AWARDS** MA. Part-time programs available. Postbaccalaureate distance learning degree programs offered (minimal on-campus study).
**Degree requirements:** For master's, thesis, fieldwork or internship, practicum.

### ■ RADFORD UNIVERSITY

**Graduate College, College of Arts and Sciences, Department of Psychology, Radford, VA 24142**
**AWARDS** Clinical psychology (MA); counseling psychology (MA); general psychology (MA, MS); industrial-organizational psychology (MA); school psychology (Ed S). Part-time programs available. Postbaccalaureate distance learning degree programs offered (minimal on-campus study).
**Faculty:** 20 full-time (6 women).
**Students:** 65 full-time (46 women), 9 part-time (8 women); includes 6 minority (2 African Americans, 3 Asian Americans or Pacific Islanders, 1 Native American), 1 international. Average age 26. 127 applicants, 83% accepted, 26 enrolled. In 2001, 40 master's, 10 other advanced degrees awarded.
**Degree requirements:** For master's, thesis (for some programs), comprehensive exam.
**Entrance requirements:** For degree, GMAT, GRE General Test, MAT, NTE, TOEFL. *Application deadline:* For fall admission, 2/15 (priority date); for spring admission, 10/15. Applications are processed on a rolling basis. *Application fee:* $25. Electronic applications accepted.
**Expenses:** Tuition, state resident: full-time $2,564; part-time $167 per credit hour. Tuition, nonresident: full-time $6,314; part-time $323 per credit hour. Required fees: $1,440.
**Financial support:** In 2001–02, 64 students received support, including 4 fellowships with tuition reimbursements available (averaging $8,060 per year), 46 research assistantships (averaging $4,401

per year), 7 teaching assistantships with tuition reimbursements available (averaging $8,680 per year); career-related internships or fieldwork, Federal Work-Study, institutionally sponsored loans, and scholarships/grants also available. Financial award application deadline: 2/1; financial award applicants required to submit FAFSA.
Dr. Alastair V. Harris, Chair, 540-831-5361, *Fax:* 540-831-6113, *E-mail:* aharris@radford.edu. *Web site:* http://www.radford.edu/

### ■ REGENT UNIVERSITY

**Graduate School, School of Psychology and Counseling, Virginia Beach, VA 23464-9800**
**AWARDS** Counseling (MA); counseling psychology (Psy D). Part-time programs available.
**Faculty:** 11 full-time (3 women), 11 part-time/adjunct (5 women).
**Students:** 248 (200 women); includes 76 minority (62 African Americans, 6 Asian Americans or Pacific Islanders, 6 Hispanic Americans, 2 Native Americans) 4 international. Average age 34. 142 applicants, 85% accepted, 92 enrolled. In 2001, 59 master's, 3 doctorates awarded.
**Degree requirements:** For master's, thesis or alternative, internship, practicum, written competency exam; for doctorate, thesis/dissertation or alternative.
**Entrance requirements:** For master's, GRE General Test or MAT, minimum undergraduate GPA of 2.75; for doctorate, GRE General Test, GRE Subject Test, minimum undergraduate GPA of 3.0. *Application deadline:* For fall admission, 4/1 (priority date); for spring admission, 11/1 (priority date). Applications are processed on a rolling basis. *Application fee:* $40.
**Expenses:** Contact institution.
**Financial support:** In 2001–02, 185 students received support, including 6 teaching assistantships (averaging $10,000 per year); career-related internships or fieldwork and scholarships/grants also available. Support available to part-time students. Financial award application deadline: 9/1.
**Faculty research:** Marriage enrichment, AIDS counseling, troubled youth. *Total annual research expenditures:* $12,000.
Dr. Rosemarie Hughes, Dean, 757-226-4255, *Fax:* 757-226-4263, *E-mail:* rosehug@regent.edu.
**Application contact:** Steve Bruce, Director of Admissions for Counseling, 800-373-5504, *Fax:* 757-226-4381, *E-mail:* admissions@regent.edu. *Web site:* http://www.regent.edu/psychology

### ■ REGIS UNIVERSITY

**School for Professional Studies, Program in Liberal Studies, Denver, CO 80221-1099**
**AWARDS** Adult learning, training and development (MLS, Certificate); language and communication (MLS); licensed professional counselor (MLS); psychology (MLS); social science (MLS); technical communication (Certificate). Part-time and evening/weekend programs available. Postbaccalaureate distance learning degree programs offered (minimal on-campus study).
**Students:** 400. Average age 35. In 2001, 136 degrees awarded.
**Degree requirements:** For master's and Certificate, thesis or alternative, research project.
**Entrance requirements:** For master's, TOEFL, resumé; for Certificate, GMAT, TOEFL, or university-based test (international applicants), resumé. *Application deadline:* For fall admission, 7/15; for spring admission, 10/15. Applications are processed on a rolling basis. *Application fee:* $75. Electronic applications accepted.
**Expenses:** Contact institution.
**Financial support:** Federal Work-Study available. Support available to part-time students. Financial award application deadline: 3/15; financial award applicants required to submit FAFSA.
**Faculty research:** Independent/nonresidential graduate study: new methods and models, adult learning and the capstone experience.
Dr. David Elliot, Chair, 303-964-5315, *Fax:* 303-964-5538.
**Application contact:** Graduate Admissions, 800-677-9270 Ext. 4080, *Fax:* 303-964-5538, *E-mail:* masters@regis.edu. *Web site:* http://www.regis.edu/spsgraduate/

### ■ RIVIER COLLEGE

**School of Graduate Studies, Department of Education, Nashua, NH 03060-5086**
**AWARDS** Counseling and psychotherapy (MA); counselor education (M Ed); early childhood education (M Ed); educational administration (M Ed); elementary education (M Ed); general education (M Ed); learning disabilities (M Ed); reading (M Ed); secondary education (M Ed). Part-time and evening/weekend programs available.
**Faculty:** 8 full-time (4 women), 26 part-time/adjunct (21 women).
**Students:** 30 full-time (25 women), 374 part-time (330 women); includes 8 minority (1 African American, 1 Asian American or Pacific Islander, 5 Hispanic Americans, 1 Native American), 23 international. Average age 36. In 2001, 18 degrees awarded.

**Degree requirements:** For master's, internships.

**Entrance requirements:** For master's, GRE General Test or MAT. *Application deadline:* Applications are processed on a rolling basis.

**Expenses:** Tuition: Part-time $360 per credit. Required fees: $25 per year. Part-time tuition and fees vary according to course level and course load.

**Financial support:** Available to part-time students. Application deadline: 2/1. Dr. Charles L. Mitsakos, Chairman, 603-888-1311 Ext. 8582.

**Application contact:** Diane Monahan, Director of Graduate Admissions, 603-897-8129, *Fax:* 603-897-8810, *E-mail:* gradadm@rivier.edu.

## ■ ROSEMONT COLLEGE

**Graduate School, Program in Counseling Psychology, Rosemont, PA 19010-1699**

**AWARDS** Human services (MA); school counseling (MA). Part-time programs available.

**Faculty:** 4 full-time (2 women), 5 part-time/adjunct (2 women).

**Students:** 78 (75 women). Average age 35. 21 applicants, 86% accepted. In 2001, 7 degrees awarded.

**Degree requirements:** For master's, thesis or alternative.

**Entrance requirements:** For master's, GRE or MAT. *Application deadline:* Applications are processed on a rolling basis. *Application fee:* $50.

**Expenses:** Contact institution.
Edward Samulewicz, Director, 610-527-0200 Ext. 2359, *Fax:* 610-526-2964.

**Application contact:** Karen Scales, Enrollment and Marketing Coordinator, 610-527-0200 Ext. 2187, *Fax:* 610-526-2964, *E-mail:* gradstudies@rosemont.edu. *Web site:* http://www.rosemont.edu/

## ■ RUTGERS, THE STATE UNIVERSITY OF NEW JERSEY, NEW BRUNSWICK

**Graduate School of Education, Department of Educational Psychology, Program in Counseling Psychology, New Brunswick, NJ 08901-1281**

**AWARDS** Ed M.

**Entrance requirements:** For master's, GRE General Test. Electronic applications accepted.

**Faculty research:** Cultural variables affecting counseling process, adult attachment theory, multicultural training.

## ■ ST. EDWARD'S UNIVERSITY

**College of Professional and Graduate Studies, Program in Counseling, Austin, TX 78704-6489**

**AWARDS** MA. Part-time and evening/weekend programs available.

**Faculty:** 2 full-time (1 woman).

**Students:** 17 full-time (14 women), 22 part-time (18 women); includes 10 minority (2 African Americans, 8 Hispanic Americans), 1 international. Average age 33. 38 applicants, 84% accepted, 27 enrolled. In 2001, 6 degrees awarded.

**Entrance requirements:** For master's, GRE General Test, TOEFL, minimum GPA of 3.0 in last 60 hours or 2.75 overall. *Application deadline:* For fall admission, 8/1; for spring admission, 12/1. Applications are processed on a rolling basis. *Application fee:* $30 ($50 for international students). Electronic applications accepted.

**Expenses:** Tuition: Full-time $7,974; part-time $443 per credit hour.

**Financial support:** In 2001–02, 22 students received support. Application deadline: 4/15.
Dr. Elizabeth Katz, Dean, 512-464-8833, *Fax:* 512-448-8492, *E-mail:* elizk@admin.stedwards.edu.

**Application contact:** Bridget Sowinski, Graduate Admissions Coordinator, 512-428-1061, *Fax:* 512-428-1032, *E-mail:* bridgets@admin.stewards.edu.

## ■ SAINT MARTIN'S COLLEGE

**Graduate Programs, Program in Counseling and Community Psychology, Lacey, WA 98503-7500**

**AWARDS** MAC. Part-time and evening/weekend programs available.

**Faculty:** 3 full-time (2 women), 4 part-time/adjunct (2 women).

**Students:** Average age 41. 32 applicants, 53% accepted. In 2001, 24 degrees awarded.

**Degree requirements:** For master's, clinical experience, interview.
*Application deadline:* For fall admission, 7/1; for spring admission, 2/15 (priority date). Applications are processed on a rolling basis. *Application fee:* $35.

**Expenses:** Tuition: Part-time $519 per credit hour. Required fees: $180; $90 per semester. One-time fee: $125 full-time.

**Financial support:** In 2001–02, 70 students received support. Career-related internships or fieldwork, Federal Work-Study, and institutionally sponsored loans available. Support available to part-time students. Financial award application deadline: 3/1.
Dr. Godfrey Ellis, Director, 360-438-4560, *E-mail:* gellis@stmartin.edu.

**Application contact:** Sandra Brandt, Administrative Assistant, 360-438-4560, *E-mail:* sbrandt@stmartin.edu.

## ■ SAINT MARY'S UNIVERSITY OF MINNESOTA

**Graduate School, Program in Counseling and Psychological Services, Winona, MN 55987-1399**

**AWARDS** MA, MA/MA. Part-time and evening/weekend programs available.

**Degree requirements:** For master's, thesis or alternative, integration papers, oral exam, practicum.

**Entrance requirements:** For master's, interview, minimum GPA of 2.75.

**Expenses:** Tuition: Full-time $4,230; part-time $235 per credit. One-time fee: $220. Tuition and fees vary according to degree level and program.

## ■ ST. MARY'S UNIVERSITY OF SAN ANTONIO

**Graduate School, Department of Counseling and Human Services, San Antonio, TX 78228-8507**

**AWARDS** Community counseling (MA); counseling (PhD, Sp C); marriage and family relations (Certificate); marriage and family therapy (MA, PhD); mental health (MA); mental health and substance abuse counseling (Certificate); substance abuse (MA). Postbaccalaureate distance learning degree programs offered (minimal on-campus study).

**Faculty:** 9 full-time (4 women), 5 part-time/adjunct (3 women).

**Students:** 125 (98 women); includes 48 minority (8 African Americans, 40 Hispanic Americans) 5 international. Average age 28. In 2001, 24 master's, 4 doctorates awarded.

**Degree requirements:** For master's, internship; for doctorate, thesis/dissertation, internship.

**Entrance requirements:** For master's, GRE General Test, MAT; for doctorate, GRE General Test. *Application deadline:* Applications are processed on a rolling basis. *Application fee:* $15. Electronic applications accepted.

**Expenses:** Tuition: Full-time $8,190; part-time $455 per credit hour. Required fees: $375.

**Financial support:** Career-related internships or fieldwork and Federal Work-Study available. Financial award application deadline: 2/15; financial award applicants required to submit FAFSA.
Dr. Dana Comstock, Graduate Program Director, 210-436-3226.

## ■ ST. THOMAS UNIVERSITY

**School of Graduate Studies, Department of Social Sciences and Counseling, Program in Mental Health Counseling, Miami, FL 33054-6459**

**AWARDS** MS. Part-time and evening/weekend programs available.

**Degree requirements:** For master's, comprehensive exam.

**Entrance requirements:** For master's, TOEFL, interview, minimum GPA of 3.0 or GRE.

## ■ SAINT XAVIER UNIVERSITY

**Graduate Studies, School of Arts and Sciences, Department of Psychology, Chicago, IL 60655-3105**

**AWARDS** Adult counseling (Certificate); child/adolescent counseling (Certificate); core counseling (Certificate); counseling psychology (MA). Part-time and evening/weekend programs available.

**Faculty:** 7.

**Students:** 18 full-time (13 women), 20 part-time (16 women); includes 8 minority (all African Americans). Average age 33. In 2001, 11 degrees awarded.

**Entrance requirements:** For master's, GRE General Test, minimum GPA of 3.0, interview. *Application deadline:* For fall admission, 8/15 (priority date). Applications are processed on a rolling basis. *Application fee:* $35.

**Expenses:** Tuition: Full-time $4,500; part-time $500 per credit. Required fees: $40 per term.

**Financial support:** Career-related internships or fieldwork available. Support available to part-time students. Financial award applicants required to submit FAFSA.
Dr. Anthony Rotatori, Director, 773-298-3477, *Fax:* 773-779-9061.

**Application contact:** Beth Gierach, Managing Director of Admission, 773-298-3053, *Fax:* 773-298-3076, *E-mail:* gierach@sxu.edu.

**Find an in-depth description at www.petersons.com/gradchannel.**

## ■ SALVE REGINA UNIVERSITY

**Graduate School, Program in Holistic Counseling, Newport, RI 02840-4192**

**AWARDS** MA, CAGS. Part-time and evening/weekend programs available.

**Faculty:** 3 full-time (1 woman), 8 part-time/adjunct (all women).

**Students:** 12 full-time (10 women), 59 part-time (53 women); includes 3 minority (2 African Americans, 1 Asian American or Pacific Islander). Average age 40. 26 applicants, 65% accepted, 3 enrolled. In 2001, 19 master's, 4 other advanced degrees awarded.

**Degree requirements:** For master's, internship. *Median time to degree:* Master's–2.5 years full-time, 3 years part-time; CAGS–1 year full-time, 1.5 years part-time.

**Entrance requirements:** For master's, GMAT, GRE General Test, or MAT; for CAGS, certificate of advanced graduate study. *Application deadline:* Applications are processed on a rolling basis. *Application fee:* $50. Electronic applications accepted.

**Expenses:** Tuition: Full-time $5,400; part-time $300 per credit. Required fees: $330; $40 per term. Tuition and fees vary according to degree level.

**Financial support:** Career-related internships or fieldwork and Federal Work-Study available. Support available to part-time students. Financial award application deadline: 3/1.
Dr. Peter Mullen, Director, 401-341-3278, *Fax:* 401-341-2977, *E-mail:* mullenp@salve.edu.

**Application contact:** Karen E. Johnson, Graduate Admissions Counselor, 401-341-2153, *Fax:* 401-341-2973, *E-mail:* graduate_studies@salve.edu. *Web site:* http://www.salve.edu/programs_grad/index.html

## ■ SAM HOUSTON STATE UNIVERSITY

**College of Education and Applied Science, Department of Psychology and Philosophy, Huntsville, TX 77341**

**AWARDS** Clinical psychology (MA); counseling (MA); forensic psychology (PhD); psychology (MA); school psychology (MA). Part-time programs available.

**Students:** 44 full-time (36 women), 17 part-time (11 women); includes 6 minority (2 African Americans, 4 Hispanic Americans), 3 international. Average age 29. In 2001, 1 degree awarded.

**Degree requirements:** For master's, thesis.

**Entrance requirements:** For master's, GRE General Test or MAT, minimum GPA of 3.0. *Application deadline:* For fall admission, 8/1; for spring admission, 12/1. Applications are processed on a rolling basis. *Application fee:* $20.

**Expenses:** Tuition, area resident: Part-time $69 per credit. Tuition, state resident: full-time $1,380; part-time $69 per credit. Tuition, nonresident: full-time $5,600; part-time $280 per credit. Required fees: $748. Tuition and fees vary according to course load.

**Financial support:** Research assistantships, teaching assistantships, career-related internships or fieldwork and institutionally sponsored loans available. Support available to part-time students. Financial award

application deadline: 5/31; financial award applicants required to submit FAFSA.

**Faculty research:** Recognition memory, embarrassment, divorce, relationship satisfaction, eyewitness testimony. *Total annual research expenditures:* $50,000.
Dr. Donna M. Desforges, Chairperson, 936-294-1174, *Fax:* 936-294-3798.

**Application contact:** Dr. Rowland Miller, Graduate Coordinator, 936-294-1176, *Fax:* 936-294-3798, *E-mail:* psy_rsm@shsu.edu. *Web site:* http://www.shsu.edu/~psy_www/

## ■ SAN FRANCISCO STATE UNIVERSITY

**Graduate Division, College of Health and Human Services, Department of Counseling, Program in Counseling, San Francisco, CA 94132-1722**

**AWARDS** MS. Part-time programs available.

**Degree requirements:** For master's, culminating written description of internship.

**Entrance requirements:** For master's, minimum GPA of 2.5 in last 60 units.

## ■ SAN JOSE STATE UNIVERSITY

**Graduate Studies, College of Social Sciences, Department of Psychology, San Jose, CA 95192-0001**

**AWARDS** Clinical psychology (MS); counseling (MS); industrial psychology (MS); research psychology (MA).

**Faculty:** 32 full-time (5 women), 13 part-time/adjunct (7 women).

**Students:** 40 full-time (32 women), 20 part-time (12 women); includes 17 minority (2 African Americans, 11 Asian Americans or Pacific Islanders, 4 Hispanic Americans), 6 international. Average age 30. 150 applicants, 32% accepted. In 2001, 25 degrees awarded.

**Degree requirements:** For master's, thesis (for some programs), comprehensive exam.

**Entrance requirements:** For master's, minimum GPA of 3.0. *Application deadline:* For fall admission, 6/29; for spring admission, 11/30. Applications are processed on a rolling basis. *Application fee:* $59. Electronic applications accepted.

**Expenses:** Tuition, nonresident: part-time $246 per unit. Required fees: $678 per semester. Tuition and fees vary according to course load.

**Financial support:** In 2001–02, 15 teaching assistantships were awarded; career-related internships or fieldwork and institutionally sponsored loans also available. Financial award application deadline: 3/1; financial award applicants required to submit FAFSA.

**Faculty research:** Drug and alcohol abuse, neurohormonal mechanisms in motion sickness, behavior modification, sleep research, genetics.

Dr. Robert Pelligrini, Chair, 408-924-5600, *Fax:* 408-924-5605.

**Application contact:** Laree Huntsman, Graduate Adviser, 408-924-5633.

---

### ■ SANTA CLARA UNIVERSITY

**Division of Counseling Psychology and Education, Program in Counseling Psychology, Santa Clara, CA 95053**

**AWARDS** MA. Part-time and evening/weekend programs available.

**Students:** 31 full-time (29 women), 56 part-time (49 women); includes 16 minority (6 Asian Americans or Pacific Islanders, 10 Hispanic Americans), 8 international. Average age 36. 62 applicants, 76% accepted. In 2001, 36 degrees awarded.

**Degree requirements:** For master's, thesis optional.

**Entrance requirements:** For master's, GRE or MAT, TOEFL, minimum GPA of 3.0, 1 year of related experience. *Application deadline:* For fall admission, 4/1; for winter admission, 11/1; for spring admission, 2/1. Applications are processed on a rolling basis. *Application fee:* $35.

**Expenses:** Tuition: Part-time $320 per unit. Tuition and fees vary according to class time, degree level, program and student level.

**Financial support:** Fellowships, teaching assistantships, career-related internships or fieldwork, Federal Work-Study, institutionally sponsored loans, and scholarships/grants available. Support available to part-time students. Financial award application deadline: 3/1; financial award applicants required to submit FAFSA.

Dr. Jerrold Shapiro, Director, 408-554-4012.

**Application contact:** Helen Valine, Assistant to the Dean, 408-554-4656, *Fax:* 408-554-2392.

**Find an in-depth description at www.petersons.com/gradchannel.**

---

### ■ SETON HALL UNIVERSITY

**College of Education and Human Services, Department of Professional Psychology and Family Therapy, Program in Counseling Psychology, South Orange, NJ 07079-2697**

**AWARDS** PhD.

**Degree requirements:** For doctorate, thesis/dissertation, internship, comprehensive exam.

**Entrance requirements:** For doctorate, GRE, interview.

**Expenses:** Tuition: Full-time $10,818; part-time $601 per credit. Required fees: $610; $185 per term. Tuition and fees vary

according to course load, program and student's religious affiliation.

**Faculty research:** Vocational indecision, coping skills, cognitive behavioral interventions, vocational development.

---

### ■ SOUTHERN CALIFORNIA BIBLE COLLEGE & SEMINARY

**Graduate and Professional Programs, El Cajon, CA 92019**

**AWARDS** Biblical studies (MA); counseling psychology (MACP); religious studies (MRS); theology (M Div). Part-time and evening/weekend programs available. Postbaccalaureate distance learning degree programs offered (no on-campus study).

Electronic applications accepted.

---

### ■ SOUTHERN CHRISTIAN UNIVERSITY

**Graduate and Professional Programs, Montgomery, AL 36117**

**AWARDS** Biblical studies (MA, D Min); Christian ministry (M Div); marriage and family therapy (M Div, D Min, PhD); ministerial leadership (MS); organizational leadership (MS); pastoral counseling (M Div, MS, PhD); practical theology (MA); professional counseling (M Div, PhD). Part-time and evening/weekend programs available. Postbaccalaureate distance learning degree programs offered (no on-campus study).

**Faculty:** 43 full-time (5 women), 18 part-time/adjunct (8 women).

**Students:** 224 full-time (86 women); includes 69 minority (64 African Americans, 3 Asian Americans or Pacific Islanders, 2 Native Americans). Average age 35. In 2001, 8 first professional degrees, 29 master's, 3 doctorates awarded.

**Degree requirements:** For master's, one foreign language, thesis (for some programs); for doctorate, thesis/dissertation.

**Entrance requirements:** For M Div, master's, and doctorate, GRE General Test or MAT. *Application deadline:* For fall admission, 9/1 (priority date); for spring admission, 1/1 (priority date). Applications are processed on a rolling basis. *Application fee:* $50. Electronic applications accepted.

**Expenses:** Tuition: Full-time $7,020; part-time $390 per semester hour. Required fees: $1,600; $400 per semester. Tuition and fees vary according to course load.

**Financial support:** Federal Work-Study and scholarships/grants available. Support available to part-time students. Financial award applicants required to submit FAFSA.

**Faculty research:** Homiletics, hermeneutics, ancient Near Eastern history.

Rick Johnson, Director of Enrollment Management, 800-351-4040 Ext. 213, *Fax:* 334-387-3878, *E-mail:* rickjohnson@southernchristian.edu.

**Application contact:** Becky Bagwell, Admissions Officer, 334-387-3877 Ext. 224, *Fax:* 334-387-3878, *E-mail:* beckybagwell@southernchristian.edu. *Web site:* http://www.southernchristian.edu/

---

### ■ SOUTHERN ILLINOIS UNIVERSITY CARBONDALE

**Graduate School, College of Liberal Arts, Department of Psychology, Carbondale, IL 62901-6806**

**AWARDS** Clinical psychology (MA, MS, PhD); counseling psychology (MA, MS, PhD); experimental psychology (MA, MS, PhD).

**Faculty:** 27 full-time (14 women), 1 part-time/adjunct (0 women).

**Students:** 79 full-time (58 women), 42 part-time (29 women); includes 28 minority (16 African Americans, 7 Asian Americans or Pacific Islanders, 4 Hispanic Americans, 1 Native American), 10 international. 128 applicants, 22% accepted. In 2001, 14 master's, 21 doctorates awarded.

**Degree requirements:** For master's and doctorate, thesis/dissertation.

**Entrance requirements:** For master's, GRE General Test, GRE Subject Test, TOEFL, minimum GPA of 2.7; for doctorate, GRE General Test, GRE Subject Test, TOEFL, minimum GPA of 3.25. *Application deadline:* For fall admission, 3/1 (priority date). Applications are processed on a rolling basis. *Application fee:* $20.

**Expenses:** Tuition, state resident: full-time $3,794; part-time $154 per hour. Tuition, nonresident: full-time $6,566; part-time $308 per hour. Required fees: $277 per hour.

**Financial support:** In 2001–02, 82 students received support, including 14 fellowships with full tuition reimbursements available, 23 research assistantships with full tuition reimbursements available, 22 teaching assistantships with full tuition reimbursements available; Federal Work-Study, institutionally sponsored loans, and tuition waivers (full) also available.

**Faculty research:** Developmental neuropsychology; smoking, affect, and cognition; personality measurement; vocational psychology; program evaluation.

Alan Vaux, Chair, 618-453-3529. *Web site:* http://www.siu.edu/departments/cola/psycho/

**Find an in-depth description at www.petersons.com/gradchannel.**

## ■ SOUTHERN METHODIST UNIVERSITY

**Dedman College, Department of Psychology, Program in Clinical and Counseling Psychology, Dallas, TX 75275**

**AWARDS** MA. Part-time programs available.

**Students:** 19 full-time (17 women), 6 part-time (5 women); includes 2 minority (1 African American, 1 Asian American or Pacific Islander), 1 international. Average age 28. In 2001, 12 degrees awarded.
**Degree requirements:** For master's, thesis, oral exam.
**Entrance requirements:** For master's, minimum GPA of 3.0. *Application deadline:* For fall admission, 2/15. *Application fee:* $50.
**Expenses:** Tuition: Part-time $285 per credit hour.
**Financial support:** Research assistantships, teaching assistantships, career-related internships or fieldwork, Federal Work-Study, and institutionally sponsored loans available. Support available to part-time students. Financial award application deadline: 3/1; financial award applicants required to submit FAFSA.
**Faculty research:** Family assessment, personality disorders, development of self-concept, learning disabilities, mood and emotion.
**Application contact:** Dr. Neil Mulligan, Director, Graduate Studies, 214-768-4385.

## ■ SOUTHERN NAZARENE UNIVERSITY

**Graduate College, School of Psychology, Bethany, OK 73008**

**AWARDS** Counseling psychology (MSCP); marriage and family therapy (MA).

**Degree requirements:** For master's, thesis optional.
**Entrance requirements:** For master's, English proficiency exam, minimum GPA of 3.0 in last 60 hours/major, 2.7 overall.

## ■ SOUTHWESTERN ASSEMBLIES OF GOD UNIVERSITY

**Thomas F. Harrison School of Graduate Studies, Program in Counseling Psychology, Waxahachie, TX 75165-2397**

**AWARDS** MS, MS/MA. Part-time programs available.

**Faculty:** 4 full-time (1 woman).
**Students:** 12 applicants, 100% accepted.
**Degree requirements:** For master's, comprehensive written and oral exams.
**Entrance requirements:** For master's, GRE General Test, minimum GPA of 2.5.
*Application deadline:* For fall admission, 7/1

(priority date); for spring admission, 11/1 (priority date). Applications are processed on a rolling basis. *Application fee:* $50. Electronic applications accepted.
**Expenses:** Tuition: Part-time $260 per hour.
**Financial support:** Application deadline: 3/1.
Dr. Calvin Carmen, Coordinator, 972-937-4010 Ext. 3328, *E-mail:* ccarmen@sagu.edu.
**Application contact:** Eddie Davis, Senior Director, Enrollment Services, 972-937-4010 Ext. 1123, *E-mail:* edavis@sagu.edu. *Web site:* http://www.sagu.edu/

## ■ SOUTHWESTERN COLLEGE

**Program in Counseling, Santa Fe, NM 87502-4788**

**AWARDS** Counseling (MA); school counseling (Certificate). Part-time and evening/weekend programs available.

**Faculty:** 5 full-time (4 women), 22 part-time/adjunct (15 women).
**Students:** 27 full-time (18 women), 62 part-time (57 women); includes 3 minority (2 African Americans, 1 Hispanic American). Average age 41. 34 applicants, 100% accepted, 24 enrolled. In 2001, 12 degrees awarded.
**Degree requirements:** For master's, internship.
**Entrance requirements:** For master's, resumé, letters of reference (3), interview. *Application deadline:* For fall admission, 6/30 (priority date); for winter admission, 9/30 (priority date); for spring admission, 1/15 (priority date). Applications are processed on a rolling basis. *Application fee:* $50.
**Expenses:** Tuition: Full-time $11,760; part-time $245 per unit.
**Financial support:** In 2001–02, 46 students received support. Career-related internships or fieldwork, institutionally sponsored loans, and scholarships/grants available. Support available to part-time students. Financial award application deadline: 6/1; financial award applicants required to submit FAFSA.
Dr. Pamela Bell, Chair, 877-471-5756 Ext. 13.
**Application contact:** Kristine Schmidt, Director of Admissions, 505-471-5756 Ext. 26, *Fax:* 505-471-4071, *E-mail:* admissions@swc.edu.

## ■ SOUTHWESTERN COLLEGE

**Program in Grief Counseling, Santa Fe, NM 87502-4788**

**AWARDS** Certificate.

**Faculty:** 1 (woman) full-time.
**Students:** Average age 41. 25 applicants, 100% accepted, 25 enrolled. In 2001, 11

degrees awarded. *Median time to degree:* 2 years part-time.
**Entrance requirements:** For degree, letters of reference (3), interview. *Application deadline:* Applications are processed on a rolling basis. *Application fee:* $25.
**Expenses:** Tuition: Full-time $11,760; part-time $245 per unit.
Dr. Janet Schreiber, Director, 877-471-5756, *Fax:* 877-471-4071.
**Application contact:** Kristine Schmidt, Director of Admissions, 877-471-5756, *Fax:* 877-471-4071, *E-mail:* admissions@swc.edu.

## ■ SPRINGFIELD COLLEGE

**School of Graduate Studies, Programs in Counseling and Psychological Services, Springfield, MA 01109-3797**

**AWARDS** Athletic counseling (M Ed, MS, CAS); general counseling (M Ed, MS, CAS); industrial/organizational psychology (MS, CAS); marriage and family therapy (M Ed, MS, CAS); mental health counseling (M Ed, MS, CAS); school guidance and counseling (M Ed, MS, CAS); student personnel in higher education (M Ed, MS, CAS). Part-time and evening/weekend programs available.

**Faculty:** 11 full-time (7 women), 20 part-time/adjunct (9 women).
**Students:** 133 full-time, 34 part-time. Average age 26. 210 applicants, 93% accepted. In 2001, 63 master's, 3 other advanced degrees awarded.
**Degree requirements:** For master's, thesis (for some programs), research project, internship, comprehensive exam.
**Entrance requirements:** For master's and CAS, interview. *Application deadline:* For fall admission, 2/1 (priority date); for spring admission, 12/1. Applications are processed on a rolling basis. *Application fee:* $40.
**Financial support:** In 2001–02, 8 fellowships with partial tuition reimbursements (averaging $2,000 per year), 2 research assistantships (averaging $4,000 per year), 7 teaching assistantships (averaging $1,800 per year) were awarded. Career-related internships or fieldwork, Federal Work-Study, institutionally sponsored loans, scholarships/grants, and tuition waivers (full and partial) also available. Financial award application deadline: 3/1.
**Faculty research:** Sport psychology, leadership and emotional intelligence, rehabilitation adherence, professional career women and caregiving. *Total annual research expenditures:* $715,109.
Dr. Barbara Mandell, Director, 413-748-3339, *Fax:* 413-748-3854, *E-mail:* barbara_mandell@spfldcol.edu.

**Application contact:** Donald James Shaw, Director of Graduate Admissions, 413-748-3225, *Fax:* 413-748-3694, *E-mail:* donald_shaw_jr@spfldcol.edu.

### ■ STANFORD UNIVERSITY

**School of Education, Program in Psychological Studies in Education, Stanford, CA 94305-9991**

**AWARDS** Child and adolescent development (PhD); counseling psychology (PhD); educational psychology (PhD).

**Degree requirements:** For doctorate, thesis/dissertation.

**Entrance requirements:** For doctorate, GRE General Test. *Application deadline:* For fall admission, 1/2. *Application fee:* $65 ($80 for international students). Electronic applications accepted.

**Application contact:** Graduate Admissions Office, 650-723-4794.

### ■ STATE UNIVERSITY OF NEW YORK AT ALBANY

**School of Education, Department of Educational and Counseling Psychology, Albany, NY 12222-0001**

**AWARDS** Counseling psychology (MS, PhD, CAS); educational psychology (Ed D); educational psychology and statistics (MS); measurements and evaluation (Ed D); rehabilitation counseling (MS); school counselor (CAS); school psychology (Psy D, CAS); special education (MS); statistics and research design (Ed D). Evening/weekend programs available.

**Students:** 149 full-time (113 women), 106 part-time (85 women); includes 22 minority (7 African Americans, 1 Asian American or Pacific Islander, 14 Hispanic Americans), 15 international. Average age 31. 169 applicants, 28% accepted. In 2001, 86 master's, 19 doctorates, 24 other advanced degrees awarded.

**Degree requirements:** For doctorate, thesis/dissertation.

**Entrance requirements:** For doctorate, GRE General Test. *Application fee:* $50.

**Expenses:** Tuition, state resident: full-time $2,550; part-time $213 per credit. Tuition, nonresident: full-time $4,208; part-time $351 per credit. Required fees: $470; $470 per year.

**Financial support:** Fellowships, career-related internships or fieldwork available. Deborah May, Chair, 518-442-5050.

### ■ STATE UNIVERSITY OF NEW YORK AT OSWEGO

**Graduate Studies, School of Education, Department of Counseling and Psychological Services, Program in Counseling Services, Oswego, NY 13126**

**AWARDS** MS, CAS, MS/CAS.

**Faculty:** 7 full-time, 6 part-time/adjunct.
**Students:** 22 full-time (20 women), 24 part-time (21 women); includes 4 minority (2 African Americans, 1 Asian American or Pacific Islander, 1 Hispanic American). Average age 31. 45 applicants, 42% accepted. In 2001, 14 master's, 1 other advanced degree awarded.

**Degree requirements:** For master's, fieldwork; for CAS, thesis or alternative, fieldwork.

**Entrance requirements:** For master's, GRE General Test, GRE Subject Test, 18 hours of course work in behavioral science or education, interview, minimum GPA of 3.0; for CAS, GRE General Test, GRE Subject Test, 18 hours of course work in behavioral science or education, interview, MA or MS, minimum GPA of 3.0. *Application deadline:* For fall admission, 2/1. *Application fee:* $50.

**Expenses:** Tuition, state resident: full-time $5,100; part-time $213 per credit. Tuition, nonresident: full-time $8,416; part-time $351 per credit.

**Financial support:** Teaching assistantships, career-related internships or fieldwork, Federal Work-Study, institutionally sponsored loans, scholarships/grants, and tuition waivers (partial) available. Support available to part-time students. Financial award application deadline: 4/1; financial award applicants required to submit FAFSA.

**Faculty research:** Psychological applications in education and human services, evaluation of standard tests for admissions criteria.

Dr. Betsy Waterman, Chair, Department of Counseling and Psychological Services, 315-312-4051.

### ■ STATE UNIVERSITY OF NEW YORK AT OSWEGO

**Graduate Studies, School of Education, Department of Counseling and Psychological Services, Program in Human Services/Counseling, Oswego, NY 13126**

**AWARDS** MS. Part-time programs available.

**Faculty:** 7 full-time (3 women), 6 part-time/adjunct.
**Students:** 7 full-time (3 women), 26 part-time (21 women); includes 3 minority (2 African Americans, 1 Asian American or Pacific Islander). Average age 31. 32

applicants, 66% accepted. In 2001, 12 degrees awarded.

**Degree requirements:** For master's, comprehensive exam.

**Entrance requirements:** For master's, GRE General Test, GRE Subject Test, interview, minimum GPA of 3.0. *Application deadline:* For fall admission, 2/1; for spring admission, 10/15. *Application fee:* $50.

**Expenses:** Tuition, state resident: full-time $5,100; part-time $213 per credit. Tuition, nonresident: full-time $8,416; part-time $351 per credit.

**Financial support:** Career-related internships or fieldwork, Federal Work-Study, institutionally sponsored loans, scholarships/grants, and tuition waivers (partial) available. Support available to part-time students. Financial award application deadline: 4/1.

Dr. Betsy Waterman, Chair, Department of Counseling and Psychological Services, 315-312-4051.

### ■ TARLETON STATE UNIVERSITY

**College of Graduate Studies, College of Education, Department of Educational Administration, Counseling, and Psychology, Program in Counseling and Psychology, Stephenville, TX 76402**

**AWARDS** Counseling (M Ed); counseling psychology (M Ed); educational psychology (M Ed). Part-time programs available.

**Degree requirements:** For master's, thesis optional.

**Entrance requirements:** For master's, GRE General Test.

### ■ TEACHERS COLLEGE COLUMBIA UNIVERSITY

**Graduate Faculty of Education, Department of Counseling and Clinical Psychology, Program in Counseling Psychology, New York, NY 10027-6696**

**AWARDS** Ed M, Ed D, PhD. Part-time programs available.

**Degree requirements:** For doctorate, thesis/dissertation.

**Entrance requirements:** For doctorate, GRE General Test.

**Expenses:** Tuition: Full-time $19,080; part-time $780 per unit. Required fees: $170 per semester.

**Faculty research:** Career development, mentoring racial identity, adult development, gender issues.

## ■ TEMPLE UNIVERSITY

**Graduate School, College of Education, Department of Psychological Studies in Education, Counseling Psychology Program, Philadelphia, PA 19122-6096**

**AWARDS** Ed M, PhD. Part-time programs available. Terminal master's awarded for partial completion of doctoral program.

**Degree requirements:** For master's, thesis or alternative; for doctorate, thesis/dissertation.
**Entrance requirements:** For master's, GRE General Test or MAT, minimum GPA of 2.8; for doctorate, GRE General Test, GRE Subject Test.
**Expenses:** Tuition, state resident: full-time $8,487; part-time $369 per credit hour. Tuition, nonresident: full-time $12,282; part-time $534 per credit hour. Required fees: $350. Tuition and fees vary according to course load, program and reciprocity agreements.
**Faculty research:** Multi-cultural and diversity training, health psychology/supervision/addictions.

## ■ TENNESSEE STATE UNIVERSITY

**Graduate School, College of Education, Department of Psychology, Nashville, TN 37209-1561**

**AWARDS** Counseling and guidance (MS), including counseling, elementary school counseling, organizational counseling, secondary school counseling; counseling psychology (PhD); psychology (MS, PhD); school psychology (MS, PhD). Part-time and evening/weekend programs available.

**Faculty:** 13 full-time (6 women), 9 part-time/adjunct (7 women).
**Students:** 43 full-time (34 women), 76 part-time (56 women). Average age 29. 75 applicants, 95% accepted. In 2001, 9 master's, 10 doctorates awarded.
**Degree requirements:** For master's, comprehensive exam or thesis; for doctorate, thesis/dissertation, comprehensive exam.
**Entrance requirements:** For master's, GRE General Test; for doctorate, GRE General Test or MAT, minimum GPA of 3.25, work experience. *Application deadline:* Applications are processed on a rolling basis. *Application fee:* $15.
**Expenses:** Tuition, state resident: full-time $3,884; part-time $247 per hour. Tuition, nonresident: full-time $10,356; part-time $517 per hour.
**Financial support:** In 2001–02, 2 fellowships (averaging $5,924 per year), 3 research assistantships (averaging $5,962

per year), 6 teaching assistantships (averaging $17,432 per year) were awarded. Financial award application deadline: 5/1.
**Faculty research:** Stress reduction, student retention, computer education, marital and family therapy, increasing of faculty effectiveness. *Total annual research expenditures:* $50,000.
Dr. Peter Millet, Head, 615-963-5139, *Fax:* 615-963-5140.
**Application contact:** Dr. Helen Barrett, Dean of the Graduate School, 615-963-5901, *Fax:* 615-963-5963, *E-mail:* hbarrett@picard.tnstate.edu.

## ■ TEXAS A&M INTERNATIONAL UNIVERSITY

**Division of Graduate Studies, College of Arts and Humanities, Department of Psychology and Sociology, Laredo, TX 78041-1900**

**AWARDS** Counseling psychology (MA); sociology (MA).

**Students:** 5 full-time (2 women), 30 part-time (21 women); includes 33 minority (all Hispanic Americans), 1 international. In 2001, 15 degrees awarded.
**Degree requirements:** For master's, thesis (for some programs).
**Entrance requirements:** For master's, GRE General Test. *Application deadline:* For fall admission, 7/15 (priority date); for spring admission, 11/12. Applications are processed on a rolling basis. *Application fee:* $0.
**Expenses:** Tuition, state resident: full-time $1,536; part-time $64 per credit. Tuition, nonresident: full-time $6,600; part-time $275 per credit. Required fees: $594; $9 per credit. $33 per term. One-time fee: $10 part-time.
**Financial support:** Application deadline: 11/1.
Dr. Marion Aguila, Chair, 956-326-2644, *Fax:* 956-326-2459, *E-mail:* maguilar@tamiu.edu.
**Application contact:** Veronica Gonzalez, Director of Enrollment Management and School Relations, 956-326-2270, *Fax:* 956-326-2269, *E-mail:* enroll@tamiu.edu.

## ■ TEXAS A&M UNIVERSITY

**College of Education, Department of Educational Psychology, Program in Counseling Psychology, College Station, TX 77843**

**AWARDS** PhD.

**Faculty:** 6 full-time (2 women).
**Students:** 31 full-time (16 women), 25 part-time (15 women); includes 6 minority (1 African American, 1 Asian American or Pacific Islander, 4 Hispanic Americans). 56 applicants, 30% accepted, 9 enrolled. In 2001, 9 degrees awarded.

**Degree requirements:** For doctorate, thesis/dissertation. *Median time to degree:* Doctorate–6 years full-time.
**Entrance requirements:** For doctorate, GRE General Test, TOEFL. *Application deadline:* For fall admission, 12/15. *Application fee:* $50 ($75 for international students). Electronic applications accepted.
**Expenses:** Tuition, state resident: full-time $11,872. Tuition, nonresident: full-time $17,892.
**Financial support:** In 2001–02, 22 research assistantships (averaging $8,400 per year), 1 teaching assistantship (averaging $8,925 per year) were awarded. Fellowships, career-related internships or fieldwork, institutionally sponsored loans, scholarships/grants, and unspecified assistantships also available. Financial award applicants required to submit FAFSA.
**Faculty research:** Gerontology, gender issues, marriage and family, psychopathology.
Dr. Donna Davenport, Director of Training, 979-845-0285, *Fax:* 979-862-1256, *E-mail:* donna-davenport@tamu.edu.
**Application contact:** Carol A. Wagner, Graduate Advisor, 979-845-1833, *Fax:* 979-862-1256, *E-mail:* c-wagner@tamu.edu. *Web site:* http://www.coe.tamu.edu/~epsy/

## ■ TEXAS A&M UNIVERSITY–COMMERCE

**Graduate School, College of Education, Department of Counseling, Commerce, TX 75429-3011**

**AWARDS** M Ed, MS, Ed D. Part-time programs available.

**Faculty:** 8 full-time (3 women), 11 part-time/adjunct (3 women).
**Students:** 46 full-time (37 women), 249 part-time (205 women); includes 77 minority (56 African Americans, 2 Asian Americans or Pacific Islanders, 14 Hispanic Americans, 5 Native Americans), 2 international. Average age 36. 84 applicants, 96% accepted. In 2001, 87 master's, 7 doctorates awarded. Terminal master's awarded for partial completion of doctoral program.
**Degree requirements:** For master's, thesis (for some programs), comprehensive exam; for doctorate, thesis/dissertation, departmental qualifying exam.
**Entrance requirements:** For master's and doctorate, GRE General Test. *Application deadline:* For fall admission, 6/1 (priority date); for spring admission, 11/1 (priority date). Applications are processed on a rolling basis. *Application fee:* $0 ($25 for international students).

**Expenses:** Tuition, state resident: full-time $2,221. International tuition: $7,285 full-time.

**Financial support:** In 2001–02, research assistantships (averaging $7,875 per year), teaching assistantships (averaging $7,875 per year) were awarded. Federal Work-Study, institutionally sponsored loans, and scholarships/grants also available. Financial award application deadline: 5/1; financial award applicants required to submit FAFSA.

**Faculty research:** Emergency responders, efficacy and effect of web-based instruction, family violence, play therapy. Dr. Phyllis Erdman, Head, 903-886-5637, *Fax:* 903-886-5780, *E-mail:* phyllis_erdman@tamu-commerce.edu.

**Application contact:** Tammi Higginbotham, Graduate Admissions Adviser, 843-886-5167, *Fax:* 843-886-5165, *E-mail:* tammi_higginbotham@tamu-commerce.edu. *Web site:* http://www.research2.tamu-commerce.edu/counseling/

### ■ TEXAS A&M UNIVERSITY–TEXARKANA

**Graduate School, College of Business and Behavioral Sciences, Texarkana, TX 75505-5518**

**AWARDS** Accounting (MSA); business administration (MBA, MS); counseling psychology (MS). Part-time and evening/weekend programs available.

**Faculty:** 13 full-time (4 women), 1 (woman) part-time/adjunct.

**Students:** 118. Average age 32. In 2001, 33 degrees awarded.

**Degree requirements:** For master's, thesis or alternative.

**Entrance requirements:** For master's, GMAT, bachelor's degree from a regionally accredited institution. *Application deadline:* For fall admission, 7/15 (priority date); for spring admission, 12/1 (priority date). Applications are processed on a rolling basis. *Application fee:* $0 ($25 for international students). Electronic applications accepted.

**Expenses:** Tuition, state resident: part-time $84 per semester hour. Tuition, nonresident: part-time $295 per semester hour. Required fees: $13 per semester hour.

**Financial support:** Career-related internships or fieldwork and scholarships/grants available. Financial award application deadline: 3/1; financial award applicants required to submit FAFSA.

Dr. Alfred Ntoko, Dean, 903-223-3106, *E-mail:* alfred.ntoko@tamut.edu.

**Application contact:** Patricia E. Black, Director of Admissions and Registrar, 903-223-3068, *Fax:* 903-223-3140, *E-mail:*

pat.black@tamut.edu. *Web site:* http://www.tamut.edu

### ■ TEXAS TECH UNIVERSITY

**Graduate School, College of Arts and Sciences, Department of Psychology, Lubbock, TX 79409**

**AWARDS** Clinical psychology (PhD); counseling psychology (PhD); general experimental (MA, PhD). Part-time programs available.

**Faculty:** 21 full-time (10 women).

**Students:** 72 full-time (50 women), 19 part-time (10 women); includes 19 minority (1 African American, 3 Asian Americans or Pacific Islanders, 14 Hispanic Americans, 1 Native American). Average age 28. 158 applicants, 20% accepted, 18 enrolled. In 2001, 9 master's, 11 doctorates awarded.

**Degree requirements:** For doctorate, thesis/dissertation.

**Entrance requirements:** For master's and doctorate, GRE General Test, GRE Subject Test. *Application deadline:* Applications are processed on a rolling basis. *Application fee:* $25 ($50 for international students). Electronic applications accepted.

**Expenses:** Tuition, state resident: full-time $1,926; part-time $107 per credit hour. Tuition, nonresident: full-time $5,724; part-time $318 per credit hour. Required fees: $779; $737 per year. Tuition and fees vary according to course level, course load and program.

**Financial support:** In 2001–02, 71 students received support, including 5 research assistantships with partial tuition reimbursements available (averaging $10,220 per year), 48 teaching assistantships with partial tuition reimbursements available (averaging $10,067 per year); fellowships, career-related internships or fieldwork, Federal Work-Study, and institutionally sponsored loans also available. Support available to part-time students. Financial award application deadline: 5/1; financial award applicants required to submit FAFSA.

**Faculty research:** Failure/success in relationships, peer rejection in school, stress and coping, group processes, use of information technology in education. *Total annual research expenditures:* $95,236. Dr. Ruth H. Maki, Chair, 806-742-3737, *Fax:* 806-742-0818.

**Application contact:** Graduate Adviser, 806-742-3737, *Fax:* 806-742-0818. *Web site:* http://www.ttu.edu/~psy/

### ■ TEXAS WOMAN'S UNIVERSITY

**Graduate Studies and Research, College of Arts and Sciences, Department of Psychology and Philosophy, Denton, TX 76201**

**AWARDS** Counseling psychology (MA, PhD); school psychology (MA, PhD).

**Faculty:** 10 full-time (6 women), 2 part-time/adjunct (0 women).

**Students:** 51 full-time (all women), 101 part-time (85 women); includes 25 minority (5 African Americans, 7 Asian Americans or Pacific Islanders, 13 Hispanic Americans). Average age 36. 121 applicants, 39% accepted, 40 enrolled. In 2001, 14 master's, 11 doctorates awarded. Terminal master's awarded for partial completion of doctoral program.

**Degree requirements:** For master's, thesis; for doctorate, variable foreign language requirement, thesis/dissertation, internship, residency. *Median time to degree:* Master's–3 years full-time, 4 years part-time; doctorate–5 years full-time, 7 years part-time.

**Entrance requirements:** For master's, GRE General Test, minimum GPA of 3.5 in psychology, 3.0 overall; for doctorate, GRE General Test, minimum graduate GPA of 3.5 in psychology, 3.0 overall, 3 letters of reference. *Application deadline:* For fall admission, 2/1. *Application fee:* $30.

**Expenses:** Tuition, state resident: part-time $90 per semester hour. Tuition, nonresident: part-time $303 per semester hour. Required fees: $24 per credit hour. $79 per semester.

**Financial support:** In 2001–02, 12 teaching assistantships (averaging $8,514 per year) were awarded; research assistantships, career-related internships or fieldwork, Federal Work-Study, and institutionally sponsored loans also available. Support available to part-time students. Financial award application deadline: 4/1. Dr. Basil Hamilton, Chair, 940-898-2303, *Fax:* 940-898-2301, *E-mail:* bhamilton@twu.edu. *Web site:* http://www.twu.edu/as/psyphil/

### ■ TOWSON UNIVERSITY

**Graduate School, Program in School Psychology, Towson, MD 21252-0001**

**AWARDS** Clinical psychology (MA); counseling psychology (MA); experimental psychology (MA); psychology (MA); school psychology (MA, CAS). Part-time and evening/weekend programs available.

**Faculty:** 13 full-time (5 women), 2 part-time/adjunct (both women).

**Students:** 195. In 2001, 64 master's, 15 other advanced degrees awarded.

**Degree requirements:** For master's, thesis (for some programs), exams.

*Towson University (continued)*

**Entrance requirements:** For master's, GRE General Test. *Application deadline:* For fall admission, 2/1; for spring admission, 10/1. *Application fee:* $40. Electronic applications accepted.

**Expenses:** Tuition, state resident: part-time $211 per credit. Tuition, nonresident: part-time $435 per credit. Required fees: $52 per credit.

**Financial support:** Fellowships, Federal Work-Study and unspecified assistantships available. Financial award application deadline: 4/1; financial award applicants required to submit FAFSA.

**Faculty research:** Cognitive behavior, issues affecting the aging, relaxation hypnosis and imagery, lesbian and gay issues.

Dr. Susan Bartels, Director, 410-704-3070, *Fax:* 410-704-3800, *E-mail:* sbartels@towson.edu.

**Application contact:** 410-704-2501, *Fax:* 410-704-4675, *E-mail:* grads@towson.edu.

### ■ TREVECCA NAZARENE UNIVERSITY

**Graduate Division, Division of Social and Behavioral Sciences, Major in Counseling Psychology, Nashville, TN 37210-2877**

**AWARDS** MA. Part-time and evening/weekend programs available.

**Students:** In 2001, 4 degrees awarded.

**Degree requirements:** For master's, thesis, comprehensive exam.

**Entrance requirements:** For master's, GRE General Test minimum 800 or MAT minimum 30, minimum GPA of 2.7. *Application deadline:* For fall admission, 8/31; for spring admission, 1/18. Applications are processed on a rolling basis. *Application fee:* $25.

**Expenses:** Tuition: Part-time $270 per credit. Tuition and fees vary according to program.

**Financial support:** Applicants required to submit FAFSA.

Dr. Peter Wilson, Director of Graduate Psychology Program, 615-248-1417, *Fax:* 615-248-1366, *E-mail:* pwilson@trevecca.edu.

**Application contact:** Joyce Houk, Division of Social and Behavior Sciences, 615-248-1417, *Fax:* 615-248-1366, *E-mail:* admissions_psy@trevecca.edu. *Web site:* http://www.treveca.edu/

### ■ TRINITY INTERNATIONAL UNIVERSITY

**Trinity Evangelical Divinity School, Deerfield, IL 60015-1284**

**AWARDS** Biblical studies (Certificate); biblical, historical and theological studies (M Div); bioethics for the chaplaincy (D Min); children's ministries (MA); Christian thought (MA), including church history, counseling psychology, educational ministries; church history (Th M); counseling ministries (MA); cultural studies (M Div); educational leadership (M Div); educational studies (PhD); evangelism (MA); general studies (MAR); intercultural studies (PhD); interdisciplinary studies (M Div); leadership and management (D Min); missiology (D Min); missions (M Div, MA); missions and evangelism (Th M); New Testament (MA, Th M); Old Testament (MA, Th M); pastoral and general church ministries (M Div); pastoral care (D Min); pastoral counseling (Th M); pastoral ministry (D Min); practical theology (Th M); preaching (D Min); systematics (Th M); theological studies (PhD); urban ministry (MAR); youth ministries (MA). Part-time programs available. Postbaccalaureate distance learning degree programs offered (minimal on-campus study).

**Entrance requirements:** For M Div, GRE, MAT, minimum GPA of 2.5; for master's, GRE, MAT, cumulative undergraduate GPA of 3.0 or higher. Electronic applications accepted.

**Expenses:** Contact institution. *Web site:* http://www.tiu.edu/

### ■ TRINITY INTERNATIONAL UNIVERSITY

**Trinity Graduate School, Program in Counseling Psychology, Deerfield, IL 60015-1284**

**AWARDS** MA, Psy D.

**Entrance requirements:** For master's, GRE General Test or MAT.

**Expenses:** Tuition: Full-time $10,440; part-time $522 per credit. Part-time tuition and fees vary according to course load and degree level.

### ■ TRINITY INTERNATIONAL UNIVERSITY, SOUTH FLORIDA CAMPUS

**Program in Counseling Psychology, Miami, FL 33132-1996**

**AWARDS** MA.

### ■ TRUMAN STATE UNIVERSITY

**Graduate School, Division of Social Science, Program in Counseling, Kirksville, MO 63501-4221**

**AWARDS** MA.

**Students:** 15 full-time (8 women), 6 part-time (all women); includes 4 minority (1 African American, 3 Hispanic Americans). 21 applicants, 62% accepted. In 2001, 8 degrees awarded.

**Degree requirements:** For master's, thesis, comprehensive exam.

**Entrance requirements:** For master's, GRE General Test, minimum GPA of 3.0.

*Application deadline:* For fall admission, 6/15 (priority date); for spring admission, 11/1. Applications are processed on a rolling basis. *Application fee:* $0.

**Expenses:** Tuition, state resident: full-time $4,072. Tuition, nonresident: full-time $7,412. Required fees: $30.

**Financial support:** Research assistantships with tuition reimbursements, teaching assistantships with tuition reimbursements, career-related internships or fieldwork and Federal Work-Study available. Financial award application deadline: 5/1; financial award applicants required to submit FAFSA.

Dr. Christopher Maglio, Coordinator, 660-785-4403, *Fax:* 660-785-4181, *E-mail:* cjmaglio@academic.truman.edu.

**Application contact:** Crista Chappell, Graduate Office Secretary, 660-785-4109, *Fax:* 660-785-7460, *E-mail:* gradinfo@truman.edu. *Web site:* http://www2.truman.edu/gradinfo/

### ■ THE UNIVERSITY OF AKRON

**Graduate School, Buchtel College of Arts and Sciences, Department of Psychology, Program in Counseling Psychology, Akron, OH 44325-0001**

**AWARDS** MA.

**Students:** 16 full-time (12 women), 19 part-time (13 women); includes 3 minority (1 African American, 1 Asian American or Pacific Islander, 1 Hispanic American), 1 international. Average age 29. 31 applicants, 16% accepted, 3 enrolled. Terminal master's awarded for partial completion of doctoral program.

**Degree requirements:** For master's, thesis or specialty exam, one foreign language.

**Entrance requirements:** For master's, GRE General Test, GRE Subject Test, minimum GPA of 2.75. *Application deadline:* For fall admission, 3/1. Applications are processed on a rolling basis. *Application fee:* $40 ($50 for international students).

**Expenses:** Tuition, state resident: full-time $6,562; part-time $219 per credit. Tuition, nonresident: full-time $9,027; part-time $383 per credit. Required fees: $272; $11 per credit. Tuition and fees vary according to course load.

**Financial support:** In 2001–02, 9 research assistantships with full tuition reimbursements, 6 teaching assistantships with full tuition reimbursements were awarded. Fellowships with full tuition reimbursements, career-related internships or fieldwork, Federal Work-Study, institutionally sponsored loans, and tuition waivers (full) also available. Financial award application deadline: 3/1.

**Faculty research:** Counseling process and outcome, expectations about counseling, health psychology and eating disorders, women's concerns, career issues.

Dr. Charles Waehler, Chair, 330-972-8379, *E-mail:* cwaehler@uakron.edu.

### ■ THE UNIVERSITY OF AKRON

**Graduate School, College of Education, Department of Counseling, Program in Counseling Psychology, Akron, OH 44325-0001**

**AWARDS** PhD.

**Students:** 19 full-time (15 women), 16 part-time (9 women); includes 3 minority (2 African Americans, 1 Asian American or Pacific Islander). Average age 33. 9 applicants, 67% accepted, 6 enrolled. In 2001, 7 degrees awarded.

**Degree requirements:** For doctorate, one foreign language, thesis/dissertation, written and oral exams.

**Entrance requirements:** For doctorate, GRE, MAT, interview, minimum GPA of 3.25. *Application deadline:* For fall admission, 8/15. Applications are processed on a rolling basis. *Application fee:* $40 ($50 for international students).

**Expenses:** Tuition, state resident: full-time $6,562; part-time $219 per credit. Tuition, nonresident: full-time $9,027; part-time $383 per credit. Required fees: $272; $11 per credit. Tuition and fees vary according to course load.

### ■ UNIVERSITY OF BALTIMORE

**Graduate School, College of Liberal Arts, Department of Psychology, Baltimore, MD 21201-5779**

**AWARDS** Applied assessment and consulting (Psy D); applied psychology (MS); counseling (MS); industrial and organizational psychology (MS). Part-time and evening/weekend programs available.

**Faculty:** 7 full-time (5 women), 7 part-time/adjunct (2 women).

**Students:** 42 full-time (31 women), 45 part-time (34 women); includes 23 minority (14 African Americans, 5 Asian Americans or Pacific Islanders, 4 Hispanic Americans), 6 international. Average age 27. 102 applicants, 79% accepted. In 2001, 40 degrees awarded.

**Degree requirements:** For master's, thesis optional; for doctorate, thesis/dissertation.

**Entrance requirements:** For master's, GRE, minimum GPA of 3.0; for doctorate, GRE. *Application deadline:* For fall admission, 7/15; for spring admission, 12/15. Applications are processed on a rolling basis. *Application fee:* $30. Electronic applications accepted.

**Expenses:** Contact institution.

**Financial support:** In 2001–02, 5 research assistantships with full and partial tuition

reimbursements were awarded; fellowships, career-related internships or fieldwork and Federal Work-Study also available. Support available to part-time students. Financial award application deadline: 4/1; financial award applicants required to submit FAFSA.

**Faculty research:** Participatory decision making, counter productive workplace behavior, organizational consulting, substance abuse treatment, cognitive functioning in head injured. *Total annual research expenditures:* $93,146.

Dr. Paul Mastrangelo, Director, Applied Psychology Program, 410-837-5352, *E-mail:* pmastrangelo@ubalt.edu.

**Application contact:** Jeffrey Zavrotny, Assistant Director of Admissions, 410-837-4777, *Fax:* 410-837-4793, *E-mail:* jzavrotny@ubalt.edu.

**Find an in-depth description at www.petersons.com/gradchannel.**

### ■ UNIVERSITY OF CALIFORNIA, SANTA BARBARA

**Graduate Division, Graduate School of Education, Program in Clinical/School/Counseling Psychology, Santa Barbara, CA 93106**

**AWARDS** Clinical/school/counseling psychology (PhD); school psychology (M Ed).

**Degree requirements:** For master's, thesis or alternative; for doctorate, thesis/dissertation.

**Entrance requirements:** For master's and doctorate, GRE General Test or MAT, TOEFL, background questionnaire, minimum GPA of 3.0. Electronic applications accepted.

### ■ UNIVERSITY OF CENTRAL ARKANSAS

**Graduate School, College of Education, Department of Counseling and Psychology, Program in Counseling Psychology, Conway, AR 72035-0001**

**AWARDS** MS.

**Faculty:** 18.

**Students:** 26 full-time (21 women), 11 part-time (9 women); includes 7 minority (6 African Americans, 1 Native American), 2 international. In 2001, 14 degrees awarded.

**Entrance requirements:** For master's, GRE General Test, minimum GPA of 2.7.

**Expenses:** Tuition, state resident: full-time $3,303; part-time $184 per hour. Tuition, nonresident: full-time $5,922; part-time $329 per hour. Required fees: $68; $24 per semester.

**Financial support:** In 2001–02, 35 students received support, including 5

research assistantships with partial tuition reimbursements available (averaging $6,000 per year)

Dr. Kevin Rowell, Head, 501-450-3193. **Application contact:** Jane Douglas, Co-Admissions Secretary, 501-450-5064, *Fax:* 501-450-5066, *E-mail:* janed@ecom.uca.edu.

### ■ UNIVERSITY OF CENTRAL OKLAHOMA

**College of Graduate Studies and Research, College of Education, Department of Psychology, Program in Counseling Psychology, Edmond, OK 73034-5209**

**AWARDS** MS.

**Entrance requirements:** For master's, GRE General Test.

### ■ UNIVERSITY OF COLORADO AT DENVER

**Graduate School, School of Education, Program in Counseling Psychology and Counselor Education, Denver, CO 80217-3364**

**AWARDS** MA. Part-time and evening/weekend programs available.

**Faculty:** 9 full-time (4 women).

**Students:** 93 full-time (78 women), 104 part-time (86 women); includes 20 minority (4 African Americans, 8 Asian Americans or Pacific Islanders, 7 Hispanic Americans, 1 Native American), 1 international. Average age 34. 55 applicants, 45% accepted, 19 enrolled. In 2001, 75 degrees awarded.

**Degree requirements:** For master's, thesis or alternative.

**Entrance requirements:** For master's, GRE or MAT, minimum GPA of 2.75. *Application deadline:* For fall admission, 4/15; for spring admission, 9/15. Applications are processed on a rolling basis. *Application fee:* $50 ($60 for international students). Electronic applications accepted.

**Expenses:** Tuition, state resident: full-time $3,284; part-time $198 per credit hour. Tuition, nonresident: full-time $13,380; part-time $802 per credit hour. Required fees: $444; $222 per semester.

**Financial support:** Research assistantships, teaching assistantships, Federal Work-Study available. Financial award application deadline: 3/1; financial award applicants required to submit FAFSA. Marsha Wiggins-Frame, Area Coordinator, 303-556-3374, *Fax:* 303-556-4479.

**Application contact:** Elizabeth Kozleski, Associate Dean, 303-556-3990, *Fax:* 303-556-6142. *Web site:* http://carbon.cudenver.edu/public/education/edschool/CPCEdesc.html

## ■ UNIVERSITY OF CONNECTICUT

**Graduate School, School of Education, Field of Counseling Psychology, Storrs, CT 06269**

AWARDS MA, PhD. Terminal master's awarded for partial completion of doctoral program.

**Degree requirements:** For master's, thesis or alternative; for doctorate, thesis/dissertation.

**Entrance requirements:** For doctorate, GRE General Test.

## ■ UNIVERSITY OF DENVER

**College of Education, Denver, CO 80208**

AWARDS Counseling psychology (MA, PhD); curriculum and instruction (MA, PhD), including curriculum leadership; educational psychology (MA, PhD, Ed S), including child and family studies (MA, PhD), quantitative research methods (MA, PhD), school psychology (PhD, Ed S); higher education and adult studies (MA, PhD); school administration (PhD). Part-time and evening/weekend programs available. Postbaccalaureate distance learning degree programs offered (no on-campus study).

**Faculty:** 25 full-time (16 women), 1 (woman) part-time/adjunct.

**Students:** 392 (312 women); includes 47 minority (10 African Americans, 11 Asian Americans or Pacific Islanders, 23 Hispanic Americans, 3 Native Americans) 12 international. Average age 31. 352 applicants, 68% accepted. In 2001, 71 master's, 27 doctorates awarded.

**Degree requirements:** For master's, comprehensive exam; for doctorate, 2 foreign languages, thesis/dissertation, comprehensive exam.

**Entrance requirements:** For master's and doctorate, GRE General Test, TSE. *Application deadline:* For fall admission, 1/1. Applications are processed on a rolling basis. *Application fee:* $45. Electronic applications accepted.

**Expenses:** Tuition: Full-time $21,456.

**Financial support:** In 2001–02, 92 students received support, including 7 fellowships with full and partial tuition reimbursements available, 1 research assistantship with full and partial tuition reimbursement available (averaging $7,785 per year), 19 teaching assistantships with full and partial tuition reimbursements available (averaging $7,677 per year); career-related internships or fieldwork, Federal Work-Study, institutionally sponsored loans, and scholarships/grants also available. Support available to part-time students. Financial award application deadline: 3/1; financial award applicants required to submit FAFSA.

**Faculty research:** Parkinson's disease, personnel training, development and assessments, gifted education, sexual functioning, service learning. *Total annual research expenditures:* $369,539.
Dr. Virginia Maloney, Dean, 303-871-3828.
**Application contact:** Linda McCarthy, Contact, 303-871-2509. *Web site:* http://www.du.edu/education/

## ■ UNIVERSITY OF GEORGIA

**Graduate School, College of Education, Department of Counseling and Human Development Services, Athens, GA 30602**

AWARDS College student affairs administration (M Ed); counseling and student personnel services (PhD); counseling psychology (PhD); education (MA); guidance and counseling (M Ed).

**Faculty:** 13 full-time (7 women).

**Students:** 94 full-time (68 women), 32 part-time (27 women); includes 40 minority (34 African Americans, 3 Asian Americans or Pacific Islanders, 3 Hispanic Americans), 5 international. 210 applicants, 18% accepted. In 2001, 33 master's, 14 doctorates awarded.

**Degree requirements:** For master's, thesis (MA); for doctorate, variable foreign language requirement, thesis/dissertation.

**Entrance requirements:** For master's, GRE General Test or MAT; for doctorate, GRE General Test. *Application deadline:* For fall admission, 7/1 (priority date); for spring admission, 11/15. *Application fee:* $30. Electronic applications accepted.

**Expenses:** Tuition, state resident: full-time $2,376; part-time $132 per credit hour. Tuition, nonresident: full-time $9,504; part-time $528 per credit hour. Required fees: $236 per semester.

**Financial support:** Fellowships, research assistantships, teaching assistantships, unspecified assistantships available.
Dr. John C. Dagley, Head and Graduate Coordinator, 706-542-1697, *Fax:* 706-542-4130, *E-mail:* jdagley@coe.uga.edu. *Web site:* http://www.coe.uga.edu/ecp/

## ■ UNIVERSITY OF GREAT FALLS

**Graduate Studies Division, Program in Counseling, Great Falls, MT 59405**

AWARDS Counseling psychology (MSC); marriage and family counseling (MSC). Part-time and evening/weekend programs available. Postbaccalaureate distance learning degree programs offered (minimal on-campus study).

**Faculty:** 4 full-time (3 women), 10 part-time/adjunct (6 women).

**Students:** 11 full-time (all women), 49 part-time (42 women); includes 6 minority (1 African American, 5 Native Americans). Average age 30. 22 applicants, 91%

accepted. In 2001, 18 degrees awarded. *Median time to degree:* Master's–2 years full-time, 3.8 years part-time.

**Entrance requirements:** For master's, GRE General Test or MAT. *Application deadline:* for fall admission, 8/15 (priority date); for winter admission, 11/15 (priority date); for spring admission, 12/15 (priority date). Applications are processed on a rolling basis. *Application fee:* $35.

**Expenses:** Tuition: Part-time $440 per credit. One-time fee: $35 full-time.

**Financial support:** In 2001–02, 50 students received support, including 2 fellowships, 8 research assistantships; career-related internships or fieldwork, Federal Work-Study, institutionally sponsored loans, and scholarships/grants also available. Support available to part-time students. Financial award application deadline: 3/1.

**Faculty research:** Head trauma and aggression, self concept and adolescent offenders, juvenile delinquency. *Total annual research expenditures:* $300,000.
Karen Low, Director, 406-791-5361, *Fax:* 406-791-5990, *E-mail:* klow01@ugf.edu.

## ■ UNIVERSITY OF HOUSTON

**College of Education, Department of Educational Psychology, Houston, TX 77204**

AWARDS Counseling psychology (M Ed, PhD); educational psychology (M Ed); educational psychology and individual differences (PhD); special education (M Ed, Ed D). Part-time and evening/weekend programs available.

**Faculty:** 15 full-time (6 women), 9 part-time/adjunct (4 women).

**Students:** 79 full-time (64 women), 133 part-time (113 women); includes 56 minority (19 African Americans, 10 Asian Americans or Pacific Islanders, 24 Hispanic Americans, 3 Native Americans), 4 international. Average age 36. In 2001, 52 master's, 18 doctorates awarded.

**Degree requirements:** For master's, comprehensive exam or thesis; for doctorate, thesis/dissertation, comprehensive exam.

**Entrance requirements:** For master's, GRE General Test or MAT, interview (counseling psychology); for doctorate, GRE General Test, interview. *Application deadline:* For fall admission, 2/1. *Application fee:* $35 ($75 for international students).

**Expenses:** Tuition, state resident: full-time $1,512. Tuition, nonresident: full-time $5,310. Required fees: $1,308. Tuition and fees vary according to program.

**Financial support:** Research assistantships, teaching assistantships available.

**Faculty research:** Cross-cultural assessment and counseling, cognitive and

psychosocial development, learning and emotional disturbances. *Total annual research expenditures:* $74,277.
Robert McPherson, Chairperson, 713-743-9827, *Fax:* 713-743-4989.
**Application contact:** Graduate Adviser, 713-743-5019, *Fax:* 713-743-4996, *E-mail:* epsy@uh.edu.

■ **UNIVERSITY OF KANSAS**

**Graduate School, School of Education, Department of Psychology and Research in Education, Program in Counseling Psychology, Lawrence, KS 66045**

AWARDS MS, PhD. Part-time programs available.

**Students:** 49 full-time (40 women), 45 part-time (35 women); includes 12 minority (4 African Americans, 4 Asian Americans or Pacific Islanders, 1 Hispanic American, 3 Native Americans). Average age 28. 79 applicants, 27% accepted, 17 enrolled. In 2001, 34 master's, 10 doctorates awarded. Terminal master's awarded for partial completion of doctoral program.
**Degree requirements:** For master's and doctorate, thesis/dissertation.
**Entrance requirements:** For master's, GRE General Test, TOEFL, minimum GPA of 3.0; for doctorate, GRE General Test, TOEFL. *Application deadline:* For fall admission, 1/15. *Application fee:* $35. Electronic applications accepted.
**Expenses:** Tuition, state resident: full-time $2,722; part-time $113 per credit. Tuition, nonresident: full-time $8,586; part-time $358 per credit. Required fees: $551; $46 per credit. Tuition and fees vary according to campus/location, program and reciprocity agreements.
**Financial support:** Fellowships, research assistantships, teaching assistantships, career-related internships or fieldwork available.
**Faculty research:** Alcohol/substance abuse, learning styles, outcomes/process research. *Total annual research expenditures:* $20,000.
James Lichtenberg, Professor and Director of Training, *E-mail:* jlicht@ku.edu.
**Application contact:** Admissions Coordinator, 785-864-3931, *Fax:* 785-864-5076. *Web site:* http://www.soe.ku.edu/pre/

■ **UNIVERSITY OF KENTUCKY**

**Graduate School, Graduate School Programs from the College of Education, Program in Educational and Counseling Psychology, Lexington, KY 40506-0032**

AWARDS MA Ed, MS Ed, Ed D, PhD, Ed S.
**Faculty:** 24 full-time (12 women).

**Students:** 119 full-time (96 women), 63 part-time (51 women); includes 23 minority (18 African Americans, 4 Asian Americans or Pacific Islanders, 1 Native American), 5 international. 166 applicants, 40% accepted. In 2001, 32 master's, 5 doctorates, 10 other advanced degrees awarded.
**Degree requirements:** For master's, thesis optional; for doctorate, thesis/dissertation, comprehensive exam.
**Entrance requirements:** For master's, GRE General Test, minimum undergraduate GPA of 2.5; for doctorate, GRE General Test, minimum graduate GPA of 3.0; for Ed S, GRE General Test. *Application deadline:* Applications are processed on a rolling basis. *Application fee:* $30 ($35 for international students).
**Expenses:** Tuition, state resident: full-time $4,075; part-time $213 per credit hour. Tuition, nonresident: full-time $11,295; part-time $614 per credit hour.
**Financial support:** In 2001–02, 3 fellowships, 24 research assistantships, 22 teaching assistantships were awarded. Career-related internships or fieldwork, Federal Work-Study, institutionally sponsored loans, and unspecified assistantships also available. Support available to part-time students.
**Faculty research:** Industrial and agricultural injury prevention, outcome evaluation in counseling and psychology, hypertension and stress in African-American youth, resilience in victims of trauma and violence, achievement motivation during adolescence.
Dr. Eric Anderman, Director of Graduate Studies, 859-257-7928, *Fax:* 859-257-5662, *E-mail:* eande1@pop.uky.edu.
**Application contact:** Dr. Jeannine Blackwell, Associate Dean, 859-257-4905, *Fax:* 859-323-1928.

■ **UNIVERSITY OF LA VERNE**

**College of Arts and Sciences, Department of Psychology, Masters Programs in Counseling, La Verne, CA 91750-4443**

AWARDS Counseling in higher education (MS); general counseling (MS); gerontology (MS); marriage, family and child counseling (MS). Part-time programs available.

**Faculty:** 9 full-time (5 women), 5 part-time/adjunct (3 women).
**Students:** 21 full-time (18 women), 45 part-time (34 women); includes 33 minority (9 African Americans, 3 Asian Americans or Pacific Islanders, 20 Hispanic Americans, 1 Native American). Average age 36. In 2001, 10 degrees awarded.
**Degree requirements:** For master's, competency exam, thesis optional.

**Entrance requirements:** For master's, undergraduate GPA of 3.0. *Application deadline:* Applications are processed on a rolling basis. *Application fee:* $40.
**Expenses:** Tuition: Full-time $4,410; part-time $245 per unit. Required fees: $60. Tuition and fees vary according to course load, degree level, campus/location and program.
**Financial support:** In 2001–02, 42 students received support, including 5 research assistantships (averaging $2,200 per year); career-related internships or fieldwork, institutionally sponsored loans, and scholarships/grants also available. Financial award application deadline: 3/2; financial award applicants required to submit FAFSA.
Dr. Errol Moultrie, Chairperson, 909-593-3511 Ext. 4169, *Fax:* 909-392-2745, *E-mail:* moultrie@ulv.edu.
**Application contact:** Jo Nell Baker, Director, Graduate Admissions and Academic Services, 909-593-3511 Ext. 4504, *Fax:* 909-392-2761, *E-mail:* bakerj@ulv.edu. *Web site:* http://www.ulaverne.edu/

■ **UNIVERSITY OF LA VERNE**

**School of Public Affairs and Health Administration, Department of Health Services Management and Gerontology, Graduate Program in Gerontology, La Verne, CA 91750-4443**

AWARDS Business administration (MS); counseling (MS); gerontology administration (MS); health services management (MS); public administration (MS). Part-time programs available.

**Faculty:** 3 full-time (2 women), 5 part-time/adjunct (all women).
**Students:** 1 (woman) full-time, 20 part-time (15 women); includes 8 minority (7 African Americans, 1 Asian American or Pacific Islander), 2 international. Average age 50. In 2001, 9 degrees awarded.
**Entrance requirements:** For master's, minimum GPA of 3.0. *Application deadline:* Applications are processed on a rolling basis. *Application fee:* $40.
**Expenses:** Tuition: Full-time $4,410; part-time $245 per unit. Required fees: $60. Tuition and fees vary according to course load, degree level, campus/location and program.
**Financial support:** In 2001–02, 8 students received support. Institutionally sponsored loans available. Financial award application deadline: 3/2; financial award applicants required to submit FAFSA.
**Application contact:** Jo Nell Baker, Director, Graduate Admissions and Academic Services, 909-593-3511 Ext. 4504, *Fax:* 909-392-2761, *E-mail:* bakerj@ulv.edu. *Web site:* http://www.ulv.edu/gerontology/

# UNIVERSITY OF LOUISVILLE

**Graduate School, College of Education and Human Development, Department of Educational and Counseling Psychology, Louisville, KY 40292-0001**

**AWARDS** College student personnel services (M Ed); community counseling (M Ed); counseling and personnel services (M Ed, Ed D); counseling psychology (M Ed, Ed D); expressive therapies (MA); school counseling (M Ed).

**Students:** 105 full-time (77 women), 169 part-time (137 women); includes 39 minority (31 African Americans, 5 Asian Americans or Pacific Islanders, 1 Hispanic American, 2 Native Americans), 5 international. Average age 34. In 2001, 63 master's, 7 doctorates awarded.

**Degree requirements:** For doctorate, thesis/dissertation.

**Entrance requirements:** For master's and doctorate, GRE General Test. *Application deadline:* Applications are processed on a rolling basis. *Application fee:* $25. Electronic applications accepted.

**Expenses:** Tuition, state resident: full-time $4,134. Tuition, nonresident: full-time $11,486.

**Financial support:** Fellowships, research assistantships, teaching assistantships, Federal Work-Study and scholarships/grants available.

Dr. Gerald Sklare, Chair, 502-852-0632, *Fax:* 502-852-0726, *E-mail:* sklare@louisville.edu.

# UNIVERSITY OF MARY HARDIN-BAYLOR

**School of Sciences and Humanities, Department of Psychology and Counseling, Program in Counseling, Belton, TX 76513**

**AWARDS** MA. Part-time and evening/weekend programs available.

**Faculty:** 4 full-time (3 women), 3 part-time/adjunct (1 woman).

**Entrance requirements:** For master's, GRE General Test, minimum GPA of 3.0 in last 60 hours or 2.75 overall. *Application deadline:* For fall admission, 6/1 (priority date); for spring admission, 11/1. Applications are processed on a rolling basis. *Application fee:* $35 ($135 for international students).

**Expenses:** Tuition: Full-time $5,940; part-time $330 per credit hour. Required fees: $554; $28 per credit hour. One-time fee: $40 part-time.

**Financial support:** Career-related internships or fieldwork and scholarship for some active duty military personnel available. Support available to part-time students.

**Application contact:** Rhonda Neuses, Secretary, 254-295-4555.

# UNIVERSITY OF MARYLAND, COLLEGE PARK

**Graduate Studies and Research, College of Education, Department of Counseling and Personnel Services, College Park, MD 20742**

**AWARDS** College student personnel (M Ed, MA); college student personnel administration (PhD); community counseling (CAGS); community/career counseling (M Ed, MA); counseling and personnel services (M Ed, MA, PhD); counseling psychology (PhD); counselor education (PhD); rehabilitation counseling (M Ed, MA); school counseling (M Ed, MA); school psychology (M Ed, MA, PhD). Part-time and evening/weekend programs available. Postbaccalaureate distance learning degree programs offered (no on-campus study).

**Faculty:** 17 full-time (10 women), 2 part-time/adjunct (1 woman).

**Students:** 127 full-time (99 women), 153 part-time (116 women); includes 91 minority (55 African Americans, 18 Asian Americans or Pacific Islanders, 16 Hispanic Americans, 2 Native Americans), 19 international. 358 applicants, 27% accepted, 57 enrolled. In 2001, 62 master's, 8 doctorates awarded.

**Degree requirements:** For master's, thesis (for some programs); for doctorate, thesis/dissertation.

**Entrance requirements:** For master's, GRE General Test or MAT, minimum GPA of 3.0; for doctorate, GRE General Test or MAT, minimum GPA of 3.5. *Application deadline:* For spring admission, 10/1. Applications are processed on a rolling basis. *Application fee:* $50 ($70 for international students). Electronic applications accepted.

**Expenses:** Tuition, state resident: part-time $289 per credit hour. Tuition, nonresident: part-time $448 per credit hour. One-time fee: $436 part-time. Full-time tuition and fees vary according to course load, campus/location and program.

**Financial support:** In 2001–02, 18 fellowships with full tuition reimbursements (averaging $7,029 per year), 13 teaching assistantships with tuition reimbursements (averaging $12,582 per year) were awarded. Research assistantships, career-related internships or fieldwork, Federal Work-Study, and scholarships/grants also available. Support available to part-time students. Financial award applicants required to submit FAFSA.

**Faculty research:** Educational psychology, counseling, health.

Dr. Dennis Kiulighan, Chairman, 301-405-2858, *Fax:* 301-405-9995.

**Application contact:** Trudy Lindsey, Director, Graduate Admissions and Records, 301-405-6991, *Fax:* 301-314-9305, *E-mail:* grschool@deans.umd.edu.

# THE UNIVERSITY OF MEMPHIS

**Graduate School, College of Education, Department of Counseling, Educational Psychology and Research, Memphis, TN 38152**

**AWARDS** Counseling and personnel services (MS, Ed D), including community agency counseling (MS), rehabilitation counseling (MS), school counseling (MS), student personnel services (MS); counseling psychology (PhD); educational psychology and research (MS, Ed D, PhD), including educational psychology (MS, Ed D), educational research (MS, Ed D).

**Degree requirements:** For master's, thesis or alternative, comprehensive exam; for doctorate, thesis/dissertation, comprehensive exam.

**Entrance requirements:** For master's, GRE General Test or MAT, minimum GPA of 2.5; for doctorate, GRE General Test.

**Expenses:** Tuition, state resident: full-time $2,026. Tuition, nonresident: full-time $4,528.

**Faculty research:** Anger management, aging and disability, supervision, multicultural counseling.

# UNIVERSITY OF MIAMI

**Graduate School, School of Education, Department of Educational and Psychological Studies, Doctoral Program in Counseling Psychology, Coral Gables, FL 33124**

**AWARDS** PhD.

**Faculty:** 9 full-time (3 women), 10 part-time/adjunct (6 women).

**Students:** 35 full-time (24 women), 2 part-time (both women); includes 9 minority (3 African Americans, 6 Asian Americans or Pacific Islanders), 2 international. Average age 30. 38 applicants, 18% accepted. In 2001, 5 degrees awarded.

**Degree requirements:** For doctorate, thesis/dissertation.

**Entrance requirements:** For doctorate, GRE General Test, GRE Subject Test, TOEFL. *Application fee:* $50. Electronic applications accepted.

**Expenses:** Tuition: Part-time $960 per credit hour. Required fees: $85 per semester. Tuition and fees vary according to program.

**Financial support:** In 2001–02, 2 fellowships with partial tuition reimbursements (averaging $17,000 per year), research assistantships with partial tuition reimbursements (averaging $11,000 per year), teaching assistantships with partial

tuition reimbursements (averaging $11,000 per year) were awarded. Career-related internships or fieldwork, Federal Work-Study, institutionally sponsored loans, and unspecified assistantships also available. Support available to part-time students. Financial award application deadline: 3/1.
**Faculty research:** Cocaine recidivism, family systems, behavior and health, nontraditional families, stress and coping, diversity and counseling process.
Dr. Blaine Fowers, Director of Training, 305-284-5261, *Fax:* 305-284-3003, *E-mail:* bfowers@miami.edu. *Web site:* http://www.education.miami.edu/

### ■ UNIVERSITY OF MINNESOTA, TWIN CITIES CAMPUS

**Graduate School, College of Liberal Arts, Department of Psychology, Program in Counseling Psychology, Minneapolis, MN 55455-0213**

AWARDS PhD.

**Students:** 30 full-time (19 women); includes 7 minority (1 African American, 5 Asian Americans or Pacific Islanders, 1 Hispanic American), 1 international. 58 applicants, 10% accepted, 4 enrolled. In 2001, 2 degrees awarded.
**Degree requirements:** For doctorate, thesis/dissertation, comprehensive exam.
**Entrance requirements:** For doctorate, GRE General Test, GRE Subject Test (recommended), TOEFL, 12 credits of upper-level psychology courses, including a course in statistics or psychological measurement. *Application deadline:* For fall admission, 1/5. *Application fee:* $55 ($75 for international students).
**Expenses:** Tuition, state resident: full-time $2,932; part-time $489 per credit. Tuition, nonresident: full-time $5,758; part-time $960 per credit. Part-time tuition and fees vary according to course load, program and reciprocity agreements.
**Financial support:** Fellowships, research assistantships, teaching assistantships, career-related internships or fieldwork and tuition waivers (partial) available. Financial award application deadline: 12/1.
**Application contact:** Coordinator, 612-624-4181, *Fax:* 612-626-2079, *E-mail:* psyapply@tc.umn.edu.

### ■ UNIVERSITY OF MISSOURI–COLUMBIA

**Graduate School, College of Education, Department of Educational and Counseling Psychology, Columbia, MO 65211**

AWARDS M Ed, MA, PhD, Ed S. Part-time programs available.
**Faculty:** 24 full-time (7 women).

**Students:** 122 full-time (87 women), 61 part-time (46 women); includes 31 minority (19 African Americans, 3 Asian Americans or Pacific Islanders, 7 Hispanic Americans, 2 Native Americans), 26 international. 123 applicants, 17% accepted. In 2001, 24 master's, 11 doctorates, 4 other advanced degrees awarded.
**Degree requirements:** For doctorate, thesis/dissertation.
**Entrance requirements:** For master's, doctorate, and Ed S, GRE General Test, minimum GPA of 3.0. *Application deadline:* For fall admission, 1/8 (priority date). Applications are processed on a rolling basis. *Application fee:* $25 ($50 for international students).
**Expenses:** Tuition, state resident: part-time $179 per credit hour. Tuition, nonresident: part-time $539 per credit hour. Required fees: $122 per semester. Tuition and fees vary according to program.
**Financial support:** Fellowships, research assistantships, teaching assistantships, institutionally sponsored loans available.
Dr. Richard Cox, Director of Graduate Studies, 573-882-7601, *E-mail:* coxrh@missouri.edu. *Web site:* http://www.coe.missouri.edu/~ecp/index.html

### ■ UNIVERSITY OF MISSOURI–KANSAS CITY

**School of Education, Division of Counseling, Educational Psychology, and Exercise Science, Kansas City, MO 64110-2499**

AWARDS Counseling and guidance (MA, Ed S); counseling psychology (PhD); education research and psychology (MA). Part-time and evening/weekend programs available.
**Faculty:** 19 full-time (7 women), 12 part-time/adjunct (7 women).
**Students:** 50 full-time (37 women), 127 part-time (93 women); includes 29 minority (16 African Americans, 6 Asian Americans or Pacific Islanders, 6 Hispanic Americans, 1 Native American), 4 international. Average age 32. 150 applicants, 21% accepted. In 2001, 26 master's, 5 doctorates awarded.
**Degree requirements:** For master's and doctorate, thesis/dissertation, internship, practicum; for Ed S, practicum.
**Entrance requirements:** For master's, MAT, minimum GPA of 2.75; for doctorate, GRE, minimum GPA of 3.0; for Ed S, minimum GPA of 3.0. *Application deadline:* For fall admission, 3/1. *Application fee:* $25.
**Expenses:** Tuition, state resident: part-time $233 per credit hour. Tuition, nonresident: part-time $623 per credit hour. Tuition and fees vary according to course load.

**Financial support:** In 2001–02, 1 research assistantship (averaging $8,190 per year), teaching assistantships (averaging $8,190 per year) were awarded. Career-related internships or fieldwork, Federal Work-Study, institutionally sponsored loans, and tuition waivers (full and partial) also available. Support available to part-time students.
**Faculty research:** Career development, reading related rates, psychotherapy process and outcome, human sexuality.
Dr. Robert Paul, Chairperson, 816-235-2722, *Fax:* 816-235-5270, *E-mail:* paul@umkc.edu.

### ■ UNIVERSITY OF NEVADA, LAS VEGAS

**Graduate College, Greenspun College of Urban Affairs, Department of Counseling, Las Vegas, NV 89154-9900**

AWARDS Community agency counseling (MS); marriage and family counseling (MS); rehabilitation counseling (MS). Part-time programs available.

**Faculty:** 19 full-time (9 women).
**Students:** 25 full-time (20 women), 22 part-time (17 women); includes 6 minority (2 African Americans, 2 Asian Americans or Pacific Islanders, 2 Hispanic Americans). In 2001, 12 degrees awarded.
**Degree requirements:** For master's, thesis (for some programs), comprehensive exam (for some programs).
**Entrance requirements:** For master's, GRE General Test, minimum GPA of 3.0 during previous 2 years, 2.75 overall. *Application deadline:* For fall admission, 2/1. *Application fee:* $40 ($55 for international students).
**Expenses:** Tuition, state resident: full-time $1,926; part-time $107 per credit. Tuition, nonresident: full-time $9,376; part-time $220 per credit. Tuition and fees vary according to course load.
**Financial support:** In 2001–02, 2 research assistantships with partial tuition reimbursements (averaging $10,000 per year), 2 teaching assistantships with partial tuition reimbursements (averaging $10,000 per year) were awarded. Financial award application deadline: 3/1.
Dr. Gerald Weeks, Chair, 702-895-1867.
**Application contact:** Graduate College Admissions Evaluator, 702-895-3320, *Fax:* 702-895-4180, *E-mail:* gradcollege@ccmail.nevada.edu. *Web site:* http://www.unlv.edu/Colleges/Urban/Counseling/

## ■ THE UNIVERSITY OF NORTH CAROLINA AT GREENSBORO

**Graduate School, School of Education, Department of Counseling and Educational Development, Greensboro, NC 27412-5001**

**AWARDS** Counseling and development (MS, Ed D, PhD); gerontological counseling (PMC); marriage and family counseling (PMC); school counseling (PMC).

**Faculty:** 9 full-time (4 women), 1 part-time/adjunct (0 women).
**Students:** 90 full-time (74 women), 32 part-time (20 women); includes 12 minority (6 African Americans, 3 Asian Americans or Pacific Islanders, 3 Hispanic Americans). 254 applicants, 24% accepted, 41 enrolled. In 2001, 20 master's, 6 doctorates, 6 other advanced degrees awarded.
**Degree requirements:** For master's, practicum, internship; for doctorate, thesis/dissertation, comprehensive exam.
**Entrance requirements:** For master's and doctorate, GRE General Test, TOEFL; for PMC, GRE General Test. *Application deadline:* For fall admission, 2/15. *Application fee:* $35.
**Expenses:** Tuition, state resident: part-time $344 per course. Tuition, nonresident: part-time $2,457 per course.
**Financial support:** In 2001–02, 57 students received support, including 4 fellowships with full tuition reimbursements available (averaging $14,000 per year), 33 research assistantships with full tuition reimbursements available (averaging $4,820 per year), 25 teaching assistantships with full tuition reimbursements available (averaging $4,240 per year); career-related internships or fieldwork, Federal Work-Study, scholarships/grants, traineeships, and unspecified assistantships also available. Support available to part-time students.
**Faculty research:** Gerontology, invitational theory, career development, marriage and family therapy, drug and alcohol abuse prevention.
Dr. DiAnne Borders, Chair, 336-334-3423, *Fax:* 336-334-4120, *E-mail:* borders@uncg.edu.
**Application contact:** Dr. James Lynch, Director of Graduate Recruitment and Information Services, 336-334-4881, *Fax:* 336-334-4424. *Web site:* http://www.uncg.edu/ced/

## ■ UNIVERSITY OF NORTH DAKOTA

**Graduate School, College of Education and Human Development, Department of Counseling, Grand Forks, ND 58202**

**AWARDS** Counseling (MA); counseling psychology (PhD).

**Faculty:** 4 full-time (3 women).
**Students:** 32 full-time (21 women), 35 part-time (26 women). 24 applicants, 71% accepted, 16 enrolled. In 2001, 10 master's, 3 doctorates awarded.
**Degree requirements:** For master's, thesis or alternative, comprehensive final examination; for doctorate, thesis/dissertation, comprehensive final examination, final examination.
**Entrance requirements:** For master's, GRE General Test or MAT, TOEFL, minimum GPA of 3.0; for doctorate, GRE General Test, GRE Subject Test, TOEFL, minimum GPA of 3.5. *Application deadline:* For fall admission, 1/15. *Application fee:* $30.
**Expenses:** Tuition, state resident: full-time $3,298. Tuition, nonresident: full-time $7,998.
**Financial support:** In 2001–02, 28 students received support, including 4 research assistantships with full tuition reimbursements available (averaging $9,282 per year), 7 teaching assistantships with full tuition reimbursements available (averaging $9,282 per year); fellowships, career-related internships or fieldwork, Federal Work-Study, institutionally sponsored loans, scholarships/grants, tuition waivers (full and partial), and unspecified assistantships also available. Support available to part-time students. Financial award application deadline: 3/15; financial award applicants required to submit FAFSA.
**Faculty research:** Group dynamics, addictive behavior, item response theory, geopsychology, women's health.
Dr. Cindy L. Juntunen, Director, Doctoral Program, 701-777-3740, *Fax:* 701-777-3184, *E-mail:* cindy_juntunen@und.nodak.edu. *Web site:* http://www.und.edu/dept/grad/depts/coun/

## ■ UNIVERSITY OF NORTHERN COLORADO

**Graduate School, College of Education, Division of Professional Psychology, Program in Counselor Education and Counseling Psychology, Greeley, CO 80639**

**AWARDS** Agency counseling (MA); counseling psychology (Psy D); counselor education (Ed D); elementary school counseling (MA);

secondary and postsecondary school counseling (MA). Part-time programs available.

**Faculty:** 6 full-time (3 women).
**Students:** 100 full-time (80 women), 34 part-time (28 women); includes 12 minority (1 African American, 3 Asian Americans or Pacific Islanders, 7 Hispanic Americans, 1 Native American), 4 international. Average age 34. 131 applicants, 57% accepted. In 2001, 87 master's, 7 doctorates awarded.
**Degree requirements:** For master's, comprehensive exam; for doctorate, thesis/dissertation, comprehensive exam.
**Entrance requirements:** For doctorate, GRE General Test. *Application deadline:* Applications are processed on a rolling basis. *Application fee:* $35.
**Expenses:** Tuition, state resident: full-time $2,549; part-time $546 per credit hour. Tuition, nonresident: full-time $10,459; part-time $581 per credit hour. Required fees: $631; $85 per year. Part-time tuition and fees vary according to course load.
**Financial support:** In 2001–02, 89 students received support, including 22 fellowships (averaging $1,781 per year), 13 research assistantships (averaging $8,683 per year), 1 teaching assistantship (averaging $1,000 per year); unspecified assistantships also available. Financial award application deadline: 3/1.
Tracy Baldo, Coordinator, 970-351-2727.

## ■ UNIVERSITY OF NORTH FLORIDA

**College of Arts and Sciences, Department of Psychology, Jacksonville, FL 32224-2645**

**AWARDS** Counseling psychology (MAC); general psychology (MA). Part-time and evening/weekend programs available.

**Faculty:** 17 full-time (7 women).
**Students:** 28 full-time (20 women), 12 part-time (11 women); includes 2 minority (1 African American, 1 Asian American or Pacific Islander). Average age 28. 106 applicants, 29% accepted, 19 enrolled. In 2001, 15 degrees awarded.
**Degree requirements:** For master's, practicum, thesis optional.
**Entrance requirements:** For master's, TOEFL, GRE General Test or minimum GPA of 3.0 in last 60 hours. *Application deadline:* For fall admission, 2/2 (priority date). Applications are processed on a rolling basis. *Application fee:* $20. Electronic applications accepted.
**Expenses:** Tuition, state resident: full-time $2,411; part-time $134 per credit hour. Tuition, nonresident: full-time $9,391; part-time $522 per credit hour. Required fees: $670; $37 per credit hour.

**Financial support:** In 2001–02, 28 students received support. Federal Work-Study and tuition waivers (partial) available. Support available to part-time students. Financial award application deadline: 4/1; financial award applicants required to submit FAFSA.
**Faculty research:** Person by situation interaction, jury decision processes, domestic violence impact on children, head-start and early childhood development, applied behavior analysis. *Total annual research expenditures:* $7,500.
Dr. Minor H. Chamblin, Chair, 904-620-2807, *E-mail:* mchambli@unf.edu.
**Application contact:** Dr. Maury Nation, Coordinator, 904-620-2807, *E-mail:* mnation@unf.edu.

■ **UNIVERSITY OF NORTH TEXAS**
**Robert B. Toulouse School of Graduate Studies, College of Arts and Sciences, Department of Psychology, Denton, TX 76203**
**AWARDS** Clinical psychology (PhD); counseling psychology (MA, MS, PhD); experimental psychology (MA, MS, PhD); health psychology and behavioral medicine (PhD); industrial psychology (MA, MS); psychology (MA, MS, PhD); school psychology (MA, MS, PhD).
**Faculty:** 29 full-time (5 women), 7 part-time/adjunct (5 women).
**Students:** 129 full-time (96 women), 98 part-time (70 women); includes 23 minority (2 African Americans, 4 Asian Americans or Pacific Islanders, 15 Hispanic Americans, 2 Native Americans), 9 international. Average age 30. In 2001, 24 master's, 17 doctorates awarded. Terminal master's awarded for partial completion of doctoral program.
**Degree requirements:** For master's, thesis or alternative, comprehensive exam; for doctorate, one foreign language, thesis/dissertation, comprehensive exam.
**Entrance requirements:** For master's and doctorate, GRE General Test, GRE Subject Test, interview. *Application deadline:* For fall admission, 2/1. *Application fee:* $25 ($50 for international students).
**Expenses:** Tuition, state resident: part-time $186 per hour. Tuition, nonresident: part-time $319 per hour. Required fees: $88; $21 per hour.
**Financial support:** Fellowships, research assistantships, teaching assistantships, career-related internships or fieldwork, Federal Work-Study, and institutionally sponsored loans available. Financial award application deadline: 8/1.
Dr. Ernest H. Harrell, Chair, 940-565-2671, *Fax:* 940-546-4682, *E-mail:* harrelle@unt.edu.

**Application contact:** Dr. Joseph Critelli, Graduate Adviser, 940-565-2671, *Fax:* 940-565-4682, *E-mail:* critelli@facstaff.cas.unt.edu.

■ **UNIVERSITY OF NOTRE DAME**
**Graduate School, College of Arts and Letters, Division of Social Science, Department of Psychology, Notre Dame, IN 46556**
**AWARDS** Cognitive psychology (PhD); counseling psychology (PhD); developmental psychology (PhD); quantitative psychology (PhD).
**Faculty:** 31 full-time (11 women).
**Students:** 60 full-time (42 women); includes 10 minority (3 African Americans, 2 Asian Americans or Pacific Islanders, 5 Hispanic Americans), 5 international. 189 applicants, 12% accepted, 15 enrolled. In 2001, 8 doctorates awarded.
**Degree requirements:** For doctorate, thesis/dissertation, comprehensive exam. *Median time to degree:* Doctorate–5.9 years full-time.
**Entrance requirements:** For doctorate, GRE General Test, GRE Subject Test (strongly recommended), TOEFL. *Application deadline:* For fall admission, 1/2. *Application fee:* $50. Electronic applications accepted.
**Expenses:** Tuition: Full-time $24,220; part-time $1,346 per credit hour. Required fees: $155.
**Financial support:** In 2001–02, 59 students received support, including 31 fellowships with full tuition reimbursements available (averaging $16,000 per year), 10 research assistantships with full tuition reimbursements available (averaging $11,400 per year), 17 teaching assistantships with full tuition reimbursements available (averaging $11,400 per year); career-related internships or fieldwork and tuition waivers (full) also available. Financial award application deadline: 1/2.
**Faculty research:** Cognitive and socioemotional development, marital discord, statistical methods and quantitative models applicable to psychology, interpersonal relations, life span development and developmental delay, childhood depression, structural equation and dynamical systems, modeling, social cognition, ecology, health psychology, aging behavior genetics. *Total annual research expenditures:* $1.8 million.
Dr. Laura Carlson, Director of Graduate Studies, 574-631-6650, *Fax:* 574-631-8883, *E-mail:* lcarlson@nd.edu.
**Application contact:** Dr. Terrence J. Akai, Director of Graduate Admissions, 574-631-7706, *Fax:* 574-631-4183, *E-mail:* gradad@nd.edu. *Web site:* http://www.nd.edu/~psych/

■ **UNIVERSITY OF OKLAHOMA**
**Graduate College, College of Education, Department of Educational Psychology, Program in Counseling Psychology, Norman, OK 73019-0390**
**AWARDS** PhD.
**Students:** 26 full-time (16 women), 17 part-time (14 women); includes 8 minority (2 African Americans, 1 Asian American or Pacific Islander, 1 Hispanic American, 4 Native Americans), 2 international. 25 applicants, 16% accepted, 4 enrolled. In 2001, 8 degrees awarded.
**Degree requirements:** For doctorate, thesis/dissertation, general exam.
**Entrance requirements:** For doctorate, GRE General Test, TOEFL, master's degree, minimum graduate GPA of 3.25. *Application fee:* $25 ($50 for international students).
**Expenses:** Tuition, state resident: full-time $2,208; part-time $92 per credit hour. Tuition, nonresident: part-time $297 per credit hour. Tuition and fees vary according to course level, course load and program.
**Financial support:** In 2001–02, 21 students received support, including 2 fellowships (averaging $2,200 per year); research assistantships with partial tuition reimbursements available, teaching assistantships with partial tuition reimbursements available, career-related internships or fieldwork, Federal Work-Study, institutionally sponsored loans, traineeships, tuition waivers (partial), and unspecified assistantships also available. Financial award application deadline: 3/1; financial award applicants required to submit FAFSA.
**Faculty research:** Marriage and family, health psychology, psychological measurement and assessment, cross-cultural, supervision and training.
**Application contact:** Dr. Cal Stoltenberg, Director of Training, 405-325-5974, *Fax:* 405-325-6655, *E-mail:* cstoltenberg@ou.edu.

■ **UNIVERSITY OF PENNSYLVANIA**
**Graduate School of Education, Division of Psychology in Education, Program in Psychological Services, Philadelphia, PA 19104**
**AWARDS** Counseling psychology (MS Ed).
**Degree requirements:** For master's, exam.
**Entrance requirements:** For master's, GRE General Test.
**Expenses:** Tuition: Part-time $12,875 per semester.
**Faculty research:** Counseling in school, college, or agency.

# ■ UNIVERSITY OF PHOENIX–NEW MEXICO CAMPUS

**College of Counseling and Human Services, Albuquerque, NM 87109-4645**

**AWARDS** Marriage and family therapy (MC); mental health counseling (MC). Evening/weekend programs available. Postbaccalaureate distance learning degree programs offered (no on-campus study).

**Students:** 34 full-time. Average age 34. In 2001, 16 degrees awarded.
**Degree requirements:** For master's, thesis or alternative.
**Entrance requirements:** For master's, TOEFL, Comprehensive Cognitive Assessment, minimum undergraduate GPA of 2.5, 3 years work experience. *Application deadline:* Applications are processed on a rolling basis. *Application fee:* $85.
**Expenses:** Tuition: Full-time $7,336; part-time $306 per credit. Full-time tuition and fees vary according to program.
**Financial support:** Applicants required to submit FAFSA.
Dr. Patrick Romine, Dean, 480-557-1074, *E-mail:* patrick.romine@phoenix.edu. *Web site:* http://www.phoenix.edu/

# ■ UNIVERSITY OF PHOENIX–PHOENIX CAMPUS

**College of Counseling and Human Services, Phoenix, AZ 85040-1958**

**AWARDS** Community counseling (MC); marriage, family, and child therapy (MC); mental health counseling (MC). Evening/weekend programs available. Postbaccalaureate distance learning degree programs offered (no on-campus study).

**Students:** 241 full-time. Average age 33. In 2001, 70 degrees awarded.
**Degree requirements:** For master's, thesis or alternative.
**Entrance requirements:** For master's, TOEFL, comprehensive cognitive assessment (COCA), portfolio. *Application deadline:* Applications are processed on a rolling basis. *Application fee:* $85.
**Expenses:** Contact institution.
**Financial support:** Applicants required to submit FAFSA.
Dr. Patrick Romine, Dean, 480-557-1074 Ext. 1074, *E-mail:* patrick.romine@phoenix.edu.
**Application contact:** 480-966-7400. *Web site:* http://www.phoenix.edu/

# ■ UNIVERSITY OF RHODE ISLAND

**Graduate School, College of Human Science and Services, Department of Human Development, Counseling, and Family Studies, Kingston, RI 02881**

**AWARDS** Guidance and counseling (MS); marriage and family therapy (MS). Evening/weekend programs available.

**Entrance requirements:** For master's, GRE or MAT. *Application deadline:* For fall admission, 4/15 (priority date); for spring admission, 11/15. Applications are processed on a rolling basis. *Application fee:* $35.
**Expenses:** Tuition, state resident: full-time $3,756; part-time $209 per credit. Tuition, nonresident: full-time $10,774; part-time $599 per credit. Required fees: $1,586; $76 per credit. One-time fee: $60 full-time.
**Financial support:** Career-related internships or fieldwork available.
Dr. Barbara Newman, Chair, 401-874-2440.

# ■ UNIVERSITY OF SAINT FRANCIS

**Graduate School, Department of Psychology and Counseling, Fort Wayne, IN 46808-3994**

**AWARDS** General psychology (MS); mental health counseling (MS); school counseling (MS Ed). Part-time and evening/weekend programs available.

**Faculty:** 3 full-time (1 woman).
**Students:** 9 full-time (7 women), 31 part-time (26 women); includes 4 minority (3 African Americans, 1 Asian American or Pacific Islander), 1 international. Average age 34. 16 applicants, 88% accepted. In 2001, 6 degrees awarded.
**Entrance requirements:** For master's, interview, minimum undergraduate GPA of 3.0. *Application deadline:* For fall admission, 7/1; for spring admission, 11/1. Applications are processed on a rolling basis. *Application fee:* $20.
**Expenses:** Tuition: Part-time $430 per hour. Required fees: $10 per hour.
**Financial support:** In 2001–02, 4 students received support. Federal Work-Study, scholarships/grants, and unspecified assistantships available.
Dr. Rolf Daniel, Chair, 260-434-3233, *Fax:* 260-434-7562, *E-mail:* rdaniel@sf.edu.
**Application contact:** David McMahan, Director of Admissions, 260-434-3264, *Fax:* 260-434-7590, *E-mail:* dmcmahan@sf.edu.

# ■ UNIVERSITY OF ST. THOMAS

**Graduate Studies, Graduate School of Professional Psychology, St. Paul, MN 55105-1096**

**AWARDS** Counseling psychology (MA, Psy D); family psychology (Certificate). Part-time and evening/weekend programs available.

**Faculty:** 8 full-time (4 women), 15 part-time/adjunct (8 women).
**Students:** 42 full-time (34 women), 124 part-time (98 women); includes 19 minority (8 African Americans, 6 Asian Americans or Pacific Islanders, 4 Hispanic Americans, 1 Native American). Average age 34. 41 applicants, 76% accepted, 29 enrolled. In 2001, 34 master's, 8 doctorates, 6 other advanced degrees awarded.
**Degree requirements:** For master's, practicum; for doctorate, thesis/dissertation, qualifying exam, practicum, internship, comprehensive exam.
**Entrance requirements:** For master's and doctorate, MAT or GRE, minimum GPA of 2.75. *Application deadline:* For fall admission, 10/1; for winter admission, 2/1; for spring admission, 4/1. *Application fee:* $50.
**Expenses:** Contact institution.
**Financial support:** In 2001–02, 91 students received support; fellowships, research assistantships, institutionally sponsored loans and scholarships/grants available. Support available to part-time students. Financial award application deadline: 4/1.
**Faculty research:** Elderly, eating disorders, anxiety.
Dr. Burton Nolan, Dean, 651-962-4650, *Fax:* 651-962-4651, *E-mail:* bnolan@stthomas.edu.
**Application contact:** Dr. Mary M. Brant, Assistant Professor, 651-962-4641, *Fax:* 651-962-4651, *E-mail:* mmbrant@stthomas.edu.

# ■ UNIVERSITY OF SAN FRANCISCO

**School of Education, Department of Counseling Psychology, San Francisco, CA 94117-1080**

**AWARDS** Counseling (MA), including educational counseling, life transitions counseling, marital and family therapy; counseling psychology (Psy D).

**Faculty:** 7 full-time (3 women), 55 part-time/adjunct (29 women).
**Students:** 131 full-time (106 women), 68 part-time (56 women); includes 58 minority (11 African Americans, 17 Asian Americans or Pacific Islanders, 27 Hispanic Americans, 3 Native Americans), 8 international. Average age 35. 165 applicants, 93% accepted, 75 enrolled. In 2001, 79 master's, 9 doctorates awarded.

**Degree requirements:** For doctorate, thesis/dissertation.
**Entrance requirements:** For doctorate, GRE General Test. *Application fee:* $55 ($65 for international students).
**Expenses:** Tuition: Full-time $14,400; part-time $800 per unit. Tuition and fees vary according to degree level, campus/location and program.
**Financial support:** In 2001–02, 134 students received support; fellowships, research assistantships, teaching assistantships available. Financial award application deadline: 3/2; financial award applicants required to submit FAFSA.
Dr. Elena Flores, Chair, 415-422-6868.

## ■ THE UNIVERSITY OF SCRANTON

**Graduate School, Department of Counseling and Human Services, Scranton, PA 18510**
**AWARDS** Community counseling (MS); professional counseling (CAGS); rehabilitation counseling (MS); school counseling (MS). Part-time and evening/weekend programs available.
**Faculty:** 8 full-time (5 women), 6 part-time/adjunct (2 women).
**Students:** 35 full-time (32 women), 97 part-time (75 women); includes 4 minority (1 African American, 2 Asian Americans or Pacific Islanders, 1 Hispanic American), 4 international. Average age 32. 60 applicants, 85% accepted. In 2001, 33 degrees awarded.
**Degree requirements:** For master's, capstone experience.
**Entrance requirements:** For master's, TOEFL, minimum GPA of 2.75. *Application deadline:* For fall admission, 3/1. *Application fee:* $50.
**Expenses:** Tuition: Part-time $539 per credit. Required fees: $25 per term.
**Financial support:** In 2001–02, 9 teaching assistantships with full tuition reimbursements (averaging $6,790 per year) were awarded; career-related internships or fieldwork, Federal Work-Study, and teaching fellowships also available. Support available to part-time students. Financial award application deadline: 3/1.
Dr. Oliver J. Morgan, Chair, 570-941-6171, *Fax:* 570-941-4201, *E-mail:* morgan1@scranton.edu. *Web site:* http://academic.uofs.edu/department/chs/

## ■ UNIVERSITY OF SOUTHERN CALIFORNIA

**Graduate School, School of Education, Department of Counseling Psychology, Los Angeles, CA 90089**
**AWARDS** College student personnel services (MS); counseling psychology (MS, PhD);

educational psychology (PhD); marriage, family and child counseling (MFCC); pupil personnel services (K–12) (MS).
**Degree requirements:** For doctorate, thesis/dissertation.
**Entrance requirements:** For master's and doctorate, GRE General Test.
**Expenses:** Tuition: Full-time $25,060; part-time $844 per unit. Required fees: $473.

## ■ THE UNIVERSITY OF TENNESSEE

**Graduate School, College of Education, Program in Education, Knoxville, TN 37996**
**AWARDS** Art education (MS); counseling education (PhD); counseling psychology (PhD); cultural studies in education (PhD); curriculum (MS, Ed S); curriculum education research and evaluation (PhD); curriculum, educational research and evaluation (Ed D); early childhood education (PhD); early childhood special education (MS); education of deaf and hard of hearing (MS); education psychology (PhD); educational administration and policy studies (Ed D, PhD); educational administration and supervision (Ed S); educational psychology (Ed D); elementary education (MS, Ed S); elementary teaching (MS); English education (MS, Ed S); exercise science (PhD); foreign language/ESL education (MS, Ed S); industrial technology (PhD); instructional technology (MS, Ed D, Ed S); literacy, language education and ESL education (PhD); literacy, language education, and ESL education (Ed D); mathematics education (MS, Ed S); modified and comprehensive special education (MS); reading education (MS, Ed S); school counseling (Ed S); school psychology (PhD, Ed S); science education (MS, Ed S); secondary teaching (MS); social foundations (MS); social science education (MS, Ed S); socio-cultural foundations of sports and education (PhD); special education (Ed S); teacher education (Ed D, PhD). Part-time and evening/weekend programs available.
**Students:** 493 full-time (365 women), 258 part-time (173 women); includes 54 minority (43 African Americans, 6 Asian Americans or Pacific Islanders, 2 Hispanic Americans, 3 Native Americans), 34 international. 420 applicants, 50% accepted. In 2001, 344 master's, 52 doctorates, 26 other advanced degrees awarded.
**Degree requirements:** For master's and Ed S, thesis optional; for doctorate, variable foreign language requirement, thesis/dissertation.
**Entrance requirements:** For master's, TOEFL, minimum GPA of 2.7; for doctorate and Ed S, GRE General Test, TOEFL, minimum GPA of 2.7. *Application deadline:* For fall admission, 2/1 (priority

date). Applications are processed on a rolling basis. *Application fee:* $35. Electronic applications accepted.
**Expenses:** Tuition, state resident: full-time $4,280; part-time $233 per hour. Tuition, nonresident: full-time $12,066; part-time $666 per hour. Tuition and fees vary according to program.
**Financial support:** In 2001–02, 4 fellowships, 9 teaching assistantships were awarded. Career-related internships or fieldwork, Federal Work-Study, institutionally sponsored loans, and unspecified assistantships also available. Financial award application deadline: 2/1; financial award applicants required to submit FAFSA.
Dr. Lester Knight, Head, 865-974-0907, *Fax:* 865-974-8718, *E-mail:* lknight@utk.edu.

## ■ THE UNIVERSITY OF TEXAS AT AUSTIN

**Graduate School, College of Education, Department of Educational Psychology, Austin, TX 78712-1111**
**AWARDS** Academic educational psychology (M Ed, MA); counseling education (M Ed); counseling psychology (PhD); human development and education (PhD); learning cognition and instruction (PhD); quantitative methods (PhD); school psychology (PhD).
**Faculty:** 30 full-time (16 women), 17 part-time/adjunct (8 women).
**Students:** 233 full-time (191 women), 55 part-time (44 women); includes 52 minority (13 African Americans, 8 Asian Americans or Pacific Islanders, 29 Hispanic Americans, 2 Native Americans), 36 international. Average age 29. 292 applicants, 47% accepted, 70 enrolled. In 2001, 20 master's, 38 doctorates awarded.
**Degree requirements:** For master's, thesis optional; for doctorate, thesis/dissertation.
**Entrance requirements:** For master's and doctorate, GRE General Test, 3 letters of recommendation. *Application deadline:* For fall admission, 1/15 (priority date); for winter admission, 3/1 (priority date); for spring admission, 10/1 (priority date). Applications are processed on a rolling basis. *Application fee:* $50 ($75 for international students).
**Expenses:** Tuition, state resident: full-time $3,159. Tuition, nonresident: full-time $6,957. Tuition and fees vary according to program.
**Financial support:** In 2001–02, 21 fellowships with full and partial tuition reimbursements (averaging $1,700 per year), 33 research assistantships (averaging $4,500 per year), 116 teaching assistantships (averaging $4,250 per year) were awarded. Career-related internships or

*The University of Texas at Austin (continued)*

fieldwork, Federal Work-Study, institutionally sponsored loans, scholarships/grants, tuition waivers (full and partial), and unspecified assistantships also available. Financial award application deadline: 1/15. Dr. Edmund T. Emmer, Department Chair, 512-471-4155 Ext. 22, *Fax:* 512-471-1288, *E-mail:* emmer@mail.utexas.edu. **Application contact:** Dr. Cindy I. Carlson, Graduate Adviser, 512-471-4155 Ext. 24, *Fax:* 512-471-1288, *E-mail:* cindy.carlson@mail.utexas.edu. *Web site:* http://www.edb.utexas.edu/coe/depts/edp/edp.html

## ■ THE UNIVERSITY OF TEXAS AT TYLER

**Graduate Studies, College of Education and Psychology, Department of Psychology, Tyler, TX 75799-0001**

**AWARDS** Clinical psychology (MS); counseling psychology (MA); interdisciplinary studies (MS, MSIS); school counseling (MA). Part-time and evening/weekend programs available.

**Faculty:** 7 full-time (4 women), 1 (woman) part-time/adjunct.

**Students:** 30 full-time (26 women), 52 part-time (48 women); includes 9 minority (5 African Americans, 1 Asian American or Pacific Islander, 2 Hispanic Americans, 1 Native American), 3 international. Average age 30. 23 applicants, 100% accepted, 16 enrolled. In 2001, 18 degrees awarded.

**Degree requirements:** For master's, comprehensive exam and/or thesis.

**Entrance requirements:** For master's, GRE General Test, GRE Subject Test, minimum GPA of 3.0. *Application deadline:* For fall admission, 2/1; for spring admission, 10/1. *Application fee:* $0 ($50 for international students). Electronic applications accepted.

**Expenses:** Tuition, state resident: part-time $44 per credit hour. Tuition, nonresident: part-time $262 per credit hour. Required fees: $58 per credit hour. $76 per semester.

**Financial support:** Teaching assistantships, career-related internships or fieldwork, Federal Work-Study, and institutionally sponsored loans available. Support available to part-time students. Financial award application deadline: 7/1.

**Faculty research:** Incest, aging, depression, neuropsychology, child psychopathology.

Dr. Henry L. Schreiber, Chairperson, 903-566-7239, *Fax:* 903-565-5656, *E-mail:* hschreiber@mail.uttyl.edu.

**Application contact:** Dr. Robert F. McClure, Graduate Adviser, 903-566-7435,

*Fax:* 903-566-7065, *E-mail:* rmcclure@mail.uttyl.edu. *Web site:* http://www.uttyl.edu/psychology/grad.htm/

## ■ UNIVERSITY OF THE PACIFIC

**Graduate School, School of Education, Department of Educational and Counseling Psychology, Stockton, CA 95211-0197**

**AWARDS** Educational counseling and psychology (MA); educational psychology (MA, Ed D); educational research (MA); school psychology (Ed D, PhD, Ed S).

**Students:** 9 full-time (8 women), 17 part-time (16 women); includes 5 minority (1 African American, 3 Hispanic Americans, 1 Native American), 2 international. Average age 35. 19 applicants, 32% accepted, 4 enrolled. In 2001, 12 master's, 1 doctorate awarded.

**Degree requirements:** For master's, thesis (for some programs); for doctorate, thesis/dissertation.

**Entrance requirements:** For master's and doctorate, GRE General Test, GRE Subject Test. *Application deadline:* For fall admission, 3/1 (priority date); for spring admission, 10/1 (priority date). Applications are processed on a rolling basis. *Application fee:* $50.

**Expenses:** Tuition: Full-time $21,150; part-time $661 per unit. Required fees: $375.

**Financial support:** In 2001–02, 6 teaching assistantships were awarded. Financial award application deadline: 3/1.

Dr. Linda Webster, Chairperson, 209-946-2559, *E-mail:* lwebster@uop.edu.

## ■ UNIVERSITY OF VERMONT

**Graduate College, College of Education and Social Services, Department of Integrated Professional Studies, Counseling Program, Burlington, VT 05405**

**AWARDS** MS.

**Entrance requirements:** For master's, GRE General Test.

**Expenses:** Tuition, state resident: part-time $335 per credit. Tuition, nonresident: part-time $838 per credit.

**Faculty research:** Women and tenure, counseling children and adolescents. *Web site:* http://www.uvm.edu/~cslgprog/

**Find an in-depth description at www.petersons.com/gradchannel.**

## ■ UNIVERSITY OF WISCONSIN–MADISON

**Graduate School, School of Education, Department of Counseling Psychology, Program in Counseling Psychology, Madison, WI 53706-1380**

**AWARDS** PhD.

**Degree requirements:** For doctorate, thesis/dissertation. *Application fee:* $38.

**Expenses:** Tuition, state resident: full-time $7,361; part-time $399 per credit. Tuition, nonresident: full-time $20,499; part-time $1,282 per credit. Required fees: $34 per credit. Full-time tuition and fees vary according to course load, program, reciprocity agreements and student level. Dr. Stephen M. Quintana, Chair, Department of Counseling Psychology, 608-262-0461.

## ■ UNIVERSITY OF WISCONSIN–STOUT

**Graduate School, College of Human Development, Program in Guidance and Counseling, Menomonie, WI 54751**

**AWARDS** MS. Part-time programs available.

**Students:** 71 full-time (56 women), 44 part-time (35 women); includes 5 minority (1 African American, 3 Asian Americans or Pacific Islanders, 1 Native American), 1 international. 47 applicants, 60% accepted, 28 enrolled. In 2001, 41 degrees awarded.

**Degree requirements:** For master's, thesis.

*Application deadline:* For fall admission, 2/1; for spring admission, 10/1. *Application fee:* $45.

**Expenses:** Tuition, state resident: full-time $4,915. Tuition, nonresident: full-time $12,553.

**Financial support:** In 2001–02, 6 research assistantships were awarded; teaching assistantships, Federal Work-Study, scholarships/grants, and tuition waivers (full and partial) also available. Support available to part-time students. Financial award application deadline: 4/1; financial award applicants required to submit FAFSA.

Dr. Mary Hopkins-Best, Director, 715-232-1168, *E-mail:* hopkinsbestm@uwstout.edu.

**Application contact:** Anne E. Johnson, Graduate Student Evaluator, 715-232-1322, *Fax:* 715-232-2413, *E-mail:* johnsona@uwstout.edu.

## ■ UNIVERSITY OF WISCONSIN–STOUT

**Graduate School, College of Human Development, Program in Mental Health Counseling, Menomonie, WI 54751**

**AWARDS** MS. Part-time programs available.

**Students:** 19 applicants, 58% accepted, 10 enrolled.

**Degree requirements:** For master's, thesis optional.

*Application deadline:* For fall admission, 2/1; for winter admission, 10/1. *Application fee:* $45.

**Expenses:** Tuition, state resident: full-time $4,915. Tuition, nonresident: full-time $12,553.

**Financial support:** In 2001–02, 5 research assistantships were awarded; teaching assistantships, Federal Work-Study and tuition waivers (full and partial) also available. Support available to part-time students. Financial award application deadline: 4/1; financial award applicants required to submit FAFSA.

Dr. Gary Rockwood, Director, 715-232-1303, *E-mail:* rockwoodg@uwstat.edu.

**Application contact:** Anne E. Johnson, Graduate Student Evaluator, 715-232-1322, *Fax:* 715-232-2413, *E-mail:* johnsona@uwstout.edu.

# ■ UTAH STATE UNIVERSITY

**School of Graduate Studies, College of Education, Department of Psychology, Logan, UT 84322**

**AWARDS** Clinical/counseling/school psychology (PhD); research and evaluation methodology (PhD); school counseling (MS); school psychology (MS). Part-time and evening/weekend programs available. Postbaccalaureate distance learning degree programs offered (no on-campus study).

**Faculty:** 18 full-time (8 women), 40 part-time/adjunct (15 women).

**Students:** 55 full-time (31 women), 80 part-time (62 women); includes 10 minority (3 Asian Americans or Pacific Islanders, 1 Hispanic American, 6 Native Americans), 3 international. Average age 34. 138 applicants, 38% accepted. In 2001, 31 master's, 7 doctorates awarded. Terminal master's awarded for partial completion of doctoral program.

**Degree requirements:** For master's, thesis (for some programs); for doctorate, thesis/dissertation.

**Entrance requirements:** For master's and doctorate, GRE General Test, TOEFL, minimum GPA of 3.5. *Application deadline:* For fall admission, 1/15; for spring admission, 10/15. Applications are processed on a rolling basis. *Application fee:* $40.

**Expenses:** Tuition, state resident: full-time $1,693. Tuition, nonresident: full-time $4,233. Required fees: $501. Tuition and fees vary according to program.

**Financial support:** In 2001–02, 5 fellowships with full and partial tuition reimbursements (averaging $12,000 per year), 25 research assistantships with full and partial tuition reimbursements (averaging $8,500 per year), 18 teaching assistantships with full and partial tuition reimbursements (averaging $7,000 per

year) were awarded. Career-related internships or fieldwork, Federal Work-Study, institutionally sponsored loans, scholarships/grants, tuition waivers (partial), and unspecified assistantships also available. Financial award application deadline: 2/1.

**Faculty research:** Hearing loss detection in infancy, ADHD, eating disorders, domestic violence, neuropsychology. David M. Stein, Head, 435-797-1460, *Fax:* 435-797-1448, *E-mail:* davids@coe.usu.edu.

**Application contact:** Sheila Jessie, Staff Assistant IV, 435-797-1449, *Fax:* 435-797-1448, *E-mail:* sheilaj@coe.usu.edu. *Web site:* http://www.coe.usu.edu/psyc/ndex.html

# ■ VALDOSTA STATE UNIVERSITY

**Graduate School, College of Education, Department of Psychology and Guidance, Valdosta, GA 31698**

**AWARDS** Clinical/counseling psychology (MS); industrial/organizational psychology (MS); school counseling (M Ed, Ed S); school psychology (M Ed, Ed S). Evening/weekend programs available.

**Faculty:** 13 full-time (2 women).

**Students:** 40 full-time (30 women), 62 part-time (54 women); includes 10 minority (7 African Americans, 1 Asian American or Pacific Islander, 1 Hispanic American, 1 Native American). Average age 26. 67 applicants, 75% accepted. In 2001, 17 degrees awarded.

**Degree requirements:** For master's, thesis or alternative, comprehensive written and/or oral exams; for Ed S, thesis.

**Entrance requirements:** For master's and Ed S, GRE General Test or MAT. *Application deadline:* For fall admission, 7/1; for spring admission, 11/15. Applications are processed on a rolling basis. *Application fee:* $20. Electronic applications accepted.

**Expenses:** Tuition, state resident: full-time $1,746; part-time $97 per hour. Tuition, nonresident: full-time $6,966; part-time $387 per hour. Required fees: $594; $297 per semester.

**Financial support:** In 2001–02, 2 research assistantships with full tuition reimbursements (averaging $2,452 per year) were awarded; institutionally sponsored loans and unspecified assistantships also available. Support available to part-time students. Financial award application deadline: 7/1; financial award applicants required to submit FAFSA.

**Faculty research:** Using Bender-Gestalt to predict graphomotor dimensions of the draw-a-person test, neurobehavioral hemispheric dominance. Dr. R. Bauer, Head, 229-333-5930, *Fax:* 229-259-5576, *E-mail:* bbauer@valdosta.edu.

# ■ VALPARAISO UNIVERSITY

**Graduate Division, Department of Psychology, Valparaiso, IN 46383-6493**

**AWARDS** Applied behavioral science (MA); clinical mental health counseling (MA); counseling (MA). Part-time and evening/weekend programs available.

**Students:** 14 full-time (10 women), 14 part-time (10 women); includes 2 minority (1 Asian American or Pacific Islander, 1 Hispanic American), 1 international. Average age 33. In 2001, 8 degrees awarded.

**Degree requirements:** For master's, thesis or alternative, internship.

**Entrance requirements:** For master's, GRE General Test (MA), minimum GPA of 3.0. *Application deadline:* Applications are processed on a rolling basis. *Application fee:* $30.

**Expenses:** Tuition: Full-time $5,400; part-time $300 per credit.

**Financial support:** Career-related internships or fieldwork, Federal Work-Study, and institutionally sponsored loans available. Financial award applicants required to submit FAFSA.

**Faculty research:** Sex roles, environmental psychology, human reproduction, treatment of adolescent assault victims, neuropsychological assessment. Dr. Jody Esper, Chair, 219-464-5443, *E-mail:* jody.esper@valpo.edu.

**Application contact:** Graduate Division Office, 219-464-5313.

# ■ VIRGINIA COMMONWEALTH UNIVERSITY

**School of Graduate Studies, College of Humanities and Sciences, Department of Psychology, Program in Counseling Psychology, Richmond, VA 23284-9005**

**AWARDS** PhD.

**Students:** 20 full-time, 18 part-time; includes 8 minority (5 African Americans, 2 Asian Americans or Pacific Islanders, 1 Hispanic American). 88 applicants, 7% accepted. In 2001, 4 doctorates awarded.

**Degree requirements:** For doctorate, thesis/dissertation.

**Entrance requirements:** For doctorate, GRE General Test, GRE Subject Test. *Application deadline:* For fall admission, 1/15. *Application fee:* $30.

**Expenses:** Tuition, state resident: full-time $4,276; part-time $238 per credit. Tuition, nonresident: full-time $12,672; part-time $704 per credit. Required fees: $1,167; $43 per credit.

**Financial support:** Fellowships, research assistantships, teaching assistantships, Federal Work-Study, institutionally

*Virginia Commonwealth University (continued)*

sponsored loans, and scholarships/grants available. Support available to part-time students.

**Faculty research:** Life span development counseling, couple/family therapy, health psychology, psychotherapy.

**Application contact:** DeWitt Pritchard, Counseling Program Assistant, 804-828-2975. *Web site:* http://www.vcu.edu/hasweb/psy/psych.html

■ **VIRGINIA COMMONWEALTH UNIVERSITY**

**School of Graduate Studies, School of Allied Health Professions, Program in Patient Counseling, Richmond, VA 23284-9005**

**AWARDS** MS, CPC.

**Students:** 11 full-time, 12 part-time; includes 6 minority (4 African Americans, 2 Asian Americans or Pacific Islanders). 13 applicants, 77% accepted. In 2001, 3 degrees awarded.

**Entrance requirements:** For master's, GRE General Test. *Application deadline:* Applications are processed on a rolling basis. *Application fee:* $30.

**Expenses:** Tuition, state resident: full-time $4,276; part-time $238 per credit. Tuition, nonresident: full-time $12,672; part-time $704 per credit. Required fees: $1,167; $43 per credit.

**Financial support:** Application deadline: 3/1.

Dr. Alexander F. Tartaglia, Director, 804-828-0540, *E-mail:* atartaglia@hsu.vcu.edu. *Web site:* http://views.vcu.edu/sahp/rehab/

■ **WALLA WALLA COLLEGE**

**Graduate School, School of Education and Psychology, Specialization in Counseling Psychology, College Place, WA 99324-1198**

**AWARDS** MA. Part-time programs available.

**Faculty:** 9 full-time (3 women), 3 part-time/adjunct (0 women).

**Students:** 4 full-time (all women), 17 part-time (12 women); includes 3 minority (2 African Americans, 1 Hispanic American). 3 applicants, 100% accepted, 2 enrolled. In 2001, 8 degrees awarded.

**Degree requirements:** For master's, thesis (for some programs). *Median time to degree:* Master's–2 years full-time.

**Entrance requirements:** For master's, GRE General Test, minimum GPA of 2.75, previous course work in education and psychology. *Application deadline:* For fall admission, 4/1 (priority date). Applications are processed on a rolling basis. *Application fee:* $50. Electronic applications accepted.

**Expenses:** Tuition: Full-time $15,561; part-time $399 per credit.

**Financial support:** In 2001–02, 3 teaching assistantships with partial tuition reimbursements (averaging $2,500 per year) were awarded. Financial award application deadline: 4/1; financial award applicants required to submit FAFSA.

**Faculty research:** Instructional psychology, moral development.

**Application contact:** Dr. Joe G. Galusha, Dean of Graduate Studies, 509-527-2421, *Fax:* 509-527-2253, *E-mail:* galujo@wwc.edu.

■ **WASHINGTON STATE UNIVERSITY**

**Graduate School, College of Education, Department of Educational Leadership and Counseling Psychology, Program in Counseling Psychology, Pullman, WA 99164**

**AWARDS** MA, PhD.

**Faculty:** 8 full-time, 4 part-time/adjunct.

**Students:** 73 full-time (48 women), 28 part-time (20 women); includes 30 minority (6 African Americans, 6 Asian Americans or Pacific Islanders, 12 Hispanic Americans, 6 Native Americans). Average age 27. In 2001, 10 master's, 3 doctorates awarded. Terminal master's awarded for partial completion of doctoral program.

**Degree requirements:** For master's, oral or written exam, thesis optional; for doctorate, thesis/dissertation, oral and written exam.

**Entrance requirements:** For master's and doctorate, GRE General Test, minimum GPA of 3.0. *Application deadline:* For fall admission, 2/1. *Application fee:* $35. Electronic applications accepted.

**Expenses:** Tuition, state resident: full-time $6,088; part-time $304 per semester. Tuition, nonresident: full-time $14,918; part-time $746 per semester. Tuition and fees vary according to program.

**Financial support:** In 2001–02, 12 research assistantships with full and partial tuition reimbursements were awarded; teaching assistantships, career-related internships or fieldwork, Federal Work-Study, institutionally sponsored loans, tuition waivers (partial), and staff assistantships, teaching associateships also available. Financial award application deadline: 4/1; financial award applicants required to submit FAFSA.

**Faculty research:** Hypnosis supervision, multicultural counseling, American Indian mental health, eating disorders. *Total annual research expenditures:* $450,000.

Brian McNeill, Associate Chair and Director of Training, 509-335-6477, *Fax:* 509-335-7977, *E-mail:* mcneill@mail.wsu.edu.

*Web site:* http://www.educ.wsu.edu/ELCP/Counseling_Psych/index.html

■ **WEBSTER UNIVERSITY**

**College of Arts and Sciences, Department of Behavioral and Social Sciences, Program in Counseling, St. Louis, MO 63119-3194**

**AWARDS** MA.

**Students:** 635 full-time (530 women), 514 part-time (425 women); includes 623 minority (530 African Americans, 8 Asian Americans or Pacific Islanders, 81 Hispanic Americans, 4 Native Americans), 17 international. Average age 35. In 2001, 338 degrees awarded.

*Application deadline:* Applications are processed on a rolling basis. *Application fee:* $25 ($50 for international students).

**Expenses:** Tuition: Full-time $7,164; part-time $398 per credit hour.

**Financial support:** Federal Work-Study available. Support available to part-time students. Financial award application deadline: 4/1; financial award applicants required to submit FAFSA.

William Huddleston Berry, Head, 314-968-6978, *Fax:* 314-963-6094.

**Application contact:** Denise Harrell, Associate Director of Graduate and Evening Student Admissions, 314-968-6983, *Fax:* 314-968-7116, *E-mail:* gadmit@webster.edu.

■ **WESTERN MICHIGAN UNIVERSITY**

**Graduate College, College of Education, Department of Counselor Education and Counseling Psychology, Kalamazoo, MI 49008-5202**

**AWARDS** Counseling psychology (PhD); counselor education (MA, Ed D, PhD); counselor education and counseling psychology (MA, PhD); counselor psychology (MA); marriage and family therapy (MA).

**Faculty:** 19 full-time (5 women), 2 part-time/adjunct.

**Students:** 328 full-time (258 women), 201 part-time (158 women); includes 57 minority (45 African Americans, 4 Asian Americans or Pacific Islanders, 6 Hispanic Americans, 2 Native Americans), 19 international. 294 applicants, 81% accepted, 101 enrolled. In 2001, 108 master's, 13 doctorates awarded.

**Degree requirements:** For doctorate, thesis/dissertation, oral exams.

**Entrance requirements:** For doctorate, GRE General Test. *Application deadline:* For fall admission, 1/15. Applications are processed on a rolling basis. *Application fee:* $25.

**Expenses:** Tuition, state resident: part-time $186 per credit hour. Tuition, nonresident: part-time $442 per credit hour. Required fees: $602. One-time fee: $132 part-time. Tuition and fees vary according to course load.
**Financial support:** Fellowships, research assistantships, teaching assistantships, Federal Work-Study available. Financial award application deadline: 2/15; financial award applicants required to submit FAFSA.
Dr. Joseph Morris, Chairperson, 616-387-5100.
**Application contact:** Admissions and Orientation, 616-387-2000, *Fax:* 616-387-2355.

## ■ WESTERN WASHINGTON UNIVERSITY

**Graduate School, College of Arts and Sciences, Department of Psychology, Program in Mental Health Counseling, Bellingham, WA 98225-5996**

AWARDS MS.

**Degree requirements:** For master's, thesis optional.
**Entrance requirements:** For master's, GRE General Test, TOEFL, minimum GPA of 3.0 in last 60 semester hours or last 90 quarter hours.

## ■ WESTFIELD STATE COLLEGE

**Division of Graduate Studies and Continuing Education, Program in Counseling/Clinical Psychology, Westfield, MA 01086**

AWARDS MA. Part-time and evening/weekend programs available.

**Faculty:** 9 part-time/adjunct (6 women).
**Students:** 22 full-time (20 women), 30 part-time (19 women). Average age 32. In 2001, 13 degrees awarded.
**Degree requirements:** For master's, comprehensive exam.
**Entrance requirements:** For master's, GRE General Test, MAT, minimum undergraduate GPA of 2.7. *Application deadline:* Applications are processed on a rolling basis. *Application fee:* $30.
**Expenses:** Tuition, state resident: part-time $155 per credit. Tuition, nonresident: part-time $165 per credit.
**Financial support:** In 2001–02, 5 research assistantships (averaging $1,600 per year) were awarded; teaching assistantships, career-related internships or fieldwork, Federal Work-Study, and tuition waivers (full and partial) also available. Support available to part-time students. Financial award application deadline: 4/1; financial award applicants required to submit CSS PROFILE.

Dr. Ricki Kantrowitz, Co-Director, 413-572-5376.
**Application contact:** Russ Leary, Admissions Clerk, 413-572-8022, *Fax:* 413-572-5227, *E-mail:* rleary@wisdom.wsc.mass.edu.

## ■ WESTFIELD STATE COLLEGE

**Division of Graduate Studies and Continuing Education, Program in Mental Health Counseling/Psychology, Westfield, MA 01086**

AWARDS MA. Part-time and evening/weekend programs available.

**Faculty:** 9 part-time/adjunct (6 women).
**Students:** 22 full-time (20 women), 30 part-time (19 women). Average age 32. In 2001, 13 degrees awarded.
**Degree requirements:** For master's, comprehensive exam.
**Entrance requirements:** For master's, GRE General Test, MAT, minimum undergraduate GPA of 2.7. *Application deadline:* Applications are processed on a rolling basis. *Application fee:* $30.
**Expenses:** Tuition, state resident: part-time $155 per credit. Tuition, nonresident: part-time $165 per credit.
**Financial support:** In 2001–02, 5 research assistantships were awarded; teaching assistantships, career-related internships or fieldwork, Federal Work-Study, and tuition waivers (full and partial) also available. Support available to part-time students. Financial award application deadline: 4/1; financial award applicants required to submit CSS PROFILE.
Dr. Robert Hayes, Co-Director, 413-572-5900.
**Application contact:** Russ Leary, Admissions Clerk, 413-572-8022, *Fax:* 413-572-5227, *E-mail:* rleary@wisdom.wsc.mass.edu.

## ■ WEST VIRGINIA UNIVERSITY

**College of Human Resources and Education, Department of Counseling, Rehabilitation Counseling, and Counseling Psychology, Program in Counseling, Morgantown, WV 26506**

AWARDS MA. Part-time and evening/weekend programs available. Postbaccalaureate distance learning degree programs offered (no on-campus study).

**Students:** 60 full-time (49 women), 57 part-time (39 women); includes 7 minority (3 African Americans, 2 Asian Americans or Pacific Islanders, 2 Native Americans), 1 international. Average age 31. In 2001, 28 degrees awarded.
**Degree requirements:** For master's, content exams.
**Entrance requirements:** For master's, TOEFL, minimum GPA of 2.7. *Application*

*deadline:* For fall admission, 3/15; for spring admission, 10/15. *Application fee:* $45.
**Expenses:** Tuition, state resident: full-time $2,791. Tuition, nonresident: full-time $8,659. Required fees: $1,002. Tuition and fees vary according to program.
**Financial support:** In 2001–02, 3 research assistantships, 11 teaching assistantships were awarded. Career-related internships or fieldwork, Federal Work-Study, institutionally sponsored loans, tuition waivers (full and partial), and graduate recital hall assistantships also available. Financial award application deadline: 2/1; financial award applicants required to submit FAFSA.
**Faculty research:** Career development and placement, family therapy, conflict resolution, interviewing technique, multicultural counseling, rehabilitation psychology.
Cynthia R. Kalodner, Associate Department Chair, 304-293-3807 Ext. 1218, *Fax:* 304-293-4082, *E-mail:* cyndee.kalodner@mail.wvu.edu. *Web site:* http://www.wvu.edu/~cvc/coun/

## ■ WEST VIRGINIA UNIVERSITY

**College of Human Resources and Education, Department of Counseling, Rehabilitation Counseling, and Counseling Psychology, Program in Counseling Psychology, Morgantown, WV 26506**

AWARDS PhD.

**Students:** 19 full-time (10 women), 20 part-time (12 women); includes 7 minority (5 African Americans, 2 Asian Americans or Pacific Islanders), 1 international. Average age 34. In 2001, 7 degrees awarded.
**Degree requirements:** For doctorate, thesis/dissertation, comprehensive exam.
**Entrance requirements:** For doctorate, GRE General Test, TOEFL, interview. *Application deadline:* For fall admission, 1/15. *Application fee:* $45.
**Expenses:** Tuition, state resident: full-time $2,791. Tuition, nonresident: full-time $8,659. Required fees: $1,002. Tuition and fees vary according to program.
**Financial support:** In 2001–02, 3 research assistantships, 8 teaching assistantships were awarded. Financial award application deadline: 2/1.
Cynthia R. Kalodner, Associate Department Chair, 304-293-3807 Ext. 1218, *Fax:* 304-293-4082, *E-mail:* cyndee.kalodner@mail.wvu.edu. *Web site:* http://www.wvu.edu/~crc/cpsyc/

## ■ WILLIAM CAREY COLLEGE

**Graduate School, Program in Psychology, Hattiesburg, MS 39401-5499**

**AWARDS** Counseling psychology (MS); industrial and organizational psychology (MS). Part-time programs available.

**Faculty:** 4 full-time (2 women), 5 part-time/adjunct (3 women).

**Students:** 105 full-time (80 women), 37 part-time (31 women); includes 49 minority (46 African Americans, 1 Asian American or Pacific Islander, 2 Hispanic Americans), 1 international. In 2001, 18 degrees awarded.

**Entrance requirements:** For master's, GRE, minimum GPA of 2.5. *Application fee:* $25.

**Expenses:** Contact institution.

**Financial support:** Fellowships with partial tuition reimbursements, Federal Work-Study available. Support available to part-time students.

**Faculty research:** Counseling, industrial organizations.

Dr. Tommy King, Director, Graduate Psychology, 601-582-6774, *Fax:* 601-582-6454, *E-mail:* tommy.king@wmcarey.edu. *Web site:* http://www.umcarey.edu/

# DEVELOPMENTAL PSYCHOLOGY

## ■ ANDREWS UNIVERSITY

**School of Graduate Studies, School of Education, Department of Educational and Counseling Psychology, Program in Educational and Developmental Psychology, Berrien Springs, MI 49104**

**AWARDS** MA.

**Students:** 6 full-time (5 women), 8 part-time (7 women); includes 2 minority (both African Americans), 9 international. Average age 33. In 2001, 11 degrees awarded.

**Degree requirements:** For master's, thesis optional.

*Application deadline:* Applications are processed on a rolling basis. *Application fee:* $40.

**Expenses:** Tuition: Full-time $12,600; part-time $525 per semester. Required fees: $268. Tuition and fees vary according to degree level.

Dr. Elsie P. Jackson, Program Coordinator, 616-471-3133.

**Application contact:** Carolyn Hurst, Supervisor of Graduate Admission, 800-253-2874, *Fax:* 616-471-3228, *E-mail:* enroll@andrews.edu.

## ■ ARIZONA STATE UNIVERSITY

**Graduate College, College of Liberal Arts and Sciences, Department of Psychology, Tempe, AZ 85287**

**AWARDS** Behavioral neuroscience (PhD); clinical psychology (PhD); cognitive/behavioral systems (PhD); developmental psychology (PhD); environmental psychology (PhD); quantitative research methods (PhD); social psychology (PhD).

**Degree requirements:** For doctorate, thesis/dissertation.

**Entrance requirements:** For doctorate, GRE General Test, GRE Subject Test.

**Faculty research:** Reduction of personal stress, cognitive aspects of motor skills training, behavior analysis and treatment of depression.

## ■ BOSTON COLLEGE

**Lynch Graduate School of Education, Department of Counseling Psychology, Developmental and Educational Psychology, Program in Developmental and Educational Psychology, Chestnut Hill, MA 02467-3800**

**AWARDS** MA, PhD.

**Students:** 24 full-time (21 women), 29 part-time (27 women); includes 8 minority (2 African Americans, 2 Asian Americans or Pacific Islanders, 4 Hispanic Americans), 7 international. 84 applicants, 64% accepted. In 2001, 19 master's, 6 doctorates awarded. Terminal master's awarded for partial completion of doctoral program.

**Degree requirements:** For master's, comprehensive exam; for doctorate, thesis/dissertation, comprehensive exam.

**Entrance requirements:** For master's, GRE General Test or MAT; for doctorate, GRE General Test. *Application fee:* $40.

**Expenses:** Tuition: Full-time $17,664; part-time $8,832 per semester.

**Financial support:** Fellowships with full and partial tuition reimbursements, research assistantships with full and partial tuition reimbursements, teaching assistantships with full and partial tuition reimbursements, career-related internships or fieldwork, Federal Work-Study, scholarships/grants, traineeships, tuition waivers (full and partial), and unspecified assistantships available. Support available to part-time students. Financial award applicants required to submit FAFSA.

**Faculty research:** Facilitating self-control, use of stories in moral development, changing role of educational psychology, prematurity, development of problem-solving strategies.

**Application contact:** Arline Riordan, Graduate Admissions Director, 617-552-4214, *Fax:* 617-552-0812, *E-mail:*

grad.ed.info@bc.edu. *Web site:* http://www.bc.edu/education

## ■ BOWLING GREEN STATE UNIVERSITY

**Graduate College, College of Arts and Sciences, Department of Psychology, Bowling Green, OH 43403**

**AWARDS** Clinical psychology (MA, PhD); developmental psychology (MA, PhD); experimental psychology (MA, PhD); industrial/organizational psychology (MA, PhD); quantitative psychology (MA, PhD).

**Faculty:** 31.

**Students:** 89 full-time (57 women), 27 part-time (18 women); includes 14 minority (3 African Americans, 7 Asian Americans or Pacific Islanders, 4 Hispanic Americans), 9 international. Average age 27. 274 applicants, 15% accepted, 24 enrolled. In 2001, 10 master's, 17 doctorates awarded. Terminal master's awarded for partial completion of doctoral program.

**Degree requirements:** For master's and doctorate, thesis/dissertation.

**Entrance requirements:** For master's and doctorate, GRE General Test, TOEFL. *Application deadline:* For fall admission, 1/15. *Application fee:* $30. Electronic applications accepted.

**Expenses:** Tuition, state resident: full-time $7,376; part-time $342 per credit hour. Tuition, nonresident: full-time $13,628; part-time $640 per credit hour.

**Financial support:** In 2001–02, 30 research assistantships with full tuition reimbursements (averaging $9,452 per year), 32 teaching assistantships with full tuition reimbursements (averaging $9,607 per year) were awarded. Career-related internships or fieldwork, Federal Work-Study, institutionally sponsored loans, tuition waivers (full), and unspecified assistantships also available. Financial award applicants required to submit FAFSA.

**Faculty research:** Personnel psychology, developmental-mathematical models, behavioral medication, brain process, child/adolescent social cognition.

Dr. Dale Klopfer, Chair, 419-372-2733. **Application contact:** Dr. Eric Dubow, Graduate Coordinator, 419-372-2556.

## ■ BRANDEIS UNIVERSITY

**Graduate School of Arts and Sciences, Department of Psychology, Waltham, MA 02454-9110**

**AWARDS** Cognitive neuroscience (PhD); general psychology (MA); social/developmental psychology (PhD). Part-time programs available.

**Faculty:** 18 full-time (4 women), 6 part-time/adjunct (3 women).

**Students:** 25 full-time (18 women); includes 8 minority (1 African American, 5 Asian Americans or Pacific Islanders, 2 Hispanic Americans). Average age 29. 69 applicants, 35% accepted. In 2001, 4 master's, 2 doctorates awarded. Terminal master's awarded for partial completion of doctoral program.
**Degree requirements:** For master's and doctorate, thesis/dissertation.
**Entrance requirements:** For master's, GRE General Test; for doctorate, GRE General Test, GRE Subject Test. *Application deadline:* Applications are processed on a rolling basis. *Application fee:* $60. Electronic applications accepted.
**Expenses:** Tuition: Full-time $27,392. Required fees: $35.
**Financial support:** In 2001–02, 16 students received support, including 12 fellowships with full tuition reimbursements available (averaging $13,600 per year), 4 research assistantships with partial tuition reimbursements available (averaging $2,000 per year); scholarships/grants, traineeships, and tuition waivers (partial) also available. Support available to part-time students. Financial award application deadline: 5/1; financial award applicants required to submit CSS PROFILE or FAFSA.
**Faculty research:** Development, cognition, social aging, perception. *Total annual research expenditures:* $2.2 million.
Margie Lachman, Director of Graduate Studies, 781-736-3255, *Fax:* 781-736-3291, *E-mail:* lachman@brandeis.edu.
**Application contact:** Janice Steinberg, Graduate Admissions Coordinator, 781-736-3303, *Fax:* 781-736-3291, *E-mail:* steinberg@brandeis.edu. *Web site:* http://www.brandeis.edu/departments/psych/

## ■ BRYN MAWR COLLEGE

**Graduate School of Arts and Sciences, Department of Psychology, Bryn Mawr, PA 19010-2899**
**AWARDS** Clinical developmental psychology (PhD). Part-time programs available.
**Students:** 14 full-time (12 women), 22 part-time (all women); includes 2 minority (both Asian Americans or Pacific Islanders). 57 applicants, 7% accepted. In 2001, 1 doctorate awarded.
**Degree requirements:** For doctorate, one foreign language, thesis/dissertation.
**Entrance requirements:** For doctorate, GRE General Test. *Application deadline:* For fall admission, 2/1. *Application fee:* $25.
**Expenses:** Tuition: Full-time $22,260.
**Financial support:** In 2001–02, 6 teaching assistantships were awarded; fellowships, career-related internships or fieldwork, Federal Work-Study, institutionally sponsored loans, and tuition awards also

available. Support available to part-time students. Financial award application deadline: 1/15.
Dr. Leslie Rescorla, Chair, 610-526-5190.
**Application contact:** Graduate School of Arts and Sciences, 610-526-5072.

## ■ CALIFORNIA STATE UNIVERSITY, SAN BERNARDINO

**Graduate Studies, College of Social and Behavioral Sciences, Department of Psychology, Program in Child Development, San Bernardino, CA 92407-2397**
**AWARDS** MA.
**Students:** 10 full-time (all women), 6 part-time (all women); includes 4 minority (1 African American, 3 Hispanic Americans). Average age 39. 24 applicants, 54% accepted. In 2001, 4 degrees awarded.
**Degree requirements:** For master's, thesis (for some programs).
**Entrance requirements:** For master's, minimum GPA of 3.0 in major. *Application deadline:* For fall admission, 8/31 (priority date). *Application fee:* $55.
**Expenses:** Tuition, nonresident: full-time $4,428. Required fees: $1,733.
Dr. Amanda Wilcox Herzog, Head.
**Application contact:** Luci Van Loon, Graduate Secretary, 909-880-5570, *Fax:* 909-880-7003, *E-mail:* lvanloon@csusb.edu.

## ■ CARNEGIE MELLON UNIVERSITY

**College of Humanities and Social Sciences, Department of Psychology, Area of Developmental Psychology, Pittsburgh, PA 15213-3891**
**AWARDS** PhD.
**Degree requirements:** For doctorate, thesis/dissertation, comprehensive exam.
**Entrance requirements:** For doctorate, GRE General Test, TOEFL, TSE.
**Faculty research:** Cognitive development, language acquisition.

## ■ CLAREMONT GRADUATE UNIVERSITY

**Graduate Programs, School of Behavioral and Organizational Sciences, Department of Psychology, Claremont, CA 91711-6160**
**AWARDS** Cognitive psychology (MA, PhD); developmental psychology (MA, PhD); organizational behavior (MA, PhD); program design, management, and evaluation (MA); social environmental psychology (PhD); social psychology (MA). Part-time programs available.
**Faculty:** 6 full-time (2 women), 7 part-time/adjunct (6 women).

**Students:** 127 full-time (93 women), 23 part-time (19 women); includes 48 minority (8 African Americans, 23 Asian Americans or Pacific Islanders, 15 Hispanic Americans, 2 Native Americans), 9 international. Average age 30. In 2001, 25 master's, 16 doctorates awarded. Terminal master's awarded for partial completion of doctoral program.
**Degree requirements:** For master's, thesis (for some programs); for doctorate, thesis/dissertation, comprehensive exam.
**Entrance requirements:** For master's and doctorate, GRE General Test. *Application deadline:* For fall admission, 2/15 (priority date). Applications are processed on a rolling basis. *Application fee:* $50. Electronic applications accepted.
**Expenses:** Tuition: Full-time $22,984; part-time $1,000 per unit. Required fees: $160; $80 per semester.
**Financial support:** Fellowships, research assistantships, teaching assistantships, career-related internships or fieldwork, Federal Work-Study, institutionally sponsored loans, and tuition waivers (full and partial) available. Support available to part-time students. Financial award application deadline: 2/15; financial award applicants required to submit FAFSA.
**Faculty research:** Social intervention, diversity in organizations, eyewitness memory, aging and cognition, drug policy.
**Application contact:** Jessica Johnson, Program Coordinator, 909-621-8084, *Fax:* 909-621-8905, *E-mail:* jessica.johnson@cgu.edu. *Web site:* http://www.cgu.edu/sbus
**Find an in-depth description at www.petersons.com/gradchannel.**

## ■ CLARK UNIVERSITY

**Graduate School, Department of Psychology, Program in Developmental Psychology, Worcester, MA 01610-1477**
**AWARDS** PhD.
**Degree requirements:** For doctorate, thesis/dissertation.
**Entrance requirements:** For doctorate, GRE General Test, TOEFL. *Application deadline:* For fall admission, 1/31 (priority date). Applications are processed on a rolling basis. *Application fee:* $40.
**Expenses:** Tuition: Full-time $24,400; part-time $763 per credit. Required fees: $10.
**Financial support:** In 2001–02, fellowships with full tuition reimbursements (averaging $10,900 per year), research assistantships with full tuition reimbursements (averaging $10,900 per year), teaching assistantships with full tuition reimbursements (averaging $10,900 per year) were awarded. Tuition waivers (full) also available.

*Clark University (continued)*
Dr. Nancy Budwig, Director, 508-793-7274.
**Application contact:** Cynthia LaRochelle, Graduate School Secretary, 508-793-7274, *Fax:* 508-793-7265, *E-mail:* clarochelle@clarku.edu. *Web site:* http://www2.clarku.edu/newsite/graduatefolder/programs/index.shtml

## ■ COLLEGE OF STATEN ISLAND OF THE CITY UNIVERSITY OF NEW YORK

**Graduate Programs, Center for Developmental Neuroscience and Developmental Disabilities, Sub-program in Learning Processes, Staten Island, NY 10314-6600**

AWARDS Biopsychology (PhD); clinical psychology (PhD); developmental psychology (PhD); environmental psychology (PhD); experimental cognition (PhD); experimental psychology (PhD); neuropsychology (PhD); psychology (PhD); social-personality psychology (PhD).

**Degree requirements:** For doctorate, one foreign language, thesis/dissertation.
**Entrance requirements:** For doctorate, GRE, TOEFL. *Application deadline:* For fall admission, 3/15 (priority date). Applications are processed on a rolling basis. *Application fee:* $40.
**Expenses:** Tuition, state resident: full-time $4,350; part-time $185 per credit. Tuition, nonresident: full-time $7,600; part-time $320 per credit. Required fees: $53 per semester.
**Financial support:** Fellowships, research assistantships, teaching assistantships, career-related internships or fieldwork and institutionally sponsored loans available. Financial award application deadline: 3/15. Dr. Nancy Hemmes, Head, 718-997-3561.

## ■ CORNELL UNIVERSITY

**Graduate School, Graduate Fields of Human Ecology, Field of Human Development, Ithaca, NY 14853-0001**

AWARDS Developmental psychology (PhD), including cognitive development, developmental psychopathology, ecology of human development, sociology and personality development; human development and family studies (PhD), including ecology of human development, family studies and the life course.

**Faculty:** 33 full-time.
**Students:** 33 full-time (23 women); includes 7 minority (4 African Americans, 1 Asian American or Pacific Islander, 2 Hispanic Americans), 6 international. 70 applicants, 16% accepted. In 2001, 6 doctorates awarded.

**Degree requirements:** For doctorate, thesis/dissertation, predoctoral research project, teaching experience.
**Entrance requirements:** For doctorate, GRE General Test, TOEFL, 2 letters of recommendation. *Application deadline:* For fall admission, 1/15. *Application fee:* $65. Electronic applications accepted.
**Expenses:** Tuition: Full-time $25,970. Required fees: $50.
**Financial support:** In 2001–02, 33 students received support, including 7 fellowships with full tuition reimbursements available, 10 research assistantships with full tuition reimbursements available, 16 teaching assistantships with full tuition reimbursements available; institutionally sponsored loans, scholarships/grants, tuition waivers (full and partial), and unspecified assistantships also available. Financial award applicants required to submit FAFSA.
**Faculty research:** Cognitive development, developmental psychopathology, ecology of human development, family studies and the life course, social and personality development.
**Application contact:** Graduate Field Assistant, 607-255-3181, *Fax:* 607-255-9856, *E-mail:* hdfs@cornell.edu. *Web site:* http://www.gradschool.cornell.edu/grad/fields_1/hdfs.html

## ■ DUKE UNIVERSITY

**Graduate School, Department of Psychology, Durham, NC 27708-0586**

AWARDS Biological psychology (PhD); clinical psychology (PhD); cognitive psychology (PhD); developmental psychology (PhD); experimental psychology (PhD); health psychology (PhD); human social development (PhD).

**Faculty:** 52 full-time, 15 part-time/adjunct.
**Students:** 66 full-time (42 women); includes 11 minority (6 African Americans, 2 Asian Americans or Pacific Islanders, 3 Hispanic Americans), 13 international. 386 applicants, 7% accepted, 15 enrolled. In 2001, 8 doctorates awarded.

**Degree requirements:** For doctorate, thesis/dissertation.
**Entrance requirements:** For doctorate, GRE General Test. *Application deadline:* For fall admission, 12/31. *Application fee:* $75.
**Expenses:** Tuition: Full-time $24,600.
**Financial support:** Fellowships, research assistantships, teaching assistantships, career-related internships or fieldwork and Federal Work-Study available. Financial award application deadline: 12/31. Reiko Mazuka, Co-Director of Graduate Studies, 919-660-5716, *Fax:* 919-660-5726,

*E-mail:* bseymore@acpub.duke.edu. *Web site:* http://www.psych.duke.edu/

## ■ DUQUESNE UNIVERSITY

**Graduate School of Liberal Arts, Department of Psychology, Pittsburgh, PA 15282-0001**

AWARDS Clinical psychology (PhD); developmental psychology (PhD).

**Faculty:** 15 full-time (5 women), 5 part-time/adjunct (2 women).
**Students:** 83 full-time (42 women), 9 part-time (5 women); includes 6 minority (4 African Americans, 1 Asian American or Pacific Islander, 1 Hispanic American), 4 international. Average age 28. 54 applicants, 56% accepted, 13 enrolled. In 2001, 13 degrees awarded.
**Degree requirements:** For doctorate, 2 foreign languages, thesis/dissertation, comprehensive exam.
**Entrance requirements:** For doctorate, GRE General Test, TOEFL, MA in psychology. *Application deadline:* For fall admission, 2/1. *Application fee:* $50.
**Expenses:** Tuition: Part-time $566 per credit. Required fees: $56 per credit. Part-time tuition and fees vary according to degree level and program.
**Financial support:** In 2001–02, 1 research assistantship with full tuition reimbursement (averaging $11,000 per year), 14 teaching assistantships with full tuition reimbursements (averaging $11,000 per year) were awarded. Fellowships with full tuition reimbursements, career-related internships or fieldwork, scholarships/grants, and tuition waivers (partial) also available. Financial award application deadline: 5/1.
**Faculty research:** Emotion, language motivation, imagination, development. Dr. Russell Walsh, Chair, 412-396-6520.

## ■ EASTERN WASHINGTON UNIVERSITY

**Graduate School Studies, College of Education and Human Development, Department of Counseling, Educational, and Developmental Psychology, Cheney, WA 99004-2431**

AWARDS Developing psychology (MS); school counseling (MS), including counseling psychology, school counseling; school psychology (MS); special education (M Ed).

**Faculty:** 14 full-time (5 women).
**Students:** 62 full-time (53 women), 13 part-time (11 women); includes 3 minority (1 African American, 2 Asian Americans or Pacific Islanders), 3 international. 48 applicants, 67% accepted, 27 enrolled. In 2001, 30 degrees awarded.
**Degree requirements:** For master's, thesis or alternative, comprehensive exam.

**Entrance requirements:** For master's, GRE General Test, minimum GPA of 3.0. *Application deadline:* For fall admission, 2/1. Applications are processed on a rolling basis. *Application fee:* $35.

**Expenses:** Tuition, state resident: full-time $1,586; part-time $159 per credit hour. Tuition, nonresident: full-time $4,677; part-time $468 per credit hour. Required fees: $222; $159 per credit. $74 per quarter.

**Financial support:** In 2001–02, 4 teaching assistantships with partial tuition reimbursements (averaging $7,000 per year) were awarded; career-related internships or fieldwork, Federal Work-Study, institutionally sponsored loans, scholarships/grants, health care benefits, tuition waivers (partial), and unspecified assistantships also available. Support available to part-time students. Financial award application deadline: 2/1; financial award applicants required to submit FAFSA. Dr. Armin Arndt, Chair, 509-359-2827, *Fax:* 509-359-4366. *Web site:* http://www.appliedpsyc.ewu.edu

■ **EMORY UNIVERSITY**

**Graduate School of Arts and Sciences, Department of Psychology, Atlanta, GA 30322-1100**

**AWARDS** Clinical psychology (PhD); cognition and development (PhD); psychobiology (PhD).

**Faculty:** 26 full-time (6 women), 2 part-time/adjunct (0 women).

**Students:** 73 full-time (55 women); includes 5 minority (1 African American, 2 Asian Americans or Pacific Islanders, 2 Hispanic Americans), 6 international. 272 applicants, 6% accepted, 13 enrolled. In 2001, 10 doctorates awarded.

**Degree requirements:** For doctorate, thesis/dissertation, comprehensive exam, registration.

**Entrance requirements:** For doctorate, GRE General Test, TOEFL, minimum GPA of 3.0. *Application deadline:* For fall admission, 1/15. *Application fee:* $50. Electronic applications accepted.

**Expenses:** Tuition: Full-time $24,770. Required fees: $100. Tuition and fees vary according to program and student level.

**Financial support:** In 2001–02, 56 fellowships were awarded; research assistantships, teaching assistantships, career-related internships or fieldwork, Federal Work-Study, institutionally sponsored loans, scholarships/grants, and tuition waivers (full and partial) also available. Financial award application deadline: 1/20.

**Faculty research:** Neurophysiology, drugs and behavior, hormones and behavior, nonverbal behavior.

Dr. Darryl Neill, Chair, 404-727-7437.

**Application contact:** Dr. Robyn Fivush, Director of Graduate Studies, 404-727-7456, *E-mail:* psyrf@emory.edu.

■ **ERIKSON INSTITUTE**

**Erikson Institute, Chicago, IL 60611-5627**

**AWARDS** Child development (MS); early childhood education (M Ed, MS, PhD). PhD offered through the Graduate School.

**Faculty:** 10 full-time (8 women), 11 part-time/adjunct (all women).

**Students:** 40 full-time (39 women), 106 part-time (100 women); includes 47 minority (33 African Americans, 6 Asian Americans or Pacific Islanders, 8 Hispanic Americans), 4 international. Average age 31. 81 applicants, 89% accepted. In 2001, 22 master's, 4 doctorates awarded.

**Degree requirements:** For master's, internship; for doctorate, one foreign language, thesis/dissertation, comprehensive exam.

**Entrance requirements:** For master's, experience working with young children, interview; for doctorate, GRE General Test, interview. *Application deadline:* For fall admission, 4/1 (priority date). Applications are processed on a rolling basis. *Application fee:* $30.

**Expenses:** Tuition: Full-time $18,852; part-time $460 per credit. Required fees: $150. One-time fee: $115 part-time. Tuition and fees vary according to course load and program.

**Financial support:** In 2001–02, 85 students received support, including 2 fellowships with tuition reimbursements available; career-related internships or fieldwork, Federal Work-Study, institutionally sponsored loans, tuition waivers (partial), and unspecified assistantships also available. Support available to part-time students. Financial award application deadline: 3/1; financial award applicants required to submit FAFSA.

**Faculty research:** Early childhood development, cognitive development, sociocultural contexts, early childhood education, family and culture, early literacy.

Barbara T. Bowman, President, 312-755-2250, *Fax:* 312-755-2255, *E-mail:* bbowman@erikson.edu.

**Application contact:** Melanie K. Miller, Associate Director of Recruitment and Financial Aid, 312-755-2250 Ext. 2276, *Fax:* 312-755-0928, *E-mail:* mmiller@erikson.edu. *Web site:* http://www.erikson.edu/

■ **FLORIDA INTERNATIONAL UNIVERSITY**

**College of Arts and Sciences, Department of Psychology, Miami, FL 33199**

**AWARDS** Developmental psychology (PhD); general psychology (MS); psychology (MS). Part-time programs available.

**Faculty:** 26 full-time (8 women).

**Students:** 73 full-time (53 women), 35 part-time (26 women); includes 41 minority (4 African Americans, 4 Asian Americans or Pacific Islanders, 33 Hispanic Americans), 13 international. Average age 29. 191 applicants, 29% accepted, 33 enrolled. In 2001, 16 master's, 9 doctorates awarded. Terminal master's awarded for partial completion of doctoral program.

**Degree requirements:** For master's and doctorate, thesis/dissertation.

**Entrance requirements:** For master's and doctorate, GRE General Test, TOEFL. *Application deadline:* For fall admission, 4/1 (priority date); for spring admission, 10/1. Applications are processed on a rolling basis. *Application fee:* $20.

**Expenses:** Tuition, state resident: full-time $2,916; part-time $162 per credit hour. Tuition, nonresident: full-time $10,245; part-time $569 per credit hour. Required fees: $168 per term.

**Financial support:** In 2001–02, 6 fellowships, 2 research assistantships were awarded. Federal Work-Study, institutionally sponsored loans, and tuition waivers (partial) also available. Support available to part-time students. Financial award application deadline: 4/1.

**Faculty research:** Community psychology. Dr. Marvin Dunn, Chairperson, 305-348-3466, *Fax:* 305-348-3879, *E-mail:* dunnm@fiu.edu.

■ **FORDHAM UNIVERSITY**

**Graduate School of Arts and Sciences, Department of Psychology, Program in Developmental Psychology, New York, NY 10458**

**AWARDS** PhD.

**Students:** 32 applicants, 47% accepted. In 2001, 6 doctorates awarded.

**Degree requirements:** For doctorate, thesis/dissertation, comprehensive exam.

**Entrance requirements:** For doctorate, GRE General Test, GRE Subject Test. *Application deadline:* For fall admission, 1/8. *Application fee:* $65. Electronic applications accepted.

**Expenses:** Tuition: Part-time $720 per credit. Required fees: $135 per semester.

**Financial support:** In 2001–02, 28 students received support, including 3 fellowships with tuition reimbursements

*Fordham University (continued)*
available (averaging $15,000 per year), 4 research assistantships with tuition reimbursements available (averaging $12,000 per year), 21 teaching assistantships with tuition reimbursements available (averaging $15,000 per year); career-related internships or fieldwork, institutionally sponsored loans, tuition waivers (full and partial), and unspecified assistantships also available. Financial award application deadline: 1/8.
Dr. Ann Higgins, Director, 718-817-3776, *Fax:* 718-817-3785, *E-mail:* higgins@ fordham.edu.
**Application contact:** Dr. Craig W. Pilant, Assistant Dean, 718-817-4420, *Fax:* 718-817-3566, *E-mail:* pilant@fordham.edu. *Web site:* http://www.fordham.edu/gsas/

### ■ GALLAUDET UNIVERSITY

**The Graduate School, College of Arts and Sciences, Department of Psychology, Program in School Psychology, Washington, DC 20002-3625**
AWARDS Developmental psychology (MA); school psychology (Psy S).

**Degree requirements:** For master's, thesis optional.
**Entrance requirements:** For master's, GRE General Test or MAT.

### ■ GEORGE MASON UNIVERSITY

**College of Arts and Sciences, Department of Psychology, Program in Developmental Psychology, Fairfax, VA 22030-4444**
AWARDS PhD.

**Degree requirements:** For doctorate, thesis/dissertation.
**Entrance requirements:** For doctorate, GRE General Test, minimum undergraduate GPA of 3.0, 3.25 in major. Electronic applications accepted.
**Expenses:** Tuition, state resident: full-time $3,168; part-time $132 per credit hour. Tuition, nonresident: full-time $11,280; part-time $470 per credit hour. Required fees: $1,416; $59 per credit hour.

### ■ GEORGE MASON UNIVERSITY

**College of Arts and Sciences, Department of Psychology, Program in Life-Span Development Psychology, Fairfax, VA 22030-4444**
AWARDS MA.

**Degree requirements:** For master's, thesis optional.
**Entrance requirements:** For master's, GRE General Test, minimum GPA of 3.0 in last 60 hours, previous undergraduate

course work in psychology. Electronic applications accepted.
**Expenses:** Tuition, state resident: full-time $3,168; part-time $132 per credit hour. Tuition, nonresident: full-time $11,280; part-time $470 per credit hour. Required fees: $1,416; $59 per credit hour.

### ■ GRADUATE SCHOOL AND UNIVERSITY CENTER OF THE CITY UNIVERSITY OF NEW YORK

**Graduate Studies, Program in Psychology, New York, NY 10016-4039**
AWARDS Basic applied neurocognition (PhD); biopsychology (PhD); clinical psychology (PhD); developmental psychology (PhD); environmental psychology (PhD); experimental psychology (PhD); industrial psychology (PhD); learning processes (PhD); neuropsychology (PhD); psychology (PhD); social personality (PhD).

**Faculty:** 119 full-time (40 women).
**Students:** 463 full-time (335 women), 4 part-time (2 women); includes 96 minority (39 African Americans, 20 Asian Americans or Pacific Islanders, 36 Hispanic Americans, 1 Native American), 47 international. Average age 33. 493 applicants, 24% accepted, 65 enrolled. In 2001, 28 degrees awarded.
**Degree requirements:** For doctorate, one foreign language, thesis/dissertation.
**Entrance requirements:** For doctorate, GRE General Test. *Application deadline:* For fall admission, 2/1. *Application fee:* $40.
**Expenses:** Tuition, state resident: part-time $245 per credit. Tuition, nonresident: part-time $425 per credit. Required fees: $72 per semester.
**Financial support:** In 2001–02, 226 students received support, including 141 fellowships, 14 research assistantships, 4 teaching assistantships; career-related internships or fieldwork, Federal Work-Study, institutionally sponsored loans, and tuition waivers (full and partial) also available. Financial award application deadline: 2/1; financial award applicants required to submit FAFSA.
Dr. Joseph Glick, Executive Officer, 212-817-8706, *Fax:* 212-817-1533, *E-mail:* jglick@gc.cuny.edu.

### ■ HARVARD UNIVERSITY

**Graduate School of Arts and Sciences, Department of Psychology, Cambridge, MA 02138**
AWARDS Psychology (AM, PhD), including behavior and decision analysis, cognition, developmental psychology, experimental psychology, personality, psychobiology, psychopathology; social psychology (AM, PhD).

**Degree requirements:** For doctorate, thesis/dissertation, general exams.
**Entrance requirements:** For master's and doctorate, GRE General Test, TOEFL.
**Expenses:** Tuition: Full-time $23,370. Required fees: $816. Full-time tuition and fees vary according to program and student level.

### ■ HOWARD UNIVERSITY

**Graduate School of Arts and Sciences, Department of Psychology, Washington, DC 20059-0002**
AWARDS Clinical psychology (PhD); developmental psychology (PhD); experimental psychology (PhD); neuropsychology (PhD); personality psychology (PhD); psychology (MS); social psychology (PhD). Part-time programs available.

**Faculty:** 16 full-time (7 women).
**Students:** 70 full-time (51 women), 20 part-time (14 women). Average age 29. 165 applicants, 15% accepted, 20 enrolled. In 2001, 10 master's, 12 doctorates awarded.
**Degree requirements:** For master's, thesis, comprehensive exam; for doctorate, thesis/dissertation, qualifying exam, comprehensive exam. *Median time to degree:* Master's–3 years full-time, 5 years part-time; doctorate–5 years full-time, 9 years part-time.
**Entrance requirements:** For master's, GRE General Test, minimum GPA of 2.5, bachelor's degree in psychology or related field; for doctorate, GRE General Test, minimum GPA of 3.0. *Application deadline:* For fall admission, 4/1; for spring admission, 11/1. Applications are processed on a rolling basis. *Application fee:* $45.
**Financial support:** In 2001–02, 19 students received support, including 3 fellowships with full tuition reimbursements available (averaging $13,500 per year), 2 research assistantships with full tuition reimbursements available (averaging $10,000 per year), 8 teaching assistantships with full tuition reimbursements available (averaging $13,000 per year); career-related internships or fieldwork, institutionally sponsored loans, and scholarships/grants also available. Financial award application deadline: 4/1; financial award applicants required to submit FAFSA.
**Faculty research:** Personality and psychophysiology, educational and social development of African-American children, child and adult psychopathology.
Dr. Albert Roberts, Chair, 202-806-6805, *Fax:* 202-806-4823, *E-mail:* aroberts@ howard.edu.
**Application contact:** Dr. Alfonso Campbell, Chairman, Graduate Admissions Committee, 202-806-6805, *Fax:* 202-806-4873, *E-mail:* acampbell@howard.edu.

## ■ ILLINOIS STATE UNIVERSITY

**Graduate School, College of Arts and Sciences, Department of Psychology, Normal, IL 61790-2200**

**AWARDS** Psychology (MA, MS), including clinical psychology, counseling psychology, developmental psychology, educational psychology, experimental psychology, measurement-evaluation, organizational-industrial psychology; school psychology (PhD, SSP).

**Faculty:** 30 full-time (10 women), 1 part-time/adjunct (0 women).

**Students:** 59 full-time (48 women), 24 part-time (13 women); includes 7 minority (3 African Americans, 3 Hispanic Americans, 1 Native American), 5 international. 81 applicants, 46% accepted. In 2001, 40 master's, 2 doctorates, 4 other advanced degrees awarded.

**Degree requirements:** For master's, thesis or alternative; for doctorate, variable foreign language requirement, thesis/dissertation, 2 terms of residency, internship, practicum.

**Entrance requirements:** For master's, GRE General Test, GRE Subject Test, minimum GPA of 3.0 in last 60 hours; for doctorate, GRE General Test. *Application deadline:* Applications are processed on a rolling basis. *Application fee:* $30.

**Expenses:** Tuition, state resident: full-time $2,691; part-time $112 per credit hour. Tuition, nonresident: full-time $5,880; part-time $245 per credit hour. Required fees: $1,146; $48 per credit hour.

**Financial support:** In 2001–02, 21 research assistantships (averaging $5,127 per year), 27 teaching assistantships (averaging $4,308 per year) were awarded. Tuition waivers (full) and unspecified assistantships also available. Financial award application deadline: 4/1.

**Faculty research:** Dialogues with children, sexual harassment in the military, mental health consultant. *Total annual research expenditures:* $248,177.

Dr. David Barone, Chairperson, 309-438-8651. *Web site:* http://www.cas.ilstu.edu/psychology/index.html

## ■ INDIANA UNIVERSITY BLOOMINGTON

**Graduate School, College of Arts and Sciences, Department of Psychology, Bloomington, IN 47405**

**AWARDS** Biology and behavior (PhD); clinical science (PhD); cognitive psychology (PhD); developmental psychology (PhD); social psychology (PhD). Offered through the University Graduate School.

**Faculty:** 40 full-time (7 women), 1 (woman) part-time/adjunct.

**Students:** 42 full-time (23 women), 37 part-time (18 women); includes 9 minority (2 African Americans, 5 Asian Americans or Pacific Islanders, 2 Hispanic Americans), 9 international. Average age 28. 222 applicants, 14% accepted. In 2001, 18 doctorates awarded.

**Degree requirements:** For doctorate, thesis/dissertation, 1st- and 2nd-year projects, 1 year as associate instructor, qualifying exam.

**Entrance requirements:** For doctorate, GRE, TOEFL. *Application deadline:* For fall admission, 12/15. *Application fee:* $45 ($55 for international students). Electronic applications accepted.

**Expenses:** Tuition, state resident: full-time $4,720; part-time $197 per credit. Tuition, nonresident: full-time $13,748; part-time $573 per credit. Required fees: $642.

**Financial support:** In 2001–02, 8 fellowships (averaging $14,000 per year), 24 teaching assistantships (averaging $11,800 per year) were awarded.

Dr. Joseph E. Steinmetz, Chairperson, 812-855-3991, *Fax:* 812-855-4691, *E-mail:* steinmet@indiana.edu.

**Application contact:** Beth Laske-Miller, Graduate Admissions Assistant, 812-855-2014, *Fax:* 812-855-4691, *E-mail:* psychgrd@indiana.edu. *Web site:* http://www.indiana.edu/~psych/

## ■ LOUISIANA STATE UNIVERSITY AND AGRICULTURAL AND MECHANICAL COLLEGE

**Graduate School, College of Arts and Sciences, Department of Psychology, Baton Rouge, LA 70803**

**AWARDS** Biological psychology (MA, PhD); clinical psychology (MA, PhD); cognitive psychology (MA, PhD); developmental psychology (MA, PhD); industrial/organizational psychology (MA, PhD); school psychology (MA, PhD).

**Faculty:** 25 full-time (7 women).

**Students:** 70 full-time (53 women), 43 part-time (24 women); includes 7 minority (3 African Americans, 2 Asian Americans or Pacific Islanders, 2 Hispanic Americans), 2 international. Average age 30. 179 applicants, 12% accepted, 20 enrolled. In 2001, 19 degrees awarded. Terminal master's awarded for partial completion of doctoral program.

**Degree requirements:** For master's, thesis; for doctorate, thesis/dissertation, 1 year internship.

**Entrance requirements:** For master's and doctorate, GRE General Test, minimum GPA of 3.0. *Application deadline:* For fall admission, 1/25 (priority date). Applications are processed on a rolling basis. *Application fee:* $25.

**Expenses:** Tuition, state resident: full-time $2,551. Tuition, nonresident: full-time $5,551. Required fees: $854. Part-time tuition and fees vary according to course load.

**Financial support:** In 2001–02, 1 fellowship (averaging $14,333 per year), 10 research assistantships with partial tuition reimbursements (averaging $14,200 per year), 33 teaching assistantships with partial tuition reimbursements (averaging $10,371 per year) were awarded. Career-related internships or fieldwork, institutionally sponsored loans, and contracts also available. Financial award applicants required to submit FAFSA. *Total annual research expenditures:* $242,157.

Dr. Irving Lane, Chair, 225-578-8745, *Fax:* 225-578-4125, *E-mail:* irvlane@unix1.sncc.lsu.edu.

**Application contact:** Dr. Janet McDonald, Coordinator of Graduate Studies, 225-578-4116, *Fax:* 225-578-4125, *E-mail:* psmcdo@lsu.edu. *Web site:* http://www.artsci.lsu.edu/psych

## ■ LOYOLA UNIVERSITY CHICAGO

**Graduate School, Department of Psychology, Program in Developmental Psychology, Chicago, IL 60611-2196**

**AWARDS** PhD.

**Faculty:** 4 full-time (2 women).

**Students:** 17 full-time (13 women); includes 2 minority (1 African American, 1 Asian American or Pacific Islander), 2 international. Average age 25. 13 applicants, 77% accepted. In 2001, 4 doctorates awarded.

**Degree requirements:** For doctorate, thesis/dissertation, internship, oral and written comprehensive exams.

**Entrance requirements:** For doctorate, GRE General Test, GRE Subject Test. *Application deadline:* For fall admission, 2/1. *Application fee:* $40.

**Expenses:** Tuition: Part-time $529 per credit hour.

**Financial support:** In 2001–02, 13 students received support, including 4 fellowships with full tuition reimbursements available (averaging $10,000 per year), 11 research assistantships with full tuition reimbursements available (averaging $10,000 per year), 3 teaching assistantships (averaging $10,000 per year); career-related internships or fieldwork and Federal Work-Study also available. Financial award application deadline: 2/1; financial award applicants required to submit FAFSA.

**Faculty research:** Cognitive development, parenting, schooling, bilingualism, aging.

*Loyola University Chicago (continued)*
Dr. David Mitchell, Acting Director, 773-508-8684, *E-mail:* dmitch@luc.edu.

# ■ MICHIGAN STATE UNIVERSITY

**Graduate School, College of Social Science, Department of Psychology, East Lansing, MI 48824**

**AWARDS** Applied developmental science (MA, PhD); infant studies (MA, PhD); neuroscience-psychology (MA, PhD); psychology (MA, PhD); psychology-urban studies (MA, PhD).

**Faculty:** 50.
**Students:** 80 full-time (53 women), 37 part-time (22 women); includes 24 minority (12 African Americans, 8 Asian Americans or Pacific Islanders, 4 Hispanic Americans), 7 international. Average age 28. 312 applicants, 5% accepted. In 2001, 20 master's, 23 doctorates awarded.
**Degree requirements:** For master's, thesis (for some programs); for doctorate, thesis/dissertation.
**Entrance requirements:** For master's, GRE General Test, TOEFL, minimum GPA of 3.25; for doctorate, GRE General Test, TOEFL, minimum GPA of 3.5. *Application deadline:* For fall admission, 1/5. *Application fee:* $30 ($40 for international students). Electronic applications accepted.
**Expenses:** Tuition, state resident: part-time $244 per credit hour. Tuition, nonresident: part-time $494 per credit hour. Required fees: $268 per semester. Tuition and fees vary according to course load, degree level and program.
**Financial support:** In 2001–02, 57 fellowships (averaging $3,788 per year), 51 research assistantships with tuition reimbursements (averaging $12,076 per year), 47 teaching assistantships with tuition reimbursements (averaging $11,555 per year) were awarded. Career-related internships or fieldwork and institutionally sponsored loans also available. Support available to part-time students. Financial award applicants required to submit FAFSA.
**Faculty research:** Hormones and behavior, cognitive processes, personnel selection, social cognition, program evaluation. *Total annual research expenditures:* $4.2 million.
Dr. Neal Schmitt, Chairperson, 517-355-9561, *Fax:* 517-432-2476.
**Application contact:** Graduate Secretary, 517-353-5258, *Fax:* 517-432-2476. *Web site:* http://psychology.msu.edu/

# ■ NEW YORK UNIVERSITY

**The Steinhardt School of Education, Department of Applied Psychology, Program in Applied Psychology, New York, NY 10012-1019**

**AWARDS** Educational psychology (MA), including measurement and evaluation, psychology of parenthood; professional child/school psychology (Psy D); psychological development (PhD); school psychologist (Advanced Certificate); school psychology (PhD). Part-time and evening/weekend programs available.
**Faculty:** 15 full-time (10 women).
**Students:** 66 full-time (55 women), 101 part-time (95 women); includes 37 minority (15 African Americans, 14 Asian Americans or Pacific Islanders, 8 Hispanic Americans). 240 applicants, 23% accepted, 39 enrolled. In 2001, 59 master's, 17 doctorates, 1 other advanced degree awarded. Terminal master's awarded for partial completion of doctoral program.
**Degree requirements:** For master's, thesis (for some programs); for doctorate, thesis/dissertation.
**Entrance requirements:** For master's and Advanced Certificate, TOEFL; for doctorate, GRE General Test, TOEFL, interview. *Application deadline:* For fall admission, 2/1 (priority date); for spring admission, 12/1. Applications are processed on a rolling basis. *Application fee:* $40 ($60 for international students).
**Expenses:** Tuition: Full-time $19,536; part-time $814 per credit. Required fees: $1,330; $38 per credit. Tuition and fees vary according to course load and program.
**Financial support:** Teaching assistantships with partial tuition reimbursements, career-related internships or fieldwork, Federal Work-Study, institutionally sponsored loans, and tuition waivers (partial) available. Support available to part-time students. Financial award application deadline: 3/1; financial award applicants required to submit FAFSA.
**Faculty research:** Infant cognition; exploration, language, and symbolic play in toddlerhood; emotional and perceptual problems in children; development of reading comprehension.
Dr. Catherine Tamis-Lemonda, Director, 212-998-5399, *Fax:* 212-995-4368.
**Application contact:** 212-998-5030, *Fax:* 212-995-4328, *E-mail:* grad.admissions@nyu.edu.

# ■ THE OHIO STATE UNIVERSITY

**Graduate School, College of Social and Behavioral Sciences, Department of Psychology, Columbus, OH 43210**

**AWARDS** Clinical psychology (PhD); cognitive/experimental psychology (PhD); counseling psychology (PhD); developmental psychology (PhD); mental retardation and developmental disabilities (PhD); psychobiology (PhD); quantitative psychology (PhD); social psychology (PhD).
**Degree requirements:** For doctorate, thesis/dissertation.
**Entrance requirements:** For doctorate, GRE General Test, TOEFL.

# ■ THE PENNSYLVANIA STATE UNIVERSITY UNIVERSITY PARK CAMPUS

**Graduate School, College of Liberal Arts, Department of Psychology, State College, University Park, PA 16802-1503**

**AWARDS** Clinical psychology (MS, PhD); cognitive psychology (MS, PhD); developmental psychology (MS, PhD); industrial/organizational psychology (MS, PhD); psychobiology (MS, PhD); social psychology (MS, PhD).
**Students:** 126 full-time (83 women), 12 part-time (7 women). In 2001, 15 master's, 14 doctorates awarded.
**Degree requirements:** For master's and doctorate, thesis/dissertation.
**Entrance requirements:** For master's and doctorate, GRE General Test, GRE Subject Test. *Application fee:* $45.
**Expenses:** Tuition, state resident: full-time $7,882; part-time $333 per credit. Tuition, nonresident: full-time $16,142; part-time $673 per credit. Required fees: $124 per semester.
**Financial support:** Fellowships, research assistantships, teaching assistantships available.
Dr. Keith Crnic, Head, 814-863-1721.

# ■ RUTGERS, THE STATE UNIVERSITY OF NEW JERSEY, NEW BRUNSWICK

**Graduate School, Program in Psychology, New Brunswick, NJ 08901-1281**

**AWARDS** Biopsychology and behavioral neuroscience (PhD); clinical psychology (PhD); cognitive psychology (PhD); interdisciplinary developmental psychology (PhD); interdisciplinary health psychology (PhD); social psychology (PhD).
**Students:** Average age 24. 423 applicants, 11% accepted. In 2001, 13 degrees awarded.
**Degree requirements:** For doctorate, thesis/dissertation.
**Entrance requirements:** For doctorate, GRE General Test. *Application deadline:* For fall admission, 12/15. *Application fee:* $50.

**Financial support:** In 2001–02, 68 students received support, including 18 fellowships with full tuition reimbursements available (averaging $15,000 per year), 13 research assistantships with full tuition reimbursements available (averaging $14,000 per year), 43 teaching assistantships with full tuition reimbursements available (averaging $13,800 per year); career-related internships or fieldwork, Federal Work-Study, scholarships/grants, and traineeships also available. Financial award application deadline: 12/15.
Dr. G. Terence Wilson, Director, 732-445-2556, *Fax:* 732-445-2263.
**Application contact:** Joan Olmizzi, Administrative Assistant, 732-445-2555, *Fax:* 732-445-2263, *E-mail:* joan@psych-b.rutgers.edu. *Web site:* http://psychology.rutgers.edu/

### ■ STANFORD UNIVERSITY

**School of Education, Program in Psychological Studies in Education, Stanford, CA 94305-9991**

AWARDS Child and adolescent development (PhD); counseling psychology (PhD); educational psychology (PhD).

**Degree requirements:** For doctorate, thesis/dissertation.
**Entrance requirements:** For doctorate, GRE General Test. *Application deadline:* For fall admission, 1/2. *Application fee:* $65 ($80 for international students). Electronic applications accepted.
**Application contact:** Graduate Admissions Office, 650-723-4794.

### ■ SUFFOLK UNIVERSITY

**College of Arts and Sciences, Department of Psychology, Boston, MA 02108-2770**

AWARDS Clinical-developmental psychology (PhD).

**Faculty:** 12 full-time (10 women), 6 part-time/adjunct (4 women).
**Students:** 41 full-time (34 women), 21 part-time (17 women); includes 6 minority (2 African Americans, 3 Asian Americans or Pacific Islanders, 1 Hispanic American), 3 international. Average age 29. 74 applicants, 45% accepted, 15 enrolled. In 2001, 6 degrees awarded.
**Degree requirements:** For doctorate, thesis/dissertation, Practicum.
**Entrance requirements:** For doctorate, GRE General Test or MAT. *Application deadline:* For fall admission, 1/15. Applications are processed on a rolling basis. *Application fee:* $50.
**Expenses:** Contact institution.
**Financial support:** In 2001–02, 50 students received support, including 42

fellowships with full and partial tuition reimbursements available (averaging $10,200 per year); career-related internships or fieldwork, Federal Work-Study, and institutionally sponsored loans also available. Support available to part-time students. Financial award application deadline: 3/15; financial award applicants required to submit FAFSA.
**Faculty research:** Cognitive, emotional, personality, and social development.
Dr. Robert Webb, Chair, 617-573-8293, *Fax:* 617-367-2924, *E-mail:* rwebb@suffolk.edu.
**Application contact:** Judith Reynolds, Director of Graduate Admissions, 617-573-8302, *Fax:* 617-523-0116, *E-mail:* grad.admission@suffolk.edu. *Web site:* http://www/cas/suffolk.edu/psych/ndonovan/phd.htm

### ■ TEACHERS COLLEGE COLUMBIA UNIVERSITY

**Graduate Faculty of Education, Department of Human Development, Program in Developmental Psychology, New York, NY 10027-6696**

AWARDS MA, Ed D, PhD.

**Degree requirements:** For doctorate, thesis/dissertation, integrative project.
**Entrance requirements:** For doctorate, GRE General Test.
**Expenses:** Tuition: Full-time $19,080; part-time $780 per unit. Required fees: $170 per semester.
**Faculty research:** Language development in infants, psychology of mathematics education, intellectual development, testing and assessment, cognitive development, adolescence in the inner city.

### ■ TEMPLE UNIVERSITY

**Graduate School, College of Liberal Arts, Department of Psychology, Program in Developmental Psychology, Philadelphia, PA 19122-6096**

AWARDS PhD.

**Degree requirements:** For doctorate, thesis/dissertation.
**Entrance requirements:** For doctorate, GRE General Test, minimum GPA of 3.0. Electronic applications accepted.
**Expenses:** Tuition, state resident: full-time $8,487; part-time $369 per credit hour. Tuition, nonresident: full-time $12,282; part-time $534 per credit hour. Required fees: $350. Tuition and fees vary according to course load, program and reciprocity agreements.

**Faculty research:** Social development, cognitive development, emotional development, research methodology.
**Find an in-depth description at www.petersons.com/gradchannel.**

### ■ TUFTS UNIVERSITY

**Division of Graduate and Continuing Studies and Research, Graduate School of Arts and Sciences, Department of Child Development, Medford, MA 02155**

AWARDS Applied developmental psychology (PhD); child development (MA, CAGS); early childhood education (MAT). Part-time programs available.

**Faculty:** 10 full-time, 12 part-time/adjunct.
**Students:** 111 (99 women); includes 15 minority (6 African Americans, 6 Asian Americans or Pacific Islanders, 2 Hispanic Americans, 1 Native American) 10 international. 141 applicants, 75% accepted. In 2001, 36 master's, 1 doctorate awarded.
**Degree requirements:** For master's, thesis (for some programs); for doctorate, thesis/dissertation.
**Entrance requirements:** For master's and doctorate, GRE General Test, TOEFL. *Application deadline:* For fall admission, 1/15. Applications are processed on a rolling basis. *Application fee:* $50. Electronic applications accepted.
**Expenses:** Tuition: Full-time $26,853. Full-time tuition and fees vary according to program.
**Financial support:** Research assistantships with full and partial tuition reimbursements, teaching assistantships with full and partial tuition reimbursements, career-related internships or fieldwork, Federal Work-Study, scholarships/grants, and tuition waivers (partial) available. Support available to part-time students. Financial award application deadline: 2/15; financial award applicants required to submit FAFSA.
Ann Easterbrooks, Head, 617-627-3355, *Fax:* 617-627-3503, *E-mail:* sbarry@emerald.tufts.edu.
**Application contact:** Fred Rothbaum, Information Contact, 617-627-3355, *Fax:* 617-627-3503, *E-mail:* sbarry@emerald.tufts.edu. *Web site:* http://ase.tufts.edu/eped/

### ■ THE UNIVERSITY OF ALABAMA AT BIRMINGHAM

**Graduate School, School of Social and Behavioral Sciences, Department of Psychology, Birmingham, AL 35294**

AWARDS Behavioral neuroscience (PhD); clinical psychology (PhD); developmental

*The University of Alabama at Birmingham (continued)*
psychology (PhD); medical psychology (PhD); psychology (MA, PhD).

**Students:** 46 full-time (27 women), 5 part-time (3 women); includes 5 minority (4 African Americans, 1 Asian American or Pacific Islander), 1 international. 143 applicants, 17% accepted. In 2001, 6 master's, 9 doctorates awarded. *Application deadline:* Applications are processed on a rolling basis. *Application fee:* $35 ($60 for international students). Electronic applications accepted.
**Expenses:** Tuition, state resident: full-time $3,058. Tuition, nonresident: full-time $5,746. Tuition and fees vary according to course load, degree level and program.
**Financial support:** Career-related internships or fieldwork available.
**Faculty research:** Biological basis of behavior structure, function of the nervous system.
Dr. Carl E. McFarland, Chairman, 205-934-3850, *E-mail:* cmcfarla@uab.edu. *Web site:* http://www.sbs.uab.edu/psyc.htm/

## ■ UNIVERSITY OF CALIFORNIA, SANTA CRUZ

**Division of Graduate Studies, Division of Social Sciences, Program in Psychology, Santa Cruz, CA 95064**

**AWARDS** Developmental psychology (PhD); experimental psychology (PhD); social psychology (PhD).

**Faculty:** 26 full-time.
**Students:** 52 full-time (39 women); includes 23 minority (1 African American, 10 Asian Americans or Pacific Islanders, 11 Hispanic Americans, 1 Native American), 4 international. 96 applicants, 21% accepted. In 2001, 4 doctorates awarded.
**Degree requirements:** For doctorate, thesis/dissertation, qualifying exam. *Median time to degree:* Doctorate–7 years full-time.
**Entrance requirements:** For doctorate, GRE General Test. *Application deadline:* For fall admission, 1/1. *Application fee:* $40.
**Expenses:** Tuition: Full-time $19,857.
**Financial support:** Fellowships, research assistantships, teaching assistantships, career-related internships or fieldwork, Federal Work-Study, and institutionally sponsored loans available. Financial award application deadline: 1/1.
**Faculty research:** Cognitive psychology, human information processing, sensation perceptions, psychobiology.
Maureen Callanan, Chairperson, 831-459-2153.
**Application contact:** Graduate Admissions, 831-459-2301. *Web site:* http://www.ucsc.edu/

## ■ UNIVERSITY OF CONNECTICUT

**Graduate School, College of Liberal Arts and Sciences, Field of Psychology, Storrs, CT 06269**

**AWARDS** Behavioral neuroscience (PhD); biopsychology (PhD); clinical psychology (PhD); cognition/instruction psychology (PhD); developmental psychology (PhD); ecological psychology (PhD); general experimental psychology (PhD); industrial and organizational psychology (PhD); language psychology (PhD); social psychology (PhD).
**Faculty:** 41 full-time (11 women), 2 part-time/adjunct (both women).
**Students:** 134 full-time (83 women), 17 part-time (9 women); includes 13 minority (9 African Americans, 1 Asian American or Pacific Islander, 3 Hispanic Americans), 17 international. Average age 28. 378 applicants, 14% accepted, 25 enrolled. In 2001, 18 degrees awarded.
**Degree requirements:** For doctorate, thesis/dissertation, internship, comprehensive exam, registration.
**Entrance requirements:** For doctorate, GRE General Test, GRE Subject Test, letters of recommendation. *Application deadline:* For fall admission, 12/31. *Application fee:* $40 ($45 for international students).
**Financial support:** In 2001–02, 45 fellowships (averaging $4,000 per year), 16 research assistantships with full tuition reimbursements (averaging $16,000 per year), 83 teaching assistantships with full tuition reimbursements (averaging $16,000 per year) were awarded. Career-related internships or fieldwork, Federal Work-Study, scholarships/grants, health care benefits, and unspecified assistantships also available. Financial award application deadline: 12/31.
**Faculty research:** Behavioral neuroscience; physiology/chemistry of memory; sensation, motor control/motivation; cognitive, social, personality and language development; infancy/person perceptions and intergroup relations. *Total annual research expenditures:* $8 million.
Charles A. Lowe, Head, *Fax:* 860-486-2760, *E-mail:* charles.lowe@uconn.edu.
**Application contact:** Gina Stuart, Graduate Admissions, 860-486-3528, *Fax:* 860-486-2760, *E-mail:* futuregr@psych.psy.uconn.edu. *Web site:* http://psych.uconn.edu/

## ■ UNIVERSITY OF ILLINOIS AT URBANA–CHAMPAIGN

**Graduate College, College of Liberal Arts and Sciences, Department of Psychology, Champaign, IL 61820**

**AWARDS** Applied measurement (MS); biological psychology (AM, PhD); clinical psychology (AM, PhD); cognitive psychology (AM, PhD); developmental psychology (AM, PhD); engineering psychology (MS); personnel psychology (MS); quantitative psychology (AM, PhD); social-personality-organizational (AM, PhD); visual cognition and human performance (AM, PhD).

**Faculty:** 41 full-time (14 women), 11 part-time/adjunct (3 women).
**Students:** 156 full-time (90 women); includes 23 minority (6 African Americans, 12 Asian Americans or Pacific Islanders, 5 Hispanic Americans, 42 international. 461 applicants, 17% accepted, 27 enrolled. In 2001, 1 master's, 25 doctorates awarded.
**Degree requirements:** For doctorate, thesis/dissertation.
**Entrance requirements:** For master's, GRE General Test, GRE Subject Test (recommended), minimum GPA of 3.0; for doctorate, GRE General Test, GRE Subject Test (recommended). *Application deadline:* For fall admission, 1/1. *Application fee:* $40 ($50 for international students).
**Expenses:** Tuition, state resident: part-time $3,227 per degree program. Tuition, nonresident: part-time $7,169 per degree program. Tuition and fees vary according to program.
**Financial support:** In 2001–02, 31 fellowships with full tuition reimbursements (averaging $15,000 per year), 21 research assistantships with full tuition reimbursements (averaging $13,585 per year), 73 teaching assistantships with full tuition reimbursements (averaging $13,585 per year) were awarded. Career-related internships or fieldwork, traineeships, and tuition waivers (full) also available. Financial award application deadline: 1/1. *Total annual research expenditures:* $4.6 million.
Dr. Edward J. Shoben, Head.
**Application contact:** Cheryl Berger, Assistant Head for Graduate Affairs, 217-333-3429, *Fax:* 217-244-5876, *E-mail:* gradstdy@s.psych.uiuc.edu. *Web site:* http://www.psych.uiuc.edu/

## ■ UNIVERSITY OF KANSAS

**Graduate School, College of Liberal Arts and Sciences, Department of Human Development and Family Life, Lawrence, KS 66045**

**AWARDS** Developmental and child psychology (PhD); early childhood education (MA, PhD); human development (MA, MHD). PhD offered jointly with the Kansas City campus.

**Faculty:** 21.
**Students:** 78 full-time (63 women), 18 part-time (9 women); includes 15 minority (6 African Americans, 2 Asian Americans or Pacific Islanders, 6 Hispanic Americans, 1 Native American), 8 international. Average age 31. 51 applicants, 27% accepted,

14 enrolled. In 2001, 10 master's, 6 doctorates awarded.

**Degree requirements:** For master's, thesis or alternative; for doctorate, thesis/dissertation, comprehensive oral and written exams.

**Entrance requirements:** For master's, TOEFL, GRE; for doctorate, GRE, TOEFL, GRE. *Application deadline:* For fall admission, 2/15 (priority date). *Application fee:* $35.

**Expenses:** Tuition, state resident: full-time $2,722; part-time $113 per credit. Tuition, nonresident: full-time $8,586; part-time $358 per credit. Required fees: $551; $46 per credit. Tuition and fees vary according to campus/location, program and reciprocity agreements.

**Financial support:** In 2001–02, 15 research assistantships with partial tuition reimbursements (averaging $9,223 per year), 27 teaching assistantships with full and partial tuition reimbursements (averaging $6,710 per year) were awarded. Fellowships, career-related internships or fieldwork also available.
Edward K. Morris, Chair, 785-864-4840, *Fax:* 785-864-5202.

**Application contact:** R. Mark Mathews, Graduate Director, 785-864-4840, *Fax:* 785-864-5202, *E-mail:* rm-mathews@ ku.edu. *Web site:* http://www.ku.edu/~hdfl/

## ■ UNIVERSITY OF KANSAS

**Graduate School, College of Liberal Arts and Sciences, Program in Child Language, Lawrence, KS 66045**

**AWARDS** MA, PhD.

**Students:** 8 full-time (7 women), 1 (woman) part-time; includes 2 minority (1 Asian American or Pacific Islander, 1 Native American), 2 international. Average age 31. 5 applicants, 60% accepted, 3 enrolled.

**Degree requirements:** For master's and doctorate, thesis/dissertation.

**Entrance requirements:** For master's, TOEFL, GRE, minimum GPA of 3.5; for doctorate, GRE, TOEFL, minimum GPA of 3.5. *Application deadline:* For fall admission, 2/1 (priority date); for spring admission, 11/1. Applications are processed on a rolling basis. *Application fee:* $35.

**Expenses:** Tuition, state resident: full-time $2,722; part-time $113 per credit. Tuition, nonresident: full-time $8,586; part-time $358 per credit. Required fees: $551; $46 per credit. Tuition and fees vary according to campus/location, program and reciprocity agreements.

**Financial support:** Fellowships, research assistantships, career-related internships or fieldwork available.

**Faculty research:** Phonology, speech disorders, etiology of language impairments, word recognition processes, cultural context and linguistic patterns.
Mabel Rice, Director, 785-864-4570, *E-mail:* mabel@ku.edu.

**Application contact:** Susan Kemper, Graduate Adviser, 785-864-0748, *E-mail:* skemper@ku.edu. *Web site:* http://www.clp.ku.edu/

## ■ UNIVERSITY OF MAINE

**Graduate School, College of Liberal Arts and Sciences, Department of Psychology, Orono, ME 04469**

**AWARDS** Clinical psychology (PhD); developmental psychology (MA); experimental psychology (MA, PhD); social psychology (MA).

**Faculty:** 21.
**Students:** 22 full-time (17 women), 13 part-time (11 women); includes 3 minority (all Native Americans), 2 international. 100 applicants, 14% accepted, 6 enrolled. In 2001, 4 degrees awarded.

**Degree requirements:** For master's and doctorate, thesis/dissertation.

**Entrance requirements:** For master's and doctorate, GRE General Test, GRE Subject Test, TOEFL. *Application deadline:* For fall admission, 2/1 (priority date). Applications are processed on a rolling basis. *Application fee:* $50. Electronic applications accepted.

**Expenses:** Tuition, state resident: full-time $3,780; part-time $210 per credit hour. Tuition, nonresident: full-time $10,782; part-time $599 per credit hour. Required fees: $9.50 per credit hour. $32 per semester. Tuition and fees vary according to reciprocity agreements.

**Financial support:** In 2001–02, 3 research assistantships with tuition reimbursements (averaging $9,010 per year), 21 teaching assistantships with tuition reimbursements (averaging $9,010 per year) were awarded. Fellowships with tuition reimbursements, Federal Work-Study, institutionally sponsored loans, and tuition waivers (full and partial) also available. Financial award application deadline: 3/1.

**Faculty research:** Social development, hypertension and aging, attitude change, self-confidence in achievement situations, health psychology.
Dr. Joel Gold, Chair, 207-581-2030, *Fax:* 207-581-6128.

**Application contact:** Scott G. Delcourt, Director of the Graduate School, 207-581-3218, *Fax:* 207-581-3232, *E-mail:* graduate@maine.edu. *Web site:* http://www.umaine.edu/graduate/

## ■ UNIVERSITY OF MARYLAND, BALTIMORE COUNTY

**Graduate School, Department of Psychology, Program in Applied Developmental Psychology, Baltimore, MD 21250-5398**

**AWARDS** PhD.

**Degree requirements:** For doctorate, thesis/dissertation.

**Entrance requirements:** For doctorate, GRE General Test, GRE Subject Test, TOEFL, minimum GPA of 3.41.

**Faculty research:** Early intervention and development, schooling and development, cultural aspects of development, parent-infant relations, development in high risk children. *Web site:* http://www.umbc.edu/psyc/grad/adp.html

## ■ UNIVERSITY OF MARYLAND, COLLEGE PARK

**Graduate Studies and Research, College of Behavioral and Social Sciences, Department of Psychology, College Park, MD 20742**

**AWARDS** Clinical psychology (PhD); developmental psychology (PhD); experimental psychology (PhD); industrial psychology (MA, MS, PhD); social psychology (PhD).

**Faculty:** 52 full-time (17 women), 10 part-time/adjunct (5 women).
**Students:** 80 full-time (50 women), 22 part-time (15 women); includes 26 minority (14 African Americans, 8 Asian Americans or Pacific Islanders, 3 Hispanic Americans, 1 Native American), 11 international. 432 applicants, 10% accepted, 18 enrolled. In 2001, 8 master's, 21 doctorates awarded.

**Degree requirements:** For master's, thesis; for doctorate, variable foreign language requirement, thesis/dissertation, comprehensive exam.

**Entrance requirements:** For master's, GRE General Test, GRE Subject Test, minimum GPA of 3.5, research and/or work experience; for doctorate, GRE General Test, GRE Subject Test. *Application deadline:* For fall admission, 12/15. Applications are processed on a rolling basis. *Application fee:* $50 ($70 for international students). Electronic applications accepted.

**Expenses:** Tuition, state resident: part-time $289 per credit hour. Tuition, nonresident: part-time $448 per credit hour. One-time fee: $436 part-time. Full-time tuition and fees vary according to course load, campus/location and program.

**Financial support:** In 2001–02, 15 fellowships with full tuition reimbursements (averaging $11,508 per year), 87 teaching assistantships with tuition reimbursements

*University of Maryland, College Park (continued)*
(averaging $12,153 per year) were awarded. Career-related internships or fieldwork, Federal Work-Study, and scholarships/grants also available. Support available to part-time students. Financial award applicants required to submit FAFSA.
**Faculty research:** Counseling and social psychology.
Dr. William Hall, Chairman, 301-405-5862, *Fax:* 301-314-9566.
**Application contact:** Trudy Lindsey, Director, Graduate Admissions and Records, 301-405-6991, *Fax:* 301-314-9305, *E-mail:* grschool@deans.umd.edu.

■ **UNIVERSITY OF MIAMI**
**Graduate School, College of Arts and Sciences, Department of Psychology, Coral Gables, FL 33124**
**AWARDS** Applied developmental psychology (PhD); behavioral neuroscience (PhD); clinical psychology (PhD); health psychology (PhD); psychology (MS).
**Faculty:** 39 full-time (18 women).
**Students:** 70 full-time (51 women); includes 23 minority (6 African Americans, 4 Asian Americans or Pacific Islanders, 13 Hispanic Americans). Average age 25. 200 applicants, 14% accepted, 18 enrolled. In 2001, 12 degrees awarded.
**Degree requirements:** For doctorate, thesis/dissertation, comprehensive exam. *Median time to degree:* Doctorate–5 years full-time.
**Entrance requirements:** For doctorate, GRE General Test, TOEFL, minimum GPA of 3.5. *Application deadline:* For fall admission, 12/1. *Application fee:* $50. Electronic applications accepted.
**Expenses:** Tuition: Part-time $960 per credit hour. Required fees: $85 per semester. Tuition and fees vary according to program.
**Financial support:** In 2001–02, 7 fellowships with full tuition reimbursements (averaging $17,000 per year), 43 research assistantships with full tuition reimbursements (averaging $16,500 per year), 19 teaching assistantships with full tuition reimbursements (averaging $12,300 per year) were awarded. Career-related internships or fieldwork, institutionally sponsored loans, scholarships/grants, and traineeships also available. Financial award applicants required to submit FAFSA.
**Faculty research:** Depression, social and emotional development, stress and coping, AIDS and psychoneuroimmunology, children's peer relations. *Total annual research expenditures:* $10 million.
Dr. A. Rodney Wellens, Chairman, 305-284-2814, *Fax:* 305-284-3402.

**Application contact:** Patricia L. Perreira, Staff Associate, 305-284-2814, *Fax:* 305-284-3402, *E-mail:* inquire@mail.psy.miami.edu. *Web site:* http://www.psy.miami.edu/

■ **UNIVERSITY OF MICHIGAN**
**Horace H. Rackham School of Graduate Studies, College of Literature, Science, and the Arts, Department of Psychology, Ann Arbor, MI 48109**
**AWARDS** Biopsychology (PhD); clinical psychology (PhD); cognition and perception (PhD); developmental psychology (PhD); organizational psychology (PhD); personality psychology (PhD); social psychology (PhD).
**Faculty:** 68 full-time, 29 part-time/adjunct.
**Students:** 166 full-time (122 women); includes 57 minority (27 African Americans, 13 Asian Americans or Pacific Islanders, 14 Hispanic Americans, 3 Native Americans), 22 international. Average age 24. 555 applicants, 8% accepted, 27 enrolled. In 2001, 25 degrees awarded.
**Degree requirements:** For doctorate, oral defense of dissertation, preliminary exam.
**Entrance requirements:** For doctorate, GRE General Test, GRE Subject Test, TOEFL. *Application deadline:* For fall admission, 12/15. *Application fee:* $55. Electronic applications accepted.
**Financial support:** Fellowships with full tuition reimbursements, research assistantships with full tuition reimbursements, teaching assistantships with full tuition reimbursements, career-related internships or fieldwork available. Financial award application deadline: 3/15.
Richard Gonzalez, Chair, 734-764-7429.
**Application contact:** 734-764-6316, *Fax:* 734-764-3520. *Web site:* http://www.lsa.umich.edu/psych/

■ **THE UNIVERSITY OF MONTANA–MISSOULA**
**Graduate School, College of Arts and Sciences, Department of Psychology, Programs in Experimental Psychology, Missoula, MT 59812-0002**
**AWARDS** Animal behavior (PhD); developmental psychology (PhD).
**Degree requirements:** For doctorate, thesis/dissertation, oral exam.
**Entrance requirements:** For doctorate, GRE General Test, minimum GPA of 3.2. *Application deadline:* For fall admission, 1/15. *Application fee:* $45.
**Expenses:** Tuition, state resident: full-time $2,482; part-time $1,700 per year. Tuition, nonresident: full-time $7,372; part-time

$5,000 per year. Required fees: $1,900. Tuition and fees vary according to degree level.
**Financial support:** In 2001–02, teaching assistantships with full tuition reimbursements (averaging $8,400 per year); fellowships, research assistantships, Federal Work-Study also available. Financial award application deadline: 3/1; financial award applicants required to submit FAFSA.
**Faculty research:** Animal learning and behavior, neurological assessment, developmental psychology.
**Application contact:** Graduate Secretary, 406-243-4523, *Fax:* 406-243-6366, *E-mail:* psycgrad@selway.umt.edu. *Web site:* http://www.cas.umt.edu/psych/

■ **UNIVERSITY OF NEBRASKA AT OMAHA**
**Graduate Studies and Research, College of Arts and Sciences, Department of Psychology, Omaha, NE 68182**
**AWARDS** Developmental psychobiology (PhD); experimental child psychology (PhD); industrial/organizational psychology (MS, PhD); psychology (MA); school psychology (MS, Ed S). Part-time programs available.
**Faculty:** 17 full-time (7 women).
**Students:** 32 full-time (22 women), 18 part-time (10 women); includes 2 minority (1 African American, 1 Hispanic American). Average age 27. 64 applicants, 44% accepted, 28 enrolled. In 2001, 23 master's, 4 other advanced degrees awarded.
**Degree requirements:** For master's, thesis (for some programs), comprehensive exam; for doctorate, thesis/dissertation.
**Entrance requirements:** For master's, GRE General Test, GRE Subject Test, previous course work in psychology, including statistics and a laboratory course; minimum GPA of 3.0; for doctorate, GRE General Test. *Application deadline:* For fall admission, 2/1. *Application fee:* $35. Electronic applications accepted.
**Expenses:** Tuition, state resident: part-time $116 per credit hour. Tuition, nonresident: part-time $291 per credit hour. Required fees: $13 per credit hour. $4 per semester. One-time fee: $52 part-time.
**Financial support:** In 2001–02, 42 students received support; fellowships, research assistantships, teaching assistantships, career-related internships or fieldwork, Federal Work-Study, institutionally sponsored loans, scholarships/grants, tuition waivers (partial), and unspecified assistantships available. Support available to part-time students. Financial award application deadline: 3/1; financial award applicants required to submit FAFSA.

Dr. Kenneth Deffenbacher, Chairperson, 402-554-2592.

## ■ UNIVERSITY OF NEW ORLEANS

**Graduate School, College of Sciences, Department of Psychology, New Orleans, LA 70148**

**AWARDS** Applied psychology (PhD), including applied biopsychology, applied developmental psychology; psychology (MS).

**Faculty:** 6 full-time (3 women).
**Students:** 25 full-time (17 women); includes 1 minority (African American), 1 international. Average age 29. 47 applicants, 23% accepted, 6 enrolled. In 2001, 3 doctorates awarded.
**Degree requirements:** For doctorate, thesis/dissertation.
**Entrance requirements:** For doctorate, GRE General Test, minimum GPA of 3.0, 21 hours of course work in psychology. *Application deadline:* For fall admission, 7/1 (priority date); for spring admission, 11/15 (priority date). Applications are processed on a rolling basis. *Application fee:* $20. Electronic applications accepted.
**Expenses:** Tuition, state resident: full-time $2,748; part-time $435 per credit. Tuition, nonresident: full-time $9,792; part-time $1,773 per credit.
**Financial support:** Fellowships, research assistantships, teaching assistantships, career-related internships or fieldwork and unspecified assistantships available. Financial award application deadline: 2/15; financial award applicants required to submit FAFSA.
**Faculty research:** Biofeedback, visual and auditory perception, psychopharmacology, neuropeptides.
Dr. Matthew Stanford, Graduate Coordinator, 504-280-6185, *Fax:* 504-280-6049, *E-mail:* mstanfor@uno.edu.
**Application contact:** Dr. Paul Frick, Graduate Coordinator, 504-280-6012, *Fax:* 504-280-6049, *E-mail:* pfrick@uno.edu.

## ■ THE UNIVERSITY OF NORTH CAROLINA AT CHAPEL HILL

**Graduate School, College of Arts and Sciences, Department of Psychology, Chapel Hill, NC 27599**

**AWARDS** Biological psychology (PhD); clinical psychology (PhD); cognitive psychology (PhD); developmental psychology (PhD); quantitative psychology (PhD); social psychology (PhD).

**Faculty:** 46 full-time (25 women), 6 part-time/adjunct (0 women).
**Students:** 116 full-time (63 women). 546 applicants, 7% accepted, 29 enrolled. In 2001, 27 doctorates awarded.
**Degree requirements:** For doctorate, thesis/dissertation, comprehensive exam.
**Entrance requirements:** For doctorate, GRE General Test, minimum GPA of 3.0. *Application deadline:* For fall admission, 12/1. *Application fee:* $55. Electronic applications accepted.
**Expenses:** Tuition, state resident: full-time $2,864. Tuition, nonresident: full-time $12,030.
**Financial support:** In 2001–02, 11 fellowships with tuition reimbursements, 28 research assistantships with tuition reimbursements, 63 teaching assistantships with tuition reimbursements were awarded. Unspecified assistantships also available. Financial award application deadline: 2/1.
**Faculty research:** Expressed emotion, cognitive development, social cognitive neuroscience, human memory personality. *Total annual research expenditures:* $605,806.
Peter A. Ornstein, Chair, 919-962-3088.
**Application contact:** Barbara Atkins, Student Services Manager, 919-962-7149, *Fax:* 919-962-2537, *E-mail:* batkins@email.unc.edu.

## ■ THE UNIVERSITY OF NORTH CAROLINA AT GREENSBORO

**Graduate School, College of Arts and Sciences, Department of Psychology, Greensboro, NC 27412-5001**

**AWARDS** Clinical psychology (MA, PhD); cognitive psychology (MA, PhD); developmental psychology (MA, PhD); social psychology (MA, PhD).

**Faculty:** 22 full-time (9 women), 1 part-time/adjunct (0 women).
**Students:** 42 full-time (35 women), 20 part-time (13 women); includes 2 African Americans, 2 Asian Americans or Pacific Islanders, 2 Hispanic Americans. In 2001, 13 master's, 5 doctorates awarded. Terminal master's awarded for partial completion of doctoral program.
**Degree requirements:** For master's, thesis, comprehensive exam; for doctorate, one foreign language, thesis/dissertation, preliminary exam.
**Entrance requirements:** For master's, GRE General Test, TOEFL; for doctorate, GRE General Test, GRE Subject Test (recommended), TOEFL. *Application deadline:* For fall admission, 2/1. *Application fee:* $35.
**Expenses:** Tuition, state resident: part-time $344 per course. Tuition, nonresident: part-time $2,457 per course.
**Financial support:** In 2001–02, 3 fellowships with full tuition reimbursements (averaging $10,833 per year), 54 research assistantships with full tuition reimbursements (averaging $8,514 per year), 2 teaching assistantships with full tuition reimbursements (averaging $3,500 per year) were awarded. Unspecified assistantships also available.
**Faculty research:** Sensory and perceptual determinants; evoked potential: disorders, deafness, and development.
Dr. Timothy Johnston, Head, 336-334-5013, *Fax:* 336-334-5066, *E-mail:* johnston@uncg.edu.
**Application contact:** Dr. James Lynch, Director of Graduate Recruitment and Information Services, 336-334-4881, *Fax:* 336-334-4424. *Web site:* http://www.uncg.edu/psy/

## ■ UNIVERSITY OF NOTRE DAME

**Graduate School, College of Arts and Letters, Division of Social Science, Department of Psychology, Notre Dame, IN 46556**

**AWARDS** Cognitive psychology (PhD); counseling psychology (PhD); developmental psychology (PhD); quantitative psychology (PhD).

**Faculty:** 31 full-time (11 women).
**Students:** 60 full-time (42 women); includes 10 minority (3 African Americans, 2 Asian Americans or Pacific Islanders, 5 Hispanic Americans), 5 international. 189 applicants, 12% accepted, 15 enrolled. In 2001, 8 doctorates awarded.
**Degree requirements:** For doctorate, thesis/dissertation, comprehensive exam. *Median time to degree:* Doctorate–5.9 years full-time.
**Entrance requirements:** For doctorate, GRE General Test, GRE Subject Test (strongly recommended), TOEFL. *Application deadline:* For fall admission, 1/2. *Application fee:* $50. Electronic applications accepted.
**Expenses:** Tuition: Full-time $24,220; part-time $1,346 per credit hour. Required fees: $155.
**Financial support:** In 2001–02, 59 students received support, including 31 fellowships with full tuition reimbursements available (averaging $16,000 per year), 10 research assistantships with full tuition reimbursements available (averaging $11,400 per year), 17 teaching assistantships with full tuition reimbursements available (averaging $11,400 per year); career-related internships or fieldwork and tuition waivers (full) also available. Financial award application deadline: 1/2.
**Faculty research:** Cognitive and socioemotional development, marital discord, statistical methods and quantitative models applicable to psychology, interpersonal relations, life span development and developmental delay, childhood depression, structural equation and dynamical systems, modeling, social cognition, ecology, health

*University of Notre Dame (continued)*
psychology, aging behavior genetics. *Total annual research expenditures:* $1.8 million. Dr. Laura Carlson, Director of Graduate Studies, 574-631-6650, *Fax:* 574-631-8883, *E-mail:* lcarlson@nd.edu.
**Application contact:** Dr. Terrence J. Akai, Director of Graduate Admissions, 574-631-7706, *Fax:* 574-631-4183, *E-mail:* gradad@nd.edu. *Web site:* http://www.nd.edu/~psych/

### ■ UNIVERSITY OF OREGON

**Graduate School, College of Arts and Sciences, Department of Psychology, Eugene, OR 97403**

**AWARDS** Clinical psychology (PhD); cognitive psychology (MA, MS, PhD); developmental psychology (MA, MS, PhD); physiological psychology (MA, MS, PhD); psychology (MA, MS, PhD); social/personality psychology (MA, MS, PhD).

**Faculty:** 27 full-time (11 women), 11 part-time/adjunct (8 women).
**Students:** 73 full-time (49 women), 3 part-time (all women); includes 7 minority (3 Asian Americans or Pacific Islanders, 2 Hispanic Americans, 2 Native Americans), 14 international. 176 applicants, 11% accepted. In 2001, 21 master's, 11 doctorates awarded. Terminal master's awarded for partial completion of doctoral program.
**Degree requirements:** For doctorate, thesis/dissertation.
**Entrance requirements:** For master's, GRE General Test, TOEFL, minimum GPA of 3.0; for doctorate, GRE General Test, TOEFL. *Application deadline:* For fall admission, 12/1. *Application fee:* $50.
**Expenses:** Tuition, state resident: full-time $4,968; part-time $501 per credit hour. Tuition, nonresident: full-time $8,400; part-time $691 per credit hour.
**Financial support:** In 2001–02, 48 teaching assistantships were awarded; research assistantships, career-related internships or fieldwork also available.
Marjorie Taylor, Head, 541-346-4921, *Fax:* 541-346-4911.
**Application contact:** Lori Olsen, Admissions Contact, 541-346-5060, *Fax:* 541-346-4911, *E-mail:* gradsec@psych.uoregon.edu. *Web site:* http://psychweb.uoregon.edu/

### ■ UNIVERSITY OF PITTSBURGH

**School of Education, Department of Psychology in Education, Program in Educational and Developmental Psychology, Pittsburgh, PA 15260**

**AWARDS** PhD.

**Students:** 13 full-time (11 women), 26 part-time (20 women); includes 4 minority (1 African American, 3 Hispanic

Americans), 6 international. 25 applicants, 36% accepted, 6 enrolled. In 2001, 3 degrees awarded.
**Degree requirements:** For doctorate, thesis/dissertation.
**Entrance requirements:** For doctorate, GRE General Test, TOEFL. *Application deadline:* For fall admission, 2/1. *Application fee:* $40. Electronic applications accepted.
**Expenses:** Tuition, state resident: full-time $9,410; part-time $385 per credit. Tuition, nonresident: full-time $19,376; part-time $797 per credit. Required fees: $480; $90 per term. Tuition and fees vary according to program.
**Financial support:** In 2001–02, fellowships (averaging $2,500 per year), research assistantships with partial tuition reimbursements (averaging $8,000 per year), teaching assistantships with partial tuition reimbursements (averaging $8,000 per year) were awarded. Career-related internships or fieldwork, tuition waivers (partial), and unspecified assistantships also available. Financial award application deadline: 5/1; financial award applicants required to submit FAFSA.
**Application contact:** Jackie Harden, Manager, 412-648-2230, *Fax:* 412-648-1899, *E-mail:* soeinfo@pitt.edu. *Web site:* http://www.pitt.edu/programs/d~psy/

### ■ UNIVERSITY OF ROCHESTER

**The College, Arts and Sciences, Department of Clinical and Social Sciences in Psychology, Rochester, NY 14627-0250**

**AWARDS** Clinical psychology (PhD); developmental psychology (PhD); psychology (MA); social-personality psychology (PhD).

**Faculty:** 14.
**Students:** 43 full-time (30 women); includes 3 minority (2 African Americans, 1 Native American), 8 international. 166 applicants, 11% accepted, 8 enrolled. In 2001, 4 master's, 7 doctorates awarded. Terminal master's awarded for partial completion of doctoral program.
**Degree requirements:** For doctorate, thesis/dissertation, qualifying exam.
**Entrance requirements:** For doctorate, GRE General Test, TOEFL. *Application deadline:* For fall admission, 2/1 (priority date). *Application fee:* $25.
**Expenses:** Tuition: Part-time $755 per credit hour.
**Financial support:** Fellowships, research assistantships, teaching assistantships, career-related internships or fieldwork and tuition waivers (full and partial) available. Financial award application deadline: 2/1.
Miron Zuckerman, Chair, 585-275-2453.
**Application contact:** Mary Ann Gilbert, Graduate Program Secretary, 585-275-8704.

### ■ UNIVERSITY OF WISCONSIN–MADISON

**Graduate School, College of Letters and Science, Department of Psychology, Program in Developmental Psychology, Madison, WI 53706-1380**

**AWARDS** PhD.

**Faculty:** 5 full-time (3 women), 1 (woman) part-time/adjunct.
**Students:** 9 full-time (6 women), 1 international. Average age 23. 34 applicants, 18% accepted, 2 enrolled. In 2001, 2 doctorates awarded.
**Degree requirements:** For doctorate, thesis/dissertation, comprehensive exam, registration. *Median time to degree:* Doctorate–5 years full-time.
**Entrance requirements:** For doctorate, GRE General Test, minimum undergraduate GPA of 3.0. *Application deadline:* For fall admission, 1/5 (priority date). Applications are processed on a rolling basis. *Application fee:* $45. Electronic applications accepted.
**Expenses:** Tuition, state resident: full-time $7,361; part-time $399 per credit. Tuition, nonresident: full-time $20,499; part-time $1,282 per credit. Required fees: $34 per credit. Full-time tuition and fees vary according to course load, program, reciprocity agreements and student level.
**Financial support:** In 2001–02, 9 students received support, including fellowships with full tuition reimbursements available (averaging $13,446 per year), 6 research assistantships with full tuition reimbursements available (averaging $13,814 per year), 2 teaching assistantships with full tuition reimbursements available (averaging $13,814 per year); institutionally sponsored loans, traineeships, health care benefits, and unspecified assistantships also available. Financial award application deadline: 1/5.
Seth Pollak, Chair, 608-265-8190, *Fax:* 608-262-4029, *E-mail:* spollak@facstaff.wisc.edu.
**Application contact:** Jane Fox-Anderson, Secretary, 608-262-2079, *Fax:* 608-262-4029, *E-mail:* jefoxand@facstaff.wisc.edu.

### ■ VIRGINIA POLYTECHNIC INSTITUTE AND STATE UNIVERSITY

**Graduate School, College of Arts and Sciences, Department of Psychology, Blacksburg, VA 24061**

**AWARDS** Bio-behavioral sciences (PhD); clinical psychology (PhD); developmental psychology (PhD); industrial/organizational psychology (PhD); psychology (MS).

**Faculty:** 22 full-time (4 women), 3 part-time/adjunct (2 women).
**Students:** 68 full-time (45 women), 8 part-time (6 women); includes 13 minority (5 African Americans, 4 Asian Americans or Pacific Islanders, 4 Hispanic Americans). Average age 23. 156 applicants, 21% accepted, 15 enrolled. In 2001, 4 master's, 8 doctorates awarded.
**Degree requirements:** For doctorate, thesis/dissertation.
**Entrance requirements:** For master's and doctorate, GRE General Test, TOEFL. *Application deadline:* For fall admission, 1/15 (priority date); for winter admission, 12/15 (priority date). Applications are processed on a rolling basis. *Application fee:* $45. Electronic applications accepted.
**Expenses:** Tuition, state resident: part-time $241 per hour. Tuition, nonresident: part-time $406 per hour. Tuition and fees vary according to program.
**Financial support:** In 2001–02, 1 fellowship with tuition reimbursement (averaging $12,500 per year), 13 research assistantships with full tuition reimbursements (averaging $11,790 per year), 52 teaching assistantships with full tuition reimbursements (averaging $7,074 per year) were awarded. Unspecified assistantships also available. Financial award application deadline: 4/1.
**Faculty research:** Infant development from electrophysical point of view, work motivation and personnel selection, EEG, ERP and hypnosis with reference to chronic pain, intimate violence.
Dr. Jack W. Finney, Chair, 540-231-6581, *Fax:* 540-231-3652, *E-mail:* finney@vt.edu. *Web site:* http://www.psyc.vt.edu/

### ■ WAYNE STATE UNIVERSITY

**Graduate School, College of Science, Department of Psychology, Program in Psychology, Detroit, MI 48202**

**AWARDS** Clinical psychology (PhD); cognitive psychology (PhD); developmental psychology (PhD); industrial/organizational psychology (PhD); psychology (MA, PhD); social psychology (PhD).

**Students:** 114. In 2001, 22 master's, 23 doctorates awarded.
**Degree requirements:** For doctorate, thesis/dissertation.
**Entrance requirements:** For doctorate, GRE General Test, GRE Subject Test. *Application deadline:* For fall admission, 2/1. *Application fee:* $20 ($30 for international students). Electronic applications accepted.
**Expenses:** Tuition, state resident: full-time $3,764. Tuition and fees vary according to degree level and program.
**Financial support:** Application deadline: 2/1.

**Application contact:** Kathryn Urberg, Graduate Director, 313-577-2820, *Fax:* 313-577-7636, *E-mail:* kurberg@sun.science.wayne.edu.

### ■ WEST VIRGINIA UNIVERSITY

**Eberly College of Arts and Sciences, Department of Psychology, Morgantown, WV 26506**

**AWARDS** Behavior analysis (PhD); clinical psychology (MA, PhD); development psychology (PhD). Part-time programs available.

**Faculty:** 23 full-time (8 women), 2 part-time/adjunct (both women).
**Students:** 53 full-time (40 women), 17 part-time (9 women); includes 6 minority (3 Asian Americans or Pacific Islanders, 2 Hispanic Americans, 1 Native American), 3 international. Average age 27. 306 applicants, 6% accepted. In 2001, 11 master's, 17 doctorates awarded. Terminal master's awarded for partial completion of doctoral program.
**Degree requirements:** For master's, thesis optional; for doctorate, thesis/dissertation, comprehensive exam.
**Entrance requirements:** For master's and doctorate, GRE General Test, TOEFL, minimum GPA of 3.0. *Application deadline:* For fall admission, 1/15. *Application fee:* $45.
**Expenses:** Tuition, state resident: full-time $2,791. Tuition, nonresident: full-time $8,659. Required fees: $1,002. Tuition and fees vary according to program.
**Financial support:** In 2001–02, 20 research assistantships, 30 teaching assistantships were awarded. Fellowships, career-related internships or fieldwork, Federal Work-Study, institutionally sponsored loans, and tuition waivers (full and partial) also available. Financial award application deadline: 1/15; financial award applicants required to submit FAFSA.
**Faculty research:** Adult and child clinical psychology, behavioral assessment and therapy, child and adolescent behavior, life span development, experimental and applied behavior analysis. *Total annual research expenditures:* $372,796.
Dr. Michael T. Perone, Chair, 304-293-2001 Ext. 604, *Fax:* 304-293-6606, *E-mail:* michael.perone@mail.wvu.edu.
**Application contact:** Dr. Katherine A. Karraker, Director, Graduate Training, 304-293-2001 Ext. 625, *Fax:* 304-293-6606, *E-mail:* katherine.karraker@mail.wvu.edu. *Web site:* http://www.as.wvu.edu/psyc/

### ■ YESHIVA UNIVERSITY

**Ferkauf Graduate School of Psychology, Program in Developmental Psychology, New York, NY 10033-3201**

**AWARDS** PhD. Part-time programs available.

**Faculty:** 2 full-time (0 women), 11 part-time/adjunct (6 women).
**Students:** 10 full-time (5 women), 3 part-time (all women); includes 2 minority (both African Americans), 3 international. Average age 28. 35 applicants, 11% accepted. In 2001, 3 degrees awarded.
**Degree requirements:** For doctorate, thesis/dissertation.
**Entrance requirements:** For doctorate, GRE General Test, GRE Subject Test. *Application deadline:* For fall admission, 1/15. *Application fee:* $50.
**Financial support:** In 2001–02, 3 fellowships (averaging $5,000 per year), 2 research assistantships (averaging $2,000 per year), 4 teaching assistantships (averaging $2,000 per year) were awarded. Career-related internships or fieldwork, Federal Work-Study, institutionally sponsored loans, and scholarships/grants also available. Support available to part-time students. Financial award application deadline: 4/15.
**Faculty research:** Early childhood learning, socio-moral development, language development.
Dr. William Arsenio, Director, 718-430-3951, *E-mail:* warsenio@wesleyan.edu.
**Application contact:** Elaine Schwartz, Assistant Director of Admissions, 718-430-3820, *Fax:* 718-430-3960, *E-mail:* eschart@ymail.yu.edu. *Web site:* http://www.yu.edu/fgs/

# EXPERIMENTAL PSYCHOLOGY

### ■ AMERICAN UNIVERSITY

**College of Arts and Sciences, Department of Psychology, Program in Experimental Psychology, Washington, DC 20016-8001**

**AWARDS** PhD.

**Students:** 5 full-time (all women), 1 part-time; includes 2 minority (both Asian Americans or Pacific Islanders).
**Degree requirements:** For doctorate, thesis/dissertation.
**Entrance requirements:** For doctorate, GRE General Test, GRE Subject Test. *Application deadline:* For fall admission, 2/1. *Application fee:* $50.
**Expenses:** Tuition: Full-time $14,274; part-time $793 per credit. Required fees: $290. Tuition and fees vary according to program.

*American University (continued)*

**Financial support:** In 2001–02, 3 research assistantships were awarded; fellowships, teaching assistantships, career-related internships or fieldwork, Federal Work-Study, institutionally sponsored loans, and tuition waivers (full and partial) also available. Support available to part-time students. Financial award application deadline: 2/1.

**Faculty research:** Psychophysics, drug discrimination learning, choice behavior, conditioning and learning, olfaction and taste.

Bryan Sanke, Professor, 202-885-1790.
**Application contact:** Dr. Anthony Riley, Chair, 202-885-1720.

■ **AMERICAN UNIVERSITY**

College of Arts and Sciences, Department of Psychology, Program in Psychology, Washington, DC 20016-8001

**AWARDS** Experimental/biological psychology (MA); general psychology (MA, PhD); personality/social psychology (MA). Part-time programs available.

**Students:** 38 full-time (31 women), 50 part-time (45 women); includes 16 minority (5 African Americans, 5 Asian Americans or Pacific Islanders, 6 Hispanic Americans), 6 international. Average age 25.

**Degree requirements:** For master's, thesis (for some programs).

**Entrance requirements:** For master's, GRE General Test, GRE Subject Test. *Application deadline:* For fall admission, 4/30. Applications are processed on a rolling basis. *Application fee:* $50.

**Expenses:** Tuition: Full-time $14,274; part-time $793 per credit. Required fees: $290. Tuition and fees vary according to program.

**Financial support:** In 2001–02, 2 students received support; teaching assistantships available. Financial award application deadline: 2/1.

**Faculty research:** Behavior therapy, cognitive behavior modification, pro-social behavior, conditioning and learning, olfaction.

Dr. Brian Yates, Director, 202-885-1727.

■ **APPALACHIAN STATE UNIVERSITY**

Cratis D. Williams Graduate School, College of Arts and Sciences, Department of Psychology, Program in General Experimental Psychology, Boone, NC 28608

**AWARDS** MA. Part-time programs available.
**Faculty:** 24 full-time (8 women).

**Students:** 6 full-time (0 women). In 2001, 2 degrees awarded.

**Degree requirements:** For master's, thesis, GRE Subject Test exit exam, comprehensive exam.

**Entrance requirements:** For master's, GRE General Test, GRE Subject Test. *Application deadline:* For fall admission, 3/1 (priority date). Applications are processed on a rolling basis. *Application fee:* $35.

**Expenses:** Tuition, state resident: full-time $1,286. Tuition, nonresident: full-time $9,354. Required fees: $1,116.

**Financial support:** In 2001–02, research assistantships (averaging $6,250 per year), teaching assistantships (averaging $6,250 per year) were awarded. Fellowships, career-related internships or fieldwork also available. Support available to part-time students. Financial award application deadline: 7/1.

Dr. Mark Zrull, Director, 828-262-2272, *E-mail:* zrullmc@appstate.edu. *Web site:* http://www.acs.appstate.edu/dept/psych/

■ **BOWLING GREEN STATE UNIVERSITY**

Graduate College, College of Arts and Sciences, Department of Psychology, Bowling Green, OH 43403

**AWARDS** Clinical psychology (MA, PhD); developmental psychology (MA, PhD); experimental psychology (MA, PhD); industrial/organizational psychology (MA, PhD); quantitative psychology (MA, PhD).

**Faculty:** 31.

**Students:** 89 full-time (57 women), 27 part-time (18 women); includes 14 minority (3 African Americans, 7 Asian Americans or Pacific Islanders, 4 Hispanic Americans), 9 international. Average age 27. 274 applicants, 15% accepted, 24 enrolled. In 2001, 10 master's, 17 doctorates awarded. Terminal master's awarded for partial completion of doctoral program.

**Degree requirements:** For master's and doctorate, thesis/dissertation.

**Entrance requirements:** For master's and doctorate, GRE General Test, TOEFL. *Application deadline:* For fall admission, 1/15. *Application fee:* $30. Electronic applications accepted.

**Expenses:** Tuition, state resident: full-time $7,376; part-time $342 per credit hour. Tuition, nonresident: full-time $13,628; part-time $640 per credit hour.

**Financial support:** In 2001–02, 30 research assistantships with full tuition reimbursements (averaging $9,452 per year), 32 teaching assistantships with full tuition reimbursements (averaging $9,607 per year) were awarded. Career-related internships or fieldwork, Federal Work-Study, institutionally sponsored loans, tuition waivers (full), and unspecified

assistantships also available. Financial award applicants required to submit FAFSA.

**Faculty research:** Personnel psychology, developmental-mathematical models, behavioral medication, brain process, child/adolescent social cognition.

Dr. Dale Klopfer, Chair, 419-372-2733.
**Application contact:** Dr. Eric Dubow, Graduate Coordinator, 419-372-2556.

■ **BROOKLYN COLLEGE OF THE CITY UNIVERSITY OF NEW YORK**

Division of Graduate Studies, Department of Psychology, Brooklyn, NY 11210-2889

**AWARDS** Experimental psychology (MA); industrial and organizational psychology (MA), including industrial and organizational psychology-human relations, psychology-organizational psychology and behavior; psychology (PhD). Part-time programs available.

**Students:** 7 full-time (4 women), 87 part-time (63 women); includes 40 minority (24 African Americans, 5 Asian Americans or Pacific Islanders, 11 Hispanic Americans), 11 international. 104 applicants, 59% accepted. In 2001, 47 degrees awarded.

**Degree requirements:** For master's, thesis or alternative, comprehensive exam.

**Entrance requirements:** For master's, TOEFL, minimum GPA of 3.0; for doctorate, GRE. *Application deadline:* For fall admission, 3/1 (priority date); for spring admission, 11/1. Applications are processed on a rolling basis. *Application fee:* $40.

**Expenses:** Tuition, state resident: full-time $4,350; part-time $185 per credit. Tuition, nonresident: full-time $7,600; part-time $320 per credit.

**Financial support:** Career-related internships or fieldwork, Federal Work-Study, institutionally sponsored loans, scholarships/grants, and tuition waivers (partial) available. Support available to part-time students. Financial award application deadline: 5/1; financial award applicants required to submit FAFSA.

Dr. Glen Hass, Chairperson, 718-951-5601, *Fax:* 718-951-4814.
**Application contact:** Dr. Benzion Chanowitz, Graduate Deputy, 718-951-5019, *Fax:* 718-951-4814, *E-mail:* psych-ma@brooklyn.cuny.edu. *Web site:* http://academic.brooklyn.cuny.edu/psych

## ■ CALIFORNIA STATE UNIVERSITY, SAN BERNARDINO

**Graduate Studies, College of Social and Behavioral Sciences, Department of Psychology, Program in General/Experimental Psychology, San Bernardino, CA 92407-2397**

AWARDS MA.

**Students:** 13 full-time (9 women), 11 part-time (9 women); includes 8 minority (1 African American, 1 Asian American or Pacific Islander, 6 Hispanic Americans), 2 international. Average age 36. 19 applicants, 42% accepted. In 2001, 5 degrees awarded.
**Entrance requirements:** For master's, minimum GPA of 3.0 in major. *Application deadline:* For fall admission, 4/1; for spring admission, 3/1. *Application fee:* $55.
**Expenses:** Tuition, nonresident: full-time $4,428. Required fees: $1,733.
**Financial support:** Unspecified assistantships available.
Dr. Sanders McDougall, Head, 909-880-5581, *Fax:* 909-880-7003, *E-mail:* smcdouga@csusb.edu.
**Application contact:** Luci Van Loon, Graduate Secretary, 909-880-5570, *Fax:* 909-880-7003, *E-mail:* lvanloon@csusb.edu.

## ■ CASE WESTERN RESERVE UNIVERSITY

**School of Graduate Studies, Department of Psychology, Program in Experimental Psychology, Cleveland, OH 44106**

AWARDS PhD.

**Degree requirements:** For doctorate, thesis/dissertation, internship.
**Entrance requirements:** For doctorate, GRE General Test, GRE Subject Test, TOEFL.
**Faculty research:** Memory and intelligence, brain function in rats.

## ■ THE CATHOLIC UNIVERSITY OF AMERICA

**School of Arts and Sciences, Department of Psychology, Program in Applied Experimental Psychology, Washington, DC 20064**

AWARDS MA, PhD.

**Students:** 4 full-time (2 women), 3 part-time (2 women); includes 2 minority (1 African American, 1 Hispanic American), 1 international. Average age 28. 5 applicants, 80% accepted, 1 enrolled. In 2001, 1 master's, 2 doctorates awarded.
**Degree requirements:** For doctorate, thesis/dissertation, comprehensive exam.

**Entrance requirements:** For doctorate, GRE General Test, GRE Subject Test. *Application deadline:* For fall admission, 2/15. Applications are processed on a rolling basis. *Application fee:* $55. Electronic applications accepted.
**Expenses:** Tuition: Full-time $20,050; part-time $770 per credit. Required fees: $430 per term. Tuition and fees vary according to program.
**Financial support:** Fellowships, research assistantships, teaching assistantships, career-related internships or fieldwork, Federal Work-Study, institutionally sponsored loans, scholarships/grants, and tuition waivers (full and partial) available. Support available to part-time students. Financial award application deadline: 2/1.
**Faculty research:** Aviation human factors, human perception and cognition, cognitive science, artificial intelligence, attention and vigilance.
Dr. Raja Parasuraman, Director, 202-319-5750.

## ■ CENTRAL MICHIGAN UNIVERSITY

**College of Graduate Studies, College of Humanities and Social and Behavioral Sciences, Department of Psychology, Program in General, Applied, and Experimental Psychology, Mount Pleasant, MI 48859**

AWARDS Applied experimental psychology (PhD); general/experimental psychology (MS).

**Degree requirements:** For master's, thesis or alternative.
**Entrance requirements:** For doctorate, GRE.
**Expenses:** Tuition, state resident: part-time $182 per unit. Tuition, nonresident: part-time $182 per unit. Required fees: $208 per semester. Part-time tuition and fees vary according to course load.

## ■ CENTRAL WASHINGTON UNIVERSITY

**Graduate Studies and Research, College of the Sciences, Department of Psychology, Program in Experimental Psychology, Ellensburg, WA 98926-7463**

AWARDS MS.

**Faculty:** 23 full-time (9 women).
**Students:** 9 full-time (8 women), 2 part-time (1 woman). 16 applicants, 44% accepted, 5 enrolled. In 2001, 3 degrees awarded.
**Degree requirements:** For master's, thesis.
**Entrance requirements:** For master's, GRE General Test, minimum GPA of 3.0. *Application deadline:* For fall admission, 4/1

(priority date). Applications are processed on a rolling basis. *Application fee:* $35.
**Expenses:** Tuition, state resident: full-time $4,848; part-time $162 per credit. Tuition, nonresident: full-time $14,772; part-time $492 per credit. Required fees: $324.
**Financial support:** In 2001–02, 3 research assistantships with partial tuition reimbursements (averaging $7,120 per year) were awarded; teaching assistantships, career-related internships or fieldwork and Federal Work-Study also available. Financial award application deadline: 3/1.
**Application contact:** Barbara Sisko, Office Assistant, Graduate Studies and Research, 509-963-3103, *Fax:* 509-963-1799, *E-mail:* masters@cwu.edu. *Web site:* http://www.cwu.edu/

## ■ CITY COLLEGE OF THE CITY UNIVERSITY OF NEW YORK

**Graduate School, College of Liberal Arts and Science, Division of Social Science, Department of Psychology, New York, NY 10031-9198**

AWARDS Clinical psychology (PhD); experimental cognition (PhD); general psychology (MA). Part-time programs available.

**Students:** 81. In 2001, 10 degrees awarded.
**Degree requirements:** For master's, one foreign language, thesis, comprehensive exam.
**Entrance requirements:** For master's, TOEFL, minimum undergraduate B average. *Application deadline:* For fall admission, 5/1; for spring admission, 12/1. *Application fee:* $40.
**Expenses:** Tuition, state resident: part-time $185 per credit. Tuition, nonresident: part-time $320 per credit. Required fees: $43 per term.
**Financial support:** Fellowships, teaching assistantships, career-related internships or fieldwork, Federal Work-Study, and tuition waivers (full and partial) available. Support available to part-time students. Financial award application deadline: 5/1.
**Faculty research:** Social/personality psychology, physiological psychology, cognition and development.
Brett Silverstein, Chair, 212-650-5442.
**Application contact:** Dr. William King, Graduate Adviser, 212-650-5723.

## ■ CLEVELAND STATE UNIVERSITY

**College of Graduate Studies, College of Arts and Sciences, Department of Psychology, Program in Research Psychology, Cleveland, OH 44115**

AWARDS MA. Part-time programs available.

*Cleveland State University (continued)*
**Faculty:** 17 full-time (6 women), 4 part-time/adjunct (1 woman).
**Students:** 3 full-time (1 woman), 7 part-time (4 women); includes 2 minority (both Asian Americans or Pacific Islanders). Average age 27. 15 applicants, 53% accepted, 2 enrolled. In 2001, 4 degrees awarded.
**Degree requirements:** For master's, thesis. *Median time to degree: Master's–2 years part-time.*
**Entrance requirements:** For master's, GRE General Test, GRE Subject Test, minimum GPA of 2.8. *Application deadline:* For fall admission, 6/1 (priority date). Applications are processed on a rolling basis. *Application fee:* $25 ($50 for international students).
**Expenses:** Tuition, state resident: full-time $6,838; part-time $263 per credit hour. Tuition, nonresident: full-time $13,526; part-time $520 per credit hour.
**Financial support:** In 2001–02, 3 students received support. Federal Work-Study and tuition waivers (full) available. Financial award application deadline: 5/1; financial award applicants required to submit FAFSA.
**Faculty research:** Cognitive processes, imagery, behavioral pharmacology, human stress reactions. *Total annual research expenditures:* $80,000.
Dr. Leslie Fisher, Director, 216-687-9386.
**Application contact:** Karen Colston, Administrative Coordinator, 216-687-2552, *E-mail:* k.colston@csuohio.edu. *Web site:* http://www.asic.csuohio.edu/psy/grad/exp.html

### ■ COLLEGE OF STATEN ISLAND OF THE CITY UNIVERSITY OF NEW YORK

**Graduate Programs, Center for Developmental Neuroscience and Developmental Disabilities, Subprogram in Learning Processes, Staten Island, NY 10314-6600**

**AWARDS** Biopsychology (PhD); clinical psychology (PhD); developmental psychology (PhD); environmental psychology (PhD); experimental cognition (PhD); experimental psychology (PhD); neuropsychology (PhD); psychology (PhD); social-personality psychology (PhD).

**Degree requirements:** For doctorate, one foreign language, thesis/dissertation.
**Entrance requirements:** For doctorate, GRE, TOEFL. *Application deadline:* For fall admission, 3/15 (priority date). Applications are processed on a rolling basis. *Application fee:* $40.
**Expenses:** Tuition, state resident: full-time $4,350; part-time $185 per credit. Tuition,

nonresident: full-time $7,600; part-time $320 per credit. Required fees: $53 per semester.
**Financial support:** Fellowships, research assistantships, teaching assistantships, career-related internships or fieldwork and institutionally sponsored loans available. Financial award application deadline: 3/15.
Dr. Nancy Hemmes, Head, 718-997-3561.

### ■ THE COLLEGE OF WILLIAM AND MARY

**Faculty of Arts and Sciences, Department of Psychology, Program in General Experimental Psychology, Williamsburg, VA 23187-8795**

**AWARDS** MA.

**Faculty:** 13 full-time (2 women).
**Students:** 15 full-time (11 women). Average age 26. 61 applicants, 41% accepted, 10 enrolled. In 2001, 10 degrees awarded.
**Degree requirements:** For master's, thesis. *Median time to degree: Master's–2 years full-time.*
**Entrance requirements:** For master's, GRE, previous course work in statistics and experimental psychology. *Application deadline:* For fall admission, 2/15. *Application fee:* $30.
**Expenses:** Tuition, state resident: full-time $3,262; part-time $175 per credit hour. Tuition, nonresident: full-time $14,768; part-time $550 per credit hour. Required fees: $2,478.
**Financial support:** In 2001–02, 2 research assistantships with full tuition reimbursements (averaging $9,000 per year), 13 teaching assistantships with full tuition reimbursements (averaging $9,000 per year) were awarded. Career-related internships or fieldwork, institutionally sponsored loans, scholarships/grants, and unspecified assistantships also available. Financial award application deadline: 2/15; financial award applicants required to submit FAFSA.
**Faculty research:** Personality, developmental, professional development, applied decision theory, social psychology.
Dr. Lee A. Kirkpatrick, Graduate Director, 757-221-3997, *Fax:* 757-221-3896, *E-mail:* lakirk@wm.edu.
**Application contact:** Barbara B. Pumilia, Secretary. *Web site:* http://www.wm.edu/psyc/

### ■ COLUMBIA UNIVERSITY

**Graduate School of Arts and Sciences, Division of Natural Sciences, Department of Psychology, New York, NY 10027**

**AWARDS** Experimental psychology (M Phil, MA, PhD); psychobiology (M Phil, MA, PhD); social psychology (M Phil, MA, PhD).

**Faculty:** 23 full-time.
**Students:** 35 full-time (19 women), 2 part-time. Average age 28. 156 applicants, 7% accepted. In 2001, 7 master's, 6 doctorates awarded.
**Degree requirements:** For master's and doctorate, thesis/dissertation.
**Entrance requirements:** For master's and doctorate, GRE General Test, TOEFL. *Application deadline:* For fall admission, 1/3. *Application fee:* $65.
**Expenses:** Tuition: Full-time $27,528. Required fees: $1,638.
**Financial support:** Fellowships, teaching assistantships, Federal Work-Study and institutionally sponsored loans available. Support available to part-time students. Financial award application deadline: 1/5; financial award applicants required to submit FAFSA.
Donald Hood, Chair, 212-854-4587, *Fax:* 212-854-3609.

### ■ CORNELL UNIVERSITY

**Graduate School, Graduate Fields of Arts and Sciences, Field of Psychology, Ithaca, NY 14853-0001**

**AWARDS** Biopsychology (PhD); general psychology (PhD); human experimental psychology (PhD); personality and social psychology (PhD).

**Faculty:** 36 full-time.
**Students:** 37 full-time (20 women); includes 2 minority (1 Asian American or Pacific Islander, 1 Hispanic American), 10 international. 144 applicants, 8% accepted. In 2001, 2 doctorates awarded.
**Degree requirements:** For doctorate, thesis/dissertation, 2 semesters of teaching experience.
**Entrance requirements:** For doctorate, GRE General Test, TOEFL, 3 letters of recommendation. *Application deadline:* For fall admission, 1/15. *Application fee:* $65. Electronic applications accepted.
**Expenses:** Tuition: Full-time $25,970. Required fees: $50.
**Financial support:** In 2001–02, 36 students received support, including 9 fellowships with full tuition reimbursements available, 27 teaching assistantships with full tuition reimbursements available; research assistantships with full tuition reimbursements available, institutionally sponsored loans, scholarships/grants, tuition waivers (full and partial) also available. Financial award applicants required to submit FAFSA.
**Faculty research:** Sensory and perceptual systems, social cognition, cognitive development, neuroscience, quantitative and computational modeling.
**Application contact:** Graduate Field Assistant, 607-255-6364, *E-mail:*

psychapp@cornell.edu. *Web site:* http://www.gradschool.cornell.edu/grad/fields_1/psych.html

# ■ DEPAUL UNIVERSITY

**College of Liberal Arts and Sciences, Department of Psychology, Program in Experimental Psychology, Chicago, IL 60604-2287**

AWARDS MA, PhD.

**Faculty:** 9 full-time (3 women), 1 (woman) part-time/adjunct.

**Students:** 6 full-time (4 women), 3 part-time (1 woman); includes 1 minority (Hispanic American). Average age 29. 18 applicants, 22% accepted, 4 enrolled. In 2001, 4 master's, 1 doctorate awarded.

**Degree requirements:** For master's, thesis, oral exam; for doctorate, thesis/dissertation, oral and written exams, comprehensive exam. *Median time to degree:* Master's–2 years full-time; doctorate–5 years full-time.

**Entrance requirements:** For master's, GRE General Test and subject test, minimum GPA of 3.5; for doctorate, GRE General Test and subject test, 24 hours or 32 quarter hours in psychology, minimum GPA of 3.5. *Application deadline:* For fall admission, 2/28. *Application fee:* $40.

**Expenses:** Tuition: Part-time $362 per credit hour. Tuition and fees vary according to program.

**Financial support:** In 2001–02, 8 students received support, including 4 research assistantships with full and partial tuition reimbursements available (averaging $6,000 per year), 3 teaching assistantships with full and partial tuition reimbursements available (averaging $6,000 per year); scholarships/grants also available. Financial award application deadline: 2/28.

**Faculty research:** Facial expressions of children, cross cultural research moods and emotions, sensorimotor development in infancy, judgement and decision making, mental imagery.

Dr. China-Fan Sheu, Director, 773-325-4255, *E-mail:* csheu@condor.depaul.edu.

**Application contact:** Information Contact, 773-325-7887, *E-mail:* lrapp@depaul.edu. *Web site:* http://www.depaul.edu/~psych/

# ■ DUKE UNIVERSITY

**Graduate School, Department of Psychology, Durham, NC 27708-0586**

AWARDS Biological psychology (PhD); clinical psychology (PhD); cognitive psychology (PhD); developmental psychology (PhD); experimental psychology (PhD); health psychology (PhD); human social development (PhD).

**Faculty:** 52 full-time, 15 part-time/adjunct.

**Students:** 66 full-time (42 women); includes 11 minority (6 African Americans, 2 Asian Americans or Pacific Islanders, 3 Hispanic Americans), 13 international. 386 applicants, 7% accepted, 15 enrolled. In 2001, 8 doctorates awarded.

**Degree requirements:** For doctorate, thesis/dissertation.

**Entrance requirements:** For doctorate, GRE General Test. *Application deadline:* For fall admission, 12/31. *Application fee:* $75.

**Expenses:** Tuition: Full-time $24,600.

**Financial support:** Fellowships, research assistantships, teaching assistantships, career-related internships or fieldwork and Federal Work-Study available. Financial award application deadline: 12/31.

Reiko Mazuka, Co-Director of Graduate Studies, 919-660-5716, *Fax:* 919-660-5726, *E-mail:* bseymore@acpub.duke.edu. *Web site:* http://www.psych.duke.edu/

# ■ FAIRLEIGH DICKINSON UNIVERSITY, COLLEGE AT FLORHAM

**Maxwell Becton College of Arts and Sciences, Department of Psychology, Programs in General Experimental Psychology, Madison, NJ 07940-1099**

AWARDS MA.

**Students:** 1 (woman) full-time, 2 part-time (1 woman). Average age 30.

**Entrance requirements:** For master's, GRE General Test. *Application deadline:* Applications are processed on a rolling basis. *Application fee:* $40.

**Expenses:** Tuition: Full-time $11,484; part-time $638 per credit. Required fees: $420. One-time fee: $97 part-time.

# ■ FAIRLEIGH DICKINSON UNIVERSITY, METROPOLITAN CAMPUS

**University College: Arts, Sciences, and Professional Studies, School of Psychology, Program in General-Theoretical Psychology, Teaneck, NJ 07666-1914**

AWARDS MA.

**Students:** 20 full-time (15 women), 20 part-time (18 women); includes 3 minority (1 Asian American or Pacific Islander, 2 Hispanic Americans), 2 international. Average age 29. 22 applicants, 91% accepted, 10 enrolled. In 2001, 26 degrees awarded. *Application deadline:* Applications are processed on a rolling basis. *Application fee:* $40.

**Expenses:** Tuition: Full-time $11,484; part-time $638 per credit. Required fees: $420; $97.

# ■ GEORGE MASON UNIVERSITY

**College of Arts and Sciences, Department of Psychology, Program in Experimental Neuropsychology, Fairfax, VA 22030-4444**

AWARDS MA.

**Degree requirements:** For master's, internship, thesis optional.

**Entrance requirements:** For master's, GRE General Test, minimum GPA of 3.0 in last 60 hours, previous undergraduate course work in psychology. Electronic applications accepted.

**Expenses:** Tuition, state resident: full-time $3,168; part-time $132 per credit hour. Tuition, nonresident: full-time $11,280; part-time $470 per credit hour. Required fees: $1,416; $59 per credit hour.

# ■ GRADUATE SCHOOL AND UNIVERSITY CENTER OF THE CITY UNIVERSITY OF NEW YORK

**Graduate Studies, Program in Psychology, New York, NY 10016-4039**

AWARDS Basic applied neurocognition (PhD); biopsychology (PhD); clinical psychology (PhD); developmental psychology (PhD); environmental psychology (PhD); experimental psychology (PhD); industrial psychology (PhD); learning processes (PhD); neuropsychology (PhD); psychology (PhD); social personality (PhD).

**Faculty:** 119 full-time (40 women).

**Students:** 463 full-time (335 women), 4 part-time (2 women); includes 96 minority (39 African Americans, 20 Asian Americans or Pacific Islanders, 36 Hispanic Americans, 1 Native American), 47 international. Average age 33. 493 applicants, 24% accepted, 65 enrolled. In 2001, 28 degrees awarded.

**Degree requirements:** For doctorate, one foreign language, thesis/dissertation.

**Entrance requirements:** For doctorate, GRE General Test. *Application deadline:* For fall admission, 2/1. *Application fee:* $40.

**Expenses:** Tuition, state resident: part-time $245 per credit. Tuition, nonresident: part-time $425 per credit. Required fees: $72 per semester.

**Financial support:** In 2001–02, 226 students received support, including 141 fellowships, 14 research assistantships, 4 teaching assistantships; career-related internships or fieldwork, Federal Work-Study, institutionally sponsored loans, and tuition waivers (full and partial) also available. Financial award application deadline: 2/1; financial award applicants required to submit FAFSA.

Dr. Joseph Glick, Executive Officer, 212-817-8706, *Fax:* 212-817-1533, *E-mail:* jglick@gc.cuny.edu.

## ■ HARVARD UNIVERSITY

**Graduate School of Arts and Sciences, Department of Psychology, Cambridge, MA 02138**

**AWARDS** Psychology (AM, PhD), including behavior and decision analysis, cognition, developmental psychology, experimental psychology, personality, psychobiology, psychopathology; social psychology (AM, PhD).

**Degree requirements:** For doctorate, thesis/dissertation, general exams.

**Entrance requirements:** For master's and doctorate, GRE General Test, TOEFL.

**Expenses:** Tuition: Full-time $23,370. Required fees: $816. Full-time tuition and fees vary according to program and student level.

## ■ HOWARD UNIVERSITY

**Graduate School of Arts and Sciences, Department of Psychology, Washington, DC 20059-0002**

**AWARDS** Clinical psychology (PhD); developmental psychology (PhD); experimental psychology (PhD); neuropsychology (PhD); personality psychology (PhD); psychology (MS); social psychology (PhD). Part-time programs available.

**Faculty:** 16 full-time (7 women).

**Students:** 70 full-time (51 women), 20 part-time (14 women). Average age 29. 165 applicants, 15% accepted, 20 enrolled. In 2001, 10 master's, 12 doctorates awarded.

**Degree requirements:** For master's, thesis, comprehensive exam; for doctorate, thesis/dissertation, qualifying exam, comprehensive exam. *Median time to degree:* Master's–3 years full-time, 5 years part-time; doctorate–5 years full-time, 9 years part-time.

**Entrance requirements:** For master's, GRE General Test, minimum GPA of 2.5, bachelor's degree in psychology or related field; for doctorate, GRE General Test, minimum GPA of 3.0. *Application deadline:* For fall admission, 4/1; for spring admission, 11/1. Applications are processed on a rolling basis. *Application fee:* $45.

**Financial support:** In 2001–02, 19 students received support, including 3 fellowships with full tuition reimbursements available (averaging $13,500 per year), 2 research assistantships with full tuition reimbursements available (averaging $10,000 per year), 8 teaching assistantships with full tuition reimbursements available (averaging $13,000 per year); career-related internships or fieldwork, institutionally sponsored loans, and scholarships/grants also available. Financial award application deadline: 4/1; financial award applicants required to submit FAFSA.

**Faculty research:** Personality and psychophysiology, educational and social development of African-American children, child and adult psychopathology.
Dr. Albert Roberts, Chair, 202-806-6805, *Fax:* 202-806-4823, *E-mail:* aroberts@ howard.edu.

**Application contact:** Dr. Alfonso Campbell, Chairman, Graduate Admissions Committee, 202-806-6805, *Fax:* 202-806-4873, *E-mail:* acampbell@howard.edu.

## ■ ILLINOIS STATE UNIVERSITY

**Graduate School, College of Arts and Sciences, Department of Psychology, Normal, IL 61790-2200**

**AWARDS** Psychology (MA, MS), including clinical psychology, counseling psychology, developmental psychology, educational psychology, experimental psychology, measurement-evaluation, organizational-industrial psychology; school psychology (PhD, SSP).

**Faculty:** 30 full-time (10 women), 1 part-time/adjunct (0 women).

**Students:** 59 full-time (48 women), 24 part-time (13 women); includes 7 minority (3 African Americans, 3 Hispanic Americans, 1 Native American), 5 international. 81 applicants, 46% accepted. In 2001, 40 master's, 2 doctorates, 4 other advanced degrees awarded.

**Degree requirements:** For master's, thesis or alternative; for doctorate, variable foreign language requirement, thesis/dissertation, 2 terms of residency, internship, practicum.

**Entrance requirements:** For master's, GRE General Test, GRE Subject Test, minimum GPA of 3.0 in last 60 hours; for doctorate, GRE General Test. *Application deadline:* Applications are processed on a rolling basis. *Application fee:* $30.

**Expenses:** Tuition, state resident: full-time $2,691; part-time $112 per credit hour. Tuition, nonresident: full-time $5,880; part-time $245 per credit hour. Required fees: $1,146; $48 per credit hour.

**Financial support:** In 2001–02, 21 research assistantships (averaging $5,127 per year), 27 teaching assistantships (averaging $4,308 per year) were awarded. Tuition waivers (full) and unspecified assistantships also available. Financial award application deadline: 4/1.

**Faculty research:** Dialogues with children, sexual harassment in the military, mental health consultant. *Total annual research expenditures:* $248,177.
Dr. David Barone, Chairperson, 309-438-8651. *Web site:* http://www.cas.ilstu.edu/ psychology/index.html

## ■ JOHNS HOPKINS UNIVERSITY

**Zanvyl Krieger School of Arts and Sciences, Department of Psychological and Brain Sciences, Baltimore, MD 21218-2699**

**AWARDS** Experimental psychology (PhD); psychology (PhD).

**Faculty:** 9 full-time (3 women).

**Students:** 17 full-time (11 women); includes 1 minority (Asian American or Pacific Islander), 7 international. Average age 24. 84 applicants, 7% accepted, 2 enrolled. In 2001, 4 degrees awarded.

**Degree requirements:** For doctorate, thesis/dissertation, research project, teaching experience.

**Entrance requirements:** For doctorate, GRE General Test, GRE Subject Test. *Application deadline:* For fall admission, 1/15 (priority date). *Application fee:* $55. Electronic applications accepted.

**Expenses:** Tuition: Full-time $27,390.

**Financial support:** In 2001–02, 16 teaching assistantships were awarded; fellowships, research assistantships, Federal Work-Study also available. Financial award application deadline: 4/15; financial award applicants required to submit FAFSA.

**Faculty research:** Biopsychology, cognitive psychology, developmental psychology, quantitative psychology. *Total annual research expenditures:* $4.1 million.
Dr. Michela Gallagher, Chair, 410-516-7057, *Fax:* 410-516-4478, *E-mail:* michela@jhu.edu.

**Application contact:** Joan Krach, Administrative Assistant, 410-516-6175, *Fax:* 410-516-4478, *E-mail:* krach@jhu.edu. *Web site:* http://www.psy.jhu.edu/

## ■ KENT STATE UNIVERSITY

**College of Arts and Sciences, Department of Psychology, Kent, OH 44242-0001**

**AWARDS** Clinical psychology (MA, PhD); experimental psychology (MA, PhD).

**Degree requirements:** For master's and doctorate, thesis/dissertation.

**Entrance requirements:** For master's, GRE Subject Test, minimum GPA of 2.75; for doctorate, GRE Subject Test, minimum GPA of 3.0.

## ■ LEHIGH UNIVERSITY

**College of Arts and Sciences, Department of Psychology, Bethlehem, PA 18015-3094**

**AWARDS** Experimental psychology (PhD).

**Faculty:** 9 full-time (4 women), 2 part-time/adjunct (0 women).

**Students:** 14 full-time (10 women); includes 1 minority (Hispanic American), 2 international. Average age 35. 24 applicants, 17% accepted, 1 enrolled.

**Degree requirements:** For doctorate, thesis/dissertation, comprehensive exam.
**Entrance requirements:** For doctorate, GRE General Test, TOEFL. *Application deadline:* For fall admission, 2/1. *Application fee:* $50. Electronic applications accepted.
**Expenses:** Contact institution.
**Financial support:** In 2001–02, 11 students received support, including 1 research assistantship with full tuition reimbursement available (averaging $12,350 per year), 8 teaching assistantships with full tuition reimbursements available (averaging $12,350 per year); scholarships/grants, tuition waivers (full), and unspecified assistantships also available. Financial award application deadline: 1/15.
**Faculty research:** Social-cognitive developmental psychology, cognition and language, social cognition.
Dr. Barbara C. Malt, Chairperson, 610-758-4702, *Fax:* 610-758-6277, *E-mail:* barbara.malt@lehigh.edu.
**Application contact:** Dr. Padraig G. O'Seaghdha, Graduate Coordinator, 610-758-3630, *Fax:* 610-758-6277. *Web site:* http://www.lehigh.edu/~inpsy/inpsy.html
**Find an in-depth description at www.petersons.com/gradchannel.**

### ■ LONG ISLAND UNIVERSITY, C.W. POST CAMPUS

**College of Liberal Arts and Sciences, Department of Psychology, Program in General Experimental Psychology, Brookville, NY 11548-1300**
AWARDS MA. Part-time programs available.
**Faculty:** 7 full-time (2 women), 2 part-time/adjunct (0 women).
**Students:** 11 full-time (9 women), 5 part-time (4 women). 22 applicants, 50% accepted, 2 enrolled. In 2001, 12 degrees awarded.
**Degree requirements:** For master's, thesis.
**Entrance requirements:** For master's, GRE General Test, GRE Subject Test, minimum GPA of 3.0 in psychology, 2.8 overall. *Application deadline:* For fall admission, 4/1 (priority date). Applications are processed on a rolling basis. *Application fee:* $30. Electronic applications accepted.
**Expenses:** Tuition: Full-time $10,296; part-time $572 per credit. Required fees: $380; $190 per semester.
**Financial support:** In 2001–02, 1 research assistantship (averaging $4,625 per year), 3 teaching assistantships were awarded. Institutionally sponsored loans and tuition waivers (partial) also available. Support available to part-time students. Financial award application deadline: 5/15; financial award applicants required to submit CSS PROFILE or FAFSA.

**Faculty research:** Operant conditioning, vision, behavioral modification influence of home environments.
**Application contact:** Dr. Ethel Matin, Graduate Advisor, 516-299-2063, *E-mail:* ethel.matin@liu.edu. *Web site:* http://www.liu.edu/postlas/

### ■ MIAMI UNIVERSITY

**Graduate School, College of Arts and Sciences, Department of Psychology, Oxford, OH 45056**
AWARDS Clinical psychology (PhD); experimental psychology (PhD); social psychology (PhD).
**Faculty:** 12 full-time (2 women), 9 part-time/adjunct (5 women).
**Students:** 73 full-time (49 women); includes 12 minority (9 African Americans, 3 Asian Americans or Pacific Islanders), 7 international. 128 applicants, 41% accepted, 17 enrolled. In 2001, 12 doctorates awarded.
**Degree requirements:** For doctorate, thesis/dissertation, final exams, comprehensive exam.
**Entrance requirements:** For doctorate, GRE General Test, GRE Subject Test, minimum GPA of 2.75 (undergraduate), 3.0 (graduate). *Application deadline:* For fall admission, 2/1. *Application fee:* $35.
**Expenses:** Tuition, state resident: full-time $7,155; part-time $295 per semester hour. Tuition, nonresident: full-time $14,829; part-time $615 per semester hour. Tuition and fees vary according to degree level and campus/location.
**Financial support:** In 2001–02, 28 fellowships (averaging $9,134 per year), 12 teaching assistantships (averaging $11,337 per year) were awarded. Research assistantships, career-related internships or fieldwork, Federal Work-Study, and tuition waivers (full) also available. Financial award application deadline: 3/1.
Dr. Karen Schilling, Chair, 513-529-2400, *Fax:* 513-529-2420, *E-mail:* psych@muohio.edu.
**Application contact:** Dr. Phillip Best, Director of Graduate Studies, 513-529-2400, *Fax:* 513-529-2420, *E-mail:* psych@muohio.edu. *Web site:* http://www.muohio.edu/~psycwis/graduate.html

### ■ MOREHEAD STATE UNIVERSITY

**Graduate Programs, College of Science and Technology, Department of Psychology, Morehead, KY 40351**
AWARDS Clinical psychology (MA); counseling psychology (MA); experimental/general psychology (MA). Part-time programs available.
**Faculty:** 7 full-time (2 women).

**Students:** 30 full-time (19 women), 1 international. Average age 25. 5 applicants, 80% accepted. In 2001, 15 degrees awarded.
**Entrance requirements:** For master's, GRE General Test, TOEFL, 18 undergraduate hours in psychology, minimum GPA of 3.0. *Application deadline:* For fall admission, 8/1 (priority date); for spring admission, 12/1. Applications are processed on a rolling basis. *Application fee:* $0.
**Expenses:** Tuition, state resident: part-time $176 per hour. Tuition, nonresident: full-time $1,584; part-time $472 per hour. International tuition: $4,247 full-time.
**Financial support:** In 2001–02, 21 research assistantships (averaging $5,000 per year) were awarded; career-related internships or fieldwork, Federal Work-Study, and institutionally sponsored loans also available. Financial award application deadline: 4/1; financial award applicants required to submit FAFSA.
**Faculty research:** Mood induction effects, serotonin receptor activity, stress, perceptual processes.
Dr. Bruce A. Mattingly, Chair, 606-783-2891, *Fax:* 606-783-5077, *E-mail:* b.mattin@moreheadstate.edu.
**Application contact:** Betty R. Cowsert, Graduate Admissions/Records Manager, 606-783-2039, *Fax:* 606-783-5061, *E-mail:* b.cowsert@moreheadstate.edu. *Web site:* http://www.moreheadstate.edu

### ■ NORTHEASTERN UNIVERSITY

**College of Arts and Sciences, Department of Psychology, Boston, MA 02115-5096**
AWARDS Experimental psychology (MA, PhD).
**Faculty:** 18 full-time (5 women).
**Students:** 25 full-time (16 women); includes 4 minority (2 African Americans, 1 Asian American or Pacific Islander, 1 Native American), 4 international. Average age 28. 72 applicants, 10% accepted. In 2001, 6 master's, 1 doctorate awarded.
**Degree requirements:** For doctorate, thesis/dissertation.
**Entrance requirements:** For doctorate, GRE General Test, TOEFL. *Application deadline:* For fall admission, 1/15. Applications are processed on a rolling basis. *Application fee:* $50.
**Expenses:** Tuition: Part-time $535 per credit hour. Required fees: $56. Tuition and fees vary according to program.
**Financial support:** In 2001–02, 20 research assistantships with full tuition reimbursements (averaging $14,325 per year) were awarded; fellowships with full tuition reimbursements, teaching assistantships with full tuition reimbursements,

*Northeastern University (continued)*
career-related internships or fieldwork and traineeships also available. Financial award application deadline: 1/15; financial award applicants required to submit FAFSA.
**Faculty research:** Language/cognition, social/personality, sensation/perception and neuropsychology.
Dr. Stephen Harkins, Chair, 617-373-3076, *Fax:* 617-373-8714, *E-mail:* psychology@neu.edu.
**Application contact:** Dr. Judith Hall, Graduate Coordinator, 617-373-3076, *Fax:* 617-373-8714, *E-mail:* psychology@neu.edu. *Web site:* http://www.psych.neu.edu/

■ **THE OHIO STATE UNIVERSITY**

**Graduate School, College of Social and Behavioral Sciences, Department of Psychology, Columbus, OH 43210**
**AWARDS** Clinical psychology (PhD); cognitive/experimental psychology (PhD); counseling psychology (PhD); developmental psychology (PhD); mental retardation and developmental disabilities (PhD); psychobiology (PhD); quantitative psychology (PhD); social psychology (PhD).
**Degree requirements:** For doctorate, thesis/dissertation.
**Entrance requirements:** For doctorate, GRE General Test, TOEFL.

■ **OHIO UNIVERSITY**

**Graduate Studies, College of Arts and Sciences, Department of Psychology, Program in Experimental Psychology, Athens, OH 45701-2979**
**AWARDS** PhD.
**Faculty:** 6 full-time (1 woman), 1 part-time/adjunct (0 women).
**Students:** 15 full-time (6 women), 3 part-time (1 woman), 4 international. Average age 28. 18 applicants, 22% accepted.
**Degree requirements:** For doctorate, one foreign language, thesis/dissertation, comprehensive exam.
**Entrance requirements:** For doctorate, GRE General Test, GRE Subject Test, minimum graduate GPA of 3.4. *Application deadline:* For fall admission, 1/15. *Application fee:* $30. Electronic applications accepted.
**Expenses:** Tuition, state resident: full-time $6,585. Tuition, nonresident: full-time $12,254.
**Financial support:** In 2001–02, 14 students received support, including 4 research assistantships with full tuition reimbursements available (averaging $8,662 per year), 4 teaching assistantships with full tuition reimbursements available (averaging $7,963 per year); fellowships with full tuition reimbursements available,

Federal Work-Study, institutionally sponsored loans, tuition waivers (full), and unspecified assistantships also available. Financial award application deadline: 1/15.
**Faculty research:** Cognitive psychology, quantitative psychology, social psychology, judgment and decision making, health psychology.
Dr. Mark D. Alicke, Director of Experimental Training, 740-593-1707, *Fax:* 740-593-0579, *E-mail:* malick1@ohiou.edu.
**Application contact:** Admissions Secretary, 740-593-0902, *Fax:* 740-593-0579, *E-mail:* pgraduate1@ohiou.edu. *Web site:* http://www.cats.ohiou.edu/~psydept/

■ **OKLAHOMA STATE UNIVERSITY**

**Graduate College, College of Arts and Sciences, Department of Psychology, Stillwater, OK 74078**
**AWARDS** Clinical psychology (PhD); experimental psychology (PhD); general psychology (MS).
**Faculty:** 16 full-time (5 women), 1 (woman) part-time/adjunct.
**Students:** 32 full-time (24 women), 17 part-time (11 women); includes 13 minority (1 African American, 2 Asian Americans or Pacific Islanders, 4 Hispanic Americans, 6 Native Americans), 1 international. Average age 27. 67 applicants, 24% accepted. In 2001, 5 master's, 10 doctorates awarded.
**Degree requirements:** For doctorate, thesis/dissertation.
**Entrance requirements:** For master's, TOEFL; for doctorate, GRE General Test, TOEFL. *Application deadline:* For fall admission, 2/1 (priority date). *Application fee:* $25.
**Expenses:** Tuition, state resident: part-time $92 per credit hour. Tuition, nonresident: part-time $297 per credit hour. Required fees: $21 per credit hour. $14 per semester. One-time fee: $20. Tuition and fees vary according to course load.
**Financial support:** In 2001–02, 30 students received support, including 12 research assistantships (averaging $12,269 per year), 22 teaching assistantships (averaging $11,551 per year); career-related internships or fieldwork, Federal Work-Study, and tuition waivers (partial) also available. Support available to part-time students. Financial award application deadline: 3/1.
Dr. Maureen A. Sullivan, Head, 405-744-6028.

■ **ST. JOHN'S UNIVERSITY**

**St. John's College of Liberal Arts and Sciences, Department of Psychology, Program in General Experimental Psychology, Jamaica, NY 11439**
**AWARDS** MA. Part-time and evening/weekend programs available.
**Students:** 4 full-time (all women), 8 part-time (4 women); includes 1 minority (Hispanic American), 3 international. Average age 26. 16 applicants, 50% accepted, 2 enrolled. In 2001, 4 degrees awarded.
**Degree requirements:** For master's, thesis optional.
**Entrance requirements:** For master's, minimum GPA of 3.0, 2 writing samples. *Application fee:* $40.
**Expenses:** Tuition: Full-time $14,520; part-time $605 per credit. Required fees: $150; $75 per term. Tuition and fees vary according to class time, course load, degree level, campus/location, program and student level.
**Financial support:** Research assistantships, career-related internships or fieldwork, scholarships/grants, and unspecified assistantships available. Support available to part-time students. Financial award application deadline: 3/1; financial award applicants required to submit FAFSA.
**Faculty research:** Learning and memory neuropsychology, perception, social psychology, developmental psychology.
Dr. Leonard Brosgole, Director, 718-990-1552, *E-mail:* brosgoll@stjohns.edu.
**Application contact:** Matthew Whelan, Director, Office of Admission, 718-990-2000, *Fax:* 718-990-2096, *E-mail:* admissions@stjohns.edu. *Web site:* http://www.stjohns.edu/

■ **SAINT LOUIS UNIVERSITY**

**Graduate School, College of Arts and Sciences, Department of Psychology, St. Louis, MO 63103-2097**
**AWARDS** Applied experimental psychology (MS(R), PhD); clinical psychology (MS(R), PhD).
**Faculty:** 28 full-time (8 women), 16 part-time/adjunct (4 women).
**Students:** 34 full-time (17 women), 65 part-time (38 women); includes 20 minority (15 African Americans, 3 Asian Americans or Pacific Islanders, 2 Hispanic Americans), 1 international. Average age 28. 160 applicants, 27% accepted, 23 enrolled. In 2001, 7 master's, 12 doctorates awarded.
**Degree requirements:** For master's, thesis, comprehensive exam; for doctorate, thesis/dissertation, internship, preliminary exams.
**Entrance requirements:** For master's and doctorate, GRE General Test, interview.

*Application deadline:* For fall admission, 1/1; for spring admission, 11/1. *Application fee:* $40.

**Expenses:** Tuition: Part-time $630 per credit hour.

**Financial support:** In 2001–02, 57 students received support, including 6 fellowships with tuition reimbursements available, 4 research assistantships with tuition reimbursements available, 2 teaching assistantships with tuition reimbursements available; career-related internships or fieldwork, tuition waivers (partial), and unspecified assistantships also available. Financial award application deadline: 4/1; financial award applicants required to submit FAFSA.

**Faculty research:** Implicit and explicit memory in older adults, cognitive processes in post-traumatic stress disorder, prejudice and attitude change, locus of control and health psychology, psychometric evaluation of cognitive impairment.

Dr. Ronald T. Kellogg, Chairperson, 314-977-2300, *Fax:* 314-977-3679, *E-mail:* kelloggr@slu.edu.

**Application contact:** Dr. Marcia Buresch, Associate Dean of the Graduate School, 314-977-2240, *Fax:* 314-977-3943, *E-mail:* bureschm@slu.edu.

### ■ SOUTHERN ILLINOIS UNIVERSITY CARBONDALE

**Graduate School, College of Liberal Arts, Department of Psychology, Carbondale, IL 62901-6806**

**AWARDS** Clinical psychology (MA, MS, PhD); counseling psychology (MA, MS, PhD); experimental psychology (MA, MS, PhD).

**Faculty:** 27 full-time (14 women), 1 part-time/adjunct (0 women).

**Students:** 79 full-time (58 women), 42 part-time (29 women); includes 28 minority (16 African Americans, 7 Asian Americans or Pacific Islanders, 4 Hispanic Americans, 1 Native American), 10 international. 128 applicants, 22% accepted. In 2001, 14 master's, 21 doctorates awarded.

**Degree requirements:** For master's and doctorate, thesis/dissertation.

**Entrance requirements:** For master's, GRE General Test, GRE Subject Test, TOEFL, minimum GPA of 2.7; for doctorate, GRE General Test, GRE Subject Test, TOEFL, minimum GPA of 3.25. *Application deadline:* For fall admission, 3/1 (priority date). Applications are processed on a rolling basis. *Application fee:* $20.

**Expenses:** Tuition, state resident: full-time $3,794; part-time $154 per hour. Tuition, nonresident: full-time $6,566; part-time $308 per hour. Required fees: $277 per hour.

**Financial support:** In 2001–02, 82 students received support, including 14 fellowships with full tuition reimbursements available, 23 research assistantships with full tuition reimbursements available, 22 teaching assistantships with full tuition reimbursements available; Federal Work-Study, institutionally sponsored loans, and tuition waivers (full) also available.

**Faculty research:** Developmental neuropsychology; smoking, affect, and cognition; personality measurement; vocational psychology; program evaluation. Alan Vaux, Chair, 618-453-3529. *Web site:* http://www.siu.edu/departments/cola/psycho/

**Find an in-depth description at www.petersons.com/gradchannel.**

### ■ STATE UNIVERSITY OF NEW YORK AT ALBANY

**College of Arts and Sciences, Department of Psychology, Albany, NY 12222-0001**

**AWARDS** Biopsychology (PhD); clinical psychology (PhD); general/experimental psychology (PhD); industrial/organizational psychology (PhD); psychology (MA); social/personality psychology (PhD).

**Students:** 69 full-time (45 women), 58 part-time (41 women); includes 12 minority (2 African Americans, 3 Asian Americans or Pacific Islanders, 7 Hispanic Americans), 13 international. Average age 28. 220 applicants, 20% accepted. In 2001, 11 master's, 6 doctorates awarded.

**Degree requirements:** For doctorate, thesis/dissertation.

**Entrance requirements:** For doctorate, GRE General Test, GRE Subject Test. *Application deadline:* For fall admission, 1/15. *Application fee:* $50.

**Expenses:** Tuition, state resident: full-time $2,550; part-time $213 per credit. Tuition, nonresident: full-time $4,208; part-time $351 per credit. Required fees: $470; $470 per year.

**Financial support:** Fellowships, research assistantships, teaching assistantships, career-related internships or fieldwork available. Financial award application deadline: 2/1.

Robert Rosellini, Chair, 518-442-4820.

**Application contact:** Glenn Sanders, Graduate Director, 518-442-4853.

### ■ STONY BROOK UNIVERSITY, STATE UNIVERSITY OF NEW YORK

**Graduate School, College of Arts and Sciences, Department of Psychology, Program in Experimental Psychology, Stony Brook, NY 11794**

**AWARDS** PhD.

**Students:** 11 full-time (6 women), 6 part-time (3 women); includes 2 minority (1 African American, 1 Asian American or Pacific Islander), 5 international. Average age 29. 21 applicants, 43% accepted. In 2001, 3 degrees awarded.

**Degree requirements:** For doctorate, thesis/dissertation.

**Entrance requirements:** For doctorate, GRE General Test, GRE Subject Test, TOEFL. *Application deadline:* For fall admission, 1/15. *Application fee:* $50.

**Expenses:** Tuition, state resident: full-time $5,100; part-time $213 per credit. Tuition, nonresident: full-time $8,416; part-time $351 per credit. Required fees: $496.

**Application contact:** Dr. Harriet Waters, Director, 631-632-7855, *Fax:* 631-632-7876, *E-mail:* hwaters@ccvm.sunysb.edu.

**Find an in-depth description at www.petersons.com/gradchannel.**

### ■ SYRACUSE UNIVERSITY

**Graduate School, College of Arts and Sciences, Department of Psychology, Program in Experimental Psychology, Syracuse, NY 13244-0003**

**AWARDS** MA, MS, PhD.

**Degree requirements:** For master's, thesis (for some programs); for doctorate, thesis/dissertation.

**Entrance requirements:** For master's and doctorate, GRE General Test.

**Expenses:** Tuition: Full-time $15,528; part-time $647 per credit. Required fees: $420; $38 per term. Tuition and fees vary according to program.

### ■ TEMPLE UNIVERSITY

**Graduate School, College of Liberal Arts, Department of Psychology, Program in Experimental Psychology, Philadelphia, PA 19122-6096**

**AWARDS** PhD.

**Degree requirements:** For doctorate, thesis/dissertation.

**Entrance requirements:** For doctorate, GRE General Test, minimum GPA of 3.0. Electronic applications accepted.

**Expenses:** Tuition, state resident: full-time $8,487; part-time $369 per credit hour. Tuition, nonresident: full-time $12,282; part-time $534 per credit hour. Required fees: $350. Tuition and fees vary according

*Temple University (continued)*
to course load, program and reciprocity agreements.

**Faculty research:** Comparative psychology, Pavlovian processes, experimental analysis of behavior, neuroscience, psychopharmacology, sociobiology.

**Find an in-depth description at www.petersons.com/gradchannel.**

## ■ TEXAS TECH UNIVERSITY

**Graduate School, College of Arts and Sciences, Department of Psychology, Lubbock, TX 79409**

**AWARDS** Clinical psychology (PhD); counseling psychology (PhD); general experimental (MA, PhD). Part-time programs available.

**Faculty:** 21 full-time (10 women).
**Students:** 72 full-time (50 women), 19 part-time (10 women); includes 19 minority (1 African American, 3 Asian Americans or Pacific Islanders, 14 Hispanic Americans, 1 Native American). Average age 28. 158 applicants, 20% accepted, 18 enrolled. In 2001, 9 master's, 11 doctorates awarded.
**Degree requirements:** For doctorate, thesis/dissertation.
**Entrance requirements:** For master's and doctorate, GRE General Test, GRE Subject Test. *Application deadline:* Applications are processed on a rolling basis. *Application fee:* $25 ($50 for international students). Electronic applications accepted.
**Expenses:** Tuition, state resident: full-time $1,926; part-time $107 per credit hour. Tuition, nonresident: full-time $5,724; part-time $318 per credit hour. Required fees: $779; $737 per year. Tuition and fees vary according to course level, course load and program.
**Financial support:** In 2001–02, 71 students received support, including 5 research assistantships with partial tuition reimbursements available (averaging $10,220 per year), 48 teaching assistantships with partial tuition reimbursements available (averaging $10,067 per year); fellowships, career-related internships or fieldwork, Federal Work-Study, and institutionally sponsored loans also available. Support available to part-time students. Financial award application deadline: 5/1; financial award applicants required to submit FAFSA.
**Faculty research:** Failure/success in relationships, peer rejection in school, stress and coping, group processes, use of information technology in education. *Total annual research expenditures:* $95,236.
Dr. Ruth H. Maki, Chair, 806-742-3737, *Fax:* 806-742-0818.
**Application contact:** Graduate Adviser, 806-742-3737, *Fax:* 806-742-0818. *Web site:* http://www.ttu.edu/~psy/

## ■ TOWSON UNIVERSITY

**Graduate School, Program in School Psychology, Towson, MD 21252-0001**

**AWARDS** Clinical psychology (MA); counseling psychology (MA); experimental psychology (MA); psychology (MA); school psychology (MA, CAS). Part-time and evening/weekend programs available.

**Faculty:** 13 full-time (5 women), 2 part-time/adjunct (both women).
**Students:** 195. In 2001, 64 master's, 15 other advanced degrees awarded.
**Degree requirements:** For master's, thesis (for some programs), exams.
**Entrance requirements:** For master's, GRE General Test. *Application deadline:* For fall admission, 2/1; for spring admission, 10/1. *Application fee:* $40. Electronic applications accepted.
**Expenses:** Tuition, state resident: part-time $211 per credit. Tuition, nonresident: part-time $435 per credit. Required fees: $52 per credit.
**Financial support:** Fellowships, Federal Work-Study and unspecified assistantships available. Financial award application deadline: 4/1; financial award applicants required to submit FAFSA.
**Faculty research:** Cognitive behavior, issues affecting the aging, relaxation hypnosis and imagery, lesbian and gay issues.
Dr. Susan Bartels, Director, 410-704-3070, *Fax:* 410-704-3800, *E-mail:* sbartels@towson.edu.
**Application contact:** 410-704-2501, *Fax:* 410-704-4675, *E-mail:* grads@towson.edu.

## ■ UNIVERSITY OF CALIFORNIA, SANTA CRUZ

**Division of Graduate Studies, Division of Social Sciences, Program in Psychology, Santa Cruz, CA 95064**

**AWARDS** Developmental psychology (PhD); experimental psychology (PhD); social psychology (PhD).

**Faculty:** 26 full-time.
**Students:** 52 full-time (39 women); includes 23 minority (1 African American, 10 Asian Americans or Pacific Islanders, 11 Hispanic Americans, 1 Native American), 4 international. 96 applicants, 21% accepted. In 2001, 4 doctorates awarded.
**Degree requirements:** For doctorate, thesis/dissertation, qualifying exam. *Median time to degree:* Doctorate–7 years full-time.
**Entrance requirements:** For doctorate, GRE General Test. *Application deadline:* For fall admission, 1/1. *Application fee:* $40.
**Expenses:** Tuition: Full-time $19,857.
**Financial support:** Fellowships, research assistantships, teaching assistantships, career-related internships or fieldwork, Federal Work-Study, and institutionally

sponsored loans available. Financial award application deadline: 1/1.
**Faculty research:** Cognitive psychology, human information processing, sensation perceptions, psychobiology.
Maureen Callanan, Chairperson, 831-459-2153.
**Application contact:** Graduate Admissions, 831-459-2301. *Web site:* http://www.ucsc.edu/

## ■ UNIVERSITY OF CINCINNATI

**Division of Research and Advanced Studies, McMicken College of Arts and Sciences, Department of Psychology, Cincinnati, OH 45221**

**AWARDS** Clinical psychology (PhD); experimental psychology (PhD).

**Faculty:** 25 full-time.
**Students:** 69 full-time, 20 part-time; includes 15 minority (12 African Americans, 2 Asian Americans or Pacific Islanders, 1 Hispanic American), 3 international. 210 applicants, 13 enrolled. In 2001, 18 degrees awarded.
**Degree requirements:** For doctorate, thesis/dissertation.
**Entrance requirements:** For doctorate, GRE General Test, GRE Subject Test. *Application deadline:* For fall admission, 1/7. *Application fee:* $35. Electronic applications accepted.
**Expenses:** Tuition, state resident: part-time $2,698 per quarter. Tuition, nonresident: part-time $4,977 per quarter.
**Financial support:** Fellowships with full tuition reimbursements, traineeships, tuition waivers (partial), and unspecified assistantships available. Financial award application deadline: 5/1. *Total annual research expenditures:* $374,651.
Dr. Kevin M. Corcoran, Head, 513-556-5569, *Fax:* 513-556-1904.
**Application contact:** Dr. Paula K. Shear, Graduate Program Director, 513-556-5577, *Fax:* 513-556-1904, *E-mail:* paula.shear@uc.edu. *Web site:* http://asweb.artsci.uc.edu/psychology

## ■ UNIVERSITY OF CONNECTICUT

**Graduate School, College of Liberal Arts and Sciences, Field of Psychology, Storrs, CT 06269**

**AWARDS** Behavioral neuroscience (PhD); biopsychology (PhD); clinical psychology (PhD); cognition/instruction psychology (PhD); developmental psychology (PhD); ecological psychology (PhD); general experimental psychology (PhD); industrial and organizational psychology (PhD); language psychology (PhD); social psychology (PhD).

**Faculty:** 41 full-time (11 women), 2 part-time/adjunct (both women).
**Students:** 134 full-time (83 women), 17 part-time (9 women); includes 13 minority

(9 African Americans, 1 Asian American or Pacific Islander, 3 Hispanic Americans), 17 international. Average age 28. 378 applicants, 14% accepted, 25 enrolled. In 2001, 18 degrees awarded.
**Degree requirements:** For doctorate, thesis/dissertation, internship, comprehensive exam, registration.
**Entrance requirements:** For doctorate, GRE General Test, GRE Subject Test, letters of recommendation. *Application deadline:* For fall admission, 12/31. *Application fee:* $40 ($45 for international students).
**Financial support:** In 2001–02, 45 fellowships (averaging $4,000 per year), 16 research assistantships with full tuition reimbursements (averaging $16,000 per year), 83 teaching assistantships with full tuition reimbursements (averaging $16,000 per year) were awarded. Career-related internships or fieldwork, Federal Work-Study, scholarships/grants, health care benefits, and unspecified assistantships also available. Financial award application deadline: 12/31.
**Faculty research:** Behavioral neuroscience; physiology/chemistry of memory; sensation, motor control/motivation; cognitive, social, personality and language development; infancy/person perceptions and intergroup relations. *Total annual research expenditures:* $8 million.
Charles A. Lowe, Head, *Fax:* 860-486-2760, *E-mail:* charles.lowe@uconn.edu.
**Application contact:** Gina Stuart, Graduate Admissions, 860-486-3528, *Fax:* 860-486-2760, *E-mail:* futuregr@psych.psy.uconn.edu. *Web site:* http://psych.uconn.edu/

### ■ UNIVERSITY OF DAYTON

**Graduate School, College of Arts and Sciences, Department of Psychology, Program in Human Factors and Research, Dayton, OH 45469-1300**

**AWARDS** MA. Part-time and evening/weekend programs available.

**Faculty:** 9 full-time (1 woman).
**Students:** 2 full-time (both women), 9 part-time (2 women). 9 applicants, 78% accepted, 2 enrolled. In 2001, 2 degrees awarded.
**Degree requirements:** For master's, thesis.
**Entrance requirements:** For master's, GRE General Test, GRE Subject Test, minimum undergraduate GPA of 3.0. *Application deadline:* For fall admission, 3/1 (priority date). *Application fee:* $30. Electronic applications accepted.
**Expenses:** Tuition: Full-time $5,436; part-time $453 per credit hour. Required fees: $50; $25 per term.

**Financial support:** In 2001–02, 3 research assistantships with full tuition reimbursements were awarded; teaching assistantships with full tuition reimbursements, career-related internships or fieldwork also available. Financial award application deadline: 3/1.
Dr. William F. Maroney, Director, 937-229-2161, *Fax:* 937-229-3900, *E-mail:* humfac@udayton.edu.

### ■ UNIVERSITY OF HARTFORD

**College of Arts and Sciences, Department of Psychology, Program in General Experimental Psychology, West Hartford, CT 06117-1599**

**AWARDS** MA. Part-time programs available.
**Faculty:** 3 full-time (2 women), 4 part-time/adjunct (1 woman).
**Students:** 7 full-time (5 women), 9 part-time (8 women), 1 international. Average age 27. 22 applicants, 68% accepted. In 2001, 2 degrees awarded.
**Degree requirements:** For master's, thesis or alternative, comprehensive exam.
**Entrance requirements:** For master's, GRE General Test, GRE Subject Test, TOEFL, minimum GPA of 3.0. *Application deadline:* For fall admission, 2/25 (priority date). Applications are processed on a rolling basis. *Application fee:* $40 ($55 for international students). Electronic applications accepted.
**Expenses:** Tuition: Part-time $300 per credit hour.
**Financial support:** In 2001–02, 2 research assistantships (averaging $2,000 per year), 1 teaching assistantship (averaging $2,550 per year) were awarded. Financial award application deadline: 6/1; financial award applicants required to submit FAFSA.
**Faculty research:** Decision making, social judgement and stereotyping, stress and health.
Dr. A. Richard Brayer, Director, 860-768-4545, *E-mail:* brayer@mail.hartford.edu.
**Application contact:** Kellie Richard Westenfeld, Assistant Director of Graduate Admissions, 860-768-4371, *Fax:* 860-768-5160, *E-mail:* westenfel@mail.hartford.edu. *Web site:* http://www.hartford.edu/

### ■ UNIVERSITY OF LOUISVILLE

**Graduate School, College of Arts and Sciences, Department of Psychology, Program in Experimental Psychology, Louisville, KY 40292-0001**

**AWARDS** PhD.
**Students:** 27 full-time (14 women), 1 (woman) part-time; includes 2 minority (1 African American, 1 Asian American or Pacific Islander), 6 international. Average age 28. In 2001, 6 doctorates awarded.

**Degree requirements:** For doctorate, thesis/dissertation.
**Entrance requirements:** For doctorate, GRE General Test. *Application deadline:* Applications are processed on a rolling basis. *Application fee:* $25.
**Expenses:** Tuition, state resident: full-time $4,134. Tuition, nonresident: full-time $11,486.
Dr. Edward Essock, Director, 502-852-5948, *E-mail:* eaesso01@louisville.edu.

### ■ UNIVERSITY OF MAINE

**Graduate School, College of Liberal Arts and Sciences, Department of Psychology, Orono, ME 04469**

**AWARDS** Clinical psychology (PhD); developmental psychology (MA); experimental psychology (MA, PhD); social psychology (MA).

**Faculty:** 21.
**Students:** 22 full-time (17 women), 13 part-time (11 women); includes 3 minority (all Native Americans), 2 international. 100 applicants, 14% accepted, 6 enrolled. In 2001, 4 degrees awarded.
**Degree requirements:** For master's and doctorate, thesis/dissertation.
**Entrance requirements:** For master's and doctorate, GRE General Test, GRE Subject Test, TOEFL. *Application deadline:* For fall admission, 2/1 (priority date). Applications are processed on a rolling basis. *Application fee:* $50. Electronic applications accepted.
**Expenses:** Tuition, state resident: full-time $3,780; part-time $210 per credit hour. Tuition, nonresident: full-time $10,782; part-time $599 per credit hour. Required fees: $9.50 per credit hour. $32 per semester. Tuition and fees vary according to reciprocity agreements.
**Financial support:** In 2001–02, 3 research assistantships with tuition reimbursements (averaging $9,010 per year), 21 teaching assistantships with tuition reimbursements (averaging $9,010 per year) were awarded. Fellowships with tuition reimbursements, Federal Work-Study, institutionally sponsored loans, and tuition waivers (full and partial) also available. Financial award application deadline: 3/1.
**Faculty research:** Social development, hypertension and aging, attitude change, self-confidence in achievement situations, health psychology.
Dr. Joel Gold, Chair, 207-581-2030, *Fax:* 207-581-6128.
**Application contact:** Scott G. Delcourt, Director of the Graduate School, 207-581-3218, *Fax:* 207-581-3232, *E-mail:* graduate@maine.edu. *Web site:* http://www.umaine.edu/graduate/

## ■ UNIVERSITY OF MARYLAND, COLLEGE PARK

**Graduate Studies and Research, College of Behavioral and Social Sciences, Department of Psychology, College Park, MD 20742**

**AWARDS** Clinical psychology (PhD); developmental psychology (PhD); experimental psychology (PhD); industrial psychology (MA, MS, PhD); social psychology (PhD).

**Faculty:** 52 full-time (17 women), 10 part-time/adjunct (5 women).
**Students:** 80 full-time (50 women), 22 part-time (15 women); includes 26 minority (14 African Americans, 8 Asian Americans or Pacific Islanders, 3 Hispanic Americans, 1 Native American), 11 international. 432 applicants, 10% accepted, 18 enrolled. In 2001, 8 master's, 21 doctorates awarded.
**Degree requirements:** For master's, thesis; for doctorate, variable foreign language requirement, thesis/dissertation, comprehensive exam.
**Entrance requirements:** For master's, GRE General Test, GRE Subject Test, minimum GPA of 3.5, research and/or work experience; for doctorate, GRE General Test, GRE Subject Test. *Application deadline:* For fall admission, 12/15. Applications are processed on a rolling basis. *Application fee:* $50 ($70 for international students). Electronic applications accepted.
**Expenses:** Tuition, state resident: part-time $289 per credit hour. Tuition, nonresident: part-time $448 per credit hour. One-time fee: $436 part-time. Full-time tuition and fees vary according to course load, campus/location and program.
**Financial support:** In 2001–02, 15 fellowships with full tuition reimbursements (averaging $11,508 per year), 87 teaching assistantships with tuition reimbursements (averaging $12,153 per year) were awarded. Career-related internships or fieldwork, Federal Work-Study, and scholarships/grants also available. Support available to part-time students. Financial award applicants required to submit FAFSA.
**Faculty research:** Counseling and social psychology.
Dr. William Hall, Chairman, 301-405-5862, *Fax:* 301-314-9566.
**Application contact:** Trudy Lindsey, Director, Graduate Admissions and Records, 301-405-6991, *Fax:* 301-314-9305, *E-mail:* grschool@deans.umd.edu.

## ■ THE UNIVERSITY OF MEMPHIS

**Graduate School, College of Arts and Sciences, Department of Psychology, Memphis, TN 38152**

**AWARDS** Clinical psychology (PhD); experimental psychology (PhD); psychology (MS); school psychology (MA, PhD). Part-time programs available.

**Faculty:** 30 full-time (2 women), 6 part-time/adjunct (3 women).
**Students:** 81 full-time (56 women), 19 part-time (11 women); includes 9 minority (8 African Americans, 1 Native American), 7 international. Average age 28. 188 applicants, 26% accepted. In 2001, 20 master's, 12 doctorates awarded. Terminal master's awarded for partial completion of doctoral program.
**Degree requirements:** For master's, thesis (for some programs), oral exam (MS), comprehensive exam; for doctorate, thesis/dissertation, internship.
**Entrance requirements:** For master's, GRE General Test, 18 undergraduate hours in psychology, minimum GPA of 2.5; for doctorate, GRE General Test, GRE Subject Test. *Application deadline:* For fall admission, 2/1. Applications are processed on a rolling basis. *Application fee:* $35 ($60 for international students).
**Expenses:** Tuition, state resident: full-time $2,026. Tuition, nonresident: full-time $4,528.
**Financial support:** In 2001–02, 2 fellowships with full tuition reimbursements (averaging $13,333 per year), 116 research assistantships with full tuition reimbursements (averaging $5,000 per year), 2 teaching assistantships with full tuition reimbursements (averaging $1,500 per year) were awarded.
**Faculty research:** Psychotherapy and psychopathology, behavioral medicine and community psychology, child and family studies, cognitive and social processes, neuropsychology and behavioral neuroscience. *Total annual research expenditures:* $2.5 million.
Dr. Andrew Meyers, Chairman and Coordinator of Graduate Studies, 901-678-2145.

## ■ UNIVERSITY OF MISSISSIPPI

**Graduate School, College of Liberal Arts, Department of Psychology, Oxford, University, MS 38677**

**AWARDS** Clinical psychology (PhD); experimental psychology (PhD); psychology (MA).

**Faculty:** 13.
**Students:** 62 full-time (40 women), 12 part-time (4 women); includes 10 minority (6 African Americans, 3 Asian Americans or Pacific Islanders, 1 Hispanic American), 1 international. In 2001, 5 master's, 5 doctorates awarded.
**Degree requirements:** For master's and doctorate, thesis/dissertation.
**Entrance requirements:** For master's, GRE General Test, TOEFL, minimum GPA of 3.0; for doctorate, GRE General Test, TOEFL. *Application deadline:* For fall admission, 8/1. Applications are processed on a rolling basis. *Application fee:* $0 ($25 for international students).
**Expenses:** Tuition, state resident: full-time $3,626; part-time $202 per hour. Tuition, nonresident: full-time $8,172; part-time $454 per hour.
**Financial support:** Application deadline: 3/1.
Dr. David S. Hargrove, Chairman, 662-915-7383, *Fax:* 662-915-5398, *E-mail:* psych@olemiss.edu.

## ■ UNIVERSITY OF MISSOURI–ST. LOUIS

**Graduate School, College of Arts and Sciences, Department of Psychology, St. Louis, MO 63121-4499**

**AWARDS** Clinical psychology (PhD); clinical psychology respecialization (Certificate); experimental psychology (PhD); general psychology (MA); industrial/organizational (PhD). Evening/weekend programs available.

**Faculty:** 18.
**Students:** 34 full-time (27 women), 38 part-time (25 women); includes 9 minority (6 African Americans, 2 Asian Americans or Pacific Islanders, 1 Hispanic American), 2 international. In 2001, 12 master's, 5 doctorates awarded. Terminal master's awarded for partial completion of doctoral program.
**Degree requirements:** For doctorate, thesis/dissertation.
**Entrance requirements:** For master's and doctorate, GRE General Test, GRE Subject Test. *Application deadline:* For fall admission, 2/1 (priority date). Applications are processed on a rolling basis. *Application fee:* $25 ($40 for international students). Electronic applications accepted.
**Expenses:** Tuition, state resident: part-time $231 per credit hour. Tuition, nonresident: part-time $621 per credit hour.
**Financial support:** In 2001–02, 2 fellowships with full tuition reimbursements (averaging $12,000 per year), 9 research assistantships with full and partial tuition reimbursements (averaging $13,585 per year), 23 teaching assistantships with full and partial tuition reimbursements (averaging $9,096 per year) were awarded.
**Faculty research:** Animal-human learning; physiological, industrial-organizational and cognitive processes; personality-social,

clinical and community psychology. *Total annual research expenditures:* $1.1 million. Dr. Gary Burger, Chair, 314-516-5391, *Fax:* 314-516-5392.

**Application contact:** Graduate Admissions, 314-516-5458, *Fax:* 314-516-5310, *E-mail:* gradadm@umsl.edu.

■ **THE UNIVERSITY OF MONTANA–MISSOULA**

**Graduate School, College of Arts and Sciences, Department of Psychology, Programs in Experimental Psychology, Missoula, MT 59812-0002**

**AWARDS** Animal behavior (PhD); developmental psychology (PhD).

**Degree requirements:** For doctorate, thesis/dissertation, oral exam.

**Entrance requirements:** For doctorate, GRE General Test, minimum GPA of 3.2. *Application deadline:* For fall admission, 1/15. *Application fee:* $45.

**Expenses:** Tuition, state resident: full-time $2,482; part-time $1,700 per year. Tuition, nonresident: full-time $7,372; part-time $5,000 per year. Required fees: $1,900. Tuition and fees vary according to degree level.

**Financial support:** In 2001–02, teaching assistantships with full tuition reimbursements (averaging $8,400 per year); fellowships, research assistantships, Federal Work-Study also available. Financial award application deadline: 3/1; financial award applicants required to submit FAFSA.

**Faculty research:** Animal learning and behavior, neurological assessment, developmental psychology.

**Application contact:** Graduate Secretary, 406-243-4523, *Fax:* 406-243-6366, *E-mail:* psycgrad@selway.umt.edu. *Web site:* http://www.cas.umt.edu/psych/

■ **UNIVERSITY OF NEBRASKA AT OMAHA**

**Graduate Studies and Research, College of Arts and Sciences, Department of Psychology, Omaha, NE 68182**

**AWARDS** Developmental psychobiology (PhD); experimental child psychology (PhD); industrial/organizational psychology (MS, PhD); psychology (MA); school psychology (MS, Ed S). Part-time programs available.

**Faculty:** 17 full-time (7 women).

**Students:** 32 full-time (22 women), 18 part-time (10 women); includes 2 minority (1 African American, 1 Hispanic American). Average age 27. 64 applicants, 44% accepted, 28 enrolled. In 2001, 23 master's, 4 other advanced degrees awarded.

**Degree requirements:** For master's, thesis (for some programs), comprehensive exam; for doctorate, thesis/dissertation.

**Entrance requirements:** For master's, GRE General Test, GRE Subject Test, previous course work in psychology, including statistics and a laboratory course; minimum GPA of 3.0; for doctorate, GRE General Test. *Application deadline:* For fall admission, 2/1. *Application fee:* $35. Electronic applications accepted.

**Expenses:** Tuition, state resident: part-time $116 per credit hour. Tuition, nonresident: part-time $291 per credit hour. Required fees: $13 per credit hour. $4 per semester. One-time fee: $52 part-time.

**Financial support:** In 2001–02, 42 students received support; fellowships, research assistantships, teaching assistantships, career-related internships or fieldwork, Federal Work-Study, institutionally sponsored loans, scholarships/grants, tuition waivers (partial), and unspecified assistantships available. Support available to part-time students. Financial award application deadline: 3/1; financial award applicants required to submit FAFSA. Dr. Kenneth Deffenbacher, Chairperson, 402-554-2592.

■ **UNIVERSITY OF NEVADA, LAS VEGAS**

**Graduate College, College of Liberal Arts, Department of Psychology, Las Vegas, NV 89154-9900**

**AWARDS** Clinical psychology (PhD); experimental psychology (PhD); general psychology (MA). Part-time programs available.

**Faculty:** 21 full-time (7 women).

**Students:** 29 full-time (22 women), 6 part-time (4 women); includes 6 minority (2 Asian Americans or Pacific Islanders, 4 Hispanic Americans). 47 applicants, 28% accepted, 12 enrolled. In 2001, 4 degrees awarded.

**Degree requirements:** For master's and doctorate, thesis/dissertation, oral exam, comprehensive exam.

**Entrance requirements:** For master's, GRE General Test, GRE Subject Test, minimum GPA of 3.2; for doctorate, GRE General Test, GRE Subject Test, minimum GPA of 3.2 in bachelor's and 3.5 in master's. *Application deadline:* For fall admission, 3/1. *Application fee:* $40 ($55 for international students).

**Expenses:** Tuition, state resident: full-time $1,926; part-time $107 per credit. Tuition, nonresident: full-time $9,376; part-time $220 per credit. Tuition and fees vary according to course load.

**Financial support:** In 2001–02, 6 research assistantships with full and partial tuition

reimbursements (averaging $11,000 per year), 18 teaching assistantships with partial tuition reimbursements (averaging $11,000 per year) were awarded. Financial award application deadline: 3/1. Dr. Charles Rusmussen, Chair, 702-895-3305.

**Application contact:** Graduate College Admissions Evaluator, 702-895-3320, *Fax:* 702-895-4180, *E-mail:* gradcollege@ccmail.nevada.edu. *Web site:* http://psychology.unlv.edu/gradinfo.html/

■ **THE UNIVERSITY OF NORTH CAROLINA AT CHAPEL HILL**

**Graduate School, College of Arts and Sciences, Department of Psychology, Chapel Hill, NC 27599**

**AWARDS** Biological psychology (PhD); clinical psychology (PhD); cognitive psychology (PhD); developmental psychology (PhD); quantitative psychology (PhD); social psychology (PhD).

**Faculty:** 46 full-time (25 women), 6 part-time/adjunct (0 women).

**Students:** 116 full-time (63 women). 546 applicants, 7% accepted, 29 enrolled. In 2001, 27 doctorates awarded.

**Degree requirements:** For doctorate, thesis/dissertation, comprehensive exam.

**Entrance requirements:** For doctorate, GRE General Test, minimum GPA of 3.0. *Application deadline:* For fall admission, 12/1. *Application fee:* $55. Electronic applications accepted.

**Expenses:** Tuition, state resident: full-time $2,864. Tuition, nonresident: full-time $12,030.

**Financial support:** In 2001–02, 11 fellowships with tuition reimbursements, 28 research assistantships with tuition reimbursements, 63 teaching assistantships with tuition reimbursements were awarded. Unspecified assistantships also available. Financial award application deadline: 2/1.

**Faculty research:** Expressed emotion, cognitive development, social cognitive neuroscience, human memory personality. *Total annual research expenditures:* $605,806. Peter A. Ornstein, Chair, 919-962-3088.

**Application contact:** Barbara Atkins, Student Services Manager, 919-962-7149, *Fax:* 919-962-2537, *E-mail:* batkins@email.unc.edu.

■ **UNIVERSITY OF NORTH DAKOTA**

**Graduate School, College of Arts and Sciences, Department of Psychology, Grand Forks, ND 58202**

**AWARDS** Clinical psychology (PhD); experimental psychology (PhD); psychology (MA).

**Faculty:** 15 full-time (3 women).

*University of North Dakota (continued)*
**Students:** 9 full-time (8 women), 37 part-time (20 women). 57 applicants, 23% accepted, 12 enrolled. In 2001, 9 master's, 8 doctorates awarded.
**Degree requirements:** For master's, thesis, final exam; for doctorate, thesis/dissertation, internship, final exam, comprehensive exam.
**Entrance requirements:** For master's, GRE General Test, GRE Subject Test, TOEFL, minimum GPA of 3.0; for doctorate, GRE General Test, GRE Subject Test, TOEFL, minimum GPA of 3.5. *Application deadline:* For fall admission, 2/1. *Application fee:* $30.
**Expenses:** Tuition, state resident: full-time $3,298. Tuition, nonresident: full-time $7,998.
**Financial support:** In 2001–02, 34 students received support, including 2 research assistantships with full tuition reimbursements available (averaging $9,282 per year), 23 teaching assistantships with full tuition reimbursements available (averaging $9,282 per year); fellowships, career-related internships or fieldwork, Federal Work-Study, institutionally sponsored loans, scholarships/grants, tuition waivers (full and partial), and unspecified assistantships also available. Support available to part-time students. Financial award application deadline: 3/15; financial award applicants required to submit FAFSA.
**Faculty research:** Developmental psychology, clinical social psychology, educational psychology, personality disorders.
Dr. Mark D. Grabe, Chair, 701-777-3920, *Fax:* 701-777-3454, *E-mail:* mark_grabe@und.nodak.edu. *Web site:* http://www.und.edu/dept/psychol/

### ■ UNIVERSITY OF NORTH TEXAS

**Robert B. Toulouse School of Graduate Studies, College of Arts and Sciences, Department of Psychology, Denton, TX 76203**

**AWARDS** Clinical psychology (PhD); counseling psychology (MA, MS, PhD); experimental psychology (MA, MS, PhD); health psychology and behavioral medicine (PhD); industrial psychology (MA, MS); psychology (MA, MS, PhD); school psychology (MA, MS, PhD).
**Faculty:** 29 full-time (5 women), 7 part-time/adjunct (5 women).
**Students:** 129 full-time (96 women), 98 part-time (70 women); includes 23 minority (2 African Americans, 4 Asian Americans or Pacific Islanders, 15 Hispanic Americans, 2 Native Americans), 9 international. Average age 30. In 2001, 24 master's, 17 doctorates awarded. Terminal master's awarded for partial completion of doctoral program.

**Degree requirements:** For master's, thesis or alternative, comprehensive exam; for doctorate, one foreign language, thesis/dissertation, comprehensive exam.
**Entrance requirements:** For master's and doctorate, GRE General Test, GRE Subject Test, interview. *Application deadline:* For fall admission, 2/1. *Application fee:* $25 ($50 for international students).
**Expenses:** Tuition, state resident: part-time $186 per hour. Tuition, nonresident: part-time $319 per hour. Required fees: $88; $21 per hour.
**Financial support:** Fellowships, research assistantships, teaching assistantships, career-related internships or fieldwork, Federal Work-Study, and institutionally sponsored loans available. Financial award application deadline: 8/1.
Dr. Ernest H. Harrell, Chair, 940-565-2671, *Fax:* 940-546-4682, *E-mail:* harrelle@unt.edu.
**Application contact:** Dr. Joseph Critelli, Graduate Adviser, 940-565-2671, *Fax:* 940-565-4682, *E-mail:* critelli@facstaff.cas.unt.edu.

### ■ UNIVERSITY OF RHODE ISLAND

**Graduate School, College of Arts and Sciences, Department of Psychology, Program in Experimental Psychology, Kingston, RI 02881**

**AWARDS** PhD.
**Students:** In 2001, 2 doctorates awarded. *Application deadline:* For fall admission, 4/15 (priority date). Applications are processed on a rolling basis. *Application fee:* $35.
**Expenses:** Tuition, state resident: full-time $3,756; part-time $209 per credit. Tuition, nonresident: full-time $10,774; part-time $599 per credit. Required fees: $1,586; $76 per credit. One-time fee: $60 full-time.
John Stevenson, Head, 401-874-2193.

### ■ UNIVERSITY OF SOUTH CAROLINA

**The Graduate School, College of Liberal Arts, Department of Psychology, Program in Experimental Psychology, Columbia, SC 29208**

**AWARDS** MA, PhD.
**Faculty:** 12 full-time (4 women), 4 part-time/adjunct (2 women).
**Students:** 15 full-time (8 women); includes 1 minority (African American), 1 international. Average age 29. 20 applicants, 30% accepted. In 2001, 2 degrees awarded. Terminal master's awarded for partial completion of doctoral program.
**Degree requirements:** For master's and doctorate, thesis/dissertation.

**Entrance requirements:** For master's, GRE General Test, minimum GPA of 3.2; for doctorate, GRE General Test. *Application deadline:* For fall admission, 2/1 (priority date). Applications are processed on a rolling basis. *Application fee:* $35. Electronic applications accepted.
**Expenses:** Tuition, state resident: full-time $4,434. Tuition, nonresident: full-time $9,854. Tuition and fees vary according to program.
**Financial support:** In 2001–02, 3 fellowships with full tuition reimbursements (averaging $15,000 per year), 5 research assistantships with full tuition reimbursements (averaging $9,000 per year), 4 teaching assistantships with full tuition reimbursements (averaging $9,000 per year) were awarded. Federal Work-Study and institutionally sponsored loans also available. Support available to part-time students.
**Faculty research:** Cognition, development, neuroscience.
Douglas H. Wedell, Director, 803-777-9342, *Fax:* 803-777-9558, *E-mail:* wedell@sc.edu.
**Application contact:** Doris Davis, Graduate Secretary, 803-777-2312, *Fax:* 803-777-9558, *E-mail:* doris@gwm.sc.edu.

### ■ UNIVERSITY OF SOUTH FLORIDA

**College of Graduate Studies, College of Arts and Sciences, Department of Psychology, Tampa, FL 33620-9951**

**AWARDS** Clinical psychology (PhD); experimental psychology (PhD); industrial/organizational psychology (PhD).

**Faculty:** 37 full-time (12 women), 2 part-time/adjunct (0 women).
**Students:** 99 full-time (67 women), 47 part-time (35 women); includes 32 minority (14 African Americans, 5 Asian Americans or Pacific Islanders, 13 Hispanic Americans), 8 international. Average age 30. 367 applicants, 7% accepted, 22 enrolled. In 2001, 5 doctorates awarded.
**Degree requirements:** For doctorate, thesis/dissertation.
**Entrance requirements:** For doctorate, GRE General Test, minimum GPA of 3.0 in last 60 hours. *Application deadline:* For fall admission, 1/15. *Application fee:* $20. Electronic applications accepted.
**Expenses:** Contact institution.
**Financial support:** Fellowships with partial tuition reimbursements, research assistantships with partial tuition reimbursements, teaching assistantships, career-related internships or fieldwork, Federal Work-Study, and institutionally

sponsored loans available. Financial award application deadline: 4/15; financial award applicants required to submit FAFSA.
**Faculty research:** Human memory, job analysis, stress, drug and alcohol abuse, neuroscience. *Total annual research expenditures:* $1.4 million.
Emanuel Donchin, Chairperson, 813-974-4066, *Fax:* 813-974-4617, *E-mail:* donchin@luna.cas.usf.edu.
**Application contact:** Michael D. Coovert, Graduate Coordinator, 813-974-0482, *Fax:* 813-974-4617, *E-mail:* coovert@luna.cas.usf.edu. *Web site:* http://www.cas.usf.edu/psychology/

■ **THE UNIVERSITY OF TENNESSEE**

**Graduate School, College of Arts and Sciences, Department of Psychology, Knoxville, TN 37996**

**AWARDS** Clinical psychology (PhD); experimental psychology (MA, PhD); psychology (MA).

**Faculty:** 23 full-time (5 women), 6 part-time/adjunct (1 woman).
**Students:** 70 full-time (40 women), 24 part-time (10 women); includes 14 minority (9 African Americans, 3 Asian Americans or Pacific Islanders, 2 Native Americans), 10 international. 116 applicants, 12% accepted. In 2001, 9 master's, 18 doctorates awarded. Terminal master's awarded for partial completion of doctoral program.
**Degree requirements:** For master's and doctorate, thesis/dissertation.
**Entrance requirements:** For master's and doctorate, GRE General Test, GRE Subject Test, TOEFL, minimum GPA of 2.7. *Application deadline:* For fall admission, 2/1. *Application fee:* $35. Electronic applications accepted.
**Expenses:** Tuition, state resident: full-time $4,280; part-time $233 per hour. Tuition, nonresident: full-time $12,066; part-time $666 per hour. Tuition and fees vary according to program.
**Financial support:** In 2001–02, 1 fellowship, 10 teaching assistantships were awarded. Research assistantships, Federal Work-Study, institutionally sponsored loans, and unspecified assistantships also available. Financial award application deadline: 2/1; financial award applicants required to submit FAFSA.
Dr. James Lawler, Head, 865-974-3328, *Fax:* 865-974-3330, *E-mail:* jlawler@utk.edu.

■ **THE UNIVERSITY OF TENNESSEE AT CHATTANOOGA**

**Graduate Division, College of Arts and Sciences, Department of Psychology, Program in Research Psychology, Chattanooga, TN 37403-2598**

**AWARDS** MS. Part-time and evening/weekend programs available.

**Students:** 14 full-time (10 women), 2 part-time (both women); includes 2 minority (both African Americans). Average age 26. 13 applicants, 92% accepted, 8 enrolled. In 2001, 4 degrees awarded.
**Degree requirements:** For master's, thesis.
**Entrance requirements:** For master's, GRE General Test. *Application deadline:* For fall admission, 8/1 (priority date); for spring admission, 12/1 (priority date). Applications are processed on a rolling basis. *Application fee:* $25.
**Expenses:** Tuition, state resident: full-time $3,752; part-time $228 per hour. Tuition, nonresident: full-time $10,282; part-time $565 per hour.
**Financial support:** Fellowships, research assistantships available. Financial award application deadline: 4/1; financial award applicants required to submit FAFSA.
Dr. Michael D. Biderman, Coordinator, 423-425-4268, *Fax:* 423-425-4284, *E-mail:* michael-biderman@utc.edu.
**Application contact:** Dr. Deborah E. Arfken, Dean of Graduate Studies, 865-425-1740, *Fax:* 865-425-5223, *E-mail:* deborah-arfken@utc.edu. *Web site:* http://www.utc.edu/

■ **THE UNIVERSITY OF TEXAS AT ARLINGTON**

**Graduate School, College of Science, Department of Psychology, Arlington, TX 76019**

**AWARDS** Experimental psychology (PhD); psychology (MS).

**Faculty:** 13 full-time (3 women), 1 part-time/adjunct (0 women).
**Students:** 33 full-time (25 women), 5 part-time (4 women); includes 9 minority (2 African Americans, 2 Asian Americans or Pacific Islanders, 4 Hispanic Americans, 1 Native American), 5 international. 27 applicants, 74% accepted, 12 enrolled. In 2001, 4 master's, 3 doctorates awarded.
**Degree requirements:** For master's, thesis, comprehensive exam or thesis; for doctorate, one foreign language, thesis/dissertation.
**Entrance requirements:** For master's and doctorate, GRE General Test, TOEFL. *Application deadline:* For fall admission, 6/16. Applications are processed on a rolling basis. *Application fee:* $25 ($50 for international students).

**Expenses:** Tuition, area resident: full-time $2,268. Tuition, nonresident: full-time $6,264. Required fees: $839. Tuition and fees vary according to course load.
**Financial support:** In 2001–02, 4 fellowships (averaging $1,000 per year), 2 research assistantships (averaging $12,000 per year), 28 teaching assistantships (averaging $12,000 per year) were awarded. Federal Work-Study also available. Financial award application deadline: 6/1; financial award applicants required to submit FAFSA.
Dr. Paul B. Paulus, Chairman, 817-272-2281, *Fax:* 817-272-2364, *E-mail:* paulus@uta.edu.
**Application contact:** Dr. David Gorfein, Graduate Advisor, 817-272-2281, *Fax:* 817-272-2364, *E-mail:* gorfein@uta.edu.

■ **THE UNIVERSITY OF TEXAS AT EL PASO**

**Graduate School, College of Liberal Arts, Department of Psychology, El Paso, TX 79968-0001**

**AWARDS** Clinical psychology (MA); experimental psychology (MA); psychology (PhD). Part-time and evening/weekend programs available.

**Students:** 42 (29 women); includes 21 minority (20 Hispanic Americans, 1 Native American) 2 international. Average age 34. 54 applicants, 98% accepted. In 2001, 2 master's, 2 doctorates awarded.
**Degree requirements:** For master's and doctorate, thesis/dissertation.
**Entrance requirements:** For master's and doctorate, GRE General Test, TOEFL. *Application deadline:* For fall admission, 2/1. Applications are processed on a rolling basis. *Application fee:* $15 ($65 for international students). Electronic applications accepted.
**Expenses:** Tuition, state resident: full-time $2,450. Tuition, nonresident: full-time $6,000.
**Financial support:** In 2001–02, 18 students received support, including research assistantships with partial tuition reimbursements available (averaging $18,625 per year), teaching assistantships with partial tuition reimbursements available (averaging $14,900 per year); fellowships with partial tuition reimbursements available, career-related internships or fieldwork, Federal Work-Study, institutionally sponsored loans, scholarships/grants, and tuition waivers (partial) also available. Financial award application deadline: 3/15; financial award applicants required to submit FAFSA.
Dr. Judith P. Goggin, Chairperson, 915-747-5551, *Fax:* 915-747-6553, *E-mail:* jgoggin@miners.utep.edu.

*The University of Texas at El Paso (continued)*

**Application contact:** Dr. Charles H. Ambler, Dean of the Graduate School, 915-747-5491 Ext. 7886, *Fax:* 915-747-5788, *E-mail:* cambler@miners.utep.edu.

## ■ THE UNIVERSITY OF TEXAS– PAN AMERICAN

**College of Social and Behavioral Sciences, Department of Psychology and Anthropology, Edinburg, TX 78539-2999**

**AWARDS** Psychology (MA), including clinical psychology, experimental psychology. Part-time and evening/weekend programs available.

**Faculty:** 11 full-time (0 women).
**Students:** 13 full-time (7 women), 29 part-time (20 women); includes 33 minority (1 Asian American or Pacific Islander, 32 Hispanic Americans). Average age 29. 18 applicants, 44% accepted. In 2001, 7 degrees awarded.
**Degree requirements:** For master's, internship, thesis optional.
**Entrance requirements:** For master's, GRE General Test. *Application deadline:* For fall admission, 2/1 (priority date); for winter admission, 10/1 (priority date). Applications are processed on a rolling basis. *Application fee:* $0. Electronic applications accepted.
**Expenses:** Tuition, state resident: part-time $212 per semester hour. Tuition, nonresident: part-time $367 per semester hour.
**Financial support:** In 2001–02, 3 teaching assistantships were awarded; career-related internships or fieldwork, Federal Work-Study, and institutionally sponsored loans also available.
**Faculty research:** Rehabilitation, biofeedback, acculturation, child development, health.
Dr. Mark Winkel, Director, 956-381-3528, *Fax:* 956-381-3333, *E-mail:* winkelm@panam.edu. *Web site:* http://www.panam.edu/dept/gsprog/

## ■ UNIVERSITY OF TOLEDO

**Graduate School, College of Arts and Sciences, Department of Psychology, Toledo, OH 43606-3398**

**AWARDS** Clinical psychology (PhD); experimental psychology (MA, PhD).
**Faculty:** 20.
**Students:** 51 full-time (43 women). Average age 28. 104 applicants, 21% accepted, 20 enrolled. In 2001, 4 master's, 7 doctorates awarded.
**Degree requirements:** For master's, thesis; for doctorate, one foreign language, thesis/dissertation.

**Entrance requirements:** For master's and doctorate, GRE General Test, GRE Subject Test. *Application deadline:* For fall admission, 1/15. *Application fee:* $30.
**Expenses:** Tuition, state resident: full-time $7,278; part-time $303 per hour. Tuition, nonresident: full-time $15,731; part-time $699 per hour. Required fees: $43 per hour.
**Financial support:** In 2001–02, 41 research assistantships were awarded; career-related internships or fieldwork, Federal Work-Study, and institutionally sponsored loans also available. Support available to part-time students. Financial award application deadline: 1/15; financial award applicants required to submit FAFSA.
**Faculty research:** Neural taste response.
Dr. Robert A. Haaf, Chair, 419-530-2717, *Fax:* 419-530-8479, *E-mail:* rhaaf@uoft02.utoledo.edu. *Web site:* http://utoledo.edu/www/psychology/graduate.html

**Find an in-depth description at www.petersons.com/gradchannel.**

## ■ UNIVERSITY OF WISCONSIN– OSHKOSH

**Graduate School, College of Letters and Science, Department of Psychology, Oshkosh, WI 54901**

**AWARDS** Experimental psychology (MS); industrial/organizational psychology (MS).
**Faculty:** 8 full-time (2 women).
**Students:** 20; includes 2 minority (1 Asian American or Pacific Islander, 1 Hispanic American). Average age 26. In 2001, 7 degrees awarded.
**Degree requirements:** For master's, thesis.
**Entrance requirements:** For master's, GRE, 10 semester hours of undergraduate course work in psychology. *Application deadline:* Applications are processed on a rolling basis. *Application fee:* $45. Electronic applications accepted.
**Expenses:** Tuition, state resident: full-time $2,236; part-time $250 per credit. Tuition, nonresident: full-time $7,148; part-time $795 per credit. Tuition and fees vary according to program.
**Financial support:** Career-related internships or fieldwork, institutionally sponsored loans, and unspecified assistantships available. Financial award application deadline: 3/15; financial award applicants required to submit FAFSA.
**Faculty research:** Performance evaluation, training, biological bases of behavior, tactile perception, aging.
Dr. Susan McFadden, Chair, 920-424-2300.
**Application contact:** 920-424-2300, *E-mail:* psychology@uwosh.edu. *Web site:*

http://www.uwosh.edu/departments/psychology/

## ■ WASHINGTON UNIVERSITY IN ST. LOUIS

**Graduate School of Arts and Sciences, Department of Psychology, St. Louis, MO 63130-4899**

**AWARDS** Clinical psychology (PhD); general experimental psychology (MA, PhD); social psychology (MA, PhD). Part-time programs available.

**Students:** 55 full-time (35 women); includes 4 minority (3 African Americans, 1 Asian American or Pacific Islander), 4 international. 171 applicants, 18% accepted. In 2001, 7 degrees awarded. Terminal master's awarded for partial completion of doctoral program.
**Degree requirements:** For master's, thesis or alternative; for doctorate, thesis/dissertation.
**Entrance requirements:** For master's and doctorate, GRE General Test. *Application deadline:* For fall admission, 1/15 (priority date). Applications are processed on a rolling basis. *Application fee:* $35. Electronic applications accepted.
**Expenses:** Tuition: Full-time $26,900.
**Financial support:** Fellowships, research assistantships, teaching assistantships, career-related internships or fieldwork, Federal Work-Study, institutionally sponsored loans, and tuition waivers (full and partial) available. Support available to part-time students. Financial award application deadline: 1/15.
Dr. Henry L. Roediger, Chairperson, 314-935-6567. *Web site:* http://artsci.wustl.edu/~psych/

## ■ WESTERN MICHIGAN UNIVERSITY

**Graduate College, College of Arts and Sciences, Department of Psychology, Kalamazoo, MI 49008-5202**

**AWARDS** Applied behavior analysis (MA, PhD); clinical psychology (MA, PhD); experimental analysis of behavior (PhD); experimental psychology (MA); industrial/organizational psychology (MA); school psychology (PhD, Ed S).
**Faculty:** 19 full-time (6 women).
**Students:** 94 full-time (68 women), 41 part-time (26 women); includes 10 minority (1 African American, 3 Asian Americans or Pacific Islanders, 6 Hispanic Americans), 12 international. 192 applicants, 31% accepted, 25 enrolled. In 2001, 21 master's, 6 doctorates, 6 other advanced degrees awarded.
**Degree requirements:** For master's, variable foreign language requirement, thesis, oral exams; for doctorate, 2 foreign

languages, thesis/dissertation, oral exams, comprehensive exam; for Ed S, thesis, oral exams.

**Entrance requirements:** For master's, doctorate, and Ed S, GRE General Test. *Application deadline:* For fall admission, 2/15. *Application fee:* $25.

**Expenses:** Tuition, state resident: part-time $186 per credit hour. Tuition, nonresident: part-time $442 per credit hour. Required fees: $602. One-time fee: $132 part-time. Tuition and fees vary according to course load.

**Financial support:** Fellowships, research assistantships, teaching assistantships, Federal Work-Study available. Financial award application deadline: 2/15; financial award applicants required to submit FAFSA.

R. Wayne Fuqua, Chairperson, 616-387-4498.

**Application contact:** Admissions and Orientation, 616-387-2000, *Fax:* 616-387-2355.

# FORENSIC PSYCHOLOGY

## ■ ALLIANT INTERNATIONAL UNIVERSITY

**School of Social and Policy Studies, Program in Forensic Psychology–Fresno, Fresno, CA 93727**

**AWARDS** PhD, Psy D.

**Faculty:** 3 full-time (1 woman), 4 part-time/adjunct (2 women).

**Students:** 74 full-time (56 women); includes 17 minority (4 African Americans, 5 Asian Americans or Pacific Islanders, 5 Hispanic Americans, 3 Native Americans). Average age 27. 114 applicants, 29% accepted.

**Degree requirements:** For doctorate, thesis/dissertation.

**Entrance requirements:** For doctorate, interview; master's degree in psychology, forensic psychology, criminology, criminal justice, social work or law; minimum GPA of 3.0 in both psychology and overall. *Application deadline:* For fall admission, 1/2 (priority date). *Application fee:* $65.

**Expenses:** Tuition: Part-time $397 per credit hour. Tuition and fees vary according to degree level, campus/location and program.

**Financial support:** Research assistantships, teaching assistantships, career-related internships or fieldwork and Federal Work-Study available. Financial award application deadline: 2/15; financial award applicants required to submit FAFSA.

**Faculty research:** Police stress, punishment and insanity defense, sexual offenders, sexual victimization, juvenile delinquency.

Dr. Bryan Myers, Interim Director, 559-456-2777 Ext. 2275, *Fax:* 559-253-2267, *E-mail:* bmyers@alliant.edu.

**Application contact:** Patricia J. Mullen, Vice President, Enrollment and Student Services, 800-457-1273 Ext. 303, *Fax:* 415-931-8322, *E-mail:* admissions@alliant.edu. *Web site:* http://www.alliant.edu/

## ■ ARGOSY UNIVERSITY-CHICAGO

**Illinois School of Professional Psychology, Doctoral Program in Clinical Psychology, Chicago, IL 60603**

**AWARDS** Child and adolescent psychology (Psy D); ethnic and racial psychology (Psy D); family psychology (Psy D); forensic psychology (Psy D); health psychology (Psy D); maltreatment and trauma (Psy D); psychoanalytic psychotherapy (Psy D); psychology and spirituality (Psy D).

**Faculty:** 21 full-time (13 women), 41 part-time/adjunct (18 women).

**Students:** 176 full-time (137 women), 185 part-time (132 women). Average age 31. 293 applicants, 61% accepted. In 2001, 92 degrees awarded.

**Degree requirements:** For doctorate, thesis/dissertation, internship, research project, clinical competency exam, comprehensive exam.

**Entrance requirements:** For doctorate, minimum GPA of 3.25. *Application deadline:* For fall admission, 1/15; for winter admission, 10/15. *Application fee:* $55. Electronic applications accepted.

**Expenses:** Tuition: Part-time $332 per credit hour. Required fees: $75 per year. $35 per term.

**Financial support:** In 2001–02, 200 students received support, including 25 fellowships with partial tuition reimbursements available (averaging $2,000 per year), 150 teaching assistantships with partial tuition reimbursements available (averaging $600 per year); research assistantships with partial tuition reimbursements available, career-related internships or fieldwork, Federal Work-Study, scholarships/grants, tuition waivers (partial), and unspecified assistantships also available. Support available to part-time students. Financial award application deadline: 5/29.

**Faculty research:** Meditation, clinical competency, family cultural patterns, sexual abuse patterns, psychosis and psychotherapy. *Total annual research expenditures:* $30,000.

Dr. Anne Marie Slobig, Director, 312-279-3911, *Fax:* 312-201-1907, *E-mail:* aslobig@argosyu.edu.

**Application contact:** Ashley Delaney, Director of Admissions, 312-279-3906, *Fax:* 312-201-1907, *E-mail:* adelaney@argosyu.edu. *Web site:* http://www.argosy.edu/

**Find an in-depth description at www.petersons.com/gradchannel.**

## ■ ARGOSY UNIVERSITY-WASHINGTON D.C.

**Professional Programs in Psychology, Arlington, VA 22209**

**AWARDS** Clinical psychology (MA, Psy D, Certificate); counseling psychology (MA); forensic psychology (MA). Part-time and evening/weekend programs available.

**Faculty:** 12 full-time (7 women), 43 part-time/adjunct (26 women).

**Students:** 304 full-time (237 women), 119 part-time (96 women); includes 112 minority (83 African Americans, 15 Asian Americans or Pacific Islanders, 11 Hispanic Americans, 3 Native Americans), 1 international. Average age 33. 341 applicants, 59% accepted. In 2001, 26 master's, 20 doctorates awarded.

**Degree requirements:** For master's, thesis (for some programs), practicum, comprehensive exam (for some programs); for doctorate, thesis/dissertation, internship, comprehensive exam. *Median time to degree:* Master's–2 years full-time, 3 years part-time; doctorate–6 years full-time.

**Entrance requirements:** For master's, clinical experience, minimum GPA of 3.0; for doctorate, clinical experience, minimum GPA of 3.25. *Application deadline:* For fall admission, 1/15 (priority date); for spring admission, 10/15. Applications are processed on a rolling basis. *Application fee:* $55. Electronic applications accepted.

**Expenses:** Tuition: Full-time $6,732; part-time $374 per credit. Required fees: $22; $90 per term. Tuition and fees vary according to course load, degree level and program.

**Financial support:** In 2001–02, 347 students received support, including 2 fellowships with tuition reimbursements available (averaging $3,600 per year), 55 teaching assistantships with full and partial tuition reimbursements available (averaging $1,530 per year); research assistantships, career-related internships or fieldwork, Federal Work-Study, and scholarships/grants also available. Support available to part-time students. Financial award application deadline: 6/30; financial award applicants required to submit FAFSA.

**Faculty research:** Psychotherapy integration, minority health, forensic assessment,

*Argosy University-Washington D.C. (continued)*

family violence, child maltreatment. *Total annual research expenditures:* $2,000.

Dr. Cynthia G. Baum, Campus President, 703-243-5300, *Fax:* 703-243-8973, *E-mail:* cbaum@argosyu.edu.

**Application contact:** Debbie Jacobs, Director of Admissions, 703-243-5300 Ext. 118, *Fax:* 703-243-8973, *E-mail:* ddmjacobs@argosyu.edu. *Web site:* http://www.argosy.edu/

**Find an in-depth description at www.petersons.com/gradchannel.**

■ **CASTLETON STATE COLLEGE**

**Division of Graduate Studies, Department of Psychology, Castleton, VT 05735**

**AWARDS** Forensic psychology (MA).

**Faculty:** 6 full-time (3 women).

**Students:** 19 full-time (all women), 4 part-time (all women). In 2001, 16 degrees awarded.

**Degree requirements:** For master's, thesis.

**Entrance requirements:** For master's, GRE General Test, minimum undergraduate GPA of 3.5, previous course work in research methodology and statistics. *Application deadline:* For fall admission, 7/1. Applications are processed on a rolling basis. *Application fee:* $30.

**Expenses:** Tuition, state resident: full-time $4,404; part-time $184 per credit. Tuition, nonresident: full-time $10,320; part-time $430 per credit. Required fees: $838; $31 per credit.

**Financial support:** In 2001–02, 8 fellowships (averaging $1,875 per year) were awarded; teaching assistantships, career-related internships or fieldwork and Federal Work-Study also available. Financial award application deadline: 2/15; financial award applicants required to submit FAFSA.

**Faculty research:** Psychology and law, juvenile delinquency, criminal psychology, correctional psychology, police psychology. Dr. Brenda Russell, Program Director, 802-468-1424, *Fax:* 802-468-5237, *E-mail:* brenda.russell@castleton.edu.

**Application contact:** Bill Allen, Dean of Enrollment, 802-468-1213, *Fax:* 802-468-1476, *E-mail:* info@castleton.edu.

■ **CHICAGO SCHOOL OF PROFESSIONAL PSYCHOLOGY**

**Graduate School, Chicago, IL 60605-2024**

**AWARDS** Clinical psychology (Psy D); forensic psychology (MA); industrial and organizational psychology (MA). Part-time programs available.

**Faculty:** 19 full-time (10 women), 43 part-time/adjunct (25 women).

**Students:** 216 full-time (162 women), 157 part-time (114 women); includes 75 minority (38 African Americans, 16 Asian Americans or Pacific Islanders, 21 Hispanic Americans), 25 international. Average age 25. 215 applicants, 74% accepted, 70 enrolled. In 2001, 48 degrees awarded.

**Degree requirements:** For doctorate, thesis/dissertation, competency exam, internship, practica.

**Entrance requirements:** For master's, 18 undergraduate hours in psychology, course work in statistics; for doctorate, GRE General Test or other graduate entrance exam, 18 hours in psychology (1 course each in statistics, abnormal psychology, and theories of personality). *Application deadline:* For fall admission, 1/15 (priority date); for spring admission, 11/1 (priority date). Applications are processed on a rolling basis. *Application fee:* $50.

**Expenses:** Tuition: Part-time $550 per credit hour. Required fees: $350 per year. Tuition and fees vary according to degree level and program.

**Financial support:** In 2001–02, 16 research assistantships with partial tuition reimbursements, 32 teaching assistantships with partial tuition reimbursements were awarded. Career-related internships or fieldwork, Federal Work-Study, scholarships/grants, and tuition waivers (partial) also available. Support available to part-time students. Financial award application deadline: 5/1; financial award applicants required to submit FAFSA.

**Faculty research:** White racial identity, work with cross-cultural clients, teaching in psychology.

Dr. Michael Horowitz, President, 312-786-9443 Ext. 3033, *Fax:* 312-322-3273, *E-mail:* mhorowitz@csopp.edu.

**Application contact:** Magdelen Kellogg, Director of Admission, 312-786-9443 Ext. 3029, *Fax:* 312-322-3273, *E-mail:* mkellogg@csopp.edu. *Web site:* http://www.csopp.edu/

**Find an in-depth description at www.petersons.com/gradchannel.**

■ **DREXEL UNIVERSITY**

**Graduate School, College of Arts and Sciences, Clinical Psychology Program, Philadelphia, PA 19104-2875**

**AWARDS** Clinical psychology (MA, MS); forensic psychology (PhD); health psychology (PhD); neuropsychology (PhD).

**Faculty:** 9 full-time (4 women).

**Students:** 120 full-time (106 women), 3 part-time (2 women); includes 12 minority (7 African Americans, 4 Asian Americans or Pacific Islanders, 1 Hispanic American),

3 international. Average age 27. 82 applicants, 18% accepted, 13 enrolled. In 2001, 22 master's, 11 doctorates awarded. Terminal master's awarded for partial completion of doctoral program.

**Degree requirements:** For master's, thesis, comprehensive exam; for doctorate, thesis/dissertation, qualifying exam. *Median time to degree:* Master's–3 years full-time; doctorate–6 years full-time.

**Entrance requirements:** For master's, GRE General Test, minimum GPA of 3.0; for doctorate, GRE General Test, GRE Subject Test, minimum GPA of 3.0. *Application deadline:* For spring admission, 1/15. *Application fee:* $30. Electronic applications accepted.

**Expenses:** Contact institution.

**Financial support:** Fellowships, research assistantships, teaching assistantships, career-related internships or fieldwork, Federal Work-Study, institutionally sponsored loans, and tuition waivers (partial) available. Support available to part-time students. Financial award application deadline: 5/1; financial award applicants required to submit FAFSA.

**Faculty research:** Cognitive behavioral therapy, stress and coping, eating disorders, substance abuse, developmental disabilities.

Dr. Kirk Heilbrun, Head, 215-895-2402, *Fax:* 215-895-1333.

**Find an in-depth description at www.petersons.com/gradchannel.**

■ **JOHN JAY COLLEGE OF CRIMINAL JUSTICE OF THE CITY UNIVERSITY OF NEW YORK**

**Graduate Studies, Program in Forensic Psychology, New York, NY 10019-1093**

**AWARDS** Forensic psychology (MA). Part-time and evening/weekend programs available.

**Students:** 181 full-time (143 women), 230 part-time (178 women); includes 96 minority (42 African Americans, 11 Asian Americans or Pacific Islanders, 42 Hispanic Americans, 1 Native American). 400 applicants, 63% accepted, 140 enrolled. In 2001, 148 degrees awarded.

**Degree requirements:** For master's, thesis or alternative, externship. *Median time to degree:* Master's–3.62 years part-time.

**Entrance requirements:** For master's, GRE General Test, TOEFL, minimum B average in major. *Application deadline:* For fall admission, 6/30 (priority date); for spring admission, 12/1. Applications are processed on a rolling basis. *Application fee:* $40.

**Expenses:** Tuition, state resident: full-time $4,350; part-time $185 per credit. Tuition, nonresident: full-time $7,600; part-time $285 per credit. Required fees: $80; $40 per semester. Tuition and fees vary according to degree level.
**Financial support:** Career-related internships or fieldwork, Federal Work-Study, institutionally sponsored loans, and scholarships/grants available. Support available to part-time students. Financial award applicants required to submit FAFSA.
Dr. James Wulach, Director, 212-237-8782, *E-mail:* jwulach@jjay.cuny.edu.
**Application contact:** Shirley Rodriguez-Melendez, Admissions Assistant, 212-237-8863, *Fax:* 212-237-8777, *E-mail:* srodrigu@jjay.cuny.edu.

## ■ JOHN JAY COLLEGE OF CRIMINAL JUSTICE OF THE CITY UNIVERSITY OF NEW YORK

**Graduate Studies, Programs in Criminal Justice, New York, NY 10019-1093**
**AWARDS** Criminal justice (MA, PhD); criminology and deviance (PhD); forensic psychology (PhD); forensic science (PhD); law and philosophy (PhD); organizational behavior (PhD); public policy (PhD). Part-time and evening/weekend programs available.
**Students:** 33 full-time (20 women), 165 part-time (86 women); includes 68 minority (36 African Americans, 11 Asian Americans or Pacific Islanders, 21 Hispanic Americans). 150 applicants, 80% accepted. In 2001, 58 degrees awarded. Terminal master's awarded for partial completion of doctoral program.
**Degree requirements:** For master's, thesis or alternative; for doctorate, one foreign language, thesis/dissertation.
**Entrance requirements:** For master's, GRE General Test, TOEFL, minimum B average; for doctorate, GRE General Test, TOEFL. *Application deadline:* For fall admission, 6/30 (priority date); for spring admission, 12/1. Applications are processed on a rolling basis. *Application fee:* $40.
**Expenses:** Tuition, state resident: full-time $4,350; part-time $185 per credit. Tuition, nonresident: full-time $7,600; part-time $285 per credit. Required fees: $80; $40 per semester. Tuition and fees vary according to degree level.
**Financial support:** Career-related internships or fieldwork, Federal Work-Study, institutionally sponsored loans, and scholarships/grants available. Support available to part-time students. Financial award applicants required to submit FAFSA.
Dr. Andrew Karmen, Co-Director, 212-237-8695, *E-mail:* akarmen@jjay.cuny.edu.

**Application contact:** Shirley Rodriguez-Melendez, Admissions Assistant, 212-237-8863, *Fax:* 212-237-8777, *E-mail:* srodrigu@jjay.cuny.edu.
**Find an in-depth description at www.petersons.com/gradchannel.**

## ■ MARYMOUNT UNIVERSITY

**School of Education and Human Services, Program in Psychology, Arlington, VA 22207-4299**
**AWARDS** Counseling psychology (MA, Certificate); forensic psychology (MA); school counseling (MA). Part-time and evening/weekend programs available.
**Students:** 80 full-time (71 women), 101 part-time (87 women); includes 28 minority (20 African Americans, 7 Hispanic Americans, 1 Native American), 3 international. Average age 32. 65 applicants, 98% accepted, 44 enrolled. In 2001, 41 degrees awarded.
**Degree requirements:** For master's, thesis or alternative.
**Entrance requirements:** For master's, GRE General Test or MAT, interview; for Certificate, master's degree in counseling. *Application deadline:* Applications are processed on a rolling basis. *Application fee:* $35. Electronic applications accepted.
**Expenses:** Tuition: Part-time $512 per credit. Required fees: $5 per credit.
**Financial support:** Research assistantships with full tuition reimbursements, career-related internships or fieldwork and scholarships/grants available. Support available to part-time students. Financial award applicants required to submit FAFSA.
Dr. Carolyn Oxenford, Chair, 703-284-1620, *Fax:* 703-284-1631, *E-mail:* carolyn.oxenford@marymount.edu. *Web site:* http://www.marymount.edu/academic/sehs/

## ■ PRAIRIE VIEW A&M UNIVERSITY

**Graduate School, School of Juvenile Justice and Psychology, Prairie View, TX 77446-0188**
**AWARDS** Juvenile forensic psychology (MSJFP); juvenile justice (MSJJ, PhD). Part-time and evening/weekend programs available.
**Faculty:** 12 full-time (4 women), 1 part-time/adjunct (0 women).
**Students:** 33 full-time (21 women), 41 part-time (24 women); includes 54 minority (52 African Americans, 2 Hispanic Americans), 5 international. Average age 34. 51 applicants, 45% accepted, 23 enrolled. In 2001, 1 degree awarded.
**Degree requirements:** For master's, thesis (for some programs), comprehensive

exam; for doctorate, thesis/dissertation, comprehensive exam.
**Entrance requirements:** For master's and doctorate, GRE. *Application deadline:* For fall admission, 4/1 (priority date); for spring admission, 11/1. Applications are processed on a rolling basis. *Application fee:* $50.
**Expenses:** Tuition, state resident: full-time $864; part-time $48 per credit hour. Tuition, nonresident: full-time $4,716; part-time $262 per credit hour. Required fees: $1,324; $59 per credit hour. $131 per term.
**Financial support:** In 2001–02, 12 students received support, including 5 research assistantships (averaging $16,000 per year), 3 teaching assistantships (averaging $16,000 per year); career-related internships or fieldwork and scholarships/grants also available. Financial award application deadline: 4/1.
**Faculty research:** Juvenile justice, juvenile forensic psychology. *Total annual research expenditures:* $700,000.
Dr. Elaine Rodney, Dean, 936-857-4938, *Fax:* 936-857-4941.
**Application contact:** Sandy Siegmund, Executive Secretary, Graduate Program, 936-857-4938, *Fax:* 936-857-4941, *E-mail:* sandy_siegmund@pvamu.edu.

## ■ SAGE GRADUATE SCHOOL

**Graduate School, Division of Psychology, Program in Forensic Psychology, Troy, NY 12180-4115**
**AWARDS** MA.
**Students:** 8 full-time (7 women), 37 part-time (31 women); includes 4 minority (1 African American, 3 Hispanic Americans). Average age 32. 38 applicants, 76% accepted, 11 enrolled.
**Degree requirements:** For master's, thesis or alternative.
**Entrance requirements:** For master's, minimum GPA of 3.0. *Application deadline:* Applications are processed on a rolling basis. *Application fee:* $40.
**Expenses:** Tuition: Full-time $7,600. Required fees: $100.
**Financial support:** Application deadline: 3/1.
Dr. Bronna Romanoff, Advisor, 518-244-2260, *E-mail:* romanb@sage.edu.
**Application contact:** Melissa M. Robertson, Associate Director of Admissions, 518-244-6878, *Fax:* 518-244-6880, *E-mail:* sgsadm@sage.edu.

## ■ SAM HOUSTON STATE UNIVERSITY

**College of Education and Applied Science, Department of Psychology and Philosophy, Huntsville, TX 77341**

**AWARDS** Clinical psychology (MA); counseling (MA); forensic psychology (PhD); psychology (MA); school psychology (MA). Part-time programs available.

**Students:** 44 full-time (36 women), 17 part-time (11 women); includes 6 minority (2 African Americans, 4 Hispanic Americans), 3 international. Average age 29. In 2001, 1 degree awarded.

**Degree requirements:** For master's, thesis.

**Entrance requirements:** For master's, GRE General Test or MAT, minimum GPA of 3.0. *Application deadline:* For fall admission, 8/1; for spring admission, 12/1. Applications are processed on a rolling basis. *Application fee:* $20.

**Expenses:** Tuition, area resident: Part-time $69 per credit. Tuition, state resident: full-time $1,380; part-time $69 per credit. Tuition, nonresident: full-time $5,600; part-time $280 per credit. Required fees: $748. Tuition and fees vary according to course load.

**Financial support:** Research assistantships, teaching assistantships, career-related internships or fieldwork and institutionally sponsored loans available. Support available to part-time students. Financial award application deadline: 5/31; financial award applicants required to submit FAFSA.

**Faculty research:** Recognition memory, embarrassment, divorce, relationship satisfaction, eyewitness testimony. *Total annual research expenditures:* $50,000.
Dr. Donna M. Desforges, Chairperson, 936-294-1174, *Fax:* 936-294-3798.

**Application contact:** Dr. Rowland Miller, Graduate Coordinator, 936-294-1176, *Fax:* 936-294-3798, *E-mail:* psy_rsm@shsu.edu. *Web site:* http://www.shsu.edu/~psy_www/

# GENETIC COUNSELING

## ■ ARCADIA UNIVERSITY

**Graduate Studies, Program in Genetic Counseling, Glenside, PA 19038-3295**

**AWARDS** MSGC.

**Students:** 21 full-time (20 women). In 2001, 9 degrees awarded.

**Degree requirements:** For master's, thesis.

**Entrance requirements:** For master's, GRE, TOEFL. *Application deadline:* For fall admission, 3/1. *Application fee:* $50.

**Expenses:** Contact institution.

**Financial support:** In 2001–02, 9 students received support. Tuition waivers (partial) and unspecified assistantships available. Deborah L. Eunpu, Coordinator, 215-572-2875.

**Application contact:** 215-572-2910, *Fax:* 215-572-4049, *E-mail:* admiss@arcadia.edu.

## ■ BRANDEIS UNIVERSITY

**Graduate School of Arts and Sciences, Program in Genetic Counseling, Waltham, MA 02454-9110**

**AWARDS** MS.

**Faculty:** 9 full-time (4 women).

**Students:** 19 full-time (18 women); includes 3 minority (2 Asian Americans or Pacific Islanders, 1 Native American). Average age 28. 99 applicants, 9% accepted. In 2001, 7 degrees awarded.

**Degree requirements:** For master's, thesis.

**Entrance requirements:** For master's, GRE General Test, resumé, 3 letters of recommendation. *Application deadline:* For fall admission, 2/1. *Application fee:* $60. Electronic applications accepted.

**Expenses:** Tuition: Full-time $27,392. Required fees: $35.

**Financial support:** In 2001–02, 19 students received support. Career-related internships or fieldwork, institutionally sponsored loans, scholarships/grants, and tuition waivers (full and partial) available. Financial award application deadline: 4/15; financial award applicants required to submit CSS PROFILE or FAFSA.
Dr. Judith Tsipis, Director, 781-736-3179, *Fax:* 781-736-3107, *E-mail:* tsipis@brandeis.edu. *Web site:* http://www.bio.brandeis.edu/gc/

## ■ CALIFORNIA STATE UNIVERSITY, NORTHRIDGE

**Graduate Studies, College of Education, Department of Educational Psychology and Counseling, Northridge, CA 91330**

**AWARDS** Counseling and guidance (MS, MFCC), including counseling (MS), marriage, family and child counseling (MFCC); educational psychology and counseling (MA); elementary education (MA); genetic counseling (MS). Part-time and evening/weekend programs available.

**Faculty:** 19 full-time, 28 part-time/adjunct.

**Students:** 318 full-time (274 women), 142 part-time (120 women); includes 156 minority (33 African Americans, 29 Asian Americans or Pacific Islanders, 89 Hispanic Americans, 5 Native Americans), 8 international. Average age 34. 170 applicants, 84% accepted, 108 enrolled. In 2001, 60 degrees awarded.

**Entrance requirements:** For master's, TOEFL, GRE General Test, MAT, or minimum GPA of 3.0. *Application deadline:* For fall admission, 11/30. *Application fee:* $55.

**Expenses:** Tuition, nonresident: part-time $631 per semester. Required fees: $246 per unit.

**Financial support:** Scholarships/grants available. Support available to part-time students. Financial award application deadline: 3/1.

**Faculty research:** Motivation, learning development, bilingual education, interpersonal relationships.
Rie Rogers Mitchell, Chair, 818-677-4976.

**Application contact:** W. Dean McCafferty, Coordinator, 818-885-2508.

## ■ CALIFORNIA STATE UNIVERSITY, NORTHRIDGE

**Graduate Studies, College of Education, Department of Special Education, Northridge, CA 91330**

**AWARDS** Early childhood special education (MA); education of the deaf and hard of hearing (MA); education of the gifted (MA); education of the learning handicapped (MA); education of the severely handicapped (MA); educational therapy (MA); genetic counseling (MS).

**Faculty:** 19 full-time, 33 part-time/adjunct.

**Students:** 73 full-time (62 women), 196 part-time (168 women); includes 60 minority (16 African Americans, 17 Asian Americans or Pacific Islanders, 26 Hispanic Americans, 1 Native American), 4 international. Average age 36. 95 applicants, 93% accepted, 51 enrolled. In 2001, 47 degrees awarded.

**Entrance requirements:** For master's, GRE General Test, TOEFL. *Application deadline:* For fall admission, 11/30. *Application fee:* $55.

**Expenses:** Tuition, nonresident: part-time $631 per semester. Required fees: $246 per unit.

**Financial support:** Application deadline: 3/1.

**Faculty research:** Teacher training, classroom aide training.
Dr. Claire Cavallaro, Chair, 818-677-2596.

**Application contact:** Dr. Ellen Schneiderman, Graduate Coordinator, 818-677-2528.

# CALIFORNIA STATE UNIVERSITY, NORTHRIDGE

**Graduate Studies, College of Science and Mathematics, Department of Biology and Department of Educational Psychology and Counseling and Department of Special Education, Genetic Counseling Program, Northridge, CA 91330**

**AWARDS** MS.

**Students:** 15 full-time (all women); includes 5 minority (1 African American, 2 Asian Americans or Pacific Islanders, 2 Hispanic Americans). Average age 26. 19 applicants, 58% accepted, 7 enrolled. In 2001, 3 degrees awarded.
**Degree requirements:** For master's, thesis, 1000 hours of clinical work, 2 laboratory rotations.
**Entrance requirements:** For master's, GRE General Test, TOEFL. *Application deadline:* For fall admission, 2/1. *Application fee:* $55.
**Expenses:** Tuition, nonresident: part-time $631 per semester. Required fees: $246 per unit.
**Financial support:** Research assistantships, teaching assistantships, Federal Work-Study, institutionally sponsored loans, scholarships/grants, and tuition waivers (partial) available. Support available to part-time students. Financial award application deadline: 3/15; financial award applicants required to submit FAFSA.
**Faculty research:** Molecular basis of heritable disease, molecular basis of cancer. *Total annual research expenditures:* $185,000.
Dr. Aida Metzenberg, Director, 818-677-3355, *Fax:* 818-677-2034, *E-mail:* aida.metzenberg@csun.edu.
**Application contact:** Lisa McCulley-Frakes, Administrative Assistant, 818-677-3356, *Fax:* 818-677-2034, *E-mail:* genetic.counseling@csun.edu. *Web site:* http://www.csun.edu/~hcbio033/

# CASE WESTERN RESERVE UNIVERSITY

**School of Medicine and School of Graduate Studies, Graduate Programs in Medicine, Department of Genetics, Program in Genetic Counseling, Cleveland, OH 44106**

**AWARDS** MS.

**Faculty:** 23 full-time (8 women).
**Students:** 9 full-time (all women); includes 1 minority (Asian American or Pacific Islander), 1 international. Average age 24. 67 applicants, 6% accepted. In 2001, 2 degrees awarded.
**Degree requirements:** For master's, thesis.

**Entrance requirements:** For master's, GRE General Test, TOEFL. *Application deadline:* For fall admission, 2/1. *Application fee:* $25.
**Financial support:** In 2001–02, 9 fellowships (averaging $8,000 per year) were awarded. Financial award application deadline: 2/28.
Dr. Anne L. Matthews, Director of Counseling Training Program, 216-368-1821, *Fax:* 216-368-3432, *E-mail:* alm14@po.cwru.edu.
**Application contact:** Dianne R. Austin, Administrative Assistant, 216-368-3433, *Fax:* 216-368-3432, *E-mail:* dra3@po.cwru.edu.

# JOHNS HOPKINS UNIVERSITY

**School of Public Health, Department of Health Policy and Management, Faculty of Social and Behavioral Sciences, Baltimore, MD 21205**

**AWARDS** Genetic counseling (Sc M); health education (MHS); social and behavioral sciences (PhD, Sc D).

**Students:** 70.
**Degree requirements:** For master's, thesis (for some programs), internship, comprehensive exam (for some programs), registration; for doctorate, thesis/dissertation, 1 year full-time residency, oral and written exam, comprehensive exam, registration.
**Entrance requirements:** For master's and doctorate, GRE General Test, TOEFL, work experience in health-related field. *Application deadline:* For fall admission, 1/2. Applications are processed on a rolling basis. *Application fee:* $60. Electronic applications accepted.
**Expenses:** Tuition: Full-time $27,390.
**Financial support:** Federal Work-Study, institutionally sponsored loans, scholarships/grants, and stipends available. Financial award application deadline: 4/15; financial award applicants required to submit FAFSA.
**Faculty research:** Health program evaluation; health education and communications, social and behavioral aspects.
Dr. Margaret Ensminger, Associate Chair, 410-955-2313, *E-mail:* mensming@jhsph.edu.
**Application contact:** Mary Sewell, Coordinator, 410-955-2488, *Fax:* 410-614-9152, *E-mail:* msewell@jhsph.edu.

# NORTHWESTERN UNIVERSITY

**The Graduate School, Program in Genetic Counseling, Chicago, IL 60611**

**AWARDS** MS.

**Faculty:** 9 full-time (6 women), 1 (woman) part-time/adjunct.

**Students:** 14 full-time (13 women). Average age 24. 97 applicants, 8% accepted, 8 enrolled. In 2001, 6 degrees awarded.
**Degree requirements:** For master's, thesis. *Median time to degree:* Master's–1.5 years full-time.
**Entrance requirements:** For master's, GRE General Test, TOEFL, interview. *Application deadline:* For fall admission, 1/15. *Application fee:* $50 ($55 for international students).
**Expenses:** Tuition: Full-time $26,526.
**Financial support:** Institutionally sponsored loans available. Support available to part-time students. Financial award application deadline: 12/31; financial award applicants required to submit FAFSA.
**Faculty research:** Preimplantation genetic diagnosis, gene expression in preimplantation embryos, fetal cells in maternal blood: a new form of prenatal diagnosis, first trimester prenatal screening for Down's Syndrome, genetic counseling efficacy and counseling issues in prenatal diagnosis. *Total annual research expenditures:* $250,000.
Kelly Elizabeth Ormond, Admissions Officer, 312-926-7466, *Fax:* 312-926-3553, *E-mail:* kormond@nmh.org.
**Application contact:** Agnes Maria Barin, Program Assistant, 312-926-7726, *Fax:* 312-926-3553, *E-mail:* a-barin@northwestern.edu. *Web site:* http://www.nums.northwestern.edu/geneticcounseling/introduction-html

# SARAH LAWRENCE COLLEGE

**Graduate Studies, Program in Genetic Counseling, Bronxville, NY 10708**

**AWARDS** Human genetics (MPS, MS).

**Degree requirements:** For master's, thesis, fieldwork.
**Entrance requirements:** For master's, previous course work in biology, chemistry, developmental biology, genetics, probability and statistics.
**Expenses:** Contact institution.
**Faculty research:** Genetics.

# UNIVERSITY OF CALIFORNIA, BERKELEY

**Graduate Division, School of Public Health, Division of Health and Medical Sciences, Berkeley, CA 94720-1500**

**AWARDS** Health and medical sciences (MS), including genetic counseling.

**Degree requirements:** For master's, comprehensive exam (MS), thesis (MD/MS).
**Entrance requirements:** For master's, GRE General Test (MS), MCAT (MD/MS), minimum GPA of 3.0.
**Expenses:** Tuition, nonresident: full-time $10,704. Required fees: $4,349.

# ■ UNIVERSITY OF CALIFORNIA, IRVINE

**College of Medicine and Office of Research and Graduate Studies, Graduate Programs in Medicine, Department of Pediatrics, Program in Genetic Counseling, Irvine, CA 92697**

**AWARDS** MS.

**Faculty:** 10.

**Students:** 12 full-time (10 women); includes 4 minority (all Asian Americans or Pacific Islanders), 1 international. 82 applicants, 11% accepted, 5 enrolled. In 2001, 2 degrees awarded.

**Degree requirements:** For master's, thesis.

**Entrance requirements:** For master's, GRE General Test. *Application deadline:* For fall and spring admission, 2/1 (priority date); for winter admission, 10/15 (priority date). Applications are processed on a rolling basis. *Application fee:* $60. Electronic applications accepted.

**Expenses:** Tuition, nonresident: full-time $10,704. Required fees: $8,396. Tuition and fees vary according to course load, program and student level.

**Financial support:** In 2001–02, 3 students received support, including 2 research assistantships, 1 teaching assistantship; career-related internships or fieldwork and institutionally sponsored loans also available. Financial award application deadline: 3/2; financial award applicants required to submit FAFSA.

**Faculty research:** Gene mapping and linkage analysis, delineation of new malformation and chromosomal syndromes, ethical and counseling issues in genetics.

Ann P. Walker, Director, 714-456-5789, *Fax:* 714-456-5330, *E-mail:* awalker@uci.edu.

**Application contact:** Evelyn Hohlfeld, Administrative Assistant, 714-456-8520, *Fax:* 714-456-5330.

# ■ UNIVERSITY OF CINCINNATI

**Division of Research and Advanced Studies, College of Allied Health Sciences, Program in Genetic Counseling, Cincinnati, OH 45221**

**AWARDS** Medical genetics (MS).

**Faculty:** 30 full-time (15 women).

**Students:** 16 full-time (all women), 1 (woman) part-time; includes 1 minority (Asian American or Pacific Islander), 2 international. Average age 23. 100 applicants, 8% accepted, 8 enrolled. In 2001, 7 degrees awarded.

**Degree requirements:** For master's, thesis.

**Entrance requirements:** For master's, GRE General Test, TOEFL, bachelor's degree in science. *Application deadline:* For fall admission, 2/1. *Application fee:* $30. Electronic applications accepted.

**Expenses:** Tuition, state resident: part-time $2,698 per quarter. Tuition, nonresident: part-time $4,977 per quarter.

**Financial support:** Unspecified assistantships available. Financial award application deadline: 5/1.

Nancy Steinberg Warren, Program Director, *Fax:* 513-636-7297, *E-mail:* warrn0@chmcc.org.

**Application contact:** Carol Turner, Graduate Program Secretary, 513-636-8448, *Fax:* 513-636-7297, *E-mail:* gcprog@chmcc.org. *Web site:* http://www.grad.uc.edu/content/programs.cfm#g/

# ■ UNIVERSITY OF COLORADO HEALTH SCIENCES CENTER

**Graduate School, Programs in Biological Sciences, Programs in Biophysics and Genetics, Program in Genetic Counseling, Denver, CO 80262**

**AWARDS** MS.

**Students:** 95 applicants, 7 enrolled. In 2001, 8 degrees awarded.

**Degree requirements:** For master's, thesis optional.

**Entrance requirements:** For master's, GRE General Test. *Application deadline:* For fall admission, 2/1. *Application fee:* $50.

**Expenses:** Contact institution.

**Financial support:** Application deadline: 3/15.

Carol Walton, Director, 303-315-7739.

# ■ UNIVERSITY OF MINNESOTA, TWIN CITIES CAMPUS

**Graduate School, Program in Molecular, Cellular, Developmental Biology and Genetics, Minneapolis, MN 55455-0213**

**AWARDS** Genetic counseling (MS); molecular, cellular, developmental biology and genetics (PhD). Part-time programs available. Terminal master's awarded for partial completion of doctoral program.

**Degree requirements:** For master's, thesis optional; for doctorate, thesis/dissertation.

**Entrance requirements:** For master's and doctorate, GRE General Test, TOEFL.

**Expenses:** Tuition, state resident: full-time $2,932; part-time $489 per credit. Tuition, nonresident: full-time $5,758; part-time $960 per credit. Part-time tuition and fees vary according to course load, program and reciprocity agreements.

**Faculty research:** Membrane receptors and membrane transport, cell interactions, cytoskeleton and cell mobility, regulation of gene expression, plant cell and molecular biology. *Web site:* http://biosci.cbs.umn.edu/mcdbg/

**Find an in-depth description at www.petersons.com/gradchannel.**

# ■ THE UNIVERSITY OF NORTH CAROLINA AT GREENSBORO

**Graduate School, Program in Interdisciplinary Studies, Greensboro, NC 27412-5001**

**AWARDS** Genetic counseling (MS); gerontology (MS). Part-time programs available.

**Faculty:** 1 (woman) full-time, 1 (woman) part-time/adjunct.

**Students:** 19 full-time (18 women), 14 part-time (all women); includes 4 minority (2 African Americans, 1 Asian American or Pacific Islander, 1 Hispanic American), 1 international. 107 applicants, 29% accepted.

**Degree requirements:** For master's, thesis or alternative, comprehensive exam.

**Entrance requirements:** For master's, GRE or MAT, TOEFL. *Application deadline:* Applications are processed on a rolling basis. *Application fee:* $35.

**Expenses:** Tuition, state resident: part-time $344 per course. Tuition, nonresident: part-time $2,457 per course.

**Financial support:** In 2001–02, 2 students received support; fellowships available.

Dr. James Lynch, Director of Graduate Recruitment and Information Services, 336-334-4881, *Fax:* 336-334-4424.

# ■ UNIVERSITY OF PITTSBURGH

**Graduate School of Public Health, Department of Human Genetics, Program in Genetic Counseling, Pittsburgh, PA 15260**

**AWARDS** MS.

**Faculty:** 19 full-time (8 women).

**Students:** 16 full-time (15 women), 3 international. Average age 23. In 2001, 9 degrees awarded.

**Degree requirements:** For master's, thesis, clinical internship.

**Entrance requirements:** For master's, GRE General Test, previous course work in biochemistry, calculus, and genetics. *Application deadline:* For fall admission, 2/1. *Application fee:* $50 ($60 for international students). Electronic applications accepted.

**Expenses:** Tuition, state resident: full-time $9,410; part-time $385 per credit. Tuition, nonresident: full-time $19,376; part-time $797 per credit. Required fees: $480; $90 per term. Tuition and fees vary according to program.

**Financial support:** In 2001–02, 15 students received support, including 15 research assistantships with full tuition reimbursements available (averaging

$15,600 per year); career-related internships or fieldwork and scholarships/grants also available.

**Faculty research:** Statistical genetics, molecular genetics, cytogenetics, gene therapy. *Total annual research expenditures:* $3.3 million.

**Application contact:** Jeanette Norbut, Administrative Secretary, 412-624-9951, *Fax:* 412-624-3020, *E-mail:* jnorbut@ helix.hgen.pitt.edu. *Web site:* http:// www.pitt.edu/~gsphhome/hgen/

■ **UNIVERSITY OF SOUTH CAROLINA**

School of Medicine and The Graduate School, Graduate Programs in Medicine, Genetic Counseling Program, Columbia, SC 29208
**AWARDS** MS.

**Faculty:** 3 full-time (1 woman), 8 part-time/adjunct (4 women).
**Students:** 12 full-time (all women); includes 1 minority (Asian American or Pacific Islander). Average age 25. 92 applicants, 7% accepted, 6 enrolled. In 2001, 6 degrees awarded.
**Degree requirements:** For master's, internship, practicum. *Median time to degree:* Master's–1.7 years full-time.
**Entrance requirements:** For master's, GRE General Test or GMAT. *Application deadline:* For fall admission, 2/1. *Application fee:* $35. Electronic applications accepted.
**Expenses:** Contact institution.
**Financial support:** In 2001–02, 12 research assistantships with partial tuition reimbursements (averaging $2,000 per year) were awarded; institutionally sponsored loans and unspecified assistantships also available. Financial award application deadline: 4/15.
**Faculty research:** Maternal serum alpha–fetoprotein screening, hospital discharge data, ethical issues in genetics, counseling effectiveness.
Janice G. Edwards, Program Coordinator, 803-779-4928 Ext. 228, *Fax:* 803-733-3168, *E-mail:* jedwards@ richmed.medpark.sc.edu. *Web site:* http:// www.med.sc.edu:88/gradstudies.htm

■ **THE UNIVERSITY OF TEXAS HEALTH SCIENCE CENTER AT HOUSTON**

Graduate School of Biomedical Sciences, Program in Genetic Counseling, Houston, TX 77225-0036
**AWARDS** MS.

**Faculty:** 14 full-time (10 women).
**Students:** 12 full-time (all women); includes 1 minority (Hispanic American).

Average age 27. 48 applicants, 10% accepted. In 2001, 3 degrees awarded.
**Degree requirements:** For master's, thesis.
**Entrance requirements:** For master's, GRE General Test, TOEFL, TWE. *Application deadline:* For fall admission, 2/1. *Application fee:* $10. Electronic applications accepted.
**Expenses:** Tuition, state resident: full-time $2,736; part-time $76 per credit hour. Tuition, nonresident: full-time $10,584; part-time $294 per credit hour. Required fees: $642.
**Financial support:** Institutionally sponsored loans available. Financial award application deadline: 1/15.
**Faculty research:** Genetics, molecular genetics, ctyogenetics, psychosocial issues associated with genetics practice, research aspects of genetics and clinical experience. Dr. Jacqueline Hecht, Director, 713-500-5764, *Fax:* 713-500-5689, *E-mail:* jacqueline.t.hecht@uth.tmc.edu.
**Application contact:** Dr. Victoria P. Knutson, Assistant Dean of Admissions, 713-500-9860, *Fax:* 713-500-9877, *E-mail:* victoria.p.knutson@uth.tmc.edu. *Web site:* http://gsbs.gs.uth.tmc.edu/

■ **VIRGINIA COMMONWEALTH UNIVERSITY**

School of Graduate Studies and School of Medicine, School of Medicine Graduate Programs, Department of Human Genetics, Richmond, VA 23284-9005
**AWARDS** Genetic counseling (MS); human genetics (PhD, CBHS); molecular biology and genetics (PhD).

**Students:** 18 full-time, 2 part-time; includes 6 minority (5 Asian Americans or Pacific Islanders, 1 Native American). 149 applicants, 13% accepted. In 2001, 2 master's, 3 doctorates, 1 other advanced degree awarded.
**Degree requirements:** For master's, thesis; for doctorate, thesis/dissertation, comprehensive oral and written exams.
**Entrance requirements:** For master's, DAT, GRE General Test, or MCAT; for doctorate, GRE General Test, DAT, MCAT. *Application deadline:* For fall admission, 2/15 (priority date). *Application fee:* $30.
**Expenses:** Tuition, state resident: full-time $4,276; part-time $238 per credit. Tuition, nonresident: full-time $12,672; part-time $704 per credit. Required fees: $1,167; $43 per credit.
**Financial support:** Fellowships available.
**Faculty research:** Genetic epidemiology, biochemical genetics, quantitative genetics, human cytogenetics, molecular genetics.

Dr. Walter E. Nance, Chair, 804-828-9632, *Fax:* 804-828-3760.
**Application contact:** Dr. Linda A. Corey, Graduate Program Director, 804-828-9632, *Fax:* 804-828-3760, *E-mail:* lacorey@ vcu.edu. *Web site:* http://views.vcu.edu/ views/genetics/

**Find an in-depth description at www.petersons.com/gradchannel.**

# HEALTH PSYCHOLOGY

■ **ALLIANT INTERNATIONAL UNIVERSITY**

California School of Professional Psychology, Program in Health Psychology–San Diego, San Diego, CA 92121
**AWARDS** PhD.

**Faculty:** 3 full-time (1 woman), 6 part-time/adjunct (1 woman).
**Students:** 30 full-time (21 women), 17 part-time (14 women); includes 14 minority (3 African Americans, 8 Asian Americans or Pacific Islanders, 2 Hispanic Americans, 1 Native American). Average age 32. 28 applicants, 68% accepted. In 2001, 3 degrees awarded.
**Degree requirements:** For doctorate, thesis/dissertation.
**Entrance requirements:** For doctorate, TOEFL, interview, minimum GPA of 3.0 in both psychology and overall. *Application deadline:* For fall admission, 2/1 (priority date). *Application fee:* $65.
**Expenses:** Tuition: Part-time $397 per credit hour. Tuition and fees vary according to degree level, campus/location and program.
**Financial support:** In 2001–02, 45 students received support; research assistantships, teaching assistantships, career-related internships or fieldwork and Federal Work-Study available. Financial award application deadline: 2/15; financial award applicants required to submit FAFSA.
**Faculty research:** Coping with chronic illness, relationship between stress and health.
Dr. Perry Nicassio, Director, 858-635-4837, *Fax:* 858-635-4585, *E-mail:* pnicassio@alliant.edu.
**Application contact:** Patricia J. Mullen, Vice President, Enrollment and Student Services, 800-457-1273 Ext. 303, *Fax:* 415-931-8322, *E-mail:* admissions@ mail.cspp.edu. *Web site:* http:// www.alliant.edu/

## ■ APPALACHIAN STATE UNIVERSITY

**Cratis D. Williams Graduate School, College of Arts and Sciences, Department of Psychology, Program in Health Psychology, Boone, NC 28608**

**AWARDS** MA. Part-time programs available.

**Faculty:** 24 full-time (8 women).
**Students:** 8 full-time (all women). In 2001, 1 degree awarded.
**Degree requirements:** For master's, GRE Subject Test exit exam, thesis optional.
**Entrance requirements:** For master's, GRE General Test, GRE Subject Test. *Application deadline:* For fall admission, 3/1 (priority date). Applications are processed on a rolling basis. *Application fee:* $35.
**Expenses:** Tuition, state resident: full-time $1,286. Tuition, nonresident: full-time $9,354. Required fees: $1,116.
**Financial support:** In 2001–02, research assistantships (averaging $6,250 per year), teaching assistantships (averaging $6,250 per year) were awarded. Fellowships, career-related internships or fieldwork also available. Support available to part-time students. Financial award application deadline: 7/1.
**Faculty research:** Eating disorders, body image, behavioral medicine, pediatric psychology, childhood depression.
Dr. Denise Martz, Director, 828-262-2272, *E-mail:* martzdm@appstate.edu. *Web site:* http://www.acs.appstate.edu/dept/psych/

## ■ ARGOSY UNIVERSITY-CHICAGO

**Illinois School of Professional Psychology, Doctoral Program in Clinical Psychology, Chicago, IL 60603**

**AWARDS** Child and adolescent psychology (Psy D); ethnic and racial psychology (Psy D); family psychology (Psy D); forensic psychology (Psy D); health psychology (Psy D); maltreatment and trauma (Psy D); psychoanalytic psychotherapy (Psy D); psychology and spirituality (Psy D).

**Faculty:** 21 full-time (13 women), 41 part-time/adjunct (18 women).
**Students:** 176 full-time (137 women), 185 part-time (132 women). Average age 31. 293 applicants, 61% accepted. In 2001, 92 degrees awarded.
**Degree requirements:** For doctorate, thesis/dissertation, internship, research project, clinical competency exam, comprehensive exam.
**Entrance requirements:** For doctorate, minimum GPA of 3.25. *Application deadline:* For fall admission, 1/15; for winter admission, 10/15. *Application fee:* $55. Electronic applications accepted.

**Expenses:** Tuition: Part-time $332 per credit hour. Required fees: $75 per year. $35 per term.
**Financial support:** In 2001–02, 200 students received support, including 25 fellowships with partial tuition reimbursements available (averaging $2,000 per year), 150 teaching assistantships with partial tuition reimbursements available (averaging $600 per year); research assistantships with partial tuition reimbursements available, career-related internships or fieldwork, Federal Work-Study, scholarships/grants, tuition waivers (partial), and unspecified assistantships also available. Support available to part-time students. Financial award application deadline: 5/29.
**Faculty research:** Meditation, clinical competency, family cultural patterns, sexual abuse patterns, psychosis and psychotherapy. *Total annual research expenditures:* $30,000.
Dr. Anne Marie Slobig, Director, 312-279-3911, *Fax:* 312-201-1907, *E-mail:* aslobig@argosyu.edu.
**Application contact:** Ashley Delaney, Director of Admissions, 312-279-3906, *Fax:* 312-201-1907, *E-mail:* adelaney@argosyu.edu. *Web site:* http://www.argosy.edu/

**Find an in-depth description at www.petersons.com/gradchannel.**

## ■ CALIFORNIA INSTITUTE OF INTEGRAL STUDIES

**Graduate Programs, School of Professional Psychology, San Francisco, CA 94103**

**AWARDS** Drama therapy (MA); expressive arts therapy (MA, Certificate), including consulting and education (Certificate), expressive arts (Certificate), expressive arts therapy (MA); integral counseling psychology (MA); psychology (Psy D), including clinical psychology; somatics (MA, Certificate), including integral health education (Certificate), somatics (MA). Part-time and evening/weekend programs available.

**Students:** 205 full-time, 236 part-time. 298 applicants, 65% accepted, 115 enrolled.
**Degree requirements:** For master's, comprehensive exam; for doctorate, thesis/dissertation, comprehensive exam.
**Entrance requirements:** For master's, TOEFL, minimum GPA of 3.0; for doctorate, TOEFL, field experience, master's degree, minimum GPA of 3.1. *Application deadline:* Applications are processed on a rolling basis. *Application fee:* $65.
**Expenses:** Tuition: Full-time $10,890; part-time $605 per unit. Tuition and fees vary according to degree level.

**Financial support:** Career-related internships or fieldwork, Federal Work-Study, institutionally sponsored loans, and scholarships/grants available. Support available to part-time students. Financial award application deadline: 6/15; financial award applicants required to submit FAFSA.
**Faculty research:** Somatic psychology.
Dr. Harrison Voigt, Head, 415-575-6218.
**Application contact:** David Towner, Admissions Officer, 415-575-6152, *Fax:* 415-575-1268, *E-mail:* dtowner@ciis.edu.

**Find an in-depth description at www.petersons.com/gradchannel.**

## ■ DREXEL UNIVERSITY

**Graduate School, College of Arts and Sciences, Clinical Psychology Program, Philadelphia, PA 19104-2875**

**AWARDS** Clinical psychology (MA, MS); forensic psychology (PhD); health psychology (PhD); neuropsychology (PhD).

**Faculty:** 9 full-time (4 women).
**Students:** 120 full-time (106 women), 3 part-time (2 women); includes 12 minority (7 African Americans, 4 Asian Americans or Pacific Islanders, 1 Hispanic American), 3 international. Average age 27. 82 applicants, 18% accepted, 13 enrolled. In 2001, 22 master's, 11 doctorates awarded. Terminal master's awarded for partial completion of doctoral program.
**Degree requirements:** For master's, thesis, comprehensive exam; for doctorate, thesis/dissertation, qualifying exam. *Median time to degree:* Master's–3 years full-time; doctorate–6 years full-time.
**Entrance requirements:** For master's, GRE General Test, minimum GPA of 3.0; for doctorate, GRE General Test, GRE Subject Test, minimum GPA of 3.0. *Application deadline:* For spring admission, 1/15. *Application fee:* $30. Electronic applications accepted.
**Expenses:** Contact institution.
**Financial support:** Fellowships, research assistantships, teaching assistantships, career-related internships or fieldwork, Federal Work-Study, institutionally sponsored loans, and tuition waivers (partial) available. Support available to part-time students. Financial award application deadline: 5/1; financial award applicants required to submit FAFSA.
**Faculty research:** Cognitive behavioral therapy, stress and coping, eating disorders, substance abuse, developmental disabilities.
Dr. Kirk Heilbrun, Head, 215-895-2402, *Fax:* 215-895-1333.

**Find an in-depth description at www.petersons.com/gradchannel.**

# ■ DREXEL UNIVERSITY

**Graduate School, College of Arts and Sciences, Program in Law-Psychology, Philadelphia, PA 19104-2875**

**AWARDS** PhD, JD/PhD.

**Students:** 22 full-time (16 women), 9 part-time (8 women); includes 4 minority (2 African Americans, 2 Hispanic Americans), 1 international. Average age 27. 11 applicants, 27% accepted, 3 enrolled. In 2001, 1 degree awarded.

**Degree requirements:** For doctorate, thesis/dissertation, qualifying exam. *Median time to degree:* Doctorate–10 years part-time.

**Entrance requirements:** For doctorate, GRE General Test, GRE Subject Test, minimum GPA of 3.0. *Application deadline:* For fall admission, 2/15. *Application fee:* $50. Electronic applications accepted.

**Expenses:** Contact institution.

**Financial support:** Fellowships, research assistantships, teaching assistantships, career-related internships or fieldwork, Federal Work-Study, and institutionally sponsored loans available. Support available to part-time students. Financial award application deadline: 5/1; financial award applicants required to submit FAFSA.

**Faculty research:** Mental health law issues, professional ethics, social science applications to law.

Dr. Kirk Heilbrun, Head, 215-895-2402, *Fax:* 215-895-1333.

**Find an in-depth description at www.petersons.com/gradchannel.**

# ■ DUKE UNIVERSITY

**Graduate School, Department of Psychology, Durham, NC 27708-0586**

**AWARDS** Biological psychology (PhD); clinical psychology (PhD); cognitive psychology (PhD); developmental psychology (PhD); experimental psychology (PhD); health psychology (PhD); human social development (PhD).

**Faculty:** 52 full-time, 15 part-time/adjunct.

**Students:** 66 full-time (42 women); includes 11 minority (6 African Americans, 2 Asian Americans or Pacific Islanders, 3 Hispanic Americans), 13 international. 386 applicants, 7% accepted, 15 enrolled. In 2001, 8 doctorates awarded.

**Degree requirements:** For doctorate, thesis/dissertation.

**Entrance requirements:** For doctorate, GRE General Test. *Application deadline:* For fall admission, 12/31. *Application fee:* $75.

**Expenses:** Tuition: Full-time $24,600.

**Financial support:** Fellowships, research assistantships, teaching assistantships,

career-related internships or fieldwork and Federal Work-Study available. Financial award application deadline: 12/31. Reiko Mazuka, Co-Director of Graduate Studies, 919-660-5716, *Fax:* 919-660-5726, *E-mail:* bseymore@acpub.duke.edu. *Web site:* http://www.psych.duke.edu/

# ■ EMPORIA STATE UNIVERSITY

**School of Graduate Studies, The Teachers College, Department of Counselor Education and Rehabilitation Programs, Program in Counselor Education, Emporia, KS 66801-5087**

**AWARDS** Counselor education (MS); mental health counseling (MS); school counseling (MS); student personnel (MS).

**Students:** 30 full-time (24 women), 38 part-time (31 women); includes 5 minority (1 African American, 3 Hispanic Americans, 1 Native American), 5 international. 10 applicants, 50% accepted. In 2001, 31 degrees awarded.

**Degree requirements:** For master's, comprehensive exam or thesis. *Application deadline:* For fall admission, 8/15 (priority date). Applications are processed on a rolling basis. *Application fee:* $30 ($75 for international students). Electronic applications accepted.

**Expenses:** Tuition, state resident: full-time $2,632; part-time $119 per credit hour. Tuition, nonresident: full-time $6,734; part-time $290 per credit hour.

**Financial support:** Career-related internships or fieldwork, Federal Work-Study, institutionally sponsored loans, health care benefits, and unspecified assistantships available. Financial award application deadline: 3/15; financial award applicants required to submit FAFSA.

**Application contact:** Dr. Marvin Kuehn, Graduate Coordinator, 620-341-5795, *E-mail:* kuehnmar@emporia.edu.

# ■ NATIONAL-LOUIS UNIVERSITY

**College of Arts and Sciences, Division of Liberal Arts and Sciences, Program in Psychology, Chicago, IL 60603**

**AWARDS** Cultural psychology (MA); health psychology (MA); human development (MA); organizational psychology (MA); psychology (Certificate). Part-time and evening/weekend programs available.

**Degree requirements:** For master's, thesis, internship (health psychology).

**Entrance requirements:** For master's, GRE, MAT, or Watson-Glaser Critical Thinking Appraisal, interview, minimum GPA of 3.0; for Certificate, GRE, MAT, or Watson-Glaser Critical Thinking Appraisal, interview, minimum GPA of 3.0, previous undergraduate course work in psychology.

**Expenses:** Tuition: Full-time $13,830; part-time $461 per credit hour.

**Faculty research:** Human development, personality theory, abnormal psychology.

# ■ NORTHERN ARIZONA UNIVERSITY

**Graduate College, College of Social and Behavioral Sciences, Department of Psychology, Flagstaff, AZ 86011**

**AWARDS** Applied health psychology (MA); general (MA). Part-time programs available.

**Students:** 19 full-time (14 women), 12 part-time (10 women); includes 3 minority (2 Hispanic Americans, 1 Native American), 2 international. Average age 26. 41 applicants, 44% accepted, 7 enrolled. In 2001, 10 degrees awarded.

**Degree requirements:** For master's, thesis, oral defense.

**Entrance requirements:** For master's, GRE General Test. *Application deadline:* For fall admission, 2/15 (priority date). Applications are processed on a rolling basis. *Application fee:* $45.

**Expenses:** Tuition, state resident: full-time $2,488. Tuition, nonresident: full-time $10,354.

**Financial support:** In 2001–02, 7 research assistantships, 7 teaching assistantships were awarded. Federal Work-Study, institutionally sponsored loans, and tuition waivers (full and partial) also available. Financial award application deadline: 2/15. Robert Till, Chair, 928-523-3063.

**Application contact:** Information Contact, 928-523-3063, *E-mail:* psychology.general@nau.edu. *Web site:* http://www.edu/~psych/psyhomepg.html

# ■ PHILADELPHIA COLLEGE OF OSTEOPATHIC MEDICINE

**Graduate and Professional Programs, Department of Psychology, Philadelphia, PA 19131-1694**

**AWARDS** Clinical health psychology (MS); clinical psychology (Psy D); organizational leadership and development (MS).

**Faculty:** 6 full-time (3 women), 1 part-time/adjunct (0 women).

**Students:** 253 full-time (186 women); includes 35 minority (23 African Americans, 7 Asian Americans or Pacific Islanders, 5 Hispanic Americans). Average age 33. 77 applicants, 86% accepted. In 2001, 1 degree awarded.

**Degree requirements:** For master's, thesis; for doctorate, thesis/dissertation, final project, fieldwork, comprehensive exam.

**Entrance requirements:** For master's, GRE, minimum GPA of 3.0, previous course work in biology, chemistry, English, physics; for doctorate, MAT. *Application*

*Philadelphia College of Osteopathic Medicine (continued)*
*deadline:* For fall admission, 1/17. Applications are processed on a rolling basis. *Application fee:* $50.
**Expenses:** Tuition: Part-time $441 per credit. Required fees: $250. Tuition and fees vary according to program.
**Faculty research:** Cognitive-behavioral therapy, coping skills.
Dr. Arthur Freeman, Chairman, 215-871-6442.
**Application contact:** Carol A. Fox, Associate Dean for Admissions, 215-871-6700, *Fax:* 215-871-6719, *E-mail:* carolf@pcom.edu.
**Find an in-depth description at www.petersons.com/gradchannel.**

■ **PONCE SCHOOL OF MEDICINE**
**Program in Clinical Psychology, Ponce, PR 00732-7004**
**AWARDS** Clinical health psychology (Psy D); consultant psychology (Psy D); pediatric psychology (Psy D); psychotherapeutic interventions (Psy D).
**Faculty:** 5 full-time (2 women).
**Students:** 114 full-time (89 women); all minorities (all Hispanic Americans). Average age 30. 63 applicants, 65% accepted, 34 enrolled.
**Degree requirements:** For doctorate, one foreign language, thesis/dissertation, comprehensive exam, registration.
**Entrance requirements:** For doctorate, GRE General Test or PAEG. *Application deadline:* For fall admission, 3/30. Applications are processed on a rolling basis. *Application fee:* $100.
**Expenses:** Tuition: Full-time $17,835. Required fees: $2,340. Full-time tuition and fees vary according to class time, course load, degree level, program and student level.
Dr. José Pons, Head, 787-840-2575, *E-mail:* jponspr@yahoo.com.
**Application contact:** Dr. Carmen Mercado, Assistant Dean of Admissions, 787-840-2575 Ext. 251, *E-mail:* cmercado@psm.edu.

■ **RUTGERS, THE STATE UNIVERSITY OF NEW JERSEY, NEW BRUNSWICK**
**Graduate School, Program in Psychology, New Brunswick, NJ 08901-1281**
**AWARDS** Biopsychology and behavioral neuroscience (PhD); clinical psychology (PhD); cognitive psychology (PhD); interdisciplinary developmental psychology (PhD); interdisciplinary health psychology (PhD); social psychology (PhD).

**Students:** Average age 24. 423 applicants, 11% accepted. In 2001, 13 degrees awarded.
**Degree requirements:** For doctorate, thesis/dissertation.
**Entrance requirements:** For doctorate, GRE General Test. *Application deadline:* For fall admission, 12/15. *Application fee:* $50.
**Financial support:** In 2001–02, 68 students received support, including 18 fellowships with full tuition reimbursements available (averaging $15,000 per year), 13 research assistantships with full tuition reimbursements available (averaging $14,000 per year), 43 teaching assistantships with full tuition reimbursements available (averaging $13,800 per year); career-related internships or fieldwork, Federal Work-Study, scholarships/grants, and traineeships also available. Financial award application deadline: 12/15.
Dr. G. Terence Wilson, Director, 732-445-2556, *Fax:* 732-445-2263.
**Application contact:** Joan Olmizzi, Administrative Assistant, 732-445-2555, *Fax:* 732-445-2263, *E-mail:* joan@psych-b.rutgers.edu. *Web site:* http://psychology.rutgers.edu/

■ **SANTA CLARA UNIVERSITY**
**Division of Counseling Psychology and Education, Program in Counseling, Santa Clara, CA 95053**
**AWARDS** Health psychology (MA); pastoral counseling (MA). Part-time and evening/weekend programs available.
**Students:** 2 full-time (both women), 12 part-time (7 women); includes 2 minority (1 African American, 1 Hispanic American). Average age 36. 8 applicants, 63% accepted. In 2001, 12 degrees awarded.
**Degree requirements:** For master's, thesis optional.
**Entrance requirements:** For master's, GRE or MAT, TOEFL, minimum GPA of 3.0, 1 year of related experience. *Application deadline:* For fall admission, 4/1; for winter admission, 11/1; for spring admission, 2/1. Applications are processed on a rolling basis. *Application fee:* $35.
**Expenses:** Tuition: Part-time $320 per unit. Tuition and fees vary according to class time, degree level, program and student level.
**Financial support:** Fellowships, teaching assistantships, career-related internships or fieldwork, Federal Work-Study, institutionally sponsored loans, and scholarships/grants available. Support available to part-time students. Financial award application deadline: 3/1; financial award applicants required to submit FAFSA.

Dr. Jerrold Shapiro, Director, 408-554-4012.
**Application contact:** Helen Valine, Assistant to the Dean, 408-554-4656, *Fax:* 408-554-2392.

■ **SAYBROOK GRADUATE SCHOOL AND RESEARCH CENTER**
**Program in Psychology, Human Science and Organizational Systems, San Francisco, CA 94133-4640**
**AWARDS** Human science (MA, PhD), including consciousness and spirituality, individualized (PhD), organizational systems, social transformation; organizational systems (MA, PhD), including individualized (PhD), organizational systems; psychology (MA, PhD), including consciousness and spirituality, humanistic and transpersonal, clinical inquiry, and health studies, individualized (PhD), licensure track (MA), organizational systems, social transformation. Postbaccalaureate distance learning degree programs offered (minimal on-campus study).
**Faculty:** 20 full-time (6 women), 83 part-time/adjunct (29 women).
**Students:** 392 full-time (246 women); includes 63 minority (28 African Americans, 16 Asian Americans or Pacific Islanders, 14 Hispanic Americans, 5 Native Americans), 17 international. Average age 42. 280 applicants, 34% accepted. In 2001, 9 master's, 35 doctorates awarded. Terminal master's awarded for partial completion of doctoral program.
**Degree requirements:** For master's, thesis or alternative; for doctorate, thesis/dissertation.
**Entrance requirements:** For master's, TOEFL; for doctorate, TOEFL, master's degree in psychology or related social science. *Application deadline:* For fall admission, 6/1 (priority date); for spring admission, 12/16 (priority date). Electronic applications accepted.
**Expenses:** Tuition: Full-time $13,800. Required fees: $2,000. One-time fee: $600 full-time.
**Financial support:** In 2001–02, 275 students received support. Scholarships/grants available. Financial award applicants required to submit FAFSA.
**Faculty research:** Humanistic theory, health studies, organizational systems, consciousness and spirituality, social transformation. *Total annual research expenditures:* $90,000.
Dr. Maureen O'Hara, President, 800-825-4480, *Fax:* 415-433-9271, *E-mail:* mohara@saybrook.edu.
**Application contact:** Mindy Myers, Vice President for Recruitment and Admissions, 800-825-4480, *Fax:* 415-433-9271, *E-mail:*

mmyers@saybrook.edu. *Web site:* http://www.saybrook.edu/

## ■ SOUTHWEST TEXAS STATE UNIVERSITY

**Graduate School, College of Liberal Arts, Department of Psychology, San Marcos, TX 78666**

AWARDS Health psychology (MA).

**Faculty:** 5 full-time (1 woman), 1 (woman) part-time/adjunct.
**Students:** 8 full-time (all women), 11 part-time (8 women); includes 2 minority (both Hispanic Americans). Average age 27. 14 applicants, 64% accepted, 7 enrolled. In 2001, 1 degree awarded.
**Degree requirements:** For master's, thesis, 450 hours of practicum courses.
**Entrance requirements:** For master's, GRE General Test, minimum GPA of 3.0 in last 60 hours, 3.0 in psychology coursework. *Application deadline:* For fall admission, 3/15. Applications are processed on a rolling basis. *Application fee:* $40 ($90 for international students).
**Expenses:** Tuition, state resident: full-time $1,512; part-time $84 per credit hour. Tuition, nonresident: full-time $5,310; part-time $295 per credit hour. Required fees: $864; $29 per credit hour. $195 per term. Full-time tuition and fees vary according to course load.
**Financial support:** In 2001–02, 6 teaching assistantships (averaging $4,656 per year) were awarded
Dr. Randall E. Osborne, Acting Chair, 512-245-8236, *Fax:* 512-245-3153, *E-mail:* ro10@swt.edu.
**Application contact:** Dr. John Davis, Graduate Advisor, 512-245-3162, *Fax:* 512-245-3153, *E-mail:* jd04@swt.edu.

## ■ STONY BROOK UNIVERSITY, STATE UNIVERSITY OF NEW YORK

**Graduate School, College of Arts and Sciences, Department of Psychology, Program in Social/Health Psychology, Stony Brook, NY 11794**

AWARDS PhD.

**Students:** 12 full-time (10 women), 10 part-time (5 women); includes 6 minority (4 African Americans, 1 Asian American or Pacific Islander, 1 Hispanic American), 1 international. Average age 29. 55 applicants, 13% accepted. In 2001, 3 degrees awarded.
**Degree requirements:** For doctorate, thesis/dissertation.
**Entrance requirements:** For doctorate, GRE General Test, GRE Subject Test, TOEFL. *Application deadline:* For fall admission, 1/15. *Application fee:* $50.

**Expenses:** Tuition, state resident: full-time $5,100; part-time $213 per credit. Tuition, nonresident: full-time $8,416; part-time $351 per credit. Required fees: $496.

**Find an in-depth description at www.petersons.com/gradchannel.**

## ■ UNIVERSITY OF CALIFORNIA, IRVINE

**Office of Research and Graduate Studies, School of Social Ecology, Department of Psychology and Social Behavior, Irvine, CA 92697**

AWARDS Health psychology (PhD); human development (PhD).

**Faculty:** 18.
**Students:** 39 full-time (30 women), 1 part-time; includes 8 minority (6 Asian Americans or Pacific Islanders, 2 Hispanic Americans). 72 applicants, 25% accepted, 7 enrolled. In 2001, 2 degrees awarded. Terminal master's awarded for partial completion of doctoral program.
**Degree requirements:** For doctorate, thesis/dissertation, research project.
**Entrance requirements:** For doctorate, GRE General Test. *Application deadline:* For fall and spring admission, 1/15 (priority date); for winter admission, 10/15 (priority date). Applications are processed on a rolling basis. *Application fee:* $60. Electronic applications accepted.
**Expenses:** Tuition, nonresident: full-time $10,704. Required fees: $8,396. Tuition and fees vary according to course load, program and student level.
**Financial support:** Fellowships, research assistantships, teaching assistantships, institutionally sponsored loans and tuition waivers (full and partial) available. Financial award application deadline: 3/2; financial award applicants required to submit FAFSA.
**Faculty research:** Psychosocial development in children, adolescents, and adults; gerontology, childhood behavior disorders, and developmental psychopathology; sex differences; attitude change; social psychology.
Chuansheng Chen, Chair, 949-824-4184.
**Application contact:** Jeanne Haynes, Academic Counselor, 949-824-5917, *Fax:* 949-824-2056, *E-mail:* jhaynes@uci.edu. *Web site:* http://www.socecol.uci.edu/~socecol/

## ■ UNIVERSITY OF FLORIDA

**Graduate School, College of Health Professions, Department of Clinical and Health Psychology, Gainesville, FL 32611**

AWARDS PhD.

**Degree requirements:** For doctorate, thesis/dissertation.

**Entrance requirements:** For doctorate, GRE General Test, minimum GPA of 3.0. Electronic applications accepted.
**Expenses:** Tuition, state resident: part-time $164 per hour. Tuition, nonresident: part-time $571 per hour. Tuition and fees vary according to course level and program.
**Faculty research:** Child psychology, pediatric psychology, health/medical psychology, neuropsychology. *Web site:* http://www.hp.ufl.edu/chp

## ■ UNIVERSITY OF MIAMI

**Graduate School, College of Arts and Sciences, Department of Psychology, Coral Gables, FL 33124**

AWARDS Applied developmental psychology (PhD); behavioral neuroscience (PhD); clinical psychology (PhD); health psychology (PhD); psychology (MS).

**Faculty:** 39 full-time (18 women).
**Students:** 70 full-time (51 women); includes 23 minority (6 African Americans, 4 Asian Americans or Pacific Islanders, 13 Hispanic Americans). Average age 25. 200 applicants, 14% accepted, 18 enrolled. In 2001, 12 degrees awarded.
**Degree requirements:** For doctorate, thesis/dissertation, comprehensive exam. *Median time to degree:* Doctorate–5 years full-time.
**Entrance requirements:** For doctorate, GRE General Test, TOEFL, minimum GPA of 3.5. *Application deadline:* For fall admission, 12/1. *Application fee:* $50. Electronic applications accepted.
**Expenses:** Tuition: Part-time $960 per credit hour. Required fees: $85 per semester. Tuition and fees vary according to program.
**Financial support:** In 2001–02, 7 fellowships with full tuition reimbursements (averaging $17,000 per year), 43 research assistantships with full tuition reimbursements (averaging $16,500 per year), 19 teaching assistantships with full tuition reimbursements (averaging $12,300 per year) were awarded. Career-related internships or fieldwork, institutionally sponsored loans, scholarships/grants, and traineeships also available. Financial award applicants required to submit FAFSA.
**Faculty research:** Depression, social and emotional development, stress and coping, AIDS and psychoneuroimmunology, children's peer relations. *Total annual research expenditures:* $10 million.
Dr. A. Rodney Wellens, Chairman, 305-284-2814, *Fax:* 305-284-3402.
**Application contact:** Patricia L. Perreira, Staff Associate, 305-284-2814, *Fax:* 305-284-3402, *E-mail:* inquire@mail.psy.miami.edu. *Web site:* http://www.psy.miami.edu/

## ■ THE UNIVERSITY OF MONTANA–MISSOULA

**Graduate School, School of Education, Department of Health and Human Performance, Missoula, MT 59812-0002**

**AWARDS** Exercise and performance psychology (MS); exercise science (MS); health promotion (MS). Part-time programs available.

**Faculty:** 10 full-time (3 women).
**Students:** 13 full-time (6 women), 5 part-time (2 women); includes 1 minority (Asian American or Pacific Islander). Average age 30. 16 applicants, 81% accepted, 10 enrolled. In 2001, 5 degrees awarded.
**Entrance requirements:** For master's, GRE General Test. *Application deadline:* For fall admission, 3/15 (priority date). Applications are processed on a rolling basis. *Application fee:* $45.
**Expenses:** Tuition, state resident: full-time $2,482; part-time $1,700 per year. Tuition, nonresident: full-time $7,372; part-time $5,000 per year. Required fees: $1,900. Tuition and fees vary according to degree level.
**Financial support:** In 2001–02, 5 teaching assistantships with full tuition reimbursements (averaging $8,665 per year) were awarded; Federal Work-Study and unspecified assistantships also available. Financial award application deadline: 3/1; financial award applicants required to submit FAFSA.
**Faculty research:** Exercise physiology, performance psychology, nutrition, pre-employment physical screening, program evaluation. *Total annual research expenditures:* $72,562.
Dr. Gene Burns, Chair, 406-243-4211.
**Application contact:** Dr. Lewis Curry, Graduate Coordinator, 406-243-5242, *E-mail:* curry58@selway.umt.edu. *Web site:* http://www.umt.edu/hhp/

## ■ UNIVERSITY OF NORTH TEXAS

**Robert B. Toulouse School of Graduate Studies, College of Arts and Sciences, Department of Psychology, Denton, TX 76203**

**AWARDS** Clinical psychology (PhD); counseling psychology (MA, MS, PhD); experimental psychology (MA, MS, PhD); health psychology and behavioral medicine (PhD); industrial psychology (MA, MS); psychology (MA, MS, PhD); school psychology (MA, MS, PhD).

**Faculty:** 29 full-time (5 women), 7 part-time/adjunct (5 women).
**Students:** 129 full-time (96 women), 98 part-time (70 women); includes 23 minority (2 African Americans, 4 Asian Americans or Pacific Islanders, 15 Hispanic Americans, 2 Native Americans),

9 international. Average age 30. In 2001, 24 master's, 17 doctorates awarded. Terminal master's awarded for partial completion of doctoral program.
**Degree requirements:** For master's, thesis or alternative, comprehensive exam; for doctorate, one foreign language, thesis/dissertation, comprehensive exam.
**Entrance requirements:** For master's and doctorate, GRE General Test, GRE Subject Test, interview. *Application deadline:* For fall admission, 2/1. *Application fee:* $25 ($50 for international students).
**Expenses:** Tuition, state resident: part-time $186 per hour. Tuition, nonresident: part-time $319 per hour. Required fees: $88; $21 per hour.
**Financial support:** Fellowships, research assistantships, teaching assistantships, career-related internships or fieldwork, Federal Work-Study, and institutionally sponsored loans available. Financial award application deadline: 8/1.
Dr. Ernest H. Harrell, Chair, 940-565-2671, *Fax:* 940-546-4682, *E-mail:* harrelle@unt.edu.
**Application contact:** Dr. Joseph Critelli, Graduate Adviser, 940-565-2671, *Fax:* 940-565-4682, *E-mail:* critelli@facstaff.cas.unt.edu.

## ■ UNIVERSITY OF THE SCIENCES IN PHILADELPHIA

**College of Graduate Studies, Program in Health Psychology, Philadelphia, PA 19104-4495**

**AWARDS** MS.

**Entrance requirements:** For master's, GRE General Test, TOEFL, bachelor's degree in related field, minimum GPA of 3.0 in major.
**Expenses:** Tuition: Full-time $17,122; part-time $713 per credit. Required fees: $26 per credit.
**Faculty research:** Stress and immune system; women's health and breast cancer, memory, health care policy.

## ■ YESHIVA UNIVERSITY

**Ferkauf Graduate School of Psychology, Program in Clinical Health Psychology, New York, NY 10033-3201**

**AWARDS** PhD. Part-time programs available.
**Faculty:** 6 full-time (1 woman), 27 part-time/adjunct (12 women).
**Students:** 53 full-time (36 women), 9 part-time (7 women); includes 9 minority (1 African American, 5 Asian Americans or Pacific Islanders, 3 Hispanic Americans), 8 international. Average age 26. 75 applicants, 20% accepted. In 2001, 17 degrees awarded.

**Degree requirements:** For doctorate, thesis/dissertation.
**Entrance requirements:** For doctorate, GRE General Test. *Application deadline:* For fall admission, 1/15. *Application fee:* $50.
**Financial support:** In 2001–02, 6 fellowships (averaging $5,000 per year), 15 research assistantships (averaging $2,000 per year), 8 teaching assistantships (averaging $2,000 per year) were awarded. Career-related internships or fieldwork, Federal Work-Study, institutionally sponsored loans, and scholarships/grants also available. Support available to part-time students. Financial award application deadline: 4/15.
**Faculty research:** Dieting, substance abuse, adolescent depression and suicide, cancer research, MS research.
Dr. Charles Swencionis, Director, 718-430-3990, *E-mail:* swencion@aecom.yu.edu.
**Application contact:** Elaine Schwartz, Assistant Director of Admissions, 718-430-3820, *Fax:* 718-430-3960, *E-mail:* eschart@ymail.yu.edu. *Web site:* http://www.yu.edu/fgs/

# HUMAN DEVELOPMENT

## ■ APPALACHIAN STATE UNIVERSITY

**Cratis D. Williams Graduate School, College of Fine and Applied Arts, Department of Family and Consumer Sciences, Boone, NC 28608**

**AWARDS** Child development (MA); family and consumer science (MA). Part-time programs available.

**Faculty:** 5 full-time (4 women).
**Students:** 19 full-time (16 women), 3 part-time (all women); includes 1 minority (Native American). 21 applicants, 90% accepted, 8 enrolled. In 2001, 7 degrees awarded.
**Degree requirements:** For master's, thesis or alternative, comprehensive exam.
**Entrance requirements:** For master's, GRE General Test. *Application deadline:* For fall admission, 7/1 (priority date); for spring admission, 11/1. *Application fee:* $35.
**Expenses:** Tuition, state resident: full-time $1,286. Tuition, nonresident: full-time $9,354. Required fees: $1,116.
**Financial support:** In 2001–02, 3 research assistantships (averaging $6,250 per year), 4 teaching assistantships (averaging $6,250 per year) were awarded. Fellowships, career-related internships or fieldwork, scholarships/grants, and unspecified

assistantships also available. Support available to part-time students. Financial award application deadline: 7/1; financial award applicants required to submit FAFSA.

**Faculty research:** Food antioxidants, preschool curriculum, children with special needs, family child care, FCS curriculum content. *Total annual research expenditures:* $138,358.

Dr. Sammie Garner, Chairperson, 828-262-2661, *E-mail:* garnersg@appstate.edu.

**Application contact:** Dr. Cindy McGaha, Graduate Director, 828-262-2698.

### ■ ARGOSY UNIVERSITY-CHICAGO

**Illinois School of Professional Psychology, Doctoral Program in Clinical Psychology, Chicago, IL 60603**

AWARDS Child and adolescent psychology (Psy D); ethnic and racial psychology (Psy D); family psychology (Psy D); forensic psychology (Psy D); health psychology (Psy D); maltreatment and trauma (Psy D); psychoanalytic psychotherapy (Psy D); psychology and spirituality (Psy D).

**Faculty:** 21 full-time (13 women), 41 part-time/adjunct (18 women).

**Students:** 176 full-time (137 women), 185 part-time (132 women). Average age 31. 293 applicants, 61% accepted. In 2001, 92 degrees awarded.

**Degree requirements:** For doctorate, thesis/dissertation, internship, research project, clinical competency exam, comprehensive exam.

**Entrance requirements:** For doctorate, minimum GPA of 3.25. *Application deadline:* For fall admission, 1/15; for winter admission, 10/15. *Application fee:* $55. Electronic applications accepted.

**Expenses:** Tuition: Part-time $332 per credit hour. Required fees: $75 per year. $35 per term.

**Financial support:** In 2001–02, 200 students received support, including 25 fellowships with partial tuition reimbursements available (averaging $2,000 per year), 150 teaching assistantships with partial tuition reimbursements available (averaging $600 per year); research assistantships with partial tuition reimbursements available, career-related internships or fieldwork, Federal Work-Study, scholarships/grants, tuition waivers (partial), and unspecified assistantships also available. Support available to part-time students. Financial award application deadline: 5/29.

**Faculty research:** Meditation, clinical competency, family cultural patterns, sexual abuse patterns, psychosis and psychotherapy. *Total annual research expenditures:* $30,000.

Dr. Anne Marie Slobig, Director, 312-279-3911, *Fax:* 312-201-1907, *E-mail:* aslobig@argosyu.edu.

**Application contact:** Ashley Delaney, Director of Admissions, 312-279-3906, *Fax:* 312-201-1907, *E-mail:* adelaney@argosyu.edu. *Web site:* http://www.argosy.edu/

**Find an in-depth description at www.petersons.com/gradchannel.**

### ■ ARIZONA STATE UNIVERSITY

**Graduate College, College of Liberal Arts and Sciences, Department of Family Resources and Human Development, Tempe, AZ 85287**

AWARDS Family resources and human development (MS); family science (PhD).

**Degree requirements:** For master's, thesis or alternative; for doctorate, thesis/dissertation.

**Entrance requirements:** For master's and doctorate, GRE.

**Faculty research:** Nutrition of the elderly, quality and stability of marital relationships.

### ■ AUBURN UNIVERSITY

**Graduate School, College of Human Sciences, Department of Human Development and Family Studies, Auburn University, AL 36849**

AWARDS MS, PhD. Part-time programs available.

**Faculty:** 14 full-time (7 women).

**Students:** 26 full-time (20 women), 20 part-time (12 women); includes 7 minority (6 African Americans, 1 Native American), 2 international. 77 applicants, 57% accepted. In 2001, 11 master's, 5 doctorates awarded.

**Degree requirements:** For master's, thesis (MS), oral exam; for doctorate, thesis/dissertation.

**Entrance requirements:** For master's, GRE General Test; for doctorate, GRE General Test, master's degree. *Application deadline:* For fall admission, 7/7; for spring admission, 11/24. Applications are processed on a rolling basis. *Application fee:* $25 ($50 for international students).

**Financial support:** Research assistantships, teaching assistantships, Federal Work-Study available. Support available to part-time students. Financial award application deadline: 3/15.

**Faculty research:** Family influences on personality and social development, parent-child relations, infancy, day care, parent education.

Dr. Marilyn Bradbard, Head, 334-844-4151, *E-mail:* mbradbar@humsci.auburn.edu.

**Application contact:** Dr. John F. Pritchett, Dean of the Graduate School, 334-844-4700, *E-mail:* hatchlb@mail.auburn.edu. *Web site:* http://www.humsci.auburn.edu/fcd/

### ■ BOSTON UNIVERSITY

**School of Education, Department of Developmental Studies and Counseling, Program in Developmental Studies, Boston, MA 02215**

AWARDS Ed M, Ed D, CAGS.

**Degree requirements:** For doctorate, thesis/dissertation, comprehensive exam.

**Entrance requirements:** For master's, doctorate, and CAGS, GRE or MAT, TOEFL. Electronic applications accepted.

**Expenses:** Tuition: Full-time $25,872; part-time $340 per credit. Required fees: $40 per semester. Part-time tuition and fees vary according to class time, course level and program.

**Faculty research:** Moral development, social and cognitive development, language and literacy development, cross-cultural development.

### ■ BOWLING GREEN STATE UNIVERSITY

**Graduate College, College of Education and Human Development, School of Family and Consumer Sciences, Bowling Green, OH 43403**

AWARDS Food and nutrition (MFCS); human development and family studies (MFCS). Part-time programs available.

**Faculty:** 24.

**Students:** 14 full-time (all women), 8 part-time (7 women), 3 international. Average age 26. 14 applicants, 57% accepted, 7 enrolled. In 2001, 6 degrees awarded.

**Degree requirements:** For master's, thesis.

**Entrance requirements:** For master's, GRE General Test, TOEFL, minimum GPA of 3.0. *Application deadline:* For fall admission, 2/15. *Application fee:* $30.

**Expenses:** Tuition, state resident: full-time $7,376; part-time $342 per credit hour. Tuition, nonresident: full-time $13,628; part-time $640 per credit hour.

**Financial support:** In 2001–02, 12 research assistantships with full tuition reimbursements (averaging $4,486 per year), 2 teaching assistantships with full tuition reimbursements (averaging $5,475 per year) were awarded. Career-related internships or fieldwork and unspecified assistantships also available. Financial award applicants required to submit FAFSA.

*Bowling Green State University*
*(continued)*

**Faculty research:** Public health, wellness, social issues and policies, ethnic foods, nutrition and aging.
Dr. Joe Williford, Acting Chair, 419-372-7823.
**Application contact:** Dr. Rebecca Pebocik, Graduate Coordinator, 419-372-6920.

### ■ BRADLEY UNIVERSITY

**Graduate School, College of Education and Health Sciences, Department of Educational Leadership and Human Development, Peoria, IL 61625-0002**

**AWARDS** Human development counseling (MA), including community agency counseling, school counseling; leadership in educational administration (MA); leadership in human services administration (MA). Part-time and evening/weekend programs available.

**Students:** 21 full-time, 121 part-time. 54 applicants, 85% accepted. In 2001, 52 degrees awarded.
**Degree requirements:** For master's, comprehensive exam.
**Entrance requirements:** For master's, MAT, TOEFL, interview. *Application deadline:* For fall admission, 7/1 (priority date); for spring admission, 11/1 (priority date). Applications are processed on a rolling basis. *Application fee:* $40 ($50 for international students).
**Expenses:** Tuition: Part-time $7,615 per semester. Tuition and fees vary according to course load.
**Financial support:** In 2001–02, 9 research assistantships with full and partial tuition reimbursements (averaging $4,600 per year) were awarded; scholarships/grants and tuition waivers (partial) also available. Financial award application deadline: 3/1.
Dr. Jenny Tripses, Chairperson, 309-677-3593.

### ■ BRIGHAM YOUNG UNIVERSITY

**Graduate Studies, College of Family, Home, and Social Sciences, Marriage, Family and Human Development Department, Provo, UT 84602-1001**

**AWARDS** MS, PhD.

**Faculty:** 26 full-time (6 women).
**Students:** 31 full-time (24 women); includes 4 minority (1 Asian American or Pacific Islander, 1 Hispanic American, 2 Native Americans), 3 international. Average age 30. 29 applicants, 52% accepted, 13 enrolled. In 2001, 2 master's, 2 doctorates awarded.
**Degree requirements:** For master's, thesis, publishable paper; for doctorate, thesis/dissertation, comprehensive exam,

registration. *Median time to degree:* Master's–3 years full-time; doctorate–6 years full-time.
**Entrance requirements:** For master's and doctorate, GRE General Test, GRE Writing Assessment, minimum GPA of 3.0 in last 60 hours. *Application deadline:* For fall admission, 1/10. *Application fee:* $50. Electronic applications accepted.
**Expenses:** Tuition: Full-time $3,860; part-time $214 per hour.
**Financial support:** In 2001–02, 27 students received support, including 19 research assistantships with partial tuition reimbursements available (averaging $5,096 per year), 8 teaching assistantships with partial tuition reimbursements available (averaging $5,096 per year); fellowships, career-related internships or fieldwork and tuition waivers (partial) also available. Financial award application deadline: 1/10.
**Faculty research:** Early childhood education, family process, family life education.
Dr. Craig H. Hart, Chair, 801-422-2069.
**Application contact:** Shauna Pitts, MFHD and Graduate Secretary, School of Family Life, 801-422-2060, *E-mail:* shauna_pitts@byu.edu. *Web site:* http://fhss.byu.edu/mfhd/main.htm

### ■ THE CATHOLIC UNIVERSITY OF AMERICA

**School of Arts and Sciences, Department of Psychology, Program in Human Development, Washington, DC 20064**

**AWARDS** PhD.

**Students:** 1 full-time (0 women), 1 (woman) part-time. Average age 52. 7 applicants, 29% accepted, 1 enrolled.
**Degree requirements:** For doctorate, thesis/dissertation, comprehensive exam.
**Entrance requirements:** For doctorate, GRE General Test, GRE Subject Test. *Application deadline:* For fall admission, 2/15. Applications are processed on a rolling basis. *Application fee:* $55. Electronic applications accepted.
**Expenses:** Tuition: Full-time $20,050; part-time $770 per credit. Required fees: $430 per term. Tuition and fees vary according to program.
**Financial support:** Fellowships, research assistantships, teaching assistantships, career-related internships or fieldwork, Federal Work-Study, institutionally sponsored loans, scholarships/grants, and tuition waivers (full and partial) available. Support available to part-time students. Financial award application deadline: 2/1.
**Faculty research:** Social interaction, adolescent development, social and intellectual development, adult development.

Dr. Deborah Clawson, Director, 202-319-5750.

### ■ CENTRAL MICHIGAN UNIVERSITY

**College of Graduate Studies, College of Education and Human Services, Department of Human Environmental Studies, Mount Pleasant, MI 48859**

**AWARDS** Human development and family studies (MA); nutrition and dietetics (MS).

**Degree requirements:** For master's, thesis or alternative.
**Entrance requirements:** For master's, GRE (MA), minimum GPA of 3.0 in last 60 hours, 15 credits in human development and family studies or related area (MA).
**Expenses:** Tuition, state resident: part-time $182 per unit. Tuition, nonresident: part-time $182 per unit. Required fees: $208 per semester. Part-time tuition and fees vary according to course load.
**Faculty research:** Human growth and development, family studies and human sexuality, nutritional food science/food services, apparel and textile retailing, computer-aided design for apparel and interior design.

### ■ CLAREMONT GRADUATE UNIVERSITY

**Graduate Programs, School of Educational Studies, Claremont, CA 91711-6160**

**AWARDS** Comparative educational studies (MA, PhD); education policy issues (MA, PhD); higher education (MA, PhD); human development (MA, PhD); linguistics and anthropology (MA, PhD); organization and administration (PhD); public school administration (MA, PhD); reading and language development (MA, PhD); teacher education (MA, PhD); teaching/learning process (PhD); urban education administration (MA, PhD). Part-time programs available.

**Faculty:** 16 full-time (8 women), 4 part-time/adjunct (3 women).
**Students:** 156 full-time (113 women), 250 part-time (181 women); includes 191 minority (46 African Americans, 38 Asian Americans or Pacific Islanders, 104 Hispanic Americans, 3 Native Americans), 11 international. Average age 35. In 2001, 124 master's, 31 doctorates awarded. Terminal master's awarded for partial completion of doctoral program.
**Degree requirements:** For master's, thesis or alternative, comprehensive exam (for some programs); for doctorate, thesis/dissertation, comprehensive exam.
**Entrance requirements:** For master's and doctorate, GRE General Test. *Application*

*deadline:* For fall admission, 2/15 (priority date). Applications are processed on a rolling basis. *Application fee:* $50. Electronic applications accepted.

**Expenses:** Tuition: Full-time $22,984; part-time $1,000 per unit. Required fees: $160; $80 per semester.

**Financial support:** Fellowships, research assistantships, Federal Work-Study and institutionally sponsored loans available. Support available to part-time students. Financial award application deadline: 2/15; financial award applicants required to submit FAFSA.

**Faculty research:** Education administration, K–12 and higher education, multicultural education, education policy, diversity in higher education, faculty issues.

David Drew, Dean, 909-621-8075, *Fax:* 909-621-8734, *E-mail:* david.drew@cgu.edu.

**Application contact:** Janet Alonzo, Secretary, 909-621-8075, *Fax:* 909-621-8734, *E-mail:* educ@cgu.edu. *Web site:* http://www.cgu.edu/ces/

**Find an in-depth description at www.petersons.com/gradchannel.**

## ■ COLORADO STATE UNIVERSITY

**Graduate School, College of Applied Human Sciences, Department of Human Development and Family Studies, Fort Collins, CO 80523-0015**

AWARDS MS. Part-time programs available.

**Faculty:** 12 full-time (6 women), 2 part-time/adjunct (1 woman).

**Students:** 23 full-time (21 women), 10 part-time (9 women); includes 5 minority (1 African American, 3 Hispanic Americans, 1 Native American), 2 international. Average age 29. 49 applicants, 47% accepted, 15 enrolled. In 2001, 7 degrees awarded.

**Degree requirements:** For master's, thesis.

**Entrance requirements:** For master's, GRE General Test, TOEFL, minimum GPA of 3.0; previous course work in human development, family studies, and statistics. *Application deadline:* For fall admission, 1/15 (priority date). *Application fee:* $30. Electronic applications accepted.

**Expenses:** Tuition, state resident: full-time $2,880; part-time $160 per credit. Tuition, nonresident: full-time $11,412; part-time $634 per credit. Required fees: $750; $34 per credit.

**Financial support:** In 2001–02, 1 fellowship, 4 research assistantships, 13 teaching assistantships were awarded. Career-related internships or fieldwork, Federal Work-Study, institutionally sponsored loans, and

traineeships also available. Support available to part-time students. Financial award application deadline: 1/15.

**Faculty research:** Development of self in the social context, risk factors in development, grief and loss, intergeneration relationships. *Total annual research expenditures:* $625,000.

Dr. Clifton E. Barber, Head, 970-491-3581, *Fax:* 970-491-7975.

**Application contact:** Dr. Karen C. Barrett, Graduate Coordinator, 970-491-7382, *Fax:* 970-491-7975, *E-mail:* barrett@cahs.colostate.edu. *Web site:* http://www.cahs.colostate.edu/Depts/HDFS/

## ■ CONCORDIA UNIVERSITY

**College of Graduate and Continuing Studies, School of Human Services, St. Paul, MN 55104-5494**

AWARDS Community education (MA Ed); criminal justice (MAHS); early childhood education (MA Ed); family studies (MAHS); leadership (MAHS); parish education (MA Ed); school-age care (MA Ed); youth development (MA Ed). Evening/weekend programs available. Postbaccalaureate distance learning degree programs offered (minimal on-campus study).

**Faculty:** 8 full-time (3 women), 98 part-time/adjunct (51 women).

**Students:** 161 full-time (136 women); includes 24 minority (20 African Americans, 2 Asian Americans or Pacific Islanders, 2 Hispanic Americans). Average age 34. 50 applicants, 90% accepted. In 2001, 18 degrees awarded.

**Degree requirements:** For master's, thesis or alternative, final project.

**Entrance requirements:** For master's, leadership portfolio, minimum GPA of 2.75. *Application deadline:* Applications are processed on a rolling basis. *Application fee:* $50. Electronic applications accepted.

**Expenses:** Tuition: Part-time $300 per semester hour. Tuition and fees vary according to program.

**Financial support:** Federal Work-Study available. Support available to part-time students. Financial award application deadline: 4/6.

James Ollhoff, Associate Dean, 651-603-6148, *E-mail:* ollhoff@csp.edu.

**Application contact:** Gail Ann Wells, Marketing Coordinator, 651-603-6186, *Fax:* 651-603-6144, *E-mail:* wells@csp.edu. *Web site:* http://www.cshs.csp.edu/

## ■ CORNELL UNIVERSITY

**Graduate School, Graduate Fields of Human Ecology, Field of Human Development, Ithaca, NY 14853-0001**

AWARDS Developmental psychology (PhD), including cognitive development, developmental psychopathology, ecology of

human development, sociology and personality development; human development and family studies (PhD), including ecology of human development, family studies and the life course.

**Faculty:** 33 full-time.

**Students:** 33 full-time (23 women); includes 7 minority (4 African Americans, 1 Asian American or Pacific Islander, 2 Hispanic Americans), 6 international. 70 applicants, 16% accepted. In 2001, 6 doctorates awarded.

**Degree requirements:** For doctorate, thesis/dissertation, predoctoral research project, teaching experience.

**Entrance requirements:** For doctorate, GRE General Test, TOEFL, 2 letters of recommendation. *Application deadline:* For fall admission, 1/15. *Application fee:* $65. Electronic applications accepted.

**Expenses:** Tuition: Full-time $25,970. Required fees: $50.

**Financial support:** In 2001–02, 33 students received support, including 7 fellowships with full tuition reimbursements available, 10 research assistantships with full tuition reimbursements available, 16 teaching assistantships with full tuition reimbursements available; institutionally sponsored loans, scholarships/grants, tuition waivers (full and partial), and unspecified assistantships also available. Financial award applicants required to submit FAFSA.

**Faculty research:** Cognitive development, developmental psychopathology, ecology of human development, family studies and the life course, social and personality development.

**Application contact:** Graduate Field Assistant, 607-255-3181, *Fax:* 607-255-9856, *E-mail:* hdfs@cornell.edu. *Web site:* http://www.gradschool.cornell.edu/grad/fields_1/hdfs.html

## ■ DUKE UNIVERSITY

**Graduate School, Department of Psychology, Durham, NC 27708-0586**

AWARDS Biological psychology (PhD); clinical psychology (PhD); cognitive psychology (PhD); developmental psychology (PhD); experimental psychology (PhD); health psychology (PhD); human social development (PhD).

**Faculty:** 52 full-time, 15 part-time/adjunct.

**Students:** 66 full-time (42 women); includes 11 minority (6 African Americans, 2 Asian Americans or Pacific Islanders, 3 Hispanic Americans), 13 international. 386 applicants, 7% accepted, 15 enrolled. In 2001, 8 doctorates awarded.

**Degree requirements:** For doctorate, thesis/dissertation.

*Duke University (continued)*
**Entrance requirements:** For doctorate, GRE General Test. *Application deadline:* For fall admission, 12/31. *Application fee:* $75.
**Expenses:** Tuition: Full-time $24,600.
**Financial support:** Fellowships, research assistantships, teaching assistantships, career-related internships or fieldwork and Federal Work-Study available. Financial award application deadline: 12/31.
Reiko Mazuka, Co-Director of Graduate Studies, 919-660-5716, *Fax:* 919-660-5726, *E-mail:* bseymore@acpub.duke.edu. *Web site:* http://www.psych.duke.edu/

■ **ERIKSON INSTITUTE**
**Academic Programs, Chicago, IL 60611-5627**
**AWARDS** Child development (MS); director's leadership (Certificate); early childhood education (MS); infant studies (Certificate). Part-time and evening/weekend programs available.
**Faculty:** 10 full-time (8 women), 11 part-time/adjunct (all women).
**Students:** 40 full-time (39 women), 106 part-time (100 women); includes 48 minority (31 African Americans, 7 Asian Americans or Pacific Islanders, 10 Hispanic Americans), 1 international. Average age 30. 102 applicants, 84% accepted, 60 enrolled. In 2001, 16 master's, 14 other advanced degrees awarded.
**Degree requirements:** For master's, internship; for Certificate, internship.
**Entrance requirements:** For master's and Certificate, minimum GPA of 2.75. *Application deadline:* For fall admission, 4/1 (priority date). Applications are processed on a rolling basis. *Application fee:* $30.
**Expenses:** Tuition: Full-time $18,852; part-time $460 per credit. Required fees: $150. One-time fee: $115 part-time. Tuition and fees vary according to course load and program.
**Financial support:** In 2001–02, 80 students received support, including 80 fellowships (averaging $3,534 per year); career-related internships or fieldwork, institutionally sponsored loans, and scholarships/grants also available. Support available to part-time students. Financial award application deadline: 4/1; financial award applicants required to submit FAFSA.
**Faculty research:** Assessment strategies from early childhood through elementary years; language, literacy, and the arts in children's development; inclusive special education; parent-child relationships; cognitive development. *Total annual research expenditures:* $3.8 million.
Dr. Fran Stott, Vice President/Dean of Academic Programs, 312-755-2250 Ext.

2280, *Fax:* 312-755-0928, *E-mail:* fstott@erikson.edu.
**Application contact:** Melanie K. Miller, Associate Director of Recruitment and Financial Aid, 312-755-2250 Ext. 2276, *Fax:* 312-755-0928, *E-mail:* mmiller@erikson.edu.

■ **FIELDING GRADUATE INSTITUTE**
**Graduate Programs, Programs in Human and Organization Development, Santa Barbara, CA 93105-3538**
**AWARDS** Human and organizational systems (PhD); human development (MA, PhD); human organization development (Ed D); human services (MA); organization development (MA). Evening/weekend programs available.
**Faculty:** 28 full-time (12 women), 15 part-time/adjunct (6 women).
**Students:** 464 full-time (299 women); includes 83 minority (53 African Americans, 10 Asian Americans or Pacific Islanders, 15 Hispanic Americans, 5 Native Americans), 10 international. Average age 47. 82 applicants, 78% accepted, 57 enrolled. In 2001, 42 master's, 51 doctorates awarded. Terminal master's awarded for partial completion of doctoral program.
**Degree requirements:** For doctorate, thesis/dissertation. *Median time to degree:* Master's–3.5 years full-time; doctorate–6 years full-time.
*Application deadline:* For fall admission, 3/5; for spring admission, 9/5. *Application fee:* $75.
**Expenses:** Tuition: Full-time $14,100.
**Financial support:** In 2001–02, 165 students received support. Career-related internships or fieldwork, institutionally sponsored loans, scholarships/grants, and diversity scholarships available. Financial award application deadline: 4/1; financial award applicants required to submit FAFSA.
Dr. Charles McClintock, Dean, 805-898-2930, *Fax:* 805-687-4590, *E-mail:* cmcclintock@fielding.edu.
**Application contact:** Alexis Long, Admissions Counselor, 805-898-4020, *Fax:* 805-687-9793, *E-mail:* along@fielding.edu.

■ **THE GEORGE WASHINGTON UNIVERSITY**
**Graduate School of Education and Human Development, Individualized Master's Program in Educational Human Development, Washington, DC 20052**
**AWARDS** MA Ed.
**Students:** 1 (woman) full-time, 14 part-time (10 women); includes 1 minority

(Hispanic American), 1 international. Average age 34. 7 applicants, 100% accepted. In 2001, 1 degree awarded.
**Degree requirements:** For master's, comprehensive exam.
**Entrance requirements:** For master's, GRE General Test or MAT, minimum GPA of 2.75. *Application deadline:* For fall admission, 3/1 (priority date); for spring admission, 10/1. Applications are processed on a rolling basis. *Application fee:* $55.
**Expenses:** Tuition: Part-time $810 per credit. Required fees: $1 per credit.
**Financial support:** Applicants required to submit FAFSA.
Dr. Janet C. Heddesheimer, Associate Dean, 202-994-6170, *E-mail:* gsehdapp@gwu.edu. *Web site:* http://www.gwu.edu/~gradinfo/

■ **HARVARD UNIVERSITY**
**Graduate School of Education, Area of Human Development and Psychology, Cambridge, MA 02138**
**AWARDS** Gender studies (Ed M); human development and psychology (Ed M, Ed D, CAS); individualized program (Ed M); language and literacy (Ed M, Ed D, CAS); mind brain and education (Ed M); risk and prevention (Ed M, CAS). Part-time programs available.
**Faculty:** 13 full-time (7 women), 33 part-time/adjunct (12 women).
**Students:** 243 full-time (204 women), 37 part-time (31 women); includes 59 minority (21 African Americans, 16 Asian Americans or Pacific Islanders, 18 Hispanic Americans, 4 Native Americans), 35 international. Average age 32. 162 applicants, 21% accepted. In 2001, 118 master's, 18 doctorates, 2 other advanced degrees awarded. Terminal master's awarded for partial completion of doctoral program.
**Degree requirements:** For doctorate, thesis/dissertation.
**Entrance requirements:** For master's, GRE General Test or MAT, TOEFL, TWE; for doctorate and CAS, GRE General Test, TOEFL, TWE. *Application deadline:* For fall admission, 1/2. *Application fee:* $65.
**Financial support:** In 2001–02, 146 students received support, including 22 fellowships (averaging $19,708 per year), 5 research assistantships, 106 teaching assistantships (averaging $3,733 per year); career-related internships or fieldwork, Federal Work-Study, and scholarships/grants also available. Support available to part-time students. Financial award application deadline: 2/3; financial award applicants required to submit FAFSA.
**Faculty research:** Educational technologies; reading, writing, and language; risk

and prevention of developmental and educational problems; bilingualism and multicultural education; gender difference in development.

Dr. Robert L. Selman, Chair, 617-495-3414.

**Application contact:** Roland A. Hence, Director of Admissions, 617-495-3414, *Fax:* 617-496-3577, *E-mail:* gseadmissions@harvard.edu. *Web site:* http://gse.harvard.edu/

### ■ HOWARD UNIVERSITY

**School of Education, Department of Human Development and Psychoeducational Studies, Program in Human Development, Washington, DC 20059-0002**

**AWARDS** MS. Offered through the Graduate School of Arts and Sciences. Part-time programs available.

**Degree requirements:** For master's, thesis, expository writing exam, comprehensive exam.

**Entrance requirements:** For master's, GRE General Test, minimum GPA of 2.7.

### ■ IOWA STATE UNIVERSITY OF SCIENCE AND TECHNOLOGY

**Graduate College, College of Family and Consumer Sciences, Department of Human Development and Family Studies, Ames, IA 50011**

**AWARDS** Human development and family studies (MFCS, MS, PhD); marriage and family therapy (PhD).

**Faculty:** 33 full-time, 3 part-time/adjunct.
**Students:** 35 full-time (27 women), 67 part-time (51 women); includes 8 minority (1 African American, 2 Asian Americans or Pacific Islanders, 5 Hispanic Americans), 16 international. 42 applicants, 64% accepted, 14 enrolled. In 2001, 10 master's, 15 doctorates awarded.
**Degree requirements:** For master's and doctorate, thesis/dissertation. *Median time to degree:* Master's–2.4 years full-time; doctorate–5.9 years full-time.
**Entrance requirements:** For master's and doctorate, GRE General Test, TOEFL or IELTS. *Application deadline:* For fall admission, 1/15 (priority date). *Application fee:* $20 ($50 for international students). Electronic applications accepted.
**Expenses:** Tuition, state resident: full-time $1,851. Tuition, nonresident: full-time $5,449. Tuition and fees vary according to program.
**Financial support:** In 2001–02, 25 research assistantships with partial tuition reimbursements (averaging $12,175 per year), 17 teaching assistantships with partial tuition reimbursements (averaging

$11,439 per year) were awarded. Fellowships, scholarships/grants also available.
**Faculty research:** Child development, early childhood education, family resource management and housing, life span studies.
Dr. Maurice M. MacDonald, Chair, 515-294-6316, *Fax:* 515-294-2502, *E-mail:* hdfs-grad-adm@iastate.edu.
**Application contact:** Dr. Dee Draper, Director of Graduate Education, 515-294-6321, *Fax:* 515-294-2502, *E-mail:* hdfs-grad-adm@iastate.edu. *Web site:* http://www.fcs.iastate.edu/hdfs/grad/default.htm/

### ■ KENT STATE UNIVERSITY

**Graduate School of Education, Department of Adult, Counseling, Health and Vocational Education, Program in Counseling and Human Development Services, Kent, OH 44242-0001**

**AWARDS** PhD.

**Students:** 74 full-time (51 women), 23 part-time (17 women); includes 17 minority (15 African Americans, 2 Hispanic Americans), 5 international. 14 applicants, 93% accepted, 10 enrolled. In 2001, 8 degrees awarded.
**Degree requirements:** For doctorate, thesis/dissertation, comprehensive exam, registration.
**Entrance requirements:** For doctorate, GRE General Test. *Application deadline:* For fall admission, 2/15. *Application fee:* $30. Electronic applications accepted.
**Financial support:** In 2001–02, fellowships with full tuition reimbursements (averaging $9,500 per year); research assistantships with full tuition reimbursements, teaching assistantships with full tuition reimbursements, career-related internships or fieldwork, Federal Work-Study, institutionally sponsored loans, scholarships/grants, health care benefits, and unspecified assistantships also available. Support available to part-time students. Financial award application deadline: 4/1; financial award applicants required to submit FAFSA.
**Faculty research:** Family/child therapy, clinical supervision, group work, experiential training methods.
Dr. John West, Coordinator, 330-672-2662, *E-mail:* jwest@kent.edu.
**Application contact:** Deborah Barber, Director, Office of Academic Services, 330-672-2862, *Fax:* 330-672-3549, *E-mail:* oas@educ.kent.edu.

### ■ LINDSEY WILSON COLLEGE

**Department of Human Services and Counseling, Columbia, KY 42728-1298**

**AWARDS** Counseling and human development (M Ed).

**Expenses:** Tuition: Part-time $396 per credit hour.

### ■ MARYWOOD UNIVERSITY

**Graduate School of Arts and Sciences, Department of Human Development, Scranton, PA 18509-1598**

**AWARDS** PhD. Part-time and evening/weekend programs available.

**Faculty:** 26 full-time (16 women).
**Students:** 2 full-time (both women), 39 part-time (27 women); includes 3 minority (2 African Americans, 1 Hispanic American). Average age 39. 32 applicants, 59% accepted.
**Degree requirements:** For doctorate, thesis/dissertation, qualifying exam.
**Entrance requirements:** For doctorate, GRE, TOEFL, interview. *Application deadline:* For fall admission, 2/1. *Application fee:* $20.
**Expenses:** Contact institution.
**Financial support:** Fellowships, research assistantships, scholarships/grants and tuition waivers (partial) available. Financial award application deadline: 2/15.
Dr. Marie Loftus, Chairperson, 570-348-6292.
**Application contact:** Deborah M. Flynn, Coordinator of Admissions, 570-340-6002, *Fax:* 570-961-4745, *E-mail:* gsas_adm@ ac.marywood.edu.

### ■ MONTANA STATE UNIVERSITY–BOZEMAN

**College of Graduate Studies, College of Education, Health, and Human Development, Department of Health and Human Development, Bozeman, MT 59717**

**AWARDS** Education (M Ed); health and human development (MS). Part-time programs available.

**Students:** 46 full-time (38 women), 21 part-time (15 women); includes 2 minority (both Asian Americans or Pacific Islanders), 3 international. Average age 33. 33 applicants, 94% accepted, 20 enrolled. In 2001, 24 degrees awarded.
**Degree requirements:** For master's, thesis or alternative.
**Entrance requirements:** For master's, GRE General Test, TOEFL, minimum GPA of 3.0. *Application deadline:* For spring admission, 11/15. Applications are processed on a rolling basis. *Application fee:* $50. Electronic applications accepted.
**Expenses:** Tuition, state resident: full-time $3,894; part-time $198 per credit. Tuition, nonresident: full-time $10,661; part-time $480 per credit. International tuition: $10,811 full-time. Tuition and fees vary according to course load and program.

*Montana State University–Bozeman (continued)*

**Financial support:** In 2001–02, 27 students received support, including 7 research assistantships with full and partial tuition reimbursements available (averaging $4,150 per year), 18 teaching assistantships with full and partial tuition reimbursements available (averaging $5,900 per year); career-related internships or fieldwork, scholarships/grants, and unspecified assistantships also available. Financial award application deadline: 3/1; financial award applicants required to submit FAFSA. *Total annual research expenditures:* $1.9 million.
Dr. Ellen Kreighbaum, Head, 406-994-4001, *Fax:* 406-994-2013, *E-mail:* ellenk@montana.edu. *Web site:* http://www.montana.edu/wwwhhd/

■ **NATIONAL-LOUIS UNIVERSITY**

**College of Arts and Sciences, Division of Liberal Arts and Sciences, Program in Psychology, Chicago, IL 60603**

**AWARDS** Cultural psychology (MA); health psychology (MA); human development (MA); organizational psychology (MA); psychology (Certificate). Part-time and evening/weekend programs available.

**Degree requirements:** For master's, thesis, internship (health psychology).
**Entrance requirements:** For master's, GRE, MAT, or Watson-Glaser Critical Thinking Appraisal, interview, minimum GPA of 3.0; for Certificate, GRE, MAT, or Watson-Glaser Critical Thinking Appraisal, interview, minimum GPA of 3.0, previous undergraduate course work in psychology.
**Expenses:** Tuition: Full-time $13,830; part-time $461 per credit hour.
**Faculty research:** Human development, personality theory, abnormal psychology.

■ **NATIONAL-LOUIS UNIVERSITY**

**National College of Education, McGaw Graduate School, Doctoral Programs in Education, Program in Human Learning and Development, Chicago, IL 60603**

**AWARDS** Ed D. Part-time and evening/weekend programs available.

**Degree requirements:** For doctorate, thesis/dissertation, internship, comprehensive exam.
**Entrance requirements:** For doctorate, GRE General Test, minimum GPA of 3.25, interview, resumé, writing sample.
**Expenses:** Tuition: Full-time $13,830; part-time $461 per credit hour.

■ **NATIONAL-LOUIS UNIVERSITY**

**National College of Education, McGaw Graduate School, Program in Educational Psychology/Human Learning and Development, Chicago, IL 60603**

**AWARDS** Educational psychology (CAS); educational psychology/human learning and development (M Ed, MS Ed); educational psychology/school psychology (M Ed). Part-time and evening/weekend programs available.

**Degree requirements:** For master's, thesis (for some programs).
**Entrance requirements:** For master's, MAT or GRE, minimum GPA of 3.0, teaching certificate; for CAS, master's degree, teaching certificate. Electronic applications accepted.
**Expenses:** Tuition: Full-time $13,830; part-time $461 per credit hour.

■ **NEW YORK INSTITUTE OF TECHNOLOGY**

**Graduate Division, School of Allied Health and Life Sciences, Program in Human Relations, Old Westbury, NY 11568-8000**

**AWARDS** MPS. Part-time and evening/weekend programs available. Postbaccalaureate distance learning degree programs offered.

**Students:** 8 full-time (7 women), 22 part-time (14 women); includes 2 minority (both African Americans), 5 international. Average age 36. 13 applicants, 38% accepted, 4 enrolled. In 2001, 33 degrees awarded.
**Degree requirements:** For master's, thesis or alternative.
**Entrance requirements:** For master's, minimum QPA of 2.85. *Application deadline:* For fall admission, 7/1 (priority date); for spring admission, 12/1 (priority date). Applications are processed on a rolling basis. *Application fee:* $50. Electronic applications accepted.
**Expenses:** Tuition: Part-time $545 per credit. Tuition and fees vary according to course load, degree level, program and student level.
**Financial support:** Fellowships, research assistantships with partial tuition reimbursements, institutionally sponsored loans, tuition waivers (full and partial), and unspecified assistantships available. Support available to part-time students. Financial award applicants required to submit FAFSA.
**Faculty research:** Distance learning delivery systems.
Dr. Maria LaPadula, Coordinator, 516-686-3869, *E-mail:* mlapadul@nyit.edu.

**Application contact:** Jacquelyn Nealon, Dean of Admissions and Financial Aid, 516-686-7925, *Fax:* 516-686-7613, *E-mail:* jnealon@nyit.edu.

■ **NORTHWESTERN UNIVERSITY**

**The Graduate School, School of Education and Social Policy, Program in Human Development and Social Policy, Evanston, IL 60208**

**AWARDS** PhD. Admissions and degrees offered through The Graduate School.

**Faculty:** 12 full-time (5 women), 5 part-time/adjunct (1 woman).
**Students:** 32 full-time (29 women); includes 7 minority (5 African Americans, 2 Asian Americans or Pacific Islanders), 4 international. Average age 33. 60 applicants, 17% accepted, 5 enrolled. In 2001, 6 degrees awarded.
**Degree requirements:** For doctorate, thesis/dissertation.
**Entrance requirements:** For doctorate, GRE General Test, sample of written work. *Application deadline:* For fall admission, 12/31 (priority date). *Application fee:* $50 ($55 for international students). Electronic applications accepted.
**Expenses:** Tuition: Full-time $26,526.
**Financial support:** In 2001–02, 32 students received support, including 5 fellowships with full tuition reimbursements available; research assistantships with full tuition reimbursements available, teaching assistantships, career-related internships or fieldwork, Federal Work-Study, institutionally sponsored loans, and scholarships/grants also available. Financial award application deadline: 12/31; financial award applicants required to submit FAFSA.
**Faculty research:** Social context of development; social policy issues affecting children, adolescents, adults, and families.
Dr. Lindsay Chase-Lansdale, Program Chair, 847-491-4329.
**Application contact:** Mary Lou Manning, Department Assistant, 847-491-4329, *Fax:* 847-491-8999, *E-mail:* mmanning@casbah.acns.northwestern.edu. *Web site:* http://www.sesp.northwestern.edu

**Find an in-depth description at www.petersons.com/gradchannel.**

■ **THE OHIO STATE UNIVERSITY**

**Graduate School, College of Human Ecology, Department of Human Development and Family Science, Columbus, OH 43210**

**AWARDS** Family and consumer sciences education (M Ed, MS, PhD); family relations and human development (MS, PhD).

**Degree requirements:** For master's, thesis optional; for doctorate, thesis/dissertation.

**Entrance requirements:** For master's and doctorate, GRE General Test.

### ■ OREGON STATE UNIVERSITY

**Graduate School, College of Home Economics, Department of Human Development and Family Sciences, Corvallis, OR 97331**

AWARDS Gerontology (MAIS); human development and family studies (MS, PhD).

**Faculty:** 19 full-time (18 women).
**Students:** 21 full-time (20 women), 7 part-time (all women); includes 4 minority (3 Asian Americans or Pacific Islanders, 1 Hispanic American), 7 international. Average age 36. In 2001, 3 master's, 4 doctorates awarded.
**Degree requirements:** For doctorate, thesis/dissertation.
**Entrance requirements:** For master's and doctorate, GRE, TOEFL, minimum GPA of 3.0 in last 90 hours. *Application deadline:* Applications are processed on a rolling basis. *Application fee:* $50.
**Expenses:** Tuition, area resident: Full-time $15,933. Tuition, state resident: full-time $28,937.
**Financial support:** Research assistantships, teaching assistantships, career-related internships or fieldwork, Federal Work-Study, and institutionally sponsored loans available. Support available to part-time students. Financial award application deadline: 2/1.
Dr. Alan Acock, Head, 541-737-4992, *Fax:* 541-737-1076, *E-mail:* alan.acock@ orst.edu.

### ■ OUR LADY OF THE LAKE UNIVERSITY OF SAN ANTONIO

**School of Education and Clinical Studies, Program in Human Sciences and Sociology, San Antonio, TX 78207-4689**

AWARDS Human sciences (MA); sociology (MA). Part-time and evening/weekend programs available.

**Degree requirements:** For master's, thesis optional.
**Entrance requirements:** For master's, GRE General Test or MAT.
**Faculty research:** Criminal justice, health care, family, Southwest studies.

### ■ PACIFIC OAKS COLLEGE

**Graduate School, Program in Human Development, Pasadena, CA 91103**

AWARDS MA. Part-time and evening/weekend programs available. Postbaccalaureate distance learning degree programs offered.

**Faculty:** 22 full-time (19 women), 37 part-time/adjunct.

**Students:** 60 full-time, 373 part-time; includes 125 minority (43 African Americans, 26 Asian Americans or Pacific Islanders, 47 Hispanic Americans, 9 Native Americans), 2 international. Average age 38. 96 applicants, 91% accepted, 64 enrolled. In 2001, 72 degrees awarded.
**Degree requirements:** For master's, thesis.
*Application deadline:* For fall admission, 4/15 (priority date); for spring admission, 10/1 (priority date). Applications are processed on a rolling basis. *Application fee:* $55.
**Expenses:** Tuition: Full-time $10,450; part-time $550 per unit. Required fees: $30 per term.
**Financial support:** Federal Work-Study and scholarships/grants available. Support available to part-time students. Financial award application deadline: 4/15; financial award applicants required to submit FAFSA.
**Faculty research:** Bicultural development, teaching adults, art education, literacy development.
Martha Cook, Acting Director, 626-583-6031, *Fax:* 626-432-5561.
**Application contact:** Marsha Franker, Director of Admissions, 626-397-1349, *Fax:* 626-577-6144, *E-mail:* admissions@ pacificoaks.edu. *Web site:* http:// www.pacificoaks.edu/

### ■ THE PENNSYLVANIA STATE UNIVERSITY UNIVERSITY PARK CAMPUS

**Graduate School, College of Health and Human Development, Department of Human Development and Family Studies, State College, University Park, PA 16802-1503**

AWARDS MS, PhD.

**Students:** 57 full-time (46 women), 4 part-time (3 women). In 2001, 11 master's, 15 doctorates awarded.
**Entrance requirements:** For master's and doctorate, GRE General Test. *Application fee:* $45.
**Expenses:** Tuition, state resident: full-time $7,882; part-time $333 per credit. Tuition, nonresident: full-time $16,142; part-time $673 per credit. Required fees: $124 per semester.
Dr. Leann Birch, Head, 814-863-0241.
**Application contact:** Dr. Lisa J. Crockett, Chair, 814-863-8000.

**Find an in-depth description at www.petersons.com/gradchannel.**

### ■ PURDUE UNIVERSITY

**Graduate School, School of Consumer and Family Sciences, Department of Child Development and Family Studies, West Lafayette, IN 47907**

AWARDS Developmental studies (MS, PhD); family studies (MS, PhD); marriage and family therapy (MS, PhD). Part-time programs available.

**Faculty:** 19 full-time (14 women).
**Students:** 46 full-time (37 women), 20 part-time (15 women); includes 6 minority (3 African Americans, 1 Asian American or Pacific Islander, 2 Hispanic Americans), 11 international. Average age 29. 82 applicants, 48% accepted. In 2001, 13 master's, 10 doctorates awarded. Terminal master's awarded for partial completion of doctoral program.
**Degree requirements:** For master's and doctorate, thesis/dissertation.
**Entrance requirements:** For master's and doctorate, GRE General Test, TWE. *Application deadline:* For fall admission, 1/10. *Application fee:* $30. Electronic applications accepted.
**Expenses:** Tuition, state resident: full-time $4,164; part-time $149 per credit hour. Tuition, nonresident: full-time $13,872; part-time $458 per credit hour. Tuition and fees vary according to campus/location and program.
**Financial support:** In 2001–02, 50 students received support, including 1 fellowship with full tuition reimbursement available (averaging $13,299 per year), 26 research assistantships with full tuition reimbursements available (averaging $9,900 per year), 26 teaching assistantships with full tuition reimbursements available (averaging $9,900 per year); career-related internships or fieldwork also available. Support available to part-time students. Financial award application deadline: 1/15; financial award applicants required to submit FAFSA.
**Faculty research:** Inclusion of children with special needs, families as learning environments, relationships in child care, work-family relations, AIDS prevention.
Dr. D. R. Powell, Head, 765-494-9511.
**Application contact:** Becky Harshman, Graduate Secretary, 765-494-2965, *Fax:* 765-494-0503, *E-mail:* harshman@ cfs.purdue.edu. *Web site:* http:// www.cfs.purdue.edu/cdfs/

### ■ SAINT JOSEPH COLLEGE

**Graduate Division, Department of Gerontology, West Hartford, CT 06117-2700**

AWARDS Human development/gerontology (MA, Certificate). Part-time and evening/weekend programs available.

*Saint Joseph College (continued)*
**Faculty:** 1 (woman) full-time, 3 part-time/ adjunct (2 women).
**Students:** 2 full-time (both women), 31 part-time (30 women), 1 international. Average age 33. In 2001, 11 degrees awarded.
**Degree requirements:** For master's, thesis or alternative. *Median time to degree:* Master's–2 years full-time, 3 years part-time.
**Entrance requirements:** For master's, GRE or MAT. *Application deadline:* For fall admission, 9/2 (priority date); for spring admission, 1/20 (priority date). Applications are processed on a rolling basis. *Application fee:* $25.
**Expenses:** Tuition: Part-time $475 per credit hour.
**Financial support:** In 2001–02, 8 students received support, including 8 fellowships with partial tuition reimbursements available (averaging $1,000 per year), 2 research assistantships with full tuition reimbursements available; tuition waivers (full) and unspecified assistantships also available. Financial award application deadline: 7/15; financial award applicants required to submit FAFSA.
**Faculty research:** Education, aging, public health.
Dr. Mary Alice Wolf, Chair, 860-231-5325, *Fax:* 860-233-5695, *E-mail:* mawolf@sjc.edu.

### ■ ST. LAWRENCE UNIVERSITY

**Department of Education, Program in Counseling and Human Development, Canton, NY 13617-1455**

**AWARDS** M Ed, CAS. Part-time and evening/weekend programs available.

**Faculty:** 3 full-time (1 woman), 6 part-time/adjunct (2 women).
**Students:** 10 full-time, 20 part-time.
**Entrance requirements:** For master's, GRE General Test. *Application deadline:* For spring admission, 3/1 (priority date). Applications are processed on a rolling basis. *Application fee:* $0.
**Expenses:** Tuition: Part-time $515 per credit.
**Financial support:** In 2001–02, 1 research assistantship was awarded. Financial award application deadline: 4/15.
**Faculty research:** Defense mechanisms and mediation.
Dr. Arthur Clark, Coordinator, 315-229-5863, *Fax:* 315-229-7423, *E-mail:* aclark@stlawu.edu.
**Application contact:** Naomi S. Ten Eyck, Senior Secretary, 315-229-5861, *Fax:* 315-229-7423, *E-mail:* nteneyck@stlawu.edu.

### ■ SAINT LOUIS UNIVERSITY

**Graduate School, College of Public Service, Department of Counseling and Family Therapy, St. Louis, MO 63103-2097**

**AWARDS** Counseling and family therapy (PhD); human development counseling (MA); marriage and family therapy (Certificate); school counseling (MA).

**Faculty:** 5 full-time (4 women).
**Students:** 16 full-time (13 women), 58 part-time (44 women); includes 20 minority (15 African Americans, 3 Asian Americans or Pacific Islanders, 1 Hispanic American, 1 Native American), 1 international. Average age 37. 46 applicants, 67% accepted, 17 enrolled. In 2001, 15 master's, 6 doctorates awarded.
**Degree requirements:** For master's, comprehensive exam; for doctorate, thesis/dissertation, preliminary oral and written exams, comprehensive exam.
**Entrance requirements:** For master's, GRE General Test or MAT, interview; for doctorate, GRE General Test, interview. *Application deadline:* For fall admission, 2/1; for spring admission, 11/1. Applications are processed on a rolling basis. *Application fee:* $40.
**Expenses:** Tuition: Part-time $630 per credit hour.
**Financial support:** In 2001–02, 18 students received support; fellowships, unspecified assistantships available. Financial award application deadline: 4/1; financial award applicants required to submit FAFSA.
**Faculty research:** Learning styles/personality differences, black males' counseling perspectives, adult-sibling relationships, clinical supervision, low-income clients.
Dr. Nancy Morrison, Chairperson, 314-977-7114, *Fax:* 314-977-3214, *E-mail:* morrisonc@slu.edu.
**Application contact:** Dr. Marcia Buresch, Associate Dean of the Graduate School, 314-977-2240, *Fax:* 314-977-3943, *E-mail:* bureschm@slu.edu.

### ■ SAINT MARY'S UNIVERSITY OF MINNESOTA

**Graduate School, Program in Human Development, Winona, MN 55987-1399**

**AWARDS** MA. Part-time and evening/weekend programs available.

**Degree requirements:** For master's, colloquium, position papers.
**Entrance requirements:** For master's, interview, minimum GPA of 2.75.
**Expenses:** Tuition: Full-time $4,230; part-time $235 per credit. One-time fee: $220. Tuition and fees vary according to degree level and program.

### ■ SARAH LAWRENCE COLLEGE

**Graduate Studies, Program in Child Development, Bronxville, NY 10708**

**AWARDS** MA.

**Degree requirements:** For master's, thesis, fieldwork.
**Entrance requirements:** For master's, minimum B average in undergraduate coursework.

### ■ SOUTHERN ILLINOIS UNIVERSITY CARBONDALE

**Graduate School, College of Education, Department of Educational Psychology and Special Education, Program in Educational Psychology, Carbondale, IL 62901-6806**

**AWARDS** Counselor education (MS Ed, PhD); educational psychology (PhD); human learning and development (MS Ed); measurement and statistics (PhD).

**Faculty:** 19 full-time (9 women), 7 part-time/adjunct (2 women).
**Students:** 44 full-time (35 women), 81 part-time (60 women); includes 13 minority (9 African Americans, 1 Asian American or Pacific Islander, 3 Hispanic Americans), 16 international. Average age 36. 42 applicants, 48% accepted. In 2001, 13 master's, 4 doctorates awarded.
**Degree requirements:** For master's and doctorate, thesis/dissertation.
**Entrance requirements:** For master's, GRE General Test, TOEFL, minimum GPA of 2.7; for doctorate, TOEFL, minimum GPA of 3.25. *Application deadline:* For fall admission, 6/15 (priority date). Applications are processed on a rolling basis. *Application fee:* $20.
**Expenses:** Tuition, state resident: full-time $3,794; part-time $154 per hour. Tuition, nonresident: full-time $6,566; part-time $308 per hour. Required fees: $277 per hour.
**Financial support:** In 2001–02, 36 students received support, including 2 fellowships with full tuition reimbursements available, 4 research assistantships with full tuition reimbursements available; teaching assistantships with full tuition reimbursements available, career-related internships or fieldwork, Federal Work-Study, institutionally sponsored loans, and tuition waivers (full) also available. Support available to part-time students. Financial award application deadline: 5/1.
**Faculty research:** Career development, problem solving, learning and instruction, cognitive development, family assessment. *Total annual research expenditures:* $10,000.

**Application contact:** Laurie Viernum, Graduate Secretary, 618-536-7763, *Fax:* 618-453-7110.

**Find an in-depth description at www.petersons.com/gradchannel.**

■ **TEXAS A&M UNIVERSITY**

**College of Education, Department of Educational Psychology, College Station, TX 77843**

**AWARDS** Counseling (MS); counseling psychology (PhD); educational technology (M Ed); gifted and talented education (M Ed, MS); intelligence, creativity, and giftedness (PhD); learning, development, and instruction (M Ed, MS, PhD); licensing specialist in school psychology (MS); research, measurement and statistics (MS); research, measurement, and statistics (M Ed, PhD); school counseling (M Ed); school psychology (PhD); special education (M Ed, PhD). Part-time and evening/weekend programs available. Postbaccalaureate distance learning degree programs offered (no on-campus study).

**Faculty:** 35 full-time (16 women), 4 part-time/adjunct (all women).
**Students:** 135 full-time (105 women), 201 part-time (167 women); includes 52 minority (9 African Americans, 3 Asian Americans or Pacific Islanders, 40 Hispanic Americans), 22 international. 301 applicants, 37% accepted. In 2001, 41 master's, 26 doctorates awarded.
**Degree requirements:** For master's, thesis optional; for doctorate, thesis/dissertation. *Median time to degree:* Master's–2 years full-time, 3 years part-time; doctorate–4.5 years full-time, 6 years part-time.
**Entrance requirements:** For master's, GRE General Test, TOEFL; for doctorate, GRE General Test, TOEFL, master's degree (counseling psychology). *Application fee:* $50 ($75 for international students). Electronic applications accepted.
**Expenses:** Tuition, state resident: full-time $11,872. Tuition, nonresident: full-time $17,892.
**Financial support:** In 2001–02, 34 fellowships (averaging $12,000 per year), 69 research assistantships (averaging $8,400 per year), 5 teaching assistantships (averaging $8,925 per year) were awarded. Career-related internships or fieldwork, institutionally sponsored loans, scholarships/grants, and unspecified assistantships also available. Financial award applicants required to submit FAFSA. *Total annual research expenditures:* $1.5 million.
Dr. Douglas J. Palmer, Head, 979-845-1831, *Fax:* 979-862-1256, *E-mail:* epsy@tamu.edu.

**Application contact:** Carol A. Wagner, Graduate Adviser, 979-845-1833, *Fax:* 979-862-1256, *E-mail:* c-wagner@tamu.edu. *Web site:* http://coe.tamu.edu/!~epsy/

■ **TEXAS SOUTHERN UNIVERSITY**

**Graduate School, College of Liberal Arts and Behavioral Sciences, Department of Human Services and Consumer Sciences, Houston, TX 77004-4584**

**AWARDS** Human services and consumer sciences (MS), including child development, comprehensive human services and consumer sciences, foods and nutrition. Part-time and evening/weekend programs available.

**Faculty:** 3 full-time (all women), 1 (woman) part-time/adjunct.
**Students:** 3 full-time (all women), 22 part-time (18 women); includes 22 minority (21 African Americans, 1 Asian American or Pacific Islander), 3 international. 6 applicants, 100% accepted. In 2001, 10 degrees awarded.
**Degree requirements:** For master's, thesis (for some programs), comprehensive exam.
**Entrance requirements:** For master's, GRE General Test, TOEFL, minimum GPA of 2.5. *Application deadline:* For fall admission, 7/15 (priority date). Applications are processed on a rolling basis. *Application fee:* $35 ($75 for international students).
**Expenses:** Tuition, state resident: full-time $1,188. Tuition, nonresident: full-time $4,644. Required fees: $900. Tuition and fees vary according to degree level.
**Financial support:** In 2001–02, 1 research assistantship was awarded; teaching assistantships, career-related internships or fieldwork and institutionally sponsored loans also available. Financial award application deadline: 5/1.
**Faculty research:** Food radiation/food for space travel, adolescent parenting, gerontology/grandparenting. *Total annual research expenditures:* $185,000.
Dr. Shirley R. Nealy, Chair, 713-313-7638, *Fax:* 713-313-7228, *E-mail:* nealy_sr@tsu.edu.

■ **TEXAS TECH UNIVERSITY**

**Graduate School, College of Human Sciences, Department of Human Development and Family Studies, Lubbock, TX 79409**

**AWARDS** Human development and family studies (MS, PhD); marriage and family therapy (MS, PhD).
**Faculty:** 21 full-time (12 women), 3 part-time/adjunct (all women).

**Students:** 49 full-time (38 women), 25 part-time (18 women); includes 11 minority (6 African Americans, 5 Hispanic Americans), 15 international. Average age 32. 49 applicants, 61% accepted, 15 enrolled. In 2001, 5 master's, 6 doctorates awarded.
**Degree requirements:** For master's and doctorate, thesis/dissertation.
**Entrance requirements:** For master's and doctorate, GRE General Test. *Application deadline:* Applications are processed on a rolling basis. *Application fee:* $25 ($50 for international students). Electronic applications accepted.
**Expenses:** Tuition, state resident: full-time $1,926; part-time $107 per credit hour. Tuition, nonresident: full-time $5,724; part-time $318 per credit hour. Required fees: $779; $737 per year. Tuition and fees vary according to course level, course load and program.
**Financial support:** In 2001–02, 57 students received support, including 26 research assistantships with partial tuition reimbursements available (averaging $11,313 per year), 24 teaching assistantships with partial tuition reimbursements available (averaging $11,641 per year); fellowships with tuition reimbursements available, career-related internships or fieldwork, Federal Work-Study, institutionally sponsored loans, and scholarships/grants also available. Support available to part-time students. Financial award application deadline: 5/1; financial award applicants required to submit FAFSA.
**Faculty research:** Parenting, marital and premarital relationships, adolescent drug abuse, early childhood, life span. *Total annual research expenditures:* $190,567.
Dr. Dean M. Busby, Chair, 806-742-3000, *Fax:* 806-742-0285, *E-mail:* dbusby@hs.ttu.edu.

**Application contact:** Graduate Adviser, 806-742-3000, *Fax:* 806-742-1849. *Web site:* http://www.hs.ttu.edu/HDFS/default.htm

■ **TROY STATE UNIVERSITY**

**Graduate School, School of Education, Program in Counseling and Human Development, Troy, AL 36082**

**AWARDS** MS. Part-time and evening/weekend programs available.

**Degree requirements:** For master's, thesis, comprehensive exam.
**Entrance requirements:** For master's, minimum GPA of 2.5. Electronic applications accepted. *Web site:* http://www.troyst.edu/

# ■ TROY STATE UNIVERSITY MONTGOMERY

**Graduate Programs, Division of Counseling, Education, and Psychology, Program in Counseling, Montgomery, AL 36103-4419**

**AWARDS** Counseling (Ed S); counseling and human development (MS, Ed S). Part-time and evening/weekend programs available.

**Students:** 116. In 2001, 41 degrees awarded.
**Degree requirements:** For master's and Ed S, thesis or alternative.
**Entrance requirements:** For master's, GRE, MAT, or NTE; TOEFL; for Ed S, GRE General Test, MAT, or NTE; TOEFL. *Application deadline:* Applications are processed on a rolling basis. *Application fee:* $30. Electronic applications accepted.
**Expenses:** Tuition, state resident: full-time $2,286; part-time $127 per semester hour. Tuition, nonresident: full-time $4,572; part-time $254 per semester hour. Required fees: $30 per term. Tuition and fees vary according to program.
Dr. John Patrick, Coordinator, 334-241-9593, *E-mail:* jpatrick@tsum.edu.

# ■ THE UNIVERSITY OF ALABAMA

**Graduate School, College of Human Environmental Sciences, Department of Human Development and Family Studies, Tuscaloosa, AL 35487**

**AWARDS** MSHES.

**Faculty:** 8 full-time (5 women).
**Students:** 11 full-time (9 women), 9 part-time (all women); includes 3 minority (2 African Americans, 1 Hispanic American). Average age 29. 2 applicants, 50% accepted, 1 enrolled. In 2001, 6 degrees awarded.
**Degree requirements:** For master's, thesis (for some programs).
**Entrance requirements:** For master's, GRE General Test or MAT, minimum GPA of 3.0. *Application deadline:* For fall admission, 7/6. Applications are processed on a rolling basis. *Application fee:* $25.
**Expenses:** Tuition, state resident: full-time $3,292; part-time $183 per credit hour. Tuition, nonresident: full-time $8,912; part-time $495 per credit hour. Tuition and fees vary according to course load, campus/location and program.
**Financial support:** In 2001–02, 7 research assistantships with full tuition reimbursements (averaging $8,100 per year), 3 teaching assistantships with full tuition reimbursements (averaging $8,100 per year) were awarded. Career-related internships or fieldwork, Federal Work-Study, and scholarships/grants also available. Financial award application deadline: 3/15.

**Faculty research:** Parent/child relationships, psychosocial care of hospitalized children, family care to elders, moral judgment development, family strengths and adolescent wildness.
Dr. Stephen J. Thoma, Chair and Professor, 205-348-8146, *Fax:* 205-348-3789, *E-mail:* sthoma@ches.ua.edu. *Web site:* http://www.ches.ua.edu/

# ■ THE UNIVERSITY OF ARIZONA

**Graduate College, College of Agriculture and Life Sciences, School of Family and Consumer Sciences, Division of Family Studies and Human Development, Tucson, AZ 85721**

**AWARDS** Family and consumer sciences (MS); family studies and human development (PhD). Terminal master's awarded for partial completion of doctoral program.

**Entrance requirements:** For master's and doctorate, GRE General Test, TOEFL, minimum undergraduate GPA of 3.0.
**Expenses:** Tuition, state resident: full-time $2,490; part-time $436 per unit. Tuition, nonresident: full-time $10,300; part-time $436 per unit. Full-time tuition and fees vary according to degree level and program. *Web site:* http://ag.arizona.edu/fcs/fshd

# ■ UNIVERSITY OF CALIFORNIA, BERKELEY

**Graduate Division, School of Education, Division of Cognition and Development, Program in Human Development and Education, Berkeley, CA 94720-1500**

**AWARDS** MA, PhD.

**Expenses:** Tuition, nonresident: full-time $10,704. Required fees: $4,349.

# ■ UNIVERSITY OF CALIFORNIA, DAVIS

**Graduate Studies, Graduate Group in Human Development, Davis, CA 95616**

**AWARDS** PhD.

**Faculty:** 34 full-time (18 women), 1 part-time/adjunct (0 women).
**Students:** 18 full-time (15 women). Average age 32. 24 applicants, 42% accepted, 4 enrolled. In 2001, 8 degrees awarded.
**Degree requirements:** For doctorate, thesis/dissertation.
**Entrance requirements:** For doctorate, GRE General Test, GRE Subject Test, minimum GPA of 3.0. *Application deadline:* For fall admission, 4/1. *Application fee:* $60. Electronic applications accepted.
**Expenses:** Tuition, state resident: full-time $4,831. Tuition, nonresident: full-time $15,725.

**Financial support:** In 2001–02, 14 students received support, including fellowships with full and partial tuition reimbursements available (averaging $4,996 per year), 4 research assistantships with full and partial tuition reimbursements available (averaging $8,632 per year), 7 teaching assistantships with partial tuition reimbursements available (averaging $13,134 per year); career-related internships or fieldwork, Federal Work-Study, institutionally sponsored loans, scholarships/grants, tuition waivers (full), and associate instructorships also available. Financial award application deadline: 1/15; financial award applicants required to submit FAFSA.
**Faculty research:** Life span socioemotional and cognitive development, individual differences, relationship between biological and behavioral development, cross-cultural and cross-generational development.
Lawrence Harper, Chair, 530-752-3624, *Fax:* 530-752-5660, *E-mail:* lharper@ucdavis.edu.
**Application contact:** Judy Erwin, Graduate Assistant, 530-752-1926, *Fax:* 530-752-5660, *E-mail:* gjerwin@ucdavis.edu. *Web site:* http://hcd.ucdavis.edu/graduate/

# ■ UNIVERSITY OF CALIFORNIA, IRVINE

**Office of Research and Graduate Studies, School of Social Ecology, Department of Psychology and Social Behavior, Irvine, CA 92697**

**AWARDS** Health psychology (PhD); human development (PhD).

**Faculty:** 18.
**Students:** 39 full-time (30 women), 1 part-time; includes 8 minority (6 Asian Americans or Pacific Islanders, 2 Hispanic Americans). 72 applicants, 25% accepted, 7 enrolled. In 2001, 2 degrees awarded. Terminal master's awarded for partial completion of doctoral program.
**Degree requirements:** For doctorate, thesis/dissertation, research project.
**Entrance requirements:** For doctorate, GRE General Test. *Application deadline:* For fall and spring admission, 1/15 (priority date); for winter admission, 10/15 (priority date). Applications are processed on a rolling basis. *Application fee:* $60. Electronic applications accepted.
**Expenses:** Tuition, nonresident: full-time $10,704. Required fees: $8,396. Tuition and fees vary according to course load, program and student level.
**Financial support:** Fellowships, research assistantships, teaching assistantships, institutionally sponsored loans and tuition waivers (full and partial) available. Financial award application deadline: 3/2;

financial award applicants required to submit FAFSA.

**Faculty research:** Psychosocial development in children, adolescents, and adults; gerontology, childhood behavior disorders, and developmental psychopathology; sex differences; attitude change; social psychology.

Chuansheng Chen, Chair, 949-824-4184. **Application contact:** Jeanne Haynes, Academic Counselor, 949-824-5917, *Fax:* 949-824-2056, *E-mail:* jhaynes@uci.edu. *Web site:* http://www.socecol.uci.edu/ ~socecol/

## ■ UNIVERSITY OF CENTRAL OKLAHOMA

**College of Graduate Studies and Research, College of Education, Department of Human Environmental Sciences, Edmond, OK 73034-5209**

AWARDS Family and child studies (MS); family and consumer science education (MS); interior design (MS); nutrition-food management (MS). Part-time programs available.

**Faculty research:** Dietetics and food science. *Web site:* http://www.ucok.edu/ graduate/human.htm/

## ■ UNIVERSITY OF CHICAGO

**Division of Social Sciences, Committee on Human Development, Chicago, IL 60637-1513**

AWARDS PhD.

**Students:** 69.

**Degree requirements:** For doctorate, one foreign language, thesis/dissertation, predoctoral written exams.

**Entrance requirements:** For doctorate, GRE General Test, GRE Subject Test, TOEFL. *Application deadline:* For fall admission, 12/28. *Application fee:* $55. Electronic applications accepted.

**Expenses:** Tuition: Full-time $16,548.

**Financial support:** Fellowships, research assistantships, teaching assistantships, Federal Work-Study and institutionally sponsored loans available. Financial award application deadline: 12/28.

Prof. Richard P. Taub, Acting Chair, 773-702-3971.

**Application contact:** Office of the Dean of Students, 773-702-8415.

## ■ UNIVERSITY OF CONNECTICUT

**Graduate School, School of Family Studies, Field of Human Development and Family Relations, Storrs, CT 06269**

AWARDS MA, PhD.

**Degree requirements:** For doctorate, thesis/dissertation.

**Entrance requirements:** For master's, GRE General Test, TOEFL.

## ■ UNIVERSITY OF DAYTON

**Graduate School, School of Education and Allied Professions, Department of Counselor Education and Human Services, Dayton, OH 45469-1300**

AWARDS College student personnel (MS Ed); community counseling (MS Ed); higher education administration (MS Ed); human development services (MS Ed); school counseling (MS Ed); school psychology (MS Ed); teacher as child/youth development specialist (MS Ed). Part-time and evening/weekend programs available.

**Faculty:** 9 full-time (4 women), 23 part-time/adjunct (13 women).

**Students:** 23 full-time (21 women), 421 part-time (323 women). Average age 32. 263 applicants, 60% accepted. In 2001, 233 degrees awarded.

**Degree requirements:** For master's, exit exam, thesis optional.

**Entrance requirements:** For master's, MAT or GRE if GPA is below 2.75, interview. *Application deadline:* For fall admission, 2/15 (priority date). Applications are processed on a rolling basis. *Application fee:* $30.

**Expenses:** Tuition: Full-time $5,436; part-time $453 per credit hour. Required fees: $50; $25 per term.

**Financial support:** In 2001–02, 3 research assistantships with partial tuition reimbursements (averaging $6,100 per year) were awarded; Federal Work-Study and institutionally sponsored loans also available.

**Faculty research:** Anger as part of the grief process, inclusion of children with severe disabilities, comparisons of school counselors in Bosnia and the U. S., graduate and professional student socialization, use of cohort groups in doctoral programs. Dr. Thomas W. Rueth, Chairperson, 937-229-3644, *Fax:* 937-229-1055, *E-mail:* thomas.rueth@notes.udayton.edu.

## ■ UNIVERSITY OF DELAWARE

**College of Human Services, Education and Public Policy, Department of Individual and Family Studies, Newark, DE 19716**

AWARDS Family studies (PhD); individual and family studies (MS). Part-time programs available.

**Faculty:** 23 full-time (16 women).

**Students:** 27 full-time (22 women), 12 part-time (11 women); includes 8 minority (7 African Americans, 1 Hispanic American), 4 international. Average age 34. 14 applicants, 64% accepted, 8 enrolled. In 2001, 10 master's, 1 doctorate awarded.

Terminal master's awarded for partial completion of doctoral program.

**Degree requirements:** For master's, thesis or alternative; for doctorate, thesis/dissertation.

**Entrance requirements:** For master's and doctorate, GRE General Test, TOEFL, letters of recommendation (3). *Application deadline:* For fall admission, 2/1. *Application fee:* $50. Electronic applications accepted.

**Expenses:** Tuition, state resident: full-time $4,770; part-time $265 per credit. Tuition, nonresident: full-time $13,860; part-time $770 per credit. Required fees: $414.

**Financial support:** In 2001–02, 20 students received support, including 1 fellowship with full tuition reimbursement available (averaging $11,000 per year), 16 research assistantships with full tuition reimbursements available (averaging $11,000 per year), 3 teaching assistantships with full tuition reimbursements available (averaging $11,000 per year); career-related internships or fieldwork and institutionally sponsored loans also available. Financial award application deadline: 2/1.

**Faculty research:** Early childhood inclusive education, relationships, family risk and resilience, disability issues, program development and evaluation. Dr. Michael Ferrari, Interim Chair, 302-831-8566, *Fax:* 302-831-8776, *E-mail:* mferrari@udel.edu.

**Application contact:** Dr. Penny Deiner, Graduate Coordinator, 302-831-6932, *Fax:* 302-831-8776, *E-mail:* pennyd@udel.edu. *Web site:* http://www.udel.edu/ifst/

## ■ UNIVERSITY OF ILLINOIS AT CHICAGO

**Graduate College, College of Associated Health Professions, Department of Disability, Disability Studies, and Human Development, Chicago, IL 60607-7128**

AWARDS Disability and human development (MS); disability studies (PhD). Part-time programs available.

**Faculty:** 12 full-time (2 women), 6 part-time/adjunct (4 women).

**Students:** 11 full-time (8 women), 28 part-time (25 women); includes 8 minority (4 African Americans, 3 Asian Americans or Pacific Islanders, 1 Hispanic American), 7 international. Average age 34. 35 applicants, 51% accepted, 14 enrolled. In 2001, 6 degrees awarded.

**Degree requirements:** For master's, thesis optional; for doctorate, thesis/dissertation.

**Entrance requirements:** For master's and doctorate, GRE General Test, TOEFL. *Application deadline:* For fall admission, 3/1 (priority date). Applications are processed

*University of Illinois at Chicago (continued)*

on a rolling basis. *Application fee:* $40 ($50 for international students). Electronic applications accepted.

**Expenses:** Tuition, state resident: full-time $3,060. Tuition, nonresident: full-time $6,688.

**Financial support:** In 2001–02, 17 students received support; fellowships with full tuition reimbursements available, research assistantships with full tuition reimbursements available, teaching assistantships with full tuition reimbursements available, career-related internships or fieldwork, Federal Work-Study, and institutionally sponsored loans available. Financial award application deadline: 3/1; financial award applicants required to submit FAFSA.

**Faculty research:** Emerging trends in disability, demography and financial structure of disability services, aging and disability, empowerment of people with disabilities, health promotion in disabilities.

Glenn Fujiura, Head, 312-413-1977, *Fax:* 312-413-1630, *E-mail:* gfujiura@uic.edu.

**Application contact:** Dr. Tamar Heller, Director of Graduate Studies, 312-413-1537, *Fax:* 312-413-1630, *E-mail:* theller@uic.edu. *Web site:* http://www.uic.edu/depts/idhd

■ **UNIVERSITY OF ILLINOIS AT SPRINGFIELD**

**Graduate Programs, College of Education and Human Services, Program in Human Development Counseling, Springfield, IL 62703-5404**

**AWARDS** MA. Part-time and evening/weekend programs available.

**Faculty:** 5 full-time (2 women), 1 (woman) part-time/adjunct.

**Students:** 13 full-time (12 women), 59 part-time (46 women). Average age 37. 40 applicants, 88% accepted, 12 enrolled. In 2001, 17 degrees awarded.

**Degree requirements:** For master's, thesis or alternative.

**Entrance requirements:** For master's, GRE General Test (recommended), minimum GPA of 2.5, previous course work in psychology. *Application deadline:* Applications are processed on a rolling basis. *Application fee:* $0.

**Expenses:** Tuition, state resident: full-time $2,680. Tuition, nonresident: full-time $8,064. Required fees: $626. One-time fee: $626.

**Financial support:** In 2001–02, 25 students received support, including 5 research assistantships with full and partial tuition reimbursements available (averaging $6,300 per year); career-related internships or fieldwork, Federal Work-Study,

scholarships/grants, tuition waivers (partial), and unspecified assistantships also available. Support available to part-time students. Financial award application deadline: 6/1; financial award applicants required to submit FAFSA.

Dr. Larry Stonecipher, Dean, 217-206-7815.

■ **UNIVERSITY OF ILLINOIS AT URBANA–CHAMPAIGN**

**Graduate College, College of Agricultural, Consumer and Environmental Sciences, Department of Human and Community Development, Champaign, IL 61820**

**AWARDS** Extension education (MS); human and community development (AM, MS, PhD).

**Faculty:** 20 full-time.

**Students:** 41 full-time (34 women); includes 7 minority (4 African Americans, 1 Asian American or Pacific Islander, 2 Hispanic Americans), 5 international. 39 applicants, 31% accepted. In 2001, 11 master's, 3 doctorates awarded.

**Degree requirements:** For doctorate, thesis/dissertation.

**Entrance requirements:** For master's, GRE, minimum GPA of 3.0. *Application deadline:* For fall admission, 1/15. Applications are processed on a rolling basis. *Application fee:* $40 ($50 for international students). Electronic applications accepted.

**Expenses:** Tuition, state resident: part-time $3,227 per degree program. Tuition, nonresident: part-time $7,169 per degree program. Tuition and fees vary according to program.

**Financial support:** In 2001–02, 11 fellowships, 9 research assistantships, 18 teaching assistantships were awarded. Tuition waivers (full and partial) also available. Financial award application deadline: 2/15.

Constance H. Shapiro, Head, 217-333-3790, *Fax:* 217-244-7877, *E-mail:* chshapir@uiuc.edu.

**Application contact:** Leann Topol, Clerk, 217-333-3869, *Fax:* 217-244-7877, *E-mail:* l-topol@uiuc.edu. *Web site:* http://w3ag.uiuc.edu/hcd/

■ **UNIVERSITY OF KANSAS**

**Graduate School, College of Liberal Arts and Sciences, Department of Human Development and Family Life, Lawrence, KS 66045**

**AWARDS** Developmental and child psychology (PhD); early childhood education (MA, PhD); human development (MA, MHD). PhD offered jointly with the Kansas City campus.

**Faculty:** 21.

**Students:** 78 full-time (63 women), 18 part-time (9 women); includes 15 minority (6 African Americans, 2 Asian Americans

or Pacific Islanders, 6 Hispanic Americans, 1 Native American), 8 international. Average age 31. 51 applicants, 27% accepted, 14 enrolled. In 2001, 10 master's, 6 doctorates awarded.

**Degree requirements:** For master's, thesis or alternative; for doctorate, thesis/dissertation, comprehensive oral and written exams.

**Entrance requirements:** For master's, TOEFL, GRE; for doctorate, GRE, TOEFL, GRE. *Application deadline:* For fall admission, 2/15 (priority date). *Application fee:* $35.

**Expenses:** Tuition, state resident: full-time $2,722; part-time $113 per credit. Tuition, nonresident: full-time $8,586; part-time $358 per credit. Required fees: $551; $46 per credit. Tuition and fees vary according to campus/location, program and reciprocity agreements.

**Financial support:** In 2001–02, 15 research assistantships with partial tuition reimbursements (averaging $9,223 per year), 27 teaching assistantships with full and partial tuition reimbursements (averaging $6,710 per year) were awarded. Fellowships, career-related internships or fieldwork also available.

Edward K. Morris, Chair, 785-864-4840, *Fax:* 785-864-5202.

**Application contact:** R. Mark Mathews, Graduate Director, 785-864-4840, *Fax:* 785-864-5202, *E-mail:* rm-mathews@ku.edu. *Web site:* http://www.ku.edu/~hdfl/

■ **UNIVERSITY OF MAINE**

**Graduate School, College of Education and Human Development, Department of Human Development and Family Relations, Orono, ME 04469**

**AWARDS** Human development (MS). Part-time programs available.

**Faculty:** 11 full-time (5 women).

**Students:** 8 full-time (all women), 8 part-time (7 women). 8 applicants, 88% accepted, 5 enrolled. In 2001, 4 degrees awarded.

**Degree requirements:** For master's, thesis.

**Entrance requirements:** For master's, GRE General Test, TOEFL. *Application deadline:* For fall admission, 2/1 (priority date). Applications are processed on a rolling basis. *Application fee:* $50. Electronic applications accepted.

**Expenses:** Tuition, state resident: full-time $3,780; part-time $210 per credit hour. Tuition, nonresident: full-time $10,782; part-time $599 per credit hour. Required fees: $9.50 per credit hour. $32 per semester. Tuition and fees vary according to reciprocity agreements.

**Financial support:** In 2001–02, 1 research assistantship with tuition reimbursement (averaging $9,010 per year), 5 teaching assistantships with tuition reimbursements (averaging $9,010 per year) were awarded. Career-related internships or fieldwork, Federal Work-Study, institutionally sponsored loans, tuition waivers (full and partial), and unspecified assistantships also available. Financial award application deadline: 3/1.

**Faculty research:** Methods to assess nutrient intake and risk, carnitine-supplemented diets for protein-calorie malnutrition, nutrition education, grandfathers' perceptions of relations to grandchildren, social participation of spouses in distressed and nondistressed marriages.
Dr. Sandra Caron, Chair, 207-581-3138, *Fax:* 207-581-3120.
**Application contact:** Scott G. Delcourt, Director of the Graduate School, 207-581-3218, *Fax:* 207-581-3232, *E-mail:* graduate@maine.edu. *Web site:* http://www.umaine.edu/graduate/

■ **UNIVERSITY OF MARYLAND, COLLEGE PARK**

**Graduate Studies and Research, College of Education, Department of Human Development, College Park, MD 20742**
**AWARDS** Early childhood/elementary education (M Ed, MA, Ed D, PhD, CAGS); human development (M Ed, MA, Ed D, PhD, CAGS). Part-time and evening/weekend programs available. Postbaccalaureate distance learning degree programs offered.
**Faculty:** 28 full-time (19 women), 8 part-time/adjunct (6 women).
**Students:** 51 full-time (45 women), 73 part-time (58 women); includes 25 minority (12 African Americans, 7 Asian Americans or Pacific Islanders, 5 Hispanic Americans, 1 Native American), 12 international. 114 applicants, 51% accepted, 33 enrolled. In 2001, 7 master's, 11 doctorates awarded.
**Degree requirements:** For master's, thesis (for some programs); for doctorate, thesis/dissertation, essay, exam, research paper.
**Entrance requirements:** For master's, GRE General Test or MAT, minimum GPA of 3.0; for doctorate, GRE General Test or MAT; for CAGS, MAT. *Application deadline:* For fall admission, 6/1; for spring admission, 10/1. Applications are processed on a rolling basis. *Application fee:* $50 ($70 for international students). Electronic applications accepted.
**Expenses:** Tuition, state resident: part-time $289 per credit hour. Tuition, nonresident: part-time $448 per credit

hour. One-time fee: $436 part-time. Full-time tuition and fees vary according to course load, campus/location and program.
**Financial support:** In 2001–02, 12 fellowships with full tuition reimbursements (averaging $12,063 per year), 3 research assistantships with tuition reimbursements (averaging $12,398 per year), 24 teaching assistantships with tuition reimbursements (averaging $13,243 per year) were awarded. Federal Work-Study and scholarships/grants also available. Support available to part-time students. Financial award applicants required to submit FAFSA.
**Faculty research:** Developmental science, educational psychology.
Dr. Charles Flatter, Acting Chair, 301-405-2827, *Fax:* 301-405-2891.
**Application contact:** Trudy Lindsey, Director, Graduate Admissions and Records, 301-405-6991, *Fax:* 301-314-9305, *E-mail:* grschool@deans.umd.edu.

■ **UNIVERSITY OF MISSOURI–COLUMBIA**

**Graduate School, College of Human Environmental Science, Department of Human Development and Family Studies, Columbia, MO 65211**
**AWARDS** MA, MS, PhD.
**Faculty:** 13 full-time (10 women).
**Students:** 22 full-time (20 women), 11 part-time (10 women); includes 3 minority (all African Americans), 5 international. 3 applicants, 33% accepted. In 2001, 17 degrees awarded.
**Entrance requirements:** For master's, GRE General Test, minimum GPA of 3.0. *Application deadline:* For fall admission, 2/1 (priority date); for winter admission, 11/15 (priority date). Applications are processed on a rolling basis. *Application fee:* $25 ($50 for international students).
**Expenses:** Tuition, state resident: part-time $179 per credit hour. Tuition, nonresident: part-time $539 per credit hour. Required fees: $122 per semester. Tuition and fees vary according to program.
**Financial support:** Research assistantships, teaching assistantships, institutionally sponsored loans available.
Dr. Marilyn Coleman, Director of Graduate Studies, 573-882-4360, *E-mail:* colemanma@missouri.edu. *Web site:* http://web.missouri.edu/~hdfswww/

■ **UNIVERSITY OF NEVADA, RENO**

**Graduate School, College of Human and Community Sciences, Department of Human Development and Family Studies, Reno, NV 89557**
**AWARDS** MS.
**Faculty:** 10.
**Students:** 9 full-time (all women), 8 part-time (all women); includes 2 minority (1 Hispanic American, 1 Native American), 1 international. Average age 36. In 2001, 3 degrees awarded.
**Degree requirements:** For master's, thesis.
**Entrance requirements:** For master's, TOEFL, GRE General Test, minimum GPA of 3.0. *Application deadline:* For fall admission, 3/1; for spring admission, 10/1. *Application fee:* $40.
**Expenses:** Tuition, state resident: full-time $2,067; part-time $108 per credit. Tuition, nonresident: full-time $9,282; part-time $109 per credit. Required fees: $57 per semester. Tuition and fees vary according to course load.
**Financial support:** In 2001–02, 10 research assistantships, 2 teaching assistantships were awarded. Financial award application deadline: 3/1.
Colleen I. Murray, Graduate Program Director, 775-784-6490, *E-mail:* cimurray@scs.unr.edu.

■ **THE UNIVERSITY OF NORTH CAROLINA AT GREENSBORO**

**Graduate School, School of Human Environmental Sciences, Department of Human Development and Family Studies, Greensboro, NC 27412-5001**
**AWARDS** Human development and family studies (M Ed, MS, PhD).
**Faculty:** 14 full-time (11 women), 1 part-time/adjunct (0 women).
**Students:** 20 full-time (15 women), 26 part-time (25 women); includes 11 minority (10 African Americans, 1 Native American), 4 international. 35 applicants, 46% accepted, 14 enrolled. In 2001, 10 master's, 3 doctorates awarded.
**Degree requirements:** For master's, one foreign language; for doctorate, one foreign language, thesis/dissertation.
**Entrance requirements:** For master's and doctorate, GRE General Test, TOEFL. *Application deadline:* For fall admission, 3/15. *Application fee:* $35.
**Expenses:** Contact institution.
**Financial support:** In 2001–02, 3 fellowships with full tuition reimbursements (averaging $4,666 per year), 29 research assistantships with full tuition reimbursements (averaging $9,767 per year), 4 teaching assistantships with full tuition

*The University of North Carolina at Greensboro (continued)*
reimbursements (averaging $8,000 per year) were awarded. Career-related internships or fieldwork, Federal Work-Study, scholarships/grants, traineeships, and unspecified assistantships also available. Support available to part-time students.
**Faculty research:** Adolescent mothers, multihandicapped, older adults.
Dr. David Demo, Chair, 336-334-5307, *Fax:* 336-334-5076, *E-mail:* dhdemo@office.uncg.edu.
**Application contact:** Dr. James Lynch, Director of Graduate Recruitment and Information Services, 336-334-4881, *Fax:* 336-334-4424. *Web site:* http://www.uncg.edu/hdf/

### ■ UNIVERSITY OF NORTH TEXAS
**Robert B. Toulouse School of Graduate Studies, College of Education, Department of Counseling, Development and Higher Education, Program in Development and Family Studies, Denton, TX 76203**

**AWARDS** MS. Evening/weekend programs available.

**Students:** 27.
**Degree requirements:** For master's, thesis optional.
**Entrance requirements:** For master's, GRE General Test. *Application deadline:* For fall admission, 7/17. *Application fee:* $25 ($50 for international students).
**Expenses:** Tuition, state resident: part-time $186 per hour. Tuition, nonresident: part-time $319 per hour. Required fees: $88; $21 per hour.
**Financial support:** Teaching assistantships, career-related internships or fieldwork, Federal Work-Study, and institutionally sponsored loans available. Financial award application deadline: 4/1.
**Application contact:** Arminta Jacobson, Adviser, 940-565-2910.

### ■ UNIVERSITY OF PENNSYLVANIA
**Graduate School of Education, Division of Psychology in Education, Interdisciplinary Studies in Human Development, Philadelphia, PA 19104**

**AWARDS** MS Ed, PhD. Part-time programs available. Terminal master's awarded for partial completion of doctoral program.

**Degree requirements:** For master's, exam; for doctorate, thesis/dissertation, exam.
**Entrance requirements:** For master's, GRE General Test; for doctorate, GRE General Test, GRE Subject Test. Electronic applications accepted.

**Expenses:** Tuition: Part-time $12,875 per semester.
**Faculty research:** Child development, risk and resilience among vulnerable youth in high-risk environments.

### ■ UNIVERSITY OF PITTSBURGH
**School of Education, Department of Psychology in Education, Program in Child Development, Pittsburgh, PA 15260**

**AWARDS** MS. Part-time and evening/weekend programs available.

**Students:** 12 full-time (11 women), 26 part-time (22 women); includes 6 minority (5 African Americans, 1 Asian American or Pacific Islander), 2 international. 29 applicants, 100% accepted, 26 enrolled. In 2001, 11 degrees awarded.
**Degree requirements:** For master's, thesis.
**Entrance requirements:** For master's, TOEFL. *Application deadline:* For fall admission, 2/1. *Application fee:* $40. Electronic applications accepted.
**Expenses:** Tuition, state resident: full-time $9,410; part-time $385 per credit. Tuition, nonresident: full-time $19,376; part-time $797 per credit. Required fees: $480; $90 per term. Tuition and fees vary according to program.
**Financial support:** Tuition waivers (partial) available. Support available to part-time students. Financial award applicants required to submit FAFSA.
**Application contact:** Jackie Harden, Manager, 412-648-2230, *Fax:* 412-648-1899, *E-mail:* soeinfo@pitt.edu. *Web site:* http://www.education.pitt.edu/programs/childdev/

### ■ UNIVERSITY OF ST. THOMAS
**Graduate Studies, School of Education, Program in Organization Learning and Development, St. Paul, MN 55105-1096**

**AWARDS** MA, Ed D, Certificate. Part-time and evening/weekend programs available.

**Faculty:** 3 full-time (1 woman), 3 part-time/adjunct (0 women).
**Students:** 2 full-time (both women), 85 part-time (66 women); includes 2 minority (both Hispanic Americans), 2 international. Average age 39. 14 applicants, 93% accepted. In 2001, 22 master's, 1 other advanced degree awarded.
**Degree requirements:** For master's, thesis (for some programs), registration; for doctorate, thesis/dissertation, registration.
**Entrance requirements:** For master's, minimum GPA of 3.0 or MAT; for doctorate, MAT, minimum GPA of 3.00, MA degree required; for Certificate, minimum

graduate GPA of 3.25. *Application deadline:* For fall admission, 6/1 (priority date); for spring admission, 11/1 (priority date). Applications are processed on a rolling basis. *Application fee:* $50.
**Expenses:** Tuition: Part-time $401 per credit. Tuition and fees vary according to degree level and program.
**Financial support:** In 2001–02, 21 students received support; fellowships, research assistantships, institutionally sponsored loans and scholarships/grants available. Support available to part-time students. Financial award application deadline: 4/1; financial award applicants required to submit FAFSA.
**Faculty research:** Leadership development, international organizational development, organizational aesthetics, organizational career development, intellectual capital.
Dr. Nick Nissley, Department Chair, *Fax:* 651-962-4169, *E-mail:* nnissley@stthomas.edu.
**Application contact:** Patricia L. Helland, Department Assistant, 651-962-4980, *Fax:* 651-962-4169, *E-mail:* plhelland@stthomas.edu.

### ■ THE UNIVERSITY OF TEXAS AT AUSTIN
**Graduate School, College of Education, Department of Educational Psychology, Austin, TX 78712-1111**

**AWARDS** Academic educational psychology (M Ed, MA); counseling education (M Ed); counseling psychology (PhD); human development and education (PhD); learning cognition and instruction (PhD); quantitative methods (PhD); school psychology (PhD).

**Faculty:** 30 full-time (16 women), 17 part-time/adjunct (8 women).
**Students:** 233 full-time (191 women), 55 part-time (44 women); includes 52 minority (13 African Americans, 8 Asian Americans or Pacific Islanders, 29 Hispanic Americans, 2 Native Americans), 36 international. Average age 29. 292 applicants, 47% accepted, 70 enrolled. In 2001, 20 master's, 38 doctorates awarded.
**Degree requirements:** For master's, thesis optional; for doctorate, thesis/dissertation.
**Entrance requirements:** For master's and doctorate, GRE General Test, 3 letters of recommendation. *Application deadline:* For fall admission, 1/15 (priority date); for winter admission, 3/1 (priority date); for spring admission, 10/1 (priority date). Applications are processed on a rolling basis. *Application fee:* $50 ($75 for international students).

**Expenses:** Tuition, state resident: full-time $3,159. Tuition, nonresident: full-time $6,957. Tuition and fees vary according to program.

**Financial support:** In 2001–02, 21 fellowships with full and partial tuition reimbursements (averaging $1,700 per year), 33 research assistantships (averaging $4,500 per year), 116 teaching assistantships (averaging $4,250 per year) were awarded. Career-related internships or fieldwork, Federal Work-Study, institutionally sponsored loans, scholarships/grants, tuition waivers (full and partial), and unspecified assistantships also available. Financial award application deadline: 1/15. Dr. Edmund T. Emmer, Department Chair, 512-471-4155 Ext. 22, *Fax:* 512-471-1288, *E-mail:* emmer@mail.utexas.edu. **Application contact:** Dr. Cindy I. Carlson, Graduate Adviser, 512-471-4155 Ext. 24, *Fax:* 512-471-1288, *E-mail:* cindy.carlson@mail.utexas.edu. *Web site:* http://www.edb.utexas.edu/coe/depts/edp/edp.html

### ■ THE UNIVERSITY OF TEXAS AT DALLAS

**School of Human Development, Program in Human Development and Communication Sciences, Richardson, TX 75083-0688**

**AWARDS** PhD. Part-time and evening/weekend programs available.

**Faculty:** 19 full-time (10 women), 8 part-time/adjunct (6 women).

**Students:** 37 full-time (26 women), 23 part-time (17 women); includes 8 minority (3 African Americans, 4 Asian Americans or Pacific Islanders, 1 Hispanic American), 9 international. Average age 34. In 2001, 6 degrees awarded.

**Degree requirements:** For doctorate, thesis/dissertation.

**Entrance requirements:** For doctorate, GRE General Test, TOEFL, minimum GPA of 3.0 in upper-level course work in field. *Application deadline:* For fall admission, 7/15; for spring admission, 11/15. Applications are processed on a rolling basis. *Application fee:* $25 ($75 for international students). Electronic applications accepted.

**Expenses:** Tuition, state resident: full-time $1,440; part-time $84 per credit. Tuition, nonresident: full-time $5,310; part-time $295 per credit. Required fees: $1,835; $87 per credit. $138 per term.

**Financial support:** In 2001–02, 10 research assistantships with tuition reimbursements (averaging $5,000 per year), 29 teaching assistantships with tuition reimbursements (averaging $4,776 per year) were awarded. Fellowships,

Federal Work-Study also available. Support available to part-time students. Financial award application deadline: 4/30; financial award applicants required to submit FAFSA.

**Faculty research:** Speech perception, auditory processing, language acquisition by young children, language development. Dr. Robert D. Stillman, Head, 972-883-3106, *Fax:* 972-883-3022, *E-mail:* stillman@utdallas.edu. *Web site:* http://www.utdallas.edu/dept/hd/

### ■ THE UNIVERSITY OF TEXAS AT DALLAS

**School of Human Development, Program in Human Development and Early Childhood Disorders, Richardson, TX 75083-0688**

**AWARDS** MS. Part-time and evening/weekend programs available.

**Faculty:** 11 full-time (7 women), 4 part-time/adjunct (2 women).

**Students:** 17 full-time (15 women), 11 part-time (10 women); includes 5 minority (1 African American, 1 Asian American or Pacific Islander, 3 Hispanic Americans), 4 international. Average age 26. 17 applicants, 47% accepted. In 2001, 6 degrees awarded.

**Degree requirements:** For master's, directed project or internship.

**Entrance requirements:** For master's, GRE General Test, TOEFL, minimum GPA of 3.0 in upper-level course work. *Application deadline:* For fall admission, 7/15; for spring admission, 11/15. Applications are processed on a rolling basis. *Application fee:* $25 ($75 for international students). Electronic applications accepted.

**Expenses:** Tuition, state resident: full-time $1,440; part-time $84 per credit. Tuition, nonresident: full-time $5,310; part-time $295 per credit. Required fees: $1,835; $87 per credit. $138 per term.

**Financial support:** In 2001–02, 4 research assistantships with tuition reimbursements (averaging $5,850 per year), 4 teaching assistantships with tuition reimbursements (averaging $4,428 per year) were awarded. Fellowships, Federal Work-Study also available. Support available to part-time students. Financial award application deadline: 4/30; financial award applicants required to submit FAFSA.

**Faculty research:** Social competence in normal and hyperactive youth, preschool number development, social-emotional development, family and peer relationships. Dr. Margaret Tresch Owen, Associate Dean and College Master, 972-883-0000, *Fax:* 972-883-2491, *E-mail:* mowen@utdallas.edu.

**Application contact:** Dr. Robert D. Stillman, Head, 972-883-3106, *Fax:* 972-883-3022, *E-mail:* stillman@utdallas.edu. *Web site:* http://www.utdallas.edu/dept/hd/

### ■ UNIVERSITY OF WASHINGTON

**Graduate School, College of Education, Program in Educational Psychology, Seattle, WA 98195**

**AWARDS** Human development and cognition (M Ed, PhD); measurement and research (M Ed, PhD); school counseling (M Ed, PhD); school psychology (M Ed, PhD).

**Degree requirements:** For master's, thesis optional; for doctorate, thesis/dissertation.

**Entrance requirements:** For master's and doctorate, GRE General Test, TOEFL, minimum GPA of 3.0.

**Expenses:** Tuition, state resident: full-time $5,539. Tuition, nonresident: full-time $14,376. Required fees: $390. Tuition and fees vary according to course load and program.

### ■ UNIVERSITY OF WISCONSIN–MADISON

**Graduate School, School of Human Ecology, Program in Human Development and Family Studies, Madison, WI 53706-1380**

**AWARDS** MS, PhD.

**Faculty:** 12 full-time (8 women), 4 part-time/adjunct (1 woman).

**Students:** 40 full-time (34 women), 4 part-time (all women); includes 6 minority (3 Asian Americans or Pacific Islanders, 3 Hispanic Americans), 10 international. Average age 32. 48 applicants, 48% accepted, 7 enrolled. In 2001, 3 master's, 4 doctorates awarded.

**Degree requirements:** For master's and doctorate, thesis/dissertation.

**Entrance requirements:** For master's and doctorate, GRE General Test, TOEFL. *Application deadline:* For fall admission, 1/15 (priority date). Applications are processed on a rolling basis. *Application fee:* $45. Electronic applications accepted.

**Expenses:** Tuition, state resident: full-time $7,361; part-time $399 per credit. Tuition, nonresident: full-time $20,499; part-time $1,282 per credit. Required fees: $34 per credit. Full-time tuition and fees vary according to course load, program, reciprocity agreements and student level.

**Financial support:** In 2001–02, 17 students received support, including 1 fellowship with full tuition reimbursement available, 2 research assistantships with full tuition reimbursements available, 14 teaching assistantships with full tuition reimbursements available; institutionally sponsored loans, scholarships/grants, and

*University of Wisconsin–Madison (continued)*

unspecified assistantships also available. Financial award application deadline: 1/15. **Faculty research:** Human development, adolescence, adulthood, prevention, intervention, marital relationships, infancy, family policy, life span, poverty. William Aquilino, Chair, 608-263-2381, *Fax:* 608-265-1172.

**Application contact:** Jane A. Weier, Program Assistant, 608-263-2381, *Fax:* 608-265-1172, *E-mail:* jaweier@facstaff.wisc.edu. *Web site:* http://sohe.wisc.edu/cfs/

■ **UTAH STATE UNIVERSITY**

**School of Graduate Studies, College of Family Life, Department of Family and Human Development, Logan, UT 84322**

AWARDS Family and human development (MFHD, MS); marriage and family therapy (MS). Part-time programs available.

**Faculty:** 13 full-time (7 women). **Students:** 21 full-time (14 women), 20 part-time (15 women); includes 2 minority (both Hispanic Americans), 2 international. 40 applicants, 25% accepted. In 2001, 9 degrees awarded. **Degree requirements:** For master's, thesis, registration. **Entrance requirements:** For master's, GRE General Test or MAT, TOEFL, minimum GPA of 3.0. *Application deadline:* For fall admission, 1/15 (priority date). Applications are processed on a rolling basis. *Application fee:* $40. **Expenses:** Tuition, state resident: full-time $1,693. Tuition, nonresident: full-time $4,233. Required fees: $501. Tuition and fees vary according to program. **Financial support:** In 2001–02, 23 students received support, including 2 fellowships (averaging $500 per year), 3 research assistantships with partial tuition reimbursements available (averaging $6,933 per year), 18 teaching assistantships with partial tuition reimbursements available (averaging $4,400 per year); Federal Work-Study, institutionally sponsored loans, scholarships/grants, and tuition waivers (full and partial) also available. Financial award application deadline: 3/1. **Faculty research:** Parent-infant attachment, marriage and family relations, intergenerational relationships, adolescent problem behavior, child and adolescent development. *Total annual research expenditures:* $983,720. Shelley K. Lindauer, Interim Head, 435-797-1501, *Fax:* 435-797-3845, *E-mail:* lindauer@cc.usu.edu.

**Application contact:** Randall M. Jones, Graduate Coordinator, 435-797-1553, *Fax:* 435-797-3845, *E-mail:* rjones@cc.usu.edu. *Web site:* http://www.usu.edu/fhd/

■ **VANDERBILT UNIVERSITY**

**Graduate School, Department of Psychology and Human Development, Nashville, TN 37240-1001**

AWARDS MS, PhD.

**Faculty:** 23 full-time (12 women), 12 part-time/adjunct (2 women). **Students:** 42 full-time (30 women), 3 part-time (all women); includes 5 minority (2 African Americans, 2 Asian Americans or Pacific Islanders, 1 Hispanic American), 5 international. Average age 30. 143 applicants, 8% accepted. In 2001, 5 master's, 10 doctorates awarded. **Degree requirements:** For master's, thesis; for doctorate, thesis/dissertation, final and qualifying exams. **Entrance requirements:** For master's and doctorate, GRE General Test. *Application deadline:* For fall admission, 1/15. *Application fee:* $40. Electronic applications accepted. **Expenses:** Tuition: Full-time $28,350. **Financial support:** In 2001–02, research assistantships with full tuition reimbursements (averaging $9,450 per year), teaching assistantships with full tuition reimbursements (averaging $9,450 per year) were awarded. Fellowships, career-related internships or fieldwork, Federal Work-Study, institutionally sponsored loans, and traineeships also available. Financial award application deadline: 1/15. **Faculty research:** Applied social, clinical, community, and developmental psychology; children and families; cognition; mental retardation. *Total annual research expenditures:* $41,108. Kathleen V. Hoover-Dempsey, Chair, 615-322-8141, *Fax:* 615-343-9494, *E-mail:* kathy.hoover-dempsey@vanderbilt.edu.

**Application contact:** David Lubinski, Director of Graduate Studies, 615-322-8141, *Fax:* 615-343-9494, *E-mail:* david.lubinski@vanderbilt.edu. *Web site:* http://peabody.vanderbilt.edu/peabody/psychhum.html

■ **VANDERBILT UNIVERSITY**

**Graduate School, Program in Education and Human Development, Nashville, TN 37240-1001**

AWARDS Educational leadership (MS, PhD); policy development and program evaluation (MS, PhD); special education (MS, PhD); teaching and learning (MS, PhD). Part-time programs available.

**Faculty:** 44 full-time (16 women), 1 (woman) part-time/adjunct.

**Students:** 101 full-time (72 women), 12 part-time (10 women); includes 16 minority (10 African Americans, 3 Asian Americans or Pacific Islanders, 3 Hispanic Americans), 10 international. Average age 36. 83 applicants, 40% accepted. In 2001, 1 master's, 24 doctorates awarded. **Degree requirements:** For master's, thesis; for doctorate, thesis/dissertation, final and qualifying exams. **Entrance requirements:** For master's and doctorate, GRE General Test. *Application deadline:* For fall admission, 1/15. *Application fee:* $40. Electronic applications accepted. **Expenses:** Tuition: Full-time $28,350. **Financial support:** In 2001–02, research assistantships with full tuition reimbursements (averaging $9,450 per year), teaching assistantships with full tuition reimbursements (averaging $9,450 per year) were awarded. Fellowships, Federal Work-Study, institutionally sponsored loans, and traineeships also available. Financial award application deadline: 1/15. **Faculty research:** Teaching, curriculum, and technology; persons with disabilities; policies in education; mental health, welfare, and criminal justice. James H. Hogge, Director, 615-322-8407, *Fax:* 615-322-8501, *E-mail:* j.hogge@vanderbilt.edu. *Web site:* http://vanderbilt.edu/

■ **VANDERBILT UNIVERSITY**

**Peabody College, Department of Human and Organizational Development, Nashville, TN 37240-1001**

AWARDS Human development counseling (M Ed); human, organizational and community development (M Ed). Part-time programs available.

**Faculty:** 18 full-time (9 women), 13 part-time/adjunct (8 women). **Students:** 38 full-time (33 women), 7 part-time (5 women); includes 5 minority (all African Americans), 2 international. Average age 28. 52 applicants, 73% accepted, 27 enrolled. In 2001, 18 degrees awarded. **Degree requirements:** For master's, thesis optional. **Entrance requirements:** For master's, GRE General Test, MAT. *Application deadline:* For fall admission, 1/15 (priority date); for spring admission, 11/1 (priority date). Applications are processed on a rolling basis. *Application fee:* $40. Electronic applications accepted. **Expenses:** Tuition: Full-time $28,350. **Financial support:** In 2001–02, 25 students received support; fellowships with full and partial tuition reimbursements available, research assistantships with full

and partial tuition reimbursements available, teaching assistantships with full and partial tuition reimbursements available, Federal Work-Study, institutionally sponsored loans, scholarships/grants, tuition waivers (partial), and unspecified assistantships available. Support available to part-time students. Financial award application deadline: 5/1.
**Faculty research:** Citizen empowerment as a change and development strategy in communities, impact of managed care on child and adolescent mental health services, role of values and ethics for human service professionals, activist and constructivist theories of education to enhancing adult learning.
Joseph Cunningham, Chair, 615-322-8484, *Fax:* 615-343-2661, *E-mail:* joe.cunningham@vanderbilt.edu.
**Application contact:** Sherrie Lane, Office Assistant, 615-322-8484, *Fax:* 615-343-2661, *E-mail:* sherrie.a.lane@vanderbilt.edu.

■ **VIRGINIA POLYTECHNIC INSTITUTE AND STATE UNIVERSITY**

**Graduate School, College of Human Resources and Education, Department of Human Development, Doctoral Program in Adult Development and Aging, Blacksburg, VA 24061**

AWARDS PhD. Part-time programs available.

**Faculty:** 4 full-time (all women).
**Students:** 1 (woman) full-time, 4 part-time (all women). Average age 35. 3 applicants, 67% accepted, 0 enrolled. In 2001, 1 degree awarded.
**Degree requirements:** For doctorate, thesis/dissertation optional.
**Entrance requirements:** For doctorate, GRE General Test, TOEFL, minimum GPA of 3.5. *Application deadline:* For fall admission, 1/2 (priority date). *Application fee:* $45. Electronic applications accepted.
**Expenses:** Tuition, state resident: part-time $241 per hour. Tuition, nonresident: part-time $406 per hour. Tuition and fees vary according to program.
**Financial support:** Unspecified assistantships available. Support available to part-time students. Financial award application deadline: 3/1; financial award applicants required to submit FAFSA.
**Faculty research:** Research on healthcare, friendship, and dementia; research of older families in rural communities; agricultural experimental study of osteoporosis; study of Alzheimer's and evaluation of public guardianship; study of Virginia-area Agencies on Aging for medical disease fraud. *Total annual research expenditures:* $180,000.

**Application contact:** Katharine Ann Surface, Administrative and Program Specialist III, 540-231-6149, *Fax:* 540-231-7012, *E-mail:* ksurface@vt.edu. *Web site:* http://www.chre.vt.edu/hd/hd.html

■ **VIRGINIA POLYTECHNIC INSTITUTE AND STATE UNIVERSITY**

**Graduate School, College of Human Resources and Education, Department of Human Development, Master's Program in Adult Development and Aging, Blacksburg, VA 24061**

AWARDS MS. Part-time programs available.

**Faculty:** 6 full-time (all women).
**Students:** 6 full-time (all women). Average age 26. 6 applicants, 83% accepted, 4 enrolled.
**Degree requirements:** For master's, thesis optional.
**Entrance requirements:** For master's, GRE General Test, TOEFL, minimum GPA of 3.0. *Application deadline:* For fall admission, 1/2 (priority date). *Application fee:* $45. Electronic applications accepted.
**Expenses:** Tuition, state resident: part-time $241 per hour. Tuition, nonresident: part-time $406 per hour. Tuition and fees vary according to program.
**Financial support:** Unspecified assistantships available. Support available to part-time students. Financial award application deadline: 3/1.
**Faculty research:** Research of healthcare, friendship, and dementia; research of older families in rural communities; agricultural experimental study of osteoporosis; study of Alzheimer's and evaluation of public guardianship; study of Virginia-area Agencies on Aging for medical disease fraud. *Total annual research expenditures:* $180,000.
**Application contact:** Katharine Ann Surface, Administrative and Program Specialist III, 540-231-6149, *Fax:* 540-231-7012, *E-mail:* ksurface@vt.edu. *Web site:* http://www.chre.vt.edu/HD/hd.html

■ **WALSH UNIVERSITY**

**Graduate Programs, Program in Counseling and Human Development, North Canton, OH 44720-3396**

AWARDS MA. Part-time and evening/weekend programs available.

**Degree requirements:** For master's, internship, practicum.
**Entrance requirements:** For master's, GRE General Test, MAT, interview, minimum GPA of 2.6, writing sample.
**Faculty research:** Multicultural issues in counseling, gender issues in counseling, family issues.

■ **WASHINGTON STATE UNIVERSITY**

**Graduate School, College of Agriculture and Home Economics, Department of Human Development, Pullman, WA 99164**

AWARDS MA. Part-time programs available.

**Faculty:** 14 full-time (10 women).
**Students:** 5 full-time (all women), 3 part-time (2 women). Average age 29. 6 applicants, 83% accepted, 5 enrolled. In 2001, 3 degrees awarded.
**Degree requirements:** For master's, thesis, oral exam.
**Entrance requirements:** For master's, GRE General Test, minimum GPA of 3.0. *Application deadline:* For fall admission, 3/1 (priority date). *Application fee:* $35. Electronic applications accepted.
**Expenses:** Tuition, state resident: full-time $6,088; part-time $304 per semester. Tuition, nonresident: full-time $14,918; part-time $746 per semester. Tuition and fees vary according to program.
**Financial support:** In 2001–02, 6 teaching assistantships with partial tuition reimbursements (averaging $10,868 per year) were awarded; research assistantships with partial tuition reimbursements, Federal Work-Study, institutionally sponsored loans, tuition waivers (partial), and teaching associateships also available. Financial award application deadline: 4/1; financial award applicants required to submit FAFSA.
**Faculty research:** Family processes, social development of children, quality child care, community collaborations, parent-child relationships. *Total annual research expenditures:* $310,090.
Thomas G Power, Chair, 509-355-9540, *Fax:* 509-335-2456, *E-mail:* tompower@wsu.edu.
**Application contact:** Dr. Thomas Power, Professor, 509-335-9540, *Fax:* 509-385-2456, *E-mail:* tompower@wsu.edu. *Web site:* http://hd.wsu.edu/

■ **WAYNE STATE UNIVERSITY**

**Graduate School, College of Science, Department of Psychology, Program in Human Development, Detroit, MI 48202**

AWARDS MA.

**Students:** 9. In 2001, 2 degrees awarded.
**Entrance requirements:** For master's, GRE General Test. *Application deadline:* For fall admission, 6/15; for spring admission, 10/15. *Application fee:* $20 ($30 for international students). Electronic applications accepted.
**Expenses:** Tuition, state resident: full-time $3,764. Tuition and fees vary according to degree level and program.

*Wayne State University (continued)*
**Financial support:** Application deadline: 2/1.
**Faculty research:** Emotional expression, peer influence in adolescence, preschool concept formation and memory, mother-infant interaction.
Dr. Melissa Kaplan-Estrin, Head, 313-577-3310.
**Find an in-depth description at www.petersons.com/gradchannel.**

# INDUSTRIAL AND ORGANIZATIONAL PSYCHOLOGY

## ■ ADLER SCHOOL OF PROFESSIONAL PSYCHOLOGY

**Programs in Psychology, Chicago, IL 60601-7203**
**AWARDS** Art therapy (Certificate); clinical hypnosis (Certificate); clinical psychology (Psy D); counseling psychology (MACP); counseling psychology/art therapy (MACAT); gerontology (MAGP, Certificate); marriage and family counseling (MAMFC); marriage and family therapy (Certificate); organizational psychology (MAO); substance abuse counseling (MASAC, Certificate). Part-time and evening/weekend programs available.
**Faculty:** 19 full-time (9 women), 48 part-time/adjunct (21 women).
**Students:** 124 full-time (78 women), 284 part-time (208 women); includes 77 minority (43 African Americans, 20 Asian Americans or Pacific Islanders, 13 Hispanic Americans, 1 Native American), 8 international. Average age 39. 253 applicants, 59% accepted, 121 enrolled. In 2001, 101 master's, 29 doctorates, 5 other advanced degrees awarded. Terminal master's awarded for partial completion of doctoral program.
**Degree requirements:** For master's, thesis or alternative, oral exam, practicum; for doctorate, thesis/dissertation, clinical exam, internship, oral exam, practicum, written qualifying exam.
**Entrance requirements:** For master's, 12 semester hours in psychology, minimum GPA of 3.0; for doctorate, 18 semester hours in psychology, minimum GPA of 3.25; for Certificate, appropriate master's or doctoral degree. *Application deadline:* For fall admission, 1/1 (priority date). Applications are processed on a rolling basis. *Application fee:* $50.
**Expenses:** Tuition: Full-time $13,680; part-time $380 per credit. Required fees: $100; $15 per credit.
**Financial support:** In 2001–02, 180 students received support. Career-related

internships or fieldwork, Federal Work-Study, scholarships/grants, and tuition waivers (full and partial) available. Support available to part-time students. Financial award application deadline: 5/15; financial award applicants required to submit FAFSA.
Dr. Frank Gruba-McCallister, Dean of Academic Affairs, 312-201-5900, *Fax:* 312-201-5917.
**Application contact:** Erene Soliman, Admissions Counselor, 312-201-5900, *Fax:* 312-201-5917.
**Find an in-depth description at www.petersons.com/gradchannel.**

## ■ ALLIANT INTERNATIONAL UNIVERSITY

**California School of Organizational Studies, Program in Organizational Behavior–Fresno, Fresno, CA 93727**
**AWARDS** Organizational behavior (MOB); organizational development (Psy D). Part-time and evening/weekend programs available.
**Faculty:** 10 part-time/adjunct (4 women).
**Students:** 15 full-time (9 women), 36 part-time (19 women); includes 14 minority (4 African Americans, 6 Asian Americans or Pacific Islanders, 4 Hispanic Americans). Average age 41. 21 applicants, 95% accepted. In 2001, 14 degrees awarded.
**Degree requirements:** For master's, thesis or alternative; for doctorate, thesis/dissertation.
**Entrance requirements:** For master's and doctorate, TOEFL, interview, minimum GPA of 3.0 in both psychology and overall. *Application deadline:* Applications are processed on a rolling basis. *Application fee:* $35.
**Expenses:** Tuition: Part-time $397 per credit hour. Tuition and fees vary according to degree level, campus/location and program.
**Financial support:** In 2001–02, 20 students received support. Career-related internships or fieldwork, Federal Work-Study, institutionally sponsored loans, and scholarships/grants available. Financial award application deadline: 2/15; financial award applicants required to submit FAFSA.
**Faculty research:** Leadership, ethics and management, career development, human resources management.
Dr. Toni Knott, Director, 559-456-2777 Ext. 2262, *Fax:* 559-253-2267, *E-mail:* tknott@alliant.edu.
**Application contact:** Patricia J. Mullen, Vice President, Enrollment and Student Services, 800-457-1273 Ext. 303, *Fax:* 415-931-8322, *E-mail:* admissions@alliant.edu. *Web site:* http://www.cspp.edu/

## ■ ALLIANT INTERNATIONAL UNIVERSITY

**California School of Organizational Studies, Programs in Industrial-Organizational Psychology–San Diego, San Diego, CA 92121**
**AWARDS** Consulting psychology (PhD); industrial-organizational psychology (PhD); organizational behavior (MA); organizational psychology (MA). Part-time and evening/weekend programs available.
**Faculty:** 5 full-time (0 women), 8 part-time/adjunct (1 woman).
**Students:** 69 full-time (46 women), 47 part-time (30 women); includes 25 minority (3 African Americans, 12 Asian Americans or Pacific Islanders, 9 Hispanic Americans, 1 Native American). Average age 32. 65 applicants, 45% accepted. In 2001, 3 master's, 8 doctorates awarded. Terminal master's awarded for partial completion of doctoral program.
**Degree requirements:** For doctorate, thesis/dissertation.
**Entrance requirements:** For master's and doctorate, TOEFL, interview, minimum GPA of 3.0 in both psychology and overall. *Application deadline:* For fall admission, 2/1 (priority date).
**Expenses:** Tuition: Part-time $397 per credit hour. Tuition and fees vary according to degree level, campus/location and program.
**Financial support:** In 2001–02, 58 students received support; research assistantships, teaching assistantships, career-related internships or fieldwork, Federal Work-Study, institutionally sponsored loans, and scholarships/grants available. Financial award application deadline: 2/15; financial award applicants required to submit FAFSA.
**Faculty research:** Cultural diversity in the workplace, work motivation, personnel, professional development.
Dr. Herbert Baker, Director, 858-623-2777 Ext. 359, *Fax:* 858-552-1974, *E-mail:* hbaker@alliant.edu.
**Application contact:** Patricia J. Mullen, Vice President, Enrollment and Student Services, 800-457-1273 Ext. 303, *Fax:* 415-931-8322, *E-mail:* admissions@ mail.cspp.edu. *Web site:* http://www.alliant.edu/

## ■ ALLIANT INTERNATIONAL UNIVERSITY

**California School of Organizational Studies, Programs in Organizational Psychology–Los Angeles, Alhambra, CA 91803-1360**
**AWARDS** Executive management (Psy D); organizational behavior (MA); organizational psychology (MA, PhD).

**Faculty:** 6 full-time (2 women), 7 part-time/adjunct (3 women).
**Students:** 100 full-time (61 women), 31 part-time (17 women); includes 67 minority (12 African Americans, 37 Asian Americans or Pacific Islanders, 18 Hispanic Americans). Average age 33. 41 applicants, 56% accepted. In 2001, 18 degrees awarded. Terminal master's awarded for partial completion of doctoral program.
**Degree requirements:** For doctorate, thesis/dissertation.
**Entrance requirements:** For master's and doctorate, TOEFL, interview, minimum GPA of 3.0 in both psychology and overall.
**Expenses:** Tuition: Part-time $397 per credit hour. Tuition and fees vary according to degree level, campus/location and program.
**Financial support:** In 2001–02, 79 students received support; research assistantships, teaching assistantships, career-related internships or fieldwork, Federal Work-Study, institutionally sponsored loans, and scholarships/grants available. Financial award application deadline: 2/15; financial award applicants required to submit FAFSA.
**Faculty research:** Organizational transitions, productivity, work force demographics, family business, management technology.
Dr. Cal Hoffman, Director, 626-284-2777 Ext. 3160, *Fax:* 626-284-0550, *E-mail:* choffman@alliant.edu.
**Application contact:** Patricia J. Mullen, Vice President, Enrollment and Student Services, 800-457-1273 Ext. 303, *Fax:* 415-931-8322, *E-mail:* admissions@ mail.cspp.edu. *Web site:* http://www.alliant.edu/

■ **ALLIANT INTERNATIONAL UNIVERSITY**
**California School of Organizational Studies, Programs in Organizational Psychology–San Francisco Bay, Alameda, CA 94501**
AWARDS Change leadership (MA); organizational consulting (Psy D); organizational development (MA); organizational psychology (MA, PhD). Part-time and evening/weekend programs available.
**Faculty:** 4 full-time (2 women), 13 part-time/adjunct (6 women).
**Students:** 66 full-time (46 women), 32 part-time (20 women); includes 35 minority (12 African Americans, 16 Asian Americans or Pacific Islanders, 5 Hispanic Americans, 2 Native Americans). Average age 34. 32 applicants, 63% accepted. In 2001, 2 degrees awarded. Terminal

master's awarded for partial completion of doctoral program.
**Degree requirements:** For doctorate, thesis/dissertation.
**Entrance requirements:** For master's and doctorate, TOEFL, interview, minimum GPA of 3.0 in both psychology and overall. *Application deadline:* For fall admission, 2/1 (priority date).
**Expenses:** Tuition: Part-time $397 per credit hour. Tuition and fees vary according to degree level, campus/location and program.
**Financial support:** In 2001–02, 71 students received support; research assistantships, teaching assistantships, career-related internships or fieldwork, Federal Work-Study, institutionally sponsored loans, and scholarships/grants available. Financial award application deadline: 2/15; financial award applicants required to submit FAFSA.
**Faculty research:** Leadership, ethics and management, career development, human relations, organizational behavior.
Dr. Kathryn Goldman-Schuyler, Director, 510-814-8597 Ext. 103, *Fax:* 510-521-3678, *E-mail:* kgschuyler@alliant.edu.
**Application contact:** Patricia J. Mullen, Vice President, Enrollment and Student Services, 800-457-1273 Ext. 303, *Fax:* 415-931-8322, *E-mail:* admissions@alliant.edu. *Web site:* http://www.alliant.edu/

■ **ANGELO STATE UNIVERSITY**
**Graduate School, College of Liberal and Fine Arts, Department of Psychology and Sociology, San Angelo, TX 76909**
AWARDS Psychology (MS), including counseling psychology, general psychology, industrial and organizational psychology. Part-time and evening/weekend programs available.
**Faculty:** 7 full-time (1 woman).
**Students:** 32 full-time (26 women), 25 part-time (21 women); includes 13 minority (2 African Americans, 1 Asian American or Pacific Islander, 9 Hispanic Americans, 1 Native American). Average age 35. 36 applicants, 53% accepted, 13 enrolled. In 2001, 14 degrees awarded.
**Degree requirements:** For master's, thesis, comprehensive exam.
**Entrance requirements:** For master's, GRE General Test, minimum GPA of 2.5. *Application deadline:* For fall admission, 8/7 (priority date); for spring admission, 1/2. Applications are processed on a rolling basis. *Application fee:* $25 ($50 for international students).
**Expenses:** Tuition, area resident: Full-time $960; part-time $40 per credit hour. Tuition, nonresident: full-time $6,120;

part-time $255 per credit hour. Required fees: $1,336; $56 per credit hour.
**Financial support:** In 2001–02, 27 students received support, including 20 fellowships, 3 teaching assistantships; career-related internships or fieldwork, Federal Work-Study, tuition waivers (partial), and unspecified assistantships also available. Support available to part-time students. Financial award application deadline: 8/1.
Dr. William Davidson, Head, 915-942-2205. *Web site:* http://www.angelo.edu/dept/psychology_sociology/

■ **APPALACHIAN STATE UNIVERSITY**
**Cratis D. Williams Graduate School, College of Arts and Sciences, Department of Psychology, Program in Industrial and Organizational Psychology, Boone, NC 28608**
AWARDS MA.
**Faculty:** 24 full-time (8 women).
**Students:** 12 full-time (8 women). In 2001, 4 degrees awarded.
**Degree requirements:** For master's, GRE Subject Test exit exam, thesis optional.
**Entrance requirements:** For master's, GRE General Test, GRE Subject Test. *Application deadline:* For fall admission, 3/1 (priority date). Applications are processed on a rolling basis. *Application fee:* $35.
**Expenses:** Tuition, state resident: full-time $1,286. Tuition, nonresident: full-time $9,354. Required fees: $1,116.
**Financial support:** In 2001–02, research assistantships (averaging $6,250 per year), teaching assistantships (averaging $6,250 per year) were awarded. Fellowships, career-related internships or fieldwork also available. Support available to part-time students. Financial award application deadline: 7/1.
**Faculty research:** Organizational behavior management, performance management, employment law and labor relations, international HRM, mood and employee performance.
Dr. Timothy Ludwig, Director, 808-262-2712, *E-mail:* ludwigtd@appstate.edu. *Web site:* http://www.acs.appstate.edu/dept/psych/

■ **BERNARD M. BARUCH COLLEGE OF THE CITY UNIVERSITY OF NEW YORK**
**Zicklin School of Business, Program in Industrial and Organizational Psychology, New York, NY 10010-5585**
AWARDS MBA, MS, PhD, Certificate. Part-time and evening/weekend programs available.

*Bernard M. Baruch College of the City University of New York (continued)*
**Faculty:** 17 full-time (7 women), 5 part-time/adjunct (2 women).
**Students:** 5 full-time (all women), 24 part-time (15 women). In 2001, 12 degrees awarded.
**Degree requirements:** For master's, thesis or alternative; for doctorate, thesis/dissertation, comprehensive exam.
**Entrance requirements:** For master's and doctorate, GMAT or GRE General Test, TOEFL, TWE. *Application deadline:* For fall admission, 4/1; for spring admission, 11/1. *Application fee:* $40.
**Expenses:** Tuition, state resident: full-time $4,350; part-time $185 per credit. Tuition, nonresident: full-time $7,600; part-time $320 per credit. Tuition and fees vary according to program.
**Financial support:** Research assistantships, career-related internships or fieldwork and Federal Work-Study available. Financial award application deadline: 5/1; financial award applicants required to submit FAFSA.
**Faculty research:** Job attitudes, power and leadership in organizations, measurement issues in organizational behavior, work motivation, fair employment practices. Harold Goldstein, Head, 646-312-3820, *Fax:* 646-312-3781, *E-mail:* harold_goldstein@baruch.cuny.edu.
**Application contact:** Frances Murphy, Office of Graduate Admissions, 646-312-1300, *Fax:* 646-312-1301, *E-mail:* zicklingradadmissions@baruch.cuny.edu.

■ **BOWLING GREEN STATE UNIVERSITY**
**Graduate College, College of Arts and Sciences, Department of Psychology, Bowling Green, OH 43403**
**AWARDS** Clinical psychology (MA, PhD); developmental psychology (MA, PhD); experimental psychology (MA, PhD); industrial/organizational psychology (MA, PhD); quantitative psychology (MA, PhD).
**Faculty:** 31.
**Students:** 89 full-time (57 women), 27 part-time (18 women); includes 14 minority (3 African Americans, 7 Asian Americans or Pacific Islanders, 4 Hispanic Americans), 9 international. Average age 27. 274 applicants, 15% accepted, 24 enrolled. In 2001, 10 master's, 17 doctorates awarded. Terminal master's awarded for partial completion of doctoral program.
**Degree requirements:** For master's and doctorate, thesis/dissertation.
**Entrance requirements:** For master's and doctorate, GRE General Test, TOEFL. *Application deadline:* For fall admission, 1/15. *Application fee:* $30. Electronic applications accepted.

**Expenses:** Tuition, state resident: full-time $7,376; part-time $342 per credit hour. Tuition, nonresident: full-time $13,628; part-time $640 per credit hour.
**Financial support:** In 2001–02, 30 research assistantships with full tuition reimbursements (averaging $9,452 per year), 32 teaching assistantships with full tuition reimbursements (averaging $9,607 per year) were awarded. Career-related internships or fieldwork, Federal Work-Study, institutionally sponsored loans, tuition waivers (full), and unspecified assistantships also available. Financial award applicants required to submit FAFSA.
**Faculty research:** Personnel psychology, developmental-mathematical models, behavioral medication, brain process, child/adolescent social cognition. Dr. Dale Klopfer, Chair, 419-372-2733.
**Application contact:** Dr. Eric Dubow, Graduate Coordinator, 419-372-2556.

■ **BROOKLYN COLLEGE OF THE CITY UNIVERSITY OF NEW YORK**
**Division of Graduate Studies, Department of Psychology, Brooklyn, NY 11210-2889**
**AWARDS** Experimental psychology (MA); industrial and organizational psychology (MA), including industrial and organizational psychology-human relations, psychology-organizational psychology and behavior; psychology (PhD). Part-time programs available.
**Students:** 7 full-time (4 women), 87 part-time (63 women); includes 40 minority (24 African Americans, 5 Asian Americans or Pacific Islanders, 11 Hispanic Americans), 11 international. 104 applicants, 59% accepted. In 2001, 47 degrees awarded.
**Degree requirements:** For master's, thesis or alternative, comprehensive exam.
**Entrance requirements:** For master's, TOEFL, minimum GPA of 3.0; for doctorate, GRE. *Application deadline:* For fall admission, 3/1 (priority date); for spring admission, 11/1. Applications are processed on a rolling basis. *Application fee:* $40.
**Expenses:** Tuition, state resident: full-time $4,350; part-time $185 per credit. Tuition, nonresident: full-time $7,600; part-time $320 per credit.
**Financial support:** Career-related internships or fieldwork, Federal Work-Study, institutionally sponsored loans, scholarships/grants, and tuition waivers (partial) available. Support available to part-time students. Financial award application deadline: 5/1; financial award applicants required to submit FAFSA.
Dr. Glen Hass, Chairperson, 718-951-5601, *Fax:* 718-951-4814.

**Application contact:** Dr. Benzion Chanowitz, Graduate Deputy, 718-951-5019, *Fax:* 718-951-4814, *E-mail:* psychma@brooklyn.cuny.edu. *Web site:* http://academic.brooklyn.cuny.edu/psych

■ **CALIFORNIA STATE UNIVERSITY, SAN BERNARDINO**
**Graduate Studies, College of Social and Behavioral Sciences, Department of Psychology, Program in Industrial Organizational Psychology, San Bernardino, CA 92407-2397**
**AWARDS** MS.
**Students:** 25 full-time (16 women), 4 part-time (2 women); includes 8 minority (1 African American, 4 Asian Americans or Pacific Islanders, 3 Hispanic Americans), 2 international. Average age 29. 42 applicants, 33% accepted. In 2001, 9 degrees awarded.
**Degree requirements:** For master's, thesis (for some programs).
**Entrance requirements:** For master's, minimum GPA of 3.0 in major. *Application deadline:* For fall admission, 8/31 (priority date). *Application fee:* $55.
**Expenses:** Tuition, nonresident: full-time $4,428. Required fees: $1,733.
Dr. Janelle Gilbert, Head, 909-880-5587, *Fax:* 909-880-7003, *E-mail:* janelle@csusb.edu.
**Application contact:** Luci Van Loon, Graduate Secretary, 909-880-5570, *Fax:* 909-880-7003, *E-mail:* lvanloon@csusb.edu.

■ **CARLOS ALBIZU UNIVERSITY**
**Graduate Programs in Psychology, San Juan, PR 00902-3711**
**AWARDS** Clinical psychology (PhD, Psy D); general psychology (PhD); industrial/organizational psychology (MS, PhD). Part-time and evening/weekend programs available.
**Degree requirements:** For master's, one foreign language, comprehensive exam; for doctorate, one foreign language, thesis/dissertation, written qualifying exams.
**Entrance requirements:** For master's, GRE General Test or PAEG, interview, minimum GPA of 3.0; for doctorate, PAEG, interview, minimum GPA of 3.0.
**Faculty research:** Psychotherapeutic techniques for Hispanics, psychology of the aged, school dropouts, stress, violence.

■ **CARLOS ALBIZU UNIVERSITY, MIAMI CAMPUS**
**Graduate Programs, Miami, FL 33172-2209**
**AWARDS** Clinical psychology (Psy D); industrial/organizational psychology (MS);

management (MBA); marriage and family therapy (MS); mental health counseling (MS); psychology (MS); school counseling (MS). Part-time and evening/weekend programs available.

**Faculty:** 19 full-time (9 women), 37 part-time/adjunct (19 women).

**Students:** 432 full-time (322 women), 32 part-time (22 women); includes 328 minority (58 African Americans, 7 Asian Americans or Pacific Islanders, 263 Hispanic Americans), 4 international. Average age 35. 189 applicants, 50% accepted, 69 enrolled. In 2001, 44 master's, 69 doctorates awarded. Terminal master's awarded for partial completion of doctoral program.

**Degree requirements:** For master's, one foreign language, comprehensive exam, integrative project (MBA); for doctorate, one foreign language, thesis/dissertation, written and oral qualifying exam, internship.

**Entrance requirements:** For master's, GMAT (MBA), letters of recommendation (3), interview, minimum GPA of 3.0, resumé; for doctorate, GRE General Test, GRE Subject Test, letters of recommendation (3), minimum GPA of 3.0. *Application deadline:* For fall admission, 8/1 (priority date); for spring admission, 11/30 (priority date). Applications are processed on a rolling basis. *Application fee:* $50.

**Expenses:** Tuition: Part-time $455 per credit. Required fees: $819; $273 per term. Tuition and fees vary according to course load and degree level.

**Financial support:** In 2001–02, 22 students received support. Federal Work-Study and scholarships/grants available. Financial award application deadline: 6/1; financial award applicants required to submit FAFSA.

**Faculty research:** Culture, psychodiagnostics, psychotherapy, forensic psychology, neuropsychology; marketing strategy, entrepreneurship.

Dr. Gerardo F. Rodriquez-Menedez, Chancellor, 305-593-1223 Ext. 120, *Fax:* 305-629-8052, *E-mail:* grodriguez@albizu.edu.

**Application contact:** Miriam Matos, Admissions Officer, 305-593-1223 Ext. 134, *Fax:* 305-593-1854, *E-mail:* mmatos@albizu.edu. *Web site:* http://www.albizu.edu/

### ■ CENTRAL MICHIGAN UNIVERSITY

College of Graduate Studies, College of Humanities and Social and Behavioral Sciences, Department of Psychology, Program in Industrial/Organizational Psychology, Mount Pleasant, MI 48859

**AWARDS** MA, PhD.

**Degree requirements:** For master's and doctorate, thesis/dissertation or alternative.

**Entrance requirements:** For master's and doctorate, GRE.

**Expenses:** Tuition, state resident: part-time $182 per unit. Tuition, nonresident: part-time $182 per unit. Required fees: $208 per semester. Part-time tuition and fees vary according to course load.

**Faculty research:** Work stress, personnel selection.

### ■ CENTRAL WASHINGTON UNIVERSITY

Graduate Studies and Research, College of the Sciences, Department of Psychology, Program in Organizational Development, Ellensburg, WA 98926-7463

**AWARDS** MS. Evening/weekend programs available.

**Faculty:** 23 full-time (9 women).

**Students:** 30 full-time (16 women), 3 part-time (2 women); includes 4 minority (3 African Americans, 1 Hispanic American). 24 applicants, 63% accepted, 12 enrolled. In 2001, 13 degrees awarded.

**Degree requirements:** For master's, thesis or alternative.

**Entrance requirements:** For master's, GRE General Test, minimum GPA of 3.0. *Application deadline:* For fall admission, 4/1. *Application fee:* $35.

**Expenses:** Tuition, state resident: full-time $4,848; part-time $162 per credit. Tuition, nonresident: full-time $14,772; part-time $492 per credit. Required fees: $324.

**Financial support:** In 2001–02, 1 research assistantship with partial tuition reimbursement (averaging $7,120 per year) was awarded; Federal Work-Study also available. Financial award application deadline: 3/1; financial award applicants required to submit FAFSA.

**Application contact:** Barbara Sisko, Office Assistant, Graduate Studies and Research, 509-963-3103, *Fax:* 509-963-1799, *E-mail:* masters@cwu.edu. *Web site:* http://www.cwu.edu/

### ■ CHICAGO SCHOOL OF PROFESSIONAL PSYCHOLOGY

Graduate School, Chicago, IL 60605-2024

**AWARDS** Clinical psychology (Psy D); forensic psychology (MA); industrial and organizational psychology (MA). Part-time programs available.

**Faculty:** 19 full-time (10 women), 43 part-time/adjunct (25 women).

**Students:** 216 full-time (162 women), 157 part-time (114 women); includes 75 minority (38 African Americans, 16 Asian Americans or Pacific Islanders, 21

Hispanic Americans), 25 international. Average age 25. 215 applicants, 74% accepted, 70 enrolled. In 2001, 48 degrees awarded.

**Degree requirements:** For doctorate, thesis/dissertation, competency exam, internship, practica.

**Entrance requirements:** For master's, 18 undergraduate hours in psychology, course work in statistics; for doctorate, GRE General Test or other graduate entrance exam, 18 hours in psychology (1 course each in statistics, abnormal psychology, and theories of personality). *Application deadline:* For fall admission, 1/15 (priority date); for spring admission, 11/1 (priority date). Applications are processed on a rolling basis. *Application fee:* $50.

**Expenses:** Tuition: Part-time $550 per credit hour. Required fees: $350 per year. Tuition and fees vary according to degree level and program.

**Financial support:** In 2001–02, 16 research assistantships with partial tuition reimbursements, 32 teaching assistantships with partial tuition reimbursements were awarded. Career-related internships or fieldwork, Federal Work-Study, scholarships/grants, and tuition waivers (partial) also available. Support available to part-time students. Financial award application deadline: 5/1; financial award applicants required to submit FAFSA.

**Faculty research:** White racial identity, work with cross-cultural clients, teaching in psychology.

Dr. Michael Horowitz, President, 312-786-9443 Ext. 3033, *Fax:* 312-322-3273, *E-mail:* mhorowitz@csopp.edu.

**Application contact:** Magdelen Kellogg, Director of Admission, 312-786-9443 Ext. 3029, *Fax:* 312-322-3273, *E-mail:* mkellogg@csopp.edu. *Web site:* http://www.csopp.edu/

**Find an in-depth description at www.petersons.com/gradchannel.**

### ■ CHRISTOPHER NEWPORT UNIVERSITY

Graduate Studies, Department of Psychology, Newport News, VA 23606-2998

**AWARDS** Applied psychology (MS), including industrial/organizational psychology. Part-time and evening/weekend programs available.

**Faculty:** 6 full-time (3 women).

**Students:** 14 full-time (11 women), 16 part-time (10 women); includes 8 minority (6 African Americans, 1 Asian American or Pacific Islander, 1 Hispanic American). Average age 32. 11 applicants, 100% accepted. In 2001, 8 degrees awarded.

**Degree requirements:** For master's, thesis, comprehensive exam.

*Christopher Newport University (continued)*

**Entrance requirements:** For master's, GRE General Test, GRE Subject Test, minimum GPA of 3.0. *Application deadline:* For fall admission, 7/1 (priority date); for spring admission, 11/15. Applications are processed on a rolling basis. *Application fee:* $40.

**Expenses:** Tuition, state resident: full-time $1,782; part-time $99 per credit. Tuition, nonresident: full-time $6,138; part-time $341 per credit. Required fees: $49 per credit hour. $20 per term.

**Financial support:** In 2001–02, 3 research assistantships with full and partial tuition reimbursements (averaging $1,700 per year) were awarded; career-related internships or fieldwork, Federal Work-Study, institutionally sponsored loans, and scholarships/grants also available. Support available to part-time students. Financial award application deadline: 3/1; financial award applicants required to submit FAFSA.

**Faculty research:** Organizational development, affirmative action attitudes, organizational justice, service organizations, organizational environment, occupational stereotyping.

Dr. Thomas Berry, Coordinator, 757-594-7934, *Fax:* 757-594-7342, *E-mail:* berry@cnu.edu.

**Application contact:** Susan R. Chittenden, Graduate Admissions, 757-594-7359, *Fax:* 757-594-7333, *E-mail:* gradstdy@cnu.edu. *Web site:* http://www.cnu.edu/

# ■ CLAREMONT GRADUATE UNIVERSITY

**Graduate Programs, School of Behavioral and Organizational Sciences, Department of Psychology, Claremont, CA 91711-6160**

**AWARDS** Cognitive psychology (MA, PhD); developmental psychology (MA, PhD); organizational behavior (MA, PhD); program design, management, and evaluation (MA); social environmental psychology (PhD); social psychology (MA). Part-time programs available.

**Faculty:** 6 full-time (2 women), 7 part-time/adjunct (6 women).

**Students:** 127 full-time (93 women), 23 part-time (19 women); includes 48 minority (8 African Americans, 23 Asian Americans or Pacific Islanders, 15 Hispanic Americans, 2 Native Americans), 9 international. Average age 30. In 2001, 25 master's, 16 doctorates awarded. Terminal master's awarded for partial completion of doctoral program.

**Degree requirements:** For master's, thesis (for some programs); for doctorate, thesis/dissertation, comprehensive exam.

**Entrance requirements:** For master's and doctorate, GRE General Test. *Application deadline:* For fall admission, 2/15 (priority date). Applications are processed on a rolling basis. *Application fee:* $50. Electronic applications accepted.

**Expenses:** Tuition: Full-time $22,984; part-time $1,000 per unit. Required fees: $160; $80 per semester.

**Financial support:** Fellowships, research assistantships, teaching assistantships, career-related internships or fieldwork, Federal Work-Study, institutionally sponsored loans, and tuition waivers (full and partial) available. Support available to part-time students. Financial award application deadline: 2/15; financial award applicants required to submit FAFSA.

**Faculty research:** Social intervention, diversity in organizations, eyewitness memory, aging and cognition, drug policy.

**Application contact:** Jessica Johnson, Program Coordinator, 909-621-8084, *Fax:* 909-621-8905, *E-mail:* jessica.johnson@cgu.edu. *Web site:* http://www.cgu.edu/sbus

**Find an in-depth description at www.petersons.com/gradchannel.**

# ■ CLEMSON UNIVERSITY

**Graduate School, College of Business and Behavioral Science, Department of Psychology, Program in Industrial/Organizational Psychology, Clemson, SC 29634**

**AWARDS** PhD.

**Students:** 11 full-time (4 women), 5 part-time (2 women); includes 1 minority (African American). 100 applicants, 5% accepted, 3 enrolled.

**Degree requirements:** For doctorate, thesis/dissertation.

**Entrance requirements:** For doctorate, GRE General Test, TOEFL. *Application deadline:* For fall admission, 3/15. *Application fee:* $40.

**Expenses:** Tuition, state resident: full-time $5,310. Tuition, nonresident: full-time $11,284.

**Financial support:** Application deadline: 3/15; *Web site:* http://hubcap.clemson.edu/psych/gradprog.htm

# ■ CLEVELAND STATE UNIVERSITY

**College of Graduate Studies, College of Arts and Sciences, Department of Psychology, Program in Consumer/Industrial Research, Cleveland, OH 44115**

**AWARDS** MA.

**Faculty:** 17 full-time (6 women), 4 part-time/adjunct (1 woman).

**Students:** 12 full-time (8 women), 8 part-time (6 women). Average age 24. 27 applicants, 41% accepted, 10 enrolled. In 2001, 4 degrees awarded.

**Degree requirements:** For master's, thesis optional. *Median time to degree:* Master's–2 years full-time.

**Entrance requirements:** For master's, GRE General Test, GRE Subject Test. *Application deadline:* For fall admission, 7/15. Applications are processed on a rolling basis. *Application fee:* $25 ($50 for international students).

**Expenses:** Tuition, state resident: full-time $6,838; part-time $263 per credit hour. Tuition, nonresident: full-time $13,526; part-time $520 per credit hour.

**Financial support:** In 2001–02, 9 students received support. Federal Work-Study and tuition waivers (full) available. Financial award application deadline: 5/1; financial award applicants required to submit FAFSA.

Dr. Brian Blake, Head, 216-687-2531.

**Application contact:** Karen Colston, Administrative Coordinator, 216-687-2552, *E-mail:* k.colston@csuohio.edu.

# ■ COLORADO STATE UNIVERSITY

**Graduate School, College of Natural Sciences, Department of Psychology, Fort Collins, CO 80523-0015**

**AWARDS** Applied social psychology (PhD); behavioral neuroscience (PhD); cognitive psychology (PhD); counseling psychology (PhD); industrial-organizational psychology (PhD).

**Faculty:** 29 full-time (8 women), 13 part-time/adjunct (7 women).

**Students:** 56 full-time (42 women), 37 part-time (29 women). Average age 29. 309 applicants, 12% accepted, 16 enrolled. In 2001, 9 doctorates awarded.

**Degree requirements:** For doctorate, thesis/dissertation.

**Entrance requirements:** For doctorate, GRE General Test, GRE Subject Test, TOEFL, minimum GPA of 3.5. *Application deadline:* For fall admission, 1/15. *Application fee:* $30. Electronic applications accepted.

**Expenses:** Tuition, state resident: full-time $2,880; part-time $160 per credit. Tuition, nonresident: full-time $11,412; part-time $634 per credit. Required fees: $750; $34 per credit.

**Financial support:** In 2001–02, 3 fellowships with full tuition reimbursements (averaging $12,120 per year), 10 research assistantships with full tuition reimbursements (averaging $9,720 per year), 52 teaching assistantships with full tuition

reimbursements (averaging $9,720 per year) were awarded. Career-related internships or fieldwork, Federal Work-Study, institutionally sponsored loans, scholarships/grants, and traineeships also available.

**Faculty research:** Environmental psychology, cognitive learning, health psychology, occupations of health. *Total annual research expenditures:* $12.5 million.

Ernest L. Chavez, Chair, 970-491-6363, *Fax:* 970-491-1032, *E-mail:* echavez@lamar.colostate.edu.

**Application contact:** Wendy Standring, Graduate Admissions Coordinator, 970-491-6363, *Fax:* 970-491-1032, *E-mail:* wendyann@lamar.colostate.edu. *Web site:* http://www.colostate.edu/Depts/Psychology/

# ■ DEPAUL UNIVERSITY

**College of Liberal Arts and Sciences, Department of Psychology, Program in Industrial/Organizational Psychology, Chicago, IL 60604-2287**

AWARDS MA, PhD.

**Faculty:** 8 full-time (3 women), 2 part-time/adjunct (both women).

**Students:** 12 full-time (7 women), 10 part-time (5 women); includes 2 minority (1 African American, 1 Asian American or Pacific Islander), 1 international. Average age 27. 64 applicants, 5% accepted. In 2001, 3 degrees awarded.

**Degree requirements:** For master's, thesis/dissertation, oral and written exams; for doctorate, thesis/dissertation, oral and written exams, comprehensive exam.

**Entrance requirements:** For master's, GRE General Test and subject test, minimum GPA of 3.5, 8 courses in psychology; for doctorate, GRE General Test and subject test, 24 hours or 32 quarter hours in psychology, minimum GPA of 3.5. *Application deadline:* For fall admission, 1/31. *Application fee:* $40. Electronic applications accepted.

**Expenses:** Tuition: Part-time $362 per credit hour. Tuition and fees vary according to program.

**Financial support:** In 2001–02, 12 students received support, including 7 research assistantships with full and partial tuition reimbursements available (averaging $5,500 per year), 5 teaching assistantships with full and partial tuition reimbursements available (averaging $5,500 per year); career-related internships or fieldwork, traineeships, tuition waivers (full and partial), and unspecified assistantships also available.

**Faculty research:** Cognitive theories of work motivation, job design, not-for-profit organizations, decision and conflict in workplace.

Dr. Jane Halpert, Director, 773-325-4265, *E-mail:* jhalpert@depaul.edu.

**Application contact:** Lucinda Rapp, Information Contact, 773-325-7887, *E-mail:* lrapp@depaul.edu. *Web site:* http://condor.depaul.edu/~psych/

# ■ EASTERN KENTUCKY UNIVERSITY

**The Graduate School, College of Arts and Sciences, Department of Psychology, Richmond, KY 40475-3102**

AWARDS Clinical psychology (MS); industrial/organizational psychology (MS); school psychology (Psy S). Part-time programs available.

**Faculty:** 21 full-time (10 women).

**Students:** 66 full-time (58 women), 4 part-time (2 women); includes 4 minority (3 African Americans, 1 Hispanic American). Average age 24. 303 applicants, 30% accepted. In 2001, 20 degrees awarded.

**Entrance requirements:** For master's and Psy S, GRE General Test, minimum GPA of 2.5. *Application deadline:* For fall admission, 3/15 (priority date). Applications are processed on a rolling basis. *Application fee:* $0.

**Expenses:** Tuition, state resident: full-time $1,468; part-time $165 per credit hour. Tuition, nonresident: full-time $4,034; part-time $450 per credit hour.

**Financial support:** In 2001–02, 30 students received support, including 16 research assistantships, 10 teaching assistantships; career-related internships or fieldwork and Federal Work-Study also available. Support available to part-time students.

**Faculty research:** Cognitive behavior therapy, therapy with the deaf, victims of drunk drivers, autism. *Total annual research expenditures:* $40,000.

Dr. Robert M. Adams, Chair, 859-622-1105, *Fax:* 859-622-5871, *E-mail:* robert.adams@eku.edu. *Web site:* http://www.psychology.eku.edu/

# ■ ELMHURST COLLEGE

**Graduate Programs, Program in Industrial/Organizational Psychology, Elmhurst, IL 60126-3296**

AWARDS MA. Part-time and evening/weekend programs available.

**Faculty:** 2 full-time (1 woman), 1 (woman) part-time/adjunct.

**Students:** 43 applicants, 65% accepted, 13 enrolled. In 2001, 13 degrees awarded.

**Degree requirements:** For master's, thesis optional.

**Entrance requirements:** For master's, GRE. *Application deadline:* For fall admission, 4/1 (priority date). Applications are processed on a rolling basis. *Application fee:* $25.

**Expenses:** Tuition: Part-time $555 per hour.

**Financial support:** Federal Work-Study and scholarships/grants available. Support available to part-time students. Financial award application deadline: 6/1; financial award applicants required to submit FAFSA.

**Application contact:** Elizabeth D. Kuebler, Director of Graduate Admission, 630-617-3069, *Fax:* 630-617-5501, *E-mail:* gradadm@elmhurst.edu.

# ■ EMPORIA STATE UNIVERSITY

**School of Graduate Studies, The Teachers College, Department of Psychology and Special Education, Program in Psychology, Emporia, KS 66801-5087**

AWARDS Clinical psychology (MS); general psychology (MS); industrial/organizational psychology (MS).

**Students:** 39 full-time (32 women), 8 part-time (6 women); includes 2 minority (both African Americans), 6 international. 23 applicants, 78% accepted. In 2001, 23 degrees awarded.

**Degree requirements:** For master's, comprehensive exam or thesis.

**Entrance requirements:** For master's, GRE General Test or MAT, TOEFL. *Application deadline:* For fall admission, 6/1 (priority date); for spring admission, 10/1. Applications are processed on a rolling basis. *Application fee:* $30 ($75 for international students). Electronic applications accepted.

**Expenses:** Tuition, state resident: full-time $2,632; part-time $119 per credit hour. Tuition, nonresident: full-time $6,734; part-time $290 per credit hour.

**Financial support:** Career-related internships or fieldwork, Federal Work-Study, institutionally sponsored loans, health care benefits, and unspecified assistantships available. Financial award application deadline: 3/15; financial award applicants required to submit FAFSA.

**Faculty research:** Driving under the influence (DUI) personality, lifestyles and imposter phenomenon.

Dr. Kenneth A. Weaver, Chair, Department of Psychology and Special Education, 620-341-5317, *E-mail:* weaverke@emporia.edu.

## ■ FAIRLEIGH DICKINSON UNIVERSITY, COLLEGE AT FLORHAM

**Maxwell Becton College of Arts and Sciences, Department of Psychology, Program in Industrial/Organizational Psychology, Madison, NJ 07940-1099**

**AWARDS** MA, MA/MBA.

**Students:** 14 full-time (8 women), 14 part-time (8 women); includes 2 minority (1 African American, 1 Asian American or Pacific Islander), 4 international. Average age 26. 17 applicants, 88% accepted, 7 enrolled. In 2001, 11 degrees awarded. **Entrance requirements:** For master's, GRE General Test. *Application deadline:* Applications are processed on a rolling basis. *Application fee:* $40. **Expenses:** Tuition: Full-time $11,484; part-time $638 per credit. Required fees: $420. One-time fee: $97 part-time.

## ■ FLORIDA INSTITUTE OF TECHNOLOGY

**Graduate Programs, School of Psychology, Program in Industrial/Organizational Psychology, Melbourne, FL 32901-6975**

**AWARDS** MS, PhD. Part-time programs available.

**Students:** Average age 29.
**Degree requirements:** For master's, preliminary exam, thesis optional; for doctorate, internship, preliminary exam.
**Entrance requirements:** For master's, GRE General Test, minimum GPA of 3.0. *Application deadline:* For fall admission, 3/15. Applications are processed on a rolling basis. Electronic applications accepted.
**Expenses:** Tuition: Part-time $650 per credit.
**Financial support:** Research assistantships with partial tuition reimbursements, teaching assistantships with partial tuition reimbursements, career-related internships or fieldwork and tuition waivers (partial) available. Financial award application deadline: 3/1; financial award applicants required to submit FAFSA.
**Faculty research:** Faking, personality measures, team performance, behavioral change, strategies for programming, analysis of verbal behavior.
Dr. Richard Griffith, Chairman, 321-674-8104, *Fax:* 321-674-7105, *E-mail:* griffith@fit.edu.
**Application contact:** Carolyn P. Farrior, Director of Graduate Admissions, 321-674-7118, *Fax:* 321-723-9468, *E-mail:* cfarrior@fit.edu. *Web site:* http://www.fit.edu/

**Find an in-depth description at www.petersons.com/gradchannel.**

## ■ GEORGE MASON UNIVERSITY

**College of Arts and Sciences, Department of Psychology, Program in Human Factors Engineering Psychology, Fairfax, VA 22030-4444**

**AWARDS** MA, PhD.

**Degree requirements:** For master's, internship, thesis optional; for doctorate, thesis/dissertation.
**Entrance requirements:** For master's, GRE General Test, minimum GPA of 3.0 in last 60 hours, previous undergraduate course work in psychology; for doctorate, GRE General Test, minimum undergraduate GPA of 3.0, 3.25 in major. Electronic applications accepted.
**Expenses:** Tuition, state resident: full-time $3,168; part-time $132 per credit hour. Tuition, nonresident: full-time $11,280; part-time $470 per credit hour. Required fees: $1,416; $59 per credit hour.

## ■ GEORGE MASON UNIVERSITY

**College of Arts and Sciences, Department of Psychology, Program in Industrial/Organizational Psychology, Fairfax, VA 22030-4444**

**AWARDS** MA, PhD.

**Degree requirements:** For master's, thesis optional; for doctorate, thesis/dissertation.
**Entrance requirements:** For master's, GRE General Test, minimum GPA of 3.0 in last 60 hours, previous undergraduate course work in psychology; for doctorate, GRE General Test, minimum undergraduate GPA of 3.0, 3.25 in major. Electronic applications accepted.
**Expenses:** Tuition, state resident: full-time $3,168; part-time $132 per credit hour. Tuition, nonresident: full-time $11,280; part-time $470 per credit hour. Required fees: $1,416; $59 per credit hour.

## ■ THE GEORGE WASHINGTON UNIVERSITY

**Columbian College of Arts and Sciences, Department of Psychology, Washington, DC 20052**

**AWARDS** Applied social psychology (PhD); clinical psychology (PhD, Psy D); cognitive neuropsychology (PhD); industrial-organizational psychology (PhD). Part-time and evening/weekend programs available.

**Faculty:** 15 full-time (8 women), 1 (woman) part-time/adjunct.
**Students:** 133 full-time (106 women), 102 part-time (82 women); includes 50 minority (22 African Americans, 13 Asian Americans or Pacific Islanders, 14 Hispanic Americans, 1 Native American), 15 international. Average age 30. 413

applicants, 18% accepted. In 2001, 32 doctorates awarded.
**Degree requirements:** For doctorate, thesis/dissertation or alternative, general exam.
**Entrance requirements:** For doctorate, GRE General Test, minimum GPA of 3.0. *Application fee:* $55.
**Expenses:** Tuition: Part-time $810 per credit. Required fees: $1 per credit.
**Financial support:** In 2001–02, 27 students received support, including 22 fellowships with tuition reimbursements available (averaging $4,700 per year), 20 teaching assistantships with tuition reimbursements available (averaging $2,900 per year); career-related internships or fieldwork and Federal Work-Study also available. Financial award application deadline: 2/1.
Dr. Rolf Peterson, Chair, 202-994-6544. *Web site:* http://www.gwu.edu/~gradinfo/

## ■ GODDARD COLLEGE

**Graduate Programs, Program in Psychology and Counseling, Plainfield, VT 05667-9432**

**AWARDS** Organizational development (MA); psychology and counseling (MA). Postbaccalaureate distance learning degree programs offered (minimal on-campus study).

**Degree requirements:** For master's, thesis.
Electronic applications accepted. *Web site:* http://www.goddard.edu/

## ■ GOLDEN GATE UNIVERSITY

**School of Professional Programs and Undergraduate Studies, Program in Applied Psychology, San Francisco, CA 94105-2968**

**AWARDS** Applied psychology (Certificate); counseling (MA); industrial/organizational psychology (MA); marriage, family and child counseling (MA).

**Entrance requirements:** For master's, TOEFL, minimum GPA of 2.5.

## ■ GRADUATE SCHOOL AND UNIVERSITY CENTER OF THE CITY UNIVERSITY OF NEW YORK

**Graduate Studies, Program in Psychology, New York, NY 10016-4039**

**AWARDS** Basic applied neurocognition (PhD); biopsychology (PhD); clinical psychology (PhD); developmental psychology (PhD); environmental psychology (PhD); experimental psychology (PhD); industrial psychology (PhD); learning processes (PhD); neuropsychology (PhD); psychology (PhD); social personality (PhD).

**Faculty:** 119 full-time (40 women).

**Students:** 463 full-time (335 women), 4 part-time (2 women); includes 96 minority (39 African Americans, 20 Asian Americans or Pacific Islanders, 36 Hispanic Americans, 1 Native American), 47 international. Average age 33. 493 applicants, 24% accepted, 65 enrolled. In 2001, 28 degrees awarded.
**Degree requirements:** For doctorate, one foreign language, thesis/dissertation.
**Entrance requirements:** For doctorate, GRE General Test. *Application deadline:* For fall admission, 2/1. *Application fee:* $40.
**Expenses:** Tuition, state resident: part-time $245 per credit. Tuition, nonresident: part-time $425 per credit. Required fees: $72 per semester.
**Financial support:** In 2001–02, 226 students received support, including 141 fellowships, 14 research assistantships, 4 teaching assistantships; career-related internships or fieldwork, Federal Work-Study, institutionally sponsored loans, and tuition waivers (full and partial) also available. Financial award application deadline: 2/1; financial award applicants required to submit FAFSA.
Dr. Joseph Glick, Executive Officer, 212-817-8706, *Fax:* 212-817-1533, *E-mail:* jglick@gc.cuny.edu.

### ■ HOFSTRA UNIVERSITY
**College of Liberal Arts and Sciences, Division of Social Sciences, Department of Psychology, Program in Industrial/Organizational Psychology, Hempstead, NY 11549**
**AWARDS** MA. Part-time programs available.
**Faculty:** 26 full-time (5 women), 14 part-time/adjunct (6 women).
**Students:** 30 full-time (15 women), 35 part-time (26 women). Average age 27. In 2001, 24 degrees awarded.
**Degree requirements:** For master's, comprehensive exam.
**Entrance requirements:** For master's, GRE General Test, minimum undergraduate GPA of 3.0. *Application deadline:* Applications are processed on a rolling basis. *Application fee:* $40 ($75 for international students).
**Expenses:** Tuition: Full-time $12,408. Tuition and fees vary according to course load and program.
**Financial support:** In 2001–02, 24 students received support, including 2 fellowships, 16 research assistantships, 6 teaching assistantships; career-related internships or fieldwork, Federal Work-Study, and institutionally sponsored loans also available. Support available to part-time students. Financial award application deadline: 5/1; financial award applicants required to submit FAFSA.

Dr. William Metlay, Director, 516-463-6343, *Fax:* 516-463-6354.
**Application contact:** Mary Beth Carey, Vice President of Enrollment Services, *Fax:* 516-560-7660, *E-mail:* hofstra@hofstra.edu.

### ■ ILLINOIS INSTITUTE OF TECHNOLOGY
**Graduate College, Institute of Psychology, Chicago, IL 60616-3793**
**AWARDS** Clinical psychology (PhD); industrial/organizational psychology (PhD); personnel/human resource development (MS); psychology (MS); rehabilitation counseling (MS); rehabilitation psychology (PhD).
**Faculty:** 17 full-time (7 women), 4 part-time/adjunct (2 women).
**Students:** 84 full-time (56 women), 75 part-time (51 women); includes 32 minority (15 African Americans, 10 Asian Americans or Pacific Islanders, 6 Hispanic Americans, 1 Native American), 15 international. Average age 30. 157 applicants, 49% accepted. In 2001, 21 master's, 15 doctorates awarded. Terminal master's awarded for partial completion of doctoral program.
**Degree requirements:** For master's, thesis (for some programs), comprehensive exam; for doctorate, thesis/dissertation, qualifying exams, comprehensive exam.
**Entrance requirements:** For master's and doctorate, GRE General Test, TOEFL, minimum GPA of 3.0. *Application deadline:* For fall admission, 1/15 (priority date); for spring admission, 11/1. Applications are processed on a rolling basis. *Application fee:* $30. Electronic applications accepted.
**Expenses:** Tuition: Part-time $590 per credit hour.
**Financial support:** In 2001–02, 32 fellowships, 18 teaching assistantships were awarded. Research assistantships, career-related internships or fieldwork, Federal Work-Study, institutionally sponsored loans, scholarships/grants, and unspecified assistantships also available. Financial award application deadline: 3/1; financial award applicants required to submit FAFSA.
**Faculty research:** Leadership, life span developmental processes, rehabilitation engineering technology, behavioral medicine, substance abuse and disability. *Total annual research expenditures:* $494,180.
Dr. M. Ellen Mitchell, Chairman, 312-567-3362, *Fax:* 312-567-3493, *E-mail:* mitchell@itt.edu.
**Application contact:** Dr. Ali Cinar, Dean of Graduate College, 312-567-3637, *Fax:* 312-567-7517, *E-mail:* gradstu@iit.edu. *Web site:* http://www.iit.edu/colleges/psych/

### ■ ILLINOIS STATE UNIVERSITY
**Graduate School, College of Arts and Sciences, Department of Psychology, Normal, IL 61790-2200**
**AWARDS** Psychology (MA, MS), including clinical psychology, counseling psychology, developmental psychology, educational psychology, experimental psychology, measurement-evaluation, organizational-industrial psychology; school psychology (PhD, SSP).
**Faculty:** 30 full-time (10 women), 1 part-time/adjunct (0 women).
**Students:** 59 full-time (48 women), 24 part-time (13 women); includes 7 minority (3 African Americans, 3 Hispanic Americans, 1 Native American), 5 international. 81 applicants, 46% accepted. In 2001, 40 master's, 2 doctorates, 4 other advanced degrees awarded.
**Degree requirements:** For master's, thesis or alternative; for doctorate, variable foreign language requirement, thesis/dissertation, 2 terms of residency, internship, practicum.
**Entrance requirements:** For master's, GRE General Test, GRE Subject Test, minimum GPA of 3.0 in last 60 hours; for doctorate, GRE General Test. *Application deadline:* Applications are processed on a rolling basis. *Application fee:* $30.
**Expenses:** Tuition, state resident: full-time $2,691; part-time $112 per credit hour. Tuition, nonresident: full-time $5,880; part-time $245 per credit hour. Required fees: $1,146; $48 per credit hour.
**Financial support:** In 2001–02, 21 research assistantships (averaging $5,127 per year), 27 teaching assistantships (averaging $4,308 per year) were awarded. Tuition waivers (full) and unspecified assistantships also available. Financial award application deadline: 4/1.
**Faculty research:** Dialogues with children, sexual harassment in the military, mental health consultant. *Total annual research expenditures:* $248,177.
Dr. David Barone, Chairperson, 309-438-8651. *Web site:* http://www.cas.ilstu.edu/psychology/index.html

### ■ INDIANA UNIVERSITY–PURDUE UNIVERSITY INDIANAPOLIS
**School of Science, Department of Psychology, Indianapolis, IN 46202-3275**
**AWARDS** Clinical rehabilitation psychology (MS, PhD); industrial/organizational psychology (MS); psychobiology of addictions (PhD). Part-time programs available.
**Students:** 22 full-time (17 women), 14 part-time (12 women); includes 2 minority (1 Asian American or Pacific Islander, 1

*Indiana University–Purdue University Indianapolis (continued)*
Hispanic American), 3 international. Average age 27. In 2001, 12 master's, 3 doctorates awarded. Terminal master's awarded for partial completion of doctoral program. **Degree requirements:** For master's and doctorate, thesis/dissertation.
**Entrance requirements:** For master's, GRE General Test, minimum undergraduate GPA of 3.0; for doctorate, GRE General Test, GRE Subject Test (clinical rehabilitation psychology), minimum undergraduate GPA of 3.2. *Application deadline:* For fall admission, 2/1 (priority date). *Application fee:* $45 ($55 for international students).
**Expenses:** Tuition, state resident: full-time $4,480; part-time $187 per credit. Tuition, nonresident: full-time $12,926; part-time $539 per credit. Required fees: $177.
**Financial support:** In 2001–02, 21 students received support, including 6 fellowships with partial tuition reimbursements available (averaging $11,000 per year), 15 research assistantships with partial tuition reimbursements available (averaging $9,000 per year), 12 teaching assistantships with partial tuition reimbursements available (averaging $9,000 per year); career-related internships or fieldwork, Federal Work-Study, and institutionally sponsored loans also available. Financial award application deadline: 3/1; financial award applicants required to submit FAFSA.
**Faculty research:** Psychiatric rehabilitation, health psychology, psychopharmacology of drugs of abuse, personnel psychology, organizational decision making.
Dr. J. Gregor Fetterman, Chairman, 317-274-6768, *Fax:* 317-274-6756, *E-mail:* gfetter@iupui.edu.
**Application contact:** Donna Miller, Graduate Program Coordinator, 317-274-6945, *Fax:* 317-274-6756, *E-mail:* dmiller1@iupui.edu. *Web site:* http://www.psynt.iupui.edu/

## ■ JOHN F. KENNEDY UNIVERSITY

**Graduate School of Professional Psychology, Program in Organizational Psychology, Orinda, CA 94563-2603**

**AWARDS** MA, Certificate. Part-time and evening/weekend programs available.

**Degree requirements:** For master's, thesis or alternative.
**Entrance requirements:** For master's, TOEFL, interview.
**Expenses:** Tuition: Full-time $9,396; part-time $348 per unit. Required fees: $9 per

quarter. Tuition and fees vary according to degree level and program.

## ■ KEAN UNIVERSITY

**College of Arts, Humanities and Social Sciences, Department of Psychology, Union, NJ 07083**

**AWARDS** Behavioral sciences (MA), including business and industry counseling, human behavior and organizational psychology, psychological services; business and industry counseling (PMC); educational psychology (MA); marriage and family therapy (Diploma); school psychology (Diploma). Part-time and evening/weekend programs available.

**Faculty:** 21 full-time (13 women), 25 part-time/adjunct.
**Students:** 25 full-time (16 women), 121 part-time (74 women); includes 38 minority (12 African Americans, 8 Asian Americans or Pacific Islanders, 18 Hispanic Americans), 3 international. Average age 30. 87 applicants, 67% accepted. In 2001, 42 master's, 12 other advanced degrees awarded.
**Degree requirements:** For master's, thesis, comprehensive exam.
**Entrance requirements:** For master's, GRE General Test. *Application deadline:* For fall admission, 6/15; for spring admission, 11/15. *Application fee:* $35.
**Expenses:** Tuition, state resident: full-time $7,372. Tuition, nonresident: full-time $9,004. Required fees: $1,006.
**Financial support:** In 2001–02, 27 research assistantships with full tuition reimbursements (averaging $3,360 per year) were awarded; career-related internships or fieldwork and unspecified assistantships also available.
Dr. Henry L. Kaplowitz, Graduate Coordinator, 908-527-2598.
**Application contact:** Joanne Morris, Director of Graduate Admissions, 908-527-2665, *Fax:* 908-527-2286, *E-mail:* grad_adm@kean.edu.

## ■ LAMAR UNIVERSITY

**College of Graduate Studies, College of Arts and Sciences, Department of Psychology, Beaumont, TX 77710**

**AWARDS** Community/clinical psychology (MS); industrial/organizational psychology (MS). Part-time programs available.

**Faculty:** 5 full-time (2 women).
**Students:** 15 full-time (8 women), 5 part-time (4 women); includes 4 minority (2 African Americans, 2 Hispanic Americans). Average age 32. 35 applicants, 80% accepted. In 2001, 9 degrees awarded.
**Degree requirements:** For master's, thesis, practicum.
**Entrance requirements:** For master's, GRE General Test, TOEFL, minimum GPA of 2.5 in last 60 hours of

undergraduate course work. *Application deadline:* For fall admission, 8/1; for spring admission, 12/1. *Application fee:* $25 ($50 for international students).
**Expenses:** Tuition, state resident: full-time $1,114. Tuition, nonresident: full-time $3,670.
**Financial support:** In 2001–02, 12 students received support, including research assistantships (averaging $6,000 per year), 7 teaching assistantships with tuition reimbursements available (averaging $3,000 per year); fellowships, career-related internships or fieldwork, Federal Work-Study, scholarships/grants, and tuition waivers (partial) also available. Support available to part-time students. Financial award application deadline: 4/1.
**Faculty research:** Counseling psychology, industrial psychology. *Total annual research expenditures:* $17,000.
Dr. Oney D. Fitzpatrick, Chair, 409-880-8285, *Fax:* 409-880-1779, *E-mail:* fitzpatrod@hal.lamar.edu. *Web site:* http://140.158.184.30/

## ■ LOUISIANA STATE UNIVERSITY AND AGRICULTURAL AND MECHANICAL COLLEGE

**Graduate School, College of Arts and Sciences, Department of Psychology, Baton Rouge, LA 70803**

**AWARDS** Biological psychology (MA, PhD); clinical psychology (MA, PhD); cognitive psychology (MA, PhD); developmental psychology (MA, PhD); industrial/organizational psychology (MA, PhD); school psychology (MA, PhD).

**Faculty:** 25 full-time (7 women).
**Students:** 70 full-time (53 women), 43 part-time (24 women); includes 7 minority (3 African Americans, 2 Asian Americans or Pacific Islanders, 2 Hispanic Americans), 2 international. Average age 30. 179 applicants, 12% accepted, 20 enrolled. In 2001, 19 degrees awarded. Terminal master's awarded for partial completion of doctoral program.
**Degree requirements:** For master's, thesis; for doctorate, thesis/dissertation, 1 year internship.
**Entrance requirements:** For master's and doctorate, GRE General Test, minimum GPA of 3.0. *Application deadline:* For fall admission, 1/25 (priority date). Applications are processed on a rolling basis. *Application fee:* $25.
**Expenses:** Tuition, state resident: full-time $2,551. Tuition, nonresident: full-time $5,551. Required fees: $854. Part-time tuition and fees vary according to course load.
**Financial support:** In 2001–02, 1 fellowship (averaging $14,333 per year), 10

research assistantships with partial tuition reimbursements (averaging $14,200 per year), 33 teaching assistantships with partial tuition reimbursements (averaging $10,371 per year) were awarded. Career-related internships or fieldwork, institutionally sponsored loans, and contracts also available. Financial award applicants required to submit FAFSA. *Total annual research expenditures:* $242,157. Dr. Irving Lane, Chair, 225-578-8745, *Fax:* 225-578-4125, *E-mail:* irvlane@unix1.sncc.lsu.edu. **Application contact:** Dr. Janet McDonald, Coordinator of Graduate Studies, 225-578-4116, *Fax:* 225-578-4125, *E-mail:* psmcdo@lsu.edu. *Web site:* http://www.artsci.lsu.edu/psych

### ■ LOUISIANA TECH UNIVERSITY

**Graduate School, College of Education, Department of Behavioral Sciences, Ruston, LA 71272**

**AWARDS** Counseling (MA, Ed S); counseling psychology (PhD); industrial/organizational psychology (MA); special education (MA). Part-time programs available.

**Degree requirements:** For master's, thesis or alternative; for doctorate, thesis/dissertation.
**Entrance requirements:** For master's and doctorate, GRE General Test.

### ■ MARSHALL UNIVERSITY

**Graduate College, College of Liberal Arts, Department of Psychology, Huntington, WV 25755**

**AWARDS** Clinical psychology (MA); general psychology (MA); industrial and organizational psychology (MA); psychology (Psy D).

**Faculty:** 15 full-time (6 women), 15 part-time/adjunct (7 women).
**Students:** 78 full-time (59 women), 88 part-time (62 women); includes 5 minority (4 African Americans, 1 Hispanic American), 3 international. In 2001, 65 degrees awarded.
**Degree requirements:** For master's, thesis optional.
**Entrance requirements:** For master's, GRE General Test or MAT. *Application deadline:* For fall admission, 3/1; for spring admission, 11/1.
**Expenses:** Tuition, state resident: part-time $147 per credit. Tuition, nonresident: part-time $468 per credit. Tuition and fees vary according to campus/location and reciprocity agreements.
**Financial support:** Teaching assistantships with tuition reimbursements available. Dr. Martin Amerikaner, Chairperson, 304-696-6446, *E-mail:* amerikan@marshall.edu.
**Application contact:** Ken O'Neal, Assistant Vice President, Adult Student

Services, 304-746-2500 Ext. 1907, *Fax:* 304-746-1902, *E-mail:* oneal@marshall.edu.

### ■ MIDDLE TENNESSEE STATE UNIVERSITY

**College of Graduate Studies, College of Education and Behavioral Science, Department of Psychology, Murfreesboro, TN 37132**

**AWARDS** Industrial/organizational psychology (MA); psychology (MA); school counseling (M Ed, Ed S); school psychology (Ed S). Part-time and evening/weekend programs available.

**Faculty:** 37 full-time (13 women).
**Students:** 28 full-time, 165 part-time; includes 24 minority (18 African Americans, 4 Asian Americans or Pacific Islanders, 2 Hispanic Americans). Average age 26. 54 applicants, 67% accepted. In 2001, 46 master's, 12 other advanced degrees awarded.
**Degree requirements:** For master's, one foreign language, thesis, comprehensive exam.
**Entrance requirements:** For master's, GRE. *Application deadline:* For fall admission, 8/1 (priority date). Applications are processed on a rolling basis. *Application fee:* $25. Electronic applications accepted.
**Expenses:** Tuition, state resident: full-time $1,716; part-time $191 per hour. Tuition, nonresident: full-time $4,952; part-time $461 per hour. Required fees: $14 per hour. $58 per semester.
**Financial support:** In 2001–02, 8 teaching assistantships were awarded; research assistantships, career-related internships or fieldwork, institutionally sponsored loans, and scholarships/grants also available. Support available to part-time students. Financial award application deadline: 5/1; financial award applicants required to submit FAFSA.
**Faculty research:** Industrial/organizational, social/personality/sports, counseling/clinical/school, cognitive/language/learning/perception, developmental/aging. *Total annual research expenditures:* $44,089.
Dr. Larry Morris, Chair, 615-898-2706, *Fax:* 615-898-5027, *E-mail:* lmorris@mtsu.edu.

### ■ MINNESOTA STATE UNIVERSITY, MANKATO

**College of Graduate Studies, College of Social and Behavioral Sciences, Department of Psychology, Mankato, MN 56001**

**AWARDS** Clinical psychology (MA); industrial psychology (MA); psychology (MT). Part-time programs available.

**Faculty:** 12 full-time (3 women).
**Students:** 31 full-time (28 women), 8 part-time (3 women). Average age 26. In 2001, 15 degrees awarded.
**Degree requirements:** For master's, one foreign language, thesis (for some programs), comprehensive exam.
**Entrance requirements:** For master's, GRE General Test, GRE Subject Test (clinical psychology), minimum GPA of 3.0 during previous 2 years. *Application deadline:* For fall admission, 3/1; for spring admission, 11/27. Applications are processed on a rolling basis. *Application fee:* $20. Electronic applications accepted.
**Expenses:** Tuition, state resident: full-time $3,253; part-time $157 per credit. Tuition, nonresident: full-time $4,893; part-time $248 per credit. Required fees: $24 per credit. Tuition and fees vary according to reciprocity agreements.
**Financial support:** Research assistantships, teaching assistantships with full tuition reimbursements, career-related internships or fieldwork, Federal Work-Study, and institutionally sponsored loans available. Support available to part-time students. Financial award application deadline: 3/15; financial award applicants required to submit FAFSA.
**Faculty research:** Professional competency in hospitals, mood disturbance, 360-degree feedback, employee selection, planning fallacy. Dr. Michael Fatis, Chairperson, 507-389-1818.
**Application contact:** Joni Roberts, Admissions Coordinator, 507-389-5244, *Fax:* 507-389-5974, *E-mail:* grad@mankato.msus.edu.

### ■ MONTCLAIR STATE UNIVERSITY

**The School of Graduate, Professional and Continuing Education, College of Humanities and Social Sciences, Department of Psychology, Program in Psychology, Upper Montclair, NJ 07043-1624**

**AWARDS** Industrial and organizational psychology (MA). Part-time and evening/weekend programs available.

**Degree requirements:** For master's, thesis, comprehensive exam.
**Entrance requirements:** For master's, GRE General Test, GRE Subject Test, previous course work in psychology. Electronic applications accepted.

### ■ NATIONAL-LOUIS UNIVERSITY

**College of Arts and Sciences, Division of Liberal Arts and Sciences, Program in Psychology, Chicago, IL 60603**

**AWARDS** Cultural psychology (MA); health psychology (MA); human development (MA);

*National-Louis University (continued)*
organizational psychology (MA); psychology (Certificate). Part-time and evening/weekend programs available.

**Degree requirements:** For master's, thesis, internship (health psychology).
**Entrance requirements:** For master's, GRE, MAT, or Watson-Glaser Critical Thinking Appraisal, interview, minimum GPA of 3.0; for Certificate, GRE, MAT, or Watson-Glaser Critical Thinking Appraisal, interview, minimum GPA of 3.0, previous undergraduate course work in psychology.
**Expenses:** Tuition: Full-time $13,830; part-time $461 per credit hour.
**Faculty research:** Human development, personality theory, abnormal psychology.

■ **NEW YORK UNIVERSITY**
**Graduate School of Arts and Science, Department of Psychology, New York, NY 10012-1019**
**AWARDS** Clinical psychology (PhD); cognition and perception (PhD); community psychology (PhD); general psychology (MA); industrial/organizational psychology (MA, PhD); psychoanalysis (Advanced Certificate); social/personality psychology (PhD). Part-time programs available.

**Faculty:** 38 full-time (13 women), 78 part-time/adjunct.
**Students:** 118 full-time (85 women), 304 part-time (235 women); includes 64 minority (14 African Americans, 27 Asian Americans or Pacific Islanders, 22 Hispanic Americans, 1 Native American), 49 international. Average age 28. 586 applicants, 44% accepted, 101 enrolled. In 2001, 67 master's, 22 doctorates awarded. Terminal master's awarded for partial completion of doctoral program.
**Degree requirements:** For master's, thesis or alternative, comprehensive exam; for doctorate, thesis/dissertation.
**Entrance requirements:** For master's, GRE General Test, minimum GPA of 3.0; for doctorate, GRE General Test, GRE Subject Test; for Advanced Certificate, doctoral degree, minimum GPA of 3.0. *Application deadline:* For fall admission, 1/4. *Application fee:* $60.
**Expenses:** Tuition: Full-time $19,536; part-time $814 per credit. Required fees: $1,330; $38 per credit. Tuition and fees vary according to course load and program.
**Financial support:** Fellowships with tuition reimbursements, research assistantships with tuition reimbursements, teaching assistantships with tuition reimbursements, career-related internships or fieldwork, Federal Work-Study, institutionally sponsored loans, and traineeships available. Financial award

application deadline: 1/4; financial award applicants required to submit FAFSA.
**Faculty research:** Vision, memory, social cognition, social and cognitive development, relationships.
Marisa Carrasco, Chair, 212-998-7900.
**Application contact:** Susan Andersen, Director of Graduate Studies, 212-998-7900, *Fax:* 212-995-4018, *E-mail:* psychquery@psych.nyu.edu. *Web site:* http://www.psych.nyu.edu/

■ **OHIO UNIVERSITY**
**Graduate Studies, College of Arts and Sciences, Department of Psychology, Program in Industrial and Organizational Psychology, Athens, OH 45701-2979**
**AWARDS** PhD.
**Faculty:** 4 full-time (2 women), 1 part-time/adjunct (0 women).
**Students:** 6 full-time (1 woman), 1 part-time, 1 international. 28 applicants, 0% accepted.
**Degree requirements:** For doctorate, one foreign language, thesis/dissertation, comprehensive exam.
**Entrance requirements:** For doctorate, GRE General Test, GRE Subject Test. *Application deadline:* For fall admission, 2/1. *Application fee:* $30.
**Expenses:** Tuition, state resident: full-time $6,585. Tuition, nonresident: full-time $12,254.
**Financial support:** In 2001–02, 1 fellowship with full tuition reimbursement (averaging $12,000 per year), 6 teaching assistantships with full tuition reimbursements (averaging $8,120 per year) were awarded. Research assistantships with full tuition reimbursements, career-related internships or fieldwork, Federal Work-Study, institutionally sponsored loans, tuition waivers (full), and unspecified assistantships also available. Financial award application deadline: 1/15.
**Faculty research:** Performance appraisal, job satisfaction, organizational entry, sexual harassment.
Paula M. Popovich, Director of Industrial/Organizational Training, 740-593-1707, *Fax:* 740-593-0579, *E-mail:* popovich@ohio.edu.
**Application contact:** Admissions Secretary, 740-593-0902, *Fax:* 740-593-0579, *E-mail:* pgraduate1@ohiou.edu. *Web site:* http://www.cats.ohiou.edu/~psydept/

■ **OLD DOMINION UNIVERSITY**
**College of Sciences, Program in Industrial/Organizational Psychology, Norfolk, VA 23529**
**AWARDS** PhD.

**Faculty:** 8 full-time (2 women), 1 part-time/adjunct (0 women).
**Students:** 32 full-time (22 women); includes 5 minority (2 African Americans, 3 Asian Americans or Pacific Islanders). Average age 29. 36 applicants, 22% accepted, 5 enrolled. In 2001, 4 degrees awarded.
**Degree requirements:** For doctorate, thesis/dissertation, internship, qualifying exam.
**Entrance requirements:** For doctorate, GRE General Test, TOEFL. *Application deadline:* For fall admission, 2/1. *Application fee:* $30. Electronic applications accepted.
**Expenses:** Tuition, state resident: part-time $202 per credit. Tuition, nonresident: part-time $534 per credit. Required fees: $76 per semester.
**Financial support:** In 2001–02, 2 research assistantships with full and partial tuition reimbursements (averaging $15,000 per year), 7 teaching assistantships with full and partial tuition reimbursements (averaging $9,000 per year) were awarded. Career-related internships or fieldwork, scholarships/grants, and tuition waivers (partial) also available. Support available to part-time students. Financial award application deadline: 2/15; financial award applicants required to submit FAFSA.
**Faculty research:** Management psychology, personnel and training psychology, human factors/ergonomics.
Dr. Mark Scerbo, Graduate Program Director, 757-683-4217, *Fax:* 757-683-5087, *E-mail:* iogpd@odu.edu. *Web site:* http://www.psychology.odu.edu/psych.htm/

■ **THE PENNSYLVANIA STATE UNIVERSITY UNIVERSITY PARK CAMPUS**
**Graduate School, College of Liberal Arts, Department of Psychology, State College, University Park, PA 16802-1503**
**AWARDS** Clinical psychology (MS, PhD); cognitive psychology (MS, PhD); developmental psychology (MS, PhD); industrial/organizational psychology (MS, PhD); psychobiology (MS, PhD); social psychology (MS, PhD).
**Students:** 126 full-time (83 women), 12 part-time (7 women). In 2001, 15 master's, 14 doctorates awarded.
**Degree requirements:** For master's and doctorate, thesis/dissertation.
**Entrance requirements:** For master's and doctorate, GRE General Test, GRE Subject Test. *Application fee:* $45.
**Expenses:** Tuition, state resident: full-time $7,882; part-time $333 per credit. Tuition, nonresident: full-time $16,142; part-time $673 per credit. Required fees: $124 per semester.

**Financial support:** Fellowships, research assistantships, teaching assistantships available.
Dr. Keith Crnic, Head, 814-863-1721.

## ■ PHILADELPHIA COLLEGE OF OSTEOPATHIC MEDICINE

**Graduate and Professional Programs, Department of Psychology, Philadelphia, PA 19131-1694**

**AWARDS** Clinical health psychology (MS); clinical psychology (Psy D); organizational leadership and development (MS).

**Faculty:** 6 full-time (3 women), 1 part-time/adjunct (0 women).

**Students:** 253 full-time (186 women); includes 35 minority (23 African Americans, 7 Asian Americans or Pacific Islanders, 5 Hispanic Americans). Average age 33. 77 applicants, 86% accepted. In 2001, 1 degree awarded.

**Degree requirements:** For master's, thesis; for doctorate, thesis/dissertation, final project, fieldwork, comprehensive exam.

**Entrance requirements:** For master's, GRE, minimum GPA of 3.0, previous course work in biology, chemistry, English, physics; for doctorate, MAT. *Application deadline:* For fall admission, 1/17. Applications are processed on a rolling basis. *Application fee:* $50.

**Expenses:** Tuition: Part-time $441 per credit. Required fees: $250. Tuition and fees vary according to program.

**Faculty research:** Cognitive-behavioral therapy, coping skills.
Dr. Arthur Freeman, Chairman, 215-871-6442.

**Application contact:** Carol A. Fox, Associate Dean for Admissions, 215-871-6700, *Fax:* 215-871-6719, *E-mail:* carolf@pcom.edu.

**Find an in-depth description at www.petersons.com/gradchannel.**

## ■ PONTIFICAL CATHOLIC UNIVERSITY OF PUERTO RICO

**Institute of Graduate Studies in Behavioral Science and Community Affairs, Ponce, PR 00717-0777**

**AWARDS** Clinical psychology (MS); clinical social work (MSW); criminology (MA); industrial psychology (MS); psychology (PhD); public administration (MA). Part-time and evening/weekend programs available.

**Faculty:** 10 full-time (7 women), 17 part-time/adjunct (12 women).

**Students:** 86 full-time (56 women), 394 part-time (266 women); all minorities (all Hispanic Americans). 141 applicants, 83% accepted, 104 enrolled. In 2001, 35 degrees awarded.

**Entrance requirements:** For master's, GRE, 2 recommendation letters, interview, minimum GPA of 2.75. *Application deadline:* For fall admission, 4/30 (priority date). Applications are processed on a rolling basis. *Application fee:* $50. Electronic applications accepted.

**Expenses:** Tuition: Full-time $2,880; part-time $160 per credit. Required fees: $360. Tuition and fees vary according to degree level and program.

**Financial support:** Federal Work-Study and tuition waivers (partial) available. Support available to part-time students. Financial award application deadline: 7/15. Dr. Nilde Cordoline, Director, 787-841-2000 Ext. 1024.

**Application contact:** Ana O. Bonilla, Director of Admissions, 787-841-2000 Ext. 1000, *Fax:* 787-840-4295. *Web site:* http://www.pucpr.edu/

## ■ RADFORD UNIVERSITY

**Graduate College, College of Arts and Sciences, Department of Psychology, Radford, VA 24142**

**AWARDS** Clinical psychology (MA); counseling psychology (MA); general psychology (MA, MS); industrial-organizational psychology (MA); school psychology (Ed S). Part-time programs available. Postbaccalaureate distance learning degree programs offered (minimal on-campus study).

**Faculty:** 20 full-time (6 women).

**Students:** 65 full-time (46 women), 9 part-time (8 women); includes 6 minority (2 African Americans, 3 Asian Americans or Pacific Islanders, 1 Native American), 1 international. Average age 26. 127 applicants, 83% accepted, 26 enrolled. In 2001, 40 master's, 10 other advanced degrees awarded.

**Degree requirements:** For master's, thesis (for some programs), comprehensive exam.

**Entrance requirements:** For degree, GMAT, GRE General Test, MAT, NTE, TOEFL. *Application deadline:* For fall admission, 2/15 (priority date); for spring admission, 10/15. Applications are processed on a rolling basis. *Application fee:* $25. Electronic applications accepted.

**Expenses:** Tuition, state resident: full-time $2,564; part-time $167 per credit hour. Tuition, nonresident: full-time $6,314; part-time $323 per credit hour. Required fees: $1,440.

**Financial support:** In 2001–02, 64 students received support, including 4 fellowships with tuition reimbursements available (averaging $8,060 per year), 46 research assistantships (averaging $4,401 per year), 7 teaching assistantships with

tuition reimbursements available (averaging $8,680 per year); career-related internships or fieldwork, Federal Work-Study, institutionally sponsored loans, and scholarships/grants also available. Financial award application deadline: 2/1; financial award applicants required to submit FAFSA.
Dr. Alastair V. Harris, Chair, 540-831-5361, *Fax:* 540-831-6113, *E-mail:* aharris@radford.edu. *Web site:* http://www.radford.edu/

## ■ RENSSELAER POLYTECHNIC INSTITUTE

**Graduate School, School of Humanities and Social Sciences, Department of Cognitive Science, Program in Psychology, Troy, NY 12180-3590**

**AWARDS** Human factors (MS); industrial-organizational psychology (MS). Part-time programs available.

**Faculty:** 7 full-time (0 women), 4 part-time/adjunct (0 women).

**Students:** 27 full-time (10 women), 3 part-time (1 woman); includes 3 minority (1 African American, 2 Asian Americans or Pacific Islanders), 2 international. Average age 22. 23 applicants, 74% accepted. In 2001, 4 degrees awarded.

**Degree requirements:** For master's, thesis.

**Entrance requirements:** For master's, GRE General Test, GRE Subject Test, TOEFL. *Application deadline:* For fall admission, 1/15 (priority date). Applications are processed on a rolling basis. *Application fee:* $45. Electronic applications accepted.

**Expenses:** Tuition: Full-time $26,400; part-time $1,320 per credit hour. Required fees: $1,437.

**Financial support:** In 2001–02, 1 fellowship with full tuition reimbursement (averaging $10,000 per year), 12 teaching assistantships with partial tuition reimbursements (averaging $4,000 per year) were awarded. Research assistantships, career-related internships or fieldwork, institutionally sponsored loans, scholarships/grants, and tuition waivers (partial) also available. Financial award application deadline: 2/1.

**Faculty research:** Cognitive psychology. *Web site:* http://www.rpi.edu/

**Find an in-depth description at www.petersons.com/gradchannel.**

## ■ RICE UNIVERSITY

**Graduate Programs, School of Social Sciences, Department of Psychology, Houston, TX 77251-1892**

**AWARDS** Industrial-organizational/social psychology (MA, PhD); psychology (MA, PhD).

**Faculty:** 21 full-time (4 women), 21 part-time/adjunct (14 women).

**Students:** 35 full-time (27 women); includes 5 minority (1 African American, 2 Asian Americans or Pacific Islanders, 2 Hispanic Americans), 9 international. Average age 29. 91 applicants, 22% accepted, 14 enrolled. In 2001, 3 master's, 9 doctorates awarded. Terminal master's awarded for partial completion of doctoral program.

**Degree requirements:** For master's and doctorate, thesis/dissertation.

**Entrance requirements:** For master's and doctorate, GRE General Test, TOEFL, minimum GPA of 3.0. *Application deadline:* For fall admission, 1/15 (priority date). Applications are processed on a rolling basis. *Application fee:* $25. Electronic applications accepted.

**Expenses:** Tuition: Full-time $17,300. Required fees: $250.

**Financial support:** In 2001–02, 22 fellowships with full tuition reimbursements (averaging $12,500 per year), 2 research assistantships with full tuition reimbursements (averaging $12,500 per year) were awarded. Federal Work-Study and tuition waivers (full) also available. Financial award applicants required to submit FAFSA.

**Faculty research:** Learning and memory, information processing, decision theory. Robert L. Dipboye, Chairman, 713-348-4764, *Fax:* 713-348-5221, *E-mail:* dpboye@rice.edu.

**Application contact:** Azelia Badruddin, Office Assistant, 713-348-4856, *Fax:* 713-348-5221, *E-mail:* psyc@rice.edu. *Web site:* http://www.ruf.rice.edu/~psyc/

## ■ ROOSEVELT UNIVERSITY

**Graduate Division, College of Arts and Sciences, School of Psychology, Chicago, IL 60605-1394**

**AWARDS** Clinical professional psychology (MA); clinical psychology (MA, Psy D); general psychology (MA); industrial/organizational psychology (MA). Part-time and evening/weekend programs available.

**Faculty:** 12 full-time (3 women), 22 part-time/adjunct (13 women).

**Students:** 97 full-time (64 women), 213 part-time (153 women); includes 39 minority (22 African Americans, 10 Asian Americans or Pacific Islanders, 6 Hispanic Americans, 1 Native American), 10 international.

**Degree requirements:** For master's, thesis or alternative; for doctorate, thesis/dissertation.

**Entrance requirements:** For master's, 18 undergraduate hours in psychology; for doctorate, GRE, master's degree in psychology. *Application deadline:* For fall admission, 6/1 (priority date). Applications are processed on a rolling basis. *Application fee:* $25 ($35 for international students).

**Expenses:** Tuition: Full-time $9,090; part-time $505 per credit hour. Required fees: $100 per term.

**Financial support:** Application deadline: 2/15.

**Faculty research:** Multicultural issues, psychotherapy research, stress, neuropsychology, psychodiagnostic assessment.

Edward Rossini, Head, 312-341-3760.

**Application contact:** Joanne Canyon-Heller, Coordinator of Graduate Admissions, 312-281-3250, *Fax:* 312-341-3523, *E-mail:* applyru@roosevelt.edu.

## ■ RUTGERS, THE STATE UNIVERSITY OF NEW JERSEY, NEW BRUNSWICK

**Graduate School of Applied and Professional Psychology, Program in Organizational Psychology, New Brunswick, NJ 08901-1281**

**AWARDS** Psy M, Psy D.

**Degree requirements:** For doctorate, thesis/dissertation, 1 year internship.

**Entrance requirements:** For doctorate, GRE General Test, GRE Subject Test (psychology), BA in psychology or equivalent. Electronic applications accepted.

**Faculty research:** Organizational assessment, managerial and organizational practice, consultation, organizational development, decision making. *Web site:* http://www.rci.rutgers.edu/~gsapp

## ■ ST. MARY'S UNIVERSITY OF SAN ANTONIO

**Graduate School, Department of Psychology, San Antonio, TX 78228-8507**

**AWARDS** Clinical psychology (MA, MS); industrial psychology (MA, MS); school psychology (MA). Part-time programs available.

**Faculty:** 5 full-time (4 women), 5 part-time/adjunct.

**Students:** 27 full-time (22 women), 35 part-time (29 women); includes 31 minority (6 African Americans, 1 Asian American or Pacific Islander, 24 Hispanic Americans), 1 international. Average age 24. In 2001, 17 degrees awarded.

**Degree requirements:** For master's, thesis (for some programs), comprehensive exam.

**Entrance requirements:** For master's, GRE General Test. *Application deadline:* Applications are processed on a rolling basis. *Application fee:* $15. Electronic applications accepted.

**Expenses:** Tuition: Full-time $8,190; part-time $455 per credit hour. Required fees: $375.

**Financial support:** Research assistantships, Federal Work-Study and institutionally sponsored loans available. Financial award application deadline: 2/15; financial award applicants required to submit FAFSA. Dr. Willibrord Silva, Graduate Program Director, 210-436-3314.

## ■ SAN DIEGO STATE UNIVERSITY

**Graduate and Research Affairs, College of Sciences, Department of Psychology, San Diego, CA 92182**

**AWARDS** Clinical psychology (MS, PhD); industrial and organizational psychology (MS); program evaluation (MS); psychology (MA). Terminal master's awarded for partial completion of doctoral program.

**Degree requirements:** For master's, thesis, oral exam; for doctorate, thesis/dissertation.

**Entrance requirements:** For master's, GRE General Test, TOEFL; for doctorate, GRE General Test, GRE Subject Test, minimum GPA of 3.5. *Web site:* http://www.phsychology.sdsu.edu/

## ■ SAN JOSE STATE UNIVERSITY

**Graduate Studies, College of Social Sciences, Department of Psychology, San Jose, CA 95192-0001**

**AWARDS** Clinical psychology (MS); counseling (MS); industrial psychology (MS); research psychology (MA).

**Faculty:** 32 full-time (5 women), 13 part-time/adjunct (7 women).

**Students:** 40 full-time (32 women), 20 part-time (12 women); includes 17 minority (2 African Americans, 11 Asian Americans or Pacific Islanders, 4 Hispanic Americans), 6 international. Average age 30. 150 applicants, 32% accepted. In 2001, 25 degrees awarded.

**Degree requirements:** For master's, thesis (for some programs), comprehensive exam.

**Entrance requirements:** For master's, minimum GPA of 3.0. *Application deadline:* For fall admission, 6/29; for spring admission, 11/30. Applications are processed on a rolling basis. *Application fee:* $59. Electronic applications accepted.

**Expenses:** Tuition, nonresident: part-time $246 per unit. Required fees: $678 per semester. Tuition and fees vary according to course load.

**Financial support:** In 2001–02, 15 teaching assistantships were awarded; career-related internships or fieldwork and institutionally sponsored loans also available. Financial award application deadline: 3/1; financial award applicants required to submit FAFSA.

**Faculty research:** Drug and alcohol abuse, neurohormonal mechanisms in motion sickness, behavior modification, sleep research, genetics.

Dr. Robert Pelligrini, Chair, 408-924-5600, *Fax:* 408-924-5605.

**Application contact:** Laree Huntsman, Graduate Adviser, 408-924-5633.

■ **SOUTHERN ILLINOIS UNIVERSITY EDWARDSVILLE**

**Graduate Studies and Research, School of Education, Department of Psychology, Edwardsville, IL 62026-0001**

**AWARDS** Clinical adult (MS); community school (MS); general academic (MA); industrial organizational (MS). Part-time programs available.

**Students:** 33 full-time (26 women), 24 part-time (20 women); includes 6 minority (4 African Americans, 2 Hispanic Americans), 3 international. Average age 33. 64 applicants, 56% accepted, 21 enrolled. In 2001, 29 degrees awarded.

**Degree requirements:** For master's, thesis, final exam.

**Entrance requirements:** For master's, GRE General Test, GRE Subject Test, MAT, TOEFL. *Application deadline:* For fall admission, 7/20; for spring admission, 12/7. *Application fee:* $25.

**Expenses:** Tuition, state resident: full-time $2,712; part-time $113 per credit hour. Tuition, nonresident: full-time $5,424; part-time $226 per credit hour. Required fees: $250; $125 per term. Tuition and fees vary according to course load, campus/location and reciprocity agreements.

**Financial support:** In 2001–02, 3 fellowships with full tuition reimbursements, 4 teaching assistantships with full tuition reimbursements were awarded. Research assistantships, career-related internships or fieldwork, Federal Work-Study, institutionally sponsored loans, traineeships, and unspecified assistantships also available. Support available to part-time students. Financial award application deadline: 3/1; financial award applicants required to submit FAFSA.

Dr. Bryce Sullivan, Chair, 618-650-2202, *E-mail:* bsulliv@siue.edu.

■ **SPRINGFIELD COLLEGE**

**School of Graduate Studies, Programs in Counseling and Psychological Services, Springfield, MA 01109-3797**

**AWARDS** Athletic counseling (M Ed, MS, CAS); general counseling (M Ed, MS, CAS); industrial/organizational psychology (MS, CAS); marriage and family therapy (M Ed, MS, CAS); mental health counseling (M Ed, MS, CAS); school guidance and counseling (M Ed, MS, CAS); student personnel in higher education (M Ed, MS, CAS). Part-time and evening/weekend programs available.

**Faculty:** 11 full-time (7 women), 20 part-time/adjunct (9 women).

**Students:** 133 full-time, 34 part-time. Average age 26. 210 applicants, 93% accepted. In 2001, 63 master's, 3 other advanced degrees awarded.

**Degree requirements:** For master's, thesis (for some programs), research project, internship, comprehensive exam.

**Entrance requirements:** For master's and CAS, interview. *Application deadline:* For fall admission, 2/1 (priority date); for spring admission, 12/1. Applications are processed on a rolling basis. *Application fee:* $40.

**Financial support:** In 2001–02, 8 fellowships with partial tuition reimbursements (averaging $2,000 per year), 2 research assistantships (averaging $4,000 per year), 7 teaching assistantships (averaging $1,800 per year) were awarded. Career-related internships or fieldwork, Federal Work-Study, institutionally sponsored loans, scholarships/grants, and tuition waivers (full and partial) also available. Financial award application deadline: 3/1.

**Faculty research:** Sport psychology, leadership and emotional intelligence, rehabilitation adherence, professional career women and caregiving. *Total annual research expenditures:* $715,109.

Dr. Barbara Mandell, Director, 413-748-3339, *Fax:* 413-748-3854, *E-mail:* barbara_mandell@spfldcol.edu.

**Application contact:** Donald James Shaw, Director of Graduate Admissions, 413-748-3225, *Fax:* 413-748-3694, *E-mail:* donald_shaw_jr@spfldcol.edu.

■ **STATE UNIVERSITY OF NEW YORK AT ALBANY**

**College of Arts and Sciences, Department of Psychology, Albany, NY 12222-0001**

**AWARDS** Biopsychology (PhD); clinical psychology (PhD); general/experimental psychology (PhD); industrial/organizational psychology (PhD); psychology (MA); social/personality psychology (PhD).

**Students:** 69 full-time (45 women), 58 part-time (41 women); includes 12 minority (2 African Americans, 3 Asian

Americans or Pacific Islanders, 7 Hispanic Americans), 13 international. Average age 28. 220 applicants, 20% accepted. In 2001, 11 master's, 6 doctorates awarded.

**Degree requirements:** For doctorate, thesis/dissertation.

**Entrance requirements:** For doctorate, GRE General Test, GRE Subject Test. *Application deadline:* For fall admission, 1/15. *Application fee:* $50.

**Expenses:** Tuition, state resident: full-time $2,550; part-time $213 per credit. Tuition, nonresident: full-time $4,208; part-time $351 per credit. Required fees: $470; $470 per year.

**Financial support:** Fellowships, research assistantships, teaching assistantships, career-related internships or fieldwork available. Financial award application deadline: 2/1.

Robert Rosellini, Chair, 518-442-4820.

**Application contact:** Glenn Sanders, Graduate Director, 518-442-4853.

■ **TEACHERS COLLEGE COLUMBIA UNIVERSITY**

**Graduate Faculty of Education, Department of Organization and Leadership, Program in Social and Organizational Psychology, New York, NY 10027-6696**

**AWARDS** Organizational psychology (MA, Ed D, PhD); social psychology (Ed D, PhD). Terminal master's awarded for partial completion of doctoral program.

**Degree requirements:** For master's, comprehensive exam; for doctorate, thesis/dissertation.

**Entrance requirements:** For master's, minimum GPA of 3.0; for doctorate, GRE General Test.

**Expenses:** Tuition: Full-time $19,080; part-time $780 per unit. Required fees: $170 per semester.

**Faculty research:** Conflict resolution, human resource and organization development, management competence, organizational culture, leadership, leader and manager competencies.

■ **TEMPLE UNIVERSITY**

**Graduate School, College of Education, Department of Psychological Studies in Education, Program in Adult and Organizational Development, Philadelphia, PA 19122-6096**

**AWARDS** Ed M. Part-time and evening/weekend programs available.

**Degree requirements:** For master's, thesis or alternative.

**Entrance requirements:** For master's, GRE General Test or MAT, minimum GPA of 2.8.

*Temple University (continued)*

**Expenses:** Tuition, state resident: full-time $8,487; part-time $369 per credit hour. Tuition, nonresident: full-time $12,282; part-time $534 per credit hour. Required fees: $350. Tuition and fees vary according to course load, program and reciprocity agreements.

■ **TEMPLE UNIVERSITY**

**Graduate School, College of Liberal Arts, Department of Psychology, Program in Social and Organizational Psychology, Philadelphia, PA 19122-6096**

**AWARDS** PhD.

**Degree requirements:** For doctorate, thesis/dissertation, preliminary exam.
**Entrance requirements:** For doctorate, GRE General Test, minimum GPA of 3.0. Electronic applications accepted.
**Expenses:** Tuition, state resident: full-time $8,487; part-time $369 per credit hour. Tuition, nonresident: full-time $12,282; part-time $534 per credit hour. Required fees: $350. Tuition and fees vary according to course load, program and reciprocity agreements.
**Faculty research:** Power and technology, organizational behavior, interpersonal dynamics, belief, consumer behavior.

**Find an in-depth description at www.petersons.com/gradchannel.**

■ **TEXAS A&M UNIVERSITY**

**College of Liberal Arts, Department of Psychology, Program in Industrial/Organizational Psychology, College Station, TX 77843**

**AWARDS** MS, PhD.

**Degree requirements:** For master's and doctorate, thesis/dissertation.
**Entrance requirements:** For master's and doctorate, GRE General Test, TOEFL. *Application deadline:* For fall admission, 1/15. *Application fee:* $50 ($75 for international students). Electronic applications accepted.
**Expenses:** Tuition, state resident: full-time $11,872. Tuition, nonresident: full-time $17,892.
**Financial support:** Fellowships, research assistantships, teaching assistantships, career-related internships or fieldwork and institutionally sponsored loans available. Financial award application deadline: 1/15; financial award applicants required to submit FAFSA.
**Faculty research:** Performance appraisal, validation and criterion development, organizational productivity, group decision making.
Dr. Winfred Arthur, Area Coordinator, 979-845-2502, *E-mail:* wea@psyc.tamu.edu.

**Application contact:** Sharon Starr, Graduate Admissions Supervisor, 979-458-1710, *Fax:* 979-845-4727, *E-mail:* gradadv@psyc.tamu.edu. *Web site:* http://psycweb.tamu.edu/

■ **THE UNIVERSITY OF AKRON**

**Graduate School, Buchtel College of Arts and Sciences, Department of Psychology, Program in Industrial/Organizational Psychology, Akron, OH 44325-0001**

**AWARDS** MA, PhD.

**Students:** 32 full-time (18 women), 20 part-time (10 women), 7 international. Average age 29. 30 applicants, 40% accepted, 8 enrolled. In 2001, 1 master's, 11 doctorates awarded. Terminal master's awarded for partial completion of doctoral program.
**Degree requirements:** For master's, thesis or specialty exam; for doctorate, one foreign language, thesis/dissertation, comprehensive exam.
**Entrance requirements:** For master's, GRE General Test, GRE Subject Test, minimum GPA of 2.75; for doctorate, GRE General Test, GRE Subject Test. *Application deadline:* For fall admission, 3/1. Applications are processed on a rolling basis. *Application fee:* $40 ($50 for international students).
**Expenses:** Tuition, state resident: full-time $6,562; part-time $219 per credit. Tuition, nonresident: full-time $9,027; part-time $383 per credit. Required fees: $272; $11 per credit. Tuition and fees vary according to course load.
**Financial support:** Fellowships with full tuition reimbursements, research assistantships with full tuition reimbursements, teaching assistantships with full tuition reimbursements available. Financial award application deadline: 3/1.
**Faculty research:** Job evaluation, comparable worth, leadership, statistical analysis, information processing.
Dr. Paul Levy, Coordinator, 330-972-8369, *E-mail:* plevy@uakron.edu.
**Application contact:** Dr. Daniel Svyantek, Head, 330-972-6705, *E-mail:* dsvyantek@uakron.edu.

■ **UNIVERSITY OF BALTIMORE**

**Graduate School, College of Liberal Arts, Department of Psychology, Baltimore, MD 21201-5779**

**AWARDS** Applied assessment and consulting (Psy D); applied psychology (MS); counseling (MS); industrial and organizational psychology (MS). Part-time and evening/weekend programs available.

**Faculty:** 7 full-time (5 women), 7 part-time/adjunct (2 women).

**Students:** 42 full-time (31 women), 45 part-time (34 women); includes 23 minority (14 African Americans, 5 Asian Americans or Pacific Islanders, 4 Hispanic Americans), 6 international. Average age 27. 102 applicants, 79% accepted. In 2001, 40 degrees awarded.
**Degree requirements:** For master's, thesis optional; for doctorate, thesis/dissertation.
**Entrance requirements:** For master's, GRE, minimum GPA of 3.0; for doctorate, GRE. *Application deadline:* For fall admission, 7/15; for spring admission, 12/15. Applications are processed on a rolling basis. *Application fee:* $30. Electronic applications accepted.
**Expenses:** Contact institution.
**Financial support:** In 2001–02, 5 research assistantships with full and partial tuition reimbursements were awarded; fellowships, career-related internships or fieldwork and Federal Work-Study also available. Support available to part-time students. Financial award application deadline: 4/1; financial award applicants required to submit FAFSA.
**Faculty research:** Participatory decision making, counter productive workplace behavior, organizational consulting, substance abuse treatment, cognitive functioning in head injured. *Total annual research expenditures:* $93,146.
Dr. Paul Mastrangelo, Director, Applied Psychology Program, 410-837-5352, *E-mail:* pmastrangelo@ubalt.edu.
**Application contact:** Jeffrey Zavrotny, Assistant Director of Admissions, 410-837-4777, *Fax:* 410-837-4793, *E-mail:* jzavrotny@ubalt.edu.

**Find an in-depth description at www.petersons.com/gradchannel.**

■ **UNIVERSITY OF CENTRAL FLORIDA**

**College of Arts and Sciences, Department of Psychology, Program in Human Factors Psychology, Orlando, FL 32816**

**AWARDS** PhD.

**Faculty:** 31 full-time (9 women), 24 part-time/adjunct (12 women).
**Students:** 23 full-time (9 women), 21 part-time (9 women); includes 6 minority (all Hispanic Americans). Average age 31. 23 applicants, 61% accepted, 13 enrolled. In 2001, 5 degrees awarded.
**Degree requirements:** For doctorate, thesis/dissertation, departmental candidacy exam.
**Entrance requirements:** For doctorate, GRE General Test, TOEFL, minimum GPA of 3.2 in last 60 hours or master's qualifying exam. *Application deadline:* For

fall admission, 2/1. *Application fee:* $20. Electronic applications accepted.
**Expenses:** Tuition, state resident: part-time $162 per hour. Tuition, nonresident: part-time $569 per hour.
**Financial support:** In 2001–02, 15 fellowships with partial tuition reimbursements (averaging $3,900 per year), 37 research assistantships with partial tuition reimbursements (averaging $4,820 per year), 8 teaching assistantships with partial tuition reimbursements (averaging $2,766 per year) were awarded. Career-related internships or fieldwork, Federal Work-Study, institutionally sponsored loans, tuition waivers (partial), and unspecified assistantships also available. Financial award application deadline: 3/1; financial award applicants required to submit FAFSA.
**Faculty research:** Visual performance, team training, controls/displays, synthetic speech, alarms/warning.
Dr. Eduardo Salas, Coordinator, 407-823-1011, *Fax:* 407-823-5862, *E-mail:* esalas@pegasus.cc.ucf.edu.
**Application contact:** Information Contact, 407-823-1011, *Fax:* 402-823-5862. *Web site:* http://www.ucf.edu/

## ■ UNIVERSITY OF CENTRAL FLORIDA

College of Arts and Sciences, Department of Psychology, Program in Industrial/Organizational Psychology, Orlando, FL 32816
**AWARDS** MS, PhD. Part-time and evening/weekend programs available.
**Faculty:** 31 full-time (9 women), 24 part-time/adjunct (12 women).
**Students:** 32 full-time (22 women), 22 part-time (14 women); includes 17 minority (9 African Americans, 1 Asian American or Pacific Islander, 7 Hispanic Americans), 1 international. Average age 30. 123 applicants, 31% accepted, 17 enrolled. In 2001, 1 degree awarded.
**Degree requirements:** For master's, thesis, practicum, comprehensive exam.
**Entrance requirements:** For master's, GRE General Test, TOEFL, minimum GPA of 3.0 in last 60 hours, resumé.
*Application deadline:* For fall admission, 2/1. *Application fee:* $20. Electronic applications accepted.
**Expenses:** Tuition, state resident: part-time $162 per hour. Tuition, nonresident: part-time $569 per hour.
**Financial support:** In 2001–02, 18 fellowships with partial tuition reimbursements (averaging $3,375 per year), 20 research assistantships with partial tuition reimbursements (averaging $3,017 per year), 22 teaching assistantships with partial tuition reimbursements (averaging

$2,527 per year) were awarded. Career-related internships or fieldwork, Federal Work-Study, institutionally sponsored loans, tuition waivers (partial), and unspecified assistantships also available. Financial award application deadline: 3/1; financial award applicants required to submit FAFSA.
**Faculty research:** Sports psychology, electronic selection systems, team training, stress effects, psychometrics.
Dr. William Wooten, Coordinator, 407-823-3478.
**Application contact:** Dr. Eugene Stone-Romero, Information Contact, 407-823-1011, *E-mail:* estone@pegasus.cc.ucf.edu. *Web site:* http://www.ucf.edu/

## ■ UNIVERSITY OF CONNECTICUT

Graduate School, College of Liberal Arts and Sciences, Field of Psychology, Storrs, CT 06269
**AWARDS** Behavioral neuroscience (PhD); biopsychology (PhD); clinical psychology (PhD); cognition/instruction psychology (PhD); developmental psychology (PhD); ecological psychology (PhD); general experimental psychology (PhD); industrial and organizational psychology (PhD); language psychology (PhD); social psychology (PhD).
**Faculty:** 41 full-time (11 women), 2 part-time/adjunct (both women).
**Students:** 134 full-time (83 women), 17 part-time (9 women); includes 13 minority (9 African Americans, 1 Asian American or Pacific Islander, 3 Hispanic Americans), 17 international. Average age 28. 378 applicants, 14% accepted, 25 enrolled. In 2001, 18 degrees awarded.
**Degree requirements:** For doctorate, thesis/dissertation, internship, comprehensive exam, registration.
**Entrance requirements:** For doctorate, GRE General Test, GRE Subject Test, letters of recommendation. *Application deadline:* For fall admission, 12/31. *Application fee:* $40 ($45 for international students).
**Financial support:** In 2001–02, 45 fellowships (averaging $4,000 per year), 16 research assistantships with full tuition reimbursements (averaging $16,000 per year), 83 teaching assistantships with full tuition reimbursements (averaging $16,000 per year) were awarded. Career-related internships or fieldwork, Federal Work-Study, scholarships/grants, health care benefits, and unspecified assistantships also available. Financial award application deadline: 12/31.
**Faculty research:** Behavioral neuroscience; physiology/chemistry of memory; sensation, motor control/motivation; cognitive, social, personality and language development; infancy/person

perceptions and intergroup relations. *Total annual research expenditures:* $8 million.
Charles A. Lowe, Head, *Fax:* 860-486-2760, *E-mail:* charles.lowe@uconn.edu.
**Application contact:** Gina Stuart, Graduate Admissions, 860-486-3528, *Fax:* 860-486-2760, *E-mail:* futuregr@psych.psy.uconn.edu. *Web site:* http://psych.uconn.edu/

## ■ UNIVERSITY OF DETROIT MERCY

College of Liberal Arts and Education, Department of Psychology, Program in Industrial/Organizational Psychology, Detroit, MI 48219-0900
**AWARDS** MA.
**Faculty:** 14 full-time (10 women).
**Students:** 4 full-time (3 women), 11 part-time (10 women); includes 3 minority (all African Americans). In 2001, 9 degrees awarded.
**Entrance requirements:** For master's, GRE General Test, minimum GPA of 3.0. *Application deadline:* For fall admission, 8/1 (priority date). Applications are processed on a rolling basis. *Application fee:* $30 ($50 for international students).
**Expenses:** Tuition: Full-time $10,620; part-time $590 per credit hour. Required fees: $400. Tuition and fees vary according to program.
Dr. Kathleen Zimmerman-Oster, Director, 313-993-1137, *Fax:* 313-993-6397, *E-mail:* zimmerka@udmercy.edu.

## ■ UNIVERSITY OF HOUSTON

College of Liberal Arts and Social Sciences, Department of Psychology, Houston, TX 77204
**AWARDS** Clinical psychology (PhD); industrial/organizational psychology (PhD); social psychology (PhD).
**Faculty:** 22 full-time (9 women), 8 part-time/adjunct (4 women).
**Students:** 82 full-time (57 women), 20 part-time (16 women); includes 12 minority (2 African Americans, 3 Asian Americans or Pacific Islanders, 7 Hispanic Americans), 2 international. Average age 29. 280 applicants, 8% accepted. In 2001, 14 doctorates awarded.
**Degree requirements:** For doctorate, thesis/dissertation.
**Entrance requirements:** For doctorate, GRE General Test, minimum GPA of 3.0. *Application deadline:* For fall admission, 1/1. *Application fee:* $40 ($75 for international students).
**Expenses:** Tuition, state resident: full-time $1,512. Tuition, nonresident: full-time $5,310. Required fees: $1,308. Tuition and fees vary according to program.

*University of Houston (continued)*

**Financial support:** In 2001–02, research assistantships with partial tuition reimbursements (averaging $12,300 per year), teaching assistantships with partial tuition reimbursements (averaging $10,800 per year) were awarded. Career-related internships or fieldwork, Federal Work-Study, institutionally sponsored loans, and teaching fellowships also available.
**Faculty research:** Health psychology, depression, child/family process, organizational effectiveness, close relationships. *Total annual research expenditures:* $4.5 million.
Dr. John P. Vincent, Chairman, 713-743-8503, *Fax:* 713-743-8588, *E-mail:* jvincent@uh.edu.
**Application contact:** Sherry A. Berun, Coordinator—Academic Affairs, 713-743-8508, *Fax:* 713-743-8588, *E-mail:* sherryr@uh.edu. *Web site:* http://firenza.uh.edu/

### ■ UNIVERSITY OF ILLINOIS AT URBANA–CHAMPAIGN

**Graduate College, College of Liberal Arts and Sciences, Department of Psychology, Champaign, IL 61820**
**AWARDS** Applied measurement (MS); biological psychology (AM, PhD); clinical psychology (AM, PhD); cognitive psychology (AM, PhD); developmental psychology (AM, PhD); engineering psychology (MS); personnel psychology (MS); quantitative psychology (AM, PhD); social-personality-organizational (AM, PhD); visual cognition and human performance (AM, PhD).
**Faculty:** 41 full-time (14 women), 11 part-time/adjunct (3 women).
**Students:** 156 full-time (90 women); includes 23 minority (6 African Americans, 12 Asian Americans or Pacific Islanders, 5 Hispanic Americans), 42 international. 461 applicants, 17% accepted, 27 enrolled. In 2001, 1 master's, 25 doctorates awarded.
**Degree requirements:** For doctorate, thesis/dissertation.
**Entrance requirements:** For master's, GRE General Test, GRE Subject Test (recommended), minimum GPA of 3.0; for doctorate, GRE General Test, GRE Subject Test (recommended). *Application deadline:* For fall admission, 1/1. *Application fee:* $40 ($50 for international students).
**Expenses:** Tuition, state resident: part-time $3,227 per degree program. Tuition, nonresident: part-time $7,169 per degree program. Tuition and fees vary according to program.
**Financial support:** In 2001–02, 31 fellowships with full tuition reimbursements (averaging $15,000 per year), 21 research assistantships with full tuition reimbursements (averaging $13,585 per year), 73 teaching assistantships with full tuition

reimbursements (averaging $13,585 per year) were awarded. Career-related internships or fieldwork, traineeships, and tuition waivers (full) also available. Financial award application deadline: 1/1. *Total annual research expenditures:* $4.6 million.
Dr. Edward J. Shoben, Head.
**Application contact:** Cheryl Berger, Assistant Head for Graduate Affairs, 217-333-3429, *Fax:* 217-244-5876, *E-mail:* gradstdy@s.psych.uiuc.edu. *Web site:* http://www.psych.uiuc.edu/

### ■ UNIVERSITY OF MARYLAND, COLLEGE PARK

**Graduate Studies and Research, College of Behavioral and Social Sciences, Department of Psychology, College Park, MD 20742**
**AWARDS** Clinical psychology (PhD); developmental psychology (PhD); experimental psychology (PhD); industrial psychology (MA, MS, PhD); social psychology (PhD).
**Faculty:** 52 full-time (17 women), 10 part-time/adjunct (5 women).
**Students:** 80 full-time (50 women), 22 part-time (15 women); includes 26 minority (14 African Americans, 8 Asian Americans or Pacific Islanders, 3 Hispanic Americans, 1 Native American), 11 international. 432 applicants, 10% accepted, 18 enrolled. In 2001, 8 master's, 21 doctorates awarded.
**Degree requirements:** For master's, thesis; for doctorate, variable foreign language requirement, thesis/dissertation, comprehensive exam.
**Entrance requirements:** For master's, GRE General Test, GRE Subject Test, minimum GPA of 3.5, research and/or work experience; for doctorate, GRE General Test, GRE Subject Test. *Application deadline:* For fall admission, 12/15. Applications are processed on a rolling basis. *Application fee:* $50 ($70 for international students). Electronic applications accepted.
**Expenses:** Tuition, state resident: part-time $289 per credit hour. Tuition, nonresident: part-time $448 per credit hour. One-time fee: $436 part-time. Full-time tuition and fees vary according to course load, campus/location and program.
**Financial support:** In 2001–02, 15 fellowships with full tuition reimbursements (averaging $11,508 per year), 87 teaching assistantships with tuition reimbursements (averaging $12,153 per year) were awarded. Career-related internships or fieldwork, Federal Work-Study, and scholarships/grants also available. Support available to part-time students. Financial award applicants required to submit FAFSA.

**Faculty research:** Counseling and social psychology.
Dr. William Hall, Chairman, 301-405-5862, *Fax:* 301-314-9566.
**Application contact:** Trudy Lindsey, Director, Graduate Admissions and Records, 301-405-6991, *Fax:* 301-314-9305, *E-mail:* grschool@deans.umd.edu.

### ■ UNIVERSITY OF MICHIGAN

**Horace H. Rackham School of Graduate Studies, College of Literature, Science, and the Arts, Department of Psychology, Ann Arbor, MI 48109**
**AWARDS** Biopsychology (PhD); clinical psychology (PhD); cognition and perception (PhD); developmental psychology (PhD); organizational psychology (PhD); personality psychology (PhD); social psychology (PhD).
**Faculty:** 68 full-time, 29 part-time/adjunct.
**Students:** 166 full-time (122 women); includes 57 minority (27 African Americans, 13 Asian Americans or Pacific Islanders, 14 Hispanic Americans, 3 Native Americans), 22 international. Average age 24. 555 applicants, 8% accepted, 27 enrolled. In 2001, 25 degrees awarded.
**Degree requirements:** For doctorate, oral defense of dissertation, preliminary exam.
**Entrance requirements:** For doctorate, GRE General Test, GRE Subject Test, TOEFL. *Application deadline:* For fall admission, 12/15. *Application fee:* $55. Electronic applications accepted.
**Financial support:** Fellowships with full tuition reimbursements, research assistantships with full tuition reimbursements, teaching assistantships with full tuition reimbursements, career-related internships or fieldwork available. Financial award application deadline: 3/15.
Richard Gonzalez, Chair, 734-764-7429.
**Application contact:** 734-764-6316, *Fax:* 734-764-3520. *Web site:* http://www.lsa.umich.edu/psych/

### ■ UNIVERSITY OF MINNESOTA, TWIN CITIES CAMPUS

**Graduate School, College of Liberal Arts, Department of Psychology, Program in Industrial/Organizational Psychology, Minneapolis, MN 55455-0213**
**AWARDS** PhD.
**Students:** 18 full-time (12 women); includes 1 minority (African American), 3 international. 72 applicants, 11% accepted, 2 enrolled.
**Degree requirements:** For doctorate, thesis/dissertation, comprehensive exam.
**Entrance requirements:** For doctorate, GRE General Test, GRE Subject Test

(recommended), TOEFL, 12 credits of upper-level psychology courses, including a course in statistics or psychological measurement. *Application deadline:* For fall admission, 1/5. *Application fee:* $55 ($75 for international students).
**Expenses:** Tuition, state resident: full-time $2,932; part-time $489 per credit. Tuition, nonresident: full-time $5,758; part-time $960 per credit. Part-time tuition and fees vary according to course load, program and reciprocity agreements.
**Financial support:** Fellowships, research assistantships, teaching assistantships, career-related internships or fieldwork and tuition waivers (partial) available. Financial award application deadline: 12/1.
**Application contact:** Coordinator, 612-624-4181, *Fax:* 612-626-2079, *E-mail:* psyapply.tc.umn.edu.

■ **UNIVERSITY OF MISSOURI–ST. LOUIS**

**Graduate School, College of Arts and Sciences, Department of Psychology, St. Louis, MO 63121-4499**

**AWARDS** Clinical psychology (PhD); clinical psychology respecialization (Certificate); experimental psychology (PhD); general psychology (MA); industrial/organizational (PhD). Evening/weekend programs available.
**Faculty:** 18.
**Students:** 34 full-time (27 women), 38 part-time (25 women); includes 9 minority (6 African Americans, 2 Asian Americans or Pacific Islanders, 1 Hispanic American), 2 international. In 2001, 12 master's, 5 doctorates awarded. Terminal master's awarded for partial completion of doctoral program.
**Degree requirements:** For doctorate, thesis/dissertation.
**Entrance requirements:** For master's and doctorate, GRE General Test, GRE Subject Test. *Application deadline:* For fall admission, 2/1 (priority date). Applications are processed on a rolling basis. *Application fee:* $25 ($40 for international students). Electronic applications accepted.
**Expenses:** Tuition, state resident: part-time $231 per credit hour. Tuition, nonresident: part-time $621 per credit hour.
**Financial support:** In 2001–02, 2 fellowships with full tuition reimbursements (averaging $12,000 per year), 9 research assistantships with full and partial tuition reimbursements (averaging $13,585 per year), 23 teaching assistantships with full and partial tuition reimbursements (averaging $9,096 per year) were awarded.
**Faculty research:** Animal-human learning; physiological, industrial-organizational and cognitive processes; personality-social,

clinical and community psychology. *Total annual research expenditures:* $1.1 million.
Dr. Gary Burger, Chair, 314-516-5391, *Fax:* 314-516-5392.
**Application contact:** Graduate Admissions, 314-516-5458, *Fax:* 314-516-5310, *E-mail:* gradadm@umsl.edu.

■ **UNIVERSITY OF NEBRASKA AT OMAHA**

**Graduate Studies and Research, College of Arts and Sciences, Department of Psychology, Omaha, NE 68182**

**AWARDS** Developmental psychobiology (PhD); experimental child psychology (PhD); industrial/organizational psychology (MS, PhD); psychology (MA); school psychology (MS, Ed S). Part-time programs available.
**Faculty:** 17 full-time (7 women).
**Students:** 32 full-time (22 women), 18 part-time (10 women); includes 2 minority (1 African American, 1 Hispanic American). Average age 27. 64 applicants, 44% accepted, 28 enrolled. In 2001, 23 master's, 4 other advanced degrees awarded.
**Degree requirements:** For master's, thesis (for some programs), comprehensive exam; for doctorate, thesis/dissertation.
**Entrance requirements:** For master's, GRE General Test, GRE Subject Test, previous course work in psychology, including statistics and a laboratory course; minimum GPA of 3.0; for doctorate, GRE General Test. *Application deadline:* For fall admission, 2/1. *Application fee:* $35. Electronic applications accepted.
**Expenses:** Tuition, state resident: part-time $116 per credit hour. Tuition, nonresident: part-time $291 per credit hour. Required fees: $13 per credit hour. $4 per semester. One-time fee: $52 part-time.
**Financial support:** In 2001–02, 42 students received support; fellowships, research assistantships, teaching assistantships, career-related internships or fieldwork, Federal Work-Study, institutionally sponsored loans, scholarships/grants, tuition waivers (partial), and unspecified assistantships available. Support available to part-time students. Financial award application deadline: 3/1; financial award applicants required to submit FAFSA.
Dr. Kenneth Deffenbacher, Chairperson, 402-554-2592.

■ **UNIVERSITY OF NEW HAVEN**

**Graduate School, College of Arts and Sciences, Program in Industrial and Organizational Psychology, West Haven, CT 06516-1916**

**AWARDS** MA, Certificate. Part-time and evening/weekend programs available.

**Students:** 44 full-time (23 women), 29 part-time (20 women); includes 6 minority (3 African Americans, 3 Hispanic Americans), 3 international. In 2001, 33 degrees awarded.
**Degree requirements:** For master's, thesis or alternative.
*Application deadline:* Applications are processed on a rolling basis. *Application fee:* $50.
**Expenses:** Tuition: Full-time $12,015; part-time $445 per credit hour. Required fees: $30. One-time fee: $100 full-time.
**Financial support:** Career-related internships or fieldwork and Federal Work-Study available. Support available to part-time students. Financial award application deadline: 5/1; financial award applicants required to submit FAFSA.
Dr. Tara L'Heureux, Coordinator, 203-932-7341.
**Application contact:** Information Contact, 800-DIAL-UNH Ext. 7341, *Fax:* 203-931-6032. *Web site:* http://www.newhaven.edu/departments/psych.htm

■ **THE UNIVERSITY OF NORTH CAROLINA AT CHARLOTTE**

**Graduate School, College of Arts and Sciences, Department of Psychology, Concentration in Industrial/ Organizational Psychology, Charlotte, NC 28223-0001**

**AWARDS** MA.

**Students:** 24 full-time (17 women), 9 part-time (6 women); includes 6 minority (3 African Americans, 2 Asian Americans or Pacific Islanders, 1 Native American), 2 international. Average age 26. 68 applicants, 18% accepted, 11 enrolled. In 2001, 8 degrees awarded.
**Degree requirements:** For master's, thesis, comprehensive exam.
**Entrance requirements:** For master's, GRE General Test, GRE Subject Test, minimum undergraduate GPA of 3.0 in major, 2.8 overall. *Application deadline:* For fall admission, 2/1. *Application fee:* $35. Electronic applications accepted.
**Expenses:** Tuition, state resident: full-time $1,483; part-time $371 per year. Tuition, nonresident: full-time $9,850; part-time $2,463 per year. Required fees: $1,043; $277 per year. Tuition and fees vary according to course load.
**Financial support:** In 2001–02, 2 research assistantships, 4 teaching assistantships were awarded. Fellowships, career-related internships or fieldwork, Federal Work-Study, institutionally sponsored loans, scholarships/grants, and unspecified assistantships also available. Support available to part-time students. Financial award application deadline: 4/1; financial award applicants required to submit FAFSA.

*The University of North Carolina at Charlotte (continued)*
Dr. William Scott Terry, Coordinator, 704-687-4751, *Fax:* 704-687-3096, *E-mail:* wsterry@email.wcc.edu.
**Application contact:** Kathy Barringer, Director of Graduate Admissions, 704-687-3366, *Fax:* 704-687-3279, *E-mail:* gradadm@email.uncc.edu.

■ **UNIVERSITY OF NORTH TEXAS**
**Robert B. Toulouse School of Graduate Studies, College of Arts and Sciences, Department of Psychology, Denton, TX 76203**

**AWARDS** Clinical psychology (PhD); counseling psychology (MA, MS, PhD); experimental psychology (MA, MS, PhD); health psychology and behavioral medicine (PhD); industrial psychology (MA, MS); psychology (MA, MS, PhD); school psychology (MA, MS, PhD).

**Faculty:** 29 full-time (5 women), 7 part-time/adjunct (5 women).
**Students:** 129 full-time (96 women), 98 part-time (70 women); includes 23 minority (2 African Americans, 4 Asian Americans or Pacific Islanders, 15 Hispanic Americans, 2 Native Americans), 9 international. Average age 30. In 2001, 24 master's, 17 doctorates awarded. Terminal master's awarded for partial completion of doctoral program.
**Degree requirements:** For master's, thesis or alternative, comprehensive exam; for doctorate, one foreign language, thesis/dissertation, comprehensive exam.
**Entrance requirements:** For master's and doctorate, GRE General Test, GRE Subject Test, interview. *Application deadline:* For fall admission, 2/1. *Application fee:* $25 ($50 for international students).
**Expenses:** Tuition, state resident: part-time $186 per hour. Tuition, nonresident: part-time $319 per hour. Required fees: $88; $21 per hour.
**Financial support:** Fellowships, research assistantships, teaching assistantships, career-related internships or fieldwork, Federal Work-Study, and institutionally sponsored loans available. Financial award application deadline: 8/1.
Dr. Ernest H. Harrell, Chair, 940-565-2671, *Fax:* 940-546-4682, *E-mail:* harrelle@unt.edu.
**Application contact:** Dr. Joseph Critelli, Graduate Adviser, 940-565-2671, *Fax:* 940-565-4682, *E-mail:* critelli@facstaff.cas.unt.edu.

■ **UNIVERSITY OF SOUTH FLORIDA**
**College of Graduate Studies, College of Arts and Sciences, Department of Psychology, Tampa, FL 33620-9951**
**AWARDS** Clinical psychology (PhD); experimental psychology (PhD); industrial/organizational psychology (PhD).
**Faculty:** 37 full-time (12 women), 2 part-time/adjunct (0 women).
**Students:** 99 full-time (67 women), 47 part-time (35 women); includes 32 minority (14 African Americans, 5 Asian Americans or Pacific Islanders, 13 Hispanic Americans), 8 international. Average age 30. 367 applicants, 7% accepted, 22 enrolled. In 2001, 5 doctorates awarded.
**Degree requirements:** For doctorate, thesis/dissertation.
**Entrance requirements:** For doctorate, GRE General Test, minimum GPA of 3.0 in last 60 hours. *Application deadline:* For fall admission, 1/15. *Application fee:* $20. Electronic applications accepted.
**Expenses:** Contact institution.
**Financial support:** Fellowships with partial tuition reimbursements, research assistantships with partial tuition reimbursements, teaching assistantships, career-related internships or fieldwork, Federal Work-Study, and institutionally sponsored loans available. Financial award application deadline: 4/15; financial award applicants required to submit FAFSA.
**Faculty research:** Human memory, job analysis, stress, drug and alcohol abuse, neuroscience. *Total annual research expenditures:* $1.4 million.
Emanuel Donchin, Chairperson, 813-974-4066, *Fax:* 813-974-4617, *E-mail:* donchin@luna.cas.usf.edu.
**Application contact:** Michael D. Coovert, Graduate Coordinator, 813-974-0482, *Fax:* 813-974-4617, *E-mail:* coovert@luna.cas.usf.edu. *Web site:* http://www.cas.usf.edu/psychology/

■ **THE UNIVERSITY OF TENNESSEE**
**Graduate School, College of Business Administration, Program in Industrial/Organizational Psychology, Knoxville, TN 37996**
**AWARDS** PhD.
**Students:** 19 full-time (12 women), 11 part-time (5 women); includes 1 minority (African American), 1 international. 36 applicants, 11% accepted. In 2001, 5 degrees awarded.
**Degree requirements:** For doctorate, thesis/dissertation.
**Entrance requirements:** For doctorate, GRE General Test, TOEFL, minimum

GPA of 2.7. *Application deadline:* For fall admission, 2/1 (priority date). Applications are processed on a rolling basis. *Application fee:* $35. Electronic applications accepted.
**Expenses:** Tuition, state resident: full-time $4,280; part-time $233 per hour. Tuition, nonresident: full-time $12,066; part-time $666 per hour. Tuition and fees vary according to program.
**Financial support:** In 2001–02, 1 fellowship was awarded; unspecified assistantships also available. Financial award application deadline: 2/1; financial award applicants required to submit FAFSA.
Dr. Robert T. Ladd, Director, 865-974-4843, *Fax:* 865-974-3163, *E-mail:* tladd@utk.edu.

■ **THE UNIVERSITY OF TENNESSEE AT CHATTANOOGA**
**Graduate Division, College of Arts and Sciences, Department of Psychology, Program in Industrial/Organizational Psychology, Chattanooga, TN 37403-2598**
**AWARDS** MS. Part-time and evening/weekend programs available.
**Students:** 23 full-time (16 women), 8 part-time (6 women); includes 5 minority (all African Americans). Average age 25. 44 applicants, 80% accepted, 12 enrolled. In 2001, 16 degrees awarded.
**Degree requirements:** For master's, thesis optional.
**Entrance requirements:** For master's, GRE General Test. *Application deadline:* For fall admission, 8/1 (priority date); for spring admission, 12/1 (priority date). Applications are processed on a rolling basis. *Application fee:* $25.
**Expenses:** Tuition, state resident: full-time $3,752; part-time $228 per hour. Tuition, nonresident: full-time $10,282; part-time $565 per hour.
**Financial support:** Fellowships, research assistantships available. Financial award application deadline: 4/1; financial award applicants required to submit FAFSA.
Dr. Michael D. Biderman, Coordinator, 423-425-4268, *Fax:* 423-425-4284, *E-mail:* michael-biderman@utc.edu.
**Application contact:** Dr. Deborah E. Arfken, Dean of Graduate Studies, 865-425-1740, *Fax:* 865-425-5223, *E-mail:* deborah-arfken@utc.edu. *Web site:* http://www.utc.edu/

■ **UNIVERSITY OF TULSA**
**Graduate School, College of Arts and Sciences, Department of Psychology, Program in Industrial/Organizational Psychology, Tulsa, OK 74104-3189**
**AWARDS** MA, PhD, JD/MA. Part-time programs available.

**Faculty:** 6 full-time (3 women).
**Students:** 31 full-time (12 women), 7 part-time (5 women); includes 4 minority (1 African American, 2 Hispanic Americans, 1 Native American), 2 international. Average age 27. 52 applicants, 40% accepted, 12 enrolled. In 2001, 20 master's, 4 doctorates awarded.
**Degree requirements:** For master's, comprehensive exam; for doctorate, thesis/dissertation, comprehensive exam.
**Entrance requirements:** For master's and doctorate, GRE General Test, TOEFL. *Application deadline:* For fall admission, 2/1 (priority date). Applications are processed on a rolling basis. *Application fee:* $30. Electronic applications accepted.
**Expenses:** Tuition: Full-time $9,540; part-time $530 per credit hour. Required fees: $80. One-time fee: $230 full-time.
**Financial support:** In 2001–02, 2 fellowships with full and partial tuition reimbursements (averaging $9,000 per year), 3 research assistantships with full and partial tuition reimbursements (averaging $7,300 per year), 11 teaching assistantships with full and partial tuition reimbursements (averaging $7,100 per year) were awarded. Career-related internships or fieldwork, Federal Work-Study, scholarships/grants, tuition waivers (partial), and unspecified assistantships also available. Support available to part-time students. Financial award application deadline: 2/1; financial award applicants required to submit FAFSA.
**Faculty research:** Personnel assessment and selection, leadership, industrial gerontology, personality factors in organizational performance.
Dr. Deidra Schleicher, Director, 918-631-2839, *Fax:* 918-631-2833, *E-mail:* deidra-schleicher@utulsa.edu. *Web site:* http://www.cas.utulsa.edu/psych.io_index.html/

## ■ UNIVERSITY OF WISCONSIN–OSHKOSH

**Graduate School, College of Letters and Science, Department of Psychology, Oshkosh, WI 54901**
**AWARDS** Experimental psychology (MS); industrial/organizational psychology (MS).
**Faculty:** 8 full-time (2 women).
**Students:** 20; includes 2 minority (1 Asian American or Pacific Islander, 1 Hispanic American). Average age 26. In 2001, 7 degrees awarded.
**Degree requirements:** For master's, thesis.
**Entrance requirements:** For master's, GRE, 10 semester hours of undergraduate course work in psychology. *Application deadline:* Applications are processed on a rolling basis. *Application fee:* $45. Electronic applications accepted.

**Expenses:** Tuition, state resident: full-time $2,236; part-time $250 per credit. Tuition, nonresident: full-time $7,148; part-time $795 per credit. Tuition and fees vary according to program.
**Financial support:** Career-related internships or fieldwork, institutionally sponsored loans, and unspecified assistantships available. Financial award application deadline: 3/15; financial award applicants required to submit FAFSA.
**Faculty research:** Performance evaluation, training, biological bases of behavior, tactile perception, aging.
Dr. Susan McFadden, Chair, 920-424-2300.
**Application contact:** 920-424-2300, *E-mail:* psychology@uwosh.edu. *Web site:* http://www.uwosh.edu/departments/psychology/

## ■ VALDOSTA STATE UNIVERSITY

**Graduate School, College of Education, Department of Psychology and Guidance, Valdosta, GA 31698**
**AWARDS** Clinical/counseling psychology (MS); industrial/organizational psychology (MS); school counseling (M Ed, Ed S); school psychology (M Ed, Ed S). Evening/weekend programs available.
**Faculty:** 13 full-time (2 women).
**Students:** 40 full-time (30 women), 62 part-time (54 women); includes 10 minority (7 African Americans, 1 Asian American or Pacific Islander, 1 Hispanic American, 1 Native American). Average age 26. 67 applicants, 75% accepted. In 2001, 17 degrees awarded.
**Degree requirements:** For master's, thesis or alternative, comprehensive written and/or oral exams; for Ed S, thesis.
**Entrance requirements:** For master's and Ed S, GRE General Test or MAT. *Application deadline:* For fall admission, 7/1; for spring admission, 11/15. Applications are processed on a rolling basis. *Application fee:* $20. Electronic applications accepted.
**Expenses:** Tuition, state resident: full-time $1,746; part-time $97 per hour. Tuition, nonresident: full-time $6,966; part-time $387 per hour. Required fees: $594; $297 per semester.
**Financial support:** In 2001–02, 2 research assistantships with full tuition reimbursements (averaging $2,452 per year) were awarded; institutionally sponsored loans and unspecified assistantships also available. Support available to part-time students. Financial award application deadline: 7/1; financial award applicants required to submit FAFSA.
**Faculty research:** Using Bender-Gestalt to predict graphomotor dimensions of the draw-a-person test, neurobehavioral hemispheric dominance.

Dr. R. Bauer, Head, 229-333-5930, *Fax:* 229-259-5576, *E-mail:* bbauer@valdosta.edu.

## ■ VIRGINIA POLYTECHNIC INSTITUTE AND STATE UNIVERSITY

**Graduate School, College of Arts and Sciences, Department of Psychology, Blacksburg, VA 24061**
**AWARDS** Bio-behavioral sciences (PhD); clinical psychology (PhD); developmental psychology (PhD); industrial/organizational psychology (PhD); psychology (MS).
**Faculty:** 22 full-time (4 women), 3 part-time/adjunct (2 women).
**Students:** 68 full-time (45 women), 8 part-time (6 women); includes 13 minority (5 African Americans, 4 Asian Americans or Pacific Islanders, 4 Hispanic Americans). Average age 23. 156 applicants, 21% accepted, 15 enrolled. In 2001, 4 master's, 8 doctorates awarded.
**Degree requirements:** For doctorate, thesis/dissertation.
**Entrance requirements:** For master's and doctorate, GRE General Test, TOEFL. *Application deadline:* For fall admission, 1/15 (priority date); for winter admission, 12/15 (priority date). Applications are processed on a rolling basis. *Application fee:* $45. Electronic applications accepted.
**Expenses:** Tuition, state resident: part-time $241 per hour. Tuition, nonresident: part-time $406 per hour. Tuition and fees vary according to program.
**Financial support:** In 2001–02, 1 fellowship with tuition reimbursement (averaging $12,500 per year), 13 research assistantships with full tuition reimbursements (averaging $11,790 per year), 52 teaching assistantships with full tuition reimbursements (averaging $7,074 per year) were awarded. Unspecified assistantships also available. Financial award application deadline: 4/1.
**Faculty research:** Infant development from electrophysical point of view, work motivation and personnel selection, EEG, ERP and hypnosis with reference to chronic pain, intimate violence.
Dr. Jack W. Finney, Chair, 540-231-6581, *Fax:* 540-231-3652, *E-mail:* finney@vt.edu. *Web site:* http://www.psyc.vt.edu/

## ■ WAYNE STATE UNIVERSITY

**Graduate School, College of Science, Department of Psychology, Program in Psychology, Detroit, MI 48202**
**AWARDS** Clinical psychology (PhD); cognitive psychology (PhD); developmental psychology (PhD); industrial/organizational psychology (PhD); psychology (MA, PhD); social psychology (PhD).

*Wayne State University (continued)*
**Students:** 114. In 2001, 22 master's, 23 doctorates awarded.
**Degree requirements:** For doctorate, thesis/dissertation.
**Entrance requirements:** For doctorate, GRE General Test, GRE Subject Test. *Application deadline:* For fall admission, 2/1. *Application fee:* $20 ($30 for international students). Electronic applications accepted.
**Expenses:** Tuition, state resident: full-time $3,764. Tuition and fees vary according to degree level and program.
**Financial support:** Application deadline: 2/1.
**Application contact:** Kathryn Urberg, Graduate Director, 313-577-2820, *Fax:* 313-577-7636, *E-mail:* kurberg@ sun.science.wayne.edu.

## ■ WEST CHESTER UNIVERSITY OF PENNSYLVANIA

**Graduate Studies, College of Arts and Sciences, Department of Psychology, West Chester, PA 19383**

**AWARDS** Clinical psychology (MA); general psychology (MA); industrial organizational psychology (MA). Part-time and evening/ weekend programs available.
**Faculty:** 11.
**Students:** 44 full-time (36 women), 23 part-time (15 women); includes 3 minority (all African Americans), 2 international. Average age 28. 107 applicants, 71% accepted. In 2001, 26 degrees awarded.
**Degree requirements:** For master's, thesis (for some programs), comprehensive exam.
**Entrance requirements:** For master's, GRE General Test or MAT, interview. *Application deadline:* For fall admission, 4/15 (priority date); for spring admission, 10/15. Applications are processed on a rolling basis. *Application fee:* $25.
**Expenses:** Tuition, state resident: full-time $4,600; part-time $256 per credit. Tuition, nonresident: full-time $7,554; part-time $420 per credit. Required fees: $44 per credit.
**Financial support:** In 2001–02, 10 research assistantships with full tuition reimbursements (averaging $5,000 per year) were awarded; unspecified assistantships also available. Support available to part-time students. Financial award application deadline: 2/15; financial award applicants required to submit FAFSA.
**Faculty research:** Animal learning and cognition.
Dr. Sandra Kerr, Chair, 610-436-2945.
**Application contact:** Dr. Deanne Bonifazi-Zotter, Graduate Coordinator, 610-436-3143, *E-mail:* dbonifazi@ wcupa.edu.

## ■ WESTERN MICHIGAN UNIVERSITY

**Graduate College, College of Arts and Sciences, Department of Psychology, Kalamazoo, MI 49008-5202**

**AWARDS** Applied behavior analysis (MA, PhD); clinical psychology (MA, PhD); experimental analysis of behavior (PhD); experimental psychology (MA); industrial/ organizational psychology (MA); school psychology (PhD, Ed S).

**Faculty:** 19 full-time (6 women).
**Students:** 94 full-time (68 women), 41 part-time (26 women); includes 10 minority (1 African American, 3 Asian Americans or Pacific Islanders, 6 Hispanic Americans), 12 international. 192 applicants, 31% accepted, 25 enrolled. In 2001, 21 master's, 6 doctorates, 6 other advanced degrees awarded.
**Degree requirements:** For master's, variable foreign language requirement, thesis, oral exams; for doctorate, 2 foreign languages, thesis/dissertation, oral exams, comprehensive exam; for Ed S, thesis, oral exams.
**Entrance requirements:** For master's, doctorate, and Ed S, GRE General Test. *Application deadline:* For fall admission, 2/15. *Application fee:* $25.
**Expenses:** Tuition, state resident: part-time $186 per credit hour. Tuition, nonresident: part-time $442 per credit hour. Required fees: $602. One-time fee: $132 part-time. Tuition and fees vary according to course load.
**Financial support:** Fellowships, research assistantships, teaching assistantships, Federal Work-Study available. Financial award application deadline: 2/15; financial award applicants required to submit FAFSA.
R. Wayne Fuqua, Chairperson, 616-387-4498.
**Application contact:** Admissions and Orientation, 616-387-2000, *Fax:* 616-387-2355.

## ■ WILLIAM CAREY COLLEGE

**Graduate School, Program in Psychology, Hattiesburg, MS 39401-5499**

**AWARDS** Counseling psychology (MS); industrial and organizational psychology (MS). Part-time programs available.

**Faculty:** 4 full-time (2 women), 5 part-time/adjunct (3 women).
**Students:** 105 full-time (80 women), 37 part-time (31 women); includes 49 minority (46 African Americans, 1 Asian American or Pacific Islander, 2 Hispanic Americans), 1 international. In 2001, 18 degrees awarded.

**Entrance requirements:** For master's, GRE, minimum GPA of 2.5. *Application fee:* $25.
**Expenses:** Contact institution.
**Financial support:** Fellowships with partial tuition reimbursements, Federal Work-Study available. Support available to part-time students.
**Faculty research:** Counseling, industrial organizations.
Dr. Tommy King, Director, Graduate Psychology, 601-582-6774, *Fax:* 601-582-6454, *E-mail:* tommy.king@wmcarey.edu. *Web site:* http://www.umcarey.edu/

## ■ WRIGHT STATE UNIVERSITY

**School of Graduate Studies, College of Science and Mathematics, Department of Psychology, Program in Human Factors and Industrial/ Organizational Psychology, Dayton, OH 45435**

**AWARDS** MS, PhD.

**Degree requirements:** For master's and doctorate, thesis/dissertation.
**Expenses:** Tuition, state resident: full-time $7,161; part-time $225 per quarter hour. Tuition, nonresident: full-time $12,324; part-time $385 per quarter hour. Tuition and fees vary according to course load, degree level and program.
Dr. John M. Flach, Director, 937-775-2391, *Fax:* 937-775-3347, *E-mail:* john.flach@wright.edu.

# MARRIAGE AND FAMILY THERAPY

## ■ ABILENE CHRISTIAN UNIVERSITY

**Graduate School, College of Biblical Studies, Program in Marriage and Family Therapy, Abilene, TX 79699-9100**

**AWARDS** MMFT.

**Faculty:** 6 part-time/adjunct (3 women).
**Students:** 29 full-time (17 women), 1 (woman) part-time; includes 2 minority (both Asian Americans or Pacific Islanders), 5 international. 27 applicants, 67% accepted, 18 enrolled. In 2001, 11 degrees awarded.
**Degree requirements:** For master's, comprehensive exam.
**Entrance requirements:** For master's, GRE General Test, interview. *Application deadline:* For fall admission, 4/1 (priority date); for spring admission, 11/1. Applications are processed on a rolling basis. *Application fee:* $25 ($45 for international students).

**Expenses:** Tuition: Full-time $8,904; part-time $371 per hour. Required fees: $520; $17 per hour.

**Financial support:** Teaching assistantships, career-related internships or fieldwork available. Support available to part-time students. Financial award application deadline: 4/1.

**Faculty research:** Overeating variables, family systems, intervention strategies. Dr. Waymon Hinson, Chairman, 915-674-3778.

**Application contact:** Dr. Roger Gee, Graduate Dean, 915-674-2122, *Fax:* 915-674-2123, *E-mail:* gradinfo@ education.acu.edu.

### ■ ADLER SCHOOL OF PROFESSIONAL PSYCHOLOGY

**Programs in Psychology, Chicago, IL 60601-7203**

**AWARDS** Art therapy (Certificate); clinical hypnosis (Certificate); clinical psychology (Psy D); counseling psychology (MACP); counseling psychology/art therapy (MACAT); gerontology (MAGP, Certificate); marriage and family counseling (MAMFC); marriage and family therapy (Certificate); organizational psychology (MAO); substance abuse counseling (MASAC, Certificate). Part-time and evening/weekend programs available.

**Faculty:** 19 full-time (9 women), 48 part-time/adjunct (21 women).

**Students:** 124 full-time (78 women), 284 part-time (208 women); includes 77 minority (43 African Americans, 20 Asian Americans or Pacific Islanders, 13 Hispanic Americans, 1 Native American), 8 international. Average age 39. 253 applicants, 59% accepted, 121 enrolled. In 2001, 101 master's, 29 doctorates, 5 other advanced degrees awarded. Terminal master's awarded for partial completion of doctoral program.

**Degree requirements:** For master's, thesis or alternative, oral exam, practicum; for doctorate, thesis/dissertation, clinical exam, internship, oral exam, practicum, written qualifying exam.

**Entrance requirements:** For master's, 12 semester hours in psychology, minimum GPA of 3.0; for doctorate, 18 semester hours in psychology, minimum GPA of 3.25; for Certificate, appropriate master's or doctoral degree. *Application deadline:* For fall admission, 1/1 (priority date). Applications are processed on a rolling basis. *Application fee:* $50.

**Expenses:** Tuition: Full-time $13,680; part-time $380 per credit. Required fees: $100; $15 per credit.

**Financial support:** In 2001–02, 180 students received support. Career-related internships or fieldwork, Federal Work-Study, scholarships/grants, and tuition

waivers (full and partial) available. Support available to part-time students. Financial award application deadline: 5/15; financial award applicants required to submit FAFSA.

Dr. Frank Gruba-McCallister, Dean of Academic Affairs, 312-201-5900, *Fax:* 312-201-5917.

**Application contact:** Erene Soliman, Admissions Counselor, 312-201-5900, *Fax:* 312-201-5917.

**Find an in-depth description at www.petersons.com/gradchannel.**

### ■ ALLIANT INTERNATIONAL UNIVERSITY

**California School of Professional Psychology, Program in Marital and Family Therapy—Irvine, San Francisco, CA 94109**

**AWARDS** MA, Psy D.

**Students:** 22.

**Expenses:** Tuition: Part-time $397 per credit hour. Tuition and fees vary according to degree level, campus/location and program.

**Financial support:** Application deadline: 2/15.

Dr. Scott Woolley, Program Director, 858-635-4785, *E-mail:* swoolley@alliant.edu.

**Application contact:** Susan Topham, Director of Admissions, 858-635-4777, *E-mail:* stopham@alliant.edu. *Web site:* http://www.alliant.edu/

### ■ ALLIANT INTERNATIONAL UNIVERSITY

**California School of Professional Psychology, Program in Marital and Family Therapy—San Diego, San Francisco, CA 94109**

**AWARDS** MA, Psy D.

**Students:** 61.

**Expenses:** Tuition: Part-time $397 per credit hour. Tuition and fees vary according to degree level, campus/location and program.

Dr. Scott Woolley, Program Director, 858-635-4785, *E-mail:* swoolley@alliant.edu.

**Application contact:** Susan Topham, Director of Admissions, 858-635-4777, *E-mail:* stopham@alliant.edu. *Web site:* http://www.alliant.edu/

### ■ ANTIOCH NEW ENGLAND GRADUATE SCHOOL

**Graduate School, Department of Applied Psychology, Program in Marriage and Family Therapy, Keene, NH 03431-3552**

**AWARDS** MA.

**Faculty:** 9 full-time (7 women), 25 part-time/adjunct (15 women).

**Students:** 24 full-time (21 women), 2 part-time (1 woman); includes 1 African American, 2 Hispanic Americans. Average age 34. 13 applicants, 85% accepted. In 2001, 11 degrees awarded.

**Degree requirements:** For master's, internship, practicum.

**Entrance requirements:** For master's, previous course work and work experience in psychology. *Application deadline:* For fall admission, 8/1. Applications are processed on a rolling basis. *Application fee:* $40.

**Expenses:** Tuition: Full-time $15,150.

**Financial support:** In 2001–02, 20 students received support, including 2 fellowships (averaging $1,150 per year); Federal Work-Study and scholarships/grants also available. Financial award applicants required to submit FAFSA.

**Faculty research:** Use of reflective team model in case teaching and in organizational consulting, executive mentoring and coaching.

Dr. David Watts, Director, 603-357-3122 Ext. 254, *Fax:* 603-357-0718, *E-mail:* dwatts@antiochne.edu.

**Application contact:** Robbie P. Hertneky, Director of Admissions, 603-357-6265, *Fax:* 603-357-0718, *E-mail:* rhertneky@ antiochne.edu. *Web site:* http:// www.antiochne.edu/

### ■ APPALACHIAN STATE UNIVERSITY

**Cratis D. Williams Graduate School, College of Education, Department of Human Development and Psychological Counseling, Program in Marriage and Family Therapy, Boone, NC 28608**

**AWARDS** MA.

**Students:** In 2001, 9 degrees awarded.

**Expenses:** Tuition, state resident: full-time $1,286. Tuition, nonresident: full-time $9,354. Required fees: $1,116.

Dr. Jon Winek, Coordinator, 828-262-4890.

### ■ ARGOSY UNIVERSITY-CHICAGO

**Illinois School of Professional Psychology, Doctoral Program in Clinical Psychology, Chicago, IL 60603**

**AWARDS** Child and adolescent psychology (Psy D); ethnic and racial psychology (Psy D); family psychology (Psy D); forensic psychology (Psy D); health psychology (Psy D); maltreatment and trauma (Psy D); psychoanalytic psychotherapy (Psy D); psychology and spirituality (Psy D).

**Faculty:** 21 full-time (13 women), 41 part-time/adjunct (18 women).

*Argosy University-Chicago (continued)*
**Students:** 176 full-time (137 women), 185 part-time (132 women). Average age 31. 293 applicants, 61% accepted. In 2001, 92 degrees awarded.
**Degree requirements:** For doctorate, thesis/dissertation, internship, research project, clinical competency exam, comprehensive exam.
**Entrance requirements:** For doctorate, minimum GPA of 3.25. *Application deadline:* For fall admission, 1/15; for winter admission, 10/15. *Application fee:* $55. Electronic applications accepted.
**Expenses:** Tuition: Part-time $332 per credit hour. Required fees: $75 per year. $35 per term.
**Financial support:** In 2001–02, 200 students received support, including 25 fellowships with partial tuition reimbursements available (averaging $2,000 per year), 150 teaching assistantships with partial tuition reimbursements available (averaging $600 per year); research assistantships with partial tuition reimbursements available, career-related internships or fieldwork, Federal Work-Study, scholarships/grants, tuition waivers (partial), and unspecified assistantships also available. Support available to part-time students. Financial award application deadline: 5/29.
**Faculty research:** Meditation, clinical competency, family cultural patterns, sexual abuse patterns, psychosis and psychotherapy. *Total annual research expenditures:* $30,000.
Dr. Anne Marie Slobig, Director, 312-279-3911, *Fax:* 312-201-1907, *E-mail:* aslobig@argosyu.edu.
**Application contact:** Ashley Delaney, Director of Admissions, 312-279-3906, *Fax:* 312-201-1907, *E-mail:* adelaney@argosyu.edu. *Web site:* http://www.argosy.edu/

**Find an in-depth description at www.petersons.com/gradchannel.**

■ **ARGOSY UNIVERSITY-HONOLULU**

**Graduate Studies, Program in Professional Counseling, Honolulu, HI 96813**

**AWARDS** Marriage and family specialty (MA); professional counseling (MA). Part-time and evening/weekend programs available.

**Faculty:** 20 part-time/adjunct (13 women).
**Students:** 70 full-time (50 women), 3 part-time (2 women); includes 36 minority (1 African American, 30 Asian Americans or Pacific Islanders, 2 Hispanic Americans, 3 Native Americans). Average age 32. 55 applicants, 100% accepted. In 2001, 45 degrees awarded.

**Degree requirements:** For master's, practica. *Median time to degree:* Master's–2 years full-time, 3 years part-time.
**Entrance requirements:** For master's, minimum GPA of 3.0 in last 60 hours. *Application deadline:* For fall admission, 6/1; for winter admission, 11/1; for spring admission, 5/1. Applications are processed on a rolling basis. *Application fee:* $50. Electronic applications accepted.
**Expenses:** Contact institution.
**Financial support:** In 2001–02, 9 students received support. Career-related internships or fieldwork and Federal Work-Study available. Support available to part-time students. Financial award application deadline: 5/1; financial award applicants required to submit FAFSA.
Addie Jackson, Coordinator, 808-536-5555, *Fax:* 808-536-5505.
**Application contact:** Eric C. Carlson, Director of Admissions, 808-536-5555, *Fax:* 808-536-5505, *E-mail:* ecarlson@argosyu.edu. *Web site:* http://www.argosyu.edu/

**Find an in-depth description at www.petersons.com/gradchannel.**

■ **ARGOSY UNIVERSITY-TWIN CITIES**

**Graduate Programs, Bloomington, MN 55437-9761**

**AWARDS** Clinical psychology (MA, Psy D); education (MA); professional counseling/marriage and family therapy (MA). Part-time programs available.

**Faculty:** 13 full-time (6 women), 33 part-time/adjunct (13 women).
**Students:** 233 full-time (192 women), 122 part-time (83 women); includes 9 minority (3 African Americans, 4 Asian Americans or Pacific Islanders, 1 Hispanic American, 1 Native American), 1 international. Average age 31. 224 applicants, 62% accepted, 95 enrolled. In 2001, 27 master's, 41 doctorates awarded. Terminal master's awarded for partial completion of doctoral program.
**Degree requirements:** For master's, thesis (for some programs); for doctorate, thesis/dissertation, internship, research project, comprehensive exam. *Median time to degree:* Master's–2 years full-time, 3 years part-time; doctorate–5 years full-time, 6 years part-time.
**Entrance requirements:** For master's, GRE or MAT, minimum GPA of 3.0 (clinical psychology), 2.8 (professional counseling/marriage and family therapy); interview; for doctorate, GRE or MAT, minimum GPA of 3.25, interview. *Application deadline:* For fall admission, 5/15 (priority date); for winter admission, 1/15 (priority date). Applications are processed

on a rolling basis. *Application fee:* $50. Electronic applications accepted.
**Expenses:** Tuition: Part-time $424 per credit hour. Required fees: $31 per year. Tuition and fees vary according to program and student level.
**Financial support:** In 2001–02, 12 fellowships with partial tuition reimbursements, 12 teaching assistantships with partial tuition reimbursements were awarded. Career-related internships or fieldwork and Federal Work-Study also available. Support available to part-time students. Financial award application deadline: 3/14; financial award applicants required to submit FAFSA.
**Faculty research:** Cognitive behavioral therapy, human development, psychological assessment, marriage and family therapy, health psychology, physical/sexual abuse.
Dr. Jack T. O'Regan, Vice President Academic Affairs, 952-252-7575, *Fax:* 952-921-9574, *E-mail:* joregan@argosyu.edu.
**Application contact:** Jennifer Radke, Graduate Admissions Representative, 952-921-9500 Ext. 353, *Fax:* 952-921-9574, *E-mail:* tcadmissions@argosyu.edu. *Web site:* http://www.aspp.edu/

**Find an in-depth description at www.petersons.com/gradchannel.**

■ **AZUSA PACIFIC UNIVERSITY**

**School of Education and Behavioral Studies, Department of Graduate Psychology, Azusa, CA 91702-7000**

**AWARDS** Clinical psychology (MA, Psy D); family therapy (MFT). Part-time and evening/weekend programs available.

**Students:** 87 full-time (65 women), 47 part-time (33 women); includes 43 minority (10 African Americans, 15 Asian Americans or Pacific Islanders, 17 Hispanic Americans, 1 Native American), 7 international.
**Degree requirements:** For master's, 250 hours of clinical experience, individual and group therapy.
**Entrance requirements:** For master's, Minnesota Multiphasic Personality Inventory, interview, minimum GPA of 3.0. *Application deadline:* For fall admission, 6/30 (priority date). Applications are processed on a rolling basis. *Application fee:* $45 ($65 for international students).
**Expenses:** Tuition: Part-time $265 per unit. Required fees: $175 per semester. Tuition and fees vary according to degree level and program.
Dr. Mark Stanton, Chair, 626-815-5008.

**Find an in-depth description at www.petersons.com/gradchannel.**

# ■ BARRY UNIVERSITY

**School of Education, Program in Marriage and Family Counseling, Miami Shores, FL 33161-6695**

**AWARDS** MS, Ed S. Part-time and evening/weekend programs available.

**Faculty:** 5 full-time (2 women), 1 (woman) part-time/adjunct.
**Students:** 16 full-time (14 women), 24 part-time (19 women); includes 25 minority (10 African Americans, 1 Asian American or Pacific Islander, 14 Hispanic Americans).
**Degree requirements:** For master's, scholarly paper.
**Entrance requirements:** For master's, GRE General Test or MAT, minimum GPA of 3.0; for Ed S, GRE General Test, minimum GPA of 3.0. *Application deadline:* For fall admission, 5/1 (priority date). Applications are processed on a rolling basis. *Application fee:* $30. Electronic applications accepted.
**Expenses:** Tuition: Full-time $12,480. Tuition and fees vary according to degree level and program.
Dr. Maureen Duffy, Chair, 305-899-3701, *Fax:* 305-899-3630, *E-mail:* mduffy@mail.barry.edu.
**Application contact:** Angela Scott, Assistant Dean, Enrollment Services, 305-899-3112, *Fax:* 305-899-3149, *E-mail:* ascott@mail.barry.edu.

# ■ BETHEL COLLEGE

**Division of Graduate Studies, Program in Counseling, Mishawaka, IN 46545-5591**

**AWARDS** Marriage and family counseling/therapy (MA); mental health counseling (MA).

**Faculty:** 6 part-time/adjunct (2 women).
**Students:** In 2001, 1 degree awarded.
**Entrance requirements:** For master's, GRE, interview, previous undergraduate course work in psychology and religion. *Application deadline:* For fall admission, 7/1 (priority date); for winter admission, 11/1 (priority date); for spring admission, 3/15 (priority date). Applications are processed on a rolling basis. *Application fee:* $25. Electronic applications accepted.
**Expenses:** Tuition: Full-time $5,940; part-time $330 per semester hour.
**Financial support:** Unspecified assistantships available. Financial award applicants required to submit FAFSA.
**Faculty research:** Counseling and religiosity, aging and hearing, cognitive schema.
Dr. Mark J. Gerig, Director, 219-257-2595, *Fax:* 219-257-3357, *E-mail:* gerigm1@bethel-in.edu.

**Application contact:** Elizabeth W. McLaughlin, Assistant Director of Graduate Admissions, 219-257-3360, *Fax:* 219-257-3357, *E-mail:* mclaughb2@bethel-in.edu.

# ■ BETHEL SEMINARY

**Graduate and Professional Programs, St. Paul, MN 55112-6998**

**AWARDS** Biblical studies (M Div, MATS); children's and family ministry (MACFM); Christian education (M Div, MACE); Christian thought (MACT); church leadership (D Min); evangelism (M Div); global missions (Certificate); historical studies (M Div, MATS); marriage and family studies (M Div, MAMFT, D Min); missions (M Div, MATS); New Testament (M Div); Old Testament (M Div); pastoral care (M Div, MATS); pastoral ministries (M Div); preaching (M Div); theological studies (M Div, MATS); transformational leadership (MATL); youth ministry (M Div, MACE). Part-time and evening/weekend programs available. Postbaccalaureate distance learning degree programs offered (minimal on-campus study).

**Faculty:** 24 full-time (4 women), 108 part-time/adjunct (15 women).
**Students:** 480 full-time (127 women), 519 part-time (218 women); includes 129 minority (61 African Americans, 51 Asian Americans or Pacific Islanders, 15 Hispanic Americans, 2 Native Americans), 19 international. Average age 36. 275 applicants, 89% accepted. In 2001, 47 first professional degrees, 62 master's, 18 doctorates awarded.
**Degree requirements:** For M Div, one foreign language; for master's, variable foreign language requirement, thesis (for some programs); for doctorate, thesis/dissertation.
**Entrance requirements:** For doctorate, M Div. *Application deadline:* For fall admission, 8/1 (priority date); for winter admission, 12/1 (priority date); for spring admission, 1/1 (priority date). Applications are processed on a rolling basis. *Application fee:* $20.
**Expenses:** Tuition: Full-time $9,420; part-time $196 per quarter hour. Required fees: $15; $5 per quarter.
**Financial support:** In 2001–02, 375 students received support, including 20 teaching assistantships; career-related internships or fieldwork, Federal Work-Study, institutionally sponsored loans, and scholarships/grants also available. Financial award application deadline: 7/15; financial award applicants required to submit FAFSA.
**Faculty research:** Nature of theology, sexuality and misconduct, evangelicalism, ethics, biblical commentaries.
Dr. Leland Eliason, Executive Vice President and Provost, 651-638-6182.

**Application contact:** Morris Anderson, Director of Admissions, 651-638-6288, *Fax:* 651-638-6002.

# ■ BRIGHAM YOUNG UNIVERSITY

**Graduate Studies, College of Family, Home, and Social Sciences, Marriage and Family Therapy Department, Provo, UT 84602-1001**

**AWARDS** MS, PhD.

**Faculty:** 9 full-time (2 women), 6 part-time/adjunct (2 women).
**Students:** 32 full-time (10 women), 12 part-time (5 women); includes 8 minority (6 Asian Americans or Pacific Islanders, 1 Hispanic American, 1 Native American), 4 international. Average age 28. 67 applicants, 15% accepted. In 2001, 13 master's, 9 doctorates awarded.
**Degree requirements:** For master's, thesis/dissertation; for doctorate, thesis/dissertation, comprehensive exam.
**Entrance requirements:** For master's and doctorate, GRE General Test, GRE Writing Assessment, minimum GPA of 3.0 in last 60 hours. *Application deadline:* For fall admission, 1/10. *Application fee:* $50. Electronic applications accepted.
**Expenses:** Tuition: Full-time $3,860; part-time $214 per hour.
**Financial support:** In 2001–02, 32 students received support, including 26 research assistantships with partial tuition reimbursements available (averaging $7,500 per year), 3 teaching assistantships with partial tuition reimbursements available (averaging $5,000 per year); fellowships, career-related internships or fieldwork and tuition waivers (partial) also available. Financial award application deadline: 1/10.
**Faculty research:** Family process, family life education, therapy outcomes.
Dr. Robert F. Stahmann, Chair, 801-422-3888 Ext. ', *Fax:* 801-422-0163.
**Application contact:** Linda Kader, Department Secretary, 801-422-5680, *Fax:* 801-422-0163, *E-mail:* linda_kader@byu.edu. *Web site:* http://byu.edu/mft/

# ■ CALIFORNIA BAPTIST UNIVERSITY

**Graduate Program in Marriage and Family Therapy, Riverside, CA 92504-3206**

**AWARDS** Counseling psychology (MS). Part-time programs available.

**Faculty:** 4 full-time (1 woman), 3 part-time/adjunct (1 woman).
**Students:** 75. 40 applicants, 78% accepted, 23 enrolled. In 2001, 18 degrees awarded.
**Degree requirements:** For master's, thesis or alternative, 24 hours (individual)

*California Baptist University (continued)* or 50 hours (group) psychotherapy, comprehensive exam.

**Entrance requirements:** For master's, Minnesota Multiphasic Personality Inventory and Myers-Briggs Personality Inventory, previous course work in developmental psychology, theories of personality, and statistics, minimum undergraduate GPA of 3.0. *Application deadline:* For fall admission, 7/15; for spring admission, 11/1. Applications are processed on a rolling basis. *Application fee:* $45.

**Expenses:** Contact institution.

**Financial support:** In 2001–02, 59 students received support. Career-related internships or fieldwork and Federal Work-Study available. Support available to part-time students. Financial award applicants required to submit FAFSA. Dr. Gary Collins, Director, 909-343-4304, *Fax:* 909-343-4569, *E-mail:* gcollins@ calbaptist.edu.

**Application contact:** Gail Ronveaux, Associate Dean, Enrollment Services, 909-343-5045, *Fax:* 909-343-5095, *E-mail:* gradservices@calbaptist.edu. *Web site:* http://www.calbaptist.edu/

### ■ CALIFORNIA LUTHERAN UNIVERSITY

**Graduate Studies, Department of Psychology, Thousand Oaks, CA 91360-2787**

**AWARDS** Clinical psychology (MS); marital and family therapy (MS). Part-time programs available.

**Degree requirements:** For master's, thesis or comprehensive exams.

**Entrance requirements:** For master's, GRE General Test, interview, minimum GPA of 3.0. *Web site:* http://www.clunet.edu/htdocs/ClinicalPsych/ClinicalPsychology.html

### ■ CALIFORNIA STATE UNIVERSITY, BAKERSFIELD

**Division of Graduate Studies and Research, School of Humanities and Social Sciences, Program in Psychology, Bakersfield, CA 93311-1099**

**AWARDS** Family and child counseling (MFCC); psychology (MS).

**Degree requirements:** For master's, thesis.

**Entrance requirements:** For master's, GRE Subject Test. *Web site:* http://www.csub.edu/Psychology/Grcourse.htm

### ■ CALIFORNIA STATE UNIVERSITY, DOMINGUEZ HILLS

**College of Arts and Sciences, Program in Marriage, Family, and Child Counseling, Carson, CA 90747-0001**

**AWARDS** MS. Evening/weekend programs available.

**Faculty:** 15 full-time, 4 part-time/adjunct.

**Students:** 36 full-time (33 women), 16 part-time (11 women); includes 27 minority (17 African Americans, 1 Asian American or Pacific Islander, 8 Hispanic Americans, 1 Native American), 1 international. Average age 36. 2 applicants, 50% accepted. In 2001, 24 degrees awarded.

**Degree requirements:** For master's, thesis or alternative.

**Entrance requirements:** For master's, minimum GPA of 3.0. *Application deadline:* For fall admission, 6/1. *Application fee:* $55.

**Expenses:** Tuition, nonresident: full-time $1,508; part-time $438 per semester. Required fees: $442; $246 per unit. $227 per semester.

**Faculty research:** Sociology of the family, clinical psychology theory, employee assistance programs, race and sport. Dr. Hal Charnofsky, Coordinator, 310-516-3439, *E-mail:* hcharnofsky@ dhvx20.csudh.edu.

### ■ CALIFORNIA STATE UNIVERSITY, FRESNO

**Division of Graduate Studies, School of Education and Human Development, Department of Counseling and Special Education, Program in Marriage and Family Therapy, Fresno, CA 93740-8027**

**AWARDS** MS. Part-time and evening/weekend programs available.

**Faculty:** 6 full-time (2 women).

**Students:** 54 full-time (44 women), 27 part-time (22 women); includes 45 minority (3 African Americans, 4 Asian Americans or Pacific Islanders, 37 Hispanic Americans, 1 Native American), 2 international. Average age 31. 14 applicants, 79% accepted, 8 enrolled. In 2001, 23 degrees awarded.

**Degree requirements:** For master's, thesis or alternative. *Median time to degree:* Master's–2.5 years full-time, 3.5 years part-time.

**Entrance requirements:** For master's, GRE General Test, MAT, TOEFL, minimum GPA of 2.75. *Application deadline:* For fall admission, 4/1 (priority date); for spring admission, 11/1. Applications are processed on a rolling basis. *Application fee:* $55. Electronic applications accepted.

**Expenses:** Tuition, nonresident: part-time $246 per unit. Required fees: $605 per semester. Tuition and fees vary according to course load.

**Financial support:** Career-related internships or fieldwork, Federal Work-Study, scholarships/grants, and research awards, travel grants available. Support available to part-time students. Financial award application deadline: 3/1; financial award applicants required to submit FAFSA.

**Faculty research:** Child abuse prevention, early childhood education. Dr. Sari Dworkin, Head, 559-278-0328, *E-mail:* sari_dworkin@csufresno.edu.

**Application contact:** Chris Lucey, Graduate Program Coordinator, 559-278-0340, *E-mail:* chris_lucey@csufresno.edu.

### ■ CALIFORNIA STATE UNIVERSITY, NORTHRIDGE

**Graduate Studies, College of Education, Department of Educational Psychology and Counseling, Program in Counseling and Guidance, Northridge, CA 91330**

**AWARDS** Counseling (MS); marriage, family and child counseling (MFCC). Part-time and evening/weekend programs available.

**Students:** 292 full-time (250 women), 94 part-time (73 women); includes 136 minority (29 African Americans, 24 Asian Americans or Pacific Islanders, 78 Hispanic Americans, 5 Native Americans), 7 international. Average age 34. 138 applicants, 85% accepted, 86 enrolled. In 2001, 60 degrees awarded.

**Degree requirements:** For master's, comprehensive exam or thesis.

**Entrance requirements:** For master's, TOEFL, GRE General Test, MAT, or minimum GPA of 3.0. *Application deadline:* For fall admission, 11/30. *Application fee:* $55.

**Expenses:** Tuition, nonresident: part-time $631 per semester. Required fees: $246 per unit.

**Financial support:** Scholarships/grants available. Financial award application deadline: 3/1.

### ■ CARLOS ALBIZU UNIVERSITY, MIAMI CAMPUS

**Graduate Programs, Miami, FL 33172-2209**

**AWARDS** Clinical psychology (Psy D); industrial/organizational psychology (MS); management (MBA); marriage and family therapy (MS); mental health counseling (MS); psychology (MS); school counseling (MS). Part-time and evening/weekend programs available.

**Faculty:** 19 full-time (9 women), 37 part-time/adjunct (19 women).

**Students:** 432 full-time (322 women), 32 part-time (22 women); includes 328 minority (58 African Americans, 7 Asian Americans or Pacific Islanders, 263 Hispanic Americans), 4 international. Average age 35. 189 applicants, 50% accepted, 69 enrolled. In 2001, 44 master's, 69 doctorates awarded. Terminal master's awarded for partial completion of doctoral program.

**Degree requirements:** For master's, one foreign language, comprehensive exam, integrative project (MBA); for doctorate, one foreign language, thesis/dissertation, written and oral qualifying exam, internship.

**Entrance requirements:** For master's, GMAT (MBA), letters of recommendation (3), interview, minimum GPA of 3.0, resumé; for doctorate, GRE General Test, GRE Subject Test, letters of recommendation (3), minimum GPA of 3.0. *Application deadline:* For fall admission, 8/1 (priority date); for spring admission, 11/30 (priority date). Applications are processed on a rolling basis. *Application fee:* $50.

**Expenses:** Tuition: Part-time $455 per credit. Required fees: $819; $273 per term. Tuition and fees vary according to course load and degree level.

**Financial support:** In 2001–02, 22 students received support. Federal Work-Study and scholarships/grants available. Financial award application deadline: 6/1; financial award applicants required to submit FAFSA.

**Faculty research:** Culture, psychodiagnostics, psychotherapy, forensic psychology, neuropsychology; marketing strategy, entrepreneurship.

Dr. Gerardo F. Rodriquez-Menedez, Chancellor, 305-593-1223 Ext. 120, *Fax:* 305-629-8052, *E-mail:* grodriguez@albizu.edu.

**Application contact:** Miriam Matos, Admissions Officer, 305-593-1223 Ext. 134, *Fax:* 305-593-1854, *E-mail:* mmatos@albizu.edu. *Web site:* http://www.albizu.edu/

### ■ CENTRAL CONNECTICUT STATE UNIVERSITY

**School of Graduate Studies, School of Education and Professional Studies, Department of Health and Human Service Professions, Program in Marriage and Family Therapy, New Britain, CT 06050-4010**

**AWARDS** MS. Part-time and evening/weekend programs available.

**Degree requirements:** For master's, thesis or alternative, special project.

**Entrance requirements:** For master's, TOEFL, minimum GPA of 2.7. *Application deadline:* For fall admission, 8/10 (priority

date); for spring admission, 12/10. Applications are processed on a rolling basis. *Application fee:* $40.

**Expenses:** Tuition, state resident: full-time $2,772; part-time $245 per credit. Tuition, nonresident: full-time $7,726; part-time $245 per credit. Required fees: $2,102. Tuition and fees vary according to course level and degree level.

**Financial support:** Application deadline: 3/15.

Dr. Ralph Cohen, Coordinator, 860-832-2122.

### ■ CHAPMAN UNIVERSITY

**Graduate Studies, Division of Psychology, Program in Marriage and Family Therapy, Orange, CA 92866**

**AWARDS** MA. Part-time and evening/weekend programs available.

**Faculty:** 11 full-time (5 women).

**Degree requirements:** For master's, comprehensive exam.

**Entrance requirements:** For master's, GRE General Test, MAT, minimum undergraduate GPA of 3.0. *Application deadline:* Applications are processed on a rolling basis. *Application fee:* $40.

**Expenses:** Tuition: Part-time $450 per credit. Tuition and fees vary according to program.

**Financial support:** Application deadline: 3/1.

**Application contact:** Susan Read-Weil, Coordinator, 714-744-7837, *E-mail:* sreadwei@chapman.edu.

### ■ CHRISTIAN THEOLOGICAL SEMINARY

**Graduate and Professional Programs, Indianapolis, IN 46208-3301**

**AWARDS** Christian education (MA); church music (MA); marriage and family (MA); pastoral care and counseling (D Min); pastoral counseling (MA); practical theology (D Min); sacred theology (STM); theological studies (MTS); theology (M Div). Part-time programs available.

**Faculty:** 20 full-time (7 women), 14 part-time/adjunct (5 women).

**Students:** 142 full-time (91 women), 138 part-time (80 women); includes 67 minority (60 African Americans, 4 Asian Americans or Pacific Islanders, 2 Hispanic Americans, 1 Native American), 4 international. 94 applicants, 95% accepted, 70 enrolled. In 2001, 27 first professional degrees, 22 master's, 6 doctorates awarded. Terminal master's awarded for partial completion of doctoral program.

**Degree requirements:** For M Div, thesis, missionary and cross-cultural experience, comprehensive exam (for some programs); for master's, thesis (for some programs),

comprehensive exam (for some programs); for doctorate, thesis/dissertation, comprehensive exam (for some programs). *Median time to degree:* M Div–4 years full-time; master's–3 years full-time; doctorate–2 years full-time.

**Entrance requirements:** For master's, GRE, MAT; for doctorate, M Div or BD. *Application deadline:* For fall admission, 7/15; for spring admission, 11/15. Applications are processed on a rolling basis. *Application fee:* $30. Electronic applications accepted.

**Expenses:** Tuition: Full-time $6,480; part-time $1,620 per semester. Required fees: $80; $20 per semester. Tuition and fees vary according to course load.

**Financial support:** In 2001–02, 156 students received support, including 15 fellowships (averaging $6,480 per year); career-related internships or fieldwork, Federal Work-Study, scholarships/grants, and tuition waivers (full and partial) also available. Financial award application deadline: 4/1; financial award applicants required to submit FAFSA.

Dr. Edward Wheeler, President, 317-931-2305, *Fax:* 317-923-1961, *E-mail:* wheeler@cts.edu.

**Application contact:** Rev. Annette Barnes, Director of Admissions, 317-931-2300, *Fax:* 317-923-1961, *E-mail:* abarnes@cts.edu. *Web site:* http://www.cts.edu/

### ■ THE COLLEGE OF NEW JERSEY

**Graduate Division, School of Education, Department of Counselor Education, Program in Marriage and Family Therapy, Ewing, NJ 08628**

**AWARDS** Ed S. Part-time and evening/weekend programs available.

*Application deadline:* For fall admission, 4/15; for spring admission, 10/15. *Application fee:* $50.

**Expenses:** Tuition, state resident: full-time $6,981; part-time $387 per credit. Tuition, nonresident: full-time $9,772; part-time $542 per credit. Required fees: $1,011.

**Financial support:** Unspecified assistantships available. Financial award application deadline: 5/1; financial award applicants required to submit FAFSA.

Dr. Charlene Alderfer, Coordinator, 609-771-2136, *Fax:* 609-637-5116, *E-mail:* alderfer@tcnj.edu.

**Application contact:** Frank Cooper, Director, Office of Graduate Studies, 609-771-2300, *Fax:* 609-637-5105, *E-mail:* graduate@tcnj.edu.

## ■ THE COLLEGE OF WILLIAM AND MARY

**School of Education, Program in Counselor Education, Williamsburg, VA 23187-8795**

**AWARDS** Community and addictions counseling (M Ed); community counseling (M Ed); educational counseling (M Ed, Ed D, PhD); family counseling (M Ed); school counseling (M Ed). Part-time and evening/weekend programs available.

**Faculty:** 5 full-time (2 women), 5 part-time/adjunct (3 women).
**Students:** 42 full-time (29 women), 26 part-time (24 women); includes 3 minority (2 African Americans, 1 Hispanic American), 1 international. Average age 32. 103 applicants, 41% accepted, 24 enrolled. In 2001, 14 master's, 1 doctorate awarded.
**Degree requirements:** For doctorate, thesis/dissertation, comprehensive exam.
**Entrance requirements:** For master's, GRE or MAT, minimum GPA of 2.5; for doctorate, GRE or MAT, minimum GPA of 3.5. *Application deadline:* For fall admission, 2/1. *Application fee:* $30.
**Expenses:** Tuition, state resident: full-time $3,262; part-time $175 per credit hour. Tuition, nonresident: full-time $14,768; part-time $550 per credit hour. Required fees: $2,478.
**Financial support:** In 2001–02, 31 research assistantships with full tuition reimbursements (averaging $9,000 per year) were awarded; fellowships with full tuition reimbursements, career-related internships or fieldwork, institutionally sponsored loans, scholarships/grants, and unspecified assistantships also available. Financial award application deadline: 2/1; financial award applicants required to submit FAFSA.
**Faculty research:** Sexuality, multicultural education, substance abuse, transpersonal psychology.
Dr. Sandra Ward, Area Coordinator, 757-221-2326, *E-mail:* scbrub@wm.edu.
**Application contact:** Patricia Burleson, Director of Admissions, 757-221-2317, *E-mail:* paburl@wm.edu. *Web site:* http://www.wm.edu/education/programs/space.html/

## ■ CONVERSE COLLEGE

**Department of Education, Education Specialist Program, Spartanburg, SC 29302-0006**

**AWARDS** Administration and supervision (Ed S); curriculum and instruction (Ed S); marriage and family therapy (Ed S). Part-time programs available.

**Entrance requirements:** For degree, GRE or MAT, minimum GPA of 3.0.

**Expenses:** Tuition: Part-time $225 per credit hour. One-time fee: $20 part-time.

## ■ DENVER SEMINARY

**Graduate and Professional Programs, Denver, CO 80250-0100**

**AWARDS** Biblical studies (MA); Christian studies (MA, Certificate); church and para church leadership (D Min); counseling licensure (MA); counseling ministry (MA); educational ministry (MA); leadership (MA, Certificate); marriage and family counseling (D Min); pastoral ministry (D Min); philosophy of religion (MA); spiritual guidance (Certificate); theology (M Div, Certificate); world Christianity (D Min); youth and family ministry (MA). Part-time and evening/weekend programs available. Postbaccalaureate distance learning degree programs offered (minimal on-campus study).

**Degree requirements:** For M Div, 2 foreign languages; for master's, 2 foreign languages, thesis (for some programs); for doctorate, 2 foreign languages, thesis/dissertation.
**Entrance requirements:** For doctorate, M Div, 3 years of ministry experience. Electronic applications accepted.

## ■ DREXEL UNIVERSITY

**College of Nursing and Health Professions, Program in Couples and Family Therapy, Philadelphia, PA 19104-2875**

**AWARDS** Couples and family therapy (PhD); family therapy (MFT). Part-time programs available.

**Faculty:** 6 full-time (5 women).
**Students:** 32 full-time (25 women), 12 part-time (10 women); includes 21 minority (15 African Americans, 3 Asian Americans or Pacific Islanders, 3 Hispanic Americans). Average age 34. 16 applicants, 69% accepted, 11 enrolled. In 2001, 6 degrees awarded. Terminal master's awarded for partial completion of doctoral program.
**Degree requirements:** For master's, thesis, comprehensive exam; for doctorate, thesis/dissertation, qualifying exam. *Median time to degree:* Master's–2 years full-time.
**Entrance requirements:** For master's, GRE General Test or MAT, minimum GPA of 2.75; for doctorate, GRE General Test, minimum GPA of 3.0. *Application deadline:* For fall admission, 3/1. Applications are processed on a rolling basis. *Application fee:* $50. Electronic applications accepted.
**Expenses:** Tuition: Full-time $20,088; part-time $558 per credit. Required fees: $78 per term. One-time fee: $200. Tuition and fees vary according to course load, degree level and program.

**Financial support:** Career-related internships or fieldwork, Federal Work-Study, and institutionally sponsored loans available. Support available to part-time students. Financial award application deadline: 5/1; financial award applicants required to submit FAFSA.
**Faculty research:** Family assessment, gender issues, chronic illness, early intervention.
Dr. Marlene Watson, Director, 215-762-6782, *E-mail:* marlene.f.watson@drexel.edu.

**Find an in-depth description at www.petersons.com/gradchannel.**

## ■ EAST CAROLINA UNIVERSITY

**Graduate School, School of Human Environmental Sciences, Department of Child Development and Family Relations, Greenville, NC 27858-4353**

**AWARDS** Child development and family relations (MS); marriage and family therapy (MS). Part-time programs available.

**Faculty:** 7 full-time (3 women).
**Students:** 42 full-time (36 women), 14 part-time (all women); includes 9 minority (8 African Americans, 1 Asian American or Pacific Islander). Average age 29. 59 applicants, 47% accepted. In 2001, 24 degrees awarded.
**Degree requirements:** For master's, thesis optional.
*Application deadline:* For fall admission, 1/15; for spring admission, 10/15. Applications are processed on a rolling basis. *Application fee:* $45.
**Expenses:** Tuition, state resident: full-time $2,636. Tuition, nonresident: full-time $11,365.
**Financial support:** Career-related internships or fieldwork and Federal Work-Study available. Support available to part-time students. Financial award application deadline: 6/1.
**Faculty research:** Child care quality, mental health delivery systems for children, family violence.
Dr. Mel Markowski, Chairperson, 252-328-1333, *E-mail:* markowskie@mail.ecu.edu.

## ■ EASTERN BAPTIST THEOLOGICAL SEMINARY

**Graduate and Professional Programs, Program in Ministry, Wynnewood, PA 19096-3430**

**AWARDS** Marriage and family (D Min). Part-time programs available.

**Degree requirements:** For doctorate, thesis/dissertation.

**Entrance requirements:** For doctorate, 3 years of experience, involvement in ministry, church endorsement.
**Expenses:** Contact institution.

### ■ EASTERN NAZARENE COLLEGE

**Graduate Studies, Program in Family Counseling, Quincy, MA 02170-2999**
**AWARDS** MS. Part-time and evening/weekend programs available.
**Faculty:** 4 full-time (1 woman), 2 part-time/adjunct (1 woman).
**Students:** 35; includes 4 minority (3 African Americans, 1 Native American), 1 international. Average age 35. 5 applicants, 100% accepted. In 2001, 24 degrees awarded.
**Entrance requirements:** For master's, TOEFL. *Application deadline:* Applications are processed on a rolling basis. *Application fee:* $35.
**Expenses:** Tuition: Part-time $360 per credit hour. Required fees: $50 per semester.
**Financial support:** Career-related internships or fieldwork and scholarships/grants available. Support available to part-time students. Financial award applicants required to submit FAFSA.
Dr. Mark Bromley, Graduate Coordinator, 617-745-3562.
**Application contact:** Cleo P. Cakridas, Assistant Director of Graduate Studies, 617-745-3870, *Fax:* 617-774-6800, *E-mail:* cakridac@enc.edu.

### ■ EAST TENNESSEE STATE UNIVERSITY

**School of Graduate Studies, College of Education, Department of Human Development and Learning, Johnson City, TN 37614**
**AWARDS** Advanced practitioner (M Ed); community agency counseling (M Ed, MA); comprehensive concentration (M Ed); counseling (M Ed, MA); early childhood education (M Ed, MA); early childhood general (M Ed); early childhood special education (M Ed); early childhood teaching (M Ed); elementary and secondary (school counseling) (M Ed, MA); marriage and family therapy (M Ed, MA); modified concentration (M Ed). Part-time programs available.
**Faculty:** 20 full-time (10 women).
**Students:** 77 full-time (64 women), 57 part-time (48 women); includes 9 minority (7 African Americans, 1 Asian American or Pacific Islander, 1 Hispanic American), 1 international. Average age 30. In 2001, 61 degrees awarded.
**Degree requirements:** For master's, thesis (for some programs), comprehensive exam.

**Entrance requirements:** For master's, GRE General Test, TOEFL, minimum GPA of 3.0. *Application deadline:* For fall admission, 7/15 (priority date); for spring admission, 11/1. Applications are processed on a rolling basis. *Application fee:* $25 ($35 for international students).
**Expenses:** Tuition, state resident: part-time $181 per hour. Tuition, nonresident: part-time $270 per hour. Required fees: $220 per term.
**Financial support:** Research assistantships with full tuition reimbursements, teaching assistantships with full tuition reimbursements, career-related internships or fieldwork, Federal Work-Study, institutionally sponsored loans, scholarships/grants, and unspecified assistantships available.
**Faculty research:** Drug and alcohol abuse, marriage and family counseling, severe mental retardation, parenting of children with disabilities. *Total annual research expenditures:* $269,024.
Dr. Patricia Robertson, Chair, 423-439-7693, *Fax:* 423-439-7790, *E-mail:* robertpe@etsu.edu.

### ■ EDGEWOOD COLLEGE

**Program in Marriage and Family Therapy, Madison, WI 53711-1997**
**AWARDS** MS. Part-time and evening/weekend programs available.
**Faculty:** 2 full-time (1 woman), 6 part-time/adjunct (4 women).
**Students:** 14 full-time (12 women), 15 part-time (13 women); includes 3 minority (1 African American, 2 Asian Americans or Pacific Islanders). Average age 32. In 2001, 9 degrees awarded.
**Degree requirements:** For master's, research project.
*Application deadline:* For fall admission, 3/1. *Application fee:* $25.
**Expenses:** Tuition: Full-time $10,200; part-time $425 per credit.
Dr. Peter Fabian, Director, 608-663-2233, *Fax:* 608-663-3291, *E-mail:* fabian@edgewood.edu.
**Application contact:** Paula O'Malley, Graduate Student Admissions Counselor, 608-663-2282, *Fax:* 608-663-3291, *E-mail:* gradprograms@edgewood.edu.

### ■ EVANGELICAL SCHOOL OF THEOLOGY

**Graduate and Professional Programs, Myerstown, PA 17067-1212**
**AWARDS** Divinity (M Div); educational ministries (MA); marriage and family therapy (MA); ministry (Certificate); religion (MAR); theology (Diploma). Part-time programs available.
**Faculty:** 6 full-time (0 women), 5 part-time/adjunct (1 woman).

**Students:** 16 full-time (5 women), 135 part-time (35 women). Average age 40. 42 applicants, 90% accepted, 38 enrolled. In 2001, 5 first professional degrees, 10 master's, 3 other advanced degrees awarded.
**Degree requirements:** For M Div, 2 foreign languages; for master's, practicum; for other advanced degree, thesis.
**Entrance requirements:** For M Div, minimum GPA of 2.5; for master's, GRE General Test or MAT, minimum GPA of 2.5. *Application deadline:* For fall admission, 6/1 (priority date); for spring admission, 11/1 (priority date). Applications are processed on a rolling basis. *Application fee:* $30. Electronic applications accepted.
**Expenses:** Tuition: Full-time $7,600; part-time $320 per credit. Required fees: $50. One-time fee: $150 full-time. Tuition and fees vary according to program.
**Financial support:** Career-related internships or fieldwork, scholarships/grants, and tuition waivers (full) available. Support available to part-time students. Financial award application deadline: 6/1; financial award applicants required to submit FAFSA.
**Faculty research:** Literary form and structure within the Hebrew and Greek scriptures; Wesley studies, esoteric biblical languages; the Mosaic law and the Christian.
Rev. Dr. Rodney H. Shearer, Vice President, Academic Affairs, 717-866-5775 Ext. 105, *Fax:* 717-866-4667, *E-mail:* rshearer@evangelical.edu.
**Application contact:** Tom M. Maiello, Dean of Admissions, 800-532-5775 Ext. 109, *Fax:* 717-866-4667, *E-mail:* admissions@evangelical.edu. *Web site:* http://www.evangelical.edu/

### ■ FAIRFIELD UNIVERSITY

**Graduate School of Education and Allied Professions, Department of Marriage and Family Therapy, Fairfield, CT 06824**
**AWARDS** MA. Part-time and evening/weekend programs available.
**Faculty:** 2 full-time (both women), 3 part-time/adjunct (1 woman).
**Students:** 19 full-time (17 women), 26 part-time (20 women); includes 2 minority (1 African American, 1 Hispanic American). Average age 28. 20 applicants, 40% accepted, 5 enrolled. In 2001, 18 degrees awarded.
**Degree requirements:** For master's, comprehensive exam.
**Entrance requirements:** For master's, TOEFL, minimum QPA of 2.67. *Application deadline:* For fall admission, 4/2; for spring admission, 10/15. *Application fee:* $55. Electronic applications accepted.
**Expenses:** Tuition: Full-time $9,550; part-time $390 per credit hour. Required fees:

*Fairfield University (continued)*
$25 per term. Tuition and fees vary according to program.
**Financial support:** Tuition waivers (partial) and unspecified assistantships available. Support available to part-time students. Financial award applicants required to submit FAFSA.
**Faculty research:** Couple therapy, professional ethics, multicultural issues in counseling, alcoholism and family structure.
Dr. Ingeborg Haug, Chair, 203-254-4000 Ext. 2540, *Fax:* 203-254-4047, *E-mail:* ihaug@fair1.fairfield.edu.
**Application contact:** Karen L Creecy, Assistant Dean, 203-254-4000 Ext. 2414, *Fax:* 203-254-4241, *E-mail:* klcreecy@mail.fairfield.edu. *Web site:* http://www.fairfield.edu/

### ■ FITCHBURG STATE COLLEGE

**Division of Graduate and Continuing Education, Programs in Counseling, Fitchburg, MA 01420-2697**
**AWARDS** Adolescent and family therapy (Certificate); child protective services (Certificate); elementary school guidance counseling (MS); forensic case work (Certificate); mental health counseling (MS); school guidance counselor (Certificate); secondary school guidance counseling (MS). Part-time and evening/weekend programs available.
**Students:** 30 full-time (24 women), 52 part-time (48 women); includes 4 minority (1 African American, 1 Asian American or Pacific Islander, 2 Hispanic Americans), 3 international. In 2001, 27 degrees awarded.
**Entrance requirements:** For master's, GRE General Test or MAT, interview, previous course work in psychology; for Certificate, master's degree. *Application deadline:* Applications are processed on a rolling basis. *Application fee:* $10.
**Expenses:** Tuition, state resident: part-time $150 per credit. Required fees: $7 per credit. $65 per term. Tuition and fees vary according to course load.
**Financial support:** In 2001–02, research assistantships with partial tuition reimbursements (averaging $5,500 per year), teaching assistantships with partial tuition reimbursements (averaging $5,500 per year) were awarded. Federal Work-Study and unspecified assistantships also available. Support available to part-time students. Financial award application deadline: 3/1; financial award applicants required to submit FAFSA.
Dr. Richard Spencer, Co-Chair, 978-665-3349, *Fax:* 978-665-3658, *E-mail:* gce@fsc.edu.
**Application contact:** Director of Admissions, 978-665-3144, *Fax:* 978-665-4540,

*E-mail:* admissions@fsc.edu. *Web site:* http://www.fsc.edu/

### ■ FLORIDA STATE UNIVERSITY

**Graduate Studies, College of Human Sciences and School of Social Work, Interdivisional Program in Marriage and the Family, Tallahassee, FL 32306**
**AWARDS** PhD. Part-time programs available.
**Faculty:** 4 full-time (1 woman).
**Students:** 21 full-time (16 women), 8 part-time (4 women); includes 6 minority (5 African Americans, 1 Hispanic American), 1 international. Average age 34. 18 applicants, 33% accepted, 3 enrolled. In 2001, 3 degrees awarded.
**Degree requirements:** For doctorate, thesis/dissertation.
**Entrance requirements:** For doctorate, GRE General Test, minimum GPA of 3.0. *Application deadline:* For fall admission, 1/31 (priority date). *Application fee:* $20. Electronic applications accepted.
**Expenses:** Tuition, state resident: part-time $163 per credit hour. Tuition, nonresident: part-time $570 per credit hour. Tuition and fees vary according to program.
**Financial support:** In 2001–02, 6 students received support, including 2 research assistantships with partial tuition reimbursements available (averaging $8,000 per year), 4 teaching assistantships with partial tuition reimbursements available (averaging $8,000 per year); institutionally sponsored loans also available. Financial award applicants required to submit FAFSA.
**Faculty research:** Families in crisis, family therapy effectiveness, family therapy relationships, post-traumatic stress.
Dr. Mary Hicks, Director, 850-644-7741, *E-mail:* mhicks@mailer.fsu.edu.
**Application contact:** Lynn LaCombe, Program Assistant, 850-644-3217, *Fax:* 850-644-3439, *E-mail:* llacomb@mailer.fsu.edu.

**Find an in-depth description at www.petersons.com/gradchannel.**

### ■ FRIENDS UNIVERSITY

**Graduate Programs, College of Arts and Sciences, Program in Family Therapy, Wichita, KS 67213**
**AWARDS** MSFT. Evening/weekend programs available.
**Faculty:** 7 full-time, 6 part-time/adjunct.
**Students:** 94 full-time.
*Application fee:* $45 ($65 for international students).
**Expenses:** Tuition: Part-time $399 per credit hour. Full-time tuition and fees vary according to campus/location and program.

Dr. Dan Lord, Director, 800-794-6945 Ext. 5617.
**Application contact:** Director of Graduate Admissions, 800-794-6945 Ext. 5583.

### ■ FULLER THEOLOGICAL SEMINARY

**Graduate School of Psychology, Department of Marriage and Family Therapy, Pasadena, CA 91182**
**AWARDS** Marital/family therapy (MS).
**Degree requirements:** For master's, practicum.
**Entrance requirements:** For master's, GRE General Test, TOEFL.
**Expenses:** Contact institution.
**Faculty research:** Marital intimacy, sex-roles, psychoanalytical theory, men's issues. *Web site:* http://www.fuller.edu/sop/

### ■ GENEVA COLLEGE

**Program in Counseling, Beaver Falls, PA 15010-3599**
**AWARDS** Marriage and family (MA); mental health (MA); school counseling (MA). Part-time and evening/weekend programs available.
**Faculty:** 5 full-time (2 women), 2 part-time/adjunct (0 women).
**Students:** 16 full-time (14 women), 31 part-time (23 women). Average age 26. In 2001, 4 degrees awarded.
**Degree requirements:** For master's, internship. *Median time to degree:* Master's–2 years full-time, 4.5 years part-time.
**Entrance requirements:** For master's, GRE General Test or MAT, minimum GPA of 3.0, letters of recommendation, faith statement. *Application deadline:* For fall admission, 7/1 (priority date); for spring admission, 11/1 (priority date). Applications are processed on a rolling basis. *Application fee:* $50. Electronic applications accepted.
**Expenses:** Tuition: Part-time $445 per credit hour.
**Financial support:** In 2001–02, 6 teaching assistantships (averaging $2,500 per year) were awarded; career-related internships or fieldwork and unspecified assistantships also available.
Dr. Carol Luce, Director, 724-847-6622, *Fax:* 724-847-6101, *E-mail:* cbluce@geneva.edu.
**Application contact:** Dr. Robin Ware, Director of Graduate Student Services, 724-847-6697, *Fax:* 724-847-6101, *E-mail:* counseling@geneva.edu. *Web site:* http://www.geneva.edu/

**Find an in-depth description at www.petersons.com/gradchannel.**

## ■ GEORGE FOX UNIVERSITY

**Graduate and Professional Studies, Graduate Department of Counseling, Newberg, OR 97132-2697**

**AWARDS** Counseling (MA); marriage and family therapy (MA). Part-time programs available.

**Faculty:** 7 full-time (3 women), 4 part-time/adjunct (3 women).

**Students:** 117 full-time (95 women), 86 part-time (71 women); includes 17 minority (2 African Americans, 7 Asian Americans or Pacific Islanders, 5 Hispanic Americans, 3 Native Americans), 3 international. 88 applicants, 69% accepted, 53 enrolled. In 2001, 25 degrees awarded.

**Degree requirements:** For master's, thesis optional.

*Application deadline:* For fall admission, 7/1; for spring admission, 10/15. Applications are processed on a rolling basis. *Application fee:* $40. Electronic applications accepted.

**Expenses:** Contact institution.

**Financial support:** Career-related internships or fieldwork available.

Dr. Karin Jordan, Director, 503-554-6141, *E-mail:* kjordan@georgefox.edu.

**Application contact:** Dr. Andrea Cook, Vice President for Enrollment Services, 800-631-0921, *Fax:* 503-554-3856, *E-mail:* acook@georgefox.edu. *Web site:* http://www.georgefox.edu

## ■ GOLDEN GATE UNIVERSITY

**School of Professional Programs and Undergraduate Studies, Program in Applied Psychology, San Francisco, CA 94105-2968**

**AWARDS** Applied psychology (Certificate); counseling (MA); industrial/organizational psychology (MA); marriage, family and child counseling (MA).

**Entrance requirements:** For master's, TOEFL, minimum GPA of 2.5.

## ■ HARDING UNIVERSITY

**College of Bible and Religion, Program in Marriage and Family Therapy, Searcy, AR 72149-0001**

**AWARDS** MS. Part-time programs available.

**Faculty:** 3 full-time (0 women), 4 part-time/adjunct (1 woman).

**Students:** 31 full-time (16 women); includes 2 minority (1 African American, 1 Asian American or Pacific Islander). Average age 28. 20 applicants, 80% accepted, 14 enrolled. In 2001, 10 degrees awarded.

**Entrance requirements:** For master's, GRE General Test. *Application deadline:* For fall admission, 4/15 (priority date). *Application fee:* $25.

**Expenses:** Tuition: Full-time $5,238; part-time $291 per credit hour. Required fees: $300. $150 per semester. Tuition and fees

vary according to course load, degree level, reciprocity agreements, student level and student's religious affiliation.

**Financial support:** Career-related internships or fieldwork, Federal Work-Study, and institutionally sponsored loans available. Financial award application deadline: 3/31.

Dr. Lewis L. Moore, Chairman, 501-279-4347, *Fax:* 501-279-4042.

## ■ HARDIN-SIMMONS UNIVERSITY

**Graduate School, Department of Psychology, Program in Family Psychology, Abilene, TX 79698-0001**

**AWARDS** MA. Part-time programs available.

**Faculty:** 7 full-time (1 woman).

**Students:** 16 full-time (12 women), 5 part-time (3 women); includes 1 minority (Hispanic American). Average age 28. 13 applicants, 100% accepted, 7 enrolled. In 2001, 15 degrees awarded.

**Degree requirements:** For master's, clinical experience, project.

**Entrance requirements:** For master's, minimum undergraduate GPA of 3.0 in major, 2.7 overall; 21 semester hours in psychology, 18 of those in upper division classes. *Application deadline:* For fall admission, 8/15 (priority date); for spring admission, 1/5 (priority date). Applications are processed on a rolling basis. *Application fee:* $25 ($100 for international students).

**Expenses:** Tuition: Full-time $6,120; part-time $340 per credit. Required fees: $750.

**Financial support:** In 2001–02, 5 fellowships with partial tuition reimbursements (averaging $1,100 per year) were awarded; career-related internships or fieldwork, Federal Work-Study, scholarships/grants, and tuition waivers (full and partial) also available. Support available to part-time students. Financial award application deadline: 3/15; financial award applicants required to submit FAFSA.

**Faculty research:** Family stress management, spirituality in marriage, intimacy and sexuality in marriage, sex education in the church, role of faith in marital satisfaction.

Dr. Sue Lucas, Head, 915-670-1531, *E-mail:* fampsyc@hsutx.edu.

**Application contact:** Dr. Gary Stanlake, Dean of Graduate Studies, 915-670-1298, *Fax:* 915-670-1564, *E-mail:* gradoff@hsutx.edu. *Web site:* http://www.hsutx.edu/

## ■ HOPE INTERNATIONAL UNIVERSITY

**School of Graduate Studies, Program in Marriage, Family, and Child Counseling, Fullerton, CA 92831-3138**

**AWARDS** Counseling (MA); marriage and family therapy (MFT); marriage, family, and child counseling (MA); psychology (MA).

**Degree requirements:** For master's, final exam, practicum.

**Entrance requirements:** For master's, minimum GPA of 3.0. Electronic applications accepted.

## ■ IDAHO STATE UNIVERSITY

**Office of Graduate Studies, College of Health Professions, Department of Counseling, Department of Counseling, Pocatello, ID 83209**

**AWARDS** Counseling (Ed S); marriage and family counseling (M Coun); mental health counseling (M Coun); school counseling (M Coun); student affairs and college counseling (M Coun).

**Students:** In 2001, 13 master's, 2 other advanced degrees awarded.

**Degree requirements:** For Ed S, thesis.

**Entrance requirements:** For master's, GRE General Test, MAT, minimum GPA of 2.75; for Ed S, GRE General Test, minimum graduate GPA of 3.0. *Application deadline:* For fall admission, 2/15 (priority date). Applications are processed on a rolling basis. *Application fee:* $55.

**Expenses:** Tuition, area resident: Full-time $3,432. Tuition, state resident: part-time $172 per credit. Tuition, nonresident: full-time $10,196; part-time $262 per credit. International tuition: $9,672 full-time. Part-time tuition and fees vary according to course load, program and reciprocity agreements.

**Financial support:** In 2001–02, 15 teaching assistantships with full and partial tuition reimbursements (averaging $10,099 per year) were awarded. Financial award application deadline: 3/15.

Dr. Steve Feit, Chair, Department of Counseling, 208-282-3156.

## ■ IDAHO STATE UNIVERSITY

**Office of Graduate Studies, College of Health Professions, Department of Family Medicine, Pocatello, ID 83209**

**AWARDS** Certificate.

**Students:** 1 full-time (0 women). Average age 27. 250 applicants, 2% accepted.

**Entrance requirements:** For degree, GRE General Test, MD. *Application fee:* $35.

**Expenses:** Tuition, area resident: Full-time $3,432. Tuition, state resident: part-time

*Idaho State University (continued)*
$172 per credit. Tuition, nonresident: full-time $10,196; part-time $262 per credit. International tuition: $9,672 full-time. Part-time tuition and fees vary according to course load, program and reciprocity agreements.
**Faculty research:** Rural medicine. *Total annual research expenditures:* $372,779.
Dr. Jonathan Cree, Director, 208-282-3253.
**Application contact:** Leslie Brassfield, Residency Coordinator, 208-282-4508. *Web site:* http://www.clinic.isu.edu/fammed.html

### ■ INDIANA STATE UNIVERSITY

**School of Graduate Studies, School of Education, Department of Counseling, Terre Haute, IN 47809-1401**

**AWARDS** Counseling psychology (PhD); counselor education (PhD); guidance (PhD, Ed S); higher education (MA, MS); marriage and family counseling (MA, MS); school counseling (M Ed). Part-time and evening/weekend programs available.

**Degree requirements:** For doctorate, 2 foreign languages, thesis/dissertation.
**Entrance requirements:** For master's, minimum undergraduate GPA of 2.5; for doctorate, GRE General Test, master's degree, minimum undergraduate GPA of 3.5; for Ed S, GRE General Test, minimum graduate GPA of 3.25. Electronic applications accepted.
**Faculty research:** Vocational development supervision.

### ■ INDIANA WESLEYAN UNIVERSITY

**College of Adult and Professional Studies, Program in Counseling, Marion, IN 46953-4974**

**AWARDS** Community counseling (MA); community/addiction counseling (MA); marriage and family counseling (MA). Part-time programs available.

**Faculty:** 3 full-time (0 women), 7 part-time/adjunct (4 women).
**Students:** 27 full-time (19 women), 30 part-time (24 women); includes 1 minority (African American). Average age 35. In 2001, 5 degrees awarded.
**Degree requirements:** For master's, thesis or alternative.
**Entrance requirements:** For master's, GRE General Test. *Application deadline:* For fall admission, 4/1 (priority date); for spring admission, 10/1 (priority date). *Application fee:* $25. Electronic applications accepted.
**Expenses:** Contact institution.
**Financial support:** In 2001–02, 1 research assistantship with tuition reimbursement, 1

teaching assistantship with partial tuition reimbursement (averaging $1,000 per year) were awarded. Financial award application deadline: 3/1; financial award applicants required to submit FAFSA.
**Faculty research:** Attachment, emotional softening, cultural reentry, third culture kids, sexuality.
Dr. Jerry Davis, Director of Graduate Counseling Studies, 765-677-2995, *Fax:* 765-677-2504, *E-mail:* jdavis@indwes.edu.
**Find an in-depth description at www.petersons.com/gradchannel.**

### ■ IONA COLLEGE

**School of Arts and Science, Department of Family and Pastoral Counseling, New Rochelle, NY 10801-1890**

**AWARDS** Family counseling (MS, Certificate); pastoral counseling (MS). Part-time and evening/weekend programs available.

**Faculty:** 4 full-time (0 women), 1 part-time/adjunct (0 women).
**Students:** 1 full-time (0 women), 35 part-time (29 women); includes 9 minority (8 African Americans, 1 Hispanic American), 1 international. Average age 36. In 2001, 16 master's awarded.
**Degree requirements:** For master's, thesis, project.
**Entrance requirements:** For master's, draw-a-person test, sentence completion test, interview, minimum GPA of 3.0. *Application deadline:* Applications are processed on a rolling basis. *Application fee:* $25.
**Expenses:** Contact institution.
**Financial support:** Career-related internships or fieldwork, tuition waivers (partial), and unspecified assistantships available. Support available to part-time students.
Dr. Robert Burns, Chair, 914-633-2418, *E-mail:* rburns@iona.edu.
**Application contact:** Alyce Ware, Associate Director of Graduate Recruitment, 914-633-2420, *Fax:* 914-633-2023, *E-mail:* aware@iona.edu. *Web site:* http://www.iona.edu/

### ■ IOWA STATE UNIVERSITY OF SCIENCE AND TECHNOLOGY

**Graduate College, College of Family and Consumer Sciences, Department of Human Development and Family Studies, Ames, IA 50011**

**AWARDS** Human development and family studies (MFCS, MS, PhD); marriage and family therapy (PhD).

**Faculty:** 33 full-time, 3 part-time/adjunct.
**Students:** 35 full-time (27 women), 67 part-time (51 women); includes 8 minority (1 African American, 2 Asian Americans or Pacific Islanders, 5 Hispanic Americans),

16 international. 42 applicants, 64% accepted, 14 enrolled. In 2001, 10 master's, 15 doctorates awarded.
**Degree requirements:** For master's and doctorate, thesis/dissertation. *Median time to degree:* Master's–2.4 years full-time; doctorate–5.9 years full-time.
**Entrance requirements:** For master's and doctorate, GRE General Test, TOEFL or IELTS. *Application deadline:* For fall admission, 1/15 (priority date). *Application fee:* $20 ($50 for international students). Electronic applications accepted.
**Expenses:** Tuition, state resident: full-time $1,851. Tuition, nonresident: full-time $5,449. Tuition and fees vary according to program.
**Financial support:** In 2001–02, 25 research assistantships with partial tuition reimbursements (averaging $12,175 per year), 17 teaching assistantships with partial tuition reimbursements (averaging $11,439 per year) were awarded. Fellowships, scholarships/grants also available.
**Faculty research:** Child development, early childhood education, family resource management and housing, life span studies.
Dr. Maurice M. MacDonald, Chair, 515-294-6316, *Fax:* 515-294-2502, *E-mail:* hdfs-grad-adm@iastate.edu.
**Application contact:** Dr. Dee Draper, Director of Graduate Education, 515-294-6321, *Fax:* 515-294-2502, *E-mail:* hdfs-grad-adm@iastate.edu. *Web site:* http://www.fcs.iastate.edu/hdfs/grad/default.htm/

### ■ JOHN BROWN UNIVERSITY

**Department of Counseling, Siloam Springs, AR 72761-2121**

**AWARDS** Licensed professional counseling (MS); marriage and family therapy (MS); school counseling (MS). Part-time and evening/weekend programs available.

**Faculty:** 7 full-time (2 women), 2 part-time/adjunct (0 women).
**Students:** 59 full-time (36 women), 39 part-time (20 women); includes 3 minority (1 African American, 2 Native Americans). Average age 32. 32 applicants, 81% accepted, 19 enrolled. In 2001, 27 degrees awarded.
**Degree requirements:** For master's, practica or internships. *Median time to degree:* Master's–2 years full-time, 3 years part-time.
**Entrance requirements:** For master's, GRE General Test, MAT, minimum GPA of 3.0. *Application deadline:* For fall admission, 8/15 (priority date); for spring admission, 1/8. Applications are processed on a rolling basis. *Application fee:* $25. Electronic applications accepted.
**Expenses:** Tuition: Full-time $5,940; part-time $330 per hour.

**Financial support:** In 2001–02, 12 students received support, including 3 research assistantships (averaging $8,100 per year); scholarships/grants, tuition waivers (full), and unspecified assistantships also available. Financial award applicants required to submit FAFSA.
Dr. John V. Carmack, Chair, 479-524-7460, *Fax:* 479-524-9548, *E-mail:* jcarmack@jbu.edu.
**Application contact:** Dr. Ida M. Adolphson, Graduate Business Coordinator, 479-524-7291, *Fax:* 479-524-9548, *E-mail:* idolphs@jbu.edu. *Web site:* http://www.jbu.edu/

### ■ JOHNSON BIBLE COLLEGE

**Department of Marriage and Family Therapy, Knoxville, TN 37998-1001**
**AWARDS** MA.
**Faculty:** 2 full-time (0 women), 3 part-time/adjunct (0 women).
**Students:** 13 full-time (6 women), 5 part-time (2 women); includes 1 minority (Asian American or Pacific Islander). Average age 32. In 2001, 7 degrees awarded.
**Degree requirements:** For master's, internship (300 client contact hours).
**Entrance requirements:** For master's, GRE General Test, Minnesota Multiphasic Personality Inventory, interview, minimum GPA of 3.0, 20 credits each in psychology/counseling, 15 credits in Bible/theology. *Application deadline:* For fall admission, 4/15. *Application fee:* $50.
**Expenses:** Tuition: Full-time $2,250. Tuition and fees vary according to program.
**Financial support:** In 2001–02, 11 students received support. Scholarships/grants available. Financial award application deadline: 8/1; financial award applicants required to submit FAFSA.
Dr. Rick Townsend, Chair, 865-573-4517, *Fax:* 865-251-2337, *E-mail:* rtownsen@jbc.edu.

### ■ KEAN UNIVERSITY

**College of Arts, Humanities and Social Sciences, Department of Psychology, Union, NJ 07083**
**AWARDS** Behavioral sciences (MA), including business and industry counseling, human behavior and organizational psychology, psychological services; business and industry counseling (PMC); educational psychology (MA); marriage and family therapy (Diploma); school psychology (Diploma). Part-time and evening/weekend programs available.
**Faculty:** 21 full-time (13 women), 25 part-time/adjunct.
**Students:** 25 full-time (16 women), 121 part-time (74 women); includes 38 minority (12 African Americans, 8 Asian

Americans or Pacific Islanders, 18 Hispanic Americans), 3 international. Average age 30. 87 applicants, 67% accepted. In 2001, 42 master's, 12 other advanced degrees awarded.
**Degree requirements:** For master's, thesis, comprehensive exam.
**Entrance requirements:** For master's, GRE General Test. *Application deadline:* For fall admission, 6/15; for spring admission, 11/15. *Application fee:* $35.
**Expenses:** Tuition, state resident: full-time $7,372. Tuition, nonresident: full-time $9,004. Required fees: $1,006.
**Financial support:** In 2001–02, 27 research assistantships with full tuition reimbursements (averaging $3,360 per year) were awarded; career-related internships or fieldwork and unspecified assistantships also available.
Dr. Henry L. Kaplowitz, Graduate Coordinator, 908-527-2598.
**Application contact:** Joanne Morris, Director of Graduate Admissions, 908-527-2665, *Fax:* 908-527-2286, *E-mail:* grad_adm@kean.edu.

### ■ KUTZTOWN UNIVERSITY OF PENNSYLVANIA

**College of Graduate Studies and Extended Learning, Program in Counseling Psychology, Kutztown, PA 19530-0730**
**AWARDS** Agency counseling (MA); marital and family therapy (MA). Part-time and evening/weekend programs available.
**Faculty:** 7 full-time (6 women).
**Students:** 10 full-time (8 women), 49 part-time (37 women); includes 1 minority (Asian American or Pacific Islander), 1 international. Average age 33. In 2001, 16 degrees awarded.
**Degree requirements:** For master's, thesis optional.
**Entrance requirements:** For master's, GRE General Test, TOEFL, TSE, interview. *Application deadline:* For fall admission, 3/1; for spring admission, 8/11. *Application fee:* $35.
**Expenses:** Tuition, state resident: full-time $4,600; part-time $256 per credit. Tuition, nonresident: full-time $7,554; part-time $420 per credit. Required fees: $835.
**Financial support:** Career-related internships or fieldwork, Federal Work-Study, and unspecified assistantships available. Financial award application deadline: 3/15; financial award applicants required to submit FAFSA.
**Faculty research:** Addicted families.
Dr. Margaret A. Herrick, Chairperson, 610-683-4204, *Fax:* 610-683-1585, *E-mail:* herrick@kutztown.edu. *Web site:* http://www.kutztown.edu/acad/

### ■ LA SALLE UNIVERSITY

**School of Arts and Sciences, Program in Psychology, Philadelphia, PA 19141-1199**
**AWARDS** Clinical geropsychology (Psy D); clinical psychology (Psy D); family psychology (Psy D); rehabilitation psychology (Psy D). Part-time and evening/weekend programs available.
**Faculty:** 8 full-time (1 woman), 10 part-time/adjunct (5 women).
**Students:** 40 full-time (25 women), 35 part-time (29 women); includes 7 minority (5 African Americans, 2 Hispanic Americans). Average age 35. 95 applicants, 48% accepted, 25 enrolled. In 2001, 1 degree awarded.
**Entrance requirements:** For doctorate, GRE, minimum GPA of 3.0. *Application deadline:* For fall admission, 3/1. *Application fee:* $30.
**Expenses:** Contact institution.
**Financial support:** Scholarships/grants available.
**Faculty research:** Cognitive therapy, attribution theory, treatment of addiction.
Dr. John A. Smith, Director, 215-951-1350, *Fax:* 215-951-1351, *E-mail:* smithj@lasalle.edu.

### ■ LOMA LINDA UNIVERSITY

**Graduate School, Department of Counseling and Family Science, Department of Marriage and Family Therapy, Loma Linda, CA 92350**
**AWARDS** MS, DMFT, PhD. Part-time programs available.
**Students:** 60 full-time (44 women), 9 part-time (5 women).
**Entrance requirements:** For master's, GRE General Test. *Application deadline:* For fall admission, 4/14. *Application fee:* $40.
**Expenses:** Tuition: Part-time $420 per unit.
**Financial support:** Teaching assistantships, career-related internships or fieldwork, Federal Work-Study, and tuition waivers (partial) available. Support available to part-time students.
Dr. Mary Moline, Chair, 909-824-4547, *Fax:* 909-824-4859.

### ■ LONG ISLAND UNIVERSITY, C.W. POST CAMPUS

**School of Education, Department of Counseling and Development, Brookville, NY 11548-1300**
**AWARDS** Marriage and family therapy (PD); mental health counseling (MS); school counseling (MS). Part-time and evening/weekend programs available.
**Faculty:** 12 full-time (5 women), 82 part-time/adjunct (40 women).

*Long Island University, C.W. Post Campus (continued)*

**Students:** 102 full-time (80 women), 194 part-time (136 women). 133 applicants, 88% accepted, 78 enrolled. In 2001, 117 degrees awarded.

**Degree requirements:** For master's, comprehensive exam or thesis, internship; for PD, internship.

**Entrance requirements:** For master's, interview, minimum GPA of 3.0. *Application deadline:* For fall admission, 8/20; for spring admission, 1/10. Applications are processed on a rolling basis. *Application fee:* $30. Electronic applications accepted.

**Expenses:** Tuition: Full-time $10,296; part-time $572 per credit. Required fees: $380; $190 per semester.

**Financial support:** In 2001–02, 8 research assistantships were awarded; career-related internships or fieldwork also available. Financial award application deadline: 5/15; financial award applicants required to submit CSS PROFILE or FAFSA.

**Faculty research:** Community prevention programs, youth gang violence, community mental health counseling.

Dr. A. Scott McGowan, Chair, 516-299-2814, *Fax:* 516-299-4167, *E-mail:* amcgowan@liu.edu.

**Application contact:** Debbie Moslin, Academic Advisor, 516-299-2995, *Fax:* 516-299-3151, *E-mail:* debbie.moslin@liu.edu. *Web site:* http://www.liu.edu/postedu/

## ■ LOYOLA MARYMOUNT UNIVERSITY

**Graduate Division, College of Liberal Arts, Department of Marital and Family Therapy, Los Angeles, CA 90045-2659**

**AWARDS** MA. Part-time programs available.

**Students:** 44 full-time (39 women); includes 9 minority (4 Asian Americans or Pacific Islanders, 4 Hispanic Americans, 1 Native American), 1 international. 40 applicants, 63% accepted, 22 enrolled. In 2001, 12 degrees awarded.

**Degree requirements:** For master's, thesis, 2 semesters of psychotherapy, project.

**Entrance requirements:** For master's, MAT, TOEFL, interview, previous course work in art and psychology. *Application deadline:* Applications are processed on a rolling basis. *Application fee:* $45. Electronic applications accepted.

**Expenses:** Contact institution.

**Financial support:** Research assistantships, career-related internships or fieldwork and scholarships/grants available. Support available to part-time students. Financial award application deadline: 7/1; financial award applicants required to submit FAFSA.

Dr. Debra Linesch, Chair, 310-338-7674, *Fax:* 310-338-4518, *E-mail:* dlinesch@lmu.edu. *Web site:* http://www.lmu.edu/acad/gd/graddiv.htm

## ■ MENNONITE BRETHREN BIBLICAL SEMINARY

**School of Theology, Program in Marriage, Family, and Child Counseling, Fresno, CA 93727-5097**

**AWARDS** MAMFCC, Diploma.

**Students:** Average age 36. 15 applicants, 80% accepted. In 2001, 5 degrees awarded.

**Degree requirements:** For master's, thesis or alternative.

**Entrance requirements:** For master's, GRE General Test, TOEFL. *Application deadline:* For fall admission, 8/1 (priority date); for spring admission, 12/1 (priority date). Applications are processed on a rolling basis. *Application fee:* $35.

**Expenses:** Tuition: Part-time $260 per unit.

**Financial support:** Career-related internships or fieldwork, institutionally sponsored loans, scholarships/grants, and tuition waivers (partial) available. Support available to part-time students. Financial award application deadline: 5/1; financial award applicants required to submit FAFSA.

**Application contact:** 559-452-1730, *Fax:* 559-251-7212, *E-mail:* mbseminary@aol.com.

## ■ MERCY COLLEGE

**Division of Social and Behavioral Sciences, Dobbs Ferry, NY 10522-1189**

**AWARDS** Alcohol and substance abuse counseling (AC); family counseling (AC); health services management (MPA, MS); psychology (MS); retirement counseling (AC); school counseling (MS), including bilingual extension; school psychology (MS), including bilingual extension.

**Students:** 51 full-time (41 women), 105 part-time (81 women); includes 104 minority (47 African Americans, 7 Asian Americans or Pacific Islanders, 50 Hispanic Americans), 10 international.

**Entrance requirements:** For master's, 8 years of healthcare management or practitioner (MS in health services management); interview; minimum GPA of 3.0. *Application fee:* $35.

**Expenses:** Tuition: Part-time $450 per credit. Part-time tuition and fees vary according to program.

Dr. Frances T.M. Mahoney, Chairperson, 914-674-7438, *Fax:* 914-674-7542, *E-mail:* fmahoney@mercy.edu.

**Application contact:** Information Contact, 800-MERCY-NY.

**Find an in-depth description at www.petersons.com/gradchannel.**

## ■ MICHIGAN STATE UNIVERSITY

**Graduate School, College of Human Ecology, Department of Family and Child Ecology, East Lansing, MI 48824**

**AWARDS** Child development (MA); community service-urban studies (MS); community services (MS); family and child ecology (PhD); family consumer sciences education (MA); family ecology (PhD); family economics and management (MA); family studies (MA); home economics education (MA); marriage and family therapy (MA). Part-time and evening/weekend programs available. Postbaccalaureate distance learning degree programs offered.

**Faculty:** 26.

**Students:** 56 full-time (50 women), 75 part-time (67 women); includes 28 minority (20 African Americans, 2 Asian Americans or Pacific Islanders, 6 Hispanic Americans), 21 international. Average age 35. 80 applicants, 61% accepted. In 2001, 39 master's, 9 doctorates awarded.

**Degree requirements:** For master's, thesis optional; for doctorate, thesis/dissertation.

**Entrance requirements:** For master's, GRE General Test, minimum GPA of 3.0 in last 2 years of undergraduate course work; for doctorate, GRE General Test. *Application deadline:* Applications are processed on a rolling basis. *Application fee:* $30 ($40 for international students). Electronic applications accepted.

**Expenses:** Tuition, state resident: part-time $244 per credit hour. Tuition, nonresident: part-time $494 per credit hour. Required fees: $268 per semester. Tuition and fees vary according to course load, degree level and program.

**Financial support:** In 2001–02, 35 fellowships with tuition reimbursements (averaging $2,480 per year), 8 research assistantships with tuition reimbursements (averaging $10,944 per year), 14 teaching assistantships with tuition reimbursements (averaging $10,845 per year) were awarded. Financial award applicants required to submit FAFSA.

**Faculty research:** Early childhood education, family dynamics, family utilization, parenting. *Total annual research expenditures:* $357,600.

Dr. Anne Soderman, Chairperson, 517-432-2953, *E-mail:* fce@msu.edu. *Web site:* http://www.he.msu.edu/fce.html/

# ■ MONTCLAIR STATE UNIVERSITY

**The School of Graduate, Professional and Continuing Education, College of Humanities and Social Sciences, Department of Psychology, Program in Educational Psychology, Upper Montclair, NJ 07043-1624**

**AWARDS** Child/adolescent clinical psychology (MA); clinical psychology for Spanish/English bilinguals (MA). Part-time and evening/weekend programs available.

**Degree requirements:** For master's, thesis optional.

**Entrance requirements:** For master's, GRE General Test, GRE Subject Test, previous course work in psychology. Electronic applications accepted.

# ■ NORTH AMERICAN BAPTIST SEMINARY

**Graduate and Professional Programs, Program in Marriage and Family Therapy, Sioux Falls, SD 57105-1599**

**AWARDS** MA.

**Students:** 6 full-time (all women).
**Entrance requirements:** For master's, minimum GPA of 3.0. *Application deadline:* For fall admission, 8/1 (priority date); for spring admission, 1/1 (priority date). Applications are processed on a rolling basis. *Application fee:* $35.
**Expenses:** Tuition: Full-time $9,900; part-time $412 per hour. Required fees: $40; $20 per semester.
**Financial support:** Scholarships/grants available.
Dr. Del Donaldson, Professor of Marriage & Family Therapy, 605-336-6588, *Fax:* 605-335-9090.
**Application contact:** Melissa M. Hiatt, Director of Admissions, 605-336-6588, *Fax:* 605-335-9090, *E-mail:* melissah@nabs.edu.

# ■ NORTHWESTERN UNIVERSITY

**The Graduate School, Program in Marital and Family Therapy, Evanston, IL 60208**

**AWARDS** MS.

**Faculty:** 18 full-time (10 women).
**Students:** 29 full-time (26 women); includes 5 minority (2 African Americans, 2 Asian Americans or Pacific Islanders, 1 Native American). Average age 28. 47 applicants, 32% accepted. In 2001, 18 degrees awarded. Terminal master's awarded for partial completion of doctoral program.
**Entrance requirements:** For master's, GRE General Test. *Application deadline:* For fall admission, 3/1 (priority date).

Applications are processed on a rolling basis. *Application fee:* $50.
**Expenses:** Tuition: Full-time $26,526.
**Financial support:** In 2001–02, 20 students received support. Career-related internships or fieldwork, Federal Work-Study, institutionally sponsored loans, and scholarships/grants available. Financial award application deadline: 7/15; financial award applicants required to submit FAFSA.
**Faculty research:** Marital and family therapy training, gender, psychotherapy outcome, adolescents and pre-school children at risk, families.
Dr. Linda Rubinowitz, Director of Graduate Education, 847-733-4300, *Fax:* 847-733-0390, *E-mail:* lrubin@northwestern.edu.
**Application contact:** Lisa Day, Program Manager, 847-733-4300 Ext. 206, *Fax:* 847-733-0390, *E-mail:* l-day1@northwestern.edu. *Web site:* http://www.family-institute.org

# ■ NOTRE DAME DE NAMUR UNIVERSITY

**Graduate School, School of Sciences, Department of Counseling and Psychology/Gerontology, Program in Marital and Family Therapy, Belmont, CA 94002-1997**

**AWARDS** MAMFT.

**Expenses:** Tuition: Full-time $9,450; part-time $525 per unit. Required fees: $35 per term.
Dr. Blair McCracken, Director, 650-508-3735.
**Application contact:** Barbara Sterner, Assistant Director of Graduate Admissions, 650-508-3527, *Fax:* 650-508-3662, *E-mail:* grad.admit@ndnu.edu.

# ■ NOVA SOUTHEASTERN UNIVERSITY

**Graduate School of Humanities and Social Sciences, Department of Family Therapy, Master's Program in Family Therapy, Fort Lauderdale, FL 33314-7721**

**AWARDS** MS, Certificate. Part-time programs available.

**Students:** 78 full-time (69 women). In 2001, 19 degrees awarded.
**Degree requirements:** For master's, comprehensive exam.
**Entrance requirements:** For master's, TOEFL, minimum GPA of 3.0, interview. *Application deadline:* For fall admission, 6/1 (priority date); for winter admission, 11/1 (priority date); for spring admission, 3/1 (priority date). Applications are processed on a rolling basis. *Application fee:* $50.
Electronic applications accepted.

**Expenses:** Tuition: Full-time $7,380; part-time $432 per credit. Required fees: $200. Tuition and fees vary according to campus/location and program.
**Financial support:** Research assistantships with partial tuition reimbursements, career-related internships or fieldwork, Federal Work-Study, institutionally sponsored loans, and scholarships/grants available. Support available to part-time students. Financial award application deadline: 4/1.
**Faculty research:** Cross-cultural counseling, family business, medical family therapy, solution-focused therapy, supervision and training.
Dr. Pat Cole, Director, 954-262-3000, *Fax:* 954-262-3968, *E-mail:* cole@nova.edu.
**Application contact:** Heidi Fisher, Graduate Admissions Office, 954-262-3000, *Fax:* 954-262-3968, *E-mail:* heidil@nova.edu.

# ■ NOVA SOUTHEASTERN UNIVERSITY

**Graduate School of Humanities and Social Sciences, Department of Family Therapy, PhD Program in Family Therapy, Fort Lauderdale, FL 33314-7721**

**AWARDS** PhD. Evening/weekend programs available.

**Students:** 77 full-time (62 women). In 2001, 5 degrees awarded.
**Degree requirements:** For doctorate, thesis/dissertation, qualifying exam.
**Entrance requirements:** For doctorate, TOEFL, master's degree in related field, minimum GPA of 3.0, interview. *Application deadline:* Applications are processed on a rolling basis. *Application fee:* $50.
**Expenses:** Tuition: Full-time $7,380; part-time $432 per credit. Required fees: $200. Tuition and fees vary according to campus/location and program.
**Financial support:** Research assistantships, teaching assistantships, career-related internships or fieldwork, Federal Work-Study, institutionally sponsored loans, scholarships/grants, and unspecified assistantships available. Support available to part-time students. Financial award application deadline: 4/1.
**Faculty research:** Cross-cultural counseling, HIV counseling, medical family therapy, solution-focused therapy, supervision and training.
Dr. Shelley Green, Director, 954-262-3000, *Fax:* 954-262-3968, *E-mail:* shelly@nova.edu.
**Application contact:** Heidi Fisher, Graduate Admissions Office, 954-262-3000, *Fax:* 954-262-3968, *E-mail:* heidil@nova.edu. *Web site:* http://www.nova.edu/shss/ft/

### ■ OKLAHOMA BAPTIST UNIVERSITY

**Graduate Studies in Marriage and Family Therapy, Shawnee, OK 74804**

**AWARDS** MS. Part-time and evening/weekend programs available. Postbaccalaureate distance learning degree programs offered (minimal on-campus study).

**Faculty:** 4 full-time (0 women), 3 part-time/adjunct (1 woman).
**Students:** 10 full-time (9 women), 10 part-time (7 women). Average age 36. 14 applicants, 86% accepted. In 2001, 9 degrees awarded.
**Degree requirements:** For master's, practicum, thesis optional.
**Entrance requirements:** For master's, GRE General Test, minimum GPA of 3.0. *Application deadline:* For fall admission, 3/31 (priority date). *Application fee:* $50.
**Expenses:** Tuition: Full-time $7,680; part-time $320 per credit. Required fees: $200; $100 per semester.
**Financial support:** In 2001–02, 16 students received support. Career-related internships or fieldwork, Federal Work-Study, and institutionally sponsored loans available. Support available to part-time students. Financial award application deadline: 3/31; financial award applicants required to submit FAFSA. *Web site:* http://www.okbu.edu/

### ■ OUR LADY OF HOLY CROSS COLLEGE

**Program in Education and Counseling, New Orleans, LA 70131-7399**

**AWARDS** Administration and supervision (M Ed); curriculum and instruction (M Ed); marriage and family counseling (MA); school counseling (M Ed, MA). Part-time and evening/weekend programs available.

**Faculty:** 7 full-time (4 women), 8 part-time/adjunct (3 women).
**Students:** 18 full-time (16 women), 79 part-time (55 women); includes 32 minority (25 African Americans, 2 Asian Americans or Pacific Islanders, 3 Hispanic Americans, 2 Native Americans). Average age 30. 20 applicants, 50% accepted. In 2001, 28 degrees awarded.
**Degree requirements:** For master's, thesis.
**Entrance requirements:** For master's, GRE General Test, minimum GPA of 2.7. *Application deadline:* For fall admission, 9/1. *Application fee:* $20.
**Expenses:** Tuition: Full-time $4,860; part-time $270 per semester hour. Required fees: $500; $250 per term.
**Financial support:** Federal Work-Study and tuition waivers (partial) available. Support available to part-time students. Financial award application deadline: 6/1.

Dr. Judith G. Miranti, Dean of Education, 504-394-7744 Ext. 214, *Fax:* 504-391-2421, *E-mail:* jmiranti@olhcc.edu.
**Application contact:** Kristine Hatfield Kopecky, Dean of Student Affairs and Admissions, 504-394-7744 Ext. 185, *Fax:* 504-391-2421, *E-mail:* kkopecky@ olhcc.edu. *Web site:* http://www.olhcc.edu/

### ■ PACIFIC LUTHERAN UNIVERSITY

**Division of Graduate Studies, Division of Social Sciences, Program in Marriage and Family Therapy, Tacoma, WA 98447**

**AWARDS** MA.
**Faculty:** 7.
**Students:** 21 full-time (17 women), 19 part-time (13 women); includes 5 minority (2 African Americans, 2 Asian Americans or Pacific Islanders, 1 Hispanic American), 3 international. Average age 27. 35 applicants, 57% accepted, 18 enrolled. In 2001, 14 degrees awarded.
**Degree requirements:** For master's, clinical competency, thesis optional.
**Entrance requirements:** For master's, TOEFL, interview for selected applicants. *Application deadline:* For fall admission, 1/31 (priority date). *Application fee:* $35.
**Expenses:** Tuition: Full-time $13,296; part-time $554 per credit. Tuition and fees vary according to course load and program.
**Financial support:** Research assistantships, Federal Work-Study and scholarships/grants available. Financial award application deadline: 3/1.
Dr. Charles York, Chair, 253-535-7599.

### ■ PACIFIC OAKS COLLEGE

**Graduate School, Program in Marriage and Family Therapy, Pasadena, CA 91103**

**AWARDS** MA. Part-time and evening/weekend programs available.

**Faculty:** 5 full-time (3 women), 8 part-time/adjunct (5 women).
**Students:** 29 full-time, 78 part-time; includes 57 minority (11 African Americans, 2 Asian Americans or Pacific Islanders, 43 Hispanic Americans, 1 Native American). Average age 38. 20 applicants, 85% accepted, 9 enrolled. In 2001, 15 degrees awarded.
**Degree requirements:** For master's, thesis.
**Entrance requirements:** For master's, interview. *Application deadline:* For fall admission, 4/15 (priority date); for spring admission, 10/1 (priority date). Applications are processed on a rolling basis. *Application fee:* $55.

**Expenses:** Tuition: Full-time $10,450; part-time $550 per unit. Required fees: $30 per term.
**Financial support:** Federal Work-Study and scholarships/grants available. Support available to part-time students. Financial award application deadline: 4/15; financial award applicants required to submit FAFSA.
**Faculty research:** Family systems, cross-cultural development, therapeutic intervention and Latino families.
Connie Destito, Chair, MFCC Department, 626-685-2527, *Fax:* 626-397-1304, *E-mail:* cdestito@pacificoaks.edu.
**Application contact:** Marsha Franker, Director of Admissions, 626-397-1349, *Fax:* 626-577-6144, *E-mail:* admissions@ pacificoaks.edu. *Web site:* http:// www.pacificoaks.edu/

### ■ PALM BEACH ATLANTIC UNIVERSITY

**School of Education and Behavioral Studies, West Palm Beach, FL 33416-4708**

**AWARDS** Counseling psychology (MSCP), including marriage and family therapy, mental health counseling, school guidance counseling; elementary education (M Ed).

**Faculty:** 4 full-time (2 women), 7 part-time/adjunct (6 women).
**Students:** 129 full-time (102 women), 64 part-time (52 women); includes 46 minority (29 African Americans, 2 Asian Americans or Pacific Islanders, 14 Hispanic Americans, 1 Native American), 6 international. Average age 34. 118 applicants, 69% accepted, 65 enrolled. In 2001, 55 degrees awarded.
**Entrance requirements:** For master's, GRE General Test, minimum GPA of 3.0 in last 60 hours. *Application deadline:* For fall admission, 7/15 (priority date); for spring admission, 11/15 (priority date). Applications are processed on a rolling basis. *Application fee:* $35. Electronic applications accepted.
**Expenses:** Tuition: Part-time $290 per credit hour.
**Financial support:** Available to part-time students. Applicants required to submit FAFSA.
Dr. Dona Thornton, Dean, 561-803-2350, *Fax:* 561-803-2186, *E-mail:* thorntond@ pbac.edu.
**Application contact:** Carolanne M. Brown, Director of Graduate Admissions, 800-281-3466, *Fax:* 561-803-2115, *E-mail:* grad@pbac.edu. *Web site:* http:// www.pbac.edu/

## ■ PHILLIPS GRADUATE INSTITUTE

**Program in Clinical Family Psychology, Encino, CA 91316-1509**

**AWARDS** Psy D.

**Faculty:** 13 full-time, 30 part-time/adjunct.

**Students:** 35 full-time (0 women), 171 part-time (1 woman); includes 61 minority (13 African Americans, 10 Asian Americans or Pacific Islanders, 38 Hispanic Americans).

**Degree requirements:** For doctorate, thesis/dissertation, registration.

**Entrance requirements:** For doctorate, minimum GPA of 3.0, interview. *Application deadline:* For fall admission, 6/1 (priority date); for spring admission, 12/1 (priority date). Applications are processed on a rolling basis. *Application fee:* $50.

**Expenses:** Tuition: Part-time $550 per unit.

**Financial support:** Tuition waivers (full and partial) available.

**Application contact:** Kim Bell, Assistant Director of Admission, 818-386-5639, *Fax:* 818-386-5699, *E-mail:* admit@pgi.edu.

## ■ PHILLIPS GRADUATE INSTITUTE

**Program in Marriage and Family Therapy, Organizational Behavior and School Counseling, Encino, CA 91316-1509**

**AWARDS** Marital and family therapy (MA); organizational behavior (MA); school counseling (MA). Evening/weekend programs available.

**Faculty:** 13 full-time, 30 part-time/adjunct.

**Students:** 384 full-time (311 women); includes 76 minority (21 African Americans, 17 Asian Americans or Pacific Islanders, 38 Hispanic Americans), 3 international. Average age 39. In 2001, 117 degrees awarded.

**Degree requirements:** For master's, thesis, comprehensive exam.

**Entrance requirements:** For master's, minimum GPA of 2.5. *Application deadline:* For fall admission, 8/15 (priority date); for spring admission, 12/15. Applications are processed on a rolling basis. *Application fee:* $0.

**Expenses:** Tuition: Part-time $550 per unit.

**Financial support:** Tuition waivers (full and partial) available. Financial award application deadline: 8/15; financial award applicants required to submit FAFSA.

**Faculty research:** Integration of interpersonal psychological theory, systems approach, firsthand experiential learning.

Dr. Lisa Porche-Burke, President, 818-386-5650, *Fax:* 818-386-5699.

**Application contact:** Kim Bell, Assistant Director of Admission, 818-386-5639, *Fax:* 818-386-5699, *E-mail:* admit@pgi.edu. *Web site:* http://www.pgi.edu/

## ■ PRAIRIE VIEW A&M UNIVERSITY

**Graduate School, College of Agriculture and Human Sciences, Prairie View, TX 77446-0188**

**AWARDS** Agricultural economics (MS); animal sciences (MS); interdisciplinary human sciences (MS); marriage and family therapy (MS); soil science (MS).

**Faculty:** 15 full-time (5 women), 1 part-time/adjunct (0 women).

**Students:** 45 full-time (28 women), 28 part-time (21 women); includes 63 minority (61 African Americans, 2 Asian Americans or Pacific Islanders), 6 international. Average age 35. 15 applicants, 100% accepted. In 2001, 20 degrees awarded.

**Entrance requirements:** For master's, GRE General Test. *Application deadline:* For fall admission, 10/2 (priority date); for spring admission, 2/19. Applications are processed on a rolling basis. *Application fee:* $25.

**Expenses:** Tuition, state resident: full-time $864; part-time $48 per credit hour. Tuition, nonresident: full-time $4,716; part-time $262 per credit hour. Required fees: $1,324; $59 per credit hour. $131 per term.

**Financial support:** In 2001–02, 10 research assistantships with tuition reimbursements (averaging $13,500 per year) were awarded; career-related internships or fieldwork, Federal Work-Study, and institutionally sponsored loans also available. Financial award application deadline: 4/1. *Total annual research expenditures:* $3 million.

Dr. Elizabeth Noel, Dean, 936-857-2996, *Fax:* 936-857-2998.

## ■ PURDUE UNIVERSITY

**Graduate School, School of Consumer and Family Sciences, Department of Child Development and Family Studies, West Lafayette, IN 47907**

**AWARDS** Developmental studies (MS, PhD); family studies (MS, PhD); marriage and family therapy (MS, PhD). Part-time programs available.

**Faculty:** 19 full-time (14 women).

**Students:** 46 full-time (37 women), 20 part-time (15 women); includes 6 minority (3 African Americans, 1 Asian American or Pacific Islander, 2 Hispanic Americans), 11 international. Average age 29. 82

applicants, 48% accepted. In 2001, 13 master's, 10 doctorates awarded. Terminal master's awarded for partial completion of doctoral program.

**Degree requirements:** For master's and doctorate, thesis/dissertation.

**Entrance requirements:** For master's and doctorate, GRE General Test, TWE. *Application deadline:* For fall admission, 1/10. *Application fee:* $30. Electronic applications accepted.

**Expenses:** Tuition, state resident: full-time $4,164; part-time $149 per credit hour. Tuition, nonresident: full-time $13,872; part-time $458 per credit hour. Tuition and fees vary according to campus/location and program.

**Financial support:** In 2001–02, 50 students received support, including 1 fellowship with full tuition reimbursement available (averaging $13,299 per year), 26 research assistantships with full tuition reimbursements available (averaging $9,900 per year), 26 teaching assistantships with full tuition reimbursements available (averaging $9,900 per year); career-related internships or fieldwork also available. Support available to part-time students. Financial award application deadline: 1/15; financial award applicants required to submit FAFSA.

**Faculty research:** Inclusion of children with special needs, families as learning environments, relationships in child care, work-family relations, AIDS prevention. Dr. D. R. Powell, Head, 765-494-9511.

**Application contact:** Becky Harshman, Graduate Secretary, 765-494-2965, *Fax:* 765-494-0503, *E-mail:* harshman@cfs.purdue.edu. *Web site:* http://www.cfs.purdue.edu/cdfs/

## ■ PURDUE UNIVERSITY CALUMET

**Graduate School, School of Liberal Arts and Sciences, Department of Behavioral Sciences, Hammond, IN 46323-2094**

**AWARDS** Marriage and family therapy (MS).

**Degree requirements:** For master's, thesis.

**Entrance requirements:** For master's, GRE, TOEFL, interview.

## ■ REFORMED THEOLOGICAL SEMINARY

**Graduate and Professional Programs, Jackson, MS 39209-3099**

**AWARDS** Bible, theology, and missions (Certificate); biblical studies (MA); Christian education (M Div, MA); counseling (M Div); divinity (M Div, Diploma); intercultural studies (PhD); marriage and family therapy (MA); ministry (D Min); missions (M Div, MA,

*Reformed Theological Seminary (continued)*

D Min); New Testament (Th M); Old Testament (Th M); theological studies (MA); theology (Th M).

**Faculty:** 16 full-time (0 women), 16 part-time/adjunct (3 women).

**Students:** 130 full-time (31 women), 77 part-time (26 women); includes 38 minority (25 African Americans, 9 Asian Americans or Pacific Islanders, 4 Hispanic Americans). In 2001, 24 first professional degrees, 26 master's, 59 doctorates awarded.

**Degree requirements:** For M Div, 2 foreign languages, thesis (for some programs); for master's, thesis (for some programs), fieldwork; for doctorate, 2 foreign languages, thesis/dissertation.

**Entrance requirements:** For M Div and master's, TOEFL, minimum GPA of 2.6; for doctorate, TOEFL, minimum GPA of 3.0. *Application deadline:* Applications are processed on a rolling basis. *Application fee:* $25.

**Expenses:** Tuition: Full-time $6,500; part-time $250 per hour. Required fees: $120. One-time fee: $120 part-time. Tuition and fees vary according to degree level.

**Financial support:** Research assistantships, career-related internships or fieldwork, scholarships/grants, and tuition waivers (full and partial) available. Financial award application deadline: 5/1.

Dr. Allen Curry, Dean, 601-922-4988, *Fax:* 601-922-1153.

**Application contact:** Brian Gault, Director of Admissions, 601-923-1600, *Fax:* 601-923-1654.

■ **SAINT JOSEPH COLLEGE**

**Graduate Division, Department of Marriage and Family Therapy, West Hartford, CT 06117-2700**

**AWARDS** MA. Part-time and evening/weekend programs available.

**Faculty:** 2 full-time (both women), 2 part-time/adjunct (both women).

**Students:** 16 full-time (11 women), 22 part-time (17 women); includes 3 minority (2 African Americans, 1 Hispanic American). Average age 33. In 2001, 13 degrees awarded.

**Degree requirements:** For master's, comprehensive exam.

**Entrance requirements:** For master's, GRE or MAT. *Application deadline:* Applications are processed on a rolling basis. *Application fee:* $25.

**Expenses:** Tuition: Part-time $475 per credit hour.

**Financial support:** In 2001–02, 2 research assistantships with full tuition reimbursements were awarded. Financial award

application deadline: 7/15; financial award applicants required to submit FAFSA.

**Faculty research:** Communication in organizations, adoptive family development, therapeutic services for adoptive families. *Total annual research expenditures:* $3,000.

Dr. Catherine K. Kikoski, Director, 860-231-5324, *Fax:* 860-231-1691, *E-mail:* ckikoski@sjc.edu.

■ **SAINT LOUIS UNIVERSITY**

**Graduate School, College of Public Service, Department of Counseling and Family Therapy, St. Louis, MO 63103-2097**

**AWARDS** Counseling and family therapy (PhD); human development counseling (MA); marriage and family therapy (Certificate); school counseling (MA).

**Faculty:** 5 full-time (4 women).

**Students:** 16 full-time (13 women), 58 part-time (44 women); includes 20 minority (15 African Americans, 3 Asian Americans or Pacific Islanders, 1 Hispanic American, 1 Native American), 1 international. Average age 37. 46 applicants, 67% accepted, 17 enrolled. In 2001, 15 master's, 6 doctorates awarded.

**Degree requirements:** For master's, comprehensive exam; for doctorate, thesis/dissertation, preliminary oral and written exams, comprehensive exam.

**Entrance requirements:** For master's, GRE General Test or MAT, interview; for doctorate, GRE General Test, interview. *Application deadline:* For fall admission, 2/1; for spring admission, 11/1. Applications are processed on a rolling basis. *Application fee:* $40.

**Expenses:** Tuition: Part-time $630 per credit hour.

**Financial support:** In 2001–02, 18 students received support; fellowships, unspecified assistantships available. Financial award application deadline: 4/1; financial award applicants required to submit FAFSA.

**Faculty research:** Learning styles/personality differences, black males' counseling perspectives, adult-sibling relationships, clinical supervision, low-income clients.

Dr. Nancy Morrison, Chairperson, 314-977-7114, *Fax:* 314-977-3214, *E-mail:* morrisonc@slu.edu.

**Application contact:** Dr. Marcia Buresch, Associate Dean of the Graduate School, 314-977-2240, *Fax:* 314-977-3943, *E-mail:* bureschm@slu.edu.

■ **SAINT MARY'S COLLEGE OF CALIFORNIA**

**School of Education, Program in Counseling, Moraga, CA 94556**

**AWARDS** General counseling (MA); marital and family therapy (MA); school counseling (MA). Part-time and evening/weekend programs available.

**Faculty:** 4 full-time (3 women), 21 part-time/adjunct (15 women).

**Students:** 35 full-time, 66 part-time; includes 18 minority (2 African Americans, 5 Asian Americans or Pacific Islanders, 7 Hispanic Americans, 4 Native Americans), 1 international. Average age 35. 56 applicants, 89% accepted, 44 enrolled. In 2001, 10 degrees awarded.

**Degree requirements:** For master's, thesis or alternative.

**Entrance requirements:** For master's, interview, minimum GPA of 3.0. *Application deadline:* Applications are processed on a rolling basis. *Application fee:* $50.

**Financial support:** In 2001–02, 5 students received support. Career-related internships or fieldwork and Federal Work-Study available. Support available to part-time students. Financial award application deadline: 2/15; financial award applicants required to submit FAFSA.

**Faculty research:** Counselor training effectiveness, multicultural development, empathy, the interface of spirituality and psychotherapy, gender issues.

Dr. Colette Fleuridas, Director, 925-631-4489, *Fax:* 925-376-8379, *E-mail:* cfleurid@stmarys-ca.edu.

■ **ST. MARY'S UNIVERSITY OF SAN ANTONIO**

**Graduate School, Department of Counseling and Human Services, San Antonio, TX 78228-8507**

**AWARDS** Community counseling (MA); counseling (PhD, Sp C); marriage and family relations (Certificate); marriage and family therapy (MA, PhD); mental health (MA); mental health and substance abuse counseling (Certificate); substance abuse (MA). Postbaccalaureate distance learning degree programs offered (minimal on-campus study).

**Faculty:** 9 full-time (4 women), 5 part-time/adjunct (3 women).

**Students:** 125 (98 women); includes 48 minority (8 African Americans, 40 Hispanic Americans) 5 international. Average age 28. In 2001, 24 master's, 4 doctorates awarded.

**Degree requirements:** For master's, internship; for doctorate, thesis/dissertation, internship.

**Entrance requirements:** For master's, GRE General Test, MAT; for doctorate, GRE General Test. *Application deadline:*

Applications are processed on a rolling basis. *Application fee:* $15. Electronic applications accepted.
**Expenses:** Tuition: Full-time $8,190; part-time $455 per credit hour. Required fees: $375.
**Financial support:** Career-related internships or fieldwork and Federal Work-Study available. Financial award application deadline: 2/15; financial award applicants required to submit FAFSA.
Dr. Dana Comstock, Graduate Program Director, 210-436-3226.

■ **ST. THOMAS UNIVERSITY**

**School of Graduate Studies, Department of Social Sciences and Counseling, Program in Marriage and Family Therapy, Miami, FL 33054-6459**
**AWARDS** MS. Part-time and evening/weekend programs available.

**Degree requirements:** For master's, comprehensive exam.
**Entrance requirements:** For master's, TOEFL, interview; minimum GPA of 3.0 or GRE.

■ **SAN FRANCISCO STATE UNIVERSITY**

**Graduate Division, College of Health and Human Services, Department of Counseling, Program in Marriage, Family, and Child Counseling, San Francisco, CA 94132-1722**
**AWARDS** Marriage and family counseling (MS). Part-time programs available.

**Degree requirements:** For master's, culminating written description of internship.
**Entrance requirements:** For master's, minimum GPA of 2.5 in last 60 units.

■ **SANTA CLARA UNIVERSITY**

**Division of Counseling Psychology and Education, Program in Marriage, Family, and Child Counseling, Santa Clara, CA 95053**
**AWARDS** MA. Part-time and evening/weekend programs available.
**Students:** 14 full-time (13 women), 37 part-time (35 women); includes 7 minority (3 Asian Americans or Pacific Islanders, 4 Hispanic Americans), 2 international. Average age 35.
**Degree requirements:** For master's, field internship/practicum, thesis optional.
**Entrance requirements:** For master's, GRE or MAT, TOEFL, minimum GPA of 3.0, 1 year of related experience. *Application deadline:* For fall admission, 4/1; for winter admission, 11/1; for spring admission, 2/1. Applications are processed on a rolling basis. *Application fee:* $35.

**Expenses:** Tuition: Part-time $320 per unit. Tuition and fees vary according to class time, degree level, program and student level.
**Financial support:** Fellowships, teaching assistantships, career-related internships or fieldwork, Federal Work-Study, institutionally sponsored loans, and scholarships/grants available. Support available to part-time students. Financial award application deadline: 3/1; financial award applicants required to submit FAFSA.
Dr. Jerrold Shapiro, Director, 408-554-4434.
**Application contact:** Helen Valine, Assistant to the Dean, 408-554-4656, *Fax:* 408-554-2392.

■ **SEATTLE PACIFIC UNIVERSITY**

**Graduate School, School of Psychology, Family and Community, Program in Marriage and Family Therapy, Seattle, WA 98119-1997**
**AWARDS** MS. Part-time programs available.
**Students:** 69 (62 women); includes 6 minority (4 African Americans, 2 Hispanic Americans) 1 international. In 2001, 22 degrees awarded.
**Degree requirements:** For master's, internship, thesis optional.
**Entrance requirements:** For master's, GRE General Test or MAT, interview. *Application deadline:* For fall admission, 3/1. *Application fee:* $50.
**Expenses:** Tuition: Part-time $300 per credit hour. Tuition and fees vary according to program.
**Financial support:** Career-related internships or fieldwork and unspecified assistantships available. Financial award applicants required to submit FAFSA.
**Faculty research:** Roles of therapists, models of collaboration, medical and mental health theories of marriage and family therapy.
Dr. Claudia Grauf-Grounds, Chair, 206-281-2632, *Fax:* 206-281-2695, *E-mail:* claudiagg@spu.edu.
**Application contact:** Vicki Vorhes, Coordinator, 206-281-2762, *Fax:* 206-281-2695, *E-mail:* vvorhes@spu.edu. *Web site:* http://www.spu.edu/depts/psych/graduate_school_in_psychology.htm

■ **SETON HALL UNIVERSITY**

**College of Education and Human Services, Department of Professional Psychology and Family Therapy, Program in Marriage and Family Counseling, South Orange, NJ 07079-2697**
**AWARDS** MS, PhD, Ed S.

**Degree requirements:** For master's, case study; for doctorate, thesis/dissertation, internship, comprehensive exam; for Ed S, internship.
**Entrance requirements:** For master's, GRE; for doctorate, GRE, interview; for Ed S, GRE or MAT, interview.
**Expenses:** Tuition: Full-time $10,818; part-time $601 per credit. Required fees: $610; $185 per term. Tuition and fees vary according to course load, program and student's religious affiliation.
**Faculty research:** Family systems.

■ **SETON HILL UNIVERSITY**

**Program in Marriage and Family Therapy, Greensburg, PA 15601**
**AWARDS** MA. Part-time and evening/weekend programs available.
**Faculty:** 3 full-time (2 women), 5 part-time/adjunct (2 women).
**Students:** 13 full-time (all women), 24 part-time (18 women). Average age 32. 26 applicants, 81% accepted, 20 enrolled.
**Entrance requirements:** For master's, TOEFL, minimum GPA of 3.0, 12 credits in psychology. *Application deadline:* For fall admission, 8/15 (priority date); for spring admission, 12/15. Applications are processed on a rolling basis. *Application fee:* $30. Electronic applications accepted.
**Expenses:** Tuition: Full-time $10,800; part-time $400 per credit. Required fees: $80; $40 per semester.
**Financial support:** Scholarships/grants available. Support available to part-time students. Financial award application deadline: 8/15; financial award applicants required to submit FAFSA.
**Faculty research:** Social cognition, feminist psychology, psychology of gender, developmental psychology.
Dr. Tracey Laszloffy, Director, 724-838-7816, *E-mail:* laszloffy@setonhill.edu.
**Application contact:** Dana Sember, Program Advisor, 724-838-4283, *Fax:* 724-830-1294, *E-mail:* sember@setonhill.edu. *Web site:* http://www.setonhill.edu

■ **SONOMA STATE UNIVERSITY**

**School of Social Sciences, Department of Counseling, Rohnert Park, CA 94928-3609**
**AWARDS** Counseling (MA); marriage, family, and child counseling (MA); pupil personnel services (MA). Part-time programs available.
**Faculty:** 5 full-time (3 women), 5 part-time/adjunct (3 women).
**Students:** 61 full-time (45 women), 34 part-time (29 women); includes 23 minority (1 African American, 5 Asian Americans or Pacific Islanders, 16 Hispanic Americans, 1 Native American), 5 international. Average age 35. 66

*Sonoma State University (continued)*
applicants, 35% accepted, 20 enrolled. In 2001, 28 degrees awarded.
**Degree requirements:** For master's, internship.
**Entrance requirements:** For master's, minimum GPA of 3.0. *Application deadline:* For fall admission, 11/30. *Application fee:* $55.
**Expenses:** Tuition, nonresident: full-time $4,428; part-time $246 per unit. Required fees: $2,084; $727 per semester.
**Financial support:** Career-related internships or fieldwork available. Support available to part-time students. Financial award application deadline: 3/2.
**Faculty research:** Self-esteem, relationship of emotion and health, at-risk youth, feminist issues, supervision strategies.
Dr. Carolyn Saarni, Chair, 707-664-2544, *E-mail:* carolyn.saarni@sonoma.edu.

■ **SOUTHERN ADVENTIST UNIVERSITY**
**School of Education and Psychology, Collegedale, TN 37315-0370**
**AWARDS** Community counseling (MS); curriculum and instruction (MS Ed); educational administration and supervision (MS Ed); inclusive education (MS Ed); marriage and family therapy (MS Ed); multiage/multigrade teaching (MS Ed); outdoor teacher education (MS Ed); school counseling (MS). Part-time and evening/weekend programs available.
**Faculty:** 11 full-time (7 women), 2 part-time/adjunct (1 woman).
**Students:** 46 full-time (25 women), 70 part-time (48 women); includes 23 minority (11 African Americans, 1 Asian American or Pacific Islander, 10 Hispanic Americans, 1 Native American), 2 international. Average age 36. 22 applicants, 91% accepted. In 2001, 29 degrees awarded.
**Degree requirements:** For master's, position paper (counseling), portfolio (MS Ed in outdoor teacher education).
**Entrance requirements:** For master's, GRE General Test, Minnesota Multiphasic Personality Inventory. *Application deadline:* Applications are processed on a rolling basis. *Application fee:* $25. Electronic applications accepted.
**Expenses:** Tuition: Full-time $5,580; part-time $310 per credit hour.
**Financial support:** In 2001–02, 11 students received support, including 1 research assistantship; career-related internships or fieldwork, scholarships/grants, and tuition waivers (partial) also available. Support available to part-time students. Financial award application deadline: 4/1; financial award applicants required to submit FAFSA.

**Faculty research:** Comparative study of education in North America and Central America, service learning and academic achievement.
Dr. Alberto dos Santos, Dean, 423-238-2779, *Fax:* 423-238-2468, *E-mail:* adossant@southern.edu.
**Application contact:** Cathy Olson, Information Contact, 423-238-2765, *Fax:* 423-238-2468, *E-mail:* cjolson@southern.edu. *Web site:* http://www.southern.edu/edupsy/homepage.html

■ **SOUTHERN CHRISTIAN UNIVERSITY**
**Graduate and Professional Programs, Montgomery, AL 36117**
**AWARDS** Biblical studies (MA, D Min); Christian ministry (M Div); marriage and family therapy (M Div, D Min, PhD); ministerial leadership (MS); organizational leadership (MS); pastoral counseling (M Div, MS, PhD); practical theology (MA); professional counseling (M Div, PhD). Part-time and evening/weekend programs available. Postbaccalaureate distance learning degree programs offered (no on-campus study).
**Faculty:** 43 full-time (5 women), 18 part-time/adjunct (8 women).
**Students:** 224 full-time (86 women); includes 69 minority (64 African Americans, 3 Asian Americans or Pacific Islanders, 2 Native Americans). Average age 35. In 2001, 8 first professional degrees, 29 master's, 3 doctorates awarded.
**Degree requirements:** For master's, one foreign language, thesis (for some programs); for doctorate, thesis/dissertation.
**Entrance requirements:** For M Div, master's, and doctorate, GRE General Test or MAT. *Application deadline:* For fall admission, 9/1 (priority date); for spring admission, 1/1 (priority date). Applications are processed on a rolling basis. *Application fee:* $50. Electronic applications accepted.
**Expenses:** Tuition: Full-time $7,020; part-time $390 per semester hour. Required fees: $1,600; $400 per semester. Tuition and fees vary according to course load.
**Financial support:** Federal Work-Study and scholarships/grants available. Support available to part-time students. Financial award applicants required to submit FAFSA.
**Faculty research:** Homiletics, hermeneutics, ancient Near Eastern history.
Rick Johnson, Director of Enrollment Management, 800-351-4040 Ext. 213, *Fax:* 334-387-3878, *E-mail:* rickjohnson@southernchristian.edu.
**Application contact:** Becky Bagwell, Admissions Officer, 334-387-3877 Ext. 224, *Fax:* 334-387-3878, *E-mail:*

beckybagwell@southernchristian.edu. *Web site:* http://www.southernchristian.edu/

■ **SOUTHERN CONNECTICUT STATE UNIVERSITY**
**School of Graduate Studies, School of Health and Human Services, Department of Marriage and Family Therapy, New Haven, CT 06515-1355**
**AWARDS** MFT.
**Faculty:** 2 full-time (1 woman).
**Students:** 35 full-time (25 women), 19 part-time (13 women); includes 6 minority (2 African Americans, 2 Asian Americans or Pacific Islanders, 2 Hispanic Americans). 46 applicants, 39% accepted. In 2001, 21 degrees awarded.
**Degree requirements:** For master's, internship.
**Entrance requirements:** For master's, minimum undergraduate QPA of 3.0 in graduate major field or 2.5 overall, interview. *Application deadline:* For fall admission, 7/15 (priority date). Applications are processed on a rolling basis. *Application fee:* $40.
**Financial support:** Application deadline: 4/15.
Dr. Edward Lynch, Chairperson, 203-392-6411, *Fax:* 203-392-6441, *E-mail:* lynch_j@southernct.edu. *Web site:* http://www.southernct.edu/

■ **SOUTHERN NAZARENE UNIVERSITY**
**Graduate College, School of Psychology, Bethany, OK 73008**
**AWARDS** Counseling psychology (MSCP); marriage and family therapy (MA).
**Degree requirements:** For master's, thesis optional.
**Entrance requirements:** For master's, English proficiency exam, minimum GPA of 3.0 in last 60 hours/major, 2.7 overall.

■ **SPRINGFIELD COLLEGE**
**School of Graduate Studies, Programs in Counseling and Psychological Services, Springfield, MA 01109-3797**
**AWARDS** Athletic counseling (M Ed, MS, CAS); general counseling (M Ed, MS, CAS); industrial/organizational psychology (MS, CAS); marriage and family therapy (M Ed, MS, CAS); mental health counseling (M Ed, MS, CAS); school guidance and counseling (M Ed, MS, CAS); student personnel in higher education (M Ed, MS, CAS). Part-time and evening/weekend programs available.
**Faculty:** 11 full-time (7 women), 20 part-time/adjunct (9 women).
**Students:** 133 full-time, 34 part-time. Average age 26. 210 applicants, 93%

accepted. In 2001, 63 master's, 3 other advanced degrees awarded.

**Degree requirements:** For master's, thesis (for some programs), research project, internship, comprehensive exam.

**Entrance requirements:** For master's and CAS, interview. *Application deadline:* For fall admission, 2/1 (priority date); for spring admission, 12/1. Applications are processed on a rolling basis. *Application fee:* $40.

**Financial support:** In 2001–02, 8 fellowships with partial tuition reimbursements (averaging $2,000 per year), 2 research assistantships (averaging $4,000 per year), 7 teaching assistantships (averaging $1,800 per year) were awarded. Career-related internships or fieldwork, Federal Work-Study, institutionally sponsored loans, scholarships/grants, and tuition waivers (full and partial) also available. Financial award application deadline: 3/1.

**Faculty research:** Sport psychology, leadership and emotional intelligence, rehabilitation adherence, professional career women and caregiving. *Total annual research expenditures:* $715,109.

Dr. Barbara Mandell, Director, 413-748-3339, *Fax:* 413-748-3854, *E-mail:* barbara_mandell@spfldcol.edu.

**Application contact:** Donald James Shaw, Director of Graduate Admissions, 413-748-3225, *Fax:* 413-748-3694, *E-mail:* donald_shaw_jr@spfldcol.edu.

### ■ STATE UNIVERSITY OF NEW YORK COLLEGE AT ONEONTA

**Graduate Studies, Division of Education, Department of Educational Psychology, Oneonta, NY 13820-4015**

**AWARDS** Community mental health (MS); marriage and family therapy (MS); school counselor K-12 (MS Ed, CAS). Part-time and evening/weekend programs available.

**Students:** 4 full-time (3 women), 50 part-time (39 women). 16 applicants, 69% accepted. In 2001, 22 master's, 8 other advanced degrees awarded.

**Degree requirements:** For master's, comprehensive exam.

**Entrance requirements:** For master's, GRE General Test. *Application deadline:* For fall admission, 3/1; for spring admission, 10/1. *Application fee:* $50.

**Expenses:** Tuition, state resident: full-time $5,100; part-time $213 per credit hour. Tuition, nonresident: full-time $8,416; part-time $351 per credit hour. Required fees: $616; $12 per credit hour.

Dr. Joanne Curran, Chair, 607-436-3554, *Fax:* 607-436-3799, *E-mail:* curranjm@oneonta.edu.

### ■ STETSON UNIVERSITY

**College of Arts and Sciences, Division of Education, Department of Counselor Education, DeLand, FL 32723**

**AWARDS** Marriage and family therapy (MS); mental health counseling (MS); school guidance and family consultation (MS). Evening/weekend programs available.

**Students:** 31 full-time (29 women), 63 part-time (52 women); includes 20 minority (15 African Americans, 1 Asian American or Pacific Islander, 4 Hispanic Americans), 1 international. Average age 34. In 2001, 31 degrees awarded.

**Entrance requirements:** For master's, GRE General Test. *Application deadline:* For fall admission, 3/1 (priority date); for spring admission, 11/1. Applications are processed on a rolling basis. *Application fee:* $25.

**Expenses:** Tuition: Part-time $430 per credit hour. Full-time tuition and fees vary according to program.

Dr. Lynn L. Landis-Long, Chair, 386-822-8992.

**Application contact:** Pat LeClaire, Office of Graduate Studies, 386-822-7075, *Fax:* 386-822-7388, *E-mail:* pat.leclaire@stetson.edu.

### ■ SYRACUSE UNIVERSITY

**Graduate School, College of Human Services and Health Professions, Marriage and Family Therapy Program, Syracuse, NY 13244-0003**

**AWARDS** MA, PhD.

**Faculty:** 2 full-time (1 woman), 2 part-time/adjunct (1 woman).

**Students:** 31 full-time (27 women), 14 part-time (11 women); includes 10 minority (5 African Americans, 2 Asian Americans or Pacific Islanders, 3 Hispanic Americans). Average age 31. 32 applicants, 28% accepted. In 2001, 16 degrees awarded.

**Degree requirements:** For doctorate, thesis/dissertation.

**Entrance requirements:** For master's, GRE General Test. *Application deadline:* For fall admission, 1/15. *Application fee:* $50.

**Expenses:** Tuition: Full-time $15,528; part-time $647 per credit. Required fees: $420; $38 per term. Tuition and fees vary according to program.

**Financial support:** Fellowships, research assistantships, teaching assistantships, Federal Work-Study, scholarships/grants, tuition waivers (partial), and unspecified assistantships available.

Dr. Linda Stone Fish, Graduate Director, 315-443-3024.

**Application contact:** Linda M. Littlejohn, Assistant Dean, Enrollment Management, 315-443-5555, *Fax:* 315-443-2562, *E-mail:* inquire@hshp.syr.edu.

### ■ TEXAS TECH UNIVERSITY

**Graduate School, College of Human Sciences, Department of Human Development and Family Studies, Lubbock, TX 79409**

**AWARDS** Human development and family studies (MS, PhD); marriage and family therapy (MS, PhD).

**Faculty:** 21 full-time (12 women), 3 part-time/adjunct (all women).

**Students:** 49 full-time (38 women), 25 part-time (18 women); includes 11 minority (6 African Americans, 5 Hispanic Americans), 15 international. Average age 32. 49 applicants, 61% accepted, 15 enrolled. In 2001, 5 master's, 6 doctorates awarded.

**Degree requirements:** For master's and doctorate, thesis/dissertation.

**Entrance requirements:** For master's and doctorate, GRE General Test. *Application deadline:* Applications are processed on a rolling basis. *Application fee:* $25 ($50 for international students). Electronic applications accepted.

**Expenses:** Tuition, state resident: full-time $1,926; part-time $107 per credit hour. Tuition, nonresident: full-time $5,724; part-time $318 per credit hour. Required fees: $779; $737 per year. Tuition and fees vary according to course level, course load and program.

**Financial support:** In 2001–02, 57 students received support, including 26 research assistantships with partial tuition reimbursements available (averaging $11,313 per year), 24 teaching assistantships with partial tuition reimbursements available (averaging $11,641 per year); fellowships with tuition reimbursements available, career-related internships or fieldwork, Federal Work-Study, institutionally sponsored loans, and scholarships/grants also available. Support available to part-time students. Financial award application deadline: 5/1; financial award applicants required to submit FAFSA.

**Faculty research:** Parenting, marital and premarital relationships, adolescent drug abuse, early childhood, life span. *Total annual research expenditures:* $190,567.

Dr. Dean M. Busby, Chair, 806-742-3000, *Fax:* 806-742-0285, *E-mail:* dbusby@hs.ttu.edu.

**Application contact:** Graduate Adviser, 806-742-3000, *Fax:* 806-742-1849. *Web site:* http://www.hs.ttu.edu/HDFS/default.htm

## ■ TEXAS WOMAN'S UNIVERSITY

**Graduate Studies and Research, College of Professional Education, Department of Family Sciences, Denton, TX 76201**

**AWARDS** Child development (MS, PhD); counseling and development (MS); early childhood education (M Ed, MA, MS); family studies (MS, PhD); family therapy (MS, PhD). Part-time and evening/weekend programs available.

**Faculty:** 15 full-time (11 women), 3 part-time/adjunct (2 women).
**Students:** 42 full-time (36 women), 213 part-time (189 women); includes 41 minority (25 African Americans, 1 Asian American or Pacific Islander, 14 Hispanic Americans, 1 Native American), 12 international. Average age 39. 40 applicants, 88% accepted. In 2001, 28 master's, 8 doctorates awarded. Terminal master's awarded for partial completion of doctoral program.
**Degree requirements:** For doctorate, thesis/dissertation.
*Application deadline:* For fall admission, 1/7 (priority date); for spring admission, 8/31 (priority date). Applications are processed on a rolling basis. *Application fee:* $30.
**Expenses:** Tuition, state resident: part-time $90 per semester hour. Tuition, nonresident: part-time $303 per semester hour. Required fees: $24 per credit hour. $79 per semester.
**Financial support:** In 2001–02, 52 students received support, including 2 research assistantships, 5 teaching assistantships; career-related internships or fieldwork, institutionally sponsored loans, scholarships/grants, tuition waivers (partial), and graders also available. Support available to part-time students. Financial award application deadline: 2/1.
**Faculty research:** Parenting/parent education, family therapy counseling, early development, education, distance education.
Dr. Linda Ladd, Chair, 940-898-2685, *Fax:* 940-898-2676, *E-mail:* lladd@twu.edu. *Web site:* http://www.twu.edu/cope/famsci/

## ■ THE UNIVERSITY OF AKRON

**Graduate School, College of Education, Department of Counseling, Program in Marriage and Family Therapy, Akron, OH 44325-0001**

**AWARDS** MA, MS.

**Students:** 19 full-time (16 women), 22 part-time (18 women); includes 3 minority (2 African Americans, 1 Asian American or Pacific Islander), 3 international. Average age 31. 10 applicants, 90% accepted, 8 enrolled. In 2001, 11 degrees awarded.

**Degree requirements:** For master's, comprehensive exam.
**Entrance requirements:** For master's, MAT, minimum GPA of 2.75. *Application deadline:* For fall admission, 8/15. Applications are processed on a rolling basis. *Application fee:* $40 ($50 for international students).
**Expenses:** Tuition, state resident: full-time $6,562; part-time $219 per credit. Tuition, nonresident: full-time $9,027; part-time $383 per credit. Required fees: $272; $11 per credit. Tuition and fees vary according to course load.

## ■ THE UNIVERSITY OF ALABAMA AT BIRMINGHAM

**Graduate School, School of Education, Department of Human Studies, Program in Counseling, Birmingham, AL 35294**

**AWARDS** Agency counseling (MA); marriage and family counseling (MA); rehabilitation counseling (MA); school counseling (MA); school psychology (MA Ed).
**Students:** 43 full-time (35 women), 103 part-time (84 women); includes 36 minority (35 African Americans, 1 Asian American or Pacific Islander), 4 international. 152 applicants, 84% accepted. In 2001, 29 degrees awarded.
**Degree requirements:** For master's, thesis optional.
**Entrance requirements:** For master's, GRE General Test, MAT, or NTE, minimum GPA of 3.0. *Application deadline:* Applications are processed on a rolling basis. *Application fee:* $35 ($60 for international students). Electronic applications accepted.
**Expenses:** Tuition, state resident: full-time $3,058. Tuition, nonresident: full-time $5,746. Tuition and fees vary according to course load, degree level and program.
**Financial support:** Career-related internships or fieldwork available.
Dr. David M. Macrina, Chairperson, Department of Human Studies, 205-934-2446, *Fax:* 205-975-8040, *E-mail:* dmacrina@uab.edu.

## ■ UNIVERSITY OF FLORIDA

**Graduate School, College of Education, Department of Counseling and Guidance, Gainesville, FL 32611**

**AWARDS** Marriage and family counseling (M Ed, Ed D, PhD, Ed S); mental health counseling (M Ed, Ed D, PhD, Ed S); school counseling and guidance (M Ed, Ed D, PhD, Ed S); student counseling and guidance (PhD); student personnel services in higher education (M Ed, Ed D, PhD, Ed S). Part-time programs available. Terminal master's awarded for partial completion of doctoral program.

**Degree requirements:** For master's, thesis optional; for doctorate, thesis/dissertation.
**Entrance requirements:** For master's and doctorate, GRE General Test, minimum GPA of 3.0 (undergraduate), 3.5 (graduate); for Ed S, GRE General Test. Electronic applications accepted.
**Expenses:** Tuition, state resident: part-time $164 per hour. Tuition, nonresident: part-time $571 per hour. Tuition and fees vary according to course level and program. *Web site:* http://www.coe.ufl.edu/counselor/counselor.html/

## ■ UNIVERSITY OF GREAT FALLS

**Graduate Studies Division, Program in Counseling, Great Falls, MT 59405**

**AWARDS** Counseling psychology (MSC); marriage and family counseling (MSC). Part-time and evening/weekend programs available. Postbaccalaureate distance learning degree programs offered (minimal on-campus study).

**Faculty:** 4 full-time (3 women), 10 part-time/adjunct (6 women).
**Students:** 11 full-time (all women), 49 part-time (42 women); includes 6 minority (1 African American, 5 Native Americans). Average age 30. 22 applicants, 91% accepted. In 2001, 18 degrees awarded. *Median time to degree:* Master's–2 years full-time, 3.8 years part-time.
**Entrance requirements:** For master's, GRE General Test or MAT. *Application deadline:* For fall admission, 8/15 (priority date); for winter admission, 11/15 (priority date); for spring admission, 12/15 (priority date). Applications are processed on a rolling basis. *Application fee:* $35.
**Expenses:** Tuition: Part-time $440 per credit. One-time fee: $35 full-time.
**Financial support:** In 2001–02, 50 students received support, including 2 fellowships, 8 research assistantships; career-related internships or fieldwork, Federal Work-Study, institutionally sponsored loans, and scholarships/grants also available. Support available to part-time students. Financial award application deadline: 3/1.
**Faculty research:** Head trauma and aggression, self concept and adolescent offenders, juvenile delinquency. *Total annual research expenditures:* $300,000.
Karen Low, Director, 406-791-5361, *Fax:* 406-791-5990, *E-mail:* klow01@ugf.edu.

## ■ UNIVERSITY OF HOUSTON– CLEAR LAKE

**School of Human Sciences and Humanities, Programs in Human Sciences, Houston, TX 77058-1098**

**AWARDS** Behavioral sciences (MA), including behavioral sciences-general, behavioral sciences-psychology, behavioral sciences-sociology; clinical psychology (MA); cross-cultural studies (MA); family therapy (MA); fitness and human performance (MA); school psychology (MA); studies of the future (MS). Part-time and evening/weekend programs available.

**Students:** 562; includes 183 minority (95 African Americans, 16 Asian Americans or Pacific Islanders, 70 Hispanic Americans, 2 Native Americans), 16 international. Average age 34. In 2001, 152 degrees awarded.
**Degree requirements:** For master's, thesis or alternative.
**Entrance requirements:** For master's, GRE General Test. *Application deadline:* For fall admission, 8/1; for spring admission, 12/1. Applications are processed on a rolling basis. *Application fee:* $30 ($70 for international students). Electronic applications accepted.
**Expenses:** Tuition, state resident: full-time $2,016; part-time $84 per credit hour. Tuition, nonresident: full-time $6,072; part-time $253 per credit hour. Tuition and fees vary according to course load.
**Financial support:** Research assistantships, teaching assistantships, career-related internships or fieldwork, Federal Work-Study, institutionally sponsored loans, and scholarships/grants available. Support available to part-time students. Financial award application deadline: 5/1.
Dr. Hilary Karp, Division Co-Chair, 281-283-3383, *E-mail:* karp@cl.uh.edu.

### ■ UNIVERSITY OF LA VERNE

**College of Arts and Sciences, Department of Psychology, Masters Programs in Counseling, La Verne, CA 91750-4443**

**AWARDS** Counseling in higher education (MS); general counseling (MS); gerontology (MS); marriage, family and child counseling (MS). Part-time programs available.

**Faculty:** 9 full-time (5 women), 5 part-time/adjunct (3 women).
**Students:** 21 full-time (18 women), 45 part-time (34 women); includes 33 minority (9 African Americans, 3 Asian Americans or Pacific Islanders, 20 Hispanic Americans, 1 Native American). Average age 36. In 2001, 10 degrees awarded.
**Degree requirements:** For master's, competency exam, thesis optional.
**Entrance requirements:** For master's, undergraduate GPA of 3.0. *Application deadline:* Applications are processed on a rolling basis. *Application fee:* $40.
**Expenses:** Tuition: Full-time $4,410; part-time $245 per unit. Required fees: $60. Tuition and fees vary according to course load, degree level, campus/location and program.

**Financial support:** In 2001–02, 42 students received support, including 5 research assistantships (averaging $2,200 per year); career-related internships or fieldwork, institutionally sponsored loans, and scholarships/grants also available. Financial award application deadline: 3/2; financial award applicants required to submit FAFSA.
Dr. Errol Moultrie, Chairperson, 909-593-3511 Ext. 4169, *Fax:* 909-392-2745, *E-mail:* moultrie@ulv.edu.
**Application contact:** Jo Nell Baker, Director, Graduate Admissions and Academic Services, 909-593-3511 Ext. 4504, *Fax:* 909-392-2761, *E-mail:* bakerj@ulv.edu. *Web site:* http://www.ulaverne.edu/

### ■ UNIVERSITY OF LOUISIANA AT MONROE

**Graduate Studies and Research, College of Education and Human Development, Department of Instructional Leadership and Counseling, Program in Marriage and Family Therapy, Monroe, LA 71209-0001**

**AWARDS** MA, PhD. Part-time and evening/weekend programs available.

**Degree requirements:** For master's, comprehensive exam; for doctorate, thesis/dissertation.
**Entrance requirements:** For master's, GRE General Test, interview, minimum GPA of 2.8; for doctorate, GRE General Test.
**Faculty research:** Family systems, substance abuse.

### ■ UNIVERSITY OF MARYLAND, COLLEGE PARK

**Graduate Studies and Research, College of Health and Human Performance, Department of Family Studies, College Park, MD 20742**

**AWARDS** Family studies (MS, PhD); marriage and family therapy (MS). Part-time and evening/weekend programs available.

**Faculty:** 11 full-time (7 women), 11 part-time/adjunct (7 women).
**Students:** 31 full-time (25 women), 13 part-time (12 women); includes 12 minority (7 African Americans, 1 Asian American or Pacific Islander, 4 Hispanic Americans), 1 international. 68 applicants, 59% accepted, 21 enrolled. In 2001, 16 master's, 1 doctorate awarded.
**Degree requirements:** For master's, thesis or alternative.
**Entrance requirements:** For master's and doctorate, GRE General Test, minimum GPA of 3.0. *Application deadline:* For fall admission, 2/1; for spring admission, 11/15. Applications are processed on a

rolling basis. *Application fee:* $50 ($70 for international students). Electronic applications accepted.
**Expenses:** Tuition, state resident: part-time $289 per credit hour. Tuition, nonresident: part-time $448 per credit hour. One-time fee: $436 part-time. Full-time tuition and fees vary according to course load, campus/location and program.
**Financial support:** In 2001–02, 12 fellowships with full tuition reimbursements (averaging $11,158 per year), 3 research assistantships with tuition reimbursements (averaging $10,153 per year), 9 teaching assistantships with tuition reimbursements (averaging $8,768 per year) were awarded. Career-related internships or fieldwork, Federal Work-Study, and scholarships/grants also available. Support available to part-time students. Financial award applicants required to submit FAFSA.
**Faculty research:** Family life quality.
Dr. Sally Koblinsky, Chairman, 301-405-4009, *Fax:* 301-314-9161.
**Application contact:** Trudy Lindsey, Director, Graduate Admissions and Records, 301-405-6991, *Fax:* 301-314-9305, *E-mail:* grschool@deans.umd.edu.

**Find an in-depth description at www.petersons.com/gradchannel.**

### ■ UNIVERSITY OF MIAMI

**Graduate School, School of Education, Department of Educational and Psychological Studies, Master's Program in Counseling, Coral Gables, FL 33124**

**AWARDS** Bilingual and bicultural counseling (Certificate); marriage and family therapy (MS Ed); mental health counseling (MS Ed). Part-time programs available.

**Faculty:** 9 full-time (3 women), 10 part-time/adjunct (6 women).
**Students:** 32 full-time (30 women), 20 part-time (all women); includes 25 minority (7 African Americans, 18 Hispanic Americans), 3 international. Average age 27. 80 applicants, 68% accepted. In 2001, 20 degrees awarded.
**Entrance requirements:** For master's, GRE General Test, TOEFL; for Certificate, enrolled or completed masters in mental health field. *Application deadline:* For fall admission, 5/1 (priority date). Applications are processed on a rolling basis. *Application fee:* $50. Electronic applications accepted.
**Expenses:** Tuition: Part-time $960 per credit hour. Required fees: $85 per semester. Tuition and fees vary according to program.
**Financial support:** Research assistantships, teaching assistantships, Federal Work-Study, institutionally sponsored loans,

*University of Miami (continued)*
scholarships/grants, unspecified assistant-ships, and employee benefits available. Support available to part-time students. Financial award application deadline: 3/1.
**Faculty research:** Cocaine recidivism, HIV, non-traditional families, health psychology, diversity.
Dr. Margaret Crosbie-Burnett, Coordina-tor, 305-284-2808, *Fax:* 305-284-3003, *E-mail:* mcrosbur@miami.edu.

■ **UNIVERSITY OF MOBILE**

**Graduate Programs, Program in Religious Studies, Mobile, AL 36663-0220**

**AWARDS** Biblical/theological studies (MA); marriage and family counseling (MA). Part-time and evening/weekend programs available.

**Faculty:** 6 full-time (0 women), 2 part-time/adjunct (0 women).
**Students:** 43 (26 women); includes 13 minority (all African Americans). Average age 41. In 2001, 5 degrees awarded.
**Degree requirements:** For master's, one foreign language, comprehensive exam.
**Entrance requirements:** For master's, GRE General Test, TOEFL. *Application deadline:* For fall admission, 8/3 (priority date); for spring admission, 12/23. Applica-tions are processed on a rolling basis. *Application fee:* $30 ($50 for international students).
**Expenses:** Tuition: Full-time $3,582; part-time $199 per semester hour.
**Financial support:** Federal Work-Study and tuition waivers (partial) available. Sup-port available to part-time students. Financial award application deadline: 8/1.
Dr. Cecil Taylor, Dean, School of Religion, 251-442-2255, *Fax:* 251-442-2523, *E-mail:* ceciltaylor@free.umobile.edu.
**Application contact:** Dr. Kaye F. Brown, Dean, Graduate Programs and Director of Institutional Effectiveness, 251-442-2289, *Fax:* 251-442-2523, *E-mail:* kayebrown@free.umobile.edu. *Web site:* http://www.umobile.edu/

■ **UNIVERSITY OF NEVADA, LAS VEGAS**

**Graduate College, Greenspun College of Urban Affairs, Department of Counseling, Las Vegas, NV 89154-9900**

**AWARDS** Community agency counseling (MS); marriage and family counseling (MS); rehabilitation counseling (MS). Part-time programs available.

**Faculty:** 19 full-time (9 women).
**Students:** 25 full-time (20 women), 22 part-time (17 women); includes 6 minority (2 African Americans, 2 Asian Americans

or Pacific Islanders, 2 Hispanic Americans). In 2001, 12 degrees awarded.
**Degree requirements:** For master's, thesis (for some programs), comprehensive exam (for some programs).
**Entrance requirements:** For master's, GRE General Test, minimum GPA of 3.0 during previous 2 years, 2.75 overall. *Application deadline:* For fall admission, 2/1. *Application fee:* $40 ($55 for international students).
**Expenses:** Tuition, state resident: full-time $1,926; part-time $107 per credit. Tuition, nonresident: full-time $9,376; part-time $220 per credit. Tuition and fees vary according to course load.
**Financial support:** In 2001–02, 2 research assistantships with partial tuition reimbursements (averaging $10,000 per year), 2 teaching assistantships with partial tuition reimbursements (averaging $10,000 per year) were awarded. Financial award application deadline: 3/1.
Dr. Gerald Weeks, Chair, 702-895-1867.
**Application contact:** Graduate College Admissions Evaluator, 702-895-3320, *Fax:* 702-895-4180, *E-mail:* gradcollege@ccmail.nevada.edu. *Web site:* http://www.unlv.edu/Colleges/Urban/Counseling/

■ **UNIVERSITY OF NEW HAMPSHIRE**

**Graduate School, School of Health and Human Services, Department of Family Studies, Durham, NH 03824**

**AWARDS** Family studies (MS); marriage and family therapy (MS). Part-time programs available.

**Faculty:** 8 full-time.
**Students:** 16 full-time (13 women), 11 part-time (10 women); includes 2 minority (1 Asian American or Pacific Islander, 1 Hispanic American), 2 international. Aver-age age 30. 12 applicants, 83% accepted, 6 enrolled.
**Degree requirements:** For master's, thesis or alternative.
**Entrance requirements:** For master's, GRE General Test. *Application deadline:* For fall admission, 4/1 (priority date); for winter admission, 12/1. Applications are processed on a rolling basis. *Application fee:* $50. Electronic applications accepted.
**Expenses:** Tuition, state resident: full-time $6,300; part-time $350 per credit. Tuition, nonresident: full-time $15,720; part-time $643 per credit. Required fees: $560; $280 per term. One-time fee: $15 part-time. Tuition and fees vary according to course load.
**Financial support:** In 2001–02, 7 teaching assistantships were awarded; fellowships, research assistantships, career-related internships or fieldwork, Federal Work-Study, scholarships/grants, and tuition

waivers (full and partial) also available. Support available to part-time students. Financial award application deadline: 2/15.
Dr. Kristine Baber, Chairperson, 603-862-2160, *E-mail:* dkmbaber@cisunix.unh.edu.
**Application contact:** Dr. Larry Hansen, Coordinator, 603-862-2146, *E-mail:* ljhansen@cisunix.unh.edu. *Web site:* http://www.unh.edu/family-studies/

■ **THE UNIVERSITY OF NORTH CAROLINA AT GREENSBORO**

**Graduate School, School of Education, Department of Counseling and Educational Development, Greensboro, NC 27412-5001**

**AWARDS** Counseling and development (MS, Ed D, PhD); gerontological counseling (PMC); marriage and family counseling (PMC); school counseling (PMC).

**Faculty:** 9 full-time (4 women), 1 part-time/adjunct (0 women).
**Students:** 90 full-time (74 women), 32 part-time (20 women); includes 12 minor-ity (6 African Americans, 3 Asian Americans or Pacific Islanders, 3 Hispanic Americans). 254 applicants, 24% accepted, 41 enrolled. In 2001, 20 master's, 6 doctorates, 6 other advanced degrees awarded.
**Degree requirements:** For master's, practicum, internship; for doctorate, thesis/dissertation, comprehensive exam.
**Entrance requirements:** For master's and doctorate, GRE General Test, TOEFL; for PMC, GRE General Test. *Application deadline:* For fall admission, 2/15. *Applica-tion fee:* $35.
**Expenses:** Tuition, state resident: part-time $344 per course. Tuition, nonresident: part-time $2,457 per course.
**Financial support:** In 2001–02, 57 students received support, including 4 fel-lowships with full tuition reimbursements available (averaging $14,000 per year), 33 research assistantships with full tuition reimbursements available (averaging $4,820 per year), 25 teaching assistantships with full tuition reimbursements available (averaging $4,240 per year); career-related internships or fieldwork, Federal Work-Study, scholarships/grants, traineeships, and unspecified assistantships also avail-able. Support available to part-time students.
**Faculty research:** Gerontology, invitational theory, career development, marriage and family therapy, drug and alcohol abuse prevention.
Dr. DiAnne Borders, Chair, 336-334-3423, *Fax:* 336-334-4120, *E-mail:* borders@uncg.edu.
**Application contact:** Dr. James Lynch, Director of Graduate Recruitment and Information Services, 336-334-4881, *Fax:*

336-334-4424. *Web site:* http://www.uncg.edu/ced/

## ■ UNIVERSITY OF PHOENIX–HAWAII CAMPUS

**College of Counseling and Human Services, Honolulu, HI 96813-4317**

**AWARDS** Community counseling (MC); marriage and family therapy (MC). Evening/weekend programs available. Postbaccalaureate distance learning degree programs offered (no on-campus study).

**Students:** 77 full-time. Average age 35.
**Degree requirements:** For master's, thesis or alternative.
**Entrance requirements:** For master's, TOEFL, Comprehensive Cognitive Assessment, minimum undergraduate GPA of 2.5, 3 years of work experience. *Application deadline:* Applications are processed on a rolling basis. *Application fee:* $85.
**Expenses:** Tuition: Full-time $8,784; part-time $366 per credit.
**Financial support:** Applicants required to submit FAFSA.
Dr. Patrick Romine, Dean, 480-557-1074, *E-mail:* patrick.romine@phoenix.edu.
**Application contact:** Campus Information Center, 808-536-2686, *Fax:* 808-536-3848.

## ■ UNIVERSITY OF PHOENIX–NEW MEXICO CAMPUS

**College of Counseling and Human Services, Albuquerque, NM 87109-4645**

**AWARDS** Marriage and family therapy (MC); mental health counseling (MC). Evening/weekend programs available. Postbaccalaureate distance learning degree programs offered (no on-campus study).

**Students:** 34 full-time. Average age 34. In 2001, 16 degrees awarded.
**Degree requirements:** For master's, thesis or alternative.
**Entrance requirements:** For master's, TOEFL, Comprehensive Cognitive Assessment, minimum undergraduate GPA of 2.5, 3 years work experience. *Application deadline:* Applications are processed on a rolling basis. *Application fee:* $85.
**Expenses:** Tuition: Full-time $7,336; part-time $306 per credit. Full-time tuition and fees vary according to program.
**Financial support:** Applicants required to submit FAFSA.
Dr. Patrick Romine, Dean, 480-557-1074, *E-mail:* patrick.romine@phoenix.edu. *Web site:* http://www.phoenix.edu/

## ■ UNIVERSITY OF PHOENIX–PHOENIX CAMPUS

**College of Counseling and Human Services, Phoenix, AZ 85040-1958**

**AWARDS** Community counseling (MC); marriage, family, and child therapy (MC); mental health counseling (MC). Evening/weekend programs available. Postbaccalaureate distance learning degree programs offered (no on-campus study).

**Students:** 241 full-time. Average age 33. In 2001, 70 degrees awarded.
**Degree requirements:** For master's, thesis or alternative.
**Entrance requirements:** For master's, TOEFL, comprehensive cognitive assessment (COCA), portfolio. *Application deadline:* Applications are processed on a rolling basis. *Application fee:* $85.
**Expenses:** Contact institution.
**Financial support:** Applicants required to submit FAFSA.
Dr. Patrick Romine, Dean, 480-557-1074 Ext. 1074, *E-mail:* patrick.romine@phoenix.edu.
**Application contact:** 480-966-7400. *Web site:* http://www.phoenix.edu/

## ■ UNIVERSITY OF PHOENIX–SACRAMENTO CAMPUS

**College of Counseling and Human Services, Sacramento, CA 95833-3632**

**AWARDS** Marriage, family and child counseling (MC). Evening/weekend programs available. Postbaccalaureate distance learning degree programs offered (no on-campus study).

**Students:** 109 full-time. Average age 34. In 2001, 46 degrees awarded.
**Degree requirements:** For master's, thesis or alternative.
**Entrance requirements:** For master's, TOEFL, comprehensive cognitive assessment (COCA), minimum undergraduate GPA of 2.5, 3 years work experience. *Application deadline:* Applications are processed on a rolling basis. *Application fee:* $85.
**Expenses:** Tuition: Full-time $9,720; part-time $405 per credit. Full-time tuition and fees vary according to program.
**Financial support:** Applicants required to submit FAFSA.
Dr. Patrick Romine, Dean, 480-557-1074, *E-mail:* patrick.romine@phoenix.edu. *Web site:* http://www.phoenix.edu/

## ■ UNIVERSITY OF PHOENIX–SAN DIEGO CAMPUS

**College of Counseling and Human Services, San Diego, CA 92130-2092**

**AWARDS** Marriage, family and child counseling (MC). Evening/weekend programs available. Postbaccalaureate distance learning degree programs offered (no on-campus study).

**Students:** 133 full-time. Average age 34. In 2001, 30 degrees awarded.
**Degree requirements:** For master's, thesis or alternative.
**Entrance requirements:** For master's, TOEFL, comprehensive cognitive assessment (COCA), minimum undergraduate GPA of 2.5, 3 years work experience. *Application deadline:* Applications are processed on a rolling basis. *Application fee:* $85.
**Expenses:** Tuition: Full-time $8,808; part-time $367 per credit.
**Financial support:** Applicants required to submit FAFSA.
Dr. Patrick Romine, Dean, 480-557-1074, *E-mail:* patrick.romine@phoenix.edu.
**Application contact:** Campus Information Center, 880-UOP-INFO. *Web site:* http://www.phoenix.edu/

## ■ UNIVERSITY OF PITTSBURGH

**School of Social Work, Program in Family and Marital Therapy, Pittsburgh, PA 15260**

**AWARDS** Certificate.

**Students:** Average age 30.
**Degree requirements:** For Certificate, thesis.
*Application deadline:* Applications are processed on a rolling basis. *Application fee:* $40.
**Expenses:** Tuition, state resident: full-time $9,410; part-time $385 per credit. Tuition, nonresident: full-time $19,376; part-time $797 per credit. Required fees: $480; $90 per term. Tuition and fees vary according to program.
**Financial support:** Application deadline: 6/1.
Tracy M. Soska, Continuing Education Director, 412-624-3711, *Fax:* 412-624-6323, *E-mail:* tsssw@pitt.edu.
**Application contact:** Dr. Grady H. Roberts, Associate Dean of Admissions, 412-624-6346, *Fax:* 412-624-6323. *Web site:* http://www.pitt.edu/~pittssw/

## ■ UNIVERSITY OF ROCHESTER

**School of Medicine and Dentistry, Graduate Programs in Medicine and Dentistry, Department of Psychiatry, Rochester, NY 14627-0250**

**AWARDS** Marriage and family therapy (MS). Part-time programs available.

*University of Rochester (continued)*
**Faculty:** 12.
**Students:** 2 full-time (both women), 4 part-time (all women); includes 1 minority (Asian American or Pacific Islander). 11 applicants, 45% accepted, 4 enrolled.
**Degree requirements:** For master's, projects.
**Entrance requirements:** For master's, GRE General Test. *Application deadline:* For fall admission, 3/15. Applications are processed on a rolling basis. *Application fee:* $25.
Pieter le Roux, Director, 585-275-9179, *Fax:* 716-271-7706, *E-mail:* pieter_leroux@urmc.rochester.edu.
**Application contact:** Patricia Atkins, Graduate Program Secretary, 585-275-6792.

**Find an in-depth description at www.petersons.com/gradchannel.**

### ■ UNIVERSITY OF ST. THOMAS

**Graduate Studies, Graduate School of Professional Psychology, St. Paul, MN 55105-1096**

**AWARDS** Counseling psychology (MA, Psy D); family psychology (Certificate). Part-time and evening/weekend programs available.

**Faculty:** 8 full-time (4 women), 15 part-time/adjunct (8 women).
**Students:** 42 full-time (34 women), 124 part-time (98 women); includes 19 minority (8 African Americans, 6 Asian Americans or Pacific Islanders, 4 Hispanic Americans, 1 Native American). Average age 34. 41 applicants, 76% accepted, 29 enrolled. In 2001, 34 master's, 8 doctorates, 6 other advanced degrees awarded.
**Degree requirements:** For master's, practicum; for doctorate, thesis/dissertation, qualifying exam, practicum, internship, comprehensive exam.
**Entrance requirements:** For master's and doctorate, MAT or GRE, minimum GPA of 2.75. *Application deadline:* For fall admission, 10/1; for winter admission, 2/1; for spring admission, 4/1. *Application fee:* $50.
**Expenses:** Contact institution.
**Financial support:** In 2001–02, 91 students received support; fellowships, research assistantships, institutionally sponsored loans and scholarships/grants available. Support available to part-time students. Financial award application deadline: 4/1.
**Faculty research:** Elderly, eating disorders, anxiety.
Dr. Burton Nolan, Dean, 651-962-4650, *Fax:* 651-962-4651, *E-mail:* bnolan@stthomas.edu.
**Application contact:** Dr. Mary M. Brant, Assistant Professor, 651-962-4641, *Fax:*

651-962-4651, *E-mail:* mmbrant@stthomas.edu.

### ■ UNIVERSITY OF SAN DIEGO

**School of Education, Program in Marital and Family Therapy, San Diego, CA 92110-2492**

**AWARDS** MA. Part-time and evening/weekend programs available.

**Faculty:** 3 full-time (1 woman), 8 part-time/adjunct (2 women).
**Students:** 48 full-time (41 women), 16 part-time (all women); includes 12 minority (1 African American, 2 Asian Americans or Pacific Islanders, 8 Hispanic Americans, 1 Native American), 2 international. Average age 27. 75 applicants, 61% accepted. In 2001, 18 degrees awarded.
**Degree requirements:** For master's, comprehensive exam.
**Entrance requirements:** For master's, GRE or MAT, TOEFL, TWE, minimum GPA of 3.0, interview with faculty. *Application deadline:* For fall admission, 5/8; for spring admission, 2/1. *Application fee:* $45.
**Financial support:** Fellowships, career-related internships or fieldwork, Federal Work-Study, institutionally sponsored loans, unspecified assistantships, and stipends available. Support available to part-time students. Financial award application deadline: 5/1; financial award applicants required to submit FAFSA.
**Faculty research:** Addictions, father-daughter incest, supervision and training.
Dr. Lee Williams, Graduate Program Director, 619-260-6889, *Fax:* 619-260-6835, *E-mail:* williams@sandiego.edu.
**Application contact:** Mary Jane Tiernan, Director of Graduate Admissions, 619-260-4524, *Fax:* 619-260-4158, *E-mail:* grads@sandiego.edu.

### ■ UNIVERSITY OF SAN FRANCISCO

**School of Education, Department of Counseling Psychology, San Francisco, CA 94117-1080**

**AWARDS** Counseling (MA), including educational counseling, life transitions counseling, marital and family therapy; counseling psychology (Psy D).

**Faculty:** 7 full-time (3 women), 55 part-time/adjunct (29 women).
**Students:** 131 full-time (106 women), 68 part-time (56 women); includes 58 minority (11 African Americans, 17 Asian Americans or Pacific Islanders, 27 Hispanic Americans, 3 Native Americans), 8 international. Average age 35. 165 applicants, 93% accepted, 75 enrolled. In 2001, 79 master's, 9 doctorates awarded.
**Degree requirements:** For doctorate, thesis/dissertation.

**Entrance requirements:** For doctorate, GRE General Test. *Application fee:* $55 ($65 for international students).
**Expenses:** Tuition: Full-time $14,400; part-time $800 per unit. Tuition and fees vary according to degree level, campus/location and program.
**Financial support:** In 2001–02, 134 students received support; fellowships, research assistantships, teaching assistantships available. Financial award application deadline: 3/2; financial award applicants required to submit FAFSA.
Dr. Elena Flores, Chair, 415-422-6868.

### ■ UNIVERSITY OF SOUTHERN CALIFORNIA

**Graduate School, College of Letters, Arts and Sciences, Department of Sociology, Program in Marriage and Family Therapy, Los Angeles, CA 90089**

**AWARDS** PhD.

**Degree requirements:** For doctorate, thesis/dissertation.
**Entrance requirements:** For doctorate, GRE General Test.
**Expenses:** Tuition: Full-time $25,060; part-time $844 per unit. Required fees: $473.

### ■ UNIVERSITY OF SOUTHERN CALIFORNIA

**Graduate School, School of Education, Department of Counseling Psychology, Los Angeles, CA 90089**

**AWARDS** College student personnel services (MS); counseling psychology (MS, PhD); educational psychology (PhD); marriage, family and child counseling (MFCC); pupil personnel services (K–12) (MS).

**Degree requirements:** For doctorate, thesis/dissertation.
**Entrance requirements:** For master's and doctorate, GRE General Test.
**Expenses:** Tuition: Full-time $25,060; part-time $844 per unit. Required fees: $473.

### ■ UNIVERSITY OF SOUTHERN MISSISSIPPI

**Graduate School, College of Health and Human Sciences, School of Family and Consumer Sciences, Hattiesburg, MS 39406**

**AWARDS** Early intervention (MS); family and consumer studies (MS); human nutrition (MS); institution management (MS); marriage and family therapy (MS); nutrition and food systems (PhD). Part-time programs available.

**Faculty:** 19 full-time (15 women), 3 part-time/adjunct (all women).

**Students:** 48 full-time (39 women), 30 part-time (29 women); includes 19 minority (14 African Americans, 3 Asian Americans or Pacific Islanders, 2 Hispanic Americans). Average age 32. 63 applicants, 54% accepted. In 2001, 26 master's, 4 doctorates awarded.
**Degree requirements:** For master's, thesis optional; for doctorate, one foreign language, thesis/dissertation.
**Entrance requirements:** For master's, GRE General Test, minimum GPA of 2.75; for doctorate, GRE General Test, minimum GPA of 3.5. *Application deadline:* For fall admission, 8/9 (priority date). Applications are processed on a rolling basis. *Application fee:* $0 ($25 for international students). Electronic applications accepted.
**Expenses:** Tuition, state resident: full-time $3,416; part-time $190 per credit hour. Tuition, nonresident: full-time $7,932; part-time $441 per credit hour.
**Financial support:** In 2001–02, 21 students received support, including research assistantships with full tuition reimbursements available (averaging $3,500 per year), teaching assistantships with full tuition reimbursements available (averaging $3,500 per year); fellowships, career-related internships or fieldwork, Federal Work-Study, institutionally sponsored loans, scholarships/grants, and unspecified assistantships also available. Financial award application deadline: 3/15.
**Faculty research:** School food service, teen pregnancy, diet and cholesterol metabolism.
Dr. Patricia Sims, Director, 601-266-4679, *Fax:* 601-266-4680.
**Application contact:** Dr. Kathy Yadrick, Graduate Coordinator, 601-266-4479, *Fax:* 601-266-4680, *E-mail:* kathy.yadrick@usm.edu. *Web site:* http://hhs.usm.edu/fcs

### ■ UNIVERSITY OF WISCONSIN–STOUT

**Graduate School, College of Human Development, Program in Marriage and Family Therapy, Menomonie, WI 54751**
AWARDS MS. Part-time programs available.
**Students:** 23 full-time (20 women), 2 part-time (both women); includes 1 minority (Asian American or Pacific Islander). 27 applicants, 56% accepted, 12 enrolled. In 2001, 10 degrees awarded.
**Degree requirements:** For master's, thesis.
*Application deadline:* For fall admission, 3/15. *Application fee:* $45.
**Expenses:** Tuition, state resident: full-time $4,915. Tuition, nonresident: full-time $12,553.

**Financial support:** In 2001–02, 2 research assistantships were awarded; teaching assistantships, Federal Work-Study and tuition waivers (full and partial) also available. Support available to part-time students. Financial award application deadline: 4/1; financial award applicants required to submit FAFSA.
Dr. Charles Barnard, Director, 715-232-2255.
**Application contact:** Anne E. Johnson, Graduate Student Evaluator, 715-232-1322, *Fax:* 715-232-2413, *E-mail:* johnsona@uwstout.edu.

### ■ UTAH STATE UNIVERSITY

**School of Graduate Studies, College of Family Life, Department of Family and Human Development, Logan, UT 84322**
AWARDS Family and human development (MFHD, MS); marriage and family therapy (MS). Part-time programs available.
**Faculty:** 13 full-time (7 women).
**Students:** 21 full-time (14 women), 20 part-time (15 women); includes 2 minority (both Hispanic Americans), 2 international. 40 applicants, 25% accepted. In 2001, 9 degrees awarded.
**Degree requirements:** For master's, thesis, registration.
**Entrance requirements:** For master's, GRE General Test or MAT, TOEFL, minimum GPA of 3.0. *Application deadline:* For fall admission, 1/15 (priority date). Applications are processed on a rolling basis. *Application fee:* $40.
**Expenses:** Tuition, state resident: full-time $1,693. Tuition, nonresident: full-time $4,233. Required fees: $501. Tuition and fees vary according to program.
**Financial support:** In 2001–02, 23 students received support, including 2 fellowships (averaging $500 per year), 3 research assistantships with partial tuition reimbursements available (averaging $6,933 per year), 18 teaching assistantships with partial tuition reimbursements available (averaging $4,400 per year); Federal Work-Study, institutionally sponsored loans, scholarships/grants, and tuition waivers (full and partial) also available. Financial award application deadline: 3/1.
**Faculty research:** Parent-infant attachment, marriage and family relations, intergenerational relationships, adolescent problem behavior, child and adolescent development. *Total annual research expenditures:* $983,720.
Shelley K. Lindauer, Interim Head, 435-797-1501, *Fax:* 435-797-3845, *E-mail:* lindauer@cc.usu.edu.
**Application contact:** Randall M. Jones, Graduate Coordinator, 435-797-1553, *Fax:*

435-797-3845, *E-mail:* rjones@cc.usu.edu.
*Web site:* http://www.usu.edu/fhd/

### ■ VALDOSTA STATE UNIVERSITY

**Graduate School, College of Arts and Sciences, Department of Sociology and Criminal Justice, Valdosta, GA 31698**
AWARDS Criminal justice (MS); marriage and family therapy (MS); sociology (MS). Part-time and evening/weekend programs available.
**Faculty:** 18 full-time (6 women).
**Students:** 35 full-time (30 women), 34 part-time (27 women); includes 7 minority (5 African Americans, 1 Asian American or Pacific Islander, 1 Hispanic American). Average age 27. 52 applicants, 90% accepted. In 2001, 27 degrees awarded.
**Degree requirements:** For master's, thesis or alternative, comprehensive written and/or oral exams.
**Entrance requirements:** For master's, GRE General Test, minimum GPA of 2.5. *Application deadline:* For fall admission, 7/1; for spring admission, 11/15. Applications are processed on a rolling basis. *Application fee:* $20. Electronic applications accepted.
**Expenses:** Tuition, state resident: full-time $1,746; part-time $97 per hour. Tuition, nonresident: full-time $6,966; part-time $387 per hour. Required fees: $594; $297 per semester.
**Financial support:** In 2001–02, 5 research assistantships with full tuition reimbursements (averaging $2,452 per year) were awarded; career-related internships or fieldwork, institutionally sponsored loans, scholarships/grants, and unspecified assistantships also available. Support available to part-time students. Financial award application deadline: 7/1; financial award applicants required to submit FAFSA.
**Faculty research:** Police-civilian ride-along project.
Dr. J. Michael Brooks, Head, 229-333-5943, *E-mail:* mbrooks@valdosta.edu.

### ■ VIRGINIA POLYTECHNIC INSTITUTE AND STATE UNIVERSITY

**Graduate School, College of Human Resources and Education, Department of Human Development, Doctoral Program in Marriage and Family Therapy, Blacksburg, VA 24061**
AWARDS PhD. MS offered jointly with Northern Virginia campus. Part-time programs available.
**Faculty:** 4 full-time (1 woman).
**Students:** 16 full-time (9 women), 10 part-time (9 women); includes 4 minority (1 African American, 2 Asian Americans or Pacific Islanders, 1 Hispanic American).

*Virginia Polytechnic Institute and State University (continued)*
Average age 33. 14 applicants, 57% accepted, 5 enrolled. In 2001, 3 degrees awarded.
**Degree requirements:** For doctorate, thesis/dissertation optional.
**Entrance requirements:** For doctorate, GRE General Test, TOEFL, minimum GPA of 3.5. *Application deadline:* For fall admission, 1/2 (priority date). *Application fee:* $45. Electronic applications accepted.
**Expenses:** Tuition, state resident: part-time $241 per hour. Tuition, nonresident: part-time $406 per hour. Tuition and fees vary according to program.
**Financial support:** In 2001–02, research assistantships (averaging $2,812 per year), 3 teaching assistantships (averaging $8,438 per year) were awarded. Unspecified assistantships also available. Support available to part-time students. Financial award application deadline: 3/1; financial award applicants required to submit FAFSA.
**Faculty research:** Medical family therapy, literature and family systems, eating disorders, qualitative and feminist research.
**Application contact:** Katharine Ann Surface, Administrative and Program Specialist III, 540-231-6149, *Fax:* 540-231-7012, *E-mail:* ksurface@vt.edu. *Web site:* http://www.chre.vt.edu/hd/hd.html

## ■ VIRGINIA POLYTECHNIC INSTITUTE AND STATE UNIVERSITY

**Graduate School, College of Human Resources and Education, Department of Human Development, Master's Program in Marriage and Family Therapy, Falls Church, VA 22043-2311**
AWARDS MS. Part-time and evening/weekend programs available.
**Faculty:** 3 full-time (2 women), 6 part-time/adjunct (5 women).
**Students:** 11 full-time (10 women), 19 part-time (13 women); includes 8 minority (5 African Americans, 2 Asian Americans or Pacific Islanders, 1 Hispanic American). 39 applicants, 26% accepted, 10 enrolled. In 2001, 10 degrees awarded.
**Degree requirements:** For master's, thesis optional.
**Entrance requirements:** For master's, GRE General Test, TOEFL, minimum GPA of 3.0. *Application deadline:* For fall admission, 1/1 (priority date). *Application fee:* $45. Electronic applications accepted.
**Expenses:** Tuition, state resident: part-time $241 per hour. Tuition, nonresident: part-time $406 per hour. Tuition and fees vary according to program.
**Financial support:** In 2001–02, 13 students received support, including 7

research assistantships with tuition reimbursements available (averaging $10,485 per year); unspecified assistantships also available. Support available to part-time students. Financial award application deadline: 4/1.
**Faculty research:** Healthy parenting initiative, U.S. Air Force Family Advocacy Research Project: Treatment of Male Batterers. *Total annual research expenditures:* $1.6 million.
Dr. Sandra M. Stith, Director, 703-538-8462, *Fax:* 703-538-8465, *E-mail:* sstith@vt.edu.
**Application contact:** Patricia A. Meneely, Administrative Specialist, 703-538-8460, *Fax:* 703-538-8465, *E-mail:* pmeneely@vt.edu. *Web site:* http://www.nvcserver.nvgc.vt.edu/mft/prog.html

## ■ WESTERN ILLINOIS UNIVERSITY

**School of Graduate Studies, College of Education and Human Services, Department of Counselor Education and College Student Personnel, Program in Counselor Education, Macomb, IL 61455-1390**
AWARDS Counseling (MS Ed); marriage and family counseling (Certificate). Part-time programs available.
**Faculty:** 4 full-time (2 women), 3 part-time/adjunct (2 women).
**Students:** 32 full-time (30 women), 112 part-time (94 women); includes 14 minority (9 African Americans, 1 Asian American or Pacific Islander, 4 Hispanic Americans), 1 international. Average age 34. 30 applicants, 27% accepted. In 2001, 33 master's, 4 Certificates awarded.
**Degree requirements:** For master's, thesis or alternative.
**Entrance requirements:** For master's, interview. *Application deadline:* Applications are processed on a rolling basis. *Application fee:* $0 ($25 for international students). Electronic applications accepted.
**Expenses:** Tuition, state resident: part-time $108 per credit hour. Tuition, nonresident: part-time $216 per credit hour. Required fees: $33 per credit hour.
**Financial support:** In 2001–02, 11 students received support, including 11 research assistantships with full tuition reimbursements available (averaging $5,720 per year). Financial award applicants required to submit FAFSA.
**Faculty research:** Conflict resolution.
**Application contact:** Dr. Barbara Baily, Director of Graduate Studies, 309-298-1806, *Fax:* 309-298-2345, *E-mail:* grad-office@wiu.edu. *Web site:* http://www.wiu.edu/

## ■ WESTERN MICHIGAN UNIVERSITY

**Graduate College, College of Education, Department of Counselor Education and Counseling Psychology, Kalamazoo, MI 49008-5202**
AWARDS Counseling psychology (PhD); counselor education (MA, Ed D, PhD); counselor education and counseling psychology (MA, PhD); counselor psychology (MA); marriage and family therapy (MA).
**Faculty:** 19 full-time (5 women), 2 part-time/adjunct.
**Students:** 328 full-time (258 women), 201 part-time (158 women); includes 57 minority (45 African Americans, 4 Asian Americans or Pacific Islanders, 6 Hispanic Americans, 2 Native Americans), 19 international. 294 applicants, 81% accepted, 101 enrolled. In 2001, 108 master's, 13 doctorates awarded.
**Degree requirements:** For doctorate, thesis/dissertation, oral exams.
**Entrance requirements:** For doctorate, GRE General Test. *Application deadline:* For fall admission, 1/15. Applications are processed on a rolling basis. *Application fee:* $25.
**Expenses:** Tuition, state resident: part-time $186 per credit hour. Tuition, nonresident: part-time $442 per credit hour. Required fees: $602. One-time fee: $132 part-time. Tuition and fees vary according to course load.
**Financial support:** Fellowships, research assistantships, teaching assistantships, Federal Work-Study available. Financial award application deadline: 2/15; financial award applicants required to submit FAFSA.
Dr. Joseph Morris, Chairperson, 616-387-5100.
**Application contact:** Admissions and Orientation, 616-387-2000, *Fax:* 616-387-2355.

## ■ WESTERN SEMINARY

**Graduate Programs, Program in Marriage and Family Counseling, Portland, OR 97215-3367**
AWARDS MA, MFT. Offered at San Jose campus only.
**Students:** 13 full-time (12 women), 8 part-time (all women); includes 4 minority (all Asian Americans or Pacific Islanders).
**Degree requirements:** For master's, practicum.
*Application deadline:* For fall admission, 8/1 (priority date); for winter admission, 12/1 (priority date); for spring admission, 3/1 (priority date). Applications are processed on a rolling basis. *Application fee:* $40.

**Expenses:** Tuition: Part-time $275 per credit hour. Tuition and fees vary according to degree level.
Dr. David Wenzel, Director, 503-517-1869.
**Application contact:** Dr. Robert W. Wiggins, Registrar/Dean of Student Development, 503-517-1820, *Fax:* 503-517-1801, *E-mail:* rwiggins@westernseminary.edu.

# REHABILITATION COUNSELING

## ■ ARKANSAS STATE UNIVERSITY

**Graduate School, College of Education, Department of Psychology and Counseling, Jonesboro, State University, AR 72467**
**AWARDS** Counselor education (MSE, Ed S), including personnel services (Ed S), psychoeducational diagnosis (Ed S), school counseling (Ed S); rehabilitation counseling (MRC). Part-time programs available.
**Faculty:** 12 full-time (4 women), 1 (woman) part-time/adjunct.
**Students:** 26 full-time (21 women), 62 part-time (56 women); includes 14 minority (all African Americans), 2 international. Average age 35. In 2001, 20 master's, 10 other advanced degrees awarded.
**Degree requirements:** For master's and Ed S, thesis or alternative, comprehensive exam.
**Entrance requirements:** For master's, GRE General Test or MAT (MSE), appropriate bachelor's degree, interview, letters of reference; for Ed S, GRE General Test, interview, master's degree, letters of reference. *Application deadline:* For fall admission, 7/1 (priority date); for spring admission, 11/15 (priority date). Applications are processed on a rolling basis. *Application fee:* $15 ($25 for international students). Electronic applications accepted.
**Expenses:** Tuition, state resident: full-time $3,384; part-time $141 per hour. Tuition, nonresident: full-time $8,520; part-time $355 per hour. Required fees: $742; $28 per hour. $25 per semester. One-time fee: $15 full-time. Tuition and fees vary according to degree level.
**Financial support:** Teaching assistantships, career-related internships or fieldwork, Federal Work-Study, and scholarships/grants available. Support available to part-time students. Financial award application deadline: 7/1; financial award applicants required to submit FAFSA.

Dr. Lynn Howerton, Chair, 870-972-3064, *Fax:* 870-972-3962, *E-mail:* howerton@astate.edu. *Web site:* http://www.clt.astate.edu/psy&coun/

## ■ ASSUMPTION COLLEGE

**Graduate School, Institute for Social and Rehabilitation Services, Worcester, MA 01609-1296**
**AWARDS** Rehabilitation counseling (MA, CAGS). Part-time and evening/weekend programs available.
**Faculty:** 13 full-time (4 women), 13 part-time/adjunct (7 women).
**Students:** 99 (76 women); includes 21 minority (6 African Americans, 7 Asian Americans or Pacific Islanders, 8 Hispanic Americans). 21 applicants, 100% accepted. In 2001, 38 master's, 15 other advanced degrees awarded.
**Degree requirements:** For master's, internship, practicum.
**Entrance requirements:** For master's, TOEFL. *Application deadline:* Applications are processed on a rolling basis. *Application fee:* $30.
**Expenses:** Tuition: Part-time $1,005 per credit.
**Financial support:** In 2001–02, 14 research assistantships with full tuition reimbursements (averaging $11,232 per year) were awarded; career-related internships or fieldwork and traineeships also available. Support available to part-time students. Financial award applicants required to submit FAFSA.
**Faculty research:** Job placement for severe disabilities, vocational counseling, conflict resolution.
Dr. David St. John, Acting Director, 508-767-7228, *Fax:* 508-798-2872, *E-mail:* dstjohn@assumption.edu.
**Application contact:** Prof. Lee Pearson, Coordinator of Graduate Program, 508-767-7063, *E-mail:* lpearson@assumption.edu.

## ■ BARRY UNIVERSITY

**School of Education, Program in Rehabilitation Counseling, Miami Shores, FL 33161-6695**
**AWARDS** MS, Ed S. Part-time and evening/weekend programs available.
**Faculty:** 5 full-time (2 women), 1 (woman) part-time/adjunct.
**Students:** Average age 35.
**Degree requirements:** For master's, scholarly paper.
**Entrance requirements:** For master's, GRE General Test or MAT, minimum GPA of 3.0; for Ed S, GRE General Test, minimum GPA of 3.0. *Application deadline:* For fall admission, 5/1 (priority date). Applications are processed on a rolling

basis. *Application fee:* $30. Electronic applications accepted.
**Expenses:** Tuition: Full-time $12,480. Tuition and fees vary according to degree level and program.
**Financial support:** Application deadline: 5/1.
Dr. Maureen Duffy, Chair, 305-899-3701, *Fax:* 305-899-3630, *E-mail:* mduffy@mail.barry.edu.
**Application contact:** Angela Scott, Assistant Dean, Enrollment Services, 305-899-3112, *Fax:* 305-899-3149, *E-mail:* ascott@mail.barry.edu.

## ■ BOSTON UNIVERSITY

**Sargent College of Health and Rehabilitation Sciences, Department of Rehabilitation Counseling, Boston, MA 02215**
**AWARDS** MS, D Sc, CAGS. Evening/weekend programs available.
**Faculty:** 1 full-time (0 women), 11 part-time/adjunct (5 women).
**Students:** 21 full-time (15 women), 16 part-time (12 women); includes 5 minority (2 African Americans, 3 Asian Americans or Pacific Islanders), 5 international. Average age 35. 25 applicants, 36% accepted. In 2001, 20 master's, 2 doctorates awarded.
**Degree requirements:** For doctorate, thesis/dissertation.
**Entrance requirements:** For master's and doctorate, GRE General Test. *Application deadline:* For fall admission, 5/1 (priority date). Applications are processed on a rolling basis. *Application fee:* $60.
**Expenses:** Tuition: Full-time $25,872; part-time $340 per credit. Required fees: $40 per semester. Part-time tuition and fees vary according to class time, course level and program.
**Financial support:** In 2001–02, 5 fellowships with full tuition reimbursements, 2 research assistantships with full tuition reimbursements, 3 teaching assistantships with full tuition reimbursements were awarded. Career-related internships or fieldwork, Federal Work-Study, institutionally sponsored loans, scholarships/grants, and tuition waivers (partial) also available. Financial award application deadline: 4/15; financial award applicants required to submit FAFSA.
**Faculty research:** Psychiatric rehabilitation, vocational evaluation, counseling the disabled.
Dr. Arthur E. Dell Orto, Chairman, 617-353-2725, *E-mail:* ado@bu.edu.
**Application contact:** Judy Skeffington, Director, Graduate Admissions and Financial Aid, 617-353-2713, *Fax:* 617-353-7500, *E-mail:* jaskeff@bu.edu.

## ■ BOWLING GREEN STATE UNIVERSITY

**Graduate College, College of Education and Human Development, School of Education and Intervention Services, Intervention Services Division, Program in Rehabilitation Counseling, Bowling Green, OH 43403**

**AWARDS** MRC. Part-time programs available.

**Students:** 32 full-time (23 women), 17 part-time (11 women); includes 11 African Americans, 3 Hispanic Americans, 2 international. Average age 35. 23 applicants, 65% accepted, 8 enrolled. In 2001, 20 degrees awarded.
**Degree requirements:** For master's, thesis or alternative.
**Entrance requirements:** For master's, GRE General Test, TOEFL, interview. *Application deadline:* Applications are processed on a rolling basis. *Application fee:* $30. Electronic applications accepted.
**Expenses:** Tuition, state resident: full-time $7,376; part-time $342 per credit hour. Tuition, nonresident: full-time $13,628; part-time $640 per credit hour.
**Financial support:** In 2001–02, 18 research assistantships with full tuition reimbursements (averaging $7,039 per year) were awarded; teaching assistantships with full tuition reimbursements, career-related internships or fieldwork, institutionally sponsored loans, tuition waivers (full), and unspecified assistantships also available. Financial award applicants required to submit FAFSA.
**Faculty research:** Depression, disability management, schizophrenia, job analysis, rehabilitation counseling curriculum.
**Application contact:** Dr. Jay Stewart, Graduate Coordinator, 419-372-7301.

## ■ CALIFORNIA STATE UNIVERSITY, FRESNO

**Division of Graduate Studies, School of Education and Human Development, Department of Counseling and Special Education, Rehabilitation Counseling Program, Fresno, CA 93740-8027**

**AWARDS** MS. Part-time and evening/weekend programs available.

**Faculty:** 2 full-time (0 women).
**Students:** 41 full-time (25 women), 8 part-time (5 women); includes 30 minority (4 African Americans, 11 Asian Americans or Pacific Islanders, 14 Hispanic Americans, 1 Native American), 1 international. Average age 31. 15 applicants, 87% accepted, 9 enrolled. In 2001, 19 degrees awarded.
**Degree requirements:** For master's, thesis optional. *Median time to degree:* Master's–2.5 years full-time, 3.5 years part-time.

**Entrance requirements:** For master's, GRE General Test, MAT, TOEFL, minimum GPA of 2.75. *Application deadline:* For fall admission, 4/1 (priority date); for spring admission, 11/1. Applications are processed on a rolling basis. *Application fee:* $55. Electronic applications accepted.
**Expenses:** Tuition, nonresident: part-time $246 per unit. Required fees: $605 per semester. Tuition and fees vary according to course load.
**Financial support:** Career-related internships or fieldwork, Federal Work-Study, scholarships/grants, and research awards, travel grants available. Support available to part-time students. Financial award application deadline: 3/1; financial award applicants required to submit FAFSA.
**Faculty research:** Aging, career development, job retention.
Dr. Charles Arokiasamy, Coordinator, 559-278-0325, *E-mail:* charles_arokiasamy@csufresno.edu.

## ■ CALIFORNIA STATE UNIVERSITY, LOS ANGELES

**Graduate Studies, Charter College of Education, Division of Administration and Counseling, Major in Counseling, Los Angeles, CA 90032-8530**

**AWARDS** Applied behavior analysis (MS); community college counseling (MS); rehabilitation counseling (MS); school counseling and school psychology (MS). Part-time and evening/weekend programs available.

**Students:** 186 full-time (136 women), 120 part-time (89 women); includes 224 minority (29 African Americans, 31 Asian Americans or Pacific Islanders, 160 Hispanic Americans, 4 Native Americans), 2 international. In 2001, 70 degrees awarded.
**Degree requirements:** For master's, project, or thesis.
**Entrance requirements:** For master's, TOEFL, interview, minimum GPA of 2.75 in last 90 units, teaching certificate. *Application deadline:* For fall admission, 6/30; for spring admission, 2/1. Applications are processed on a rolling basis. *Application fee:* $55.
**Expenses:** Tuition, nonresident: part-time $164 per unit.
**Financial support:** Career-related internships or fieldwork and Federal Work-Study available. Support available to part-time students. Financial award application deadline: 3/1.
Dr. Marcee Soriano, Chair, Division of Administration and Counseling, 323-343-4250.

## ■ CALIFORNIA STATE UNIVERSITY, SAN BERNARDINO

**Graduate Studies, College of Education, Program in Special Education and Rehabilitation Counseling, San Bernardino, CA 92407-2397**

**AWARDS** Rehabilitation counseling (MA); special education (MA). Part-time and evening/weekend programs available.

**Faculty:** 10 full-time (7 women), 4 part-time/adjunct (1 woman).
**Students:** 98 full-time (70 women), 110 part-time (77 women); includes 69 minority (34 African Americans, 4 Asian Americans or Pacific Islanders, 28 Hispanic Americans, 3 Native Americans), 1 international. Average age 40. 68 applicants, 87% accepted. In 2001, 59 degrees awarded.
**Degree requirements:** For master's, thesis or alternative.
**Entrance requirements:** For master's, minimum GPA of 3.0 in education. *Application deadline:* For fall admission, 8/31 (priority date). *Application fee:* $55.
**Expenses:** Tuition, nonresident: full-time $4,428. Required fees: $1,733.
**Financial support:** Career-related internships or fieldwork and Federal Work-Study available. Support available to part-time students.
Dr. Jeff McNair, Chair, 909-880-5685, *Fax:* 909-880-7040, *E-mail:* jmcnair@csusb.edu.

## ■ CENTRAL CONNECTICUT STATE UNIVERSITY

**School of Graduate Studies, School of Education and Professional Studies, Department of Health and Human Service Professions, New Britain, CT 06050-4010**

**AWARDS** Marriage and family therapy (MS); rehabilitation/mental counseling (MS); school counseling (MS); student development in higher education (MS). Part-time and evening/weekend programs available.

**Faculty:** 11 full-time (8 women), 9 part-time/adjunct (6 women).
**Students:** 68 full-time (48 women), 199 part-time (160 women); includes 39 minority (20 African Americans, 4 Asian Americans or Pacific Islanders, 13 Hispanic Americans, 2 Native Americans). Average age 34. 72 applicants, 69% accepted. In 2001, 66 degrees awarded.
**Degree requirements:** For master's, thesis or alternative, special project.
**Entrance requirements:** For master's, TOEFL, minimum GPA of 2.7. *Application deadline:* For fall admission, 8/10 (priority

date); for spring admission, 12/10. Applications are processed on a rolling basis. *Application fee:* $40.

**Expenses:** Tuition, state resident: full-time $2,772; part-time $245 per credit. Tuition, nonresident: full-time $7,726; part-time $245 per credit. Required fees: $2,102. Tuition and fees vary according to course level and degree level.

**Financial support:** In 2001–02, 2 research assistantships were awarded; career-related internships or fieldwork and Federal Work-Study also available. Financial award application deadline: 3/15; financial award applicants required to submit FAFSA.

**Faculty research:** Elementary/secondary school counseling, marriage/family therapy, rehabilitation counseling, counseling in higher educational settings.

Dr. James Malley, Chair, 860-832-2117.

■ **COPPIN STATE COLLEGE**

**Division of Graduate Studies, Division of Arts and Sciences, Department of Applied Psychology and Rehabilitation Counseling, Baltimore, MD 21216-3698**

**AWARDS** Rehabilitation (M Ed). Part-time and evening/weekend programs available.

**Faculty:** 2 full-time (both women), 7 part-time/adjunct (4 women).

**Students:** 7 full-time (5 women), 82 part-time (65 women); includes 85 minority (84 African Americans, 1 Hispanic American), 1 international. 39 applicants, 87% accepted. In 2001, 9 degrees awarded.

**Degree requirements:** For master's, thesis, comprehensive exam.

**Entrance requirements:** For master's, GRE, minimum GPA of 3.0, interview. *Application deadline:* For fall admission, 7/15 (priority date); for spring admission, 12/15 (priority date). Applications are processed on a rolling basis. *Application fee:* $25.

**Expenses:** Tuition, state resident: full-time $3,576; part-time $149 per credit. Tuition, nonresident: full-time $6,360; part-time $265 per credit. Required fees: $589; $589 per year.

**Financial support:** In 2001–02, 10 fellowships (averaging $1,600 per year), 1 research assistantship (averaging $2,000 per year) were awarded. Federal Work-Study, institutionally sponsored loans, scholarships/grants, and traineeships also available. Support available to part-time students. Financial award application deadline: 4/1; financial award applicants required to submit FAFSA.

Dr. Janet Spry, Co-Chairperson, 410-951-3510, *E-mail:* jspry@coppin.edu.

**Application contact:** Vell Lyles, Associate Vice President for Enrollment Management, 410-951-3575, *E-mail:* vlyles@

coppin.edu. *Web site:* http://www.coppin.edu/

■ **EAST CENTRAL UNIVERSITY**

**Graduate School, Department of Human Resources, Ada, OK 74820-6899**

**AWARDS** Administration (MSHR); counseling (MSHR); criminal justice (MSHR); rehabilitation counseling (MSHR). Part-time and evening/weekend programs available.

**Degree requirements:** For master's, thesis optional.

**Entrance requirements:** For master's, GRE General Test, MAT, minimum GPA of 2.5.

**Expenses:** Tuition, state resident: part-time $96 per credit hour. Tuition, nonresident: part-time $225 per credit hour. Full-time tuition and fees vary according to course load.

■ **EDINBORO UNIVERSITY OF PENNSYLVANIA**

**Graduate Studies, School of Education, Department of Counseling and Human Development, Edinboro, PA 16444**

**AWARDS** Counseling (MA, Certificate), including counseling-community counseling (MA), counseling-elementary guidance (MA), counseling-rehabilitation (MA), counseling-secondary guidance (MA), counseling-student personnel services (MA). Part-time and evening/weekend programs available.

**Faculty:** 6 full-time (4 women).

**Students:** 70 full-time (52 women), 46 part-time (25 women); includes 11 minority (8 African Americans, 2 Asian Americans or Pacific Islanders, 1 Hispanic American), 1 international. Average age 31. In 2001, 25 degrees awarded.

**Degree requirements:** For master's, thesis or alternative, competency exam.

**Entrance requirements:** For master's, GRE or MAT, minimum QPA of 2.5. *Application deadline:* Applications are processed on a rolling basis. *Application fee:* $25. Electronic applications accepted.

**Expenses:** Tuition, state resident: full-time $4,600; part-time $256 per credit. Tuition, nonresident: full-time $7,554; part-time $420 per credit. Required fees: $68 per credit.

**Financial support:** In 2001–02, 21 students received support, including research assistantships with full and partial tuition reimbursements available (averaging $3,150 per year); career-related internships or fieldwork, Federal Work-Study, institutionally sponsored loans, scholarships/grants, and unspecified assistantships also available. Support available to part-time students. Financial award

application deadline: 5/1; financial award applicants required to submit FAFSA. Dr. Salene Cowher, Chairperson, 814-732-2421, *E-mail:* scowher@edinboro.edu.

**Application contact:** Dr. Mary Margaret Bevevino, Dean of Graduate Studies, 814-732-2856, *Fax:* 814-732-2611, *E-mail:* mbevevino@edinboro.edu.

■ **EMPORIA STATE UNIVERSITY**

**School of Graduate Studies, The Teachers College, Department of Counselor Education and Rehabilitation Programs, Program in Rehabilitation Counseling, Emporia, KS 66801-5087**

**AWARDS** MS.

**Students:** 14 full-time (10 women), 4 part-time (all women); includes 1 minority (African American), 3 international. 3 applicants, 33% accepted. In 2001, 3 degrees awarded.

**Degree requirements:** For master's, comprehensive exam or thesis. *Application deadline:* For fall admission, 8/15 (priority date). Applications are processed on a rolling basis. *Application fee:* $30 ($75 for international students). Electronic applications accepted.

**Expenses:** Tuition, state resident: full-time $2,632; part-time $119 per credit hour. Tuition, nonresident: full-time $6,734; part-time $290 per credit hour.

**Financial support:** Career-related internships or fieldwork, Federal Work-Study, institutionally sponsored loans, health care benefits, and unspecified assistantships available. Financial award application deadline: 3/15; financial award applicants required to submit FAFSA.

**Application contact:** Dr. Marvin Kuehn, Graduate Coordinator, 620-341-5795, *E-mail:* kuehnmar@emporia.edu.

■ **FLORIDA STATE UNIVERSITY**

**Graduate Studies, College of Education, Department of Special Education, Tallahassee, FL 32306**

**AWARDS** Emotional disturbance/learning disabilities (MS); mental retardation (MS); rehabilitation counseling (MS, PhD, Ed S); special education (PhD, Ed S); visual disabilities (MS).

**Faculty:** 13 full-time (7 women), 1 (woman) part-time/adjunct.

**Students:** 69 full-time (64 women), 61 part-time (56 women); includes 32 minority (21 African Americans, 7 Asian Americans or Pacific Islanders, 4 Hispanic Americans), 1 international. 63 applicants, 59% accepted. In 2001, 21 master's, 1 doctorate awarded.

*Florida State University (continued)*
**Degree requirements:** For master's, thesis optional; for doctorate, thesis/dissertation, comprehensive exam.
**Entrance requirements:** For master's, doctorate, and Ed S, GRE General Test, minimum GPA of 3.0. *Application deadline:* For fall admission, 7/1; for spring admission, 11/1. Applications are processed on a rolling basis. *Application fee:* $20.
**Expenses:** Tuition, state resident: part-time $163 per credit hour. Tuition, nonresident: part-time $570 per credit hour. Tuition and fees vary according to program.
**Financial support:** In 2001–02, 1 fellowship was awarded; research assistantships, teaching assistantships, career-related internships or fieldwork and traineeships also available. Financial award applicants required to submit FAFSA.
Dr. Mary Frances Hanline, Chair, 850-644-4880, *Fax:* 850-644-8715, *E-mail:* hanline@mail.coe.fsu.edu.
**Application contact:** Admission Secretary, 850-644-4880, *Fax:* 850-644-8715. *Web site:* http://fsu.edu/~coe/

■ **FORT VALLEY STATE UNIVERSITY**

**Graduate Division, Department of Counseling Psychology, Program in Vocational Rehabilitation Counseling, Fort Valley, GA 31030-4313**
AWARDS MS. Part-time programs available.
**Degree requirements:** For master's, thesis optional.
**Entrance requirements:** For master's, GRE General Test or MAT.

■ **THE GEORGE WASHINGTON UNIVERSITY**

**Graduate School of Education and Human Development, Department of Counseling, Human and Organizational Services, Program in Counseling: School, Community and Rehabilitation, Washington, DC 20052**
AWARDS MA Ed, PhD.
**Faculty:** 6 full-time (2 women).
**Students:** 72 full-time (56 women), 65 part-time (56 women); includes 41 minority (28 African Americans, 10 Asian Americans or Pacific Islanders, 3 Hispanic Americans), 7 international. 51 applicants, 94% accepted. In 2001, 39 degrees awarded.
**Degree requirements:** For master's, comprehensive exam; for doctorate, thesis/dissertation, comprehensive exam.
**Entrance requirements:** For master's, GRE General Test or MAT, minimum GPA of 2.75; for doctorate, GRE General

Test, interview, minimum GPA of 3.3. *Application deadline:* For fall admission, 1/15 (priority date); for spring admission, 10/1. Applications are processed on a rolling basis. *Application fee:* $55.
**Expenses:** Tuition: Part-time $810 per credit. Required fees: $1 per credit.
**Financial support:** Fellowships, research assistantships, teaching assistantships, career-related internships or fieldwork, Federal Work-Study, and tuition waivers (full and partial) available.
**Faculty research:** Adjustment to disability, head injury rehabilitation, cross-cultural counseling.
Dr. Donald Linkowski, Director, 202-994-7204, *Fax:* 202-994-3436, *E-mail:* dcl@gwu.edu. *Web site:* http://www.gwu.edu/~gradinfo/

■ **GEORGIA STATE UNIVERSITY**

**College of Education, Department of Counseling and Psychological Services, Program in Rehabilitation Counseling, Atlanta, GA 30303-3083**
AWARDS MS, Ed S. Part-time and evening/weekend programs available.
**Students:** 12 full-time (11 women), 11 part-time (8 women); includes 6 minority (4 African Americans, 1 Asian American or Pacific Islander, 1 Hispanic American). Average age 31. 20 applicants, 95% accepted. In 2001, 9 degrees awarded.
**Degree requirements:** For master's, comprehensive exam.
**Entrance requirements:** For master's, GRE General Test, minimum GPA of 2.5; for Ed S, GRE General Test, minimum graduate GPA of 3.25. *Application deadline:* For fall admission, 3/1. *Application fee:* $25.
**Financial support:** Career-related internships or fieldwork and scholarships/grants available. Financial award application deadline: 4/1.
**Faculty research:** Catastrophic injuries, private sector rehabilitation, closed head injuries, persons with multiple handicaps.
Dr. Joanna White, Chairperson, Department of Counseling and Psychological Services, 404-651-2550.

■ **HOFSTRA UNIVERSITY**

**School of Education and Allied Human Services, Department of Counseling, Research, Special Education and Rehabilitation, Program in Rehabilitation Counseling, Hempstead, NY 11549**
AWARDS Rehabilitation administration (Professional Diploma); rehabilitation counseling (MS Ed). Part-time and evening/weekend programs available.
**Faculty:** 13 full-time (5 women), 22 part-time/adjunct (12 women).

**Students:** 14 full-time (11 women), 16 part-time (14 women); includes 2 minority (both African Americans). Average age 33. In 2001, 19 degrees awarded.
**Degree requirements:** For master's, internship.
**Entrance requirements:** For master's, interview, minimum undergraduate GPA of 2.8; for Professional Diploma, interview, minimum graduate GPA of 3.0, master's degree. *Application deadline:* Applications are processed on a rolling basis. *Application fee:* $40 ($75 for international students).
**Expenses:** Tuition: Full-time $12,408. Tuition and fees vary according to course load and program.
**Financial support:** Career-related internships or fieldwork, Federal Work-Study, institutionally sponsored loans, and scholarships/grants available. Support available to part-time students. Financial award application deadline: 7/1; financial award applicants required to submit FAFSA.
Dr. Joseph S. Lechowicz, Director, 516-463-5782, *Fax:* 516-463-6503, *E-mail:* edajsl@hofstra.edu.
**Application contact:** Mary Beth Carey, Vice President of Enrollment Services, *Fax:* 516-560-7660, *E-mail:* hofstra@hofstra.edu.

■ **HUNTER COLLEGE OF THE CITY UNIVERSITY OF NEW YORK**

**Graduate School, School of Education, Department of Educational Foundations and Counseling Programs, Program in Rehabilitation Counseling, New York, NY 10021-5085**
AWARDS MS Ed.
**Faculty:** 1 full-time (0 women), 4 part-time/adjunct (3 women).
**Students:** 21 full-time (16 women), 38 part-time (26 women); includes 15 minority (11 African Americans, 4 Hispanic Americans), 1 international. Average age 36. 65 applicants, 42% accepted. In 2001, 26 degrees awarded.
**Degree requirements:** For master's, 1 year practicum, internship, research seminar.
**Entrance requirements:** For master's, TOEFL, TSE, TWE, interview, minimum GPA of 2.7. *Application deadline:* For fall admission, 4/28; for spring admission, 11/21. Applications are processed on a rolling basis. *Application fee:* $40.
**Expenses:** Tuition, state resident: full-time $2,175; part-time $185 per credit. Tuition, nonresident: full-time $3,800; part-time $320 per credit.
**Faculty research:** Traumatic brain injury, HIV/AIDS, supported employment.
Dr. John O'Neill, Coordinator, 212-772-4720, *E-mail:* joneil@shiva.hunter.cuny.edu.

**Application contact:** William Zlata, Director for Graduate Admissions, 212-772-4288, *Fax:* 212-650-3336, *E-mail:* admissions@hunter.cuny.edu.

### ■ ILLINOIS INSTITUTE OF TECHNOLOGY

**Graduate College, Institute of Psychology, Chicago, IL 60616-3793**

AWARDS Clinical psychology (PhD); industrial/organizational psychology (PhD); personnel/human resource development (MS); psychology (MS); rehabilitation counseling (MS); rehabilitation psychology (PhD).

**Faculty:** 17 full-time (7 women), 4 part-time/adjunct (2 women).
**Students:** 84 full-time (56 women), 75 part-time (51 women); includes 32 minority (15 African Americans, 10 Asian Americans or Pacific Islanders, 6 Hispanic Americans, 1 Native American), 15 international. Average age 30. 157 applicants, 49% accepted. In 2001, 21 master's, 15 doctorates awarded. Terminal master's awarded for partial completion of doctoral program.
**Degree requirements:** For master's, thesis (for some programs), comprehensive exam; for doctorate, thesis/dissertation, qualifying exams, comprehensive exam.
**Entrance requirements:** For master's and doctorate, GRE General Test, TOEFL, minimum GPA of 3.0. *Application deadline:* For fall admission, 1/15 (priority date); for spring admission, 11/1. Applications are processed on a rolling basis. *Application fee:* $30. Electronic applications accepted.
**Expenses:** Tuition: Part-time $590 per credit hour.
**Financial support:** In 2001–02, 32 fellowships, 18 teaching assistantships were awarded. Research assistantships, career-related internships or fieldwork, Federal Work-Study, institutionally sponsored loans, scholarships/grants, and unspecified assistantships also available. Financial award application deadline: 3/1; financial award applicants required to submit FAFSA.
**Faculty research:** Leadership, life span developmental processes, rehabilitation engineering technology, behavioral medicine, substance abuse and disability. *Total annual research expenditures:* $494,180.
Dr. M. Ellen Mitchell, Chairman, 312-567-3362, *Fax:* 312-567-3493, *E-mail:* mitchell@itt.edu.
**Application contact:** Dr. Ali Cinar, Dean of Graduate College, 312-567-3637, *Fax:* 312-567-7517, *E-mail:* gradstu@iit.edu. *Web site:* http://www.iit.edu/colleges/psych/

### ■ INDIANA UNIVERSITY–PURDUE UNIVERSITY INDIANAPOLIS

**School of Science, Department of Psychology, Indianapolis, IN 46202-3275**

AWARDS Clinical rehabilitation psychology (MS, PhD); industrial/organizational psychology (MS); psychobiology of addictions (PhD). Part-time programs available.

**Students:** 22 full-time (17 women), 14 part-time (12 women); includes 2 minority (1 Asian American or Pacific Islander, 1 Hispanic American), 3 international. Average age 27. In 2001, 12 master's, 3 doctorates awarded. Terminal master's awarded for partial completion of doctoral program.
**Degree requirements:** For master's and doctorate, thesis/dissertation.
**Entrance requirements:** For master's, GRE General Test, minimum undergraduate GPA of 3.0; for doctorate, GRE General Test, GRE Subject Test (clinical rehabilitation psychology), minimum undergraduate GPA of 3.2. *Application deadline:* For fall admission, 2/1 (priority date). *Application fee:* $45 ($55 for international students).
**Expenses:** Tuition, state resident: full-time $4,480; part-time $187 per credit. Tuition, nonresident: full-time $12,926; part-time $539 per credit. Required fees: $177.
**Financial support:** In 2001–02, 21 students received support, including 6 fellowships with partial tuition reimbursements available (averaging $11,000 per year), 15 research assistantships with partial tuition reimbursements available (averaging $9,000 per year), 12 teaching assistantships with partial tuition reimbursements available (averaging $9,000 per year); career-related internships or fieldwork, Federal Work-Study, and institutionally sponsored loans also available. Financial award application deadline: 3/1; financial award applicants required to submit FAFSA.
**Faculty research:** Psychiatric rehabilitation, health psychology, psychopharmacology of drugs of abuse, personnel psychology, organizational decision making.
Dr. J. Gregor Fetterman, Chairman, 317-274-6768, *Fax:* 317-274-6756, *E-mail:* gfetter@iupui.edu.
**Application contact:** Donna Miller, Graduate Program Coordinator, 317-274-6945, *Fax:* 317-274-6756, *E-mail:* dmiller1@iupui.edu. *Web site:* http://www.psynt.iupui.edu/

### ■ JACKSON STATE UNIVERSITY

**Graduate School, School of Education, Department of Special Education and Rehabilitative Services, Jackson, MS 39217**

AWARDS Rehabilitative counseling service (MS Ed); special education (MS Ed, Ed S). Evening/weekend programs available.

**Degree requirements:** For master's, thesis or alternative, comprehensive exam.
**Entrance requirements:** For master's, GRE General Test, TOEFL.

### ■ KENT STATE UNIVERSITY

**Graduate School of Education, Department of Educational Foundations and Special Services, Program in Rehabilitation Counseling, Kent, OH 44242-0001**

AWARDS M Ed, MA, Ed S.

**Faculty:** 4 full-time (2 women), 2 part-time/adjunct (0 women).
**Students:** 24 full-time (20 women), 19 part-time (11 women); includes 9 minority (all African Americans). 15 applicants, 67% accepted, 10 enrolled. In 2001, 19 degrees awarded.
**Degree requirements:** For master's, thesis (for some programs), registration.
**Entrance requirements:** For master's and Ed S, GRE General Test. *Application deadline:* Applications are processed on a rolling basis. *Application fee:* $30. Electronic applications accepted.
**Financial support:** In 2001–02, fellowships with full tuition reimbursements (averaging $9,500 per year); research assistantships with full tuition reimbursements, teaching assistantships with full tuition reimbursements, career-related internships or fieldwork, Federal Work-Study, institutionally sponsored loans, scholarships/grants, health care benefits, and unspecified assistantships also available. Support available to part-time students. Financial award application deadline: 4/1; financial award applicants required to submit FAFSA.
Dr. Phil Rumrill, Coordinator, 330-672-2662, *E-mail:* prumrill@kent.edu.
**Application contact:** Deborah Barber, Director, Office of Academic Services, 330-672-2862, *Fax:* 330-672-3549, *E-mail:* oas@educ.kent.edu.

### ■ LA SALLE UNIVERSITY

**School of Arts and Sciences, Program in Psychology, Philadelphia, PA 19141-1199**

AWARDS Clinical geropsychology (Psy D); clinical psychology (Psy D); family psychology (Psy D); rehabilitation psychology (Psy D). Part-time and evening/weekend programs available.

*La Salle University (continued)*

**Faculty:** 8 full-time (1 woman), 10 part-time/adjunct (5 women).

**Students:** 40 full-time (25 women), 35 part-time (29 women); includes 7 minority (5 African Americans, 2 Hispanic Americans). Average age 35. 95 applicants, 48% accepted, 25 enrolled. In 2001, 1 degree awarded.

**Entrance requirements:** For doctorate, GRE, minimum GPA of 3.0. *Application deadline:* For fall admission, 3/1. *Application fee:* $30.

**Expenses:** Contact institution.

**Financial support:** Scholarships/grants available.

**Faculty research:** Cognitive therapy, attribution theory, treatment of addiction. Dr. John A. Smith, Director, 215-951-1350, *Fax:* 215-951-1351, *E-mail:* smithj@lasalle.edu.

---

■ **LOUISIANA STATE UNIVERSITY HEALTH SCIENCES CENTER**

**School of Allied Health Professions, Department of Rehabilitation Counseling, New Orleans, LA 70112-2262**

**AWARDS** MHS. Part-time programs available.

**Faculty:** 8 full-time (3 women).

**Students:** 27 full-time (25 women); includes 3 minority (2 African Americans, 1 Asian American or Pacific Islander). Average age 23. 20 applicants, 90% accepted, 15 enrolled. In 2001, 9 degrees awarded.

**Degree requirements:** For master's, clinical internship.

**Entrance requirements:** For master's, GRE General Test, minimum GPA of 2.5. *Application deadline:* For fall admission, 4/15 (priority date). Applications are processed on a rolling basis. *Application fee:* $50.

**Expenses:** Tuition, state resident: full-time $3,146. Tuition, nonresident: full-time $6,270.

**Financial support:** In 2001–02, 9 fellowships with full tuition reimbursements (averaging $6,000 per year) were awarded **Faculty research:** Job placement, clinical judgement, counseling process, consumer satisfaction, vocational assessment. *Total annual research expenditures:* $10,000. Dr. Douglas C. Strohmer, Head, 504-568-4315, *Fax:* 504-568-4324, *E-mail:* dstroh@lsuhsc.edu.

**Application contact:** Doris E. Cather, Clinical Instructor, 504-568-4315, *Fax:* 504-568-4324, *E-mail:* dcathe@lsuhsc.edu. *Web site:* http://alliedhealth.lsuhsc.edu

---

■ **MARYVILLE UNIVERSITY OF SAINT LOUIS**

**School of Health Professions, Program in Rehabilitation Counseling, St. Louis, MO 63141-7299**

**AWARDS** MARC. Part-time and evening/weekend programs available.

**Students:** In 2001, 8 degrees awarded.

**Degree requirements:** For master's, internship, oral examination.

*Application deadline:* Applications are processed on a rolling basis. *Application fee:* $20. Electronic applications accepted.

**Expenses:** Tuition: Full-time $14,400; part-time $408 per credit hour. Required fees: $120; $30 per semester.

**Financial support:** Career-related internships or fieldwork, Federal Work-Study, and campus employment available. Financial award application deadline: 7/31. Dr. Lance Carluccio, Director, 314-529-9625, *E-mail:* lcarlucc@maryville.edu. *Web site:* http://www.maryville.edu/

---

■ **MICHIGAN STATE UNIVERSITY**

**Graduate School, College of Education, Department of Counseling, Educational Psychology and Special Education, East Lansing, MI 48824**

**AWARDS** Counseling (MA, Ed D, Ed S); counseling psychology (MA, PhD); counselor education (PhD); educational psychology (MA, Ed D, PhD, Ed S); educational system design (Ed S); educational system development (MA, Ed D); educational technology and instructional design (MA); educational technology and system design (MA); measurement and quantitative methods (MA, PhD); measurement, evaluation and research design (Ed D, PhD); rehabilitation counseling (MA); rehabilitation counseling and school counseling (PhD); school psychology (PhD, Ed S); special education (MA, Ed D, PhD, Ed S). Part-time programs available.

**Faculty:** 37.

**Students:** 174 full-time (134 women), 145 part-time (104 women); includes 38 minority (24 African Americans, 11 Asian Americans or Pacific Islanders, 3 Hispanic Americans), 47 international. Average age 32. 359 applicants, 38% accepted. In 2001, 99 master's, 28 doctorates, 7 other advanced degrees awarded.

**Degree requirements:** For doctorate, thesis/dissertation.

**Entrance requirements:** For master's and doctorate, GRE General Test. *Application deadline:* For fall admission, 2/15 (priority date). Applications are processed on a rolling basis. *Application fee:* $30 ($40 for international students). Electronic applications accepted.

**Expenses:** Tuition, state resident: part-time $244 per credit hour. Tuition, nonresident: part-time $494 per credit hour. Required fees: $268 per semester. Tuition and fees vary according to course load, degree level and program.

**Financial support:** In 2001–02, 104 fellowships (averaging $3,880 per year), 26 research assistantships with tuition reimbursements (averaging $12,108 per year), 36 teaching assistantships with tuition reimbursements (averaging $11,963 per year) were awarded. Career-related internships or fieldwork and Federal Work-Study also available. Financial award applicants required to submit FAFSA.

**Faculty research:** Longitudinal and multilevel research, international mathematics and science curriculum, early intervention for non readers/writers, predictions and consequences of exposure to violence. *Total annual research expenditures:* $2.7 million. Dr. Richard Prawat, Chairperson, 517-353-7863.

**Application contact:** Graduate Admissions, 517-355-6683, *Fax:* 517-353-6393. *Web site:* http://ed-web3.educ.msu.edu/CEPSE/

---

■ **MINNESOTA STATE UNIVERSITY, MANKATO**

**College of Graduate Studies, College of Allied Health and Nursing, Department of Rehabilitation Counseling, Mankato, MN 56001**

**AWARDS** MS.

**Faculty:** 3 full-time (1 woman).

**Students:** 14 full-time (all women), 18 part-time (14 women). Average age 33. In 2001, 13 degrees awarded.

**Degree requirements:** For master's, comprehensive exam.

**Entrance requirements:** For master's, GRE General Test, minimum GPA of 3.0 during previous 2 years. *Application deadline:* For fall admission, 7/9 (priority date); for spring admission, 11/27. Applications are processed on a rolling basis. *Application fee:* $20.

**Expenses:** Tuition, state resident: full-time $3,253; part-time $157 per credit. Tuition, nonresident: full-time $4,893; part-time $248 per credit. Required fees: $24 per credit. Tuition and fees vary according to reciprocity agreements.

**Financial support:** Research assistantships with full tuition reimbursements, teaching assistantships with full tuition reimbursements available. Financial award application deadline: 3/15; financial award applicants required to submit FAFSA. Dr. Patricia Hargrove, Chairperson, 507-389-1415.

**Application contact:** Joni Roberts, Admissions Coordinator, 507-389-5244, *Fax:* 507-389-5974, *E-mail:* grad@mankato.msus.edu. *Web site:* http://

www.mankato.msus.edu/cgi-bin/
deptPage?Rehabilitation+Counseling/

# ■ MONTANA STATE UNIVERSITY–BILLINGS

**College of Education and Human Services, Department of Counseling and Human Services, Program in Rehabilitation Counseling, Billings, MT 59101-0298**

AWARDS MSRC. Part-time programs available.

**Degree requirements:** For master's, thesis or professional paper and/or field experience.
**Entrance requirements:** For master's, GRE General Test or MAT, minimum GPA of 3.0, both undergraduate and graduate.
**Expenses:** Tuition, state resident: full-time $3,560; part-time $1,164 per semester. Tuition, nonresident: full-time $8,498; part-time $2,810 per semester.

# ■ NEW YORK UNIVERSITY

**The Steinhardt School of Education, Department of Applied Psychology, Program in Rehabilitation Counseling, New York, NY 10012-1019**

AWARDS MA, PhD. Part-time and evening/weekend programs available.

**Faculty:** 1 full-time (0 women).
**Students:** 33 full-time (23 women), 19 part-time (15 women); includes 33 minority (26 African Americans, 3 Asian Americans or Pacific Islanders, 4 Hispanic Americans). 42 applicants, 55% accepted, 21 enrolled. In 2001, 9 degrees awarded. Terminal master's awarded for partial completion of doctoral program.
**Degree requirements:** For master's, thesis (for some programs); for doctorate, thesis/dissertation.
**Entrance requirements:** For master's, TOEFL; for doctorate, GRE General Test, TOEFL, interview. *Application deadline:* For fall admission, 2/1 (priority date); for spring admission, 12/1. Applications are processed on a rolling basis. *Application fee:* $40 ($60 for international students).
**Expenses:** Tuition: Full-time $19,536; part-time $814 per credit. Required fees: $1,330; $38 per credit. Tuition and fees vary according to course load and program.
**Financial support:** Career-related internships or fieldwork, Federal Work-Study, institutionally sponsored loans, scholarships/grants, and tuition waivers (partial) available. Support available to part-time students. Financial award application deadline: 3/1; financial award applicants required to submit FAFSA.

**Faculty research:** Medical and psychological aspects of disability, sexuality and disability, technology.
Dr. David Peterson, Director, 212-998-5290, *Fax:* 212-995-4368.
**Application contact:** 212-998-5030, *Fax:* 212-995-4328, *E-mail:* grad.admissions@nyu.edu.

# ■ NORTHEASTERN UNIVERSITY

**Bouvé College of Health Sciences Graduate School, Department of Counseling and Applied Educational Psychology, Program in Rehabilitation Counseling, Boston, MA 02115-5096**

AWARDS MS. Part-time programs available.
**Faculty:** 1 full-time (0 women), 1 (woman) part-time/adjunct.
**Students:** 3 full-time (all women), 1 (woman) part-time. 10 applicants, 80% accepted. In 2001, 3 degrees awarded.
**Entrance requirements:** For master's, GRE General Test or MAT. *Application deadline:* Applications are processed on a rolling basis. *Application fee:* $50.
**Expenses:** Tuition: Part-time $535 per credit hour. Required fees: $56. Tuition and fees vary according to program.
**Financial support:** Career-related internships or fieldwork, Federal Work-Study, tuition waivers (partial), and unspecified assistantships available. Support available to part-time students. Financial award application deadline: 3/1; financial award applicants required to submit FAFSA.
**Faculty research:** Substance abuse and treatment.
Dr. James Scorzelli, Director, 617-373-5919, *Fax:* 617-373-8892, *E-mail:* j.scorzelli@neu.edu.
**Application contact:** Bill Purnell, Director of Graduate Admissions, 617-373-2708, *Fax:* 617-373-4701, *E-mail:* w.purnell@neu.edu.

**Find an in-depth description at www.petersons.com/gradchannel.**

# ■ OHIO UNIVERSITY

**Graduate Studies, College of Education, Department of Counseling and Higher Education, Athens, OH 45701-2979**

AWARDS College student personnel (M Ed); community/agency counseling (M Ed); counselor education (PhD); higher education (M Ed, PhD); rehabilitation counseling (M Ed); school counseling (M Ed). Part-time and evening/weekend programs available.
**Faculty:** 11 full-time (5 women), 9 part-time/adjunct (3 women).
**Students:** 110 full-time (75 women), 105 part-time (70 women); includes 21 minority (16 African Americans, 1 Asian American or Pacific Islander, 3 Hispanic

Americans, 1 Native American), 58 international. 123 applicants, 75% accepted, 52 enrolled. In 2001, 20 master's, 19 doctorates awarded. Terminal master's awarded for partial completion of doctoral program.
**Degree requirements:** For master's, thesis or alternative; for doctorate, thesis/dissertation.
**Entrance requirements:** For master's, GRE General Test or MAT, TOEFL; for doctorate, GRE General Test, MAT, TOEFL, minimum GPA of 3.0, work experience. *Application deadline:* For fall admission, 3/1. *Application fee:* $30.
**Expenses:** Tuition, state resident: full-time $6,585. Tuition, nonresident: full-time $12,254.
**Financial support:** In 2001–02, 68 students received support, including 39 research assistantships with full tuition reimbursements available (averaging $6,500 per year), 6 teaching assistantships with full tuition reimbursements available (averaging $7,200 per year); Federal Work-Study, institutionally sponsored loans, tuition waivers (full), and unspecified assistantships also available. Financial award application deadline: 3/15. *Total annual research expenditures:* $527,983.
Dr. Robert Young, Chair, 740-593-0847, *Fax:* 740-593-0799, *E-mail:* young@ohiou.edu.
**Application contact:** Lynn Graham, Assistant Director, Graduate Services, 740-593-4420, *Fax:* 740-593-9310, *E-mail:* graham-m@ohio.edu.

# ■ ST. CLOUD STATE UNIVERSITY

**School of Graduate Studies, College of Education, Department of Counselor Education and Educational Psychology, Program in Rehabilitation Counseling, St. Cloud, MN 56301-4498**

AWARDS MS.

**Degree requirements:** For master's, thesis or alternative.
**Entrance requirements:** For master's, GRE General Test, minimum GPA of 2.75. *Application deadline:* For fall admission, 4/15. *Application fee:* $20.
**Expenses:** Tuition, state resident: part-time $156 per credit. Tuition, nonresident: part-time $244 per credit. Required fees: $20 per credit.
**Financial support:** Career-related internships or fieldwork, Federal Work-Study, and unspecified assistantships available. Financial award application deadline: 3/1.
Dr. John Hotz, Coordinator, 320-255-2240.
**Application contact:** Ann Anderson, Graduate Studies Office, 320-255-2113, *Fax:* 320-654-5371, *E-mail:* aeanderson@stcloudstate.edu.

### ■ ST. JOHN'S UNIVERSITY

The School of Education, Division of Human Services and Counseling, Program in Rehabilitation Counseling, Jamaica, NY 11439

**AWARDS** MS Ed, PD. Part-time and evening/weekend programs available.

**Students:** 2 full-time (1 woman), 21 part-time (18 women); includes 4 minority (2 African Americans, 1 Asian American or Pacific Islander, 1 Hispanic American), 1 international. Average age 36. 10 applicants, 60% accepted, 3 enrolled. In 2001, 12 degrees awarded.
**Degree requirements:** For master's, internship, practicum; for PD, internship, practicum.
**Entrance requirements:** For master's, interview, minimum GPA of 3.0; for PD, minimum GPA of 3.0. *Application deadline:* Applications are processed on a rolling basis. *Application fee:* $40.
**Expenses:** Tuition: Full-time $14,520; part-time $605 per credit. Required fees: $150; $75 per term. Tuition and fees vary according to class time, course load, degree level, campus/location, program and student level.
**Financial support:** Research assistantships, career-related internships or fieldwork and scholarships/grants available. Support available to part-time students. Financial award application deadline: 3/1; financial award applicants required to submit FAFSA.
**Faculty research:** Counseling techniques, communication skills, computers in counseling, psychiatric rehabilitation. Dr. Gene Sampson, Coordinator, 718-990-1559, *Fax:* 718-990-1614, *E-mail:* sampson@stjohns.edu.
**Application contact:** Kelly Ronayne, Assistant Dean, 718-990-2303, *Fax:* 718-990-6069, *E-mail:* admissions@stjohns.edu. *Web site:* http://www.stjohns.edu/

### ■ SAN DIEGO STATE UNIVERSITY

Graduate and Research Affairs, College of Education, Department of Administration, Rehabilitation and Post-Secondary Education, Program in Rehabilitation Counseling, San Diego, CA 92182

**AWARDS** MS.

**Entrance requirements:** For master's, GRE General Test, TOEFL, interview.

### ■ SAN FRANCISCO STATE UNIVERSITY

Graduate Division, College of Health and Human Services, Department of Counseling, Program in Rehabilitation Counseling, San Francisco, CA 94132-1722

**AWARDS** MS. Part-time programs available.

**Degree requirements:** For master's, culminating written description of internship.
**Entrance requirements:** For master's, minimum GPA of 2.5 in last 60 units.

### ■ SOUTH CAROLINA STATE UNIVERSITY

School of Graduate Studies, School of Applied Professional Sciences, Department of Human Services, Orangeburg, SC 29117-0001

**AWARDS** Rehabilitation counseling (MA). Part-time and evening/weekend programs available.

**Degree requirements:** For master's, departmental qualifying exam, internship, thesis optional.
**Entrance requirements:** For master's, GRE, MAT, minimum GPA of 2.7.
**Faculty research:** Handicap, disability, rehabilitation evaluation, vocation.

### ■ SOUTHERN ILLINOIS UNIVERSITY CARBONDALE

Graduate School, College of Education, Rehabilitation Institute, Carbondale, IL 62901-6806

**AWARDS** Behavioral analysis and therapy (MS); communication disorders and sciences (MS); rehabilitation (Rh D); rehabilitation administration and services (MS); rehabilitation counseling (MS). Part-time programs available.

**Faculty:** 12 full-time (2 women), 1 part-time/adjunct (0 women).
**Students:** 59 full-time (39 women), 110 part-time (77 women); includes 49 minority (45 African Americans, 2 Asian Americans or Pacific Islanders, 1 Hispanic American, 1 Native American), 18 international. 45 applicants, 64% accepted. In 2001, 49 master's, 5 doctorates awarded.
**Degree requirements:** For master's and doctorate, thesis/dissertation.
**Entrance requirements:** For master's, GRE, TOEFL; for doctorate, GRE or MAT, TOEFL, minimum GPA of 3.25. *Application fee:* $20.
**Expenses:** Tuition, state resident: full-time $3,794; part-time $154 per hour. Tuition, nonresident: full-time $6,566; part-time $308 per hour. Required fees: $277 per hour.

**Financial support:** In 2001–02, 90 students received support, including 2 fellowships with full tuition reimbursements available, 48 research assistantships with full tuition reimbursements available, 43 teaching assistantships with full tuition reimbursements available; career-related internships or fieldwork, Federal Work-Study, institutionally sponsored loans, traineeships, and tuition waivers (full) also available. Support available to part-time students.
**Faculty research:** Professional ethics. Dr. Jim Bordier, Director, 618-536-7704.

**Find an in-depth description at www.petersons.com/gradchannel.**

### ■ SOUTHERN UNIVERSITY AND AGRICULTURAL AND MECHANICAL COLLEGE

Graduate School, College of Sciences, Department of Psychology and Rehabilitation Counseling, Program in Rehabilitation Counseling, Baton Rouge, LA 70813

**AWARDS** MS.

**Faculty:** 7 full-time (5 women).
**Students:** 25 full-time (21 women), 5 part-time (4 women); includes 23 minority (all African Americans), 1 international. Average age 32. 51 applicants, 45% accepted. In 2001, 13 degrees awarded.
**Degree requirements:** For master's, thesis optional.
**Entrance requirements:** For master's, GMAT or GRE General Test, TOEFL. *Application deadline:* For fall admission, 6/1 (priority date); for spring admission, 11/1. Applications are processed on a rolling basis. *Application fee:* $25.
**Expenses:** Tuition, state resident: full-time $1,323. Tuition, nonresident: full-time $2,583. International tuition: $2,613 full-time. Tuition and fees vary according to program.
**Financial support:** In 2001–02, 20 research assistantships (averaging $11,500 per year) were awarded; scholarships/grants also available. Financial award application deadline: 4/15.
**Faculty research:** Cultural diversity, professional preparation and participation of minorities, needs and satisfaction of students with disabilities, prediction model for rehabilitation outcome, diabetes. Dr. Madan Kundu, Coordinator, 225-771-2990, *Fax:* 225-771-2082, *E-mail:* kundusubr@aol.com.

**Find an in-depth description at www.petersons.com/gradchannel.**

# ■ SPRINGFIELD COLLEGE

**School of Graduate Studies, Programs in Rehabilitation Services, Springfield, MA 01109-3797**

**AWARDS** Alcohol rehabilitation/substance abuse counseling (M Ed, MS, CAS); deaf counseling (M Ed, MS, CAS); developmental disabilities (M Ed, MS, CAS); general counseling and casework (M Ed, MS, CAS); psychiatric rehabilitation/mental health counseling (M Ed, MS, CAS); special services (M Ed, MS, CAS); vocational evaluation and work adjustment (M Ed, MS, CAS). Part-time and evening/weekend programs available.

**Faculty:** 8 full-time (2 women), 1 (woman) part-time/adjunct.

**Students:** 27 full-time, 13 part-time; includes 6 minority (3 African Americans, 1 Asian American or Pacific Islander, 2 Hispanic Americans). Average age 26. 29 applicants, 100% accepted. In 2001, 14 master's awarded.

**Degree requirements:** For master's, thesis (for some programs), comprehensive exam.

**Entrance requirements:** For master's and CAS, interview. *Application deadline:* For spring admission, 12/1. Applications are processed on a rolling basis. *Application fee:* $40.

**Financial support:** In 2001–02, 4 teaching assistantships with partial tuition reimbursements were awarded; fellowships with partial tuition reimbursements, career-related internships or fieldwork, Federal Work-Study, institutionally sponsored loans, traineeships, and tuition waivers (full and partial) also available. Financial award application deadline: 3/1.

**Faculty research:** Mental health, multicultural counseling, alcohol and substance abuse, developmental disabilities, families and disabilities, rehabilitation treatment outcomes.

Thomas J. Ruscio, Director, 413-748-3318.

**Application contact:** Donald James Shaw, Director of Graduate Admissions, 413-748-3225, *Fax:* 413-748-3694, *E-mail:* donald_shaw_jr@spfldcol.edu.

# ■ STATE UNIVERSITY OF NEW YORK AT ALBANY

**School of Education, Department of Educational and Counseling Psychology, Program in Rehabilitation Counseling, Albany, NY 12222-0001**

**AWARDS** MS. Evening/weekend programs available.

**Entrance requirements:** For master's, GRE General Test. *Application deadline:* For fall admission, 2/15. *Application fee:* $50.

**Expenses:** Tuition, state resident: full-time $2,550; part-time $213 per credit. Tuition, nonresident: full-time $4,208; part-time $351 per credit. Required fees: $470; $470 per year.

**Financial support:** Career-related internships or fieldwork available.

Sheldon Grand, Coordinator, 518-442-5041.

# ■ SYRACUSE UNIVERSITY

**Graduate School, School of Education, Counseling and Human Services Program, Program in Rehabilitation Counseling, Syracuse, NY 13244-0003**

**AWARDS** MS, Ed D, PhD.

**Students:** 24 full-time (21 women), 5 part-time (4 women); includes 2 minority (both African Americans), 2 international. Average age 39. 10 applicants, 80% accepted, 6 enrolled. In 2001, 12 master's, 1 doctorate awarded.

**Degree requirements:** For master's, thesis or alternative; for doctorate, thesis/dissertation.

**Entrance requirements:** For master's and doctorate, GRE. *Application deadline:* For fall admission, 2/1 (priority date); for spring admission, 10/15 (priority date). Applications are processed on a rolling basis. *Application fee:* $50. Electronic applications accepted.

**Expenses:** Tuition: Full-time $15,528; part-time $647 per credit. Required fees: $420; $38 per term. Tuition and fees vary according to program.

**Application contact:** Graduate Admission Recruiter, 315-443-2505, *Fax:* 315-443-5732, *E-mail:* gradrcrt@gwmail.syr.edu.

# ■ THOMAS UNIVERSITY

**Department of Rehabilitation Counseling, Thomasville, GA 31792-7499**

**AWARDS** MRC.

**Faculty:** 3 full-time (1 woman).

**Students:** 23 full-time (17 women), 40 part-time (28 women). Average age 33. 6 applicants, 83% accepted.

**Entrance requirements:** For master's, MAT, GRE General Test. *Application deadline:* Applications are processed on a rolling basis. *Application fee:* $50 ($75 for international students).

**Expenses:** Tuition: Full-time $4,950; part-time $3,300 per year. Required fees: $93 per term. Tuition and fees vary according to course load.

Dr. Shirley Chandler, Chair of Human Services Division.

**Application contact:** Lourena Maxwell, Recruiter, 229-226-1621, *Fax:* 229-227-6919, *E-mail:* lmaxwell@thomasu.edu.

# ■ UNIVERSITY AT BUFFALO, THE STATE UNIVERSITY OF NEW YORK

**Graduate School, Graduate School of Education, Department of Counseling, School, and Educational Psychology, Buffalo, NY 14260**

**AWARDS** Counseling school psychology (PhD); counselor education (PhD); educational psychology (MA, PhD); rehabilitation counseling (MS); school counseling (Ed M, Certificate); school psychology (MA). Part-time programs available.

**Faculty:** 15 full-time (5 women), 4 part-time/adjunct (2 women).

**Students:** 137 full-time (106 women), 90 part-time (63 women); includes 30 minority (19 African Americans, 3 Asian Americans or Pacific Islanders, 7 Hispanic Americans, 1 Native American), 7 international. Average age 25. 203 applicants, 43% accepted. In 2001, 37 master's, 14 doctorates, 13 other advanced degrees awarded.

**Degree requirements:** For master's, thesis (for some programs); for doctorate, thesis/dissertation, comprehensive exam.

**Entrance requirements:** For master's and doctorate, GRE General Test, TOEFL, interview. *Application deadline:* For fall admission, 2/1 (priority date). *Application fee:* $50. Electronic applications accepted.

**Expenses:** Tuition, state resident: full-time $6,118. Tuition, nonresident: full-time $9,434.

**Financial support:** In 2001–02, 30 students received support, including 10 fellowships with full tuition reimbursements available (averaging $10,000 per year), 16 research assistantships with full tuition reimbursements available (averaging $8,000 per year); teaching assistantships, career-related internships or fieldwork, Federal Work-Study, institutionally sponsored loans, and unspecified assistantships also available. Financial award application deadline: 2/1; financial award applicants required to submit FAFSA.

**Faculty research:** Counseling process, vocational psychology, assessment and evaluation, learning and development, grief counseling. *Total annual research expenditures:* $1.1 million.

Dr. Timothy P. Janikowski, Chairperson, 716-645-2484 Ext. 1055, *Fax:* 716-645-6616, *E-mail:* tjanikow@buffalo.edu. *Web site:* http://www.gse.buffalo.edu/dc/cep/

# ■ THE UNIVERSITY OF ALABAMA AT BIRMINGHAM

**Graduate School, School of Education, Department of Human Studies, Program in Counseling, Birmingham, AL 35294**

**AWARDS** Agency counseling (MA); marriage and family counseling (MA); rehabilitation counseling (MA); school counseling (MA); school psychology (MA Ed).

**Students:** 43 full-time (35 women), 103 part-time (84 women); includes 36 minority (35 African Americans, 1 Asian American or Pacific Islander), 4 international. 152 applicants, 84% accepted. In 2001, 29 degrees awarded.

**Degree requirements:** For master's, thesis optional.

**Entrance requirements:** For master's, GRE General Test, MAT, or NTE, minimum GPA of 3.0. *Application deadline:* Applications are processed on a rolling basis. *Application fee:* $35 ($60 for international students). Electronic applications accepted.

**Expenses:** Tuition, state resident: full-time $3,058. Tuition, nonresident: full-time $5,746. Tuition and fees vary according to course load, degree level and program.

**Financial support:** Career-related internships or fieldwork available.

Dr. David M. Macrina, Chairperson, Department of Human Studies, 205-934-2446, *Fax:* 205-975-8040, *E-mail:* dmacrina@uab.edu.

# ■ THE UNIVERSITY OF ARIZONA

**Graduate College, College of Education, Department of Special Education, Rehabilitation and School Psychology, Tucson, AZ 85721**

**AWARDS** M Ed, MA, MS, Ed D, PhD, Ed S. Part-time programs available.

**Faculty:** 28 full-time (14 women), 9 part-time/adjunct (all women).

**Students:** 180 full-time (142 women), 47 part-time (34 women); includes 60 minority (10 African Americans, 6 Asian Americans or Pacific Islanders, 29 Hispanic Americans, 15 Native Americans), 18 international. Average age 35. 132 applicants, 70% accepted, 57 enrolled. In 2001, 85 master's, 6 doctorates, 2 other advanced degrees awarded. Terminal master's awarded for partial completion of doctoral program.

**Degree requirements:** For master's, thesis optional; for doctorate, thesis/dissertation, comprehensive exam, registration.

**Entrance requirements:** For master's and Ed S, TOEFL; for doctorate, GRE General Test or MAT, TOEFL. *Application deadline:* For fall admission, 2/15 (priority

date); for spring admission, 9/1 (priority date). Applications are processed on a rolling basis. *Application fee:* $45.

**Expenses:** Tuition, state resident: full-time $2,490; part-time $436 per unit. Tuition, nonresident: full-time $10,300; part-time $436 per unit. Full-time tuition and fees vary according to degree level and program.

**Financial support:** In 2001–02, 5 fellowships (averaging $12,500 per year), 2 teaching assistantships (averaging $9,414 per year) were awarded. Research assistantships, career-related internships or fieldwork, institutionally sponsored loans, and tuition waivers (full) also available.

**Faculty research:** Teacher assistant teams, self-advocacy, language development in preschool, the deaf, comprehension of the learning disabled.

Dr. Lawrence M. Aleamoni, Head, 520-621-7822, *Fax:* 520-621-3821.

**Application contact:** Cecilia Carlon, Coordinator, 520-621-7822, *Fax:* 520-621-3821, *E-mail:* sergrad@mail.ed.arizona.edu. *Web site:* http://www.ed.arizona.edu/html/sersp.html

# ■ UNIVERSITY OF ARKANSAS

**Graduate School, College of Education and Health Professions, Department of Rehabilitation Education and Research, Program in Rehabilitation, Fayetteville, AR 72701-1201**

**AWARDS** MS, PhD.

**Students:** 37 full-time (30 women), 11 part-time (9 women); includes 10 minority (all African Americans), 1 international. 19 applicants, 95% accepted. In 2001, 21 degrees awarded.

**Degree requirements:** For doctorate, thesis/dissertation.

*Application fee:* $40 ($50 for international students).

**Expenses:** Tuition, state resident: full-time $3,553; part-time $197 per credit. Tuition, nonresident: full-time $8,411; part-time $467 per credit. Required fees: $42 per credit. Tuition and fees vary according to course load and program.

**Financial support:** Research assistantships, teaching assistantships, career-related internships or fieldwork and Federal Work-Study available. Support available to part-time students. Financial award application deadline: 4/1; financial award applicants required to submit FAFSA.

Dr. Jason Andrew, Chair, Department of Rehabilitation Education and Research, 479-575-3658, *E-mail:* jandrew@comp.uark.edu.

# ■ UNIVERSITY OF FLORIDA

**Graduate School, College of Health Professions, Department of Rehabilitation Counseling, Gainesville, FL 32611**

**AWARDS** MHS. Part-time programs available.

**Entrance requirements:** For master's, GRE General Test, minimum GPA of 3.0. Electronic applications accepted.

**Expenses:** Tuition, state resident: part-time $164 per hour. Tuition, nonresident: part-time $571 per hour. Tuition and fees vary according to course level and program.

**Faculty research:** Overcoming mental, physical, or emotional handicaps toward personal/vocational independence. *Web site:* http://www.hp.ufl.edu/

# ■ UNIVERSITY OF ILLINOIS AT URBANA–CHAMPAIGN

**Graduate College, College of Applied Life Studies, Department of Community Health, Division of Rehabilitation Education Services, Champaign, IL 61820**

**AWARDS** Rehabilitation (MS).

**Students:** 9 full-time (7 women); includes 1 minority (African American). 7 applicants, 100% accepted.

**Degree requirements:** For master's, 600 clock hours of fieldwork.

**Entrance requirements:** For master's, GRE General Test, minimum GPA of 3.0 during last 60 hours. *Application deadline:* For fall admission, 4/15 (priority date). Applications are processed on a rolling basis. *Application fee:* $40 ($50 for international students). Electronic applications accepted.

**Expenses:** Tuition, state resident: part-time $3,227 per degree program. Tuition, nonresident: part-time $7,169 per degree program. Tuition and fees vary according to program.

**Financial support:** Fellowships, research assistantships, teaching assistantships, career-related internships or fieldwork, Federal Work-Study, institutionally sponsored loans, and tuition waivers (full) available. Financial award application deadline: 2/15.

**Faculty research:** Transitions of severely disabled to work in independent living, psychosocial aspects of disabling conditions, multiculturalism.

Bradley N. Hedrick, Director, 217-333-4601, *Fax:* 217-333-0248, *E-mail:* bhedrick@uiuc.edu.

**Application contact:** Judith Thorpe, Staff Secretary, 217-333-4602, *Fax:* 217-333-0248. *Web site:* http://www.rehab.uiuc.edu/

## ■ THE UNIVERSITY OF IOWA

**Graduate College, College of Education, Division of Counseling, Rehabilitation, and Student Development, Iowa City, IA 52242-1316**

**AWARDS** Counselor education (MA, PhD); rehabilitation counseling (MA, PhD).

**Faculty:** 13 full-time.
**Students:** 68 full-time (53 women), 39 part-time (27 women); includes 20 minority (11 African Americans, 4 Asian Americans or Pacific Islanders, 4 Hispanic Americans, 1 Native American), 3 international. 69 applicants, 64% accepted, 20 enrolled. In 2001, 36 master's, 4 doctorates awarded.
**Degree requirements:** For master's, exam, thesis optional; for doctorate, thesis/dissertation, comprehensive exam.
**Entrance requirements:** For master's, GRE General Test, TOEFL; for doctorate, GRE General Test, TOEFL, minimum GPA of 3.0. *Application fee:* $30 ($50 for international students). Electronic applications accepted.
**Expenses:** Tuition, state resident: full-time $3,702; part-time $206 per semester hour. Tuition, nonresident: full-time $11,924; part-time $206 per semester hour. Required fees: $101 per semester. Tuition and fees vary according to course load and program.
**Financial support:** In 2001–02, 18 research assistantships, 13 teaching assistantships were awarded. Fellowships Financial award applicants required to submit FAFSA.
Dr. Dennis R. Maki, Chair, 319-335-5275.

## ■ UNIVERSITY OF KENTUCKY

**Graduate School, Graduate School Programs from the College of Education, Program in Rehabilitation Counseling, Lexington, KY 40506-0032**

**AWARDS** MRC. Evening/weekend programs available.

**Faculty:** 3 full-time (2 women).
**Students:** 13 full-time (9 women), 18 part-time (15 women); includes 7 minority (6 African Americans, 1 Asian American or Pacific Islander), 1 international. 23 applicants, 87% accepted. In 2001, 24 degrees awarded.
**Degree requirements:** For master's, comprehensive exam.
**Entrance requirements:** For master's, GRE General Test, minimum undergraduate GPA of 2.5. *Application deadline:* For fall admission, 7/19 (priority date). *Application fee:* $30 ($35 for international students).
**Expenses:** Tuition, state resident: full-time $4,075; part-time $213 per credit hour.

Tuition, nonresident: full-time $11,295; part-time $614 per credit hour.
**Financial support:** In 2001–02, 3 fellowships, 1 research assistantship, 3 teaching assistantships were awarded. Career-related internships or fieldwork, Federal Work-Study, institutionally sponsored loans, and unspecified assistantships also available. Support available to part-time students.
**Faculty research:** School to work transition/transition for criminal offenders, cultural mistrust and rehabilitation service provision, alcohol counseling among African-American ministers, persons living with HIV/AIDS, career counseling issues for persons with disabilities. *Total annual research expenditures:* $106,000.
Dr. Sonja Feist-Price, Director, 859-257-4270, *Fax:* 859-257-3835, *E-mail:* smfeis@pop.uky.edu.
**Application contact:** Dr. Jeannine Blackwell, Associate Dean, 859-257-4905, *Fax:* 859-323-1928.

## ■ UNIVERSITY OF LOUISIANA AT LAFAYETTE

**Graduate School, College of Liberal Arts, Department of Psychology, Program in Rehabilitation Counseling, Lafayette, LA 70504**

**AWARDS** MS.

**Faculty:** 2 full-time (1 woman).
**Students:** 15 full-time (12 women), 10 part-time (8 women); includes 3 minority (all African Americans). Average age 32. 22 applicants, 55% accepted, 8 enrolled. In 2001, 10 degrees awarded.
**Entrance requirements:** For master's, GRE General Test, minimum GPA of 3.0. *Application deadline:* For fall admission, 5/15. *Application fee:* $20 ($30 for international students).
**Expenses:** Tuition, state resident: full-time $2,317; part-time $79 per credit. Tuition, nonresident: full-time $8,882; part-time $369 per credit. International tuition: $9,018 full-time.
**Financial support:** In 2001–02, 1 research assistantship with full tuition reimbursement (averaging $5,500 per year) was awarded; Federal Work-Study also available. Financial award application deadline: 5/1.
**Faculty research:** Vocational assessment, psychology.
Dr. Kathryn Elliott, Coordinator, 337-482-6595.

## ■ UNIVERSITY OF MARYLAND, COLLEGE PARK

**Graduate Studies and Research, College of Education, Department of Counseling and Personnel Services, College Park, MD 20742**

**AWARDS** College student personnel (M Ed, MA); college student personnel administration (PhD); community counseling (CAGS); community/career counseling (M Ed, MA); counseling and personnel services (M Ed, MA, PhD); counseling psychology (PhD); counselor education (PhD); rehabilitation counseling (M Ed, MA); school counseling (M Ed, MA); school psychology (M Ed, MA, PhD). Part-time and evening/weekend programs available. Postbaccalaureate distance learning degree programs offered (no on-campus study).

**Faculty:** 17 full-time (10 women), 2 part-time/adjunct (1 woman).
**Students:** 127 full-time (99 women), 153 part-time (116 women); includes 91 minority (55 African Americans, 18 Asian Americans or Pacific Islanders, 16 Hispanic Americans, 2 Native Americans), 19 international. 358 applicants, 27% accepted, 57 enrolled. In 2001, 62 master's, 8 doctorates awarded.
**Degree requirements:** For master's, thesis (for some programs); for doctorate, thesis/dissertation.
**Entrance requirements:** For master's, GRE General Test or MAT, minimum GPA of 3.0; for doctorate, GRE General Test or MAT, minimum GPA of 3.5. *Application deadline:* For spring admission, 10/1. Applications are processed on a rolling basis. *Application fee:* $50 ($70 for international students). Electronic applications accepted.
**Expenses:** Tuition, state resident: part-time $289 per credit hour. Tuition, nonresident: part-time $448 per credit hour. One-time fee: $436 part-time. Full-time tuition and fees vary according to course load, campus/location and program.
**Financial support:** In 2001–02, 18 fellowships with full tuition reimbursements (averaging $7,029 per year), 13 teaching assistantships with tuition reimbursements (averaging $12,582 per year) were awarded. Research assistantships, career-related internships or fieldwork, Federal Work-Study, and scholarships/grants also available. Support available to part-time students. Financial award applicants required to submit FAFSA.
**Faculty research:** Educational psychology, counseling, health.
Dr. Dennis Kiulighan, Chairman, 301-405-2858, *Fax:* 301-405-9995.
**Application contact:** Trudy Lindsey, Director, Graduate Admissions and

*University of Maryland, College Park (continued)*
Records, 301-405-6991, *Fax:* 301-314-9305, *E-mail:* grschool@deans.umd.edu.

# ■ UNIVERSITY OF MEDICINE AND DENTISTRY OF NEW JERSEY

**School of Health Related Professions, Department of Psychiatric Rehabilitation and Behavioral Health Care, Program in Psychiatric Rehabilitation, Newark, NJ 07107-3001**

**AWARDS** MS, PhD.

**Entrance requirements:** For doctorate, GRE General Test. *Application deadline:* For fall admission, 6/1; for spring admission, 11/15.
**Expenses:** Tuition, state resident: part-time $292 per credit. Tuition, nonresident: part-time $440 per credit. Full-time tuition and fees vary according to degree level, program and student level.
**Financial support:** Traineeships available. Dr. Carlos W. Pratt, Director, 908-889-2461, *E-mail:* pratt@umdnj.edu.

# ■ UNIVERSITY OF MEDICINE AND DENTISTRY OF NEW JERSEY

**School of Health Related Professions, Department of Psychiatric Rehabilitation and Behavioral Health Care, Program in Rehabilitation Counseling, Newark, NJ 07107-3001**

**AWARDS** Psychiatric rehabilitation (MS); vocational rehabilitation (MS). Programs offered at Scotch Plains and Stratford campuses.

**Degree requirements:** For master's, internship, practicum, minimum GPA of 2.5.
**Entrance requirements:** For master's, minimum 2 years of psychiatric rehabilitation or related professional experience or GRE General Test; interview. *Application deadline:* For fall admission, 6/15; for spring admission, 11/15.
**Expenses:** Tuition, state resident: part-time $292 per credit. Tuition, nonresident: part-time $440 per credit. Full-time tuition and fees vary according to degree level, program and student level.
Dr. Carlos W. Pratt, Director, 908-889-2461, *E-mail:* pratt@umdnj.edu.
**Application contact:** Francis W. Ulrich, Information Contact, Stratford Campus, 609-566-6455, *E-mail:* ulrichfw@umdnj.edu.

# ■ THE UNIVERSITY OF MEMPHIS

**Graduate School, College of Education, Department of Counseling, Educational Psychology and Research, Memphis, TN 38152**

**AWARDS** Counseling and personnel services (MS, Ed D), including community agency counseling (MS), rehabilitation counseling (MS), school counseling (MS), student personnel services (MS); counseling psychology (PhD); educational psychology and research (MS, Ed D, PhD), including educational psychology (MS, Ed D), educational research (MS, Ed D).

**Degree requirements:** For master's, thesis or alternative, comprehensive exam; for doctorate, thesis/dissertation, comprehensive exam.
**Entrance requirements:** For master's, GRE General Test or MAT, minimum GPA of 2.5; for doctorate, GRE General Test.
**Expenses:** Tuition, state resident: full-time $2,026. Tuition, nonresident: full-time $4,528.
**Faculty research:** Anger management, aging and disability, supervision, multicultural counseling.

# ■ UNIVERSITY OF NEVADA, LAS VEGAS

**Graduate College, Greenspun College of Urban Affairs, Department of Counseling, Las Vegas, NV 89154-9900**

**AWARDS** Community agency counseling (MS); marriage and family counseling (MS); rehabilitation counseling (MS). Part-time programs available.

**Faculty:** 19 full-time (9 women).
**Students:** 25 full-time (20 women), 22 part-time (17 women); includes 6 minority (2 African Americans, 2 Asian Americans or Pacific Islanders, 2 Hispanic Americans). In 2001, 12 degrees awarded.
**Degree requirements:** For master's, thesis (for some programs), comprehensive exam (for some programs).
**Entrance requirements:** For master's, GRE General Test, minimum GPA of 3.0 during previous 2 years, 2.75 overall. *Application deadline:* For fall admission, 2/1. *Application fee:* $40 ($55 for international students).
**Expenses:** Tuition, state resident: full-time $1,926; part-time $107 per credit. Tuition, nonresident: full-time $9,376; part-time $220 per credit. Tuition and fees vary according to course load.
**Financial support:** In 2001–02, 2 research assistantships with partial tuition reimbursements (averaging $10,000 per year), 2 teaching assistantships with partial tuition reimbursements (averaging $10,000

per year) were awarded. Financial award application deadline: 3/1.
Dr. Gerald Weeks, Chair, 702-895-1867.
**Application contact:** Graduate College Admissions Evaluator, 702-895-3320, *Fax:* 702-895-4180, *E-mail:* gradcollege@ccmail.nevada.edu. *Web site:* http://www.unlv.edu/Colleges/Urban/Counseling/

# ■ THE UNIVERSITY OF NORTH CAROLINA AT CHAPEL HILL

**School of Medicine and Graduate School, Graduate Programs in Medicine, Chapel Hill, NC 27599**

**AWARDS** Allied health sciences (MS, Au D, PhD), including human movement science (PhD), occupational science (MS), speech and hearing sciences; biochemistry and biophysics (MS, PhD); biomedical engineering (MS, PhD); cell and developmental biology (PhD); cell and molecular physiology (PhD); genetics and molecular biology (MS, PhD); microbiology and immunology (MS, PhD), including immunology, microbiology; neurobiology (PhD); pathology and laboratory medicine (PhD), including experimental pathology; pharmacology (PhD); rehabilitation psychology and counseling (PhD); speech and hearing sciences (PhD), including speech and hearing sciences (MS, Au D, PhD). Postbaccalaureate distance learning degree programs offered.

**Faculty:** 551 full-time (202 women), 138 part-time/adjunct (44 women).
**Students:** 574 full-time (355 women), 16 part-time (12 women); includes 65 minority (25 African Americans, 28 Asian Americans or Pacific Islanders, 6 Hispanic Americans, 6 Native Americans), 60 international. In 2001, 160 master's, 43 doctorates awarded. Terminal master's awarded for partial completion of doctoral program.
**Degree requirements:** For master's, comprehensive exam; for doctorate, thesis/dissertation.
**Entrance requirements:** For master's and doctorate, GRE General Test. *Application deadline:* Applications are processed on a rolling basis. *Application fee:* $55. Electronic applications accepted.
**Expenses:** Contact institution.
**Financial support:** In 2001–02, 86 fellowships with full and partial tuition reimbursements, 187 research assistantships with full tuition reimbursements, 29 teaching assistantships with full tuition reimbursements were awarded. Career-related internships or fieldwork, Federal Work-Study, institutionally sponsored loans, traineeships, tuition waivers (full and partial), and unspecified assistantships also available. Support available to part-time students. Financial award applicants required to submit FAFSA.

Dr. Jeffrey L. Houpt, Dean, 919-966-4161, *Fax:* 919-966-6354. *Web site:* http://www.med.unc.edu/

**Find an in-depth description at www.petersons.com/gradchannel.**

■ **THE UNIVERSITY OF NORTH CAROLINA AT CHAPEL HILL**

**School of Medicine and Graduate School, Graduate Programs in Medicine, Department of Allied Health Sciences, Division of Rehabilitation Psychology and Counseling, Chapel Hill, NC 27599**

**AWARDS** PhD.

**Faculty:** 3 full-time (all women), 2 part-time/adjunct (1 woman).
**Students:** 26 full-time (24 women), 5 part-time (3 women). 30 applicants, 47% accepted.
**Degree requirements:** For doctorate, thesis/dissertation.
**Entrance requirements:** For doctorate, GRE General Test, MS in related field, minimum GPA of 3.0. *Application deadline:* For fall admission, 1/1 (priority date). *Application fee:* $50. Electronic applications accepted.
**Expenses:** Tuition, state resident: full-time $2,864. Tuition, nonresident: full-time $12,030.
**Financial support:** In 2001–02, 17 fellowships with full tuition reimbursements (averaging $2,250 per year), 1 research assistantship (averaging $5,300 per year) were awarded. Teaching assistantships with tuition reimbursements, Federal Work-Study, institutionally sponsored loans, traineeships, and unspecified assistantships also available. Financial award application deadline: 1/1.
**Faculty research:** Motor development, motor control; treatment of sports/orthopedic patient problems; movement in older adults; postural control across the lifespan; research in clinical practice; fetal, preterm, and infant movement; functional assessment across the lifespan. *Total annual research expenditures:* $140,750.
**Application contact:** Terita Sutton-Williams, Office Assistant, 919-966-3351, *Fax:* 919-966-3678, *E-mail:* twill@med.unc.edu. *Web site:* http://www.alliedhealth.unc.edu/hmsc/

■ **UNIVERSITY OF NORTHERN COLORADO**

**Graduate School, College of Health and Human Sciences, Department of Human Services, Program in Rehabilitation Counseling, Greeley, CO 80639**

**AWARDS** MA, PhD.

**Faculty:** 2 full-time (0 women).
**Students:** 28 full-time (22 women), 6 part-time (5 women); includes 2 minority (both Hispanic Americans), 3 international. Average age 36. 11 applicants, 91% accepted. In 2001, 4 master's, 4 doctorates awarded.
**Degree requirements:** For master's, thesis or alternative, comprehensive exam; for doctorate, thesis/dissertation, comprehensive exam.
**Entrance requirements:** For doctorate, GRE General Test. *Application deadline:* Applications are processed on a rolling basis. *Application fee:* $35.
**Expenses:** Tuition, state resident: full-time $2,549; part-time $546 per credit hour. Tuition, nonresident: full-time $10,459; part-time $581 per credit hour. Required fees: $631; $85 per year. Part-time tuition and fees vary according to course load.
**Financial support:** In 2001–02, 27 students received support, including 1 fellowship (averaging $595 per year), 2 research assistantships (averaging $9,748 per year); teaching assistantships, unspecified assistantships also available. Financial award application deadline: 3/1.

■ **UNIVERSITY OF NORTH TEXAS**

**Robert B. Toulouse School of Graduate Studies, School of Community Service, Center for Rehabilitation Studies, Denton, TX 76203**

**AWARDS** Rehabilitation counseling (MS); rehabilitation studies (MS); vocational evaluation (MS); work adjustment services (MS). Part-time programs available.

**Faculty:** 8 full-time (3 women), 3 part-time/adjunct (2 women).
**Students:** 62. Average age 29. In 2001, 15 degrees awarded.
**Degree requirements:** For master's, thesis optional.
**Entrance requirements:** For master's, GRE General Test, minimum GPA of 3.0 during last 60 hours, 2.8 overall. *Application deadline:* For fall admission, 7/17; for spring admission, 12/1. Applications are processed on a rolling basis. *Application fee:* $25 ($50 for international students).
**Expenses:** Tuition, state resident: part-time $186 per hour. Tuition, nonresident: part-time $319 per hour. Required fees: $88; $21 per hour.
**Financial support:** Career-related internships or fieldwork, Federal Work-Study, institutionally sponsored loans, and scholarships/grants available. Financial award application deadline: 4/1.
**Faculty research:** Biofeedback, job placement and development, adjustment services for handicapped. *Total annual research expenditures:* $55,000.

Dr. Celia Williamson, Chair, 940-565-2488, *Fax:* 940-565-3960.
**Application contact:** Dr. Eugenia Bodenhamer, Graduate Adviser, 940-565-3467, *Fax:* 940-565-3960, *E-mail:* genie@scs.cmm.unt.edu.

■ **UNIVERSITY OF PUERTO RICO, RÍO PIEDRAS**

**College of Social Sciences, Graduate School of Rehabilitation Counseling, San Juan, PR 00931**

**AWARDS** MRC. Part-time and evening/weekend programs available.

**Faculty:** 8.
**Students:** 93 full-time (80 women), 7 part-time (6 women); all minorities (all Hispanic Americans). In 2001, 8 degrees awarded.
**Degree requirements:** For master's, thesis, internship, comprehensive exam.
**Entrance requirements:** For master's, GRE, PAEG, interview, minimum GPA of 3.0. *Application deadline:* For fall admission, 2/1. *Application fee:* $17.
**Expenses:** Students that provide official evidence of private medicine insurance or service are exempt of the payment of $529 per academic year.
**Financial support:** Fellowships, research assistantships, teaching assistantships, career-related internships or fieldwork, Federal Work-Study, institutionally sponsored loans, and tuition waivers (partial) available. Financial award application deadline: 5/31.
**Faculty research:** Rehabilitation process in Puerto Rico, profile of the rehabilitation counselor in Puerto Rico.
Dr. Marilyn Mendoza-Lugo, Interim Chairperson, 787-764-0000 Ext. 4206, *Fax:* 787-764-0000 Ext. 1212.
**Application contact:** Luz M. Rivera, Administrative Officer, 787-764-0000 Ext. 2177, *Fax:* 787-764-0000 Ext. 1212.

■ **THE UNIVERSITY OF SCRANTON**

**Graduate School, Department of Counseling and Human Services, Program in Rehabilitation Counseling, Scranton, PA 18510**

**AWARDS** MS. Part-time and evening/weekend programs available.

**Students:** 5 full-time (all women), 20 part-time (15 women); includes 1 minority (African American). Average age 36. 6 applicants, 100% accepted. In 2001, 6 degrees awarded.
**Degree requirements:** For master's, capstone experience.

*The University of Scranton (continued)*
**Entrance requirements:** For master's, TOEFL, minimum GPA of 2.75. *Application deadline:* For fall admission, 3/1. *Application fee:* $50.
**Expenses:** Tuition: Part-time $539 per credit. Required fees: $25 per term.
**Financial support:** Teaching assistantships, career-related internships or fieldwork and Federal Work-Study available. Support available to part-time students. Financial award application deadline: 3/1.
Dr. Lori A. Bruch, Director, 570-941-4308, *Fax:* 570-941-4201, *E-mail:* bruchl1@scranton.edu.

# UNIVERSITY OF SOUTH CAROLINA

**School of Medicine and The Graduate School, Graduate Programs in Medicine, Program in Rehabilitation Counseling, Columbia, SC 29208**
**AWARDS** Psychiatric rehabilitation (Certificate); rehabilitation counseling (MRC). Part-time and evening/weekend programs available.
**Faculty:** 3 full-time (2 women), 2 part-time/adjunct (1 woman).
**Students:** 6 full-time (5 women), 27 part-time (18 women); includes 7 minority (all African Americans). Average age 32. 35 applicants, 40% accepted. In 2001, 9 master's, 1 Certificate awarded.
**Degree requirements:** For master's, internship, practicum. *Median time to degree:* Master's–1.5 years full-time, 3 years part-time; Certificate–1.5 years part-time.
**Entrance requirements:** For master's, GRE General Test or GMAT; for Certificate, GRE General Test or CMAT. *Application deadline:* For fall admission, 5/30 (priority date). *Application fee:* $35. Electronic applications accepted.
**Expenses:** Contact institution.
**Financial support:** In 2001–02, 11 students received support, including 10 fellowships with full tuition reimbursements available (averaging $4,800 per year), 5 research assistantships with partial tuition reimbursements available (averaging $6,000 per year); career-related internships or fieldwork, institutionally sponsored loans, and unspecified assistantships also available.
**Faculty research:** Quality of life, alcohol dependency, technology for disabled, psychiatric rehabilitation, women with disabilities.
Dr. Linda L. Leech, Graduate Director, 803-434-4296, *Fax:* 803-434-4231, *E-mail:* lleech@richmed.medpark.sc.edu.
**Application contact:** Linda Howell, Administrative Support Specialist, 803-434-4296, *Fax:* 803-434-4231, *E-mail:*

linda@richmed.medpark.sc.edu. *Web site:* http://www.med.sc.edu:88/gradstudies.htm

# UNIVERSITY OF SOUTH FLORIDA

**College of Graduate Studies, College of Arts and Sciences, Department of Rehabilitation and Mental Health Counseling, Tampa, FL 33620-9951**
**AWARDS** MA. Part-time and evening/weekend programs available.
**Faculty:** 7 full-time (2 women).
**Students:** 68 full-time (57 women), 70 part-time (53 women); includes 28 minority (13 African Americans, 1 Asian American or Pacific Islander, 14 Hispanic Americans). Average age 38. 53 applicants, 68% accepted, 31 enrolled. In 2001, 13 degrees awarded.
**Entrance requirements:** For master's, GRE General Test, minimum GPA of 3.0 in last 60 hours. *Application deadline:* For fall admission, 3/30; for spring admission, 10/15. *Application fee:* $20. Electronic applications accepted.
**Expenses:** Tuition, state resident: part-time $166 per credit hour. Tuition, nonresident: part-time $573 per credit hour. Required fees: $17 per term.
**Financial support:** Fellowships with partial tuition reimbursements, career-related internships or fieldwork, Federal Work-Study, institutionally sponsored loans, and tuition waivers (partial) available. Financial award application deadline: 4/1; financial award applicants required to submit FAFSA.
**Faculty research:** Allied health, multiculturalism, couples therapy, addictions. *Total annual research expenditures:* $8,017.
William G. Emener, Chairperson, 813-974-0966, *Fax:* 813-974-8080, *E-mail:* emener@chuma1.cas.usf.edu.
**Application contact:** Shari Allen, Office Manager, 813-974-0970, *Fax:* 813-974-8080, *E-mail:* allen@chuma1.cas.usf.edu. *Web site:* http://www.cas.usf.edu/rehab_counseling/index.html

# THE UNIVERSITY OF TENNESSEE

**Graduate School, College of Education, Program in Counseling, Knoxville, TN 37996**
**AWARDS** Mental health counseling (MS); rehabilitation counseling (MS); school counseling (MS). Part-time and evening/weekend programs available.
**Students:** 50 full-time (41 women), 17 part-time (12 women); includes 4 minority (2 African Americans, 2 Asian Americans or Pacific Islanders), 4 international. 69

applicants, 33% accepted. In 2001, 24 degrees awarded.
**Degree requirements:** For master's, thesis optional.
**Entrance requirements:** For master's, GRE General Test, TOEFL, minimum GPA of 2.7. *Application deadline:* For fall admission, 2/1 (priority date). Applications are processed on a rolling basis. *Application fee:* $35. Electronic applications accepted.
**Expenses:** Tuition, state resident: full-time $4,280; part-time $233 per hour. Tuition, nonresident: full-time $12,066; part-time $666 per hour. Tuition and fees vary according to program.
**Financial support:** In 2001–02, 1 research assistantship, 2 teaching assistantships were awarded. Financial award application deadline: 2/1; financial award applicants required to submit FAFSA.
Dr. Olga Welch, Head, 865-974-5131, *Fax:* 865-974-8674, *E-mail:* owelch@utk.edu.

# THE UNIVERSITY OF TEXAS–PAN AMERICAN

**College of Health Sciences and Human Services, Program in Rehabilitative Services, Edinburg, TX 78539-2999**
**AWARDS** Rehabilitation counseling (MS). Part-time and evening/weekend programs available.
**Faculty:** 5 full-time (2 women).
**Students:** 24 full-time (17 women), 31 part-time (25 women); includes 49 minority (all Hispanic Americans). 35 applicants, 94% accepted. In 2001, 8 degrees awarded.
**Degree requirements:** For master's, one foreign language, comprehensive exam.
**Entrance requirements:** For master's, minimum GPA of 3.0. *Application deadline:* For fall admission, 5/1 (priority date); for winter admission, 11/1 (priority date); for spring admission, 11/1.
**Expenses:** Tuition, state resident: part-time $212 per semester hour. Tuition, nonresident: part-time $367 per semester hour.
**Financial support:** In 2001–02, 15 students received support, including 12 fellowships with full tuition reimbursements available (averaging $7,200 per year), 3 teaching assistantships (averaging $7,008 per year); career-related internships or fieldwork, institutionally sponsored loans, and scholarships/grants also available.
**Faculty research:** Attitudes and disability, substance abuse, multicultural counseling, Hispanics and disability, Social Security beneficiary characteristics. *Total annual research expenditures:* $2,000.
Dr. Bruce J. Reed, Associate Professor and Program Coordinator, 956-316-7036 Ext.

7038, *Fax:* 956-318-5237, *E-mail:* bjreed@panam.edu.
**Application contact:** Dr. Irmo D. Marini, Associate Professor and Graduate Coordinator, 956-316-7036 Ext. 7035, *Fax:* 956-318-5237, *E-mail:* imarini@panam.edu. *Web site:* http://www.panam.edu/dept/rehabser/

### ■ THE UNIVERSITY OF TEXAS SOUTHWESTERN MEDICAL CENTER AT DALLAS

**Southwestern Graduate School of Biomedical Sciences, Rehabilitation Counseling Psychology Program, Dallas, TX 75390**
AWARDS MS.

**Faculty:** 10 full-time (2 women).
**Students:** 28 full-time (21 women); includes 7 minority (3 Asian Americans or Pacific Islanders, 3 Hispanic Americans, 1 Native American). Average age 30. 16 applicants. In 2001, 9 degrees awarded.
**Degree requirements:** For master's, thesis.
**Entrance requirements:** For master's, GRE General Test, minimum GPA of 3.0. *Application deadline:* For fall admission, 5/1. Applications are processed on a rolling basis. *Application fee:* $0.
**Expenses:** Tuition, state resident: full-time $990. Tuition, nonresident: full-time $6,062. Required fees: $843.
**Financial support:** Career-related internships or fieldwork and institutionally sponsored loans available. Financial award application deadline: 3/15; financial award applicants required to submit FAFSA.
**Faculty research:** Psychophysiology of stress and emotion, psychosocial rehabilitation, assessment of learning disabilities.
Dr. Maurice Korman, Chair, 214-648-5267, *Fax:* 214-648-1771, *E-mail:* maurice.korman@email.swmed.edu.
**Application contact:** Dr. Donald Pool, Director of Training, 214-648-1740, *Fax:* 214-648-1771, *E-mail:* donald.pool@email.swmed.edu.

### ■ UNIVERSITY OF WISCONSIN–MADISON

**Graduate School, School of Education, Department of Rehabilitation Psychology and Special Education, Program in Rehabilitation Psychology, Madison, WI 53706-1380**
AWARDS MA, MS, PhD.

**Degree requirements:** For doctorate, thesis/dissertation.
*Application fee:* $38.
**Expenses:** Tuition, state resident: full-time $7,361; part-time $399 per credit. Tuition, nonresident: full-time $20,499; part-time

$1,282 per credit. Required fees: $34 per credit. Full-time tuition and fees vary according to course load, program, reciprocity agreements and student level.
Dr. Ruth Torkelson Lynch, Chair, Department of Rehabilitation Psychology and Special Education, 608-262-5860.

### ■ UNIVERSITY OF WISCONSIN–STOUT

**Graduate School, College of Human Development, Program in Vocational Rehabilitation, Menomonie, WI 54751**
AWARDS MS. Part-time programs available.

**Students:** 25 full-time (16 women), 11 part-time (10 women); includes 4 minority (2 African Americans, 2 Asian Americans or Pacific Islanders), 1 international. 8 applicants, 100% accepted, 7 enrolled. In 2001, 6 degrees awarded.
**Degree requirements:** For master's, thesis.
*Application deadline:* Applications are processed on a rolling basis. *Application fee:* $45.
**Expenses:** Tuition, state resident: full-time $4,915. Tuition, nonresident: full-time $12,553.
**Financial support:** In 2001–02, 1 research assistantship was awarded; teaching assistantships, Federal Work-Study, scholarships/grants, and tuition waivers (full and partial) also available. Support available to part-time students. Financial award application deadline: 4/1; financial award applicants required to submit FAFSA.
Dr. Kathleen Deery, Director, 715-232-2233, *E-mail:* deeryk@uwstout.edu.
**Application contact:** Information Contact, 715-232-1983.

### ■ UTAH STATE UNIVERSITY

**School of Graduate Studies, College of Education, Department of Special Education and Rehabilitation, Program in Rehabilitation Counselor Education, Logan, UT 84322**
AWARDS MRC. Part-time programs available. Postbaccalaureate distance learning degree programs offered (minimal on-campus study).

**Faculty:** 3 full-time (1 woman), 3 part-time/adjunct (1 woman).
**Students:** 21 full-time (11 women), 63 part-time (45 women); includes 4 minority (1 Asian American or Pacific Islander, 3 Hispanic Americans), 2 international. 39 applicants, 72% accepted. In 2001, 21 degrees awarded.
**Entrance requirements:** For master's, GRE General Test or MAT, TOEFL, minimum GPA of 3.0. *Application deadline:* For fall admission, 6/15 (priority date); for spring admission, 10/15 (priority date).

Applications are processed on a rolling basis. *Application fee:* $40.
**Expenses:** Tuition, state resident: full-time $1,693. Tuition, nonresident: full-time $4,233. Required fees: $501. Tuition and fees vary according to program.
**Financial support:** Fellowships, scholarships/grants and traineeships available. Support available to part-time students.
**Faculty research:** Distance education, Hispanic rehabilitation, transition from school to work.
Julie F. Smart, Coordinator, 435-797-0449, *Fax:* 435-797-3572, *E-mail:* jsmart@cc.usu.edu.
**Application contact:** Patricia Huff, Administrative Secretary, 435-797-0449, *Fax:* 435-797-3572, *E-mail:* pathuff@cc.usu.edu. *Web site:* http://www.rce.usu.edu/

### ■ VIRGINIA COMMONWEALTH UNIVERSITY

**School of Graduate Studies, School of Allied Health Professions, Department of Rehabilitation Counseling, Richmond, VA 23284-9005**
AWARDS MS, CPC.

**Students:** 141 full-time, 36 part-time; includes 44 minority (36 African Americans, 4 Asian Americans or Pacific Islanders, 4 Hispanic Americans). 71 applicants, 86% accepted. In 2001, 27 degrees awarded.
**Entrance requirements:** For master's, GRE General Test or MAT. *Application deadline:* For fall admission, 8/1; for spring admission, 12/1. Applications are processed on a rolling basis. *Application fee:* $30.
**Expenses:** Tuition, state resident: full-time $4,276; part-time $238 per credit. Tuition, nonresident: full-time $12,672; part-time $704 per credit. Required fees: $1,167; $43 per credit.
**Financial support:** Fellowships, research assistantships, teaching assistantships, career-related internships or fieldwork and tuition waivers (full and partial) available. Financial award application deadline: 3/1.
**Faculty research:** Substance abuse/addictions, lifelong disabilities, consumer empowerment, counseling models, adjustment to disability.
Dr. Christine A. Reid, Chairman, 804-828-1132, *Fax:* 801-828-1321. *Web site:* http://views.vcu.edu/sahp/rehab/

### ■ WAYNE STATE UNIVERSITY

Graduate School, College of Education, Division of Theoretical and Behavioral Foundations, Detroit, MI 48202

AWARDS Counseling (M Ed, MA, Ed D, PhD, Ed S); educational evaluation and research (M Ed, Ed D, PhD); educational psychology (M Ed, Ed D); rehabilitation counseling and community inclusion (MA); school and community psychology (Ed S). Evening/weekend programs available.

Faculty: 14 full-time.
Students: 473. 178 applicants, 45% accepted, 62 enrolled. In 2001, 87 master's, 8 doctorates awarded.
Degree requirements: For doctorate, thesis/dissertation.
Entrance requirements: For master's, GRE (school psychology); for doctorate, GRE (educational psychology), interview, minimum GPA of 3.0. *Application deadline:* For fall admission, 7/1. *Application fee:* $20 ($30 for international students). Electronic applications accepted.
Expenses: Tuition, state resident: full-time $3,764. Tuition and fees vary according to degree level and program.
Financial support: In 2001–02, 1 research assistantship, 2 teaching assistantships were awarded. Career-related internships or fieldwork, Federal Work-Study, and institutionally sponsored loans also available.
Faculty research: Adolescents at risk, supervision of counseling.
Dr. JoAnne Holbert, Deputy Dean, 313-577-1805, *Fax:* 313-577-5235, *E-mail:* jholbert@wayne.edu.

### ■ WAYNE STATE UNIVERSITY

Graduate School, Interdisciplinary Program in Developmental Disabilities, Detroit, MI 48202

AWARDS Certificate.

Students: In 2001, 1 degree awarded.
Entrance requirements: For degree, master's degree. *Application deadline:* Applications are processed on a rolling basis. *Application fee:* $0. Electronic applications accepted.
Expenses: Tuition, state resident: full-time $3,764. Tuition and fees vary according to degree level and program.
Application contact: Dr. Barbara Leroy, Director, 313-577-2654, *Fax:* 313-577-3770.

### ■ WESTERN MICHIGAN UNIVERSITY

Graduate College, College of Health and Human Services, Department of Blind Rehabilitation, Kalamazoo, MI 49008-5202

AWARDS MA.

Faculty: 8 full-time (4 women).
Students: 46 full-time (34 women), 25 part-time (20 women); includes 4 minority (1 African American, 1 Asian American or Pacific Islander, 2 Hispanic Americans), 3 international. 39 applicants, 87% accepted, 33 enrolled. In 2001, 31 degrees awarded. *Application deadline:* For fall admission, 2/15 (priority date). Applications are processed on a rolling basis. *Application fee:* $25.
Expenses: Tuition, state resident: part-time $186 per credit hour. Tuition, nonresident: part-time $442 per credit hour. Required fees: $602. One-time fee: $132 part-time. Tuition and fees vary according to course load.
Financial support: Fellowships, research assistantships, teaching assistantships, Federal Work-Study available. Financial award application deadline: 2/15; financial award applicants required to submit FAFSA.
Dr. Paul Ponchillia, Interim Chairperson, 616-387-3453.
Application contact: Admissions and Orientation, 616-387-2000, *Fax:* 616-387-2355.

### ■ WESTERN OREGON UNIVERSITY

Graduate Programs, College of Education, Division of Teacher Education, Division of Special Education, Program in Rehabilitation Counseling, Monmouth, OR 97361-1394

AWARDS MS Ed.

Faculty: 3 full-time (2 women), 2 part-time/adjunct (1 woman).
Students: 25 full-time (22 women), 1 (woman) part-time; includes 7 minority (1 Asian American or Pacific Islander, 4 Hispanic Americans, 2 Native Americans). Average age 36. 18 applicants, 50% accepted. In 2001, 13 degrees awarded.
Degree requirements: For master's, oral exam, portfolio, thesis optional.
Entrance requirements: For master's, interview, minimum GPA of 3.0. *Application deadline:* For fall admission, 4/15 (priority date). Applications are processed on a rolling basis. *Application fee:* $50.
Financial support: In 2001–02, 5 research assistantships with full tuition reimbursements (averaging $1,057 per year) were

awarded; teaching assistantships with full tuition reimbursements, career-related internships or fieldwork, Federal Work-Study, and tuition waivers (full and partial) also available. Support available to part-time students. Financial award application deadline: 3/1; financial award applicants required to submit FAFSA.
Faculty research: Deafness, rehabilitation counseling.
Dr. Linda Keller, Coordinator, 503-838-8746, *Fax:* 503-838-8228, *E-mail:* kellerl@wou.edu.
Application contact: Alison Marshall, Director of Admissions, 503-838-8211, *Fax:* 503-838-8067, *E-mail:* marshaa@wou.edu.

### ■ WESTERN WASHINGTON UNIVERSITY

Graduate School, Woodring College of Education, Department of Adult and Higher Education, Program in Rehabilitation Counseling, Bellingham, WA 98225-5996

AWARDS MA. Part-time and evening/weekend programs available. Postbaccalaureate distance learning degree programs offered (minimal on-campus study).

Degree requirements: For master's, research project.
Entrance requirements: For master's, GRE General Test or MAT, TOEFL, GPA of 3.0 in last 60 semester hours or last 90 quarter hours.

### ■ WEST VIRGINIA UNIVERSITY

College of Human Resources and Education, Department of Counseling, Rehabilitation Counseling, and Counseling Psychology, Program in Rehabilitation Counseling, Morgantown, WV 26506

AWARDS MS. Part-time programs available.

Students: 29 full-time (21 women), 8 part-time (7 women); includes 5 minority (2 African Americans, 2 Hispanic Americans, 1 Native American). Average age 30. 47 applicants, 38% accepted. In 2001, 14 degrees awarded.
Degree requirements: For master's, content exams.
Entrance requirements: For master's, TOEFL, minimum GPA of 2.5, interview. *Application deadline:* For fall admission, 3/15 (priority date). *Application fee:* $45.
Expenses: Tuition, state resident: full-time $2,791. Tuition, nonresident: full-time $8,659. Required fees: $1,002. Tuition and fees vary according to program.
Financial support: In 2001–02, 2 research assistantships, 2 teaching assistantships were awarded. Career-related internships or fieldwork, Federal Work-Study,

institutionally sponsored loans, and tuition waivers (full and partial) also available. Financial award application deadline: 2/1; financial award applicants required to submit FAFSA.

**Faculty research:** Work adjustment, job modification for the handicapped, computer resource networks, vocational evaluation.

Dr. Margaret K. Glenn, Coordinator, 304-293-3807 Ext. 1203, *Fax:* 304-293-4082, *E-mail:* margaret.glenn@mail.wvu.edu. *Web site:* http://www.wvu.edu/~crc/rehab/

### ■ WRIGHT STATE UNIVERSITY

**School of Graduate Studies, College of Education and Human Services, Department of Human Services, Program in Rehabilitation Counseling, Dayton, OH 45435**

**AWARDS** Chemical dependency (MRC); severe disabilities (MRC).

**Students:** 19 full-time (13 women), 11 part-time (10 women); includes 4 minority (all African Americans). Average age 35. 10 applicants, 90% accepted. In 2001, 9 degrees awarded.

**Degree requirements:** For master's, comprehensive exam.

**Entrance requirements:** For master's, GRE General Test, MAT, TOEFL, interview. *Application fee:* $25.

**Expenses:** Tuition, state resident: full-time $7,161; part-time $225 per quarter hour. Tuition, nonresident: full-time $12,324; part-time $385 per quarter hour. Tuition and fees vary according to course load, degree level and program.

**Financial support:** Career-related internships or fieldwork, institutionally sponsored loans, and tuition waivers (full and partial) available. Support available to part-time students. Financial award applicants required to submit FAFSA.

Dr. Stephen B. Fortson, Chair, 937-775-2075, *Fax:* 937-775-2042, *E-mail:* stephen.fortson@wright.edu.

**Application contact:** Gerald C. Malicki, Assistant Dean and Director of Graduate Admissions and Records, 937-775-2976, *Fax:* 937-775-2453, *E-mail:* jerry.malicki@wright.edu.

# SCHOOL PSYCHOLOGY

### ■ ABILENE CHRISTIAN UNIVERSITY

**Graduate School, College of Arts and Sciences, Department of Psychology, Program in School Psychology, Abilene, TX 79699-9100**

**AWARDS** MS.

**Faculty:** 12 part-time/adjunct (2 women).

**Students:** 7 full-time (5 women), 5 part-time (3 women); includes 2 minority (both Hispanic Americans). 7 applicants, 86% accepted, 6 enrolled. In 2001, 1 degree awarded.

**Degree requirements:** For master's, comprehensive exam.

**Entrance requirements:** For master's, GRE General Test. *Application deadline:* For fall admission, 4/1 (priority date); for spring admission, 11/1. Applications are processed on a rolling basis. *Application fee:* $25 ($45 for international students).

**Expenses:** Tuition: Full-time $8,904; part-time $371 per hour. Required fees: $520; $17 per hour.

**Financial support:** Federal Work-Study available. Support available to part-time students. Financial award application deadline: 4/1.

Dr. Larry Norsworthy, Graduate Adviser, 915-674-2280, *Fax:* 915-674-6968, *E-mail:* norsworthyl@acu.edu.

**Application contact:** Dr. Roger Gee, Graduate Dean, 915-674-2122, *Fax:* 915-674-2123, *E-mail:* gradinfo@education.acu.edu.

### ■ ALABAMA AGRICULTURAL AND MECHANICAL UNIVERSITY

**School of Graduate Studies, School of Education, Department of Counseling and Special Education, Huntsville, AL 35811**

**AWARDS** Communicative disorders (M Ed, MS); psychology and counseling (MS, Ed S), including clinical psychology (MS), counseling and guidance, counseling psychology (MS), personnel management (MS), psychometry (MS), school psychology (MS); special education (M Ed, MS). Part-time and evening/weekend programs available.

**Faculty:** 38 full-time (20 women).

**Students:** 21 full-time (all women), 119 part-time (90 women); includes 65 minority (64 African Americans, 1 Hispanic American), 2 international. In 2001, 55 master's, 2 other advanced degrees awarded.

**Degree requirements:** For master's, comprehensive exam.

**Entrance requirements:** For master's, GRE General Test. *Application deadline:* For fall admission, 5/1. *Application fee:* $15 ($20 for international students).

**Expenses:** Tuition, state resident: full-time $1,380. Tuition, nonresident: full-time $2,500.

**Financial support:** Career-related internships or fieldwork available. Support available to part-time students. Financial award application deadline: 4/1.

**Faculty research:** Increasing numbers of minorities in special education and speech-language pathology. *Total annual research expenditures:* $300,000.

Dr. Terry L. Douglas, Chair, 256-851-5533.

### ■ ALFRED UNIVERSITY

**Graduate School, Program in School Psychology, Alfred, NY 14802-1205**

**AWARDS** MA, Psy D, CAS.

**Students:** 35 full-time (31 women), 29 part-time (26 women). Average age 23. 52 applicants, 69% accepted. In 2001, 18 master's, 7 doctorates awarded.

**Degree requirements:** For master's, internship; for doctorate, thesis/dissertation, internship.

**Entrance requirements:** For master's and doctorate, GRE General Test, TOEFL. *Application deadline:* For fall admission, 1/15 (priority date). *Application fee:* $50. Electronic applications accepted.

**Expenses:** Tuition: Full-time $23,554. Required fees: $698. One-time fee: $116 part-time. Full-time tuition and fees vary according to program.

**Financial support:** Research assistantships, career-related internships or fieldwork, tuition waivers (full and partial), and unspecified assistantships available. Financial award applicants required to submit FAFSA.

**Faculty research:** Family processes, alternative assessment approaches, behavior disorders in children, parent involvement, school psychology training issues.

Dr. John D. Cerio, Acting Chair, 607-871-2212, *E-mail:* fgaughan@alfred.edu.

**Application contact:** Cathleen R. Johnson, Coordinator of Graduate Admissions, 607-871-2141, *Fax:* 607-871-2198, *E-mail:* johnsonc@alfred.edu. *Web site:* http://www.alfred.edu/gradschool

**Find an in-depth description at www.petersons.com/gradchannel.**

### ■ ALLIANT INTERNATIONAL UNIVERSITY

**Graduate School of Education, Program in School Psychology–Los Angeles, Alhambra, CA 91803-1360**

**AWARDS** MA, Psy D.

**Faculty:** 2 part-time/adjunct (both women).

**Students:** 7 full-time (all women), 6 part-time (2 women); includes 3 minority (1 African American, 1 Asian American or Pacific Islander, 1 Hispanic American). Average age 35.

**Degree requirements:** For doctorate, thesis/dissertation.

**Entrance requirements:** For doctorate, TOEFL, interview; master's degree in

*Alliant International University (continued)*

school psychology, educational psychology, counseling, or related field; minimum GPA of 3.0 in both psychology and overall. *Application fee:* $65.

**Expenses:** Tuition: Part-time $397 per credit hour. Tuition and fees vary according to degree level, campus/location and program.

**Financial support:** Applicants required to submit FAFSA.

Dr. Rhonda Brinkley-Kennedy, Director, 626-284-2777, *Fax:* 626-284-0550, *E-mail:* rbrinkleykennedy@alliant.edu.

**Application contact:** Patricia J. Mullen, Vice President, Enrollment and Student Services, 800-457-1273 Ext. 303, *Fax:* 415-931-8322, *E-mail:* admissions@ mail.cspp.edu. *Web site:* http:// www.alliant.edu/

### ■ ALLIANT INTERNATIONAL UNIVERSITY

**Graduate School of Education, Programs in Education–Fresno, Fresno, CA 93727**

**AWARDS** BCLAD (Credential), including Hmong, Lao, and Cambodian, Spanish; CLAD (Credential); educational leadership (Ed D); school psychology (MA, Ed D).

**Entrance requirements:** For degree, TOEFL, interview, minimum GPA of 3.0. *Application deadline:* For fall admission, 8/1. *Application fee:* $20.

**Expenses:** Tuition: Part-time $397 per credit hour. Tuition and fees vary according to degree level, campus/location and program.

**Application contact:** Patricia J. Mullen, Vice President, Enrollment and Student Services, 800-457-1273 Ext. 303, *Fax:* 415-931-8322, *E-mail:* admissions@alliant.edu. *Web site:* http://www.alliant.edu/

### ■ ALLIANT INTERNATIONAL UNIVERSITY

**Graduate School of Education, Programs in Education –San Francisco Bay, Alameda, CA 94501**

**AWARDS** BCLAD (Credential); CLAD (Credential); cross-cultural studies (MA, Ed D); educational leadership (Ed D); school psychology (MA, Ed D).

**Faculty:** 1 (woman) full-time, 4 part-time/adjunct (3 women).

**Students:** Average age 30. 8 applicants, 88% accepted.

**Entrance requirements:** For degree, TOEFL, interview, minimum GPA of 3.0. *Application deadline:* For fall admission, 8/1. *Application fee:* $20.

**Expenses:** Tuition: Part-time $397 per credit hour. Tuition and fees vary according to degree level, campus/location and program.

**Financial support:** Teaching assistantships available.

**Application contact:** Patricia J. Mullen, Vice President, Enrollment and Student Services, 800-457-1273 Ext. 303, *Fax:* 415-931-8322, *E-mail:* admissions@alliant.edu. *Web site:* http://www.alliant.edu/

### ■ AMERICAN INTERNATIONAL COLLEGE

**School of Continuing Education and Graduate Studies, School of Psychology and Education, Department of Psychology, Program in School Psychology, Springfield, MA 01109-3189**

**AWARDS** MA, CAGS, MA/CAGS. Part-time and evening/weekend programs available.

**Degree requirements:** For master's, practicum.

**Entrance requirements:** For master's, minimum C average in undergraduate course work.

### ■ ANDREWS UNIVERSITY

**School of Graduate Studies, School of Education, Department of Educational and Counseling Psychology, Program in School Counseling, Berrien Springs, MI 49104**

**AWARDS** MA.

**Students:** 7 full-time (4 women), 16 part-time (10 women); includes 10 minority (4 African Americans, 6 Hispanic Americans), 2 international. Average age 37. In 2001, 4 degrees awarded.

**Degree requirements:** For master's, thesis optional.

*Application fee:* $40.

**Expenses:** Tuition: Full-time $12,600; part-time $525 per semester. Required fees: $268. Tuition and fees vary according to degree level.

Dr. Lenore S. Branfley, Program Coordinator, 616-471-3133.

**Application contact:** Carolyn Hurst, Supervisor of Graduate Admission, 800-253-2874, *Fax:* 616-471-3228, *E-mail:* enroll@andrews.edu.

### ■ ANDREWS UNIVERSITY

**School of Graduate Studies, School of Education, Department of Educational and Counseling Psychology, Program in School Psychology, Berrien Springs, MI 49104**

**AWARDS** Ed S. Part-time programs available.

**Students:** 2 full-time (1 woman), 5 part-time (2 women), 1 international. Average age 39. In 2001, 4 degrees awarded. *Application deadline:* Applications are processed on a rolling basis. *Application fee:* $40.

**Expenses:** Tuition: Full-time $12,600; part-time $525 per semester. Required fees: $268. Tuition and fees vary according to degree level.

Dr. Sheryl A. Gregory, Program Coordinator, 616-471-3133.

**Application contact:** Carolyn Hurst, Supervisor of Graduate Admission, 800-253-2874, *Fax:* 616-471-3228, *E-mail:* enroll@andrews.edu.

### ■ APPALACHIAN STATE UNIVERSITY

**Cratis D. Williams Graduate School, College of Arts and Sciences, Department of Psychology, Program in School Psychology, Boone, NC 28608**

**AWARDS** MA, CAS.

**Faculty:** 24 full-time (8 women).

**Students:** 29 full-time (25 women); includes 2 minority (1 Asian American or Pacific Islander, 1 Hispanic American). In 2001, 8 master's, 9 other advanced degrees awarded.

**Degree requirements:** For master's and CAS, GRE Subject Test exit exam, thesis optional.

**Entrance requirements:** For master's, GRE General Test, GRE Subject Test. *Application deadline:* For fall admission, 3/1 (priority date). Applications are processed on a rolling basis. *Application fee:* $35.

**Expenses:** Tuition, state resident: full-time $1,286. Tuition, nonresident: full-time $9,354. Required fees: $1,116.

**Financial support:** In 2001–02, research assistantships (averaging $6,250 per year), teaching assistantships (averaging $6,250 per year) were awarded. Fellowships, career-related internships or fieldwork also available. Support available to part-time students. Financial award application deadline: 7/1.

**Faculty research:** School-based consultation, child behavior management, parent education.

Dr. James Deni, Director, 828-262-2728, *E-mail:* denijr@appstate.edu. *Web site:* http://www.acs.appstate.edu/dept/psych/

# ■ APPALACHIAN STATE UNIVERSITY

**Cratis D. Williams Graduate School, College of Education, Department of Human Development and Psychological Counseling, Program in School Counseling, Boone, NC 28608**

AWARDS MA.

**Expenses:** Tuition, state resident: full-time $1,286. Tuition, nonresident: full-time $9,354. Required fees: $1,116.

**Financial support:** In 2001–02, research assistantships (averaging $6,250 per year), teaching assistantships (averaging $6,250 per year) were awarded. Career-related internships or fieldwork, Federal Work-Study, scholarships/grants, and unspecified assistantships also available.

**Faculty research:** Supervision and diversity, consultation and ecotherapy, multiculturalism.

Dr. Laurie Williamson, Coordinator, 828-262-6046, *E-mail:* wmsonll@appstate.edu.

# ■ ARCADIA UNIVERSITY

**Graduate Studies, Department of Psychology, Glenside, PA 19038-3295**

AWARDS Counseling (MAC), including community counseling, school counseling. Part-time programs available.

**Faculty:** 4 full-time (2 women), 6 part-time/adjunct (4 women).

**Students:** 18 full-time (all women), 28 part-time (22 women); includes 4 minority (all African Americans), 2 international. In 2001, 14 degrees awarded.

**Degree requirements:** For master's, practicum.

**Entrance requirements:** For master's, GRE General Test or MAT. *Application deadline:* Applications are processed on a rolling basis. *Application fee:* $35.

**Expenses:** Tuition: Part-time $420 per credit. Tuition and fees vary according to degree level and program.

**Financial support:** Research assistantships, career-related internships or fieldwork and unspecified assistantships available. Support available to part-time students. Financial award application deadline: 8/15.

Samuel Cameron, Program Director, 215-572-2181.

**Application contact:** 215-572-2925, *Fax:* 215-572-2126, *E-mail:* grad@arcadia.edu.

# ■ ARGOSY UNIVERSITY-SARASOTA

**School of Psychology and Behavioral Sciences, Sarasota, FL 34235-8246**

AWARDS Counseling psychology (Ed D); guidance counseling (MA); mental health counseling (MA); organizational leadership (Ed D); pastoral community counseling (Ed D); school counseling (Ed S). Part-time and evening/weekend programs available. Postbaccalaureate distance learning degree programs offered (minimal on-campus study).

**Faculty:** 13 full-time (4 women), 19 part-time/adjunct (9 women).

**Students:** 265 full-time (180 women), 220 part-time (149 women); includes 163 minority (138 African Americans, 9 Asian Americans or Pacific Islanders, 12 Hispanic Americans, 4 Native Americans). Average age 45. In 2001, 25 master's, 24 doctorates, 5 other advanced degrees awarded.

**Degree requirements:** For master's, thesis optional; for doctorate, thesis/dissertation, comprehensive exam.

**Entrance requirements:** For master's and doctorate, TOEFL. *Application deadline:* Applications are processed on a rolling basis. *Application fee:* $50.

**Expenses:** Contact institution.

**Financial support:** Federal Work-Study available. Support available to part-time students. Financial award applicants required to submit FAFSA.

Dr. Douglas G. Riedmiller, Dean, 800-331-5995, *Fax:* 941-379-9464, *E-mail:* douglas_griedmiller@embanet.com.

**Application contact:** Admissions Representative, 800-331-5995 Ext. 221, *Fax:* 941-371-8910. *Web site:* http://www.sarasota.edu/

# ■ AUBURN UNIVERSITY

**Graduate School, College of Education, Department of Counseling and Counseling Psychology, Auburn University, AL 36849**

AWARDS Community agency counseling (M Ed, MS, Ed D, PhD, Ed S); counseling psychology (PhD); counselor education (Ed D, PhD); school counseling (M Ed, MS, Ed D, PhD, Ed S); school psychometry (M Ed, MS, Ed D, PhD, Ed S). Part-time programs available.

**Faculty:** 9 full-time (5 women).

**Students:** 57 full-time (51 women), 53 part-time (37 women); includes 32 minority (28 African Americans, 1 Asian American or Pacific Islander, 2 Hispanic Americans, 1 Native American), 4 international. 105 applicants, 57% accepted. In 2001, 19 master's, 8 doctorates awarded.

**Degree requirements:** For master's, thesis (for some programs); for doctorate, thesis/dissertation; for Ed S, thesis or alternative.

**Entrance requirements:** For master's and Ed S, GRE General Test; for doctorate, GRE General Test, GRE Subject Test. *Application deadline:* For fall admission, 5/15. *Application fee:* $25 ($50 for international students). Electronic applications accepted.

**Financial support:** Research assistantships, Federal Work-Study and traineeships available. Support available to part-time students. Financial award application deadline: 3/15.

**Faculty research:** At-risk students, substance abuse, gender roles, AIDS, professional ethics.

Dr. Holly Stadler, Head, 334-844-5160.

**Application contact:** Dr. John F. Pritchett, Dean of the Graduate School, 334-844-4700, *E-mail:* hatchlb@mail.auburn.edu. *Web site:* http://www.auburn.edu/academic/education/ccp/an_ccp.html

# ■ AUSTIN PEAY STATE UNIVERSITY

**Graduate School, College of Arts and Sciences, Department of Psychology, Clarksville, TN 37044-0001**

AWARDS Clinical psychology (MA); guidance and counseling (MS); psychological science (MA); school psychology (MA). Part-time programs available.

**Degree requirements:** For master's, thesis.

**Entrance requirements:** For master's, GRE General Test, minimum GPA of 3.0. *Web site:* http://www.apsu.edu/

# ■ BALL STATE UNIVERSITY

**Graduate School, Teachers College, Department of Educational Psychology, Program in School Psychology, Muncie, IN 47306-1099**

AWARDS MA, PhD, Ed S.

**Students:** 34 full-time (28 women), 14 part-time (11 women). Average age 29. 83 applicants, 41% accepted. In 2001, 8 master's, 7 doctorates, 1 other advanced degree awarded.

**Degree requirements:** For doctorate and Ed S, thesis/dissertation.

**Entrance requirements:** For master's and Ed S, GRE General Test; for doctorate, GRE General Test, interview, minimum graduate GPA of 3.2. *Application fee:* $25 ($35 for international students).

**Expenses:** Tuition, state resident: full-time $4,068; part-time $2,542. Tuition, nonresident: full-time $10,944; part-time $6,462. Required fees: $1,000; $500 per term.

**Financial support:** Application deadline: 3/1.

Dr. Betty Gridley, Head, 785-285-8500, *Fax:* 785-285-3653. *Web site:* http://www.bsu.edu/teachers/departments/edpsy/

# ■ BARRY UNIVERSITY

**School of Arts and Sciences, Department of Psychology, Miami Shores, FL 33161-6695**

**AWARDS** Clinical psychology (MS); school psychology (MS, SSP). Part-time and evening/weekend programs available.

**Faculty:** 9 full-time (5 women).

**Students:** 61. Average age 29. In 2001, 32 master's, 7 other advanced degrees awarded.

**Degree requirements:** For master's, thesis, practicum.

**Entrance requirements:** For master's, GRE General Test, minimum GPA of 3.0, previous course work in psychology. *Application deadline:* Applications are processed on a rolling basis. *Application fee:* $30. Electronic applications accepted.

**Expenses:** Tuition: Full-time $12,480. Tuition and fees vary according to degree level and program.

**Financial support:** In 2001–02, 38 students received support, including 5 research assistantships with partial tuition reimbursements available (averaging $3,000 per year); career-related internships or fieldwork and tuition waivers (partial) also available. Support available to part-time students. Financial award application deadline: 5/1; financial award applicants required to submit FAFSA.

**Faculty research:** Closed head injury, memory and aging, infant/mother interaction, evolutionary aspects of behavior, gender roles.

Dr. Linda Peterson, Chair, 305-899-3274, *Fax:* 305-899-3279, *E-mail:* lpeterson@ mail.barry.edu.

**Application contact:** Dave Fletcher, Director of Graduate Admissions, 305-899-3113, *Fax:* 305-899-2971, *E-mail:* dfletcher@mail.barry.edu.

# ■ BOWLING GREEN STATE UNIVERSITY

**Graduate College, College of Education and Human Development, School of Education and Intervention Services, Intervention Services Division, Program in School Psychology, Bowling Green, OH 43403**

**AWARDS** M Ed, SP. Part-time programs available.

**Students:** 21 full-time (18 women), 3 part-time (2 women); includes 2 minority (both African Americans), 1 international. Average age 29. 30 applicants, 67% accepted, 7 enrolled. In 2001, 10 degrees awarded.

**Degree requirements:** For master's, thesis or alternative, internship.

**Entrance requirements:** For master's, GRE General Test, TOEFL. *Application deadline:* Applications are processed on a

rolling basis. *Application fee:* $30. Electronic applications accepted.

**Expenses:** Tuition, state resident: full-time $7,376; part-time $342 per credit hour. Tuition, nonresident: full-time $13,628; part-time $640 per credit hour.

**Financial support:** In 2001–02, 12 research assistantships with full tuition reimbursements (averaging $4,062 per year) were awarded; teaching assistantships with full tuition reimbursements, career-related internships or fieldwork, Federal Work-Study, and unspecified assistantships also available. Financial award applicants required to submit FAFSA.

**Faculty research:** Family therapists/ multicultural issues, pre-school readiness skills, family relations, multifaceted evaluation, multidisciplinary decision-making.

**Application contact:** Dr. Audrey Ellenwood, Graduate Coordinator, 419-372-9848.

# ■ BRIGHAM YOUNG UNIVERSITY

**Graduate Studies, David O. McKay School of Education, Department of Counseling Psychology and Special Education, Provo, UT 84602-1001**

**AWARDS** Counseling and school psychology (MS); counseling psychology (PhD); special education (MS).

**Faculty:** 15 full-time (8 women), 7 part-time/adjunct (2 women).

**Students:** 57 full-time (37 women), 14 part-time (9 women); includes 5 minority (1 African American, 3 Asian Americans or Pacific Islanders, 1 Hispanic American), 4 international. Average age 31. 77 applicants, 31% accepted, 24 enrolled. In 2001, 14 master's, 3 doctorates awarded.

**Degree requirements:** For master's, thesis optional; for doctorate, thesis/ dissertation, comprehensive exam. *Median time to degree:* Master's–2.3 years full-time; doctorate–4.8 years full-time.

**Entrance requirements:** For master's, GRE General Test or MAT, minimum GPA of 3.0 in last 60 hours; for doctorate, GRE General Test, minimum GPA of 3.4 in last 60 hours. *Application deadline:* For fall admission, 2/1. *Application fee:* $50. Electronic applications accepted.

**Expenses:** Tuition: Full-time $3,860; part-time $214 per hour.

**Financial support:** In 2001–02, 42 students received support, including 20 research assistantships with partial tuition reimbursements available (averaging $5,500 per year), 3 teaching assistantships with partial tuition reimbursements available (averaging $5,500 per year); career-related internships or fieldwork, institutionally sponsored loans, and tuition waivers (partial) also available.

**Faculty research:** Values and mental health, distance education, career counselors, special education.

Dr. Ronald D. Bingham, Chair, 801-422-3857, *Fax:* 801-422-0198, *E-mail:* ron_ bingham@byu.edu.

**Application contact:** Diane E. Hancock, Executive Secretary, 801-422-3859, *Fax:* 801-422-0198, *E-mail:* diane_hancock@ byu.edu. *Web site:* http://www.byu.edu/cse/

# ■ BROOKLYN COLLEGE OF THE CITY UNIVERSITY OF NEW YORK

**Division of Graduate Studies, School of Education, Program in School Psychology, Brooklyn, NY 11210-2889**

**AWARDS** School psychology (MS Ed, CAS); school psychology-bilingual (CAS). Part-time and evening/weekend programs available.

**Students:** 26 full-time (24 women), 73 part-time (60 women); includes 35 minority (18 African Americans, 2 Asian Americans or Pacific Islanders, 15 Hispanic Americans). 87 applicants, 38% accepted. In 2001, 21 master's, 19 CASs awarded.

**Degree requirements:** For master's, internship.

**Entrance requirements:** For master's, TOEFL, GRE or liberal arts and sciences test, interview, previous course work in education and psychology, teaching certificate; for CAS, master's degree, teaching experience. *Application deadline:* For fall admission, 3/1; for spring admission, 11/1. *Application fee:* $40.

**Expenses:** Tuition, state resident: full-time $4,350; part-time $185 per credit. Tuition, nonresident: full-time $7,600; part-time $320 per credit.

**Financial support:** Career-related internships or fieldwork, Federal Work-Study, institutionally sponsored loans, scholarships/grants, and tuition waivers (partial) available. Support available to part-time students. Financial award application deadline: 5/1; financial award applicants required to submit FAFSA.

Dr. Laura Barbanel, Head, 718-951-5876, *Fax:* 718-951-4816.

**Application contact:** Michael Lovaglio, Assistant Director of Graduate Admissions, 718-951-5914, *E-mail:* adminqry@ brooklyn.cuny.edu.

# ■ BUCKNELL UNIVERSITY

**Graduate Studies, College of Arts and Sciences, Department of Education, Specialization in School Psychology, Lewisburg, PA 17837**

**AWARDS** MS Ed.

**Degree requirements:** For master's, thesis or alternative.

**Entrance requirements:** For master's, GRE General Test, TOEFL, minimum GPA of 2.8. *Application deadline:* For fall admission, 6/1 (priority date); for spring admission, 12/1 (priority date). Applications are processed on a rolling basis. *Application fee:* $25.
**Expenses:** Tuition: Part-time $2,875 per course.
**Financial support:** Unspecified assistantships available. Financial award application deadline: 3/1.

## ■ CALIFORNIA STATE UNIVERSITY, LOS ANGELES

**Graduate Studies, Charter College of Education, Division of Administration and Counseling, Major in Counseling, Los Angeles, CA 90032-8530**

**AWARDS** Applied behavior analysis (MS); community college counseling (MS); rehabilitation counseling (MS); school counseling and school psychology (MS). Part-time and evening/weekend programs available.

**Students:** 186 full-time (136 women), 120 part-time (89 women); includes 224 minority (29 African Americans, 31 Asian Americans or Pacific Islanders, 160 Hispanic Americans, 4 Native Americans), 2 international. In 2001, 70 degrees awarded.
**Degree requirements:** For master's, project, or thesis.
**Entrance requirements:** For master's, TOEFL, interview, minimum GPA of 2.75 in last 90 units, teaching certificate. *Application deadline:* For fall admission, 6/30; for spring admission, 2/1. Applications are processed on a rolling basis. *Application fee:* $55.
**Expenses:** Tuition, nonresident: part-time $164 per unit.
**Financial support:** Career-related internships or fieldwork and Federal Work-Study available. Support available to part-time students. Financial award application deadline: 3/1.
Dr. Marcee Soriano, Chair, Division of Administration and Counseling, 323-343-4250.

## ■ CALIFORNIA STATE UNIVERSITY, SACRAMENTO

**Graduate Studies, College of Education, Department of Special Education, Rehabilitation, and School Psychology, Sacramento, CA 95819-6048**

**AWARDS** School psychology (MS); special education (MA); vocational rehabilitation (MS). Part-time programs available.

**Students:** 156 full-time (128 women), 210 part-time (170 women); includes 47 minority (14 African Americans, 14 Asian Americans or Pacific Islanders, 16 Hispanic Americans, 3 Native Americans), 2 international.
**Degree requirements:** For master's, thesis or alternative, writing proficiency exam.
**Entrance requirements:** For master's, TOEFL, minimum GPA of 2.5. *Application fee:* $55.
**Expenses:** Tuition, state resident: full-time $1,965; part-time $668 per semester. Tuition, nonresident: part-time $246 per unit.
**Financial support:** Career-related internships or fieldwork and Federal Work-Study available. Support available to part-time students. Financial award application deadline: 3/1.
Dr. William Harris, Chair, 916-278-6622.

## ■ CALIFORNIA UNIVERSITY OF PENNSYLVANIA

**School of Graduate Studies, School of Education, Program in School Psychology, California, PA 15419-1394**

**AWARDS** MS. Part-time and evening/weekend programs available.

**Faculty:** 8 part-time/adjunct (3 women).
**Students:** 27 full-time (all women), 8 part-time (4 women). In 2001, 14 degrees awarded.
**Degree requirements:** For master's, internship, thesis optional.
**Entrance requirements:** For master's, TOEFL, MAT or minimum GPA of 3.0; work experience in psychology. *Application deadline:* Applications are processed on a rolling basis. *Application fee:* $25.
**Expenses:** Tuition, state resident: full-time $4,600. Tuition, nonresident: full-time $7,554.
**Financial support:** Tuition waivers (full) and unspecified assistantships available.
Dr. Kirk John, Coordinator, 724-938-4100, *E-mail:* john@cup.edu. *Web site:* http://www.cup.edu/graduate

## ■ CARLOS ALBIZU UNIVERSITY, MIAMI CAMPUS

**Graduate Programs, Miami, FL 33172-2209**

**AWARDS** Clinical psychology (Psy D); industrial/organizational psychology (MS); management (MBA); marriage and family therapy (MS); mental health counseling (MS); psychology (MS); school counseling (MS). Part-time and evening/weekend programs available.

**Faculty:** 19 full-time (9 women), 37 part-time/adjunct (19 women).

**Students:** 432 full-time (322 women), 32 part-time (22 women); includes 328 minority (58 African Americans, 7 Asian Americans or Pacific Islanders, 263 Hispanic Americans), 4 international. Average age 35. 189 applicants, 50% accepted, 69 enrolled. In 2001, 44 master's, 69 doctorates awarded. Terminal master's awarded for partial completion of doctoral program.
**Degree requirements:** For master's, one foreign language, comprehensive exam, integrative project (MBA); for doctorate, one foreign language, thesis/dissertation, written and oral qualifying exam, internship.
**Entrance requirements:** For master's, GMAT (MBA), letters of recommendation (3), interview, minimum GPA of 3.0, resumé; for doctorate, GRE General Test, GRE Subject Test, letters of recommendation (3), minimum GPA of 3.0. *Application deadline:* For fall admission, 8/1 (priority date); for spring admission, 11/30 (priority date). Applications are processed on a rolling basis. *Application fee:* $50.
**Expenses:** Tuition: Part-time $455 per credit. Required fees: $819; $273 per term. Tuition and fees vary according to course load and degree level.
**Financial support:** In 2001–02, 22 students received support. Federal Work-Study and scholarships/grants available. Financial award application deadline: 6/1; financial award applicants required to submit FAFSA.
**Faculty research:** Culture, psychodiagnostics, psychotherapy, forensic psychology, neuropsychology; marketing strategy, entrepreneurship.
Dr. Gerardo F. Rodriquez-Menedez, Chancellor, 305-593-1223 Ext. 120, *Fax:* 305-629-8052, *E-mail:* grodriguez@albizu.edu.
**Application contact:** Miriam Matos, Admissions Officer, 305-593-1223 Ext. 134, *Fax:* 305-593-1854, *E-mail:* mmatos@albizu.edu. *Web site:* http://www.albizu.edu/

## ■ CENTRAL CONNECTICUT STATE UNIVERSITY

**School of Graduate Studies, School of Education and Professional Studies, Department of Health and Human Service Professions, New Britain, CT 06050-4010**

**AWARDS** Marriage and family therapy (MS); rehabilitation/mental counseling (MS); school counseling (MS); student development in higher education (MS). Part-time and evening/weekend programs available.

**Faculty:** 11 full-time (8 women), 9 part-time/adjunct (6 women).

*Central Connecticut State University (continued)*

**Students:** 68 full-time (48 women), 199 part-time (160 women); includes 39 minority (20 African Americans, 4 Asian Americans or Pacific Islanders, 13 Hispanic Americans, 2 Native Americans). Average age 34. 72 applicants, 69% accepted. In 2001, 66 degrees awarded.

**Degree requirements:** For master's, thesis or alternative, special project.

**Entrance requirements:** For master's, TOEFL, minimum GPA of 2.7. *Application deadline:* For fall admission, 8/10 (priority date); for spring admission, 12/10. Applications are processed on a rolling basis. *Application fee:* $40.

**Expenses:** Tuition, state resident: full-time $2,772; part-time $245 per credit. Tuition, nonresident: full-time $7,726; part-time $245 per credit. Required fees: $2,102. Tuition and fees vary according to course level and degree level.

**Financial support:** In 2001–02, 2 research assistantships were awarded; career-related internships or fieldwork and Federal Work-Study also available. Financial award application deadline: 3/15; financial award applicants required to submit FAFSA.

**Faculty research:** Elementary/secondary school counseling, marriage/family therapy, rehabilitation counseling, counseling in higher educational settings.

Dr. James Malley, Chair, 860-832-2117.

## ■ CENTRAL MICHIGAN UNIVERSITY

**College of Graduate Studies, College of Humanities and Social and Behavioral Sciences, Department of Psychology, Program in School Psychology, Mount Pleasant, MI 48859**

**AWARDS** PhD, S Psy S.

**Degree requirements:** For doctorate, thesis/dissertation or alternative; for S Psy S, thesis.

**Entrance requirements:** For doctorate, GRE.

**Expenses:** Tuition, state resident: part-time $182 per unit. Tuition, nonresident: part-time $182 per unit. Required fees: $208 per semester. Part-time tuition and fees vary according to course load.

**Faculty research:** Psychology and education foundations, psychology and education assessment, intervention strategies.

## ■ CENTRAL WASHINGTON UNIVERSITY

**Graduate Studies and Research, College of the Sciences, Department of Psychology, Program in School Psychology, Ellensburg, WA 98926-7463**

**AWARDS** M Ed.

**Faculty:** 23 full-time (9 women).

**Students:** 13 full-time (10 women), 3 part-time (2 women); includes 1 minority (Hispanic American). 18 applicants, 56% accepted, 10 enrolled. In 2001, 5 degrees awarded.

**Degree requirements:** For master's, thesis, internship.

**Entrance requirements:** For master's, GRE General Test, minimum GPA of 3.0. *Application deadline:* For fall admission, 4/1 (priority date). Applications are processed on a rolling basis. *Application fee:* $35.

**Expenses:** Tuition, state resident: full-time $4,848; part-time $162 per credit. Tuition, nonresident: full-time $14,772; part-time $492 per credit. Required fees: $324.

**Financial support:** In 2001–02, 6 research assistantships with partial tuition reimbursements (averaging $7,120 per year) were awarded; career-related internships or fieldwork and Federal Work-Study also available. Financial award application deadline: 3/1; financial award applicants required to submit FAFSA.

**Application contact:** Barbara Sisko, Office Assistant, Graduate Studies and Research, 509-963-3103, *Fax:* 509-963-1799, *E-mail:* masters@cwu.edu. *Web site:* http://www.cwu.edu/

## ■ THE CITADEL, THE MILITARY COLLEGE OF SOUTH CAROLINA

**College of Graduate and Professional Studies, Department of Education, Program in School Psychology, Charleston, SC 29409**

**AWARDS** Ed S. Part-time and evening/weekend programs available.

**Students:** 34 full-time (30 women), 28 part-time (22 women); includes 12 minority (10 African Americans, 2 Asian Americans or Pacific Islanders). Average age 29. In 2001, 7 Ed Ss awarded.

**Entrance requirements:** For degree, GRE General Test. *Application deadline:* For fall admission, 3/15; for spring admission, 10/15. Applications are processed on a rolling basis. *Application fee:* $25.

**Expenses:** Tuition, state resident: full-time $1,314; part-time $141 per credit hour. Tuition, nonresident: full-time $2,619; part-time $285 per credit hour.

**Financial support:** In 2001–02, 5 students received support; research assistantships, teaching assistantships, career-related internships or fieldwork available.

**Faculty research:** Childhood depression, violence against women, developmental disorders, eyewitness testimony.

Dr. Michael Politano, Coordinator, 843-953-5321, *Fax:* 843-953-7084, *E-mail:* politano@citadel.edu.

**Application contact:** Patricia Ezell, Assistant Dean, College of Graduate and Professional Studies, 843-953-5089, *Fax:* 843-953-7630, *E-mail:* ezellp@citadel.edu. *Web site:* http://www.citadel.edu/

## ■ CITY UNIVERSITY

**Graduate Division, Gordon Albright School of Education, Bellevue, WA 98005**

**AWARDS** Curriculum and instruction (M Ed); education technology (M Ed); educational leadership and principal certification (M Ed, Certificate); guidance and counseling (M Ed); professional certification-teachers (Certificate); reading and literacy (M Ed); teacher certification (MIT, Certificate). Part-time and evening/weekend programs available. Postbaccalaureate distance learning degree programs offered (no on-campus study).

**Faculty:** 23 full-time (13 women), 345 part-time/adjunct (212 women).

**Students:** 540 full-time, 981 part-time; includes 125 minority (47 African Americans, 37 Asian Americans or Pacific Islanders, 24 Hispanic Americans, 17 Native Americans). Average age 36. 645 applicants, 100% accepted, 217 enrolled. In 2001, 612 degrees awarded.

**Degree requirements:** For master's, thesis (for some programs). *Application deadline:* Applications are processed on a rolling basis. *Application fee:* $75 ($175 for international students). Electronic applications accepted.

**Expenses:** Tuition: Part-time $324 per credit.

**Financial support:** In 2001–02, 77 students received support. Federal Work-Study available. Support available to part-time students. Financial award applicants required to submit FAFSA.

Dr. Margaret M. Davis, Dean, 425-637-1010 Ext. 5412, *Fax:* 425-709-5363, *E-mail:* mdavis@cityu.edu.

**Application contact:** 800-426-5596, *Fax:* 425-709-5363, *E-mail:* info@cityu.edu. *Web site:* http://www.cityu.edu/

## ■ CLEVELAND STATE UNIVERSITY

**College of Graduate Studies, College of Arts and Sciences, Department of Psychology, School Psychology Program, Cleveland, OH 44115**

**AWARDS** Psy S.

**Faculty:** 17 full-time (6 women), 4 part-time/adjunct (1 woman).
**Students:** 18 full-time (12 women); includes 1 minority (African American). Average age 24. 50 applicants, 14% accepted, 7 enrolled. In 2001, 8 degrees awarded.
**Degree requirements:** For Psy S, thesis optional. *Median time to degree:* 3 years full-time.
**Entrance requirements:** For degree, GRE General Test, GRE Subject Test. *Application fee:* $25 ($50 for international students).
**Expenses:** Tuition, state resident: full-time $6,838; part-time $263 per credit hour. Tuition, nonresident: full-time $13,526; part-time $520 per credit hour.
**Financial support:** In 2001–02, 7 students received support. Federal Work-Study and tuition waivers (full) available. Financial award applicants required to submit FAFSA.
Dr. Kathy McNamara, Director, 216-687-2521, *Fax:* 216-687-9294.

■ **THE COLLEGE OF NEW ROCHELLE**

**Graduate School, Division of Human Services, Program in Community-School Psychology, New Rochelle, NY 10805-2308**
AWARDS MS.

**Degree requirements:** For master's, clinical fieldwork, journal.
**Entrance requirements:** For master's, interview, minimum GPA of 3.0, previous course work in psychology, sample of written work.

■ **COLLEGE OF ST. JOSEPH**

**Graduate Program, Division of Psychology and Human Services, Program in School Guidance Counseling, Rutland, VT 05701-3899**
AWARDS MS.

**Faculty:** 3 full-time (0 women), 6 part-time/adjunct (3 women).
**Students:** 4 full-time, 4 part-time; includes 1 minority (Asian American or Pacific Islander). Average age 34.
**Degree requirements:** For master's, thesis optional.
**Entrance requirements:** For master's, GRE General Test, interview. *Application fee:* $35.
**Expenses:** Tuition: Full-time $9,000; part-time $250 per credit. Required fees: $45 per semester. Part-time tuition and fees vary according to course load.
**Financial support:** Unspecified assistantships available. Financial award application deadline: 3/1.

**Application contact:** Steve Soba, Dean of Admissions, 802-773-5900 Ext. 3206, *Fax:* 802-773-5900, *E-mail:* ssoba@csj.edu.

■ **THE COLLEGE OF SAINT ROSE**

**Graduate Studies, School of Education, Educational and School Psychology Department, Program in School Psychology, Albany, NY 12203-1419**
AWARDS MS Ed, Certificate. Part-time and evening/weekend programs available.

**Faculty:** 8 full-time (4 women).
**Students:** 39 full-time (31 women), 38 part-time (29 women); includes 4 minority (2 Hispanic Americans, 2 Native Americans), 1 international. Average age 26. 32 applicants, 100% accepted, 26 enrolled. In 2001, 15 master's, 6 Certificates awarded.
**Degree requirements:** For master's, thesis or alternative, comprehensive exam.
**Entrance requirements:** For master's, minimum undergraduate GPA of 3.0. *Application deadline:* For fall admission, 7/15 (priority date); for spring admission, 12/1 (priority date). Applications are processed on a rolling basis. *Application fee:* $30.
**Expenses:** Tuition: Full-time $8,712. Required fees: $190.
**Financial support:** Research assistantships, tuition waivers (partial) available. Support available to part-time students. Financial award application deadline: 3/1; financial award applicants required to submit FAFSA.
Dr. Gerald Fishman, Head, 518-454-5261. **Application contact:** 518-454-5136, *Fax:* 518-458-5479, *E-mail:* ace@ mail.strose.edu.

■ **THE COLLEGE OF WILLIAM AND MARY**

**School of Education, Program in School Psychology, Williamsburg, VA 23187-8795**
AWARDS M Ed, Ed S.

**Faculty:** 4 full-time (2 women), 2 part-time/adjunct (both women).
**Students:** 20 full-time (15 women), 12 part-time (10 women); includes 2 minority (1 African American, 1 Asian American or Pacific Islander), 2 international. Average age 26. 74 applicants, 45% accepted, 19 enrolled. In 2001, 8 master's, 11 other advanced degrees awarded.
**Degree requirements:** For Ed S, internship. *Median time to degree:* Master's–1 year full-time; Ed S–2 years full-time.
**Entrance requirements:** For master's, GRE, minimum GPA of 3.0; for Ed S,

GRE, minimum GPA of 3.5. *Application deadline:* For fall admission, 2/1. *Application fee:* $30.
**Expenses:** Tuition, state resident: full-time $3,262; part-time $175 per credit hour. Tuition, nonresident: full-time $14,768; part-time $550 per credit hour. Required fees: $2,478.
**Financial support:** In 2001–02, 19 research assistantships (averaging $8,000 per year) were awarded; career-related internships or fieldwork, Federal Work-Study, institutionally sponsored loans, scholarships/grants, and unspecified assistantships also available. Financial award application deadline: 2/1; financial award applicants required to submit FAFSA.
**Faculty research:** Home schooling, gifted preschoolers, inclusive schools, ability testing.
Dr. Sandra Ward, Area Coordinator, 757-221-2326, *E-mail:* scbrub@wm.edu.
**Application contact:** Patricia Burleson, Director of Admissions, 757-221-2317, *E-mail:* paburl@wm.edu. *Web site:* http:// www.wm.edu/education/

■ **DUQUESNE UNIVERSITY**

**School of Education, Department of Counseling, Psychology, and Special Education, Program in School Psychology, Pittsburgh, PA 15282-0001**
AWARDS MS Ed, CAGS. Part-time and evening/weekend programs available.

**Degree requirements:** For master's, thesis optional.
**Entrance requirements:** For master's, MAT, minimum GPA of 2.50; for CAGS, MAT, interview.
**Expenses:** Tuition: Part-time $566 per credit. Required fees: $56 per credit. Part-time tuition and fees vary according to degree level and program.
**Faculty research:** Neuropsychology.

■ **EAST CAROLINA UNIVERSITY**

**Graduate School, College of Arts and Sciences, Department of Psychology, Program in School Psychology, Greenville, NC 27858-4353**
AWARDS MA/CAS. Part-time and evening/ weekend programs available.

**Students:** 16 full-time (all women), 5 part-time (all women), 2 international. Average age 28. 30 applicants, 37% accepted. *Application deadline:* For fall admission, 3/15 (priority date). Applications are processed on a rolling basis. *Application fee:* $45.
**Expenses:** Tuition, state resident: full-time $2,636. Tuition, nonresident: full-time $11,365.

*East Carolina University (continued)*
**Financial support:** Available to part-time students. Application deadline: 6/1. Dr. Michael Brown, Interim Chairperson, 252-328-6800, *Fax:* 252-328-6283. **Application contact:** Dr. Paul D. Tschetter, Senior Associate Dean of the Graduate School, 252-328-6012, *Fax:* 252-328-6071, *E-mail:* gradschool@ mail.ecu.edu.

## ■ EASTERN ILLINOIS UNIVERSITY

**Graduate School, College of Sciences, Department of Psychology, Program in School Psychology, Charleston, IL 61920-3099**
**AWARDS** SSP.

**Degree requirements:** For SSP, thesis.
**Entrance requirements:** For degree, GRE General Test.

## ■ EASTERN KENTUCKY UNIVERSITY

**The Graduate School, College of Arts and Sciences, Department of Psychology, Richmond, KY 40475-3102**
**AWARDS** Clinical psychology (MS); industrial/organizational psychology (MS); school psychology (Psy S). Part-time programs available.

**Faculty:** 21 full-time (10 women).
**Students:** 66 full-time (58 women), 4 part-time (2 women); includes 4 minority (3 African Americans, 1 Hispanic American). Average age 24. 303 applicants, 30% accepted. In 2001, 20 degrees awarded.
**Entrance requirements:** For master's and Psy S, GRE General Test, minimum GPA of 2.5. *Application deadline:* For fall admission, 3/15 (priority date). Applications are processed on a rolling basis. *Application fee:* $0.
**Expenses:** Tuition, state resident: full-time $1,468; part-time $165 per credit hour. Tuition, nonresident: full-time $4,034; part-time $450 per credit hour.
**Financial support:** In 2001–02, 30 students received support, including 16 research assistantships, 10 teaching assistantships; career-related internships or fieldwork and Federal Work-Study also available. Support available to part-time students.
**Faculty research:** Cognitive behavior therapy, therapy with the deaf, victims of drunk drivers, autism. *Total annual research expenditures:* $40,000.
Dr. Robert M. Adams, Chair, 859-622-1105, *Fax:* 859-622-5871, *E-mail:* robert.adams@eku.edu. *Web site:* http://www.psychology.eku.edu/

## ■ EASTERN WASHINGTON UNIVERSITY

**Graduate School Studies, College of Education and Human Development, Department of Counseling, Educational, and Developmental Psychology, Cheney, WA 99004-2431**
**AWARDS** Developing psychology (MS); school counseling (MS), including counseling psychology, school counseling; school psychology (MS); special education (M Ed).
**Faculty:** 14 full-time (5 women).
**Students:** 62 full-time (53 women), 13 part-time (11 women); includes 3 minority (1 African American, 2 Asian Americans or Pacific Islanders), 3 international. 48 applicants, 67% accepted, 27 enrolled. In 2001, 30 degrees awarded.
**Degree requirements:** For master's, thesis or alternative, comprehensive exam.
**Entrance requirements:** For master's, GRE General Test, minimum GPA of 3.0. *Application deadline:* For fall admission, 2/1. Applications are processed on a rolling basis. *Application fee:* $35.
**Expenses:** Tuition, state resident: full-time $1,586; part-time $159 per credit hour. Tuition, nonresident: full-time $4,677; part-time $468 per credit hour. Required fees: $222; $159 per credit. $74 per quarter.
**Financial support:** In 2001–02, 4 teaching assistantships with partial tuition reimbursements (averaging $7,000 per year) were awarded; career-related internships or fieldwork, Federal Work-Study, institutionally sponsored loans, scholarships/grants, health care benefits, tuition waivers (partial), and unspecified assistantships also available. Support available to part-time students. Financial award application deadline: 2/1; financial award applicants required to submit FAFSA. Dr. Armin Arndt, Chair, 509-359-2827, *Fax:* 509-359-4366. *Web site:* http://www.appliedpsyc.ewu.edu

## ■ EASTERN WASHINGTON UNIVERSITY

**Graduate School Studies, College of Social and Behavioral Sciences, Department of Psychology, Cheney, WA 99004-2431**
**AWARDS** Psychology (MS); school psychology (MS).
**Faculty:** 9 full-time (2 women).
**Students:** 27 full-time (18 women), 6 part-time (3 women); includes 2 minority (1 Asian American or Pacific Islander, 1 Native American). 23 applicants, 87% accepted, 14 enrolled. In 2001, 10 degrees awarded.
**Degree requirements:** For master's, thesis or alternative, comprehensive exam.

**Entrance requirements:** For master's, GRE General Test, minimum GPA of 3.0. *Application deadline:* For fall admission, 3/1. Applications are processed on a rolling basis. *Application fee:* $35.
**Expenses:** Tuition, state resident: full-time $1,586; part-time $159 per credit hour. Tuition, nonresident: full-time $4,677; part-time $468 per credit hour. Required fees: $222; $159 per credit. $74 per quarter.
**Financial support:** In 2001–02, 8 teaching assistantships with partial tuition reimbursements (averaging $7,000 per year) were awarded; career-related internships or fieldwork, Federal Work-Study, institutionally sponsored loans, scholarships/grants, health care benefits, tuition waivers (partial), and unspecified assistantships also available. Support available to part-time students. Financial award application deadline: 2/1; financial award applicants required to submit FAFSA.
**Application contact:** Dr. Mahlon Dalley, Chair, 509-359-6174, *Fax:* 509-359-6325.

## ■ EDINBORO UNIVERSITY OF PENNSYLVANIA

**Graduate Studies, School of Education, Department of Special Education and School Psychology, Program in School Psychology, Edinboro, PA 16444**
**AWARDS** Certificate. Evening/weekend programs available.

**Students:** 16 full-time (13 women), 6 part-time (all women); includes 1 minority (African American), 2 international. Average age 30.
**Degree requirements:** For Certificate, competency exam.
**Entrance requirements:** For degree, GRE or MAT, master's degree in educational psychology or related field, minimum QPA of 2.5. *Application deadline:* Applications are processed on a rolling basis. *Application fee:* $25. Electronic applications accepted.
**Expenses:** Tuition, state resident: full-time $4,600; part-time $256 per credit. Tuition, nonresident: full-time $7,554; part-time $420 per credit. Required fees: $68 per credit.
**Financial support:** In 2001–02, 3 students received support. Career-related internships or fieldwork, Federal Work-Study, institutionally sponsored loans, scholarships/grants, and unspecified assistantships available. Support available to part-time students. Financial award application deadline: 5/1; financial award applicants required to submit FAFSA. Dr. Joel Erion, Coordinator, 814-732-2287, *Fax:* 814-732-2268, *E-mail:* jerion@ edinboro.edu.

Application contact: Dr. Mary Margaret Bevevino, Dean of Graduate Studies, 814-732-2856, *Fax:* 814-732-2611, *E-mail:* mbevevino@edinboro.edu.

■ **EMPORIA STATE UNIVERSITY**

**School of Graduate Studies, The Teachers College, Department of Psychology and Special Education, Program in School Psychology, Emporia, KS 66801-5087**

**AWARDS** MS, Ed S.

**Students:** 13 full-time (12 women), 10 part-time (6 women); includes 2 minority (both African Americans). 8 applicants, 63% accepted. In 2001, 4 master's, 8 other advanced degrees awarded.

**Degree requirements:** For master's, comprehensive exam or thesis; for Ed S, thesis or alternative.

**Entrance requirements:** For master's, GRE General Test or MAT, TOEFL. *Application deadline:* For fall admission, 8/15 (priority date). Applications are processed on a rolling basis. *Application fee:* $30 ($75 for international students). Electronic applications accepted.

**Expenses:** Tuition, state resident: full-time $2,632; part-time $119 per credit hour. Tuition, nonresident: full-time $6,734; part-time $290 per credit hour.

**Financial support:** Career-related internships or fieldwork, Federal Work-Study, institutionally sponsored loans, health care benefits, and unspecified assistantships available. Financial award application deadline: 3/15; financial award applicants required to submit FAFSA.

Dr. Kenneth A. Weaver, Chair, Department of Psychology and Special Education, 620-341-5317, *E-mail:* weaverke@emporia.edu.

■ **FAIRFIELD UNIVERSITY**

**Graduate School of Education and Allied Professions, Department of Psychology and Special Education, Fairfield, CT 06824**

**AWARDS** Applied psychology (MA); school psychology (MA, CAS); special education (MA, CAS). Part-time and evening/weekend programs available.

**Faculty:** 4 full-time (2 women), 9 part-time/adjunct (4 women).

**Students:** 34 full-time (24 women), 103 part-time (88 women); includes 19 minority (4 African Americans, 2 Asian Americans or Pacific Islanders, 13 Hispanic Americans), 3 international. Average age 28. 91 applicants, 69% accepted, 45 enrolled. In 2001, 39 master's, 9 other advanced degrees awarded.

**Degree requirements:** For master's, educational technology course required.

**Entrance requirements:** For master's, PRAXIS I (CBT), TOEFL, minimum QPA of 2.67. *Application deadline:* Applications are processed on a rolling basis. *Application fee:* $55. Electronic applications accepted.

**Expenses:** Tuition: Full-time $9,550; part-time $390 per credit hour. Required fees: $25 per term. Tuition and fees vary according to program.

**Financial support:** Scholarships/grants, tuition waivers (partial), and unspecified assistantships available. Support available to part-time students. Financial award applicants required to submit FAFSA.

**Faculty research:** School university collaboration, special education consultation, child neuropsychology, disabilities, effect of pretreatment orientation on treatment. Dr. Daniel Geller, Chair, 203-254-4000 Ext. 2324, *Fax:* 203-254-4047, *E-mail:* dgeller@fair1.fairfield.edu.

**Application contact:** Karen L Creecy, Assistant Dean, 203-254-4000 Ext. 2414, *Fax:* 203-254-4241, *E-mail:* klcreecy@mail.fairfield.edu. *Web site:* http://www.fairfield.edu/

■ **FAIRLEIGH DICKINSON UNIVERSITY, METROPOLITAN CAMPUS**

**University College: Arts, Sciences, and Professional Studies, School of Psychology, Program in School Psychology, Teaneck, NJ 07666-1914**

**AWARDS** MA, Psy D.

**Students:** 48 full-time (36 women), 18 part-time (17 women); includes 9 minority (3 African Americans, 1 Asian American or Pacific Islander, 5 Hispanic Americans), 1 international. Average age 32. 60 applicants, 68% accepted, 16 enrolled. In 2001, 9 master's, 4 doctorates awarded. *Application deadline:* Applications are processed on a rolling basis. *Application fee:* $40.

**Expenses:** Tuition: Full-time $11,484; part-time $638 per credit. Required fees: $420; $97.

■ **FLORIDA AGRICULTURAL AND MECHANICAL UNIVERSITY**

**Division of Graduate Studies, Research, and Continuing Education, College of Arts and Sciences, Department of Psychology, Program in School Psychology, Tallahassee, FL 32307-3200**

**AWARDS** MS.

**Degree requirements:** For master's, thesis.

**Entrance requirements:** For master's, GRE General Test, minimum GPA of 3.0.

■ **FLORIDA INTERNATIONAL UNIVERSITY**

**College of Education, Department of Educational Psychology, Research, and Special Education, Program in School Psychology, Miami, FL 33199**

**AWARDS** Ed S. Part-time and evening/weekend programs available.

**Students:** 28 full-time (25 women), 26 part-time (23 women); includes 36 minority (4 African Americans, 2 Asian Americans or Pacific Islanders, 30 Hispanic Americans), 1 international. Average age 30. 27 applicants, 22% accepted, 6 enrolled. In 2001, 12 degrees awarded.

**Degree requirements:** For Ed S, internship.

**Entrance requirements:** For degree, TOEFL, GRE General Test or minimum GPA of 3.0 in last 60 undergraduate credits. *Application deadline:* For fall admission, 4/1 (priority date); for spring admission, 10/1. Applications are processed on a rolling basis. *Application fee:* $20.

**Expenses:** Tuition, state resident: full-time $2,916; part-time $162 per credit hour. Tuition, nonresident: full-time $10,245; part-time $569 per credit hour. Required fees: $168 per term.

**Financial support:** In 2001–02, 3 research assistantships were awarded

**Faculty research:** Incidence assessment, personality evaluation, psychopathology in children and adolescents, school psychology licensure, biased assessment. Dr. Patricia M. Barbetta, Chairperson, Department of Educational Psychology, Research, and Special Education, 305-348-2551, *Fax:* 305-348-4125, *E-mail:* barbetta@fiu.edu.

■ **FLORIDA STATE UNIVERSITY**

**Graduate Studies, College of Education, Department of Educational Psychology and Learning Systems, Program in School Psychology, Tallahassee, FL 32306**

**AWARDS** MS, Ed S.

**Faculty:** 2 full-time (1 woman).

**Students:** 20 full-time (14 women), 1 part-time; includes 12 minority (9 African Americans, 3 Hispanic Americans). 140 applicants, 22% accepted. In 2001, 10 degrees awarded.

**Degree requirements:** For master's, comprehensive exam; for Ed S, thesis, comprehensive exam.

**Entrance requirements:** For master's and Ed S, GRE General Test, minimum GPA of 3.0. *Application deadline:* For fall admission, 7/1 (priority date); for spring admission, 11/1. Applications are processed on a rolling basis. *Application fee:* $20.

*Florida State University (continued)*
**Expenses:** Tuition, state resident: part-time $163 per credit hour. Tuition, nonresident: part-time $570 per credit hour. Tuition and fees vary according to program.
**Financial support:** Fellowships, career-related internships or fieldwork available. Financial award applicants required to submit FAFSA.

## ■ FORDHAM UNIVERSITY

**Graduate School of Education, Division of Psychological and Educational Services, New York, NY 10023**
**AWARDS** Counseling and personnel services (MSE, Adv C); counseling psychology (PhD); educational psychology (MSE, PhD); school psychology (PhD); urban and urban bilingual school psychology (Adv C).
**Students:** 89 full-time (76 women), 307 part-time (257 women); includes 114 minority (41 African Americans, 20 Asian Americans or Pacific Islanders, 52 Hispanic Americans, 1 Native American). Average age 30. 506 applicants, 56% accepted, 111 enrolled. In 2001, 73 master's, 14 doctorates, 24 other advanced degrees awarded.
**Degree requirements:** For doctorate, thesis/dissertation.
**Entrance requirements:** For doctorate, GRE General Test. *Application fee:* $65.
**Financial support:** Applicants required to submit FAFSA.
Dr. Giselle Esquivel, Chairman, 212-636-6460.

## ■ FORT HAYS STATE UNIVERSITY

**Graduate School, College of Arts and Sciences, Department of Psychology, Program in School Psychology, Hays, KS 67601-4099**
**AWARDS** Ed S.
**Faculty:** 7 full-time (1 woman).
**Students:** 3 full-time (all women), 1 (woman) part-time. Average age 33. 7 applicants, 100% accepted. In 2001, 3 degrees awarded.
**Degree requirements:** For Ed S, thesis, comprehensive exam.
**Entrance requirements:** For degree, GRE Subject Test. *Application deadline:* For fall admission, 3/1 (priority date). Applications are processed on a rolling basis. *Application fee:* $25 ($35 for international students). Electronic applications accepted.
**Expenses:** Tuition, state resident: full-time $927; part-time $103 per credit hour. Tuition, nonresident: full-time $2,466; part-time $247 per credit hour.

**Financial support:** Research assistantships, teaching assistantships available.
Dr. Steve Duvall, Coordinator, 785-628-5855.

## ■ FRANCIS MARION UNIVERSITY

**Graduate Programs, Department of Psychology, Florence, SC 29501-0547**
**AWARDS** Applied clinical psychology (MS); applied community psychology (MS); school psychology (MS). Part-time and evening/weekend programs available.
**Faculty:** 12 full-time (3 women), 2 part-time/adjunct (1 woman).
**Students:** 57. Average age 36. In 2001, 12 degrees awarded.
**Degree requirements:** For master's, internship.
**Entrance requirements:** For master's, GRE General Test. *Application deadline:* For fall admission, 4/15; for spring admission, 10/15. Applications are processed on a rolling basis. *Application fee:* $30.
**Expenses:** Tuition, state resident: full-time $3,820; part-time $191 per semester hour. Tuition, nonresident: full-time $7,640; part-time $382 per semester hour. Required fees: $170; $4 per semester hour. $30 per semester.
**Financial support:** In 2001–02, fellowships (averaging $6,000 per year); career-related internships or fieldwork and unspecified assistantships also available. Support available to part-time students. Financial award application deadline: 3/1; financial award applicants required to submit FAFSA.
**Faculty research:** Critical thinking, spatial localization, cognition and aging, family psychology.
Dr. John R. Hester, Coordinator, 843-661-1635, *Fax:* 843-661-1628.
**Application contact:** Ginger Ridgill, Administrative Assistant, 843-661-1378, *Fax:* 843-661-1628, *E-mail:* gridgill@fmarion.edu.

## ■ FRESNO PACIFIC UNIVERSITY

**Graduate School, Programs in Education, Fresno, CA 93702-4709**
**AWARDS** Administration (MA Ed), including administrative services; foundations, curriculum and teaching (MA Ed), including curriculum and teaching, school library and information technology; language, literacy, and culture (MA Ed), including bilingual/cross-cultural education, language development, reading; mathematics/science/computer education (MA Ed), including educational technology, integrated mathematics/science education, mathematics education; multilingual contexts (MA Ed); pupil personnel (MA Ed), including school counseling, school psychology; special education (MA Ed), including learning handicapped, physical and

health impairments, severely handicapped. Part-time and evening/weekend programs available.
**Faculty:** 21 full-time (9 women), 33 part-time/adjunct (16 women).
**Students:** 45 full-time (36 women), 411 part-time (299 women); includes 88 minority (6 African Americans, 14 Asian Americans or Pacific Islanders, 65 Hispanic Americans, 3 Native Americans), 1 international. Average age 40. 114 applicants, 70% accepted, 75 enrolled. In 2001, 143 degrees awarded.
**Degree requirements:** For master's, thesis (for some programs), registration. *Median time to degree:* Master's–2 years full-time, 4 years part-time.
**Entrance requirements:** For master's, interview; GMAT, GRE, MAT, or 6 units of course work with a faculty recommendation. *Application deadline:* Applications are processed on a rolling basis. *Application fee:* $90. Electronic applications accepted.
**Expenses:** Tuition: Full-time $5,760; part-time $320 per unit. Tuition and fees vary according to course level and program.
**Financial support:** In 2001–02, 135 students received support. Career-related internships or fieldwork, scholarships/grants, and tuition waivers (full and partial) available. Support available to part-time students. Financial award applicants required to submit FAFSA.
**Application contact:** Edith D. Thiessen, Director of Graduate Admissions, 559-453-2256, *Fax:* 559-453-2001, *E-mail:* edthiess@fresno.edu.

## ■ FRESNO PACIFIC UNIVERSITY

**Graduate School, Programs in Education, Division of Pupil Personnel, Program in School Psychology, Fresno, CA 93702-4709**
**AWARDS** MA Ed. Part-time and evening/weekend programs available.
**Students:** 33 full-time (26 women), 17 part-time (all women); includes 14 minority (3 Asian Americans or Pacific Islanders, 11 Hispanic Americans). Average age 33. 10 applicants, 70% accepted, 7 enrolled. In 2001, 8 degrees awarded.
**Degree requirements:** For master's, thesis or alternative, registration. *Median time to degree:* Master's–2 years full-time, 4 years part-time.
*Application deadline:* Applications are processed on a rolling basis. *Application fee:* $90.
**Expenses:** Tuition: Full-time $5,760; part-time $320 per unit. Tuition and fees vary according to course level and program.
**Financial support:** In 2001–02, 30 students received support. Scholarships/grants and tuition waivers (full and partial)

available. Support available to part-time students. Financial award applicants required to submit FAFSA.

**Application contact:** Edith D. Thiessen, Director of Graduate Admissions, 559-453-2256, *Fax:* 559-453-2001, *E-mail:* edthiess@fresno.edu.

## ■ GALLAUDET UNIVERSITY

**The Graduate School, College of Arts and Sciences, Department of Psychology, Program in School Psychology, Washington, DC 20002-3625**

**AWARDS** Developmental psychology (MA); school psychology (Psy S).

**Degree requirements:** For master's, thesis optional.

**Entrance requirements:** For master's, GRE General Test or MAT.

## ■ GARDNER-WEBB UNIVERSITY

**Graduate School, Department of Psychology, Program in School Counseling, Boiling Springs, NC 28017**

**AWARDS** MA. Part-time and evening/weekend programs available.

**Faculty:** 5 full-time (3 women), 2 part-time/adjunct (1 woman).

**Students:** Average age 34. In 2001, 14 degrees awarded.

**Degree requirements:** For master's, comprehensive exam.

**Entrance requirements:** For master's, GRE General Test, MAT, minimum GPA of 2.7. *Application deadline:* For fall admission, 7/1 (priority date). Applications are processed on a rolling basis. *Application fee:* $25. Electronic applications accepted.

**Expenses:** Tuition: Part-time $210 per hour. Part-time tuition and fees vary according to program.

**Financial support:** Unspecified assistantships available.

Dr. Pat Partin, Coordinator, 704-406-4242, *Fax:* 704-406-4329, *E-mail:* ppartin@gardner-webb.edu.

## ■ GEORGE MASON UNIVERSITY

**College of Arts and Sciences, Department of Psychology, Program in School Psychology, Fairfax, VA 22030-4444**

**AWARDS** MA.

**Degree requirements:** For master's, internship, thesis optional.

**Entrance requirements:** For master's, GRE General Test, minimum GPA of 3.0 in last 60 hours, previous undergraduate course work in psychology. Electronic applications accepted.

**Expenses:** Tuition, state resident: full-time $3,168; part-time $132 per credit hour. Tuition, nonresident: full-time $11,280;

part-time $470 per credit hour. Required fees: $1,416; $59 per credit hour.

## ■ GEORGIA SOUTHERN UNIVERSITY

**Jack N. Averitt College of Graduate Studies, College of Education, Department of Leadership, Technology, and Human Development, Program in School Psychology, Statesboro, GA 30460**

**AWARDS** M Ed, Ed S. Part-time and evening/weekend programs available.

**Students:** 10 full-time (all women), 23 part-time (19 women); includes 7 minority (6 African Americans, 1 Hispanic American). Average age 33. 15 applicants, 73% accepted, 8 enrolled. In 2001, 7 master's, 5 other advanced degrees awarded.

**Degree requirements:** For master's and Ed S, exams.

**Entrance requirements:** For master's, GRE General Test or MAT, minimum GPA of 2.5; for Ed S, GRE General Test or MAT, minimum graduate GPA of 3.25. *Application deadline:* For fall admission, 4/1 (priority date); for spring admission, 8/15 (priority date). Applications are processed on a rolling basis. *Application fee:* $0. Electronic applications accepted.

**Expenses:** Tuition, state resident: full-time $1,746; part-time $97 per credit hour. Tuition, nonresident: full-time $6,966; part-time $387 per credit hour. Required fees: $294 per semester.

**Financial support:** In 2001–02, 13 students received support, including 4 research assistantships with partial tuition reimbursements available (averaging $4,900 per year); career-related internships or fieldwork and Federal Work-Study also available. Support available to part-time students. Financial award application deadline: 4/15; financial award applicants required to submit FAFSA.

**Application contact:** Dr. John R. Diebolt, Associate Graduate Dean, 912-681-5384, *Fax:* 912-681-0740, *E-mail:* gradschool@gasou.edu.

## ■ GEORGIA STATE UNIVERSITY

**College of Education, Department of Counseling and Psychological Services, Program in School Psychology, Atlanta, GA 30303-3083**

**AWARDS** M Ed, PhD, Ed S.

**Students:** 37 full-time (35 women), 39 part-time (37 women); includes 12 minority (11 African Americans, 1 Hispanic American). Average age 32. 55 applicants, 55% accepted. In 2001, 9 master's, 2 doctorates, 12 other advanced degrees awarded.

**Degree requirements:** For master's, comprehensive exam; for doctorate, thesis/dissertation, comprehensive exam.

**Entrance requirements:** For master's, GRE General Test, minimum GPA of 2.5; for doctorate, GRE General Test, minimum GPA of 3.3; for Ed S, GRE General Test, minimum graduate GPA of 3.25. *Application fee:* $25.

**Financial support:** Career-related internships or fieldwork and scholarships/grants available. Financial award application deadline: 4/1.

**Faculty research:** School reform, reading (early intervention), school violence.

Dr. Joanna White, Chairperson, Department of Counseling and Psychological Services, 404-651-2550.

## ■ HOFSTRA UNIVERSITY

**College of Liberal Arts and Sciences, Division of Social Sciences, Department of Psychology, Program in Clinical and School Psychology, Hempstead, NY 11549**

**AWARDS** MA, PhD, Post-Doctoral Certificate.

**Faculty:** 26 full-time (5 women), 14 part-time/adjunct (6 women).

**Students:** 59 full-time (48 women), 71 part-time (46 women); includes 4 minority (1 African American, 3 Asian Americans or Pacific Islanders). Average age 29. In 2001, 20 master's, 23 doctorates awarded.

**Degree requirements:** For doctorate, thesis/dissertation.

**Entrance requirements:** For master's, GRE General Test, GRE Subject Test; for doctorate, GRE General Test, GRE Subject Test, letters of recommendation (3), interview, minimum GPA of 3.0 in psychology. *Application deadline:* For fall admission, 2/1. *Application fee:* $40 ($75 for international students).

**Expenses:** Tuition: Full-time $12,408. Tuition and fees vary according to course load and program.

**Financial support:** Career-related internships or fieldwork available.

Dr. Kurt Salzinger, Director, 516-463-5219, *Fax:* 516-463-6052, *E-mail:* psykzs@hofstra.edu.

**Application contact:** Mary Beth Carey, Vice President of Enrollment Services, *Fax:* 516-560-7660, *E-mail:* hofstra@hofstra.edu.

## ■ HOFSTRA UNIVERSITY

**College of Liberal Arts and Sciences, Division of Social Sciences, Department of Psychology, Program in School-Community Psychology, Hempstead, NY 11549**

**AWARDS** MS, Psy D.

*Hofstra University (continued)*
**Faculty:** 26 full-time (5 women), 14 part-time/adjunct (6 women).
**Students:** 27 full-time (21 women), 59 part-time (49 women); includes 1 minority (Asian American or Pacific Islander). Average age 30. In 2001, 11 master's, 9 doctorates awarded.
**Degree requirements:** For master's, comprehensive exam; for doctorate, thesis/dissertation, comprehensive exam.
**Entrance requirements:** For master's, GRE General Test; for doctorate, GRE General Test, GRE Subject Test, interview, minimum GPA of 3.0 in psychology. *Application deadline:* Applications are processed on a rolling basis. *Application fee:* $40 ($75 for international students).
**Expenses:** Tuition: Full-time $12,408. Tuition and fees vary according to course load and program.
Dr. Robert Motta, Assistant Director, 516-463-5295, *E-mail:* psyrwm@hofstra.edu.
**Application contact:** Mary Beth Carey, Vice President of Enrollment Services, *Fax:* 516-560-7660, *E-mail:* hofstra@hofstra.edu.

■ **HOWARD UNIVERSITY**
**School of Education, Department of Human Development and Psychoeducational Studies, Program in School Psychology, Washington, DC 20059-0002**
**AWARDS** M Ed, MA, Ed D, PhD, CAGS. MA and PhD offered through the Graduate School of Arts and Sciences.

**Degree requirements:** For master's, thesis (MA), expository writing exam, practicum; for doctorate, one foreign language, thesis/dissertation, expository writing exam, internship, comprehensive exam.
**Entrance requirements:** For master's, GRE General Test, minimum GPA of 2.7; for doctorate, GRE General Test, minimum GPA of 3.4; for CAGS, GRE General Test, minimum graduate GPA of 3.0, master's degree.

■ **IDAHO STATE UNIVERSITY**
**Office of Graduate Studies, College of Education, Department of Education, Pocatello, ID 83209**
**AWARDS** Child and family studies (M Ed); curriculum and instruction (M Ed); educational administration (M Ed); human exceptionality (M Ed), including early childhood education, school psychological examiner, special education; instructional technology (M Ed); literacy (M Ed); school psychology (Ed S); special education (Ed S).
**Faculty:** 23 full-time (13 women).
**Students:** 32 full-time (28 women), 141 part-time (87 women); includes 7 minority

(1 African American, 5 Hispanic Americans, 1 Native American), 7 international. Average age 38. In 2001, 49 master's, 6 other advanced degrees awarded.
*Application fee:* $35.
**Expenses:** Tuition, area resident: Full-time $3,432. Tuition, state resident: part-time $172 per credit. Tuition, nonresident: full-time $10,196; part-time $262 per credit. International tuition: $9,672 full-time. Part-time tuition and fees vary according to course load, program and reciprocity agreements.
**Financial support:** In 2001–02, 16 teaching assistantships with full and partial tuition reimbursements (averaging $8,272 per year) were awarded
Dr. Alan Frantz, Chair, 208-282-2976. *Web site:* http://www.isu.edu/

■ **IDAHO STATE UNIVERSITY**
**Office of Graduate Studies, College of Health Professions, Department of Counseling, Department of Counseling, Pocatello, ID 83209**
**AWARDS** Counseling (Ed S); marriage and family counseling (M Coun); mental health counseling (M Coun); school counseling (M Coun); student affairs and college counseling (M Coun).
**Students:** In 2001, 13 master's, 2 other advanced degrees awarded.
**Degree requirements:** For Ed S, thesis.
**Entrance requirements:** For master's, GRE General Test, MAT, minimum GPA of 2.75; for Ed S, GRE General Test, minimum graduate GPA of 3.0. *Application deadline:* For fall admission, 2/15 (priority date). Applications are processed on a rolling basis. *Application fee:* $55.
**Expenses:** Tuition, area resident: Full-time $3,432. Tuition, state resident: part-time $172 per credit. Tuition, nonresident: full-time $10,196; part-time $262 per credit. International tuition: $9,672 full-time. Part-time tuition and fees vary according to course load, program and reciprocity agreements.
**Financial support:** In 2001–02, 15 teaching assistantships with full and partial tuition reimbursements (averaging $10,099 per year) were awarded. Financial award application deadline: 3/15.
Dr. Steve Feit, Chair, Department of Counseling, 208-282-3156.

■ **ILLINOIS STATE UNIVERSITY**
**Graduate School, College of Arts and Sciences, Department of Psychology, Program in School Psychology, Normal, IL 61790-2200**
**AWARDS** PhD, SSP.

**Students:** 33 full-time (28 women), 18 part-time (15 women); includes 5 minority (1 African American, 1 Asian American or Pacific Islander, 2 Hispanic Americans, 1 Native American), 1 international. 36 applicants, 67% accepted. In 2001, 2 doctorates, 4 other advanced degrees awarded.
**Degree requirements:** For doctorate, variable foreign language requirement, thesis/dissertation, 2 terms of residency, internship, practicum.
**Entrance requirements:** For doctorate, GRE General Test. *Application deadline:* Applications are processed on a rolling basis. *Application fee:* $30.
**Expenses:** Tuition, state resident: full-time $2,691; part-time $112 per credit hour. Tuition, nonresident: full-time $5,880; part-time $245 per credit hour. Required fees: $1,146; $48 per credit hour.
**Financial support:** In 2001–02, 25 research assistantships (averaging $5,927 per year), 19 teaching assistantships (averaging $4,993 per year) were awarded. Tuition waivers (full) also available. Financial award application deadline: 4/1.
Dr. David Barone, Chairperson, Department of Psychology, 309-438-8651. *Web site:* http://www.cas.ilstu.edu/psychology/schpsy.html/

■ **IMMACULATA UNIVERSITY**
**College of Graduate Studies, Department of Psychology, Immaculata, PA 19345**
**AWARDS** Clinical psychology (Psy D); counseling psychology (MA, Certificate), including school guidance counselor (Certificate), school psychologist (Certificate); school psychology (Psy D). Part-time and evening/weekend programs available.

**Students:** 57 full-time (45 women), 220 part-time (188 women). Average age 34. 88 applicants, 80% accepted, 41 enrolled. In 2001, 36 master's, 9 doctorates awarded.
**Degree requirements:** For master's, thesis optional; for doctorate, thesis/dissertation, comprehensive exam.
**Entrance requirements:** For master's, GRE General Test or MAT, TOEFL, minimum GPA of 3.0; for doctorate, GRE General Test, TOEFL, minimum GPA of 3.5. *Application deadline:* Applications are processed on a rolling basis. *Application fee:* $25.
**Expenses:** Tuition: Part-time $390 per credit.
**Financial support:** Application deadline: 5/1.
**Faculty research:** Supervision ethics, psychology of teaching, gender.
Dr. Jed A. Yalof, Chair, 610-647-4400 Ext. 3503, *E-mail:* jyalof@immaculate.edu.

**Application contact:** Office of Graduate Admission, 610-647-4400 Ext. 3211.

# ■ INDIANA STATE UNIVERSITY

**School of Graduate Studies, School of Education, Department of Educational and School Psychology, Terre Haute, IN 47809-1401**

**AWARDS** Educational psychology (MA, MS); school psychology (M Ed, PhD, Ed S).

**Degree requirements:** For doctorate, thesis/dissertation; for Ed S, research project.

**Entrance requirements:** For master's, GRE General Test, minimum undergraduate GPA of 2.5; for doctorate, GRE General Test, minimum graduate GPA of 3.5; for Ed S, GRE General Test, minimum graduate GPA of 3.25. Electronic applications accepted.

**Faculty research:** Cognitive behavior modification, moral development, emotional handicaps, personality assessments, human development.

# ■ INDIANA UNIVERSITY BLOOMINGTON

**School of Education, Department of Counseling and Educational Psychology, Bloomington, IN 47405**

**AWARDS** Counseling/counselor education (MS Ed, Ed D, PhD); educational psychology (MS Ed, Ed D, PhD); school psychology (Ed S). PhD offered through the University Graduate School.

**Students:** 117 full-time (90 women), 130 part-time (90 women); includes 35 minority (18 African Americans, 7 Asian Americans or Pacific Islanders, 9 Hispanic Americans, 1 Native American), 31 international. Average age 30. In 2001, 89 master's, 15 doctorates awarded. Terminal master's awarded for partial completion of doctoral program.

**Degree requirements:** For master's, thesis optional; for doctorate, thesis/dissertation; for Ed S, comprehensive exam or project.

**Entrance requirements:** For master's, doctorate, and Ed S, GRE General Test. *Application deadline:* For fall admission, 6/1; for winter admission, 11/1. Applications are processed on a rolling basis. *Application fee:* $45 ($55 for international students). Electronic applications accepted.

**Expenses:** Tuition, state resident: full-time $4,720; part-time $197 per credit. Tuition, nonresident: full-time $13,748; part-time $573 per credit. Required fees: $642.

**Financial support:** In 2001–02, 10 fellowships with partial tuition reimbursements (averaging $14,000 per year), research assistantships with partial tuition reimbursements (averaging $8,888 per

year), 25 teaching assistantships with partial tuition reimbursements (averaging $10,605 per year) were awarded. Career-related internships or fieldwork, Federal Work-Study, institutionally sponsored loans, tuition waivers (full and partial), and unspecified assistantships also available. Support available to part-time students.

**Faculty research:** Affective and maturational factors in learning complex cognitive tasks, children's strategies for representing depth, prime time evaluation, rural school psychology.

Dr. Jack Cummings, Chairperson, 812-856-8300, *Fax:* 812-856-8333.

**Application contact:** Dinorah Sapp, Department Secretary, 812-856-8300, *Fax:* 812-856-8333, *E-mail:* cep@indiana.edu. *Web site:* http://education.indiana.edu/cep/

# ■ INDIANA UNIVERSITY OF PENNSYLVANIA

**Graduate School and Research, College of Education and Educational Technology, Department of Educational and School Psychology, Program in School Psychology, Indiana, PA 15705-1087**

**AWARDS** D Ed. Part-time programs available.

**Students:** 24 full-time (14 women), 26 part-time (21 women); includes 4 minority (2 African Americans, 1 Asian American or Pacific Islander, 1 Hispanic American). Average age 38. 32 applicants, 66% accepted. In 2001, 8 degrees awarded.

**Degree requirements:** For doctorate, thesis/dissertation, comprehensive exam.

**Entrance requirements:** For doctorate, GRE General Test, GRE Subject Test, TOEFL, letters of recommendation (2). *Application deadline:* For fall admission, 1/10. Applications are processed on a rolling basis. *Application fee:* $30.

**Expenses:** Tuition, state resident: full-time $4,600; part-time $256 per credit hour. Tuition, nonresident: full-time $7,554; part-time $420 per credit hour. Required fees: $800. Part-time tuition and fees vary according to course load.

**Financial support:** In 2001–02, 2 fellowships (averaging $5,000 per year), 7 research assistantships with full and partial tuition reimbursements (averaging $6,170 per year), 5 teaching assistantships with partial tuition reimbursements (averaging $17,001 per year) were awarded. Career-related internships or fieldwork and Federal Work-Study also available. Support available to part-time students. Financial award application deadline: 3/15; financial award applicants required to submit FAFSA.

Dr. Edward Levinson, Graduate Coordinator, 724-357-3785, *E-mail:* emlevins@iup.edu.

# ■ INTER AMERICAN UNIVERSITY OF PUERTO RICO, SAN GERMÁN CAMPUS

**Graduate Programs, Department of Social Sciences, San Germán, PR 00683-5008**

**AWARDS** Counseling psychology (PhD); psychology (MA, MS); school psychology (PhD). Part-time and evening/weekend programs available.

**Faculty:** 5 full-time (4 women), 8 part-time/adjunct (4 women).

**Students:** 48 full-time (40 women), 48 part-time (41 women). In 2001, 11 degrees awarded.

**Degree requirements:** For master's and doctorate, thesis/dissertation, comprehensive exam.

**Entrance requirements:** For master's, GRE General Test or PAEG, minimum GPA of 3.0; for doctorate, GRE, PAEG or MAT, minimum GPA of 3.0. *Application deadline:* For fall admission, 4/30 (priority date); for spring admission, 11/15. Applications are processed on a rolling basis. *Application fee:* $31.

**Expenses:** Tuition: Part-time $165 per credit. Required fees: $390. Tuition and fees vary according to degree level and program.

**Financial support:** Teaching assistantships available.

Carmen Rodriguez, Graduate Coordinator, 787-264-1912 Ext. 7646, *Fax:* 787-892-6350, *E-mail:* carrod@sg.inter.edu.

**Application contact:** Dr. Waldemar Velez, Director of Graduate Program Center, 787-892-4300 Ext. 7358, *Fax:* 787-892-6350, *E-mail:* wvelez@sg.inter.edu.

# ■ IONA COLLEGE

**School of Arts and Science, Department of Psychology, New Rochelle, NY 10801-1890**

**AWARDS** Psychology (MA); school counseling (MA); school psychologist (MA).

**Faculty:** 7 full-time (4 women).

**Students:** 12 full-time (11 women), 33 part-time (28 women); includes 9 minority (4 African Americans, 1 Asian American or Pacific Islander, 3 Hispanic Americans, 1 Native American). Average age 27. In 2001, 8 degrees awarded.

**Degree requirements:** For master's, thesis.

**Entrance requirements:** For master's, GRE or minimum GPA of 3.0. *Application deadline:* Applications are processed on a rolling basis. *Application fee:* $25.

**Expenses:** Tuition: Part-time $525 per credit.

**Financial support:** Career-related internships or fieldwork, tuition waivers (partial),

*Iona College (continued)*
and unspecified assistantships available. Support available to part-time students. Dr. Paul Greene, Chair, 914-633-2048, *E-mail:* pgreene@iona.edu.
**Application contact:** Alyce Ware, Associate Director of Graduate Recruitment, 914-633-2420, *Fax:* 914-633-2023, *E-mail:* aware@iona.edu. *Web site:* http://www.iona.edu/

### ■ JAMES MADISON UNIVERSITY

**College of Graduate and Professional Programs, College of Integrated Science and Technology, Department of Psychology, Program in School Psychology, Harrisonburg, VA 22807**
**AWARDS** MA, Ed S. Part-time and evening/weekend programs available.

**Students:** 18 full-time (16 women), 8 part-time (4 women); includes 5 minority (2 African Americans, 1 Asian American or Pacific Islander, 2 Hispanic Americans), 1 international. Average age 29. In 2001, 6 master's, 7 other advanced degrees awarded.
**Degree requirements:** For Ed S, thesis.
**Entrance requirements:** For master's, GRE General Test. *Application deadline:* For fall admission, 7/1 (priority date). Applications are processed on a rolling basis. *Application fee:* $55.
**Expenses:** Tuition, state resident: part-time $143 per credit hour. Tuition, nonresident: part-time $465 per credit hour.
**Financial support:** In 2001–02, 3 teaching assistantships with full tuition reimbursements (averaging $7,170 per year) were awarded; career-related internships or fieldwork, Federal Work-Study, and unspecified assistantships also available. Financial award application deadline: 3/1; financial award applicants required to submit FAFSA.
Dr. Jane Halonen, Director, Department of Psychology, 540-568-2555.

### ■ KEAN UNIVERSITY

**College of Arts, Humanities and Social Sciences, Department of Psychology, Union, NJ 07083**
**AWARDS** Behavioral sciences (MA), including business and industry counseling, human behavior and organizational psychology, psychological services; business and industry counseling (PMC); educational psychology (MA); marriage and family therapy (Diploma); school psychology (Diploma). Part-time and evening/weekend programs available.

**Faculty:** 21 full-time (13 women), 25 part-time/adjunct.
**Students:** 25 full-time (16 women), 121 part-time (74 women); includes 38 minority (12 African Americans, 8 Asian

Americans or Pacific Islanders, 18 Hispanic Americans), 3 international. Average age 30. 87 applicants, 67% accepted. In 2001, 42 master's, 12 other advanced degrees awarded.
**Degree requirements:** For master's, thesis, comprehensive exam.
**Entrance requirements:** For master's, GRE General Test. *Application deadline:* For fall admission, 6/15; for spring admission, 11/15. *Application fee:* $35.
**Expenses:** Tuition, state resident: full-time $7,372. Tuition, nonresident: full-time $9,004. Required fees: $1,006.
**Financial support:** In 2001–02, 27 research assistantships with full tuition reimbursements (averaging $3,360 per year) were awarded; career-related internships or fieldwork and unspecified assistantships also available.
Dr. Henry L. Kaplowitz, Graduate Coordinator, 908-527-2598.
**Application contact:** Joanne Morris, Director of Graduate Admissions, 908-527-2665, *Fax:* 908-527-2286, *E-mail:* grad_adm@kean.edu.

### ■ KENT STATE UNIVERSITY

**Graduate School of Education, Department of Educational Foundations and Special Services, Program in School Psychology, Kent, OH 44242-0001**
**AWARDS** M Ed, PhD, Ed S.

**Faculty:** 3 full-time (2 women), 1 (woman) part-time/adjunct.
**Students:** 58 full-time (51 women), 6 part-time (5 women); includes 7 minority (4 African Americans, 2 Asian Americans or Pacific Islanders, 1 Hispanic American), 1 international. 6 applicants, 83% accepted, 3 enrolled. In 2001, 13 master's, 3 doctorates, 12 other advanced degrees awarded.
**Degree requirements:** For master's and Ed S, registration; for doctorate, thesis/dissertation, comprehensive exam, registration.
**Entrance requirements:** For master's and doctorate, GRE General Test; for Ed S, GRE General Test, MAT or minimum graduate GPA of 3.5. *Application deadline:* For fall admission, 7/15; for spring admission, 11/15. *Application fee:* $30. Electronic applications accepted.
**Financial support:** In 2001–02, fellowships with full tuition reimbursements (averaging $9,500 per year); research assistantships with full tuition reimbursements, teaching assistantships with full tuition reimbursements, career-related internships or fieldwork, Federal Work-Study, institutionally sponsored loans, scholarships/grants, health care benefits, and unspecified assistantships also available. Support available to part-time

students. Financial award application deadline: 4/1; financial award applicants required to submit FAFSA.
**Faculty research:** Special education policy and practice, treatment fidelity, school-based consultation.
Dr. Cathy Telzrow, Coordinator, 330-672-2928, *E-mail:* ctelzrow@kent.edu.
**Application contact:** Deborah Barber, Director, Office of Academic Services, 330-672-2862, *Fax:* 330-672-3549, *E-mail:* oas@educ.kent.edu.

### ■ LA SIERRA UNIVERSITY

**School of Education, Department of Educational Psychology and Counseling, Riverside, CA 92515-8247**
**AWARDS** Counseling (MA); educational psychology (Ed S); school psychology (Ed S). Part-time and evening/weekend programs available.

**Degree requirements:** For master's, thesis optional; for Ed S, practicum (educational psychology).
**Entrance requirements:** For master's, California Basic Educational Skills Test, NTE, minimum GPA of 3.0; for Ed S, minimum GPA of 3.3.
**Faculty research:** Equivalent score scales, self perception.

### ■ LEHIGH UNIVERSITY

**College of Education, Department of Education and Human Services, Program in School Psychology, Bethlehem, PA 18015-3094**
**AWARDS** PhD, Certificate, Ed S. Part-time and evening/weekend programs available.

**Faculty:** 4 full-time (1 woman).
**Students:** 32 full-time (24 women), 19 part-time (18 women). 91 applicants, 25% accepted, 12 enrolled. In 2001, 5 doctorates, 6 other advanced degrees awarded.
**Degree requirements:** For doctorate, thesis/dissertation, internship, research qualifying exam; for other advanced degree, internship.
**Entrance requirements:** For doctorate, GRE General Test or MAT, TOEFL; for other advanced degree, GRE General Test or MAT, TOEFL, minimum GPA of 2.75. *Application deadline:* For fall admission, 1/15. *Application fee:* $50. Electronic applications accepted.
**Expenses:** Tuition: Part-time $468 per credit hour. Required fees: $200; $100 per semester. Tuition and fees vary according to program.
**Financial support:** Fellowships, research assistantships, career-related internships or fieldwork, Federal Work-Study, institutionally sponsored loans, and tuition waivers (full and partial) available. Financial award application deadline: 1/31.

**Faculty research:** Applied behavior, analysis development disabilities, psychology of the mildly handicapped.
Dr. George J. DuPaul, Coordinator, 610-758-3256, *Fax:* 610-758-6223, *E-mail:* gjd3@lehigh.edu.

### ■ LENOIR-RHYNE COLLEGE

**The Graduate School, School of Social and Behavioral Sciences, Program in School Counseling, Hickory, NC 28603**
**AWARDS** MA.

**Students:** 1 (woman) full-time, 20 part-time (17 women). In 2001, 5 degrees awarded.
**Entrance requirements:** For master's, GRE General Test, minimum GPA of 2.7.
**Expenses:** Tuition: Full-time $8,100; part-time $225 per credit hour. Required fees: $50; $25 per semester. Tuition and fees vary according to program.
**Application contact:** Gabriela Abad, Administrative Assistant, 828-328-7275, *Fax:* 828-328-7368, *E-mail:* abadg@lre.edu.

### ■ LESLEY UNIVERSITY

**Graduate School of Arts and Social Sciences, Cambridge, MA 02138-2790**
**AWARDS** Clinical mental health counseling (MA), including expressive therapies counseling, holistic counseling, school and community counseling; counseling psychology (MA, CAGS), including school counseling (MA); creative arts in learning (M Ed, CAGS), including individually designed (M Ed, MA), multicultural education (M Ed, MA), storytelling (M Ed), theater studies (M Ed); ecological literacy (MS); environmental education (MS); expressive therapies (MA, PhD, CAGS), including art therapy (MA), dance therapy (MA), individually designed (M Ed, MA), mental health counseling (MA), music therapy (MA); independent studies (M Ed); independent study (MA); intercultural relations (MA, CAGS), including development project administration (MA), individually designed (M Ed, MA), intercultural conflict resolution (MA), intercultural health and human services (MA), intercultural relations (CAGS), intercultural training and consulting (MA), international education exchange (MA), international student advising (MA), managing culturally diverse human resources (MA), multicultural education (M Ed, MA); interdisciplinary studies (MA); visual arts and creative writing (MFA). MS (environmental education) offered jointly with the Audubon Society Expedition Institute. Part-time and evening/weekend programs available. Postbaccalaureate distance learning degree programs offered (minimal on-campus study).

**Faculty:** 73 full-time (58 women), 137 part-time/adjunct (95 women).
**Students:** 108 full-time (97 women), 1,190 part-time (1,084 women); includes 134 minority (81 African Americans, 23 Asian Americans or Pacific Islanders, 26 Hispanic Americans, 4 Native Americans), 16 international. Average age 36. 639 applicants, 91% accepted, 313 enrolled. In 2001, 1106 degrees awarded.
**Degree requirements:** For master's, internship, practicum, thesis (expressive therapies); for doctorate and CAGS, thesis/dissertation, arts apprenticeship, field placement; for CAGS, thesis, internship (counseling psychology, expressive therapies).
**Entrance requirements:** For master's, MAT (counseling psychology), TOEFL, interview; for doctorate, GRE or MAT; for CAGS, interview, master's degree. *Application deadline:* Applications are processed on a rolling basis. *Application fee:* $50.
**Expenses:** Tuition: Part-time $330 per credit. Required fees: $15 per term. Part-time tuition and fees vary according to campus/location and program.
**Financial support:** In 2001–02, 47 students received support; research assistantships, teaching assistantships, career-related internships or fieldwork, Federal Work-Study, and unspecified assistantships available. Support available to part-time students. Financial award application deadline: 4/1; financial award applicants required to submit FAFSA.
**Faculty research:** Developmental psychology, women's issues, health psychology, limited supervision group psychology.
Dr. Martha B. McKenna, Dean, 617-349-8467, *Fax:* 617-349-8366.
**Application contact:** Hugh Norwood, Dean of Admissions and Enrollment Planning, 800-999-1959, *Fax:* 617-349-8366, *E-mail:* hnorwood@mail.lesley.edu. *Web site:* http://www.lesley.edu/gsass.html

### ■ LEWIS & CLARK COLLEGE

**Graduate School of Professional Studies, Department of Counseling Psychology, Program in School Psychology, Portland, OR 97219-7899**
**AWARDS** MS. Part-time and evening/weekend programs available.

**Degree requirements:** For master's, thesis.
**Entrance requirements:** For master's, GRE General Test.
**Faculty research:** Peer rejection, social skills, consultation, sexual abuse.

### ■ LONG ISLAND UNIVERSITY, BROOKLYN CAMPUS

**School of Education, Department of Human Development and Leadership, Program in School Psychology, Brooklyn, NY 11201-8423**
**AWARDS** MS Ed. Part-time and evening/weekend programs available.

**Degree requirements:** For master's, thesis optional.
Electronic applications accepted.

### ■ LONG ISLAND UNIVERSITY, WESTCHESTER GRADUATE CAMPUS

**Program in Education-School Counselor and School Psychologist, Purchase, NY 10577**
**AWARDS** School counselor (MS Ed); school psychologist (MS Ed).

**Students:** 15 full-time (11 women), 17 part-time (14 women).
*Application fee:* $30.
**Expenses:** Tuition: Part-time $572 per credit.
Prof. Michael Axelrad, Program Coordinator, 914-251-6510, *Fax:* 914-251-5959.
**Application contact:** Carol A. Messar, Director of Admissions, 914-251-6510, *Fax:* 914-251-5959, *E-mail:* cmessar@liu.edu. *Web site:* http://www.liu.edu/westchester/

### ■ LOUISIANA STATE UNIVERSITY AND AGRICULTURAL AND MECHANICAL COLLEGE

**Graduate School, College of Arts and Sciences, Department of Psychology, Baton Rouge, LA 70803**
**AWARDS** Biological psychology (MA, PhD); clinical psychology (MA, PhD); cognitive psychology (MA, PhD); developmental psychology (MA, PhD); industrial/organizational psychology (MA, PhD); school psychology (MA, PhD).

**Faculty:** 25 full-time (7 women).
**Students:** 70 full-time (53 women), 43 part-time (24 women); includes 7 minority (3 African Americans, 2 Asian Americans or Pacific Islanders, 2 Hispanic Americans), 2 international. Average age 30. 179 applicants, 12% accepted, 20 enrolled. In 2001, 19 degrees awarded. Terminal master's awarded for partial completion of doctoral program.
**Degree requirements:** For master's, thesis; for doctorate, thesis/dissertation, 1 year internship.
**Entrance requirements:** For master's and doctorate, GRE General Test, minimum GPA of 3.0. *Application deadline:* For fall admission, 1/25 (priority date). Applications are processed on a rolling basis. *Application fee:* $25.
**Expenses:** Tuition, state resident: full-time $2,551. Tuition, nonresident: full-time $5,551. Required fees: $854. Part-time tuition and fees vary according to course load.
**Financial support:** In 2001–02, 1 fellowship (averaging $14,333 per year), 10

*Louisiana State University and Agricultural and Mechanical College (continued)*

research assistantships with partial tuition reimbursements (averaging $14,200 per year), 33 teaching assistantships with partial tuition reimbursements (averaging $10,371 per year) were awarded. Career-related internships or fieldwork, institutionally sponsored loans, and contracts also available. Financial award applicants required to submit FAFSA. *Total annual research expenditures:* $242,157.
Dr. Irving Lane, Chair, 225-578-8745, *Fax:* 225-578-4125, *E-mail:* irvlane@unix1.sncc.lsu.edu.
**Application contact:** Dr. Janet McDonald, Coordinator of Graduate Studies, 225-578-4116, *Fax:* 225-578-4125, *E-mail:* psmcdo@lsu.edu. *Web site:* http://www.artsci.lsu.edu/psych

## ■ LOUISIANA STATE UNIVERSITY IN SHREVEPORT

**College of Education, Program in School Psychology, Shreveport, LA 71115-2399**

AWARDS SSP. Part-time programs available.
**Faculty:** 9 full-time (5 women), 2 part-time/adjunct (both women).
**Students:** 33 full-time (25 women), 25 part-time (22 women); includes 17 minority (all African Americans). Average age 34. 11 applicants, 100% accepted, 11 enrolled. In 2001, 4 degrees awarded.
**Degree requirements:** For SSP, comprehensive exam.
**Entrance requirements:** For degree, GRE General Test, minimum GPA of 2.75. *Application deadline:* For fall admission, 6/1 (priority date); for spring admission, 11/1. *Application fee:* $10.
**Expenses:** Tuition, area resident: Full-time $1,890; part-time $105 per credit. Tuition, nonresident: full-time $6,000; part-time $175 per credit. Required fees: $220; $55 per credit.
**Financial support:** In 2001–02, 2 students received support; research assistantships, teaching assistantships, career-related internships or fieldwork and Federal Work-Study available. Support available to part-time students. Financial award application deadline: 6/1; financial award applicants required to submit FAFSA.
**Faculty research:** Alternatives to violence, behavioral interventions, psychological-social basis of cancer, classroom management, self-esteem, depression.
Dr. Jean Hollenshead, Chair, Department of Psychology, 318-797-5044, *Fax:* 318-798-4171, *E-mail:* jhollens@pilot.lsus.edu.
**Application contact:** Dr. Patricia Stanley, Director, 318-797-5044, *Fax:* 318-798-4171, *E-mail:* pstanley@pilot.lsus.edu.

## ■ LOYOLA MARYMOUNT UNIVERSITY

**Graduate Division, School of Education, Program in Educational Psychology, Los Angeles, CA 90045-2659**

AWARDS School psychology (MA). Part-time and evening/weekend programs available.
**Students:** 26 full-time (25 women), 1 (woman) part-time; includes 11 minority (2 African Americans, 2 Asian Americans or Pacific Islanders, 7 Hispanic Americans). In 2001, 19 degrees awarded.
**Degree requirements:** For master's, comprehensive exam.
**Entrance requirements:** For master's, GRE General Test, TOEFL, interview. *Application deadline:* For fall admission, 7/15; for spring admission, 11/15. *Application fee:* $45. Electronic applications accepted.
**Expenses:** Tuition: Part-time $612 per credit hour. Required fees: $86 per term. Tuition and fees vary according to program.
**Financial support:** In 2001–02, 5 students received support. Scholarships/grants available. Support available to part-time students. Financial award application deadline: 7/1; financial award applicants required to submit FAFSA.
Dr. Scott Kester, Coordinator, 310-338-7308, *E-mail:* skester@lmu.edu. *Web site:* http://www.lmu.edu/acad/gd/graddiv.htm

## ■ LOYOLA UNIVERSITY CHICAGO

**School of Education, Department of Curriculum, Instruction and Educational Psychology, Program in School Psychology, Chicago, IL 60611-2196**

AWARDS M Ed, PhD, Ed S. PhD offered through the Graduate School. Part-time and evening/weekend programs available.
**Faculty:** 7 full-time (5 women), 11 part-time/adjunct (8 women).
**Students:** 82 full-time (75 women), 85 part-time (72 women); includes 44 minority (13 African Americans, 6 Asian Americans or Pacific Islanders, 25 Hispanic Americans). Average age 26. 112 applicants, 61% accepted, 40 enrolled. In 2001, 19 master's, 8 doctorates awarded. Terminal master's awarded for partial completion of doctoral program.
**Degree requirements:** For master's, comprehensive exam; for doctorate, thesis/dissertation, comprehensive exam. *Median time to degree:* Master's–3 years full-time, 4 years part-time; doctorate–5 years full-time, 7 years part-time.
**Entrance requirements:** For master's, GRE; for doctorate, GRE, interview.

*Application deadline:* For fall admission, 2/15; for spring admission, 10/15. *Application fee:* $35. Electronic applications accepted.
**Expenses:** Tuition: Part-time $529 per credit hour.
**Financial support:** In 2001–02, 8 students received support, including 5 fellowships with full and partial tuition reimbursements available, 3 research assistantships with full and partial tuition reimbursements available; institutionally sponsored loans, scholarships/grants, and tuition waivers (full and partial) also available. Financial award application deadline: 3/15.
**Faculty research:** Learning theory and teaching, school reform, instructional intervention, violence prevention, mental health programming in schools and communities. *Total annual research expenditures:* $125,000.
Dr. Nancy Scott, Director, 312-915-6218, *E-mail:* nscott1@luc.edu.
**Application contact:** Marie Rosin-Dittmar, Information Contact, 312-915-6722, *E-mail:* schleduc@luc.edu.

## ■ MARIST COLLEGE

**Graduate Programs, School of Social/Behavioral Sciences, Poughkeepsie, NY 12601-1387**

AWARDS Counseling/community psychology (MA); education psychology (MA); school psychology (MA, Adv C). Part-time and evening/weekend programs available.
**Faculty:** 8 full-time (3 women), 20 part-time/adjunct (11 women).
**Students:** 66 full-time (49 women), 149 part-time (113 women); includes 11 minority (5 African Americans, 1 Asian American or Pacific Islander, 4 Hispanic Americans, 1 Native American). Average age 30. 104 applicants, 79% accepted. In 2001, 62 degrees awarded.
**Degree requirements:** For master's, thesis optional.
**Entrance requirements:** For master's, GRE General Test. *Application deadline:* For fall admission, 8/1 (priority date); for spring admission, 12/15. Applications are processed on a rolling basis. *Application fee:* $30.
**Expenses:** Tuition: Full-time $4,320; part-time $480 per credit. Required fees: $30 per semester.
**Financial support:** Career-related internships or fieldwork, Federal Work-Study, and tuition waivers (partial) available. Support available to part-time students. Financial award application deadline: 8/15; financial award applicants required to submit FAFSA.

**Faculty research:** Obsessive-compulsive disorders/eating disorders, AIDS prevention, educational intervention, humanistic counseling research, program evaluation research.

Margaret Calista, Dean, 845-575-3000 Ext. 2960, *E-mail:* margaret.calista@marist.edu.

**Application contact:** Dr. John DeJoy, Acting Dean of Graduate and Continuing Education, 845-575-3530, *Fax:* 845-575-3640, *E-mail:* john.dejoy@marist.edu.

# ■ MARSHALL UNIVERSITY

**Graduate College, College of Education and Human Services, Graduate School of Education and Professional Development, Program in School Psychology, Huntington, WV 25755**

**AWARDS** Ed S. Part-time and evening/weekend programs available.

**Students:** 11 full-time (8 women), 26 part-time (19 women); includes 3 minority (all African Americans). Average age 34. In 2001, 8 degrees awarded.

**Entrance requirements:** For degree, master's degree in psychology. *Application fee:* $0.

**Expenses:** Tuition, state resident: part-time $147 per credit. Tuition, nonresident: part-time $468 per credit. Tuition and fees vary according to campus/location and reciprocity agreements.

**Financial support:** Career-related internships or fieldwork and tuition waivers (full) available. Support available to part-time students. Financial award applicants required to submit FAFSA.

Dr. Steven O'Keefe, Head, 800-642-9842 Ext. 1937, *E-mail:* sokeefe@marshall.edu.

# ■ MERCY COLLEGE

**Division of Social and Behavioral Sciences, Dobbs Ferry, NY 10522-1189**

**AWARDS** Alcohol and substance abuse counseling (AC); family counseling (AC); health services management (MPA, MS); psychology (MS); retirement counseling (AC); school counseling (MS), including bilingual extension; school psychology (MS), including bilingual extension.

**Students:** 51 full-time (41 women), 105 part-time (81 women); includes 104 minority (47 African Americans, 7 Asian Americans or Pacific Islanders, 50 Hispanic Americans), 10 international.

**Entrance requirements:** For master's, 8 years of healthcare management or practitioner (MS in health services management); interview; minimum GPA of 3.0. *Application fee:* $35.

**Expenses:** Tuition: Part-time $450 per credit. Part-time tuition and fees vary according to program.

Dr. Frances T.M. Mahoney, Chairperson, 914-674-7438, *Fax:* 914-674-7542, *E-mail:* fmahoney@mercy.edu.

**Application contact:** Information Contact, 800-MERCY-NY.

**Find an in-depth description at www.petersons.com/gradchannel.**

# ■ MIAMI UNIVERSITY

**Graduate School, School of Education and Allied Professions, Department of Educational Psychology, Program in School Psychology, Oxford, OH 45056**

**AWARDS** MS, Ed S.

**Students:** 34 full-time (30 women); includes 4 minority (1 African American, 3 Asian Americans or Pacific Islanders). 38 applicants, 47% accepted, 12 enrolled. In 2001, 16 degrees awarded.

**Degree requirements:** For master's, thesis or alternative, oral or written exam; for Ed S, oral or written exam.

**Entrance requirements:** For master's, GRE General Test or MAT, minimum undergraduate GPA of 3.0 during previous 2 years or 2.75 overall; for Ed S, GRE General Test or MAT. *Application deadline:* For fall admission, 3/1 (priority date); for spring admission, 12/1. Applications are processed on a rolling basis. *Application fee:* $35.

**Expenses:** Tuition, state resident: full-time $7,155; part-time $295 per semester hour. Tuition, nonresident: full-time $14,829; part-time $615 per semester hour. Tuition and fees vary according to degree level and campus/location.

**Financial support:** Fellowships, research assistantships, teaching assistantships, career-related internships or fieldwork, Federal Work-Study, and tuition waivers (full) available. Financial award application deadline: 3/1.

**Application contact:** Dr. Ray Witte, Director of Graduate Studies. *Web site:* http://www.muohio.edu/~edpcwis/gradprog.htmlx#schpsych

# ■ MICHIGAN STATE UNIVERSITY

**Graduate School, College of Education, Department of Counseling, Educational Psychology and Special Education, East Lansing, MI 48824**

**AWARDS** Counseling (MA, Ed D, Ed S); counseling psychology (MA, PhD); counselor education (PhD); educational psychology (MA, Ed D, PhD, Ed S); educational system design (Ed S); educational system development (MA, Ed D); educational technology and instructional design (MA); educational technology and system design (MA); measurement and quantitative methods (MA, PhD); measurement, evaluation and research design (Ed D, PhD); rehabilitation counseling (MA); rehabilitation counseling and school

counseling (PhD); school psychology (PhD, Ed S); special education (MA, Ed D, PhD, Ed S). Part-time programs available.

**Faculty:** 37.

**Students:** 174 full-time (134 women), 145 part-time (104 women); includes 38 minority (24 African Americans, 11 Asian Americans or Pacific Islanders, 3 Hispanic Americans), 47 international. Average age 32. 359 applicants, 38% accepted. In 2001, 99 master's, 28 doctorates, 7 other advanced degrees awarded.

**Degree requirements:** For doctorate, thesis/dissertation.

**Entrance requirements:** For master's and doctorate, GRE General Test. *Application deadline:* For fall admission, 2/15 (priority date). Applications are processed on a rolling basis. *Application fee:* $30 ($40 for international students). Electronic applications accepted.

**Expenses:** Tuition, state resident: part-time $244 per credit hour. Tuition, nonresident: part-time $494 per credit hour. Required fees: $268 per semester. Tuition and fees vary according to course load, degree level and program.

**Financial support:** In 2001–02, 104 fellowships (averaging $3,880 per year), 26 research assistantships with tuition reimbursements (averaging $12,108 per year), 36 teaching assistantships with tuition reimbursements (averaging $11,963 per year) were awarded. Career-related internships or fieldwork and Federal Work-Study also available. Financial award applicants required to submit FAFSA.

**Faculty research:** Longitudinal and multilevel research, international mathematics and science curriculum, early intervention for non readers/writers, predictions and consequences of exposure to violence. *Total annual research expenditures:* $2.7 million.

Dr. Richard Prawat, Chairperson, 517-353-7863.

**Application contact:** Graduate Admissions, 517-355-6683, *Fax:* 517-353-6393. *Web site:* http://ed-web3.educ.msu.edu/CEPSE/

# ■ MIDDLE TENNESSEE STATE UNIVERSITY

**College of Graduate Studies, College of Education and Behavioral Science, Department of Psychology, Murfreesboro, TN 37132**

**AWARDS** Industrial/organizational psychology (MA); psychology (MA); school counseling (M Ed, Ed S); school psychology (Ed S). Part-time and evening/weekend programs available.

**Faculty:** 37 full-time (13 women).

**Students:** 28 full-time, 165 part-time; includes 24 minority (18 African

*Middle Tennessee State University (continued)*

Americans, 4 Asian Americans or Pacific Islanders, 2 Hispanic Americans). Average age 26. 54 applicants, 67% accepted. In 2001, 46 master's, 12 other advanced degrees awarded.
**Degree requirements:** For master's, one foreign language, thesis, comprehensive exam.
**Entrance requirements:** For master's, GRE. *Application deadline:* For fall admission, 8/1 (priority date). Applications are processed on a rolling basis. *Application fee:* $25. Electronic applications accepted.
**Expenses:** Tuition, state resident: full-time $1,716; part-time $191 per hour. Tuition, nonresident: full-time $4,952; part-time $461 per hour. Required fees: $14 per hour. $58 per semester.
**Financial support:** In 2001–02, 8 teaching assistantships were awarded; research assistantships, career-related internships or fieldwork, institutionally sponsored loans, and scholarships/grants also available. Support available to part-time students. Financial award application deadline: 5/1; financial award applicants required to submit FAFSA.
**Faculty research:** Industrial/organizational, social/personality/sports, counseling/clinical/school, cognitive/language/learning/perception, developmental/aging. *Total annual research expenditures:* $44,089.
Dr. Larry Morris, Chair, 615-898-2706, *Fax:* 615-898-5027, *E-mail:* lmorris@mtsu.edu.

### ■ MILLERSVILLE UNIVERSITY OF PENNSYLVANIA

**Graduate School, School of Education, Department of Psychology, Program in Psychology, Millersville, PA 17551-0302**

**AWARDS** Clinical psychology (MS); school psychology (MS). Part-time and evening/weekend programs available.

**Faculty:** 20 full-time (14 women), 5 part-time/adjunct (3 women).
**Students:** 37 full-time (31 women), 58 part-time (49 women); includes 7 minority (3 African Americans, 2 Asian Americans or Pacific Islanders, 2 Hispanic Americans). Average age 28. 54 applicants, 65% accepted, 32 enrolled. In 2001, 30 degrees awarded.
**Degree requirements:** For master's, departmental exam, thesis optional.
**Entrance requirements:** For master's, GRE General Test, minimum undergraduate GPA of 2.75, 18 undergraduate hours in psychology, group interview, letters of recommendation, writing sample. *Application deadline:* For fall admission, 3/31; for

spring admission, 11/1. Applications are processed on a rolling basis. *Application fee:* $30.
**Expenses:** Tuition, state resident: part-time $256 per credit. Tuition, nonresident: full-time $7,554; part-time $420 per credit. Required fees: $1,037; $44 per credit.
**Financial support:** In 2001–02, 44 research assistantships with full tuition reimbursements (averaging $4,250 per year) were awarded; career-related internships or fieldwork, Federal Work-Study, institutionally sponsored loans, and unspecified assistantships also available. Support available to part-time students. Financial award application deadline: 3/15; financial award applicants required to submit FAFSA.
Dr. Helena Tuleya-Payne, Chair, 717-872-3925, *Fax:* 717-871-2480, *E-mail:* helena.tuleya-payne@millersville.edu.
**Application contact:** Dr. Duncan M. Perry, Dean of Graduate Studies, Professional Training and Education, 717-872-3030, *E-mail:* duncan.perry@millersville.edu.

### ■ MILLERSVILLE UNIVERSITY OF PENNSYLVANIA

**Graduate School, School of Education, Department of Psychology, Program in School Counseling, Millersville, PA 17551-0302**

**AWARDS** M Ed. Part-time and evening/weekend programs available.

**Faculty:** 20 full-time (14 women), 5 part-time/adjunct (3 women).
**Students:** 5 full-time (4 women), 53 part-time (36 women); includes 3 minority (2 Asian Americans or Pacific Islanders, 1 Hispanic American). Average age 30. 17 applicants, 47% accepted, 7 enrolled. In 2001, 15 degrees awarded.
**Degree requirements:** For master's, departmental exam, thesis optional.
**Entrance requirements:** For master's, GRE General Test, group interview, minimum undergraduate GPA of 2.75, 6 undergraduate hours in education and psychology, letters of recommendation, writing sample. *Application deadline:* For fall admission, 3/31; for spring admission, 11/1. Applications are processed on a rolling basis. *Application fee:* $30.
**Expenses:** Tuition, state resident: part-time $256 per credit. Tuition, nonresident: full-time $7,554; part-time $420 per credit. Required fees: $1,037; $44 per credit.
**Financial support:** In 2001–02, 12 research assistantships with full tuition reimbursements (averaging $4,000 per year) were awarded; career-related internships or fieldwork, Federal Work-Study, institutionally sponsored loans, and unspecified assistantships also available.

Support available to part-time students. Financial award application deadline: 3/15; financial award applicants required to submit FAFSA.
Dr. Ruth J. Benns-Suter, Director, 717-872-3098, *Fax:* 717-871-2480, *E-mail:* ruth.benns-suter@millersville.edu.
**Application contact:** Dr. Duncan M. Perry, Dean of Graduate Studies, Professional Training and Education, 717-872-3030, *E-mail:* duncan.perry@millersville.edu.

### ■ MINNESOTA STATE UNIVERSITY MOORHEAD

**Graduate Studies, Department of Psychology, Moorhead, MN 56563-0002**

**AWARDS** School psychology (MS, Psy S).

**Faculty:** 8.
**Students:** 17 (11 women). 23 applicants, 52% accepted.
**Degree requirements:** For master's, thesis, final oral and written comprehensive exams.
**Entrance requirements:** For master's, GRE General Test, TOEFL, interview, minimum GPA of 3.0, letters of recommendation (3); for Psy S, MS in school psychology. *Application deadline:* For fall admission, 2/15. *Application fee:* $20 ($35 for international students). Electronic applications accepted.
**Expenses:** Tuition, area resident: Part-time $148 per credit. Tuition, nonresident: part-time $234 per credit.
**Financial support:** Career-related internships or fieldwork, Federal Work-Study, and unspecified assistantships available. Financial award application deadline: 7/15; financial award applicants required to submit FAFSA.
Dr. Gary Nickell, Chairperson, 218-236-4080.
**Application contact:** Margaret Potter, Coordinator, 218-236-2805. *Web site:* http://www.mnstate.edu/gradpsyc/

### ■ NATIONAL-LOUIS UNIVERSITY

**National College of Education, McGaw Graduate School, Doctoral Programs in Education, Program in Educational Psychology/School Psychology, Chicago, IL 60603**

**AWARDS** Educational psychology/school psychology (Ed D). Part-time and evening/weekend programs available.

**Degree requirements:** For doctorate, thesis/dissertation, internship, comprehensive exam.
**Entrance requirements:** For doctorate, GRE General Test, minimum GPA of 3.25, interview, resumé, writing sample.

**Expenses:** Tuition: Full-time $13,830; part-time $461 per credit hour.

■ **NATIONAL-LOUIS UNIVERSITY**

National College of Education, McGaw Graduate School, Program in Educational Psychology/Human Learning and Development, Chicago, IL 60603

**AWARDS** Educational psychology (CAS); educational psychology/human learning and development (M Ed, MS Ed); educational psychology/school psychology (M Ed). Part-time and evening/weekend programs available.

**Degree requirements:** For master's, thesis (for some programs).
**Entrance requirements:** For master's, MAT or GRE, minimum GPA of 3.0, teaching certificate; for CAS, master's degree, teaching certificate. Electronic applications accepted.
**Expenses:** Tuition: Full-time $13,830; part-time $461 per credit hour.

■ **NATIONAL-LOUIS UNIVERSITY**

National College of Education, McGaw Graduate School, Programs in Educational Psychology/School Psychology, Chicago, IL 60603

**AWARDS** Educational psychology/school psychology (M Ed, Ed S).

**Degree requirements:** For master's and Ed S, internship.
**Entrance requirements:** For master's, MAT or GRE, minimum GPA of 3.0; for Ed S, GRE, interview, master's degree, writing sample.
**Expenses:** Tuition: Full-time $13,830; part-time $461 per credit hour.

■ **NATIONAL UNIVERSITY**

Academic Affairs, School of Education, Department of Specialized Programs, La Jolla, CA 92037-1011

**AWARDS** Educational administration (MS); educational counseling (MS); educational technology (MS); school psychology (MS); special education (MS). Part-time and evening/weekend programs available. Postbaccalaureate distance learning degree programs offered (minimal on-campus study).

**Faculty:** 19 full-time (10 women), 414 part-time/adjunct (227 women).
**Students:** 1,345 full-time (928 women), 768 part-time (483 women); includes 725 minority (261 African Americans, 119 Asian Americans or Pacific Islanders, 326 Hispanic Americans, 19 Native Americans), 6 international. 485 applicants, 100% accepted. In 2001, 445 degrees awarded.

**Entrance requirements:** For master's, interview, minimum GPA of 2.5. *Application deadline:* Applications are processed on a rolling basis. *Application fee:* $60 ($100 for international students).
**Expenses:** Tuition: Part-time $221 per quarter hour.
**Financial support:** Institutionally sponsored loans, scholarships/grants, and tuition waivers (full and partial) available. Support available to part-time students. Financial award application deadline: 5/1; financial award applicants required to submit FAFSA.
Dr. Jane Duckett, Chair, 858-642-8346, *Fax:* 858-642-8724, *E-mail:* jduckett@nu.edu.
**Application contact:** Nancy Rohland, Director of Enrollment Management, 858-642-8180, *Fax:* 858-642-8710, *E-mail:* advisor@nu.edu. *Web site:* http://www.nu.edu/

■ **NEW JERSEY CITY UNIVERSITY**

Graduate Studies, College of Arts and Sciences, Department of Psychology, Program in School Psychology, Jersey City, NJ 07305-1597

**AWARDS** PD.

**Faculty:** 3 full-time (2 women).
**Students:** Average age 35. 3 applicants, 100% accepted. In 2001, 4 degrees awarded.
**Degree requirements:** For PD, summer internship or externship.
**Entrance requirements:** For degree, GRE General Test, TOEFL. *Application deadline:* For fall admission, 8/1 (priority date); for spring admission, 12/1. Applications are processed on a rolling basis. *Application fee:* $0.
**Expenses:** Tuition, state resident: full-time $5,062. Tuition, nonresident: full-time $8,663.
Dr. James Lennon, Director, 201-200-3309.

■ **NEW YORK UNIVERSITY**

The Steinhardt School of Education, Department of Applied Psychology, Program in Applied Psychology, New York, NY 10012-1019

**AWARDS** Educational psychology (MA), including measurement and evaluation, psychology of parenthood; professional child/school psychology (Psy D); psychological development (PhD); school psychologist (Advanced Certificate); school psychology (PhD). Part-time and evening/weekend programs available.

**Faculty:** 15 full-time (10 women).

**Students:** 66 full-time (55 women), 101 part-time (95 women); includes 37 minority (15 African Americans, 14 Asian Americans or Pacific Islanders, 8 Hispanic Americans). 240 applicants, 23% accepted, 39 enrolled. In 2001, 59 master's, 17 doctorates, 1 other advanced degree awarded. Terminal master's awarded for partial completion of doctoral program.
**Degree requirements:** For master's, thesis (for some programs); for doctorate, thesis/dissertation.
**Entrance requirements:** For master's and Advanced Certificate, TOEFL; for doctorate, GRE General Test, TOEFL, interview. *Application deadline:* For fall admission, 2/1 (priority date); for spring admission, 12/1. Applications are processed on a rolling basis. *Application fee:* $40 ($60 for international students).
**Expenses:** Tuition: Full-time $19,536; part-time $814 per credit. Required fees: $1,330; $38 per credit. Tuition and fees vary according to course load and program.
**Financial support:** Teaching assistantships with partial tuition reimbursements, career-related internships or fieldwork, Federal Work-Study, institutionally sponsored loans, and tuition waivers (partial) available. Support available to part-time students. Financial award application deadline: 3/1; financial award applicants required to submit FAFSA.
**Faculty research:** Infant cognition; exploration, language, and symbolic play in toddlerhood; emotional and perceptual problems in children; development of reading comprehension.
Dr. Catherine Tamis-Lemonda, Director, 212-998-5399, *Fax:* 212-995-4368.
**Application contact:** 212-998-5030, *Fax:* 212-995-4328, *E-mail:* grad.admissions@nyu.edu.

■ **NICHOLLS STATE UNIVERSITY**

Graduate Studies, College of Education, Department of Psychology and Counselor Education, Thibodaux, LA 70310

**AWARDS** Counselor education (M Ed); psychological counseling (MA); school psychology (SSP). Part-time and evening/weekend programs available.

**Faculty:** 8 full-time (2 women).
**Students:** 26 full-time (23 women), 63 part-time (56 women); includes 14 minority (13 African Americans, 1 Asian American or Pacific Islander). In 2001, 15 master's, 3 other advanced degrees awarded.
**Degree requirements:** For master's, comprehensive exam.
**Entrance requirements:** For master's, GRE General Test. *Application deadline:*

*Nicholls State University (continued)*
For fall admission, 6/17 (priority date); for spring admission, 11/15 (priority date). Applications are processed on a rolling basis. *Application fee:* $20 ($30 for international students). Electronic applications accepted.

**Financial support:** In 2001–02, research assistantships with tuition reimbursements (averaging $4,000 per year), teaching assistantships with tuition reimbursements (averaging $6,000 per year) were awarded. Financial award application deadline: 6/17. Dr. J. Steven Welsh, Head, 985-448-4371, *E-mail:* gred-jtb@mail.nich.edu.

■ **NORTHEASTERN UNIVERSITY**

**Bouvé College of Health Sciences Graduate School, Department of Counseling and Applied Educational Psychology, Program in Applied Educational Psychology, Boston, MA 02115-5096**

**AWARDS** School counseling (MS); school psychology (MS). Part-time programs available.

**Faculty:** 5 full-time (3 women), 4 part-time/adjunct (2 women).
**Students:** 71 full-time (67 women), 10 part-time (all women). Average age 26. 109 applicants, 81% accepted. In 2001, 83 degrees awarded.
**Entrance requirements:** For master's, GRE General Test or MAT. *Application deadline:* Applications are processed on a rolling basis. *Application fee:* $50.
**Expenses:** Tuition: Part-time $535 per credit hour. Required fees: $56. Tuition and fees vary according to program.
**Financial support:** Career-related internships or fieldwork, Federal Work-Study, tuition waivers (partial), and unspecified assistantships available. Support available to part-time students. Financial award application deadline: 3/1; financial award applicants required to submit FAFSA.
**Faculty research:** Multicultural issues, assessment, early intervention, bilingual education.
Dr. Louis J. Kruger, Director, 617-373-5897, *Fax:* 617-373-4701.
**Application contact:** Bill Purnell, Director of Graduate Admissions, 617-373-2708, *Fax:* 617-373-4701, *E-mail:* w.purnell@neu.edu.

**Find an in-depth description at www.petersons.com/gradchannel.**

■ **NORTHEASTERN UNIVERSITY**

**Bouvé College of Health Sciences Graduate School, Department of Counseling and Applied Educational Psychology, Program in School Psychology, Boston, MA 02115-5096**

**AWARDS** PhD, CAGS. Part-time programs available.

**Faculty:** 4 full-time (2 women), 3 part-time/adjunct (all women).
**Students:** 28 full-time (22 women), 1 (woman) part-time. Average age 29. 7 applicants, 57% accepted. In 2001, 2 doctorates, 11 other advanced degrees awarded.
**Degree requirements:** For doctorate, thesis/dissertation, qualifying exams, comprehensive exam.
**Entrance requirements:** For doctorate, GRE General Test, school psychologist certificate; for CAGS, GRE General Test or MAT, MS in school psychology or related field. *Application deadline:* Applications are processed on a rolling basis. *Application fee:* $50.
**Expenses:** Tuition: Part-time $535 per credit hour. Required fees: $56. Tuition and fees vary according to program.
**Financial support:** Research assistantships, career-related internships or fieldwork, Federal Work-Study, tuition waivers (partial), and unspecified assistantships available. Financial award application deadline: 3/1; financial award applicants required to submit FAFSA.
**Faculty research:** Multicultural education, early intervention.
Dr. Louis J. Kruger, Director, 617-373-5897, *Fax:* 617-373-4701.
**Application contact:** Bill Purnell, Director of Graduate Admissions, 617-373-2708, *Fax:* 617-373-4701, *E-mail:* w.purnell@neu.edu.

**Find an in-depth description at www.petersons.com/gradchannel.**

■ **NORTHERN ARIZONA UNIVERSITY**

**Graduate College, Center for Excellence in Education, Program in Educational Psychology, Flagstaff, AZ 86011**

**AWARDS** Counseling psychology (Ed D); learning and instruction (Ed D); school psychology (Ed D).

**Students:** 33 full-time (26 women), 28 part-time (19 women); includes 10 minority (5 African Americans, 1 Asian American or Pacific Islander, 3 Hispanic Americans, 1 Native American), 2 international. Average age 35. 13 applicants, 69% accepted, 7 enrolled. In 2001, 1 degree awarded.

**Degree requirements:** For doctorate, thesis/dissertation, internship, comprehensive exam.
**Entrance requirements:** For doctorate, GRE General Test. *Application deadline:* For fall admission, 1/15. *Application fee:* $45.
**Expenses:** Tuition, state resident: full-time $2,488. Tuition, nonresident: full-time $10,354.
Dr. Ramona Mellott, Chair, 928-523-7103, *E-mail:* ramona.mellott@nau.edu.
**Application contact:** Marcia Couch, Secretary, 928-523-7103. *Web site:* http://www.nau.edu/~cee/academics/

■ **NORTHERN ARIZONA UNIVERSITY**

**Graduate College, Center for Excellence in Education, Program in School Psychology, Flagstaff, AZ 86011**

**AWARDS** School psychology (MA).

**Students:** 19 full-time (16 women), 6 part-time (all women); includes 5 minority (all Hispanic Americans). Average age 30. 24 applicants, 63% accepted, 11 enrolled. In 2001, 12 degrees awarded.
**Degree requirements:** For master's, internship.
**Entrance requirements:** For master's, GRE General Test. *Application deadline:* For fall admission, 2/15.
**Expenses:** Tuition, state resident: full-time $2,488. Tuition, nonresident: full-time $10,354.
Dr. Ramona Mellott, Chair, 928-523-7103, *E-mail:* ramona.mellott@nau.edu.
**Application contact:** Marcia Couch, Secretary, 928-523-7103. *Web site:* http://www.nau.edu/cee/academics/

■ **NOVA SOUTHEASTERN UNIVERSITY**

**Center for Psychological Studies, Master's Program in Counseling, Mental Health, and School Guidance, Fort Lauderdale, FL 33314-7721**

**AWARDS** Mental health counseling (MS); school guidance and counseling (MS). Part-time and evening/weekend programs available.

**Faculty:** 33 full-time (10 women), 19 part-time/adjunct (10 women).
**Students:** 468 full-time (410 women). In 2001, 155 degrees awarded.
**Degree requirements:** For master's, 3 practica.
*Application deadline:* For fall admission, 6/11; for spring admission, 10/19. Applications are processed on a rolling basis. *Application fee:* $50.
**Expenses:** Tuition: Full-time $7,380; part-time $432 per credit. Required fees: $200.

Tuition and fees vary according to campus/location and program.

**Financial support:** Career-related internships or fieldwork, Federal Work-Study, and institutionally sponsored loans available. Financial award application deadline: 4/1.

**Faculty research:** Clinical and child clinical psychology, geriatrics, interpersonal violence.

**Application contact:** Nancy L. Smith, Supervisor, 954-262-5760, *Fax:* 954-262-3893, *E-mail:* cpsinfo@cps.nova.edu. *Web site:* http://www.cps.nova.edu/

## ■ PACE UNIVERSITY

**Dyson College of Arts and Sciences, Department of Psychology, Program in School-Community Psychology, New York, NY 10038**

**AWARDS** MS Ed, Psy D.

**Students:** 70 full-time (62 women), 14 part-time (12 women); includes 15 minority (3 African Americans, 6 Asian Americans or Pacific Islanders, 5 Hispanic Americans, 1 Native American), 1 international. Average age 25. 170 applicants, 43% accepted. In 2001, 25 master's, 22 doctorates awarded. Terminal master's awarded for partial completion of doctoral program.

**Degree requirements:** For master's, qualifying exams, internship; for doctorate, qualifying exams, externship, internship, project.

**Entrance requirements:** For master's and doctorate, GRE General Test, GRE Subject Test, interview. *Application deadline:* For fall admission, 2/1 (priority date). Applications are processed on a rolling basis. *Application fee:* $65. Electronic applications accepted.

**Expenses:** Tuition: Part-time $545 per credit.

**Financial support:** Research assistantships, teaching assistantships, career-related internships or fieldwork, Federal Work-Study, and tuition waivers (partial) available. Support available to part-time students. Financial award applicants required to submit FAFSA.

Dr. Barbara Mowder, Director, 212-346-1506.

**Application contact:** Joanna Broda, Director of Admissions, 212-346-1652, *Fax:* 212-346-1585, *E-mail:* gradnyc@pace.edu. *Web site:* http://www.pace.edu/

**Find an in-depth description at www.petersons.com/gradchannel.**

## ■ THE PENNSYLVANIA STATE UNIVERSITY UNIVERSITY PARK CAMPUS

**Graduate School, College of Education, Department of Educational and School Psychology and Special Education, Program in School Psychology, State College, University Park, PA 16802-1503**

**AWARDS** M Ed, MS, PhD.

**Students:** 35 full-time (27 women), 19 part-time (17 women). In 2001, 3 degrees awarded.

**Entrance requirements:** For master's and doctorate, GRE General Test or MAT. *Application fee:* $45.

**Expenses:** Tuition, state resident: full-time $7,882; part-time $333 per credit. Tuition, nonresident: full-time $16,142; part-time $673 per credit. Required fees: $124 per semester.

Dr. Marley W. Watkins, Professor in Charge, 814-865-1881.

## ■ PITTSBURG STATE UNIVERSITY

**Graduate School, College of Education, Department of Psychology and Counseling, Program in School Psychology, Pittsburg, KS 66762**

**AWARDS** Ed S.

**Degree requirements:** For Ed S, thesis or alternative.

**Entrance requirements:** For degree, GRE General Test, minimum GPA of 3.0. *Application fee:* $0 ($40 for international students).

**Expenses:** Tuition, state resident: full-time $2,676; part-time $114 per credit hour. Tuition, nonresident: full-time $6,778; part-time $285 per credit hour.

**Financial support:** Teaching assistantships, career-related internships or fieldwork and Federal Work-Study available.

**Application contact:** Marvene Darraugh, Administrative Officer, 620-235-4220, *Fax:* 620-235-4219, *E-mail:* mdarraug@pittstate.edu.

## ■ PLATTSBURGH STATE UNIVERSITY OF NEW YORK

**Faculty of Arts and Science, Department of Psychology, Plattsburgh, NY 12901-2681**

**AWARDS** School psychology (MA, CAS). Part-time programs available.

**Students:** 12 full-time (8 women), 5 part-time (all women); includes 1 minority (Hispanic American).

**Degree requirements:** For master's, thesis, internship.

**Entrance requirements:** For master's, GRE General Test, minimum GPA of 3.0. *Application deadline:* For fall admission, 3/1 (priority date). Applications are processed on a rolling basis. *Application fee:* $50.

**Expenses:** Tuition, state resident: part-time $213 per credit hour. Tuition, nonresident: part-time $351 per credit hour.

**Financial support:** Federal Work-Study available. Support available to part-time students. Financial award application deadline: 4/15; financial award applicants required to submit FAFSA.

**Faculty research:** Alzheimer's disease, adolescent behavior, intellectual assessment, learning disabilities, reading skill acquisition.

Dr. William Gaeddert, Chair, 518-564-3076.

**Application contact:** Dr. Ronald Dumont, Chair, Graduate Admissions Committee.

## ■ PONTIFICAL CATHOLIC UNIVERSITY OF PUERTO RICO

**College of Education, Ponce, PR 00717-0777**

**AWARDS** Commercial education (MRE); curriculum instruction (M Ed); education (PhD); education-general (MRE); english as a second language (MRE); religious education (MA Ed); scholar psychology (MRE). Part-time and evening/weekend programs available.

**Faculty:** 7 full-time (5 women), 8 part-time/adjunct (6 women).

**Students:** 67 full-time (53 women), 255 part-time (193 women); all minorities (all Hispanic Americans). Average age 37. 158 applicants, 99% accepted, 109 enrolled. In 2001, 25 degrees awarded.

**Degree requirements:** For master's, thesis (for some programs), comprehensive exam.

**Entrance requirements:** For master's, GRE, 2 recommendation letters, interview, minimum GPA of 2.5. *Application deadline:* For fall admission, 4/30 (priority date). Applications are processed on a rolling basis. *Application fee:* $25. Electronic applications accepted.

**Expenses:** Tuition: Full-time $2,880; part-time $160 per credit. Required fees: $360. Tuition and fees vary according to degree level and program.

**Financial support:** Fellowships, career-related internships or fieldwork, Federal Work-Study, and tuition waivers (partial) available. Support available to part-time students. Financial award application deadline: 7/15.

**Faculty research:** Teaching English as a second language, learning styles, leadership styles.

Dr. Myvian Zayas, Chairperson, 787-841-2000 Ext. 1742.

*Pontifical Catholic University of Puerto Rico (continued)*
**Application contact:** Ana O. Bonilla, Director of Admissions, 787-841-2000 Ext. 1000, *Fax:* 787-840-4295. *Web site:* http://www.pucpr.edu/

## ■ QUEENS COLLEGE OF THE CITY UNIVERSITY OF NEW YORK

**Division of Graduate Studies, Division of Education, Department of Educational and Community Programs, Program in School Psychology, Flushing, NY 11367-1597**

**AWARDS** MS Ed, AC. Part-time programs available.

**Faculty:** 4 full-time (3 women), 5 part-time/adjunct (4 women).
**Students:** 23 full-time (18 women), 72 part-time (64 women). 127 applicants, 48% accepted. In 2001, 20 master's, 2 ACs awarded.
**Degree requirements:** For master's, internship, research project; for AC, internship, thesis optional.
**Entrance requirements:** For master's, TOEFL, minimum GPA of 3.0; for AC, TOEFL, master's degree or equivalent. *Application deadline:* For fall admission, 4/1; for spring admission, 11/1. Applications are processed on a rolling basis. *Application fee:* $40.
**Expenses:** Tuition, state resident: full-time $2,175; part-time $185 per credit. Tuition, nonresident: full-time $3,800; part-time $320 per credit. Required fees: $114; $57 per semester. Tuition and fees vary according to course load.
**Financial support:** Career-related internships or fieldwork, Federal Work-Study, institutionally sponsored loans, and tuition waivers (partial) available. Support available to part-time students. Financial award application deadline: 4/1; financial award applicants required to submit FAFSA.
Dr. Elizabeth Erwin, Coordinator and Graduate Adviser, 718-997-5230, *E-mail:* elizabeth_erwin@qc.edu.
**Application contact:** Mario Caruso, Director of Graduate Admissions, 718-997-5200, *Fax:* 718-997-5193, *E-mail:* graduate_admissions@qc.edu.

## ■ RADFORD UNIVERSITY

**Graduate College, College of Arts and Sciences, Department of Psychology, Program in School Psychology, Radford, VA 24142**

**AWARDS** Ed S. Part-time programs available. Postbaccalaureate distance learning degree programs offered (minimal on-campus study).
**Students:** 12 full-time (9 women), 7 part-time (5 women). Average age 24. 19

applicants, 100% accepted, 4 enrolled. In 2001, 10 degrees awarded.
**Degree requirements:** For Ed S, comprehensive exam.
**Entrance requirements:** For degree, GMAT, GRE General Test, MAT, NTE, TOEFL. *Application deadline:* For fall admission, 2/1 (priority date); for spring admission, 10/1. Applications are processed on a rolling basis. *Application fee:* $25. Electronic applications accepted.
**Expenses:** Tuition, state resident: full-time $2,564; part-time $167 per credit hour. Tuition, nonresident: full-time $6,314; part-time $323 per credit hour. Required fees: $1,440.
**Financial support:** In 2001–02, 16 students received support, including 4 research assistantships (averaging $4,263 per year); fellowships with tuition reimbursements available, teaching assistantships with tuition reimbursements available, career-related internships or fieldwork, Federal Work-Study, institutionally sponsored loans, and scholarships/grants also available. Financial award application deadline: 2/1; financial award applicants required to submit FAFSA.
Dr. Dianne Friedman, Director, 540-831-5361, *Fax:* 540-831-6113, *E-mail:* dfriedma@radford.edu. *Web site:* http://www.radford.edu/

## ■ RHODE ISLAND COLLEGE

**School of Graduate Studies, Feinstein School of Education and Human Development, Department of Counseling and Educational Psychology, Program in School Psychology, Providence, RI 02908-1991**

**AWARDS** CAGS.

**Faculty:** 2 full-time (0 women), 9 part-time/adjunct (5 women).
**Students:** 8 full-time (7 women), 4 part-time (all women). Average age 29. In 2001, 9 degrees awarded.
**Degree requirements:** For CAGS, thesis.
**Entrance requirements:** For degree, MAT. *Application deadline:* For fall admission, 4/1. Applications are processed on a rolling basis. *Application fee:* $25.
**Expenses:** Tuition, state resident: full-time $3,060; part-time $170 per credit. Tuition, nonresident: full-time $6,390; part-time $355 per credit.
**Financial support:** Application deadline: 4/1.
Dr. Murray H. Finley, Chair, Department of Counseling and Educational Psychology, 401-456-8023, *E-mail:* mfinley@ric.edu.

## ■ ROCHESTER INSTITUTE OF TECHNOLOGY

**Graduate Enrollment Services, College of Liberal Arts, Department of Behavioral Science, Program in School Psychology, Rochester, NY 14623-5698**

**AWARDS** MS, AC.

**Students:** 38 full-time (34 women), 7 part-time (all women); includes 2 minority (1 Asian American or Pacific Islander, 1 Hispanic American). 57 applicants, 58% accepted, 22 enrolled. In 2001, 30 master's, 18 other advanced degrees awarded.
*Application deadline:* For fall admission, 3/1 (priority date). Applications are processed on a rolling basis. Electronic applications accepted.
**Expenses:** Tuition: Full-time $20,928; part-time $587 per hour. Required fees: $162. Tuition and fees vary according to program.
Dr. Virginia Costenbader, Director, 585-475-2765, *E-mail:* vkcgsp@rit.edu.

## ■ ROWAN UNIVERSITY

**Graduate School, College of Education, Department of Special Educational Services/Instruction, Program in School Psychology, Glassboro, NJ 08028-1701**

**AWARDS** MA, Ed S. Part-time and evening/weekend programs available.

**Students:** 17 full-time (13 women), 57 part-time (46 women); includes 17 minority (9 African Americans, 4 Asian Americans or Pacific Islanders, 4 Hispanic Americans). Average age 32. 38 applicants, 76% accepted, 28 enrolled. In 2001, 35 degrees awarded.
**Degree requirements:** For master's, thesis, comprehensive exam; for Ed S, thesis or alternative.
**Entrance requirements:** For master's and Ed S, GRE General Test, GRE Subject Test, interview, minimum GPA of 3.0. *Application deadline:* For winter admission, 12/1 (priority date); for spring admission, 4/1 (priority date). Applications are processed on a rolling basis. *Application fee:* $50. Electronic applications accepted.
**Expenses:** Tuition, state resident: full-time $7,080; part-time $295 per semester hour. Tuition, nonresident: full-time $11,328; part-time $472 per semester hour. Required fees: $855; $39 per semester hour. Tuition and fees vary according to degree level.
**Financial support:** Career-related internships or fieldwork, Federal Work-Study, and unspecified assistantships available. Support available to part-time students.

Dr. John Klanderman, Adviser, 856-256-4500 Ext. 3797.

# ■ RUTGERS, THE STATE UNIVERSITY OF NEW JERSEY, NEW BRUNSWICK

**Graduate School of Applied and Professional Psychology, Program in School Psychology, New Brunswick, NJ 08901-1281**

AWARDS Psy M, Psy D.

**Degree requirements:** For doctorate, thesis/dissertation, 1 year internship.
**Entrance requirements:** For doctorate, GRE General Test, GRE Subject Test, bachelor's degree in psychology or equivalent.
**Faculty research:** Consultation, program evaluation, applied educational psychology, exceptional children, crisis intervention. *Web site:* http://www.rci.rutgers.edu/~gsapp

# ■ ST. JOHN'S UNIVERSITY

**St. John's College of Liberal Arts and Sciences, Department of Psychology, Program in School Psychology, Jamaica, NY 11439**

AWARDS MS, Psy D. Part-time programs available.

**Students:** 82 full-time (66 women), 60 part-time (47 women); includes 23 minority (6 African Americans, 4 Asian Americans or Pacific Islanders, 13 Hispanic Americans), 5 international. Average age 28. 140 applicants, 55% accepted, 46 enrolled. In 2001, 17 degrees awarded.
**Degree requirements:** For master's, comprehensive exam; for doctorate, thesis/dissertation, internship, comprehensive exam.
**Entrance requirements:** For master's, GRE General Test, GRE Subject Test, minimum GPA of 3.0, 2 writing samples; for doctorate, GRE General Test, GRE Subject Test, interview, minimum GPA of 3.0. *Application deadline:* For fall admission, 4/15. *Application fee:* $40.
**Expenses:** Contact institution.
**Financial support:** Fellowships with full tuition reimbursements, research assistantships, career-related internships or fieldwork, scholarships/grants, and unspecified assistantships available. Support available to part-time students. Financial award application deadline: 3/1; financial award applicants required to submit FAFSA.
**Faculty research:** Therapeutic alliance, intelligence testing, multicultural assessment, neuropsychological assessment, adolescent suicide.
Dr. Dawn Flanagan, Director, 718-990-5388.

**Application contact:** Matthew Whelan, Director, Office of Admission, 718-990-2000, *Fax:* 718-990-2096, *E-mail:* admissions@stjohns.edu. *Web site:* http://www.stjohns.edu/

# ■ ST. MARY'S UNIVERSITY OF SAN ANTONIO

**Graduate School, Department of Psychology, San Antonio, TX 78228-8507**

AWARDS Clinical psychology (MA, MS); industrial psychology (MA, MS); school psychology (MA). Part-time programs available.

**Faculty:** 5 full-time (4 women), 5 part-time/adjunct.
**Students:** 27 full-time (22 women), 35 part-time (29 women); includes 31 minority (6 African Americans, 1 Asian American or Pacific Islander, 24 Hispanic Americans), 1 international. Average age 24. In 2001, 17 degrees awarded.
**Degree requirements:** For master's, thesis (for some programs), comprehensive exam.
**Entrance requirements:** For master's, GRE General Test. *Application deadline:* Applications are processed on a rolling basis. *Application fee:* $15. Electronic applications accepted.
**Expenses:** Tuition: Full-time $8,190; part-time $455 per credit hour. Required fees: $375.
**Financial support:** Research assistantships, Federal Work-Study and institutionally sponsored loans available. Financial award application deadline: 2/15; financial award applicants required to submit FAFSA.
Dr. Willibrord Silva, Graduate Program Director, 210-436-3314.

# ■ SAM HOUSTON STATE UNIVERSITY

**College of Education and Applied Science, Department of Psychology and Philosophy, Program in School Psychology, Huntsville, TX 77341**

AWARDS MA. Part-time programs available.

**Students:** 1 (woman) full-time, 3 part-time (all women). Average age 26. In 2001, 4 degrees awarded.
**Degree requirements:** For master's, thesis, practicum.
**Entrance requirements:** For master's, GRE General Test or MAT, minimum GPA of 3.0. *Application deadline:* For fall admission, 8/1; for spring admission, 12/1. Applications are processed on a rolling basis. *Application fee:* $20.
**Expenses:** Tuition, area resident: Part-time $69 per credit. Tuition, state resident: full-time $1,380; part-time $69 per credit. Tuition, nonresident: full-time $5,600;

part-time $280 per credit. Required fees: $748. Tuition and fees vary according to course load.
**Financial support:** Teaching assistantships, career-related internships or fieldwork and institutionally sponsored loans available. Financial award application deadline: 5/31; financial award applicants required to submit FAFSA.
**Faculty research:** Malingering, eyewitness testimony. *Total annual research expenditures:* $7,500.
**Application contact:** Dr. Rowland Miller, Graduate Coordinator, 936-294-1176, *Fax:* 936-294-3798, *E-mail:* psy-rsm@shsu.edu. *Web site:* http://www.shsu.edu/~psy_www/school/

# ■ SAN DIEGO STATE UNIVERSITY

**Graduate and Research Affairs, College of Education, Department of Counseling and School Psychology, San Diego, CA 92182**

AWARDS MS. Evening/weekend programs available.

**Entrance requirements:** For master's, GRE General Test, TOEFL, interview.
**Faculty research:** Multicultural and cross-cultural counseling and training, AIDS counseling.

# ■ SEATTLE PACIFIC UNIVERSITY

**Graduate School, School of Education, Program in School Psychology, Seattle, WA 98119-1997**

AWARDS Ed S. Part-time programs available.

**Students:** 5 (4 women); includes 2 minority (1 Asian American or Pacific Islander, 1 Hispanic American). In 2001, 1 degree awarded.
**Degree requirements:** For Ed S, internship.
**Entrance requirements:** For degree, master's degree. *Application deadline:* Applications are processed on a rolling basis. *Application fee:* $50.
**Expenses:** Tuition: Part-time $300 per credit hour. Tuition and fees vary according to program.
**Financial support:** Applicants required to submit FAFSA.
Dr. William Rowley, Chair, 206-281-2671, *Fax:* 206-281-2756, *E-mail:* wrowley@spu.edu.
**Application contact:** Dr. Carol Stuen, Associate Director, 206-281-2710, *Fax:* 206-281-2756, *E-mail:* cstuen@spu.edu.

## ■ SEATTLE UNIVERSITY

School of Education, Program in Educational Diagnostics/School Psychology, Seattle, WA 98122

AWARDS Ed S. Part-time and evening/weekend programs available.

Students: 8 full-time (7 women), 30 part-time (24 women); includes 8 minority (2 African Americans, 3 Asian Americans or Pacific Islanders, 2 Hispanic Americans, 1 Native American). Average age 37. 13 applicants, 69% accepted, 7 enrolled. In 2001, 13 degrees awarded.
Degree requirements: For Ed S, comprehensive exam.
Entrance requirements: For degree, GRE or MAT, interview, 1 year of related experience. *Application deadline:* For fall admission, 7/1; for spring admission, 2/20. Applications are processed on a rolling basis. *Application fee:* $55.
Financial support: Career-related internships or fieldwork and Federal Work-Study available. Support available to part-time students. Financial award applicants required to submit FAFSA.
Dr. Kristen Guest, Coordinator, 206-296-5750, *E-mail:* kguest@seattleu.edu.
Application contact: Janet Shandley, Associate Dean of Graduate Admissions, 206-296-5900, *Fax:* 206-298-5656, *E-mail:* grad_admissions@seattleu.edu.

## ■ SETON HALL UNIVERSITY

College of Education and Human Services, Department of Professional Psychology and Family Therapy, Program in School Psychology, South Orange, NJ 07079-2697

AWARDS Ed S.

Degree requirements: For Ed S, thesis, internship, comprehensive exam.
Entrance requirements: For degree, GRE or MAT, interview.
Expenses: Tuition: Full-time $10,818; part-time $601 per credit. Required fees: $610; $185 per term. Tuition and fees vary according to course load, program and student's religious affiliation.
Faculty research: Family systems, ethical behavior, childhood depression.

## ■ SOUTHERN CONNECTICUT STATE UNIVERSITY

School of Graduate Studies, School of Education, Department of Counseling and School Psychology, New Haven, CT 06515-1355

AWARDS Community counseling (MS); counseling (Diploma); school counseling (MS); school psychology (MS, Diploma).

Faculty: 6 full-time (2 women), 11 part-time/adjunct.

Students: 85 full-time (67 women), 141 part-time (110 women); includes 22 minority (17 African Americans, 1 Asian American or Pacific Islander, 4 Hispanic Americans), 3 international. 194 applicants, 29% accepted. In 2001, 57 master's, 21 other advanced degrees awarded.
Degree requirements: For master's, comprehensive exam.
Entrance requirements: For master's, interview, previous course work in behavioral sciences, minimum QPA of 2.7. *Application deadline:* For fall admission, 1/15; for spring admission, 10/15. *Application fee:* $40.
Financial support: Teaching assistantships, career-related internships or fieldwork available. Financial award application deadline: 4/15; financial award applicants required to submit FAFSA.
Dr. Michael Martin, Chair, 203-392-5912, *E-mail:* martin_m@southernct.edu.
Application contact: Dr. Uchenna Nwachuku, Graduate Coordinator, Community Counseling Program, 203-392-5914, *E-mail:* nwachuku@southernct.edu. *Web site:* http://www.southernct.edu/

## ■ SOUTHERN ILLINOIS UNIVERSITY EDWARDSVILLE

Graduate Studies and Research, School of Education, Program in School Psychology, Edwardsville, IL 62026-0001

AWARDS Ed S. Part-time programs available.

Students: Average age 33. 10 applicants, 70% accepted, 2 enrolled. In 2001, 5 degrees awarded.
Degree requirements: For Ed S, thesis, registration. *Median time to degree:* 2.5 years full-time, 4 years part-time. *Application deadline:* For fall admission, 7/20; for spring admission, 12/7. *Application fee:* $25.
Expenses: Tuition, state resident: full-time $2,712; part-time $113 per credit hour. Tuition, nonresident: full-time $5,424; part-time $226 per credit hour. Required fees: $250; $125 per term. Tuition and fees vary according to course load, campus/location and reciprocity agreements.
Financial support: Fellowships, research assistantships, teaching assistantships, career-related internships or fieldwork, Federal Work-Study, institutionally sponsored loans, traineeships, and unspecified assistantships available. Financial award application deadline: 3/1; financial award applicants required to submit FAFSA.
Dr. Bryce Sullivan, Chair, 618-650-2202, *E-mail:* bsulliv@siue.edu.

## ■ SOUTHWEST TEXAS STATE UNIVERSITY

Graduate School, College of Education, Department of Educational Administration and Psychological Services, Program in School Psychology, San Marcos, TX 78666

AWARDS MA. Part-time programs available.

Students: 28 full-time (24 women), 15 part-time (13 women); includes 19 minority (4 African Americans, 15 Hispanic Americans). Average age 26. 31 applicants, 68% accepted, 13 enrolled. In 2001, 10 degrees awarded.
Degree requirements: For master's, comprehensive exam.
Entrance requirements: For master's, GRE General Test, TOEFL, interview, minimum GPA of 2.75 in last 60 hours. *Application deadline:* For fall admission, 6/15; for spring admission, 10/15. Applications are processed on a rolling basis. *Application fee:* $40 ($90 for international students).
Expenses: Tuition, state resident: full-time $1,512; part-time $84 per credit hour. Tuition, nonresident: full-time $5,310; part-time $295 per credit hour. Required fees: $864; $29 per credit hour. $195 per term. Full-time tuition and fees vary according to course load.
Financial support: Career-related internships or fieldwork, Federal Work-Study, and institutionally sponsored loans available. Support available to part-time students. Financial award application deadline: 4/1; financial award applicants required to submit FAFSA.
Dr. Alicia Scribner, Graduate Advisor, 512-245-8682, *Fax:* 512-245-8872, *E-mail:* as08@swt.edu. *Web site:* http://www.swt.edu/

## ■ STATE UNIVERSITY OF NEW YORK AT ALBANY

School of Education, Department of Educational and Counseling Psychology, Albany, NY 12222-0001

AWARDS Counseling psychology (MS, PhD, CAS); educational psychology (Ed D); educational psychology and statistics (MS); measurements and evaluation (Ed D); rehabilitation counseling (MS); school counselor (CAS); school psychology (Psy D, CAS); special education (MS); statistics and research design (Ed D). Evening/weekend programs available.

Students: 149 full-time (113 women), 106 part-time (85 women); includes 22 minority (7 African Americans, 1 Asian American or Pacific Islander, 14 Hispanic Americans), 15 international. Average age 31. 169 applicants, 28% accepted. In 2001,

86 master's, 19 doctorates, 24 other advanced degrees awarded.

**Degree requirements:** For doctorate, thesis/dissertation.

**Entrance requirements:** For doctorate, GRE General Test. *Application fee:* $50.

**Expenses:** Tuition, state resident: full-time $2,550; part-time $213 per credit. Tuition, nonresident: full-time $4,208; part-time $351 per credit. Required fees: $470; $470 per year.

**Financial support:** Fellowships, career-related internships or fieldwork available. Deborah May, Chair, 518-442-5050.

## ■ STATE UNIVERSITY OF NEW YORK AT OSWEGO

**Graduate Studies, School of Education, Department of Counseling and Psychological Services, Program in School Psychology, Oswego, NY 13126**

**AWARDS** MS, CAS, MS/CAS.

**Faculty:** 7 full-time, 6 part-time/adjunct. **Students:** 28 full-time (23 women), 23 part-time (16 women); includes 3 minority (2 African Americans, 1 Hispanic American). Average age 31. 33 applicants, 64% accepted. In 2001, 16 master's, 1 other advanced degree awarded.

**Degree requirements:** For master's, fieldwork; for CAS, fieldwork.

**Entrance requirements:** For master's, GRE General Test, GRE Subject Test, interview, minimum GPA of 3.0; for CAS, GRE General Test, GRE Subject Test, interview, MA or MS, minimum GPA of 3.0. *Application deadline:* For fall admission, 2/1. *Application fee:* $50.

**Expenses:** Tuition, state resident: full-time $5,100; part-time $213 per credit. Tuition, nonresident: full-time $8,416; part-time $351 per credit.

**Financial support:** Teaching assistantships, career-related internships or fieldwork, Federal Work-Study, institutionally sponsored loans, scholarships/grants, and tuition waivers (partial) available. Support available to part-time students. Financial award application deadline: 4/1; financial award applicants required to submit FAFSA.

**Faculty research:** Psychological applications in education and human services, evaluation of standard tests for admissions criteria.

Dr. Betsy Waterman, Chair, Department of Counseling and Psychological Services, 315-312-4051.

## ■ STEPHEN F. AUSTIN STATE UNIVERSITY

**Graduate School, College of Education, Department of Human Services, Nacogdoches, TX 75962**

**AWARDS** Counseling (MA); school psychology (MA); special education (M Ed); speech pathology (MS).

**Faculty:** 24 full-time (11 women). **Students:** 82 full-time (75 women), 120 part-time (110 women); includes 17 minority (11 African Americans, 1 Asian American or Pacific Islander, 4 Hispanic Americans, 1 Native American). 120 applicants, 48% accepted. In 2001, 71 degrees awarded.

**Degree requirements:** For master's, thesis (for some programs), comprehensive exam.

**Entrance requirements:** For master's, GRE General Test, TOEFL, minimum GPA of 2.8. *Application deadline:* For fall admission, 3/1; for spring admission, 10/1. *Application fee:* $25 ($50 for international students).

**Expenses:** Tuition, state resident: full-time $1,008; part-time $42 per credit. Tuition, nonresident: full-time $6,072; part-time $253 per credit. Required fees: $1,248; $52 per credit. Tuition and fees vary according to course load.

**Financial support:** In 2001–02, 4 research assistantships (averaging $6,633 per year), 2 teaching assistantships (averaging $6,633 per year) were awarded. Career-related internships or fieldwork, Federal Work-Study, institutionally sponsored loans, and traineeships also available. Support available to part-time students. Financial award application deadline: 3/1.

Dr. Anna Bradfield, Chair, 936-468-2906.

## ■ SYRACUSE UNIVERSITY

**Graduate School, College of Arts and Sciences, Department of Psychology, Program in School Psychology, Syracuse, NY 13244-0003**

**AWARDS** PhD.

**Degree requirements:** For doctorate, thesis/dissertation.

**Entrance requirements:** For doctorate, GRE General Test.

**Expenses:** Tuition: Full-time $15,528; part-time $647 per credit. Required fees: $420; $38 per term. Tuition and fees vary according to program.

## ■ TARLETON STATE UNIVERSITY

**College of Graduate Studies, College of Education, Department of Educational Administration, Counseling, and Psychology, Program in Counseling and Psychology, Stephenville, TX 76402**

**AWARDS** Counseling (M Ed); counseling psychology (M Ed); educational psychology (M Ed). Part-time programs available.

**Degree requirements:** For master's, thesis optional.

**Entrance requirements:** For master's, GRE General Test.

## ■ TEACHERS COLLEGE COLUMBIA UNIVERSITY

**Graduate Faculty of Education, Department of Health and Behavioral Studies, Program in Applied Educational Psychology—School Psychology, New York, NY 10027-6696**

**AWARDS** Ed M, MA, Ed D, PhD.

**Degree requirements:** For master's, integrative paper; for doctorate, thesis/dissertation, integrative project.

**Entrance requirements:** For doctorate, GRE General Test.

**Expenses:** Tuition: Full-time $19,080; part-time $780 per unit. Required fees: $170 per semester.

**Faculty research:** Psychoeducational assessment, observation and concept acquisition in young children, reading, mathematical thinking, memory, cognition and instruction.

## ■ TEMPLE UNIVERSITY

**Graduate School, College of Education, Department of Psychological Studies in Education, Program in School Psychology, Philadelphia, PA 19122-6096**

**AWARDS** Ed M, PhD. Part-time and evening/weekend programs available. Terminal master's awarded for partial completion of doctoral program.

**Degree requirements:** For master's, thesis or alternative; for doctorate, thesis/dissertation.

**Entrance requirements:** For master's, GRE General Test or MAT, minimum GPA of 2.8; for doctorate, GRE General Test or MAT, minimum GPA of 3.0 during previous 2 years, 2.8 overall.

**Expenses:** Tuition, state resident: full-time $8,487; part-time $369 per credit hour. Tuition, nonresident: full-time $12,282; part-time $534 per credit hour. Required fees: $350. Tuition and fees vary according to course load, program and reciprocity agreements.

## ■ TENNESSEE STATE UNIVERSITY

**Graduate School, College of Education, Department of Psychology, Nashville, TN 37209-1561**

**AWARDS** Counseling and guidance (MS), including counseling, elementary school counseling, organizational counseling, secondary school counseling; counseling psychology (PhD); psychology (MS, PhD); school psychology (MS, PhD). Part-time and evening/weekend programs available.

**Faculty:** 13 full-time (6 women), 9 part-time/adjunct (7 women).
**Students:** 43 full-time (34 women), 76 part-time (56 women). Average age 29. 75 applicants, 95% accepted. In 2001, 9 master's, 10 doctorates awarded.
**Degree requirements:** For master's, comprehensive exam or thesis; for doctorate, thesis/dissertation, comprehensive exam.
**Entrance requirements:** For master's, GRE General Test; for doctorate, GRE General Test or MAT, minimum GPA of 3.25, work experience. *Application deadline:* Applications are processed on a rolling basis. *Application fee:* $15.
**Expenses:** Tuition, state resident: full-time $3,884; part-time $247 per hour. Tuition, nonresident: full-time $10,356; part-time $517 per hour.
**Financial support:** In 2001–02, 2 fellowships (averaging $5,924 per year), 3 research assistantships (averaging $5,962 per year), 6 teaching assistantships (averaging $17,432 per year) were awarded. Financial award application deadline: 5/1.
**Faculty research:** Stress reduction, student retention, computer education, marital and family therapy, increasing of faculty effectiveness. *Total annual research expenditures:* $50,000.
Dr. Peter Millet, Head, 615-963-5139, *Fax:* 615-963-5140.
**Application contact:** Dr. Helen Barrett, Dean of the Graduate School, 615-963-5901, *Fax:* 615-963-5963, *E-mail:* hbarrett@picard.tnstate.edu.

## ■ TEXAS A&M UNIVERSITY

**College of Education, Department of Educational Psychology, Program in School Psychology, College Station, TX 77843**

**AWARDS** PhD.

**Faculty:** 2 full-time (both women), 6 part-time/adjunct (2 women).
**Students:** 32 full-time (25 women), 28 part-time (24 women); includes 24 minority (5 African Americans, 4 Asian Americans or Pacific Islanders, 15 Hispanic Americans), 1 international. 26

applicants, 54% accepted, 9 enrolled. In 2001, 5 degrees awarded.
**Degree requirements:** For doctorate, thesis/dissertation. *Median time to degree:* Doctorate–5.5 years full-time.
**Entrance requirements:** For doctorate, GRE General Test, TOEFL. *Application deadline:* For fall admission, 12/15. *Application fee:* $50 ($75 for international students). Electronic applications accepted.
**Expenses:** Tuition, state resident: full-time $11,872. Tuition, nonresident: full-time $17,892.
**Financial support:** In 2001–02, 5 fellowships (averaging $12,000 per year), 19 research assistantships (averaging $8,400 per year), 1 teaching assistantship (averaging $9,000 per year) were awarded. Scholarships/grants and unspecified assistantships also available. Financial award applicants required to submit FAFSA.
**Faculty research:** Assessment, child therapy, bilingual, neuropsychology.
Dr. Michael J. Ash, Director of Training, 979-845-1875, *Fax:* 979-862-1256, *E-mail:* mash@tamu.edu.
**Application contact:** Carol A. Wagner, Graduate Advisor, 979-845-1833, *Fax:* 979-862-1256, *E-mail:* c-wagner@tamu.edu.

## ■ TEXAS WOMAN'S UNIVERSITY

**Graduate Studies and Research, College of Arts and Sciences, Department of Psychology and Philosophy, Denton, TX 76201**

**AWARDS** Counseling psychology (MA, PhD); school psychology (MA, PhD).

**Faculty:** 10 full-time (6 women), 2 part-time/adjunct (0 women).
**Students:** 51 full-time (all women), 101 part-time (85 women); includes 25 minority (5 African Americans, 7 Asian Americans or Pacific Islanders, 13 Hispanic Americans). Average age 36. 121 applicants, 39% accepted, 40 enrolled. In 2001, 14 master's, 11 doctorates awarded. Terminal master's awarded for partial completion of doctoral program.
**Degree requirements:** For master's, thesis; for doctorate, variable foreign language requirement, thesis/dissertation, internship, residency. *Median time to degree:* Master's–3 years full-time, 4 years part-time; doctorate–5 years full-time, 7 years part-time.
**Entrance requirements:** For master's, GRE General Test, minimum GPA of 3.5 in psychology, 3.0 overall; for doctorate, GRE General Test, minimum graduate GPA of 3.5 in psychology, 3.0 overall, 3 letters of reference. *Application deadline:* For fall admission, 2/1. *Application fee:* $30.

**Expenses:** Tuition, state resident: part-time $90 per semester hour. Tuition, nonresident: part-time $303 per semester hour. Required fees: $24 per credit hour. $79 per semester.
**Financial support:** In 2001–02, 12 teaching assistantships (averaging $8,514 per year) were awarded; research assistantships, career-related internships or fieldwork, Federal Work-Study, and institutionally sponsored loans also available. Support available to part-time students. Financial award application deadline: 4/1.
Dr. Basil Hamilton, Chair, 940-898-2303, *Fax:* 940-898-2301, *E-mail:* bhamilton@twu.edu. *Web site:* http://www.twu.edu/as/psyphil/

## ■ TOWSON UNIVERSITY

**Graduate School, Program in School Psychology, Towson, MD 21252-0001**

**AWARDS** Clinical psychology (MA); counseling psychology (MA); experimental psychology (MA); psychology (MA); school psychology (MA, CAS). Part-time and evening/weekend programs available.

**Faculty:** 13 full-time (5 women), 2 part-time/adjunct (both women).
**Students:** 195. In 2001, 64 master's, 15 other advanced degrees awarded.
**Degree requirements:** For master's, thesis (for some programs), exams.
**Entrance requirements:** For master's, GRE General Test. *Application deadline:* For fall admission, 2/1; for spring admission, 10/1. *Application fee:* $40. Electronic applications accepted.
**Expenses:** Tuition, state resident: part-time $211 per credit. Tuition, nonresident: part-time $435 per credit. Required fees: $52 per credit.
**Financial support:** Fellowships, Federal Work-Study and unspecified assistantships available. Financial award application deadline: 4/1; financial award applicants required to submit FAFSA.
**Faculty research:** Cognitive behavior, issues affecting the aging, relaxation hypnosis and imagery, lesbian and gay issues.
Dr. Susan Bartels, Director, 410-704-3070, *Fax:* 410-704-3800, *E-mail:* sbartels@towson.edu.
**Application contact:** 410-704-2501, *Fax:* 410-704-4675, *E-mail:* grads@towson.edu.

## ■ TRINITY UNIVERSITY

**Division of Behavioral and Administrative Studies, Department of Education, Program in School Psychology, San Antonio, TX 78212-7200**

**AWARDS** MA.

**Faculty:** 2 full-time (1 woman), 9 part-time/adjunct (4 women).
**Students:** 22 full-time (19 women), 15 part-time (12 women); includes 13 minority (1 Asian American or Pacific Islander, 12 Hispanic Americans), 1 international. Average age 25. In 2001, 15 degrees awarded.
**Entrance requirements:** For master's, GRE General Test, minimum GPA of 3.0, interview. *Application deadline:* For fall admission, 4/1. Applications are processed on a rolling basis. *Application fee:* $30.
**Expenses:** Tuition: Full-time $16,410; part-time $684 per credit hour. Required fees: $6 per credit hour.
**Financial support:** Fellowships, research assistantships, career-related internships or fieldwork, Federal Work-Study, and institutionally sponsored loans available. Support available to part-time students. Financial award application deadline: 4/1. Dr. Terry Migliore, Director, 210-999-7501, *Fax:* 210-999-7592, *E-mail:* terry.migliore@trinity.edu. *Web site:* http://www.trinity.edu/departments/education/ma.htm

## ■ TUFTS UNIVERSITY

**Division of Graduate and Continuing Studies and Research, Graduate School of Arts and Sciences, Department of Education, Program in School Psychology, Medford, MA 02155**

**AWARDS** MA, CAGS.

**Faculty:** 12 full-time, 5 part-time/adjunct.
**Students:** 44 (40 women); includes 5 minority (2 African Americans, 3 Asian Americans or Pacific Islanders) 1 international. 56 applicants, 66% accepted. In 2001, 15 master's, 15 other advanced degrees awarded.
**Entrance requirements:** For master's, GRE General Test, TOEFL. *Application deadline:* For fall admission, 2/15; for spring admission, 10/15. Applications are processed on a rolling basis. *Application fee:* $50. Electronic applications accepted.
**Expenses:** Tuition: Full-time $26,853. Full-time tuition and fees vary according to program.
**Financial support:** Federal Work-Study, scholarships/grants, and tuition waivers (full and partial) available. Financial award application deadline: 2/15.
**Application contact:** Caroline Wandle, Professor, 617-627-2343, *Fax:* 617-627-3901. *Web site:* http://www.ase.tufts.edu/education/proginfo.html

## ■ UNIVERSITY AT BUFFALO, THE STATE UNIVERSITY OF NEW YORK

**Graduate School, Graduate School of Education, Department of Counseling, School, and Educational Psychology, Buffalo, NY 14260**

**AWARDS** Counseling school psychology (PhD); counselor education (PhD); educational psychology (MA, PhD); rehabilitation counseling (MS); school counseling (Ed M, Certificate); school psychology (MA). Part-time programs available.

**Faculty:** 15 full-time (5 women), 4 part-time/adjunct (2 women).
**Students:** 137 full-time (106 women), 90 part-time (63 women); includes 30 minority (19 African Americans, 3 Asian Americans or Pacific Islanders, 7 Hispanic Americans, 1 Native American), 7 international. Average age 25. 203 applicants, 43% accepted. In 2001, 37 master's, 14 doctorates, 13 other advanced degrees awarded.
**Degree requirements:** For master's, thesis (for some programs); for doctorate, thesis/dissertation, comprehensive exam.
**Entrance requirements:** For master's and doctorate, GRE General Test, TOEFL, interview. *Application deadline:* For fall admission, 2/1 (priority date). *Application fee:* $50. Electronic applications accepted.
**Expenses:** Tuition, state resident: full-time $6,118. Tuition, nonresident: full-time $9,434.
**Financial support:** In 2001–02, 30 students received support, including 10 fellowships with full tuition reimbursements available (averaging $10,000 per year), 16 research assistantships with full tuition reimbursements available (averaging $8,000 per year); teaching assistantships, career-related internships or fieldwork, Federal Work-Study, institutionally sponsored loans, and unspecified assistantships also available. Financial award application deadline: 2/1; financial award applicants required to submit FAFSA.
**Faculty research:** Counseling process, vocational psychology, assessment and evaluation, learning and development, grief counseling. *Total annual research expenditures:* $1.1 million.
Dr. Timothy P. Janikowski, Chairperson, 716-645-2484 Ext. 1055, *Fax:* 716-645-6616, *E-mail:* tjanikow@buffalo.edu. *Web site:* http://www.gse.buffalo.edu/dc/cep/

## ■ THE UNIVERSITY OF AKRON

**Graduate School, College of Education, Department of Counseling, Program in Classroom Guidance for Teachers, Akron, OH 44325-0001**

**AWARDS** MA, MS.

**Students:** Average age 32. In 2001, 22 degrees awarded.
**Degree requirements:** For master's, thesis optional.
**Entrance requirements:** For master's, MAT, minimum GPA of 2.75. *Application deadline:* For fall admission, 8/15. Applications are processed on a rolling basis. *Application fee:* $25 ($50 for international students).
**Expenses:** Tuition, state resident: full-time $6,562; part-time $219 per credit. Tuition, nonresident: full-time $9,027; part-time $383 per credit. Required fees: $272; $11 per credit. Tuition and fees vary according to course load.

## ■ THE UNIVERSITY OF AKRON

**Graduate School, College of Education, Department of Counseling, Program in Guidance and Counseling, Akron, OH 44325-0001**

**AWARDS** PhD.

**Students:** 18 full-time (13 women), 16 part-time (12 women); includes 4 minority (2 African Americans, 2 Asian Americans or Pacific Islanders). Average age 37. 13 applicants, 85% accepted, 8 enrolled. In 2001, 2 degrees awarded.
**Degree requirements:** For doctorate, one foreign language, thesis/dissertation, written and oral exams, other language alternatives.
**Entrance requirements:** For doctorate, GRE, MAT, interview, minimum GPA of 3.25. *Application deadline:* For fall admission, 8/15. Applications are processed on a rolling basis. *Application fee:* $40 ($50 for international students).
**Expenses:** Tuition, state resident: full-time $6,562; part-time $219 per credit. Tuition, nonresident: full-time $9,027; part-time $383 per credit. Required fees: $272; $11 per credit. Tuition and fees vary according to course load.
**Financial support:** Fellowships, research assistantships, teaching assistantships, career-related internships or fieldwork and unspecified assistantships available.

## ■ THE UNIVERSITY OF ALABAMA AT BIRMINGHAM

**Graduate School, School of Education, Department of Human Studies, Program in Counseling, Birmingham, AL 35294**

**AWARDS** Agency counseling (MA); marriage and family counseling (MA); rehabilitation

*The University of Alabama at Birmingham (continued)*
counseling (MA); school counseling (MA); school psychology (MA Ed).

**Students:** 43 full-time (35 women), 103 part-time (84 women); includes 36 minority (35 African Americans, 1 Asian American or Pacific Islander, 4 international. 152 applicants, 84% accepted. In 2001, 29 degrees awarded.
**Degree requirements:** For master's, thesis optional.
**Entrance requirements:** For master's, GRE General Test, MAT, or NTE, minimum GPA of 3.0. *Application deadline:* Applications are processed on a rolling basis. *Application fee:* $35 ($60 for international students). Electronic applications accepted.
**Expenses:** Tuition, state resident: full-time $3,058. Tuition, nonresident: full-time $5,746. Tuition and fees vary according to course load, degree level and program.
**Financial support:** Career-related internships or fieldwork available.
Dr. David M. Macrina, Chairperson, Department of Human Studies, 205-934-2446, *Fax:* 205-975-8040, *E-mail:* dmacrina@uab.edu.

■ **UNIVERSITY OF CALIFORNIA, BERKELEY**

**Graduate Division, School of Education, Division of Cognition and Development, Program in School Psychology, Berkeley, CA 94720-1500**

AWARDS PhD.

**Expenses:** Tuition, nonresident: full-time $10,704. Required fees: $4,349. *Web site:* http://www-gse.berkeley.edu/

■ **UNIVERSITY OF CALIFORNIA, SANTA BARBARA**

**Graduate Division, Graduate School of Education, Program in Clinical/School/Counseling Psychology, Santa Barbara, CA 93106**

AWARDS Clinical/school/counseling psychology (PhD); school psychology (M Ed).

**Degree requirements:** For master's, thesis or alternative; for doctorate, thesis/dissertation.
**Entrance requirements:** For master's and doctorate, GRE General Test or MAT, TOEFL, background questionnaire, minimum GPA of 3.0. Electronic applications accepted.

■ **UNIVERSITY OF CENTRAL ARKANSAS**

**Graduate School, College of Education, Department of Counseling and Psychology, Program in School Psychology, Conway, AR 72035-0001**

AWARDS MS, PhD.

**Faculty:** 18.
**Students:** 19 full-time (18 women), 6 part-time (all women); includes 2 minority (both African Americans). In 2001, 15 degrees awarded.
**Degree requirements:** For master's, thesis optional.
**Entrance requirements:** For master's, GRE General Test, minimum GPA of 2.7. *Application deadline:* For fall admission, 3/1 (priority date); for spring admission, 10/1. Applications are processed on a rolling basis. *Application fee:* $25 ($40 for international students).
**Expenses:** Tuition, state resident: full-time $3,303; part-time $184 per hour. Tuition, nonresident: full-time $5,922; part-time $329 per hour. Required fees: $68; $24 per semester.
**Financial support:** In 2001–02, 14 students received support, including 4 research assistantships with partial tuition reimbursements available (averaging $6,000 per year); career-related internships or fieldwork, Federal Work-Study, and scholarships/grants also available. Financial award application deadline: 2/15.
Dr. John Murphy, Coordinator, 501-450-3193, *Fax:* 501-450-5424, *E-mail:* jmurphy@mail.uca.edu.
**Application contact:** Jane Douglas, Co-Admissions Secretary, 501-450-5064, *Fax:* 501-450-5066, *E-mail:* janed@ecom.uca.edu.

■ **UNIVERSITY OF CENTRAL FLORIDA**

**College of Education, Department of Child, Family and Community Sciences, Program in School Psychology, Orlando, FL 32816**

AWARDS Ed S. Part-time and evening/weekend programs available.

**Students:** 43 full-time (40 women), 6 part-time (5 women); includes 9 minority (1 African American, 3 Asian Americans or Pacific Islanders, 4 Hispanic Americans, 1 Native American). Average age 29. 35 applicants, 54% accepted, 18 enrolled. In 2001, 16 degrees awarded.
**Degree requirements:** For Ed S, thesis or alternative, practicum, internship.
**Entrance requirements:** For degree, GRE General Test, TOEFL, minimum GPA of 3.0, resumé, interview. *Application deadline:* For fall admission, 3/1. *Application fee:* $20. Electronic applications accepted.

**Expenses:** Tuition, state resident: part-time $162 per hour. Tuition, nonresident: part-time $569 per hour.
**Financial support:** In 2001–02, 10 fellowships with partial tuition reimbursements (averaging $3,150 per year), 50 research assistantships with partial tuition reimbursements (averaging $2,442 per year) were awarded. Teaching assistantships with partial tuition reimbursements, career-related internships or fieldwork, Federal Work-Study, institutionally sponsored loans, tuition waivers (partial), and unspecified assistantships also available. Financial award application deadline: 3/1; financial award applicants required to submit FAFSA.
Dr. Carl Balado, Coordinator, 407-823-2054, *E-mail:* cbalado@mail.ucf.edu. *Web site:* http://www.ucf.edu/

■ **UNIVERSITY OF CINCINNATI**

**Division of Research and Advanced Studies, College of Education, Division of Human Services, Program in School Psychology, Cincinnati, OH 45221**

AWARDS M Ed, PhD. Part-time programs available.

**Faculty:** 5 full-time (2 women), 5 part-time/adjunct (4 women).
**Students:** 37 full-time (33 women), 20 part-time (18 women). 57 applicants, 30% accepted, 15 enrolled. In 2001, 7 master's, 5 doctorates awarded.
**Degree requirements:** For master's, thesis or alternative, comprehensive exam; for doctorate, thesis/dissertation, comprehensive exam. *Median time to degree:* Master's–1.75 years full-time; doctorate–6 years full-time.
**Entrance requirements:** For master's, GRE General Test; for doctorate, GRE General Test, GRE Subject Test. *Application deadline:* For fall admission, 2/1. *Application fee:* $30. Electronic applications accepted.
**Expenses:** Tuition, state resident: part-time $2,698 per quarter. Tuition, nonresident: part-time $4,977 per quarter.
**Financial support:** In 2001–02, 9 research assistantships with full tuition reimbursements (averaging $10,000 per year) were awarded; fellowships, career-related internships or fieldwork, scholarships/grants, and tuition waivers (partial) also available. Financial award application deadline: 2/15.
**Faculty research:** School psychology services delivery, direct assessment and intervention.
**Application contact:** Dr. Janet Graden, Graduate Coordinator, 513-556-3337, *Fax:* 513-556-3898, *E-mail:* janet.graden@uc.edu. *Web site:* http://www.education.uc.edu/

## ■ UNIVERSITY OF CONNECTICUT

**Graduate School, School of Education, Field of School Psychology, Storrs, CT 06269**

**AWARDS** MA, PhD. Terminal master's awarded for partial completion of doctoral program.

**Degree requirements:** For master's, thesis or alternative; for doctorate, thesis/dissertation.

**Entrance requirements:** For doctorate, GRE General Test.

## ■ UNIVERSITY OF DAYTON

**Graduate School, School of Education and Allied Professions, Department of Counselor Education and Human Services, Dayton, OH 45469-1300**

**AWARDS** College student personnel (MS Ed); community counseling (MS Ed); higher education administration (MS Ed); human development services (MS Ed); school counseling (MS Ed); school psychology (MS Ed); teacher as child/youth development specialist (MS Ed). Part-time and evening/weekend programs available.

**Faculty:** 9 full-time (4 women), 23 part-time/adjunct (13 women).
**Students:** 23 full-time (21 women), 421 part-time (323 women). Average age 32. 263 applicants, 60% accepted. In 2001, 233 degrees awarded.
**Degree requirements:** For master's, exit exam, thesis optional.
**Entrance requirements:** For master's, MAT or GRE if GPA is below 2.75, interview. *Application deadline:* For fall admission, 2/15 (priority date). Applications are processed on a rolling basis. *Application fee:* $30.
**Expenses:** Tuition: Full-time $5,436; part-time $453 per credit hour. Required fees: $50; $25 per term.
**Financial support:** In 2001–02, 3 research assistantships with partial tuition reimbursements (averaging $6,100 per year) were awarded; Federal Work-Study and institutionally sponsored loans also available.
**Faculty research:** Anger as part of the grief process, inclusion of children with severe disabilities, comparisons of school counselors in Bosnia and the U. S., graduate and professional student socialization, use of cohort groups in doctoral programs.
Dr. Thomas W. Rueth, Chairperson, 937-229-3644, *Fax:* 937-229-1055, *E-mail:* thomas.rueth@notes.udayton.edu.

## ■ UNIVERSITY OF DELAWARE

**College of Human Services, Education and Public Policy, Program in College Counseling/Student Affairs Practice in Higher Education, Newark, DE 19716**

**AWARDS** College counseling (M Ed); student affairs practice in higher education (M Ed).
**Faculty:** 1 full-time (0 women), 9 part-time/adjunct (4 women).
**Students:** 20 full-time (16 women), 1 (woman) part-time; includes 3 minority (2 African Americans, 1 Native American). Average age 30. 23 applicants, 35% accepted, 4 enrolled. In 2001, 4 degrees awarded.
**Entrance requirements:** For master's, GRE, on-campus interview. *Application deadline:* Applications are processed on a rolling basis. *Application fee:* $50.
**Expenses:** Tuition, state resident: full-time $4,770; part-time $265 per credit. Tuition, nonresident: full-time $13,860; part-time $770 per credit. Required fees: $414.
**Financial support:** In 2001–02, 21 students received support, including 2 research assistantships with full tuition reimbursements available (averaging $5,500 per year), 21 teaching assistantships with full tuition reimbursements available (averaging $10,500 per year)
John Bishop, Associate Vice President, Student Life and Associate Professor, 302-831-8107, *Fax:* 302-831-2148.

## ■ UNIVERSITY OF DELAWARE

**College of Human Services, Education and Public Policy, School of Education, Newark, DE 19716**

**AWARDS** Cognition and instruction (MA); cognition, development, and instruction (PhD); curriculum and instruction (M Ed, PhD); educational leadership (M Ed, Ed D); educational policy (MA, PhD); English as a second language/bilingualism (MA); exceptional children (M Ed); exceptionality (PhD); instruction (MI); measurements, statistics, and evaluation (MA, PhD); school counseling (M Ed); school psychology (MA); secondary education (M Ed). Part-time and evening/weekend programs available.
**Faculty:** 45 full-time (23 women), 1 part-time/adjunct (0 women).
**Students:** 99 full-time (71 women), 233 part-time (177 women); includes 36 minority (27 African Americans, 3 Asian Americans or Pacific Islanders, 5 Hispanic Americans, 1 Native American), 9 international. 317 applicants, 65% accepted. In 2001, 77 master's, 19 doctorates awarded. Terminal master's awarded for partial completion of doctoral program.
**Degree requirements:** For master's, thesis (for some programs), comprehensive exam (for some programs), registration; for doctorate, thesis/dissertation,

comprehensive exam (for some programs), registration.
**Entrance requirements:** For master's and doctorate, GRE, letters of recommendation (3), goal statement. *Application deadline:* For fall admission, 7/1; for spring admission, 1/15. Applications are processed on a rolling basis. *Application fee:* $50.
**Expenses:** Tuition, state resident: full-time $4,770; part-time $265 per credit. Tuition, nonresident: full-time $13,860; part-time $770 per credit. Required fees: $414.
**Financial support:** In 2001–02, 65 students received support, including 2 fellowships with full tuition reimbursements available (averaging $11,000 per year), 28 research assistantships with full tuition reimbursements available (averaging $11,200 per year), 19 teaching assistantships with full tuition reimbursements available (averaging $11,000 per year); career-related internships or fieldwork, Federal Work-Study, tuition waivers (partial), and unspecified assistantships also available. Financial award application deadline: 3/1.
**Faculty research:** Conceptual change and teaching, infant language development, curriculum theory and development, covariance structure modeling theory, achievement testing. *Total annual research expenditures:* $4.9 million.
Dr. Christopher M. Clark, Director, 302-831-2573, *Fax:* 302-831-4421, *E-mail:* cmclark@udel.edu.
**Application contact:** Dr. Gail S. Rys, Assistant Director, 302-831-1165, *Fax:* 302-831-4421, *E-mail:* gailrys@udel.edu. *Web site:* http://www.udel.edu/educ

## ■ UNIVERSITY OF DENVER

**College of Education, Denver, CO 80208**

**AWARDS** Counseling psychology (MA, PhD); curriculum and instruction (MA, PhD), including curriculum leadership; educational psychology (MA, PhD, Ed S), including child and family studies (MA, PhD), quantitative research methods (MA, PhD), school psychology (PhD, Ed S); higher education and adult studies (MA, PhD); school administration (PhD). Part-time and evening/weekend programs available. Postbaccalaureate distance learning degree programs offered (no on-campus study).
**Faculty:** 25 full-time (16 women), 1 (woman) part-time/adjunct.
**Students:** 392 (312 women); includes 47 minority (10 African Americans, 11 Asian Americans or Pacific Islanders, 23 Hispanic Americans, 3 Native Americans) 12 international. Average age 31. 352 applicants, 68% accepted. In 2001, 71 master's, 27 doctorates awarded.
**Degree requirements:** For master's, comprehensive exam; for doctorate, 2

*University of Denver (continued)*
foreign languages, thesis/dissertation, comprehensive exam.
**Entrance requirements:** For master's and doctorate, GRE General Test, TSE. *Application deadline:* For fall admission, 1/1. Applications are processed on a rolling basis. *Application fee:* $45. Electronic applications accepted.
**Expenses:** Tuition: Full-time $21,456.
**Financial support:** In 2001–02, 92 students received support, including 7 fellowships with full and partial tuition reimbursements available, 1 research assistantship with full and partial tuition reimbursement available (averaging $7,785 per year), 19 teaching assistantships with full and partial tuition reimbursements available (averaging $7,677 per year); career-related internships or fieldwork, Federal Work-Study, institutionally sponsored loans, and scholarships/grants also available. Support available to part-time students. Financial award application deadline: 3/1; financial award applicants required to submit FAFSA.
**Faculty research:** Parkinson's disease, personnel training, development and assessments, gifted education, sexual functioning, service learning. *Total annual research expenditures:* $369,539.
Dr. Virginia Maloney, Dean, 303-871-3828.
**Application contact:** Linda McCarthy, Contact, 303-871-2509. *Web site:* http:// www.du.edu/education/

■ **UNIVERSITY OF DETROIT MERCY**

**College of Liberal Arts and Education, Department of Psychology, Program in School Psychology, Detroit, MI 48219-0900**

**AWARDS** Spec.

**Faculty:** 14 full-time (10 women).
**Students:** 14 full-time (13 women), 22 part-time (21 women); includes 8 minority (6 African Americans, 1 Hispanic American, 1 Native American). In 2001, 10 degrees awarded.
*Application deadline:* For fall admission, 8/1 (priority date). Applications are processed on a rolling basis. *Application fee:* $30 ($50 for international students).
**Expenses:** Tuition: Full-time $10,620; part-time $590 per credit hour. Required fees: $400. Tuition and fees vary according to program.
Dr. Mary Hannah, Head, 313-993-6167, *Fax:* 313-993-6397, *E-mail:* hannahme@ udmercy.edu.

■ **UNIVERSITY OF FLORIDA**

**Graduate School, College of Education, Department of Educational Psychology, Gainesville, FL 32611**

**AWARDS** Educational psychology (M Ed, MAE, Ed D, PhD, Ed S); school psychology (MAE, Ed D, PhD, Ed S); statistics, measurement and evaluation methodology (Ed S); statistics, measurement, and evaluation methodology (M Ed, MAE, Ed D, PhD). Terminal master's awarded for partial completion of doctoral program.

**Degree requirements:** For master's, thesis (MAE); for doctorate, variable foreign language requirement, thesis/dissertation.
**Entrance requirements:** For master's and doctorate, GRE General Test, minimum GPA of 3.0; for Ed S, GRE General Test. Electronic applications accepted.
**Expenses:** Tuition, state resident: part-time $164 per hour. Tuition, nonresident: part-time $571 per hour. Tuition and fees vary according to course level and program.
**Faculty research:** School improvement, teaching and learning, item response theory. *Web site:* http://www.coe.ufl.edu/ Foundations/Foundations.html

■ **UNIVERSITY OF GEORGIA**

**Graduate School, College of Education, Department of Educational Psychology, Athens, GA 30602**

**AWARDS** Education of the gifted (Ed D); educational psychology (M Ed, MA, PhD); school psychology and school psychometry (Ed S).

**Faculty:** 21 full-time (8 women).
**Students:** 64 full-time (44 women), 37 part-time (33 women); includes 11 minority (9 African Americans, 1 Asian American or Pacific Islander, 1 Hispanic American), 15 international. 123 applicants, 30% accepted. In 2001, 14 master's, 21 doctorates awarded.
**Degree requirements:** For master's, thesis (MA); for doctorate, variable foreign language requirement, thesis/dissertation.
**Entrance requirements:** For master's and Ed S, GRE General Test or MAT; for doctorate, GRE General Test. *Application deadline:* For fall admission, 7/1 (priority date); for spring admission, 11/15. *Application fee:* $30. Electronic applications accepted.
**Expenses:** Tuition, state resident: full-time $2,376; part-time $132 per credit hour. Tuition, nonresident: full-time $9,504; part-time $528 per credit hour. Required fees: $236 per semester.
**Financial support:** Fellowships, research assistantships, teaching assistantships, unspecified assistantships available.

Dr. Randy W. Kamphaus, Graduate Coordinator, 706-542-4110, *Fax:* 706-542-4240, *E-mail:* rkamp@coe.uga.edu.
**Application contact:** Dr. Bonnie Cramond, Information Contact, 706-542-4248, *Fax:* 706-542-4240, *E-mail:* bonnie@ coe.uga.edu. *Web site:* http:// www.coe.uga.edu/edpsych/

■ **UNIVERSITY OF HARTFORD**

**College of Arts and Sciences, Department of Psychology, Program in School Psychology, West Hartford, CT 06117-1599**

**AWARDS** MS. Part-time programs available.

**Faculty:** 4 full-time (1 woman), 6 part-time/adjunct (1 woman).
**Students:** 15 full-time (13 women), 13 part-time (10 women). Average age 27. 27 applicants, 78% accepted. In 2001, 11 degrees awarded.
**Degree requirements:** For master's, comprehensive exam.
**Entrance requirements:** For master's, GRE General Test, GRE Subject Test, TOEFL, minimum GPA of 3.0. *Application deadline:* For fall admission, 2/15 (priority date). *Application fee:* $40 ($55 for international students). Electronic applications accepted.
**Expenses:** Tuition: Part-time $300 per credit hour.
**Financial support:** In 2001–02, 2 research assistantships (averaging $2,000 per year), 2 teaching assistantships (averaging $2,550 per year) were awarded. Federal Work-Study also available. Support available to part-time students. Financial award application deadline: 6/1; financial award applicants required to submit FAFSA.
**Faculty research:** Family therapy, child developments, clinical supervision.
Dr. Tony Crespi, Director, 860-768-5081, *E-mail:* crespi@mail.hartford.edu.
**Application contact:** Kellie Richard Westenfeld, Assistant Director of Graduate Admissions, 860-768-4371, *Fax:* 860-768-5160, *E-mail:* westenfel@mail.hartford.edu. *Web site:* http://www.hartford.edu/

■ **UNIVERSITY OF HOUSTON– CLEAR LAKE**

**School of Human Sciences and Humanities, Programs in Human Sciences, Houston, TX 77058-1098**

**AWARDS** Behavioral sciences (MA), including behavioral sciences-general, behavioral sciences-psychology, behavioral sciences-sociology; clinical psychology (MA); cross-cultural studies (MA); family therapy (MA); fitness and human performance (MA); school psychology (MA); studies of the future (MS). Part-time and evening/weekend programs available.

**Students:** 562; includes 183 minority (95 African Americans, 16 Asian Americans or Pacific Islanders, 70 Hispanic Americans, 2 Native Americans), 16 international. Average age 34. In 2001, 152 degrees awarded.
**Degree requirements:** For master's, thesis or alternative.
**Entrance requirements:** For master's, GRE General Test. *Application deadline:* For fall admission, 8/1; for spring admission, 12/1. Applications are processed on a rolling basis. *Application fee:* $30 ($70 for international students). Electronic applications accepted.
**Expenses:** Tuition, state resident: full-time $2,016; part-time $84 per credit hour. Tuition, nonresident: full-time $6,072; part-time $253 per credit hour. Tuition and fees vary according to course load.
**Financial support:** Research assistantships, teaching assistantships, career-related internships or fieldwork, Federal Work-Study, institutionally sponsored loans, and scholarships/grants available. Support available to part-time students. Financial award application deadline: 5/1.
Dr. Hilary Karp, Division Co-Chair, 281-283-3383, *E-mail:* karp@cl.uh.edu.

### ■ UNIVERSITY OF IDAHO
**College of Graduate Studies, College of Education, Division of Adult, Counselor, and Technology Education, Moscow, ID 83844-2282**
**AWARDS** Adult education (M Ed, MS, Ed D, PhD); business education (M Ed); counseling and human services (M Ed, MS, Ed D, PhD, CHSS); industrial technology education (M Ed, MS, Ed D, PhD); professional-technical education (M Ed, Ed D, PhD, Ed Sp PTE); school psychology (SPS); vocational education (MS).
**Faculty:** 16 full-time (8 women), 2 part-time/adjunct (1 woman).
**Students:** 72 full-time (44 women), 177 part-time (113 women); includes 8 minority (1 African American, 1 Asian American or Pacific Islander, 5 Hispanic Americans, 1 Native American), 2 international. 27 applicants, 59% accepted. In 2001, 57 master's, 7 other advanced degrees awarded.
**Degree requirements:** For doctorate, thesis/dissertation.
**Entrance requirements:** For master's, minimum GPA of 2.8; for doctorate, minimum undergraduate GPA of 2.8, 3.0 graduate. *Application deadline:* For fall admission, 8/1; for spring admission, 12/15. *Application fee:* $35 ($45 for international students).
**Expenses:** Tuition, state resident: full-time $1,613. Tuition, nonresident: full-time $3,000.
**Financial support:** In 2001–02, 1 teaching assistantship (averaging $9,001 per year)

was awarded; research assistantships available. Financial award application deadline: 2/15.
Dr. James Gregson, Director, 208-885-6556.
**Find an in-depth description at www.petersons.com/gradchannel.**

### ■ UNIVERSITY OF KANSAS
**Graduate School, School of Education, Department of Psychology and Research in Education, Program in School Psychology, Lawrence, KS 66045**
**AWARDS** PhD, Ed S.
**Students:** 19 full-time (17 women), 13 part-time (11 women); includes 3 minority (all Hispanic Americans). Average age 31. 30 applicants, 17% accepted, 5 enrolled. In 2001, 8 degrees awarded.
**Degree requirements:** For doctorate, variable foreign language requirement, thesis/dissertation.
**Entrance requirements:** For doctorate, GRE General Test, TOEFL; for Ed S, TOEFL, minimum GPA of 3.0. *Application deadline:* For fall admission, 2/15; for spring admission, 11/15. *Application fee:* $35.
**Expenses:** Tuition, state resident: full-time $2,722; part-time $113 per credit. Tuition, nonresident: full-time $8,586; part-time $358 per credit. Required fees: $551; $46 per credit. Tuition and fees vary according to campus/location, program and reciprocity agreements.
**Financial support:** Research assistantships with partial tuition reimbursements, teaching assistantships with full and partial tuition reimbursements available.
Steven W. Lee, Director of Training, 785-864-3931, *E-mail:* swlee@ku.edu.

### ■ UNIVERSITY OF LOUISIANA AT MONROE
**Graduate Studies and Research, College of Education and Human Development, Department of Psychology, Program in School Psychology, Monroe, LA 71209-0001**
**AWARDS** SSP.
**Degree requirements:** For SSP, thesis.
**Entrance requirements:** For degree, GRE General Test, minimum GPA of 2.75.

### ■ UNIVERSITY OF MARYLAND, COLLEGE PARK
**Graduate Studies and Research, College of Education, Department of Counseling and Personnel Services, College Park, MD 20742**
**AWARDS** College student personnel (M Ed, MA); college student personnel administration

(PhD); community counseling (CAGS); community/career counseling (M Ed, MA); counseling and personnel services (M Ed, MA, PhD); counseling psychology (PhD); counselor education (PhD); rehabilitation counseling (M Ed, MA); school counseling (M Ed, MA); school psychology (M Ed, MA, PhD). Part-time and evening/weekend programs available. Postbaccalaureate distance learning degree programs offered (no on-campus study).
**Faculty:** 17 full-time (10 women), 2 part-time/adjunct (1 woman).
**Students:** 127 full-time (99 women), 153 part-time (116 women); includes 91 minority (55 African Americans, 18 Asian Americans or Pacific Islanders, 16 Hispanic Americans, 2 Native Americans), 19 international. 358 applicants, 27% accepted, 57 enrolled. In 2001, 62 master's, 8 doctorates awarded.
**Degree requirements:** For master's, thesis (for some programs); for doctorate, thesis/dissertation.
**Entrance requirements:** For master's, GRE General Test or MAT, minimum GPA of 3.0; for doctorate, GRE General Test or MAT, minimum GPA of 3.5. *Application deadline:* For spring admission, 10/1. Applications are processed on a rolling basis. *Application fee:* $50 ($70 for international students). Electronic applications accepted.
**Expenses:** Tuition, state resident: part-time $289 per credit hour. Tuition, nonresident: part-time $448 per credit hour. One-time fee: $436 part-time. Full-time tuition and fees vary according to course load, campus/location and program.
**Financial support:** In 2001–02, 18 fellowships with full tuition reimbursements (averaging $7,029 per year), 13 teaching assistantships with tuition reimbursements (averaging $12,582 per year) were awarded. Research assistantships, career-related internships or fieldwork, Federal Work-Study, and scholarships/grants also available. Support available to part-time students. Financial award applicants required to submit FAFSA.
**Faculty research:** Educational psychology, counseling, health.
Dr. Dennis Kiulighan, Chairman, 301-405-2858, *Fax:* 301-405-9995.
**Application contact:** Trudy Lindsey, Director, Graduate Admissions and Records, 301-405-6991, *Fax:* 301-314-9305, *E-mail:* grschool@deans.umd.edu.

### ■ UNIVERSITY OF MASSACHUSETTS AMHERST
**Graduate School, School of Education, Program in School Psychology, Amherst, MA 01003**
**AWARDS** PhD.

*University of Massachusetts Amherst (continued)*
**Students:** 12 full-time (7 women), 18 part-time (16 women); includes 7 minority (5 African Americans, 2 Asian Americans or Pacific Islanders), 2 international. Average age 36. 57 applicants, 21% accepted. In 2001, 3 degrees awarded.
**Degree requirements:** For doctorate, thesis/dissertation.
**Entrance requirements:** For doctorate, GRE General Test. *Application deadline:* For fall admission, 1/15. Applications are processed on a rolling basis. *Application fee:* $40 ($50 for international students).
**Expenses:** Tuition, state resident: full-time $1,980; part-time $110 per credit. Tuition, nonresident: full-time $7,456; part-time $414 per credit. Required fees: $4,112. One-time fee: $115 full-time.
**Financial support:** Fellowships with full tuition reimbursements, research assistantships with full tuition reimbursements, teaching assistantships with full tuition reimbursements, career-related internships or fieldwork, Federal Work-Study, scholarships/grants, traineeships, and unspecified assistantships available. Support available to part-time students. Financial award application deadline: 1/15. Dr. Gary Stoner, Head, 413-545-3610.

■ **UNIVERSITY OF MASSACHUSETTS BOSTON**
**Office of Graduate Studies and Research, Graduate College of Education, Counseling and School Psychology Department, Program in School Psychology, Boston, MA 02125-3393**
**AWARDS** M Ed, CAGS. Part-time and evening/weekend programs available.
**Degree requirements:** For master's, practicum, final project.
**Entrance requirements:** For master's, GRE General Test or MAT, minimum GPA of 3.0; for CAGS, minimum GPA of 2.75.
**Faculty research:** School psychology services, assessment of children, cultural and gender differences on psychological adjustment to disabilities.

■ **THE UNIVERSITY OF MEMPHIS**
**Graduate School, College of Arts and Sciences, Department of Psychology, Memphis, TN 38152**
**AWARDS** Clinical psychology (PhD); experimental psychology (PhD); psychology (MS); school psychology (MA, PhD). Part-time programs available.
**Faculty:** 30 full-time (2 women), 6 part-time/adjunct (3 women).

**Students:** 81 full-time (56 women), 19 part-time (11 women); includes 9 minority (8 African Americans, 1 Native American), 7 international. Average age 28. 188 applicants, 26% accepted. In 2001, 20 master's, 12 doctorates awarded. Terminal master's awarded for partial completion of doctoral program.
**Degree requirements:** For master's, thesis (for some programs), oral exam (MS), comprehensive exam; for doctorate, thesis/dissertation, internship.
**Entrance requirements:** For master's, GRE General Test, 18 undergraduate hours in psychology, minimum GPA of 2.5; for doctorate, GRE General Test, GRE Subject Test. *Application deadline:* For fall admission, 2/1. Applications are processed on a rolling basis. *Application fee:* $35 ($60 for international students).
**Expenses:** Tuition, state resident: full-time $2,026. Tuition, nonresident: full-time $4,528.
**Financial support:** In 2001–02, 2 fellowships with full tuition reimbursements (averaging $13,333 per year), 116 research assistantships with full tuition reimbursements (averaging $5,000 per year), 2 teaching assistantships with full tuition reimbursements (averaging $1,500 per year) were awarded.
**Faculty research:** Psychotherapy and psychopathology, behavioral medicine and community psychology, child and family studies, cognitive and social processes, neuropsychology and behavioral neuroscience. *Total annual research expenditures:* $2.5 million.
Dr. Andrew Meyers, Chairman and Coordinator of Graduate Studies, 901-678-2145.

■ **UNIVERSITY OF MINNESOTA, TWIN CITIES CAMPUS**
**Graduate School, College of Education and Human Development, Department of Educational Psychology, Program in School Psychology, Minneapolis, MN 55455-0213**
**AWARDS** MA, PhD, Ed S.
**Students:** In 2001, 11 master's, 2 doctorates, 8 other advanced degrees awarded.
**Expenses:** Tuition, state resident: full-time $2,932; part-time $489 per credit. Tuition, nonresident: full-time $5,758; part-time $960 per credit. Part-time tuition and fees vary according to course load, program and reciprocity agreements.
**Application contact:** Dr. Mary Bents, Assistant Dean, 612-625-6501, *Fax:* 612-626-1580, *E-mail:* mbents@tc.umn.edu.

■ **UNIVERSITY OF MINNESOTA, TWIN CITIES CAMPUS**
**Graduate School, College of Education and Human Development, Institute of Child Development, Minneapolis, MN 55455-0213**
**AWARDS** Child psychology (MA, PhD); early childhood education (M Ed, MA, PhD); school psychology (MA, PhD).
**Students:** 56 full-time (49 women), 3 part-time (2 women); includes 5 minority (1 African American, 2 Asian Americans or Pacific Islanders, 2 Hispanic Americans), 3 international. 57 applicants, 30% accepted, 10 enrolled. In 2001, 2 master's, 10 doctorates awarded.
**Expenses:** Tuition, state resident: full-time $2,932; part-time $489 per credit. Tuition, nonresident: full-time $5,758; part-time $960 per credit. Part-time tuition and fees vary according to course load, program and reciprocity agreements.
**Faculty research:** Cognitive development, psychobiology, psychopathology, perceptual development.
Ann S. Masten, Director, 612-624-0526, *Fax:* 612-624-6373, *E-mail:* amasten@umn.edu.
**Application contact:** Claudia Johnston, Information Contact, 612-624-2576, *Fax:* 612-624-6373, *E-mail:* johnstc@staff.tc.umn.edu. *Web site:* http://www.education.umn.edu/icd/

■ **UNIVERSITY OF MINNESOTA, TWIN CITIES CAMPUS**
**Graduate School, College of Liberal Arts, Department of Psychology, Minneapolis, MN 55455-0213**
**AWARDS** Biological psychopathology (PhD); clinical psychology (PhD); cognitive and biological psychology (PhD); counseling psychology (PhD); differential psychology/behavior genetics (PhD); industrial/organizational psychology (PhD); personality research (PhD); psychometric methods (MA, PhD); school psychology (PhD); social psychology (PhD).
**Faculty:** 37 full-time (8 women), 34 part-time/adjunct (11 women).
**Students:** 141 full-time (82 women); includes 21 minority (5 African Americans, 12 Asian Americans or Pacific Islanders, 4 Hispanic Americans), 12 international. 336 applicants, 15% accepted, 24 enrolled. In 2001, 2 master's, 13 doctorates awarded.
**Degree requirements:** For doctorate, thesis/dissertation, comprehensive exam.
**Entrance requirements:** For master's and doctorate, GRE General Test, GRE Subject Test (recommended), TOEFL, 12 credits of upper-level psychology courses, including a course in statistics or psychological measurement. *Application*

*deadline:* For fall admission, 1/5. *Application fee:* $55 ($75 for international students).
**Expenses:** Tuition, state resident: full-time $2,932; part-time $489 per credit. Tuition, nonresident: full-time $5,758; part-time $960 per credit. Part-time tuition and fees vary according to course load, program and reciprocity agreements.
**Financial support:** In 2001–02, fellowships with full tuition reimbursements (averaging $13,500 per year), research assistantships with full tuition reimbursements (averaging $10,234 per year), teaching assistantships with full tuition reimbursements (averaging $10,234 per year) were awarded. Career-related internships or fieldwork, traineeships, and tuition waivers (partial) also available. Financial award application deadline: 12/1. *Total annual research expenditures:* $3.9 million. John Campbell, Chairman, 612-625-7873, *Fax:* 612-626-2079.
**Application contact:** Coordinator, 612-624-4181, *Fax:* 612-626-2079, *E-mail:* psyapply@tc.umn.edu. *Web site:* http://www.psych.umn.edu/

## ■ THE UNIVERSITY OF MONTANA–MISSOULA

**Graduate School, College of Arts and Sciences, Department of Psychology, Program in School Psychology, Missoula, MT 59812-0002**

**AWARDS** MA, Ed S.

**Degree requirements:** For master's, oral exam, professional paper; for Ed S, thesis.
**Entrance requirements:** For master's, GRE General Test, GRE Subject Test, minimum GPA of 3.25 during previous 2 years; for Ed S, GRE General Test. *Application deadline:* For fall admission, 2/15. *Application fee:* $45.
**Expenses:** Tuition, state resident: full-time $2,482; part-time $1,700 per year. Tuition, nonresident: full-time $7,372; part-time $5,000 per year. Required fees: $1,900. Tuition and fees vary according to degree level.
**Financial support:** Career-related internships or fieldwork, Federal Work-Study, institutionally sponsored loans, and unspecified assistantships available. Financial award application deadline: 3/1; financial award applicants required to submit FAFSA.
**Faculty research:** Child development and creativity, psychological measurement. Dr. George Camp, Director, 406-243-4521. *Web site:* http://www.cas.umt.edu/psych/

## ■ UNIVERSITY OF NEBRASKA AT KEARNEY

**College of Graduate Study, College of Education, Department of Counseling and School Psychology, Kearney, NE 68849-0001**

**AWARDS** Counseling (MS Ed, Ed S); school psychology (Ed S). Part-time and evening/weekend programs available.

**Faculty:** 6 full-time (2 women).
**Students:** 41 full-time (all women), 121 part-time (101 women); includes 4 minority (1 African American, 1 Hispanic American, 2 Native Americans), 1 international. 60 applicants, 88% accepted. In 2001, 48 master's, 7 Ed Ss awarded.
**Degree requirements:** For master's, thesis optional; for Ed S, thesis.
**Entrance requirements:** For master's and Ed S, GRE General Test, interview. *Application deadline:* For fall admission, 8/1 (priority date); for spring admission, 12/15 (priority date). Applications are processed on a rolling basis. *Application fee:* $35. Electronic applications accepted.
**Expenses:** Tuition, state resident: part-time $102 per hour. Tuition, nonresident: part-time $201 per hour. Required fees: $12 per hour.
**Financial support:** In 2001–02, 7 research assistantships with full tuition reimbursements (averaging $5,694 per year), 3 teaching assistantships with full tuition reimbursements (averaging $5,694 per year) were awarded. Career-related internships or fieldwork and scholarships/grants also available. Support available to part-time students. Financial award application deadline: 3/1; financial award applicants required to submit FAFSA.
**Faculty research:** Multicultural counseling and diversity issues, team decision making, adult development, women's issues, brief therapy. Dr. Kent Estes, Chair, 308-865-8508, *E-mail:* estesk@unk.edu.

## ■ UNIVERSITY OF NEBRASKA AT OMAHA

**Graduate Studies and Research, College of Arts and Sciences, Department of Psychology, Omaha, NE 68182**

**AWARDS** Developmental psychobiology (PhD); experimental child psychology (PhD); industrial/organizational psychology (MS, PhD); psychology (MA); school psychology (MS, Ed S). Part-time programs available.

**Faculty:** 17 full-time (7 women).
**Students:** 32 full-time (22 women), 18 part-time (10 women); includes 2 minority (1 African American, 1 Hispanic American). Average age 27. 64 applicants,

44% accepted, 28 enrolled. In 2001, 23 master's, 4 other advanced degrees awarded.
**Degree requirements:** For master's, thesis (for some programs), comprehensive exam; for doctorate, thesis/dissertation.
**Entrance requirements:** For master's, GRE General Test, GRE Subject Test, previous course work in psychology, including statistics and a laboratory course; minimum GPA of 3.0; for doctorate, GRE General Test. *Application deadline:* For fall admission, 2/1. *Application fee:* $35. Electronic applications accepted.
**Expenses:** Tuition, state resident: part-time $116 per credit hour. Tuition, nonresident: part-time $291 per credit hour. Required fees: $13 per credit hour. $4 per semester. One-time fee: $52 part-time.
**Financial support:** In 2001–02, 42 students received support; fellowships, research assistantships, teaching assistantships, career-related internships or fieldwork, Federal Work-Study, institutionally sponsored loans, scholarships/grants, tuition waivers (partial), and unspecified assistantships available. Support available to part-time students. Financial award application deadline: 3/1; financial award applicants required to submit FAFSA. Dr. Kenneth Deffenbacher, Chairperson, 402-554-2592.

## ■ UNIVERSITY OF NEVADA, LAS VEGAS

**Graduate College, College of Education, Department of Special Education, Las Vegas, NV 89154-9900**

**AWARDS** Assessment and evaluation techniques for the exceptional (Ed D); emotional disturbance (Ed D); general special education (Ed D); learning disabilities (Ed D); mental retardation (Ed D); school psychology (Ed S); special education (M Ed, MS, PhD, Ed S). Part-time and evening/weekend programs available.

**Faculty:** 24 full-time (16 women).
**Students:** 112 full-time (93 women), 191 part-time (164 women); includes 71 minority (33 African Americans, 11 Asian Americans or Pacific Islanders, 25 Hispanic Americans, 2 Native Americans), 5 international. 94 applicants, 86% accepted, 68 enrolled. In 2001, 84 master's, 3 doctorates awarded.
**Degree requirements:** For master's, thesis (for some programs), oral exam, comprehensive exam (for some programs); for doctorate, thesis/dissertation, oral exam, comprehensive exam. *Median time to degree:* Doctorate–4.1 years full-time.
**Entrance requirements:** For master's, minimum GPA of 3.0; for doctorate, GRE General Test, minimum graduate GPA of

*University of Nevada, Las Vegas (continued)*

3.0; for Ed S, GRE General Test or MAT, minimum graduate GPA of 3.0. *Application deadline:* For fall admission, 6/15; for spring admission, 11/15. Applications are processed on a rolling basis. *Application fee:* $40 ($55 for international students).
**Expenses:** Tuition, state resident: full-time $1,926; part-time $107 per credit. Tuition, nonresident: full-time $9,376; part-time $220 per credit. Tuition and fees vary according to course load.
**Financial support:** In 2001–02, 2 research assistantships with partial tuition reimbursements (averaging $10,000 per year), 12 teaching assistantships with partial tuition reimbursements (averaging $11,000 per year) were awarded. Financial award application deadline: 3/1.
Dr. Tom Pierce, Chair, 702-895-3205, *E-mail:* pierce@nevada.edu.
**Application contact:** Graduate College Admissions Evaluator, 702-895-3320, *Fax:* 702-895-4180, *E-mail:* gradcollege@ccmail.nevada.edu. *Web site:* http://www.unlv.edu/colleges/education/special_ed/

### ■ THE UNIVERSITY OF NORTH CAROLINA AT CHAPEL HILL

**Graduate School, School of Education, Program in School Psychology, Chapel Hill, NC 27599**
**AWARDS** M Ed, MA, PhD.

**Degree requirements:** For master's, thesis (for some programs), comprehensive exam; for doctorate, thesis/dissertation, comprehensive exam.
**Entrance requirements:** For master's and doctorate, GRE General Test, minimum GPA of 3.0 during last 2 years of undergraduate course work.
**Expenses:** Tuition, state resident: full-time $2,864. Tuition, nonresident: full-time $12,030.

### ■ THE UNIVERSITY OF NORTH CAROLINA AT GREENSBORO

**Graduate School, School of Education, Department of Counseling and Educational Development, Greensboro, NC 27412-5001**
**AWARDS** Counseling and development (MS, Ed D, PhD); gerontological counseling (PMC); marriage and family counseling (PMC); school counseling (PMC).

**Faculty:** 9 full-time (4 women), 1 part-time/adjunct (0 women).
**Students:** 90 full-time (74 women), 32 part-time (20 women); includes 12 minority (6 African Americans, 3 Asian Americans or Pacific Islanders, 3 Hispanic Americans). 254 applicants, 24% accepted,

41 enrolled. In 2001, 20 master's, 6 doctorates, 6 other advanced degrees awarded.
**Degree requirements:** For master's, practicum, internship; for doctorate, thesis/dissertation, comprehensive exam.
**Entrance requirements:** For master's and doctorate, GRE General Test, TOEFL; for PMC, GRE General Test. *Application deadline:* For fall admission, 2/15. *Application fee:* $35.
**Expenses:** Tuition, state resident: part-time $344 per course. Tuition, nonresident: part-time $2,457 per course.
**Financial support:** In 2001–02, 57 students received support, including 4 fellowships with full tuition reimbursements available (averaging $14,000 per year), 33 research assistantships with full tuition reimbursements available (averaging $4,820 per year), 25 teaching assistantships with full tuition reimbursements available (averaging $4,240 per year); career-related internships or fieldwork, Federal Work-Study, scholarships/grants, traineeships, and unspecified assistantships also available. Support available to part-time students.
**Faculty research:** Gerontology, invitational theory, career development, marriage and family therapy, drug and alcohol abuse prevention.
Dr. DiAnne Borders, Chair, 336-334-3423, *Fax:* 336-334-4120, *E-mail:* borders@uncg.edu.
**Application contact:** Dr. James Lynch, Director of Graduate Recruitment and Information Services, 336-334-4881, *Fax:* 336-334-4424. *Web site:* http://www.uncg.edu/ced/

### ■ UNIVERSITY OF NORTHERN COLORADO

**Graduate School, College of Education, Division of Professional Psychology, Program in School Psychology, Greeley, CO 80639**
**AWARDS** PhD, Ed S. Part-time programs available.

**Faculty:** 4 full-time (2 women).
**Students:** 40 full-time (31 women), 9 part-time (6 women); includes 5 minority (1 Asian American or Pacific Islander, 3 Hispanic Americans, 1 Native American). Average age 28. 70 applicants, 40% accepted. In 2001, 6 doctorates, 9 other advanced degrees awarded.
**Degree requirements:** For doctorate, one foreign language, thesis/dissertation, comprehensive exam; for Ed S, thesis, comprehensive exam.
**Entrance requirements:** For doctorate, GRE General Test. *Application deadline:* Applications are processed on a rolling basis. *Application fee:* $35.

**Expenses:** Tuition, state resident: full-time $2,549; part-time $546 per credit hour. Tuition, nonresident: full-time $10,459; part-time $581 per credit hour. Required fees: $631; $85 per year. Part-time tuition and fees vary according to course load.
**Financial support:** In 2001–02, 42 students received support, including 4 fellowships (averaging $3,270 per year), 10 research assistantships (averaging $7,755 per year), 3 teaching assistantships (averaging $10,075 per year); unspecified assistantships also available. Financial award application deadline: 3/1.
Dr. Ellis Copeland, Coordinator, 970-351-2731.

### ■ UNIVERSITY OF NORTHERN IOWA

**Graduate College, College of Education, Department of Educational Psychology and Foundations, Cedar Falls, IA 50614**

**AWARDS** Educational psychology (MAE), including professional development for teachers; school psychology (Ed S). Part-time and evening/weekend programs available.

**Students:** 26 full-time (18 women), 20 part-time (16 women); includes 5 minority (4 African Americans, 1 Hispanic American), 7 international. 35 applicants, 86% accepted. In 2001, 8 master's, 3 other advanced degrees awarded.
**Degree requirements:** For master's and Ed S, thesis or alternative.
**Entrance requirements:** For master's, GRE General Test, GRE Subject Test, 3 years of educational experience, minimum GPA of 3.5; for Ed S, GRE General Test, GRE Subject Test. *Application deadline:* For fall admission, 8/1 (priority date). Applications are processed on a rolling basis. *Application fee:* $20 ($50 for international students).
**Expenses:** Tuition, state resident: full-time $3,704; part-time $206 per credit hour. Tuition, nonresident: full-time $9,122; part-time $501 per credit hour. Required fees: $324; $108 per semester. Part-time tuition and fees vary according to course load.
**Financial support:** Career-related internships or fieldwork, Federal Work-Study, scholarships/grants, and tuition waivers (full and partial) available. Support available to part-time students. Financial award application deadline: 3/1.
Dr. Barry J. Wilson, Head, 319-273-2694, *Fax:* 319-273-7732, *E-mail:* barry.wilson@uni.edu. *Web site:* http://www.uni.edu/coe/epf/

# ■ UNIVERSITY OF NORTH TEXAS

**Robert B. Toulouse School of Graduate Studies, College of Arts and Sciences, Department of Psychology, Denton, TX 76203**

**AWARDS** Clinical psychology (PhD); counseling psychology (MA, MS, PhD); experimental psychology (MA, MS, PhD); health psychology and behavioral medicine (PhD); industrial psychology (MA, MS); psychology (MA, MS, PhD); school psychology (MA, MS, PhD).

**Faculty:** 29 full-time (5 women), 7 part-time/adjunct (5 women).

**Students:** 129 full-time (96 women), 98 part-time (70 women); includes 23 minority (2 African Americans, 4 Asian Americans or Pacific Islanders, 15 Hispanic Americans, 2 Native Americans), 9 international. Average age 30. In 2001, 24 master's, 17 doctorates awarded. Terminal master's awarded for partial completion of doctoral program.

**Degree requirements:** For master's, thesis or alternative, comprehensive exam; for doctorate, one foreign language, thesis/dissertation, comprehensive exam.

**Entrance requirements:** For master's and doctorate, GRE General Test, GRE Subject Test, interview. *Application deadline:* For fall admission, 2/1. *Application fee:* $25 ($50 for international students).

**Expenses:** Tuition, state resident: part-time $186 per hour. Tuition, nonresident: part-time $319 per hour. Required fees: $88; $21 per hour.

**Financial support:** Fellowships, research assistantships, teaching assistantships, career-related internships or fieldwork, Federal Work-Study, and institutionally sponsored loans available. Financial award application deadline: 8/1.

Dr. Ernest H. Harrell, Chair, 940-565-2671, *Fax:* 940-546-4682, *E-mail:* harrelle@unt.edu.

**Application contact:** Dr. Joseph Critelli, Graduate Adviser, 940-565-2671, *Fax:* 940-565-4682, *E-mail:* critelli@facstaff.cas.unt.edu.

# ■ UNIVERSITY OF PENNSYLVANIA

**Graduate School of Education, Division of Psychology in Education, Program in School, Community, and Clinical Child Psychology, Philadelphia, PA 19104**

**AWARDS** PhD.

**Degree requirements:** For doctorate, thesis/dissertation, exams.

**Entrance requirements:** For doctorate, GRE General Test, GRE Subject Test. Electronic applications accepted.

**Expenses:** Tuition: Part-time $12,875 per semester.

**Faculty research:** Therapeutic interventions at a preschool level, childhood stress, college psychology, school and community psychology.

# ■ UNIVERSITY OF RHODE ISLAND

**Graduate School, College of Arts and Sciences, Department of Psychology, Program in School Psychology, Kingston, RI 02881**

**AWARDS** MS, PhD.

**Students:** In 2001, 3 master's, 6 doctorates awarded.

*Application deadline:* For spring admission, 2/15. *Application fee:* $35.

**Expenses:** Tuition, state resident: full-time $3,756; part-time $209 per credit. Tuition, nonresident: full-time $10,774; part-time $599 per credit. Required fees: $1,586; $76 per credit. One-time fee: $60 full-time. Paul Demesquita, Director, 401-874-2193.

# ■ UNIVERSITY OF SOUTH CAROLINA

**The Graduate School, College of Liberal Arts, Department of Psychology, Program in School Psychology, Columbia, SC 29208**

**AWARDS** PhD.

**Faculty:** 5 full-time (1 woman), 4 part-time/adjunct (2 women).

**Students:** 38 full-time (33 women), 6 part-time (all women); includes 4 African Americans. Average age 28. 65 applicants, 11% accepted. In 2001, 6 doctorates awarded.

**Degree requirements:** For doctorate, thesis/dissertation.

**Entrance requirements:** For doctorate, GRE General Test, minimum GPA of 3.0. *Application deadline:* For fall admission, 2/1 (priority date). Applications are processed on a rolling basis. *Application fee:* $35. Electronic applications accepted.

**Expenses:** Tuition, state resident: full-time $4,434. Tuition, nonresident: full-time $9,854. Tuition and fees vary according to program.

**Financial support:** In 2001–02, 3 fellowships (averaging $16,000 per year), 5 research assistantships (averaging $9,400 per year), 4 teaching assistantships (averaging $9,400 per year) were awarded. Career-related internships or fieldwork, Federal Work-Study, institutionally sponsored loans, traineeships, and unspecified assistantships also available. Support available to part-time students.

**Faculty research:** Preschool services, families and diversity life satisfaction, ADHD intervention, attachment.

Dr. E. Scott Huebner, Director, 803-777-2700, *Fax:* 803-777-9558, *E-mail:* huebner@sc.edu.

**Application contact:** Doris Davis, Graduate Secretary, 803-777-2312, *Fax:* 803-777-9558, *E-mail:* doris@gwm.sc.edu.

# ■ UNIVERSITY OF SOUTHERN MAINE

**College of Education and Human Development, Program in School Psychology, Portland, ME 04104-9300**

**AWARDS** MS. Part-time and evening/weekend programs available.

**Degree requirements:** For master's, thesis or alternative, portfolio, comprehensive exam.

**Entrance requirements:** For master's, interview.

**Expenses:** Tuition, state resident: part-time $200 per credit. Tuition, nonresident: part-time $560 per credit. *Web site:* http://www.usm.maine.edu/~coe/

# ■ UNIVERSITY OF SOUTH FLORIDA

**College of Graduate Studies, College of Education, Department of Psychological and Social Foundations of Education, Program in School Psychology, Tampa, FL 33620-9951**

**AWARDS** PhD, Ed S. Part-time and evening/weekend programs available.

**Students:** 21 full-time (16 women), 9 part-time (8 women); includes 8 minority (4 African Americans, 1 Asian American or Pacific Islander, 2 Hispanic Americans, 1 Native American). Average age 30. 6 applicants, 100% accepted, 6 enrolled. In 2001, 1 degree awarded.

**Degree requirements:** For doctorate, thesis/dissertation, 2 tools of research in foreign language, statistics, and/or computers.

**Entrance requirements:** For doctorate, GRE General Test, minimum undergraduate GPA of 3.0 or 3.5 graduate; for Ed S, GRE General Test. *Application deadline:* For fall admission, 1/15. *Application fee:* $20. Electronic applications accepted.

**Expenses:** Tuition, state resident: part-time $166 per credit hour. Tuition, nonresident: part-time $573 per credit hour. Required fees: $17 per term.

**Financial support:** Federal Work-Study and institutionally sponsored loans available. Support available to part-time students. Financial award applicants required to submit FAFSA.

**Faculty research:** Academic and behavioral interventions, collaborative planning and problem solving,

*University of South Florida (continued)* organizational and systems change, school violence, social skills and conflict resolution.

**Application contact:** George Bafsche, Information Contact, 813-974-9472, *Fax:* 813-974-5814, *E-mail:* bafsche@ tempest.coedu.usf.edu. *Web site:* http:// www.coedu.usf.edu/behavior/

## ■ THE UNIVERSITY OF TENNESSEE

**Graduate School, College of Education, Program in Education, Knoxville, TN 37996**

**AWARDS** Art education (MS); counseling education (PhD); counseling psychology (PhD); cultural studies in education (PhD); curriculum (MS, Ed S); curriculum education research and evaluation (PhD); curriculum, educational research and evaluation (Ed D); early childhood education (PhD); early childhood special education (MS); education of deaf and hard of hearing (MS); education psychology (PhD); educational administration and policy studies (Ed D, PhD); educational administration and supervision (Ed S); educational psychology (Ed D); elementary education (MS, Ed S); elementary teaching (MS); English education (MS, Ed S); exercise science (PhD); foreign language/ESL education (MS, Ed S); industrial technology (PhD); instructional technology (MS, Ed D, Ed S); literacy, language education and ESL education (PhD); literacy, language education, and ESL education (Ed D); mathematics education (MS, Ed S); modified and comprehensive special education (MS); reading education (MS, Ed S); school counseling (Ed S); school psychology (PhD, Ed S); science education (MS, Ed S); secondary teaching (MS); social foundations (MS); social science education (MS, Ed S); socio-cultural foundations of sports and education (PhD); special education (Ed S); teacher education (Ed D, PhD). Part-time and evening/weekend programs available.

**Students:** 493 full-time (365 women), 258 part-time (173 women); includes 54 minority (43 African Americans, 6 Asian Americans or Pacific Islanders, 2 Hispanic Americans, 3 Native Americans), 34 international. 420 applicants, 50% accepted. In 2001, 344 master's, 52 doctorates, 26 other advanced degrees awarded. **Degree requirements:** For master's and Ed S, thesis optional; for doctorate, variable foreign language requirement, thesis/dissertation. **Entrance requirements:** For master's, TOEFL, minimum GPA of 2.7; for doctorate and Ed S, GRE General Test, TOEFL, minimum GPA of 2.7. *Application deadline:* For fall admission, 2/1 (priority

date). Applications are processed on a rolling basis. *Application fee:* $35. Electronic applications accepted.

**Expenses:** Tuition, state resident: full-time $4,280; part-time $233 per hour. Tuition, nonresident: full-time $12,066; part-time $666 per hour. Tuition and fees vary according to program.

**Financial support:** In 2001–02, 4 fellowships, 9 teaching assistantships were awarded. Career-related internships or fieldwork, Federal Work-Study, institutionally sponsored loans, and unspecified assistantships also available. Financial award application deadline: 2/1; financial award applicants required to submit FAFSA.

Dr. Lester Knight, Head, 865-974-0907, *Fax:* 865-974-8718, *E-mail:* lknight@ utk.edu.

## ■ THE UNIVERSITY OF TENNESSEE AT CHATTANOOGA

**Graduate Division, College of Arts and Sciences, Department of Psychology, Chattanooga, TN 37403-2598**

**AWARDS** Industrial/organizational psychology (MS); research psychology (MS); school psychology (MS). Part-time and evening/weekend programs available.

**Faculty:** 9 full-time (3 women).
**Students:** 37 full-time (26 women), 11 part-time (9 women); includes 7 minority (all African Americans). Average age 25. 57 applicants, 82% accepted, 20 enrolled. In 2001, 35 degrees awarded.
**Entrance requirements:** For master's, GRE General Test. *Application deadline:* For fall admission, 8/1 (priority date); for spring admission, 12/1 (priority date). Applications are processed on a rolling basis. *Application fee:* $25.
**Expenses:** Tuition, state resident: full-time $3,752; part-time $228 per hour. Tuition, nonresident: full-time $10,282; part-time $565 per hour.
**Financial support:** Fellowships, research assistantships, Federal Work-Study available. Financial award application deadline: 4/1; financial award applicants required to submit FAFSA.
Dr. David Pittenger, Head, 423-425-4262, *Fax:* 423-425-4279.
**Application contact:** Dr. Deborah E. Arfken, Dean of Graduate Studies, 865-425-1740, *Fax:* 865-425-5223, *E-mail:* deborah-arfken@utc.edu. *Web site:* http:// www.utc.edu/

## ■ THE UNIVERSITY OF TEXAS AT AUSTIN

**Graduate School, College of Education, Department of Educational Psychology, Austin, TX 78712-1111**

**AWARDS** Academic educational psychology (M Ed, MA); counseling education (M Ed); counseling psychology (PhD); human development and education (PhD); learning cognition and instruction (PhD); quantitative methods (PhD); school psychology (PhD).

**Faculty:** 30 full-time (16 women), 17 part-time/adjunct (8 women).
**Students:** 233 full-time (191 women), 55 part-time (44 women); includes 52 minority (13 African Americans, 8 Asian Americans or Pacific Islanders, 29 Hispanic Americans, 2 Native Americans), 36 international. Average age 29. 292 applicants, 47% accepted, 70 enrolled. In 2001, 20 master's, 38 doctorates awarded.
**Degree requirements:** For master's, thesis optional; for doctorate, thesis/dissertation.
**Entrance requirements:** For master's and doctorate, GRE General Test, 3 letters of recommendation. *Application deadline:* For fall admission, 1/15 (priority date); for winter admission, 3/1 (priority date); for spring admission, 10/1 (priority date). Applications are processed on a rolling basis. *Application fee:* $50 ($75 for international students).
**Expenses:** Tuition, state resident: full-time $3,159. Tuition, nonresident: full-time $6,957. Tuition and fees vary according to program.
**Financial support:** In 2001–02, 21 fellowships with full and partial tuition reimbursements (averaging $1,700 per year), 33 research assistantships (averaging $4,500 per year), 116 teaching assistantships (averaging $4,250 per year) were awarded. Career-related internships or fieldwork, Federal Work-Study, institutionally sponsored loans, scholarships/grants, tuition waivers (full and partial), and unspecified assistantships also available. Financial award application deadline: 1/15.
Dr. Edmund T. Emmer, Department Chair, 512-471-4155 Ext. 22, *Fax:* 512-471-1288, *E-mail:* emmer@mail.utexas.edu.
**Application contact:** Dr. Cindy I. Carlson, Graduate Adviser, 512-471-4155 Ext. 24, *Fax:* 512-471-1288, *E-mail:* cindy.carlson@mail.utexas.edu. *Web site:* http://www.edb.utexas.edu/coe/depts/edp/ edp.html

## ■ THE UNIVERSITY OF TEXAS AT TYLER

**Graduate Studies, College of Education and Psychology, Department of Psychology, Tyler, TX 75799-0001**

**AWARDS** Clinical psychology (MS); counseling psychology (MA); interdisciplinary studies (MS, MSIS); school counseling (MA). Part-time and evening/weekend programs available.

**Faculty:** 7 full-time (4 women), 1 (woman) part-time/adjunct.

**Students:** 30 full-time (26 women), 52 part-time (48 women); includes 9 minority (5 African Americans, 1 Asian American or Pacific Islander, 2 Hispanic Americans, 1 Native American), 3 international. Average age 30. 23 applicants, 100% accepted, 16 enrolled. In 2001, 18 degrees awarded.

**Degree requirements:** For master's, comprehensive exam and/or thesis.

**Entrance requirements:** For master's, GRE General Test, GRE Subject Test, minimum GPA of 3.0. *Application deadline:* For fall admission, 2/1; for spring admission, 10/1. *Application fee:* $0 ($50 for international students). Electronic applications accepted.

**Expenses:** Tuition, state resident: part-time $44 per credit hour. Tuition, nonresident: part-time $262 per credit hour. Required fees: $58 per credit hour. $76 per semester.

**Financial support:** Teaching assistantships, career-related internships or fieldwork, Federal Work-Study, and institutionally sponsored loans available. Support available to part-time students. Financial award application deadline: 7/1.

**Faculty research:** Incest, aging, depression, neuropsychology, child psychopathology.

Dr. Henry L. Schreiber, Chairperson, 903-566-7239, *Fax:* 903-565-5656, *E-mail:* hschreiber@mail.uttyl.edu.

**Application contact:** Dr. Robert F. McClure, Graduate Adviser, 903-566-7435, *Fax:* 903-566-7065, *E-mail:* rmcclure@ mail.uttyl.edu. *Web site:* http://www.uttyl.edu/psychology/grad.htm/

## ■ THE UNIVERSITY OF TEXAS– PAN AMERICAN

**College of Education, Department of Educational Psychology, Edinburg, TX 78539-2999**

**AWARDS** Counseling and guidance (M Ed); educational diagnostics (M Ed); educational psychology (D Phil); gifted and talented education (M Ed); school psychology (MA); special education (M Ed).

**Degree requirements:** For master's, thesis optional.

**Entrance requirements:** For master's, GRE General Test, interview.

**Expenses:** Tuition, state resident: part-time $212 per semester hour. Tuition, nonresident: part-time $367 per semester hour.

**Faculty research:** Psychoeducational factors of gifted, writing to read, topographic brain mapping, learning disabilities, unbiased testing.

## ■ UNIVERSITY OF THE PACIFIC

**Graduate School, School of Education, Department of Educational and Counseling Psychology, Stockton, CA 95211-0197**

**AWARDS** Educational counseling and psychology (MA); educational psychology (MA, Ed D); educational research (MA); school psychology (Ed D, PhD, Ed S).

**Students:** 9 full-time (8 women), 17 part-time (16 women); includes 5 minority (1 African American, 3 Hispanic Americans, 1 Native American), 2 international. Average age 35. 19 applicants, 32% accepted, 4 enrolled. In 2001, 12 master's, 1 doctorate awarded.

**Degree requirements:** For master's, thesis (for some programs); for doctorate, thesis/dissertation.

**Entrance requirements:** For master's and doctorate, GRE General Test, GRE Subject Test. *Application deadline:* For fall admission, 3/1 (priority date); for spring admission, 10/1 (priority date). Applications are processed on a rolling basis. *Application fee:* $50.

**Expenses:** Tuition: Full-time $21,150; part-time $661 per unit. Required fees: $375.

**Financial support:** In 2001–02, 6 teaching assistantships were awarded. Financial award application deadline: 3/1.

Dr. Linda Webster, Chairperson, 209-946-2559, *E-mail:* lwebster@uop.edu.

## ■ UNIVERSITY OF TOLEDO

**Graduate School, College of Health and Human Services, Department of School Psychology, Toledo, OH 43606-3398**

**AWARDS** ME, Ed S.

**Students:** 2 full-time (both women), 4 part-time (3 women). 1 applicant, 0% accepted. In 2001, 4 degrees awarded. *Application deadline:* For fall admission, 3/1 (priority date). *Application fee:* 30 Albanian leks.

**Expenses:** Tuition, state resident: full-time $7,278; part-time $303 per hour. Tuition, nonresident: full-time $15,731; part-time $699 per hour. Required fees: $43 per hour.

Dr. Jerome M. Sulivan, Dean, College of Health and Human Services, 419-530-4180.

## ■ UNIVERSITY OF WASHINGTON

**Graduate School, College of Education, Program in Educational Psychology, Seattle, WA 98195**

**AWARDS** Human development and cognition (M Ed, PhD); measurement and research (M Ed, PhD); school counseling (M Ed, PhD); school psychology (M Ed, PhD).

**Degree requirements:** For master's, thesis optional; for doctorate, thesis/dissertation.

**Entrance requirements:** For master's and doctorate, GRE General Test, TOEFL, minimum GPA of 3.0.

**Expenses:** Tuition, state resident: full-time $5,539. Tuition, nonresident: full-time $14,376. Required fees: $390. Tuition and fees vary according to course load and program.

## ■ UNIVERSITY OF WISCONSIN– EAU CLAIRE

**College of Arts and Sciences, Department of Psychology, Eau Claire, WI 54702-4004**

**AWARDS** School psychology (MSE, Ed S).

**Faculty:** 18 full-time (7 women).

**Students:** 18 full-time (14 women), 2 part-time (1 woman); includes 1 minority (Asian American or Pacific Islander). Average age 24. 40 applicants, 50% accepted, 18 enrolled. In 2001, 16 degrees awarded.

**Degree requirements:** For master's, thesis, comprehensive exam.

**Entrance requirements:** For master's, GRE. *Application deadline:* For fall admission, 3/1. Applications are processed on a rolling basis. *Application fee:* $45.

**Expenses:** Tuition, state resident: full-time $4,481; part-time $249 per credit. Tuition, nonresident: full-time $14,305; part-time $795 per credit.

**Financial support:** In 2001–02, 8 students received support, including 6 teaching assistantships (averaging $3,600 per year); Federal Work-Study also available. Financial award application deadline: 4/15; financial award applicants required to submit FAFSA.

Dr. Larry Morse, Chair, 715-836-5733, *Fax:* 715-836-2214, *E-mail:* morsela@ uwec.edu. *Web site:* http://www.uwec.edu/

## ■ UNIVERSITY OF WISCONSIN– LA CROSSE

**Graduate Studies, College of Liberal Studies, Department of Psychology, Program in School Psychology, La Crosse, WI 54601-3742**

**AWARDS** MS Ed, CAGS.

*University of Wisconsin–La Crosse (continued)*

**Degree requirements:** For master's, thesis, seminar, or comprehensive exams.
**Entrance requirements:** For master's, GRE General Test, minimum GPA of 2.85, interview, sample of written work, resumé.
**Faculty research:** Assessment, cognitive strategies, personality assessment. *Web site:* http://www.uwlax.edu/LS/Psych/spgrad.htm

■ **UNIVERSITY OF WISCONSIN– RIVER FALLS**

**Outreach and Graduate Studies, College of Education and Professional Studies, Department of Counseling and School Psychology, River Falls, WI 54022-5001**

**AWARDS** Counseling (MSE); school psychology (MSE, Ed S). Part-time programs available.

**Faculty:** 6 full-time (2 women).
**Students:** 108 (85 women). In 2001, 39 degrees awarded.
**Entrance requirements:** For master's, minimum GPA of 2.75, resumé, 3 letters of reference. *Application deadline:* For fall admission, 2/1. *Application fee:* $45. Electronic applications accepted.
**Expenses:** Tuition, state resident: full-time $2,257; part-time $278 per credit. Tuition, nonresident: full-time $7,169; part-time $824 per credit. Tuition and fees vary according to reciprocity agreements.
**Financial support:** Research assistantships, Federal Work-Study available. Financial award application deadline: 3/1.
Dr. Donald Lee Stovall, Chair, 715-425-3281, *Fax:* 715-425-3242, *E-mail:* donald.lee.stovall@uwrh.edu.
**Application contact:** Julia M. Persico, Program Assistant III, 715-425-3843, *Fax:* 715-425-3185, *E-mail:* julia.m.persico@uwrf.edu.

■ **UNIVERSITY OF WISCONSIN– STOUT**

**Graduate School, College of Human Development, Program in School Psychology, Menomonie, WI 54751**

**AWARDS** MS Ed, Ed S. Part-time programs available.

**Students:** 17 full-time (14 women), 6 part-time (5 women); includes 1 minority (Hispanic American). 32 applicants, 34% accepted, 9 enrolled. In 2001, 13 degrees awarded.
**Degree requirements:** For master's and Ed S, thesis.

*Application deadline:* For fall admission, 1/15 (priority date). Applications are processed on a rolling basis. *Application fee:* $45.
**Expenses:** Tuition, state resident: full-time $4,915. Tuition, nonresident: full-time $12,553.
**Financial support:** In 2001–02, 8 research assistantships were awarded; teaching assistantships, Federal Work-Study and tuition waivers (full and partial) also available. Support available to part-time students. Financial award application deadline: 4/1; financial award applicants required to submit FAFSA.
Dr. Denise Maricle, Director, 715-232-2229, *E-mail:* maricled@uwstout.edu.
**Application contact:** Anne E. Johnson, Graduate Student Evaluator, 715-232-1322, *Fax:* 715-232-2413, *E-mail:* johnsona@uwstout.edu.

■ **UNIVERSITY OF WISCONSIN– WHITEWATER**

**School of Graduate Studies, College of Education, Department of Counselor Education, Whitewater, WI 53190-1790**

**AWARDS** Community counseling (MS); higher education (MS); school counseling (MS). Part-time and evening/weekend programs available.

**Students:** 6 full-time (all women), 156 part-time (130 women); includes 15 minority (8 African Americans, 2 Asian Americans or Pacific Islanders, 4 Hispanic Americans, 1 Native American). Average age 27. 19 applicants, 84% accepted, 15 enrolled. In 2001, 20 degrees awarded.
**Degree requirements:** For master's, thesis or alternative.
**Entrance requirements:** For master's, resumé, 2 letters of reference. *Application deadline:* For fall admission, 3/15; for spring admission, 10/15. *Application fee:* $45. Electronic applications accepted.
**Expenses:** Tuition, state resident: full-time $4,511; part-time $251 per credit. Tuition, nonresident: full-time $14,335; part-time $797 per credit. One-time fee: $45. Tuition and fees vary according to course load and program.
**Financial support:** In 2001–02, 4 research assistantships (averaging $8,889 per year) were awarded; Federal Work-Study, unspecified assistantships, and out of state fee waiver also available. Support available to part-time students. Financial award application deadline: 3/15; financial award applicants required to submit FAFSA.
**Faculty research:** Alcohol and other drug prevention/intervention.
Dr. Anene Okocha, Coordinator, 262-472-1940, *Fax:* 262-472-2841, *E-mail:* okochaa@uww.edu.

**Application contact:** Sally A. Lange, School of Graduate Studies, 262-472-1006, *Fax:* 262-472-5027, *E-mail:* gradschl@uww.edu.

■ **UNIVERSITY OF WISCONSIN– WHITEWATER**

**School of Graduate Studies, College of Letters and Sciences, Department of Psychology, Whitewater, WI 53190-1790**

**AWARDS** School psychology (MS Ed). Part-time and evening/weekend programs available.

**Students:** 11 full-time (8 women), 3 part-time (all women); includes 2 minority (both African Americans). Average age 27. 25 applicants, 88% accepted, 20 enrolled. In 2001, 14 degrees awarded.
**Degree requirements:** For master's, comprehensive exam or thesis.
**Entrance requirements:** For master's, MAT or GRE, interview, minimum GPA of 3.0, 3 letters of recommendation.
*Application deadline:* For fall and spring admission, 3/1. Applications are processed on a rolling basis. *Application fee:* $45. Electronic applications accepted.
**Expenses:** Tuition, state resident: full-time $4,511; part-time $251 per credit. Tuition, nonresident: full-time $14,335; part-time $797 per credit. One-time fee: $45. Tuition and fees vary according to course load and program.
**Financial support:** In 2001–02, 6 research assistantships with partial tuition reimbursements (averaging $8,889 per year) were awarded; Federal Work-Study, unspecified assistantships, and out of state fee waiver also available. Support available to part-time students. Financial award application deadline: 3/15; financial award applicants required to submit FAFSA.
**Faculty research:** Neural substrate of reward.
Dr. James Larson, Coordinator, 262-472-5412, *Fax:* 262-472-1863, *E-mail:* larsonj@uww.edu.
**Application contact:** Sally A. Lange, School of Graduate Studies, 262-472-1006, *Fax:* 262-472-5027, *E-mail:* gradschl@uww.edu.

■ **UNIVERSITY OF WISCONSIN– WHITEWATER**

**School of Graduate Studies, College of Letters and Sciences, Program in School Psychology, Whitewater, WI 53190-1790**

**AWARDS** Ed S.

**Students:** 9 full-time (8 women), 24 part-time (16 women); includes 4 minority (1 African American, 2 Hispanic Americans, 1

Native American). Average age 26. 9 applicants, 100% accepted, 9 enrolled.
**Entrance requirements:** For degree, master's in school psychology from an accredited school. *Application deadline:* For fall and spring admission, 3/1. Applications are processed on a rolling basis. *Application fee:* $45. Electronic applications accepted.
**Expenses:** Tuition, state resident: full-time $4,511; part-time $251 per credit. Tuition, nonresident: full-time $14,335; part-time $797 per credit. One-time fee: $45. Tuition and fees vary according to course load and program.
Dr. James Larson, Coordinator, 262-472-5412, *Fax:* 262-472-1863, *E-mail:* larsonj@uww.edu.
**Application contact:** Sally A. Lange, School of Graduate Studies, 262-472-1006, *Fax:* 262-472-5027, *E-mail:* gradschl@uww.edu.

## ■ UTAH STATE UNIVERSITY

**School of Graduate Studies, College of Education, Department of Psychology, Logan, UT 84322**

**AWARDS** Clinical/counseling/school psychology (PhD); research and evaluation methodology (PhD); school counseling (MS); school psychology (MS). Part-time and evening/weekend programs available. Postbaccalaureate distance learning degree programs offered (no on-campus study).
**Faculty:** 18 full-time (8 women), 40 part-time/adjunct (15 women).
**Students:** 55 full-time (31 women), 80 part-time (62 women); includes 10 minority (3 Asian Americans or Pacific Islanders, 1 Hispanic American, 6 Native Americans), 3 international. Average age 34. 138 applicants, 38% accepted. In 2001, 31 master's, 7 doctorates awarded. Terminal master's awarded for partial completion of doctoral program.
**Degree requirements:** For master's, thesis (for some programs); for doctorate, thesis/dissertation.
**Entrance requirements:** For master's and doctorate, GRE General Test, TOEFL, minimum GPA of 3.5. *Application deadline:* For fall admission, 1/15; for spring admission, 10/15. Applications are processed on a rolling basis. *Application fee:* $40.
**Expenses:** Tuition, state resident: full-time $1,693. Tuition, nonresident: full-time $4,233. Required fees: $501. Tuition and fees vary according to program.
**Financial support:** In 2001–02, 5 fellowships with full and partial tuition reimbursements (averaging $12,000 per year), 25 research assistantships with full and partial tuition reimbursements (averaging $8,500 per year), 18 teaching assistantships with full and partial tuition reimbursements (averaging $7,000 per

year) were awarded. Career-related internships or fieldwork, Federal Work-Study, institutionally sponsored loans, scholarships/grants, tuition waivers (partial), and unspecified assistantships also available. Financial award application deadline: 2/1.
**Faculty research:** Hearing loss detection in infancy, ADHD, eating disorders, domestic violence, neuropsychology. David M. Stein, Head, 435-797-1460, *Fax:* 435-797-1448, *E-mail:* davids@coe.usu.edu.
**Application contact:** Sheila Jessie, Staff Assistant IV, 435-797-1449, *Fax:* 435-797-1448, *E-mail:* sheilaj@coe.usu.edu. *Web site:* http://www.coe.usu.edu/psyc/ndex.html

## ■ VALDOSTA STATE UNIVERSITY

**Graduate School, College of Education, Department of Psychology and Guidance, Valdosta, GA 31698**

**AWARDS** Clinical/counseling psychology (MS); industrial/organizational psychology (MS); school counseling (M Ed, Ed S); school psychology (M Ed, Ed S). Evening/weekend programs available.

**Faculty:** 13 full-time (2 women).
**Students:** 40 full-time (30 women), 62 part-time (54 women); includes 10 minority (7 African Americans, 1 Asian American or Pacific Islander, 1 Hispanic American, 1 Native American). Average age 26. 67 applicants, 75% accepted. In 2001, 17 degrees awarded.
**Degree requirements:** For master's, thesis or alternative, comprehensive written and/or oral exams; for Ed S, thesis.
**Entrance requirements:** For master's and Ed S, GRE General Test or MAT. *Application deadline:* For fall admission, 7/1; for spring admission, 11/15. Applications are processed on a rolling basis. *Application fee:* $20. Electronic applications accepted.
**Expenses:** Tuition, state resident: full-time $1,746; part-time $97 per hour. Tuition, nonresident: full-time $6,966; part-time $387 per hour. Required fees: $594; $297 per semester.
**Financial support:** In 2001–02, 2 research assistantships with full tuition reimbursements (averaging $2,452 per year) were awarded; institutionally sponsored loans and unspecified assistantships also available. Support available to part-time students. Financial award application deadline: 7/1; financial award applicants required to submit FAFSA.
**Faculty research:** Using Bender-Gestalt to predict graphomotor dimensions of the draw-a-person test, neurobehavioral hemispheric dominance.
Dr. R. Bauer, Head, 229-333-5930, *Fax:* 229-259-5576, *E-mail:* bbauer@valdosta.edu.

## ■ VALPARAISO UNIVERSITY

**Graduate Division, Department of Education, Program in School Psychology, Valparaiso, IN 46383-6493**

**AWARDS** MA, M Ed/Ed S. Part-time and evening/weekend programs available.

**Students:** 14 full-time (12 women), 9 part-time (all women); includes 2 minority (1 African American, 1 Hispanic American). Average age 35. In 2001, 6 degrees awarded.
**Entrance requirements:** For master's, minimum GPA 3.0. *Application deadline:* For fall admission, 8/15. Applications are processed on a rolling basis. *Application fee:* $30.
**Expenses:** Tuition: Full-time $5,400; part-time $300 per credit.
**Financial support:** Career-related internships or fieldwork, Federal Work-Study, and institutionally sponsored loans available. Financial award applicants required to submit FAFSA.
Dr. Jeffrey Daley, Chair, Department of Education, 219-464-5474, *E-mail:* jeffrey.daley@valpo.edu.

## ■ WAYNE STATE UNIVERSITY

**Graduate School, College of Education, Division of Theoretical and Behavioral Foundations, Detroit, MI 48202**

**AWARDS** Counseling (M Ed, MA, Ed D, PhD, Ed S); educational evaluation and research (M Ed, Ed D, PhD); educational psychology (M Ed, Ed D); rehabilitation counseling and community inclusion (MA); school and community psychology (Ed S). Evening/weekend programs available.

**Faculty:** 14 full-time.
**Students:** 473. 178 applicants, 45% accepted, 62 enrolled. In 2001, 87 master's, 8 doctorates awarded.
**Degree requirements:** For doctorate, thesis/dissertation.
**Entrance requirements:** For master's, GRE (school psychology); for doctorate, GRE (educational psychology), interview, minimum GPA of 3.0. *Application deadline:* For fall admission, 7/1. *Application fee:* $20 ($30 for international students). Electronic applications accepted.
**Expenses:** Tuition, state resident: full-time $3,764. Tuition and fees vary according to degree level and program.
**Financial support:** In 2001–02, 1 research assistantship, 2 teaching assistantships were awarded. Career-related internships or fieldwork, Federal Work-Study, and institutionally sponsored loans also available.
**Faculty research:** Adolescents at risk, supervision of counseling.

*Wayne State University (continued)*
Dr. JoAnne Holbert, Deputy Dean, 313-577-1805, *Fax:* 313-577-5235, *E-mail:* jholbert@wayne.edu.

## ■ WESTERN CAROLINA UNIVERSITY

**Graduate School, College of Education and Allied Professions, Department of Psychology, Program in School Psychology, Cullowhee, NC 28723**

**AWARDS** MA. Part-time and evening/weekend programs available.

**Faculty:** 18 full-time (9 women).
**Students:** 16 full-time (10 women), 3 part-time (all women); includes 1 minority (Hispanic American). 15 applicants, 93% accepted, 8 enrolled. In 2001, 4 degrees awarded.
**Degree requirements:** For master's, thesis, comprehensive exam.
**Entrance requirements:** For master's, GRE General Test. *Application deadline:* For fall admission, 2/1. *Application fee:* $35.
**Expenses:** Tuition, state resident: full-time $1,072. Tuition, nonresident: full-time $8,704. Required fees: $1,171.
**Financial support:** In 2001–02, 8 students received support, including 8 teaching assistantships with full and partial tuition reimbursements available (averaging $4,691 per year); research assistantships with full and partial tuition reimbursements available, Federal Work-Study and scholarships/grants also available. Financial award application deadline: 3/15; financial award applicants required to submit FAFSA.
**Application contact:** Josie Bewsey, Assistant to the Dean, 828-227-7398, *Fax:* 828-227-7480, *E-mail:* jbewsey@email.wcu.edu. *Web site:* http://www.wcu.edu/ceap/psychology/psyhome.htm

## ■ WESTERN ILLINOIS UNIVERSITY

**School of Graduate Studies, College of Arts and Sciences, Department of Psychology, Macomb, IL 61455-1390**

**AWARDS** Clinical/community mental health (MS); general psychology (MS); psychology (MS, SSP); school psychology (SSP). Part-time programs available.

**Faculty:** 22 full-time (8 women).
**Students:** 45 full-time (34 women), 13 part-time (9 women), 1 international. Average age 33. 54 applicants, 54% accepted. In 2001, 12 master's, 5 other advanced degrees awarded.
**Degree requirements:** For master's, thesis or alternative.

**Entrance requirements:** For master's and SSP, GRE General Test. *Application deadline:* Applications are processed on a rolling basis. *Application fee:* $0 ($25 for international students). Electronic applications accepted.
**Expenses:** Tuition, state resident: part-time $108 per credit hour. Tuition, nonresident: part-time $216 per credit hour. Required fees: $33 per credit hour.
**Financial support:** In 2001–02, 40 students received support, including 40 research assistantships with full tuition reimbursements available (averaging $5,720 per year). Financial award applicants required to submit FAFSA.
**Faculty research:** Geriatric psychology, social psychology, psychology of women, embarrassability.
Dr. James Ackil, Chairperson, 309-298-1593.
**Application contact:** Dr. Barbara Baily, Director of Graduate Studies, 309-298-1806, *Fax:* 309-298-2345, *E-mail:* gradoffice@wiu.edu. *Web site:* http://www.wiu.edu/

## ■ WESTERN KENTUCKY UNIVERSITY

**Graduate Studies, College of Education and Behavioral Sciences, Department of Psychology, Bowling Green, KY 42101-3576**

**AWARDS** Psychology (MA); school psychology (Ed S).

**Faculty:** 17 full-time (12 women), 1 (woman) part-time/adjunct.
**Students:** In 2001, 15 master's, 6 other advanced degrees awarded.
**Degree requirements:** For master's, thesis (for some programs), comprehensive exam; for Ed S, thesis, oral exam.
**Entrance requirements:** For master's, GRE General Test; for Ed S, GRE General Test, minimum GPA of 3.5. *Application deadline:* For fall admission, 7/1 (priority date); for spring admission, 11/1 (priority date). Applications are processed on a rolling basis. *Application fee:* $30.
**Expenses:** Tuition, area resident: Part-time $167 per credit. Tuition, state resident: full-time $2,490. Tuition, nonresident: full-time $6,660; part-time $399 per credit. Required fees: $554. Part-time tuition and fees vary according to campus/location and reciprocity agreements.
**Financial support:** Research assistantships with partial tuition reimbursements, teaching assistantships with partial tuition reimbursements, career-related internships or fieldwork, Federal Work-Study, institutionally sponsored loans, and service awards available. Support available to part-time students. Financial award application

deadline: 4/1; financial award applicants required to submit FAFSA.
**Faculty research:** Neural regeneration, enhancing mobility in the elderly, improvement in visual processing in older adults, lifespan development. *Total annual research expenditures:* $164,147.
Dr. Steven Haggbloom, Head, 270-745-2696, *Fax:* 270-745-6934, *E-mail:* steven.haggbloom@wku.edu.

## ■ WESTERN MICHIGAN UNIVERSITY

**Graduate College, College of Arts and Sciences, Department of Psychology, Kalamazoo, MI 49008-5202**

**AWARDS** Applied behavior analysis (MA, PhD); clinical psychology (MA, PhD); experimental analysis of behavior (PhD); experimental psychology (MA); industrial/organizational psychology (MA); school psychology (PhD, Ed S).

**Faculty:** 19 full-time (6 women).
**Students:** 94 full-time (68 women), 41 part-time (26 women); includes 10 minority (1 African American, 3 Asian Americans or Pacific Islanders, 6 Hispanic Americans), 12 international. 192 applicants, 31% accepted, 25 enrolled. In 2001, 21 master's, 6 doctorates, 6 other advanced degrees awarded.
**Degree requirements:** For master's, variable foreign language requirement, thesis, oral exams; for doctorate, 2 foreign languages, thesis/dissertation, oral exams, comprehensive exam; for Ed S, thesis, oral exams.
**Entrance requirements:** For master's, doctorate, and Ed S, GRE General Test. *Application deadline:* For fall admission, 2/15. *Application fee:* $25.
**Expenses:** Tuition, state resident: part-time $186 per credit hour. Tuition, nonresident: part-time $442 per credit hour. Required fees: $602. One-time fee: $132 part-time. Tuition and fees vary according to course load.
**Financial support:** Fellowships, research assistantships, teaching assistantships, Federal Work-Study available. Financial award application deadline: 2/15; financial award applicants required to submit FAFSA.
R. Wayne Fuqua, Chairperson, 616-387-4498.
**Application contact:** Admissions and Orientation, 616-387-2000, *Fax:* 616-387-2355.

# ◾ WICHITA STATE UNIVERSITY

**Graduate School, College of Education, Department of Administration, Counseling, Educational and School Psychology, Wichita, KS 67260**

**AWARDS** Counseling (M Ed); education administration (M Ed, Ed D); educational psychology (M Ed); school psychology (Ed S). Part-time and evening/weekend programs available.

**Faculty:** 14 full-time (8 women).
**Students:** 23 full-time (16 women), 234 part-time (156 women); includes 23 minority (11 African Americans, 2 Asian Americans or Pacific Islanders, 6 Hispanic Americans, 4 Native Americans). Average age 40. 29 applicants, 38% accepted, 9 enrolled. In 2001, 52 master's, 5 doctorates awarded.
**Degree requirements:** For master's, thesis optional; for doctorate, one foreign language, thesis/dissertation; for Ed S, internship, practicum.
**Entrance requirements:** For master's, TOEFL, minimum GPA of 2.75; for doctorate, GRE General Test, TOEFL. *Application deadline:* For fall admission, 7/1 (priority date); for spring admission, 1/1. Applications are processed on a rolling basis. *Application fee:* $25 ($40 for international students). Electronic applications accepted.
**Expenses:** Tuition, state resident: full-time $1,888; part-time $105 per credit. Tuition, nonresident: full-time $6,129; part-time $341 per credit. Required fees: $345; $19 per credit. $17 per semester. Tuition and fees vary according to course load and program.
**Financial support:** In 2001–02, 5 research assistantships (averaging $4,800 per year), 1 teaching assistantship with full tuition reimbursement (averaging $3,000 per year) were awarded. Career-related internships or fieldwork, Federal Work-Study, institutionally sponsored loans, scholarships/grants, traineeships, and unspecified assistantships also available. Support available to part-time students. Financial award application deadline: 4/1; financial award applicants required to submit FAFSA.
Dr. Chuck Romig, Chairperson, 316-978-3326, *Fax:* 316-978-3102, *E-mail:* chuck.romig@wichita.edu. *Web site:* http://www.wichita.edu/

# ◾ WILMINGTON COLLEGE

**Division of Behavioral Science, New Castle, DE 19720-6491**

**AWARDS** Community counseling (MS); criminal justice studies (MS); student affairs and college counseling (MS). Part-time and evening/weekend programs available.

**Faculty:** 6 full-time (2 women), 35 part-time/adjunct (15 women).
**Students:** 9 full-time (6 women), 79 part-time (64 women); includes 21 minority (19 African Americans, 2 Hispanic Americans). In 2001, 25 degrees awarded. *Median time to degree:* Master's–3 years full-time, 4 years part-time.
*Application deadline:* For fall admission, 4/15. *Application fee:* $25.
**Expenses:** Tuition: Full-time $4,788; part-time $266 per credit. Required fees: $50; $25 per semester. Tuition and fees vary according to course level, course load, degree level, campus/location and program.
**Financial support:** Applicants required to submit FAFSA.
James Wilson, Chair, 302-328-9401 Ext. 154, *Fax:* 302-328-5164, *E-mail:* jwils@wilmcoll.edu.
**Application contact:** Michael Lee, Director of Admissions and Financial Aid, 302-328-9407 Ext. 102, *Fax:* 302-328-5164, *E-mail:* inquire@wilmcoll.edu.

# ◾ YESHIVA UNIVERSITY

**Ferkauf Graduate School of Psychology, Program in School/Clinical-Child Psychology, New York, NY 10033-3201**

**AWARDS** Psy D. Part-time programs available.

**Faculty:** 8 full-time (6 women), 13 part-time/adjunct (7 women).
**Students:** 93 full-time (62 women), 32 part-time (19 women); includes 23 minority (8 African Americans, 3 Asian Americans or Pacific Islanders, 12 Hispanic Americans), 9 international. Average age 27. 135 applicants, 24% accepted. In 2001, 34 degrees awarded.
**Degree requirements:** For doctorate, thesis/dissertation.
**Entrance requirements:** For doctorate, GRE General Test. *Application deadline:* For fall admission, 1/15. *Application fee:* $50.
**Financial support:** In 2001–02, 85 students received support, including 15 fellowships (averaging $5,000 per year), research assistantships (averaging $2,000 per year), 25 teaching assistantships (averaging $2,000 per year); career-related internships or fieldwork, Federal Work-Study, institutionally sponsored loans, and scholarships/grants also available. Support available to part-time students. Financial award application deadline: 4/15.
**Faculty research:** Testing, early childhood intervention, child and adolescent psychotherapy, clinical child psychology.
Dr. Abraham Givner, Director, 718-430-3945, *E-mail:* givner@aecom.yu.edu.

**Application contact:** Elaine Schwartz, Assistant Director of Admissions, 718-430-3820, *Fax:* 718-430-3960, *E-mail:* eschart@ymail.yu.edu. *Web site:* http://www.yu.edu/fgs/

# SOCIAL PSYCHOLOGY

# ◾ ALLIANT INTERNATIONAL UNIVERSITY

**School of Social and Policy Studies, Program in Culture and Human Behavior–San Diego, San Diego, CA 92121**

**AWARDS** Psy D.

**Faculty:** 5 full-time (0 women), 1 (woman) part-time/adjunct.
**Students:** 13 full-time (11 women), 11 part-time (8 women); includes 15 minority (11 African Americans, 3 Asian Americans or Pacific Islanders, 1 Hispanic American). Average age 36. 22 applicants, 59% accepted.
**Degree requirements:** For doctorate, thesis/dissertation.
**Entrance requirements:** For doctorate, interview. *Application deadline:* Applications are processed on a rolling basis. *Application fee:* $65.
**Expenses:** Tuition: Part-time $397 per credit hour. Tuition and fees vary according to degree level, campus/location and program.
**Financial support:** In 2001–02, 19 students received support; research assistantships, teaching assistantships, career-related internships or fieldwork and Federal Work-Study available. Financial award application deadline: 2/15.
**Faculty research:** Culture, emotion, and thought; multicultural competency development.
Dr. Linda Swanson, Interim Director, 858-635-4713, *Fax:* 858-635-4730, *E-mail:* lswanson@alliant.edu.
**Application contact:** Patricia J. Mullen, Vice President, Enrollment and Student Services, 800-457-1273 Ext. 303, *Fax:* 415-931-8322, *E-mail:* admissions@mail.cspp.edu. *Web site:* http://www.alliant.edu/

# ◾ AMERICAN UNIVERSITY

**College of Arts and Sciences, Department of Psychology, Program in Psychology, Washington, DC 20016-8001**

**AWARDS** Experimental/biological psychology (MA); general psychology (MA, PhD); personality/social psychology (MA). Part-time programs available.

*American University (continued)*
**Students:** 38 full-time (31 women), 50 part-time (45 women); includes 16 minority (5 African Americans, 5 Asian Americans or Pacific Islanders, 6 Hispanic Americans), 6 international. Average age 25.
**Degree requirements:** For master's, thesis (for some programs).
**Entrance requirements:** For master's, GRE General Test, GRE Subject Test. *Application deadline:* For fall admission, 4/30. Applications are processed on a rolling basis. *Application fee:* $50.
**Expenses:** Tuition: Full-time $14,274; part-time $793 per credit. Required fees: $290. Tuition and fees vary according to program.
**Financial support:** In 2001–02, 2 students received support; teaching assistantships available. Financial award application deadline: 2/1.
**Faculty research:** Behavior therapy, cognitive behavior modification, pro-social behavior, conditioning and learning, olfaction.
Dr. Brian Yates, Director, 202-885-1727.

■ **ANDREWS UNIVERSITY**
**School of Graduate Studies, School of Education, Department of Educational and Counseling Psychology, Program in Community Counseling, Berrien Springs, MI 49104**
**AWARDS** MA.
**Students:** 19 full-time (15 women); includes 6 minority (5 African Americans, 1 Asian American or Pacific Islander), 9 international. Average age 29. In 2001, 14 degrees awarded.
**Degree requirements:** For master's, thesis optional.
*Application fee:* $40.
**Expenses:** Tuition: Full-time $12,600; part-time $525 per semester. Required fees: $268. Tuition and fees vary according to degree level.
Dr. Frederick A. Kosinski, Program Coordinator, 616-471-3133.
**Application contact:** Carolyn Hurst, Supervisor of Graduate Admission, 800-253-2874, *Fax:* 616-471-3228, *E-mail:* enroll@andrews.edu.

■ **APPALACHIAN STATE UNIVERSITY**
**Cratis D. Williams Graduate School, College of Education, Department of Human Development and Psychological Counseling, Program in Community Counseling, Boone, NC 28608**
**AWARDS** MA.

**Expenses:** Tuition, state resident: full-time $1,286. Tuition, nonresident: full-time $9,354. Required fees: $1,116.
**Financial support:** In 2001–02, research assistantships (averaging $6,250 per year), teaching assistantships (averaging $6,250 per year) were awarded.
Dr. Diana Quealy Berge, Coordinator, 828-262-2055, *E-mail:* quealybrgdp@appstate.edu.

■ **ARCADIA UNIVERSITY**
**Graduate Studies, Department of Psychology, Glenside, PA 19038-3295**
**AWARDS** Counseling (MAC), including community counseling, school counseling. Part-time programs available.
**Faculty:** 4 full-time (2 women), 6 part-time/adjunct (4 women).
**Students:** 18 full-time (all women), 28 part-time (22 women); includes 4 minority (all African Americans), 2 international. In 2001, 14 degrees awarded.
**Degree requirements:** For master's, practicum.
**Entrance requirements:** For master's, GRE General Test or MAT. *Application deadline:* Applications are processed on a rolling basis. *Application fee:* $35.
**Expenses:** Tuition: Part-time $420 per credit. Tuition and fees vary according to degree level and program.
**Financial support:** Research assistantships, career-related internships or fieldwork and unspecified assistantships available. Support available to part-time students. Financial award application deadline: 8/15. Samuel Cameron, Program Director, 215-572-2181.
**Application contact:** 215-572-2925, *Fax:* 215-572-2126, *E-mail:* grad@arcadia.edu.

■ **ARIZONA STATE UNIVERSITY**
**Graduate College, College of Liberal Arts and Sciences, Department of Psychology, Tempe, AZ 85287**
**AWARDS** Behavioral neuroscience (PhD); clinical psychology (PhD); cognitive/behavioral systems (PhD); developmental psychology (PhD); environmental psychology (PhD); quantitative research methods (PhD); social psychology (PhD).
**Degree requirements:** For doctorate, thesis/dissertation.
**Entrance requirements:** For doctorate, GRE General Test, GRE Subject Test.
**Faculty research:** Reduction of personal stress, cognitive aspects of motor skills training, behavior analysis and treatment of depression.

■ **AUBURN UNIVERSITY**
**Graduate School, College of Education, Department of Counseling and Counseling Psychology, Auburn University, AL 36849**
**AWARDS** Community agency counseling (M Ed, MS, Ed D, PhD, Ed S); counseling psychology (PhD); counselor education (Ed D, PhD); school counseling (M Ed, MS, Ed D, PhD, Ed S); school psychometry (M Ed, MS, Ed D, PhD, Ed S). Part-time programs available.
**Faculty:** 9 full-time (5 women).
**Students:** 57 full-time (51 women), 53 part-time (37 women); includes 32 minority (28 African Americans, 1 Asian American or Pacific Islander, 2 Hispanic Americans, 1 Native American), 4 international. 105 applicants, 57% accepted. In 2001, 19 master's, 8 doctorates awarded.
**Degree requirements:** For master's, thesis (for some programs); for doctorate, thesis/dissertation; for Ed S, thesis or alternative.
**Entrance requirements:** For master's and Ed S, GRE General Test; for doctorate, GRE General Test, GRE Subject Test. *Application deadline:* For fall admission, 5/15. *Application fee:* $25 ($50 for international students). Electronic applications accepted.
**Financial support:** Research assistantships, Federal Work-Study and traineeships available. Support available to part-time students. Financial award application deadline: 3/15.
**Faculty research:** At-risk students, substance abuse, gender roles, AIDS, professional ethics.
Dr. Holly Stadler, Head, 334-844-5160.
**Application contact:** Dr. John F. Pritchett, Dean of the Graduate School, 334-844-4700, *E-mail:* hatchlb@mail.auburn.edu. *Web site:* http://www.auburn.edu/academic/education/ccp/an_ccp.html

■ **BALL STATE UNIVERSITY**
**Graduate School, Teachers College, Department of Counseling Psychology and Guidance Services, Program in Social Psychology, Muncie, IN 47306-1099**
**AWARDS** MA.
**Students:** 4 full-time (2 women), 11 part-time (9 women). Average age 27. 21 applicants, 81% accepted. In 2001, 5 degrees awarded.
**Entrance requirements:** For master's, GRE General Test. *Application fee:* $25 ($35 for international students).
**Expenses:** Tuition, state resident: full-time $4,068; part-time $2,542. Tuition,

nonresident: full-time $10,944; part-time $6,462. Required fees: $1,000; $500 per term.
**Financial support:** Application deadline: 3/1.
Dr. Michael White, Head, 765-285-8040, *Fax:* 765-285-2067, *E-mail:* oomjwhite@exchange.sts. *Web site:* http://www.bsu.edu/teachers/departments/cpsy/

## ■ BOWLING GREEN STATE UNIVERSITY

**Graduate College, College of Arts and Sciences, Department of Sociology, Bowling Green, OH 43403**

**AWARDS** Criminology/deviant behavior (MA, PhD); demography and population studies (MA, PhD); family studies (MA, PhD); social psychology (MA, PhD). Part-time programs available.

**Faculty:** 17.
**Students:** 32 full-time (22 women), 12 part-time (8 women); includes 3 minority (2 African Americans, 1 Hispanic American), 6 international. Average age 28. 53 applicants, 53% accepted, 12 enrolled. In 2001, 7 master's, 4 doctorates awarded.
**Degree requirements:** For master's, thesis or alternative; for doctorate, thesis/dissertation, comprehensive exam.
**Entrance requirements:** For master's and doctorate, GRE General Test, TOEFL. *Application deadline:* For fall admission, 2/15. *Application fee:* $30. Electronic applications accepted.
**Expenses:** Tuition, state resident: full-time $7,376; part-time $342 per credit hour. Tuition, nonresident: full-time $13,628; part-time $640 per credit hour.
**Financial support:** In 2001–02, 26 research assistantships with full tuition reimbursements (averaging $9,134 per year), 6 teaching assistantships with full tuition reimbursements (averaging $11,000 per year) were awarded. Career-related internships or fieldwork, Federal Work-Study, institutionally sponsored loans, and unspecified assistantships also available. Financial award applicants required to submit FAFSA.
**Faculty research:** Applied demography, criminology and deviance, family studies, population studies, social psychology.
Dr. Gary Lee, Chair, 419-372-2294.
**Application contact:** Dr. Steve Cernkovich, Graduate Coordinator, 419-372-2743.

## ■ BRANDEIS UNIVERSITY

**Graduate School of Arts and Sciences, Department of Psychology, Waltham, MA 02454-9110**

**AWARDS** Cognitive neuroscience (PhD); general psychology (MA); social/

developmental psychology (PhD). Part-time programs available.

**Faculty:** 18 full-time (4 women), 6 part-time/adjunct (3 women).
**Students:** 25 full-time (18 women); includes 8 minority (1 African American, 5 Asian Americans or Pacific Islanders, 2 Hispanic Americans). Average age 29. 69 applicants, 35% accepted. In 2001, 4 master's, 2 doctorates awarded. Terminal master's awarded for partial completion of doctoral program.
**Degree requirements:** For master's and doctorate, thesis/dissertation.
**Entrance requirements:** For master's, GRE General Test; for doctorate, GRE General Test, GRE Subject Test. *Application deadline:* Applications are processed on a rolling basis. *Application fee:* $60. Electronic applications accepted.
**Expenses:** Tuition: Full-time $27,392. Required fees: $35.
**Financial support:** In 2001–02, 16 students received support, including 12 fellowships with full tuition reimbursements available (averaging $13,600 per year), 4 research assistantships with partial tuition reimbursements available (averaging $2,000 per year); scholarships/grants, traineeships, and tuition waivers (partial) also available. Support available to part-time students. Financial award application deadline: 5/1; financial award applicants required to submit CSS PROFILE or FAFSA.
**Faculty research:** Development, cognition, social aging, perception. *Total annual research expenditures:* $2.2 million.
Margie Lachman, Director of Graduate Studies, 781-736-3255, *Fax:* 781-736-3291, *E-mail:* lachman@brandeis.edu.
**Application contact:** Janice Steinberg, Graduate Admissions Coordinator, 781-736-3303, *Fax:* 781-736-3291, *E-mail:* steinberg@brandeis.edu. *Web site:* http://www.brandeis.edu/departments/psych/

## ■ BROOKLYN COLLEGE OF THE CITY UNIVERSITY OF NEW YORK

**Division of Graduate Studies, Department of Psychology, Brooklyn, NY 11210-2889**

**AWARDS** Experimental psychology (MA); industrial and organizational psychology (MA), including industrial and organizational psychology-human relations, psychology-organizational psychology and behavior; psychology (PhD). Part-time programs available.

**Students:** 7 full-time (4 women), 87 part-time (63 women); includes 40 minority (24 African Americans, 5 Asian Americans or Pacific Islanders, 11 Hispanic Americans), 11 international. 104 applicants, 59% accepted. In 2001, 47 degrees awarded.

**Degree requirements:** For master's, thesis or alternative, comprehensive exam.
**Entrance requirements:** For master's, TOEFL, minimum GPA of 3.0; for doctorate, GRE. *Application deadline:* For fall admission, 3/1 (priority date); for spring admission, 11/1. Applications are processed on a rolling basis. *Application fee:* $40.
**Expenses:** Tuition, state resident: full-time $4,350; part-time $185 per credit. Tuition, nonresident: full-time $7,600; part-time $320 per credit.
**Financial support:** Career-related internships or fieldwork, Federal Work-Study, institutionally sponsored loans, scholarships/grants, and tuition waivers (partial) available. Support available to part-time students. Financial award application deadline: 5/1; financial award applicants required to submit FAFSA.
Dr. Glen Hass, Chairperson, 718-951-5601, *Fax:* 718-951-4814.
**Application contact:** Dr. Benzion Chanowitz, Graduate Deputy, 718-951-5019, *Fax:* 718-951-4814, *E-mail:* psych-ma@brooklyn.cuny.edu. *Web site:* http://academic.brooklyn.cuny.edu/psych

## ■ CALIFORNIA STATE UNIVERSITY, FULLERTON

**Graduate Studies, College of Humanities and Social Sciences, Department of Psychology, Fullerton, CA 92834-9480**

**AWARDS** Clinical/community psychology (MS); psychology (MA). Part-time programs available.

**Faculty:** 24 full-time (11 women), 28 part-time/adjunct.
**Students:** 50 full-time (41 women), 7 part-time (6 women); includes 19 minority (1 African American, 8 Asian Americans or Pacific Islanders, 10 Hispanic Americans), 1 international. Average age 28. 70 applicants, 61% accepted, 33 enrolled. In 2001, 18 degrees awarded.
**Degree requirements:** For master's, thesis.
**Entrance requirements:** For master's, GRE General Test, GRE Subject Test, undergraduate major in psychology or related field. *Application deadline:* For fall admission, 3/15. *Application fee:* $55.
**Expenses:** Tuition, nonresident: part-time $246 per unit. Required fees: $964.
**Financial support:** Teaching assistantships, career-related internships or fieldwork, Federal Work-Study, institutionally sponsored loans, and scholarships/grants available. Support available to part-time students. Financial award application deadline: 3/1.
Dr. David Perkins, Chair, 714-278-3514.

## ■ CARNEGIE MELLON UNIVERSITY

College of Humanities and Social Sciences, Department of Psychology, Program in Social/Personality Psychology, Pittsburgh, PA 15213-3891

AWARDS PhD.

Degree requirements: For doctorate, thesis/dissertation, comprehensive exam.
Entrance requirements: For doctorate, GRE General Test, TOEFL, TSE.

## ■ CENTRAL CONNECTICUT STATE UNIVERSITY

School of Graduate Studies, School of Arts and Sciences, Department of Psychology, New Britain, CT 06050-4010

AWARDS Community psychology (MA); psychology (MA). Part-time and evening/weekend programs available.

Faculty: 19 full-time (7 women), 15 part-time/adjunct (5 women).
Students: 8 full-time (5 women), 12 part-time (9 women); includes 5 minority (4 African Americans, 1 Hispanic American). Average age 30. 9 applicants, 67% accepted. In 2001, 7 degrees awarded.
Degree requirements: For master's, thesis, comprehensive exam or special project.
Entrance requirements: For master's, TOEFL, minimum GPA of 2.7. *Application deadline:* For fall admission, 8/10 (priority date); for spring admission, 12/10. Applications are processed on a rolling basis. *Application fee:* $40.
Expenses: Tuition, state resident: full-time $2,772; part-time $245 per credit. Tuition, nonresident: full-time $7,726; part-time $245 per credit. Required fees: $2,102. Tuition and fees vary according to course level and degree level.
Financial support: In 2001–02, 1 research assistantship was awarded; career-related internships or fieldwork and Federal Work-Study also available. Financial award application deadline: 3/15; financial award applicants required to submit FAFSA.
Faculty research: Clinical psychology, general psychology, child development, cognitive development, drugs/behavior. Dr. Frank Donis, Chair, 860-832-3100.

## ■ CLAREMONT GRADUATE UNIVERSITY

Graduate Programs, School of Behavioral and Organizational Sciences, Department of Psychology, Claremont, CA 91711-6160

AWARDS Cognitive psychology (MA, PhD); developmental psychology (MA, PhD);

organizational behavior (MA, PhD); program design, management, and evaluation (MA); social environmental psychology (PhD); social psychology (MA). Part-time programs available.

Faculty: 6 full-time (2 women), 7 part-time/adjunct (6 women).
Students: 127 full-time (93 women), 23 part-time (19 women); includes 48 minority (8 African Americans, 23 Asian Americans or Pacific Islanders, 15 Hispanic Americans, 2 Native Americans), 9 international. Average age 30. In 2001, 25 master's, 16 doctorates awarded. Terminal master's awarded for partial completion of doctoral program.
Degree requirements: For master's, thesis (for some programs); for doctorate, thesis/dissertation, comprehensive exam.
Entrance requirements: For master's and doctorate, GRE General Test. *Application deadline:* For fall admission, 2/15 (priority date). Applications are processed on a rolling basis. *Application fee:* $50. Electronic applications accepted.
Expenses: Tuition: Full-time $22,984; part-time $1,000 per unit. Required fees: $160; $80 per semester.
Financial support: Fellowships, research assistantships, teaching assistantships, career-related internships or fieldwork, Federal Work-Study, institutionally sponsored loans, and tuition waivers (full and partial) available. Support available to part-time students. Financial award application deadline: 2/15; financial award applicants required to submit FAFSA.
Faculty research: Social intervention, diversity in organizations, eyewitness memory, aging and cognition, drug policy.
Application contact: Jessica Johnson, Program Coordinator, 909-621-8084, *Fax:* 909-621-8905, *E-mail:* jessica.johnson@cgu.edu. *Web site:* http://www.cgu.edu/sbus

Find an in-depth description at www.petersons.com/gradchannel.

## ■ CLARK UNIVERSITY

Graduate School, Department of Psychology, Program in Social-Personality Psychology, Worcester, MA 01610-1477

AWARDS PhD.

Degree requirements: For doctorate, thesis/dissertation.
Entrance requirements: For doctorate, GRE General Test, TOEFL. *Application deadline:* For fall admission, 1/31 (priority date). Applications are processed on a rolling basis. *Application fee:* $40.
Expenses: Tuition: Full-time $24,400; part-time $763 per credit. Required fees: $10.
Financial support: In 2001–02, fellowships with full tuition reimbursements

(averaging $10,900 per year), research assistantships with full tuition reimbursements (averaging $10,900 per year), teaching assistantships with full tuition reimbursements (averaging $10,900 per year) were awarded.
Dr. Joseph deRivera, Director, 508-793-7274.
Application contact: Cynthia LaRochelle, Graduate School Secretary, 508-793-7274, *Fax:* 508-793-7265, *E-mail:* clarochelle@clarku.edu. *Web site:* http://www2.clarku.edu/newsite/graduatefolder/programs/index.shtml

## ■ THE COLLEGE OF NEW ROCHELLE

Graduate School, Division of Human Services, Program in Community-School Psychology, New Rochelle, NY 10805-2308

AWARDS MS.

Degree requirements: For master's, clinical fieldwork, journal.
Entrance requirements: For master's, interview, minimum GPA of 3.0, previous course work in psychology, sample of written work.

## ■ COLLEGE OF ST. JOSEPH

Graduate Program, Division of Psychology and Human Services, Rutland, VT 05701-3899

AWARDS Clinical psychology (MS); community counseling (MS); school guidance counseling (MS). Part-time and evening/weekend programs available.

Faculty: 3 full-time (0 women), 6 part-time/adjunct (3 women).
Students: 14 full-time, 32 part-time; includes 3 minority (2 African Americans, 1 Asian American or Pacific Islander). Average age 34. In 2001, 7 degrees awarded.
Degree requirements: For master's, thesis, comprehensive exam, registration.
Entrance requirements: For master's, GRE General Test, interview. *Application deadline:* Applications are processed on a rolling basis. *Application fee:* $35.
Expenses: Tuition: Full-time $9,000; part-time $250 per credit. Required fees: $45 per semester. Part-time tuition and fees vary according to course load.
Financial support: Career-related internships or fieldwork, Federal Work-Study, and unspecified assistantships available. Support available to part-time students. Financial award application deadline: 3/1.
Dr. Craig Knapp, Chair, 802-773-5900 Ext. 3219, *Fax:* 802-773-5900, *E-mail:* cknapp@csj.edu.

**Application contact:** Steve Soba, Dean of Admissions, 802-773-5900 Ext. 3206, *Fax:* 802-773-5900, *E-mail:* ssoba@csj.edu.

### ■ COLLEGE OF STATEN ISLAND OF THE CITY UNIVERSITY OF NEW YORK

**Graduate Programs, Center for Developmental Neuroscience and Developmental Disabilities, Sub-program in Learning Processes, Staten Island, NY 10314-6600**

**AWARDS** Biopsychology (PhD); clinical psychology (PhD); developmental psychology (PhD); environmental psychology (PhD); experimental cognition (PhD); experimental psychology (PhD); neuropsychology (PhD); psychology (PhD); social-personality psychology (PhD).

**Degree requirements:** For doctorate, one foreign language, thesis/dissertation.

**Entrance requirements:** For doctorate, GRE, TOEFL. *Application deadline:* For fall admission, 3/15 (priority date). Applications are processed on a rolling basis. *Application fee:* $40.

**Expenses:** Tuition, state resident: full-time $4,350; part-time $185 per credit. Tuition, nonresident: full-time $7,600; part-time $320 per credit. Required fees: $53 per semester.

**Financial support:** Fellowships, research assistantships, teaching assistantships, career-related internships or fieldwork and institutionally sponsored loans available. Financial award application deadline: 3/15. Dr. Nancy Hemmes, Head, 718-997-3561.

### ■ COLORADO STATE UNIVERSITY

**Graduate School, College of Natural Sciences, Department of Psychology, Fort Collins, CO 80523-0015**

**AWARDS** Applied social psychology (PhD); behavioral neuroscience (PhD); cognitive psychology (PhD); counseling psychology (PhD); industrial-organizational psychology (PhD).

**Faculty:** 29 full-time (8 women), 13 part-time/adjunct (7 women).

**Students:** 56 full-time (42 women), 37 part-time (29 women). Average age 29. 309 applicants, 12% accepted, 16 enrolled. In 2001, 9 doctorates awarded.

**Degree requirements:** For doctorate, thesis/dissertation.

**Entrance requirements:** For doctorate, GRE General Test, GRE Subject Test, TOEFL, minimum GPA of 3.5. *Application deadline:* For fall admission, 1/15. *Application fee:* $30. Electronic applications accepted.

**Expenses:** Tuition, state resident: full-time $2,880; part-time $160 per credit. Tuition,

nonresident: full-time $11,412; part-time $634 per credit. Required fees: $750; $34 per credit.

**Financial support:** In 2001–02, 3 fellowships with full tuition reimbursements (averaging $12,120 per year), 10 research assistantships with full tuition reimbursements (averaging $9,720 per year), 52 teaching assistantships with full tuition reimbursements (averaging $9,720 per year) were awarded. Career-related internships or fieldwork, Federal Work-Study, institutionally sponsored loans, scholarships/grants, and traineeships also available.

**Faculty research:** Environmental psychology, cognitive learning, health psychology, occupations of health. *Total annual research expenditures:* $12.5 million.

Ernest L. Chavez, Chair, 970-491-6363, *Fax:* 970-491-1032, *E-mail:* echavez@lamar.colostate.edu.

**Application contact:** Wendy Standring, Graduate Admissions Coordinator, 970-491-6363, *Fax:* 970-491-1032, *E-mail:* wendyann@lamar.colostate.edu. *Web site:* http://www.colostate.edu/Depts/Psychology/

### ■ COLUMBIA UNIVERSITY

**Graduate School of Arts and Sciences, Division of Natural Sciences, Department of Psychology, New York, NY 10027**

**AWARDS** Experimental psychology (M Phil, MA, PhD); psychobiology (M Phil, MA, PhD); social psychology (M Phil, MA, PhD).

**Faculty:** 23 full-time.

**Students:** 35 full-time (19 women), 2 part-time. Average age 28. 156 applicants, 7% accepted. In 2001, 7 master's, 6 doctorates awarded.

**Degree requirements:** For master's and doctorate, thesis/dissertation.

**Entrance requirements:** For master's and doctorate, GRE General Test, TOEFL. *Application deadline:* For fall admission, 1/3. *Application fee:* $65.

**Expenses:** Tuition: Full-time $27,528. Required fees: $1,638.

**Financial support:** Fellowships, teaching assistantships, Federal Work-Study and institutionally sponsored loans available. Support available to part-time students. Financial award application deadline: 1/5; financial award applicants required to submit FAFSA.

Donald Hood, Chair, 212-854-4587, *Fax:* 212-854-3609.

### ■ CORNELL UNIVERSITY

**Graduate School, Graduate Fields of Arts and Sciences, Field of Psychology, Ithaca, NY 14853-0001**

**AWARDS** Biopsychology (PhD); general psychology (PhD); human experimental psychology (PhD); personality and social psychology (PhD).

**Faculty:** 36 full-time.

**Students:** 37 full-time (20 women); includes 2 minority (1 Asian American or Pacific Islander, 1 Hispanic American), 10 international. 144 applicants, 8% accepted. In 2001, 2 doctorates awarded.

**Degree requirements:** For doctorate, thesis/dissertation, 2 semesters of teaching experience.

**Entrance requirements:** For doctorate, GRE General Test, TOEFL, 3 letters of recommendation. *Application deadline:* For fall admission, 1/15. *Application fee:* $65. Electronic applications accepted.

**Expenses:** Tuition: Full-time $25,970. Required fees: $50.

**Financial support:** In 2001–02, 36 students received support, including 9 fellowships with full tuition reimbursements available, 27 teaching assistantships with full tuition reimbursements available; research assistantships with full tuition reimbursements available, institutionally sponsored loans, scholarships/grants, tuition waivers (full and partial), and unspecified assistantships also available. Financial award applicants required to submit FAFSA.

**Faculty research:** Sensory and perceptual systems, social cognition, cognitive development, neuroscience, quantitative and computational modeling.

**Application contact:** Graduate Field Assistant, 607-255-6364, *E-mail:* psychapp@cornell.edu. *Web site:* http://www.gradschool.cornell.edu/grad/fields_1/psych.html

### ■ CORNELL UNIVERSITY

**Graduate School, Graduate Fields of Arts and Sciences, Field of Sociology, Ithaca, NY 14853-0001**

**AWARDS** Economy and society (MA, PhD); gender and life course (MA, PhD); organizations (MA, PhD); political sociology/social movements (MA, PhD); racial and ethnic relations (MA, PhD); social networks (MA, PhD); social psychology (MA, PhD); social stratification (MA, PhD).

**Faculty:** 19 full-time.

**Students:** 33 full-time (17 women); includes 3 minority (1 African American, 1 Asian American or Pacific Islander, 1 Hispanic American), 17 international. 126 applicants, 13% accepted. In 2001, 2 master's, 3 doctorates awarded. Terminal

*Cornell University (continued)*
master's awarded for partial completion of doctoral program.

**Degree requirements:** For master's, thesis; for doctorate, thesis/dissertation, 1 year of teaching experience.

**Entrance requirements:** For master's and doctorate, GRE General Test, TOEFL. *Application deadline:* For fall admission, 1/15. *Application fee:* $65. Electronic applications accepted.

**Expenses:** Tuition: Full-time $25,970. Required fees: $50.

**Financial support:** In 2001–02, 32 students received support, including 13 fellowships with full tuition reimbursements available, 10 research assistantships with full tuition reimbursements available, 9 teaching assistantships with full tuition reimbursements available; institutionally sponsored loans, scholarships/grants, tuition waivers (full and partial), and unspecified assistantships also available. Financial award applicants required to submit FAFSA.

**Faculty research:** Comparative societal analysis, work and family, simulations, social class and mobility, racial segregation and inequality.

**Application contact:** Graduate Field Assistant, 607-255-4266, *Fax:* 607-255-8473, *E-mail:* sociology@cornell.edu. *Web site:* http://www.gradschool.cornell.edu/grad/fields_1/socio.html

■ **DEPAUL UNIVERSITY**

**College of Liberal Arts and Sciences, Department of Psychology, Program in Clinical Psychology, Chicago, IL 60604-2287**

**AWARDS** Child clinical psychology (MA, PhD); community clinical psychology (MA, PhD).

**Faculty:** 17 full-time (10 women), 3 part-time/adjunct (2 women).

**Students:** 24 full-time (17 women), 31 part-time (23 women); includes 14 African Americans, 8 Asian Americans or Pacific Islanders, 4 Hispanic Americans, 1 international. Average age 29. 158 applicants, 5% accepted. In 2001, 5 master's, 10 doctorates awarded.

**Degree requirements:** For master's, thesis, oral exam; for doctorate, thesis/dissertation, internship, oral and written exams, comprehensive exam. *Median time to degree:* Master's–2 years full-time; doctorate–6 years full-time.

**Entrance requirements:** For master's and doctorate, GRE General Test, 32 quarter hours in psychology, minimum GPA of 3.5. *Application deadline:* For fall admission, 1/10. *Application fee:* $40. Electronic applications accepted.

**Expenses:** Tuition: Part-time $362 per credit hour. Tuition and fees vary according to program.

**Financial support:** In 2001–02, 24 students received support, including 20 research assistantships with full and partial tuition reimbursements available (averaging $7,000 per year), 4 teaching assistantships with full and partial tuition reimbursements available (averaging $7,000 per year); career-related internships or fieldwork, scholarships/grants, traineeships, tuition waivers (partial), and unspecified assistantships also available. Financial award application deadline: 1/10.

**Faculty research:** Urban issues, child family issues, diversity, at risk youth, homeless and Latino/a HIV/AIDS.

Dr. Karen Budd, Director of Clinical Training, *E-mail:* rbudd@depaul.edu.

**Application contact:** Lucinda Rapp, Information Contact, 773-325-7887, *E-mail:* lrapp@wppost.depaul.edu. *Web site:* http://condor.depaul.edu/~psych/

■ **DEPAUL UNIVERSITY**

**College of Liberal Arts and Sciences, Department of Psychology, Program in Community Psychology, Chicago, IL 60604-2287**

**AWARDS** PhD.

**Faculty:** 17 full-time (10 women), 3 part-time/adjunct (2 women).

**Students:** 2 full-time (1 woman). Average age 29. 18 applicants, 11% accepted.

**Degree requirements:** For doctorate, thesis/dissertation, internships, oral and written exams, comprehensive exam.

**Entrance requirements:** For doctorate, GRE General Test, minimum GPA of 3.5. *Application deadline:* For fall admission, 1/10. Electronic applications accepted.

**Expenses:** Tuition: Part-time $362 per credit hour. Tuition and fees vary according to program.

**Financial support:** In 2001–02, 2 students received support, including 2 research assistantships (averaging $6,000 per year); career-related internships or fieldwork, scholarships/grants, and traineeships also available. Financial award application deadline: 1/10.

Dr. Leonard Jason, Director, 773-325-2018, *E-mail:* ljason@depaul.edu.

**Application contact:** Lucinda Rapp, Information Contact, 773-325-7887, *E-mail:* lrapp@depaul.edu. *Web site:* http://condor.depaul.edu/~psych/

■ **FAIRLEIGH DICKINSON UNIVERSITY, COLLEGE AT FLORHAM**

**Maxwell Becton College of Arts and Sciences, Department of Psychology, Program in Applied Social and Community Psychology, Madison, NJ 07940-1099**

**AWARDS** MA.

**Students:** 1 full-time (0 women), 2 part-time (both women); includes 1 minority (African American). Average age 26. 2 applicants, 50% accepted, 1 enrolled. In 2001, 4 degrees awarded.

**Entrance requirements:** For master's, GRE General Test. *Application deadline:* Applications are processed on a rolling basis. *Application fee:* $40.

**Expenses:** Tuition: Full-time $11,484; part-time $638 per credit. Required fees: $420. One-time fee: $97 part-time.

■ **FLORIDA AGRICULTURAL AND MECHANICAL UNIVERSITY**

**Division of Graduate Studies, Research, and Continuing Education, College of Arts and Sciences, Department of Psychology, Program in Community Psychology, Tallahassee, FL 32307-3200**

**AWARDS** MS.

**Degree requirements:** For master's, thesis, internship.

**Entrance requirements:** For master's, GRE General Test, minimum GPA of 3.0.

**Faculty research:** African-American personality and mental health, racism in the socialization of black children.

■ **FRANCIS MARION UNIVERSITY**

**Graduate Programs, Department of Psychology, Florence, SC 29501-0547**

**AWARDS** Applied clinical psychology (MS); applied community psychology (MS); school psychology (MS). Part-time and evening/weekend programs available.

**Faculty:** 12 full-time (3 women), 2 part-time/adjunct (1 woman).

**Students:** 57. Average age 36. In 2001, 12 degrees awarded.

**Degree requirements:** For master's, internship.

**Entrance requirements:** For master's, GRE General Test. *Application deadline:* For fall admission, 4/15; for spring admission, 10/15. Applications are processed on a rolling basis. *Application fee:* $30.

**Expenses:** Tuition, state resident: full-time $3,820; part-time $191 per semester hour. Tuition, nonresident: full-time $7,640; part-time $382 per semester hour. Required fees: $170; $4 per semester hour. $30 per semester.

**Financial support:** In 2001–02, fellowships (averaging $6,000 per year); career-related internships or fieldwork and unspecified assistantships also available. Support available to part-time students. Financial award application deadline: 3/1; financial award applicants required to submit FAFSA.

**Faculty research:** Critical thinking, spatial localization, cognition and aging, family psychology.

Dr. John R. Hester, Coordinator, 843-661-1635, *Fax:* 843-661-1628.

**Application contact:** Ginger Ridgill, Administrative Assistant, 843-661-1378, *Fax:* 843-661-1628, *E-mail:* gridgill@ fmarion.edu.

## ■ THE GEORGE WASHINGTON UNIVERSITY

**Columbian College of Arts and Sciences, Department of Psychology, Washington, DC 20052**

AWARDS Applied social psychology (PhD); clinical psychology (PhD, Psy D); cognitive neuropsychology (PhD); industrial-organizational psychology (PhD). Part-time and evening/weekend programs available.

**Faculty:** 15 full-time (8 women), 1 (woman) part-time/adjunct.
**Students:** 133 full-time (106 women), 102 part-time (82 women); includes 50 minority (22 African Americans, 13 Asian Americans or Pacific Islanders, 14 Hispanic Americans, 1 Native American), 15 international. Average age 30. 413 applicants, 18% accepted. In 2001, 32 doctorates awarded.
**Degree requirements:** For doctorate, thesis/dissertation or alternative, general exam.
**Entrance requirements:** For doctorate, GRE General Test, minimum GPA of 3.0. *Application fee:* $55.
**Expenses:** Tuition: Part-time $810 per credit. Required fees: $1 per credit.
**Financial support:** In 2001–02, 27 students received support, including 22 fellowships with tuition reimbursements available (averaging $4,700 per year), 20 teaching assistantships with tuition reimbursements available (averaging $2,900 per year); career-related internships or fieldwork and Federal Work-Study also available. Financial award application deadline: 2/1.
Dr. Rolf Peterson, Chair, 202-994-6544. *Web site:* http://www.gwu.edu/~gradinfo/

## ■ GRADUATE SCHOOL AND UNIVERSITY CENTER OF THE CITY UNIVERSITY OF NEW YORK

**Graduate Studies, Program in Psychology, New York, NY 10016-4039**

AWARDS Basic applied neurocognition (PhD); biopsychology (PhD); clinical psychology (PhD); developmental psychology (PhD); environmental psychology (PhD); experimental psychology (PhD); industrial psychology (PhD); learning processes (PhD); neuropsychology (PhD); psychology (PhD); social personality (PhD).

**Faculty:** 119 full-time (40 women).
**Students:** 463 full-time (335 women), 4 part-time (2 women); includes 96 minority (39 African Americans, 20 Asian Americans or Pacific Islanders, 36 Hispanic Americans, 1 Native American), 47 international. Average age 33. 493 applicants, 24% accepted, 65 enrolled. In 2001, 28 degrees awarded.
**Degree requirements:** For doctorate, one foreign language, thesis/dissertation.
**Entrance requirements:** For doctorate, GRE General Test. *Application deadline:* For fall admission, 2/1. *Application fee:* $40.
**Expenses:** Tuition, state resident: part-time $245 per credit. Tuition, nonresident: part-time $425 per credit. Required fees: $72 per semester.
**Financial support:** In 2001–02, 226 students received support, including 141 fellowships, 14 research assistantships, 4 teaching assistantships; career-related internships or fieldwork, Federal Work-Study, institutionally sponsored loans, and tuition waivers (full and partial) also available. Financial award application deadline: 2/1; financial award applicants required to submit FAFSA.
Dr. Joseph Glick, Executive Officer, 212-817-8706, *Fax:* 212-817-1533, *E-mail:* jglick@gc.cuny.edu.

## ■ HARVARD UNIVERSITY

**Graduate School of Arts and Sciences, Department of Psychology, Cambridge, MA 02138**

AWARDS Psychology (AM, PhD), including behavior and decision analysis, cognition, developmental psychology, experimental psychology, personality, psychobiology, psychopathology; social psychology (AM, PhD).

**Degree requirements:** For doctorate, thesis/dissertation, general exams.
**Entrance requirements:** For master's and doctorate, GRE General Test, TOEFL.
**Expenses:** Tuition: Full-time $23,370. Required fees: $816. Full-time tuition and fees vary according to program and student level.

## ■ HENDERSON STATE UNIVERSITY

**Graduate Studies, School of Education, Department of Counselor Education, Arkadelphia, AR 71999-0001**

AWARDS Community counseling (MS); elementary school counseling (MSE); secondary school counseling (MSE). Part-time programs available.

**Faculty:** 5 full-time (1 woman).
**Students:** 14 full-time (12 women), 62 part-time (45 women); includes 17 minority (15 African Americans, 1 Asian American or Pacific Islander, 1 Native American). Average age 35. 6 applicants, 17% accepted. In 2001, 10 degrees awarded.
**Entrance requirements:** For master's, GRE General Test or MAT, letters of recommendation, minimum GPA of 2.7, teacher certification. *Application deadline:* For fall admission, 5/1 (priority date); for spring admission, 12/1 (priority date). Applications are processed on a rolling basis. *Application fee:* $0 ($30 for international students).
**Expenses:** Tuition, state resident: part-time $150 per credit hour. Tuition, nonresident: part-time $300 per credit hour. Required fees: $120 per semester.
**Financial support:** In 2001–02, 3 teaching assistantships with full tuition reimbursements (averaging $4,000 per year) were awarded; Federal Work-Study and institutionally sponsored loans also available. Support available to part-time students. Financial award application deadline: 7/31.
Dr. Richard Schmid, Chairperson, 870-230-5226, *Fax:* 870-230-5455, *E-mail:* schmidr@hsu.edu.

## ■ HOFSTRA UNIVERSITY

**College of Liberal Arts and Sciences, Division of Social Sciences, Department of Psychology, Program in School-Community Psychology, Hempstead, NY 11549**

AWARDS MS, Psy D.

**Faculty:** 26 full-time (5 women), 14 part-time/adjunct (6 women).
**Students:** 27 full-time (21 women), 59 part-time (49 women); includes 1 minority (Asian American or Pacific Islander). Average age 30. In 2001, 11 master's, 9 doctorates awarded.
**Degree requirements:** For master's, comprehensive exam; for doctorate, thesis/dissertation, comprehensive exam.
**Entrance requirements:** For master's, GRE General Test; for doctorate, GRE General Test, GRE Subject Test, interview, minimum GPA of 3.0 in psychology.

*Hofstra University (continued)*
*Application deadline:* Applications are processed on a rolling basis. *Application fee:* $40 ($75 for international students).
**Expenses:** Tuition: Full-time $12,408. Tuition and fees vary according to course load and program.
Dr. Robert Motta, Assistant Director, 516-463-5295, *E-mail:* psyrwm@hofstra.edu.
**Application contact:** Mary Beth Carey, Vice President of Enrollment Services, *Fax:* 516-560-7660, *E-mail:* hofstra@hofstra.edu.

## ■ HOWARD UNIVERSITY

**Graduate School of Arts and Sciences, Department of Psychology, Washington, DC 20059-0002**

**AWARDS** Clinical psychology (PhD); developmental psychology (PhD); experimental psychology (PhD); neuropsychology (PhD); personality psychology (PhD); psychology (MS); social psychology (PhD). Part-time programs available.

**Faculty:** 16 full-time (7 women).
**Students:** 70 full-time (51 women), 20 part-time (14 women). Average age 29. 165 applicants, 15% accepted, 20 enrolled. In 2001, 10 master's, 12 doctorates awarded.
**Degree requirements:** For master's, thesis, comprehensive exam; for doctorate, thesis/dissertation, qualifying exam, comprehensive exam. *Median time to degree:* Master's–3 years full-time, 5 years part-time; doctorate–5 years full-time, 9 years part-time.
**Entrance requirements:** For master's, GRE General Test, minimum GPA of 2.5, bachelor's degree in psychology or related field; for doctorate, GRE General Test, minimum GPA of 3.0. *Application deadline:* For fall admission, 4/1; for spring admission, 11/1. Applications are processed on a rolling basis. *Application fee:* $45.
**Financial support:** In 2001–02, 19 students received support, including 3 fellowships with full tuition reimbursements available (averaging $13,500 per year), 2 research assistantships with full tuition reimbursements available (averaging $10,000 per year), 8 teaching assistantships with full tuition reimbursements available (averaging $13,000 per year); career-related internships or fieldwork, institutionally sponsored loans, and scholarships/grants also available. Financial award application deadline: 4/1; financial award applicants required to submit FAFSA.
**Faculty research:** Personality and psychophysiology, educational and social development of African-American children, child and adult psychopathology.

Dr. Albert Roberts, Chair, 202-806-6805, *Fax:* 202-806-4823, *E-mail:* aroberts@howard.edu.
**Application contact:** Dr. Alfonso Campbell, Chairman, Graduate Admissions Committee, 202-806-6805, *Fax:* 202-806-4873, *E-mail:* acampbell@howard.edu.

## ■ HUNTER COLLEGE OF THE CITY UNIVERSITY OF NEW YORK

**Graduate School, School of Arts and Sciences, Department of Psychology, New York, NY 10021-5085**

**AWARDS** Applied and evaluative psychology (MA); biopsychology and comparative psychology (MA); social, cognitive, and developmental psychology (MA). Part-time and evening/weekend programs available.

**Faculty:** 21 full-time (10 women), 8 part-time/adjunct (4 women).
**Students:** 3 full-time (2 women), 14 part-time (11 women); includes 5 minority (1 African American, 4 Hispanic Americans), 1 international. Average age 27. 53 applicants, 47% accepted, 5 enrolled. In 2001, 5 degrees awarded.
**Degree requirements:** For master's, thesis, comprehensive exam. *Median time to degree:* Master's–3.5 years part-time.
**Entrance requirements:** For master's, GRE General Test, TOEFL, minimum 12 credits in psychology, including statistics and experimental psychology. *Application deadline:* For fall admission, 4/1; for spring admission, 11/1. Applications are processed on a rolling basis. *Application fee:* $40.
**Expenses:** Tuition, state resident: full-time $2,175; part-time $185 per credit. Tuition, nonresident: full-time $3,800; part-time $320 per credit.
**Faculty research:** Personality, cognitive and linguistic development, hormonal and neural control of behavior, gender and culture, social cognition of health and attitudes.
Dr. Darlene DeFour, Acting Chairperson.
**Application contact:** William Zlata, Director for Graduate Admissions, 212-772-4288, *Fax:* 212-650-3336, *E-mail:* admissions@hunter.cuny.edu. *Web site:* http://maxweber.hunter.cuny.edu/psych/

## ■ INDIANA UNIVERSITY BLOOMINGTON

**Graduate School, College of Arts and Sciences, Department of Psychology, Bloomington, IN 47405**

**AWARDS** Biology and behavior (PhD); clinical science (PhD); cognitive psychology (PhD); developmental psychology (PhD); social psychology (PhD). Offered through the University Graduate School.

**Faculty:** 40 full-time (7 women), 1 (woman) part-time/adjunct.

**Students:** 42 full-time (23 women), 37 part-time (18 women); includes 9 minority (2 African Americans, 5 Asian Americans or Pacific Islanders, 2 Hispanic Americans), 9 international. Average age 28. 222 applicants, 14% accepted. In 2001, 18 doctorates awarded.
**Degree requirements:** For doctorate, thesis/dissertation, 1st- and 2nd-year projects, 1 year as associate instructor, qualifying exam.
**Entrance requirements:** For doctorate, GRE, TOEFL. *Application deadline:* For fall admission, 12/15. *Application fee:* $45 ($55 for international students). Electronic applications accepted.
**Expenses:** Tuition, state resident: full-time $4,720; part-time $197 per credit. Tuition, nonresident: full-time $13,748; part-time $573 per credit. Required fees: $642.
**Financial support:** In 2001–02, 8 fellowships (averaging $14,000 per year), 24 teaching assistantships (averaging $11,800 per year) were awarded.
Dr. Joseph E. Steinmetz, Chairperson, 812-855-3991, *Fax:* 812-855-4691, *E-mail:* steinmet@indiana.edu.
**Application contact:** Beth Laske-Miller, Graduate Admissions Assistant, 812-855-2014, *Fax:* 812-855-4691, *E-mail:* psychgrd@indiana.edu. *Web site:* http://www.indiana.edu/~psych/

## ■ INDIANA WESLEYAN UNIVERSITY

**College of Adult and Professional Studies, Program in Counseling, Marion, IN 46953-4974**

**AWARDS** Community counseling (MA); community/addiction counseling (MA); marriage and family counseling (MA). Part-time programs available.

**Faculty:** 3 full-time (0 women), 7 part-time/adjunct (4 women).
**Students:** 27 full-time (19 women), 30 part-time (24 women); includes 1 minority (African American). Average age 35. In 2001, 5 degrees awarded.
**Degree requirements:** For master's, thesis or alternative.
**Entrance requirements:** For master's, GRE General Test. *Application deadline:* For fall admission, 4/1 (priority date); for spring admission, 10/1 (priority date). *Application fee:* $25. Electronic applications accepted.
**Expenses:** Contact institution.
**Financial support:** In 2001–02, 1 research assistantship with tuition reimbursement, 1 teaching assistantship with partial tuition reimbursement (averaging $1,000 per year) were awarded. Financial award application deadline: 3/1; financial award applicants required to submit FAFSA.

**Faculty research:** Attachment, emotional softening, cultural reentry, third culture kids, sexuality.
Dr. Jerry Davis, Director of Graduate Counseling Studies, 765-677-2995, *Fax:* 765-677-2504, *E-mail:* jdavis@indwes.edu.

**Find an in-depth description at www.petersons.com/gradchannel.**

## ■ IOWA STATE UNIVERSITY OF SCIENCE AND TECHNOLOGY

**Graduate College, College of Liberal Arts and Sciences, Department of Psychology, Ames, IA 50011**

**AWARDS** Cognitive psychology (PhD); counseling psychology (PhD); general psychology (MS); social psychology (PhD). Terminal master's awarded for partial completion of doctoral program.

**Degree requirements:** For master's, thesis or alternative; for doctorate, thesis/dissertation.
**Entrance requirements:** For master's and doctorate, GRE General Test, GRE Subject Test (psychology), TOEFL. Electronic applications accepted.
**Expenses:** Tuition, state resident: full-time $1,851. Tuition, nonresident: full-time $5,449. Tuition and fees vary according to program.
**Faculty research:** Counseling psychology, cognitive psychology, social psychology, health psychology, psychology and public policy. *Web site:* http://psych-server.iastate.edu/

## ■ LAMAR UNIVERSITY

**College of Graduate Studies, College of Arts and Sciences, Department of Psychology, Beaumont, TX 77710**

**AWARDS** Community/clinical psychology (MS); industrial/organizational psychology (MS). Part-time programs available.

**Faculty:** 5 full-time (2 women).
**Students:** 15 full-time (8 women), 5 part-time (4 women); includes 4 minority (2 African Americans, 2 Hispanic Americans). Average age 32. 35 applicants, 80% accepted. In 2001, 9 degrees awarded.
**Degree requirements:** For master's, thesis, practicum.
**Entrance requirements:** For master's, GRE General Test, TOEFL, minimum GPA of 2.5 in last 60 hours of undergraduate course work. *Application deadline:* For fall admission, 8/1; for spring admission, 12/1. *Application fee:* $25 ($50 for international students).
**Expenses:** Tuition, state resident: full-time $1,114. Tuition, nonresident: full-time $3,670.
**Financial support:** In 2001–02, 12 students received support, including research assistantships (averaging $6,000

per year), 7 teaching assistantships with tuition reimbursements available (averaging $3,000 per year); fellowships, career-related internships or fieldwork, Federal Work-Study, scholarships/grants, and tuition waivers (partial) also available. Support available to part-time students. Financial award application deadline: 4/1.
**Faculty research:** Counseling psychology, industrial psychology. *Total annual research expenditures:* $17,000.
Dr. Oney D. Fitzpatrick, Chair, 409-880-8285, *Fax:* 409-880-1779, *E-mail:* fitzpatrod@hal.lamar.edu. *Web site:* http://140.158.184.30/

## ■ LESLEY UNIVERSITY

**Graduate School of Arts and Social Sciences, Cambridge, MA 02138-2790**

**AWARDS** Clinical mental health counseling (MA), including expressive therapies counseling, holistic counseling, school and community counseling; counseling psychology (MA, CAGS), including school counseling (MA); creative arts in learning (M Ed, CAGS), including individually designed (M Ed, MA), multicultural education (M Ed, MA), storytelling (M Ed), theater studies (M Ed); ecological literacy (MS); environmental education (MS); expressive therapies (MA, PhD, CAGS), including art therapy (MA), dance therapy (MA), individually designed (M Ed, MA), mental health counseling (MA), music therapy (MA); independent studies (M Ed); independent study (MA); intercultural relations (MA, CAGS), including development project administration (MA), individually designed (M Ed, MA), intercultural conflict resolution (MA), intercultural health and human services (MA), intercultural relations (CAGS), intercultural training and consulting (MA), international education exchange (MA), international student advising (MA), managing culturally diverse human resources (MA), multicultural education (M Ed, MA); interdisciplinary studies (MA); visual arts and creative writing (MFA). MS (environmental education) offered jointly with the Audubon Society Expedition Institute. Part-time and evening/weekend programs available. Postbaccalaureate distance learning degree programs offered (minimal on-campus study).

**Faculty:** 73 full-time (58 women), 137 part-time/adjunct (95 women).
**Students:** 108 full-time (97 women), 1,190 part-time (1,084 women); includes 134 minority (81 African Americans, 23 Asian Americans or Pacific Islanders, 26 Hispanic Americans, 4 Native Americans), 16 international. Average age 36. 639 applicants, 91% accepted, 313 enrolled. In 2001, 1106 degrees awarded.
**Degree requirements:** For master's, internship, practicum, thesis (expressive therapies); for doctorate and CAGS, thesis/dissertation, arts apprenticeship,

field placement; for CAGS, thesis, internship (counseling psychology, expressive therapies).

**Entrance requirements:** For master's, MAT (counseling psychology), TOEFL, interview; for doctorate, GRE or MAT; for CAGS, interview, master's degree. *Application deadline:* Applications are processed on a rolling basis. *Application fee:* $50.
**Expenses:** Tuition: Part-time $330 per credit. Required fees: $15 per term. Part-time tuition and fees vary according to campus/location and program.
**Financial support:** In 2001–02, 47 students received support; research assistantships, teaching assistantships, career-related internships or fieldwork, Federal Work-Study, and unspecified assistantships available. Support available to part-time students. Financial award application deadline: 4/1; financial award applicants required to submit FAFSA.
**Faculty research:** Developmental psychology, women's issues, health psychology, limited supervision group psychology.
Dr. Martha B. McKenna, Dean, 617-349-8467, *Fax:* 617-349-8366.
**Application contact:** Hugh Norwood, Dean of Admissions and Enrollment Planning, 800-999-1959, *Fax:* 617-349-8366, *E-mail:* hnorwood@mail.lesley.edu. *Web site:* http://www.lesley.edu/gsass.html

## ■ LOYOLA UNIVERSITY CHICAGO

**Graduate School, Department of Psychology, Program in Applied Social Psychology, Chicago, IL 60611-2196**

**AWARDS** MA, PhD.

**Faculty:** 8 full-time (2 women).
**Students:** 24 full-time (20 women), 13 part-time (8 women); includes 4 minority (1 African American, 1 Asian American or Pacific Islander, 2 Hispanic Americans), 6 international. Average age 26. 46 applicants, 30% accepted. In 2001, 5 master's, 3 doctorates awarded. Terminal master's awarded for partial completion of doctoral program.
**Degree requirements:** For master's, thesis, comprehensive exam; for doctorate, thesis/dissertation, internship, comprehensive exam.
**Entrance requirements:** For master's and doctorate, GRE General Test, GRE Subject Test, sample of written work. *Application deadline:* For fall admission, 2/1 (priority date). Applications are processed on a rolling basis. *Application fee:* $40.
**Expenses:** Tuition: Part-time $529 per credit hour.
**Financial support:** In 2001–02, 1 fellowship with tuition reimbursement (averaging $10,000 per year), 4 research assistantships

*Loyola University Chicago (continued)*
with tuition reimbursements (averaging $10,000 per year), 3 teaching assistantships (averaging $10,000 per year) were awarded. Career-related internships or fieldwork, Federal Work-Study, and scholarships/grants also available. Financial award application deadline: 2/1; financial award applicants required to submit FAFSA.
**Faculty research:** Program evaluation, attitudes and prejudice, psychological well-being, mass media, groups and organizations and communities. *Total annual research expenditures:* $200,000.
Dr. R. Scott Tindale, Director, 773-508-3014, *Fax:* 773-508-8713, *E-mail:* rtindal@luc.edu.
**Application contact:** Jacquie Hamilton, Secretary, 773-508-6018, *Fax:* 773-508-8713, *E-mail:* jhamilt@luc.edu. *Web site:* http://www.luc.edu/depts/Psychology/grad/

## ■ MARIST COLLEGE

**Graduate Programs, School of Social/Behavioral Sciences, Poughkeepsie, NY 12601-1387**

AWARDS Counseling/community psychology (MA); education psychology (MA); school psychology (MA, Adv C). Part-time and evening/weekend programs available.

**Faculty:** 8 full-time (3 women), 20 part-time/adjunct (11 women).
**Students:** 66 full-time (49 women), 149 part-time (113 women); includes 11 minority (5 African Americans, 1 Asian American or Pacific Islander, 4 Hispanic Americans, 1 Native American). Average age 30. 104 applicants, 79% accepted. In 2001, 62 degrees awarded.
**Degree requirements:** For master's, thesis optional.
**Entrance requirements:** For master's, GRE General Test. *Application deadline:* For fall admission, 8/1 (priority date); for spring admission, 12/15. Applications are processed on a rolling basis. *Application fee:* $30.
**Expenses:** Tuition: Full-time $4,320; part-time $480 per credit. Required fees: $30 per semester.
**Financial support:** Career-related internships or fieldwork, Federal Work-Study, and tuition waivers (partial) available. Support available to part-time students. Financial award application deadline: 8/15; financial award applicants required to submit FAFSA.
**Faculty research:** Obsessive-compulsive disorders/eating disorders, AIDS prevention, educational intervention, humanistic counseling research, program evaluation research.

Margaret Calista, Dean, 845-575-3000 Ext. 2960, *E-mail:* margaret.calista@marist.edu.
**Application contact:** Dr. John DeJoy, Acting Dean of Graduate and Continuing Education, 845-575-3530, *Fax:* 845-575-3640, *E-mail:* john.dejoy@marist.edu.

## ■ MARTIN UNIVERSITY

**Division of Psychology, Indianapolis, IN 46218-3867**

AWARDS Community psychology (MS). Part-time and evening/weekend programs available.

**Faculty:** 4 full-time (1 woman), 2 part-time/adjunct (1 woman).
**Students:** 35 full-time (23 women), 17 part-time (13 women); includes 42 minority (all African Americans), 1 international. Average age 41. In 2001, 11 degrees awarded.
**Degree requirements:** For master's, thesis, comprehensive exam.
**Entrance requirements:** For master's, GRE General Test, GRE Subject Test. *Application deadline:* Applications are processed on a rolling basis. *Application fee:* $55.
**Expenses:** Tuition: Part-time $275 per credit hour.
**Financial support:** In 2001–02, 9 students received support. Applicants required to submit FAFSA.
**Faculty research:** Social and educational issues in minority and low income communities.
Dr. Richard L. Elder, Chairperson, 317-917-3321, *Fax:* 317-543-4790, *E-mail:* relder@martin.edu.
**Application contact:** Brenda Shaheed, Director of Enrollment Management, 317-543-3237, *Fax:* 317-543-4790, *E-mail:* rlelder@iupui.edu.

## ■ MIAMI UNIVERSITY

**Graduate School, College of Arts and Sciences, Department of Psychology, Oxford, OH 45056**

AWARDS Clinical psychology (PhD); experimental psychology (PhD); social psychology (PhD).

**Faculty:** 12 full-time (2 women), 9 part-time/adjunct (5 women).
**Students:** 73 full-time (49 women); includes 12 minority (9 African Americans, 3 Asian Americans or Pacific Islanders), 7 international. 128 applicants, 41% accepted, 17 enrolled. In 2001, 12 doctorates awarded.
**Degree requirements:** For doctorate, thesis/dissertation, final exams, comprehensive exam.
**Entrance requirements:** For doctorate, GRE General Test, GRE Subject Test,

minimum GPA of 2.75 (undergraduate), 3.0 (graduate). *Application deadline:* For fall admission, 2/1. *Application fee:* $35.
**Expenses:** Tuition, state resident: full-time $7,155; part-time $295 per semester hour. Tuition, nonresident: full-time $14,829; part-time $615 per semester hour. Tuition and fees vary according to degree level and campus/location.
**Financial support:** In 2001–02, 28 fellowships (averaging $9,134 per year), 12 teaching assistantships (averaging $11,337 per year) were awarded. Research assistantships, career-related internships or fieldwork, Federal Work-Study, and tuition waivers (full) also available. Financial award application deadline: 3/1.
Dr. Karen Schilling, Chair, 513-529-2400, *Fax:* 513-529-2420, *E-mail:* psych@muohio.edu.
**Application contact:** Dr. Phillip Best, Director of Graduate Studies, 513-529-2400, *Fax:* 513-529-2420, *E-mail:* psych@muohio.edu. *Web site:* http://www.muohio.edu/~psycwis/graduate.html

## ■ MONTCLAIR STATE UNIVERSITY

**The School of Graduate, Professional and Continuing Education, College of Humanities and Social Sciences, Department of Psychology, Program in Educational Psychology, Upper Montclair, NJ 07043-1624**

AWARDS Child/adolescent clinical psychology (MA); clinical psychology for Spanish/English bilinguals (MA). Part-time and evening/weekend programs available.

**Degree requirements:** For master's, thesis optional.
**Entrance requirements:** For master's, GRE General Test, GRE Subject Test, previous course work in psychology. Electronic applications accepted.

## ■ NEW COLLEGE OF CALIFORNIA

**School of Psychology, San Francisco, CA 94102-5206**

AWARDS Feminist clinical psychology (MA); social-clinical psychology (MA). Evening/weekend programs available.

**Faculty:** 6 full-time (3 women), 10 part-time/adjunct (7 women).
**Students:** 43 full-time (32 women). Average age 28. 60 applicants, 77% accepted, 40 enrolled.
**Degree requirements:** For master's, 3 trimesters of fieldwork.
**Entrance requirements:** For master's, letters of recommendation. *Application deadline:* For fall admission, 4/1 (priority

date). Applications are processed on a rolling basis. *Application fee:* $50 ($75 for international students).

**Expenses:** Contact institution.

**Financial support:** In 2001–02, 4 students received support, including 2 teaching assistantships (averaging $900 per year); career-related internships or fieldwork and Federal Work-Study also available. Financial award application deadline: 7/15; financial award applicants required to submit FAFSA.

**Faculty research:** AIDS and therapy, dynamics of unemployment, self-psychology, sexuality and gender issues, multicultural therapy.

Dr. Ali Chavoshian, Dean, 415-437-3435.

**Application contact:** Carmen Gonzalez, Admissions Director, 415-437-3421. *Web site:* http://www.newcollege.edu/psychology/

■ **NEW ENGLAND COLLEGE**

**Program in Organizational Management, Henniker, NH 03242-3293**

AWARDS Business (MS); community mental health counseling (MS); health care (MS); health care management (Certificate); human resource management (Certificate); human services (MS). Part-time and evening/weekend programs available.

**Degree requirements:** For master's, independent research project.

Electronic applications accepted. *Web site:* http://www.nec.edu

**Find an in-depth description at www.petersons.com/gradchannel.**

■ **NEW YORK UNIVERSITY**

**Graduate School of Arts and Science, Department of Psychology, New York, NY 10012-1019**

AWARDS Clinical psychology (PhD); cognition and perception (PhD); community psychology (PhD); general psychology (MA); industrial/organizational psychology (MA, PhD); psychoanalysis (Advanced Certificate); social/personality psychology (PhD). Part-time programs available.

**Faculty:** 38 full-time (13 women), 78 part-time/adjunct.

**Students:** 118 full-time (85 women), 304 part-time (235 women); includes 64 minority (14 African Americans, 27 Asian Americans or Pacific Islanders, 22 Hispanic Americans, 1 Native American), 49 international. Average age 28. 586 applicants, 44% accepted, 101 enrolled. In 2001, 67 master's, 22 doctorates awarded. Terminal master's awarded for partial completion of doctoral program.

**Degree requirements:** For master's, thesis or alternative, comprehensive exam; for doctorate, thesis/dissertation.

**Entrance requirements:** For master's, GRE General Test, minimum GPA of 3.0; for doctorate, GRE General Test, GRE Subject Test; for Advanced Certificate, doctoral degree, minimum GPA of 3.0. *Application deadline:* For fall admission, 1/4. *Application fee:* $60.

**Expenses:** Tuition: Full-time $19,536; part-time $814 per credit. Required fees: $1,330; $38 per credit. Tuition and fees vary according to course load and program.

**Financial support:** Fellowships with tuition reimbursements, research assistantships with tuition reimbursements, teaching assistantships with tuition reimbursements, career-related internships or fieldwork, Federal Work-Study, institutionally sponsored loans, and traineeships available. Financial award application deadline: 1/4; financial award applicants required to submit FAFSA.

**Faculty research:** Vision, memory, social cognition, social and cognitive development, relationships.

Marisa Carrasco, Chair, 212-998-7900.

**Application contact:** Susan Andersen, Director of Graduate Studies, 212-998-7900, *Fax:* 212-995-4018, *E-mail:* psychquery@psych.nyu.edu. *Web site:* http://www.psych.nyu.edu/

■ **NORFOLK STATE UNIVERSITY**

**School of Graduate Studies, School of Liberal Arts, Department of Psychology, Program in Community/Clinical Psychology, Norfolk, VA 23504**

AWARDS MA.

**Entrance requirements:** For master's, minimum GPA of 2.7.

**Expenses:** Tuition, area resident: Part-time $197 per credit. Tuition, nonresident: part-time $503 per credit.

■ **NORTH GEORGIA COLLEGE & STATE UNIVERSITY**

**Graduate School, Program in Community Counseling, Dahlonega, GA 30597-1001**

AWARDS MS.

**Faculty:** 1 full-time (0 women), 2 part-time/adjunct (both women).

**Students:** 6 full-time (5 women), 21 part-time (16 women); includes 1 minority (African American). Average age 31. 20 applicants, 65% accepted. In 2001, 10 degrees awarded.

**Degree requirements:** For master's, one foreign language, thesis. *Median time to degree:* Master's–2 years part-time.

**Entrance requirements:** For master's, GRE General Test, minimum GPA of

2.75. *Application deadline:* For fall admission, 7/1 (priority date); for spring admission, 12/1 (priority date). Applications are processed on a rolling basis. *Application fee:* $25.

**Expenses:** Tuition, state resident: full-time $1,160. Tuition, nonresident: full-time $4,640.

**Financial support:** Application deadline: 5/1.

Dr. Mary Lou Frank, Chair, Department of Psychology and Sociology, 706-864-1442, *E-mail:* mfrank@ngcsu.edu. *Web site:* http://www.ngcsu.edu/

■ **NORTHWESTERN UNIVERSITY**

**The Graduate School, Judd A. and Marjorie Weinberg College of Arts and Sciences, Department of Psychology, Evanston, IL 60208**

AWARDS Brain, behavior and cognition (PhD); clinical psychology (PhD); cognitive psychology (PhD); personality (PhD); social psychology (PhD). Admissions and degrees offered through The Graduate School. Part-time programs available.

**Faculty:** 22 full-time (6 women).

**Students:** 45 full-time (26 women); includes 4 minority (2 Asian Americans or Pacific Islanders, 2 Hispanic Americans), 14 international. Average age 25. 197 applicants, 14% accepted. In 2001, 5 doctorates awarded.

**Degree requirements:** For doctorate, thesis/dissertation. *Median time to degree:* Doctorate–5 years full-time.

**Entrance requirements:** For doctorate, GRE General Test, GRE Subject Test, TOEFL, TSE. *Application deadline:* For fall admission, 12/31. *Application fee:* $50 ($55 for international students). Electronic applications accepted.

**Expenses:** Tuition: Full-time $26,526.

**Financial support:** In 2001–02, 12 fellowships with full tuition reimbursements (averaging $16,800 per year), 3 research assistantships with partial tuition reimbursements (averaging $13,419 per year), 22 teaching assistantships with full tuition reimbursements (averaging $13,419 per year) were awarded. Career-related internships or fieldwork, Federal Work-Study, institutionally sponsored loans, and tuition waivers (full and partial) also available. Financial award application deadline: 12/31; financial award applicants required to submit FAFSA.

**Faculty research:** Memory and higher order cognition, anxiety and depression, effectiveness of psychotherapy, social cognition, molecular basis of memory. *Total annual research expenditures:* $2.6 million.

*Northwestern University (continued)*
Douglas L. Medin, Chair, 847-491-7406, *Fax:* 847-491-7859, *E-mail:* medin@northwestern.edu.
**Application contact:** Florence S. Sales, Secretary, 847-491-7406, *Fax:* 847-491-7859, *E-mail:* f-sales@northwestern.edu. *Web site:* http://www.psych.northwestern.edu/

### ■ THE OHIO STATE UNIVERSITY

**Graduate School, College of Social and Behavioral Sciences, Department of Psychology, Columbus, OH 43210**

**AWARDS** Clinical psychology (PhD); cognitive/experimental psychology (PhD); counseling psychology (PhD); developmental psychology (PhD); mental retardation and developmental disabilities (PhD); psychobiology (PhD); quantitative psychology (PhD); social psychology (PhD).

**Degree requirements:** For doctorate, thesis/dissertation.

**Entrance requirements:** For doctorate, GRE General Test, TOEFL.

### ■ PACE UNIVERSITY

**Dyson College of Arts and Sciences, Department of Psychology, Program in School-Community Psychology, New York, NY 10038**

**AWARDS** MS Ed, Psy D.

**Students:** 70 full-time (62 women), 14 part-time (12 women); includes 15 minority (3 African Americans, 6 Asian Americans or Pacific Islanders, 5 Hispanic Americans, 1 Native American), 1 international. Average age 25. 170 applicants, 43% accepted. In 2001, 25 master's, 22 doctorates awarded. Terminal master's awarded for partial completion of doctoral program.

**Degree requirements:** For master's, qualifying exams, internship; for doctorate, qualifying exams, externship, internship, project.

**Entrance requirements:** For master's and doctorate, GRE General Test, GRE Subject Test, interview. *Application deadline:* For fall admission, 2/1 (priority date). Applications are processed on a rolling basis. *Application fee:* $65. Electronic applications accepted.

**Expenses:** Tuition: Part-time $545 per credit.

**Financial support:** Research assistantships, teaching assistantships, career-related internships or fieldwork, Federal Work-Study, and tuition waivers (partial) available. Support available to part-time students. Financial award applicants required to submit FAFSA.

Dr. Barbara Mowder, Director, 212-346-1506.

**Application contact:** Joanna Broda, Director of Admissions, 212-346-1652, *Fax:* 212-346-1585, *E-mail:* gradnyc@pace.edu. *Web site:* http://www.pace.edu/

**Find an in-depth description at www.petersons.com/gradchannel.**

### ■ THE PENNSYLVANIA STATE UNIVERSITY HARRISBURG CAMPUS OF THE CAPITAL COLLEGE

**Graduate Center, School of Behavioral Sciences and Education, Program in Community Psychology and Social Change, Middletown, PA 17057-4898**

**AWARDS** MA. Evening/weekend programs available.

**Students:** 5 full-time (all women), 17 part-time (11 women). Average age 33. In 2001, 8 degrees awarded.

**Degree requirements:** For master's, thesis, fieldwork.

**Entrance requirements:** For master's, minimum GPA of 2.5. *Application deadline:* For fall admission, 7/26. *Application fee:* $45.

**Expenses:** Tuition, state resident: full-time $7,882; part-time $333 per credit. Tuition, nonresident: full-time $14,384; part-time $600 per credit.

**Financial support:** Career-related internships or fieldwork available.

**Faculty research:** Community liaison, neighborhood organization, special population issues (e.g., women, the aging).

Dr. Steve Couch, Coordinator, 717-948-6036.

### ■ THE PENNSYLVANIA STATE UNIVERSITY UNIVERSITY PARK CAMPUS

**Graduate School, College of Liberal Arts, Department of Psychology, State College, University Park, PA 16802-1503**

**AWARDS** Clinical psychology (MS, PhD); cognitive psychology (MS, PhD); developmental psychology (MS, PhD); industrial/organizational psychology (MS, PhD); psychobiology (MS, PhD); social psychology (MS, PhD).

**Students:** 126 full-time (83 women), 12 part-time (7 women). In 2001, 15 master's, 14 doctorates awarded.

**Degree requirements:** For master's and doctorate, thesis/dissertation.

**Entrance requirements:** For master's and doctorate, GRE General Test, GRE Subject Test. *Application fee:* $45.

**Expenses:** Tuition, state resident: full-time $7,882; part-time $333 per credit. Tuition,

nonresident: full-time $16,142; part-time $673 per credit. Required fees: $124 per semester.

**Financial support:** Fellowships, research assistantships, teaching assistantships available.

Dr. Keith Crnic, Head, 814-863-1721.

### ■ RUTGERS, THE STATE UNIVERSITY OF NEW JERSEY, NEWARK

**Graduate School, Department of Psychology, Newark, NJ 07102**

**AWARDS** Cognitive science (PhD); perception (PhD); psychobiology (PhD); social cognition (PhD). Part-time and evening/weekend programs available.

**Students:** 34 applicants, 59% accepted. In 2001, 2 doctorates awarded.

**Degree requirements:** For doctorate, thesis/dissertation, comprehensive exam.

**Entrance requirements:** For doctorate, GRE Subject Test, minimum undergraduate B average. *Application deadline:* For fall admission, 2/1 (priority date); for spring admission, 11/1. Applications are processed on a rolling basis. *Application fee:* $50. Electronic applications accepted.

**Financial support:** In 2001–02, 12 students received support, including 11 fellowships with full tuition reimbursements available (averaging $13,000 per year), 9 teaching assistantships with full tuition reimbursements available (averaging $13,700 per year); research assistantships, career-related internships or fieldwork, Federal Work-Study, and minority scholarships also available. Support available to part-time students. Financial award application deadline: 3/1.

**Faculty research:** Visual perception (luminance, motion), neuroendocrine mechanisms in behavior (reproduction, pain), attachment theory, connectionist modeling of cognition. *Total annual research expenditures:* $300,000.

Dr. Maggie Shiffrar, Director, 973-353-5971, *Fax:* 973-353-1171, *E-mail:* mag@psychology.rutgers.edu. *Web site:* http://www.psych.rutgers.edu/

**Find an in-depth description at www.petersons.com/gradchannel.**

### ■ RUTGERS, THE STATE UNIVERSITY OF NEW JERSEY, NEW BRUNSWICK

**Graduate School, Program in Psychology, New Brunswick, NJ 08901-1281**

**AWARDS** Biopsychology and behavioral neuroscience (PhD); clinical psychology (PhD); cognitive psychology (PhD); interdisciplinary developmental psychology

(PhD); interdisciplinary health psychology (PhD); social psychology (PhD).

**Students:** Average age 24. 423 applicants, 11% accepted. In 2001, 13 degrees awarded.

**Degree requirements:** For doctorate, thesis/dissertation.

**Entrance requirements:** For doctorate, GRE General Test. *Application deadline:* For fall admission, 12/15. *Application fee:* $50.

**Financial support:** In 2001–02, 68 students received support, including 18 fellowships with full tuition reimbursements available (averaging $15,000 per year), 13 research assistantships with full tuition reimbursements available (averaging $14,000 per year), 43 teaching assistantships with full tuition reimbursements available (averaging $13,800 per year); career-related internships or fieldwork, Federal Work-Study, scholarships/grants, and traineeships also available. Financial award application deadline: 12/15.

Dr. G. Terence Wilson, Director, 732-445-2556, *Fax:* 732-445-2263.

**Application contact:** Joan Olmizzi, Administrative Assistant, 732-445-2555, *Fax:* 732-445-2263, *E-mail:* joan@psych-b.rutgers.edu. *Web site:* http://psychology.rutgers.edu/

■ **SAGE GRADUATE SCHOOL**

**Graduate School, Division of Psychology, Program in Community Psychology, Troy, NY 12180-4115**

**AWARDS** Chemical dependence (MA); child care and children's services (MA); community counseling (MA); community health (MA); general psychology (MA); visual art therapy (MA).

**Students:** 10 full-time (9 women), 46 part-time (39 women); includes 2 minority (both African Americans). Average age 32. 20 applicants, 100% accepted, 14 enrolled. In 2001, 15 degrees awarded.

**Degree requirements:** For master's, thesis or alternative.

**Entrance requirements:** For master's, minimum GPA of 2.75. *Application deadline:* Applications are processed on a rolling basis. *Application fee:* $40.

**Expenses:** Tuition: Full-time $7,600. Required fees: $100.

**Financial support:** Application deadline: 3/1.

Dr. Pat O'Connor, Director, 518-244-2221, *E-mail:* oconnp@sage.edu.

**Application contact:** Melissa M. Robertson, Associate Director of Admissions, 518-244-6878, *Fax:* 518-244-6880, *E-mail:* sgsadm@sage.edu.

■ **ST. CLOUD STATE UNIVERSITY**

**School of Graduate Studies, College of Education, Department of Educational Leadership and Community Psychology, Program in Community Counseling, St. Cloud, MN 56301-4498**

**AWARDS** MS.

**Degree requirements:** For master's, thesis or alternative.

**Entrance requirements:** For master's, GRE General Test, minimum GPA of 2.75. *Application deadline:* Applications are processed on a rolling basis. *Application fee:* $35.

**Expenses:** Tuition, state resident: part-time $156 per credit. Tuition, nonresident: part-time $244 per credit. Required fees: $20 per credit.

John Mason, Coordinator, 320-255-2160.

■ **SAINT JOSEPH COLLEGE**

**Graduate Division, Department of Counseling, West Hartford, CT 06117-2700**

**AWARDS** Community counseling (MA), including child welfare, pastoral counseling; spirituality (Certificate). Part-time and evening/weekend programs available.

**Faculty:** 3 full-time (1 woman), 3 part-time/adjunct (2 women).

**Students:** 11 full-time (all women), 69 part-time (62 women); includes 7 minority (6 African Americans, 1 Hispanic American). Average age 33. In 2001, 24 degrees awarded.

**Degree requirements:** For master's, thesis optional.

**Entrance requirements:** For master's, GRE or MAT. *Application deadline:* Applications are processed on a rolling basis. *Application fee:* $25.

**Expenses:** Tuition: Part-time $475 per credit hour.

**Financial support:** In 2001–02, 2 research assistantships with full tuition reimbursements were awarded; tuition waivers (partial) and unspecified assistantships also available. Financial award application deadline: 7/15; financial award applicants required to submit FAFSA.

Dr. Richard W. Halstead, Chair, 860-231-5213, *E-mail:* rhalstead@sjc.edu. *Web site:* http://www.sjc.edu/

■ **SAINT MARTIN'S COLLEGE**

**Graduate Programs, Program in Counseling and Community Psychology, Lacey, WA 98503-7500**

**AWARDS** MAC. Part-time and evening/weekend programs available.

**Faculty:** 3 full-time (2 women), 4 part-time/adjunct (2 women).

**Students:** Average age 41. 32 applicants, 53% accepted. In 2001, 24 degrees awarded.

**Degree requirements:** For master's, clinical experience, interview.

*Application deadline:* For fall admission, 7/1; for spring admission, 2/15 (priority date). Applications are processed on a rolling basis. *Application fee:* $35.

**Expenses:** Tuition: Part-time $519 per credit hour. Required fees: $180; $90 per semester. One-time fee: $125 full-time.

**Financial support:** In 2001–02, 70 students received support. Career-related internships or fieldwork, Federal Work-Study, and institutionally sponsored loans available. Support available to part-time students. Financial award application deadline: 3/1.

Dr. Godfrey Ellis, Director, 360-438-4560, *E-mail:* gellis@stmartin.edu.

**Application contact:** Sandra Brandt, Administrative Assistant, 360-438-4560, *E-mail:* sbrandt@stmartin.edu.

■ **SOUTHEAST MISSOURI STATE UNIVERSITY**

**School of Graduate Studies and Research, Department of Educational Administration and Counseling, Program in Guidance and Counseling, Cape Girardeau, MO 63701-4799**

**AWARDS** Community counseling (MA); guidance and counseling (MA). Part-time and evening/weekend programs available.

**Students:** 23 full-time (21 women), 77 part-time (69 women); includes 4 minority (all African Americans), 2 international. Average age 34. In 2001, 23 degrees awarded.

**Degree requirements:** For master's, thesis or alternative.

**Entrance requirements:** For master's, GRE General Test, minimum GPA of 3.0. *Application deadline:* For fall admission, 4/1 (priority date); for spring admission, 11/21. Applications are processed on a rolling basis. *Application fee:* $20 ($100 for international students).

**Expenses:** Tuition, state resident: full-time $1,242; part-time $138 per hour. Tuition, nonresident: full-time $2,268; part-time $252 per hour.

**Financial support:** In 2001–02, 4 research assistantships (averaging $6,100 per year) were awarded; career-related internships or fieldwork also available.

Dr. Zaidy Mohd Zain, Head, 573-651-2137, *Fax:* 573-986-6812, *E-mail:* zmohdzain@semo.edu.

**Application contact:** Marsha L. Arant, Office of Graduate Studies, 573-651-2192, *Fax:* 573-651-2001, *E-mail:* marant@semovm.semo.edu.

## ■ SOUTHERN ILLINOIS UNIVERSITY EDWARDSVILLE

**Graduate Studies and Research, School of Education, Department of Psychology, Edwardsville, IL 62026-0001**

**AWARDS** Clinical adult (MS); community school (MS); general academic (MA); industrial organizational (MS). Part-time programs available.

**Students:** 33 full-time (26 women), 24 part-time (20 women); includes 6 minority (4 African Americans, 2 Hispanic Americans), 3 international. Average age 33. 64 applicants, 56% accepted, 21 enrolled. In 2001, 29 degrees awarded.
**Degree requirements:** For master's, thesis, final exam.
**Entrance requirements:** For master's, GRE General Test, GRE Subject Test, MAT, TOEFL. *Application deadline:* For fall admission, 7/20; for spring admission, 12/7. *Application fee:* $25.
**Expenses:** Tuition, state resident: full-time $2,712; part-time $113 per credit hour. Tuition, nonresident: full-time $5,424; part-time $226 per credit hour. Required fees: $250; $125 per term. Tuition and fees vary according to course load, campus/location and reciprocity agreements.
**Financial support:** In 2001–02, 3 fellowships with full tuition reimbursements, 4 teaching assistantships with full tuition reimbursements were awarded. Research assistantships, career-related internships or fieldwork, Federal Work-Study, institutionally sponsored loans, traineeships, and unspecified assistantships also available. Support available to part-time students. Financial award application deadline: 3/1; financial award applicants required to submit FAFSA.
Dr. Bryce Sullivan, Chair, 618-650-2202, *E-mail:* bsulliv@siue.edu.

## ■ STATE UNIVERSITY OF NEW YORK AT ALBANY

**College of Arts and Sciences, Department of Psychology, Albany, NY 12222-0001**

**AWARDS** Biopsychology (PhD); clinical psychology (PhD); general/experimental psychology (PhD); industrial/organizational psychology (PhD); psychology (MA); social/personality psychology (PhD).

**Students:** 69 full-time (45 women), 58 part-time (41 women); includes 12 minority (2 African Americans, 3 Asian Americans or Pacific Islanders, 7 Hispanic Americans), 13 international. Average age 28. 220 applicants, 20% accepted. In 2001, 11 master's, 6 doctorates awarded.
**Degree requirements:** For doctorate, thesis/dissertation.

**Entrance requirements:** For doctorate, GRE General Test, GRE Subject Test. *Application deadline:* For fall admission, 1/15. *Application fee:* $50.
**Expenses:** Tuition, state resident: full-time $2,550; part-time $213 per credit. Tuition, nonresident: full-time $4,208; part-time $351 per credit. Required fees: $470; $470 per year.
**Financial support:** Fellowships, research assistantships, teaching assistantships, career-related internships or fieldwork available. Financial award application deadline: 2/1.
Robert Rosellini, Chair, 518-442-4820.
**Application contact:** Glenn Sanders, Graduate Director, 518-442-4853.

## ■ STATE UNIVERSITY OF NEW YORK COLLEGE AT ONEONTA

**Graduate Studies, Division of Education, Department of Educational Psychology, Oneonta, NY 13820-4015**

**AWARDS** Community mental health (MS); marriage and family therapy (MS); school counselor K-12 (MS Ed, CAS). Part-time and evening/weekend programs available.

**Students:** 4 full-time (3 women), 50 part-time (39 women). 16 applicants, 69% accepted. In 2001, 22 master's, 8 other advanced degrees awarded.
**Degree requirements:** For master's, comprehensive exam.
**Entrance requirements:** For master's, GRE General Test. *Application deadline:* For fall admission, 3/1; for spring admission, 10/1. *Application fee:* $50.
**Expenses:** Tuition, state resident: full-time $5,100; part-time $213 per credit hour. Tuition, nonresident: full-time $8,416; part-time $351 per credit hour. Required fees: $616; $12 per credit hour.
Dr. Joanne Curran, Chair, 607-436-3554, *Fax:* 607-436-3799, *E-mail:* curranjm@oneonta.edu.

## ■ STONY BROOK UNIVERSITY, STATE UNIVERSITY OF NEW YORK

**Graduate School, College of Arts and Sciences, Department of Psychology, Program in Social/Health Psychology, Stony Brook, NY 11794**

**AWARDS** PhD.

**Students:** 12 full-time (10 women), 10 part-time (5 women); includes 6 minority (4 African Americans, 1 Asian American or Pacific Islander, 1 Hispanic American), 1 international. Average age 29. 55 applicants, 13% accepted. In 2001, 3 degrees awarded.
**Degree requirements:** For doctorate, thesis/dissertation.

**Entrance requirements:** For doctorate, GRE General Test, GRE Subject Test, TOEFL. *Application deadline:* For fall admission, 1/15. *Application fee:* $50.
**Expenses:** Tuition, state resident: full-time $5,100; part-time $213 per credit. Tuition, nonresident: full-time $8,416; part-time $351 per credit. Required fees: $496.
**Find an in-depth description at www.petersons.com/gradchannel.**

## ■ SYRACUSE UNIVERSITY

**Graduate School, College of Arts and Sciences, Department of Psychology, Program in Social Psychology, Syracuse, NY 13244-0003**

**AWARDS** PhD.

**Degree requirements:** For doctorate, thesis/dissertation.
**Entrance requirements:** For doctorate, GRE General Test.
**Expenses:** Tuition: Full-time $15,528; part-time $647 per credit. Required fees: $420; $38 per term. Tuition and fees vary according to program.

## ■ TEACHERS COLLEGE COLUMBIA UNIVERSITY

**Graduate Faculty of Education, Department of Organization and Leadership, Program in Social and Organizational Psychology, New York, NY 10027-6696**

**AWARDS** Organizational psychology (MA, Ed D, PhD); social psychology (Ed D, PhD). Terminal master's awarded for partial completion of doctoral program.

**Degree requirements:** For master's, comprehensive exam; for doctorate, thesis/dissertation.
**Entrance requirements:** For master's, minimum GPA of 3.0; for doctorate, GRE General Test.
**Expenses:** Tuition: Full-time $19,080; part-time $780 per unit. Required fees: $170 per semester.
**Faculty research:** Conflict resolution, human resource and organization development, management competence, organizational culture, leadership, leader and manager competencies.

## ■ TEMPLE UNIVERSITY

**Graduate School, College of Liberal Arts, Department of Psychology, Program in Social and Organizational Psychology, Philadelphia, PA 19122-6096**

**AWARDS** PhD.

**Degree requirements:** For doctorate, thesis/dissertation, preliminary exam.

**Entrance requirements:** For doctorate, GRE General Test, minimum GPA of 3.0. Electronic applications accepted.

**Expenses:** Tuition, state resident: full-time $8,487; part-time $369 per credit hour. Tuition, nonresident: full-time $12,282; part-time $534 per credit hour. Required fees: $350. Tuition and fees vary according to course load, program and reciprocity agreements.

**Faculty research:** Power and technology, organizational behavior, interpersonal dynamics, belief, consumer behavior.

**Find an in-depth description at www.petersons.com/gradchannel.**

■ **UNIVERSITY AT BUFFALO, THE STATE UNIVERSITY OF NEW YORK**

**Graduate School, College of Arts and Sciences, Department of Psychology, Buffalo, NY 14260**

**AWARDS** Behavioral neuroscience (PhD); clinical psychology (PhD); cognitive psychology (PhD); general psychology (MA); social-personality (PhD). Part-time programs available.

**Faculty:** 28 full-time (13 women), 2 part-time/adjunct (1 woman).

**Students:** 88 full-time (52 women), 13 part-time (8 women); includes 11 minority (5 African Americans, 3 Asian Americans or Pacific Islanders, 3 Hispanic Americans), 12 international. Average age 25. 122 applicants, 31% accepted, 16 enrolled. In 2001, 13 master's, 6 doctorates awarded. Terminal master's awarded for partial completion of doctoral program.

**Degree requirements:** For master's, project; for doctorate, thesis/dissertation.

**Entrance requirements:** For master's and doctorate, GRE General Test, TOEFL. *Application deadline:* For fall admission, 1/5. *Application fee:* $35. Electronic applications accepted.

**Expenses:** Tuition, state resident: full-time $6,118. Tuition, nonresident: full-time $9,434.

**Financial support:** In 2001–02, 37 students received support, including 4 fellowships with full tuition reimbursements available (averaging $14,000 per year), 10 research assistantships with full tuition reimbursements available (averaging $9,512 per year), 37 teaching assistantships with full tuition reimbursements available (averaging $8,400 per year); career-related internships or fieldwork, Federal Work-Study, institutionally sponsored loans, tuition waivers (partial), and minority fellowships also available. Financial award application deadline: 1/15; financial award applicants required to submit FAFSA.

**Faculty research:** Neural, endocrine, and molecular bases of behavior; adult mood and anxiety disorders; relationship dysfunction; behavioral medicine; attention deficit/hyperactivity disorder. *Total annual research expenditures:* $2.1 million.

Dr. Jack A. Meacham, Chair, 716-645-3650 Ext. 203, *Fax:* 716-645-3801, *E-mail:* meacham@acsu.buffalo.edu.

**Application contact:** Michele Nowacki, Coordinator of Admissions, 716-645-3650 Ext. 209, *Fax:* 716-695-3801, *E-mail:* psych@acsu.buffalo.edu. *Web site:* http://wings.buffalo.edu/psychology/

■ **UNIVERSITY OF ALASKA FAIRBANKS**

**Graduate School, College of Liberal Arts, Department of Psychology, Fairbanks, AK 99775-7480**

**AWARDS** Community psychology (MA). Part-time programs available.

**Faculty:** 6 full-time (2 women), 5 part-time/adjunct (4 women).

**Students:** 17 full-time (12 women), 9 part-time (6 women); includes 7 minority (all Native Americans), 1 international. Average age 37. 26 applicants, 54% accepted, 11 enrolled. In 2001, 2 degrees awarded.

**Degree requirements:** For master's, thesis or alternative, comprehensive exam.

**Entrance requirements:** For master's, GRE General Test, TOEFL. *Application deadline:* For fall admission, 4/1 (priority date); for spring admission, 11/1. *Application fee:* $35. Electronic applications accepted.

**Expenses:** Tuition, state resident: full-time $4,272; part-time $178 per credit. Tuition, nonresident: full-time $8,328; part-time $347 per credit. Required fees: $960; $60 per term. Part-time tuition and fees vary according to course load.

**Financial support:** In 2001–02, fellowships with tuition reimbursements (averaging $10,000 per year); research assistantships with tuition reimbursements, teaching assistantships with tuition reimbursements, Federal Work-Study and scholarships/grants also available.

**Faculty research:** Vocational guidance counseling, entrepreneurship training, adult and youth training, rural community psychology, models of healing.

Dr. Gerald Mohatt, Head, 907-474-7007.

■ **UNIVERSITY OF CALIFORNIA, SANTA CRUZ**

**Division of Graduate Studies, Division of Social Sciences, Program in Psychology, Santa Cruz, CA 95064**

**AWARDS** Developmental psychology (PhD); experimental psychology (PhD); social psychology (PhD).

**Faculty:** 26 full-time.

**Students:** 52 full-time (39 women); includes 23 minority (1 African American, 10 Asian Americans or Pacific Islanders, 11 Hispanic Americans, 1 Native American), 4 international. 96 applicants, 21% accepted. In 2001, 4 doctorates awarded.

**Degree requirements:** For doctorate, thesis/dissertation, qualifying exam. *Median time to degree:* Doctorate–7 years full-time.

**Entrance requirements:** For doctorate, GRE General Test. *Application deadline:* For fall admission, 1/1. *Application fee:* $40.

**Expenses:** Tuition: Full-time $19,857.

**Financial support:** Fellowships, research assistantships, teaching assistantships, career-related internships or fieldwork, Federal Work-Study, and institutionally sponsored loans available. Financial award application deadline: 1/1.

**Faculty research:** Cognitive psychology, human information processing, sensation perceptions, psychobiology.

Maureen Callanan, Chairperson, 831-459-2153.

**Application contact:** Graduate Admissions, 831-459-2301. *Web site:* http://www.ucsc.edu/

■ **UNIVERSITY OF CENTRAL ARKANSAS**

**Graduate School, College of Education, Department of Counseling and Psychology, Program in Community Service Counseling, Conway, AR 72035-0001**

**AWARDS** Community service counseling (MS); student personnel services in higher education (MS).

**Faculty:** 18.

**Students:** 6 full-time (5 women), 3 part-time (1 woman).

**Degree requirements:** For master's, thesis optional.

**Entrance requirements:** For master's, GRE General Test, minimum GPA of 2.7. *Application deadline:* For fall admission, 3/1 (priority date); for spring admission, 10/1 (priority date). Applications are processed on a rolling basis. *Application fee:* $25 ($40 for international students).

**Expenses:** Tuition, state resident: full-time $3,303; part-time $184 per hour. Tuition, nonresident: full-time $5,922; part-time $329 per hour. Required fees: $68; $24 per semester.

**Financial support:** In 2001–02, 4 research assistantships with partial tuition reimbursements (averaging $6,000 per year) were awarded; career-related internships or fieldwork, Federal Work-Study, and scholarships/grants also available. Financial award application deadline: 2/15.

*University of Central Arkansas (continued)*
Dr. Linda Glenn, Coordinator, 501-450-5409, *Fax:* 501-450-5424, *E-mail:* lglenn@mail.uca.edu.
**Application contact:** Jane Douglas, Co-Admissions Secretary, 501-450-5064, *Fax:* 501-450-5066, *E-mail:* janed@ecom.uca.edu.

## ■ UNIVERSITY OF CONNECTICUT

**Graduate School, College of Liberal Arts and Sciences, Field of Psychology, Storrs, CT 06269**

**AWARDS** Behavioral neuroscience (PhD); biopsychology (PhD); clinical psychology (PhD); cognition/instruction psychology (PhD); developmental psychology (PhD); ecological psychology (PhD); general experimental psychology (PhD); industrial and organizational psychology (PhD); language psychology (PhD); social psychology (PhD).

**Faculty:** 41 full-time (11 women), 2 part-time/adjunct (both women).
**Students:** 134 full-time (83 women), 17 part-time (9 women); includes 13 minority (9 African Americans, 1 Asian American or Pacific Islander, 3 Hispanic Americans), 17 international. Average age 28. 378 applicants, 14% accepted, 25 enrolled. In 2001, 18 degrees awarded.
**Degree requirements:** For doctorate, thesis/dissertation, internship, comprehensive exam, registration.
**Entrance requirements:** For doctorate, GRE General Test, GRE Subject Test, letters of recommendation. *Application deadline:* For fall admission, 12/31. *Application fee:* $40 ($45 for international students).
**Financial support:** In 2001–02, 45 fellowships (averaging $4,000 per year), 16 research assistantships with full tuition reimbursements (averaging $16,000 per year), 83 teaching assistantships with full tuition reimbursements (averaging $16,000 per year) were awarded. Career-related internships or fieldwork, Federal Work-Study, scholarships/grants, health care benefits, and unspecified assistantships also available. Financial award application deadline: 12/31.
**Faculty research:** Behavioral neuroscience; physiology/chemistry of memory; sensation, motor control/motivation; cognitive, social, personality and language development; infancy/person perceptions and intergroup relations. *Total annual research expenditures:* $8 million.
Charles A. Lowe, Head, *Fax:* 860-486-2760, *E-mail:* charles.lowe@uconn.edu.
**Application contact:** Gina Stuart, Graduate Admissions, 860-486-3528, *Fax:* 860-486-2760, *E-mail:* futuregr@psych.psy.uconn.edu. *Web site:* http://psych.uconn.edu/

## ■ UNIVERSITY OF DAYTON

**Graduate School, School of Education and Allied Professions, Department of Counselor Education and Human Services, Dayton, OH 45469-1300**

**AWARDS** College student personnel (MS Ed); community counseling (MS Ed); higher education administration (MS Ed); human development services (MS Ed); school counseling (MS Ed); school psychology (MS Ed); teacher as child/youth development specialist (MS Ed). Part-time and evening/weekend programs available.

**Faculty:** 9 full-time (4 women), 23 part-time/adjunct (13 women).
**Students:** 23 full-time (21 women), 421 part-time (323 women). Average age 32. 263 applicants, 60% accepted. In 2001, 233 degrees awarded.
**Degree requirements:** For master's, exit exam, thesis optional.
**Entrance requirements:** For master's, MAT or GRE if GPA is below 2.75, interview. *Application deadline:* For fall admission, 2/15 (priority date). Applications are processed on a rolling basis. *Application fee:* $30.
**Expenses:** Tuition: Full-time $5,436; part-time $453 per credit hour. Required fees: $50; $25 per term.
**Financial support:** In 2001–02, 3 research assistantships with partial tuition reimbursements (averaging $6,100 per year) were awarded; Federal Work-Study and institutionally sponsored loans also available.
**Faculty research:** Anger as part of the grief process, inclusion of children with severe disabilities, comparisons of school counselors in Bosnia and the U. S., graduate and professional student socialization, use of cohort groups in doctoral programs.
Dr. Thomas W. Rueth, Chairperson, 937-229-3644, *Fax:* 937-229-1055, *E-mail:* thomas.rueth@notes.udayton.edu.

## ■ UNIVERSITY OF DELAWARE

**College of Arts and Science, Department of Psychology, Newark, DE 19716**

**AWARDS** Behavioral neuroscience (PhD); clinical psychology (PhD); cognitive psychology (PhD); social psychology (PhD).

**Faculty:** 25 full-time (6 women), 3 part-time/adjunct (0 women).
**Students:** 41 full-time (24 women); includes 3 minority (1 African American, 2 Hispanic Americans). Average age 28. 129 applicants, 13% accepted, 8 enrolled. In 2001, 7 degrees awarded.
**Degree requirements:** For doctorate, thesis/dissertation.
**Entrance requirements:** For doctorate, GRE General Test. *Application deadline:*

For fall admission, 1/7 (priority date). *Application fee:* $50. Electronic applications accepted.
**Expenses:** Tuition, state resident: full-time $4,770; part-time $265 per credit. Tuition, nonresident: full-time $13,860; part-time $770 per credit. Required fees: $414.
**Financial support:** In 2001–02, 41 students received support, including 5 fellowships with full tuition reimbursements available (averaging $11,637 per year), 8 research assistantships with full tuition reimbursements available (averaging $11,637 per year), 15 teaching assistantships with full tuition reimbursements available (averaging $11,637 per year); career-related internships or fieldwork, Federal Work-Study, institutionally sponsored loans, scholarships/grants, tuition waivers (full and partial), and minority fellowships also available. Financial award application deadline: 1/7.
**Faculty research:** Emotion development, neural and cognitive aspects of memory, neural control of feeding, intergroup relations, social cognition and communication. *Total annual research expenditures:* $1 million.
Dr. Brian P. Ackerman, Chairperson, 302-831-2271, *Fax:* 302-831-3645, *E-mail:* bpa@udel.edu.
**Application contact:** Information Contact, 302-831-2271, *Fax:* 302-831-3645, *E-mail:* bpa@udel.edu. *Web site:* http://www.udel.edu/catalog/current/as/psyc/grad.html

## ■ UNIVERSITY OF HAWAII AT MANOA

**Graduate Division, College of Arts and Sciences, College of Social Sciences, Department of Psychology, Program in Community and Culture, Honolulu, HI 96822**

**AWARDS** MA, PhD.

**Faculty:** 6 full-time (1 woman).
**Students:** 12 full-time (8 women); includes 5 minority (3 Asian Americans or Pacific Islanders, 1 Hispanic American, 1 Native American). Average age 30. 15 applicants, 27% accepted, 2 enrolled. In 2001, 2 master's, 1 doctorate awarded. Terminal master's awarded for partial completion of doctoral program.
**Degree requirements:** For master's, thesis/dissertation, registration; for doctorate, thesis/dissertation, comprehensive exam, registration. *Median time to degree:* Master's–2 years full-time; doctorate–6 years full-time.
**Entrance requirements:** For master's and doctorate, GRE. *Application deadline:* For fall admission, 1/1. *Application fee:* $25 ($50 for international students). Electronic applications accepted.

**Expenses:** Tuition, state resident: full-time $2,160; part-time $1,980 per year. Tuition, nonresident: full-time $5,190; part-time $4,829 per year.
**Financial support:** In 2001–02, 7 students received support, including 6 research assistantships with full tuition reimbursements available (averaging $12,000 per year), 1 teaching assistantship with full tuition reimbursement available (averaging $12,000 per year); health care benefits, tuition waivers (full), and part-time employment also available. Financial award application deadline: 4/1.
**Faculty research:** Delinquency, youth violence, culture and development, cross-culture training, disabilities, culture and psycopathology. *Total annual research expenditures:* $500,000.
Clifford R. O'Donnell, Director and Professor, 808-956-6271, *Fax:* 808-956-4700, *E-mail:* cliffo@hawaii.edu. *Web site:* http://www2.soc.hawaii.edu/psy/canoc.html

## ■ UNIVERSITY OF HOUSTON

**College of Liberal Arts and Social Sciences, Department of Psychology, Houston, TX 77204**

**AWARDS** Clinical psychology (PhD); industrial/organizational psychology (PhD); social psychology (PhD).

**Faculty:** 22 full-time (9 women), 8 part-time/adjunct (4 women).
**Students:** 82 full-time (57 women), 20 part-time (16 women); includes 12 minority (2 African Americans, 3 Asian Americans or Pacific Islanders, 7 Hispanic Americans), 2 international. Average age 29. 280 applicants, 8% accepted. In 2001, 14 doctorates awarded.
**Degree requirements:** For doctorate, thesis/dissertation.
**Entrance requirements:** For doctorate, GRE General Test, minimum GPA of 3.0. *Application deadline:* For fall admission, 1/1. *Application fee:* $40 ($75 for international students).
**Expenses:** Tuition, state resident: full-time $1,512. Tuition, nonresident: full-time $5,310. Required fees: $1,308. Tuition and fees vary according to program.
**Financial support:** In 2001–02, research assistantships with partial tuition reimbursements (averaging $12,300 per year), teaching assistantships with partial tuition reimbursements (averaging $10,800 per year) were awarded. Career-related internships or fieldwork, Federal Work-Study, institutionally sponsored loans, and teaching fellowships also available.
**Faculty research:** Health psychology, depression, child/family process, organizational effectiveness, close relationships. *Total annual research expenditures:* $4.5 million.

Dr. John P. Vincent, Chairman, 713-743-8503, *Fax:* 713-743-8588, *E-mail:* jvincent@uh.edu.
**Application contact:** Sherry A. Berun, Coordinator—Academic Affairs, 713-743-8508, *Fax:* 713-743-8588, *E-mail:* sherryr@uh.edu. *Web site:* http://firenza.uh.edu/

## ■ UNIVERSITY OF ILLINOIS AT URBANA–CHAMPAIGN

**Graduate College, College of Liberal Arts and Sciences, Department of Psychology, Champaign, IL 61820**

**AWARDS** Applied measurement (MS); biological psychology (AM, PhD); clinical psychology (AM, PhD); cognitive psychology (AM, PhD); developmental psychology (AM, PhD); engineering psychology (MS); personnel psychology (MS); quantitative psychology (AM, PhD); social-personality-organizational (AM, PhD); visual cognition and human performance (AM, PhD).

**Faculty:** 41 full-time (14 women), 11 part-time/adjunct (3 women).
**Students:** 156 full-time (90 women); includes 23 minority (6 African Americans, 12 Asian Americans or Pacific Islanders, 5 Hispanic Americans), 42 international. 461 applicants, 17% accepted, 27 enrolled. In 2001, 1 master's, 25 doctorates awarded.
**Degree requirements:** For doctorate, thesis/dissertation.
**Entrance requirements:** For master's, GRE General Test, GRE Subject Test (recommended), minimum GPA of 3.0; for doctorate, GRE General Test, GRE Subject Test (recommended). *Application deadline:* For fall admission, 1/1. *Application fee:* $40 ($50 for international students).
**Expenses:** Tuition, state resident: part-time $3,227 per degree program. Tuition, nonresident: part-time $7,169 per degree program. Tuition and fees vary according to program.
**Financial support:** In 2001–02, 31 fellowships with full tuition reimbursements (averaging $15,000 per year), 21 research assistantships with full tuition reimbursements (averaging $13,585 per year), 73 teaching assistantships with full tuition reimbursements (averaging $13,585 per year) were awarded. Career-related internships or fieldwork, traineeships, and tuition waivers (full) also available. Financial award application deadline: 1/1. *Total annual research expenditures:* $4.6 million.
Dr. Edward J. Shoben, Head.
**Application contact:** Cheryl Berger, Assistant Head for Graduate Affairs, 217-333-3429, *Fax:* 217-244-5876, *E-mail:* gradstdy@s.psych.uiuc.edu. *Web site:* http://www.psych.uiuc.edu/

## ■ UNIVERSITY OF MAINE

**Graduate School, College of Liberal Arts and Sciences, Department of Psychology, Orono, ME 04469**

**AWARDS** Clinical psychology (PhD); developmental psychology (MA); experimental psychology (MA, PhD); social psychology (MA).

**Faculty:** 21.
**Students:** 22 full-time (17 women), 13 part-time (11 women); includes 3 minority (all Native Americans), 2 international. 100 applicants, 14% accepted, 6 enrolled. In 2001, 4 degrees awarded.
**Degree requirements:** For master's and doctorate, thesis/dissertation.
**Entrance requirements:** For master's and doctorate, GRE General Test, GRE Subject Test, TOEFL. *Application deadline:* For fall admission, 2/1 (priority date). Applications are processed on a rolling basis. *Application fee:* $50. Electronic applications accepted.
**Expenses:** Tuition, state resident: full-time $3,780; part-time $210 per credit hour. Tuition, nonresident: full-time $10,782; part-time $599 per credit hour. Required fees: $9.50 per credit hour. $32 per semester. Tuition and fees vary according to reciprocity agreements.
**Financial support:** In 2001–02, 3 research assistantships with tuition reimbursements (averaging $9,010 per year), 21 teaching assistantships with tuition reimbursements (averaging $9,010 per year) were awarded. Fellowships with tuition reimbursements, Federal Work-Study, institutionally sponsored loans, and tuition waivers (full and partial) also available. Financial award application deadline: 3/1.
**Faculty research:** Social development, hypertension and aging, attitude change, self-confidence in achievement situations, health psychology.
Dr. Joel Gold, Chair, 207-581-2030, *Fax:* 207-581-6128.
**Application contact:** Scott G. Delcourt, Director of the Graduate School, 207-581-3218, *Fax:* 207-581-3232, *E-mail:* graduate@maine.edu. *Web site:* http://www.umaine.edu/graduate/

## ■ UNIVERSITY OF MARYLAND, COLLEGE PARK

**Graduate Studies and Research, College of Behavioral and Social Sciences, Department of Psychology, College Park, MD 20742**

**AWARDS** Clinical psychology (PhD); developmental psychology (PhD); experimental psychology (PhD); industrial psychology (MA, MS, PhD); social psychology (PhD).

*University of Maryland, College Park (continued)*

**Faculty:** 52 full-time (17 women), 10 part-time/adjunct (5 women).

**Students:** 80 full-time (50 women), 22 part-time (15 women); includes 26 minority (14 African Americans, 8 Asian Americans or Pacific Islanders, 3 Hispanic Americans, 1 Native American), 11 international. 432 applicants, 10% accepted, 18 enrolled. In 2001, 8 master's, 21 doctorates awarded.

**Degree requirements:** For master's, thesis; for doctorate, variable foreign language requirement, thesis/dissertation, comprehensive exam.

**Entrance requirements:** For master's, GRE General Test, GRE Subject Test, minimum GPA of 3.5, research and/or work experience; for doctorate, GRE General Test, GRE Subject Test. *Application deadline:* For fall admission, 12/15. Applications are processed on a rolling basis. *Application fee:* $50 ($70 for international students). Electronic applications accepted.

**Expenses:** Tuition, state resident: part-time $289 per credit hour. Tuition, nonresident: part-time $448 per credit hour. One-time fee: $436 part-time. Full-time tuition and fees vary according to course load, campus/location and program.

**Financial support:** In 2001–02, 15 fellowships with full tuition reimbursements (averaging $11,508 per year), 87 teaching assistantships with tuition reimbursements (averaging $12,153 per year) were awarded. Career-related internships or fieldwork, Federal Work-Study, and scholarships/grants also available. Support available to part-time students. Financial award applicants required to submit FAFSA.

**Faculty research:** Counseling and social psychology.

Dr. William Hall, Chairman, 301-405-5862, *Fax:* 301-314-9566.

**Application contact:** Trudy Lindsey, Director, Graduate Admissions and Records, 301-405-6991, *Fax:* 301-314-9305, *E-mail:* grschool@deans.umd.edu.

### ■ UNIVERSITY OF MASSACHUSETTS LOWELL

**Graduate School, College of Arts and Sciences, Department of Psychology, Lowell, MA 01854-2881**

**AWARDS** Community and social psychology (MA). Part-time programs available.

**Degree requirements:** For master's, thesis optional.

**Entrance requirements:** For master's, GRE General Test or MAT. Electronic applications accepted.

**Faculty research:** Domestic violence, youth sports, teen pregnancy, substance abuse, family and work roles.

### ■ UNIVERSITY OF MICHIGAN

**Horace H. Rackham School of Graduate Studies, College of Literature, Science, and the Arts, Department of Psychology, Ann Arbor, MI 48109**

**AWARDS** Biopsychology (PhD); clinical psychology (PhD); cognition and perception (PhD); developmental psychology (PhD); organizational psychology (PhD); personality psychology (PhD); social psychology (PhD).

**Faculty:** 68 full-time, 29 part-time/adjunct.

**Students:** 166 full-time (122 women); includes 57 minority (27 African Americans, 13 Asian Americans or Pacific Islanders, 14 Hispanic Americans, 3 Native Americans), 22 international. Average age 24. 555 applicants, 8% accepted, 27 enrolled. In 2001, 25 degrees awarded.

**Degree requirements:** For doctorate, oral defense of dissertation, preliminary exam.

**Entrance requirements:** For doctorate, GRE General Test, GRE Subject Test, TOEFL. *Application deadline:* For fall admission, 12/15. *Application fee:* $55. Electronic applications accepted.

**Financial support:** Fellowships with full tuition reimbursements, research assistantships with full tuition reimbursements, teaching assistantships with full tuition reimbursements, career-related internships or fieldwork available. Financial award application deadline: 3/15.

Richard Gonzalez, Chair, 734-764-7429. **Application contact:** 734-764-6316, *Fax:* 734-764-3520. *Web site:* http://www.lsa.umich.edu/psych/

### ■ UNIVERSITY OF MINNESOTA, TWIN CITIES CAMPUS

**Graduate School, College of Liberal Arts, Department of Psychology, Program in Social Psychology, Minneapolis, MN 55455-0213**

**AWARDS** PhD.

**Students:** 16 full-time (9 women); includes 3 minority (1 African American, 1 Asian American or Pacific Islander, 1 Hispanic American), 1 international. 50 applicants, 18% accepted, 2 enrolled. In 2001, 3 degrees awarded.

**Degree requirements:** For doctorate, thesis/dissertation, comprehensive exam.

**Entrance requirements:** For doctorate, GRE General Test, GRE Subject Test (recommended), TOEFL, 12 credits of upper-level psychology courses, including a course in statistics or psychological measurement. *Application deadline:* For fall

admission, 1/5. *Application fee:* $55 ($75 for international students).

**Expenses:** Tuition, state resident: full-time $2,932; part-time $489 per credit. Tuition, nonresident: full-time $5,758; part-time $960 per credit. Part-time tuition and fees vary according to course load, program and reciprocity agreements.

**Financial support:** Fellowships, research assistantships, teaching assistantships, career-related internships or fieldwork and tuition waivers (partial) available. Financial award application deadline: 12/1.

**Application contact:** Coordinator, 612-624-4181, *Fax:* 612-626-2079, *E-mail:* psyapply@tc.umn.edu.

### ■ UNIVERSITY OF MISSOURI–KANSAS CITY

**College of Arts and Sciences, Department of Psychology, Doctoral Program in Psychology, Kansas City, MO 64110-2499**

**AWARDS** Community psychology (PhD).

**Students:** Average age 34. 24 applicants, 17% accepted.

**Degree requirements:** For doctorate, thesis/dissertation, comprehensive exam.

**Entrance requirements:** For doctorate, GRE, minimum GPA of 3.25. *Application deadline:* For fall admission, 2/1. *Application fee:* $25.

**Expenses:** Tuition, state resident: part-time $233 per credit hour. Tuition, nonresident: part-time $623 per credit hour. Tuition and fees vary according to course load.

**Financial support:** In 2001–02, 5 fellowships with partial tuition reimbursements, 6 research assistantships, 12 teaching assistantships with partial tuition reimbursements (averaging $9,000 per year) were awarded. Career-related internships or fieldwork, Federal Work-Study, institutionally sponsored loans, scholarships/grants, and tuition waivers (partial) also available.

**Faculty research:** Prevention and health promotion, community organizing and development, program evaluation, child maltreatment, children and youth issues, health psychology.

Dr. Leah K. Gensheimer, Director, 816-235-1067, *Fax:* 816-235-1062. **Application contact:** 816-235-1111.

### ■ UNIVERSITY OF NEVADA, RENO

**Graduate School, College of Arts and Science, Interdisciplinary Program in Social Psychology, Reno, NV 89557**

**AWARDS** PhD.

**Faculty:** 9.

**Students:** 23 full-time (12 women), 7 part-time (5 women); includes 4 minority (2 Asian Americans or Pacific Islanders, 2 Hispanic Americans), 3 international. Average age 34. In 2001, 4 degrees awarded.
**Degree requirements:** For doctorate, one foreign language, thesis/dissertation.
**Entrance requirements:** For doctorate, GRE General Test, GRE Subject Test (psychology or sociology), TOEFL, minimum GPA of 3.0. *Application deadline:* For fall admission, 3/1 (priority date). Applications are processed on a rolling basis. *Application fee:* $40.
**Expenses:** Tuition, state resident: full-time $2,067; part-time $108 per credit. Tuition, nonresident: full-time $9,282; part-time $109 per credit. Required fees: $57 per semester. Tuition and fees vary according to course load.
**Financial support:** In 2001–02, 2 research assistantships, 2 teaching assistantships were awarded. Unspecified assistantships also available. Financial award application deadline: 3/1.
**Faculty research:** Social psychological theory, social psychology of law.
Dr. Martha Elliott, Graduate Program Director, 775-784-1878, *E-mail:* gpg@scs.unr.edu.

■ **UNIVERSITY OF NEW HAVEN**

**Graduate School, College of Arts and Sciences, Program in Community Psychology, West Haven, CT 06516-1916**

**AWARDS** MA, Certificate.

**Students:** 3 full-time (1 woman), 11 part-time (9 women); includes 2 minority (both African Americans), 2 international. In 2001, 4 degrees awarded.
**Degree requirements:** For master's, thesis or alternative.
*Application deadline:* Applications are processed on a rolling basis. *Application fee:* $50.
**Expenses:** Tuition: Full-time $12,015; part-time $445 per credit hour. Required fees: $30. One-time fee: $100 full-time.
**Financial support:** Career-related internships or fieldwork and Federal Work-Study available. Support available to part-time students. Financial award application deadline: 5/1; financial award applicants required to submit FAFSA.
Dr. Robert Hoffnung, Coordinator, 203-932-7281.

■ **THE UNIVERSITY OF NORTH CAROLINA AT CHAPEL HILL**

**Graduate School, College of Arts and Sciences, Department of Psychology, Chapel Hill, NC 27599**

**AWARDS** Biological psychology (PhD); clinical psychology (PhD); cognitive psychology (PhD); developmental psychology (PhD); quantitative psychology (PhD); social psychology (PhD).
**Faculty:** 46 full-time (25 women), 6 part-time/adjunct (0 women).
**Students:** 116 full-time (63 women). 546 applicants, 7% accepted, 29 enrolled. In 2001, 27 doctorates awarded.
**Degree requirements:** For doctorate, thesis/dissertation, comprehensive exam.
**Entrance requirements:** For doctorate, GRE General Test, minimum GPA of 3.0. *Application deadline:* For fall admission, 12/1. *Application fee:* $55. Electronic applications accepted.
**Expenses:** Tuition, state resident: full-time $2,864. Tuition, nonresident: full-time $12,030.
**Financial support:** In 2001–02, 11 fellowships with tuition reimbursements, 28 research assistantships with tuition reimbursements, 63 teaching assistantships with tuition reimbursements were awarded. Unspecified assistantships also available. Financial award application deadline: 2/1.
**Faculty research:** Expressed emotion, cognitive development, social cognitive neuroscience, human memory personality. *Total annual research expenditures:* $605,806.
Peter A. Ornstein, Chair, 919-962-3088.
**Application contact:** Barbara Atkins, Student Services Manager, 919-962-7149, *Fax:* 919-962-2537, *E-mail:* batkins@email.unc.edu.

■ **THE UNIVERSITY OF NORTH CAROLINA AT CHARLOTTE**

**Graduate School, College of Arts and Sciences, Department of Psychology, Concentration in Community/Clinical Psychology, Charlotte, NC 28223-0001**

**AWARDS** MA.

**Students:** 14 full-time (all women), 12 part-time (11 women); includes 3 minority (all African Americans). Average age 28. 55 applicants, 20% accepted, 10 enrolled. In 2001, 5 degrees awarded.
**Degree requirements:** For master's, thesis, comprehensive exam.
**Entrance requirements:** For master's, GRE General Test, GRE Subject Test, minimum GPA of 3.0 in undergraduate major, 2.8 overall. *Application deadline:* For fall admission, 3/1. *Application fee:* $35. Electronic applications accepted.
**Expenses:** Tuition, state resident: full-time $1,483; part-time $371 per year. Tuition, nonresident: full-time $9,850; part-time $2,463 per year. Required fees: $1,043; $277 per year. Tuition and fees vary according to course load.
**Financial support:** In 2001–02, 2 research assistantships, 5 teaching assistantships were awarded. Fellowships, career-related internships or fieldwork, Federal Work-Study, institutionally sponsored loans, scholarships/grants, and unspecified assistantships also available. Support available to part-time students. Financial award application deadline: 4/1; financial award applicants required to submit FAFSA.
Dr. William Scott Terry, Coordinator, 704-687-4751, *Fax:* 704-687-3096, *E-mail:* wsterry@email.wcc.edu.
**Application contact:** Kathy Barringer, Director of Graduate Admissions, 704-687-3366, *Fax:* 704-687-3279, *E-mail:* gradadm@email.uncc.edu.

■ **THE UNIVERSITY OF NORTH CAROLINA AT GREENSBORO**

**Graduate School, College of Arts and Sciences, Department of Psychology, Greensboro, NC 27412-5001**

**AWARDS** Clinical psychology (MA, PhD); cognitive psychology (MA, PhD); developmental psychology (MA, PhD); social psychology (MA, PhD).
**Faculty:** 22 full-time (9 women), 1 part-time/adjunct (0 women).
**Students:** 42 full-time (35 women), 20 part-time (13 women); includes 2 African Americans, 2 Asian Americans or Pacific Islanders, 2 Hispanic Americans. In 2001, 13 master's, 5 doctorates awarded. Terminal master's awarded for partial completion of doctoral program.
**Degree requirements:** For master's, thesis, comprehensive exam; for doctorate, one foreign language, thesis/dissertation, preliminary exam.
**Entrance requirements:** For master's, GRE General Test, TOEFL; for doctorate, GRE General Test, GRE Subject Test (recommended), TOEFL. *Application deadline:* For fall admission, 2/1. *Application fee:* $35.
**Expenses:** Tuition, state resident: part-time $344 per course. Tuition, nonresident: part-time $2,457 per course.
**Financial support:** In 2001–02, 3 fellowships with full tuition reimbursements (averaging $10,833 per year), 54 research assistantships with full tuition reimbursements (averaging $8,514 per year), 2 teaching assistantships with full tuition reimbursements (averaging $3,500 per year) were awarded. Unspecified assistantships also available.
**Faculty research:** Sensory and perceptual determinants; evoked potential: disorders, deafness, and development.

*The University of North Carolina at Greensboro (continued)*
Dr. Timothy Johnston, Head, 336-334-5013, *Fax:* 336-334-5066, *E-mail:* johnston@uncg.edu.
**Application contact:** Dr. James Lynch, Director of Graduate Recruitment and Information Services, 336-334-4881, *Fax:* 336-334-4424. *Web site:* http://www.uncg.edu/psy/

### ■ UNIVERSITY OF OKLAHOMA

**Graduate College, College of Education, Department of Educational Psychology, Program in Community Counseling, Norman, OK 73019-0390**

AWARDS M Ed. Part-time programs available.
**Students:** 28 full-time (22 women), 4 part-time (3 women); includes 6 minority (1 African American, 1 Asian American or Pacific Islander, 2 Hispanic Americans, 2 Native Americans), 2 international. 5 applicants, 20% accepted, 0 enrolled. In 2001, 13 degrees awarded.
**Entrance requirements:** For master's, TOEFL, 12 hours of course work in education, minimum GPA of 3.0. *Application fee:* $25 ($50 for international students).
**Expenses:** Tuition, state resident: full-time $2,208; part-time $92 per credit hour. Tuition, nonresident: part-time $297 per credit hour. Tuition and fees vary according to course level, course load and program.
**Financial support:** In 2001–02, 23 students received support; research assistantships with partial tuition reimbursements available, teaching assistantships with partial tuition reimbursements available, career-related internships or fieldwork, Federal Work-Study, institutionally sponsored loans, and tuition waivers (partial) available. Financial award applicants required to submit FAFSA.
**Faculty research:** Health psychology, training and supervision, psychological measurement and assessment, cross-cultural, marriage and family.
**Application contact:** Dr. Cal Stoltenberg, Director of Training, 405-325-5974, *Fax:* 405-325-6655, *E-mail:* cstoltenberg@ou.edu.

### ■ UNIVERSITY OF OREGON

**Graduate School, College of Arts and Sciences, Department of Psychology, Eugene, OR 97403**

AWARDS Clinical psychology (PhD); cognitive psychology (MA, MS, PhD); developmental psychology (MA, MS, PhD); physiological psychology (MA, MS, PhD); psychology (MA, MS, PhD); social/personality psychology (MA, MS, PhD).

**Faculty:** 27 full-time (11 women), 11 part-time/adjunct (8 women).
**Students:** 73 full-time (49 women), 3 part-time (all women); includes 7 minority (3 Asian Americans or Pacific Islanders, 2 Hispanic Americans, 2 Native Americans), 14 international. 176 applicants, 11% accepted. In 2001, 21 master's, 11 doctorates awarded. Terminal master's awarded for partial completion of doctoral program.
**Degree requirements:** For doctorate, thesis/dissertation.
**Entrance requirements:** For master's, GRE General Test, TOEFL, minimum GPA of 3.0; for doctorate, GRE General Test, TOEFL. *Application deadline:* For fall admission, 12/1. *Application fee:* $50.
**Expenses:** Tuition, state resident: full-time $4,968; part-time $501 per credit hour. Tuition, nonresident: full-time $8,400; part-time $691 per credit hour.
**Financial support:** In 2001–02, 48 teaching assistantships were awarded; research assistantships, career-related internships or fieldwork also available.
Marjorie Taylor, Head, 541-346-4921, *Fax:* 541-346-4911.
**Application contact:** Lori Olsen, Admissions Contact, 541-346-5060, *Fax:* 541-346-4911, *E-mail:* gradsec@psych.uoregon.edu. *Web site:* http://psychweb.uoregon.edu/

### ■ UNIVERSITY OF PENNSYLVANIA

**Graduate School of Education, Division of Psychology in Education, Program in School, Community, and Clinical Child Psychology, Philadelphia, PA 19104**

AWARDS PhD.
**Degree requirements:** For doctorate, thesis/dissertation, exams.
**Entrance requirements:** For doctorate, GRE General Test, GRE Subject Test. Electronic applications accepted.
**Expenses:** Tuition: Part-time $12,875 per semester.
**Faculty research:** Therapeutic interventions at a preschool level, childhood stress, college psychology, school and community psychology.

### ■ UNIVERSITY OF PHOENIX–HAWAII CAMPUS

**College of Counseling and Human Services, Honolulu, HI 96813-4317**

AWARDS Community counseling (MC); marriage and family therapy (MC). Evening/weekend programs available. Postbaccalaureate distance learning degree programs offered (no on-campus study).
**Students:** 77 full-time. Average age 35.

**Degree requirements:** For master's, thesis or alternative.
**Entrance requirements:** For master's, TOEFL, Comprehensive Cognitive Assessment, minimum undergraduate GPA of 2.5, 3 years of work experience. *Application deadline:* Applications are processed on a rolling basis. *Application fee:* $85.
**Expenses:** Tuition: Full-time $8,784; part-time $366 per credit.
**Financial support:** Applicants required to submit FAFSA.
Dr. Patrick Romine, Dean, 480-557-1074, *E-mail:* patrick.romine@phoenix.edu.
**Application contact:** Campus Information Center, 808-536-2686, *Fax:* 808-536-3848.

### ■ UNIVERSITY OF PHOENIX–PHOENIX CAMPUS

**College of Counseling and Human Services, Phoenix, AZ 85040-1958**

AWARDS Community counseling (MC); marriage, family, and child therapy (MC); mental health counseling (MC). Evening/weekend programs available. Postbaccalaureate distance learning degree programs offered (no on-campus study).
**Students:** 241 full-time. Average age 33. In 2001, 70 degrees awarded.
**Degree requirements:** For master's, thesis or alternative.
**Entrance requirements:** For master's, TOEFL, comprehensive cognitive assessment (COCA), portfolio. *Application deadline:* Applications are processed on a rolling basis. *Application fee:* $85.
**Expenses:** Contact institution.
**Financial support:** Applicants required to submit FAFSA.
Dr. Patrick Romine, Dean, 480-557-1074 Ext. 1074, *E-mail:* patrick.romine@phoenix.edu.
**Application contact:** 480-966-7400. *Web site:* http://www.phoenix.edu/

### ■ UNIVERSITY OF ROCHESTER

**The College, Arts and Sciences, Department of Clinical and Social Sciences in Psychology, Rochester, NY 14627-0250**

AWARDS Clinical psychology (PhD); developmental psychology (PhD); psychology (MA); social-personality psychology (PhD).
**Faculty:** 14.
**Students:** 43 full-time (30 women); includes 3 minority (2 African Americans, 1 Native American), 8 international. 166 applicants, 11% accepted, 8 enrolled. In 2001, 4 master's, 7 doctorates awarded. Terminal master's awarded for partial completion of doctoral program.
**Degree requirements:** For doctorate, thesis/dissertation, qualifying exam.

**Entrance requirements:** For doctorate, GRE General Test, TOEFL. *Application deadline:* For fall admission, 2/1 (priority date). *Application fee:* $25.
**Expenses:** Tuition: Part-time $755 per credit hour.
**Financial support:** Fellowships, research assistantships, teaching assistantships, career-related internships or fieldwork and tuition waivers (full and partial) available. Financial award application deadline: 2/1. Miron Zuckerman, Chair, 585-275-2453.
**Application contact:** Mary Ann Gilbert, Graduate Program Secretary, 585-275-8704.

## ■ THE UNIVERSITY OF SCRANTON

**Graduate School, Department of Counseling and Human Services, Program in Community Counseling, Scranton, PA 18510**

AWARDS MS. Part-time and evening/weekend programs available.

**Students:** 16 full-time (15 women), 33 part-time (27 women); includes 2 minority (1 Asian American or Pacific Islander, 1 Hispanic American), 2 international. Average age 34. 20 applicants, 90% accepted. In 2001, 14 degrees awarded.
**Degree requirements:** For master's, capstone experience.
**Entrance requirements:** For master's, TOEFL, minimum GPA of 2.75. *Application deadline:* For fall admission, 3/1. *Application fee:* $50.
**Expenses:** Tuition: Part-time $539 per credit. Required fees: $25 per term.
**Financial support:** Teaching assistantships, career-related internships or fieldwork and Federal Work-Study available. Support available to part-time students. Financial award application deadline: 3/1.
Dr. Thomas M. Collins, Director, 570-941-4129, *Fax:* 570-941-4201, *E-mail:* collinst1@scranton.edu.

## ■ UNIVERSITY OF SOUTH CAROLINA

**The Graduate School, College of Liberal Arts, Department of Psychology, Program in Clinical/Community Psychology, Columbia, SC 29208**

AWARDS PhD.

**Faculty:** 14 full-time (3 women), 1 (woman) part-time/adjunct.
**Students:** 71 full-time (55 women), 7 part-time (1 woman); includes 15 minority (12 African Americans, 1 Asian American or Pacific Islander, 2 Hispanic Americans). Average age 31. In 2001, 6 degrees awarded.

**Degree requirements:** For doctorate, thesis/dissertation.
**Entrance requirements:** For doctorate, GRE General Test, minimum GPA of 3.2. *Application deadline:* For fall admission, 1/4 (priority date). Applications are processed on a rolling basis. *Application fee:* $35. Electronic applications accepted.
**Expenses:** Tuition, state resident: full-time $4,434. Tuition, nonresident: full-time $9,854. Tuition and fees vary according to program.
**Financial support:** In 2001–02, 3 fellowships, 6 research assistantships, 6 teaching assistantships were awarded. Career-related internships or fieldwork, Federal Work-Study, and institutionally sponsored loans also available. Support available to part-time students.
Diane Follingstad, Director, 803-777-2836, *Fax:* 803-777-9558.
**Application contact:** Doris Davis, Graduate Secretary, 803-777-2312, *Fax:* 803-777-9558, *E-mail:* doris@gwm.sc.edu.

## ■ UNIVERSITY OF WISCONSIN–MADISON

**Graduate School, College of Letters and Science, Department of Psychology, Program in Social and Personality Psychology, Madison, WI 53706-1380**

AWARDS PhD.

**Faculty:** 6 full-time (2 women), 1 part-time/adjunct (0 women).
**Students:** 11 full-time (7 women), 1 international. Average age 23. 47 applicants, 13% accepted, 2 enrolled.
**Degree requirements:** For doctorate, thesis/dissertation, comprehensive exam, registration.
**Entrance requirements:** For doctorate, GRE General Test, minimum undergraduate GPA of 3.0. *Application deadline:* For fall admission, 1/5 (priority date). Applications are processed on a rolling basis. *Application fee:* $45. Electronic applications accepted.
**Expenses:** Tuition, state resident: full-time $7,361; part-time $399 per credit. Tuition, nonresident: full-time $20,499; part-time $1,282 per credit. Required fees: $34 per credit. Full-time tuition and fees vary according to course load, program, reciprocity agreements and student level.
**Financial support:** In 2001–02, 8 students received support, including 1 fellowship with full tuition reimbursement available (averaging $13,446 per year), 1 research assistantship with full tuition reimbursement available (averaging $13,814 per year), 6 teaching assistantships with full tuition reimbursements available (averaging $13,814 per year); institutionally sponsored loans, traineeships, health care

benefits, and unspecified assistantships also available. Financial award application deadline: 1/5.
James Shah, Chair, 608-262-0908, *Fax:* 608-262-2049, *E-mail:* jshah@facstaff.wisc.edu.
**Application contact:** Jane Fox-Anderson, Secretary, 608-262-2079, *Fax:* 608-262-4029, *E-mail:* jefoxand@facstaff.wisc.edu.

## ■ UNIVERSITY OF WISCONSIN–SUPERIOR

**Graduate Division, Department of Counseling and Psychological Professions, Superior, WI 54880-4500**

AWARDS Community counseling (MSE); elementary school counseling (MSE); human relations (MSE); secondary school counseling (MSE). Part-time and evening/weekend programs available.

**Faculty:** 8 full-time (3 women), 4 part-time/adjunct (3 women).
**Students:** 33 full-time (27 women), 54 part-time (38 women); includes 2 minority (both Native Americans), 1 international. Average age 27. 25 applicants, 100% accepted. In 2001, 38 degrees awarded.
**Degree requirements:** For master's, position paper, practicum.
**Entrance requirements:** For master's, California Psychological Inventory, GRE and/or MAT, minimum GPA of 2.75. *Application deadline:* For fall admission, 4/1 (priority date); for spring admission, 10/15 (priority date). Applications are processed on a rolling basis. *Application fee:* $45.
**Expenses:** Tuition, state resident: part-time $2,238 per semester. Tuition, nonresident: part-time $7,150 per semester.
**Financial support:** In 2001–02, 10 fellowships with partial tuition reimbursements (averaging $6,500 per year), 2 research assistantships with partial tuition reimbursements (averaging $5,000 per year) were awarded. Career-related internships or fieldwork, Federal Work-Study, institutionally sponsored loans, scholarships/grants, traineeships, and tuition waivers (partial) also available. Support available to part-time students. Financial award application deadline: 4/15; financial award applicants required to submit FAFSA.
**Faculty research:** Women and power, intrafamily dynamics.
Dr. Clyde Ekbom, Chairperson, 715-394-8149.
**Application contact:** Evelyn Hagfeldt, Program Assistant/Status Examiner, 715-394-8295, *Fax:* 715-394-8040, *E-mail:* ehagfeld@uwsuper.edu.

### ■ UNIVERSITY OF WISCONSIN–WHITEWATER

**School of Graduate Studies, College of Education, Department of Counselor Education, Whitewater, WI 53190-1790**

**AWARDS** Community counseling (MS); higher education (MS); school counseling (MS). Part-time and evening/weekend programs available.

**Students:** 6 full-time (all women), 156 part-time (130 women); includes 15 minority (8 African Americans, 2 Asian Americans or Pacific Islanders, 4 Hispanic Americans, 1 Native American). Average age 27. 19 applicants, 84% accepted, 15 enrolled. In 2001, 20 degrees awarded. **Degree requirements:** For master's, thesis or alternative. **Entrance requirements:** For master's, resumé, 2 letters of reference. *Application deadline:* For fall admission, 3/15; for spring admission, 10/15. *Application fee:* $45. Electronic applications accepted. **Expenses:** Tuition, state resident: full-time $4,511; part-time $251 per credit. Tuition, nonresident: full-time $14,335; part-time $797 per credit. One-time fee: $45. Tuition and fees vary according to course load and program. **Financial support:** In 2001–02, 4 research assistantships (averaging $8,889 per year) were awarded; Federal Work-Study, unspecified assistantships, and out of state fee waiver also available. Support available to part-time students. Financial award application deadline: 3/15; financial award applicants required to submit FAFSA. **Faculty research:** Alcohol and other drug prevention/intervention. Dr. Anene Okocha, Coordinator, 262-472-1940, *Fax:* 262-472-2841, *E-mail:* okochaa@uww.edu. **Application contact:** Sally A. Lange, School of Graduate Studies, 262-472-1006, *Fax:* 262-472-5027, *E-mail:* gradschl@uww.edu.

### ■ VALPARAISO UNIVERSITY

**Graduate Division, Department of Theology, Valparaiso, IN 46383-6493**

**AWARDS** Theology (MALS); theology and ministry (MALS). Part-time and evening/weekend programs available.

**Students:** 3 full-time (2 women), 2 part-time (both women). Average age 52. In 2001, 1 degree awarded. **Entrance requirements:** For master's, minimum GPA of 3.0. *Application deadline:* Applications are processed on a rolling basis. *Application fee:* $30. **Expenses:** Tuition: Full-time $5,400; part-time $300 per credit.

**Financial support:** Federal Work-Study and institutionally sponsored loans available. Financial award applicants required to submit FAFSA. Dr. David Truemper, Chairman, 219-464-5340, *E-mail:* david.truemper@valpo.edu.

### ■ WASHINGTON UNIVERSITY IN ST. LOUIS

**Graduate School of Arts and Sciences, Department of Psychology, St. Louis, MO 63130-4899**

**AWARDS** Clinical psychology (PhD); general experimental psychology (MA, PhD); social psychology (MA, PhD). Part-time programs available.

**Students:** 55 full-time (35 women); includes 4 minority (3 African Americans, 1 Asian American or Pacific Islander), 4 international. 171 applicants, 18% accepted. In 2001, 7 degrees awarded. Terminal master's awarded for partial completion of doctoral program. **Degree requirements:** For master's, thesis or alternative; for doctorate, thesis/dissertation. **Entrance requirements:** For master's and doctorate, GRE General Test. *Application deadline:* For fall admission, 1/15 (priority date). Applications are processed on a rolling basis. *Application fee:* $35. Electronic applications accepted. **Expenses:** Tuition: Full-time $26,900. **Financial support:** Fellowships, research assistantships, teaching assistantships, career-related internships or fieldwork, Federal Work-Study, institutionally sponsored loans, and tuition waivers (full and partial) available. Support available to part-time students. Financial award application deadline: 1/15. Dr. Henry L. Roediger, Chairperson, 314-935-6567. *Web site:* http://artsci.wustl.edu/~psych/

### ■ WAYNE STATE UNIVERSITY

**Graduate School, College of Science, Department of Psychology, Program in Psychology, Detroit, MI 48202**

**AWARDS** Clinical psychology (PhD); cognitive psychology (PhD); developmental psychology (PhD); industrial/organizational psychology (PhD); psychology (MA, PhD); social psychology (PhD).

**Students:** 114. In 2001, 22 master's, 23 doctorates awarded. **Degree requirements:** For doctorate, thesis/dissertation. **Entrance requirements:** For doctorate, GRE General Test, GRE Subject Test. *Application deadline:* For fall admission, 2/1. *Application fee:* $20 ($30 for international students). Electronic applications accepted.

**Expenses:** Tuition, state resident: full-time $3,764. Tuition and fees vary according to degree level and program. **Financial support:** Application deadline: 2/1. **Application contact:** Kathryn Urberg, Graduate Director, 313-577-2820, *Fax:* 313-577-7636, *E-mail:* kurberg@sun.science.wayne.edu.

### ■ WESTERN ILLINOIS UNIVERSITY

**School of Graduate Studies, College of Arts and Sciences, Department of Psychology, Macomb, IL 61455-1390**

**AWARDS** Clinical/community mental health (MS); general psychology (MS); psychology (MS, SSP); school psychology (SSP). Part-time programs available.

**Faculty:** 22 full-time (8 women). **Students:** 45 full-time (34 women), 13 part-time (9 women), 1 international. Average age 33. 54 applicants, 54% accepted. In 2001, 12 master's, 5 other advanced degrees awarded. **Degree requirements:** For master's, thesis or alternative. **Entrance requirements:** For master's and SSP, GRE General Test. *Application deadline:* Applications are processed on a rolling basis. *Application fee:* $0 ($25 for international students). Electronic applications accepted. **Expenses:** Tuition, state resident: part-time $108 per credit hour. Tuition, nonresident: part-time $216 per credit hour. Required fees: $33 per credit hour. **Financial support:** In 2001–02, 40 students received support, including 40 research assistantships with full tuition reimbursements available (averaging $5,720 per year). Financial award applicants required to submit FAFSA. **Faculty research:** Geriatric psychology, social psychology, psychology of women, embarrassability. Dr. James Ackil, Chairperson, 309-298-1593. **Application contact:** Dr. Barbara Baily, Director of Graduate Studies, 309-298-1806, *Fax:* 309-298-2345, *E-mail:* grad-office@wiu.edu. *Web site:* http://www.wiu.edu/

### ■ WICHITA STATE UNIVERSITY

**Graduate School, Fairmount College of Liberal Arts and Sciences, Department of Psychology, Wichita, KS 67260**

**AWARDS** Community/clinical psychology (PhD); human factors (PhD); psychology (MA). Part-time programs available.

**Faculty:** 15 full-time (4 women).

**Students:** 44 full-time (35 women), 25 part-time (18 women); includes 6 minority (4 African Americans, 2 Asian Americans or Pacific Islanders), 1 international. Average age 33. 4 applicants, 0% accepted. In 2001, 9 master's, 8 doctorates awarded.
**Degree requirements:** For doctorate, thesis/dissertation.
**Entrance requirements:** For doctorate, GRE, TOEFL. *Application deadline:* For fall admission, 3/1 (priority date); for spring admission, 1/1. Applications are processed on a rolling basis. *Application fee:* $25 ($40 for international students). Electronic applications accepted.
**Expenses:** Tuition, state resident: full-time $1,888; part-time $105 per credit. Tuition, nonresident: full-time $6,129; part-time $341 per credit. Required fees: $345; $19 per credit. $17 per semester. Tuition and fees vary according to course load and program.
**Financial support:** In 2001–02, 14 research assistantships (averaging $6,202 per year), 53 teaching assistantships with full tuition reimbursements (averaging $4,062 per year) were awarded. Career-related internships or fieldwork, Federal Work-Study, institutionally sponsored loans, and unspecified assistantships also available. Support available to part-time students. Financial award application deadline: 4/1; financial award applicants required to submit FAFSA.
**Faculty research:** Behavioral evolution, women and alcohol, behavioral medicine, delinquency prevention.
Dr. Charles Burdsal, Chairperson, 316-978-3170, *Fax:* 316-978-3006, *E-mail:* charles.burdsal@wichita.edu. *Web site:* http://www.wichita.edu/

## ■ WILMINGTON COLLEGE

**Division of Behavioral Science, New Castle, DE 19720-6491**
**AWARDS** Community counseling (MS); criminal justice studies (MS); student affairs and college counseling (MS). Part-time and evening/weekend programs available.
**Faculty:** 6 full-time (2 women), 35 part-time/adjunct (15 women).
**Students:** 9 full-time (6 women), 79 part-time (64 women); includes 21 minority (19 African Americans, 2 Hispanic Americans). In 2001, 25 degrees awarded. *Median time to degree:* Master's–3 years full-time, 4 years part-time.
*Application deadline:* For fall admission, 4/15. *Application fee:* $25.
**Expenses:** Tuition: Full-time $4,788; part-time $266 per credit. Required fees: $50; $25 per semester. Tuition and fees vary according to course level, course load, degree level, campus/location and program.

**Financial support:** Applicants required to submit FAFSA.
James Wilson, Chair, 302-328-9401 Ext. 154, *Fax:* 302-328-5164, *E-mail:* jwils@wilmcoll.edu.
**Application contact:** Michael Lee, Director of Admissions and Financial Aid, 302-328-9407 Ext. 102, *Fax:* 302-328-5164, *E-mail:* inquire@wilmcoll.edu.

# SPORT PSYCHOLOGY

## ■ ARGOSY UNIVERSITY-PHOENIX

**Program in Sport–Exercise Psychology, Phoenix, AZ 85021**
**AWARDS** Clinical psychology (Psy D); sport–exercise psychology (MA, Post-Doctoral Certificate).
**Faculty:** 3 full-time (0 women), 2 part-time/adjunct (1 woman).
**Students:** 20 full-time (10 women), 1 (woman) part-time. Average age 24. 25 applicants, 60% accepted, 10 enrolled. In 2001, 18 degrees awarded.
**Degree requirements:** For master's, practicum; for doctorate, thesis/dissertation, practicum, internship; for Post-Doctoral Certificate, practicum. *Median time to degree:* Master's–2 years full-time, 3 years part-time.
**Entrance requirements:** For master's, minimum GPA of 3.0; for doctorate, minimum GPA of 3.25; for Post-Doctoral Certificate, doctoral degree in psychology or related profession. *Application deadline:* For fall admission, 1/15 (priority date); for winter admission, 10/15 (priority date). Applications are processed on a rolling basis. *Application fee:* $50. Electronic applications accepted.
**Expenses:** Tuition: Full-time $16,000; part-time $640 per credit. Required fees: $500; $250 per term. Full-time tuition and fees vary according to program.
**Financial support:** Career-related internships or fieldwork, Federal Work-Study, and institutionally sponsored loans available. Support available to part-time students.
**Faculty research:** Sport psychology, personality assessment and psychological correlates of success in professional sports, performance enhancement techniques.
Dr. Douglas Jowdy, Director, 602-216-2600, *Fax:* 602-216-2601, *E-mail:* djowdy@argosyu.edu.
**Application contact:** Gail L. Bartkovich, Director of Admissions, 866-216-2777 Ext. 209, *Fax:* 602-216-2601, *E-mail:* gbartkovich@argosyu.edu.

## ■ CLEVELAND STATE UNIVERSITY

**College of Graduate Studies, College of Education, Department of Health, Physical Education, Recreation and Dance, Cleveland, OH 44115**
**AWARDS** Community health education (M Ed); exercise science (M Ed); health education (M Ed); human performance (M Ed); pedagogy (M Ed); sport and exercise psychology (M Ed); sport management (M Ed); sport management/exercise science (M Ed). Part-time programs available.
**Faculty:** 10 full-time (6 women), 3 part-time/adjunct (1 woman).
**Students:** 3 full-time (1 woman), 68 part-time (38 women); includes 14 minority (12 African Americans, 2 Asian Americans or Pacific Islanders), 2 international. Average age 30. 9 applicants, 89% accepted. In 2001, 37 degrees awarded.
**Degree requirements:** For master's, thesis optional.
**Entrance requirements:** For master's, GRE General Test or MAT, minimum undergraduate GPA of 2.75. *Application deadline:* For fall admission, 7/15 (priority date); for spring admission, 12/15 (priority date). Applications are processed on a rolling basis. *Application fee:* $25. Electronic applications accepted.
**Expenses:** Tuition, state resident: full-time $6,838; part-time $263 per credit hour. Tuition, nonresident: full-time $13,526; part-time $520 per credit hour.
**Financial support:** In 2001–02, 6 students received support, including 6 teaching assistantships with tuition reimbursements available (averaging $8,700 per year); career-related internships or fieldwork and tuition waivers (full) also available. Financial award application deadline: 3/31.
**Faculty research:** Mental imagery in motor learning, biomechanical analysis of motor skill, improvement of speed in running, instructional design. *Total annual research expenditures:* $78,000.
Dr. Vincent Melograno, Chairman, 216-687-4875, *Fax:* 216-687-5410, *E-mail:* v.melograno@csuohio.edu.

## ■ FLORIDA STATE UNIVERSITY

**Graduate Studies, College of Education, Department of Educational Psychology and Learning Systems, Program in Educational Psychology, Tallahassee, FL 32306**
**AWARDS** Learning and cognition (MS, PhD, Ed S); measurement and statistics (MS, PhD, Ed S); program evaluation (MS, PhD, Ed S); sports psychology (MS, PhD, Ed S).
**Faculty:** 8 full-time (2 women).
**Students:** 25 full-time (11 women), 14 part-time (10 women); includes 3 minority

*Florida State University (continued)*
(1 African American, 2 Hispanic Americans), 4 international. 55 applicants, 24% accepted. In 2001, 2 master's, 4 doctorates, 2 other advanced degrees awarded.

**Degree requirements:** For master's and Ed S, thesis optional; for doctorate, thesis/dissertation, comprehensive exam.

**Entrance requirements:** For master's, doctorate, and Ed S, GRE General Test, minimum GPA of 3.0. *Application deadline:* For fall admission, 7/1 (priority date); for spring admission, 11/1. Applications are processed on a rolling basis. *Application fee:* $20.

**Expenses:** Tuition, state resident: part-time $163 per credit hour. Tuition, nonresident: part-time $570 per credit hour. Tuition and fees vary according to program.

**Financial support:** In 2001–02, 1 fellowship was awarded; research assistantships, teaching assistantships, career-related internships or fieldwork also available. Financial award applicants required to submit FAFSA.

### ■ JOHN F. KENNEDY UNIVERSITY

**Graduate School of Professional Psychology, Program in Sport Psychology, Orinda, CA 94563-2603**

**AWARDS** MA. Part-time and evening/weekend programs available.

**Degree requirements:** For master's, thesis or alternative.

**Entrance requirements:** For master's, TOEFL, interview.

**Expenses:** Tuition: Full-time $9,396; part-time $348 per unit. Required fees: $9 per quarter. Tuition and fees vary according to degree level and program.

### ■ PURDUE UNIVERSITY

**Graduate School, School of Liberal Arts, Department of Health and Kinesiology, West Lafayette, IN 47907**

**AWARDS** Exercise, human physiology of movement and sport (PhD); health and fitness (MS); health promotion (MS); health promotion and disease prevention (PhD); movement and sport science (MS); pedagogy and administration (MS); pedagogy of physical activity and health (PhD); psychology of sport and exercise, and motor behavior (PhD). Part-time programs available.

**Faculty:** 19 full-time (7 women).

**Students:** 53 full-time (25 women), 20 part-time (14 women); includes 5 minority (2 African Americans, 2 Asian Americans or Pacific Islanders, 1 Hispanic American), 8 international. Average age 28. 145

applicants, 32% accepted. In 2001, 10 master's, 5 doctorates awarded.

**Degree requirements:** For master's, thesis (for some programs); for doctorate, thesis/dissertation.

**Entrance requirements:** For master's and doctorate, GRE General Test, TOEFL. *Application deadline:* For fall admission, 2/1 (priority date). *Application fee:* $30. Electronic applications accepted.

**Expenses:** Tuition, state resident: full-time $4,164; part-time $149 per credit hour. Tuition, nonresident: full-time $13,872; part-time $458 per credit hour. Tuition and fees vary according to campus/location and program.

**Financial support:** In 2001–02, 4 fellowships with partial tuition reimbursements (averaging $12,000 per year), 2 research assistantships with partial tuition reimbursements (averaging $10,000 per year), 22 teaching assistantships with partial tuition reimbursements (averaging $10,000 per year) were awarded. Federal Work-Study also available. Support available to part-time students. Financial award applicants required to submit FAFSA.

**Faculty research:** Wellness, motivation, teaching effectiveness, learning and development. *Total annual research expenditures:* $141,026.

Dr. T. J. Templin, Head, 765-494-3178, *Fax:* 765-496-1239, *E-mail:* ttemplin@ purdue.edu.

**Application contact:** W. A. Harper, Graduate Committee Chair, 765-494-1518, *Fax:* 765-496-1239, *E-mail:* wharper@ purdue.edu. *Web site:* http:// www.sla.purdue.edu/academic/hkls/ sections/grad.html

### ■ SOUTHERN CONNECTICUT STATE UNIVERSITY

**School of Graduate Studies, School of Education, Department of Exercise Science, New Haven, CT 06515-1355**

**AWARDS** Human performance (MS); physical education (MS); sport psychology (MS). Part-time and evening/weekend programs available.

**Faculty:** 8 full-time (2 women), 1 part-time/adjunct.

**Students:** 14 full-time (9 women), 58 part-time (31 women); includes 1 minority (Asian American or Pacific Islander), 1 international. 97 applicants, 35% accepted. In 2001, 10 degrees awarded.

**Degree requirements:** For master's, thesis or alternative.

**Entrance requirements:** For master's, interview. *Application deadline:* For fall admission, 7/15 (priority date). Applications are processed on a rolling basis. *Application fee:* $40.

**Financial support:** In 2001–02, 8 teaching assistantships were awarded. Financial award application deadline: 4/15; financial award applicants required to submit FAFSA.

Dr. Joan Barbarich, Chair, 203-392-6088, *Fax:* 203-392-6093, *E-mail:* barbarich@ southernct.edu.

**Application contact:** Dr. Robert Axtell, Coordinator, 203-392-6037, *Fax:* 203-392-6093, *E-mail:* axtell@southernct.edu. *Web site:* http://www.southernct.edu/

### ■ SPRINGFIELD COLLEGE

**School of Graduate Studies, Programs in Counseling and Psychological Services, Springfield, MA 01109-3797**

**AWARDS** Athletic counseling (M Ed, MS, CAS); general counseling (M Ed, MS, CAS); industrial/organizational psychology (MS, CAS); marriage and family therapy (M Ed, MS, CAS); mental health counseling (M Ed, MS, CAS); school guidance and counseling (M Ed, MS, CAS); student personnel in higher education (M Ed, MS, CAS). Part-time and evening/weekend programs available.

**Faculty:** 11 full-time (7 women), 20 part-time/adjunct (9 women).

**Students:** 133 full-time, 34 part-time. Average age 26. 210 applicants, 93% accepted. In 2001, 63 master's, 3 other advanced degrees awarded.

**Degree requirements:** For master's, thesis (for some programs), research project, internship, comprehensive exam.

**Entrance requirements:** For master's and CAS, interview. *Application deadline:* For fall admission, 2/1 (priority date); for spring admission, 12/1. Applications are processed on a rolling basis. *Application fee:* $40.

**Financial support:** In 2001–02, 8 fellowships with partial tuition reimbursements (averaging $2,000 per year), 2 research assistantships (averaging $4,000 per year), 7 teaching assistantships (averaging $1,800 per year) were awarded. Career-related internships or fieldwork, Federal Work-Study, institutionally sponsored loans, scholarships/grants, and tuition waivers (full and partial) also available. Financial award application deadline: 3/1.

**Faculty research:** Sport psychology, leadership and emotional intelligence, rehabilitation adherence, professional career women and caregiving. *Total annual research expenditures:* $715,109.

Dr. Barbara Mandell, Director, 413-748-3339, *Fax:* 413-748-3854, *E-mail:* barbara_ mandell@spfldcol.edu.

**Application contact:** Donald James Shaw, Director of Graduate Admissions, 413-748-3225, *Fax:* 413-748-3694, *E-mail:* donald_shaw_jr@spfldcol.edu.

## ■ SPRINGFIELD COLLEGE

**School of Graduate Studies, Programs in Physical Education, Springfield, MA 01109-3797**

**AWARDS** Adapted physical education (M Ed, MPE, MS, CAS); advanced level coaching (M Ed, MPE, MS, CAS); athletic administration (M Ed, MPE, MS, CAS); clinical masters in physical education (M Ed, MPE, MS); general physical education (DPE); sport management (M Ed, MPE, MS, CAS); sport psychology (M Ed, MPE, MS, DPE, CAS); sport studies (M Ed, MPE, MS, CAS); teaching and administration (M Ed, MPE, MS, CAS). Part-time and evening/weekend programs available.

**Faculty:** 25 full-time (13 women), 2 part-time/adjunct (0 women).

**Students:** 78 full-time, 14 part-time. Average age 26. 145 applicants, 79% accepted. In 2001, 38 master's, 1 doctorate, 1 other advanced degree awarded. Terminal master's awarded for partial completion of doctoral program.

**Degree requirements:** For master's, research project; for doctorate, thesis/dissertation.

**Entrance requirements:** For master's, GRE General Test; for doctorate, GRE General Test, interview. *Application deadline:* For fall admission, 2/1 (priority date); for spring admission, 12/1. Applications are processed on a rolling basis. *Application fee:* $40.

**Financial support:** Fellowships with partial tuition reimbursements, teaching assistantships with partial tuition reimbursements, career-related internships or fieldwork, Federal Work-Study, institutionally sponsored loans, and tuition waivers (full and partial) available. Financial award application deadline: 3/1.

**Faculty research:** Pedagogy, motor learning, history of physical education.

Dr. Lynn E. Couturier, Director, 413-748-3173.

**Application contact:** Donald James Shaw, Director of Graduate Admissions, 413-748-3225, *Fax:* 413-748-3694, *E-mail:* donald_shaw_jr@spfldcol.edu.

## ■ UNIVERSITY OF FLORIDA

**Graduate School, College of Health and Human Performance, Program in Health and Human Performance, Gainesville, FL 32611**

**AWARDS** Athletics training/sport medicine (PhD); biomechanics (PhD); exercise physiology (PhD); health behavior (PhD); motor learning control (PhD); natural resource recreation (PhD); sport and exercise psychology (PhD); therapeutic recreation (PhD); tourism (PhD).

**Degree requirements:** For doctorate, thesis/dissertation.

**Entrance requirements:** For doctorate, GRE General Test. Electronic applications accepted.

**Expenses:** Tuition, state resident: part-time $164 per hour. Tuition, nonresident: part-time $571 per hour. Tuition and fees vary according to course level and program.

## ■ WEST VIRGINIA UNIVERSITY

**School of Physical Education, Morgantown, WV 26506**

**AWARDS** Athletic coaching (MS); athletic training (MS); exercise physiology (Ed D); physical education/teacher education (MS, Ed D), including administration of physical education (Ed D); curriculum and instruction (Ed D); motor development (Ed D); special physical education (Ed D); sport management (MS); sport psychology (MS, Ed D).

**Faculty:** 21 full-time (6 women), 14 part-time/adjunct (0 women).

**Students:** 78 full-time (26 women), 26 part-time (12 women); includes 9 minority (8 African Americans, 1 Hispanic American), 8 international. Average age 26. 140 applicants, 71% accepted. In 2001, 49 master's, 4 doctorates awarded.

**Degree requirements:** For doctorate, thesis/dissertation, oral exam, comprehensive exam.

**Entrance requirements:** For master's, GRE or MAT, TOEFL, minimum GPA of 3.0; for doctorate, GRE General Test or MAT, TOEFL, minimum GPA of 3.5. *Application deadline:* For fall admission, 3/1 (priority date). *Application fee:* $45.

**Expenses:** Tuition, state resident: full-time $2,791. Tuition, nonresident: full-time $8,659. Required fees: $1,002. Tuition and fees vary according to program.

**Financial support:** In 2001–02, 4 research assistantships, 58 teaching assistantships were awarded. Career-related internships or fieldwork, Federal Work-Study, institutionally sponsored loans, tuition waivers (full and partial), and graduate administrative assistantships also available. Support available to part-time students. Financial award application deadline: 2/1; financial award applicants required to submit FAFSA.

**Faculty research:** Sport psychosociology, teacher education, exercise psychology, counseling.

**Application contact:** Carol Straight, Student Records Assistant, 304-293-3295 Ext. 5265, *Fax:* 304-293-4641, *E-mail:* cstraight@mail.wvu.edu. *Web site:* http://www.physed.wvu.edu/

# THANATOLOGY

## ■ BROOKLYN COLLEGE OF THE CITY UNIVERSITY OF NEW YORK

**Division of Graduate Studies, Department of Health and Nutrition Science, Program in Community Health, Brooklyn, NY 11210-2889**

**AWARDS** Community health (MA, MPH); computer science and health science (MS); health care management (MA, MPH); health care policy and administration (MA, MPH); thanatology (MA).

**Students:** 1 (woman) full-time, 63 part-time (46 women); includes 35 minority (26 African Americans, 4 Asian Americans or Pacific Islanders, 5 Hispanic Americans). 59 applicants, 39% accepted. In 2001, 13 degrees awarded.

**Degree requirements:** For master's, thesis or alternative.

**Entrance requirements:** For master's, TOEFL, GRE (MPH), 18 credits in health-related areas. *Application deadline:* For fall admission, 3/1; for spring admission, 11/1. *Application fee:* $40.

**Expenses:** Tuition, state resident: full-time $4,350; part-time $185 per credit. Tuition, nonresident: full-time $7,600; part-time $320 per credit.

**Financial support:** Federal Work-Study, institutionally sponsored loans, and scholarships/grants available. Support available to part-time students. Financial award application deadline: 5/1; financial award applicants required to submit FAFSA.

**Faculty research:** Diet restriction, religious practices in bereavement, diabetes, stress management, palliative care.

Dr. Jerrold Mirotznik, Deputy Chairperson for Graduate Studies, 718-951-4197, *Fax:* 718-951-4670, *E-mail:* jerrym@brooklyn.cuny.edu.

**Application contact:** Michael Lovaglio, Assistant Director of Graduate Admissions, 718-951-5914, *E-mail:* adminqry@brooklyn.cuny.edu.

## ■ THE COLLEGE OF NEW ROCHELLE

**Graduate School, Division of Human Services, Program in Thanatology, New Rochelle, NY 10805-2308**

**AWARDS** Certificate.

**Degree requirements:** For Certificate, internship.

# ■ HOOD COLLEGE

**Graduate School, Programs in Human Sciences, Frederick, MD 21701-8575**

**AWARDS** Psychology (MA); thanatology (MA). Part-time and evening/weekend programs available.

**Faculty:** 5 full-time (2 women), 3 part-time/adjunct (1 woman).

**Students:** 6 full-time (4 women), 43 part-time (37 women); includes 4 minority (1 African American, 1 Asian American or Pacific Islander, 2 Native Americans), 1 international. Average age 33. 24 applicants, 79% accepted, 15 enrolled. In 2001, 18 master's awarded.

**Degree requirements:** For master's, thesis or alternative, comprehensive exam, registration.

**Entrance requirements:** For master's, minimum GPA of 2.5. *Application deadline:* Applications are processed on a rolling basis. *Application fee:* $30.

**Expenses:** Tuition: Full-time $5,670; part-time $315 per credit. Required fees: $20 per term.

**Financial support:** Institutionally sponsored loans available. Financial award applicants required to submit FAFSA.

**Faculty research:** Mind-body medicine and multicultural healing, the New Orleans jazz funeral, death practices in African-American culture, bereavement theories and gender differences, Piaget's theory of cognitive development as a formal mathematical model.

Dr. Dana G. Cable, Chairperson, 301-696-3758, *Fax:* 301-696-3597, *E-mail:* cable@hood.edu.

**Application contact:** 301-696-3600, *Fax:* 301-696-3597, *E-mail:* hoodgrad@hood.edu.

# TRANSPERSONAL AND HUMANISTIC PSYCHOLOGY

# ■ ATLANTIC UNIVERSITY

**Program in Transpersonal Studies, Virginia Beach, VA 23451-2061**

**AWARDS** MA. Part-time and evening/weekend programs available. Postbaccalaureate distance learning degree programs offered (no on-campus study).

**Faculty:** 11 part-time/adjunct (5 women).

**Students:** 233. 52 applicants, 69% accepted. In 2001, 20 degrees awarded.

**Degree requirements:** For master's, thesis. *Median time to degree:* Master's–2.5 years full-time, 5 years part-time.

**Entrance requirements:** For master's, minimum undergraduate GPA of 2.5. *Application deadline:* Applications are

processed on a rolling basis. *Application fee:* $25. Electronic applications accepted.

H. A. Stokely, Chief Executive Officer, 757-631-8101, *Fax:* 757-631-8096, *E-mail:* info@atlanticuniv.edu.

**Application contact:** Dr. Robert Danner, Director of Admissions, 757-631-8101 Ext. 210, *Fax:* 757-631-8096, *E-mail:* info@atlanticuniv.edu. *Web site:* http://www.atlanticuniv.edu/

# ■ CENTER FOR HUMANISTIC STUDIES

**Programs in Humanistic, Clinical, and Educational Psychology, Detroit, MI 48202-3802**

**AWARDS** Humanistic and clinical psychology (MA, Psy D).

**Faculty:** 4 full-time (2 women), 12 part-time/adjunct (5 women).

**Students:** 83 full-time (60 women); includes 15 minority (13 African Americans, 2 Asian Americans or Pacific Islanders). Average age 38. 90 applicants, 83% accepted. In 2001, 30 degrees awarded.

**Degree requirements:** For master's, thesis, practicum; for doctorate, thesis/dissertation, internship, practicum.

**Entrance requirements:** For master's, 1 year of work experience, interview, minimum GPA of 3.0; for doctorate, 3 years work experience, 2 interviews, minimum GPA of 3.0 in graduate course work. *Application deadline:* For fall admission, 9/1 (priority date). Applications are processed on a rolling basis. *Application fee:* $75.

**Expenses:** Tuition: Full-time $14,060.

**Financial support:** In 2001–02, 39 students received support. Application deadline: 6/30.

**Faculty research:** Qualitative research, existential-phenomenological psychology, applications to clinical practice.

**Application contact:** Ellen F. Blau, Admissions Adviser, 313-875-7440, *Fax:* 313-875-2610, *E-mail:* eblau@humanpsych.edu.

# ■ INSTITUTE OF TRANSPERSONAL PSYCHOLOGY

**Global Division, Palo Alto, CA 94303**

**AWARDS** Creative expression (Certificate); spiritual psychology (Certificate); transpersonal psychology (MTP, PhD); transpersonal studies (MA, Certificate); wellness counseling and body-mind consciousness (Certificate); women's spiritual development (Certificate). Postbaccalaureate distance learning degree programs offered (minimal on-campus study).

**Faculty:** 3 full-time (1 woman), 31 part-time/adjunct (25 women).

**Students:** 83 full-time (67 women), 20 part-time (15 women); includes 9 minority (2 African Americans, 1 Asian American or Pacific Islander, 3 Hispanic Americans, 3 Native Americans), 12 international. Average age 43. 80 applicants, 78% accepted. In 2001, 16 degrees awarded.

**Degree requirements:** For master's, thesis (for some programs). *Median time to degree:* Master's–2 years full-time.

**Entrance requirements:** For master's, 8 hours in psychology; for doctorate, bachelor's degree with 18 quarter or 12 semester units in psychology, master's degree in psychology (advanced standing). *Application deadline:* Applications are processed on a rolling basis. *Application fee:* $55.

**Expenses:** Contact institution.

**Financial support:** In 2001–02, 55 students received support. Federal Work-Study available. Support available to part-time students. Financial award application deadline: 6/30; financial award applicants required to submit FAFSA.

Prof. Kurtick Patel, Dean, 650-493-4430, *Fax:* 650-493-6835, *E-mail:* kpatel@itp.edu.

**Application contact:** Edith Parker, Admissions Assistant, 650-493-4430 Ext. 40, *Fax:* 650-493-6835, *E-mail:* itpinfo@itp.edu. *Web site:* http://www.itp.edu/

# ■ INSTITUTE OF TRANSPERSONAL PSYCHOLOGY

**Residential Division, Palo Alto, CA 94303**

**AWARDS** Counseling psychology (MA); transpersonal psychology (MA, PhD). Part-time and evening/weekend programs available.

**Faculty:** 18 full-time (10 women), 22 part-time/adjunct (7 women).

**Students:** 236 full-time (173 women), 12 part-time (10 women); includes 30 minority (7 African Americans, 9 Asian Americans or Pacific Islanders, 11 Hispanic Americans, 3 Native Americans), 13 international. Average age 41. 122 applicants, 78% accepted, 58 enrolled. In 2001, 48 master's, 12 doctorates awarded. Terminal master's awarded for partial completion of doctoral program.

**Degree requirements:** For doctorate, thesis/dissertation.

**Entrance requirements:** For master's, 8 hours in psychology; for doctorate, 12 hours in psychology. *Application deadline:* For fall admission, 4/15 (priority date). Applications are processed on a rolling basis. *Application fee:* $55.

**Expenses:** Tuition: Full-time $17,784. Required fees: $30. Tuition and fees vary according to degree level, campus/location and program.

**Financial support:** In 2001–02, 141 students received support; teaching assistantships, career-related internships or fieldwork and Federal Work-Study available. Support available to part-time students. Financial award application deadline: 7/1; financial award applicants required to submit FAFSA.
Dr. Paul Roy, Academic Dean, 650-493-4430, *Fax:* 650-493-6835, *E-mail:* proy@itp.edu.
**Application contact:** John Hofmann, Admissions Office, 650-493-4430 Ext. 30, *Fax:* 650-493-6835, *E-mail:* itpinfo@itp.edu. *Web site:* http://www.itp.edu/

### ■ JOHN F. KENNEDY UNIVERSITY

**Graduate School for Holistic Studies, Program in Transpersonal Counseling Psychology, Orinda, CA 94563-2603**
**AWARDS** MA. Part-time and evening/weekend programs available.
**Degree requirements:** For master's, thesis or alternative.
**Entrance requirements:** For master's, TOEFL, interview.
**Expenses:** Tuition: Full-time $9,396; part-time $348 per unit. Required fees: $9 per quarter. Tuition and fees vary according to degree level and program.

### ■ NAROPA UNIVERSITY

**Graduate Programs, Program in Transpersonal Psychology, Boulder, CO 80302-6697**
**AWARDS** MA.
**Faculty:** 3 full-time (1 woman), 6 part-time/adjunct (2 women).
**Entrance requirements:** For master's, interview. *Application deadline:* Applications are processed on a rolling basis. Electronic applications accepted.
**Expenses:** Tuition: Full-time $10,766; part-time $489 per credit. Required fees: $560; $280 per semester. Tuition and fees vary according to course load and campus/location.
**Financial support:** Career-related internships or fieldwork, Federal Work-Study, scholarships/grants, health care benefits, and tuition waivers (partial) available. Support available to part-time students. Financial award application deadline: 3/1.

Dr. John Davis, Coordinator, 303-245-4654, *Fax:* 303-546-4044, *E-mail:* jdavis@naropa.edu.
**Application contact:** Alice Di Tullio, Admissions Counselor, 303-546-3598, *Fax:* 303-546-3583, *E-mail:* aliced@naropa.edu. *Web site:* http://www.naropa.edu/matrans.html/

### ■ SAYBROOK GRADUATE SCHOOL AND RESEARCH CENTER

**Program in Psychology, Human Science and Organizational Systems, San Francisco, CA 94133-4640**
**AWARDS** Human science (MA, PhD), including consciousness and spirituality, individualized (PhD), organizational systems, social transformation; organizational systems (MA, PhD), including individualized (PhD), organizational systems; psychology (MA, PhD), including consciousness and spirituality, humanistic and transpersonal, clinical inquiry, and health studies, individualized (PhD), licensure track (MA), organizational systems, social transformation. Postbaccalaureate distance learning degree programs offered (minimal on-campus study).
**Faculty:** 20 full-time (6 women), 83 part-time/adjunct (29 women).
**Students:** 392 full-time (246 women); includes 63 minority (28 African Americans, 16 Asian Americans or Pacific Islanders, 14 Hispanic Americans, 5 Native Americans), 17 international. Average age 42. 280 applicants, 34% accepted. In 2001, 9 master's, 35 doctorates awarded. Terminal master's awarded for partial completion of doctoral program.
**Degree requirements:** For master's, thesis or alternative; for doctorate, thesis/dissertation.
**Entrance requirements:** For master's, TOEFL; for doctorate, TOEFL, master's degree in psychology or related social science. *Application deadline:* For fall admission, 6/1 (priority date); for spring admission, 12/16 (priority date). Electronic applications accepted.
**Expenses:** Tuition: Full-time $13,800. Required fees: $2,000. One-time fee: $600 full-time.
**Financial support:** In 2001–02, 275 students received support. Scholarships/grants available. Financial award applicants required to submit FAFSA.

**Faculty research:** Humanistic theory, health studies, organizational systems, consciousness and spirituality, social transformation. *Total annual research expenditures:* $90,000.
Dr. Maureen O'Hara, President, 800-825-4480, *Fax:* 415-433-9271, *E-mail:* mohara@saybrook.edu.
**Application contact:** Mindy Myers, Vice President for Recruitment and Admissions, 800-825-4480, *Fax:* 415-433-9271, *E-mail:* mmyers@saybrook.edu. *Web site:* http://www.saybrook.edu/

### ■ SEATTLE UNIVERSITY

**College of Arts and Sciences, Department of Psychology, Seattle, WA 98122**
**AWARDS** Existential and phenomenological therapeutic psychology (MA Psych).
**Faculty:** 8 full-time (3 women), 4 part-time/adjunct (3 women).
**Students:** 37 full-time (23 women), 4 part-time (3 women); includes 3 minority (all Asian Americans or Pacific Islanders), 2 international. Average age 35. 51 applicants, 57% accepted, 23 enrolled. In 2001, 15 degrees awarded.
**Degree requirements:** For master's, thesis.
**Entrance requirements:** For master's, interview, minimum GPA of 3.0, previous undergraduate course work in psychology. *Application deadline:* For fall admission, 1/15. *Application fee:* $55.
**Expenses:** Tuition: Full-time $7,740; part-time $430 per credit hour. Tuition and fees vary according to course load, degree level and program.
**Financial support:** Career-related internships or fieldwork and Federal Work-Study available. Support available to part-time students. Financial award applicants required to submit FAFSA.
**Faculty research:** Healing, transformations in relationships, therapy, dialogical research.
Dr. Lane Gerber, Director, 206-296-5400, *Fax:* 206-296-2141.
**Application contact:** Janet Shandley, Associate Dean of Graduate Admissions, 206-296-5900, *Fax:* 206-298-5656, *E-mail:* grad_admissions@seattleu.edu. *Web site:* http://www.seattleu.edu/artsci/departments/psychology/

# School Index

# School Index

# School Index

# Index of
## Directories in This Book

# Your everything education destination...
## the *all-new* Petersons.com

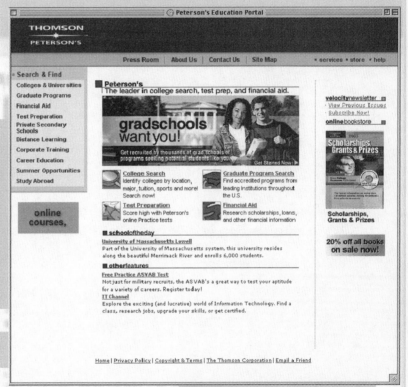